KU-397-245

ENCYCLOPEDIA OF

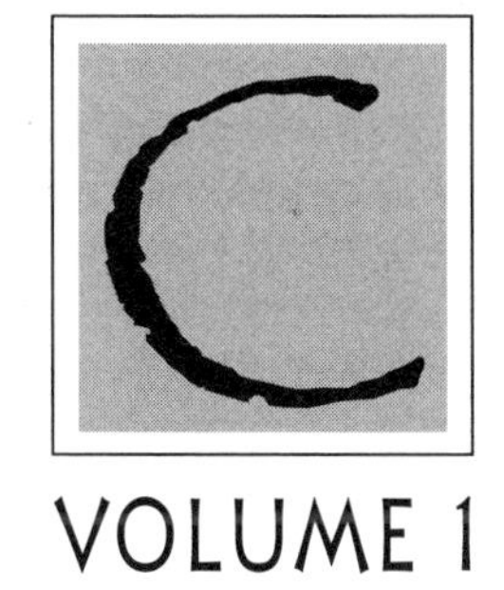

HRISTIAN THEOLOGY

VOLUME 1

ENCYCLOPEDIA OF

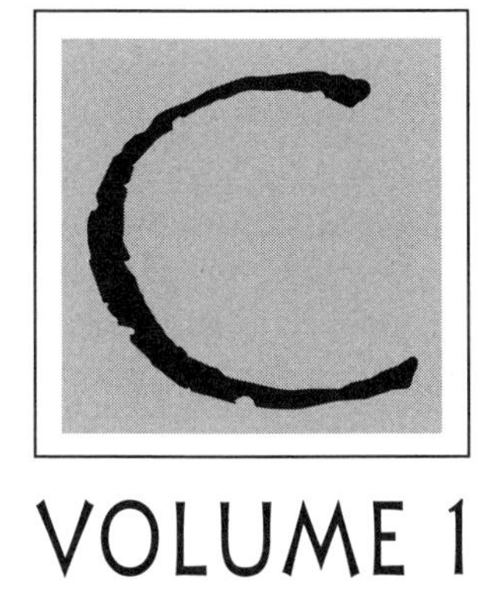

HRISTIAN THEOLOGY

VOLUME 1

JEAN-YVES LACOSTE
EDITOR

A-F

ROUTLEDGE
New York • London

Published in 2005 by
Routledge
270 Madison Avenue
New York, NY 10016

Published in Great Britain by
Routledge
2 Park Square
Milton Park, Abingdon
Oxon, OX14 4RN

Originally published as *Dictionnaire critique de théologie (Nouvelle Edition),* edited by Jean-Yves Lacoste (Paris: Presses Universitaires de France, 1999), ISBN 2–13–048825–0

Published with the participation of the *Ministère français chargé de la Culture–Centre National du Livre* (French Ministry of Culture–National Book Center)

10 9 8 7 6 5 4 3 2 1

Library of Congress Cataloging-in-Publication Data

Dictionnaire critique de théologie. English.
Encyclopedia of Christian theology / Jean-Yves Lacoste, editor.
p. cm.
Includes bibliographical references and index.
ISBN 1–57958–250–8 (set: alk. paper)—ISBN 1–57958–236–2 (v. 1: alk. paper)—ISBN 1–57958–239–7 (v. 2: alk. paper)—ISBN 1–57958–332–6 (v. 3: alk. paper) 1. Theology—Encyclopedias. I. Lacoste, Jean-Yves. II. Title.
BR95.D5313 2004
230'.03—dc22
2004004150

Printed in the United States of America on acid-free paper.

Contents

Foreword

A reader about to venture into a thick reference work (especially one dealing with theology) has the right to ask for additional mercy from its editor: that is, that the editor specifies the aim and use of the work. A few glosses about the title will answer this request. First and foremost, this is an encyclopedia of theology, meaning, in a restrictive sense that is also a precise sense, the massive amount of discourse and doctrines that Christianity has assembled about God and its experience of God. There are other discourses on God, and theology was often the first to champion their rationality. By selecting one term to refer to one practice (historically circumscribed) of the logos and one call (historically circumscribed) in the name of God, we do not pretend to deny the existence or the rationality of other practices or calls—we are only offering to make use of *theological* to name the fruits of a kind of covenant between the Greek logos and the Christian restructuring of the Jewish experience. When the philosopher discusses God, it rarely appears that his interest is theological, in the fixed sense of the term. Because Judaism was able to tie in the richest things it had to say without pillaging the theoretical legacy of classical antiquity, it is also unlikely that *theological* needs to be applied to its doctrines. Likewise, because the Islamic Kalam itself follows some rather original structuration rules, it is inadequate to baptize it "Islamic theology," unless one accepts a certain vagueness. As for the rigorous comparative study of all the discourses in which the signifier *God* (whether its intervention be that of name, concept, or other) appears, it is still in its infancy.

Second, this is an encyclopedia, by which we mean an academic tool serving knowledge. It is one thing to produce knowledge and another to transmit it. Thus, we will not expect from this collegiate effort, which the present foreword concludes, that it was a work of creation. In the organized disorder presided over by the alphabetical order of the entries, its ambition was modest: to provide readers with a starting point for the main theological objects. Events, doctrines, contributors, theories and metatheories, over five hundred objects are to be found within the pages of this encyclopedia. The reader who wants to browse through the pages following a question will always find stand-alone entries and the point about the question. The reader who prefers long explorations can rely on the navigational tools provided to learn, one entry after another, for example, about Biblical theology in general or about medieval theology or about Lutheran theology or more. For want of a consensus among scholars, which cannot be found anywhere, this work is expected to keep the promises inherent to its scientific genre: legibility, intellectual honesty, and historical precision.

Last, this intends to be a critical work, which doesn't bound its fate to some deconstructing temerity but rather emphasizes the native condition of any academic endeavor at the service of truth. The first task of critical reasoning is to criticize itself. Although it was critical of the objects it inherited from tradition, the reason of the Enlightenment was less critical of itself, its powers, duties, and agents. One demand remains, which we owe and of which we should not be afraid: we will expect from the "critical" history of the doctrines or from the "critical" presentation of the theological traditions that they wanted to identify their own objects so that they appear as they are, in all their diachronic or synchronic complexity, sometimes in all indecision. Theology concerns itself mostly with phenomena that never demand intellection without also demanding adhesion, and the historical work of discernment that the encyclopedia undertook will not deprive anybody of the necessity to forge a personal opinion. One never believes, however, without knowing slightly. If one wants to forge a straight opinion, then it is best to know critically rather than precritically.

The editor has one pleasant remaining task: that of giving thanks. Firstly, he wishes to thank the 250 contributors, from about one hundred institutions and representing about fifteen nationalities. They made this encyclopedia and accepted the many constraints imposed by such an exercise. All graciously complied with the editorial goal of global cohesiveness, and their good will allowed the work to be more than a collection of stand-alone entries. All used their own voice, however, and this allows the work to let its authors speak with the accents peculiar to their cultural and scientific traditions.

Secondly, the editor wishes to thank all colleagues and friends who, flying to the rescue at the last minute, helped fill gaps, update bibliographies, refine translations, and verify thousands of references. I thus burn the incense of my gratitude to Daniel Bourgeois, Rémi Brague, Michel Cagin, Olivier de Champris, Michel Corbin, Michel Gitton, Jérôme de Gramont, Yves-Jean Harder, Max Huot de Longchamp, Goulven Madec, Thaddée Matura, Cyrille Michon, Bruno Neveu, Jacqueline de Proyart, and Daniel de Reynal. The members of the editorial board know how dear their collaboration was to me as well as the pleasure I had working with them. It is fair that the reader should know about them, too. My thanks turn superlative for Marie-Béatrice Mesnet, who bore the final responsibility of the French manuscript, from disks to proofs, including the organization of the bibliographies, cross-references, and abbreviations: I fear to think what we would have published without her help. As for Jacqueline Champris, she allowed for this work to be published while its editor was alive, or that its editor would not die in the process: each reader will judge its merit.

Our first French edition owed its index to Georges Leblanc, and we kindly remember Edith Migo providing us with secretarial help early on. The logistical support from Françós de Vorges and Didier Le Riche greatly eased the work of the editorial board. Françoise Muckensturm and Renza Arrighi also provided their biblical knowledge. The published work bore the mark of their labors.

Some members of the editorial board and the like spent more time than others in compiling the second French edition: my hat off thus to Paul Beauchamp, Olivier Boulnois, Vincent Carraud, Irène Fernandez, Marie-Béatrice Mesnet, Oliver O'Donovan, and Françoise Vinel as well as to the knowledgeable and devoted editor of the encyclopedia. As with the first, the second edition also had many benefactors who wrote entries in a few days, suggested useful amendments, and published encouraging notices. I cannot name them all, but I do want to name Cyrille Michon, Hervé Barreau, Rémi Brague, Claude Bressolette, Yves Delorme, Henri de L'Éprevier, Bernard de Guibert, Dominique Le Tourneau, Roger Pouivet, Émile Poulat, Michel Sales, Yves Tourenne, and Claude Villemot. The first French edition was honored by the Académie des Sciences Morales et Politiques, which awarded it the Chanoine Delpeuch Prize. As for Tabatha, finally, she knows what we owe her: a lot.

Jean-Yves Lacoste

Introduction

The *Dictionnaire critique de théologie* was first published in French in 1998. When in 1999 work began on an anglophone presentation, the U.S. publishers had at their disposal the French additions and modifications to the original text undertaken with a view to its second edition. The present work is a translation of the second edition of the French original.

Users of the *Encyclopedia of Christian Theology,* whether chiefly interested in consulting it for specific information or in browsing more widely, may well wish to begin with the index. The French editorial committee and the editorial director have achieved the not inconsiderable feat of containing very nearly all the material falling within the ambit of a critical work of theology, as those terms are defined in the foreword, within some five hundred entries.

Theology remains the rationally structured discussion of the Christianized experience of Hebrew monotheism, as it was originally elaborated with the help of Greek philosophical categories and considerations familiar to the early Christian Greek-speaking world and subsequently developed during two millennia of Christian thought.

This has meant paying little more than passing attention to other important aspects of Christian life as it developed. Its liturgies, its widely diverging spiritualities, its administrative hierarchy, and its noncore teaching even about important moral and social issues occurring in response to the often political constraints that arose in the course of history are not central to its theology as here understood. Attention is concentrated on such matters as Trinitarian theology, Christology, the Incarnation, the Redemption, revelation, ecclesiology, and the understanding of the workings of the divine plan for humanity. The definition also excludes formal consideration of eastern religions and even of Islam, immensely powerful in its own right and also the vehicle for carrying the thought of Aristotle, heavily contaminated by Neoplatonism, to the Christian scholastic theologians of the High Middle Ages.

Philosophy itself, as an intellectual discipline, does not fall within the ambit of the reference function of the *Encyclopedia,* but its exclusion poses more difficult problems. As the editor of the French original, Jean-Yves Lacoste, points out in his own entry on philosophy, it is still possible in the twentieth century with Barth or Heidegger to conduct philosophical discussion without reference to any theological position. In fact, however, the possibility of the autonomous conduct of philosophical investigation, although it is not discussed in the *Encyclopedia,* looks today increasingly fragile.

Christian theology as a discipline, particularly on account of the Greco-Roman legacy still woven into it, is much more difficult to insulate from its philosophical substructure. In many of its entries, the *Encyclopedia,* having expounded the theology with which they are concerned, concludes them with philosophical considerations. Philosophically speaking, Christian theology has for centuries relied on a *philosophia perennis,* drawing its categories and premises largely from Aristotelian and Platonist traditions.

Certain aspects of that traditional substructure, notably its anthropology, its epistemology, and its ontology, are no longer generally considered useful and at least in non-English-speaking Europe have been replaced by a newer tradition. In the *Encyclopedia,* no attempt has been made to diminish the reliance on philosophical reflections developed from the mainstream European, mostly German-language tradition as it has emerged from Kant and the German idealists and subsequently been developed by Hegel, Husserl, and Heidegger, and from more recent variations of an essentially phenomenological approach to the subject such as appear also in the work of some modern theologians like Karl Rahner.

The content of the work, as indicated in the foreword, is laid out alphabetically, and anglophone readers will have no difficulty finding the keyword for many of the most important themes, events, people, and topics discussed. There is an elaborate system of cross-referencing, but, as the relative length of the entries and the bibliographies makes clear, a format of relatively long entries and essays, still within the scope of what is known as a *dictionnaire* in French, has been chosen rather than that of a high number of short entries generally denoted by the word *dictionary* in English.

Some of the new entries, like that for Moses, fill lacunae in the original text, and very few important topics will be found to have been altogether neglected, although to locate the several treatments of such themes as transsubstantiation or of theologians as important as Melanchthon, it is necessary to refer first to the index. It is even possible that certain readers will feel that occasionally, like the original eighteenth-century French *Encyclopédie,* this *Encyclopedia* advances views or developments that it purports merely to transmit or that it gives an acceptably ecumenical doctrinal spin to the historical record by omitting to dwell on or even to note some of the harsher reactions perceivable in the decrees of the council of Trent or of Vatican I or in the decisions of the Pontifical Biblical Commission. Theologians of the last fifty years are not unreasonably accorded a prominence that implies a value judgment about their work, which is inevitably less certain to endure than judgments made about theologians from centuries earlier than the twentieth whose historical contribution to the development of today's theology cannot be challenged.

It will not be difficult for users to identify the corporate viewpoint of the editorial committee of the *Encyclopedia.* It is, however, as the third paragraph of the foreword makes clear, important to preserve the work's intellectual integrity. That means identifying and acknowledging what its point of view is, especially on account of the probability that here and there the more speculative essays may seem to be urging Catholic theology to develop in a particular direction and the further probability that any such direction will be one with which the original French readership may feel more at ease than theologians brought up in some of the traditions at present current in different degrees in the various anglophone regions of the globe.

The university level that determines the amount and type of information contained in the *Encyclopedia* requires its content to be not only historically accurate, deep enough for university-level reflection, and well enough written to be readily intelligible but also useful in a university context, that is, one in which reasonably ample library resources are available. Users wishing to follow up references to patristic works, the scholastics, or modern books and articles will often require the bibliographic resources normally found only in theological colleges or in large, general academic institutions.

Because the *Encyclopedia* is intended also to serve outside a formal university context as an initial guide to the state of theological discussion on all major topics covered by its definition of theology, the references to reviews, editions, and relatively small-circulation journals are included simply for the convenience of those who wish to pursue further research. Further investigation into most of the topics covered is likely to require access to good editions of the Fathers of the Church and, where there are any, of the scholastics, as well as to more recent theologians from the nineteenth and twentieth centuries. The entries are written with a view to being easily intelligible even where there is no immediate access to the cited sources.

Some topics, like the Dead Sea Scrolls, have primarily been discussed only in languages other than English and chiefly in specialist journals. In such instances, the *Encyclopedia* attempts primarily to do service as a handbook or guide to the present state of discussion, giving only pointers in its references to places or sources where the discussion has been further developed or on which advocates of different views have relied. In all cases, and in spite of its inevitable point of view, the *Encyclopedia* attempts an objective exposition of the facts and arguments, without bias, prejudice, or any viewpoint that could be interpreted as sectarian.

The *Encyclopedia* does not aspire to be historical in that it does not undertake to cover the history of the theology of the topics that it includes except incidentally, in order to explain and contextualize them, and except insofar as the sources for contemporary theological views are necessarily grounded in the historic sources of the Christian revelation. The method adopted is, however, critical. At every point it goes out of its way to confront doctrines and views with the sources and traditions on which they rely, and it is relentless in its pursuit of theological truth as warranted by the sources and the historical facts. This criticism is not destructive of anything but falsehood, although when applied as rigorously as it is here to the legitimacy of some of the emphases of medieval theology, it produces results that are likely to surprise many brought up on a precritical tradition. The critical account of the tradition reveals, for instance, that the notion of an individual judgment at the moment of death appeared only relatively late in eastern theology and shows that the virginity of Mary has a less strong scriptural basis than is often assumed.

Without a doubt, the critical expertise of the theologians on whom the editorial committee has drawn for the entries is where this work's serious theological interest primarily lies. Whatever services may be rendered by the utility of its reference function, the most significant achievement of the entries in the work consists overwhelmingly in the critical acumen applied by its authors to their subject matter, invariably through a rigorous treatment of the sources and tradition underlying the historical and contemporary theological discussion of all theology's major issues. To this critical treatment of the tradition is often appended a more speculative section, as in the entry on being, pointing to tasks remaining to be accomplished and to directions in which theological discussion appears to be moving.

The critical method used is essentially based on a balanced appraisal of the theological sources that time, tradition, and individual religious spiritualities, such as those developed within the great religious orders or outside them by popular devotion, have inevitably tended to obscure. By confronting patterns of Christian religious belief and behavior with the sources of the Christian revelation and with the major developments in theological tradition, the *Encyclopedia* no doubt implicitly calls for a reevaluation of some views and attitudes that may at different periods have been too uncritically, and perhaps wrongly, assumed to have been dictated by fundamental theological dogma. The critical function of the *Encyclopedia* lies not in criticizing them but in confronting them with a more authentic understanding of the Christian revelation, leaving it to individuals to mold the moral and religious commitments that best both fulfil their own spiritual needs and accord with the revelation. Insofar as the *Encyclopedia* fulfils the task it has taken on itself, it must promote a pluralism of religious attitudes, both moral and devotional, capable of fulfilling the individual hunger for spiritual nourishment on the basis of a critical understanding of genuine theological truth.

It is difficult to think of any earlier attempt to produce a comprehensive critical theological handbook in the sense in which the *Encyclopedia* defines theology. There are no doubt historical reasons why this should be so, and the appearance of the *Encyclopedia* marks an important stage in the diminution of sectarian slants on theological discussion as well as a hope that a point has been reached when all those whose experience is enhanced by a spirituality situated within the Judeo-Christian religious tradition can look forward to agreeing on the theology that lies at its center. The *Encyclopedia,* in giving, however succinctly, a fully critical account of that tradition, is a product of progress already made as well as a pointer to what questions still urgently await their resolution and an indicator of the most promising paths to be followed. It summarizes the present state of theological discussion without dwelling on what has recently been achieved or laying down firm paths for the future. It may well constitute a milestone in the progress toward a truly critical theology and therefore also toward promoting a religious awareness and providing the basis for an intelligently reflective religious commitment without laying down new orthodoxies. Its task is to present the critical summary of Judeo-Christian theology necessary to further the personal and corporate attitudes of those who seek to live by the norms it promotes.

Anthony Levi

Alphabetical List of Entries

Volume 2

Abbreviations

A. Usual Abbreviations

a.	articulus
ACFEB	Association catholique française pour l'étude de la Bible
adv.	adversus
anath.	anathema
anon.	anonymous
Apos. Const.	Apostolic Constitution
ap.	*apud* (according to)
ARCIC	Anglican-Roman Catholic International Commission
arg.	argumentum
art.	article
BHK	Biblia Hebraica, ed. Kittel
BHS	Biblia Hebraica Stuttgartensia
bibl.	includes a bibliography
c.	circa
CADIR	Centre pour l'analyse du discours religieux, Lyon
can.	canon
CEPOA	Centre d'étude du Proche-Orient ancien, Louvain
ch(ap).	chapter
COE	Conseil œcuménique des Églises (see WWC)
col.	column
coll.	collection
comm.	*Commentum,* commentary
concl.	conclusio
d.	distinctio
Decr.	Decretal
diss.	dissertatio
dub.	dubium
ed.	edidit, editio
ed.	editor
ep.	epistula(e), letters
f	next verse (biblical citations)
ff	two following verses (biblical citations)
FS	Festschrift
GA	Gesamtausgabe
gr.	Greek
GS	Gesammelte Schriften
GW	Gesammelte Werke
hb, hebr.	Hebrew
hom.	homily
l.	*liber*
lat.	latin
lect.	*lectio*
MA	Middle Ages
ms.	manuscript
mss	manuscripts
n.	note/*numerus*
NT	New Testament
O.P.	Order of Preachers (Dominicans)
O.S.B.	Order of Saint Benedict (Benedictines)
OC	Œuvres complètes; Complete Works
Op.	*Opera* (Works)
OT	Old Testament
par.	parallel passages (in synoptic gospels)
Ps.-	Pseudo-
q.	quaestio
qla	quaestiuncula
quod.	quodlibet
quod sic	videtur quod sic
resp.	responsio, solutio
sess.	session
SIDC	Société internationale de droit canonique
S.J.	*Societatis Jesu* (Jesuits)
Sq	*sequen(te)s,* and following
SW	Sämtliche Werke
syr.	syriac
tract.	tractatus
v.	verse
Vulg.	Vulgate, Latin version latine of the Bible, by Jerome
vv.	verses
WWC	World Council of Churches
WW	Werke
Ia Iiae	Thomas Aquina, Summa Theologiae,

	prima secundae, first part of the second part
IIa Iiae	*Ibid., secunda secundae,* second part of the second part
LXX	Septuagint, Greek version of the Hebrew Bible

B. Biblical Texts

The Hebrew and Greek transcription of biblical texts come from the *Concordance de la Traduction œcuménique de la Bible.*

Biblical References

Colon(:) between chapter and verse. For example, Dt 24:17 refers to Deuteronomy, chapter 24:verse 17.

Hyphen: indicates the verses. For example, Dt 24:17–22 (from v. 17 to 22).

The letter *f* next to a verse refers to this verse and the following one. For example, Dt 24:17f (chapter 24:verses 17 and 18).

The letters *ff* refers to the verse and the following two. For example, Dt 24:17ff (chapter 24:verses 17, 18, and 19).

Acts	Acts of the Apostles
Am	Amos
Bar	Baruch
1 Chr	1 Chronicles
2 Chr	2 Chronicles
Col	Colossians
1 Cor	1 Corinthians
2 Cor	2 Corinthians
Dn	Daniel
Dt	Deuteronomy
Eccl	Ecclesiastes
Eph	Ephesians
Est	Esther
Ex	Exodus
Ez	Ezekiel
Ezr	Ezra
Gal	Galatians
Gn	Genesis
Hb	Habakkuk
Heb	Hebrews
Hg	Haggai
Hos	Hosea
Is	Isaiah
Jas	James
Jb	Job
Jdt	Judith
Jer	Jeremiah
Jgs	Judges
Jl	Joel
Jn	John
Jon	Jonah
Jos	Joshua
1 Jn	1 John
2 Jn	2 John
3 Jn	3 John
Jude	Jude
1 Kgs	1 Kings
2 Kgs	2 Kings
Lam	Lamentations
Lk	Luke
Lv	Leviticus
1 Macc	1 Maccabees
2 Macc	2 Maccabees
Mal	Malachi
Mi	Micah
Mk	Mark
Mt	Matthew
Na	Nahum
Neh	Nehemiah
Nm	Numbers
Ob	Obadiah
Phil	Philippians
Phlm	Philemon
Prv	Proverbs
Ps	Psalms
1 Pt	1 Peter
2 Pt	2 Peter
Rev	Revelation
Rom	Romans
Ru	Ruth
Sg	Song of Songs
Sir	Sirach
1 Sm	1 Samuel
2 Sm	2 Samuel
Tb	Tobit
1 Thes	1 Thessalonians
2 Thes	2 Thessalonians
Ti	Titus
1 Tm	1 Timothy
2 Tm	2 Timothy
Wis	Wisdom
Zep	Zepaniah

C. Writings from Ancient Judaism

a) Qumran Writings

11QT	The Temple Scroll
1QH	Hodayot, Hymns
1Qisa	Great Isaiah Scroll (Is 1–66)
1Qisb	Qumran Scroll of Isaiah
1QM	Serekh ha-Milhamah, The War Rule

1QpHab	Pesher on Habakkuk (Commentary)
1QS	Serek ha-Yachad, the Rule of the Community
1Qsa	The Rule of the Congregation
4QapMess	Messianic Apocrypha (= 4Q521)
4QDeutero-Ez	Deutero-Ezekiel (= 4Q385)
4Qenastr	Astronomical fragment from the Book of Enoch
4Qflor	Pesharim, 4Qflorilegium (= 4Q174)
4QMMT	Miqsat ma'ase ha-torah (= 4Q394–399)
4Qps-Danc	Pseudo-Daniel, ms c (= 4Q245)
4QtestQah	Testament of Qahat
4QtgJob	Targum de Job
4QviscAmrf	Visions of Amram
CD	Ciaro Damascus Document

(The numeral preceding the letter "Q" indicates the Grotto number)

b) Other Writings

Ant	Antiquitates judaicae (Flavius Josephus)
Ap	Contra Apionem (Id.)
2 Ba	Syriac Apocalypse of Baruch
Bell	De bello judaico (Flavius Josephus)
3 Esd/4 Esd	3rd/4th book of Esdras
Hen	Henoch
Lib Ant	*Biblical Antiquities* (Pseudo-Philo)
Or Sib	*Sibylline Oracles*
Ps Sal	*Psalm of Solomon*
T	Targum
TB	Talmud of Babylon
TJ	Talmud of Jerusalem
Test	Testament
Test XII	*Testaments of the Twelve Patriarchs*
Test Zab	*Testament of Zebulon*
Vita	Vita Josephi (Flavius Josephus)

D. Documents from the Second Vatican Ecumenical Council

AA	*Apostolicam Actuositatem,* decree on the apostolate of the laity, November 18, 1965
AG	*Ad Gentes,* decree on the mission activity of the Church, December 7, 1965
CD	*Christus Dominus,* decree concerning the pastoral office of bishops in the Church, October 28, 1965
DH	*Dignitatis Humanae,* declaration on religious freedom, December 7, 1965
DV	*Dei Verbum,* dogmatic constitution on divine revelation, November 18, 1965
GE	*Gravissimum Educationis,* declaration on Christian education, October 28, 1965
GS	*Gaudium et Spes*, pastoral constitution on the Church in the modern world, December 7, 1965
IM	*Inter Mirifica,* decree on the media of social communication, December 4, 1963
LG	*Lumen Gentium,* dogmatic constitution on the Church, November 21, 1964
NA	*Nostra Aetate,* declaration on the relation of the Church to non-Christian religions, October 28, 1965
OE	*Orientalium Ecclesiarum,* decree on the Catholic Churches of the Eastern rite, November 21, 1964
OT	*Optatam Totius,* decree on priestly training, October 28, 1965
PC	*Perfectae Caritatis,* decree on the adaptation and renewal of religious life, October 28, 1965
PO	*Presbyterorum Ordinis,* decree on the ministry and life of priests, December 7, 1965
SC	*Sacrosanctum Concilium,* constitution on the sacred liturgy, December 4, 1963
UR	*Unitatis Redintegratio,* decree on ecumenism, November 21, 1964

E. Editions, Collections, and Classic Works

The journal and collections abbreviations are from *Abkürzungsverzeichnis* from the *TRE* (rev. ed. 1994).

AA	Kant, Akademie Ausgabe
AAS	Acta apostolicae sedis, *Vatican City, 1909 (ASS, 1865–1908)*
AAWLM	Abhandlungen der Akademie der Wissenschaften und der Literatur in Mainz, Mainz
AAWLM.G	—Geistes- und Sozialwissenschaftliche Klasse, 1950–
ABAW	Abhandlungen der (k.) bayerischen Akademie der Wissenschaften, Munich
ABAW. PH	—Philosophisch-historische Abteilung, NS, 1929–
ABAW. PPH	—Philosophisch-philologische und historische Klasse, 1909–1928
ABC	Archivum bibliographicum carmelitanum, Rome, 1956–1982
ABG	*Archiv für Begriffsgeschichte,* Bonn, 1955–
ACan	*L'Année canonique,* Paris, 1952–
ACar	Analecta Cartusiana, Berlin, etc., 1970–1988; NS, 1989–
ACHS	American Church History Series, New York, 1893–1897
Aci	*Analecta Cisterciensa,* Rome, 1965–

ACO	*Acta conciliorum œcumenicorum,* Berlin, 1914–
Adv. Haer.	Irenaeus, *Adversus Haereses* (Against Heresies)
AF	*Archivio di filosofia,* Rome, 1931–
AFH	*Archivum Fransciscanum historicum,* Florence, 1908–
AFP	*Archivum Fratrum Praedicatorum,* Rome, 1930–
AGJU	Arbeiten zur Geschichte des antiken Judentums und des Urchristentums, Leiden, 8, 1970–15, 1978
AGPh	*Archiv für Geschichte der Philosophie und Soziologie,* Berlin, 1888–
AHC	*Annuarium historiae conciliorum,* Amsterdam, etc., 1969–
AHDL	*Archives d'histoire doctrinale et littéraire du Moyen Age,* Paris, 1926/1927–
AHP	*Archivum historiae pontificiae,* Rome, 1963–
AISP	*Archivio italiano per la storia della pietà,* Rome, 1951–
AkuG	*Archiv für Kulturgeschichte,* Berlin, 1903–
ALKGMA	Archiv für Literatur- und Kirchengeschichte des Mittelalters, Berlin, etc., 1885–1900
Aloi.	Aloisiana, Naples, 1960–
ALW	*Archiv für Liturgiewissenschaft,* Ratisbonne, 1950–
AmA	*American Anthropologist,* Menasha, Wis., 1888–1898; NS, 1899–
AnBib	Analecta biblica, Rome, 1952–
AncBD	*Anchor Bible Dictionary,* New York: Doubleday, 1992
AnCl	*Antiquité classique,* Bruxelles, 1932–
Ang.	*Angelicum,* Rome, 1925–
AnGr	Analecta Gregoriana, Rome, 1930–
ANRW	*Aufstieg und Niedergang des römischen Welt,* Berlin, 1972–
Anton.	*Antonianum,* Rome, 1926–
AphC	*Annales de philosophie chrétienne,* Paris, 1830–1913
Apol.	Luther, *Apologia confessionis Augustanae* (Apology of the Augsburg Confession)
Aquinas	*Aquinas. Revista internazionale de filosofia,* Rome, 1958–
ARMo	*L'actualité religieuse dans le monde,* Paris, 1983–
ArPh	*Archives de philosophie,* Paris, 1923–
AsbTJ	*The Asbury Theological Journal,* Wilmore, Ky, 1986–
ASCOV	*Acta synodalia sacrosancti Concilii Œcumenici Vaticani II,* Vatican City, 1970–1983
ASEs	*Annali di storia dell'esegesi,* Bologna, 1984–
ASI	*Archivio storico italiano,* Florence, 1852–
ASOC	*Analecta Sacri Ordinis Cisterciensis,* Rome, 1945–1964 (= *ACi,* 1965–)
ASS	*Acta sanctae sedis,* Rome, 1865–1908
ASSR	*Archives de sciences sociales des religions,* Paris, 1973–
A-T	Descartes, *Œuvres* (Works), eds. C. Adam and P. Tannery
ATA	Alttestamentliche Abhandlungen, Munich, 1908–1940
Ath	*L'année théologique,* Paris, 1940–1951
AthA	*Année théologique augustinienne,* Paris, 1951–1954 (= *REAug,* 1955–)
AThANT	Abhandlungen zur Theologie des Alten und Neuen Testaments, Zurich, 1944–
Aug.	*Augustinianum,* Rome, 1961–
Aug(L)	*Augustiniana,* Louvain, 1951–
AUGL	*Augustinus-Lexicon,* edited by C. Mayer, Basel, etc., 1986–
AugM	*Augustinus Magister,* Année théologique. Supplement, 3 vols., Paris: Études augustiniennes, 1954–1955
BAug	Bibliothèque augustinienne, Paris, 1936–
BBB	Bonner biblische Beiträge, Bonn, 1950–
BBKL	Biographish-bibliographisches Kirchenlexicon, edited by F. W. Bautz, Hamm, 1970–
BCG	Buchreihe der Cusanus-Gesellschaft, Münster, 1964–
BCNH	Bibliothèque copte de Nag Hammadi, Quebec.
BCPE	*Bulletin du Centre protestant d'études,* Geneva, 1949–
BEAT	Beiträge zur Erforschung des Alten Testaments und des antiken Judentums, Frankfurt, 1984–
BEL.S	Bibliotheca (Ephemerides Liturgicae), Subsidia, Rome 1975–
BEM	COE, Foi et Constitution, *Baptême, eucharistie, ministère. Convergence de la foi* (Lima, January 1982), Paris, 1982

BEThL	Bibliotheca ephemeridum theologicarum Lovaniensium, Louvain, 1947–
BevTh	Beiträge zur evangelischen Theologie, Munich, 1940–
BGLRK	Beiträge zur Geschichte und Lehre der reformierten Kirche, Neukirchen, 1937–
BGPhMA	Beiträge zur Geschichte der Philosophie (1928) und Theologie des Mittelalters, Münster, 1891–
BHK	Biblia Hebraica, ed. R. Kittel. Stuttgart, 1905/1906; 16th ed., 1973
BHS	Biblia Hebraica Stuttgartensia, Stuttgart, 1969–1975; 2nd ed., 1984
BHSA	*Bulletin historique et scientifique de l'Auvergne.* Clermont-Ferrand, 1881–
BHTh	Beiträge zur historischen Theologie, Tübingen, 1929–
Bib	*Biblica.* Commentarii periodici ad rem biblicam scientifice investigandam, Rome, 1920–
BICP	*Bulletin de l'Institut catholique de Paris,* Paris, 2nd ser., 1910–
Bidi	Bibliotheca dissidentium, Baden-Baden, 1980–
BIHBR	*Bulletin de l'Institut historique belge de Rome,* Rome, etc., 1919–
Bijdr	*Bijdragen.* Tijdschrift voor philosophie en theologie, Nimègue, etc., 1953–
BIRHT	*Bulletin de l'Institut de recherche et d'histoire des textes,* Paris, 1964–1968 (= RHT, 1971–)
BJ	*La Bible de Jérusalem* (Jerusalem Bible)
BJRL	*Bulletin of the John Rylands Library,* Manchester, 1903–
BLE	*Bulletin de littérature ecclésiastique,* Toulouse, 1899–
BN	Catalogue général des livres imprimés de la bibliothèque nationale, Paris, 1897 (General catalog of printed works from the Bibliothèque Nationale in Paris)
BN	*Biblische Notizen. Beiträge zur exegetischen Diskussion,* Bamberg, 1976–
BPhM	*Bulletin de philosophie médiévale,* Louvain, 1964–
Br	Pascal, Blaise. *Pensées.* Brunschvig.
BS	*Bibliotheca sacra,* London, 1843 (= *BSTR,* Andower, Mass.; 1844–1851 = *BSABR*; 1851–1863 = BS, Dallas, etc. 1864–)
BSFP	*Bulletin de la Société française de philosophie,* Paris, 1901–
BSGR	*Bibliothek der Symbole und Glaubensregeln der Alten Kirche,* edited by A. and C.L. Hahn, Breslau, 1842; reprinted 1962, Hildesheim
BSHPF	*Bulletin de la Société d'histoire du protestantisme français.* Paris, 1852–
BSKORK	*Bekenntnisschriften und Kirchenordnungen der nach Gottes Wort reformierten Kirche,* edited by W. Niesel, Zollikon, etc., 1937–1938; 2nd ed., 1938 (etc.) (*CCFR,* Geneva, 1986)
BSLK	*Bekenntnisschriften der evangelisch-lutherischen Kirche,* Göttingen, 1930; 10th ed., 1986; 11th ed., 1992 (FEL, Paris-Geneva, 1991)
BSS	*Bulletin de Saint-Sulpice.* Revue internationale de la Compagnie des prêtres de Saint-Sulpice, Paris, 1975–
BSSV	*Bollettino della Società di studi Valdesi,* Torre Pellice, 1934–
BSt	Biblische Studien. Neukirchen, 1951–
BT.B	Bibliothèque de théologie. 3rd ser. Théologie biblique, Paris, 1954–
BTB	*Biblical Theology Bulletin,* New York, 1971–
BTB(F)	—French ed.
BThom	*Bulletin thomiste,* Étiolles, etc., 1924–1965
BThW	*Bibeltheologisches Wörterbuch,* Graz, etc., 1–2, 19673 (Eng. Ed. *EBT*)
BTT	Bible de tous les temps, Paris, 8 vol., 1984–1989
BullFr	*Bullarium Franciscanum,* Rome, etc., 1929–1949
BWANT	Beiträge zum Wissenschaft vom Alten und Neuen Testament, Stuttgart, 1926 (= BWAT, 1908–1926)
BWAT	*Beiträge zum Wissenschaft vom Alten Testament,* Stuttgart, 1908–1926
Byz	*Byzantion,* Bruxelles, 1924–
BZ	*Biblische Zeitschrift,* Paderborn, etc., 1903–1938; NF 1957–
BZAW	Beihefte zur Zeitschrift für die alttestamentliche Wissenschaft, Berlin, 1896–
BZNW	Beihefte zur Zeitschrift für die neutestamentliche Wisssenschaft, Berlin, etc., 1923–
BZRGG	Beihefte der Zeitschrift für Religions- und Geistesgeschichte, Leyden, 1953–
CA	*Confession of Augsburg*

CAG Commentaria in Aristotelem Graeca, Berlin, 1883
CAR Cahiers de l'actualité religieuse, Tournai, 1954–1969 [Continued after 1969 as *Cahiers pour croire aujourd'hui*]
CAT Commentaire de l'Ancien Testament, Neuchatel, 1963
Cath (M) *Catholica. Jahrbuch für Kontroverstheologie,* Munster, etc. 1932–39, 1952/53–
Cath *Catholicisme. Hier, aujourd'hui, demain,* Paris, 1948–
CBFV Cahiers bibliques de *Foi et Vie,* Paris, 1936–
CBiPA Cahiers de Biblia Patristica, Strasbourg, 1987–
CBQ *Catholic Biblical Quarterly,* Washington, DC, 1939–
CCEO *Codex Canonum ecclesiarum orientalium.* Rome, 1990
CCFR Confessions et catéchismes de la foi reformée, ed., Oliver Fatio, Geneva, 1986 (*BSKORK,* Zollikon)
CCG Codices Chrysostomi Graeci, Paris, 1968–
CChr Corpus Christianorum, Turnhout
CChr.CM —Continuatio mediaevalis, 1966
CChr.SA —Series Apocryphorum, 1983–
CChr.SG —Series Graeca, 1977
CChr.SL —Series Latina, 1953
CCist *Collecteana Cisterciensia,* Westmalle, Forges, etc. 1934–
CCMéd *Cahiers de civilisation médiévale.* X^{e}–XIIe *siecles,* Poitiers, 1958–
CDTor *Collationes Diocesis Tornacensis,* Tournai, 1853–
CEC *Catéchisme de l'Eglise catholique (Catechism of the Catholic Church),* Paris, 1992 (Typical Latin text, Vatican City, 1992; rev. ed., 1997.
CEv Cahiers évangile, Paris, 1972–
CFan Cahiers de Fangeaux, Fanjeaux, etc., 1966–
CFi Cogitatio fidei, Paris, 1961
CFr Collecteana franciscana, Rome, etc.,1931–
CG *Summa Contra Gentiles*
CGG *Christlicher Glaube in moderner Gesellschaft,* Fribourg, 1981–1984
CHFMA Classiques de l'histoire de France au Moyen Age, Paris, 1923–
ChGimG see *CGG*
ChH *Church History,* Chicago: American Society of Church History, 1932–
ChPR *Chroniques de Port-Royal,* Paris, 1950–
CIC *Codex iuris canonici,* Rome, 1917 and Rome, 1983
CIC(B).C *Corpus iuris civilis,* ed. P. Krueger, T. Mommsen, Berlin, -2. *Codex Iustianus,* 1874–1877; 2nd ed., 1880, etc.
CIC(L) *Corpus iuris canonici,* ed. E. Friedberg, Leipzig, 1837–1839; Graz, 1955 (reprint)
CILL Cahiers de l'Institut de linguistique de Louvain, Louvain, 1972–
Cîteaux *Citeaux: commentarii cistercienses,* Westmalle, 1959–
Citeaux, SD —*Studia et documenta,* 1971–
COD *Conciliorum oecumenicorum Decreta,* eds. Albergio and Jedin, Bologna, 3rd ed., 1973 (*DCO,* 1994)
Com(F) *Communio. Revue catholique internationale,* Paris, 1975/76–
Com(US) *Communio. International Catholic Review,* Spokane, Wash., 1974–
Con *Contemporain,* Paris, 1866–
Conc(D) *Concilium. Internazionale Zeitschrift für Theologie,* Einsiedeln, 1965–
Conc(F) *Concilium. Revue internationale de théologie,* Paris, 1965–
Conc(US) *Concilium. Theology in the Age of Renewal,* New York, 1965–
ConscLib *Conscience et Liberté,* Paris, 1971–
Corp IC see *CIL (L)*
CPG Clavis Patrum Graecorum, Turnhout, 1974– (= CChr.SG)
CPIUI *Communio. Pontificium Institutum Utriusque Juris,* Rome, 1957–
CPPJ Cahiers de philosophie politique et juridique, Caen, 1982–
CR Corpus reformatorum, Berlin, 1834–
CRB Cahiers de la *Revue Biblique,* Paris, etc., 1964–
CrSt *Cristianesimo nella storia,* Bologna, 1980–
CR.Th.Ph *Cahiers de la Revue de théologie et de philosophie,* Geneva, 1977–
CSCO Corpus scriptorum Christianorum orientalum, Rome, etc., 1903–
CSEL Corpus scriptorum ecclesiasticorum Latinorum, Vienna, 1866–
CT *Concilium Tridentinum. Diarium, actorum, epistularum, tractatum nova collectio,* Fribourg, 1901–1981
CTh Cahiers théologiques, Neuchâtel, etc., 27, 1949– (= CthAP, 1923–1949)
CTh.HS —*Hors série,* 1945– (Special edition)

CTJ	*Calvin Theological Journal,* Grand Rapids, Mich, 1966–
CUFr	Collection des Universités de France (Les Belle Lettres), Paris, 1920–
DA	*Deutsches Archiv für Erforschung des Mittelalters,* Marburg, etc., 1937–
DACL	*Dictionnaire d'archéologie chrétienne et de liturgie,* Paris, 1924–53
DAFC	*Dictionnaire apologétique de la foi catholique,* Paris, 1889; 4th ed., 1909–1931
DB	*Dictionnaire de la Bible,* Paris, 1895–1928
DBS	*Dictionnaire de la Bible. Supplément,* Paris, 1928–
DBW	*Dietrich Bonhoeffer, Werke,* ed. E. Bethge *et al.*, Munich, 1986–
DC	*Documentation Catholique,* Paris: 1919–
DCO	*Conciliorum oecumenicorum Decreta; Les Conciles Oecuméniques,* II, 1 and 2. *Les Décrets.* ed. Albergio, Paris, 1994 (trans. of *COD*)
DCTh	*Dictionnaire critique de théologie.* ed. Jean-Yves Lacoste, Paris, 1998; 2nd revised ed., 1999
DDC	*Dictionnaire de droit canonique,* Paris, 1924–1965
DEB	*Dictionnaire encyclopédique de la Bible,* Turnhout, 2 vols., 1956–1987
DECA	*Dictionnaire encyclopédique du christianisme ancien.* ed. A. di Bernardino, Paris, 2 vols., 1990. (Trans. of *DPAC*)
DEPhM	*Dictionnaire d'éthique et de philosophie morale,* edited by M. Canto Sperber, Paris, 1996
DH	*Enchiridion Symbolorum.* Eds. H. Denzinger and P. Hunerman, Fribourg, 37th ed., 1991
DHGE	*Dictionnaire d'histoire et de géographie ecclésiastiques.* Paris, 1912–
DHOP	Dissertationes historicae. Institutum historicum FF. Praedicatorum, Rome, etc., 1931–
DJD	*Discoveries in the Judean Desert,* Oxford, 1955–
DK	*Die Fragmente der Vorsokratiker,* eds. H. Diels and W. Kranz, Berlin, 1903; 13th ed., 1972 (= *FVS*)
DMA	*Dictionary of the Middle Ages,* ed. R. Strayer, New York, 1982–
DoC	*Doctor Communis,* Rome, 1948–
Doc.-épisc.	*Documents-épiscopat,* Bulletin du secrétariat de la Conférence des évêques de France, Paris, 1965–
DOP	*Dumbarton Oaks Papers,* Cambridge, Mass., 1941–
DOPol	*Dictionnaire des oeuvres politiques,* Paris, 1986
DPAC	*Dizionario patristico e di antichità cristiane,* edited by A. di Berardino, Casale Monferrato, 1–3, 1983–1988 (French trans. *DECA*)
DPhP	*Dictionnaire de philosophie politique,* eds. Ph. Raynaud and St. Rials, Paris, 1997
DR	*Downside Review,* Bath, 1880–
DS	*Enchiridion Symbolorum,* eds. H. Denzinger and A. Schönmetzer, Freiburg, 36th ed., 1976
DSp	*Dictionnaire de spiritualité ascétique et mystique,* Paris, 1932–1995
DT	*Divus Thomas. Jahrbuch für Philosophie und spekulative Theologie,* Fribourg, 1914–1953
DT(P)	*Divus Thomas. Commentarium de philosophia et theologia,* Plaisance, 1880–
DTF	*Dizionario di Teologia Fondamentale,* eds. R. Latourelle et R. Fisichella, Assisi, 1990. (*Dictionnaire de Théologie Fondamentale,* Paris, 1992)
DThC	*Dictionnaire de Théologie Catholique,* Paris, 1–15, 1903–1950 + tables 1–3, 1951–1972
Dumeige	*La Foi Catholique,* G. Dumeige, Paris, 1975
DViv	*Dieu Vivant,* Paris, 1945–1955
EAug	Études augustiniennes, Paris, 1954– (Studies on Augustine)
EBT	*Encyclopedia of Biblical Theology,* London, 1970, etc. (Eng. ed. of *BThW*)
ECQ	*Eastern Churches Quarterly,* Ramsgate, 1936–1964 (= *OiC,* 1965–)
ECR	*Eastern Churches Review,* Oxford, 1966–1978
EdF	Erträge der Forschung, Darmstadt, 1970–
EE	Estudios ecclesiásticos, Madrid, 1922–
EeT	*Église et théologie,* Paris, 1958–1962 (= *BFLTP,* 1934–1958)
EETS	Early English Text Society, London, 1864–
EFV	*Enchiridion fontium valdensium,* Torre Pelice, 1958

EI(F) — *Encyclopedia of Islam,* French ed, Leyden. 1913–1936; new ed. 1954–
EJ — *Encyclopaedia Judaica,* Jerusalem 1–16, 1971; 17, 1982–
EKK — Evangelisch-katholischer Kommentar zum Neuen Testament, Neukirchen, 1975–
EKL — *Evangelisches Kirchenlexikon,* Göttingen, 1956–1961; 2nd ed., 1961–1962; 3rd ed., 1986–1997
EN — *Ethica nicomachea* Aristotle
En. Ps. — *Enarrationes in Psalmos,* Augustine
EnchB — *Enchiridion Biblicum,* Rome, 1927; 4th ed., 1961
EnchP — *Enchiridion patristicum,* M.J. Rouët de Journel, Fribourg, 1911; 25th ed., 1981
EncProt — *Encyclopédie du Protestantisme,* edited by P. Gisel, Paris-Geneva, 1995
EncRel(E) — *The Encyclopedia of Religion,* edited by M. Eliade, New York, 1–16, 1987
EncRel(I) — *Enciclopedia delle religioni,* edited by M. Gozzini, Florence, 1970–1976
Enn. — *Enneads,* Plotinus
EO — *Ecclesia orans.* Periodica de scientiis liturgicis, Rome, 1984–
EOr — *Échos d'Orient,* Bucharest, 1897/1898–1942/1943 (= *EtByz,* 1943–1946; *REByz,* 1946–)
Eos — Eos. Commentarii societatis philologae Polonorum, Wroclaw, etc., 1894–
Eph — *Études philosophiques,* Paris, 1927–
EPRO — Études préliminaires aux religions orientales dans l'Empire romain, Leyden, 1961–
ER — *Ecumenical Review,* Lausanne, 1948–
ErIs — *Eretz Israel,* Jerusalem, 1951–
EstB — *Estudios biblicos,* Madrid, 1929–
EStL — *Evangelisches Staatslexikon,* Stuttgart, 3rd ed., 1987
EstLul — *Estudios lulianos,* Palma de Mallorca, 1957–
EtB — Études bibliques, Paris, 1903–
EtCarm — *Études carmélitaines,* Paris, 1911–1964
Eth. à Nic. — *Ethica nicomachea,* Aristotle (Éthique à Nicomaque; Nichomachean Ethics)
Éthique — *Éthique. La vie en question,* Paris, 1991–1996 (22 issues)
EthL — *Ephemerides theologicae Lovanienses,* Louvain, etc., 1924–
EtMar — *Études mariales,* Paris, 1947–
ETR — *Études théologiques et religieuses,* Montpellier, 1926–
EU — *Encyclopaedia Universalis,* Paris, 1968–1986, 1985–1988
EvTh — *Evangelische Theologie,* Munich, 1934–1938; NS, 1946/1947–
EWNT — *Exegetisches Wörterbuch zum Neuen Testament,* Stuttgart, etc., 1–3, 1980–1983
FEL — La foi des Églises luthériennes: confessions et catéchismes, eds. A. Birmele and M. Lienhard, Paris-Geneva, 1991 (*BSLK* Göttingen)
FOP — Faith and Order Paper(s), World Council of Churches, Geneva, NS, 1949–
FKTh — *Forum katholische Theologie,* Aschaffenburg, 1985–
FRLANT — Forschungen zur Religion und Literatur des Alten und Neuen Testaments, Göttingen, 1903–
FrSA — *Fransciscan Studies Annual,* St. Bonaventure, NY, 1963– (= *FrS,* 1924–1962)
FS — Franziskanische Studien, Münster, etc., 1914–
FS.B — —Beiheft, 1915–
FSÖTh — Forschungen zur systematischen und ökumenischen Theologie, Göttingen, 1962–
FThSt — Freiburger theologische Studien, Fribourg, 1910–
FTS — Frankfurter theologische Studien, Frankfurt, 1969–
FV — *Foi et Vie,* Paris, 1898–
FVS — *Die Fragmente der Vorsokratiker,* eds. H. Diels and W. Kranz, Berlin, 1903; 13th ed., 1972 (= *DK*)
FZPhTh — *Freiburger Zeitschrift für Philosophie und Theologie,* Freibourg (Switzerland), 1954–
GCFI — *Giornale critico della filosofia italiana,* Florence, etc., 1920–
GCS — Die griechischen christlichen Schriftsteller der ersten drei Jahrhunderte, Berlin, 1897–
GNO — *Gregorii Nysseni Opera,* ed. Werner Jaeger, Berlin then Leiden (= Jaeger), 1921
GOTR — *Greek Orthodox Theological Review,* Brookline (Mass.), 1954–
Gr — *Gregorianum,* Rome, 1920–
GRBS — Greek, Roman and Byzantine Studies, Cambridge, Mass., 1958–

Grundfr. syst. Th. *Grundfragen systematischer Theologie,* W. Pannenberg, Göttingen, 1967, vol 2, 1980
GS Germanische Studien, Berlin, etc., 1919–
GuV *Glauben und Verstehen, Gesammelte Aufsätze,* R. Bultmann, 4 vol., Tübingen, 1933–1965
GVEDL Die geltenden Verfassungsgesetze der evangelisch-deutschen Landeskirchen, edited by Emil Friedberg, Fribourg, 1885 and suppl. 1–4, 1888–1904
HadSt *Haddock Studies,* Moulinsart, 1953–
Hahn see *BSGR*
HBT *Horizons in Biblical Theology,* Pittsburg, Pa, 1979–
HCO *Histoire des conciles œcuméniques,* ed. G. Dumeige, Paris, 1962–
HDG *Handbuch der Dogmengeschichte,* edited by M. Schmaus, A. Grillmeier, *et al.,* Fribourg, etc., 1951–
HDThG *Handbuch der Dogmen- und Theologiegeschichte,* edited by C. Andresen, Göttingen, 1982–1984
HE *Historia ecclesiastica.* Eusebius
Hermes *Hermes. Zeitschrift für klassische Philologie,* Wiesbaden, 1866–1944, 1952–
HeyJ *Heythrop Journal,* Oxford then London, 1960–
HFTh *Handbuch der Fundamentaltheologie,* edited by W. Kern *et al.,* 4 vol., Fribourg, 1985–1988
Hier. eccl. *Hiérarchie ecclésiastique (Ecclesiastica hierarchia)*
HistDog *Histoire des dogmes,* Paris, 1953–1971 (unfinished trans. by *HDG*)
HJ *Historisches Jahrbuch der Görresgesellschaft,* Munich, etc., 1880–
HKG(J) *Handbuch der Kirchengeschichte,* edited by H. Jedin, Fribourg, etc., 1962–1979
HMO *Handbook of Metaphysics and Ontology,* eds. H. Burkhardt and B. Smith, Munich-Philadelphia-Vienna, 1991
HST *Handbuch systematischer Theologie,* Gütersloh, 1979–
HThK Herders theologisches Kommentar zum Neuen Testament, Fribourg, 1953–
HThR *Harvard Theological Review,* Cambridge, Mass., 1908–
HThS Harvard Theological Studies, Cambridge, Mass., 1916–
HTTL *Herders theologisches Taschenlexikon,* edited by K. Rahner, 8 vol., Fribourg, 1972–1973
HUCA *Hebrew Union College Annual,* Cincinnati, Ohio, 1924–
HWP *Historisches Wörterbuch der Philosophie,* Basel-Stuttgart, 1971–
HZ *Historische Zeitschrift,* Munich, etc., 1859–
IDB *The Interpreter's Dictionary of the Bible,* New York, 1/4, 1962 +suppl., 1976
IkaZ *Internationale katholische Zeitschrift Communio,* Frankfurt, 1972–
IKZ *Internationale kirchliche Zeitschrift. Revue Internationale ecclésiastique. International Church Review,* Berne, 1911–
In Sent. *Commentary on the Sentences*
Inst. *Institutes of the Christian Religion,* Calvin
Irén Irénikon, Chèvetogne, etc., 1926–
Ist *Istina,* Boulogne-sur-Seine, etc., 1954–
JAAR *Journal of the American Academy of Religion,* Boston, Mass., etc., 1967–
JAC *Jahrbuch für Antike und Christentum,* Münster, 1958–
JAC.E *—Ergänzungsband,* 1964–
Jaeger *Gregorii Nysseni Opera,* ed. W. Jaeger, Berlin then Leyden (= *GNO*), 1921–
JBL *Journal of Biblical Literature,* Philadelphia, Pa., 1890–
JCSW *Jahrbuch für christliche Sozialwissenschaften,* Münster, 1968–
JEH *Journal of Ecclesiastical History,* London, etc., 1950–
JES *Journal of Ecumenical Studies,* Philadelphia, etc., 1964–
JHI *Journal of the History of Ideas,* New York, etc., 1940–
JJS *Journal of Jewish Studies,* London, 1948–
JLW *Jahrbuch für Liturgiewissenschaft,* Münster, 1921–1941
JÖBG *Jahrbuch der österreichischen byzantinischen Gesellschaft,* Vienna, etc., 1951–1968 (= *JÖB,* 1969–)
JRE *Journal of Religious Ethics,* Waterloo, Ont., etc., 1973–
JSNTSS *Journal for the Study of the New Testament,* Supplement series, Sheffield, 1980–

JSOT	*Journal for the Study of the Old Testament,* Sheffield, 1976–
JSOT.S	—Supplements Series, 1976–
JSPE.*S*	Journal for the Study of the Pseudepigrapha. Supplement series, Sheffield, 1987–
JThS	*Journal of Theological Studies,* Oxford, etc., 1899–1949; NS, 1950–
KD	*Die Kirchliche dogmatik,* K. Barth, Zollikon-Zurich, vol. I to IV, 1932–1967 + Index, 1970 (*Dogmatique,* 26 vol., Geneva, 1953–1974, + Index, 1980)
KiKonf	Kirche und Konfession, Göttingen, 1962–
Kirch	*Enchiridion fontium historiae ecclesiasticae,* ed. C. Kirch, Freibourg, 1910; 6th ed., 1947
KKD	*Kleine Katholische Dogmatik,* edited by J. Auer and J. Ratzinger, Ratisbonne, 1978–1988
KJ	*Kirchliches Jahrbuch für die Evangelische Kirche in Deutschland,* Gütersloh, 1900– (= *ThJb,* 1873–1899)
KL	*Kirchenlexikon oder Encyklopädie der katholischen Theologie und ihrer Hilfswissenschaften,* edited by H. J. Wetzer and B. Welte, Fribourg, 1847–1860; 2nd ed., 1882–1903
Kotter	*Die Schriften des Johannes von Damaskus,* ed. B. Kotter, Berlin, 1969–
KrV	*Kritik der reinenVErnunft,* Kant
KSA	*Kritische Studienausgabe,* Nietzsche; edited by Colli and Montinari, ed. minor
KuD	*Kerygma und Dogma,* Göttingen, 1955–
Lat	Lateranum, Rome, NS, 1935–
LCL	Loeb Classical Library, London, 1912–
LeDiv	Lectio divina, Paris, 1946–
Leit	*Leiturgia. Handbuch des evangelischen Gottesdienstes,* Kassel, 1952–1970
Liddell-Scott	*A Greek-English Lexicon,* Liddell-Scott-Jones, Oxford
LJ	*Liturgisches Jahrbuch,* Münster, 1951–
LNPh	*Les notions philosophiques,* edited by S. Auroux, vol. II of the *Encyclopédie philosophique universelle,* edited by A. Jacob, Paris, 2 vol., 1990
LO	Lex orandi, Paris, 1944–
LouvSt	*Louvain Studies,* Louvain, 1966/1967–
LR	*Lutherische Rundschau,* Stuttgart, etc., 1951–1977
LSEO	Libri symbolici Ecclesiae orientalis, ed. E. J. Kimmel, Iéna, 1843; 2nd ed., 1850
LThK	*Lexikon für Theologie und Kirche,* Fribourg-Basel-Vienna, 1930–1938; 2nd ed., 1957–1967; 3rd ed., 1993
LTP	*Laval théologique et philosophique,* Quebec, 1944/1945–
LuJ	*Luther-Jahrbuch,* Leipzig, etc., 1919–
LV(L)	*Lumière et vie,* Lyon, 1951–
LWF.R	*Lutheran World Federation Report,* 1978–
Mansi	*Sacrorum conciliorum nova et amplissima collectio,* edited by J. D. Mansi, Florence, 1759–1827; Paris-Leipzig, 1901–1927
Mar.	*Marianum. Ephemerides Mariologiae,* Rome, 1939–
Maria	*Maria. Études sur la Sainte Vierge,* edited by H. du Manoir, 8 vol., Paris, 1949–1971
MCS	Monumenta christiana selecta, Tournai, etc., 1954–
MD	*La Maison-Dieu. Revue de pastorale liturgique,* Paris, 1945–
MDom	*Memorie Domenicane,* Florence, etc., NS, 1970–
MethH	*Methodist History,* Lake Junaluska, NC, 1962–
MF	*Miscellanea francescana,* Rome, etc., 1936– (= *MFS,* 1886–1935)
MFEO	Monumenta fidei Ecclesiae orientalis, ed. H. J. C. Weissenborn, Iéna, 1850
MFCG	Mitteilungen und Forschungsbeiträge der Cusanus-Gesellschaft, Mainz, 1961–
MGH	Monumenta Germaniae historica inde ab a. C. 500 usque ad a. 1500, Hanover, etc.
MGH.Conc	—Concilia, 1893–
MGH.Ep	—Epistolae, 1887–
MGH.L	—Leges, 1835–1889
MHP	*Miscellanea historiae pontificae,* Rome, 1939–
MHSJ	Monumenta historica Societatis Jesu, Rome, etc., 1894–
MiHiEc	*Miscellanea historiae ecclesiasticae,* Congrès... de Louvain, 1960–
ML.T	Museum Lessianum. Theological section, Bruxelles, 1922–

MM Miscellanea mediaevalia, Berlin, etc., 1962–
MS *Mediaeval Studies,* Toronto, 1939–
MSR *Mélanges de science religieuse,* Lille, 1944–
MSSNTS Monograph Series. Society for New Testament Studies, Cambridge, 1965–
MThZ *Münchener theologische Zeitschrift,* Munich, etc., 1950–1984
MySal *Mysterium Salutis,* Grundriß heilsgeschichtlicher Dogmatik, vol. I to V, edited by J. Feiner and M. Löhrer, Einsiedeln, etc., 1965–1976 + supplements, 1981, etc. (*Dogmatique de l'histoire du salut,* vol. I–III/2 and IV/1 (p. 457–599), 14 vol., 1969–1975)
NBL *Neues Bibel-Lexikon,* Zurich, 1991
NCE *New Catholic Encyclopaedia,* New York, 1967–1979
NHThG *Neues Handbuch Theologischer Grundbegriffe,* edited by P. Eicher, 2nd ed. augm., Freibourg-Basel-Vienna, 1991
Not *Notitiae. Commentarii ad nuntia et studia de re liturgica,* Vatican City, 1975–
NRTh *Nouvelle revue théologique,* Louvain, 1869–1940; 1945–
NSchol *New Scholasticism,* Washington D.C., 1927–
NStB Neukirchener Studienbücher, Neukirchen, 1962–
NT *Novum Testamentum,* Leyden, 1956–
NTA Neutestamentliche Abhandlungen, Münster, 1908–
NTS *New Testament Studies,* Cambridge, 1954–
NTTS New Testament Tools and Studies, Leyden, 1960–
Numen *Numen. International Review for the History of Religions,* Leyden, 1954–
NV *Nova et vetera,* Geneva, 1926–
OBO Orbis biblicus et orientalis, Fribourg (Switzerland), 1973–
OCA Orientalia christiana analecta, Rome, 1935–
OCP *Orientalia christiana periodica,* Rome, 1935–
Oec. *Œcumenica. Jahrbuch für ökumenische Forschung,* Gütersloh, etc., 1966–1971/1972
ODCC *Oxford Dictionary of the Christian Church,* edited by F.L. Cross, London, 1957; 2nd ed., 1974 (F.L. Cross and E.A. Livingstone); 3rd ed. rev. and augm., 1997 (by E.A. Livingstone)
OED *The Oxford English Dictionary*
OGE *Ons geestelijk erf,* Anvers, etc., 1927–
OiC *One in Christ,* London, 1965–
OR *L'Osservatore romano,* Vatican City, 1849–
ÖR *Ökumenische Rundschau,* Stuttgart, 1952–
Or. *Orientalia,* Rome, 1920–
OrChr *Oriens Christianus,* Rome, 1901–
OrChrA see OCA
OrChrP see *OCP*
OS Ostkirchliche Studien, Würzburg, 1952–
OstKSt *Ostkirchliche Studien,* Würzburg, 1952–
ÖTh Ökumenische Theologie, Zurich, etc., 1978–
OTS Oudtestamentische Studien, Leyden, etc., 1942–
Par. Paradosis. Études de littérature et de théologie ancienne, Fribourg (Switzerland), 1947–
PAS *Proceedings of the Aristotelian Society,* London, 1887; NS, 1900/1901–
PatSor Patristica Sorbonensia, Paris, 1957–
PG Patrologia Graeca, ed. J.-P. Migne, Paris, 1857–1866
PGL *Patristic Greek Lexicon,* ed. G.W.H. Lampe, Oxford, 1961–1968
Ph *Philologus. Zeitschrift für das klassische Altertum,* Wiesbaden, etc., 1846–
Phil. *Philosophy,* London, 1916–
PhJ *Philosophisches Jahrbuch der Görres-Gesellschaft,* Fulda, etc., 1888–
PiLi Pietas liturgica. Studia, St. Ottilien, 1983–
PL Patrologia Latina, ed. J.-P. Migne, Paris, 1841–1864
PLS Patrologiae Latinae supplementum, Paris, 1958–1970
PO Patrologia Orientalis, Paris, etc., 1907–
POC *Proche-Orient chrétien,* Jerusalem, 1951–
PosLuth *Positions luthériennes,* Paris, 1953–
PoTh Point théologique, Institut catholique de Paris, 1971–
PPR *Philosophy and Phenomenological Research,* Buffalo, NY, 1940/1941–
PRMCL *Periodica de re morali,* canonica, liturgica, Rome, 1907–

PuN	*Pietismus und Neuzeit,* Göttingen, 1974–
PTS	Patristische Texte und Studien, Berlin, 1964–
QD	Quaestiones Disputatae, Fribourg-Basel-Vienna, 1958–
QFRG	*Quellen und Forschungen zur Reformationsgeschichte,* Gütersloh 1921–, includes *QGT*
QGT	*Quellen zur Geschichte der Taüfer,* Gütersloh 1951–
QRT	*Quaker religious Thought,* New Haven, Conn., 1959–
Qschr	*Quartalschrift,* Milwaukee, Wis., 1947–
QuLi	*Questions liturgiques,* Louvain, 1910–
RAC	*Reallexikon für Antike und Christentum,* Stuttgart, 1950–
RAM	*Revue d'ascétique et de mystique,* Toulouse, 1920–1971
RB	*Revue biblique,* Paris, 1892–1894; NS, 1915–
RBen	*Revue bénédictine de critique, d'histoire et de littérature religieuses,* Maredsous, 1890–
RDC	*Revue de droit canonique,* Strasbourg, 1951–
RDCCIF	Recherches et débats du Centre catholique des intellectuels français, Paris, 1948–1952; NS, 1952–1980
RdQ	*Revue de Qumrân,* Paris, 1958–
RE	*Realencyklopädie für protestantische Theologie und Kirche,* Gotha, 3rd ed., 1896–1913
REAug	*Revue des études augustiniennes,* Paris, 1955– (= *AThA,* 1951–1954)
REByz	*Revue des études byzantines,* Paris, 1946–
RECA	*Real-Encyclopädie der classischen Altertumswissenschaft,* edited by A. Pauly, Stuttgart, 1839–1852
RechAug	*Recherches augustiniennes*, Paris, 1958–
RechBib	Recherches bibliques, Bruges, etc., 1954–
RecL	*Revue ecclésiastique de Liège,* Liège, 1905–1967
REG	*Revue des études grecques,* Paris, 1888–
REL	*Revue des études latines,* Paris, 1923–
RelSt	*Religious Studies,* London, etc., 1965/1966–
RET	*Revista española de teología,* Madrid, 1940–
RevBib	*Revista biblica,* Buenos Aires, 1939–
RevPhil	*Revue de philosophie,* Paris, 1900–1940
RevSR	*Revue des sciences religieuses,* Strasbourg, 1921–
RFNS	*Rivista di filosofia neoscolastica,* Milan, 1909–
RGG	*Die Religion in Geschichte und Gegenwart,* Tübingen, 1909–1913; 2nd ed., 1927–1932; 3rd ed., 1956–1965
RH	*Revue historique,* Paris, 1876–
RHDF	*Revue historique de droit français et étranger,* Paris, 1855–1869; 1922–
RHE	*Revue d'histoire ecclésiastique,* Louvain, 1900–
RHEF	*Revue de l'histoire de l'Église de France,* Paris, 1910–
RHMo	*Revue d'histoire moderne,* Paris, 1926–1940 (= 1899–1914, 1954–, *RHMC*)
RHMC	*Revue d'histoire moderne et contemporaine,* Paris, 1899–1914, 1954– (= 1926–1940, *RHMo*)
RHPhR	*Revue d'histoire et de philosophie religieuses,* Strasbourg, etc., 1921–
RHR	*Revue de l'histoire des religions,* Paris, 1880
RHSp	*Revue d'histoire de la spiritualité,* Paris, 1972–1977
RHT	*Revue d'histoire des textes,* Paris, 1971– (= *BIRHT*)
RICP	*Revue de l'Institut catholique de Paris,* Paris, 1896–1910 (= *BICP,* 1910–)
RIPh	*Revue Internationale de Philosophie,* Bruxelles, 1938–
RITh	*Revue internationale de théologie,* Berne, 1893–1910
RivBib	*Rivista biblica,* Rome, 1953–
RLT	*Rassegna di letteratura tomistica,* Naples, 1966–
RMAL	*Revue du Moyen Age latin,* Paris, etc., 1945–
RMM	*Revue de métaphysique et de morale,* Paris, 1893–
ROC	*Revue de l'Orient chrétien,* Paris, 1896–1936
RPFE	*Revue Philosophique de la France et de l'étranger,* Paris, 1876–
RPL	*Revue philosophique de Louvain,* Louvain, etc., 1946–
RSF	*Rivista di storia della filosofia,* Rome, 1946; NS, 1984–

RSHum — *Revue des sciences humaines,* Lille, NS, 45, 1947–
RSLR — *Rivista di storia e letteratura religiosa,* Florence, 1965–
RSPhTh — *Revue des sciences philosophiques et théologiques,* Paris, 1907–
RSR — *Recherches de science religieuse,* Paris, 1910–
RThAM — *Recherches de théologie ancienne et médiévale,* Louvain, 1929–
RThom — *Revue thomiste,* Bruges, etc., Toulouse, 1893–
RThPh — *Revue de théologie et de philosophie,* Lausanne, 1868–1911; 3rd ser., 1951–
RTL — *Revue théologique de Louvain,* Louvain, 1970–
RTLu — *Revue théologique de Lugano,* Facoltà di teologia di Lugano, 1996–
Sal — *Salesianum,* Turin, 1939
SBAB — Stuttgarter biblische Aufsatzbände, Stuttgart, 1988–
SBi — Sources Bibliques, Paris, 1963–
SBS — Stuttgarter Bibelstudien, Stuttgart, 1965–
SC — Sources Chrétiennes, Paris, 1941–
ScC — *Scuola Cattolica,* Milan, 1873, 6th ser., 1923–
SCA — Studies in Christian Antiquity, Washington, D.C., 1941–
SCE — *Studies in Christian Ethics,* Edinburgh, 1988–
ScEc — *Sciences écclesiastiques: Revue philosophique et théologique,* Bruges, 1948–1967 (= *ScEs,* 1968–)
ScEs — *Science et esprit,* Bruges, 1968–
SCH(L) — Studies in Church History, London, 1964–
Schol. — *Scholastik. Vierteljahresschrift fur Theologie und Philosophie.* Fribourg, 1926–1965 (= *ThPh,* 1966–)
Schr.zur Th. — *Schriften zur Theologie,* K. Rahner. Einsiedeln-Zürich-Cologne, 1954–1983
SE — *Sacris erudiri,* Steenbrugge, etc., 1948–
SecCent — *The Second Century.* Abilene, Tex., 1981
SémBib — *Sémiotique et Bible,* Lyon, 1975–
Semeia — *Semeia.* An Experimental Journal for Biblical Criticism. Atlanta, Ga, 1974–
SemSup — Semeia Supplements. Philadelphia, Pa., etc., 1975–
Sent. — *Sententiarum Libri IV,* Peter Lombard
SESJ — Suomen Eksegeettisen Seuran julkaisuja. Helsinki, 1966–
SHCSR — *Spicilegium historicum Congregationis SSmi Redemptoris.* Rome, 1953–
SHCT — Studies in the History of Christian Thought. Leyden, 1966–
SJP — *Salzburger Jahrbuch für Philosophie und Psychologie,* Salzburg, 1957–
SJTh — *Scottish Journal of Theology.* Edinburgh, 1948–
SKG — Schriften der Königsberger Gelehrten Gesellschaft. Halle
SKG.G — —Geisteswissenschaftliche Klasse, 1924–1944
SM (D) — *Sacramentum Mundi. Theologisches Lexikon für die Praxis.* ed. K. Rahner. Fribourg, 1967–1969
SM (E) — *Sacramentum Mundi. An Encyclopedia of Theology.* New York, 1968–1970
SO — Symbolae Osloenses. Oslo, 1923–
Sob — *Sobornost.* London, 1979–
Sommervogel — Bibliothèque de la Compagnie de Jésus, new edition by C. Sommervogel, Bruxelles, 1890–1930; 3rd ed., 1960–1963
SOr — Sources orientales. Paris, 1959–
SPAMP — Studien zur Problemgeschichte der antiken und mittelalterlichen Philosophie, Leyden, 1966–
SpOr — Spiritualité orientale, Bégrolles-en-Mauges, 1966–
SSL — Spicilegium sacrum Lovaniense, Louvain, 1922–
SST — *Studies in Sacred Theology.* Washington, D.C., 1895–1947; 2nd ser. 1947–
ST — *Summa Theologica,* Thomas Aquinas
StA — *Werke in Auswahl* (Studien Ausgabe), P. Melanchthon, edited by R. Stupperich, Gütersloh, 1951–1955
StAns — Studia Anselmiana. Rome, 1933–
StANT — Studien zum Alten und Neuen Testament. Munich, 1960–1975
StCan — *Studia Canonica,* Ottawa, 1967–
StEv — Studia Evangelica, Berlin, 1959–1982 (= TU 73, etc.)
StGen — *Studium Generale,* Berlin, 1947–1971
STGMA — Studien und Texte zur Geistesgeschichte des Mittelalters, Leyden, 1950–
StMed — *Studi medievali,* Turin, etc.; NS, 1960–
StMiss — *Studia missionalia.* Rome, 1943
StMor — *Studia moralia,* Rome, 1963–

STMP	Studia theologiae moralis et pastoralis, Salzburg, 1956–
StPatr	Studia patristica, Berlin, 1957–
StPh	*Studia philosophica,* Basel, 1946–
STPIMS	Studies and texts, Pontifical Institute of Mediaeval Studies, Toronto, 1955–
Strom.	*Stromata,* Clement of Alexandria
StSS	Studia scholastico-scotistica. Rome, 1968–
StT	Studi e testi, Biblioteca Apostolica Vaticana, Vatican City, 1900–
StTom	Studi tomistici, Vatican City, 1974–MMMM
StZ	*Stimmen der Zeit,* Fribourg, 1914–
SVF	*Stoicorum Veterum Fragmenta,* ed. J. von Arnim, Stuttgart. 3 vol. + index, 1903–1924, etc.
SVTQ	*St. Vladimir's Theological Quarterly,* New York, 1969–
Symb. Ath.	Symbol of Athanasius
TAPhS	*Transactions of the American Philosophical Society,* Philadelphia, Pa, 1769–1809; NS, 1818–
TDNT	*Theological Dictionary of the New Testament,* Grand Rapids, Mich., 1964–1977 (trans. of *ThWNT*)
TEH	Theologische Existenz heute, edited by K. Barth *et al.*, Munich, 1933–1941; NS, 1946–
TFil	*Tijdschrift voor filosofie.* Louvain, 1962– (= *TPh,* 1939–1961)
THAT	*Theologisches Handwörterbuch zum Alten Testament,* ed. E. Jenni and C. Westermann, Munich, 1971–1976
Theos. H.	*Theosophical History.* A Quarterly Journal of Research, London, 1985–1989; Fullerton, Calif., 1990–
ThGl	*Theologie und Glaube,* Paderborn, 1909–
ThH	Théologie historique, Paris, 1963–
ThJb	*Theologisches Jahrbuch,* Gütersloh, 1873–1899 (= *KJ,* 1900–)
ThJb(L)	*Theologisches Jahrbuch.* Leipzig, 1957–
ThLZ	*Theologische Literaturzeitung,* Leipzig, 1876–
Thom	*Thomist,* Washington, D.C., 1939–
ThPh	*Theologie und Philosophie,* Fribourg, 1966–
THPQ	*Theologisch-praktische Quartalschrift,* Linz, 1848–
ThQ	*Theologische Quartalschrift,* Tübingen, etc., 1819– (1960–1968 = *TThQ*)
ThR	*Theologische Rundschau.* Tübingen, 1897–1917; NF 1929–
ThSt(B)	Theologische Studien, edited by K. Barth *et al.*, Zurich, 1938–
ThTo	*Theology Today.* Princeton, N.J., etc., 1944/1945–
ThW	*Theologische Wissenschaft,* Stuttgart, etc., 1972–
ThWA	*Theorie Werkausgabe,* Hegel, Frankfurt, 1970, 20 vols.
ThWAT	*Theologisches Wörterbuch zum Alten Testament,* edited by G. J. Botterweck and H. Ringgren, Stuttgart, etc., 1973–
ThWNT	*Theologisches Wörterbuch zum Neuen Testament,* edited by G. Kittel, Stuttgart, 1933–1979
ThZ	*Theologische Zeitschrift,* Basel, 1945–
TKTG	Texte zur Kirchen und Theologiegeschichte, Gütersloh, 1966–
TOB	Traduction oecuménique de la Bible
TPh	*Tijdschrift voor philosophie,* Louvain, 1939–1961 (= *Tfil,* 1962–)
Tr	Traditio. Studies in Ancient and Medieval History, Thought and Religion, New York, etc., 1943–
TRE	*Theologische Realenzyklopädie,* edited by G. Krause and G. Muller, Berlin, 1976–
Trin	*De Trinitate,* Augustine
TS	*Theological Studies,* Woodstock, Md., etc., 1940–
TSTP	Tubinger Studien zur Theologie und Philosophie, Mainz, 1991–
TTh	*Tijdschrift voor theologie,* Nimègue, 1961–
TThQ	*Tübinger theologische Quartalschrift,* Stuttgart, 1960–1968 (= ThQ)
TThZ	*Trierer Theologische Zeitschrift,* Trier, 1947–
TTS	Tübinger theologische Studien, Mainz, 1973–1990
TU	Texte und Untersuchungen zur Geschichte der altchrislichen Literatur, Berlin, 1882–
TuG	Theologie und Gemeinde, Munich, 1958–
UB	Urban-Bücher, Stuttgart, 1953–
UnSa	Unam Sanctam, Paris, 1937–
VC	*Verbum Caro. Revue théologique et ecclésiastique œcuménique,* Taizé, etc., 1947–1969
VerLex	*Deutsche Literatur des Mittelalters. Verfasserlexikon,* Berlin, etc, 1933–1955; 2nd ed., 1978–

VetChr — *Vetera Christianorum,* Bari, 1964–
VieCon — *Vie consacrée,* Bruxelles, 1966–
VigChr — *Vigiliae Christianae,* Amsterdam, 1947–
VS — *Vie spirituelle,* Paris, 1946–
VT — *Vetus Testamentum,* Leyden, 1951–
VT.S — —Suppl., 1953–
VThB — *Vocabulaire de théologie biblique,* edited by X. Léon-Dufour, Paris, 1962; 2nd ed., 1970
WA — *Werke. Kristiche Gesamtausgabe,* Luther (Weimarer Ausgabe), 1883–
WA.B — *—Briefwechsel,* 1930–
WA.DB — *—Deutsche Bibel,* 1906–
WA.TR — *—Tischreden,* 1912–
WBS — Wiener byzantinistische Studien, Graz, etc., 1964–
WdF — Wege der Forschung, Darmstadt, 1956–
Weischedel — *Werkausgabe,* Kant, edited by W. Weischedel, Frankfurt, 1958–1964
WMANT — Wissenschaftliche Monographien zum Alten und Neuen Testament, Neukirchen, 1960–
WSAMA.T — Walberger Studien der Albertus-Magnus-Akademie, Mainz, Theologische Reihe, 1964–
WUNT — Wissenschaftliche Untersuchungen zum Neuen Testament, Tübingen, 1950–
WuW — *Wort und Wahrheit,* Vienna, etc., 1946–1973
ZAW — *Zeitschrift für die alttestamentliche Wissenschaft und die Kunde des nachbiblischen Judentums,* Berlin, 1881–
ZDP — *Zeitschrift für deutsche Philologie,* Berlin, etc., 1869–
ZDPV — *Zeitschrift des deutschen Palästina-Vereins,* Wiesbaden, 1978–
ZevKR — *Zeitschrift für evangelisches Kirchenrecht,* Tübingen, 1951–
ZKG — *Zeitschrift für Kirchengeschichte,* Stuttgart, 1877–
ZKTh — *Zeitschrift für katholische Theologie,* Vienna, etc., 1877–
ZNW — *Zeitschrift für die neutestamentliche Wissenschaft und die Kunde der älteren Kirche,* Berlin, etc., 1900–
ZSRG.K — *Zeitschrift der Savigny-Stiftung für Rechtsgeschichte. Kanonistische Abteilung,* Weimar, 1911–
ZPE — *Zeitschrift für Papyrologie und Epigraphik,* Bonn, 1967–
ZThK — Zeitschrift für Theologie und Kirche, Tübingen, 1891–

Frankfurt = Frankfurt am Main
Fribourg = Fribourg-en-Brisgau
Fribourg-Paris = Fribourg (Switzerland)—Paris
A hyphenated date (1963–) means that the publishing is not complete or that the collection or journal is still ongoing.

Abelard, Peter

1079–1142

a) Life. Peter Abelard studied dialectics first with Roscelin de Compiègne, whose nominalism* led him to dispute the realism of William of Champeaux. After a short period of studies in theology* under Anselm of Laon, Abelard started teaching these two subjects at the cathedral school of Paris. Following the scandal of his affair with Heloise, he decided to become a monk at Saint-Denis (c. 1117). His teaching sought to lead toward theology through the study of secular authors. His first treatise on the Trinity* (*Theologia summi boni,* c. 1120) was condemned at the Council* of Soissons (1121). Between 1122 and 1127 he developed his concepts on the philosophical foundations of theology in an oratory dedicated by him to the Holy Trinity (it later became the Paraclete). In 1129, two years after becoming abbot of Saint-Gildas-de-Rhuys, he asked Heloise to transform this oratory into a monastic community. He started teaching again in Paris at the beginning of the 1130s, in the midst of controversy. In 1139 William of Saint Thierry drew Bernard* of Clairvaux's attention to a number of opinions expressed by Abelard. William accused Abelard of assigning full omnipotence only to the Father*, and thus denying that Christ* had become incarnate to free humanity from the devil. Bernard of Clairvaux took up these accusations in his turn, sent a treatise to Pope Innocent II, and succeeded in having Abelard excommunicated at the Council of Sens (1140). This excommunication was canceled thanks to the intervention of Peter the Venerable, who welcomed Abelard at Cluny and had him correct the controversial writings, thus obtaining an end to Bernard of Clairvaux's attacks.

b) Theological Contribution. Abelard's main contribution to theology is the systematic analysis of the traditional doctrines from a philosophical point of view. For him, Father, Son, and Holy* Spirit are names that signify the divine attributes* of power, wisdom*, and goodness that pagan philosophers and Jewish prophets* also recognize in their own way. He criticizes Roscelin's argument that the divine Persons* must be separate realities in order to be different from each other. He is particularly concerned for the aptitude of divine names* to create the intelligence *(intellectus)* of what they designate, according to a theme studied in his *Dialecta* and his *Logica Ingredientibus* regarding words *(voces)* in general. It is with their own specific words that the pagan philosophers gave rise to an intelligence of divinity similar to that of the prophets. Abelard suggests that the relationship between Father and Son is analogous to that existing between power and wisdom (capacity to discern), or between genus and species. His Trinitarian theology is more interested in the economy of God* in the world, above all through the Holy Spirit, than in his eternal nature. In his *Christian Theology* (1122–27) he outlines ideas on the rationality of divine action; these ideas are subsequently developed in the *Introduction* *to Theology* (*Theologia Scholarium,* started in the early 1130s). One of the most controversial theses was the idea that God cannot act any differently than he does.

On many points of his teaching, in questions regarding God, Christ, the sacraments*, or ethics*, Abelard starts from the *Sic et Non* (composed probably c. 1120–21); this list of patristic opinions, which are apparently contradictory, is preceded by a definition of his theological method. According to him it is essential always to make sure that one is not led into error by writings that are, after all, human and therefore fallible. Disagreements among the Fathers* should induce us to go all the deeper in the search for truth. In his *Dialogue* (generally dated 1140–42, but also perhaps 1125–27; Mews 1985), which is the debate of a philosopher with a Jew and a Christian about which road to take toward the Sovereign Good*, and on the nature of Good and Evil*, Abelard talks about the superiority of natural law* over written law and about the essential compatibility between the philosopher's ethical approach *(ethica)* and the Christian's theological approach *(divinitas).* But he does not give the Christian's answer regarding the road to follow in order to reach the Sovereign Good. It is only in his commentary on the Epistle to the Romans (c. 1135?) that Abelard develops the thesis that the redeeming action of Christ does not consist in freeing man from servitude to the devil, but in inspiring in him the true love* of God through the example of his life and his death. Abelard deals again with moral questions in his *Know Thyself (Scito teipsum):* sin* is no longer bad will, as in the *Dialogue* and the commentary on *Rm,* but it is the consent to bad will through contempt of God. Abelard did not write a systematic treatise on all the questions raised in the *Sic et Non,* but his students kept notes of his *Sentences,* where he addresses faith* in God and in Christ, the sacraments, and charity as the root of all ethics.

• PL 178; *Petri Abaelardi Opera,* Ed. V. Cousin, 1849 (2nd Ed. 1859), G. Olms, Hildesheim, 1970.
Philosophische Schriften, Ed. B. Geyer, BGPhMA 21, 14, 1919–33.
Scritti di Logica, Ed. M. Dal Pra, Florence, 1954 (2nd Ed., 1969).
Dialectica, Ed. L. M. de Rijk, Assen, 1956 (2nd Ed., 1970).
Historia calamitatum, Ed. J. Monfrin, Paris, 1959.
Opera theologica I–II, Ed. E. M. Buytaert, CChrCM 11–12.
III, Ed. E. M. Buytaert, C. J. Mews, CChrCM 13.
Dialogus inter Philosophum, Judaeum et Christianum, Ed. R. Thomas, Stuttgart-Bad Canstatt, 1970.
Peter Abelard's Ethics, Ed. D. E. Luscombe, Oxford, 1971.
Sic et Non, Ed. B. Boyer, R. McKeon, Chicago-London, 1976, 1977.
Des intellections, Ed. P. Morin, Paris, 1994.
♦ J. Jolivet (1969), *Arts du langage et théologie chez Abélard,* Paris (New Ed. 1982).
D. E. Luscombe (1969), *The School of Peter Abelard,* Cambridge.
R. Weingart (1970), *The Logic of Divine Love: A Critical Analysis of the Soteriology of Peter Abelard,* Oxford.
C. J. Mews (1985), "On Dating the Works of Peter Abelard," *AHDL* 52, 73–134.
J. Jolivet (1994), *Abélard ou la philosophie dans le langage,* Paris-Fribourg.
C. J. Mews (1995), *Peter Abelard,* London (bibl.).
J. Jolivet (1997), *La théologie d'Abélard,* Paris.

Constant Mews

See also **Language, Theological; Philosophy; Reason; Salvation; Tritheism**

Abortion

Scripture is silent about abortion. Along with infanticide, abortion is only obliquely related to the biblical prohibition of child sacrifice (Lv 18:21, 20:2–5; 2 Kgs 21:6) and the liability incurred by those who cause a miscarriage by brawling (Ex 21:22).

a) Jewish Antecedents and Early Christian Doctrine. The question first emerged as an issue when the Jews confronted the Hellenistic world, where both abortion and infanticide were widespread. Jewish moralists of the Diaspora began to urge parents not to abort their unwanted children, or to leave them exposed. Thus Hecataeus of Abdera (300 B.C.) (in Diodorus Siculus 40, 3, 8) writes: "[Moses] required those who dwelt in the land to rear their children" (in contrast with the Greeks who exposed unwanted newborns). Somewhat later, Pseudo-Phocylides takes up the theme (first century A.D.) (*Sentences* 184–85): "A woman should not destroy the unborn babe in her belly; nor after its birth throw it before the dogs and the vultures as a prey." Even more emphatically, Flavius Josephus (first century A.D.) (*Contra Apionem* 2, 245, 4–5) writes: "The Law ordains that all offspring are to be brought up, and forbids women either to cause abortion or to do away with the fetus. A woman convicted of this is regarded as an infanticide, because she destroys a soul and diminishes the race" (*see also* Philo of Alexandria, *Hypothetica* 7, 7.) This conviction in Hellenistic Judaism also found expression in the Septuagint. Exodus 21:22 had imposed a fine on anyone who by misadventure caused a woman to miscarry. The Greek translation required that "if the child is formed," the principle of "life for life" must be applied and the death penalty exacted.

Christianity eagerly renewed this antipathy toward abortion as part of its larger moral agenda. Christians had inherited from Israel the duty to offer communal protection to four categories of defenseless people: kinless widows and orphans, resident aliens, and the indigent poor. Christian writers quickly broadened this doctrine by extending protection to four further sets of people at risk. Beyond widowhood, the wife was now protected by Jesus' rejection of divorce (Mt 5:31–32, 19:3–15; Mk 10:1–12; Lk 16:18). The ethos of solidarity that had treated the resident alien as a neighbor was extended by Jesus' injunction to love the enemy (Rom 12:14–21; Mt 5:43–48; Lk 6:27–36). Special consideration for the pauper was now enlarged by a call to consider slaves and masters as brothers in the Lord (Philemon). And the protection for orphans took bolder form in a defense of children whose parents wanted to eliminate them: the unborn were now protected against abortion, and the newborn against infanticide.

Within a Roman rather than a Jewish cultural context, Christians came to adopt the concept of inviolability, and to apply this to the case of the abandoned child. The *Didache* (first to second century A.D.) offers the earliest Christian example: "You shall not... murder a child by abortion, kill a newborn." "Killers of children, destroyers of God's handiwork," were walking the "way of death" (2,2–3; 5,2. *See also Ep. Barn.* 19,5; 20,2).

The apologists* followed suit. Minucius Felix accuses the Romans of butchery: "You expose your own children to birds and wild beasts, or at times smother and strangle them—a pitiful way to die... and there are women who swallow drugs to stifle in their womb the burgeoning human life—committing infanticide even before they give birth to their infant" (30,1–2).

Athenagoras of Athens denied the rumor that Christians committed acts of cannibalism and slew infants to obtain blood for their eucharistic rites: "In our view, those who have recourse to methods of abortion commit murder, and they are answerable to God for this. How then could we commit such murders ourselves? The same person cannot regard that which a woman carries in her womb as a living creature, and therefore as an object of value to God, and then proceed to slay this creature once it has come forth into the light of day." Tertullian* in Rome assailed the Stoic* belief that one's first breath marks the beginning of life. To prevent the birth of a child is simply a swifter way to murder (*de anima* 38.1). The Apocalypse of Peter (Eth. 8) prescribes eternal torments for mothers who have aborted. Clement of Alexandria* writes that "women who resort to some sort of abortion drug slay not only the embryo but, along with it, all human love [*philanthropia*]" (*Paidagogos* 96). By the end of the second century it was established doctrine that abortion and infanticide were especially perverse forms of homicide.

Throughout the Christian world of the fourth century there were calls for severe church penalties against abortion. The Councils of Elvira in Spain (c. 305) and Ancyra in Galatia (314), as well as Basil* the Great in Cappadocia, Epiphanius in Cyprus, Ambrose* in Lombardy, Chrysostom* in Constantinople, and Augustine (*De nupt. et con.* 1,17) in Africa all witness to a broad repudiation of abortion. In Chrysostom's words, it was "worse than murder" (*Homiliae in Ep. Rom.* 24).

b) Developments in Discipline and Doctrine. Since antiquity had no knowledge of the female ovum, it was thought that reproduction followed solely from the planting of the male seed, which then germinated and grew. Augustine's supposition (based on Aristotle's biology), that the beginning of life came only after the embryo had developed to some degree, justified continued speculation that fetal life began sometime after intercourse. This theory had practical consequences. If the youngest unborn were not yet humans then the disciplinary penalties for early abortion might be justifiably more lenient. Some canonists, including Gratian (1160) (C.J.C. i 1121–22) and Innocent III (1216) (C.J.C. ii 81) began to reserve the charge of homicide for later abortion—that is, abortion procured after the "infusion" of the human soul. Others, such as Raymond of Penafort (†1275) (C.J.C. ii 794) dissented. Since abortion was a capital offense before the civil courts, where the rules of evidence were correspondingly rigorous, it was commonly pled in the ecclesiastical courts, where sworn testimony was accepted and where there was a quite different penitential discipline.

This development in church discipline influenced theologians, and the idea of delayed ensoulment was taken up by Peter Lombard (†1160) (4,31,11), Bonaventure* (†1274) (in lib. iv *Sent.* 31, dub.4) and Thomas* Aquinas (*Sent.* 3, 3, 1.5 a.2, ST 2a 2ae 64, 8, ad2). It was only a question of deciding whether abortion could be regarded as homicide in a formal sense, though it was believed that abortion at any time was seriously sinful in intent and effect. By the 17th century opinion had turned away from the Aristotelian theory of delayed ensoulment in favor of believing that the soul was present from the moment of conception. These were the terms of the discussion that was pursued by casuists, from the 17th to the 19th century.

c) 19th and 20th Centuries. The existence of the female ovum was scientifically established in 1827, and by 1875 it had been proved that conception involves the joining of onc gamete from each parent. This effectively quieted speculation about any later moment when the human fetus might undergo substantial change.

In the meantime another question arose: if an early pregnancy threatened inevitable death to both mother and non-viable child, would it be licit (perhaps dutiful) to save at least the mother by dismembering and removing her doomed child? The principle of double effect seemed unworkable, yet many theologians pursued an intuitive conviction that removing a child from the mother would be justified if it could not be saved and if her life could thus be spared. Others sympathized, but could not bring themselves to acquiesce in what seemed to be direct killing. When the question was formally proposed to the Vatican's Holy Office, the reply was hedged: it "could not safely be taught."

The Vatican then took the doctrinal initiative in abortion-related questions. In 1869 Pius IX removed an old restriction that withheld excommunication if the fetus were not yet "ensouled." In *Casti Connubii* (1930) he condemned all abortion and denied that any necessity could justify direct killing.

After World War II Japan adopted a population policy with abortion as a principal means of birth control. Throughout the Communist bloc, abortion was legalized, and indeed was often enforced when state population policy took an antinatal turn. In 1968 Planned Parenthood-World Federation reversed prior policy and approved of using abortion to curb population growth. Within 20 years, and despite various legal conditions, most industrial countries had adopted what was in effect abortion on demand.

Sympathy for feminism, as well as fears about population growth, led some Christian denominations to accept abortion as a moral and legal liberty rightfully due to women. The issue intensified when medical scientists began calling for tissues and organs obtained through abortion and infanticide to be used for research and transplantation.

Today, Catholics oppose abortion more than ever. In 1995 Pope John Paul II issued an encyclical letter entitled *Evangelium Vitae,* which speaks of a Christian "culture of life" facing a contemporary "culture of death."

• Sigrid Undset (1934), *Saga of Saints,* London.

J. Crahay (1941), "Les moralistes anciens et l'avortement," *AnCl* 10, 9–23.

J. Noonan (Ed.) (1970), *The Morality of Abortion: Legal and Historical Perspectives,* Cambridge (Mass.).

J.T. Burtchaell (1972), *Rachel Weeping and Other Essays on Abortion,* Kansas City.

J. Connery (1977), *Abortion: The Development of the Roman Catholic Perspective,* Chicago.

O. O'Donovan (1984), *Begotten or Made?* Oxford.

M.A. Glendon (1987), *Abortion and Divorce in Western Law,* Cambridge, Mass. London.

D. Folscheid (1992), "L'embryon, notre plus-que-prochain," *Éthique* 4, 20–43.

J.-Y. Lacoste (1993), "Être, vivre, exister: Note sur le commencement de l'homme," *RMM* 198, 347–66.

V. Bourguet (1999), *L'être en gestation: Réflexions bioéthiques sur l'embryon humain,* Paris.

James Tunstead Burtchaell

See also **Casuistry; Church and State; Ethics, Medical; Ethics, Sexual; Family; Procreation; Soul-Heart-Body**

Achard of Saint-Victor. *See* **Saint-Victor, School of**

Action

1. Definition

The theory of human action starts with a distinction between events and actions: an event happens, an action is done. Various theories have tried to reduce the actions of humans to mechanistic, biological, or divine causalities, but these reductive accounts do not explain the reality of choice and responsibility in our actions, things of which we are convinced and that are expressed in law*, theology*, and common language.

The critical element in a theory of action is whether the agent has a reason behind what he or she does, a purpose in mind when performing the action. The distinguishing feature of actions is that they are events performed by people for reasons. An act with the same physical description can be a different human act entirely by the various purposes that may be served. Cutting off a person's hand, for example, could be an instance of torture, or legitimate punishment* (as in certain Islamic countries), or saving life (where the limb is affected by gangrene).

2. Historical Conceptions

a) Aristotle and the Stoics. Aristotle (384–322 B.C.) made a lasting contribution to the theory of human action in his *Nicomachean Ethics.* He distinguishes actions that are freely chosen (voluntary) from actions that are made under compulsion, and describes the elements of actions as acting in accordance with a purpose *(telos),* using deliberation *(bouleusis)* to determine the means, and choice *(prohairesis),* which results in the actions. The choice leading to the act is produced by neither intellect *(nous)* nor desire *(orexis)* alone, but is a combination of both. Most subsequent theories are elaborations of this one, with a changing emphasis on the importance of the rational or affective elements of action.

Stoic thinkers tended to modify Aristotle in several respects. They were not averse to the deterministic implications of theories of universal law, and practical reasoning was often reduced to attitudes of obedience to laws. More attention was given to "impulse" and other irrational factors in actions.

b) Scriptures. Beginning with the story of Adam and Eve, the Bible* emphasizes liberty*, responsibility, and obedience to God*. The importance of right intention* is illustrated by the story of Cain and Abel (Gn 4), and the need for wisdom* and prudence* in living according to God's will is a major theme of the Psalms* and Proverbs.

The teaching of Jesus deepens the connection between external actions and inner disposition. Many examples, including the parables of the two sons (Mt 21:28–32), the good and bad fruit (Mt 7:16–20), and the pearl of great price (Mt 13:45–46), illustrate these points about actions: neither good attitude without action, nor action without proper motivation, is sufficient; there should be complete harmony between inner attitude and external action; such harmony is based on love* of God and his kingdom*; and it presupposes complete change in mind and heart. The pictures of abiding in Christ (Jn 15:4–5), being conformed to the image of Christ (2 Cor 3:17–18), or walking in the Spirit (Gal 5:16–26) all describe the dependence of a Christian's actions on identification and union with Christ in mind and heart.

c) Patristic and Medieval Periods. Augustine (354–430) summarizes the Christian life by emphasizing knowledge of God's will informed by the Scriptures, and the ordering of love under love for God. Some Greek theologians retained an interest in the philosophical analysis of action, including Nemesius (late fourth century) and John of Damascus (eighth century). Thomas* Aquinas was able to make use of these enrichments in his combination of Aristotelian theory with an Augustinian view of the will, balancing cognitive and affective functions in action. This balance was upset by an emphasis on the will in later thinkers (John Duns* Scotus [c. 1266–1308] and William of Ockham [c. 1285–1347/49]), with these results: Will is responsible for choice and execution; reason* is restricted to deliberation; action is disconnected from the final end, and the importance of the moral virtues is minimized.

d) Modern Times. Distortions produced by voluntarism* affected the theology of the 16th and 17th centuries, even in the commentators on Saint Thomas, such as Cajetan (1469–1534) and the Salmanticenses. Actions came to be considered as discrete occasions of the will's obedience or disobedience to conscience*, weakening the classical and biblical emphasis on moral wisdom and development of character*. In secular ethics, severed from obedience to God, action became even more atomistic, as in John Locke (1632–1704), lacking any connection to a final end, whether emphasis was put on the passions* (David Hume, 1711–76) or on rationality (Gottfried Wilhelm Leibniz* [1646–1716] or Immanuel Kant* [1724–1804]).

In the early 20th century, two influences on the theory of action may be noted. First is the innovative approach of Blondel*, who explored the dynamic quality of the will as the tension between necessity and freedom. He also put the discussion of action in a very broad context of science, art, and social life, and considered action the basis for contemplating our relationship with the divine. Next, the work of Freud* contributed to an understanding of the several levels of motivation. Actions may have a superficial explanation in terms of avowed purpose, but they may also be an expression of underlying subconscious or unconscious attitudes.

e) Contemporaries. Dissatisfied with behaviorism and other reductionist approaches, thinkers such as Anscombe and Davidson see the limitations of theories emphasizing irrational factors and, along Aristotelian lines, affirm the importance of reason in action, with descriptions combining belief and desire. The "causal" theory associated with Davidson, for example, takes the view that the total action includes belief, desire, and the exterior action. The chief contribution here has been to show how "having a reason" can be part of the description of the cause of an action. Although some (*see* Hornsby 1980) have argued for a notion of "trying" as part of mental action, most have agreed with the causal theory, which is also simpler and is compatible with Aristotle and Aquinas.

A continuing point of debate is the extent of an action, whether it is limited to the immediate "physical" action or includes direct effects. In an example from Anscombe (1963), a man pumps water from a poisoned well to a house. If he knows about the poison, then the description of his action should include more than the ensemble of his movements; it should mention the fact that they involve attacking the inhabitants of the house. Goldman (1970) argues for the limited version of the action description, but Davidson, as well as D'Arcy and Anscombe, argue for a more comprehensive view, claiming that the more restricted view is only a partial and incomplete description (summary in Neuberg 1993). This question is important for moral theology, because the question of responsibility often hinges on the correct description of an action; this is essential if deception and rationalizing are to be avoided.

3. Principles of Human Action

a) Motivation. All creatures act for an end: to fulfill a need or to reach a stage of completion. The dogma* of creation* allows us to place all these activities, originally without defect, under the plan and providence* of God. Human beings are self-acting because they can generate their own plans and have a wide range of purposes. Of course, people are often mistaken about real good and evil. Some actions, such as eating or talking with friends, are valuable in themselves and need no outside purpose to render them good or understandable; but often an action serves an end or purpose that may be remote from the action itself: undergoing painful surgery, for example, so that one's health will be improved.

b) Mental Factors. Intellect and will (or, in biblical terms, mind and heart) are central to action. Intellect and will activate each other, and thus each expresses the unified attitudes, beliefs, and desires of a person*. Human freedom cannot be reduced to the will alone, since free choice is a function of both intellect and will.

c) Dispositions. Human action is not just a succession of occasional choices, but also expresses dispositions of the mind and emotions established in a person's character. These dispositions *(habitus)* are acquired not mechanically but by patterns of thought and desire; by connection to goals and values, they become the foundation for virtues*.

d) Law and Grace. These are not interior principles of action, but exterior principles. Laws, both human and divine, direct action to the common good*, applying in situations where individual choices need to be harmonized, or where action is unclear. Grace* is the help given to the mind through the Holy* Spirit to enable the agent to see more clearly, and to be better attracted to genuine good.

4. Process of Action

Human action goes through stages of general desire, planning, deciding, and acting. In many accounts of Scholastic* theory, a multiplication of up to 12 stages can be found. However, when intellect and will are seen to be complementary, then it is possible to arrange the process of action in four steps: intention, deliberation, decision, and execution. Many actions are much simpler, and require little or no deliberation. In other cases, the decision is easy to reach, but the execution itself is difficult, and perhaps delayed or compromised. It becomes clear that a person's attitudes and purposes need to be good; that the deliberation must be open and accurate; that decisions must be made with wisdom; and that actions are to be executed in the right way.

5. Moral Assessment of Actions

a) End, Object, and Circumstances. From the moral perspective, voluntary actions are either good or bad (with a narrow range of trivial or inadvertent actions) depending on their ends and means. Taking a nap is good or bad depending on the circumstances: resting, or trying to avoid an unpleasant task.

It is useful to distinguish between the object and the end of an act. The object, the *finis operis* (end of the action), is what gives the act its species or definition; it is the description that the agent would give when asked what he has proposed to do. The end is the further purpose of the action, relating to the interior act of the will of the agent, referred to as *finis operantis* (end of acting). Both are part of the intention. For example, handing someone money is a neutral or physical description, which becomes a moral act when given a description, such as paying a debt, offering a bribe, or presenting a gift to the poor. These specifications of action are still affected in turn by the larger purposes that the agent may have: to cultivate a certain reputation, to further his interests, or to fulfill the terms of a will. Even a good act, such as giving money to the poor, may serve questionable purposes, including the enhancement of pride or silencing a guilty conscience. The money will still help the poor, but as an action of the giver it is defective. Or, the donor may have the right intention, but he may not recognize obligations to family or other responsibilities that he has, and under the circumstances the action becomes bad. If there is a defect in the object, purpose, or circumstances, then the act is vitiated, for all must be correct.

b) Consequences of Action. Some effects are direct and must be considered part of the action, since they are part of the intention. Other effects are subsequent results of the action and should not determine the morality of the act itself. Unlike theories that assess the goodness of actions in terms of consequences (consequentialism, utilitarianism*), the Christian view understands the criteria of good and bad as necessarily present in the agent's moral reasoning in the light of God's law. The consequences, however, are not irrelevant; they must be considered in a correct estimate of an action, and they may intensify the goodness or badness of an act.

c) Responsibility. The theory of action is very important for the notion of responsibility, and our assessment of praise and blame. The man pumping poisoned water cannot limit his responsibility to mere pumping if he knows that the result is likely to harm people in the house. But what of cases where the intention is for something good, but an accident or some other factor changes the expected outcome? To the extent that other factors should have been taken into account, the agent cannot excuse himself from his responsibility by saying that the outcome was not his intention. Thus, the scope of responsibility should be expanded from what is our will or intention to what is within our power. In taking a group of children on a hike, for example, one is not responsible for falling branches or sudden storms, but one is responsible for checking weather forecasts, having extra clothing or food for emergencies, and providing adequate supervision.

It must be pointed out that one cannot avoid responsibility by not acting, as is shown by the problem of negligence or omission. All negligence involves some failure to take due care; but sometimes this consists in a person's not taking care in the way he acts, sometimes in the way in which he prepares to act, and sometimes in not having thought at all. Having the correct desires and intentions is crucial, and shows why the virtues of prudence and charity are of prime importance for Christian action. Sometimes, the failure to act, or carelessness in execution, reveal a greater lack of charity than more obvious sins* do.

• Aristotle, *Nicomachean Ethics.*
Augustine, *De Doctrina Christiana,* BAug 11, 149–541.
M. Blondel, *L'Action,* Paris, 1893.
Nemesius, *De natura hominis,* PG 40.
Salmanticenses, *Cursus theologicus,* 20 vols., Paris, 1870–83, vol. III, tract. II.
Thomas Aquinas, *Summa Theologica,* Ia IIae, q. 17–21.
♦ A. Gardeil (1902), "Acte humain," *DThC* 1, 339–46.
E. Anscombe (1957), *Intention,* Oxford.
E. D'Arcy (1963), *Human Acts:* An *Essay in Their Moral Evaluation,* Oxford.
A. Goldman (1970), *A Theory of Human Actions,* Princeton.
D. Davidson (1980), *Essays on Actions and Events,* Oxford.
J. Hornsby (1980), *Actions,* London.
G. Grisez (1983), *The Way of the Lord Jesus,* Chicago.
S. Pinckaers (1985), *Les sources de la morale chrétienne,* Paris.
R. Cessario (1991), *The Moral Virtues and Theological Ethics,* Notre Dame, Ind.
M. Neuberg (1993), *Philosophie de l'action,* Gembloux.
D. Westberg (1994), *Right Practical Reason: Aristotle, Action, and Prudence in Aquinas,* Oxford.
R. Ogien (1996), "Action," *DEPhM,* 4–14.

Daniel Westberg

See also **Angels; Animals; Anthropology; Augustinianism; Cosmos; Creation; Death; Demons; Filiation; Myth; Pauline Theology; Sin, Original; Temptation; Woman**

Adam

A. Biblical Theology

a) Adam in Hebrew. The Hebrew word *adam* has several meanings. 1) Used collectively, it means "humanity" (Gn 1:26–27). Ordinarily preceded by the article (*ha-*) in prose, but not in poetry, it signifies "human" as a complement to a substantive. 2) It is used to designate every individual member of the human race*, individualized or typical. 3) It is the proper name of the first man, and as such its first certain occurrence is in Genesis 5:1.

b) First Creation Narrative. *Ha-'adam* of Genesis 1:26–7 is a collective noun covering both sexes; it is literally "the adam," but is usually translated as "man" or "humankind." The words "God created *ha-'adam* in his own image" do not refer to a rational or spiritual essence, but rather to the power conferred on Adam over other creatures and, directly, over the animals*. According to W. H. Schmidt and, in particular, Wildberger, God manifests himself in Genesis 1 with the kingly qualities of power, wisdom*, and goodness, of which his "image" is the reflection. *Tselem* (clarified by the Babylonian *tsalmu,* applied to kings and to the priests of Marduk) implies the attributes of a viceroy of God.

c) Second Creation Narrative. Genesis 2:4–25, which is of a mythic type of narrative with a more ancient Yahwist source, is rich in subtle instruction. The creation* of *ha-'adam* out of the *'adamah* (soil) opens a drama of the fragility and dignity of man, the proximity of animal and God. Prohibition and sanction presuppose responsibility, albeit limited. Does the creation of the woman* out of the man transpose the myth* of a primeval androgyny? In any case, the woman is desired as a "helper," and *kenegedo,* the term used to describe her as such, expresses a reciprocity that excludes an inferior status (Gn 2:18–20).

The story of the first couple* is presented as a tragic case of innocence exploited. The first parents are said to be *'arummim* (naked—here denoting vulnerability), and the serpent is said to be *'arum* (subtle). At first, therefore, man and woman are victims. According to Irenaeus* and other Fathers*, they are not yet adults. The principal responsibility is imputed to the serpent, and it is he who speaks of becoming "like God" (the *hubris* of superhuman creatures is an ancient theme, *see* Gn 14:12–20 and Ez 28:1–19). The exegesis* that proceeds by decoding sexual allegories denies the importance of what is said and what is left unsaid, notably in the dialogue in Genesis 3:1–5. In fact, the word *sin** does not appear. The serpent is cursed, not the man. The soil is also cursed, in relation to human work*. Nothing obliges us to see the expulsion from paradise as a punishment, since Adam and Eve are thus preserved, to remain without end in the condition in which they have been placed. Death* is the sanction for disobedience, but the myth does not say that man was created immortal, although Genesis 6:3 could suggest that. A parabola or paradigm of human weakness and its consequences, Genesis 2 and 3 should serve as a mirror, calling each reader to a better understanding of himself (*see* the comments on 2 Bar, below). In fact, it may have been conceived in order to fulfill this function.

d) Other Texts of the Old Testament and Ancient Judaism. Another myth of the entry of evil* into the world—the Fall of the "Sons of God," who have intercourse with women in Genesis 6:1–4—has been left to us in a truncated form. Genesis 6:3 leaves the evil tendency of man unexplained. The narrative sequence has gaps; 1 Enoch 6–8 (of which the ancient core dates from the third century B.C.) adds that the angels* gave instruction to men. This motif (as seen, e.g., in Ps 82) is undoubtedly anterior to Genesis 3 and 6. Genesis 3 transforms it in order to maintain human responsibility. Later, the writer of Wisdom of Solomon 2:24 replaced the serpent with "the jealousy of the devil." Overall, Jewish and Christian tradition* have held that Adam was the direct addressee of the prohibition, and therefore had the principal responsibility. The misogynistic diatribe of Sirach 25:17–26 (*see* especially verse 24) has no doctrinal weight. According to 1 Timothy 2:14 it was "Adam who was not deceived, but the woman was deceived and became a transgressor." Although this is without authority, harmful consequences have been derived from it.

At a later stage, Adam was exalted in Sirach 49:16: the collective Adam of Genesis 1:26–27 is thus assimilated to the father* of humanity in Genesis 2 (already an individual in Gn 5:3, but not yet an individual in Gn 5:1–2), with the implications of kingly dignity that Philo Judaeus (c. 15 to 10–c. 45 to 50) recognizes. Tobit 8:6 evokes the sanctity of marriage* with the figures of Adam and Eve. The Wisdom of Solomon 10:1 has Wisdom intervening immediately after Adam's transgression: "she delivered him from his transgression, and gave him strength to rule all things"; he remains "the first-formed father of the world." Conversely, the negative role of Adam is accentuated, notably at the end of the first century of our era. First and foremost, this role is a *causal* one. According to (the extracanonical) 4 Ezra 3:7, evil has prevailed because of Adam, even though the law* was also present in his "evil heart" (4 Ezr 3:20–22). This pessimistic version of the doctrine of the two "inclinations," which occupies a position within Judaism analogous to that of original sin in Christianity, comes closest to Romans 5, which very likely predates it. This role can also be reduced to that of an *example.* When (the extracanonical) 2 Baruch (which is contemporaneous with 2 Ez) declares: "O Adam, what have you done to the whole of your posterity?" (2 Bar 48:42), the reference is to death and other evils (2 Bar 56:6), but each person is responsible for his own destiny. Put on guard by the story of the first transgression, "everyone is his own Adam" (2 Bar 54:15), this doctrine prefigures the opinions of Eastern theology, rather than Augustinian views.

e) New Testament. References to Adam are to be found mainly in Paul's Letters to the Corinthians and the Romans, in which several allusions are made, forming the basis of moral exhortations.

In Matthew 19:4 ff. and Mark 10:5–8 Jesus*, questioned about divorce, refers once to Genesis 1:27 ("male and female he created them") and to 2:24 ("they become one flesh"). The name of Adam does not appear in the Gospels, except at Luke 3:38, where the genealogy of Jesus is traced back to Adam and, through him, to God.

Paul (c. 10–c. 67) presents Adam and Christ* as two contrasting archetypes. Death, sin, and the deprivation of grace* have come through one of them; through the other, there is a reentry into grace, a "new creation," and the promise* of life. However, the grace received infinitely exceeds the evil caused. Paul has no interest in speculating about Adam. Living at the time when the typology was being developed, Paul did not need to explain his theology with a "Gnostic myth of a Redeemer" (gnosis*). In 1 Corinthians 15, the parallel between Adam and Christ (the "first" and "second" Adams) takes two forms. In 15:21, the first brings death, the second life. Later (15:45–49), the first is made from dust by God, the other is a "man of heaven" (15:48) who has become a "life-giving spirit" (15:45) to the benefit of a renewed humanity. In Romans 5:12–21, Paul returns to the parallel between Adam and Christ, and the asymmetry between the consequences of their actions. This text is the principal scriptural source of the Christian theology of original sin and of justification*, but three centuries separated Augustine* (354–430) from Paul: his words must be read for themselves, while taking account of his rhetorical models. In Paul's eyes, Adam is certainly a historical figure in the same sense as Jesus is (Rom 5:14), but both continue to be conceived in a symbolic mode, as type and antitype. It is difficult to reach a conclusion about the type of causality attributed to Adam's act, because of the obscurity of *eph' ho pantes hemarton* (Rom 5:12), but in Romans 5:1–8, 39, the emphasis is placed on the *experience** of sin, as of Salvation*, which is incommensurably greater. Romans 5:12–21 sheds more light on sin than on Adam himself, thanks to the rabbinical formula of *qal ve-chômer* (a fortiori, or "much more shall," used four times in 5:9–21). In spite of everything, Paul takes a more somber view of Adam's act than his Jewish predecessors did.

References to Adam are not always definite. In Romans 7:7–13, Paul describes the first person's experience of moral distress. Is he speaking of Adam, of himself before his conversion*, or of himself after it? The problem seems to be insoluble. In Philippians 2:5–11, the obedience of Christ is celebrated as the inverse of a compelled act by a creature in revolt against God. Is this a reference to Adam, to Lucifer, as in Isaiah 14:12, or to the angels in 1 Enoch 5–6? The text, which is poetic, may have more than one interpretation.

• R. Scroggs (1946), *The Last Adam,* Oxford.
H. Wildberger (1965), "Das Abbild Gottes, Gen 1, 26–30," *ThZ* 21, 245–59, 481–501.
W.H. Schmidt (1964), *Die Schöpfungsgeschichte der Priesterschrift,* WMANT.
J. Barr (1968), "The Image of God in the Book of Genesis," *BJRL* 51, 11–26; (1972), "Man and Nature—The Ecological Controversy and the Old Testament," *BJRL* 55, 9–32.
C. Westermann (1974), *Genesis 1–11,* Neukirchen-Vluyn.
R. Murray (1975), *Symbols of Church and Kingdom: A Study in Early Syriac Tradition,* Cambridge.
J. Vermeylen (1980), "Le récit du paradis et la question des origines du Pentateuque," *Bijdr* 41, 230–50.
R. Martin (1983^2), *Carmen Christi,* Grand Rapids.
P. Beauchamp (1987), "Création et fondation de la Loi," in *La création dans l'Orient ancien* (coll.), Paris, 139–80.
J. Briend (1987), "Gn 2–3 et la création du couple humain," ibid., 123–38.
P. Beauchamp (1990), *L'un et l'autre Testament,* vol. 2: *Accomplir les Écritures,* chap. 3: "L'homme, la femme et le serpent," Paris.
P. O'Brien (1991), *The Epistle to the Philippians,* Grand Rapids.

J. Procopé (1991), "Hochmut," *RAC* 15, 795–858.
R. Murray (1992), *The Cosmic Covenant,* London.

Robert Murray

See also **Angels; Animals; Anthropology; Augustinianism; Cosmos; Creation; Death; Demons; Filiation; Myth; Pauline Theology; Sin, Original; Temptation; Woman**

B. Historical and Systematic Theology

a) Patristic and Medieval Theology. The figure of Adam took on an increasing importance over the course of the first Christian centuries. A growing number of apocryphal works dealt with him, or carried his name; rabbinical thought developed a whole mythic elaboration of his character; and there were many Gnostic myths* of a protological orientation. Within patristic theology*, Adam was above all the occasion for treatments of general anthropological themes; and when the primitive church* began to take an even greater interest in Adam himself, and in his creation*, this was chiefly out of a concern to define the true nature of humanity. Indeed, it was Adam before the Fall, with the gifts and qualities that he lost as a result of his transgression, that defined an ideal humanity, the condition that humanity would rediscover at the moment of resurrection*.

The Apostolic* Fathers and the apologists* make several references to Adam, but the first to study him seriously was Irenaeus* (c. 120 to 140–c. 200 to 203), in the course of his struggle against gnosis*. Like Theophilus of Antioch (late second century), Irenaeus represents Adam and Eve as children. However, by contrast to Theophilus, for whom Adam was neither mortal nor immortal, but capable of becoming one or the other depending on his attitude to God*, Irenaeus thinks that Adam was immortal in the beginning and became mortal because of his disobedience, his refusal to recognize God as Lord. Before the Fall, Adam had self-confidence *(parresia)* before God, and was endowed with liberty* and knowledge. His domination of the earth extended to the angels*, but it was not yet manifested because he was still a child. Adam and Eve were not yet old enough to have children, and were entirely unaware of concupiscence. Irenaeus attributes this fact as much to the breath that had given them life (a breath in direct relation with the Holy* Spirit), as to that "robe of sanctity" that Adam "wore from the Spirit" but lost because of his disobedience. Although they were allowed to stray "from the beginning" *(ab initio),* Adam and Eve were not annihilated, but were "recapitulated" in Christ*, the new Adam, and Mary*, the new Eve, and their salvation* is evidence for the universal nature of the economy of salvation.

Other Greek Fathers* emphasize Adam's perfection before the Fall. Clement of Alexandria* (150–c. 211 to 215) also regards Adam and Eve as children, but after him this conception of them disappeared, and Saint Ephraem Syrus (c. 306–73) criticizes it as "pagan." Clement links the idea that Adam was a child to that of his development: Adam had certainly been created perfect, but that meant that he was perfectly capable of acquiring virtue* through the application of his free will, not that he already possessed a plenitude of virtue. This point of view is peculiar to Clement. John of Damascus (c. 675–c. 749) summarizes the teachings of the Fathers by writing that God created man innocent, righteous, free from all sadness and anxiety, and endowed with every virtue and goodness. Clement also has a personal conception of the action* of disobedience that constitutes the Fall: he sees in it a premature use of sexuality, even though, in itself, sexuality is natural to human beings. This specifically sexual notion of Adam's sin* is a rare one among the Fathers. It is true that some of the Greek Fathers seem to have believed that human sexuality was originally latent and was not experienced until after the Fall, for it had been created solely because of it. In general, however, the Fathers tend to conceive the Fall as an apostasy, an act of turning away from God, and, sometimes, in a more Platonic context (*see* Platonism*, Christian), as an act of turning toward the things of the body and the senses (e.g., *see* Gregory of Nyssa, PG 44; Maximus* the Confessor, PG 90). The idea that death* is a consequence of the Fall, and that Adam was therefore originally endowed with immortality, can be found in all the texts. According to Athanasius*, Adam, filled with grace from the beginning, had self-confidence before God and devoted himself to intellectual contemplation*. According to Cyril* of Alexandria and John of Damascus, Adam lived in the contemplation of God so far as his nature permitted him to do so. According to the homilies attributed to Macarius, the Holy Spirit was present with Adam in paradise, instructing him and inspiring his behavior—but this did not remove from Adam either his "natural thoughts" or his desire to realize them. According to John of Damascus, grace was the original condition of humanity, and was given so that humanity could live in communion* with God. One finds everywhere the idea that Adam possessed knowledge and wisdom*, which is why he received the privilege to call the animals* (Gn 2:19–20), but no special attention was paid to the question of the "infused" nature of this knowledge (*see* Sir 17:6 f.). According to Cyril of Alexandria, however, Adam did not acquire this knowledge with the passage of time, as we do, but had it from the beginning. According to other Fathers, Adam knew of the existence of good* and evil* even before the Fall, but thereafter this knowledge became a matter of experience (e.g., John Chrysostom*).

For the most part, the earliest Latin authors, above all Tertullian*, limit themselves to reprising these views. It was the Pelagian controversy that led the West, and principally Augustine*, to undertake a more profound reflection upon Adam. According to Augustine, Adam was fully adult. He had direct experience* of God, who appeared to him and spoke with him, although this does not necessarily mean that he perceived God through his physical senses. In paradise, Adam and Eve experienced neither spiritual disturbance nor physical disorder, since, in the natural condition of humanity before the Fall, all the parts of the body and all the motions of the soul* were subject to the will, which was itself subject to God, so much so that even procreation* would have taken place by voluntary decision, in the tranquillity of the spirit, and not in a state of passionate excitation. This harmonious submission of the body to the soul was due to the divine grace that Adam enjoyed in paradise. When he lost it because of his disobedience, he became subject to the desires of the flesh*: since he had not wished to obey, it was just that his desires no longer obeyed him. The Second Council* of Orange (529) confirmed that Adam had been created in a state of grace (can. 19).

Scholasticism* offered a systematic theology of the original condition of Adam. According to Thomas* Aquinas, Adam was created in full maturity of spirit and body, ready to have children, and endowed with an infused knowledge, comprising both knowledge of natural things and knowledge of supernatural* purposes. Aquinas accepts that Adam did not ordinarily see God in his essence, even if, perhaps, he experienced this sort of ecstasy during the sleep into which God plunged him (Gn 2:21), but, according to Aquinas, Adam had a much greater knowledge* of God than we do. He also thinks that, if Adam had not sinned, he would not have known error. Peter Lombard (c. 1100–1160) and Alexander of Hales (c. 1186–1245) distinguish between two types of grace: the assistance given at the moment of creation—which made man capable of avoiding evil and living without sin, but not of doing good—and sanctifying grace, which makes man capable of doing good, living spiritually, and attaining eternal life*. By contrast, according to Aquinas Adam possessed sanctifying grace from his creation, and this was associated, as it was in Augustine, with the harmonious submission of the body to the soul, of the inferior powers to reason*, and of reason to God, making Adam capable of meritorious acts. However, Aquinas does not identify sanctifying grace with original justice*: the first is the efficient cause of the second, not its formal constituent. In his original condition, Adam was not disturbed by any ungovernable passions*, and had all the virtues appropriate to his condition: he was therefore capable of committing only venial sins. The Council of Trent* affirmed that Adam possessed "sanctity and justice" before the Fall (fifth session, cans. 1 and 2), but did not raise the question of the moment when he received sanctifying grace: in this regard it followed in the mainstream of the councils, which were always more reserved than the theologians on the subject of Adam.

b) Modern and Contemporary Theology. While the general acceptance of the theory of evolution*, originally proposed by Darwin, has forced theologians to rethink much of the teaching concerning the creation and original state of man, the required change of perspective occurred earlier, in the 18th and early 19th centuries, when Johann Gottfried von Herder (1744–1803), for example, reworked the concept of the image of God in terms of destiny: that is, the image is not something that mankind once had and has since lost, but something toward which we are progressing. This idea of the gradual and historical "humanizing" of man was complemented by a renewed attention to biblical criticism, especially by J. G. Eichhorn (1752–1827), which began to see the creation narratives in terms of myth* or saga. These two developments, later combined with Darwinism, prompted Protestant* theologians from Friedrich Schleiermacher* to Ernst Troeltsch (1865–1923) to abandon the idea of an original perfect estate of Adam, which was subsequently lost by the Fall, and to propose, in their various ways, alternatives that equated human perfection with the destiny or goal that man still has to attain.

One of the most important and interesting attempts to reinstate the doctrine of the original state, by giving it a new form, is that of Kierkegaard*. This is elaborated not so much in terms of an original historical beginning, a "fantastic assumption" of theology, but as a suprahistorical state. Kierkegaard wanted to explain the relation between the first sin and hereditary sin (*see* original sin*), and so needed to recall the figure of Adam, for to explain Adam's sin is to explain hereditary sin. This is due to the basic character of human existence: "man is an individual, and as such simultaneously himself and the whole race," so that the individual participates in the race and vice versa. As a state, this is the perfection of man. But it is also a contradiction, for the individual is not the race, and, as such, it is "the expression of a task." In the opening pages of *Sygdommen til døden* (1849; *The Sickness unto Death*), Kierkegaard describes how this task cannot be accomplished, and so produces despair. The "task" of reconciling the individual nature of man's self to his identity with the race of men results in the consciousness of a lost identity. The "original state" of man, together with the "Fall," thus becomes suprahistorical, but no less real.

With the leitmotiv of man "caught in contradiction," E. Brunner (1889–1966) develops Kierkegaard's thought as he also seeks to understand an original state based on an analysis of anxiety. Theology proposes to interpret man's dual experience of "grandeur" and "misery" as the conflict that sets man's origin against the contradiction (the Fall) opposed to this origin.

Brunner accepts the idea that there is "nothing left" of the traditional Christian picture of man's "origin." When he refers to the "origin state," he speaks of a man who has his original state in the thought, the will, and the creative action of God. The original state must thus be differentiated (yet not cut off) from man's empirical beginnings (individually, in the womb; as a race, in earliest "man"). It is only by this "origin" that we can understand the present state of man, who is living in opposition to it. Thus, for Brunner, the original state is not a historical or prehistorical period, but a "historic moment," that of the divinely created origin, which we know only in the conflict we experience with its opposite, that is, with sin.

In these and similar attempts, such as those of R. Niebuhr and H. Thielicke, to give a new sense to the concept of the original state, although man has in some sense lost his original identity or vocation, this is not explained in strictly historical terms, but is postulated as a suprahistorical presupposition explaining man's present existence. While these "existential" reinterpretations of the original state and Fall evade the problems raised by the theory of evolution*, doubts have been raised as to whether they offer a sustainable version of the traditional teaching. What, for instance, does recasting the term *origin,* from a historical beginning to the source of creation, imply for the figure of Adam? Furthermore, does not the concept of the "loss" of an original perfection imply the initial possession of that perfection, and, moreover, a chronological sequence of events?

Rather than elaborate such existential interpretations, modern Roman Catholic theology, on the other hand, has tended to attempt to establish a harmony between traditional theology and science (the sciences* of nature). While some theories of evolutionism, such as the multiple origin of the human race (monogenesis*/polygenesis), have been challenged as being incompatible with the teaching on original sin*, the basic framework of the traditional doctrine is maintained by pointing out that paleontology cannot disprove divine intervention in history. Thus, the direct creation by God of each human soul can be reaffirmed. Similarly, the special friendship between the first man and God need not be excluded on account of the supposedly primitive existence of the first man, while his special endowments can be interpreted as possibilities rather than realized perfections.

Abandoning both the existential interpretation and the program of demythologizing the Scriptures initiated by Rudolf Bultmann*, which considers the use of myth to reflect a mode of conception obsolete for the scientific thinking of modern man, and building on the work done in the field of comparative religion (especially by M. Éliade), contemporary theology has seen a return to viewing the Genesis accounts of the creation of Adam and his original state in terms of myth, or more precisely, as an etiological narrative. The location of myth in the primal age enables it to function as the basis for the present world order, as its legitimization rather than as a primitive explanation (understood by analogy to modern explanation). Moreover, an essential element in the structure of myth is its connection with the cult through which it is represented and reexperienced. However, the various elements of Babylonian mythology that supplied the imagery for the Genesis accounts, by being incorporated into the chronology of these accounts, lost the ability to be reenacted in a cult. There occurred what Pannenberg describes as a "historicization of myth." The mythical elements are used as images for the purpose of explanation: the desire of man and woman for each other, the pains of childbirth, the toil involved in our experience of work*, and, finally, death (Gn 2:23, 3:16–19). Mythical imagery is used to depict, by contrast with our present experience, a different and better mode of life, which man originally had and lost. More important, however, is the correspondence between the original state and the idea of an eschatological perfection. Within the Bible, the imagery used for paradise and Adam's original state is also used to describe the future age of the Messiah. But rather than being a simple return to the primal age, as the cyclical nature of myth would demand, the original state is not simply repeated in the eschatological age, but is itself surpassed and brought to perfection. Thus, instead of viewing the Genesis account of Adam in terms of the historical origins of the human race, contemporary theology has inscribed its protology within eschatology*, so that Adam is again understood in terms of the Pauline* typology of Adam and Christ*.

• S. Kierkegaard (1844), *Begrebet angest.* (English trans., *The Concept of Anxiety,* Tr. R. Thomte, Princeton, 1980); (1849), *Sygdommen til døden.* (English trans., *The Sickness unto Death,* Tr. H. V. Hong, Princeton, 1980).

J.B. Kors (1922), *La justice primitive et le péché originel d'après saint Thomas,* Kain (Belgium).

A. Slomkowski (1928), *L'état primitif de l'homme dans la tradition de l'Église avant saint Augustin,* Paris.

I. Onings (1936), "Adam," in *DSp* 1, 187–95.

E. Brunner (1937), *Der Mensch im Widerspruch,* Berlin.

M. Éliade (1949), *Le mythe de l'éternel retour: Archétypes et répétitions,* Paris. (English trans., *The Myth of the Eternal Return: Cosmos and History,* London, 2nd Ed. 1965, Repr. 1989.)

B.S. Childs (1960), *Myth and Reality in the Old Testament,* London.

G.W.H. Lampe (Ed.) (1961), "Adam," in *PGL,* 26–29.

A. Patfoort (Tr.), H.D. Gardeil (Comm.) (1963), *ST* Ia, q. 90–102: *Les origines de l'homme,* Paris.

W. Pannenberg (1972), *Christentum und Mythos,* Gütersloh; (1983), *Anthropologie in theologischer Perspektive,* Göttingen.

JOHN BEHR

See also **Anthropology; Creation; Death; Evolution; Monogenesis/Polygenesis; Sin, Original; Soul-Heart-Body; Woman**

Adam of Saint-Victor. *See* **Saint-Victor, School of**

Adam of Wodeham. *See* **Nominalism**

Adoptionism

The word *adoptionism* originated in the eighth century, at the time of the Spanish controversy (*see* below); the meaning of this word was extended to characterize what may be considered more as a (permanent) temptation of theology* than a heresy*. It is the temptation of those whose conception of God cannot allow that, while yet remaining God, he might communicate himself to the extent of introducing a creature within the mystery* of divine generation. Christ*, therefore, whatever his dignity, remains a creature who has been adopted and chosen. The interest inherent in the study of adoptionism can be found in identifying the reasons that led some Christians to yield to the above-mentioned temptation.

There are three important stages in the adoptionist temptation: ancient church*, Spanish crisis, and Scholastic controversy. In the early days of the church, which had to develop its own formulas of faith within milieus as various as the Judaist, the Hellenistic, and the Gnostic (gnosis*) ones, the trends were very complex.

In Judeo-Christianity of the ebionitic form, adoptionism is perhaps to be associated with a particularly high evaluation of Christian baptism*, which is considered to bestow filial adoption *(huiothesia)* at the end of the symbolic fight against the forces of evil*. In this context, Christ appears as the man in whom such an adoption has materialized in an exemplary manner, making him the Messiah*, and in a certain sense the root of all baptismal sanctification to come. Such ideas are also found, though with no apparent liturgical influence, in the early forms of Hellenistic Christianity, from Theodotus "the Byzantine" to Theodotus "the Banker," Artemon, and Paul of Samosata. Here the ideas are given a more intellectual support thanks to Greek logic, which leads to an emphasis on the disjunction between God and man based on the irreducibility of univocal concepts. However, as J. Wolinsky remarks, "reducing Christ to being only one man went much too directly against the faith of Christians for adoptionism to have had a profound impact on the history of doctrines" (Sesboüé [Ed.] , *History of Dogmas* I, Paris, 1994).

The Spanish adoptionism of the end of the eighth century is associated with the Spanish tradition of fighting for Nicene orthodoxy* (Councils* of Toledo). In order to better establish the divine nature of the Son of God, whether against Arianism* or, inversely, against some residual forms of modalism*, Christ's humanity and divinity are separated from one another. His humanity is thus considered to be "adopted." Christ's filiation* is considered natural as far as his divinity is concerned, but adoptive and the result of grace* as far as his humanity is concerned: *unigenitus in natura, primogenitus in adoptione et gratia* (PL 101, 1324). Adoptionism is here associated with the names of Elipandus of Toledo and Felix of Urgel. Its refutation (*propter unitatem personae, unus Dei Filius et idem hominis filius, perfectus Deus, perfectus homo,* ibid., 1337) belongs to the body of dogmatic options of the Council of Frankfurt (794).

Scholastic adoptionism may have a more philosophical origin, being associated with the use of certain inadequately mastered logical categories that had been recently rediscovered in theological thinking. Schematically, Scholastic thinking in this area unfolds in the following way: 1) It is not possible to put "God" and "man" in an attributive relationship in such a way that formulas such as "God is man, man is God" are improper. 2) That being stated, since "God" is unquestionably substance and can be the subject of attribution, it is not possible to say that "man" designates substance; in technical terms, he is neither *persona* nor *aliquid.* 3) How then is it possible to speak of the union of God and man in Christ? This thought process is at the root of the three positions put forward by Peter Lombard in the *Sentences* (l. III, d. 6–11), and the masters of early Scholasticism from Abelard fall within any of these three positions. First there is the theory of the *habitus,* which considers Christ's humanity to be the "clothing" of his divinity. Second, the theory of the *assumptus* proposes that it is a man who is being assumed. Finally, there is the theory of subsistence. While this last theory heralds the thinking of high Scholasticism* on hypostatic* union, the first two favor a resurgence of the theme of adoption.

The early Scholastic masters in all likelihood lacked an in-depth analysis of the distinction between person* and nature, which might have allowed them to see clearly that, on the one hand, filiation always concerns the person and that, on the other hand, logical attributes have their own specific economy where Christ is concerned (communication of the idioms).

Can we say that modernity produces a revival of the adoptionist "temptation," precisely on account of the crisis affecting our thinking on God? It does not appear to be so. Newton's christological thinking, for instance, is consciously Arian. Spinoza's and Lessing's vision of Christ is that of the *Summus Philosophus,* perfect educator of humankind, outside of any Trinitarian vision of God (Trinity*), and thus of any perspective of incarnation*, even by adoption. The contemporary Scotist school, with which the names of Déodat de Basly and Léon Seiller are associated, takes up again the theme of the *assumptus homo,* but does not fall formally into adoptionism. Nowadays, the adoptionist temptation could well play into certain types of "humanistic Christology*" which are notable for the difficulty they have in expressing the divine aspect of Jesus Christ in proper and direct terms (that is, not only by allusion or imagery), perhaps precisely because such Christologies do not have at their disposal a language for speaking about God.

• E. Portalié (1902), "Adoptionisme," *DThC* 1, 403–21.

Déodat de Basly (1928), "L'assumptus homo: L'emmêlement de trois conflits, Pélage, Nestorius, Apollinaire," *La France franciscaine* XI, 265–313.

G. Bardy (1933), "Paul de Samosate," *DThC* 12, 46–51.

L. Seiller (1944), *L'activité humaine du Christ selon Duns Scot,* Paris.

L. Ott (1953), "Das Konzil von Chalkedon in der Frühscholastik," in Grillmeier-Bacht (Ed.), *Das Konzil von Chalkedon, Geschichte und Gegenwart,* vol. II, Würzburg, 909–10.

J. Daniélou (1958), *Théologie du judéo-christianisme,* Paris (2nd Ed. 1991), 284–93.

A. Landgraf (1965), *Dogmengeschichte der Frühscholastik* II, 1, Regensburg, 116–37.

A. Grillmeier (1979), *Jesus der Christus im Glauben der Kirche* I, Freiburg-Basel-Vienna.

A. Orbe (intr.) (1985), *Il Cristo,* Milan, xlvii-lviii.

Ghislain Lafont

See also **Christ/Christology; Incarnation**

Aelred of Rievaulx. *See* **Bernard of Clairvaux**

Agape

From the end of the apostolic era (Jude 12 and Ignatius of Antioch, *Letter to the Smyrnians* 8:1), Christians had given the name *agape* to communal meals that were distinct from the Eucharist* and were accompanied by prayers*. The word *agape* was taken from the Greek word for charity, with its emphasis on the communal aspect.

New Testament narratives of the Eucharist show that a link originally existed between the celebration of the Eucharist and a fraternal meal (on the subject of the wine cup blessed after the meal, *see* 1 Cor 11:25 and Lk 22:20). But there is no further evidence of this link after the New Testament, except perhaps in the milk and honey that, according to the *Apostolic Tradition,* were offered to the newly baptized between the taking of the bread and the taking of the wine (Gy 1959). These were perhaps also offered on the evening of Maundy Thursday, though this particular hypothesis has not been proved. In the time of transition between the apostolic era and the period that followed it, the brief text entitled the *Didache (Teaching of the Twelve Apostles)* mentions religious meals, though historians disagree about their nature.

Agape is frequently mentioned in writings of the second and third centuries, and it is described in the *Apostolic Tradition* (chap. 26). Thereafter, it seems to have gradually lost its importance.

- P.-M. Gy (1959), "Die Segnung von Milch und Honig in der Osternacht," in B. Fischer, J. Wagner (Ed.), *Paschatis Sollemnia: Festschrift J.A. Jungmann,* Freiburg, 206–12.

W.-D. Hauschild (1977), "Agapen," *TRE* 1, 748–53.

W. Rordorf, A. Tuillier (1978), *La doctrine des douze Apôtres (Didachè),* Paris.

E. Mazza (1992), *L'anafora eucaristica: Studi sulle origini,* Rome.

Pierre-Marie Gy

See also **Eucharist**

Agnosticism

1. Overview

Appearing late in French, being adopted from English (T. H. Huxley 1869), the word *agnosticism,* in the literal sense, denotes the thesis that God* is unknowable, a tenet that leads to a suspension of judgment as to his existence. In this respect, agnosticism is related to skepticism and attempts to establish a distinction between the dogmatic negation of the existence of God and a simple refusal to decide. The critical dimension characteristic of the agnostic suspension of judgment is, however, ambivalent. By placing God above the order of the knowable, it may simply be a way of recognizing his eminence. But by saying of God that he has no existence for thought, there is also a possibility of denying him any kind of existence at all. Historically, it is the affinities between agnosticism and atheism* that have prevailed.

2. Philosophical Background

a) Skepticism. In ancient Pyrrhonism, skeptical doubt extends as far as knowledge of the gods, although Sextus Empiricus "asserts without dogmatism that the gods exist" (Hypotoposes III:2). This assertion is based on the simple anthropological fact of piety: it would be impossible for the divine not to exist. But the assertion defies demonstration, and we can form no concept of God (Hypotoposes III:3): "Similarly, since we are ignorant of the essence of God, we are incapable of knowing or conceiving of his attributes*" (Hypotoposes III:4).

In Hume's *Dialogues Concerning Natural Religion,* the critique of proofs by analogy* on which metaphysical theism (Deism*/Theism) is based leads to an agnosticism that seems compatible with fideism*.

b) Rationalism. Although Immanuel Kant* explicitly asserts the possibility of knowledge* of God based on analogy (*Prolegomena* §58), his critique of speculative proofs of the existence* of God, principally of the "ontological" proof, leads to the assertion that the Absolute is unknowable. The novelty of Kantianism in this regard is that it makes possible a new form of agnosticism, one that no longer depends on assuming a skeptical position toward knowledge in general, but is the corollary of an affirmation of scientific knowledge of the phenomenal world. If God is unknowable, this is because he is not an object, in the sense that modern natural science gives to the term. Once the determinism of the necessary laws of nature is accepted, God becomes an unnecessary hypothesis (Laplace).

3. Theological and Anthropological Aspects

Agnosticism cannot appeal to the *theos agnotos* of Paul (Acts 17:23), who is an "unknown god" of the Greeks and not an unknowable God. It was against agnosticism and other positions that the Second Vatican Council, relying on traditional affirmations (such as Rom 1:19–23), defined the possibility of a natural access by man to God. It insisted that whether it is ultimately joined to atheism or in solidarity with fideism, agnosticism is not only refuted by a God who reveals himself, it is also contrary to reason*, which needs no divine illumination to recognize the existence of a creator of all things.

Agnosticism may also call upon the theological argument that aims to establish the radical transcendence of the divine essence by denying the possibility of attributing to God the names that are suitable for created things. Indeed, for a discursive knowledge of God to be possible, it has to be shown that the use of divine names* derived from human language does not lead to complete ambiguity (*see* Thomas* Aquinas, *Summa contra Gentiles* I: chaps. 33–34 and 290–98). Thomas uses analogy as a solution.

The Catechism of the Catholic Church (1992) places agnosticism in the perspective of atheism and (in §2128) attributes to it a fundamental ambivalence: "Agnosticism can sometimes include a certain search for God, but it can equally express indifferentism, a flight from the ultimate question of existence, and a sluggish moral conscience. Agnosticism is all too often equivalent to practical atheism."

Arising, at least in its modern form, in the context of the scientific objectification of reality, agnosticism might nevertheless, as a reaction against that context, maintain a resolutely positive meaning in both theological and anthropological terms. A product of nature, having become an object for the sciences* of nature, humankind may save its dignity only by presenting a dimension inaccessible to scientific knowledge. Unknowing then becomes the distinctive characteristic of religion and metaphysics, in an agnosticism that might refer to "learned ignorance" (Nicholas* of Cusa) or to Wittgenstein's *Tractatus.* But it is really not certain that the limits of objective knowledge are the limits of the knowable, or that what we cannot speak about objectively we must pass over in silence.

• T. H. Huxley (1894), *Science and Christian Tradition,* London.
R. Flint (1903), *Agnosticism,* Edinburgh and London.
A. Angénieux (1948), "Agnosticisme," *Cath* 1, 219–23.
F. L. Baumer (1960), *Religion and the Rise of Skepticisms,* New York.
J. Splett (1969), "Agnostizismus," *SM(D)* 1, 52–55.
W. Stegmüller (1969), *Metaphysik, Skepsis, Wissenschaft,* Berlin.
J. P. Reid (1971), *Man without God: An Introduction to Unbelief,* London-New York.
A. Ström, B. Gustafsson (1976), "Agnostizismus," *TRE* 2, 91–100.
H. R. Schlette (1979), *Der moderne Agnostizismus,* Düsseldorf.
L. Kolakowski (1982), *Religion: If There Is No God...,* London.
G. MacGregor (1983), "Doubt and Belief," *EncRel(E)* 4, 424–30.
Catéchisme de l'Église catholique (1992), Paris, §2127–28.

Philibert Secretan

See also **Atheism; Existence of God, Proofs of; Knowledge of God; Skepticism, Christian**

Agony. *See* **Passion**

Alain of Lille. *See* **Scholasticism**

Albert the Great

1200–1280

The Dominican Albert the Great was the first Scholastic interpreter of the works of Aristotle and teacher of Thomas* Aquinas both in Paris and at the Köln *studium.* He defended the mendicant orders in response to attacks by secular leaders and was consecrated bishop* of Regensburg (Ratisbon). In 1277 he was behind a last-minute attempt to avoid the condemnation of the Aristotelian theses by Étienne Tempier (naturalism*). Albert left a body of theological works that was as impressive as his philosophical works. His biblical commentaries (on Job, Isaiah, Jeremiah, Ezekiel, Baruch, Daniel, and the minor prophets*) stand beside sermons and systematic theological works: *Commentaires des sentences* by Pierre Lombard, *De Natura Boni, De Bono, Somme de Théologie* called "from Paris," *Summa de Mirabili Scientia Dei,* called "from Köln" (SC), Commentaries on *Divine Names (DN),* and the *Mystic Theology* of Dionysius* the Pseudo-Areopagite.

a) Scientific Status of Theology. A militant Aristotelian who acquired encyclopedic scientific knowledge, Albert played a large role in developing a theology conceived as a science, in the philosophical sense of that term. However, although Albert's theology is modeled on the canons of Aristotelian science, it nevertheless cannot be reduced to the "natural" theology of philosophers. It is a practical science that considers "truth" not as simple truth, but as the "supreme source of beatitude" *(summe beatificans)* pursued by the "pious intention in the affect and works" (SC I, 3,3; Siedler 13, 65–72). Therefore, if Albert invokes Aristotle in order to explain the "contemplative bliss" that is the goal of a theology understood as "moral and practical" science, it is so that he can make an irreducible distinction between the practical philosophical sciences, which focus on works that are "perfect through the perfection of acquired virtues," and theology, which involves works "that are perfect through the perfection of virtues instilled by grace*."

More generally speaking, sacred theology is distinguished from philosophical theology in three ways. First, the "principal object of its principal part" is the God* of the Bible* and not Aristotle's primary cause or primary motive. Second, the determinations *(passiones)* of its goal are not the being and its "properties" (to be) but "the Word* incarnate, together with the totality of the sacraments* that is carried out in the Church." Third, sacred theology is distinguished by the principles of "probation" upon which its arguments are based. With reference to the last of these, what "confirms" a theological argument is not a "maxim" or a "well-known" suggestion, as it is in the case of philosophy, but faith* itself (the content of which established in the conviction defining what is "believed") and what "precedes faith" as a logical antecedent: that is, the knowledge of

Scripture*—in short, "revelation*." If all sciences, even philosophical sciences, come from God as creator of the "connatural light" in the human mind, theological science is unique in that it comes from God who "reveals through faith." Thus, theology is ultimately distinguished by the fact that it stems from "another light," "supra-worldly," which "shines" and illuminates "within the article of faith," whereas the light inspiring philosophers shines in the proposition "known to one": It is, therefore, a science of piety, in the literal sense of the term, *scientia secundum pietatem* (SC I, 3, 1; Siedler, 47–54, after Ti 1:1): that is, a science founded on the knowledge of theological faith.

b) From Theological Faith to Mystical Theology. The role played by the knowledge* of faith, "the undoubted knowledge of spiritual realities" (*DN* 2, §76), in Albert's theology allows him to surmount the traditional debate relating to the superiority of love* over the intellect, something which was affirmed in the 12th century by the school of Saint*-Victor (voluntarism*). Indeed, by rendering the light of faith a theophany* that has an anagogical function (Scripture*, senses of), and by placing faith at the top of the "habitus of grace," Albert establishes continuity between the "viatic" state (pilgrimage on earth) and celestial bliss. Often described as "intellectualist," the theology of Albert the Great is rather a theology of the intellect, which, in the same "noetic" framework, involves knowledge of theological faith, the blessed vision, and mystical union. Describing the knowledge of faith in the viatic man *(vision fidei in via)* as "information of the intellect by the light of faith," Albert the Great defines the beatific vision* with the theoretical instruments of Peripatetic noesis. The vision of the chosen people in the heavens is a "junction" between man's intellect and divine essence, an "intellectual" union, in that "he who is united to the Lord becomes one spirit with him" (1 Cor 6:17), of God and the intellect agent. However, the mystical union, the "theopathic" state that Pseudo-Dionysius the Areopagite attributes to his teacher, Hierotheus, is also intellectual. In the theophany of mystical darkness the intellect receives "an impulse stemming from the light of glory," which "converts" it and "brings it back into the unity of the Father." The theology of the intellect is thus the central piece in the theology of grace and the theology of the divine missions (Trinity*). The gift of infused wisdom* and the love of charity, in their very connection, bring about the fulfillment of theological faith in mystical contemplation*.

• *Sancti doctoris Ecclesiae Alberti Magni, Ordinis Praedicatorum, Episcopi Opera omnia* (Köln Ed.), Münster, Aschendorff, 1951.

Commentary on "Mytical Theology" Dionysius the Pseudo-Areopagite, Tr. É.-H. Wéber (1993)

Both editions by P. Jammy (Lyon, 1651) and A. Borgnet (repr. of the former, Paris, 1890–99) are incomplete, faulty, and feature nonauthentic texts.

♦ F. Ruello (1963), *Les "Noms divins" et leurs "raisons" selon saint Albert le Grand commentateur du* De Divinis nominibus, Paris.

A. de Libera (1984), *La Mystique rhénane: D'Albert le Grand à Maître Eckhart,* Paris (2nd Ed. 1994); (1990), *Albert le Grand et la philosophie,* Paris.

Alain de Libera

See also **Aristotelianism, Christian; Deity; Intellectualism; Rhineland-Flemish Mysticism; Scholasticism; Thomas Aquinas**

Albigensian. *See* **Catharism**

Alexander of Hales. *See* **Scholasticism**

Alexandria, School of

It is customary to contrast the School of Alexandria to the School* of Antioch, but these two expressions conceal a great variety of phenomena. The expression "School of Alexandria" (*see* Le Boulluec, "L'école d'Alexandrie: De quelques aventures d'un concept historiographique," in coll. 1987) refers on the one hand to a certain method of exegesis* and on the other to strictly theological questions connected successively to the very origins of Alexandrian Christianity, to the fight against Arianism*, and to the Nestorian crisis.

a) Historical Background. Around the second century B.C., the large Jewish community of Alexandria produced the translation* of the Hebrew Bible into Greek, known as the Septuagint. According to a tradition recorded by Eusebius of Caesarea (*HE* II, 16), the apostle* Mark was the first to evangelize Egypt, but very little is known about the earliest Christian community of Alexandria. Pagan and Christian philosophers succeeded one another in Alexandria, among them Pantaenus and Clement, before the establishment of the Didaskaleion, a catechetical school that was officially dependent on the church*. Origen was its first leader, during the episcopate of Demetrius (189–231), and Didymus was his distant successor in the late fourth century. Hellenism, Judeo-Christianity, and Gnosticism, with its two illustrious representatives, Basilides and Valentinus (*see* Ritter in coll. 1987), thus formed the crucible in which Christians both appropriated and challenged ways of thought and modes of expression that were fruitful for the development of Christian orthodoxy. Although the influence of Alexandria was soon recognized, so that it was even made a patriarchate*, its relations with the Christianity of the Egyptian interior—and in the fourth century with nascent monasticism*—were sometimes difficult. Crises and schisms* followed one after another in Alexandria, as witnessed in particular by the troubled history of the episcopate of Athanasius*.

b) Alexandrian Exegesis. This was not limited, as a simplistic contrast between Alexandria and Antioch might lead one to believe, to a triumph of allegory over the literal meaning of the Scriptures*. To begin with, it was rooted in the secular philosophical tradition. The Neoplatonist commentators on Plato and Aristotle had established rules of interpretation that the Christians adopted (*see* Hadot 1987, on Origen's commentary on The Song of Songs). For their part, Gnostic influences, also bearing the stamp of Platonism, oriented the understanding of Scripture in an esoteric direction. For example, Clement frequently referred to the Eleusinian mysteries to illustrate by analogy the way in which the teachings of Christ* should be transmitted and understood (*Strom.* VI, 15). Knowledge was not given to everyone (*Strom.* V, 3), and for Clement as for Origen, there were hidden meanings in Scripture, so that recourse to allegorical exegesis was necessary in order to reveal them. If Origen, who became very influential in both East and West, was the master of this technique (*Treatise of Principles* IV, 1–3; *see* Lubac* 1950), he was principally indebted to Philo of Alexandria (first century B.C.), himself heir to the dual Jewish and Greek tradition (*see* Nikiprowetzky 1977 and Runnia 1995).

The exegetical work of Hilary of Poitiers follows in the tradition of Origen, and it was thanks to the Latin translations of Origen's works, made by Rufinus and Jerome as early as the fourth century, that Alexandrian hermeneutics* was disseminated in the West. The doctrine of the four senses of Scripture, put forward by Cassian and later by Gregory* the Great, was also derived from the triple sense defined by Origen (*see* Simonetti, "Quelques considérations sur l'influence et la destinée de l'alexandrinisme en Occident," in coll. 1987).

c) Alexandrian Theologies of the Logos. The central place given by the Alexandrians to the doctrine of the Logos (Word*) had two consequences: Alexandrian thought played a decisive role in Christology*, and there was a recurring risk of heterodox deviations. The Johannine uses of the term *Logos* certainly provided a scriptural basis, but the complex philosophical heritage of the notion and its use (in the plural) by the Gnostics gave rise to ambiguities from the outset. Clement's discourse on the eternal Logos of God* and its manifestation in the flesh opposed the singleness of the Logos to the Gnostic systems, but it could seem very much like Docetism*. After Clement, Origen seems not to have tied the mediating role of the Logos solely to the Incarnation* (*see* his commentary on 1 Tm 2:5 in *Princ.* II, 6, 1; *Contra Celsum* III, 34). Athanasius, relying similarly on an affirmation of the preeminence of the Logos in redemption as well as in creation, confined himself to a theology of the Logos-sarx (Grillmeier 1979) and in a sense left in suspension the questions of the soul* and of human knowledge of Christ. These Christologies took their place within a cultural model that was primarily Platonic (Simonetti 1992), and it was only later developments in Cappadocia which were to free them from this.

• R. Cadiou (1935), *La jeunesse d'Origène: Histoire de l'école d'Alexandrie au début du IIIe s.*, Paris.

C. Mondésert (1944), *Clément d'Alexandrie: Introduction à l'étude de sa pensée religieuse à partir de l'Écriture,* Paris.

J. Guillet (1947), "Les exégèses d'Alexandrie et d'Antioche, conflit ou malentendu?" *RSR* 34, 257–302.

H. de Lubac (1950), *Histoire et Esprit: L'intelligence de l'Écriture d'après Origène,* Paris.

V. Nikiprowetzki (1977), *L'interprétation de l'Écriture chez Philon d'Alexandrie: Son caractère et sa portée,* Leyden.

A. Grillmeier (1979), *Jesus der Christus im Glauben der Kirche,* vol. 1, Freiburg-Basel-Vienna.

M. Simonetti (1985), *Lettera e/o allegoria: Un contributo alla storia dell'esegesi patristica,* Rome.

B.A. Pearson, J.E. Goehring (Ed.) (1986), *The Roots of Egyptian Christianity: Studies in Antiquity and Christianity,* Philadelphia.

I. Hadot (1987), "Les introductions aux commentaires exégétiques chez les auteurs néoplatoniciens et les auteurs chrétiens," in M. Tardieu (Ed.), *Les règles de l'interprétation,* Paris, 99–122.

Coll. (1987), *Alexandrina: Hellénisme, judaïsme et christianisme à Alexandrie.* Offered to P.C. Mondésert, Paris.

M. Simonetti (1992), "Modelli culturali nella cristianità orientale del II-III secolo," in *De Tertullien aux Mozarabes.* Offered to J. Fontaine, Ed. J.-C. Fredouille, Paris, 381–92.

B. Pouderon (1994), "Le témoignage du Codex Barrocianus 142 sur Athénagore et les origines du Didaskaleion d'Alexandrie," in G. Argoud (Ed.), *Science et vie intellectuelle à Alexandrie. (Ier-IIIe s. ap. J.-C.), Mémoires XIV,* Saint-Étienne, 163–224.

D.T. Runnia (1995), *Philo and the Church Fathers,* Leyden-New York-Köln.

Françoise Vinel

See also **Antioch, School of; Gnosis; Patriarchate; Platonism, Christian; Scripture, Senses of; Stoicism, Christian**

Allegory. *See* **Narrative; Scripture, Senses of**

Almightiness. *See* **Omnipotence, Divine**

Alphonsus Liguori

1696–1787

Alphonsus Liguori was a precocious child. From an affluent family, he received a classical education at home and matriculated in the faculty of law* at the age of 12. In 1713 he received a doctorate *in utroque jure* (civil and canon* law) and began practicing law. In 1723 he left the bar and entered a seminary where he studied moral theology*, particularly in the treatise tinged with Jansenist austerity of François Genet (1640–1702), "the leader of the probabiliorists" (*Morale de Grenoble,* 1677). Ordained as a priest* on 21 December 1726, Liguori's first parish was in Naples, among the "debauched and dissolute," then in a backward rural area where there was great ignorance about matters of faith*. In order to foster the evangelization of the countryside, in 1732 Liguori established a congregation of missionary priests, approved in 1749–50 by Benedict XIV under the name of the Institute of the Most Holy Redeemer (the Redemptorists). Addressing the pope* in 1748, he described its purpose: "With the help of missions, teaching, and other exercises, to serve the souls* of the rural poor who are most deprived of spiritual aid, for they often lack ministers, sacraments*, and the divine Word*."

His pastoral activities, and particularly the practice of confession, led Liguori from probabiliorism to probabilism and then to equiprobabilism. In the seminary and as a young priest, he was an advocate of probabiliorism, which required the adoption in every moral dilemma of the "most probable" opinion: that is to say, in effect, the most certain opinion (tutiorism) or the most rigid (rigorism). Along with his rural ministry, Liguori's move from probabiliorism to probabilism was shaped by the study he made of the *Medulla theologiae moralis* by the German Jesuit Herman Busenbaum (1600–1688), a balanced probabilist. The *Medulla,* a fundamental text in the history of casuistry*, was reprinted more than 200 times between 1645, the date of its first edition, and 1776. From this period, after 1748, date several *Dissertations* and *Annotations* of the *Medulla* (which make up the first edition of the *Theologia moralis*).

Probabilism was introduced by a Dominican of Salamanca, B. Medina (†1580), and consists in maintaining that, in doubtful cases, it is legitimate to follow *probable* opinion, that is, an articulated opinion supported by strong reasons and *approved* by the authority of experts (one or more "solemn doctors"). A probable opinion may be followed even if the opposite opinion is more probable. Probability does not refer to mere possibility, but to a proof, in its original meaning: *Probabilis* means "plausible" or "provable," in the sense of *approvable.* In 1762 Liguori published a treatise in Italian, *On the Moderate Use of Probable Opinion (Dissertazione sull'uso moderato dell'opinione probabile),* in which his doctrine reached its definitive form. It sets forth his system, called "equiprobabilism," which is based on three major principles. The first states: "If the opinion that is in support of the law* *(pro lege)* seems certainly more probable, we are obliged to follow it, and we cannot follow the opposite opinion which is in support of liberty*." This principle brings out the primacy of truth*, insofar as human action must be based on an authentic search for that truth. The second principle asserts: "If the opinion that is in support of liberty is merely probable, or as probable *(aeque probabilis)* as the one that supports the law, we cannot follow it merely because it is probable." Liguori emphasizes that a very weak probability is no longer a probability, but only a false appearance of probability. He thus refutes the principle widely accepted in modern times: *Qui probabiliter agit, prudenter agit* (Whoever acts probably, acts prudently). The third principle holds: "When two opposite opinions are equally probable *(aeque probabiles),* the opinion in support of liberty enjoys the same probability as the one in support of the law. Consequently, the existence of the law is doubtful." In order to create obligation, the law must be promulgated in such a way that it establishes the conviction that such a law does indeed exist. If this promulgation is lacking, the law is doubtful and therefore creates no obligation. Liguori thus defends the traditional principle: *Lex dubia non obligat.*

With equiprobabilism, he brings out three basic notions that, far from being in conflict, balance and mutually support one another: truth, liberty, and conscience. Conscience is here defined as "judgment or diktat" (*dictamen;* the word comes from Thomas* Aquinas, *ST* Ia, q. 79, a. 13), a practice of reason* by means of which we judge what is good and to be done or evil and to be avoided.

Through his original development of the primordial role of conscience, Liguori was not merely showing himself to be a follower of the casuists of the century before, whose equiprobabilist system was the latest embodiment of the doctrine of probability, but rather a contemporary of Jean-Jacques Rousseau. Liguori set out his system in the *Theologia moralis.* Adding original exposition to his *Annotationes* on the *Medulla* of Busenbaum (1 vol., 1748), he published the two volumes of the second edition in Naples in 1753–55. It was, in effect, an original work. The *Theologia moralis,* continually revised and expanded, went through several editions during the author's lifetime (the ninth edition, Venice, 1785, was in three volumes) and many in the 19th century. Indeed, it had considerable influence throughout that century, in particular on the attitude of confessors toward the sexual life of married people and the conditions of procreation*.

Appointed bishop* of Sant'Agata dei Goti in 1762, Liguori did not wish to write a specialist work of theological speculation but to develop a theology at the service of pastoral work and to strengthen the piety of the faithful. Among the many works he wrote, in both Italian and Latin, and ranging from the most highly technical to the most popular, there are 50 devotional texts, including the celebrated *The Glories of Mary,* one of the most important books of Marian devotion. After the *Theologia moralis* Liguori composed a number of short treatises, among which should be mentioned *The Confessor of Country People* (1764; a work preceded by *Practical Instruction for Confessors*, 1757, an abridgment of *Theologia moralis* for the use of confessors). It was specifically designed for rural priests, "who are little versed in the study of morals and who cannot buy expensive books, to make them capable of hearing the confessions of country people."

The practice of confession constitutes an essential aspect of Liguori's moral theology, which aims to reestablish a relationship of confidence between confessor and penitent and to restore to confession its character of an act of love*. From this point of view it is easy to understand why Liguori opposed the Jansenist practice of delay in sacramental absolution. The postponement of absolution was justified by the frequent relapses of sinners into the same sins*. Liguori took up the distinction between "habitudinary" and "recidivist" that moral theology had developed. The habitudinary confesses for the first time a sin that he has often committed, whereas the recidivist is one who falls into the same sin after confessing it. Refining this distinction, Liguori has no hesitation for the first case: The habitudinary must be absolved if he manifests sincere repentance. The case of the recidivist is more delicate. Liguori observes that, in general, relapses, even if they are frequent, are not incompatible with the resolution to sin no more and are thereby susceptible to absolution. An expert in humanity, Liguori observes that giving absolution is often a better remedy than delaying it. In addition, he was in favor of penance in proportion to the nature of the sin, penance that would not impel the penitent to stay away from the confessional. And in order the better to move toward God*, Liguori favored frequent, indeed daily communion*.

Liguori's major distinction is that he helped stem austerity within Catholicism and opened the way to a broader moral theology that is more understanding of human weakness. He was canonized in 1839 and declared a doctor* of the church* in 1871. His *Theologia moralis,* for which he was granted the status of doctor, is no doubt the last major monument of the doctrine of probability. After Liguori, casuistry seems to have entered on an irremediable decline.

• M. de Meulemeester (1933–39), *Bibliographie générale des écrivains rédemptoristes* (up to 1939), 3 vols., The Hague-Louvain.

A. Sampers (1953), *Bibliographia alphonsiana* 1938–53, *SHCSR* 1; (1957) *Bio-bibliographia* C.SS.R., 1938–56, ibid., 5; (1960), *Bibliographia scriptorum de systemate morali S. Alfonsi et de probalismo,* 1787–1922, ibid., 8; (1971), *Bibliographia alfonsiana,* 1953–71, ibid., 19; (1972), 1971–72, ibid., 20; (1974), 1972–74, ibid., 22; (1978), 1974–78, ibid., 26.

Critical edition of the ascetic works by Redemptorists; 7 vols., Rome, 1933 (to be reprinted in 18 vols. by Edizioni di Storia e Letteratura di Roma).

♦ J. J.I. von Dollinger, F.H. Reusch (1889), *Geschichte des Moralstreitigkeiten in der römischkatholischen Kirche,* 2 vols., Nördlingen (repr. Aalen: Scientia Verlag, 1968), vol. I, 356–476.

C. Liévin (1937), "Alphonse de Liguori," *DSp* 1, 357–89.

J. Guerer (1973), *Le ralliement du clergé français à la morale liguorienne: L'abbé Gousset et ses précurseurs* (1785–1832), Rome.

A. Dimatteo (1980), "Il differimento dell'assoluzione in S. Alfonso: Gli abituati o consuetudinari e i recidivi," *SHCSR* 28, 353–450.

T. Rey-Mermet (1982), *Le saint du siècle des Lumières: Alphonse de Liguori,* Paris.

L. Vereecke (1986), *De Guillaume d'Ockham à saint Alphonse de Liguori: Études d'histoire de la théologie morale moderne,* Rome.

M. Vidal (1986), *Frente al rigorismo morale: Benignidad pastoral: Alfonso de Liguori (1696–1787),* Madrid.

D. Capone (1987), "La Theologia moralis di S. Alfonso: Prudenzialità nella scienza casistica per la prudenza nella coscienza," *StMor* 25, 27–77.

T. Rey-Mermet (1987), *La morale selon saint Alphonse de Liguori,* Paris.

Coll. (1988), *Alphonse de Liguori, pasteur et docteur,* Paris.

Massimo Marcocchi

See also **Casuistry; Conscience; Ethics, Sexual; Intention; Jansenism; Mission/Evangelization; Penance; Prudence; Suarez, Francisco**

Ambrose of Milan

(337 or 339–97)

Around 370, Ambrose, who belonged to a senatorial family, became governor of the Roman province of Emilia and Liguria. The capital of the province was Milan, and in 374, while the Christians of that city* contested with one another concerning an episcopal election, he intervened to reestablish order and found himself being acclaimed as bishop*. Being only a catechumen at that time, he was baptized hastily and then ordained at the end of the year. During the 22 years of his episcopacy, and boosted by his political experience, he asserted himself, as one of the West's most influential personalities. He played a decisive role in Augustine*'s conversion. Well served by his mastery of Greek, he took inspiration from Philo of Alexandria (first century A.D.), Origen*, Athanasius*, and Basil* the Great, but he still showed real originality in matters concerning spirituality, pastoral work, and ethics*. The recent bilingual edition (Latin-Italian) of his Complete Works (*SAEMO, see* bibliography) is made up of 13 volumes of exegesis* (practiced according to the allegorical method of the School of Alexandria*), three volumes of moral philosophy and asceticism*, three volumes of dogmatic* texts, four volumes of speeches and letters, and one volume of poetry.

a) Doctrinal Controversies. Ambrose was at first an adversary of the western advocates of Arianism*, as much through his actions as through his writings. Between 377 and 380 he sent Emperor Gratian his major theological treaty, the *De fide*. For this work, Ambrose borrowed ideas from Athanasius and Hilary* of Poitiers, as well as from Basil, Gregory* of Nazianzus, and Gregory* of Nyssa, but did show himself to be original in places (Simonetti 1975). In 386, when Emperor Valentinian II ordered him to hand over one of Milan's basilicas to the Arians, Ambrose occupied it. In order to inspire courage in his followers, he made them sing hymns of his own composition, more popular than Hilary's. It was because of these hymns that Ambrose came to be regarded as the founder of Latin hymnology.

In his *De Spiritu Sancto* (381) he championed the divinity of the Holy* Spirit, notably by relying on the baptismal formula of Matthew 28:19 and on the mention of the Spirit in Genesis 1:2, as his Greek masters had done. He fought against Apollinarianism* by reaffirming Genesis in his *De Incarnationis dominicae sacramento* (382), the integrity of the humanity assumed by Christ*.

b) Eulogy to Virginity. Ambrose exalted virginity and widowhood in five works that marked a new stage in the history of Western spirituality. Like Athanasius, he saw in virginity a way of transcending nature, a "celestial pattern of living" made possible by the Incarnation* (*SAEMO* 14/1, 110, 116). The virgins already receive in this world the benefits of resurrection* (ibid., 152, inspired by Cyprian*). They are a "priesthood of chastity," a "living temple*" (*SAEMO* 14/1, 134; 14/2, 270). They must preserve *integritas* (integrity, purity*), not only that of the body but also that of the spirit (*SAEMO* 14/2, 24), and lead a life of prayer*, work*, poverty, and charity.

Ambrose does not condemn second marriages, but he disapproves of multiple remarriages (*SAEMO* 14/1, 300). He does not advise against marriage*, and in fact he attacks its detractors (*SAEMO* 14/1, 126; 14/2, 34). Listing the difficulties of family life, in order to exhort young ladies to preserve their virginity, he stops himself in his tracks for fear of discouraging those who are already "saintly parents" (*SAEMO* 14/1, 128). Marriage, widowhood, and virginity are but three ways of practicing chastity, because while *integritas* is only recommended, *castitas* is required of all Christians (*SAEMO* 14/1, 266; 306).

From eulogizing virginity, Ambrose goes on to eulogizing women (woman*). The widows who wish to remarry on account of the "vulnerability of women" are reminded by him that some women were able to reign as queens (*SAEMO* 14/1, 288). He refutes those who use the stories of the Creation* and the Fall to disparage women, and in Mary*, whose perpetual virginity he champions, he exalts all of womanhood (*SAEMO* 14/2, 122–34).

c) Theory and Practice of Penance. In his *De paenitentia* (SC 179) Ambrose fights against the belated followers of Novatianism*, who admit the perpetrators of grave sins* (apostasy, homicide, adultery) to penance* without the crowning step of reconciliation: "It is in vain that you claim you are preaching penance, when you are doing away with the fruit of penance" (SC 179, 125). Ambrose emphasizes divine mercy*: "even Judas could have managed... not to be excluded from forgiveness if he had done penance" (SC 179, 151). He champions above all the right of the church* to absolve sinners or not to absolve them, finding particular support for his arguments in Matthew 16:19 and John 20:22–23. On this same point, he accuses his adversaries of contradicting themselves by accepting baptism but not penance (SC 179, 85). Ambrose, however, allows Christians to resort to canonical penance only once in a lifetime; according to R. Gryson (SC 179, 48), this is a contradiction of his own principle, namely that no sin can be totally out of the church's power to absolve or not to absolve.

Beyond its polemical character, the *De paenitentia* is intended both for the bishops who impose penance and for the believers who submit to it. It asks from the former a willingness "to share the sinners' affliction from the bottom of their hearts" (SC 179, 181); and from the latter, it requires that they should know how to confess, weep, humble themselves, then live reconciliation as a total change (SC 179, 193). Heading a community not of pure people but of forgiven sinners, Ambrose says of himself that he is one of them (SC 179, 177): "I confess... that I was given more forgiveness myself when I was rescued from the quarrels of the madding crowd and from the formidable responsibilities of public administration to be called to the priesthood*."

d) Attitude in the Face of Political Authorities. In 384 Ambrose exhorted Valentinian II not to yield to the pagan senators who wanted to reestablish the altar of the goddess Victory in the Roman Curia, and in 386 he again resisted Valentinian, who was demanding a basilica for the Arians (*see* above). In 388 he asked Theodosius not to force the bishop of Callinicum, a city in the region of the Upper Euphrates River, to rebuild a synagogue set on fire by monks. And when, in 390, the same emperor ordered the massacre of thousands of Thessalonians as punishment for the lynching of an officer, Ambrose forced him to do penance publicly.

With regard to the second of the events listed above, basing his decision on Matthew 22:21, Ambrose writes: "In matters of faith*, I do mean in matters of faith, it is up to bishops to pass judgment on Christian emperors, and not up to emperors to pass judgment on bishops" (*SAEMO* 21, 108). In the case of the other three events, he reminds the monarchs of their duties as believers. As a Christian, Valentinian "has learnt to honor only the altar of Christ" (*SAEMO* 21, 68), while with regard to the situation at Callinicum, Theodosius had to give preference to the "cause of religion" over an "appearance of public order" (*SAEMO* 21, 92). In 390 Theodosius had to do penance, just as King David had done in ancient times (*SAEMO* 21, 236). Ambrose does not make a distinction between the emperor as a Christian and the imperial function as an institution. He does not see himself in an abstract fashion as a spokesman for religious authorities in the face of political authorities, but presents himself as a spiritual adviser concerned for the sovereign's salvation* (*SAEMO* 21, 86).

e) Social Morality. Ambrose, an aristocrat, wanted to reform the socioeconomic behavior of his milieu. His works draw an ideal profile of the Christian landlord at the head of a large estate. He does not practice usury (De Tobia), does not evict his neighbors from their humble properties (De Nabuthae). He does not overburden his feudal tenants with excessive charges (*De officiis* II, 16, 81). He remunerates fairly the day laborers he employs (*SAEMO* 6, 284), and he does not endanger the lives of those who work for him by assigning them hazardous tasks (*SAEMO* 6, 142–44). He does not hide his harvest in order to speculate on the price of wheat (*De officiis* III, 6, 37–44). On the contrary, he does the opposite: knowing that the fruits of nature are intended for all human beings, he opens his granary generously to the poor (*SAEMO* 6, 154). In short, he behaves as a protector of the weak (*SAEMO* 9, 258).

Displaying originality in his pastoral concern for virginity and penance, and in his actions and ideas in the face of political authorities, it is Ambrose, among all the Latin Fathers, who presents the most coherent teaching on social matters.

• *Opera omnia di Sant'Ambrogio: Sancti Ambrosii Episcopi Mediolanensis Opera (SAEMO),* Milan-Rome (the complete works—Latin texts and Italian trans.—were published in 24 vols. between 1979–94)

In SC: *Des sacrements; Des mystère; Explication du symbole* (25 *bis*); *Traité sur l'Évangile de saint Luc* (45 and 52); *La pénitence* (179); *Apologie de David* (239).

Les devoirs (De officiis), 2 vols., CUFr.

♦ G. Madec (1974), *Saint Ambroise et la philosophie,* Paris.

M. Simonetti (1975), *La crisi ariana nel IV secolo,* Rome, 435–552.

Coll. (1976), *Ambrosius episcopus: Atti del congresso internazionale di studi ambrosiani,* Milan.

H. Savon (1977), *Saint Ambroise devant l'exégèse de Philon le Juif,* 2 vols., Paris.

E. Dassmann (1978), "Ambrosius," *TRE* 2, 362–86.

Coll. (1981), *Cento anni di bibliografia ambrosiana (1874–1974),* Milan.

P. Brown (1988), *The Body and Society: Men, Women and Sexual Renunciation in Early Christianity,* New York, chap. 17.

R.A. Markus (1988), chap. VI of J.H. Burns (Ed.), *The Cambridge History of Medieval Political Thought, c. 350–c. 1450,* Cambridge.

S. Mazzarino (1989), *Storia sociale del vescovo Ambrogio,* Rome.
P. Brown (1992), *Power and Persuasion in Late Antiquity,* Madison.
J.-M. Salamito (1992), "Aut villa aut negotiatio," diss., University of Paris-Sorbonne.
C. Markschies (1993), *Ambrosius von Mailand und die Trinitätstheologie,* Tübingen.
N.B. McLynn (1994), *Ambrose of Milan: Church and Court in a Christian Capital,* Berkeley.
C. and L. Pietri (Ed.) (1995), *Naissance d'une chrétienté (250–430),* Paris.
D.H. Williams (1995), *Ambrose of Milan and the End of the Arian-Nicene Conflict,* Oxford.
H. Savon (1997), *Ambroise de Milan,* Paris.

JEAN-MARIE SALAMITO

See also **Arianism; Church and State; Novatianism; Penance; Platonism, Christian; Precepts; Property; Spiritual Direction**

Amish. *See* **Anabaptists**

Anabaptists

Anabaptism arose amidst the ferment of ideas and movements that marked the beginnings of the Reformation of the 16th century. Around this time, several attempts at reform received political support and were institutionalized. But some who wanted to reform the church*, and who were not (or were no longer) in agreement with Luther*, Zwingli*, or Calvin*, became dissidents. For polemical reasons, these Protestant dissidents have often been characterized as "Anabaptists." Contemporary historians, however, have pointed out the multiplicity and variety of this "left wing of the Reformation," or "radical Reformation," and have made distinctions among revolutionaries, spiritualists, Anabaptists, and anti-Trinitarians, which in the past had been seen as a homogeneous dissident whole. Anabaptism in the strict sense comprises various movements that arose in 1520–30 in several regions of Europe.

The earliest organized Anabaptism arose in Switzerland with Zwingli. Taking their inspiration from ideas coming from Luther, Zwingli, Erasmus, Carlstadt, or the peasant movement of 1524–25, men such as Conrad Grebel, Felix Mantz, and Balthasar Hubmaier came to reject the baptism* of infants and to formulate the idea of a "pre-Constantinian" church made up of members who had made a deliberate Christian commitment. Taking up the *sola scriptura* and the *sola fide* of the Reformation, these Swiss Anabaptists rejected the symbiosis between church* and state that the Reformers did not question. This rejection was accompanied by a Christocentric and communitarian ethics* and ecclesiology* advocating the practice of *Nachfolge Christi* (*sequela Christi,* imitation* of Jesus Christ) and, most often, a return to Christian "nonviolence." A series of theological disputes with Zwingli did not succeed in resolving all disagreements. The first baptisms on the basis of a profession of faith* (hence the name *Anabaptist*) took place in Zurich in January 1525 and led to the formation of a "Protestant" church lacking in political support. This church was able to survive only clandestinely, and it was in large part thanks to a former Benedictine, Michael Sattler, who drafted the seven articles adopted by the Swiss Anabaptist communities at Schleitheim in February 1527, that it persisted through harsh rejection and persecution. These articles confessed the baptism of adults, the necessity for a church discipline in conformity with Matthew 18:15–18, the impossibility of a Christian being a magistrate or using violence*, and a radical separation between the church and the world*.

Another Anabaptist movement arose around the same time in southern Germany and Austria. With leaders such as Hans Hut and Hans Denck, this Anabaptism was strongly marked at the outset by Rhenish mysticism*. The lay theologian Pilgram Marpeck developed a theology based on the humanity of Christ*. This influence was to survive lastingly, particularly in Moravia, under the leadership of Jakob Hutter. In the 1530s Hutter established an Anabaptism that was more radically communitarian than the Swiss movement and that practiced communal ownership of property. This Hutterite movement had a golden age during the second half of the 16th century, but was hard pressed to resist the Counter-Reformation.

A third movement, located in the Netherlands, was strongly influenced in its beginnings by the millenarian and spiritualist theology of Melchior Hoffman (†1534 in Strasbourg). This thinking met with popular support and contributed a good deal to the events in Münster in Westphalia (1534–35) where, under the leadership of Bernhard Rothmann and Jan van Leyden, an attempt was made to establish a Reformation based on Anabaptist ecclesiology and to prepare for the imminent return of Christ (Parousia*). Ending in bloodshed, the episode assisted the anti-Protestant polemic of the Catholic Church and drove Protestants to dissociate themselves as much as possible from any form of dissidence arising in their ranks. Dutch Anabaptism nevertheless survived in a pacific form thanks to the former priest Menno Simons, who assembled a large number of the refugees from Münster under a theology close to that of the Swiss Anabaptism coming out of Schleitheim.

Rejected and persecuted by "official" Protestants as well as by Catholics, thousands of Anabaptists were killed (especially in the 16th century) or driven into exile or emigration. Only in the Netherlands did the Mennonites experience a fairly peaceful cultural assimilation from the 17th century onward (the painter Rembrandt was close to Mennonite circles, although it is not known whether he was actually a member). By the 17th century many Swiss, Alsatian, and German Anabaptists found a more welcoming atmosphere in North America. Emigration to the Americas continued as late as the period after the Second World War*. Finally, with the recent collapse of communism, many Russian Mennonites of Dutch or German origin have now settled in Germany. Thus, the spiritual descendants of the 16th-century Anabaptists are now living in many countries, including countries in Africa and Asia. They call themselves Mennonites, Hutterites, or Amish.

• Menno Simons (1681), *Opera omnia theologica...*, Amsterdam; The complete writings, Tr. L. Verdun, Ed. C. Wenger, Scottdale, Penn., 1956.

Mennonitisches Lexicon, Ed. C. Hege, C. Neff, continued by H. S. Bender, E. Crous, 1913–57, Frankfurt, 1958–, Karlsruhe.

Bibl. in *The Mennonite Quarterly Review,* Goshen, Ind., 1927–.

H. J. Hillerbrand (1962), *Bibliographie des Täufertums* (1520–1630), Gütersloh (*QFRG,* 30–*QGT,* 10).

N. P. Springer, A. J. Klassen (Ed.) (1977), *Mennonite Bibliography (1631–1961),* Scottdale, Penn.

Bibliotheca dissidentium: Répertoire des non-conformistes religieux des XVIe et XVIIe s., Ed. A. Seguenny, Baden-Baden, 1980–.

♦ *The Mennonite Encyclopedia* (1955–90), 5 vols., Scottdale, Penn.

G. H. Williams (1962), *The Radical Reformation,* Philadelphia.

U. Gastaldi (1972), *Storia dell'anabattismo,* I: *Dalle origine a Münster (1525–1535);* (1981), II: *Da Münster ai giorni nostri,* Turin.

C. Bornhäuser (1973), *Leben und Lehre Menno Simons. Ein Kampf um das Fundament des Glaubens (etwa 1496–1561),* Neukirchen-Vluyn.

M. Lienhard (Ed.) (1977), *The Origins and Characteristics of Anabaptism / Les débuts et les caractéristiques de l'anabaptisme,* The Hague.

J. Séguy (1977), *Les assemblées anabaptistes-mennonites de France,* Paris-The Hague.

N. Blough (1984), *Christologie anabaptiste,* Geneva.

R. MacMaster (1985), *Land, Piety, Peoplehood: The Establishment of Mennonite Communities in America, 1683–1790,* Scottdale, Penn.

J.-G. Rott, S. L. Verheus (1987), *Anabaptistes et dissidents au XVIe s.,* Baden-Baden– Bouxwiller.

C. Baecher (1990), *L'affaire Sattler,* Méry-sur-Oise–Montbéliard.

N. Blough (Ed.) (1992), *Jésus-Christ aux marges de la Réforme,* Paris.

M. Lienhard (1992), "Les anabaptistes," in M. Vénard (Ed.), *Le temps des confessions,* vol. 8: *Histoire du christianisme,* Paris, 119–81.

G. Williams (1992), *The Radical Reformation,* Kirksville.

N. Blough (1994), "Secte et modernité: Réflexions sur l'évolution historique de l'anabaptisme aux États-Unis," *BSHPF* 140, 581–602.

A. Hamilton, S. Voolstra, P. Visser (Ed.) (1994), *From Martyr to Muppy: A Historical Introduction to Cultural Assimilation Processes of a Religious Minority in the Netherlands: The Mennonites,* Amsterdam.

M. Lienhard (1994), "Réformateurs radicaux," in M. Vénard, *De la Réforme à la Réformation,* vol. 7: *Histoire du christianisme,* 805–29.

NEAL BLOUGH

See also **Analogy; Baptists; Calvinism; Millenarianism; Protestantism; Unitarianism**

Anagogy. *See* **Mysticism; Scripture, Senses of; Trace (Vestige)**

Analogy

In theology*, analogy designates the gap between human knowledge* of God* and God himself. It expresses two requirements: respect for the absolute transcendence of God, who is ineffable and unknowable, and the preservation of a minimal intelligible pertinence in the discourse of faith*. The combination of these antagonistic elements has given rise to diverse syntheses embodying the vicissitudes of theological language*.

a) Proportion and Participation. The original meaning of analogy has to do with mathematical proportion, and represents a mid-point between total resemblance and complete dissimilarity. Etymologically, *analogia* (in Greek) is a simple relationship *(logos),* which is a logos of a logos, a relationship of relationships, a mediated identity. Prefigured in Parmenides and Heraclitus (Jüngel 1964), developed by the Pythagorean school, *analogia* is attested in Archytas of Tarentum in the sense of a mathematical proportion (a/b = c/d). Extended to all aspects of philosophy* (Boulnois 1990), it gradually came to be applied to relations between the sensible and the divine. The analogical method was disseminated by Middle Platonism as a path towards knowledge of the unknowable God, being understood also in relation to the paths of eminence *(huperokhè)* and retrenchment *(aphairesis).* Such teaching is found in Celsus (True Discourse VII, 42; Glöckner 59), Maximus of Tyre (Dübner XVII, 9) and Albinos (*Epitomè tôn Platônos dogmatôn* X, 5; Louis 61). For Proclus, analogy assures the real continuity of degrees of being, each of which participates in the next higher degree; it no longer means a proportion, but a one to one relationship, a capacity to receive participative being* (*In Timaeum* II, 27, 13). For Damascius, on the contrary, analogy demonstrates our inability to know the ineffable God: "the analogy of being" leads us to the One established above the being, but attains it as unknowable (Of First Principles, the Ineffable, and the One, Werterink-Combès 69).

b) From the Creation to the Creator. Analogy entered Jewish and then Christian theology through the Wisdom of Solomon 13:5: "From the greatness and beauty of created things comes a corresponding perception of their Creator." This verse echoes philosophical reflections asserting that the invisible divinity can be contemplated thanks to its visible works, for example in Pseudo-Aristotle, *De Mundo* VI, 399b 19–22: "Although invisible to any mortal nature, his works themselves manifest him." Often linked by the Fathers* of the Church to Romans 1:20, analogy enables us to have knowledge of God through his creation*. For Athanasius*, *Against the Pagans* 44 (SC 18 *bis*, 199), the Word*, "being the head and king and the union of all beings, performs everything for the glory* and the knowledge of the Father and teaches us through his works." According to Cyril* of Alexandria, in his treatise on the Trinity IV, 538b (SC 237, 240): "For God, it is the most beautiful and best part of his illustriousness and his glory to be able to create, because it is precisely in that way that we know who and what He is."

Knowledge of God needs the analogical method: that is, the movement upward from works to the Principle. There is no theology, however, that does not rely on divine economy. Theology is not some kind of pure reasoning on the divine nature, but must rely on tangible manifestations in order to ascend toward the Creator. Moreover, analogy even makes it possible to think about the relation among the divine Persons: as creation manifests its author, so the divine Word* in turn reveals the Father* (Boulnois 1994, 44–49). Among the Fathers of the Church, Pseudo-Dionysius adopts the interpretation of Proclus: "God is known by analogy with those things of which He is the cause"

(*Divine Names* VII, 7; PG 3, 872), but he is not a being as such. Analogy further implies the diversity of hierarchical degrees, but it means that each existent has the capacity to receive God (*Celestial Hierarchy* III, 2; PG 3, 165). In the New Testament, Romans 12:6 requires that gifts be exercised "in proportion to our faith" according to the *analogia fidei.* Origen* emphasizes the gratuitousness of God's gift, remarking that among the graces granted according to the analogy of faith "is included faith" itself (*In Rom.* III, 5-V, 7; Scherer 204). From now on, he adds, analogy is an incalculable relationship between two terms, because it includes both the divine gift and the relationship of humankind to that gift.

c) Semantics and Logic. Porphyry reduces the unit of reference among existents to an intelligible relationship by associating it with Aristotle's *paronymy* and by justifying the relationships of meanings by the inflections of a word (*In Categorias Aristotelis* VI, 1, 133); between homonymy and synonymy, analogy becomes a mode of preaching. Alexander of Aphrodisias interprets this unity as a participation, which permits the deduction of categories (*In Metaphysicam* I, 243–44). In the Latin tradition*, Boethius* transforms the mathematical usage by translating *logos* (the relation between two terms) as *proportio* and *analogia* (in Greek) by *proportionalitas* (*De institutione arithmeticae* II, 40). Thus, *analogia* (derived from Dionysius by John the Scot Eriugena) might be a simple resemblance and *proportio* a simple relation between two terms. Applied to God, this grammatical and logical apparatus joins with a strong Dionysian trend for which contemplation of created beings makes possible the ascent to God. The Fourth Lateran* Council did this in Neoplatonic terms: between God and created beings, "however great the resemblance, the dissimilarity is even greater" (Mansi 23, 986; *see* Augustine*, *De Trin.* XV. xi. 21, BAug 16, 476; Proclus, Commentary on *Parmenides,* Cousin 1864).

Other shifts come from translations from the Arabic. Arabic authors interpret *paronymie* as a form of ambiguity *(convenientia):* "The *convenants* are intermediary between the univocal and the equivocal, as existence is attributed to substance and to accident" (Algazel, *Logica* chap. 3, ed. Liechtenstein 1506, 3 vo a). But the Arabic term was also translated as *analoga.* Hence, semantically, analogy occupies the midpoint between the univocal—the single meaning of a term applied to several referents—and the equivocal—difference in meaning according to difference in referents. But grammatical analysis is coupled with a logical problem: The question arises whether an equivocal term corresponds to several concepts (equivocity); to a relation between the anterior and the posterior (analogy); or to a single concept concealed beneath various modes of signifying (univocity; *see* Ashworth 1992).

Thus, Alexander of Hales (1186–1245) thinks of the relationship of created beings to God not as a *convenientia secundum univocationem,* which presupposes at least that they are of the same type, but as a *convenientia secundum analogiam,* which refers to the relationship between substance and accidents. In the plurality of meanings of being*, there is a primary meaning—"substance"—and the others are articulated with reference to that meaning in a sequence from posterior to anterior. The Good is said first of God by nature, then of created beings through participation (*Summa Theologica* I, Intr. q. 2, membr. 3, chap. 2 [§21]; Quaracchi, I, 1924, 32 a). But analogy did not impose itself on everyone who approached the question of the relationship between God and created beings. Divine attributes, such as justice, were said to be univocal to God and the creature (Prevotinus of Cremona, quoted by Schlenker 1938), as indeed being itself had been (Peter of Capua, ibid., 58, n. 107). For Alexander of Hales himself, the notion of person is thought of as univocal (op. cit., Pars II, Inq. 2, tract. 2, sect. 1, q. 1, a. 1 [§388]; 573). In the context of this terminological uncertainty, Albert* the Great connected the unity of perfections that God causes in each order with the finite receptive capacity of each created being, invoking the concept of *univocitas analogiae* (*In de Div. Nom.*, chap. 1, 1 a). Bonaventure*, for his part, contrasted God, as pure act of unparticipated being, with the created thing which participates in it, *esse analogum* (*Journey of the Soul toward God,* Duméry 84).

Thomas* Aquinas argues against Maimonides (1135–1204), for whom there is nothing in common between God and created beings, which leads him to attribute being to God by a "simple homonymy" (*Guide for the Perplexed* I, chap. 56). For Thomas, nothing can be attributed to God univocally either, because there is no "reason" common to God and created beings: God is his own being, incommunicable. The attribution is therefore made by analogy (*De Veritate,* q. 2, a. 11; *ST* I, q. 13, a.5). To justify this analysis, Thomas advances various classifications of analogies, which had divided the commentators. However, at least the analogy of created beings to God is that of the multiple to the one, of the posterior to its center of reference (Montagnes 1963; Boulnois 1990). Thomas thus eliminates all the symbolic or metaphorical names, retaining only those that designate pure perfections (God* A. III).

The logical thought of Duns Scotus, while accepting the real analogy between God and created beings, displaces the problem of the knowledge of God. God is reached within the univocal concept of *ens,* by the articulation of this concept and its mode, which is infinity (infinite*). Negativity and eminence are absorbed in the affirmation of positive divine perfections: "We do not supremely love negations" (*Ordinatio* I, d. 3, §10). From then on, the analogy between (created) being and God becomes an analogy within being, and God is reached within the concept of being—this is designated by the *analogia entis,* which arose in the Thomist school in the 14th century (Thomas Sutton, *Contra Robert Cowton*). For Wycliffe (Hus*), the notion of analogous being—that is, the notion of going from created beings to their idea in God—confirms this unification of being in a representation. The solutions proposed by Cajetan (Thomism*) and Suarez* were unable to free themselves from this primacy of the concept.

d) Analogy of Faith and Analogy of Being. Following Cajetan, the question of analogy became the *pons asinorum* of Neoscholasticism. Metaphysics, apologetics, and natural theology* were supposed to stand or fall with analogy. The fourth of the 24 allegedly Thomist theses imposed on the clergy in 1914 thus included the analogy of the Creator to created beings (*DS* 3604). This hypertrophy provoked an absolute rejection by Barth*, according to whom analogy is an "invention of the Antichrist" because it lays claim to knowledge of God outside revelation* (which is true of Neoscholasticism but not of Scholasticism*). He contrasts it to *analogia fidei* (Rom 12:6): the grace* of God alone provides the conditions for knowledge of him (*KD* I/1, 1932, 239 ff.).

For Erich Przywara, by contrast, *analogia entis* is "the fundamental form" of Catholicism*. It provides a philosophy of religion*, as well as an answer to Protestantism*, to modern thought on subjectivity, and to transcendental theology. Integrating pure logic and making analogy dialectical by a series of oppositions calling for their own overcoming, Przywara makes Western thought, in all its polarities, the content of analogy. Reality is merely provisional and awaits its accomplishment in God, with the overcoming of all contradictions. This historical and systematic work is rooted in a meditation on the text of thc Fourth Lateran Council: dissimilarity greater than resemblance makes possible the avoidance of any "idolatrous" notion of analogy as affirmative knowledge.

Przywara was born in 1889 in Katowice, Upper Silesia, on the border of Germany and Poland. He joined the Company of Jesus in 1908 and studied in the Netherlands. From 1913 to 1917 he was director of music in Feldkirch, Austria. Ordained as a priest in 1920, he contributed to the journal *Stimmen der Zeit* from 1921 until it was banned in 1941. He pursued a dialogue with Barth, Buber, Husserl, Heidegger*, and Edith Stein, and inspired Rahner* and Balthasar*. Chaplain to the students of Munich from 1941, he gave lectures in Munich, Berlin, Vienna, and other cities. He died in 1972.

Przywara's method consists of drawing from the most important writers an objective meaning, in order to understand them better than they understood themselves, according to the principle of hermeneutics*. Augustine*, the Rhineland*-Flemish mystics, the German romantics, Nietzsche*, Scheler, and Newman thus form nodes who oppose and answer one another in the history of thought, following an internal rhythm and reciprocal polarities. Their unity goes beyond these oppositions and is expressed in terms of *analogia entis,* transforming a Neoscholastic concept into a concord of opposites and a fundamental structure of universal (Catholic) truth*. The history* of thought thereby escapes from historicism, without being trapped in the Hegelian logic of irreversible progress (Hegel*) or in simple Christian apologetics. In the spirit of the *Spiritual Exercises,* Przywara wrote *Christliche Existenz* (1934), *Heroisch* (1936), *Deus semper maior* (1938), and *Crucis mysterium: Das christliche Heute* (1939), which also attests to the resistance to Nazism. He develops the question of the foundations of religion in *Religionsphilosophie der katholische Theologie* (1927), *Das Geheimnis Kierkegaards* (1929), *Ringen der Gegenwart* (1929), *Kant heute* (1930), and *Augustinus: Gestalt als Gefüge* (1934). His debate with Luther* is set out in *Humanitas* (1952).

From a more detached standpoint, Hans Urs von Balthasar attempts to reconcile positions. Analogy is not a principle of natural knowledge but the condition of the created being, and yet this is recognized only through faith. In this way, *analogia entis* is integrated into *analogia fidei* (*Karl Barth: Darstellung und Deutung seiner Theologie,* 1962). From a Protestant perspective, Bonhoeffer* criticizes Przywara's application of analogy to being (*Akt und Sein, DBW* 2, 67–70), but he outlines his own theory of *analogia relationis* to designate the relationship between humankind (the image of God) to its model (*Schöpfung und Fall, DBW* 3, 58 ff.). The analogy of relation was to be taken up and orchestrated by Barth (*KD* III/1, 218–20; III/2, 226 ff., 390 ff.). More recently, E. Jüngel (1977) has proposed a return to analogy as a way of thinking of God in his transcendence, while at the same time emphasizing the opposite pole, which is God's mercy in revealing himself. He thereby proposes to reverse the formulation of the Fourth Lateran

Council and to see "in dissimilarity an even greater resemblance."

• E. Przywara (1932), *Analogia entis,* Einsiedeln, 1962.
Cajetan, *De l'analogie des noms* (text and tr. B. Pinchard, *Métaphysique et sémantique,* 1987).
♦ E. Schlenker (1938), *Die Lehre von der göttlichen Namen in der Summa Alexanders von Hales,* Freiburg.
J. Hellin (1947), *La analogia del ser y el conocimiento de Dios en Suarez,* Madrid.
E.L. Mascall (1949), *Existence and Analogy,* London.
A.-J. Festugière (1954), *Révélation d'Hermès Trismégiste,* IV: *Le Dieu inconnu et la gnose,* Paris, 92–140.
E. Jüngel (1962), "Die Möglichkeit theologischer Anthropologie auf dem Grunde der Analogie. Eine Untersuchung zum Analogieverständnis Karl Barths," Barth-Studien, ÖTh 9, 1982, 210–32.
B. Montagnes (1963), *La doctrine de l'analogie de l'être d'après Thomas d'Aquin,* Louvain-Paris.
E. Jüngel (1964), "Zum Ursprung des Analogie bei Parmenides und Heraklit," *Entsprechungen,* Münich, 1980, 52–102.
J.M. Bochénski (1965), *The Logic of Religion,* New York, §37 and 50 (*Die Logik der Religion,* 2nd Ed., Paderborn, 1981).
S. George (1965), "Der Begriff analogos im Buch der Weisheit," *Parusia, Festschrift J. Hirschberger,* 189–97.
G. Siewerth (1965), *Analogie des Seienden,* Einsiedeln.
W. Pannenberg (1967), "Analogie und Doxologie," *Grundfr. syst. Th.*, 181–201.
B. Gertz (1969), *Glaubenswelt und Analogie,* Düsseldorf.
L.B. Püntel (1969), *Analogie und Geschichtlichkeit,* Freiburg.
R. Mortley (1971), "Analogia chez Clément d'Alexandrie," *REG* 84, 80–93.
D. Burrell (1973), *Analogy and Philosophical Language,* London-New Haven.
E. Jüngel (1977), *Gott als Geheimnis der Welt,* Tübingen, 357–408.
P. Secretan, P. Gisel (Ed.) (1982), *Analogie et dialectique,* Geneva.
R. Mortley (1986), *From Word to Silence,* vol. II: *The Way of Negation, Christian and Greek,* Bonn.
E. Naab (1987), *Zur Begründung der analogia entis bei Erich Przywara,* Regensburg.
O. Boulnois (1990), "Analogie," *Encyclopédie philosophique universelle: Les notions philosophiques,* Ed. S. Auroux, vol. I, Paris, 80–83.
E.J. Ashworth (1992), "Analogy and Equivocation in Thirteenth-Century Logic: Aquinas in Context," *MS* 54, 94–135.
M.-O. Boulnois (1994), *Le paradoxe trinitaire chez Cyrille d'Alexandrie,* Paris.
O. Boulnois (1996), "Duns Scot, théoricien de l'analogie," *John Duns Scotus, Metaphysics and Ethics,* Ed. L. Honnefelder, Leyden, 293–315.

OLIVIER BOULNOIS

See also **Attributes, Divine; Language, Theological; Name; Negative Theology**

Andrew of Saint-Victor. *See* **Saint-Victor, School of**

Angels

1. Biblical Tradition

a) Old Testament and Postbiblical Tradition. With ancient civilizations, the Bible* acknowledges the existence of spirits, including angels and demons, but, in its strict monotheism, ranks them as creatures. There are superior spirits that serve God*—hence, the Hebrew title *mal'ak* (Greek: *aggelos,* Latin *calque: angelus,* meaning "envoy," or "messenger [of God]"). Then there are spirits that are evil and in revolt against God.

The subordination of good angels to God can be seen in their role as executors of divine will. Genesis speaks of sentinel angels at the entrance of the garden of Eden (Gn 3:24) and of an intervening angel at the time of Isaac's sacrifice* (Gn 22:11). Angels are called "sons of god" and form his court (Jb 1:6); some of them are called *seraphim* (Is 6:2), which means "burning." Often angels are reduced to simple literary symbols that lend authority to the message they deliver through a vision or a thought (as in Dn 7:16). Hence, the more critical expression *Angel of YHWH* wherever the context suggests that it is God himself who is involved (Gn 32:24–30; Ex 14:19, etc.). It would be a later correction of the text that would safeguard divine transcendence in its immediate manifestation. The prophets*, rather silent on the theme of angels until exile, when it developed because of the Persian contract, insist on their condition as loyal servants and worshipers of God. Among the "thousand thousands . . . and ten thousand times ten thousand" angels (Dn 7:10) are distinguished "seven holy angels who present the prayers of the saints" (Tb 12:15), constantly worshipping God, as are three principal angels, or archangels, Raphael (Tb 12:15), Michael, and Gabriel (Dn 8:16, 9:21, and 10:13).

The pseudoepigrapha of the New Testament and postbiblical writings introduce many more angels, but without systematizing them. Philo combines angels with Greek winged spirits. Late Jewish literature, and especially the Talmud and the Midrash, claim that angels have flaming bodies and attribute numerous roles to them in relation to human beings. Sometimes angels are sent to punish, while on other occasions they communicate God's favor. In addition to the few proper names for angels that can be found in the canonical books, there are many others, more than 250 general titles for good and bad angels, such as the Accusing Angel, the Angel of Darkness, and the Angel of Death. A certain dualism appears, with the good angels, who had been created on the first day, finding themselves at war with the rebellious angels, those ruled by the bad angel, who had been created on the ill-fated second day. Islam borrows from Jewish angelology and demonology, which has Christian connections. It assigns a large role to angels (Koran XXXV), including Gabriel, Michael (Mika'il), Cherubim, al-Hafaza, Throne Carrier, and Isrâfîl. Among the innumerable angels, angel Djibril, "the loyal spirit," is ranked up with Mika'il.

b) New Testament. Like the Old Testament, the New Testament refers to angels. Paul uses a number of accepted titles for angels, including: *thrones, sovereigns, authorities, powers* (Col 1:16, 2:14–15; Eph 1:21; and Rom 8:38). The Evangelists do the same (Lk 1:11, 1:26; Mt 1:20–21, 1:2, 1:13, and 4:11). Jesus* mentions angels quite a few times, notably in John 1:51, in Matthew 18:10 (a passage that has been understood as alluding to guardian angels), in Matthew 22:30, 25:31, and 26:53, and in Luke 12:8 and 15:10. Angels are clearly present in the accounts of the Passion* and the Resurrection* (Lk 24:4; Mt 28.2; and Jn 20:12). It is an angel, according to Paul, who gives the signal of judgment* (1 Thes 4:16). It is also an angel who frees Peter* in Acts 5:18, and an angel who addresses the deacon*, Philip, in Acts 8:26, and so forth. In the account of Paul's appearance before the Sanhedrin the disagreement between Pharisees and Sadducees over angels is brought up (Acts 23:8).

2. Christian Theology

a) Liturgy and Magisterium. Early Judeo-Christianity initially gave to Christ* the title of *Angel,* but Paul, followed by Hebrews and Apocalypse, specifies that the incarnate Christ-Son has primacy over all the angels, which are created by him and for him and are integrated into his body (Col 1:15–18). Christian liturgy, both Greek and Latin, honors angels as servants of God and friends of human beings: Michael, Gabriel, Raphael, and all the anonymous angels. It associates its own celebrations with their heavenly liturgy. This can be seen, for example, in the *Trisagion* of John Chrysostom, and in the threefold Sanctus of the Latin liturgy. The Fathers* all believed that God confided missions to his angels to help human beings on their way to salvation*. The theme of guardian angels, as instruments of divine providence, is found in the writings of Clement of Alexandria (c. 150–c. 215), Irenaeus, Origen*, Ambrose*, Augustine*, and Jerome (c. 342–420), with a few hesitations when it comes to the question of how long these angels are assigned for, and to whom (only to the only converted, to the baptized, to every human being?).

Because the question of angels is secondary from the point of view of salvation, the ecclesiastical magisterium (thus Lateran* IV) only defined their creaturely status. However, since angels did not belong to the temporal order as experienced by human beings, the ancient councils ruled out the theory of the final conversion of fallen angels during the renovation (apocatastasis*) promised for all things, a theory supported by certain disciples of Origen.

b) Patristic Era. If the desert monks referred to angels according to the mentality of their own time, the first major theologians—men such as Irenaeus, Gregory* of Nyssa, Gregory* of Nazianzus, Basil of Caesarea, and John Chrysostom—offered more deeply considered discussions. In his critique of gnosis*, Clement of Alexandria teaches that the angels only know God the Father if they are "baptized in the Name*" ("above all names"), that is, in the Son (Extracts of Theodotus 27:2. SC 23, 101s). Irenaeus specifies that the angels only contemplate the Father* while contemplating the Son, and inasmuch as the Son reveals him to them (*Adv. Haer.* II, 30, 9, SX 294, 322). Augustine also says that only grace* allows angels to reach final bliss (*City of God* XII, 9 BAug 35, 174). This sovereignty of grace for their salvation explains Mary's superiority, as mother of the incarnate Word*, over all the angels, something which was affirmed as early as the Greek Fathers.

The fact the Paul gave them different names led to a hierarchization of angels. There was no system before Pseudo-Dionysius (Irenaeus talks of six degrees; Basil, five; Athanasius*, five; and Augustine, eight). It is Pseudo-Dionysius who, while relying on Proclus, creates a hierarchy of angels (*Celestial Hierarchy,* c. 6) in three triads of increasing dignity: angels, archangels, principalities; powers, virtues, dominions; thrones, cherubim, seraphim. This hierarchy would be borrowed by John Damascene and the entire tradition*. The whole hierarchy of angels, writes Pseudo-Dionysius, constitutes the theocracy that is ruled by the divine Trinity, its function being to assure the deifying salvation of believers. Origen accounts for this hierarchy of angels in terms of their individual merits (*Principles* 1, 8, 4, SC 252, 206), but Augustine declares himself to be ignorant on this point (*Manual* 15, 58, BAug 9, 206).

Although the Fathers were in agreement on the function of angels, they were not of one view when it came to their nature. Some, it seems, acknowledged individual spirit in the angels through a certain subtle corporeal state known as spiritual. Angels were thought to have an internal life that was greater than cosmic time, but less than the divine eternity, the latter being defined by Boethius* as "the simultaneity of all moments." It is named *aevum,* eviternity. Opposing Manichean dualism (Manicheanism*), Augustine specified that the creation* of angels came before the moment they choose, therefore before their sanctification or before their reprobation. He distinguished three levels of angelic intellection. First, there was knowledge of the thing known in itself. Then there was knowledge according to two stages of transcendental illumination by the creating Word: vision in the morning light (the creating idea in the Word), and vision in the fading light of evening or in accordance with the unique nature of the angel (*De Genesis ad litt.* IV, 22, BAug 9–48, 334f.).

c) Middle Ages. The angelology of Pseudo-Dionysius, known in the West since the time of John the Scot Eriugena (c. 810–77), was common to all the medieval theologians. These scholars strove for ever greater rigor in their doctrine of angels. In his *Sentences,* Peter Lombard (c. 1100–c. 1160) brings together the teachings of Augustine, Jerome (an expert on the Greeks), Ambrose, Gregory* the Great, and Dionysius. The theory of an angel-creator is rejected and the theme of their fallible freedom, already examined by Anselm (the fall of the devil), is studied. With the theme of separated Intellects (independent of the corporeal level), which was borrowed from Greco-Arab philosophy*, critical demands increased. There were important essays on the noetics of pure spirit, which went all the deeper in that they provided an occasion for the development of a theory of knowledge in general, with angels representing a borderline case with regard to man. Albert* the Great hesitates to identify Intellects and angels. While he does draw comparisons with regard to their purely intellectual nature and their function in ruling the world, he thinks, following the Bible and Pseudo-Dionysius, that only angels transmitted the divine light of grace. From Pseudo-Dionysius, Albert the Great borrows the theme of the seraphim's immediate knowledge of God, and he extends this to the deifying illumination granted to human beings in eternal life*. Bonaventure* acknowledges philosophers' view on angels as pure Intelligence, and he applies the Pseudo-Dionysian idea of hierarchy to the human soul*. The soul is given a "hierarchical" character by its access to the light of revealed wisdom*, the illuminations of which it receives in accordance with an ascending order defined by Pseudo-Dionysius. This order becomes a series of stages in the progress of the soul, in which the angels cooperate in an occasional manner, by lifting obstacles (*In Hexaem.* III, 32; XX, 22–25, XXII, 24–34). For Thomas* Aquinas, the recognition of the existence of angels—identified with the separated Intellects in terms of their nature, but not in terms of the function in the order of grace—is necessary for philosophical reasons. Between God, Intellect or pure and infinite* thought, and man with his reason* linked to the palpable, one must, according to Thomas, acknowledge the reality of beings equipped. The nature of these beings remains unknown; one only makes out something through human intellection and desire, and by the corrections provided by negative theology. Only the Bible speaks of their contribution to the salvation of humanity. Like all free creatures, they had to convert to God in response to divine grace, of which Christ is "the efficient cause and example in his eternal mystery* of incarnation*" (*In Ep.,* c. 1, lect. 3; *In Col.,* c. 1, lect. 4–5).

All angels, according to Thomas, are strictly incorporeal. They are immaterial, being by nature exclusively intelligence and will. Each one is unique in its kind: the generic category of "angel" is a product merely of our own divisive way of reasoning. The multiplicity of angels does not form a homogeneous whole, or a univocal meaning, and is not to be specified like the things of this order. They can only be made into a hierarchy according to their relative distance from the divine essence; since we do not know it, we give them a mutual order because of the eminence of such a gift of grace, although all the gifts of grace are in all of us, but in varying degrees (*In Col.* c. 1, lect. 4). Having a simple spiritual nature, angels nevertheless have an ontological composition. Their essence (or nature) must be distinguished from their being* in action. The latter is truly in addition to the essence, for this being in action (in an entirely different way than the traditional meaning of existence) is both granted by the Creator and acquired during noetic and volitional operations that are referred to a reality that is superior to angels themselves. Not needing palpable knowledge like man, angels know through a transcendent illumination and in accordance with a priori principles, having more or less synthetic characters depending on how close they are to the absolute unity of divine thought.

Duns Scotus, for whom there are angelic genres, applies his own theory of knowledge to the intelligence of angels and therefore rejects the Thomist noetics of pure spirit (*Ordin.* II, 3, 2, 3, §388 f.). The nominalist theologians (nominalism*) continued in this vein.

d) Modern and Contemporary Theology. During the Reformation, Calvin* saw angels as administrators of divine providence and as friends of man (*Inst.* 1, 14, 1–12). Petau (1583–1652) summed up the tradition, as did Suarez* in his vast treatise on theme of angels and demons. More recently, Karl Barth*, while noting the difficult questions that the question of angels raises, underlined its importance in the Scriptures* and the revelation of salvation. The Bultmannian platform (Bultmann*) of demythologization led Karl Rahner* (1957) toward a radical critique of angelology: not only do angels have no place in the modern world, but those theological developments of which angels have been the object are incompatible with the fundamental doctrine of salvation by Christ alone. He denounces the rationalist hypothesis, adopted by Suarez, of the possibility of a natural salvation. But Paul and the first Greek Fathers, in their critique of the Gnostics, had already dismissed this by emphasizing the subordination of angelic spirits to the incarnate Son. The modern radical negation of the reality of angels stems from an easy rationalism* that biblical exegesis does not share, even when it interprets scriptural expressions, often as metaphors—something L. Scheffczyk has recently underlined (1993). From a strictly philosophical point of view, Leibniz* borrows the notion of pure spirit which he defines as monadic. Husserl (1859–1938), who took an interest in Thomas's treatise on angels, uses this theme of the monad in his analysis of the world of interpersonal relationships (*Médit. cartés.* V).

• Albert the Great, *In De caelesti hierarchia, Opera* XXXVI/1, Münster, 1993.
Augustine, *De Genesi ad litt.,* BAug 48.
Bonaventure, *In Hexaemeron* (*Les six jours de la création,* 1991).
J. Calvin, *Inst.* I, 14, no. 3–12.
John Duns Scotus, *Ordinatio* VII.
E. Husserl, *Cartesianische Meditationen und Pariser Vortrage, Husserliana,* vol. I, 5th med., §55.
Peter Lombard, II *Sententiae* 2, PL 192, 655–57.
D. Petau, *Theologica Dogmata* (I-III, 1644; IV, 1650), III, 603–705 and IV, 1–121 (Ed. Vivès, Paris, 1865–66).
Pseudo-Dionysius, *Celestial Hierarchy,* SC 58 *bis.*
F. Suarez, *Opera omnia* II, 1–1099 (Ed. Vivès, Paris, 1866).
Thomas Aquinas, *ST* Ia, q. 10, a. 4–6 (ævum); q. 50–64; q. 106–14; CG II, 46–91; *In Ep. S. Pauli ad Ephesios; In Ep. ad Colossenses.*
♦ J. Touzard, A. Lemonnyer (1928), "Ange," *DBS* 1, 242–62.
G. Kittel (1933), "Aggelos," *ThWNT* 1, 72–87.
E. Peterson (1935), *Das Buch von den Engeln,* Leipzig, repr. in *Theologische Traktate,* Munich, 1950, 323–407.
J. Duhr (1937), "Anges," *DSp* 1, 580–626.
J. Collins (1947), *The Thomistic Philosophy of the Angels,* Washington.
K. Barth (1950), *KD* III/3, §51 (*Dogmatique,* Geneva, 1963).
J. Daniélou (1952), *Les anges et leur mission d'après les Pères de l'Église,* Paris.
K. Rahner (1957), "Angelologie," *LThK2* 1, 533–38.
P.R. Régamey (1959), *Les anges au ciel et parmi nous,* Paris.
H. Schlier (1963), *Mächte und Gewalten im NT,* Freiburg.
M. Seemann (1967), "Die Welt der Engel und Dämonen als heilsgeschichtliche Mit- und Umwelt des Menschen," *MySal* II, 943–95.
P.L. Berger (1970), *A Rumour of Angels,* Harmondsworth, Middlesex.
G. Tavard (1971), *Les anges,* Paris.
S. Breton (1980), "Faut-il parler des anges?" *RSPhTh* 64, 225–40.
U. Mann, et al. (1982), "Engel," *TRE* 9, 580–615 (bibl.).
J.-M. Vernier (1986), *Les anges chez saint Thomas d'Aquin (Angelologia III),* Paris.
W. Madelung (1987), "Mala'ika," *EI(F)* 6, 200 b2–04 a.
P. Faure (1988), *Les anges,* Paris.
L. Scheffczyk (1993), "Angelologie," *LThK3* 1, 649–51.
B. Faes de Mottoni (1995), *S. Bonaventura e la Scala di Giacobbe: Letture di angelologia,* Naples.
E. Falque (1995), "L'altérité angélique ou l'angélologie thomiste au fil des 'Méditations cartésiennes' de Husserl," *LTP* 51, 625–46.
A. Paus, et al. (1995), "Engel," *LThK3* 3, 646–54.
S. Pinckaers (1996), "Les anges, garants de l'expérience spirituelle selon saint Thomas d'Aquin," *RTLu* 2, 179–92.

Édouard-Henri Weber

See also **Demons; Hierarchy; Praise**

Angelus Silesius. *See* **Negative Theology; Rhineland-Flemish Mysticism**

See **Negative Theology; Rhineland-Flemish Mysticism**

Anglican Church. *See* **Anglicanism**

Anglicanism

a) Definition. Anglicanism is the body of beliefs and practices of those Christians who are in communion* with the see of Canterbury, and in particular insofar as they distinguish themselves from other Christian confessions by virtue of their ties to England. But Anglicanism is not only English, and it includes the members of all churches that belong to the Anglican Communion.

b) Origins and History. According to the Oxford English Dictionary, the term *Anglicanism* was first used in English by Newman* in 1838, although it appeared in French as early as 1801. Some date the concept of Anglicanism much earlier, locating it at the origins of Christianity in the British Isles, punning on the origin of the adjective *Anglican: anglicanus,* English, from the Latin *Angli* "angles," the source of the name *England* (*Anglia* in Late Latin), which appeared by the late ninth century. The present-day Anglican Communion, made up of autonomous churches in full communion with the see of Canterbury, includes 65 to 70 million members scattered throughout the world. Although Anglicanism was present outside England by the 16th century, thanks to English colonization and emigration, and later due to the efforts of missionaries, the Anglican Communion itself came into being in 1851. It was formalized with the 1867 convocation of the first Lambeth Conference, a meeting of all Anglican bishops* at the London residence of the archbishop of Canterbury. The conference meets every ten years. Conference resolutions, however, have legal force in a church only if that church confirms them. If it does not do so, they have only advisory value. Finally, the Church of England alone in the Anglican Communion is a state church.

c) The Idea Anglicans Have of Themselves. Conceptions of Anglicanism differ substantially depending on notions of its historical origin. The current tendency is to reverse the perspective and, instead of beginning with the 19th century and the first appearance of the term *Anglicanism,* to locate its beginnings in the early centuries of Christianity. For example, J. Macquarrie (1970): "Anglicanism has never considered itself to be a sect or denomination originating in the 16th century. It continues without a break the *Ecclesia Anglicana* founded by Saint Augustine thirteen centuries and more ago, though nowadays that branch of the Church has spread far beyond the borders of England." Similarly, H. R. McAdoo (1965): "The absence of an official theology in Anglicanism is something deliberate which belongs to its essential nature, for it has always regarded the teaching and practice of the first five centuries as a criterion." Thus, while some see Anglicanism as dating from the 16th or the 17th century, others assert its fundamental continuity with the early church.

And although it is true that *Anglican* was used as a geographical term for centuries before taking on its current meaning, the real problem arises from the fact that Anglicanism thinks of itself as both a Reformation and a pre-Reformation church, both Catholic and Protestant. This stance is not without its difficulties. (The adjective *Protestant* is found neither in the Book of Common Prayer nor in the Thirty-nine Articles, but most Anglicans generally consider themselves Protestants.)

d) Doctrine and Basic Texts. Anglicans profess the Catholic and apostolic faith*, based on Scripture* and interpreted in the light of tradition* and reason*. They proclaim the lordship of the dead and resurrected Christ*, recognizing him as the second Person* of the Trinity*. This faith finds its principal expression in the celebration of the Eucharist*, the chief act of Christian worship. The essential texts expressing the Anglican faith are the Bible*, followed by the ritual of the Anglican liturgy* in the Book of Common Prayer (a major doctrinal source), and the document called the Lambeth Quadrilateral (*see* j below), which summarizes the principal dogmas*. To these should be added the Thirty-nine Articles and various collections of Anglican canon* law. The Book of Common Prayer exists in various forms today, but the 1662 version is still authoritative for the Church of England.

e) Theological Method. In a sense it was Queen Elizabeth I (1533–1603) who first formulated what was to become the normative principle of Anglican theology. According to her, neither her people nor herself were practicing a new and strange religion, but rather the very religion prescribed by Christ, sanctioned by the primitive Catholic Church, and approved by all the early Fathers* of the Church. It was thus a matter of finding a *via media,* a middle way between Catholicism* and Protestantism*, by relying on Scripture, reason, and tradition. Richard Hooker (1554–1600), the greatest of the Elizabethan theologians, defined the relationships of these three elements in his *Ecclesiastical Polity* (V. 8. 2): "What scripture doth plainelie deliver, to that the first place both of creditt and obedience is due; the next whereunto is whatsoever anie man can necessarelie conclude by force of reason; after these the voice of the Church succeedeth." In this, Hooker showed his opposition to the Puritans (Puritanism*), for whom Scripture alone could define faith, and he defended the right of the church to propose its own laws*, provided they were not contrary to Scripture. The following formulations permit an understanding of what this principle means for Anglicanism. According to R. P. C. Hanson, for a given subject, "we must study as completely as possible the documents and the historical context; and if we have to come to theoretical or doctrinal conclusions, we should do so with the greatest circumspection." And for A. R. Vidler: "Anglican theology is faithful to its spirit when it seeks to reconcile opposed systems, not considering them mutually exclusive but showing that the principle represented by each one has its place in the body of Christian faith and is truly assured... only if it is understood in the tension it maintains with apparently contrary but really complementary principles." According to Anglicans themselves, this openness to all points of view is characteristic of Anglicanism.

f) Church of England before the Reformation. Very little written evidence of early English Christianity of the third and fourth centuries has remained. The earliest surviving documents date from the Celtic period of the fifth and sixth centuries, and these are essentially spiritual, consisting principally of prayers* and hymns. The theology found in them closely links redemption and creation*. After the Synod* of Whitby (664), Roman ecclesiology achieved dominance, an eventuality welcomed by the Venerable Bede (673–735) in his *Ecclesiastical History.* (Bede also produced an elaborate theology of history*, miracles*, providence*, and evangelization.) Later, there were poems such as *The Dream of the Rood* (c. 750) and, in the late 10th and early 11th centuries, theological works on kingship, monasticism*, the priesthood*, the liturgy, penitence, and pastoral duties—see the works of Aelfric (c. 955–c. 1020) and Wulfstan (†1023), *The Law of Northumbrian Priests* and the *Monastic Agreement of the Monks and Nuns of the English Nation* (c. 970). After the Norman Conquest (1066) the same themes reappear in the monastic constitutions of Lanfranc (c. 1010–89), the work of the Norman Anonymous, in various coronation rituals, and in treatises on relations between church* and state.

The greatest theologian of the medieval English church was Anselm*, Archbishop of Canterbury from 1093 on, but there was in fact no lack of excellent theologians. The humanist John of Salisbury (c. 1115–80) wrote the *Policraticus* in which he describes the ideal state, where spiritual and temporal power are in balance. Robert Grosseteste (c. 1175–1253), bishop of Lincoln, studied Scripture and the origins of Christianity. Then there was a remarkable series of archbishops of Canterbury. These included Cardinal Stephen Langton (†1228), who wrote commentaries on most books of the Bible and who is credited with dividing its books into chapters; the Dominican Robert Kilwardby (archbishop 1273, †1279), author of remarkable indexes of the Fathers of the Church; the Franciscan John Pecham (c. 1225–92); and Thomas Bradwardine (c. 1290–1349, archbishop 1349), whose work on theological determinism was interrupted by the Black Death. Other major theological figures were Duns* Scotus and William of Ockham (c. 1285–1347). In maintaining that it was impossible to present rational proofs* of the existence* of God or of the creation of the world, the latter produced a climate of theological thought in which all one could really do was assert that God makes himself known barely enough for salvation* to be possible—as did, for example, the Dominican Robert Holcot (†1349). This was the context for the work of John Wycliffe (c. 1330–84), whose philosophical ideas led him to attack the possession of earthly goods by the church and the reality of eucharistic transubstantiation. He had disciples, known as Lollards, and the Reformers of the 15th century found precedents in his work for their favorite doctrines, except for that of justification.

The 14th century also witnessed the flourishing of an English school of spirituality, notably including the hermit Richard Rolle (c. 1300–49) in *Emendatio vitae et Incendium amoris;* the poet and minor cleric William Langland (†1396) in *The Vision of Piers Plowman;* Walter Hilton (†1396) in *The Scale of Perfection;* the anchoress Julian of Norwich (c. 1342–c. 1417) in *Revelations of Divine Love;* the anonymous *The Cloud of Unknowing* (c. 1370); Margery Kempe (c. 1373–after 1433); and the solitary monk of the Isle of Farne. (In this context one might even mention Chaucer [c. 1343–c. 1400]: among other things, his *Canterbury Tales* does have some strictly theological content.) The *Cloud of Unknowing* is remarkable for its negative theology*, and the work of Julian of Norwich for its optimism and its doctrine of the maternity of God. In the late Middle Ages Reginald Pecock (c. 1393–1461) was the first English bishop to be condemned for heresy*. Even though his *Repressor of Overmuch Blaming the Clergy* (1455) had the aim of refuting the Lollards, he had placed the authority of reason above that of Scripture and tradition. By the late 15th and early 16th centuries, however, humanism* was in the wings. In relation to this latter we must mention the figures of John Colet (c. 1466–1519), one of the first to deny the literal inspiration of Scripture and to replace allegorical interpretation with a more critical reading; and Thomas More (1478–1535), beheaded for his rejection of the Act of Supremacy.

g) Reformation. The Church of England has been officially separated from Rome since the time of Henry VIII (reigned 1509–47), in the course of which it rejected the sovereignty of the pope* and represented itself as the local form of the universal Church. Henry VIII's repudiation of Catherine of Aragon was certainly one of the causes of the Reformation in England, but not the only one. In any event, it gave king and Parliament the opportunity to reject the primacy of the pope and to assert the supremacy of the crown over the church. The first phases of the Reformation, moreover, consisted essentially in emancipating the church from the authority* of the pope. Theological change was already in the air. However, because institutional emancipation was carried out before it was fully articulated, the actual change in theological thinking was generally more limited than it was elsewhere. The almost complete acceptance by the episcopate of the break with Rome, following the archbishop of Canterbury, Thomas Cranmer (1489–1556), gave Anglicanism a more conservative character than the other European churches that had willingly accepted the Reformation. Because this change was embodied in a ritual, the first Book of Common Prayer (1549, produced almost entirely by Cranmer), Anglican liturgy generally serves as a doctrinal reference for Anglican theology, by virtue of the ancient principle *lex orandi lex credendi.*

The same period witnessed the rewriting of the history* of the church in England with the aim of presenting the change as a restoration. Church and state were to be considered as forming a single national body in which a quasi-episcopal king replaced the pope. In this way, Anglicanism was later able to assert that the Reformation had merely purified the existing church and not created a new one. But the Reformation was also responsible for the Bible in English, the dissolution of the monasteries (although the reasons for that were more economic than religious), the marriage* of priests*, vernacular liturgy (new Books of Common Prayer were published in 1552, 1559, and 1662), and reform of canon* law to make it independent of papal jurisdiction* (*see* in particular the canons of 1604). The sense of all these changes is clear.

Edward VI (reigned 1547–53) attempted to make the Anglican Church more Protestant. After his death his sister Mary Tudor (reigned 1553–58) tried, by contrast, to bring it back to Catholicism. Her policies engendered a suspicion of Catholicism that was to last in England and the Anglican world for centuries. Reformers like Hugh Latimer (1485–1555), Nicholas Ridley (1500–1555), and Cranmer himself were executed during her reign, while many of those who had sought refuge in Europe exerted pressure to make the Church of England more Protestant. With the accession of Elizabeth I to the throne in 1558, and thanks to her moderating influence, Anglicanism began to take on the form in which it is now known. That is to say that it represented a synthesis of Protestantism and Catholicism in a single national church whose cohesion derived from the monarch as "Supreme Head," and from a general adherence to the Book of Common Prayer. There were protests, nevertheless, from more radical Protestants and from the Calvinists, who were soon to be called Puritans (Puritanism*).

Although there was an official collection of homilies by 1547 and acceptance of the Thirty-nine Articles of 1563–71 soon became obligatory for ordained clergy and holders of benefices (a requirement that lasted with few modifications until late in the 19th century), there was no Anglican "confession of faith" comparable to those of other churches. Similarly, although the works of J. Jewel (1522–71; *Apology of the Church of England,* 1562) and Richard Hooker (*Ecclesiastical Polity,* 1594–97) clearly define the Anglicanism of their period, there was no dominant Anglican theologian comparable to Luther* or Calvin*. Indeed, in the church that took shape under Elizabeth I in the 16th century, the national experience of the unity of worship in the vernacular was much more important than theological passion. The Elizabethan Book of Common Prayer of 1559 was based on that of 1552, with a few inflections toward a moderate Protestantism. These positions were justified by Hooker, who even argued for their superiority over other forms of Protestantism.

h) 17th Century. James I (reigned 1603–25) pursued the same policies as Elizabeth. A new cause of conflict appeared, however, when the movement known as "High Church," with its predilection for the primitive church and liturgical ceremony began to take shape around the figure of William Laud (1573–1645). Laud is also known for his argument with the Jesuit John Fisher (1569–1641; *A Relation of the Conference between William Laud and Mr. Fisher the Jesuit,* 1639). In it he argued that the Anglican Church and the Roman Church were both parts of the Catholic Church. During the Civil War and under Cromwell (1599–1658), Parliament abolished the episcopate and banned the Book of Common Prayer, but the Restoration of the monarchy in 1660 once again "established" the Church of England, and a revised edition of the Book of Common Prayer appeared in 1662. The new rite of ordinations, in particular, made ordination* by a bishop obligatory. During the reigns of James I, Charles I, and Charles II, the Church of England was the only acceptable form of Christianity in the kingdom. But with the accession of William and Mary in 1689, one of the first decisions of Parliament was passage of the Act of Toleration, which granted liberty of worship to all Protestants, with certain conditions. "Nonconformity" was thereafter tolerated in Anglican theology.

The 17th century is generally considered the golden age of Anglicanism, its thinking being particularly well expressed by the theologians of the Caroline period. A simple list of their names and works is eloquent: Lancelot Andrewes (1555–1626), *Preces Privatae;* Richard Field (1561–1616), *Of the Church;* Joseph Hall (1574–1656), *Episcopacy by Divine Right;* James Ussher (1581–1656), *Britannicarum Ecclesiarum Antiquitates;* John Bramhall (1594–1663), *A Just Vindication of the Church of England;* John Cosin (1594–1672), *Collection of Private Devotions;* Herbert Thorndike (1598–1672), *Discourse of the Government of Churches;* William Chillingworth (1602–44), *Religion of Protestants;* Henry Hamond (1605–60), *Practical Catechism;* Thomas Fuller (1608–61), *Church History of Britain;* Anthony Sparrow (1612–85), *Rationale or Practical Exposition of the Book of Common Prayer;* Jeremy Taylor (1613–67), *Holy Living and Holy Dying;* Isaac Barrow (1630–77), *Treatise on the Pope's Supremacy;* George Bull (1634–1710), *Defensio Fidei Nicaenae;* Edward Stillingfleet (1635–99), *Origines Britannicae;* Thomas Ken (1637–1711), *Exposition on the Church Catechism; or, The Practice of Divine Love;* and finally, Thomas Comber (1645–99), *Companion to the Temple.*

In general, the *via media* sought by these writers was not that of a compromise, but an intellectual and spiritual attempt to recover the simplicity and purity of the primitive church. Some of them were inclined to recognize that the Church of Rome (which remained outlawed through the kingdom) did not teach only error, and in this they differed from the Puritans, who saw "papistry" as the very opposite of Christianity. And despite their attachment to the episcopacy and the apostolic* succession, they also displayed an irenic attitude toward the Protestant churches of Europe. Also of theological importance in the 17th century were the "metaphysical" poets: John Donne (1572–1631), Thomas Traherne (1636–74), and Henry Vaughan (1622–95). A major poet who did not belong to this group, George Herbert (1593–1633), a priest of the Church of England, gave an ideal image of what a parish priest* should be in *A Priest to the Temple, or The Country Parson.*

These theologians generally belonged to the High Church, but they also included "latitudinarians," who attached little importance to dogma and ecclesiastical organization and granted so much value to reason that they sometimes seemed to deify it. In addition to Edward Stillingfleet, mentioned above, these included Simon Patrick (1625–1707), the historian David Wilkins

(1685–1745), and Archbishop John Tillotson (1630–94). Liberal in spirit, they had contempt for "enthusiasm" and emphasized principally the ethical implications of Christian faith and the harmony between revealed religion and natural* theology. Some of them were close to the Cambridge Platonists, a group of mystical philosophers of the mid-17th century (the best known are Henry More [1614–87] and Ralph Cudworth [1617–88]), for whom reason was the very presence of the spirit of God in humankind—"the lamp of the Lord," in the words of Benjamin Whichcote (1609–83), a reference to Proverbs 20:27. Heirs of the humanist tradition of Colet and More, they applied all the moral seriousness of the Puritans in search of a union of philosophy* and theology, faith and reason, Christianity and Platonism. John Locke (1632–1704) was much more reductive. For him Christianity was summed up in a small number of simple truths* accessible to reason (*see Essay Concerning Human Understanding,* 1690, and *The Reasonableness of Christianity,* 1695). He was an advocate of total religious liberty* within a national church that had a very broad confessional foundation.

i) 18th Century. Anglicanism went through a crisis in the 18th century when a certain number of High Church dissidents chose to separate from the established Church rather than swear allegiance to William of Orange and his successors (Nonjurors). Their knowledge of orthodoxy* and of the Fathers of the Church had a major influence on the Scottish liturgy, which served as a model for the Communion liturgy of the Anglican Prayer Book in North America. One of them, William Law (1686–1715), is the author of one of the classics of English spiritual literature, *A Serious Call to a Devout and Holy Life* (1728); and another, Robert Nelson (1656–1715), wrote a long popular book, a *Companion for the Festivals and Fasts of the Church of England* (1704). Anglican theology of the early 18th century also had to deal with a deism* that was close to pantheism* and to Unitarianism*, something already seen in the previous century, for example in the works of Lord Herbert of Cherbury (1583–1648).

Locke was a deist, as was John Toland (1670–1722), who advocated a Christianity without a supernatural* dimension (*Christianity Not Mysterious,* 1696); and so too was Matthew Tindal (1655–1733), for whom Christianity added nothing to what nature had already revealed (*Christianity as Old as the Creation,* 1730). William Law combated deism in *The Case for Reason* (1731). The most important religious event of the 18th century, however, was the movement of evangelical Revival, characterized by a return to the Bible and to justification by faith, by an insistence on personal conversion* and social reform, and finally by a Christianity turned toward action. Although the movement led by John Wesley (1703–91), his brother Charles (1707–88), and George Whitefield (1714–70) ended by separating from Anglicanism (Methodism*), the evangelical strain was important in Anglicanism itself, being given impetus by laymen* like Lord Shaftesbury (1801–85) and William Wilberforce (1759–1833), as well as the other members of the "Clapham Sect." The struggle of the latter against slavery (liberty*) helped to bring about its abolition. We may also mention Charles Simeon (1759–1836), one of the founders of the Church Missionary Society (CMS), and Hannah More (1745–1833), whose religious books were widely read.

The century also produced bishops who were theologians and philosophers, such as George Berkeley (1685–1753), who relied on natural theology to combat deism (*The Analogy of Religion,* 1736). The theologian Daniel Waterland (1683–1740) wrote influential works on the divinity of Christ and on the Eucharist. And we must not forget the poets, Blake (1757–1827), Coleridge (1772–1834), and Wordsworth (1770–1850), who were also in their way religious writers.

j) 19th and 20th Centuries. The Church of England was in a sad state in the early 19th century, with clergy holding multiple positions, as well as problems with nepotism, nonresident pastors, and a very inegalitarian distribution of church wealth. Reform was urgently needed. Thomas Arnold (1795–1842), headmaster of Rugby, was one of the first to react with his *Principles of Church Reform* (1833), but spiritual and theological renewal came from the Oxford Movement, the key figures of which were John Keble (1792–1866), John Henry Newman, and Edward Pusey (1800–1882). Keble's 1833 sermon on national apostasy was the movement's founding act. It is well known that Newman for a time thought it possible to reconcile Anglicanism and Catholicism (*see* the famous Tract 90), but he joined the Catholic Church in 1845. It was Pusey who led the movement thereafter. These writers, known as Tractarians because of the theological tracts they published, were High Church supporters: as such, they advocated a return to the Fathers of the Church and Catholic tradition, and stressed the notions of apostolic succession, sacramental grace*, and ascetic sanctity.

The Oxford Movement, which took its inspiration from the Caroline theologians, but also from the romantic opposition to liberalism, transformed Anglicanism both in external appearance and in spirit. In this context, the term *Anglo-Catholic* appeared for the first time in 1838 and designated those who were seeking to establish "concords" that were as close as possible with the other "branches" of Catholic Christianity (particularly the Roman and Orthodox Churches). The keen interest in the liturgy (sometimes to the point of ritualism) that the Oxford Movement advocated had first appeared in 1832 with the *Origines Liturgicae* of W. Palmer (1803–85). John Mason Neale (1818–66), for example, took an interest in rites, founded a religious community, was an active writer of hymns, and wrote a history of the Orthodox Church. A certain strain of High Church existed in American Anglicanism before the Oxford Movement, thanks to people like John Henry Hobart, Bishop of New York from 1816 to 1830, who was looking for a synthesis, and according to whom "the High Church must be evangelical."

From the mid-19th century on, Anglican theology took an ever greater interest in social problems. The goal of Frederick Denison Maurice (1805–72), for one example, was to socialize Christianity and Christianize socialism (*see The Kingdom of Christ,* 1838). His ecclesiology links the family*, the state, and the church. Biblical criticism developed around the same time, particularly at Cambridge under the influence of J. B. Lightfoot (1829–89), B. F. Westcott (1825–1901), and F. J. A. Hort (1828–92). A very controversial work called *Essays and Reviews* appeared in 1860 and was a milestone in liberal Anglican theology. It was condemned by the ecclesiastical authorities in 1864. Its authors defended freedom of research in the religious realm and favored an opening to the intellectual and social movements of modernity. They rendered obsolete the distinction made by the latitudinarians between fundamental doctrines and secondary doctrines by extending critical method to the interpretation of Scripture and the creeds. For example, Benjamin Jowett (1817–93) argued that Scripture should be read "like any other book." Similar positions were expressed in the "liberal Catholicism" of Charles Gore (1853–1932) and his coauthors of *Lux mundi* (1889). Their goal was to bring together the theology of the Tractarians, modern critical methods, and social concern. For example, they accepted the evolutionist point of view (evolution*) and a kenotic concept of the human science of Jesus*. These concerns can be found in two important collections: *Foundations* (1912) and *Essays Catholic and Critical* (1926). The interest in social problems was particularly evident in the work of William Temple (1881–1944), which dealt with the relationship between theology and human experience: *see Mens Creatrix* (1917), *Christus Veritas* (1924), *Nature, Man and God* (1934), and *Christianity and Social Order* (1942). In America during the same period, William Porcher DuBose (1836–1918) was pursuing important research into soteriology, the history of the ecumenical councils*, and the notions of high priest and sacrifice. This was also the period of a bitter debate on the Thirty-nine Articles: should the members of the clergy adhere to them literally? In any event, this requirement was substantially softened in 1865.

On the basis of the works of William Reed Huntington (1838–1909; *The Church-Idea,* 1870), in 1886 the American Episcopalian (Anglican) Church formulated four fundamental principles that were approved by the Lambeth Conference in 1888. This is what is known as the Lambeth Quadrilateral: 1) Scripture (Old and New Testaments) "contains everything needed for salvation." 2) The Apostles' Creed* and the Nicene Creed* provide a sufficient definition of Christian faith. 3) The church recognizes the sacraments of baptism* and Communion, administered with the very words and instruments used by Christ himself. 4) The institution of the episcopacy is essential to the church and is to be adapted to the needs of different nations. The Quadrilateral remains the basis for ecumenical discussions within Anglicanism today. A commission was charged with examining the state of doctrine in Anglicanism, and its report *(Doctrine in the Church of England)* was published in 1938. However, because it did not define that doctrine, it contributed little to establishing the boundaries of permissible diversity.

As in other Christian churches, liturgical renewal made itself felt from 1950 on, and this influenced theology as well as the revision of the Book of Common Prayer. The book by A. G. Herbert, *Liturgy and Society* (1935), and the conference whose proceedings he published as *The Parish Communion* (1937), played a decisive role, as did *The Shape of Liturgy* by the Anglican Benedictine Gregory Dix (1945). A specialist in mysticism*, Evelyn Underhill (1875–1941; *Mysticism,* 1911; *Worship,* 1936), also had considerable influence.

Anglican theology of the 20th century was marked by Anglo-Catholicism and a moderate neobiblicism up to the period of Vatican* II. On the other hand, since the 1960s, liberalism and radicalism have taken the upper hand, as evidenced by the publication of *Honest to God* (J. A. T. Robinson) in 1960 and of *The Secular Meaning of the Gospel* (Paul van Buren) in 1963. The debate on the ordination of women (woman*) was heated until the synod* of the Church of England approved it on 11 November 1992 (following many other churches of the Anglican Communion). The first ordinations of women took place on 12 March 1994. The problem of the status of sexual minorities and that of the separation of church and state continues to be troublesome. Nevertheless, a revival of the charismatic movement (Pentecostalism) has been witnessed, as well as a renewal of evangelism, but in a form that is more learned, sacramental, and ecumenical than that of its 19th century predecessors.

*k) Ecumenism**. The coexistence within Anglicanism of Protestant and Catholic characteristics and its participation in the formation of the Ecumenical Council* of Churches in 1948 have made it possible for it to play an active role in the ecumenical movement, for which the Lambeth Quadrilateral provides an excellent basis. The birth of the Church of South India in 1947, the product of the union of a million members on the basis of the Quadrilateral, provides a good example. The ecumenical patriarch (patriarchate*) of Constantinople recognized the validity of Anglican orders in 1922, and there is an active dialogue (although without intercommunion*) with the Orthodox churches. Since the Bonn agreement of 1932 there has been intercommunion with most of the old Catholic churches. The work of the Anglican-Roman Catholic International Commission (ARCIC) from 1960 to 1980 also gave rise to much hope, until it received a negative reaction from Rome. Discussions are in progress with the Reformed churches and the Methodists, as well as with the Lutherans.

• *Certain Sermons and Homilies Appointed to Be Read in Churches in the Time of Queen Elizabeth,* London, 1899.

J.V. Bullard (Ed.), *Constitutions and Canons Ecclesiastical,* 1604, London, 1934.

Anglican Roman Catholic International Commission. The final report: Windsor, September 1981.

J.R. Wright (Ed.), *Prayer Book Spirituality,* New York, 1989.

G.R. Evans, J.R. Wright (Ed.) *The Anglican Tradition: A Handbook of Sources,* Minneapolis, 1991.

♦ J.H.R. Moorman (1953), *A History of the Church in England,* London (3rd Ed. 1980).

F.L. Cross, E.A. Livingstone (Ed.) (1958, 3rd Rev. Ed., 1997), *ODCC.*

S. Neill (1958), *Anglicanism,* Harmondsworth (4th Ed., New York, 1978).

A. M. Ramsey (1960), *An Era in Anglican Theology: From Gore to Temple,* New York.

R.J. Page (1965), *New Directions in Anglican Theology: A Survey from Temple to Robinson,* New York.

J. Macquarrie (1966), *Principles of Christian Theology,* New York (2nd Ed. 1977).

T.A. Langford (1969), *In Search of Foundations: English Theology, 1900–1920,* Nashville, Tenn.

S.W. Sykes (1978), *The Integrity of Anglicanism,* London.

L.J. Rataboul (1982), *L'anglicanisme,* Paris.

M.D. Bryant (1984), *The Future of Anglican Theology,* New York-Toronto.

A.A. Vogel (Ed.) (1984), *Theology in Anglicanism,* Wilton, Conn.

N. Lossky (1986), *Lancelot Andrewes le prédicateur (1555–1626): Aux sources de la théologie mystique de l'Église d'Angleterre,* Paris.

S.W. Sykes (Ed.) (1987), *Authority in the Anglican Communion,* Toronto.

S.W. Sykes, J. Booty (Ed.) (1988), *The Study of Anglicanism,* London-Philadelphia (2nd Ed. 1996).

G. Rowell (Ed.) (1992), *The English Religious Tradition and the Genius of Anglicanism,* Nashville, Tenn.

J. ROBERT WRIGHT

See also **Calvinism; Congregationalism; Lutheranism; Methodism; Puritanism**

Anhypostasy

The terms *anhypostasy* and *enhypostasy* have been used since the 16th century by Scholastic theologians, both Catholic and Protestant, to designate the particular ontological status of the humanity of Christ*. What they mean to indicate is that the man Jesus* is not a hypostasis or concrete individual existing separately, but that his humanity receives its concrete reality, or is "en-hypostasized," in the personal being* of the second Person* of the Trinity*. As Karl Barth* says, "as a man, he thus exists in and with the one God*, according to the mode of existence of the Son and the eternal Logos, and not otherwise" (*Die kirchliche Dogmatik* 1932–67; *Church Dogmatics*).

a) Patristic Context. The terms *enhypostasy* and *anhypostasy,* which evoke a process and a state, did not exist in classical or patristic Greek. However, the corresponding adjectives, *enhypostatos* and *anhypostatos,* were common; they meant simply "subsisting" or "not subsisting," having a specific concrete reality or not. In Christian theology* they began to be widely used in the Trinitarian debates of the fourth century, to affirm that Father*, Son, and Holy* Spirit were not words corresponding to no reality *(anhypostatoi),* simple divine modalities, but possessed a real being *(enhypostaton),* although they were defined by their relations.

Anhypostasy and *enhypostasy* became technical terms in the christological controversies of the sixth century. Starting from the classic conception of the Cappadocians, according to which essence *(ousia)* or nature *(physis)* designates a universal reality, and *hypostasis* or *prosōpon* (Latin *persona*) a concrete individual substance, person, or thing, the adversaries of the Christology* of Chalcedon* seem to have relied on an anti-Platonic axiom that was probably widespread at the time and to have maintained that "a nature/essence that is not subsisting does not exist" *(ouk esti physis/ousia anhypostatos):* in other words, that universals have no reality apart from the concrete things in which they are embodied. From this they concluded that the Chalcedonian conception of Christ as a hypostasis existing simultaneously "in two natures" was contradictory. In order to avoid the "Nestorian" consequence, which would then make Christ two hypostases or two individuals—a man united by grace and divine favor to the divine hypostasis of the Son—the anti-Chalcedonians maintained that he could be conceived of only as a single nature and a "composite" hypostasis; according to the phrasing dear to Cyril* of Alexandria, "a single incarnate nature of the Word*."

To answer them, an advocate of the Chalcedonian position, Leontius of Byzantium (c. 490–c. 545), distinguished between *hypostasis* and *hypostatic (to enhypostaton).* The latter term did not apply to concrete individuals as such, but to universals (essence, nature) that were found in them, and it indicated that they were concretely embodied. It must therefore be said that divinity and humanity, as complete and functional natures, are both "hypostatic" *(enhypostata)* in the person of Christ, but that they are not hypostases. Leontius also conceded what the supporters of Cyril considered most important, namely, that the humanity of Christ comes to concrete or hypostatic existence by being assumed "into" the person of the Word of God. This meaning is not directly indicated by the *en-* of *enhypostatos,* which is simply the opposite of an *a-,* meaning "privation." In *Ekdosis tes orthodoxou pisteos (Exposition of the Orthodox Faith),* John of Damascus (c. 750–c. 850) gave a characteristically precise expression to this conception.

The flesh of the Word of God has no specific subsistence, it is not another hypostasis beside the hypostasis of the Word, but by subsisting in the latter, it is hypostatic *(enhypostatos),* and not a hypostasis subsisting by itself. Hence, it can be said neither that it is without subsistence *(anhypostatos)* nor that it introduces another hypostasis into the Trinity.

b) Modern Usage. Modern theologians who have adopted this terminology have not always fully understood it. They believe that, for the patristic tradition*, the divine Person of the Logos assumed a generic or "impersonal" human nature (this is how they understand *anhypostatos*) and gave it a personal existence "in" him (which, in fact, no ancient writer maintains). The position of Leontius of Byzantium has been summed up by Baillie (1956) saying that, for Leontius, "although the humanity of Christ is not impersonal, it does not have an independent personality.... Human nature is personalized in the divine Logos that assumes it, it is thus not impersonal *(anhypostatos)* but 'in-personal' *(enhypostatos).*" Some 20th-century Protestant theologians consider the idea of an "anhypostatic" humanity of Christ very important because it gives rightful place to divine initiative in the work of salvation and avoids granting too much autonomy to the created order. Torrance, echoing Augustine* and Barth, sees in these two terms the basic structure of the relationship between God and humanity: "*Anhypostasia* asserts the unconditional priority of grace*, that everything in theological knowledge derives from God's grace.... But *enhypostasia,* asserts that God's grace acts only as grace. God does not override us, but makes us free. In merciful and loving condescension, he gathers us into union with himself, constituting us as his dear children, who share his life and love."

A Catholic writer, critical of Scholasticism, maintains on the other hand that a Christology that uses the concept of anhypostasy by that very fact denies the full humanity of Christ, and he therefore proposes a reconsideration of all the Chalcedonian terminology. But whether one is for or against the use of these concepts, it is always the modern notion of existence as a person that is sought beneath this ancient vocabulary of hypostasis and nature. It is therefore inappropriate to make affirmations about the economy of salvation on the basis of the subtle ontological dialectic of the universal and the particular characteristic of the sixth century. From the point of view of Chalcedonian Christology this both exaggerates the importance of the terms and fails to see their precise meaning and import.

• Anon. (6th c.), De sectis, PG 86, 1240 A1–1241 C12.

Euloge d'Alexandrie, Sunègoriai (frag.), in F. Diekamp, *Doctrina Patrum de incarnatione Verbi,* Münster, repr. 1981, 193–98.

John of Damascus, *Expositio fidei,* Ed. B. Kotter, II, Berlin, 1973, 128.

John of Damascus *De fide contra Nestorianos* 6, Ed. Kotter, IV, 1981, 413 *Sq.*

Leontius of Byzantium, *Contra Nestorianos et Eutychianos,* PG 86, 1277 C14–1280 B10.
Leontius of Byzantium, *Epiluseis,* PG 86, 1944 C1–945 B2.
Pamphilus, *Quaestiones et responsiones* 7, CCG 19, 173–77.
♦ H.M. Relton (1917), *A Study in Christology,* London.
A. Michel (1922), "Hypostase,", *DThC* 7/1, 369–437; "Hypostatique (union)," ibid., 437–568, especially 528 *Sq.*
K. Barth (1938), *KD* I/2, §15, 178 *Sq* (*Dogmatique,* Geneva, vol. 3, 1954).
D.M. Baillie (1956), *God Was in Christ,* London, 85–93.
P. Schoonenberg (1959), *Hij een God van Mensen,* Malmberg NV (He is the God of Man, CFi 71).
T.F. Torrance (1969), *Theological Science,* London, 216–19 (New Ed. 1990, 238–40).

BRIAN E. DALEY

See also **Constantinople II, Council of; Hypostatic Union; Nestorianism**

Animals

I. Old Testament

1. Main Texts

a) Narrative of Origins. In Genesis 1–3 and 7–9, man is associated with animals, which are seen by God* as "good" (Gn 1:21–25). It is in his capacity as image of God that he receives an authority* over them, which nevertheless excludes violence* or exploitation (Beauchamp 1987). Genesis 1:29f. implies that the diet of human beings as well as of animals was originally vegetarian (another opinion can be found in Dequeker, *Bijdr*). In Genesis 2:19f., where the creation of woman is also described, man is invited to "name" the animals, an act of knowledge and power. The negative role of the snake, creature of God (3:1), remains unexplained. The accounts given by Abel (Gn 4:4) and Noah (Gn 8:20f.) recognize sacrifice* to be a universal custom (cf. with Ps 50:9–14, e.g.). With Noah's help, God guarantees reproduction for all species (Gn 6:9ff., 7–9 passim). After the Flood, he modifies the status of human beings by granting them the right to eat the flesh of animals. The two texts which record this change are followed by a third from the same source (Gn 9:8–17), which describes the Covenant* between God and all living creatures, and still places cosmic peace* above any other value. Animals and human beings are coparticipants in the divine Covenant: although rarely put explicitly, this concept (Hos 2:20: Murray 1992) and Job 5:23 (obscure: ibid.) takes over from the archetypes that inspired Genesis 1–2, 9.

b) Legislative Texts. These texts codify the distinction between pure and impure animals (Lv 11; Dt 14:3–20) and the sacrificial rites (Lv 1–7; etc.). According to Exodus 21–23, Leviticus 22–25, and Deuteronomy 14–22, animals (and even trees) will be treated humanely. Contrary to 1 Corinthians 9:9, Philo does not resort to allegory to comment on these laws* (De Virt.) (Carmichael 1976; Murray 1992).

c) Other Texts. Human beings share with animals the condition of being creatures, but also that of being mortals (Pury 1985) (Ps 49:13–21; plants: *see* Ps 103:15f.). God takes care of all creatures (Ps 104:10–30) and knows their ways (Jb 39). Sparrows nest near him in the temple (Ps 84:4). Directives and reprimands may come to human beings through animals (e.g., Is 1:3; Jer 8:7), and bonds of affection are frequent between them (Balaam's female donkey: Nm 22:28ff.; the ewe lamb of the poor in Nathan's parable*: 2 Sm 12:3). Compassion for the suffering of animals (Jer 14:5f.; Jl 1:18–20; *see* Prv 2:10). The study of animals (of plants, of the cosmos*) is part of wisdom* (1 Kgs 5:13; Wis 7:20).

2. Personifications

Whether it is a question of the faithfulness of cattle (Is 1:3), or the ant's haste (Prv 6:6ff.), or the ostrich's insensitivity (Jb 39:13–18), virtues or vices are attributed to animals, who, together with all creatures, praise the Lord (Ps 148; Dn 3 [LXX]; *see* the "chapter on hymns"; *see Encyclopaedia Judaica,* "Pereq shirah"; and Beit-Arié 1966 and Francis of Assisi). Poetic imagination expresses here, better than science, the solidarity of what is created (Murray 1992).

3. Metaphors

An inexhaustible reserve of meanings, the world of animals expresses beauty (Sg 4); or animosity: for example in the guise of dogs (anonymous enemies): Psalms

59:6f., 14f.; lions (Assyrians): Isaiah 5:29; a dragon (Pharaoh): Ezekiel 29:3ff.; 32:2–8; grasshoppers (unstoppable destruction on the Day of YHWH: Jl 2:1–11) (Beauchamp, Creation and separation, 1969); or wild animals (wrath of God): Hosea 13:7f., and so on.

Peace* is consented to by dangerous animals (Ez 34:25–28); or, more accurately, it prevails between wild animals and humans. This is the myth of a golden age, taken up by Isaiah 11:6–9, probably to represent the social peace that is expected with the imminent advent of an ideal king (Murray 1992). Various rereadings influenced by the theme of a "messianic age," then made these aspirations appear more distant and hazier. Central to all this is the representation of the king as a shepherd (Gilgamesh; Homer: *poimenè laôn*), applied first to God (Ps 23, 80:2, 100:3, 78:52), to his tenderness (Is 40:1; *see* Ez 34:11–31). God bestows this function on the king, of which David is the paradigm (Ps 78:70f.). Conversely, the "bad shepherds" are the bad rulers (Ez 34:2–10). Notwithstanding the proscription imposed on the making of pictures (Ez 20:7, etc.), the *kéroubîm* have their place in the temple*. The human-animal characters that bear the weight of the divine chariot in Ezekiel 1 may suggest that the interconnection between humans and animals is modeled on what is in heaven.

II. New Testament

Jesus affirms that God takes care of sparrows (Mt 10:29), flowers (Mt 6:28 ff.), and lost sheep (Lk 15:3–7). According to the majority of exegetes, Mark 1:12f. ("He [Jesus] was with the wild beasts") does not refer to the (Pauline) theme of a second Adam*. However, those who concede more room to the midrashic allusions, as well as some poets, do accept such an interpretation (Murray 1992). Peter*'s vision (Acts 10:10–16), in which he sees both pure and impure animals gathered together ("What God has made clean, do not call common"), interpreting this as a metaphor for the welcoming of Gentiles into the church*, is based more widely on a concept of the universal sanctity of what has been created. By way of contrast, the rigid anthropocentrism of Paul's denial that God could take care of oxen (1 Cor 9:9; *see* Dt 25:4) comes as quite a shock. In the apocalypse, animal metaphors principally denote evil* and destruction. An angel* shouts, however: "Do not harm the earth or the sea or the trees, until we have sealed the servants of our God on their foreheads" (Rev 7:3). It is the repeated image of the shepherd-lamb* (7:17), pasturing his flock in the temple-paradise, that evokes the positive aspect of the biblical symbolism of animals.

• Philon, *De opificio mundi,* in *Œuvres,* vol. 1, Paris; *De Virtutitus,* in *Œuvres,* vol. 26.

♦ Beit-Arié (1966), *Pereq Shirah,* Critical Ed., 2 vols., Jerusalem.

C. Carmichael (1976), "On Separating Life and Death: An Explanation of Some Biblical Laws," *HThR* 69, 1–7.

A. de Pury (1985), "Animalité de l'homme et humanité de l'animal dans la pensée israélite," in *L'animal, l'homme, le Dieu dans le Proche-Orient ancien,* coll., Cahiers du CEPOA, Louvain, 47–70.

P. Beauchamp (1987), "Création et fondation de la loi en Gn 1, 1–2, 4a," in L. Derousseaux (Ed.), *La création dans l'Orient Ancien,* Paris, 139–82.

R. Murray (1992), *The Cosmic Covenant: Biblical Themes of Justice, Peace and the Integrity of Creation,* London.

Robert Murray

See also **Adam; Cosmos; Creation; Ecology; Purity/Impurity; Sacrifice; Violence**

Anointing of the Sick

a) Early Christianity. In early Christianity a certain number of liturgical accounts, as well as accounts of other types, bear witness to the existence of a blessing with oil for the sick, or the practice of anointing them in accordance with the recommendation of James 5:14–15. The most important liturgical accounts are the Roman blessing of the oil for the sick, which took place at the end of the eucharistic prayer; and a prayer*, in Egypt, from a compendium called the *Euchologion* (c. 350; *Sacramentary*) of Serapion. The Roman blessing was already in existence in the Greek language, in the *Apostolike paradosis (Apostolic Tra-*

dition) attributed to Hippolytus (c. 170–c. 236) (and this textual continuity is one of the elements of the complex debate regarding the specifically Roman nature of tradition). The text of the prayer for the blessing of the oil did not see much variation until the present time; but during the Middle Ages, the ministry* of this blessing came to be reserved for the bishop*, who consecrates the three holy* oils on Maundy Thursday in the course of the Mass of the Chrism. In the Greek-speaking East the prayer was already in existence in the fourth to fifth centuries in the *Euchologion* of Serapion, and has never ceased to be part of the Byzantine ritual of anointing, called the *euchelaion,* which meant, at first, "prayer on the oil," then, more recently, "prayer oil." The anointing of the sick is also mentioned in a letter addressed in 416 by Pope Innocent I to Decentius, bishop of Gubbio in central Italy. This anointing, which he relates to the Epistle of James, is intended for the care of the baptized who are sick (with the exception of public penitents). The oil is blessed by the bishop and may be brought to the sick by a priest or by a lay* person, and the Roman custom includes an internal as well as an external use of the oil. Similar customs were practiced in various Western countries until about the eighth century.

b) Middle Ages. From the Carolingian period at the very latest, the anointing was done exclusively by priests*. Since the custom was to wait until the last moment to resort to the sacrament* of penance*, the anointing was deferred, and what was expected from it was mainly the forgiveness of sins*, a conditional effect that is mentioned at the end of James's text ("if he is a sinner, his sins will be forgiven"). After the middle of the 12th century, when the Latin list of the seven sacraments was established, the anointing of the sick was included. During the 12th and 13th centuries this anointing was commonly given the name *extreme unction* and dubbed "the sacrament of those who go away *(exeuntium).*" The liturgy* of the monks of Cluny, then that of the Papal Chapel, spread a custom whereby the sacramental anointing was applied to the organs of the five senses. In each case there was a formula asking "that you be forgiven for the sins you have committed with such or such sense." In this perspective, any bodily effect of the sacrament is considered exceptional and nonessential. It became necessary, then, to distinguish between the effect of extreme unction and that of penance; the theologians of the later Middle Ages did this by stating that anointing had its own effect: it removed the remnants of the sin, and thus prepared the soul to appear before God. This opinion led to the practice of performing extreme unction after the viaticum; this became the rule of the Roman liturgy from the end of the Middle Ages until the liturgical reform of Vatican* II.

The liturgies of Eastern Christianity have different customs on this point. Copts, Western Syrians, Greeks, and Russians insist on the bodily effect of the sacrament (something that led Simeon of Thessalonica, the great Greek liturgical commentator to protest, in the 15th century, against the Western idea of extreme unction). Armenians and Eastern Syrians have, on the other hand, abandoned the practice of anointing the sick.

c) Protestant Reformers and the Council of Trent. Anointing of the sick is one of the sacramental rites accepted by the Roman Church* that the Reformers refused to include among the sacraments. In his treaty *Von der babylonischen Gefängniss der Kirche* (1520; *On the Babylonian Captivity of the Church*) Luther* thus puts in opposition the healing* ritual mentioned in the Epistle of James and the rite intended for the dying in the Roman Church. As for Calvin*, he thinks the gift of healing attested by the New Testament was not preserved beyond the apostolic era. The churches born of the Reformation were to maintain the blessing of the sick and the dying, while restricting it to an imposition of the hands to avoid any suggestion of a sacrament.

Contrary to this, in 1551 the Council* of Trent* passed a doctrinal decree on extreme unction. In a comprehensive account and in four canons, the Catholic Church formally declared that there was true homogeneity between the sacrament and the practice recommended by the Epistle of James, and it affirmed the sacerdotal identity of the minister of the sacrament. While designating the sacrament as extreme unction, however, the conciliar document avoided saying that such a designation belonged to the deposit of faith*. The Roman Ritual of 1614 includes a section on extreme unction corresponding to the teachings of the Council of Trent, and the practice there outlined has become more or less general in the Latin church.

In the liturgies of the Anglican Communion the first Booke of the Common Prayer and Administracion of the Sacramentes (1549) offered a rite of unction, which later disappeared. Similar rites would appear again in the 20th century, especially after Vatican* II. The Episcopalian Book of Common Prayer of the United States (1977) provides a good example.

d) Second Vatican Council and Liturgical Reform. Vatican II's constitution on the liturgy (*Sacrosanctum Concilium* 73; 1963), whose exact phrasing led to much debate, prefers the designation "anointing of the sick," but it does not conclude in a really decisive way whether this sacrament is to be reserved for the sick who are in danger. Coming after the rite of the blessing of the holy oils (1971), a new rite for the anointing of the sick (1972) implemented the conciliar decision and replaced the anointing of the five senses, together with the corresponding sacramental formula, with anointing of the forehead and the hands. This new rite is accompanied by a formula directly inspired by the Epistle of James, which implies that the remission of sins through this sacrament is a conditional effect and not its main effect. The rite also offers also a choice of prayers adapted to the particular condition of each sick individual. This rite can be celebrated in a communal fashion, for sick or old people assembled together.

In the Orthodox churches the blessing before Easter of the oils intended for the sick is followed by the anointing of the congregation with the holy oil. This custom may have originated in an ancient ritual of reconciliation for penitents.

• A. Chavasse (1942), *Étude sur l'onction des malades dans l'Église latine du IIIe au XIe s.*, vol. I: *Du IIIe s. à la réforme carolingienne* (vol. II was not published).

J. Dauvillier (1953), "Extrême-onction dans les Églises orientales," *DDC* 5, 725–89.

E. Doronzo (1954), *Tractatus dogmaticus de Extrema-Unctione,* 2 vols., Milwaukee.

A. Duval (1970), "L'extrême-onction au concile de Trente: Sacrement des mourants ou sacrement des malades?" *MD* 101, 127–72 (Repr. in *Des sacrements au concile de Trente,* Paris, 1985, 223–79).

R. Cabié (1973), *La lettre du pape Innocent Ier à Décentius de Gubbio,* Louvain.

P.-M. Gy (1973), "Le nouveau Rituel romain des malades," *MD* 113, 29–49.

H. Vorgrimler (1978), *Buße und Krankensalbung, HDG* IV/3.

M. Dudley, G. Rowell (Ed.) (1993), *The Oil of Gladness: Anointing in the Christian Tradition,* London.

P.-M. Gy (1996), "La question du ministre de l'onction des malades," *MD* 205, 15–24.

Pierre-Marie Gy

See also **Baptism; Eucharist; Holy Oils; Marriage; Ordination/Order; Penance; Sacrament**

Anselm of Canterbury

(c. 1033–1109)

An eminent representative of monastic theology*, Anselm principally looked for the reasons that would help elucidate the mysteries* of the faith*. His rational method led to him being seen as the "father of Scholasticism*."

a) Life. Anselm was born in Aosta (Italy) around 1033 and at a very young age formed the intention of joining the Benedictine monastery of his region. After his mother's death* Anselm left the family manor because of a difference of opinion with his father. After three years in Burgundy (1053–56) he decided to join Lanfranc, a famous scholar of that time, at the recently founded abbey of Bec in Normandy. As a monk at Bec from 1060 on Anselm was entrusted with teaching duties by Lanfranc. He became prior of the community in 1063, exercising that function for 15 years. Elected as the second abbot of Bec in 1078, for another 15 years he governed an abbey with estates and priories that were rapidly spreading, on the Continent as well as in recently conquered England. During a journey to England in 1093 Anselm was forced by King William the Red (Rufus) to become archbishop of Canterbury. Anselm had to hold simultaneously the two functions of Primate of England and of First Baron of the Realm in a climate of perpetual tension, under two successive monarchs who governed as absolute rulers. In the face of royal power and at risk to his own life, he asserted and defended the primacy of spiritual power and the freedom of the church*. This cost him two exiles. During the first of these he lived in Rome*, attended the Council of Rome and also the Council of Bari (1098), at which the Latin church's doctrine of the procession of the Holy Spirit *(Filioque*)* was pitted against the Greek position. Having started *Cur Deus homo* (1098; *Why God Was Made Man*) at Canterbury at the height of persecution, Anselm completed it near Capua. After the death of William the Red he went back to England (1100), but the attitude of King Henry I Beauclerc obliged him to choose exile a second time (1103). After the meeting of l'Aigle (1105), where he threatened the King with excommunication, Anselm went back definitively to England and convened the Council of London in order to clarify the difficult situation of the Church of England. He died in Canterbury on 21 April 1109.

b) God. Anselm was approximately 40 years old when he wrote his first meditations: the *Meditatio de redemptione humana (Meditation on Human Redemption).* He was a highly valued lecturer in monastic circles, and his first spiritual writings spread rapidly. In these writings Anselm introduces a new method of meditating and praying*, one that has recourse to reason*. His methodological research *sola ratione* (through reasoning alone) was, in fact, the result of monastic exhortations *(collationes),* long discussions, and the teaching given at the school of Bec. It was there that Anselm started practicing the sort of research that so fascinated his listeners that they begged their master to put his unusual meditations in writing. The result was the *Monologion* of 1076. In it, Anselm reflects on the divine essence so that nothing will be imposed by the authority* of the Scripture*.

Anselm starts by proving that there exists something supremely good and supremely great, which is the summit *(summum)* of all that is. He establishes his thesis for the benefit of those who have never heard of a similar thing or who do not believe in it. With the latter in mind, he declares that each human being will be able to prove, through reason alone *(saltem sola ratione),* everything we necessarily believe about God* and his creatures. Anselm starts with the various degrees of kindness that lead necessarily to the assertion that there is such a thing as Sovereign Good*. The meditation deals next with the nature of God and of his absolute being*. This process, which is purely rational *(disputatio),* is applied to all the divine attributes*. It reaches its peak in the study of the Trinity* and ends with the question of the knowledge of the Ineffable. Borrowing generously from Augustine*, Anselm condenses in a dialectical synthesis everything we can know about God, except the Incarnation*. God is presented as Spirit.

Anselm's thinking is certainly that of a monk, but it would be a mistake to classify it with monastic thinking in general. Indeed, the mainstream monastic thinking of Anselm's time, as represented by Peter Damien and others (Gérard de Csanàd, Rupert of Deutz) is more or less a tendency to resist the intrusion of the profane sciences such as grammar and dialectics into the *lectio sacra* (sacred Word). Even Lanfranc avoids using dialectics for the elucidation of the *sacra pagina* (sacred page), except when he wishes to show that he is capable of mastering it when facing its champions, who resort to it in order to question certain dogmas*.

Anselm's attitude is totally different. In his first meditation on the divine essence *(Monologion)* he makes full use of every intellectual resources, not only of dialectics *(disputatio),* but also of introspection, to clarify the Christian mystery of the triune God with a philosophical framework. Anselm makes generous use of the fundamental philosophical notions accessible at the time and even deploys a radical ontology. This entails exploring in depth the problem of the God called *Summus Spiritus,* who is also presented as *Summum Omnium*—having absolute power, independent of anyone else, needed by all beings for their welfare and indeed for their mere existence. This ontology goes to the very roots of being: the sovereign being alone *is,* and all the rest is quasi-nothingness*. Anselm returns to the problem of nothingness in one of his letters (Epistle 91), in which he places it in relation to the definition of evil*; the deepest discussion of that problem is to be found in the *De casu diaboli (On the Fall of Satan).*

Because of the novelty of his method—the use of "necessary reasons" intended to prove what it is that faith says of God, and even of the mystery of the Trinity—Anselm could not avoid giving rise to severe disquiet and indeed criticism among his entourage, mainly from his old master Lanfranc, who in the meantime had become archbishop of Canterbury. To defend his orthodoxy Anselm invokes the authority of the Fathers*, and most particularly Augustine's (354–430) *De Trinitate (On the Holy Trinity).*

To the external criticism coming from those around him was soon added Anselm's critique of his own thinking. The rational approach he had deployed in the *Monologion* started to appear too complicated to him. He had the idea to put an end to what he called *multorum concatenatione contextum argumentorum* (the sequence of numerous arguments that are intertwined) and to replace the complicated arguments unfolded in the *Monologion* with a single argument. This produced the *Proslogion* in 1077–78, the work of a contemplative mind in search of a supremely logical synthesis of all our knowledge* about God, incorporating the irrefutable proof of his existence* and of his essence and attributes*. In the *Proslogion,* initially called *Fides quaerens intellectum (Faith Seeking Understanding),* a title that reveals a great deal about his entire program, one can find simultaneously the expression of the adoration of God, which has been revealed through faith; and a dialectical approach by the mind, which is attempting to understand the object of contemplation*, and engaging, in order to do so, its whole rational capacity *(cogitari posse).*

This dialectical approach is undertaken by means of the "principle of greatness": *aliquid quo nihil maius cogitari potest* (something in relation to which nothing greater can be thought). If God is "the one in relation to whom nothing greater can be thought," he is "the one who exists not only in thought, but also in reality." This dialectics leads us at first to the obvious: there are things that exist only in thought, and there are also things that exist in thought as well as in reality. According to the hierarchy of dignities that this dialectics presupposes, what exists in reality is greater than what exists only in thought. Thus, if God is "the one in relation to whom nothing greater can be thought," he must exist not only in thought but also in reality.

Anselm's approach stems from two presuppositions: First, that God is "The one in relation to whom nothing greater can be imagined." And second, that all that exists also in reality is greater than that which exists only in thought. Each of these two presuppositions implies an outlook that considers all things in the perspective of greatness.

Anselm ends up not only with the assertion that "God really is," but also with the logical impossibility of negating the existence of God. That leads us to the following conclusion from the *Proslogion:* "That which you first gave me to believe, I now conceive in such a way, enlightened by you, that even if I did not want to believe it, I would be unable to unthink it." For from the moment one poses the problem of God in the perspective of "the one in relation to whom nothing greater can be thought," any denial of the characteristic "greater," represented by the real existence of God in relation to the idea that we make of him, becomes a logical impossibility. When the "fool" of Psalms 14:1 and 53:1, who says in his heart that "there is no God," hears that God is "the one in relation to whom nothing greater can be thought," he finds himself in the logical impossibility of denying the real existence of God. The dialectical opposition between faith and reason reaches its climax. On the one hand, faith is placed inside brackets; on the other hand, it is impossible not to think that God does exist.

Most commentators on the *Proslogion*—from the monk Gaunilon, a contemporary of Anselm, to the commentators of our own time—stop at the proof of the existence of God, mistakenly called, since Kant*, the "ontological argument," whereas it should be called the "dialectical proof through greatness." And yet, Anselm's project goes much further: it proposes to include everything we believe regarding the divine substance in that same dialectics of greatness.

According to this logic one is led to assert about God all that is better if he exists than if he does not, namely eternity*, omnipresence*, truth*, kindness (good*): in brief, all the perfections that might be said to constitute his essence and his attributes. In this first stage of the dialectical approach intelligence scours the whole of creation*. It undertakes to transcend the finite by means of logic, in order to dwell only on the perfections that represent a "plus," something greater, in relation to the imperfections to which they are opposed. In this perspective what is eternal is greater than what is ephemeral: it follows that God must be eternal, not only in thought, but in reality.

However, the first stage of the dialectics of greatness considers everything in relation to intelligence, and so one might be tempted to identify God with "something" that is indeed in reality, but that can be "grasped" by intelligence. And yet, this is not the case in Anselm's thought. By means of his dialectics he is able to transcend intelligence with intelligence by applying to human intelligence the same dialectical principle that had brought him to criticize the finite being. God is not only greater than what intelligence is capable of grasping, but greater than the concept itself. As he had done at his starting point, Anselm, now at the peak of his dialectical approach, addresses God directly to spell out his principle: God is not only that which completes the capacity of our intelligence, he is also that which transcends it. God, therefore, can only be pure surplus, pure excess, for had he not been surplus, one would be able to think of a being greater than him; and had he not been real—existing really as excess—one would be able to think of a being still greater than him. It is in this way that Anselmian dialectics arrives at its goal, with the assertion of God's reality; this reality goes beyond anything the human mind can conceive and goes even beyond the boundaries of human intelligence.

The *Proslogion* was criticized by the monk Gaunilon in terms that foreshadowed the kind of criticism Kant would later make of the "ontological argument." For Gaunilon, Anselm's thought implies that one can talk about what precisely cannot be talked about: dealing with that topic is doing what is an antinomy of the undescribable. In his reply Anselm tried to strengthen his argument with a series of demonstrations by contradiction, which are evidence of a subtle dialectical mind. He categorically rejected Gaunilon's suggestion that it would be sufficient to imagine something greater than everything—such as "the lost island"—and deduce from this that it is in existence.

c) Salvation. After the *Proslogion,* Anselm, already an abbot, between 1082 and 1090 composed several dialogues, three of which—*De veritate (Concerning Truth), De libertate arbitrii (On Freedom of Choice),* and *De casu diaboli* (*The Fall of Satan*)—are designed to aid understanding of the Scriptures. They are not, however, biblical commentaries. What these dialogues do is explain a small number of biblical statements, the most important being: "God is truth." *Concerning Truth* stems from the confrontation of traditional Augustinianism* (or from Augustinian Platonism*) with the Aristotelianism* of the logic corpus translated by Boethius*, the *logica vetus,* whose revival at the end of the 10th century brought about a rationalization of theology. *Deus est veritas* (God is truth) seems contrary to the Aristotelian definition of truth. Anselm solves the problem by insisting on the transcendental nature of the Truth that is God: the *summa veritas* causes the *veritas essentiae rerum* which, in turn, causes the *veritas enuntiationis,* the truth according to Aristotle.

On Freedom of Choice, as well as *The Fall of Satan,* discuss the Augustinian problem of freedom* and responsibility by proposing a totally new definition of freedom. Human beings are free not only because they can choose one thing rather than another, but also because they are capable of morality *(iustitia).* They can evade the determination of nature* only if they are morally good. Since God could not have determined that human beings can give up their just will (because in doing so he would be wanting what he does not want human beings to want, which would mean wanting what he himself does not want), the persistence of a just will in human beings is the result of an act of perfect self-determination, something praiseworthy and therefore responsible. God's grace* does not change this, but it explains how human beings (who on their own, can only choose what seems pleasant to them) can be just, or morally good (how they can love God for his own sake): his justice* is always a gift of God.

De grammatico (De Grammatico: How Expert-in-Grammar Is Both a Substance and a Quality)—the only nonreligious writing by Anselm—dates from this period. In this original study on the problems of language he initiates his disciples into subtle exercises of logic, introduces a new terminology that allows raising the problem of the reference, and recognizes the usefulness of such exercise, in accordance with rules familiar to the dialecticians of the time.

Cur Deus Homo (Why God Made Man) is the third work among the most famous by Anselm. He started it in England right in the midst of persecution and completed it in Capua (1098) during his first exile. It outlines a bold soteriology—a theory of vicarious satisfaction—in which Anselm attempts to find the necessary reasons to justify the Incarnation. In the *Monologion* and the *Proslogion* Anselm had wanted to support, by purely rational means, the truth of revealed faith regarding the divine substance, with the exception of the Incarnation. He had left open the opportunity to treat this mystery separately, in the *Why God Made Man,* in the form of a diptych.

Why God Made Man is a dialogue between Anselm and Boson, a monk of Bec. Answering the question: For what reason or necessity did God decide to make himself man?, he inaugurated a literary genre that later had great success in the Middle Ages (Gilbert Crispin, disciple of Anselm, Abelard*, Nicholas* of Cusa). This important work is divided into two parts. The first contains the objections of the infidels who reject the Christian faith—because, according to them, it goes against reason—and the answers of the believers. In this work Anselm shows by means of necessary reasons that no human being can be saved without Jesus Christ*. In the second part he proves, still by rational means—as if nothing were known of Christ *(remoto Christo)*—on the one hand that human nature was created for eternal bliss and that human beings were meant to enjoy that bliss in both body and soul*, and on the other hand that this bliss can be realized only by the grace of the Man-God. As a consequence, all that we believe about Christ necessarily had to be realized before reason. Thus, those reasons that we seek will at the same time constitute the common point between the believer and the unbeliever. The object of the search is therefore common, and that is why a genuine dialogue can be established.

The fundamental question of the Incarnation is, at the same time, the challenge, the main objection *(obicere)* of the infidels, who ridicule "Christian naivety." It also gives rise to many queries, from well-read people and uncultivated ones alike, who all ask for the reason behind that question *(rationem eius).*

The complete wording of the question comes from Boson: "For what necessity and for what reason, has God, who is nonetheless all powerful, assumed the humble condition and the infirmity of human nature in view of its restoration?" According to Anselm, in order to obtain a correct solution, it is indispensable to clarify certain fundamental notions, such as necessity, power, will, and the like, which, moreover, cannot be considered separately. Given that human beings are meant for beatitude*, given that they cannot avoid sinning in their present condition, and that they need the remission of sins*, it was necessary, "death having become part of human condition through the disobedience of a man, that in turn, life be reestablished through the obedience of a man." It was fitting then (a necessity of appropriateness), given this premise, that "divine and human nature meet each other in the form of one sole person." The Father* therefore wants humankind to be restored by the human act of the death* of Christ, greater than the sin of human beings, and the Son "prefers to suffer rather than leave humankind without salvation*." Through that, he settles humanity's debt and reestablishes divine honor. The satisfaction of sin is commensurate with the divine honor that has been injured; and as a consequence it cannot be done by a human being alone: "The sinner owes to the help of God what he cannot turn around by himself, and failing that help, he cannot be saved." It is then necessary that someone "should pay to God, for man's sin, something greater than anything that is, except God." The author of the satisfaction must therefore be "a God-man," because "nobody can do it, except a real God, and nobody should do it, except a real man": the same one must be perfect God and perfect man.

Anselm also composed a few occasional works: *Epistola de incarnatione Verbi* (1095; *The Incarnation of the Word*) to refute the errors of Roscelin de Compiègne (tritheism*); *De processione Spiritus Sancti (Concerning the Procession of the Holy Spirit).* In this opuscule, which resembles a dialectical exercise, advancing by means of continual objections (questions) and answers, Anselm hopes to be able, by means of reason *(rationabiliter),* to bring the Greeks to recognize the procession of the Holy Spirit according to the doctrine of the Latin church*.

De conceptu virginali et de originali peccato (Concerning Virginal Conception and Original Sin) is a complement to *Why God Made Man.* Indeed, Boson, Anselm's interlocutor, does not seem entirely satisfied with the reasons proposed by Anselm to explain how God, who is without sin, could have assumed his role as man, while mankind sins. *De concordia praescientiae et praedestinationis et gratiae dei cum libero arbitrio (On the Harmony of Foreknowledge, Predestination, and the Grace of God with Free Will)* deals with the problem of predestination*. This question originates in the apparent contradiction between the different biblical texts: some of them seem to imply that free will plays no part in salvation, and some others seem to suggest that salvation rests entirely on it. Thus the question of free will springs up like a real *Sic et Non* (Yes and No) a short time before Abelard.

Letters. Anselm left an abundant correspondence: 372 letters recognized to be authentic and covering some 30 years of his life. Some deal with doctrinal problems, but most are precious testimonies to his religious and political commitments, and accounts of his fights against abuses and royal tyranny and for the freedom of the church.

Anselm maintained assiduous relations with the most important personalities of his time, both political and religious: bishops*, abbots, popes*, dukes, counts, countesses, kings and the people close to them, but also ordinary monks, young students, and members of his own family. All of these looked to him for advice and regarded him as a trusted counselor. His letters show his limpid writerly style, marked by simplicity and conciseness; they focus on what is essential and guide his correspondents toward God.

d) Method: Faith in Search of Understanding. Anselm's argumentation aims to be convincing "at least *(saltem)* through reasoning alone." The addition of *saltem* to *sola ratione* makes us understand that, for him, the hierarchy of knowledge remains intact: the rational approach should always respect the superiority of faith. For, *nisi credideritis, non intelligetis* (if you do not believe, you will not understand): faith remains the starting point of all rational knowledge, even as far as the dialectical principle of the *Proslogion* is concerned. Throughout Anselm's work, it is faith that pursues the search, it is faith that calls for intelligibility: *Fides quaerens intellectum.* Faith remains the starting point of the dialectical search, but not of all natural knowledge, because Anselm will always continue to pretend to the ability to convince even the pagans. He has therefore changed the original title *Fides quaerens intellectum* into *Monologion,* which indicates a certain philosophical intention.

In the *Monologion* Anselm does not invoke the help of any authority and does not quote the Scriptures. In *Why God Made Man* he neglects the fact of Christ *(remoto Christo)* and looks for "necessary" reasons to explain the necessity of the Incarnation by nevertheless finding support in the Scriptures. The *rationes* (reasons) are natural reasons as well as quotations from the Scriptures. However, as with the God of the *Proslogion,* the redemptive work of God here appears, in its greatness, to go beyond the human mind.

The expression *sola ratione* can be found in Augustine; the method it designates is, however, well and truly Anselmian. Anselm makes full use of all the resources of reason by drawing heavily on the philosophical arsenal of his time. He wants to arrive at a purely rational synthesis of the object of faith through the logical sequence of a series of necessary reasons. However, the rational approach as founded on faith relies on introspection as well as on concrete examples that are likely to clarify the mysteries.

The full use of reason is carried along by the momentum of an unending quest, a *quaerere* whose dramatic shape is mapped out by Augustine at the end of *De Trinitate.* That momentum is motivated by the *quaerite faciem eius semper,* the invitation of Psalm 105 to "seek his presence continually." That search may be realized by means of *rationes necessariae* (necessary reasons), and it is here that dialectics, the use of logic and of the resources of logic, come into the picture (in the use of invincible arguments, of reductio ad absurdum, of philosophical notions, and in the deepening of the *usus communis loquendi*). Anselm attempts to adjust and purify these resources through a metaphysical form of thinking and through the use of *similitudines* drawn from experience*. He does this in order to render intelligible the question being asked, and to illustrate the truth that is to be sought and found.

Anselm recognizes, however, the possibility of finding better and more convincing reasons. *Why God Made Man* is a typical case of the extreme determination of Anselmian inquiry to explore matters to the fullest: having undertaken a prolonged search for reasons, Anselm leaves the door open, and he actually reexamines the same question in *Concerning Virginal Conception and Original Sin* because he feels that his interlocutor Boson is not satisfied.

On the other hand, the momentum of this search does not retreat in the face of any mystery that faith may pose: there is an a priori readiness to tackle any object. *Fides quaerens intellectum* is not only the statement of a method, it is also a research program, a program for a life nurtured by prayer.

Anselm's method was hailed by his contemporaries as a real liberation. William of Malmesbury makes a comparison between Anselm and the other theologians of his time, who were attempting "to extort their disciples' credulity by means of authority." Anselm, on the other hand, attempted "to corroborate their faith through reason, by demonstrating with invincible arguments that everything we believe is in accordance with reason and that it cannot be otherwise."

• Anselm, *Opera Omnia,* Ed. F.S. Schmitt, 6 vols., Seckau-Rome-Edinburgh, 1938–61.

Eadmer, *Historia Novorum in Anglia, et Opuscula Duo De Vita Sancti Anselmi et Quibusdam Miraculis Ejus,* Ed. M. Rule, London, 1884 (2nd Ed. 1965).

F.S. Schmitt, *Ein neues unvollendetes Werk des hl. Anselm von Canterbury,* BGPhMA, vol. 33/3, 1936.

M. Corbin (Ed.), *L'œuvre de saint Anselme de Cantorbéry,* 10 vols. planned (6 published) (bilingual edition), Paris, 1986–.

R.W. Southern, F.S. Schmitt, *Memorials of St. Anselm,* Oxford, 1991.

Collections

Spicilegium Beccense, I: *Congrès international du IXe centenaire de l'arrivée d'Anselme au Bec,* 1959; II: *Les mutations socioculturelles au tournant des XI-XIIe siècles,* 1984.

Analecta Anselmiana, 5 vols., Frankfurt, I: 1969; II: 1970; III: 1972; IV: 1975; V: 1976.

Anselm Studies I: *Anselm at Canterbury,* London, 1983; II: *Episcopi ad saecula—Saint Anselm and Saint Augustine,* Villanova, Penn., 1988; III: Lewiston, N.Y., 1996.

♦ C. Filliatre (1920), *La philosophie de saint Anselme: Ses principes, sa nature, son influence,* Paris.

A. Koyré (1923), *L'idée de Dieu dans la philosophie de saint Anselme,* Paris.

K. Barth (1931), *Fides quaerens intellectum: Anselms Beweis der Existenz Gottes im Zusammenhang seines theologischen Programms,* Zurich.

F.S. Schmitt (1932), "Zur Chronologie der Werke des hl. Anselm von Canterbery," *RBen* 44, 322–50.

É. Gilson (1934), "Sens et nature de l'argument de saint Anselme," *AHDL* 9, 5–51.

J. Rivière (1936), "La question du Cur deus Homo," *RevSR* 16, 1–32.

P. Vignaux (1947), "Structure et sens du 'Monologion,'" *RSPhTh* 31, 192–212.

D. Heinrich (1959), *Der ontologische Gottesbeweis,* Tübingen.

R. Roques (1962), "La méthode de saint Anselme dans le 'Cur deus Homo'," *Aquinas* 5, 3–57; (1963), *Anselme de Cantorbéry: Pourquoi Dieu s'est fait homme,* SC 91 (bibl.).

C. Viola (1970), "La dialectique de la grandeur: Une interprétation du 'Proslogion'," *RThAM* 37, 23–55.

J. Vuillemin (1971), *Le Dieu d'Anselme et les apparences de la raison,* Paris.

Eadmer. (1972), *The Life of St. Anselm Archbishop of Canterbury,* Ed. R.W. Southern, Oxford.

H. Kohlenberger (1972), *"Similitudo und Ratio," Überlegungen zur Methode bei Anselm von Canterbury,* Bonn.

H. de Lubac (1976), "Seigneur, je cherche ton visage": On chap. XIV of St. Anselm's 'Proslogion,'" *ArPh* 39, 201–25, 407–25.

G.S. Kane (1981), *Anselm's Doctrine of Freedom of the Will,* New York-Toronto.

K. Kienzler (1981), *Glauben und Denken bei Anselm von Canterbury,* Freiburg-Basel-Vienna.

G.R. Evans (1984), *A Concordance to the Works of St. Anselm,* 4 vols., Millwood.

P. Gilbert (1984), *Dire l'Ineffable: Lecture du* Monologion *de saint Anselme.*

Y. Cattin (1986), *La preuve de Dieu: Introduction à la lecture du* Proslogion *d'Anselme de Canterbury,* Paris.

S. Vanni Rovighi (1987), *Introduzione a Anselmo d'Aosta,* Bari (bibl.).

M. Parodi (1988), *Il conflitto dei pensieri: Studio su Anselmo d'Aosta,* Bergame.

I. Biffi, C. Marabelli (Ed.) (1989) *Anselmo d'Aosta: Figura europea. Convegno di studi, Aosta 1988,* Milan.

P. Gilbert (1990), *Le "Proslogion" de saint Anselme: Silence de Dieu et joie de l'homme,* Rome (bibl.).

R.W. Southern (1990), *Saint Anselm: A Portrait in a Landscape,* Cambridge.

I. Sciuto (1991), *La ragione della Fede: Il* Monologion *e il programma filosofico di Anselmo d'Aosta,* Genoa.

M. Corbin (1992), *Prière et raison de la foi: Introduction à l'œuvre de saint Anselme de Cantorbéry,* Paris.

C. Viola (1992), "Origine et portée du principe dialectique du 'Proslogion' de saint Anselme De l' 'argument ontologique' à l' 'argument mégalogique'," *RFNS* 83, 339–84; (1992), "'hoc est enim Deo esse, quod est magnum esse': Approche augustinienne de la grandeur divine," in *Chercheurs de sagesse.* Hommage à Jean Pépin, Ed. M.-O. Goulet-Cazé, et al., EAug 131, 403–20.

J. Zumr, V. Herold (1993), *The European Dimensions of St. Anselm's Thinking,* Prague.

D.E. Luscombe, G.R. Evans (Ed.) (1996), *Anselm: Aosta, Bec, Canterbury, Sheffield.*

R.W. Southern (1996), *Saint Anselm and His Biographer: A Study of Monastic Life and Thought 1059–c. 1130,* Cambridge.

Coloman Viola

See also **Bonaventure; Chartres, School of; Duns Scotus, John; Existence of God, Proofs of; Saint-Victor, School of; Scholasticism; Thomas Aquinas**

Anthony the Great. *See* **Monasticism**

Anthropology

1. Biblical Origins

a) Old Testament. The principal sources of a biblical anthropology are the passages from Genesis relating to the creation of man. In the priestly account, the creation of man in the image and likeness of God (Gn 1:26–27) is the result of a divine deliberation without equivalent in the history of religions. Similarly unique is the assertion that man exists as male and female. Man appears as the culmination of creation and is accorded dominion over the earth. In the Yahwist account (Gn 2:4b–25), man is described as being fashioned from clay, emphasizing his earthly reality and kinship with the rest of creation, and animated by the breath of God, making him "a living being" (Gn 2:7), and indicating a relationship to God. In this account, human sexual bipolarity is the result of God's act of forming Eve from the side of Adam, and man's dominion over the rest of creation is expressed in terms of his naming the creatures. Also of importance from Genesis is chapter 3, which describes the Fall*, the introduction of death*, the clothing of Adam and Eve in garments of skin, and their expulsion from paradise, with the consequent change in the conditions of human existence. The dependency of human life upon God, and his Spirit, is repeated throughout the Old Testament, especially in the Psalms (e.g., Ps 104:29–30). The Wisdom of Solomon introduces the further idea that man is created as the image of God's eternity, and that it was toward this immortality, or incorruptibility, that God created man (Wis 2:23).

b) New Testament. While the Gospels emphasize the intrinsic dignity of the human being, it is Saint Paul who develops a more considered anthropology. The most important aspect of Pauline anthropology is its Christological perspective: the first Adam was a "living being," animated by the breath of God, while the second and last Adam, the risen Christ, is "a life-giving spirit," giving spiritual life to mankind; men who have shared in the existence of the first, earth-born Adam, can, in the resurrection, come to share in the heavenly, spiritual existence of the second Adam (1 Cor 15:42–50). Adam was created as a "type of the one to come" (Rom 5:14). The creation of man in the image of God is thus referred to Christ, who is himself the likeness and image of the invisible God (2 Cor 4:4 and Col 1:15), and so Paul's anthropology has an eschatological orientation, unlike the protological mythologizing of the Gnostics (gnosis*). The continuity of man from his original creation to his future spiritual existence is guaranteed, for Paul, by the body *(soma),* an essential dimension of human existence (*see* 1 Thes 5:23, which refers to man as "spirit and soul and body"), and which is to be distinguished from the flesh* *(sarx),* the hardened state of man turned away from God.

2. Extrabiblical Origins

The larger context of Paul's anthropology, and the background for later patristic developments, was that of Judaism, especially as represented by Philo (c. 20 B.C.–C. A.D. 50), Hellenism, and Gnosticism. Philo, interpreting Genesis with the philosophy of Middle Platonism, contrasts the two accounts of creation and elaborates a distinction between the heavenly, immaterial man (Gn 1:26), who exists before, and is the image for, the earthly man (Gn 2:7), who is identified with the mind *(nous),* which itself is the essential element of actual man. Hellenism, in its various forms, generally accepted the idea that the noblest part of man's constitution, the soul or mind, is essentially divine, and, due to its kinship *(syngeneia)* with the divine, enables man, through knowledge, to know the divine. It is the soul, and not the composite of soul and body, that defines man, leaving man's relationship to his body always uneasy. Gnosticism, in all its various manifestations, further deprecated the bodily nature of man. In its Christianized form, Valentinianism, for instance, differentiated between three classes of men: the hylic (material), the psychic, and the spiritual. Only the spiritual element of the last group will be saved, by nature, from destruction; the psychic can either become spiritual or return to the hylic state, in which, with those of the hylic class, they will be utterly destroyed. The Valentinians also differentiated between the man created in the image of the demiurge, and the psychic man created in the likeness, into whom had been breathed the spiritual seed that, through gnosis, can return to the divine. The fleshly bodies that can be perceived by the senses are the "garments of skins" added to the true human nature to enable its continuation in the fallen world (Gn 3:21), so giving the spiritual seed time to grow in gnosis and ultimately return to the Pleroma.

3. Patristic Era

While faith* in the reality of the Incarnation and the Resurrection of the body ensured that the generally accepted Greek body-soul polarity never became hardened into an unresolvable dualist separation, the expressions of this faith were so varied that one must distinguish among three different anthropologies, those of Antioch*, Alexandria*, and the West.

a) School of Antioch. The Antiochene tradition united the two creation accounts, so that the man made from clay is the same man as the one created in the image, and developed this within the Pauline framework of an anthropology grafted onto Christology. This approach begins with Theophilus of Antioch (late second century) and is most fully expounded by Saint Irenaeus*. Irenaeus adopts the eschatological orientation of Pauline anthropology, and, in his battle with the Gnostics, further emphasizes the earthly reality of man by describing him as essentially flesh rather than body. For Irenaeus, there is an intimate link between theology proper and anthropology: the truth of man is revealed in the Incarnation, which at the same time is the primary, if not the sole, revelation of God. Adam was created as a type of the One to come, and the manifestations of God in the Old Testament were always prophetic revelations of the Incarnate Son. Adam was animated by the breath of life, which prefigured the future vivification of the sons of God by the Spirit: initially, of the Incarnate Son and, subsequently, through baptism* of those adopted as sons. Christ revealed the full truth of man, vivified by the Spirit; in the present, adopted sons possess a pledge of "part" of the Spirit, preparing them for their full vivification in the resurrection. Thus, the truth of man is still "hid with Christ in God" (Col 3:3); it is an eschatological reality, anticipated in Christian life, and revealed most fully in the confession of martyrdom. The Spirit, though not a constituent of created human nature, is nevertheless essential to man to be what God intended: man lives in communion with God, partaking of the Spirit, and this living man is the glory of God. As the Incarnate Son is the model for man, Irenaeus locates the "image of God" in man's corporeality, his flesh. This leads him to differentiate between the "image" and the "likeness": the latter is revealed when man lives, in the Spirit, directed toward God. This likeness was lost in the Fall, breaking the communion between God and man, and so introducing death. The likeness can, however, be regained, in Christ, the true image and likeness of God, provisionally as adopted sons, and more completely in the Resurrection. While enabling the restoration of the likeness, the Incarnation does not simply return man to Adam's original state: through the adoption that it makes possible, the Incarnation enables man to acquire the status of sons of God, growing ever closer to the stature of the Son. The potentiality of man's original state is exemplified in Irenaeus's depiction of Adam and Eve as children in paradise. Irenaeus thus inscribes anthropology within a dynamic understanding of salvation history: anthropology does not simply look at man as he was created, in some protological past, but strains ahead to what man is called to become.

A similar position with regard to the image of God in man can be found in Tertullian*, according to whom "the clay that was putting on the image of Christ, who was to come in the flesh, was not only the work but the pledge of God." The later Antiochene tradition did not locate the image of God so concretely in the flesh. Diodorus of Tarsus († c. 390), polemicizing against the Alexandrians, refuses to refer to the image of man's possession of an invisible soul, his intellectual faculty: for Diodorus, the image of God refers to man's dominion. That is, the whole man, body and soul, in his vocation as lord of creation, is in the image of God.

b) School of Alexandria and Its Posterity. Alexandrian anthropology initally developed along the lines of Philo: the image of God has no reference to the body, but, as the image of the preincarnate Logos (i.e., "without flesh," *asarkos*), it is located in the highest element of man, his intellectual *(logikos)* soul or *nous,* which is then used as the definition for the true man. This spiritual man nevertheless exists concretely as the earthly man of Genesis 2:7, from whose limitations the spiritual man must endeavor to free himself by asceticism*, and so achieve likeness to God. Christ, realizing both the image and the likeness, is the model or teacher for

Christians, showing us the way by which to achieve this likeness. Origen*, further elaborating Philo's idea of double creation within his own system of an eternal creation, considers Genesis 1:26 to refer to the creation of the true, original man, who must be recovered, and Genesis 2:7 to indicate the fallen man, the *nous* clad in garments of skin. For Saint Athanasius*, it is man as a rational *(logikos)* being who is in the image of the Logos, and the Incarnate Logos who gives fallen man the possibility of regaining his true relationship to the Logos and hence his character as an image.

The Cappadocians inherited the basic tendency of Alexandrian anthropology to refer the image of God in man to the Logos. The most comprehensive anthropology was developed by Saint Gregory* of Nyssa (c. 330–c. 395), who wrote a treatise specifically on the topic, *Peri kataskeues anthropon* (also known as *De hominis opificio;* translated as *On the Creation of Humanity*). Gregory begins this treatise by setting the appearance of man within the creation of the cosmos as a whole: man appears as the culmination of the ascent made by creation from the lower levels of inert matter, vegetative life, animal life, to the rational animal, man. Man thus encompasses all previous levels of existence and, by virtue of his rationality, can fulfill their potential: for instance, all animals have the power of sensation and movement, but humans, who have bodies suitable for their rational souls (as they have dexterous hands, their mouths are adapted for speech rather than tearing meat), can use these capacities in a manner befitting a rational being. However, the true dignity of man is not in his existence as a microcosm, but in his being created in the image and likeness of God, terms that Gregory does not distinguish. Moreover, for Gregory the image is not to be located in a static ontological element of man, but is instead manifested in man's free exercise of virtue. Gregory also goes further than other Fathers in explaining the rationale of man created as male and female (Gn 1:27). Gregory teaches a dual Creation: first, man (meaning the whole of mankind) made in the image; second, the additional distinction of male and female, which has no reference to the Divine Archetype, but was added by God in foresight of the Fall. Although this is the order of God's intended creation, its temporal realization occurs in reverse: for Gregory, unlike Philo and Origen, man (the whole of mankind) created in the image (and neither male or female) preexists the actual appearance of mankind as male and female *only* in God's foreknowledge, and will be finally realized only at the end of time. While mankind was male and female in paradise, their sexuality was not as yet operative, but was, rather, latent, "in view of the Fall." Prior to the Fall, mankind would have multiplied as the angels*. Human sexuality, along with the characteristics of the flesh as we now know it, was realized in the "garments of skins" (Gn 3:21). These garments of skins are remedial, rather than punitive, enabling mankind to continue in existence in exile from paradise, and, as it is through these garments that mankind now reaches the foreordained number, they have a positive role to play in the fallen world. In the final consummation, when the fullness of mankind has been reached, God's originally intended creation will be realized, without the economic addition of the garments of skin.

The idea of man as a microcosm was further elaborated by Saint Maximus* the Confessor, who inherited much of his anthropology from the Cappadocians, including a position on human sexuality similar to that of Gregory of Nyssa. According to Maximus, man was intended to mediate within the five divisions of creation: between the sexes, paradise and the inhabited world, heaven and earth, intelligible and sensible creation, and, finally, God and creation. Man, as a microcosm, had the vocation of uniting these divisions *(diaireseis),* through the exercise of virtue, so manifesting the theophanic character of the universe. Adam failed in this task. Only the man Jesus, because he is also God, was able to achieve this mediation. He is the new Adam, and only in him does the creation find its true harmony and communion with its Creator.

c) Western Tradition. In the West, anthropology (with the exception of the basically Asiatic position of Tertullian) developed as a form of Christian Platonism*, which referred the image of God in man to the unity and Trinity* of divine Persons*. The most important and influential person in this tradition was Saint Augustine* (354–430). Augustine detaches anthropology from its earlier Christological and cosmological settings. He uses the idea of man as a composite of soul and body, an "amazing" conjunction, and emphasizes their diverse roles, without denigrating either. Perhaps following Tertullian, Augustine differentiates between the breath *(flatus)* of Genesis 2:7, which is the soul of man, and the Spirit *(spiritus),* in terms of the created and Creator. However, Augustine's most important contribution to anthropology was to reorient the question of man as a call to a reflexive return inward: "Return within yourself; in the inward man dwells truth." The fundamental distinction, for Augustine, is not that between spirit and matter, or higher and lower, but that between inner and outer. While God can be known through the created order, our principal route to God lies "in" ourselves. The path leads from the exterior to the interior and thence to the superior, God, who is "more interior than my inmost self and more superior than my highest self."

Thus, through this reflexive approach, God is found to be the ground of the person, in the intimacy of their self-presence. Despite the route of this conclusion being anthropocentric, man is inconceivable without God, his proper end. This is the basis of Augustine's Trinitarian description of the image of God in the soul and its activity: as mind/self-knowledge/love* of self, or memory/intelligence/will. Memory (related to the Father) is the soul's implicit knowledge of itself. To be made explicit and full knowledge it needs to be formulated, put into words (the Word), which constitutes intelligence. Yet to understand one's true self fully is to love it, and so from intelligence comes will, and from self-knowledge comes self-love (the Spirit). Thus, man is most fully in the image of God through the intimacy of his self-presence and self-love.

Of further importance for Augustine's anthropology is his dissociation of the will from knowledge. Greek philosophy tended to make the will a function of knowledge: men act well and desire the good, unless they are led to evil through ignorance of the good. Augustine's teaching on the two loves allows for the possibility that our disposition may be radically perverse. Weakness of the will *(akrasia)* was a central problem for Greek philosophy; for Augustine it is the basic experience of fallen man. Because of original sin*, we have all lost the supernatural grace* and gifts that Adam originally enjoyed in paradise. These supernatural gifts enabled Adam to live righteously and in tranquility, himself subject to God, his lower appetites subject to his own reason and his will. Having been disobedient to God in the use of his sexual nature, it is fitting, Augustine argues, that human sexuality should be man's most unruly drive. Against the Pelagian* emphasis on the autonomy and capacity of man, Augustine stresses our need for grace, which for him is never opposed to human liberty*, but rather is its support. We need to be healed by grace before we can do good. Augustine thus differentiates between free will *(velle)* and ability *(posse):* it is grace that establishes free will as ability and so as true liberty. The Incarnation has the function of restoring the original condition of grace that Adam lost at the Fall; by a detour, our original destiny is fulfilled, but not transcended.

4. Scholastic Theology

With the reintroduction of Aristotelian philosophy in the West, a more holistic anthropology began to be developed, finding its most complete synthesis in the work of Saint Thomas* Aquinas (c. 1125–c. 1274). For Aquinas, man is more than a simple conjunction of a soul and body, two disparate elements, as for Plato and Augustine. The body is an essential element in the human constitution, yet it does not exists through itself, but by the intellectual soul, which is the form of the body, a form, moreover, that possesses and confers substantiality. The soul is act and itself a substance, but without the body it cannot fulfill its actuality; it would remain destitute without the body and its senses, while the body has neither actuality nor substantiality apart from that conferred by the soul. Thus, man is not a substance constructed from two self-subsisting substances, but is himself a concrete and complete substance. This implies a type of dualism, but one that does not impair man's substantial unity as a complex being: a unity of soul, which substantiates his body, and body, in which his soul concretely exists. Nevertheless, man's existence as a complex substance derives from the intellectual soul, which has in itself adequate reason for its own existence. In this way, without denigrating the importance of the body, the traditional priority of the spiritual over the material is maintained. Furthermore, it enables Aquinas to explain the immortality of the soul: the corruption of the body, when it is separated from the soul, that which gives it its actual being, cannot affect the soul itself. Despite Aquinas's emphasis on the complex unity of man, there is a novel departure from the biblical view as represented by Genesis 2:7. The latter describes the whole man, clay animated by the breath of life, as a living soul; for Aquinas, the concrete reality of man is governed by the intellectual soul *(anima intellectiva),* which has an autonomous existence as a substance. Moreover, Aquinas, following Augustine, rejects the connection between the breath of life mentioned in Genesis 2:7 and the Holy Spirit (as upheld, for instance, by Irenaeus), preferring to see, in the contrast that Paul draws in 1 Corinthians 15:45, two distinct and unrelated realities.

Following Saint John of Damascus, Aquinas distinguishes between the image and the likeness of God in man, and couples this with Augustine's teaching on the original state of grace: the image is the intellectual nature of man and his possession of free will, while the likeness was the gift of grace given to Adam, which was lost through sin and restored in Christ. Although it is by virtue of having a rational nature that man is considered to be in the image, as also are the angels, there is no connection between man's possession of *logos* and the divine Logos, as in Alexandrian anthropology. Man is said to be in the image with reference to both the divine Nature and the Trinity of Persons. Thus, the theology of the image is fully detached from Christology*. Existence as the image of God is an essential characteristic of man, enduring even after the Fall: for Aquinas, if man had lost his character as the image of God, his rationality and freedom, he would only be an animal, not a human responsible for his action and sin.

Possession of the image of God is, therefore, a presupposition for the likeness, the additional gift of grace, that is, the actual communion with God proper to the original, and the recreated, state. Thus, while generally following Augustine, Aquinas lays more emphasis on the free will and enduring dignity of man.

5. Reformation

The anthropology of the Reformation is based upon a radicalizing renewal of Augustine's doctrine of original sin and grace. Whereas Latin Scholasticism taught that the image of God was a formal property of human nature, a presupposition for the likeness, the Reformation did not differentiate between "image" and "likeness," but considered them to be equivalent to original righteousness, as Martin Luther writes: "The likeness and image of God consists in the true and perfect knowledge of God, supreme delight in God, eternal life, eternal righteousness, eternal freedom from care." In this perspective, the image of God in man is not a set of static ontological properties, but the complete orientation of life toward God. Inevitably, therefore, the Fall entailed a loss of both the likeness and the image. Fallen man is "totally depraved"; there is no aspect of man that remains unaffected by his sin. Man still possesses free will and reason, but as his will has lost the grace that constituted and empowered it, it has lost its true liberty. The loss of the image did not (despite Matthias Flacius Illyricus [1520–75]) affect our created nature as humans: man's faculties may be seriously weakened or leprous, but one can still call a leprous man a man. This ultimately led the later Reformation dogmaticians to consider both the image and likeness, as well as human sinfulness, as accidental determinations of human nature.

Man can still perform good acts and keep the law, but these will be done with a depraved motivation (for instance, selfishness), rather than in the love that alone fulfills the law. In this situation, Luther denies philosophy the possibility of either understanding or defining the essential characteristics of man: it can only achieve an autonomous self-understanding, overvaluing the (for it, naturally immortal) soul and reason, or claiming full liberty. It is possible to comprehend the true nature of man, *homo theologicus,* a created and fallen being, only because, by the grace of God, we have the Scriptures. Through the gospel, the image is restored and man begins to be re-created, prepared for the truly spiritual life, in which man will exist in flesh and bones, not with an animal mode of life (eating, drinking, resting), but from God alone. Adam was also destined for this spiritual life and, if he had not sinned, he would, in due course, have been translated to it. Luther describes man of this present life as the matter out of which God will fashion the glorious form of eschatological man. However, while man is freed from bondage and restored to the original state of the image by Christ, the spiritual existence of eschatological man is not so intimately connected with the Incarnate Christ, as it was for instance, with Irenaeus, nor, consequently, does the work of Christ have the same eschatological orientation: ultimately, there predominates an understanding of the effect of the Incarnation—the return of man to his original relationship to God.

Calvin* vehemently opposed the idea that Adam was created as an image or type of the Incarnate Christ, as Osiander (1498–1552) claimed. The image and likeness are located in the integrity, righteousness, and sanctity of Adam's first estate. Calvin, however, maintains that the image was not totally effaced at the Fall, but "was so corrupted that anything that remains is a horrible deformity." The purpose of regeneration in Christ is to renew man in the image of God, but again, this identity does not lie in the Incarnate Christ. The later Calvinist tradition distinguished between a "narrower" and a "broader" sense of the image: in the narrower sense, it refers to man's original condition in paradise; in the broader sense, it refers to those characteristics of man that make him a human rather than a beast. The image, in the narrower sense, was lost at the Fall; while in the broader sense, it remains, though deformed.

6. 18th and 19th Centuries

A reorientation occurred in the 18th century, partly as a development from the humanism of the Renaissance and the Enlightenment, which recaptured the insight and perspective of Irenaeus. In the 15th century Giovanni Pico della Mirandola (1463–94) had suggested that Adam was created with an imprecise form, able to fix his own destiny through his free will; the fulfillment of this destiny lies in assimilation to God, which was only fully achieved by Christ. Herder (1744–1803) develops this idea, but, reacting against the Promethean pretension to human perfectibility through self-improvement, inscribes man's self-determination within divine providence*. While God gave instincts to animals, in man he carved his own image: religion and humanity. The outline of the statue is still obscure, lying deep within the block. Man cannot carve it out for himself; rather, God has given us tradition, learning, reason, and experience to this end. Thus, the image has a teleological function: it is something toward which we are working, rather than something that we once had and hope to regain. This perspective, moreover, applies to our status as human: "we are not yet men, but are daily becoming so."

Herder himself, however, does not relate the fulfillment of this vocation to the Incarnation of Christ. This was done, soon after, by Schleiermacher*, for whom Christ was "the completion of the creation of man."

This reorientation had significant implications for the whole of the Protestant theology of the 19th century. Combined with the developments in biblical criticism, especially of J. G. Eichhorn (1752–1827), which tended more and more to remove any descriptive value from the accounts of the Creation, and then the first repercussions of Darwinist theories upon theology, 19th-century Protestant theology therefore necessarily came to understand the image in terms of the destiny or vocation completed in Christ, rather than the perfection of the original state that was lost in the Fall and regained in Christ.

♦ É. Gilson (1932), *L'esprit de la philosophie médiévale,* Paris.
E. Dinkler (1934), *Die Anthropologie Augustins,* Stuttgart.
T. F. Torrance (1949), *Calvin's Doctrine of Man,* Grand Rapids (2nd Ed. 1967).
J. A. T. Robinson (1952), *The Body: A Study in Pauline Theology,* London.
H. Crouzel (1956), *Théologie de l'image de Dieu chez Origène,* Paris.
G. B. Ladner (1958), "The Philosophical Anthropology of St. Gregory of Nyssa," *DOP* 12, 61–94.
A. Burghart (1962), *Gottes Ebenbild und Gleichnis,* Freiburg.
L. Thunberg (1965), *Microcosm and Mediator: The Theological Anthropology of Maximus the Confessor,* Lund.
W. Joest (1967), *Ontologie der Person bei Luther,* Göttingen.
C. E. Trinkhaus (1970), *In Our Image and Likeness: Humanity and Divinity in Italian Humanist Thought,* London.
J. Pépin (1971), *Idées grecques sur l'homme et sur Dieu,* Paris.
H. W. Wolff (1973), *Anthropologie des Alten Testaments,* Munich.
J.-M. Garrigues (1976), *Maxime le Confesseur: La charité avenir divin de l'homme,* ThH 38.
H. Köster (1979), *HDG* II. 3. b.
A. Peters (1979), *Der Mensch, HST* 8.
U. Bianchi (Ed.) (1981), Archè *e* telos: *L'anthropologia di Origene e di Gregorio di Nissa, Analisi storico-religiosa,* Milan.
L. Scheffczyk (1981), *HDG* II . 3 . a . 1.
M. Schmaus, et al. (1982), *HDG* II . 3 . c.
Y. de Andia (1986), Homo vivens: *Incorruptibilité et divinisation de l'homme selon Irénée de Lyon,* Paris.
P. Brown (1989), *The Body and Society: Men, Women and Sexual Renunciation in Early Christianity,* London.
H. Wißmann, et al. (1992), "Mensch I-VII," *TRE* 22, 458–529.

JOHN BEHR

7. 20th Century

All the theological anthropologies of the 20th century seem to have one point in common: the recourse to the concept of "relation," understood in the narrow sense of an intersubjective or interpersonal relation, as a key category. The main themes are: the widespread influence of philosophies of the "person," of "dialogue" or of "existence"; the manifest reluctance to make any appeal to the idea of "nature"; the subordination of human being to human becoming, and the suspension of this becoming into an absolute future, which must be thought of in a christological manner; and, accordingly, the concern to give anthropology a strictly theological treatment.

It is probably in the work of Karl Barth* that these themes are most powerfully deployed, within a theology that perceives the covenant* precisely as the location of fully human existence. Understood in its theological sense, the humanity of man—and therefore the "likeness"—is not at all ontic, is neither a property nor a natural faculty, and therefore cannot be linked to a natural state of integrity that man has lost. In the covenant, a "pledge and promise" to which God has called man, man never "possesses" this likeness and therefore cannot be said to have lost it; and, as God's promise, it is not even subject to partial destruction. Barth does, however, retain a correspondence between our created nature and our divine destiny. Man's prototype is the relationship and differentiation between the *I* and the *Thou* in the Trinity: man was created as a *Thou* that can be addressed by God, and an *I* responsible to God. Based in the final instance on internal relations with the divine life and intended first and foremost as a conception of man as a being *before* God, this anthropology also names other relationships and gives them theological importance: the relationship between man and woman, social relations, and, above all, ecclesial relations, in which the being-before-God is accomplished in the form of a *communion* with Christ.

Emil Brunner (1889–1966) also related the idea of the image to relationships and to existence as a person, but he remained closer to the classic Protestant positions. Even though, like Barth, he abandoned the idea of original perfection, Brunner by contrast to Barth distinguished two primordial theological traits, liberty and the capacity to enter into a loving relationship with God. The second can be lost, but not the first, which is an essential trait of the personality.

Catholic and Orthodox theology frequently adopt similar language: the rooting of Christian experience* in communion is not a concern limited to just one Christian confession, having been present in the *Catholicisme* (1938) of H. de Lubac* and in the ecclesiologies* of the "mystical body" (cf. Mersch); outlined as a very prominent aspect in the few remaining texts by J. Monchanin; made into a program in the work of V. Lossky; and brought to its first synthesis by J. Zizioulas. The ontological language used to raise "being-with" *(Mitsein)* to the rank of a theological category is certainly a language in which Protestant theology has traditionally had very little confidence. However, the purpose for which this language is used is no longer to draw up a chart of human properties, in relation to believers in particular, but to give names to theological realities: being-in-the-church, communion, which finds its paradigm in the life of the Trinity—"We have to live in circumincession* with all our brothers" (Monchanin); the absolutely primordial character of personal existence, in the image of the Father, *fons et origo totius divinitatis* (fount and origin of complete divinity) (Zizioulas); the Christological theory of anhypostasy* as the keystone of a theological doctrine of the person (Lacoste); and so on. It should be remembered that within recent theology there remain a number of anthropological beliefs that lack any theological basis for their affirmation, such as the notion that anthropology is a constant of which Christology is the variable (H. Braun).

The theological status of the religious fact remains a source of discord between the different creeds. In a period in which there has been little concern with the "virtue of religion," but a spectacular development of "religious sciences," philosophy of religion*, and theology of religions*, there has been no lack of pronouncements on man perceived as *animal religiosus* (a religious animal), in a variety of styles. In the a priori theologies that began with J. Maréchal, and above all in the work of Karl Rahner*, the religious dimension of existence is interpreted in terms of transcendental aptitude. To be "spirit" in the "world" is to exist, in fact, as the addressee of a possible word spoken by the "free unknown," of whom one may have a premonition that he governs the "mystery*" of being*. Among a posteriori theologies, responses diverge, ranging from a massive challenge to the religious fact (as in Barth) to a conceptual strategy of Christological criticism and integration (as in Balthasar*), or to descriptive analyses of the human condition in which the religious appears as the human experience that is the richest in possibilities (Pannenberg; Martelet). Theories of the religious as "experience" have been constructed, in a variety of ways, whether in response to William James or Rudolph Otto, or in response to Schleiermacher*'s *Über die Religion: Reden an die Gebildeten unter ihren Verächtern* (1799; *On Religion: Speeches to Its Cultured Despisers*), perceived as a common ancestor; during the 20th century, there has been a tendency to combine such theories with a Christian hermeneutic* of the great religious traditions. While there may be an "aptitude for experience" (R. Schaeffler), and there may be some justification for a general theological evaluation of the behaviors that display this aptitude, it is nonetheless as "Jewish experience," "Hindu experience," and so on that religious experience is captured in any more precise description. Indeed, Vatican* II came to different conclusions about different religious commitments.

An epoch in theology that began with Weiss's reopening of the case of eschatology* could not fail to put forward, as well, an eschatological position on the question of man. Indeed, in many different ways 20th-century theology has emphasized the paradox of an object, man, who exists here and now, within the finite limits of the world, only in an inchoate and provisional mode. As Barth says, "Human existence is ontologically determined by the fact that among all human beings, one of them is the man Jesus*." Man is a creature for whom Christ, and his life in Christ, is part of his existence. While this idea accounts for the present experience of the believer, it suggests, nonetheless, that the meaning of what man is to be apprehended on the basis of his future. This future is certainly what theological experience anticipates. According to Luther, *fides facit personam* (faith makes the person), and the existence of the believer has eschatological meanings that have been considered soberly within the framework of a doctrine of justification* and of liberty liberated (e.g., Jüngel; *see also* Pesch), or in a more exuberant manner, based on a doctrine of divinization (e.g., Lossky). However, these meanings, to which theology alone has access, are only the penultimate word of anthropology. Here and now, the definitive has not been realized. It is not, therefore, in his own visage that man can scrutinize his humanity, but in the visage of Christ resurrected, "in" whom believers already live an authentically human existence, while hoping for an absolute future of which they do not yet possess more than a deposit.

Some theologians, such as Bultmann*, have believed that the historical and worldly present of experience is capable of integrally providing a basis for man's access to his "authentic" humanity. However, thinking of man on the basis of his accomplishment—and thinking of being on the basis of the *eschaton*—necessarily leads us to highlight the definitive realities, understood as parts of an economy of the provisional. The anthropology of relations uses the language of being but cannot conceal the fact that the most humanizing relationships—the *esse ad Deum,* the communion of persons—are works of liberty. Man is the being who can exist face to face with God (in G. Ebeling's "*coram* relationship"), but first and foremost he necessarily exists within the world in a mode of opening up to the world. While an anthropology rooted in Christology must certainly reject every type of thinking that permits death to have the last word, the resurrected Christ should not make us forget that the disciples were not greater than their master and had to live, at first, with the image of Christ crucified.

What we shall be "does not yet appear" (1 Jn 3:2), and the definitive is no more at the disposal of theology than it is at the disposal of the believer. As against a factuality, or facticity, that can be interpreted completely without naming God, the whole of theology must object that man surpasses all that he is "in fact" because he is the bearer of a vocation. Whatever concepts one may adopt in thinking about the "being of vocation," the definitive, the *eschaton,* the absolute future, and so on, and even though there is no shortage of biblical images for expressing what "resurrection" or the "reign of God" may mean, the *problem* of man leads back, in every sense, to the *mystery* of God—and the problematic, the "question," that man represents for himself (Augustine) thus itself becomes part of the mystery. Man is the image of God in several different ways, one of which encourages us not to want to say too much about it: in the image of an incomprehensible God, man is also a being that we know without understanding. Man is also *homo absconditus* (Moltmann).

• E. Brunner (1937), *Der Mensch im Widerspruch,* Berlin.
R. Guardini (1939), *Welt und Person,* Mainz-Paderborn (6th Ed. 1988).
A. Gehlen (1940), *Der Mensch,* Frankfurt.
R. Niebuhr (1941), *The Nature and Destiny of Man,* New York.
K. Barth (1948), *KD* III/2 (*Dogmatique,* Vols. 11 and 12, Geneva, 1961).
E. Mersch (1949), "Dans le Christ," *La théologie du corps mystique,* vol. 2, Paris-Brussels, 165–398.
K. Rahner (1957), *Geist in Welt,* 2nd Ed., Munich; (1963), *Hörer des Wortes, neu bearbeitet von J.B. Metz,* Munich (SW 4, Freiburg-Düsseldorf, 1994).
P. Tillich (1957), *Systematic Theology* 2, Chicago; (1963), *Systematic Theology* 3, Chicago, 11–282.
J. Macquarrie (1966), *Principles of Christian Theology,* London (2nd Ed. Rev. 1977, 226–33).
V. Lossky (1967), *A l'image et à la ressemblance de Dieu,* Paris, chaps. 5, 6, 10, and 12.
E. Barbotin (1970 *a*), *Humanité de l'homme,* Paris; (1970 *b*), *Humanité de Dieu,* Paris.
G. Martelet (1972), *Résurrection, eucharistie, genèse de l'homme,* Paris.
E. Coreth (1973), *Was ist der Mensch? Grundzüge einer philosophischen Anthropologie,* Innsbruck-Vienna-Munich (3rd Ed. 1980).
P.J. Jewitt (1975), *Man as Male and Female,* Grand Rapids.
H.U. von Balthasar (1978), *Theodramatik II/2: Die Personen in Christus,* Einsiedeln.
G. Ebeling (1979), *Dogmatik des christlichen Glaubens,* 3 vols., Tübingen; vol. 1, §14–16; vol. 2, passim; vol. 3, §31–33, 40–42.
J.B. Lotz (1979), *Person und Freiheit,* QD 83.
E. Jüngel (1980), "Der Gott entsprechende Mensch. Bemerkungen zur Ebenbildlichkeit des Menschen als Grundfigur theologischer Anthropologie," in *Entsprechungen,* BEvTh 88, 290–317.
J. Macquarrie (1982), *In Search of Humanity: A Theological and Philosophical Approach,* London.
G. Martelet (1982), "Christologie et anthropologie," in R. Latourelle and G. O'Collins (Ed.), *Problèmes et perspectives de théologie fondamentale,* Tournai-Montréal, 211–30.
W. Pannenberg (1983), *Anthropologie in theologischer Perspektive,* Göttingen.
O.H. Pesch (1983), *Frei sein aus Gnade: Theologische Anthropologie,* Freiburg-Basel-Vienna.
J.-Y. Lacoste (1984), "Nature et personne de l'homme: D'un paradoxe christologique," in *La politique de la mystique,* offered to Mgr. M. Charles, Paris-Limoges, 129–38.
J. Moltmann (1985), *Gott in der Schöpfung,* Munich.
J.D. Zizioulas (1985), *Being as Communion,* Crestwood, N.Y.
N. Lash (1988), *Easter in Ordinary: Reflections on Human Experience and the Knowledge of God,* London.
T. Koch, W. Hirsch (1992), "Mensch VIII-X," *TRE* 22, 530–77.
J.-Y. Lacoste (1994), *Expérience et Absolu: Questions disputés sur l'humanité de l'homme,* Paris.
Th. De Koninck (1995), *De la dignité humaine,* Paris.
O. González de Cardedal (1997), "El Hombre y Dios," *La entraña del cristianismo,* Salamanca, 103–342.

Jérôme de Gramont

See also **Adam; Creation; Death; Evolution; Monogenesis/Polygenesis; Resurrection of the Dead; Soul-Heart-Body**

Anthropomorphism

In its broadest sense, anthropomorphism consists of representing in human form beings other than, and considered superior to, humans. Angels* and Wisdom* might thus fall into this category. But usage tends to confine the term to the problem of the representation of the divine, both in polytheism and monotheism*, and it is in this latter case that it has real force and interest.

1. General Characteristics of Biblical Anthropomorphism

Biblical anthropomorphism has two aspects. God* has a corporeal form. For example, in the myth of Adam he hears and walks. He also experiments (Gn 2:19) and comes down to find out what is happening on earth (Gn 11:5, 18:21). He "smelled the pleasing odor" of burnt offerings (Gn 8:21; *see also* Nm 15:24) and writes with his finger (Ex 31:18). Above all, he is "a man of war" (Ex 15:3), a "dread warrior" (Jer 20:11).

The second aspect of biblical anthropomorphism consists in attributing human passions and feelings to God. God takes pleasure in offerings (Gn 4). He shows anger and is jealous (Dt 5:9). He changes his mind (Gn 6:6–7; 1 Sm 15:11). These characteristics should not be seen as expressions that lay no claim to being assertions about reality (as would be the case, for example, if it were a question of setting the scene for a parable; *see* 1 Kgs 22:18–23 and the first two chapters of Jb), nor as what are often called poetic images (such as those in Ps 104:32). In fact, even when they come from ancient literary strata, they correspond to a perception of divine essence that will not be denied—for example, "Let us make man in our image, after our likeness" (Gn 1:26). But anthropomorphism has limits. Treachery is never attributed to God, and any sexual representation is ruled out. It is noteworthy that the Old Testament is very parsimonious in its attribution of the character of Father* to God; whereas Adam begot Seth "in his own likeness" (Gn 5:3), Genesis 1:26 does not say that Adam was begotten by God (but cf. this passage with Lk 3:38).

2. Correctives to Anthropomorphism in a Construct of Transcendence

If we agree that there are two basic forms in which the imagination can structure a universe, one tending to abolish borders (the extreme case being a world in fusion), the other emphasizing their distinctness (the extreme being a dualism with no possible passage between the two aspects), then the biblical representation of God avoids the former and provides correctives to anthropomorphism within the latter. These correctives can be reduced to three types. 1) The distance between human beings and God is marked out by intermediaries, no doubt creating a link but delaying contact: for example the angels, especially the "Angel of the Lord" who appears at those decisive moments when divine action is revealed to humankind (Gn 22:15; Ex 3:2; Nm 20:16, 22:22–35; and Jgs 2:4). Celestial beings intervene in visions of the Temple* (*serafim* in Is 6:2, 6:6 and *kerubim* in Ez 10:2), evoking the forms that had already been present in the Temple of Solomon (1 Kgs 6–8), carved images of Mesopotamian origin that were partially theriomorphic. 2) Instead of an angel, or along with him, there sometimes appear mysterious "men"—for example, the men at Mamre in Genesis 18, Jacob's adversary in Genesis 32, and the even more mysterious adversary of Moses in Exodus 4:24. 3) Jacob's combat ends with the request, "Tell me, I pray, your name*" (Gn 32:29), to which no other answer but a blessing* is given. Later texts mark a greater distance, particularly in two narratives* of similar inspiration that take up once again the Sinai theophanies*. In Exodus 33:18–23 Moses sees God's back, and only as he passes by. Later, Elijah hears the voice of God that has become *qol demamah daqqah*—"a still small voice" (1 Kgs 19:12). God "is not a man that he should repent" (1 Sm 15:29), although he is said to have repented of having made Saul king (1 Sm 15:11). The Septuagint version of Isaiah 63:9 favors "face" and "Holy Spirit" over "messenger" and "angel."

3. Word, Covenant, Partisan God

a) The Name. Jewish tradition* was very sensitive with respect to the ineffable name: it was forbidden to speak it. For the Deuteronomist, the Temple is simply "a house for my name" (2 Sm 7:13).

b) The Word. The current importance of philosophies of language encourages us to regard the word ("God speaks") as being at the root of biblical anthropomorphism. This conception gives rise to two variants, one oriented toward heaven the other toward earth. On one hand the "Word" is presented as a distinct and eternal entity. On the other, the Word* of God comes out of the mouths of human beings, the prophets*, who say: "Thus says YHWH," along the lines of a word of covenant*, the promise* of a homeland made to Abraham and later renewed, a covenant within which God may be represented as a bridegroom (Hos 2:16, 3:1; Is 62:4–5; Jer 2:2, 31:21–22; and Ez 16:8–60).

c) Critical Point. Anthropomorphism is put to the test when the notion of the chosen people makes God a partisan in human struggles, something that culminates in the extermination of the first-born of Egypt. The narrative wavers, sometimes attributing the deed to God himself, sometimes to a "destroyer" (Ex 12:23) distinct from him, whereas Psalm 136:10 sees the event only as a sign of God's "steadfast love" *(chesed)* of his people*.

d) The Incarnation. With Jesus* Christ*, God takes on human form (Phil 2:7): the "true man, true God" is at the center of the confession of faith. But the corrective that untangles the obscurity and overcomes the impasse of a partisan God is the fact that Christ's human form is one of weakness and humiliation, even unto death*. This death is not only the ritual, familiar to ethnology, of the king of fools; it also establishes the solidarity of this king with all humanity. As the first-born, the image of the invisible God, Christ is the restoration of man in the image of his Creator (Col 1:15–20). "And whatever you did to one of the least of these my brethren, you did it to me" (Mt 25:40).

4. Ambivalence of Anthropomorphism

a) Representation or Relation? Augustine* played a decisive role in the way Western thought has posed the question of anthropomorphism. In fact he gave the name *anthropomorphites* to the disciples of Audius who "in carnal thought, represent God in the form of a corruptible man." Augustine thereby doubly cut through an ambivalence of anthropomorphism, as it had been developed at the crossroads of the biblical and Greek traditions. On the one hand, Augustine denies all that, in anthropomorphism, may reduce God to man or to draw man toward God in whose image he is made. On the other hand, to the negation of an anthropomorphism conceived in terms of being, he adds the negation of an anthropomorphism conceived in terms of representation—an anthropomorphism whose most famous formulation was given by Xenophanes: "If cattle, horses, and lions had hands like men, if they could paint like men and produce works of art, then horses would paint even the images of the gods as horses, cattle as cattle, and each would establish the corporeal form of its gods according to its own appearance."

The Renaissance of the 13th century followed Augustine's lead. Although analogy, a process used to answer the question, "What is God?," played a role in the discussion of "divine names," this relational dimension was set aside to enable these concepts to be used later, legitimately, provided that their lack of adequacy is taken into account.

b) Kant. Immanuel Kant* occupies a special place because of the particular way in which he approaches the ambivalence of anthropomorphism. Discussing "the determination of the limits of reason," he observes that Hume's skepticism toward all theology hardly affects deism* (dealing with the "supreme Being") but does affect theism (Deism*/Theism) (which postulates a personal God); and only theism is of interest to man as a morally responsible being, but it is inevitably tainted with anthropomorphism. There is no solution if we rely on a "dogmatic anthropomorphism," claiming to say something about what God is "in himself." But it is proper to use a "symbolic anthropomorphism" that "concerns only language and not the object itself." An analogy is at work in this instance. What is important here is the connection with the symbol, the problematics of which, in contemporary thought, originates with Kant. And what is most fruitful is the intuition of a link with language. In the case of anthropomorphism, this meant a return to the problematics of relation. It is in fact a question of freedom* as it is experienced in the awareness of the moral law*, which finds its true development only in interpersonal relations (Kant speaks of respect). This requires that we speak of God as we would of a person (hence, in contrast to deism). The symbol derives from an effort of the imagination, linked to the tangible world, which is not to be left behind because it provides the living experience of those words that remain necessary to express what God is for us. As É. Weil correctly observed, Kantian problematics are indeed those of theomorphic man.

c) Hegel and Kierkegaard. Fichte, Schelling*, and Schleiermacher follow in Kant's footsteps. Kierkegaard* argues for a "vigorous and powerful anthropomorphism." He is thereby opposed to Hegel*, whose interest in anthropomorphism is expressed in his emphasis on the way in which Christian forms depart from pagan forms through a critique of representation. The truth of this inevitable passage through man in order to express God is the identity of identity and difference, the heart of the Hegelian "concept," the highest point of which is the idea of the Incarnation. But we can see that the emphasis returns to representation, even though this is done to criticize its inadequacy, whereas it is a struggle to maintain the weightiness of the tangible world.

d) Contemporary Thought. E. Jüngel follows a Hegelian line when he justifies anthropomorphism both through man made in the image of God and through the Incarnation, a proximity of man and God that is, as it were, "the 'result' of an identity of God and man subsuming any difference." Paul Ricœur is among those who has grasped what is of interest in Kant's analysis of the symbol. He comes up with the programmatic formulation, "The symbol provokes thought." Its first form is a reading of myths (including the myth of Adam) "with sympathy and imagination." This procedure gives imagination its rightful place, but sets it in a relation of "sympathy." As Ricœur says in an essay on the imagination, "Our images are spoken before being seen."

e) Conclusion. Karl Barth* noted as a challenge to theology the obligation to speak in those circumstances in which speech knows that it is irremediably inadequate. This opens onto "negative* theology," which is one of the fruits of the confrontation of the biblical and Greek traditions, leading toward the "beyond of being" that Plato set at the pinnacle of his dialectic. Kant's "symbolic anthropomorphism" is in some sense a negative theology reduced to modest proportions. It authorizes a reading of the Bible that does not hesitate to spend time in work on images. Whereas the negative theology deriving from Dionysius approaches mysticism* and the "night of the senses," the patient path through the tangible world is the road to "spiritual meanings." This is the attitude of one who listens, whose eyes are open, who learns to feel and taste, touching with great respect the word of God.

• A. Sertillanges (1908), *Agnosticisme ou anthropomorphisme?* Paris.
A. Abd El-Fattah (1951), "Introduction à l'anthropomorphisme," diss., Paris.
E. Amado-Lévy-Valensi (1957), "L'homme a-t-il créé Dieu à son image?" *Eph* 1957, fasc. 3, 19–24.
F. Marty (1980), *La naissance de la métaphysique chez Kant: Une étude sur la notion kantienne d'analogie,* Paris.
F. Christ (1982), *Menschlich von Gott reden: Das Problem des Anthropomorphismus bei Schleiermacher,* Einsiedeln.
K. Heinrich (1986), *Anthropomorphe: Zum Problem des Anthropomorphismus in der Religionsphilosophie,* Basel-Frankfurt.
J. Derrida (1987), "Comment ne pas parler: Dénégations," in *Psyché: Inventions de l'autre,* Paris, 535–95.
E. Jüngel (1990), "Anthropomorphismus als Grundproblem neuzeitlicher Hermeneutik" (1982 text), in *Wertlose Wahrheit,* Munich, 110–31.
J. Briend (1992), *Dieu dans l'Écriture,* Paris.

FRANÇOIS MARTY

See also **Analogy; Angels; Bible; God; Idolatry; Immutability/Impassibility, Divine; Incarnation; Love; Myth; Name; Scripture, Senses of; Theophany; Word of God**

Antinomianism

Antinomianism is the term for Christian rejection of the law* in the name of the Gospels. Antinomianism was already present in the apostolic age (*see* Rom 3:8), and it has been associated with Gnostic sects (Nicolites, Ophites). The sharp distinction between law and gospel promulgated by the Reformation led to a revival of antinomianism, particularly in the "radical Reformation" (the polemic by J. Agricola [1492–1566] against Luther*, the Anabaptist* movement). The Lutheran theory of the "uses of the law" constitutes a moderate position, probably acceptable in Catholic terms.

• O. H. Pesch (1993), "A.," *LThK3,* 1, 762–66 (bibl.).

JEAN-YVES LACOSTE

See also **Law and Christianity; Luther, Martin**

Antinomy

The concept of antinomy comes from philosophy and designates, for example in Kant*, the presence of two contradictory assertions both of which have legitimacy and a solid basis, making it impossible to apply to them the principle of the excluded middle. Antinomy has become a central theological term in recent Orthodoxy*. Examples of antinomic assertions include the unity of the divine Trinity* or of human freedom* and divine predestination*. The concept of antinomy holds a key position, alongside that of mystery*, in the organization of Orthodox theology* as an apophatic theology. The word does not belong to the vocabulary of contemporary Catholic or Protestant theology. On the other hand, the doctrine is a part of the common Christian heritage. Moreover, contemporary logic has shown renewed interest for antinomy ("dialethic" or "paraconsistent" logic).

• P. Evdokimov (1965), *L'Orthodoxie,* Paris (2nd Ed. 1979), 48–56.

J. Meyendorff (1975), *Initiation à la théologie byzantine,* Paris, 297–300.

G. Priest (1987), *In Contradiction: A Study of the Transconsistent,* Dordrecht.

K. Wuchterl, et al., "Paradox," *TRE* 25, 726–37.

Jean-Yves Lacoste

See also **Negative Theology; Orthodoxy, Modern and Contemporary**

Antioch, School of

a) Exegesis and Theology. The expression *School of Antioch* is merely a convenient name for designating the representatives of a form of exegesis* that favors the letter and the historical reality of Scripture*, in reaction against the tendency of Origen* and the Alexandrians toward what was considered an excessive reliance on allegory. The term should not, therefore, be given too narrow a meaning, nor should we posit too radical an opposition between the exegetical practices of Antioch and Alexandria. In each camp, however, use was made of different terminology to indicate closely related realities. What was true in the realm of exegesis was also true of theology* and Christology*. But here too, from Diodorus of Tarsus to Theodore of Mopsuestia and John Chrysostom*, and from Nestorius to Theodoret of Cyrrhus, despite the affinities of certain patterns of thought, positions evolved and differentiated themselves. So it is not possible to speak of an "Antiochene Christology*" without making distinctions.

b) Early Antiochenes. Diodorus, whom Cyril* of Alexandria tried to depict, along with Theodore of Mopsuestia, as an ancestor of Nestorianism, seems to have been principally concerned with preserving in Christ* the divinity of the Logos, first against the attacks of the Emperor Julian and the Arians; and then against the danger represented for him by Apollinaris's concept of a "substantial union" between the Logos and an incomplete humanity. He therefore avoided attributing to the Logos the human weaknesses of Christ, even if it meant giving the impression of a loose union with the flesh the Logos had assumed. Contrary to received notions, his Christology relied initially on a *Logos-sarx* (word-flesh) schema derived from Eusebius of Emesa, and much closer to Alexandrian Christology than that of Antioch, since it was shared by Athanasius*. Subsequently, as a consequence of the Apollinarian controversy, Diodorus argued more and more along the lines of the "Logos-man" schema, although without making of the soul* of Christ a "theological factor": this was not the point on which his refutation of Apollinaris's positions was focused.

In his almost exclusive concern with shielding the divinity of Christ from the attacks of the Arians, John Chrysostom in fact subordinated all Christ's human and psychological activity to the control of the Logos, the only real principle of decision. So on this point he remained very close to his master Diodorus. In reality it was not until Theodore of Mopsuestia that the human soul of Christ really became a "theological factor." Because the Logos had assumed the form of a perfect man—that is, a body and a rational soul—that human soul, endowed with immutability* by divine grace*, not only "animated" the person of Christ but also held the power of decision and action in him, something which in Apollinaris's system was attributed to the Logos alone. With that assumption, how was it possible to prevent this union of God* and a perfect man from appearing to introduce into Christ a duality of persons* *(prosōpa),* or from allowing for the supposition of a loose and purely mental union? Theodore might very well propose the analogy of body and soul in order to explain that the distinction of natures in Christ did not entail recognition of two persons, but he failed to express in a satisfactory manner a unity which did not proceed, as in Apollinaris, from a close but natural union. The notion of "single *prosōpon,*" used to express the result of the union of two natures, is evidence, despite the ambiguity of the term in Antioch at the time, that he had an intuition of the true unity of Christ.

c) Nestorian Crisis and Theodoret of Cyrrhus. One positive aspect of the Nestorian crisis was that it forced the representatives of Antioch and Alexandria to refine their christological terminology and correct its inadequacies. Beginning with his refutation of the anathemas of Cyril against Nestorius, Theodoret (393–460) was led into a long and painful debate that, from the Council* of Ephesus to that of Chalcedon*, made him the major theologian of the School of Antioch. However, like Theodore of Mopsuestia, nicknamed "the interpreter," he was primarily an exegete, and it was in this capacity that he challenged Cyril's christological formulations—"union by hypostasis," or "single nature of God the incarnate Word*"—which he considered devoid of any basis in Scripture. In his Christology, close to that of Theodore, the human soul of Christ also played a genuine role, as shown, for example, in his exegesis of Christ's temptation in the desert in *Scholia de incarnatione unigeniti (Scholia on the Incarnation).* Because the "union by hypostasis" of which Cyril spoke meant for him a union by "nature" *(physis)* or "substance" *(ousia),* and seemed thereby to imply the idea of "mixture" *(krasis),* which called into question the divinity of the Logos, he was always careful in his commentaries to make a clear distinction between the divine nature and human nature. His reaction was therefore close to that of Theodore against the Christology of Apollinaris. It also explains his reticence toward the term *theotokos* (God-bearer) (although he recognized its legitimacy). Above all it led him to place so much emphasis on the duality in Christ that he might give the impression of distinguishing in him not two natures but two persons. This was all the more true because, until the Council of Ephesus, he frequently used concrete expressions to designate them.

After 431 (Ephesus), aware of the ambiguity of this terminology, Theodoret gave up speaking of the "Word assuming" or the "man assumed," in favor of purely abstract formulations with which he was equally familiar. Despite an evident desire to emphasize dyophysitism, he was careful to state that it was a matter of a close and indissoluble union *(henōsis),* and not a mere juxtaposition, even less an "inhabitation" in the sense understood by Nestorius. Accomplished from the moment of conception, this union of divine and human natures remained close, even at the time of the Passion*, when impassive divinity "appropriated" the sufferings of our humanity, fully assumed by that divinity in Christ. It is therefore impossible to call into question Theodoret's good faith when he asserted that he had never "divided Christ in two" or professed the existence of "two Sons." Clearly, for him the distinction between natures occurred within a "single *prosōpon,*" within a unified subject, although he used this concept, at least until the Council of Chalcedon, in a sense close to the one it had for Theodore of Mopsuestia.

While never failing to assert the nonfusion of the two natures, in the course of the debate with Cyril, Theodoret no doubt arrived at a better understanding of the need to proclaim the unity of the person. The abandonment of concrete designations, the care taken to make Christ the only active subject, and the choice of the term *henōsis* to express union, rather than the term *synapheia* (conjunction) preferred by Nestorius, all revealed an evolution of his terminology more than of his Christology. He could thus assert that he had never professed any doctrine but the one that distinguishes in Christ the humanity from the divinity, without separating them, and that recognizes only one imputed subject, "the only Son himself, clothed in our nature." Although the form of this expression, on the eve of Chalcedon, does not express a real doctrinal evolution, it at least makes it possible to recognize the deepening in his christological thinking since Ephesus. In this area, as in that of exegesis, this last major representative of the School of Antioch had thus managed to reach a proper balance, thereby contributing, as he already had at the time of the Act of Union (433), to the acceptance of the fact that, regardless of the different formulations bequeathed by tradition*, representatives of Alexandria and Antioch expressed the same faith*.

- M. Richard (1934), "Un écrit de Théodoret sur l'unité du Christ après l'incarnation," *RSR* 24, 34–61.
- J. Montalverne (1948), *Theodoreti Cyrensis doctrina antiquior de Verbo "inhumanato,"* Rome.
- J. Liebaert (1966), *L'incarnation* I: *Des origines au concile de Chalcédoine,* Paris.
- A. Grillmeier (1979), *Jesus der Christus im Glauben der Kirche* I, Freiburg-Basel-Vienna.
- J.-N. Guinot (1995), *L'exégèse de Théodoret de Cyr,* Paris.

Jean-Noël Guinot

See also **Alexandria, School of; Apollinarianism; Arianism; Immutability/Impassibility, Divine; Mary; Nestorianism**

Antitrinitarism. *See* **Unitarianism**

Apocalyptic Literature

The literature genre of apocalypse (from the Greek *apokalupsis,* "revelation") takes its name from the title of the last book* of the New Testament. The Book of Daniel is the only other apocalyptic book in the Bible*. The genre is widely represented, however, in both Jewish and Christian pseudepigrapha, from the Hellenistic period down to the Middle Ages. Some similar kinds of literature are found in Persia as well as in the Greek and Roman worlds, but it is not clear whether they significantly influenced Jewish and Christian apocalypses.

I. Definition

Apocalypse may be defined as a story type in which a supernatural being acts as the intermediary to communicate a revelation* to a human being. The object of such a revelation is a reality that transcends both time (as it discusses eschatological salvation) and space (the scene takes place in another world). Usually, apocalypses are pseudonymous: they are attributed to famous figures such as Enoch or Ezra, instead of their real authors. The supernatural mediator is usually an angel* in the Jewish apocalypses. In Christian works, this role is sometimes taken by Christ. The eschatological salvation can take various forms, and may involve the restoration of Israel* or a new creation*, but it invariably involves reward and punishment for individuals after death.

II. Typology

1. Historical Apocalypses

Two types of apocalypse may be distinguished. The first, exemplified by the Book of Daniel, may be called "historical." In this kind of apocalypse, the revelation is given in the form of a symbolic vision, such as Daniel's vision of four great beasts coming up out of the sea (Dn 7:3). This vision is then interpreted by an angel with reference to historical events. Sometimes, the revelation takes the form of a speech by the angel rather than a vision, or a dialogue between angel and visionary. In Daniel 9, the revelation arises from the explanation of a biblical prophecy (Dn 9:2; *see also* Jer 25:11–12 and 29:10). Often, history is divided into a set number of periods. Daniel speaks of 70 weeks of years. At the end, there is a great crisis, marked by war* and persecution. Then there is a divine intervention, followed by resurrection* and the judgment* of the dead. Besides Daniel, this kind of apocalypse is found in the Animal Apocalypse (1 En 85–90), the Apocalypse of Weeks (1 En 93, 91:12–17), 4 Ezra, 2 Baruch, and the Book of Revelation.

2. Ascent into Heaven

The second type of apocalypse is characterized by the motif of ascent to heaven. Enoch is the prototypical apocalyptic visionary of this kind. In these apocalypses, the revelation takes the form of a trip to heaven with the angel serving as a guide. The emphasis is on the geography of the heavens; the classical model typically includes the realm of the dead, the place of judgment, and a vision of the divine throne. There may be also the prediction of the world's destruction, and at times a trip across history as in the historical apocalypses. The eschatological expectation deals primarily with the afterlife of individuals. Apocalypses of this kind are found in the Book of the Watchers (1 En 1–36), the Similitudes of Enoch (1 En 37–72), 2 Enoch, 3 Baruch, the Apocalypse of Zephaniah, and the Apocalypse of Abraham. This kind of apocalypse enjoyed great popularity in early Christianity (Ascension of Isaiah, Apocalypse of Paul, Apocalypse of Mary, etc.).

III. Origins of Apocalypticism

1. Precedents

Apocalypticism is a literary genre that developed late (third century B.C.—intertestament*). The historical apocalypse has obvious roots in Old Testament prophecy, especially in the later prophetic books. Isaiah 24–27, a postexilic addition to the Book of Isaiah, is often called the "Apocalypse of Isaiah," although it lacks the usual "revelation." These chapters of Isaiah make heavy use of mythological imagery, much of it drawn from ancient traditions now known through Ugaritic texts from the second millennium B.C. The ancient myths often recount a battle between a god and a monster at the time of creation (Marduk and Tiamat in Babylonian myth, Baal and Mot [Death], or Yamm [Sea], in Ugaritic). The prophetic/apocalyptic texts project this battle into the future. Isaiah 25:7 says that God will swallow up death *(Mot)* forever, and Isaiah 27:1 says that God will punish Leviathan and slay the dragon that is in the sea. Daniel's vision of beasts rising from the sea continues this tradition. The battle with the dragon is a central motif in the Book of Revelation, which also conjures up beasts from the sea in chapter 13.

Isaiah 26:19 uses the imagery of resurrection for the restoration of the Jewish people* after the exile. Isaiah 65:17 speaks of a new heaven and a new earth, a theme that also appears in Revelation 21:1. The formal side of the apocalypse also had a precedent in postexilic prophecy. The Book of Zechariah presents its revelations in the form of symbolic visions interpreted by an angel.

2. Original Characteristics

a) Daniel. The Book of Daniel goes beyond the prophetic tradition in several respects. First, there is the use of pseudonymity. The passages we have cited from the Book of Isaiah are anonymous oracles that were added to the book of the eighth-century prophet. With Daniel, and with Enoch, we have a new phenomenon, where books are ascribed to legendary characters. Daniel probably never existed. The first six chapters of the Book of Daniel describe the careers of Daniel and his friends at the Babylonian court during the exile. Daniel is supposedly a wise man who distinguishes himself by his ability to interpret dreams and mysterious signs. Enoch is also characterized as a scribe and a wise man, rather than as a prophet. Yet the Books of Daniel and Enoch bear little resemblance to Proverbs or Sirach. The Old Testament wisdom books have an empirical approach to life and avoid claims to special revelation. Apocalyptic wisdom, in contrast, is by definition inaccessible to normal human reasoning and relies completely on a supernatural revelation with mystery as its object.

Daniel also differs from the prophetic tradition in paying much more attention to angels. The divine throne in Daniel 7 is surrounded by thousands upon thousands of celestial beings. An angel explains Daniel's visions. In the end, the salvation of Israel is achieved by the heavenly victory of the archangel Michael over the "prince of Greece" (Dn 10:20; *see also* Dn 11:2). The main difference between Daniel and the Hebrew prophets, however, may be the belief in the resurrection and judgment of the dead. This belief opened the way to a set of values quite different from those in the Hebrew Bible. In the earlier prophets and in Deuteronomy, salvation means that the days will be many in the land and prosperity of the people. From the apocalyptic perspective, salvation comes after death and so it is acceptable to lose life in this world to gain it in the next. In historical reality, the heroes of the Book of Daniel are the martyrs* who lay down their lives during the persecution of the Maccabean era.

b) Enoch. The ascent apocalypses associated with Enoch show less continuity with biblical prophecy than is the case of Daniel. The figure of Enoch seems to be modeled to a large extent after a Mesopotamian legend, Enmeduranki, who was taken up to heaven before the Flood. The Enochic Book of the Watchers is older than the Book of Daniel, probably dating from the third century B.C. Unlike Daniel, it is not associated with a particular crisis, such as the persecutions of the Maccabean era. It addresses the problem of the origin of evil* by expanding the story of the sons of God who come down from heaven and married the daughters of men (Gn 6:1–4). These "Watchers," as they are called, are destroyed by divine decree. Enoch is then taken up to heaven and guided through a trip to the end of the earth.

The Book of the Watchers resembles Daniel in its interest in the heavenly world. The description of the divine throne in 1 Enoch 14 is very similar to Daniel 7. Both apocalyptic visions differ from older prophetic throne visions (such as Is 6) in emphasizing the number of celestial beings around the throne. Enoch, like Daniel, suggests that salvation* is not to be found on earth, but in a blessed life beyond death. A later section of the Book of Enoch (1 En 91–105) describes the afterlife in terms of life companionship with the stars and the angels (1 En 104:2, 4, and 6). This imagery is close to Daniel, who sees the wise shine like stars after the resurrection (Dn 12:3). Some apocalypses in the name of Enoch were also composed at the time of the

Maccabean revolt (the Animal Apocalypse and the Apocalypse of Weeks). These apocalypses are of the historical type and closer to Daniel than to the Book of the Watchers.

IV. Qumran

Both Daniel and Enoch had a profound influence on the literature found in the Qumran writings. They represent the literature of a sectarian movement that should probably be identified with the Essenes, although the identification is disputed. They also include Enoch, Daniel, and other books that were not composed within the sect. There is no clear case of a sectarian apocalypse in the writings, but nonetheless they often exhibit an apocalyptic worldview. The specifically sectarian viewpoint is most clearly set out in the rule books, especially in the Community Rule (1 QS). According to the treatise on the Two Spirits in 1 QS 3–4, humanity is divided between Spirits of Light and Darkness, and these do battle within people's hearts. The ways of the Spirit of Light have their goal in eternal life*; those of the Spirit of Darkness in fiery destruction without end. God has set a limit to the time of this conflict, and in the end he will destroy the forces of Darkness. This dualistic view of the world is expressed in a number of sectarian writings. The Testament of Amran is one of the older sectarian writings, and appears to come from the second century B.C. According to this document, the Angel of Light is known by various names (Michael, Melchizedek) and so is the Angel of Darkness (Melchiresha, Belial). The most colorful dualistic document from the writings is the Rule of the War, which describes the final battle between the Sons of Light and the Sons of Darkness. The Sons of Light, the true Israelites, are helped by the celestial forces, and they do battle with the Kittim (probably the Romans, but possibly the Greeks) and with the forces of Belial. In the end, God exalts the princely power of Michael among the angels and the kingdom of Israel on Earth (1 QM 17). This is very similar to what is found in the apocalypses, and was probably influenced by Persian dualism.

The Qumran writings also show the influence of the more mystical side of apocalyptic tradition. The *Hodayot* (Thanksgiving Hymns) express the belief that the members of the community are already mingling with the angelic army in this life. The Songs of Sabbath Sacrifice describe the liturgy* of the angels. Because of this belief in present participation in the heavenly world, the writings pay little attention to resurrection.

V. Early Christianity

Apocalyptic traditions also had a profound influence on early Christianity. Ernst Käsemann's claim that "Apocalyptic literature is the mother of Christian theology" may be too simple, since Christian theology had many sources. Nonetheless, apocalyptic expectation played a crucial part in the formation of the church*. According to the synoptic Gospels, Jesus* affirmed Daniel's vision of the "Son of Man coming in clouds with great power and glory" (Mk 13:26). There is no consensus in modern scholarship as to whether Jesus actually made such predictions. There is no doubt, however, that the early Christians believed that Jesus himself would come again as the Son of Man on the clouds. The Resurrection* of Jesus was not perceived as an isolated miracle. Rather, in the words of Saint Paul, Christ is "the first fruits of those who have fallen asleep" (1 Cor 15:20), and his Resurrection marks the beginning of the general resurrection. Paul is confident that the process will be completed within a generation (1 Thes 4:14–16). This kind of scenario (archangel, trumpet call, dead in Christ rising into heaven, etc.) only made sense within the context of the apocalyptic traditions that had developed in Judaism in the preceding 200 years.

The Book of Revelation (Johannine* theology, Lamb of God/Paschal Lamb*), composed toward the end of the first century A.D., was not an aberration in early Christianity, but the culmination of trend that is well attested in Paul and the synoptic Gospels. It differs from Jewish apocalypses in not carrying a pseudonym, but is inspired by the imagery of Daniel. It was also inspired by the ancient myths of conflict. Satan is a dragon cast out of heaven. The Roman Empire is a beast rising out of the sea, or the great whore seated on the seven-headed beast. At the end, Christ appears as a heavenly warrior who strikes down the nations with the sword of his mouth. One of the principal purposes of this apocalypse was to support persecuted Christians and assure them of victory even though they were subjected to martyrdom, following the example of Christ, who conquered from the cross. The intensity of the apocalyptic expectations of certain currents within early Christianity can also be seen in 2 Peter 2:1–3 and 3.

VI. Later Developments

In Judaism*, apocalypticism seems to have faded in the second century A.D., probably because Jewish hopes of divine deliverance had been bitterly disappointed in the great revolts against Rome. We do, however, find occasional revivals of apocalyptic expectation down to the Middle Ages. The apocalypses had an important bearing on the history of Jewish mysticism.

In Christianity, too, the mystical side of the tradition continued to flourish. The influence of the ascent to heaven (and descent to hell) apocalypses can be seen in the great poems of Dante*. Over the centuries, apocalypses of the historical type were repeatedly revived by millenarian movements, notably Joachimism (millenarianism*). Today, millenarianism has fallen into disrepute mostly because of its connection to Christian fundamentalism*, which interprets biblical prophecies in an unduly literal manner, and which lacks a sense of the mystery of the ways of God.

VII. Permanent Value

Whatever meaning they had in their historical contexts, the apocalypses, with their imaginative force and their powerful symbolic content, have been a source of hope* for the victims of oppression and alienation. Both Daniel and the Revelation of Saint John, written during persecutions, deny their approval to those who seek to oppose persecution with violence*. Their visions have inspired a view of the world in which it is better to lay down one's life than to renounce the principles of one's faith. It is true that John's Apocalypse has often been criticized because of the role that it gives to the vengeance of God*. Its depiction of the destruction of Babylon (in fact, Rome) is not, perhaps, entirely charitable, but it should be placed in its original context. It provides a means of expression for irrepressible feelings of anger and resentment toward the oppressor, but it leaves vengeance in God's hands. The decision to include this book in the canon* of Scriptures has long been contested, but is justified by the symbolic force of its images. Apocalyptic literature still contains elements that can console the oppressed, provided that it is never forgotten that we see only an enigma, as in a mirror (1 Cor 13:12), and that it is not in our power to calculate the day or the hour when God will come (Mt 25:13).

• Coll. (1977), *Apocalypses et théologies de l'espérance,* LeDiv 95.

J. Lambrecht (Ed.) (1979), *L'Apocalypse johannique et l'apocalyptique dans le Nouveau Testament,* BEThL 80, Gembloux.

B. McGinn (1979), *Apocalyptic Spirituality,* New York.

C. Rowland (1982), *The Open Heaven: A Study of Apocalyptic in Judaism and Early Christianity,* New York.

J.H. Charlesworth (1983–85), *The Old Testament Pseudepigrapha,* New York.

D. Hellholm (Ed.) (1983), *Apocalypticism in the Mediterranean World and the Near East,* Tübingen.

A. Yarbro Collins (1984), *Crisis and Catharsis in the Book of Revelation,* Westminster.

J. J. Collins (1984), *The Apocalyptic Imagination,* New York.

C. Kappler (Ed.) (1987), *Apocalypses et voyages dans l'au-delà,* Paris.

P. Sacchi (1990), *L'Apocalittica giudaica e la sua Storia,* Brescia.

J.J. Collins, J.H. Charlesworth (1991), *Mysteries and Revelations,* Sheffield.

F. Garcia Martinez (1992), *Qumran and Apocalyptic,* Leyden; *Textos de Qumrán,* Madrid.

D.S. Russel (1992), *Divine Disclosure: An Introduction to Jewish Apocalyptic,* Minneapolis.

M. Himmelfarb (1993), *Ascent to Heaven in Jewish and Christian Apocalypses,* New York-Oxford.

John J. Collins

See also **Angels; Bible; Canon of Scriptures; Death; Eschatology; Intertestament; Judgment; Mystery; Prophet and Prophecy; Resurrection of the Dead; Revelation; Violence; Wisdom**

Apocatastasis

Apocatastasis, a Greek word meaning "establishment" or "restoration," is normally used in the language of Christian theology* to denote universal salvation*, principally because Origen* and other early Christian writers used the term to express a hope* for the restoration of all creatures endowed with reason* to their original state of unity with God*.

a) Scripture. Although the Hebrew Bible*, unlike other, earlier Semitic texts, does not conceive of human history* in terms of a cyclic conception of falls followed by restorations of cosmic well-being, a number of Old Testament passages express the hope that God will one day restore the security of Israel*, as he once brought the exiles back from captivity (Hos

11:11; Jer 16:15, 27:22; Dn 9:25; and Ps 126). The word *apocatastasis* is not used by the Septuagint, and appears in the New Testament only once, in Acts 3:21, where it seems to mean simply the "establishment" of the messianic kingdom* in fulfillment of God's promise* (*see also* Acts 1:6). It is undeniable that many texts of the New Testament evoke the perspective of judgment* and eternal punishment for sinners, a number of others at least suggest that God's "original" plan is to establish, through the risen Jesus*, a new life and a new cosmic unity that will include all people (e.g., Rom 11:32; Phil 2:9–11; Eph 1:3–10; Col 1:17–20; 1 Tm 2:3–6, 4:10; Ti 2:11; 2 Pt 3:9; and Jn 12:32).

b) Patristic Theories. Clement of Alexandria († before 215) was the first Christian theologian to suggest that the punishment of sinners, whether in this life or after death, is always therapeutic and therefore temporary. It is the only conceivable punishment. Once the soul* has been purified of its passionate attachments, it can accede to that eternal contemplation* of God that Clement calls its "restoration" or apocatastasis.

Origen came from the same cultural milieu as Clement and was surely influenced by his thought, but he developed an eschatology* that is at once more consciously biblical and more cautious in its speculation. Origen often mentions, but does not comment on, the biblical threats of the judgment and the eternal punishment of sinners, but he suggests that punishment must ultimately be psychological rather than material, and medicinal rather than vengeful. This leads him to develop, at least as a possibility, the doctrine of universal salvation usually associated with his name. Since, according to him, in God's desired history "the end is always in the beginning," and both God's mercy* and human liberty* are indestructible, it is logical to think that all creatures endowed with reason will ultimately come, by God's leading yet of their own choice, to lasting union with God. At times, Origen even seems to suggest that Satan and other evil spirits will be included in the final salvation, although in his "letter to friends in Alexandria" he denies having ever held this position (cf. Rufinus, *De adulteratione librorum Origenis* [397; On the Adoration of the Books of Origen]). In any case, Origen always expresses his theory of apocatastasis with great caution; as was said, he considered it "not as a certainty but as a great hope" (Crouzel 1978).

In the late fourth century, the same hope for universal salvation was expressed, even more cautiously, by Gregory* of Nazianzus. By contrast, Gregory of Nazianzus's friend and contemporary, Gregory* of Nyssa, taught it quite openly in a number of his writings, as grounded both in the ontological finitude of evil* and in the natural dynamism that impels all creatures endowed with reason toward God. Beginning with the resurrection* of the body, final salvation will not be "restoration" in the sense of the regaining of a precorporeal state of the soul, but the realization of God's eternal design for his angelic and human creatures, who will finally attain his image and likeness.

A revival of interest in the Origenist tradition—more precisely, in the extreme forms that it had taken in the writings of Evagrius Ponticus (late fourth century)—occurred among Palestinian monks in the sixth century, leading to conflicts and, ultimately, the condemnation of a number of Origenist doctrines during the reign of Justinian (527–65). Among the theses rejected by the Synod* of Constantinople in 543 (the condemnation of the synod was apparently confirmed, in an expanded form, by the assembly of bishops* before the start of the Second Council of Constantinople* in 553), was the following: "If anyone says or holds that the punishment of demons and of impious men is temporary, and that it will have an end at some time, or that there will be a complete restoration *apocatastasis* of demons and impious men, that is anathema." This condemnation, which does not have the clear status of a decision of an ecumenical council*, is generally taken to be a rejection of the idea that one can know certainly that no one will be eternally damned.

c) Modern Theology. The doctrine of apocatastasis has continued to fascinate Christian theologians, even though it has never been a dominant opinion among them. Schleiermacher* considered the idea of eternal damnation to be incompatible with faith* in a just and good God, and thought that "a milder view" of salvation for all also had a scriptural foundation, with "at least equal rights" to credibility. According to Barth*, since our resistance to God is always temporal and finite, "the Eternal One cannot, as such, cease to negate that persistence in disbelief," and that therefore "it is impossible to expect too much from God"; just as we cannot be certain that all will be elect of God, so we cannot exclude the possibility that God, in his freedom, will save all human beings. In recent Catholic theology, Balthasar* has been the most determined supporter of the thesis that, while one can never be absolutely certain of the final salvation of all, it belongs both to Christian hope* and to Christian love* to hold that it is possible, in the mystery* of God's saving grace*. Ultimately, the question is whether human freedom is capable of definitively frustrating God's purpose, or, put another way, whether the universal triumph of grace would mean the destruction of the created freedom that it justly seeks to transform and heal. It remains today a disputed question.

• Anti-Origenean canon of 543, *ACO* III, 213 *Sq;* of 553, *ACO* IV/1, 248 *Sq.*
H.U. von Balthasar, *Was Dürfen wir Hoffen?* Einsiedeln, 1986; *Kleiner Diskurs über die Hölle,* Ostfildern, 1987; "Apokatastasis," *TThZ* 97, 1988, 169–82.
K. Barth, *KD* II/2, Zurich-Zollikon, 1942, 286–563.
E. Brunner, *Die christliche Lehre von der Kirche, vom Glauben, und von der Vollendung (Dogmatik III),* Zurich, 1960, 464–74; *see Die christliche Lehre von Gott (Dogmatik I),* Zurich, 1946, 375–81.
Gregory of Nyssa, *De anima et resurrectione,* PG 46, 104 B11–105 A2, 152 A1–11, 157 B7–160 C12; *De mortuis, GNO* 9, Leyden, 1992, 28–68; *Oratio catechetica,* Ed. J. Srawley, Cambridge, 1903, 26, 100; 35, 138.
Origen, *De principiis* I, 6, 1–3, SC 252, 194–204; I, 8, 3, ibid., 226 *Sq;* III, 5, 6–6, 9, SC 268, 228–54.
F. Schleiermacher, *Der christliche Glaube II,* §163, Berlin, repr. 1960, 437 *Sq.*
Thomas Aquinas, *Summa Theologica Suppl.,* q. 93.
♦ J. Daniélou (1940), "L'apocatastase chez saint Grégoire de Nysse," *RSR* 30, 328–47.
A. Méhat (1956), "'Apocatastase': Origène, Clément d'Alexandrie, Ac 3, 21," *VigChr* 10, 196–214.
G. Müller (1958), "Origen und die Ap.," *ThZ* 14, 174–90; (1969), *Apokatastasis pantôn. A Bibliography,* Basel.
P. Siniscalco (1961), "Ap., apokathistèmi nella tradizione della grande chiesa fine ad Ireneo," StPatr 3, 380–96.
H. Crouzel (1978), "L'Hadès et la Géhenne selon Origène," *Gr* 59, 293–309.
C. Tsirpanlis (1979), "The Concept of Universal Salvation in Saint Gregory of Nyssa," in *Greek Patristic Theology: Basic Doctrine in Eastern Church Fathers* I, New York, 141–56.
L. Scheffczyk (1985), "Ap.: Faszination und Aporie," in *IKaZ* 14, 34–46.
H. Crouzel (1987), "L'apocatastase chez Origène," in L. Lies (Ed.), *Origeniana Quarta,* Innsbruck, 282–90.
J. Ambaum (1991), "An Empty Hell? The Restoration of All Things? Balthasar's Concept of Hope for Salvation (ap.)," *Com(US)* 18, 35–52.
B.E. Daley (1991), *The Hope of the Early Church: A Handbook of Patristic Eschatology,* Cambridge.
J.R. Sachs (1991), "Current Eschatology: Universal Salvation and the Problem of Hell," *TS* 52, 227–54; (1993), "Apocatastasis in Patristic Theology," *TS* 54, 617–40.

BRIAN E. DALEY

See also **Hell; Hope; Salvation; Universalism**

Apocrypha

a) Definition. The term *apocrypha* (secret, hidden), as applied to texts, has had varied meanings in the course of history and still seems resistant to any precise, stable, and widely accepted definition (Junod 1992).

In antiquity, the name *apocrypha* was given to certain books to which only the initiated were allowed access, or which were not supposed to be read in public. By the fourth century—that is, after the "canon*" of the Scripture had been definitively established—the term took on a negative connotation in the Christian church*, as well as a rather imprecise meaning. The term *apocrypha* was applied to noncanonical books said to have been written or used by heretics and supposed to have been written later than the canonical texts.

In the 16th century Catholics and Protestants raised questions about the status and the name to be used for a particular category of works that included Judith, Tobit, 1 and 2 Maccabees, The Wisdom of Solomon, Sirach, Baruch, A Letter of Jeremiah, and passages in Esther and Daniel. The connection of these texts to the Old Testament had been discussed over time, particularly by Jerome, because they were not part of the Hebrew Bible*. Protestants called these works the Apocrypha, whereas Catholics designated them as "deuterocanonical" (made canonical in a second stage), a designation that gradually became standard. Even with the deuterocanonical works removed, the diffuse mass of the Apocrypha remained difficult to identify. From the 18th century on, scholars undertook the task of assembling and classifying texts in collections of Apocrypha of the Old Testament and Apocrypha of the New Testament. The title given to these collections, however, did not secure unanimous assent. To designate noncanonical Jewish texts composed in the Hellenistic period, the currently preferred terms are *pseudepigrapha* of the Old Testament and *intertestamentary writings.* As for Christian works, they are categorized as "Apocryphal Christian literature." This article deals exclusively with the latter.

Apocryphal Christian literature is made up of:

- Texts of Jewish origin, but Christianized in the early centuries A.D., including the Ascension of Isaiah, Odes of Solomon, Sibylline Oracles, and Testaments of the Twelve Patriarchs.
- Christian texts composed in the first three centuries A.D.—that is, before the closing of the canon. They include various Gospels*, legendary acts of particular apostles or heroes, apocalypses, and conversations of the risen Christ with disciples.
- Christian texts composed after the establishment of the Christian canon, including narratives of the childhood of Jesus*, dormitions of Mary*, hagiographic lives of apostles and biblical figures, as well as chronicles, revelations, visions, and writings composed for liturgical purposes.

There has, in fact, been no interruption in the production of such texts between late antiquity and the present time.

The cultural connections of these texts, particularly the earliest ones, are various and include Jewish, Judeo-Christian, pagan-Christian and Gnostic communities, ecclesiastical circles in East and West, heterodox movements, and Manicheans. They all have in common two principal characteristics: 1) They are anonymous or pseudepigraphical (attributed to a saint or Church Father); and 2) they each have some connection to the books of either the New Testament or the Old Testament or both. This sometimes tenuous connection will be one of various kinds, the texts displaying one or the other of the following characteristics:

- They relate to events recounted or evoked in biblical books—for example, to the Transfiguration or the Passion*.
- They are situated before or after events recounted or evoked in those books—for example, the life of Mary before the Nativity or after the Passion and the narrative of Christ's descent* into hell.
- They are centered on characters who appear in those books—for example, the prophets* or the apostles.
- Their literary genre is similar to that of biblical writings—for example, letters and apocalypses.

b) History and Transmission of the Apocrypha. The ancient Apocrypha are badly preserved. To take the case of the gospels, it is known that, in addition to the four that were later included in the New Testament, a good dozen other gospels were circulating in Christian communities in the second century. But only fragments of these various narratives* survive: the Gospel of Thomas (in Coptic), Greek fragments of the Gospel of Peter, and a few gospel scraps that are rarely identifiable.

This partial transmission was an effect of the ecclesiastical condemnation that weighed on the ancient Apocrypha from the fourth century on. Certain marginal or heretical circles were suspected—not without reason, in the case of the Manicheans, the Priscillianists, and the Encratites of Asia Minor—of relying heavily on these texts, and so they were banned or destroyed. Nevertheless, the popularity they enjoyed among the people and the monks, combined with the fact that they had been translated very early from their original language (often Greek) into several other languages (Latin, Coptic, Syriac, Armenian, Arabic, Georgian, Irish, etc.), and thereby spread through various cultures, assured the survival of some of them. However, these texts rarely survived in their complete form and in their original language. Some of them managed to survive through the centuries only because they were rewritten, either to be purged of suspect elements or to be revised in line with current tastes.

The state of conservation of the texts, whether in the original language or in translation, in their ancient form or in one of their revised forms, represents a serious obstacle to the knowledge and use of ancient apocryphal literature.

c) Principal Types of Ancient Apocrypha. The division of ancient Christian apocryphal literature into four major genres (Gospels, acts, letters, and apocalypses) corresponding to the literary* genres of New Testament writings is seriously reductive and deceptive. On the one hand, the Apocrypha exhibit a much greater variety of genres and literary forms than is found in the New Testament; and on the other, division into four genres means that texts with little in common are grouped under a single heading. For example, the various apocryphal "Acts" of John, Andrew, Thomas, Peter*, and Paul do not belong to a defined literary genre identical to that of the Acts of the Apostles composed by Luke. Frequently, moreover, texts represent several genres. For example, the *Epistle of the Apostles* has the title of letter, whereas its form is related to the discourse of revelation and to conversation. The *Clavis apocryphorum Novi Testamenti* (Geerard 1992) provides a catalogue of the Christian Apocrypha of the first five centuries A.D.

Among the oldest Apocrypha, four genres seem to predominate:

- Gospels—either very similar to the synoptic Gospels, as in the case of the *Gospel of Peter,* or a collection of "sayings" *(logia)*, as in the case of the *Gospel of Thomas.*

- Conversations of the risen Christ with disciples (and sometimes Mary*), as in the *Epistle of the Apostles, Questions of Bartholomew,* and so forth.
- Apostolic novels—for example, the *Journeys of Peter* (a pseudo-Clementine novel) and the *Acts of John, Acts of Andrew, Acts of Peter, Acts of Paul, Acts of Thomas,* and *Acts of Philip.*
- Apocalypses (centered on the Last Judgment* and hell*), including the *Apocalypse of Peter* and the *Apocalypse of Paul.*

d) New Perspective of Contemporary Research. Contemporary historical research has endeavored to reappraise the discredit that still weighs on the Apocrypha and to appreciate each text on its own terms. In particular it has modified the idea that the oldest Christian Apocrypha, by definition, propagated legendary traditions that were aberrant or clearly of secondary value (Koester 1990). It attempts to treat them as historical documents that provide invaluable evidence about the various circles in which they were written and which accepted them, as well as about the way in which the early Christians prolonged and enriched their memory of the founding heroes and events (Picard 1990). Finally, it seeks to bring to light the direct or indirect influence (in particular through the liturgy* and through iconography) that these texts have exerted on theology* and piety over the centuries.

• J.H. Charlesworth, J.R. Mueller (1987), *The New Testament Apocrypha and Pseudepigrapha: A Guide to Publications, with Excursuses on Apocalypses,* Metuchen-London.
M. Geerard (1992), *Clavis Apocryphorum Novi Testamenti,* Tournai.

Editions
J.-C. Thilo (1832), *Codex apocryphus Novi Testamenti,* Leipzig.
C. von Tischendorf (1866), *Apocalypses apocryphæ,* Leipzig (Hildesheim, 1966); (1876), *Evangelia apocrypha,* Leipzig (Hildesheim, 1966).
R.A. Lipsius, M. Bonnet (1891–1903), *Acta apostolorum apocrypha,* Vols. 1–2, Leipzig (Darmstadt, 1959).
(1983–), CChr.SA, Turnhout (text and translation).

Translations
J.-P. Migne (1856–58), *Dictionnaire des Apocryphes ou collection de tous les livres ap. relatifs à l'Ancien et au Nouveau Testament,* Vols. I–II, Paris (Tournai, 1989).
M. Erbetta (1966–81), *Gli Apocrifi del Nuovo Testamento,* vol. I, 1–2, vols. II and III, Turin.
F. Quéré (1983), *Évangiles apocryphes,* Paris.
W. Schneemelcher (1987–89), *Neutestamentliche Apokryphen,* vols. I–II, Tübingen.
J.K. Elliott (1993), *The Apocryphal New Testament,* Oxford.
F. Bovon, P. Geoltrain (Ed.) (1997), *Écrits apocryphes chrétiens,* I, Paris.
♦ F. Bovon (Ed.) (1981), *Les Actes apocryphes des apôtres: Christianisme et monde païen,* Geneva.
É. Junod, J.-D. Kaestli (1982), *L'histoire des Actes apocryphes des apôtres du IIIe au IXe siècle,* Lausanne; (1983), *Gli Apocrifi cristiani e cristianizzati, Aug.* 33; (1986), *The Apocryphal Acts of Apostles, SemSup* 38.
A.Y. Collins (1988), "Early Christian Apocalyptic Literature," *ANRW* II, 25, 6, 4665–4711.
(1990–), *Apocrypha: Revue internationale des littératures ap.,* Paris-Turnhout.
H. Koester (1990), *Ancient Christian Gospels,* Philadelphia-London.
J.-C. Picard (1990), "L'apocryphe à l'étroit: Notes historiographiques sur les corpus d'apocryphes bibliques," *Apocrypha* 1, 69–117.
É. Junod (1992), "'Apocryphe du Nouveau Testament': Une appellation erronée et une collection artificielle," *Apocrypha* 3, 17–46.
J.H. Charlesworth (1997), "Pseudepigraphen des Alten Testaments," *TRE* 27, 639–45.
P. Pokornq, G. Stemberger (1997), "Pseudepigraphie," ibid., 645–59.

Éric Junod

See also **Apocalyptic Literature; Gnosis; Heresy; Intertestament; Judeo-Christianity**

Apollinarianism

This doctrine takes its name from Apollinarius of Laodicea (c. 315–92), author of several books, many of which are completely or partially lost, or exist under an assumed name. His writings are apologetic, dogmatic (including *Apodeixis,* or *Demonstration* of divine Incarnation* by man's resemblance), polemical, and exegetical (numerous passages in the *Chains:* Apollinarius had a particularly strong reputation as an exegete). Apollinarius was ordained bishop* of the Nicaean community of Laodicea in Syria around 360 and his doctrines on Christ* soon provoked condemnation: from Athanasius in 372, in his Letter to Epictetus; and then from Epiphany, in 374. Furthermore, an investigation was conducted at Antioch, after which a warning on Apollinarist doctrine was included in the *Panarion* in 377). Several councils* condemned these doctrines: the Council of Rome (377 and 382), the Council of Antioch (379), and the Council of Constantinople* I (381 and 382). Gregory* of Nazianzus, Gregory* of Nyssa, in 385 and 387, as well as Diodorus of Tarsus and Theodore of Mopsuestia wrote refutations.

Apollinarius wanted to safeguard the unity of Christ—God* incarnate, Word* made flesh*—against a viewpoint that saw in him the union of two Persons*. But true also to his Nicene instincts, he wanted to uphold the doctrine of Christ's divinity. Apollinarius therefore first challenged all views that saw Christ as a man favored by divine grace* *(anthrôpos entheos),* any theology of the man who had been "adopted" *(homo assumptus)* by God. But in order to assert the substantial unity of flesh and Word*, he excluded the *noûs,* the mind, the rational intellect from the being* of Christ, insofar as he is able to determine himself: it is the divine element, divinity, the Spirit* of God, that takes this particular place (Apollinarius's anthropology* usually has a tripartite character—mind, soul, flesh—but it is expressed at times as bipartite, and it is then said that Christ's divinity serves as his soul).

It was his notion of fallen man and of salvation* that led Apollinarius to this Christology*. In fallen man the *noûs* has become carnal, and therefore no longer rules the passions* that are housed in the soul. But it is through the passions that sin* finds an entry into the person, and with sin comes death*. Things are quite different with Christ: in his case, the *noûs* is not conquered by flesh, because he is not human but divine, heavenly. As a result, sin and death are destroyed. Christ thus appears as a perfect man, in whom the divine Spirit prevails perfectly over flesh, which has been made divine, and over the passions of the soul. Taking up this position also allows Apollinarius to affirm, against Arius, Christ's perfect immutability* during his life. There is, therefore, a substantial unity within him between Spirit and flesh, a unity that would be impossible between Spirit and a mind. In the latter case, there would only be a union of energy, as when the grace of God acts upon a human being. But in Christ there cannot be any action of grace since this would mean that he had need of salvation. And so we have the substantial unity of a perfectly unified being, which Apollinarius expressed in his famous formula: "One is the *nature (physis)* of the Word that has been incarnated." Here the word *nature** signifies concrete reality, hypostasis, person: because he is a strict Nicene, Apollinarius gives the same meaning to *physis, ousia,* and *hypostasis.* In Apollinarius's theology, pneumatology therefore has a crucial role. The major argument that opposed Apollinarianism is well expressed by Gregory of Nazianzus: "What has not been assumed by Christ, in the incarnation has not been healed" (Letter 101: 32). Christ must therefore be a whole person body and spirit, if he is to save the whole of humanity.

- E. Muehlenberg (Ed.) "Apollinarios von Laodicea zu Ps 1–150," in *Psalmenkommentare aus der Katenenüberlieferung 1,* PTS 15, 1975, 1–118.

É. Cattaneo (Ed.) *Trois homélies pseudo-chrysostomiennes comme œuvre d'Ap. de Laodicée,* ThH 58, 1980.

♦ G. Voisin (1901), *L'apollinarisme: Étude historique, littéraire et dogmatique sur le début des controverses christologiques au IVe siècle,* Louvain-Paris.

H. Lietzman (1904), *Apollinaris von L. und seine Schule,* Tübingen.

E. Muehlenberg (1969), *Apollinarios von L.,* Göttingen.

A. Grillmeier (1977), "Apollinarios," *TRE* 3, 370–71; (1979), *Jesus der Christus im Glauben der Kirche,* I, Freiburg-Basel-Vienna; F. R. Gahbauer (1984), *Das anthropologische Modell,* Würzburg, 127–224.

A. Grillmeier (1990), *Le Christ dans la tradition chrétienne,* CFi 72, 257–72.

Pierre Maraval

See also **Adoptionism; Antioch, School of; Arianism; Consubstantial; Nicaea I, Council of**

Apologetics. *See* **Fundamental Theology**

Apologists

a) Authors and Texts. Traditionally, *apologists* is the name given to Christian authors from the second century who sought to defend *(apologein)* their religion against pagan hostility, and less frequently, Jewish opposition.

Most of them were lay* people*, converted from Hellenism, educated in rhetoric and philosophy* in the main cultural centers of the empire. They addressed the pagan world in the second person, either directly to emperors, the Roman Senate, or individuals, or in the form of an open letter to the Greeks in general. The following are major examples of such apologetic writings: Aristides of Athens, *Apology* addressed to Hadrian (c. 145); Justin, *Apologies,* the first of which is notably addressed to Antonin (between 155 and 157) (*I Ap.* and *II Ap.*); Tatian, *Discourse to the Greeks* (between 152 and 177) (Tat.); Athenagoras of Athens, *Petition about the Christians* addressed to Marcus Aurelius and Commodus (177) (Ath.); Theophilus of Antioch, *Three Books To Autolycum* (after 180; perhaps in 181) (Theoph.); Letter/Epistle to Diognetus (between 12 and 200–210) (Dg.); Hermias, *Satire on Pagan Philosophers* (end of the second century?); Clement of Alexandria, *Exhortation to the Greeks* (195? 202?) (Clem.); Tertullian*, *Apologetic,* addressed to the magistrates of the Roman Empire (197) (Tert.) and *Ad Nationes* (197); Minucius Felix, *Octavius* (end of second century) (Minuc.). Several apologias addressed to emperors are entirely or partially lost. These include: *Quadratus* to Hadrian (c. 124–25); Apollinaris of Hierapolis, to Marcus Aurelius (c. 175–76); Melito of Sardis, to Marcus Aurelius (176 or 177); Militiade to the princes of this world (after 178). Other works contain apologetic elements, but do not belong to the second century context: *Prediction of Peter* (between 110–20?) and the pseudo-Justinian treaties; *Oratio ad Graecos* (end of the second century); *Cohortatio ad Graecos* (end of the second century or middle of the third century?) *(Coh.);* and *De Monarchia* (beginning of the third century?). The later apologists, while finding themselves in a rather different historical context from that of the second century, nevertheless developed themes that had often been proposed by the first apologists. Among the Greeks, we can name: Origen*, *Against Celsus* (246) and, after 313, Eusebius of Caesarea, Athanasius* of Alexandria, Theodoret of Cyr, and others; and among the Latins: Cyprian of Carthage, Arnobius of Sicca, Lactance, Firmicus Maternus, Prudentius, and Augustine* (Barnard 1978).

With the Jews, the apologists adopted a dialogue form, or else wrote their treatises in the third person: Justin, *Dialogue with Trypho* (after *I Ap.*) (*D.*); Tertullian, *Against the Jews* (c. 200).

The Discussion between Jason and Papiscus on the subject of Christ (c. 140) by Ariston of Pella has only partially survived.

b) Relationship to Judaism. By connecting Christianity to the Old Testament, the apologists hoped to demonstrate the great age of their religion to the pagans, thereby refuting accusations of its essential novelty (Tat. 31 and 35–411; Theoph. 3, 24–29; *Coh.* 9 and 12; Tert. 19, 1–8 and 47, 1). But they especially wanted to show that the fulfillment of the Old Testament prophecies* was the foundation of the truth* of Christianity and ignited faith* (Theoph, 1:14; *see* Justin, *I Ap.* 31–53; *D.* 8, 1 and 35, 2; Tat. 29; Tert. 20, 1–4). This argument also had significance for the Jews, since once the prophecies were realized, Jewish law* had to be considered as belonging to a preliminary time and henceforth no longer valid.

Underlying this vision and undoubtedly already in the New Testament, were collections of *Testimonia* relating to messianic prophecies, to the legal custom of Judaism*, to God's rejection of Israel* and to the calling of the pagans. Both Justin and Irenaeus made use of these. There were also Christian *Midrashim* that saw in the Old Testament a baptismal typology of paradise, of earth and water, of the Last Supper and the Passion*, and there are traces of these in the *Epistle of Barnaby* and in Justin (Prigent 1961). Theophilus tacitly acknowledges the same typology (Zeegers 1975 b).

From the Old Testament, the apologists adopted the notion of a single God* (Clem. 8, 77, 1–81, 4), of God as Creator (a nihilo: Theoph. 1,4; *Coh.* 22), and who provides for his creatures. God is transcendent, without a name* (*Coh.* 211; Minuc. 18,10). He is not diffused through matter (Tat. 4, 2), nor is he contained in a single place (Ath. 8, 4–7), for God is greater than all places (Justin, *D.* 127, 2–3; Theoph. 1, 3 and 2, 22; Minuc. 32, 1). They also retained from the Old Testament a sense of the prefigurations of the Christ: Wisdom* created by God before the world* so as to be associated with his creative work (Prv 8:22–31); and the Word* produced by God (Ps 44:2) in view of the creation* of the world (Ps 33:6) (Justin, *II Ap.* 6, 3 and *D.* 61, 1–5; Tat. 5, 1–2; Ath. 10, 1; Theoph. 2, 10 and 2, 22; Dg. 7, 2; Clem. 1, 5, 3 and passim; Minuc. 18, 7), charged with completing the divine missions on earth and with safeguarding the transcendence of God (Theoph. 2, 22). The events of the life of Christ also deserve faith because they were predicted (Justin).

Certain apologists drew inspiration from rabbinical exegeses* in order to interpret the *hexameron* (Grant 1947), notably to find a personal category (the Son or the Logos) (Zeegers 1975 b) in the *en arkhè* of Genesis 1:1.

c) Relationship to the Pagan World. First and foremost, the apologists sought to defend themselves against recurring accusations of immorality, atheism*, noncivic spirit, newness, of having blind faith in a crucified man, and an irrational hope* in the resurrection* of the body.

They also sought to justify their refusal to offer the emperor the worship that was due to God alone (Theoph. 1, 11; Tat. 4, 1; Tert. 27, 1 and 28, 3–34, 4). Some continued to pray for the prosperity of the empire and hoped for harmony between church* and state (Ath. 37, 2–3), by underlining the coincidence between the prosperity of the empire and the advent of Christianity (Melito in Eusebius, *HE* 2, 4, 26, 7–11).

Asserting all the while that Christianity was the only true philosophy, the apologists nonetheless recognized common points between the two thought systems. Most explained this harmony through the Greek "small thefts." Others explained it more positively, in terms of the action of the Word *(logos spermatikos),* which instilled in all human beings the seeds of truth (Justin, *I Ap.* 44, 10; *II Ap.* 8, 1. 3 and 13, 5; Clem. 6, 68, 2 and 7, 74, 7). They went as far as asserting that those who have lived in accordance with the Word belonged to Christ (Justin, *I Ap.* 46, 3–4; *see* Ath. 7, 2; Minuc. 20, 1).

Notable points in common are the dualism of body-soul*, the rejection of idolatry*, the sign of universal cataclysm through fire, the just retribution for good and evil. Similarly, God is presented with features borrowed from Middle Platonism and Stoicism (*see* Spanneut 1957). He has negative attributes*, but he is also *provident.* His works, together with the harmony of the cosmos, reveal him as the Creator and Father of all things (*see* Plato, *Timaeus* 28 C). The Stoic terminology of *logos endiathetos* and *logos prophorikos* allows the two states of the Word to be expressed: it is simultaneously immanent to God and engendered in view of the creation (Theoph. 2, 10, and 2, 22). It is often also in Stoic terms that the *pneuma* (Holy* Spirit) is described. This presentation certainly ran the risk of erasing the specific contribution of the New Testament.

d) Relationship to the New Testament and Christian Doctrines. Some apologists cite Christ specifically. Aristides, for example, gives a summary of his life (15, 1–3; *see* Tert. 21, 14–23; in an anti-Jewish argument), while Justin asserts that the Immaculate Conception, miracles*, death*, and the Resurrection are fulfillments of prophecy (*I Ap* 22, 2 and 23, 2.) The *Cohortatio ad Graecos* stresses that the coming of the Savior was predicted by the Sibylle (38). They do not insist on the folly of the cross or on its redemptive action. With the exception of Clement (9–12), they hardly refer to "a god who took flesh in accordance with the divine economy" (Ath. 21,4), "a god born in the form of man" (Tat. 21,1) and "the God who suffered" (Tat. 13,3). Most designate Christ using Old Testament titles, such as Word (Jn 1:1) and Wisdom (1 Cor 1:24) (Justin, *D.* 61, 1–3; 62, 4; 129, 3; Tat. 5, 1; Theoph. 2, 10; Dg., 7, 2); and when they describe the Word of the Son of God, it is in this same Old Testament context (Theoph. 2, 22; Ath. 10, 2–4 and 24, 2; Dg. 7, 4; Tert. 21, 11–14).

The Trinitarian formulations are sometimes specified (Aristides, 15, 1; Justin, *I Ap.* 6, 2; 13, 3; 61, 2 and 65, 3; Ath. 10, 5; 12, 3 and 24, 2). The term *trias* is found for the first time in Theophilus (2, 15), but it designates a less Trinitarian group than has been supposed (Zeegers 1975 a).

The apologists do not all offer the same anthropology*. Most adopt the dual body-soul scheme, whereas others employ the tripartite body-soul-spirit scheme (Justin, *D.* 6,2), asserting that the soul is not necessarily immortal (Tat. 13, 1–3). To refute the objection of God's responsibility for the death of human beings (Tat. 11, 2; Theoph. 2, 27), they emphasize that God created human beings in an intermediate state between mortal and immortal (Theoph. 2, 24 and 2, 27) and granted them free choice between good* and evil*, between life and death, and therefore gave them responsibility for their own destiny (Justin, *I Ap.* 28, 3 and 43, 3–8; *II Ap.* 7, 3–6; Tat. 7, 2–3 and 11, 2; Theoph. 2, 24 and 2, 27). So they stress the reality of free will, but also humanity's need of grace* (Justin, *I Ap.* 14, 2–3 and *D.* 116, 1; *see D.* 7, 2 and 58, 1; Dg., 8, 7–9, 6) and faith (Tat. 15, 4; Clem. 9, 87, 1). They assert that the salvation* of human beings is a gift from God (Theoph. 2, 26; Clem. 10, 94, 1) and that their vocation matches their dignity. Human beings, that is, are created by God's own hands (Theoph. 2, 18), in his image and likeness (Tat. 15, 1–2; Clem. 10, 98, 1). They are called to contemplation* (Justin, *I Ap.* 23, 3), to immortality in sharing divine life (Theoph. 2, 17; Clem. 1, 8, 4 and 10, 107, 1) and to divine filiation* (Clem. 10, 99, 3). The fundamental precepts* are those of the Decalogue*. Several apologists underline the stricter character of evangelical morality in conjugal matters (Mt 5:44–46; *see* Is 66:5; Aristide 15, 5–9; Justin, *I Ap.* 14, 3; 15, 9–13 and 16, 1–3; Ath. 11, 2–3 and 12, 3; Theoph. 3, 14; Dg. 10, 5–6; Tert. 39, 7–11; Clem. 10; 108, 5), the ideal of virginity (Justin, *I Ap.* 61, 1–13 and 66, 1; *D.* 13, 1–14, 2; 43, 2) and the precept of charity (Mt 5:44–46; *see also* Is 66:5; Aristide 15, 5–9; Justin, *I Ap.* 14, 3; 15, 9–13 and 16, 1–3; Ath. 11, 2–3 and 12, 3; Theoph. 3, 14; Dg. 10, 5–6; Tert. 39, 7–11; Clem. 10; 108, 5). With regard to these points, they readily highlight the contrast between pagan and Christian behavior (Tat. 32) and more generally the paradox of Christians' attitudes in the world (Dg. 5). The only sacraments* described are those of Christian initiation*: baptism* (Justin, *I Ap.* 61, 1–13 and 66, 1; *D.* 13, 1–14, 2; 43, 2) and the Eucharist* (Justin, *I Ap.* 65–67; *D.* 41, 1–3; 70, 4 and 117, 1–3).

In terms of eschatology*, the apologists do not base the resurrection of the body on the Resurrection of Christ, and rarely on the realization of Old Testament prophecies (*see* Ez 37:7–8; Justin, *I Ap.* 52, 5–6). Rather, they look to the omnipotence of God (Lk 18:27), who is capable of recreating what he created from nothing (Justin, *I Ap.* 19, 5–6; Tat. 6, 1–2; Tert. 48, 5–7; Minuc. 34, 9–10); to the soul's need to find an identical body (Tert. 48, 2–3); and to the analogies offered by nature* (Theoph. 1, 13 and 2, 14; Tert. 48, 8; Minuc. 34, 11) and in human procreation (Justin, *I Ap.* 19, 1–4). Here again the distinctive Christian dimension is sidestepped.

e) Conclusion. The apologist polemic against paganism*, both its writings and its rituals, was caustic. Stripped of any attempt to interpret, it was more likely to annoy than convince. The claim of apologists to be the only guardians of truth could not have been well received by the pagans, whom these same apologists regarded as thieves of truth, or by the Jews, who were said to have an outdated religion. If the apologists were at all successful in making the pagans reflect, it was perhaps because their writers were intellectuals, educated in the same school as the pagans themselves, and because their attempt to defend a banned religion naturally provoked an examination of it.

The apologists are important in that they attempted to present Christianity as a coherent doctrine, venerable because of its great age, and compatible with philosophy. They undoubtedly reduced the specific dimension of the gospel and did not answer the real pagan question: that of the scandal of the cross. But they did not intend to expound the whole of the gospel. They only wanted to show the pagans that revelation* contained acceptable philosophical foundations. From this point of view, the apologists were pioneers in transmitting the Christian message.

• M. Geerard, *Clauis patrum graecorum,* I, Turnhout, 1983.
Corpus apologetarum christianorum saeculi secundi, Ed. I. C. T. Otto, 9 vols., Jena, 1847–72; 3rd Ed. 1876–81 (repr. 1969).
PG 6.
Athenagoras, *Supplique au sujet des chrétiens,* Ed. and trans. B. Pouderon (SC 379), Paris, 1992.
Clement of Alexandria, *Protrepticus.*
Épître à Diognète, Ed. and trans. H.-I. Marrou (SC 33 *bis*), Paris, 1965.
Hermias, *Mockery of the Heathen Philosophers.*
Justin, *Apologies; Dialogue with Trypho.*
Minucius Felix, *Octavius,* Ed. and trans. J. Beaujeu (CUFr), Paris, 1964.
Pseudo-Justin, *Cohortatio ad Graecos, De Monarchia, Oratio ad Graecos,* Ed. M. Marcovich (PTS 52), Berlin, 1990.
Tatian, *Oratio ad Greacos.*
Tertullian, *Apologeticum.*
Theophilus of Antioch, *Three Books to Autolycus,* Ed. and Tr. R. M. Grant, Oxford, 1970.
♦ E. J. Goodspeed (1912), *Index apologeticus siue clauis Iustini martyris operum aliorumque apologetarum pristinorum* [Theophilus omitted], Leipzig (repr. 1969).
A. Puech (1912), *Les apologistes grecs du IIe siècle de notre ère,* Paris (old and at times partial; remains useful).
R. M. Grant (1947), "Theophilus of Antioch to Autolycus," *HThR* 40, 227–56; (1955), "The Chronology of the Greek Apologists," *VigChr* 9, 25–33.
M. Spanneut (1957), *Le stoïcisme des Pères de l'Église, de Clément de Rome à Clément d'Alexandrie,* PatSor 1, Paris.
P. Prigent (1961), *Les testimonia dans le christianisme primitif: L'Épître de Barnabé I-XVI et ses sources,* Paris.
N. Zeegers (1975 *a*), "Quelques aspects judaïsants du *Logos* chez Théophile d'Antioche," in *Acts from the 12th Classical Studies Conference EIRENE (Cluj-Napoca, 2–7 October 1972),* Amsterdam, 69–87; (1975 *b*), "Les citations du NT dans les *Livres à Autolycus* de Théophile d'Antioche," TU 115, Berlin, 371–81.
L. W. Barnard (1978), "Apologetik, I: Alte Kirche," *TRE* 3, 371–411.
R. M. Grant (1988), *Greek Apologists of the Second Century,* Philadelphia.
N. Zeegers (1990), "Théophile d'Antioche," *DSp* 15, 530–42.
C. Munier (1994), *L'Apologie de saint Justin philosophe et martyr,* Fribourg.
B. Pouderon, J. Doré (Ed.) (1998), *Les Apologistes chrétiens et la culture grecque,* Paris.

Nicole Zeegers-Vander Vorst

See also **Gnosis; Judeo-Christianity; Marcionism; Messianism/Messiah; Philosophy; Platonism, Christian; Stoicism, Christian; Trinity; Word**

Apophasia. *See* **Negative Theology**

Apostasy. *See* **Cyprian of Carthage; Heresy**

Apostle

1. History of the Concept

In secular Greek the word *apostolos* had a relatively broad range of meanings. Most often it designated the accomplishment of a mission (dispatch of a fleet, naval expedition) or the document authorizing the mission (passport, letter of escort, notice of delivery). It was only rarely applied to people (e.g., Herodotus I. 21, V. 38). In using *apostolos* from the outset as an established term designating a "plenipotentiary envoy," early Christian literature was in fact recycling an Old Jewish Testament. This usage was rooted in the concrete framework of ancient Eastern law*, according to which an envoy represented and stood in for his representative throughout the duration of a particular mission. This legal principle is attested on several occasions in the Old Testament (e.g., 1 Sm 25:40 and 2 Sm 10:1–3), though the term *apostolos* itself appears only in 1 Kings 14:6 (Septuagint). Its classic expression is found in *Mishna Berakhot* 5, 5: "A man's envoy is like that man himself." Judaism* did not, however, institutionalize the function until after the catastrophe of A.D. 70, when the new central authority* created a body of commissioners charged with inspecting the communities of the Diaspora and collecting taxes from them. The official name of these functionaries was provided by the Aramaic verbal substantive *shâlîach;* and as Jerome correctly conjectured (*ad* Ga 1, 1), it corresponds exactly in form and content to the Christian term *apostolos.* The Christian idea of apostle chronologically preceded this fixing of the Jewish concept of *shâlîach,* and thus cannot be the result of a direct borrowing from Judaism. The two terms must rather be seen as parallel formations, derived from the same legal notion. The first uses of the word *apostleship* (Greek *apostolè*), as a Christian technical term designating a charge attached to the person of the apostle as a permanent agent of a mission*, are found in Paul (Gal 2:8; 1 Cor 9:2; and Rom 1:5; *see also* Acts 1:25).

2. The Two Sources of Christian Apostleship

a) Scholars are now in agreement in attributing a postpaschal origin to Christian apostleship. The identification of the prepaschal circle of the "Twelve" with the apostles—an identification that is merely incidental in Mark 3:14 and 6:30 and Matthew 10:2, and developed systematically only in Luke 9:10, 22:14, and 24:10—is the result of retrospective harmonization. The Twelve did not have the function of legal representatives of Jesus*, but that of a kerygmatic sign for Israel*. Their institution by Jesus was a significant act which illustrated the essence and the purpose of his mission to the people* of God*. The number 12, symbolizing the totality and integrity of that people, referred to the fact that Jesus had been given the task of reuniting all of Israel and leading it to its eschatological fulfillment. The Twelve then appeared, so to speak, as the founding fathers and the points of crystallization around which the people of salvation* were to gather at the end of time (Mt 19:28). They did not, however, represent an assembly in which certain functions had been institutionalized.

The circle of disciples who followed Jesus, within a community of vocation and service set under the sign of the imminent advent of the kingdom* of God, was not at all limited to the Twelve. Even after Easter, the circle of Twelve maintained for a time its meaning as a sign addressed to Israel. Having designated a new member (Acts 1:15–26) to take the place left vacant by the betrayal of Judas—who was "one of the Twelve" (Mk 14:10 and 14:43)—they took a public position in Jerusalem* by presenting themselves as the kernel around which the people of God should gather at the end of time (Acts 2). But the role of the Twelve began to decline by the mid-30s. The "apostles" then became the decisive group in the primitive community of Jerusalem (Gal 1:17), which no doubt reflects a change in the ecclesiological and missionary paradigm. The expectation of the reunion of Israel in Jerusalem was replaced by the awareness of a *mission,* which was to be actively assumed: a mission to Israel, and beyond that to the pagans.

Apostleship was founded on the apparitions of the risen Christ* (1 Cor 9:1 and 15:5–11). But not all the witnesses of the Resurrection* were considered apostles. For the church* of Jerusalem, only appearances that had the character of call and mission could legitimate those who experienced them as plenipotentiary envoys of Jesus Christ. Because Paul manifestly satisfied this criterion, he was recognized as the last apostle to be called (1 Cor 15:9–11).

The circle of those apostles called by the risen Christ was thus limited in number (1 Cor 15:7). We cannot clearly identify all its members. Peter*, first witness of the Resurrection, was thereby the leading apostle. The Twelve, named as witnesses of the Resurrection, were also without doubt apostles. To them should probably be added James the brother of Jesus and Barnabas, as well as Andronicus and Junias (Rom 16:7).

b) In addition to this clearly defined type of apostleship, as it was represented in Jerusalem, we find traces of a more open apostleship of a pneumatic and charismatic character in Antioch and its Syrian hinterland. Here the decisive factor was not the mandate of the risen Christ but the teaching of the Holy* Spirit. According to an ancient tradition (repeated in Acts 13:1–3, 14:4, and 14:14), it was through a prophetic testimony inspired by the Holy Spirit that Paul and Barnabas were invested with the charge of missionary envoys of the community of Antioch and thereby considered to be apostles. As a young man Paul had understood himself to be an apostle in this broad sense, and it was only after having established closer contacts with Jerusalem that he came to redefine his apostleship according to the criteria applied in that community. The origin of this second type of apostleship remains obscure. However, it may be presumed that it was rooted in the circle of itinerant Galilean-Syrian missionaries that came out of the prepaschal Christian community, a circle to which is connected the Q source, or *Source of the Logia* (Bible*, Gospels) (Mt 10:5–16 and Lk 10:1–12). The *Didache* (11:3–6), for example, attests to the continued existence in Syria in the early second century of itinerant charismatic preachers who were considered apostles. It is among these that we must look for the adversaries designated by Paul as "superlative apostles" (2 Cor 11:5 and 12:11) or "false apostles" (2 Cor 11:13). According to Paul, these individuals sought to legitimate their spiritual mandate by inspired speech (2 Cor 10:10 and 11:6), forcing Paul to compare himself with regard to visions (2 Cor 12:1) and the "signs of a true apostle" (2 Cor 12:12). The false apostles of Ephesus mentioned (in post-Pauline times) in Revelation 2:2 can also be included here.

3. Paul and the Pauline Tradition

a) Paul deserves particular recognition: in his vast theological reflection, he deepened the understanding of apostleship and developed it in different directions. Taking up the concept of apostleship based on the experience of the risen Christ, he interpreted his *vocation* as the act by which God "was pleased to reveal his Son" to him (Gal 1:16). He describes this revelation by making an obvious analogy with the calling of the Old Testament prophets* (Is 49:1 and Jer 1:16), and attributes a salvatory place in history to apostleship as a bearer and messenger of the eschatological, self-manifestation of God, where the prophets' message is absorbed (Rom 1:2).

Elsewhere he emphasizes *the essential relation between apostleship and the gospel.* The apostle is "set apart for the gospel of God" (Rom 1:1). As final messenger of God, charged with proclaiming to the world the saving message of God's imminent reign (Rom 10:14–17), Paul is an instrument for the fulfillment of the gospel. When, as an envoy of Christ, he implores, "be reconciled to God" (2 Cor 5:20), it is God himself who implores through Paul. He is not only the bearer and the messenger, but also the representative and personification of the gospel. His entire person and his way of life show the imprint of the gospel, of which Christ crucified forms the heart and the content. His sufferings (2 Cor 4:7–18), his weakness (2 Cor 12:9–10), and his life in the service of others (2 Cor 4:5) all reflect the structure of the gospel, founded on the journey of Christ. It is through its conformity with the gospel that the behavior of the apostle constitutes an ethical (ethics*) model (1 Cor 4:16 and 11:1; Gal 4:12).

Paul strongly emphasizes the *ecclesiological dimension* of apostleship. It is the apostle's task to bring together the community of salvation made up of Jews and pagans, to make of it the location for the presence of the gospel in history*. He has been called and sent "to bring about the obedience of faith for the sake of his name among all the nations" (Rom 1:5). This founding function distinguishes the ministry* of the apostle from the other ministries of the community: these latter, by contrast, are charisms through which the Holy Spirit acts within the Church. In the perspective of the history of salvation, the apostle's ministry is placed before all other ministries (1 Cor 12:28). He is the one who lays the foundations for the sacred edifice of the Church, a foundation on which others will build (1 Cor 3:9–17). He is the father who, in bringing the gospel, has engendered the Church (1 Cor 4:15 and Gal 4:12–20). In conformity with this founding function, the apostolic duty is not attached to a particular community but is connected to the *universal Church.* In relation to particular communities, their duties, and their services, the apostle is the one who sets down the basic foundations and establishes norms. And so it was that Paul, during the founding period of the Christian communities with which he was associated, exercised in exemplary fashion all the ministries that would later be attributed to different authorities. He was the master who transmitted the traditions and taught the basic doctrines (1 Cor 15:3–11, passim). He was the prophet who, according to the portion of the Holy Spirit that had been granted to him, interpreted Scripture and revealed what Christ, now ascended into heaven, wanted for the present (1 Cor 7:40 and 13:2). Finally, he was the leader of the community, charged with settling questions of organization (1 Cor 11:23). Through his Epistles, Paul continued to exercise all these functions after the establishment of the community, insofar as was necessary.

b) Paul's reflections are developed in the Deutero-Pauline writings (Colossians, Ephesians, pastoral Epistles), with the accent principally on the ecclesiological meaning of apostleship. Apostles are now considered founders and guarantors of the tradition on which the Church is based. According to Ephesians 2:20 (and in contrast to 1 Cor 3:10) they are, with the prophets, the solid basis on which the sanctified house of the Church stands. In the same spirit, the pastoral Epistles see Paul as the bearer and guarantor of the doctrinal treasure that the Church of future generations will have to preserve (1 Tm 6:20 and 2 Tm 1:14). In addition, Paul appears here as the normative authority in pastoral matters. Community leaders are required to follow the apostle in teaching and spiritual direction (1 Tm 4:11, 5:7, and 6:2), in the maintenance of community order (1 Tm 5:14), as well as in the witness given by their lives (2 Tm 2:8–13). They must consider themselves in all this as his successors and his replacements (1 Tm 3:15 and 4:13).

4. Other New Testament Writings

a) Luke also proposes a strong concept of apostleship in his work in two parts, Luke and Acts. In his view, apostles are above all the initiators and guarantors of the tradition* to which the Church must conform (Acts 2:42). In his concern with reporting the words and acts of Jesus by setting them out in a verifiable way, he limits the circle of apostles to those who accompanied Jesus from the beginning of his ministry and who witnessed both his life and his Resurrection (Acts 1:21–22). He thus repeats the notion, which Christians probably borrowed from Judaism (Rev 21:14), of the twelve apostles. In this perspective, which was integrated into the common understanding of the Church, Paul was to be sure a privileged witness of the gospel (Acts 26:16), but not an apostle.

b) John 13:16, 17:3, 7:18, and 7:25 and Hebrews 3:1 present an independent tradition that refers to the Jewish legal conception of the apostle as a plenipotentiary envoy (*see* 1 above). Jesus himself appears here as the envoy of God, charged with representing him in the eyes of the world. These two writings recognize no other disciple than Jesus.

5. Later Tendencies

From the second century on, apostles have generally been identified with the founding personalities of the earliest times of the church, those who established the norms of the tradition in matters of government* and doctrine.

a) The *First Epistle of Clement* (42; 44:2–4) thus relates ecclesiastical duties to a divine order, which extends from God to Christ and to the apostles, then to the bishops* and deacons* instituted by the apostles. We can see taking shape here the idea of an apostolic* succession. This would become the keystone of a hierarchy, and therefore the principal legitimizing source of authorities. On the other hand, Ignatius of Antioch believed that the presbyters* of communities, gathered around the bishop, reproduced the heavenly model of the "senate" of apostles assembled around God himself (*Letter to the Trallians* 3:1).

b) The adjective *apostolikos* (apostolic) appears for the first time in Ignatius's *Letter to the Trallians;* which first refers to the model of the apostles, and then more generally to the norms established in their doctrine as in *The Martyrdom of Polycarp* 16:2. From then on, any doctrine was considered apostolic if it could be traced back to the origins of the Church, on the grounds of its being recorded in the New Testament witness of the apostles. The concept of apostolicity, which appears only in modern dogmatic terminology, also served to express this relationship to an original norm.

• G. Klein (1961), *Die zwölf Apostel: Ursprung und Gehalt einer Idee,* FRLANT 77.
J. Roloff (1965), *Apostolat—Verkündigung—Kirche: Ursprung, Inhalt und Funktion des kirchlichen Apostelamtes nach Paulus, Lukas und den Pastoralbriefen,* Gütersloh.
K. Kertelge (1970), "Das Apostelamt des Paulus, sein Ursprung und seine Bedeutung," *BZ* 14, 161–81.
J. Delorme (Ed.) (1974), *Le ministère et les ministères selon le Nouveau Testament,* Paris.
F. Hahn (1974), "Der Apostolat im Urchristentum: Seine Eigenart und seine Voraussetzungen," *KuD* 20, 1974, 54–77.
J. H. Schütz (1975), *Paul and the Anatomy of Apostolic Authority,* MSSNTS 26.
F. Agnew (1976), "On the Origin of the Term 'Apostolos,'" *CBQ* 38, 49–53.
J. Roloff, G. G. Blum, F. Mildenberger (1978), "Apostel/Apostolat/Apostolizität," *TRE* 3, 430–83.
E. Fuchs (1980), "La faiblesse, gloire de l'apostolat selon Paul," *ETR* 55, 231–53.
K. Kertelge (Ed.) (1981), *Paulus in den neutestamentlichen Spätschriften,* QD 89.

Jürgen Roloff

See also **Apostolic Succession; Church; Gospels; Israel; Jesus, Historical; Mission/Evangelization; People of God**

Apostles, Symbols of. *See* **Creeds**

Apostolic Fathers

Introduced by scholars at the end of the 17th century, the expression *Apostolic Fathers* suggests that this generation of writers was in direct contact with the apostles*. This title initially designated the following set of writings: the *Letter of Barnabas,* the two letters of Clement of Rome, the letters of Ignatius of Antioch and Polycarp of Smyrna, and *The Shepherd* of Hermas. Later were added the passages of Papias of Hierapolis, the Letter to Diognetus, and the *Didache.* These writings have different origins, come from different eras, and vary in composition and style. For the most part, they are dated before A.D. 150 and tend to share a pastoral emphasis.

a) First Group. The *Letter of Barnabas* is a pseudepigraphon, probably written in Alexandria between A.D. 70 and 100. It contains severe criticism of Judaism, particularly of its ritual and ceremonial requirements: the sacrifices* (§2), fasting (§3), circumcision (§9), the Sabbath* (§15), the temple* (§16). The Letter criticizes Jews for applying the Scriptures* literally instead of interpreting them allegorically. The work ends with an essay on the doctrine of two paths (§18–20). Clement of Rome's *Letter to the Corinthians* was written around A.D. 96 by Peter*'s third successor, and in the name of the Christian community in Rome*. Meticulous in style, the letter describes the virtues* necessary for community life (repentance, faith*, humility, harmony: §4–36). It reminds the reader that the apostles themselves established their successors as *episcopi* and presbyters* (§44), and ends with a long prayer* that is filled with lightly Christianized references to the Old Testament (§59–61). Clement does not scruple about combining pagan themes, like the harmony of the cosmos* (§20), with several biblical citations. The so-called *Second Letter of Clement* is, in fact, an anonymous second-century homily on Christ as judge and Redeemer.

Around 110 Ignatius, bishop* of Antioch, wrote several letters in the course of his journey to Rome*, where he was martyred. Three of these were pre-served in a Syriac summary. In addition to the seven letters generally considered authentic, there were six other Apocrypha* from the fourth century. In an impassioned and sometimes uneven style, they assert the principle of the monarchical episcopate (*Magnesians* 6:1), of the necessary unity* of the community around its bishop (*Philadelphians* 4). The Eucharist, over which only the bishop can preside, is truly the body of Christ (*Smyriniotes* 1:1). They present martyrdom* as the supreme form of imitation* of Christ (*Romans* 5–6).

Ignatius's friend, Polycarp, bishop of Smyrna, wrote a *Letter to the Philippians*. The story of his *Martyrdom,* which served as a model for this literary genre, explains the veneration offered to victims of persecution and bears the traces of ancient Christian prayers (§14). Hermas, perhaps the brother of Pope* Pius I, probably wrote *The Shepherd* around 150, the first text to explicitly refer to the possibility of a (single) penitence—after baptism. The visions, which have an apocalyptic* quality, present the Church* either as an old woman (*Vision* II), or a large tower (*Vision* III and *Similitude* IX). There are also long moral lessons (*Precepts* I–XII). Sometimes Christ is called the Venerable Angel* (*Vision* V), other times, the Master of the Tower (*Similitude* IX). This work is often considered an example of Judeo-Christian theology*.

b) Added Works. Papias, bishop of Hierapolis, gathered all the information on the apostles that their disciples could convey. His work, which seems to have been rather anecdotal, is lost. Only a few passages survive. In them, Papias defends the millenarian thesis and reports that Saint Matthew first gathered the words of Christ in Hebrew.

The Letter to Diognetus is an apologia for Christianity, addressed to a cultured pagan. Both its author and intended recipient are unknown, as are the date and place of composition. Elegant in style, and attaining a remarkably high spiritual level, this work criticizes above all the idolatry* of the pagans and the formal ritualism of the Jews (§2–4). It then refers to the supernatural* life of Christians (§5–6). The work is sometimes placed among those of the Christian apologists of the second century.

The *Didache,* or *Teaching of the Twelve Apostles,* is a collection of moral doctrines and church rules and is probably from Syria. The date of composition is unknown. After having developed the doctrine of the two ways (§1–6), the text explains the liturgical procedure of baptism* (§7) and of the Eucharist* (§9–10). It also tackles disciplinary problems associated with the place of prophets* and apostles (§11 and 13). In all these areas, the *Didache* seems to represent a particular or archaic stage in the organization of the cult and communities.

• K. Bihlmeyer, W. Schneemelcher (1970), *Die Apostolischen Väter,* 3rd Ed., Tübingen.
SC 10, 33, 53, 167, 172, 248 *bis.*
♦ R. Brändle (1975), *Die Ethik der Schrift an Diognet,* Zurich.
B. Dehandschutter (1979), *Martyrium Polycarpi,* Louvain.
J. Kürzinger (1983), *Papias von Hierapolis und die Evangelien des Neuen Testaments,* Regensburg.
W.R. Schoedel (1985), *Ignatius of Antioch,* Philadelphia.
K. Niederwimmer (1989), *Der Didache,* Göttingen.
N. Brox (1992), *Der Hirt der Hermas,* Göttingen.
P. Henne (1992), *La christologie chez Clément d'Alexandrie et dans le* Pasteur *d'Hermas,* Par. 33, Fribourg.
J.-C. Paget (1994), *The Epistle of Barnabas,* Tübingen.

PHILIPPE HENNE

See also **Apocalyptic Literature; Judeo-Christianity; Millenarianism**

Apostolic Succession

a) Definition. *Apostolic succession* refers to the continuity of the church* in its character as apostolic, the permanence of the ministry from generation to generation, and the teachings of the Apostles. Apostolic succession applies above all to the church as whole, since it is the church that is apostolic.

The phrase *apostolic succession* is often used more narrowly to refer to a succession of bishops* (episcopal succession) or of priests or presbyters (presbyteral succession) reaching straight back to the apostles. Such a succession can be "local" *(successio localis),* and consist of all the persons holding the same office (e.g., the line of bishops of Rome* or Alexandria, reaching back to the first bishop, ordained by an apostle) or "personal" *(successio personalis);* in this case it refers to a sequence of persons, each having ordained the next, reaching back to the first ordained by an apostle. While apostolic succession is often reduced to a "personal succession" of bishops, recent ecumenical discussions have emphasized the importance of a more comprehensive understanding of apostolic succession.

b) Biblical Background. Elements of the concept of apostolic succession can be found in the New Testament, although it is not explicitly developed. Paul already speaks of a tradition* that he has received and must transmit intact, for example, in relation to the Resurrection* (1 Cor 15:3) or the Eucharist* (1 Cor 11:23). In later texts, greater emphasis is placed on "the faith that was once for all delivered to the saints" (Jude 3). The recipients of the pastoral epistles are particularly admonished to hand on the tradition faithfully (1 Tm 6:20; 2 Tm 1:14 and 2:2; Ti 1:9). Second, Jesus* is depicted, both before the Resurrection (Lk 10:1) and after it (Mt 28:18–20), as sending out the apostles on a mission* in which they will exercise an authority derived from his (Lk 10:16; Jn 20:21–23). The post-Resurrection sending is to continue through history (Mt 28:19). Lastly, while the meaning of the word *apostle* varies in the New Testament, the apostles are referred to many times as the foundation of the Church (Eph 2:20; Rev 21:15). In Titus 1:5 the idea appears of a transfer of authority from Paul to the next generation.

c) Patristic Era. In the second century, the concept of apostolic succession was used to fight against Gnostic heresies. Already, Ignatius had stressed the key role of the bishop in the local church (Letter to the Magnesians 6) without, however, any notion of succession, and Clement of Rome had introduced the idea of a succession from Christ* to the apostles, then to the successors of the apostles and so on (1 Clem. 42). Irenaeus* then developed apostolic succession as an aspect of the apostolic tradition that distinguishes the true churches from their Gnostic competitors. Christ did not keep anything from his apostles, his closest disciples, and taught them the whole truth*, which the apostles in turn transmitted "above all to those to whom they confided the churches themselves," that is, to the first bishops (*Adv. Haer.* III. 3.1). For the most important churches, most notably that of Rome, the line of bishops can be traced back to the apostles, "by which line and succession the Tradition of the church, beginning with the apostles, and the preaching of the truth, have come down to us" (ibid., III. 3.3). While Irenaeus does say of "the presbyters" that "with the succession in the episcopacy, they have received the certain charisma of truth" (ibid., IV. 26.2), his emphasis is on a *successio localis* as the sign of a continuity of apostolic tradition within a specific church, and thus as a criterion for identifying this tradition. Tertullian *(De Praescriptione haereticorum; Adversus Marcionem)* has a similar understanding of apostolic succession for the same anti-Gnostic reasons.

In Cyprian*, the succession of the entire episcopate from its single source in the apostles, and especially Peter*, is decisive both for the unity* of the entire church (*De unitate Ecclesiae* 5) and for the authority of each bishop over his church (*Ep.* 68). Nevertheless, apostolic succession still belongs to the church rather than to individuals. A bishop who, through heresy* or schism*, has left the unity of the church has also left the apostolic succession. The foundation for a more individually focused conception of apostolic succession was laid during the fourth and fifth centuries by an increased willingness to recognize the validity* of sacraments* and ordinations* performed outside the communion* of the church. If such ordinations were valid, they were then ordinations in apostolic succession, and bishops in heresy or schism simply were not outside this succession. It follows that apostolic succession must be less a characteristic of the church, focused in its leaders, and more a characteristic of persons ordained in a *successio personalis,* which these persons continue to possess even in heresy or schism. Augustine* laid the basis for this change, although his own explicit discussions of apostolic succession still generally follow the earlier lines.

Apostolic succession was self-evident and was not extensively debated during the Middle Ages. However, the development within Scholasticism* of a theology of orders, with its concepts of a power *(potestas)* and an indelible nature *(character indelibilis)* granted in ordination, strengthened the more individualistic understanding of apostolic succession. The absence of debate led to remaining imprecision. While it was agreed that apostolic succession was transmitted through the bishops, most Scholastic theologians held that no sacramental difference existed between bishops and priests. The grounds for denying a valid presbyteral succession were thus not clear.

d) Reformation and Post-Reformation Disputes. The various branches of the Reformation (Lutheran, Calvinist, and Anglican) rejected the contention that apostolic succession, in the sense of an episcopal *successio personalis,* was essential for a valid or effective ministry* of Word and sacrament. Luther's rejection of the ideas of a *potestas* or *character indelibilis* passed on in ordination undercut apostolic succession as it had come to be understood in medieval theology. True apostolic succession lay in holding to the apostolic gospel (*WA* 39 II, 176). While Melanchthon was more favorable to episcopal order, he nonetheless thought that episcopal apostolic succession was not essential to the church (CR 23, 595–642). The Lutheran states, however, consistently maintained that they were willing to submit to the Catholic bishops, and thus accept an episcopal apostolic succession, if the bishops would permit the preaching of the gospel and certain Lutheran reforms (*BSLK* 296, 14 ff.). An episcopal *successio personalis* remained in the Swedish and Finnish Lutheran churches.

The Calvinist tradition likewise held that an episcopal apostolic succession is not essential to the church. In placing greater emphasis on the equality of all ordained ministers (e.g., in the Second Helvetic Confession, chap. 18), however, Reformed churches have usually been less open to traditional episcopal order than the Lutheran churches, and thus more opposed to apostolic succession as traditionally understood.

Episcopal apostolic succession was preserved in the Church of England during the Reformation and defended theologically against those who preferred a presbyterian polity. All Anglican churches have an episcopal order in a *successio personalis.* Most Anglican theologians and authorities have not held that churches that lose an episcopal apostolic succession are no longer true churches. Nevertheless, this question does not lead to unanimity, especially since the Oxford movement. The Anglican Church has always had the ecumenical policy (Lambeth Quadrilateral 1888) of rejecting full communion with churches not willing at least to reenter episcopal apostolic succession.

The Council of Trent* said little explicitly about apostolic succession, but implicitly reasserted the Scholastic doctrine. The Decree on the Sacrament of Order states that "the bishops who have succeeded the apostles belong in a special way to the hierarchical order" (*ad hunc hierarchicum ordinem praecipue pertinere,* XXIII, 4). Vatican* II is more explicit: "the bishops, by virtue of divine institution, are the successors of the apostles as pastors of the Church, in such a way that those who hear them hear Christ, while those who reject them reject Christ and him who has sent Christ" (*LG* 20). While apostolic succession is realized through an ordination in a *successio personalis* that transmits a spiritual gift (*LG* 21), emphasis falls on the collective succession of the entire body of bishops, as successors of the apostles in their office of teaching, sanctifying, and governing. The apostolic succession links the Catholic Church to the Orthodox churches (*UR* 15), while what is lacking in the sacrament of orders in the Protestant churches, presumably due to the absence of an episcopal apostolic succession, means that they lack "all the reality belonging to the eucharistic Mystery" (*UR* 22).

The Orthodox churches have not shared the debate over apostolic succession. They maintain that episcopal apostolic succession is an essential aspect of the church, but often criticize Western theology for conceptually separating continuity in ministry from the total continuity of the church (Zizioulas).

e) Ecumenical Issues. Apostolic succession has been one of the most difficult ecumenical topics. Disagreements over apostolic succession have become one factor blocking a mutual recognition of ministries between Catholic, Orthodox, and Anglican churches, on the one hand, and between the various Protestant churches, on the other. Recent discussions have given hope for a resolution of the differences.

The text *Baptism, Eucharist, Ministry,* issued by the World Council of Churches in 1982, finds the "primary manifestation of apostolic succession... in the apostolic tradition of the whole church" (M §35). "The succession of the bishops became one of the modes... by which the apostolic tradition of the church was expressed" (M §36). Appealing to the reality of the *episkope,* the oversight over ministry, in all churches, the text then seeks to understand episcopal apostolic succession as "a sign, rather than a guarantee, of the continuity and unity of the church" (M §38).

The concept of "sign" is further elaborated in the Anglican-Lutheran dialogue (*Niagara Report* 1988). The apostolic continuity of the church is maintained by the faithfulness of God*, despite human failings (28), through various means: the Bible*, the creed, and the continuity of the ordained ministry* (29). Since apostolic continuity is a feature of the entire church, the presence or absence of any single criterion (e.g., an episcopal *successio personalis*) is not sufficient to judge whether a church stands in the true apostolic succession. A more comprehensive judgment must be made, taking various factors into account (20). On this basis, Anglican churches might be made to see Lutheran churches that lack such an episcopal *successio personalis* as within apostolic succession, and the Lutheran churches that stand outside such a *successio personalis* might be able to see it as a useful sign of succession in the apostolic gospel. These arguments paved the way for the Porvoo Agreement (1994), which reconciles ministries among the Anglican churches, and the Nordic and Baltic Lutheran churches.

• Y. Congar (1966), "Composantes et idée de la succession apostolique," *Oecumenica 1,* 61–80.

E. Schlink (1961), "Die apostolische Sukzession," *Der kommende Christus und die kirchlichen Traditionen,* Göttingen.

G. Blum (1978), "Apostel/Apostolat/Apostolizitat, II Alte Kirche," *TRE* 3, 445–66.

J. Zizioulas (1981), *L'être écclesial,* Geneva.

Baptême, Euchariste, Ministère (1982), Paris.

Rapport de Niagara (1988) in *Accords et Dialogues Oecuméniques,* Ed. A. Birmelé, J. Terme, Paris.

Michael Root

See also **Authority; Bishop; Irenaeus of Lyons; Ministry**

Apostolicity of the Church. *See* **Apostle; Apostolic Succession**

Appropriation

The term *appropriation* is used in Christology and Trinitarian theology.

a) In Christology, appropriations are an aspect of the communication of idioms* and correspond to communications proper. In the first case, the divine Person* of the Word* appropriates the realities of the human condition and the events experienced by Christ* (his birth, his kenosis*, his cross, etc.). In the second case, the divine Person of the Word communicates to humanity what is distinctive of divinity.

b) In Trinitarian theology, appropriations are a language* phenomenon that constitutes a third term between the essential attributes* or activities that are proper to the divine nature as such and the personal characteristics of the Father*, the Son, and the Holy* Spirit. To appropriate is to make a common noun serve as a proper noun. Trinitarian appropriation consists in applying an essential attribute to a person, as if it were his own, so as to "manifest" him. The language of the Scriptures* and tradition* appropriates to a particular person an attribute or an activity that is common to all the Trinity. Paul thus calls Christ the "power of God and the wisdom of God" (1 Cor 1:24). The Father is called "the Almighty" (Rev 1:8, chaps. 4, 8, etc.). Appropriation is commonly found in the liturgy. Thomas* Aquinas comments on four expressions of traditional appropriation. First there is that of Hilary* of Poitiers: "Eternity* is in the Father, beauty in the Image, joy in the gift that is offered to us [Holy Spirit]." Then there are those of Augustine*: "Unity is in the Father, equality in the Son, harmony between unity and equality in the Holy Spirit"; "The Father is power, the Son is wisdom, the Holy Spirit is goodness"; "'From him' it is said of the Father; 'through him,' of the Son; 'in him' of the Holy Ghost" (*ST* Ia, q. 39, a. 7–8). Similarly, the Trinity's indwelling of the justified man is appropriated to the Holy Spirit. The basis of appropriation is the resemblance or the affinity of the considered attribute with the suitability of each person, an affinity that has its roots in the knowledge* that we can have of God, and therefore of his essential attributes, starting with the creatures. Appropriations involve conveniences and do not give way to any proofs. Their danger is that, on one hand, they continue to create confusion between properties and essential attributes, and on the other hand that, lacking referents, they represent nothing more than a language game. Nevertheless, they are not without value for a spiritual understanding of the Trinity.

• M.J. Scheeben (1865), *Die Mysterien des Christentums* (3rd Ed. 1958), Freiburg, §23–31.
A. Chollet (1903), "Appropriation aux personnes de la Trinité," *DThC* 1, 1708–17.
J. Rabeneck (1949), *Das Geheimnis des dreipersonalen Gottes,* Freiburg.
J. Auer (1978), *Gott der Eine und Dreieine, KKD* 2, 305–11.
H.U. von Balthasar (1985), *Theologik* II, Einsiedeln, 117–38.
E. Salmann (1986), *Neuzeit und Offenbarung,* Rome, 307–12.

Bernard Sesboüé

See also **Father; Idioms; Trinity**

Architecture

The earliest Christians had no special buildings devoted to the cult*; they worshipped in synagogues and the Temple*, and their distinctively Christian agape (love feast) meals were held in private houses. Christian worship does not require a particular kind of building, but from early times the church* has encouraged the provision of special places, to enhance solemnity and to use the building itself as a teaching resource.

I. Early Church

Already by the end of the first century, Christian communities had grown too large to meet in private houses and required a large hall with one altar, at which the bishop* presided. By the mid-second century, the eucharistic assembly had been separated from the agape meal and had been stylized into liturgy*. We know that there were buildings referred to by special names, including *ecclesia* (assembly) and *domus dei* (House of God*), but there is little direct evidence of what these were like, except that they tended to have ancillary rooms for cultic purposes, the major of which was the baptistery. The church at Dura Europos, converted from a private house in about 240–41, had been set aside to serve the needs of the congregation by being carefully decorated with images illustrating the meaning of the rites taking place within it. Archeological evidence in Rome suggests that the second-century dwelling on the side of the basilica of San Clemente had undergone such a process of adaptation in the third century, as had some of the other titular basilicas. By the beginning of the fourth century, larger hall churches were being built in other parts of the empire (Parentium, Qirkbize in Syria). It is not known whether there was any characteristic Christian architectural style before the fourth century. Pagan temples were unsuitable models because they were not designed to house large groups of worshippers. Christian churches, like synagogues, were built for large gatherings of the faithful. After 312, when the emperor Constantine converted to Christianity, the basilica form was most frequently adopted for churches. Basilicas were large, generally aisled halls used for a variety of secular and religious purposes. They were well lit by rows of windows in the side walls and above the internal arcades: some had a rounded apse protruding from the center of a long side or from one end. Basilica churches had the apse with an altar at one end and many were provided with an atrium at the other, entrance end. Some of the latter contained fountains, symbolizing the source of life, which could be used for ablutions before entering the church. By the fourth century, most churches were oriented with the entrance at the western end and the altar in the eastern end. In this way, at the morning service the congregation faced the rising sun, symbol of the Parousia* of Christ*, the Sun of Justice*.

During Constantine's lifetime were built not only the church of the bishop of Rome, on the supposed site of Peter*'s grave, but also the basilica of the Lateran, the first official church building of Christianity, begun c. 313, as well as several memorial chapels in cemeteries. In Rome, most of these churches featured an ambulatory—that is, a gallery linking the aisles and allowing to go around the altar (Santa Agnese, mid-fourth century)—but many others had centralized structures, modeled on pagan mausoleums. In Jerusalem*, the Anastasis ("Resurrection*") Rotunda was built over the Holy Sepulcher, and in Bethlehem an octagonal chapel was erected over the Nativity grotto. The palace-church of Antioch (327–41) was also octagonal. Under Justinian the domed, centralized church of Saint Sophia in Constantinople was built. In Rome in the fourth century, the popes* founded the basilica of Santa Maria Maggiore and the church of San Stefano Rotondo, whose plan is a cross inscribed in a circle. In the late fourth and early fifth centuries, pilgrimage* churches began to be built with (or existing ones supplemented with) galleries to provide extra accommodation, especially for women or for catechumens (the basilica of Trier, as rebuilt by Gratian c. 380). Saint Peter's in Rome had a choir enclosure: such enclosures became a standard way of providing space for the clergy (Saint Thecla, Milan, mid-fourth century). In the following years, this feature spread all over the Mediterranean. Some early basilicas had transepts isolated from the nave, giving a cruciform ground plan. The earliest true cruciform church, in which all four arms are of equal height, may have been the Apostles* church in Constantinople. In a church to which crowds of pilgrims came, Saint Simeon Stylites at Kal'ar Sem'an in Syria, an unroofed octagonal building surrounded the saint's column. The cruciform plan became very popular because it turned the entire building into an embodiment of the cross. In the fifth century were built the first churches with cupolas over central spaces, and also basilica complexes, such as that adjoining the Anastasis.

In some places, for example in Aquilera and Trier, double basilicas (in effect two churches placed side by side) were built. This strange form can be explained in terms of function. In addition to the churches required for regular worship, there arose a need for places in which to commemorate the martyrs. Structures were built over or near their tombs in cemeteries outside the city walls. As the number of pilgrims increased, these churches were added to, and by the fifth century some of them were connected with monastic complexes. The monastic communities were set up to minister to the needs of pilgrims, to ensure that continual prayer* was made over the graves of the martyrs, and also to serve as bases for missionary activity. After the Goth invasions of the fifth century, the bodies of the martyrs had to be moved from the cemeteries outside Rome into the city churches for safety and access. The relics* of the saints were spread among regular churches, and soon every church was required to own some relic. In Jerusalem, Rome, and Constantinople, "stational" liturgy gained importance. The bishop and the people processed from church to church, celebrating the Eucharist* and other services, with the purpose of sanctifying the whole city*. Such public processions were hardly possible before Christianity became the state religion. Processions within church buildings, so ubiquitous throughout the Middle Ages, seem to have developed from these. Various parts of the church, such as the baptismal font or the main doorway, provided stations where the procession paused for prayer, by analogy with the use of different churches as stopping points in outside processions.

II. Medieval Church

The medieval church building was considered a representation of the heavenly Jerusalem, as envisioned in the Apocalypse. From the 10th century, at the latest, the liturgy for the consecration of a church made this quite clear. The form and decoration of the building were designed to inspire the worshippers with a sense of the transcendence and nearness of God. This notion was common to all of Christendom, but the forms in which it was realized differed between the Eastern and Western churches.

1. Byzantium

In the East, the centralized domed church predominated for nearly a millennium. The form was probably inspired by centrally planned early structures such as martyrs' sanctuaries, baptisteries, and memorial buildings (Santa Constanza in Rome, the Anastasis Rotunda in Jerusalem), themselves inspired by the domed Pantheon in Rome. The Byzantine use of the dome, however, rapidly developed into new and exciting forms, straining Roman technology to the limits, particularly during the reign of Justinian. The first masterwork of this period is San Vitale in Ravenna (526–47), with an octagonal central dome surrounded by an aisle and galleries. There were many other early forms; one frequently copied in later, smaller churches was that of Saint John at Ephesus, which had a Greek cross plan with a central dome and domes over each arm. Saint Sophia in Constantinople (532–37, altered 558–63) became the paradigm of the imperial church. It had a huge dome, carried on the first large-scale pendentives (spherical triangular segments of the vault—the first ones to be this scale), which are graceful and carry the weight of the dome efficiently down to the pillars. The dome represents the heavens, covering without enclosing. In the ninth century, after the Iconoclast controversy, a new church plan was developed. More modest in size, it consisted of a barrel-vaulted cross inscribed in a rectangle, with a dome over the center, which later came to be raised on a drum.

All of these churches were decorated with mosaics or paintings, many of which were destroyed during the Iconoclast debate. The Ravenna mosaics are especially noteworthy. With the triumph of the icons from the mid-ninth century on, imagery began to be systematically applied to church interiors. The colonnade separating nave from the sanctuary was hung with icons and developed into the iconostasis, completely kept the Eucharist hidden, except when the center doors were opened.

The mosaics represented the heavenly hierarchy, with Christ in the central dome and a descending progression of the choir of angels*, patriarchs, and apostles, down to the local saints. The building became an earthly heaven in which God was mysteriously present. This style of architecture was preserved and developed in Greece through the Middle Ages. It spread also to Russia and the Balkans. Russia developed clusters of domes raised on tall drums; the domes were eventually transformed into the characteristic onion profile. Later, these forms were translated into wooden structures, thus combining the Byzantine esthetic with native building traditions. In the West, Byzantine influence is found in the churches of Norman Sicily. Saint Mark in Venice follows the pattern of Saint John at Ephesus and (as with the Sicilian churches) is decorated with mosaics.

2. The West

The majority of churches built in the West during the medieval period were inspired by basilicas. Important exceptions are those that copied early central structures, especially the Anastasis Rotunda. During the troubled centuries that followed the breakdown of the western Roman Empire, only small churches could be built. With more settled conditions and the advent of the Romanesque style, churches began to rival the Constantinian churches of Rome. Liturgy and ceremonial became more complex; the ruling that each priest* must say his own mass every day required multiple altars in cathedrals and monasteries where there were many priests. From the sixth century on, churches might possess more than one altar. By the mid-12th century, there were 20 in Saint Denis, Paris. Each altar was dedicated to a particular saint. The dual use of these great churches, for the continual prayer of divine office and mass, and for lay pilgrimage, led to the choir and sanctuary being more completely separated from the nave and ambulatory. Such separations survive in the cathedrals of Lincoln and Paris, both 13th-century. It was during this period that the classic design of monasteries was developed: a rectangular cloister surrounding a garden. Around the cloister were the church, the chapter house, the refectory, and the dormitory, with other domestic structures set with no particular order outside the walls. Freestanding baptisteries survived in many Italian towns; they were used for multiple baptisms* at Easter and Pentecost. In northern Europe, children were baptized individually soon after birth; each parish church had its own font, usually prominently placed inside the main door as a reminder that baptism is the sacrament* of entrance into the Christian community.

a) Romanesque. Romanesque was the major western European style from around 950 to 1150, so called because it was based on the use of the Roman semicircular arch. From 950 to 1050, its formative period, there were many regional styles. Later, Romanesque became an international style because of monasticism, which helped to spread ideas, blueprints, and masons along the great pilgrimage routes, and also those opened by the Crusades. The most common form was an expanded basilica plan, with the addition of bays. There was much experiment with vaulting and structural articulation. Lombard-Catalan architecture of the early 11th century was based on a direct revival of Roman techniques, with heavy tunnel vaults (Saint Martin-du-Canigou, 1001–26; Saint Maria Ripoll, 1020–88). Interiors were dark and unadorned, but exteriors were enriched with delicate blank arcading. The great pilgrimage churches developed ambulatory and radiating chapels around the eastern end, with an exterior effect of compact massing and multiple towers. German early Romanesque used a double-apsed plan and timber ceilings rather than stone vaults. At Gernrode (c. 980) and Saint Michael in Hildesheim, the interiors were articulated by systems of alternating supports forming double bays.

The international high Romanesque style flourished

from around 1050 to around 1150. Major French pilgrimage abbeys (Tours, Conques, Limoges, Toulouse), modeled after Santiago de Compostela (c. 1075–1150), turned the basilica plan into a Latin cross with a transept, an ambulatory and chapels, a three-story elevation, and a double barrel vault with transverse ribs. Burgundian churches experimented with different vaulting (e.g., Vezelay, with its groin vaults). The third church at Cluny (1088–1130) seems to anticipate Gothic style with its height, light barrel vaults, buttressed by transverse ribs that carry the weight down on to compound piers, and the stilted pointed arches of the nave arcade. In western France, hall churches developed: Notre-Dame-la-Grande in Poitiers (c. 1130–45) and Saint Savin-sur-Gartempe (c. 1060–1115) have barrel-vaulted naves and aisles at almost equal height. In Aquitaine, under Byzantine influence, aisleless churches were covered in a series of domes on pendentives (cathedrals of Angoulême, c. 1105–25, and Périgueux, c. 1120). In Normandy and England, there were many structural experiments. Eleventh-century churches (e.g., Jumièges, 1040–67, Saint Étienne at Caen, 1066–77) used Germanic double bays and timber roofs. Most English churches also retained timber roofs.

b) Gothic. The Gothic style began in the early to mid-12th century in northern France (Saint Denis ambulatory and chapels, 1140–44); it lasted until the 15th century and, some would say, until the 16th century in France, and the 17th in England and Germany. Characterized by ribbed vaulting, deep buttresses, and tall piers, it made use of the pointed arch, which is more stable than the round arch: the angle and stilting of the arch can easily be varied to allow irregular spaces to be vaulted at uniform heights. There was thus no need for heavy walling, allowing gradual development of larger windows. Most Gothic churches have a strong vertical emphasis. In late 12th-century northern France, there were various experiments to find a satisfying bay design (Laon and Paris, c. 1160), but the rebuilding of Chartres (begun c. 1195) seems to have provided a pattern for classic Gothic: a three-story elevation, arcades, triforium passage, and tall clerestory, four-part vaults supported on buttresses, ambulatory, and radiating chapels. Thirteenth-century cathedrals in France strove for great height: the choir at Beauvais is the highest, at over 156 feet. In England, by contrast, the emphasis was on length, textural and color effects, size of windows, and complexity of vault ribbing (Lincoln, 1190s–1287; Salisbury, 1220–58). Tall spires heightened the impact. Germany and Spain did not adopt Gothic style before the mid-13th century, and then used its French form (Köln, begun 1248; Leon, 1254–1303; Toledo, begun 1227). Italy developed its own form of Gothic, retaining Romanesque techniques, using pointed arches and ribbed vaults to achieve broad, open spaces (Santa Maria Novella in Florence, begun c. 1278).

Later Gothic, from c. 1300 onward, developed decorative effects, openness, and lightness. In England the decorated Gothic style elaborated vault and tracery patterns. This was taken over in France and Germany as the flamboyant Gothic of the late 14th century, just as in England more austere effects were sought by using a perpendicular style. However, lightly decorated effects became popular again in the early 16th century with the use of the fan vault, a uniquely English form. Throughout western Europe, the interior of the late medieval church tended to be subdivided into a multiplicity of private and semiprivate chapels dedicated to various saints, or to praying for the souls* of the dead.

c) Renaissance. In Italy, beginning in the 15th century, the Renaissance style, which again looked back to the architecture of ancient Rome, gained some its impetus from the reconstruction of the early basilicas in Rome under the pontificate of Martin V (1417–31). San Lorenzo and San Spirito in Florence are the earliest examples. Appeal was made to antique precedents and principles, based on a rereading of Vitruvius. San Sebastiano in Mantua stems from designs of Roman baths; the facade includes elements of temples and triumphal arches. Centralized designs with domes were built (Pazzi chapel in San Spirito, San Biagio in Montepulciano, Bramante's "Tempietto" in Rome). Although the new style was certainly known north of the Alps, because of pilgrimages to Rome, it did not really catch on. However, Renaissance details were sometimes added to a Gothic design (Saint Eustache in Paris, the Fugger chapel in Augsburg, the screen and stalls in King's College, Cambridge).

III. Reformation and Counter-Reformation

1. Protestantism

An emphasis on preaching* and Bible* commentary, together with the rejection of the Catholic theology* of the Eucharist, transformed church interiors. Churches were built with galleries and tall pulpits to accommodate large congregations that could see and hear the preacher. Seating was arranged facing the pulpit rather than the Communion table. The Reformers rejected the idea that the building itself was holy, but this was frequently undercut by references to the Jerusalem Temple. The Anglican Church, however, retained the public singing in cathedral and college churches of morning and evening prayer, based respectively on the hours of Lauds and Prime, and on Vespers and Compline. This was reflected in the retention in such churches of medieval choir screens, which allowed nonparticipant visitors access to the nave without disrupting the office taking place in the choir.

In Lutheran Germany, as in England, the chancels of parish churches were used as Communion rooms, the communicants moving there from the nave before the prayer of consecration and gathering around the altar table. Luther* allowed many images and statues to remain; Calvin* and Zwingli* required their total removal. In Germany, castle chapels led the style of Lutheran churches (Torgau, centralized plan with galleries). Reformed churches in the Netherlands and France also often used centralized designs (La Rochelle, 1577–1603; Willemstad, 1597–1607), and these influenced Reformed churches in Germany and, later, in England. Only in the second half of the 17th century did the Renaissance style (baroque or classical) become the norm in Germany (after the Thirty Years' War) and England (after the Restoration). New churches built with this plan provided only a very small chancel for the altar table. Instances of this are the various small churches built to Wren's designs in London after the Great Fire of 1666. These display a wide variety of styles and plans, the most interesting being probably Saint Stephen Wallbrook, a rectangle in which classical columns inscribe what can be seen as either a Latin cross or a Greek cross with narthex, surmounted by a circular coffered dome. Wren's major work, Saint Paul's Cathedral in London, is the result of a compromise between the domed centralized structure that he favored and the Latin cross shape required by the chapter. Wren's work was influential throughout the 18th century in England, and also in North America, especially through the works of his pupil Gibbs (Saint Martin-in-the-Fields, 1722–26).

2. Catholicism

The Council of Trent* encouraged using fine arts. In 1576–77 Carlo Borromeo, archbishop of Milan, issued instructions for church building, referring to early Christianity. There were no stained-glass windows, since light is a symbol in itself; clear glass windows also allowed a better view of the works of art inside the church. Centralized designs were considered heathen, but this had little effect in practice. Chapels were needed along the sides of the church to provide for the cult of saints and the priests' private masses. The pulpit had to be seen in conjunction with the altar, symbolizing the unity of word* and sacrament. Robert Bellarmine* also emphasized this unity. His ideal church was divided into three parts—narthex, nave, and choir—after the pattern of Solomon's Temple. He stressed the significance of decoration to attract the faithful.

Baroque and rococo architecture both sought to engage the subjective experience of the beholder, either through the dynamic of the building or through its ornamentation. The epitome of baroque is Bernini's Andrea al Quirinale in Rome, which has a carefully orchestrated movement upward to the heavenly light of the dome. Rococo architecture tends to be simpler, with an emphasis rather on the complexity of its decoration. In France, the architecture of the 17th and 18th centuries was in a sober baroque, under strong Renaissance and Palladian influence (François Mansart's Val-de-Grâce, begun 1645; Jules-Hardouin Mansard's Dôme des Invalides, 1680–91). This "classical" style in turn influenced most of the countries of northern Europe (Prandtauer's Melk Abbey in Austria; Wren in England).

Rococo became most theatrical in Neumann's Vierzehnheiligen in Germany (1743–72). In Spain, the style tended to show an abundance of ornamentation, as in the facade of Santiago de Compostela (1738–49). This style also traveled to the New World, as can be seen in Ocotlán, Mexico (c. 1745).

At the same time, partly under the influence of Wren (Soufflot's Ste. Geneviève, now the Pantheon, 1755–95), France developed a neoclassical style arising from the arts of antiquity, especially those of Greece.

IV. 19th Century

At the beginning of the 19th century, church architecture in the West was still largely classical. Pierre Vignon's La Madeleine in Paris (1806–42) is still of Greco-Roman inspiration. However, interest in the medieval past had already begun in the previous century with romanticism, and an ever more serious study of medieval building techniques led to the revival of the Gothic style. Scholarly research and restoration were combined in the work of Viollet-le-Duc in France and George Gilbert Scott in England. Their restorations were controversial, and often overdone, but they did save a number of churches from destruction. England was the heart of the Gothic revival style, with the work of the Cambridge Camden (later Ecclesiological) Society and of the Pugins, father and son. It became the most widely used style in England, and spread to other English-speaking countries. The Catholic Cathedral of Saint Patrick's in Melbourne, Australia, begun in 1858, was designed in 13th-century style by Wardell, a pupil of the younger Pugin. The change in architecture became the physical expression of a renewed interest in medieval liturgy and ceremonial. In Anglican churches, the altar, now set against the east wall of an elongated chancel, became again the major feature of the church. Pews in medieval style faced east. The art of stained glass was revived to fill the windows with biblical scenes and figures of saints. Processions were also held once again by Protestants.

V. Contemporary Period

The liturgical movement and Vatican* II have changed the understanding of the liturgy, which is reflected in the design of churches. In many Protestant churches, the Eucharist has become more central and more often celebrated. In most major Protestant denominations, the font, pulpit, and altar are brought into visual relation with each other, to display the connection between word and sacraments. This has lessened the emphasis on the pulpit. The font, if not placed near the altar, is often given its own chapel. The rulings of Vatican II transformed the Catholic understanding of the mass. No longer is the priest leading the people* toward, and representing them before, God; instead, the laity gather before the altar, or sometimes around the altar, and participate fully in the liturgical action. This has created a tendency toward centralized structures.

Interestingly, in the late 20th century Protestant and Catholic churches have become less easily distinguishable from each other. There has also been an occasional return to the idea of the "house-church" *(domus ecclesiae),* producing small churches, often indistinguishable from surrounding houses. Many new churches are being designed for a wider range of functions and contain all sorts of ancillary installations.

Finally, together with the new theological approach to the liturgy, the 20th century has also witnessed a revolution in building materials and techniques. The new materials—iron, reinforced concrete, and glass—have been known since the middle of the 19th century: concrete was used by Bardot for Saint Jean-l'Evangéliste in Montmartre (1894–1902), iron by Boileau for Saint Eugène (1854–55) and by Baltard for Saint Augustin (1860–71). However, it was not until the 1920s or 1930s that they were extensively used to create new forms. Auguste Perret's Notre-Dame-du-Raincy (1922–23) is one of the earliest examples. Its concrete roof rests on columns of reinforced cement, and the altar is raised on a platform. Reinforced concrete permits large spaces without supports, large glass surfaces, and parabolic vaults (Dominicus Böhm's Saint Engelbert, Köln-Riehl, 1930). More recently, such materials have been used for Gothic churches, with shell vaults (Felix Candela's Miraculous Virgin of Mexico, 1954; Gudjon Samuelson's Hallgrim church in Reykjavik, Iceland, begun in 1945).

The crucial question for recent liturgical reforms has been the *participatio actuosa* (active participation, SC 14) of the whole congregation, instead of the "spectacle" performed by the clergy (and the choir). Nevertheless, the popularity of religious television programs suggests that the spectacular element of the liturgy still fulfills a real need for those who are unable or unwilling to go to church. Moreover, an excessive emphasis on the congregation normally leads to a restriction of the role played by the sense of divine transcendence, or to a forgetting of the dialectic that should be established between communal prayer and individual prayer. Finally, the assembly of the faithful around the altar may give the impression of a closed circle that excludes the seeker and the outsider. The way of the future may be to accept a plurality of liturgical conceptions and architectural solutions.

• I

H.C. Butler (1929), *Early Churches in Syria,* Princeton, N.J. (repr. 1969).

A. Grabar (1946), *Martyrium,* Paris.

T. Bayley (1971), *The Processions of Sarum and the Western Church,* Toronto.

T.F. Mathews (1971), *The Early Churches of Constantinople: Architecture and Liturgy,* University Park, Pa.

C. Heitz (1974), "Architecture et liturgie processionnelle à l'époque préromaine," *Revue de l'art* 24, 30–47.

R. Krautheimer (1975), *Early Christian and Byzantine Architecture,* 2nd Ed., Harmondsworth.

P.-M. Gy (1978), "Espace et célébration comme question théologique," *MD* 136, 39–46.

A. Chavasse (1982), "L'organisation stationnale du carême romain, avant le VIIIe s: Une organisation pastorale," *RSR* 56, 17–32.

J.F. Baldovin (1987), *The Urban Character of Christian Worship,* Rome.

L. Michael White (1990), *Building God's House in the Roman World,* Baltimore.

II

P. Frankl (1926), *Die frühmittelalterliche und romanische Baukunst,* Potsdam.

R.C. de Lasteyrie du Saillant (1929), *L'architecture religieuse en France à l'époque romane,* 2nd Ed.

H. Focillon (1938), *Art d'Occident,* Paris.

P. Frankl (1960), *The Gothic: Literary Sources and Interpretations through Eight Centuries,* Princeton.

K.J. Conant (1966), *Carolingian and Romanesque Architecture 800–1200,* 2nd Ed., London.

W. Braunfels (1972), *Monasteries of Western Europe,* London.

C. Mango (1976), *Byzantine Architecture,* New York.

J. Bony (1983), *French Gothic Architecture of the XIIth and XIIIth Centuries,* Berkeley.

III

A.W.N. Pugin (1841), *The True Principles of Pointed or Christian Architecture,* London; (1843), *An Apology for the Revival of Christian Architecture in England,* London.

E.E. Viollet-le-Duc (1854–68), *Dictionnaire raisonné de l'architecture française du XIe au XIVe siècle,* Paris.

C. Eastlake (1872), *A History of the Gothic Revival,* London.

K. Clark (1928), *The Gothic Revival,* London (repr. 1962).
L. Hautecœur (1943–57), *Histoire de l'architecture classique en France,* Paris.
N. Lieb (1953), *Barockkirchen zwischen Donau und Alpen,* Munich.
J. Summerson (1953), *Architecture in Britain, 1530–1850,* Harmondsworth (repr. 1977).
R. Wittkover (1958), *Art and Architecture in Italy, 1600–1750,* Harmondsworth (repr. 1977).
E. Hempel (1965), *Baroque Art and Architecture in Central Europe,* Harmondsworth.
N. Yates (1991), *Buildings, Faith and Worship,* Oxford (unreliable for the pre-1700 period).

IV
O. Bartning (1919), *Vom neuen Kirchbau,* Berlin.
H. R. Hitchcock (1958), *Architecture, Nineteenth and Twentieth Centuries,* Harmondsworth (repr. 1968).
P. Hammond (1961), *Liturgy and Architecture,* New York.
A. Christ-Janer, M. M. Foley (1962), *Modern Church Architecture,* New York.
G. Mercier (1968), *Architecture religieuse contemporaine en France,* Tours.

LYNNE BROUGHTON

See also **Cult; Images; Liturgy; Music**

Arianism

1. History

a) Arius (c. 260–336). Arius, of Libyan origin, was accepted to the diaconate by Bishop* Peter I of Alexandria (300–311) and then to the presbyterate by Achillas, before being put in charge of the parish of Baucalis under Alexander (312–28). He was soon denounced for his ideas on the Son of God*, whom he said was inferior to the Father*. Around 318–20, a local synod* excluded him from the church community. Despite considerable support from eastern bishops, he was also condemned in Antioch in early 325, then in Nicaea* in June 325. Exiled, and then called back from exile, Arius was not able to have himself reintroduced into the ranks of Alexandrian clergy. He died in Constantinople on a Saturday in 336. Two letters, a profession of faith*, a passage from a pamphlet in both verse and prose entitled *Thalia,* are his only writings that remain (Opitz, Boularand, Sesboüé), especially thanks to the citations offered by Athanasius* of Alexandria (Kannengiesser 1983).

b) Arians. Arius was excommunicated from the Alexandrian synod, around 319, along with five priests*, six deacons*, and two bishops, Theonas of Marmarica and Secundus of Ptolemais. At the Antioch synod, from the beginning of 325, three bishops were sentenced, including the famous Eusebius of Caesarea; however, these bishops sympathized less with the personal ideas of Arius than they disapproved of the blatant authoritarianism of their Alexandrian colleague. At the Council* of Nicaea, Theonas and Secundus were excommunicated again at the same time as Arius. Eusebius of Nicomedia, Arius's main champion, was exiled soon after the Council ended; but this was only for a lapse of time and because he pursued friendship with the condemned bishops, not because of heresy*. Moreover, he very quickly persuaded Constantine to initiate appeasement politics in the face of Nicene intransigence. He formed a coalition of eastern bishops, concerned with showing to the imperial court that religious peace* was more successfully maintained in the provinces without the Nicene protagonists. Eustathius of Antioch, Marcellus of Ancyra, and especially Athanasius of Alexandria, Alexander's successor, were sent into exile. After Constantine's death in 337, Athanasius became an unavoidable obstacle in the way of the political strategy of the Episcopal coalition, hostile to the Alexandrian reign. Because this strategy included revision, if not abolition, dogmatic decisions from Nicaea, all the while envisaging ecclesiastical hegemony supported by the imperial court, there is nothing surprising about the fact that Athanasius denounced his adversaries as "Arians," a polemical title having no precise doctrinal connotations.

One can get an idea of these more or less nominal "Arians" by studying their synods, which flourished everywhere after Nicaea until the Second Ecumenical Council, Constantinople* I, in 381 (Duchesne, Brennecke). Diverging doctrines soon complicated the advancements of the coalition. The "Homoeans," who supported the idea of only one Son "similar *(homoios)* in every way" to the Father, therefore, non "consubstantial*," seemed to dominate in Sirmium in 359. The "Anomoeans," who were strict "neo-Arians" like Aetius the Syrian, or the Cappadocian Eunomius, for whom the Son bore "no resemblance *(anhomoios)* in accordance with the essence," had their hour of glory around 360. They were quickly replaced by the "Homoousians," or "Semi-Arians," grouped around Basil of Ancyra. Their definition of the Son was "similar *(homoios)* in terms of substance *(kat'ousian).*" These moderates disapproved of the excessive ways of the more or less fanatic factions, always ready to seize a political opportunity in order to take power in churches*; they sought to get along with the Nicaeans, the undisputed chief of whom was Athanasius, remaining all the while reserved on the subject of consubstantiality. From the depths of the Egyptian desert where he was then hiding, Athanasius agreed to this union. The synod of union and reconciliation that he was able to organize in Alexandria in 362 facilitated the final victory of the Nicene "consubstantial," which was gained with the advent of Theodosius in 380.

The spread of Arianism in the west marked the Visigothic and Vandalic invasions. Indeed, it was Eusebius of Nicomedia, then reigning in Constantinople, who, around 341, consecrated Ulfilas as bishop of the Goths. His mission was to evangelize the Gothic people, who had recently settled in Roman territory.

c) The Imperial Court. Arianism in the fourth century would never have represented such a long and complex crisis without imperial interference. As Pontifex Maximus responsible for religion throughout the empire, Constantine favored the Christian bishops; in return, he expected them to actively contribute to the moral well-being of, and social peace among, his subjects. The Arian controversy, persisting after Nicaea, caused this plan to fail. Constantine died in 337, baptized on his deathbed by Eusebius of Nicomedia. His youngest son, Constantius II, was his successor, less than 30 years old and entirely unaware of Nicene issues. He was convinced that his most urgent task was to eliminate Athanasius of Alexandria, the declared enemy of the politics of compromise and appeasement, which was advocated by the episcopal coalition. The duel between these two men that resulted was unique in all of the empire's history. Constantius died in 361, and after the intermediary court ruled by Julian, Athanasius had only to endure Valens, the Arian emperor (364–78), to drain Arianism to the last drop, which had become reason of state.

2. Arian Doctrine and Its Refutation

Arius's personal doctrine was more orthodox than Origen's teaching on the hierarchical functions of the Father, Son, and the Holy* Spirit in terms of salvation. He transposed this hierarchy into the divine hypostases themselves: only the Father is God, strictly speaking; the Son, along with everything that exists, is created into being* through the will of the Father; like the Holy Spirit, he is not called God only as metaphor. Arius, as theologian, focused on the origin of the Son, with philosophical rigor reminiscent of Plotinus; this origin was to be considered without any anthropomorphism, like the kind he saw irreparably connected to *homoousios* (Williams). Arius's strict rationalism* was not shared by his Episcopal champions, who continued to oppose the "consubstantial" concept in the name of their own form of traditional Origenism. Around 355, a neo-Arian movement was launched in Alexandria by Aetius, who was then deacon. Eunomius, Aetius's secretary and disciple, soon overshadowed his teacher. Their "Anomoean" doctrine, which rejected all resemblance between the substance of the Father and that of the Son, strove to have "Inengendered" the proper name* of divinity and emphasized the radical transcendence of the Father, of whom even the Son's knowledge was imperfect.

Athanasius of Alexandria, still at the heart of Origen tradition, developed the notion of divine "generation," which was already favored by his predecessor, Alexander. By removing cosmological connotations that still existed in Origen's work, he showed that one could assert the communication of substance of the Father to the Son without broaching Sabellius's modalism*. He adopted this thesis from the point of view of the concrete realization of salvation* in the Church. His doctrine of saving "divinization" through the incarnate Word* formed his retort to Arian Christology*. According to Arius, the Word, incarnated into the body without soul*, replaced it: when Jesus* is hungry or thirsty, when he suffers or is unaware, is in anguish and dies, it is the inferiority of the divine Word that is revealed. This heroic savior needs to save himself in order to arrive at the full dignity of God. In response, Athanasius explained that the divine Word could not be affected by the inferiority of its incarnated condition; in his flesh, Christ accepted the Passion* and the cross so that we could rise with him in a transfigured human condition. The Platonist realism of this Athanasiusian conception of salvation would be borrowed by Basil* of Caesarea, Gregory of Nyssa, and Cyril of Alexandria. It offered an adequate response to Arianism within a framework of Christian Platonism* in the Alexandrian tradition.

• H.-G. Opitz (Ed.) (1934), *Athanasius-Werke* III, 1/2: *Urkunden zur Geschichte des arianischen Streites,* Berlin; (1935), *Athanasius-Werke* II, 1/2, 231–78.

Athanasius of Alexandria, *De synodis,* PG 26, 682–794.

♦ L. Duchesne (1911), *Histoire ancienne de l'Église* II, 5th Ed., Paris.

E. Schwartz (1959), *Gesammelte Schriften* III, Berlin.

E. Boularand (1972), *L'hérésie d'Arius et la "foi" de Nicée,* Paris.
M. Simonetti (1975), *La crisi ariana nel IV secolo,* Rome.
A. Ritter (1978), "Arianismus," *TRE* 3, 692–712 (bibl.).
T. A. Kopecek (1979), *A History of Neo-Arianism,* Cambridge, Mass.
C. Kannengiesser (1983), *Athanase d'Alexandrie évêque et écrivain: Une lecture des traités Contre les ariens,* Paris.
R. D. Williams (1987), *Arius, Heresy and Tradition,* London.
H. C. Brennecke (1988), *Studien zur Geschichte der Homöer,* Tübingen.
R. P. C. Hanson (1988), *The Search for the Christian Doctrine of God: The Arian Controversy,* Edinburgh.
C. Kannengiesser (1991), *Arius and Athanasius: Two Alexandrian Theologians,* Aldershot.
T. D. Barnes (1993), *Athanasius and Constantius: Theology and Politics in the Constantinian Empire,* Cambridge, Mass.
B. Sesboüé, B. Meunier (1993), *Dieu peut-il avoir un Fils? Le débat trinitaire du IVe siècle,* Paris.
M. Vinzent (1993), *Asterius von Kappadokien: Die theologischen Fragmente,* Leyden.
P. Maraval (1997), "Le débat sur les rapports du Père et du Fils: La crise arienne," *Le Christianisme de Constantin à la conquête arabe,* Paris, 313–48.

CHARLES KANNENGIESSER

See also **Consubstantial; Nicaea I, Council of; Trinity**

Aristotelianism, Christian

The encounter between Aristotle and the Aristotelianism of the disciples and commentators with Christian thought began with ignorance, and then turned to hostility. Some concepts deriving from Aristotelianism would subsequently be introduced into theological syntheses, but still at the cost of radical corrections.

a) A Threat to the Fathers. Initially Aristotelianism was coolly received. During the period when Christianity was coming into being, Aristotelianism was not dominant. Popular philosophy* was Epicurean or Stoic. Moreover, the central themes of Aristotelianism seemed hardly compatible with Christian dogma*. For example, was the eternity of the world, defended in *De Caelo* (II), compatible with the Creation* story in Genesis? And the idea of a God* who knew nothing of the world*, being its final cause but not its efficient cause (*Metaphysica* Λ,7 and 9), was inadmissible in a Christian context. Platonism*, on the other hand, seemed at first sight to be more acceptable. The figure of the Demiurge, in Timaeus, could be interpreted as a foreshadowing of the Creator in Genesis, while the idea of the immortal soul* was easier to extract from Pheidon. Even so, Plato, like Aristotle, was not accepted by the Fathers* without radical adaptation (Ivánka 1964).

For the first Fathers, Aristotle was above all the one who dared to limit divine Providence* to the world above the lunar sphere, thus denying the possibility of divine intervention in the sublunary (Festugière 1932).

The situation did not improve while the Trinitarian and christological dogmas sought rigorously to be expressed. They did so against thinkers who, like Lucian of Antioch, Arius's teacher, used Aristotelian logic in favor of heterodox solutions. Aristotle was therefore the "father of heresy*" (Clement of Alexandria, *Protreptic* V, 66, 4) and Basilides, the Gnostic, was Aristotle's disciple (Hippolytus, *Refutation* I, 20). From here came a certain recurring disingenuousness in the Fathers, who claimed to not understand Aristotelian language, but—in an allusion to Peter* the apostle*'s first trade—to be expressing themselves as fishermen *(halieutikôs, ouk aristotelikôs)* (Gr. Naz., *Or.* 23, 12; PG 35, 1164 *c;* Ambr., *De inc.* IX, 89; PL 16, 876). Nevertheless, even they would use the conceptual tool of philosophy, but only borrowing such as was needed to express a message that had come from elsewhere. Because of this there arose an eclecticism in which the Aristotelian sense of concepts was never exclusive, but always counterbalanced by their meaning in other systems—such as in the Stoic one. This is the case, for example, with the concept of substance *(ousia).* What the divine hypostases share is the same "substance," but the sense of this term is larger, less technical, than it is in Aristotle (Stead 1977).

Aristotle was directly attacked by the Pseudo-Justin, probably Diodorus of Tarsus († before 394), "Refutation of Certain Aristotelian Theses" (J. C. T. Otto, *Corpus apologetarum christianorum saeculi secundi,*

Jena, 1849, vol. IV, 88–207 and PG 6, 1491 a 1564 c). After a short preface, in which the prophets*' agreement about the Creation is contrasted with the contradictions of philosophers, the author cites and refutes, to various extent, 65 passages of *Physica* (from I, 7 to V, 1, then VIII, 1 and 6–8) and the first three books of *De caelo.*

At the beginning of the sixth century, the Alexandrian Johannes Philoponos (Böhm 1967; Sorabji 1987) launched a systematic attack against Aristotelian physics, but using the very weapons of Aristotelianism. He asserts the creation of the world in time* in two books. One of the books is directed against Proclus (*De aeternitate mundi contra Proclum,* ed. Rabe, Leipzig, 1899), while the other, of which only fragments remain, is directed against Aristotle himself, and is cited especially by Simplicius (*Against Aristotle on the Eternity of the World,* trans. C. Widberg, Ithaca and London, 1987). He denies that there is a difference between the fifth celestial element—quintessence or ether—and earthly fire. He acknowledges the existence of emptiness. He explains the movement of projectiles by an *impetus (rhopè)* which is internal to these projectiles. As a result of his doctrinal heterodoxy (he was a Monophysite and would be accused of tritheism), Simplicius's work was given only a modest reception in orthodox circles. It had more impact in the Christian Syriac East, where Simplicius was one of the "black-sheep" of the *falāsifa,* who were strict Aristotelians. He could be seen as the father of modern physics: his concept of *impetus* would be a distant foreshadowing of inertia.

b) A Tamed Aristotle. Neither the association of Aristotelianism with heresy, nor its refutations, would stop Leo of Byzantium and especially John Damascene from adopting it. Certain doctrines would still have to be made more acceptable through their refraction among commentators who were pagans. Themistios, for example, introduced the idea according to which God, in knowing himself, knows all things (Pines 1987; Brague 1991). Similarly, he extended to the individual soul the immortality that Aristotle had allowed only as impersonal identification with the agent intellect. At the same time, the Arisotelian corpus was expanded with apocrypha stemming from Neoplatonism. Among these apocryphal writings we find Aristotle's *Theology,* Plotinus's cento, very influential in Islam, or the *Book of Causes,* cento of Proclus's *Elements of Theology,* especially popular in Europe. In its final stages, antiquity made Aristotelianism the logical and physical foundation of a Neoplatonic metaphysics. The Greek Orient also pursued this path, and until the end of the Byzantine Empire the works of Aristotle were studied and commented upon (Benakis 1987).

The Syriac Orient applied itself intensely to translating and commenting on Aristotle's logical writings. The *Categories* was translated three times. Ninth-century translations of Aristotle into Arabic were simply a continuation of this effort.

For a long time, Latin Christendom only studied Aristotle in the form of the *Dialectica* and the *Decem categoriae,* both attributed to Augustine*, or else through the work of Martianus Capella (McKeon 1939), or in what Boethius* (†524) had translated, that is, the *logica vetus:* the *Categories* and *Of Interpretation,* introduced in Porphyry's Isagog. Theology* would lean on this logic that was still incomplete, but was never bound to it. For example, the eucharistic dogma of the real presence of the risen body of Christ* in the consecrated bread and wine would, following Paschasius Radbertus (†865), be expressed in terms of substance, until the idea of transubstantiation was conceived around 1140 and subsequently promulgated by Lateran* IV in 1215. But that of substance/species, a pairing unknown to him, superseded the substance/accidents pairing, classic in Aristotelianism. Indeed, it was devised in order to express a theory—species endure while substance changes—that, expressed in terms of the first opposition, would have seemed absurd to Aristotle.

In the 12th century the Toledo translators introduced a more complete Aristotle from the Arab world into Christendom, as well as commentaries by Averroes. The physics and epistemology that were thus discovered, together with the ideal of philosophical beatitude* developed by the Arabs, constituted a threat to Christian faith* and life. The theological authorities* began with a few preventive measures in the form of numerous bans on or restrictions of teaching (1210, 1215, 1231, 1263). Then they chose the riskier path of seeking to reexpress the whole dogma. Thomas* Aquinas (1225–74) played a central role in this. Basing himself on the Latin translation of William of Moerbeke, completed directly from the Greek, Aquinas commented on Aristotle's principal works (1267–73). Against Averroes, he sought an interpretation of Aristotle's psychology that would safeguard the individual style of knowing each soul*, and therefore its unique destiny (*De unitate intellectus,* Paris, 1270). He "forestalled" the question of the eternity of the world. For Aquinas, the doctrine of creation signifies that the world at every moment depends on divine will, as light depends on the sun. That there was a beginning in time is a matter of faith (*De aeternitate mundi,* Paris, spring 1271). In a rather general way, Aquinas conceives the world in an Aristotelian manner, the objects that form this world each have a stable and autonomous nature, and God created them to grant them an act of being. The idea of Providence can be found here: God gives each creature what it needs in order to attain the perfection that is proper to it. And the economy of salvation* is replaced, as an adaptation of Providence to man's nature*, led by his liberty* into a fall that only an intervention in history could redeem.

c) A Nuanced Integration. In opposition to the first condemnations, the study of Aristotle became mandatory in theological training. In this sense Christendom was distinct from the Muslim and Jewish worlds in two ways, the coexistence of which may seem paradoxical:

1) Never did Christendom consider, like al-Farabi, that after Aristotle there was nothing else to look for, and that it was only matter of teaching (Kitàb al-hurùf, §143, ed. Mahdi); or, like Averroes, that Aristotle was the unsurpassable summit of human possibility, a gift from God who only yielded such a gift to the prophets (Commentary on "*De gen. an.*" I: Ed. Des Juntes, vol. VI-2, Venice, 1562; "*De anima*" III, §14, Ed. Crawford; *Tahàfut al-tahàfut* III, §83, Ed. Bouyges). Rather, it followed Maimonides, who seemed to limit the validity of Aristotelianism to the sublunary domain; what is above—metaphysics—escapes him (Guide II, 22, Ed. Joël, Tr. Munk). Albert* the Great, for example, writes: "He who thinks that Aristotle was a God must think that he never made a mistake. But if one thinks he was a man, then, without a doubt, he could have made mistakes like us" (Physique VIII, Ed. P. Hossfeld, *Opera Omnia,* IV-2).
2) The Muslim and Jewish worlds never introduced the study of all of Aristotle's philosophy into the education of their elite. At most, Islam trained its jurists *(fuqahā),* cadis, and the like in the use of basic logic inspired in part by Aristotle. The primitive apologetic *(kalàm)* most often rested on a discontinuous vision of the world, with material and temporal atoms, which are not so much borrowed from Aristotle as from his adversaries. As for the Aristotelian *falāsifa,* it was never able to get out of the private domain to acquire social legitimacy, and even less to enter into dialogue with something like a "theology."

In Latin Christendom after the 13th century, Aristotelianism would be known above all within the context of Scholasticism. In similar fashion, after the 12th century Islam knew Aristotelianism in the form of Avicenna's synthesis, and Judaism* knew it through Maimonides, with whom Averroes would very soon be associated. In Greek Christendom, two factors were added: 1) The persistence of the Platonic tradition, starting with the Platonic dialogues, which Latin Christendom and Islam only knew in part; it constituted a counterbalance to Aristotelianism, the influence of which was therefore less exclusive; and 2) the Fathers' suspicion of the "logical subtleties" lasted to the end for the Byzantine theologians, who readily left Aristotle to mere philosophers.

Thinkers of the Italian Renaissance attempted to revive a more authentic Aristotle, sometimes borrowing the interpretation, more or less well known, of Alexander of Aphrodisias. This seemed to pose a threat to dogma, especially on the question of the soul's immortality (the Paduans, Pomponazzi). The Reformation began, and with that came Luther*'s systematic attack on Aristotle's role in theology: "It is a mistake to say: without Aristotle one cannot become theologian.... On the contrary, one does become a theologian unless one does so against Aristotle.... All of Aristotle is to theology what darkness is to light" (*Disputatio contra scholsticam theologiam,* 1517, §43 *Sq,* 50, WA, v. 1). Nor did Luther shy away from the lewd in making his attack: philosophy, he says, is "the whore of Aristotle." This did not stop Melanchthon from quickly making Aristotle a supreme authority of philosophy taught in Protestant universities, even to the point that the *Disputationes Metaphysicae* (1597) of the Jesuit Spaniard Francisco Suarez*, modeled on Aristotle's *Metaphysics,* became one of the basic books of German academic philosophy (Peterson 1921).

At the end of the 19th century, the Catholic world underwent a Thomist renaissance. In 1879 the encyclical *Aeterni Patris* of Pope* Leo XIII recommended the study of Saint Thomas. For some this was the occasion to reduce the Thomist theological synthesis—from which one attempts to extract a theory—to what comes from Aristotle, by eliminating Neoplatonic elements from it. Hence was formed an "Aristotelian-Thomist" philosophy, systematized in manuals and taught in seminaries in quasi-official fashion.

• P. Petersen (1921), *Geschichte der Aristotelischen Philosophie im protestantischen Deutschland,* Leipzig.
A.-J. Festugière (1932), "Aristote dans la littérature grecque chrétienne jusqu'à Théodoret," *L'idéal religieux des Grecs et l'Évangile,* Paris, 221–63.
R.P. McKeon (1939), "Aristotelianism in Western Christianity," in J.T. McNeill (Ed.), *Environmental Factors in Christian History,* Chicago, 206–31.
J.H. Waszink, W. Heffening (1950), "Aristoteles," *RAC* 1, col. 657–67.
E. von Ivánka (1964), *Plato Christianus: Übernahme und Umgestaltung des Platonismus durch die Väter,* Einsiedeln.
W. Böhm (1967), *Johannes Philoponos* (...), Ausgewählte Schriften (...), Munich, etc.
C. Stead (1977), *Divine Substance,* Oxford.

S. Lilla (1983), "Aristotelismo," *DPAC* 1, col. 349–63.
C.B. Schmitt (1983), *Aristotle and the Renaissance,* Cambridge, Mass.
L.G. Benakis (1987), "Grundbibliographie zum Aristoteles-Studium in Byzanz," in J. Wiesner (Ed.), *Aristoteles Werk und Wirkung: Paul Moraux gewidmet,* vol. 2, Berlin, etc., 352–79.
S. Pines (1987), "Some Distinctive Metaphysical Conceptions in Themistius' Commentary on Book Lambda and Their Place in the History of Philosophy," ibid., 177–204.
R. Sorabji (1987) (Ed.), *Philoponus and the Rejection of Aristotelian Science,* London.
R. Brague (1991), "Le destin de la "pensée de la pensée" des origines au début du Moyen Age," in T. de Koninck, G. Planty-Bonjour (Ed.), *La question de Dieu chez Aristote et Hegel,* Paris, 153–86.

RÉMI BRAGUE

See also **Maximus the Confessor; Naturalism; Platonism, Christian; Stoicism, Christian; Thomas Aquinas; Thomism**

Arminianism

Jacobus Arminius (1560–1609), a theologian from Leyden, was led by the study of the Epistle to the Romans to call into question the Calvinist doctrine of predestination*. In Leyden he encountered opposition from his colleague Francis Gomar (1563–1641), who accused him of Pelagianism* and Socinianism, accusations from which Arminius exculpated himself in a public debate in The Hague in 1603. He attempted without success to secure the revision of the two basic confessional documents of Dutch Calvinism*, the *Confessio Belgica* and the *Catechism of Heidelberg.* Arminius's doctrines were systematically set out in the "Remonstrance" of 1610: compatibility of divine omnipotence with human freedom*; Jesus died for all, not only for the elect; rejection of predestination, both after the Fall ("infralapsarian" predestination) and before the Fall ("supralapsarian" predestination). Orthodox Calvinist opposition to Arminius was led for a long time by Gomar. In 1618–19, the Synod of Dordrecht condemned Arminianism. The "remonstrants," also accused of collusion with Spain, were at first persecuted, then eventually tolerated. Arminianism exercised considerable influence on High Church Anglicans (notably on Archbishop Laud and the Erastianism* of his associates). It also exercised a decisive influence on John Wesley (Methodism*).

• G.J. Hoenderdaal (1979), "Arminius/Arminianism," *TRE* 4, 63–69 (bibl.).
A. F. L. Sell (1982), *The Great Debate: Calvinism, Arminianism and Salvation,* Worthing.

JEAN-YVES LACOSTE

See also **Calvinism; Erastianism**

Art. *See* **Architecture; Images; Music**

Ascension. *See* **Christ/Christology**

Asceticism

I. Definitions

The word *asceticism* is derived from the Greek *askèsis* (from the verb *askeô*), meaning "training" or "exercise," originally of an athletic nature. Already in Plato, the word had acquired the meaning of moral or philosophical training, or practice. Although the word is not used in the New Testament, it is found very early in the Apostolic* Fathers, in the philosophical sense (to practice patience: Ignatius of Antioch, *Polycarp* 9, 1), and also applied to martyrdom *(Martyrdom of Polycarp).* In later Christian writers, both the verb and the noun are used very generally in the sense of training the soul* to practice virtues* and overcome temptation, or to designate one who leads a life of self-denial, especially as a hermit or monk, that is, an "ascetic" *(askètès). Askèsis* comes to be used generally to mean "austerity," or a regime of austerity (as well as retaining the important meaning of "study," especially of Scripture*), and an *askètèrion,* or place of *askèsis,* was a monastery. This brief survey of the use of the Greek root-word reveals three things: the link quickly established between asceticism and monasticism*; the philosophical background of the term and concept; and an original link between asceticism and martyrdom.

II. Origins of Christian Asceticism

1. Asceticism and Eschatology: Martyrdom

The link between asceticism and martyrdom lies behind certain distinctive and lasting features of Christian asceticism. The use of the language of asceticism in relation to martyrdom was something inherited by the early Christian Church* from the Jewish experience, especially from 4 Maccabees, a late work of reflection on the experience of the Jewish martyrs under Judas Maccabaeus (†161 B.C.) that had a powerful influence on early Christian reflection on martyrdom, as can be seen in the early Christian accounts of persecutions and in the letters written by Ignatius of Antioch on his way to his own martyrdom. The text of 4 Maccabees uses the language of training and athletic effort in relation to the Jewish martyrs, because it considers these martyrs as soldiers enlisted in a holy war* against the powers of evil*, represented by the idolatrous government of Antiochus IV Epiphanes, who sought to stamp out the Jewish religion. Similar ideas are found in the writings of the Qumran community, which also saw itself as a kind of standing army-in-training for the coming final outbreak of warfare between the powers of Good* (the faithful Israelites) and the powers of Evil (the occupying forces of the Romans). This notion of preparation for eschatological warfare, the holy war against the powers of Evil, meant that those in training for it observed the regulations for fighting a holy war, which included abstinence from sexual contact. Such abstinence had huge symbolic significance: it indicated that one was prepared for the end of history* and the coming of the kingdom* of God*, quite apart from any significance it might have as a mark of individual austerity. This has remained the case with Christian monasticism and Christian asceticism in general.

2. Protological Justification of Asceticism

The most important reason for early Christian asceticism was without doubt *eschatological.* There were, however, two other justifications, either given or implied, in much early Christian practice. Alongside the obvious *moral* or *moralistic* justification, which regards austerity as leading to personal self-control, there was another widespread justification that might be regarded as *protological:* that is, concerned with the restoration of the original state of humankind that has been overthrown by sin and the Fall (original sin*). This attempt to find one's way back to the beginning, to the original state, was a concern that Christians shared with many of their contemporaries, both pagan and Jewish, and like them they saw the beginning as characterized by unity, distance from that unity being characterized by increasing multiplicity. Marriage* and procreation* could obviously be regarded as participating in multiplicity, and even adding to it; so, too, could alimentation, as prolonging into a cumulative future beings that had already wandered far from their origin. Sexual abstinence and rejection of marriage, together with abstinence from food and drink, could therefore be regarded as an attempt to stem further progress into multiplicity, and to mark the beginning of an attempt to trace one's way back to the undivided unity of the origin (even though marriage, in itself, could certainly also be regarded as something unitive). Because sexual congress between Adam and Eve is first recorded after their expulsion from paradise (Gn 4:1), it became very generally held that in paradise itself there was no sexual activity, nor had sexual activity ever been intended for man in his unfallen state, despite Genesis 1:28; those who held this view also held that unfallen propagation would not have involved sexuality. Among the Fathers*, only Augustine (perhaps following the shadowy "Ambrosiaster": *Quaestiones* 127) seriously and explicitly questioned this, upholding in the works of his maturity (e.g., *De Gen. ad litt.* 9, 3, 6) that marriage and procreation were part of God's plan for the original paradisal life (Irenaeus also perhaps envisaged something like this: *see Demonstratio* 14). This general acceptance that sexual differentiation and propagation of the species pointed away from the human primordial state provided a fertile intellectual context for the enthusiasm for sexual continence that was an aspect of Christianity.

III. New Testament

The idea of asceticism, of ascetic training, needs to be distinguished from the practice of the virtues as such. Asceticism means training for some purpose, whereas practice of the virtues, especially the practice of love*, is seen in the New Testament, and Christianity in general, as a manifestation of the fruits of the Spirit* (Gal 6:22).

1. Jesus Christ

The commandment to love (Mt 22:37–40 par.) is not primarily ascetic: it points to the essential nature of Christian community, which is itself a response to God's love for mankind. Nonetheless, in a later Christian tradition*, even love is sometimes regarded in an ascetic light, as we shall see. Properly ascetic doctrine in the teaching of Jesus and in the rest of the New Testament is nearly always—like the understanding of martyrdom outlined above—eschatological: in other words, it concerns training for the end, the *eschaton,* the coming of the kingdom of God. The key themes in this teaching are patient endurance (*hupomonè,* which also has the sense of patient expectation) and vigilance. Following Christ* means "taking up one's cross" (Mt 16:24): it is not a momentary decision, but a matter of one's whole life. The "synoptic apocalypse" (Mt 24:4–36 par.), the teaching that Jesus gave to his disciples immediately before his final days, speaks constantly of patience and watchfulness, as do the parables* that follow it in the account in Matthew. It is these themes that are developed in the rest of the New Testament.

2. Paul

Paul puts patient endurance in a sequence that leads the Christian to openness to God's love: "tribulation works patient endurance, endurance leads to testing, and testing to hope, and hope does not disappoint, because the love of God is poured out into our hearts by the Holy Spirit that has been given to us" (Rom 5:3 ff.).

In the New Testament, the word *tribulation (thlipsis)* usually suggests troubles that are signs of the final conflict between the forces of good and the forces of evil, and that might lead to martyrdom: throughout the New Testament, martyrdom and the expectation of the end (more precisely, the Second Coming of Christ) provide the horizon against which Christian action is played out.

3. Imitation of Christ

Jesus Christ is, of course, the model for such asceticism. His patient endurance is an example to those who seek to follow him (Ignatius of Antioch, *Polycarp* 8, 2): those who have been granted to become martyrs have been given the grace of special closeness to him. The martyr is the archetypal saint. However, although the New Testament presents Jesus as an example, as one to follow, the real goal is something much more inward, more intimate. Both Paul and John speak of indwelling: Christ dwelling in the hearts of Christians (Eph 3:17) or, more commonly, an indwelling of all Christians "in Christ" (Rom 12:5, but very commonly in the other Pauline epistles), and even the indwelling of the Trinity* in the disciples (Jn 14:23). On one striking occasion, Paul speaks of bearing the cross as an ascesis that leads to the manifestation of the life of the Risen Christ in one's own life: "always carrying in the body the death of Jesus, so that the life of Jesus may also be manifested in our bodies" (2 Cor 4:10).

IV. Development of Christian Asceticism

Early Christianity was enthusiastically ascetic: the origins of this asceticism were, we have argued, primarily eschatological, although protological considerations were powerfully supportive. Two features of Christianity were regularly cited by the apologists of the second century in favor of the truth* of the Christian religion: martyrdom and virginity (*see* Justin, *1 Apol.* 15 f.). Martyrdom was evident witness to the truth of Christianity, and virginity, much prized by the philosophers though less commonly embraced by them, demonstrated the power of Christianity, a power that sprang from its truth. In some branches of early Christianity (e.g., in Syria, it is argued), a vow of celibacy may even have been a requirement for baptism*. Christianity was hard pressed to prevent Christian asceticism from leading to an outright rejection of the material in the name of a metaphysical dualism. Throughout Christian history, the attractions of dualistic movements (Manicheanism, Paulicianism, Bogomilism, Catharism) have posed serious problems.

1. Clement and Origen

The development of Christian ascetic theory has been largely the preserve of monasticism, but the ground was prepared by the Christian Platonists of Alexandria*, Clement and Origen* (Christian Platonism*). Clement, in particular, developed the ideal of martyrdom in the direction of an inward ascetic struggle, which he called "spiritual martyrdom" (spiritual life*, III), and made use of the ideas of classical philosophy, especially Platonic and Stoic philosophy, in his working out of this ideal. Clement seems to have been a favorite author with the more intellectually inclined monks of the desert, especially with Evagrius (†399), who was the theorist of this early monasticism. Also influential was Origen, although certain aspects of the Origenist influence led to controversy. Despite Evagrius's condemnation as an Origenist—formally in the East, by the Patriarch of Alexandria, Theophilus, in 400, and by the Emperor Justinian in the sixth century, and informally, though much more effectively, in the West, explicitly by Jerome and implicitly by Augustine—the influence of Evagrius's rationale of ascetic theology* had vast influence.

2. Evagrius

For Evagrius, the monastic life could be divided into three stages: *praktikè,* the active effort to form the virtues and to fight temptation; *phusikè,* natural contemplation*, that is, contemplation of the inner meaning and structure of the created order, including God's design for humankind (his "economy"), which was worked out through that order; and, finally, *theologia,* the contemplation of the blessed Trinity*. What Evagrius has to say about asceticism is mainly found in his substantial teaching on *praktikè,* and draws, through Clement and Origen, on the psychological wisdom of the philosophers.

a) Platonic Doctrine of the Soul. Fundamental to Evagrius's understanding of the soul is Plato's division of it into three parts: intellect *(noûs),* aggressivity *(thumos),* and desire *(epithumia).* The true self, as with Plato, is the intellect, and its purpose is contemplation. Evagrius, however, puts this in a somewhat different way: for him, the natural state of the intellect is prayer *(Practicos).* Asceticism therefore concerns the training needed for the uninterrupted pursuit of prayer. He uses the Platonic tripartite understanding of the soul to elucidate what this involves. The lower parts of the soul can prevent the intellect from engaging in prayer, either by distracting it from its purpose or by blocking its activity.

The desiring part of the soul produces images of desirable things that draw the attention of the intellect away from God. What is involved here is more complex and more profound than is apparent. It is not just a matter of desirable objects, but rather the nexus of activities that absorb one's energies as one seeks to satisfy desire. The resulting "distraction" breaks the intellect's attention and withdraws it from prayer. Much of Evagrius's ascetic theology is concerned with understanding the psychic mechanisms involved in desire and its satisfaction, but the purpose of all this understanding of the soul is to enable it to attain a state of perpetual prayer. The aggressive part of the soul hinders the intellect from prayer, not so much by distracting it, but, more fundamentally, by blocking it. Anger, Evagrius says, is like a cloud cutting off the soul from God. In both cases, Evagrius suggests various remedies for dealing with these distracting or blocking mechanisms (e.g., *De oratione* 9, 19–27, 31, 83, 90, 98, 105).

b) The Eight Logismoi. At this stage, Evagrius introduces a much more elaborate understanding of the temptations and propensities of the human person. Temptations play on the natural reactions, called in Greek *pathè,* or "passions*." These passions are brought into play by thoughts or images, which Evagrius calls *logismoi:* perhaps not so much "thoughts" as "series of thoughts." Particularly in the case of hermits (with whom Evagrius is mainly concerned), passions are aroused through the stimulation of trains of thought by demons*. In the case of monks living in communities, and even more so in the case of Christians living in the world*, the passions are aroused by friction with other people. These passions, or the *logismoi* associated with them, are grouped by Evagrius into eight categories: gluttony, fornication, avarice, grief, anger, listlessness, vanity, and pride. (This is the origin of the later Western doctrine of the seven deadly sins*.) Some of these passions are directly associated with one of the parts of the soul—gluttony, fornication, and avarice with the desiring part, anger with the aggressive part—but there is no strict correlation, and some of the passions affect more than one part of the soul (e.g., listlessness affects all three parts). Evagrius's discussion of these passions (e.g., in *Practicos*) and, even more, the treatment of these passions in the sayings of the Desert Fathers (some collections of which have been organized around Evagrius's leading notions), show a profound awareness of the kind of games that we play with ourselves. Gluttony, for instance, is not just greed for too much food, or for especially delectable food, but may also include worries about diet, and the way in which food itself, or the rituals of eating, can become a focus for deep-seated anxieties. Nor is fornication simple lust: dealing with fornication includes also acceptance of the fact that, however habitual one's austerity, one's body can still remind one of the realm within oneself that cannot be easily subjugated to the dictates of reason*, as well as being aware that the quest for a sexual relationship can be part of the longing for family life. Evagrius envisages the austere life of the hermit, but the principles that he discerns in his discussion of the ways in which the passions tend to make our lives reactive could easily be given a wider application.

c) Apatheia. For Evagrius, the intellect needs to be freed from the disturbance of the passions if it is to engage in prayer. Ascetic practice is aimed at preventing such disturbance, or at least rendering the intellect invulnerable to such disturbance. Central to Evagrius's discussion is the notion of *apatheia* (state of nonpassion, of "impassivity"), borrowed from the Stoics by way of Clement of Alexandria. Possession of *apatheia* means that the soul is free from reactive behavior and is able to direct its attention as it wants, which will mean primarily to God, but it also means that the soul will be able to tend effectively and disinterestedly to the needs of others. It is often misunderstood as a bleak lack of passion, not least by Jerome, whose misunderstanding meant that the term was never adopted in the West. Evagrius's disciple Cassian, who brought the wisdom of his master to the Latin world, spoke instead of "purity of heart," which has a very different resonance. The whole purpose of *praktikè* is, for Evagrius, to create a state of *apatheia* that will make it possible for the soul to love selflessly and pray undistractedly. However, natural contemplation (the object of *phusikè*) also has ascetic functions. First, in natural contemplation the intellect learns to contemplate, by learning how to behold the world without being attached to it. Second, the intellect begins to understand the constitution of the created order, and especially the human person. This understanding is an important quality in a spiritual father (spiritual life* IV 2 e) who is concerned to help others in finding their way to pure prayer.

d) Synergy. If there is very little said explicitly about grace* in Evagrius's ascetic theology, this is neither because Evagrius has a defective understanding of grace, nor because he understands asceticism to be a purely human activity, but rather because Evagrius, along with much of the Eastern tradition, takes for granted that any human striving toward God is, in fact, a human response to God, and thus a working together *(sunergeia)* with God. Asceticism then, in the Eastern tradition, presupposes grace. In the West, by contrast, the relationship between ascetic practice and grace poses a problem. Even before the Pelagian controversy, Augustine had come to mistrust the claims made for asceticism by some of his contemporaries: his self-analysis in the second half of Book X of the *Confessions* exposes in detail how deeply he is in need of grace, of the Mediator, and, rather than indicating any ascetic remedies, he makes clear how impossible it would be for any discipline to bring him to a fit state to behold God. This mistrust of asceticism was only deepened in Augustine's conflict with Pelagianism*, and in his final exchange with the monks of Provence he seems to set no store by asceticism at all. In his own life, however, Augustine was extremely austere, and in his monastic rule asceticism has an important place—not, however, as self-cultivation of the individual, but rather as setting down ground rules for a life of brotherhood.

3. Asceticism of the Common Life

a) Monasticism. In the practice of monasticism, the inexorable asceticism imposed by life in community quickly came to be regarded as being at least as important as austerity, as the way by which the individual sought to restore the image-likeness to God. In both the *Rule* of Basil and that of Benedict, the surrender of one's self-will for the sake of the common life, symbolized in the acceptance of obedience to the abbot, comes to be regarded as the center of the monk's inner asceticism. The monastic round of prayer, and especially the importance attached to vigil and prayer during the night, also preserves the eschatological root of asceticism. The danger that ascetic prowess may lead to a self-control that verges on pride is one that is fully recognized in the traditions of communal ("cenobitic") monasticism.

b) Overcoming the Isolation of the Fall. The deepest meaning of asceticism in a Christian sense is to work toward and restore the perfection of the image of God in human beings. It is therefore an attempt to restore the damage done by the Fall. As such, it is affected by how that Fall has been understood. If the Fall is understood as Adam's deception by Eve, then asceticism will stress avoidance of the bonds of sexual companionship and family. If the Fall is seen as submission to the pleasure of the senses (for the fruit of the tree was "a delight to the eyes"), the denial of sensuous pleasure will become an important feature of asceticism (encouraged by Platonic dualism). Both these views are found among Christian thinkers, but a much more general and fundamental understanding of the Fall sees it as an act of disobedience toward God, or as an assertion of self in place of God, or, more philosophically, as acquiescence in the illusion, which each human being has, that he or she is the center of the world. Hence the importance, found in all Christian asceticism, of self-denial, humility, and loving service toward others (in this sense, love assumes an ascetic role). Throughout the Christian tradition, the heart of asceticism is found in acceptance of the reality and claims of the "other," the refusal to exploit the other, and, indeed, an acknowledgment of encounter with the other as encounter with Christ himself (Mt 25:31–45). In monasticism, the discipline of community life dwarfs other ascetic "disciplines." The *Rule of St. Benedict* does not include chastity or poverty among the monastic vows: the monk vows himself to stability, conversion* of life, and obedience—that is, staying in the monastery, conforming his life to that of the community, and obedience to the abbot and the *Rule.* Chastity and poverty are the inevitable corollaries of such a communal life. Humility and repentance are the requirements of recognizing the other in each of one's brothers. Such principles of asceticism could readily be worked out in relation to married life, where the relationship itself becomes the primary discipline, demanding humility and repentance if it is to last.

V. External Forms of Asceticism

To the modern ear, the word *asceticism* suggests nothing so apparently humdrum as faithfulness and putting the other first. One thinks of hair shirts, flagellation, or extreme fasts and sleep deprivation. All of these have had their place in the history of Christian asceticism, although in fact none of the classical monastic rules ever makes much mention of them (except to forbid excessive asceticism as exhibitionism, or, worse, a breach of obedience). They are also sometimes misunderstood. In general, mortification—especially in the form of flagellation, which was popular well into the 20th century—is muted in much modern practice. Insofar as this is a recognition of the ambiguity of any form of self-inflicted pain, with dangers of exhibitionism (always recognized) and sadomasochism (perhaps less so, although Saint John* of the Cross was well aware of this danger), it is hardly to be discouraged.

a) Fasting. Fasting, which has ceased to be a general requirement in modern Christianity, save for the Orthodox, is not a matter of food deprivation. One does not feel hungry during the Lenten fast, but food lacks variety and is less distracting: it also serves a symbolic function, in marking out Lent as a preparation for Easter. To put it bluntly: unless one fasts, feasting ceases to be feasting, a joyful celebration of days or periods as special.

b) Almsgiving. Almsgiving is one of the forms of asceticism most commonly recommended by the Fathers to those who live in the world. In the early centuries, and indeed well into the modern period, the almsgiving of Christians living in the world enabled the church, and institutions under the aegis of the church, to provide for the poor, the disabled, and the sick. In the modern world, in many countries such welfare provision has been taken over by the state. It is, however, precisely those countries where many Christians are comfortably off and need to regard almsgiving as an ascetic discipline.

c) Pilgrimage. Pilgrimage* is another ascetic practice, involving as it does, to some degree, an uprooting from comfortable familiarity, and a recognition of the need to go in search of the *unum necessarium.*

d) Fool for Christ. A further individual way of asceticism, commonly associated with the Byzantine East, though by no means confined to it, is the way of the "innocent." Perhaps our modern technological society* has more need of this witness than of any other, since it runs counter to all its values. Christian asceticism may have a prophetic value, not simply being directed toward individual sanctification, but presenting a challenge to the accepted norms of society. However, the example of the fool for Christ brings out another aspect of asceticism, namely that, because each human being is a unique image of God, there cannot and should not be uniformity in ascetic practices.

• F. X. Funk, K. Bihlmeyer, W. Schneemelcher (Ed.), *Die Apostolischen Väter,* 3rd Ed., Tübingen, 1970.
"Ambrosiaster" (unknown Roman priest whose exegesis was attributed to Ambrose), *Quaestiones veteris et novi testamenti,* CSEL 50.
Augustine, *Confessions,* BAug 13–14; *De Genesi ad litteram,* BAug 48–49.
Basil of Caesarea, *Asceticon magnum,* PG 31, 905–1305.
Evagrius, *Practicos,* SC 170 and 171; *De oratione,* in Nicodème l'Hagiorite (Ed.), *Philokalia,* 5 vols., Athens, 1957 (3rd Ed. 1963), I, 176–89.
Irenaeus, *The Demonstration of the Apostolic Preaching,* SC 62.
Justin Martyr, *Apologia,* in E. J. Goodspeed, *Die ältesten Apologeten,* Göttingen, 1914, 26–89.
♦ A. Stolz (1948), *L'ascèse chrétienne,* Chèvetogne.

H. von Campenhausen (1960 *a*), "Die Askese im Urchristentum," in *Tradition und Leben: Kräfte der Kirchengeschichte,* Tübingen, 114–56; (1960 *b*), "Die asketische Heimatlosigkeit im altkirchlichen und frühmittelalterlichen Mönchtum," ibid., 290–317.
S. Brock (1973), "Early Syrian Asceticism," *Numen* 20, 1–19.
R. Murray (1975), "The Features of the Earliest Christian Asceticism," in Peter Brook (Ed.), *Christian Spirituality: Essays in Honour of Gordon Rupp,* London, 63–77.
V. and E. Turner (1978), *Image and Pilgrimage in Christian Culture,* Oxford.
J. Saward (1980), *Perfect Fools: Folly for Christ's Sake in Catholic and Orthodox Spirituality,* Oxford.
U. Bianchi (Ed.) (1985), *La Tradizione dell'encrateia: Motivazioni ontologiche e protologiche,* Rome.
R. Brague (1985), "L'image et l'acédie," *RThom* 87, 197–228.
C. W. Bynum (1987), *Holy Feast and Holy Fast: The Religious Significance of Food to Mediaeval Women,* Berkeley.
P. Brown (1988), *The Body and Society: Men, Women and Sexual Renunciation in Early Christianity,* New York.
V. Wimbush, R. Valentarsis (Ed.) (1995), *Asceticism,* New York.

Andrew Louth

See also **Contemplation; Life, Spiritual; Mysticism; Prayer; Spiritual Theology**

Aseitas

a) Definition. The Latin word *aseitas* is the abstract form of *ens a se. Aseitas* is the fact of existing in oneself, of having *esse* by oneself, and can therefore be applied only to God*. The term is used in Latin ontological theology. In parallel with the division of being* by categories taught by Aristotle (substance and accident, *per se* and *per aliud*), this theology proposes another division based on the idea of the creation*: to the Creator corresponds the *ens a se* and to created beings the *ens ab alio (abalietas). Aseitas* thus negatively designates the absence of any ontological dependence, and positively the fullness of divine sovereignty. Although the idea of *aseitas* is present in various forms in Latin theology*, the term itself is recent and has been in frequent use only since the 19th century, within the Neoscholastic movement and particularly in philosophy* and theology influenced by Suarez*.

b) Patristics and Medieval Theology. The Greek fathers of the church* used several terms to indicate the absolute sovereignty of God, such as *anarkhos* (Tatian) and *agennètos* (Irenaeus*, Cyril of Jerusalem).

Augustine* is the distant herald of the notion of *aseitas* insofar as he rejects any comprehension of the Principle as *causa sui*: "Nothing exists that engenders itself" (*De Trinitate* I. i. 1; BAug 15. 89). The Neoplatonists, for their part, had no hesitation in attributing this property to the Principle: "He is self-producing" (Plotinus, *Enneads* VI. 8. 15); "he is himself the cause of himself *(aition heautou),* of himself and by himself" (ibid., 14, *see* 16). And Proclus even extended this eternal reflection to existences and intelligences that enjoy sufficient perfection to give themselves means of existence. "He is himself his own cause" *(aition heautô)* (Proclus, *Elements of Theology* no. 46, *see* no. 43). This proposition marked the birth of the *causa sui* in the Latin version of the *Book of Causes:* "And he becomes cause of himself *(causa sui)* only by his relation to his cause; and this relation is his very formation" (*Book of Causes* prop. 26, comm.). Some Fathers of the Church, such as Marius Victorinus, took up the concept. Cyril* of Alexandria, citing the Orphic Hymns (Kern Ed. 254), says of God that he is *autogennètos* (*Contra Julian* 35 c, SC 322, 176).

Augustine's opposition was thus a break with Neoplatonism. In order to name what absolutely distinguishes the Creator from created beings, Augustine uses the expression *habens esse ut sit* (*De Genesi ad litteram* 5. 16, PL 34, col. 333, no. 34): God possesses in himself the being through which he is. The Augustinian principle was systematized by Nicholas of Amiens, *De arte fidei* I. 8 (PL 210, 600a): *Nihil est causa sui* (Nothing is the cause of itself). This would be quoted by all medieval theologians to support the interpretation of divine *aseitas.* The Augustinian formulation is nuanced in Anselm*. On the one hand, Anselm says *a se* instead of *in se;* on the other, he does not pose the problem from the point of view of *esse* (being, existence), but from the point of view of the divine nature (*habeat a se sine alterius naturæ auxilio esse quidquid est; Monol.* c. 26; *see* Schmitt I. 44). Following Augustine, Anselm emphasizes the absence of ontological indignation (*nullo alio indigens; Prosl.*, Prooemium, *see* Schmitt I. 93; *Ep. de Incarnatione* I, c. 11; *see* Schmitt I. 290), and positively asserts the idea of supreme perfection (*esse perfectum; Monol.* c. 28; *see* Schmitt I. 112).

Hugh and Richard of Saint Victor attributed to God *esse a smetipso.* Thomas* Aquinas proposed a primary division of being: "being by essence" (CG 2, c. 15, 4um) and "being by participation." He proposed a secondary division corresponding to the division of being according to the categories of Aristotle: "being by itself" (substance) and "being by accident" (accidents). Even though the term *aseitas* is absent from his works (*see Index Thomisticus*), the equivalent is found in the expression "God is his own being" (*De Ver.* q. 2, a. 1, resp.; *ST* Ia, q. 3, a. 4, resp.), which constitutes the raison d'être of divine simplicity* (*De Ver.* q. 2, a. 1, resp.). The perspective chosen, that of being, *esse,* excludes any idea of "possession," *habere.* And by saying that "God is his own being," Thomas establishes the infinite nature of divine essence, as such radically different from any quantitative infinity (*De Ver.* q. 2, a. 2, ad 5). Analogous formulations can be found in Duns* Scotus. As for Nicholas* of Cusa, he associates and distinguishes at the same time *causa sui* and subsistence by oneself *(auhupostaton),* in a context inspired by Proclus: "All things that do not subsist by themselves, as they are not causes of themselves... are by a cause, which is their reason for being subsisting by itself" (*Philosophisch-theologische Schriften,* vol. 2, Vienna, 1966).

c) Modern Philosophy and Theology. The idea of *aseitas* is diametrically opposed to the idea of *ens causa sui* (Descartes, Spinoza), to that of a being that would be its own "cause." Avicenna had already dismissed any idea of causality within the First (God), for the reason that God has no essence *(quidditas).* And Bonaventure* had excluded the idea of a God who was the product of himself, *a se ipso*[*fieri*]. Descartes*, however, authorized the rule of *causa sui* by bringing together the two meanings of the expression, sovereign freedom and self-production, and attributing them to God. By virtue of the principle of reason, divine *aseitas* was therefore expressed in terms of reflexive causality: "This name [*causa sui*] can be no more usefully employed than to demonstrate the existence of God" (Descartes, *Réponses aux quatrièmes objections*). Thus God is himself through the identification of his power with the principle of reason, an ambivalent act in which is indicated both a submission to the principle and an absolute transcendence.

Having become the engendering of existence from essence, *causa sui* was to be the keystone of Spinoza's *Ethics:* "By cause of itself I understand that whose essence envelops existence" (I. 1, def. 1). And in German idealism, even when the absolute is no longer substance but subject, the term "cause of itself" is still appropriate: "Spinoza's error did not lie in this idea, but in the simple fact of positing it outside of any self" (Schelling*, *On the Self*). The absolute self, "being conditioned by itself" (Schelling, *The Form of Philosophy in General*), is both omnipotence and ontological proof, and the *causa sui* presides over the completion of ontology and theology, as set forth by Hegel* in the self-effectuation of the Absolute: it is "the absolute truth of the cause" (*Encyclopedia of Philosophical Sciences* I, *Science of Logic* §153). But *causa sui* has been distinctly rejected as contradictory in theology (Kleutgen) as well as in philosophy (Nietzsche*, Sartre). The notion of causality is of value within the realm of the created and does not apply to the Creator.

The two aspects, negative and positive, of *aseitas* have been brought to the fore by many representatives of Neoscholasticism (Billot, Farges, Scheeben*). For some (Billuart, Kleutgen, Lehmen, Lennerz), *aseitas* is the principal divine attribute*, or the metaphysical essence of God, *essentia Dei metaphysica,* from which all the other attributes logically flow. Debates on the "metaphysical essence of God" have also led to a distinction (Lafosse) between an "inadequate *aseitas,*" denoting the negative aspect, which is the exclusion of any causality; and an "adequate *aseitas,*" a concept designating the divine plenitude of Being. It is in this dual sense that Franzelin, for example, interprets the notion of *ens a se:* its content implies simultaneously the negation of any participation, and the affirmation of an Absolute Being that was already present in Anselm (*"absolutum," "absolute esse," "solum esse"; Monol.* c. 28; *see* Schmitt I. 46).

• C.R. Billuart (1754), *Summa Summae S. Thomae, sive compendium theologiae...,* I, diss. II, a. 1, §1 *Sq,* Liège.
Lafosse (1839), *Theologiae cursus completus* (Migne) vol. 7, Paris, 83.
J. Kleutgen (1867), *Die Theologie der Vorzeit,* vol. 1, Münster, 226–36.
J.B. Franzelin (1876), *Tractatus de Deo uno,* sect. III, c. I, Rome, 259.
A. Farges (1894), *L'idée de Dieu d'après la raison et la science,* Paris, 287.
L. Billot (1897), *De Deo uno et trino,* Rome, 81.
A. Lehmen, H. Lennerz (1923), *Lehrbuch der Philosophie,* vol. 3: *Theodizee,* 148–54.
P. Descoqs (1925), *Institutiones metaphysicae generalis: Éléments d'ontologie,* Paris.
E. Przywara (1932), *Analogia entis,* Munich (2nd Ed. Einsiedeln, 1962).
M. Blondel (1935), *L'Être et les êtres,* Paris, 174–75.
N. Hartmann (1935), *Zur Grundlegung der Ontologie,* Berlin.
É. Gilson (1948), *L'être et l'essence,* Paris.
C. Nink (1952), *Ontologie: Versuch einer Grundlegung,* Freiburg.

É. Gilson (1964), *Le thomisme. Introduction à la philosophie de saint Thomas d'Aquin,* 6th Ed., rev., Paris.
J. de Finance (1966), *Connaissance de l'Être: Traité d'ontologie,* Paris-Bruges.
L. de Raeymaeker (1970), *Philosophie de l'Être: Essai de synthèse métaphysique,* 3rd Ed., Louvain-Paris.
B. Weissmahr (1983), *Philosophische Gotteslehre,* Stuttgart.
S. Breton (1986), "Réflexions sur la *causa sui,*" *RSPhTh* 70, 349–64.
C. Viola (1992), "'*hoc est enim Deo esse, quod est magnum esse*': Approche augustinienne de la grandeur divine," in M.-O. Goulet-Cazé, et al. (Ed.), *Chercheurs de sagesse, Hommage à Jean Pépin,* EAug (Antiquité) 131, 403–20.

COLOMAN VIOLA

See also **Attributes, Divine; Being; Immutability/Impassibility, Divine; Justice, Divine; Knowledge, Divine; Omnipotence, Divine; Omnipresence, Divine**

Assumption. *See* **Mary**

Athanasius of Alexandria

(c. 299–373)

a) Life. Probably born in 299 (the *Index of Festal Letters,* established by his Chancery shortly after his death, states that he was not yet 30 years of age when he was consecrated in 328) to a Greek family in Alexandria*, Athanasius started, in 325, to serve as deacon* and secretary to bishop* Alexander, whom he accompanied to the Council* of Nicaea*. He was consecrated as "pope" (then a common title for the bishops of Alexandria) on 8 June 328. The first five years of his episcopate were marked by long pastoral visits to the monks of the Thebaid, the Pentapole and the Ammon deserts, or in the Delta regions. He was probably looking there for spiritual nourishment, which he greatly needed to assume his episcopal duties. These duties were weighty: the decrees of Nicaea regarding the reintegration of the Melitians to the ranks of the Catholic clergy (Melitius, bishop of Lycopolis, was opposed to Peter of Alexandria's patriarch about the reintegration into a Christian Church which had been apostatized during the Diocletian persecution, and whose bishops had been illegitimately ordained) had hardly been implemented by the old Alexander, and the opposition to the Nicene Creed persisted in the Eastern churches under a coalition directed by Eusebius of Nicomedia against the episcopal seat of Alexandria. An alliance among the schismatic Melitians, who had a slight majority in Egypt, and the vast coalition favorable to Arius (Arianism*) signified a premature end to the much too young bishop of Alexandria's episcopal ministry.

At the beginning of 331, Constantine summoned Athanasius to appear before his court because accusations had been made against him, but he was found to be innocent. The alarm sounded again in 334, when Athanasius received an order to present himself in front of a synod* apparently presided over by Eusebius of Caesarea. He refused to abide by that order. In 335, forced by another order from Constantine, he could not avoid the imperial Synod of Tyre, in Phoenicia. That synod, which sealed the alliance among Melitians and Arians, deposed him. He sought help in Constantinople from the emperor in person, who banished him at once to Trier, where his son Constantine II was residing. The emperor did not replace Athanasius, who therefore kept his seat; he was merely keeping him away from the commotion of clerical intrigues.

In Trier, the exile struck a friendship with the bishop Maximinus and the caesar Constantine. He touted the marvels of the monastic rise in the Egyptian deserts known to all around him, as a seed from which the oldest monasticism* would take germ. After the death of the emperor on 22 May 337, Constantine II authorized Athanasius to go back to Alexandria, which he did "in great triumph," according to the *Index* of 23 November of the same year.

The episcopal coalition, hostile to the Alexandrian seat, did not tolerate this comeback. The Cappadocian Gregory, chosen as Athanasius's replacement, was imposed to take the seat by force. Trouble arose; obliging Athanasius to withdraw underground on 18 March 339. Immediately after 15 April, which was Easter Sunday, the bishop left secretly for Rome*. He was received there by Pope* Julius I, whose synod soon recognized him, in 340, as the sole legitimate bishop of Alexandria. After an encounter in Trier with the Western emperor, Constans, whose support he obtained, Athanasius participated in 343 in the Council of Sardica (Sofia), where the episcopates of the East and the West refused to sit together, but where a fratricidal war between the two emperors, Constans and Constantius, was barely avoided. Marcellus of Ancyra, another victim of the Nicene after-council, who had the reputation of renewing the modalism* of Sabellius, had joined Athanasius in Rome. The two of them together had against them the unanimity of the Eastern bishops. In 346, the death of Bishop Gregory and his own precarious situation with the Persians finally justified, in the eyes of Constantius II, the recall of Athanasius and his return to the seat of Alexandria. His Alexandrine compatriots, Christians and pagans alike, celebrated the bishop as a national hero: "He was even honored with a triumphal reception before the one hundred thousandth," notes the *Index.* But the Eastern coalition remained inflexible and the emperor Constantius was biased more than ever against Athanasius. When, in 350, Constans succumbed under the assaults of usurper Magnentius, Constantius II succeeded in getting rid of him and had nothing more urgent to do than organizing synods, at Arles in 353 and at Milan in 355, with the avowed purpose of obtaining Athanasius's eviction from the seat of Alexandria and of setting up a regime of Christianity conforming to the Eastern coalition's wishes. During the nights of 8 and 9 February 356, the church where the bishop was celebrating was stormed by troops headed by the *dux* of Syrianos. Once more, Athanasius succeeded in escaping. After bloody unrest in the Christian parts of town, the Arian bishop George of Cappadocia occupied the seat of Alexandria, while Athanasius sought refuge in the desert, where he was able to hide under the monks' protection. Hidden until Constantius's sudden death in 361, Athanasius did not wait for the authorization of Julian, the new emperor, to return to Alexandria. Around the summer of 362, he organized a synod known as the "synod of the confessors," where people with different pro-Nicene tendencies decided to support the Homoousians grouped around Basil of Ancyra, which hastened the final victory of the "consubstantial*." In the meantime, Athanasisus had to, once more, go briefly into exile under Julian in 363 and under the Arian emperor Valens during the winter of 365–66. Having outlived all his adversaries, he was able to find some peace, build a few churches and carry on some epistolary exchanges before passing away at the beginning of 373.

b) Works and Doctrine. Athanasisus's literary activity, like his political career, remains marked by an astonishing continuity. Every year, circumstances allowing, the bishop published a festal letter, through which he announced the dates for Lent and Easter, with the appropriate spiritual and pastoral considerations. The first letters are marked by Origenist and monastic spirituality; from 340 on, the evangelical realism particular to Athanasius becomes the dominant feature. The first doctrinal writing of the young pastor, dating probably from 335, is entitled *De Incarnatione.* That essay, appended to an apology entitled *Contra Gentes,* which is based on older notes and has a more conventional structure, is the first of its kind to be composed by a church leader; and to diametrically oppose Arian theology*, although without naming it. Contrary to Arius's assumption, the evangelical figure of Jesus* does not purport to reveal a weak and inferior Word* that has to earn its own divine exaltation through suffering. On the contrary, the divine Word has taken upon itself, within its own flesh, all of mankind's distress, with the goal of transfiguring this distress, of "deifying" it, by changing its condition. Thus the mystery* of divine Incarnation* becomes central to Athanasius's theological synthesis. Around 339, Athanasius composed the double *Treatises Against the Arians,* intended, according to the accompanying letter, *To Monks,* for the monks. Here, he sets the foundations of a Trinitarian theology in keeping with the Nicene dogma*, by insisting above all on the principles of an anti-Arian interpretation of the Scriptures*. In 339, an *Encyclical Letter,* which was in fact a long shout of horror and protest, denounced the assaults inflicted on Athanasius at the time he had to flee to Rome. After he came back from his second exile in 346, the bishop produced a vast documentary compilation, the *Defense against the Arians,* intended to prove the legitimacy of his episcopal title. Around 350 there followed a *Letter on the Opinions of Dionysius,* the predecessor from the previous century whose formulas the Arians believed they could lay some claim to, and an essay in epistolary form, *On the Nicene Degrees.* At the time of the riots in 356, Athanasius wrote—under a miraculous state of serene concentration—an *Encyclical Letter to the Bishops of Egypt and Libya* in which he offered his best synthesis of biblical* theology against the Arian *Thalia*'s theses as he understood them. His desert exile inspired the following: the *Apology to Constance,* his only work in the polished style of the scholar, which was never made public during Constantius's lifetime; the *Defence of His Flight;* the *Epistles to Serapion;* a real cornerstone in dogmatic discussions preceding the First Council of Constantinople* (381); the long *Letter on the Synods of Rimini and Seleucia,* his longest written work, a documentary monument that is indispensable to the understanding of the Nicene after-council, and which serves as a direct preparation for the 362 synod of union, itself known thanks to the *Volume to the Antiochenes;* and above all, the *Life of Anthony,* perhaps written in its final stage after the end of the third exile, and intended to glorify, for centuries to come, the heroes of Egyptian eremitism, whose perfect model was, in Athanasius's eyes, represented by Anthony. The *Letter to Epictetus,* bishop of Corinth; the *Letter to Adolphus,* addressed to a longtime companion who had been at his side during some of his struggles; and a charming essay on the use of the Psalter, impossible to date, the *Letter to Marcellin,* complete Athanasius's literary legacy.

Centered on the mystery of divine Incarnation, Athanasius's synthesis examines notions of Trinitarian theology in more depth, without ever losing sight of the living experience* of faith. That synthesis, after many vicissitudes, led to a clear conscience of the separation between church* and state.

• *Apologies* (SC 56 *bis*).
H.-G. Opitz (Ed.) (1934–41), *Athanasius-Werke,* Berlin.
Epistles to Serapion (SC 15).
A. Martin, M. Albert (1985), *Histoire "acéphale" et Index syriaque des Lettres festales d'Athanase d'Alexandrie,* SC 317
Life of Anthony (SC 400).
On the Incarnation of the Word (SC 199).
(works by Athanasius): PG 25–27.
♦ E. Schwartz (1959), *Gesammelte Schriften,* III: *Zur Geschichte des Athanasius,* Berlin.
C. Kannengiesser (Ed.) (1974), *Politique et théologie chez Athanase d'Alexandrie,* Paris; (1983), *Athanase d'Alexandrie évêque et écrivain: Une lecture des traités* Contre les ariens, Paris; (1990), *Le Verbe de Dieu selon Athanase d'Alexandrie,* Paris.
D.W. H. Arnold (1991), *The Early Career of Athanasius of Alexandria,* Notre Dame (bibl.).
T.D. Barnes (1993), *Athanasius and Constantius,* Cambridge, Mass.
A. Martin (1996), *Athanase d'Alexandrie et l'Église d'Égypte au IVe siècle (328–373),* Paris.

Charles Kannengiesser

See also **Arianism; Consubstantial; Incarnation; Nicaea I, Council of; Trinity**

Athanasius, Symbol of. *See* **Creeds**

Atheism

A. Philosophical Problematics

1. General Definition

An atheist is one who denies the existence of God*. This nominal definition is insufficient because it leaves indeterminate not only the nature of the God that is denied, but, more importantly, the precise manner of the denial. If God is identified with an idol, denying his existence may be a way of affirming the existence of the true God: what presents itself as atheism is in truth theism. In this case, the denial is limited: a particular God is denied in order to affirm another one. But it is also possible to deny that any being whatever can exist for which the name* *God* is fitting. This denial still presupposes an idea of what is denied, and that would be enough for some to demonstrate its existence. The only coherent way of denying God or of affirming that God is nothing would be to reduce the idea of God to that of nothingness*—a delicate operation, for the idea of God is not of the same imaginary nature as that of a chimera.

From this difficulty, indeed impossibility, of denying the existence of God, it would be rash to deduce a proof* of his existence*. It is not possible, as for another being, to be indifferent about affirming or denying the existence of God. As Kant* has shown, although reason* enters into conflict with itself with respect to the world, there is on the other hand no rational antinomy concerning the existence of God. It is possible to deny that the existence of God is demonstrable; it is not possible to demonstrate that God does not exist. The metaphysical definition of God, as supreme Being, is such that atheism is not the simple antithesis of theism. In other words, atheism is not primarily an opposition to a rational thesis concerning the existence of God. Conversely, it is quite possible to have an idea of God, and even to come to a rational conclusion that he exists, and still be called an "atheist."

If atheism, in its primary usage, is not a doctrinal or speculative position, this is because it is first of all defined in relation to a belief. An atheist is one who does not believe in God, who does not share the belief accepted in a community with a relatively wide social foundation. When the community is identical to the city* or the state, the definition of atheism is political: not to believe is to place oneself outside the state. The equation for atheism represents the reverse side of official religion. To be sure, there is also a rational atheism, but its belated appearance can be explained by the modern reversal that transformed a negative meaning, indicating an exclusion, into a positive meaning, associated with an idea of humanity. It is only after this reversal that theology* itself can make atheism an object of reflection and not simply of condemnation.

2. Accusation of Atheism

The theoretical determination of atheism is sought in order to meet political and juridical requirements: it is necessary to be able to define the one who, in not respecting the state's gods, commits an act of rebellion against the state and its laws. The charge of impiety *(asebeia)* allowed the Athenians to institute proceedings against atheism. The most celebrated was the trial of Socrates in 399 B.C. The philosopher was accused of corrupting the young by "teaching them to believe in new deities instead of the gods recognized by the state" (Plato, *Apology* 26b). Strictly speaking, this formulation means that Socrates recognizes gods and that he is therefore not an atheist but merely an infidel (this might be called "weak" atheism). However, this difference appears subtle to the accuser Meletus, who has no hesitation in expressing the accusation in a radical form: "Yes, I say that you disbelieve in gods altogether" (26c). Thereafter, Socrates has no difficulty in refuting the accusation, since it is based on a contradiction: he is charged both with believing (in new gods, in *daimonia* [27d]) and with not believing (in the gods of the state). The defense is clever: while showing that he is not an atheist (in the strict sense), Socrates refrains from denying that he is an atheist (in the weak sense), that is, from affirming that he recognizes the gods of the state.

Trials for atheism are characterized by this argumentative structure. On one hand, the accuser claims that what must be condemned is not the theoretical position of atheism but its disastrous moral consequences for society*. On the other, the defendant denies that he is an atheist by invoking an idea of divinity superior to that of the accusers. The accusation can thus be turned against its proponent: the real atheist is not the one you think. Rather, he is the one who reduces God to an idol, and true religion to superstition. To clarify the concept of atheism it is therefore necessary to distinguish between the theologico-political point of view of the accuser and the dogmatic point of view of the accused. In one sense, the atheist is defined by opposition to an obligation both to believe and to practice the rituals of piety; in another, by opposition to the truth of the concept or the idea of God. There is not necessarily any connection between the two meanings.

3. The Theologico-Political Argument

a) Danger for Morality and Society. Both the obligation to believe in the existence of the gods, and its corollary, the prohibition of atheism, have a political basis, something which Plato makes explicit in Book X of the *Laws.* There the Athenian indicates the reason why it is necessary to conform to the requirements of state law in believing that the gods exist. It is a matter of countering the prejudicial objection through which the enemies of the laws might ruin the order of the state: if the gods do not exist or are not concerned with humankind (another form of atheism), everything is permitted (887e, 889e). The mob that obeys the laws because it anticipates heavenly retribution will cease to do so. "No man who believes in gods as the law would have him believe has ever yet of his own free will done unhallowed deed or let slip lawless discourse" (885b). Only atheism can lead humankind to transgress the laws. The Athenian does not assert that the atheism of the learned—that is, of the materialists, justly condemned for their impiety—is false. Rather, he considers it dangerous for the state as a whole because it provides arguments for the injustice of the ignorant. This position is symmetrical to that of Socrates: by affirming the necessity of a legislated theism, the question of theoretical atheism is left undecided. The only thing that is important for the state is that atheism not be allowed to spread, that it be censored; the question of its truth or falsity does not belong to the political order. The dissociation between opinion (or belief, which governs politics) and truth has as a consequence for the historical relativity of definitions of atheism: theism on one side of a border, atheism on the other. The contours of atheism match the contingencies of geography and history*. The Jews and the early Christians—"deadly superstition" (Tacitus, *Annals* XV: 44)—were condemned by the Roman emperors up to Constantine as denigrators of the gods of the official Roman religion. But after Constantine it was paganism that was prohibited (391). The political justification of religion contains in itself the very possibility of an intellectual challenge to religious truth.

b) Paradox of Atheist Theism. Even a philosopher such as Spinoza, who by means of demonstration reaches the mathematical certainty of the existence of God (*Ethics* I, Prop. 11), was considered an atheist during his lifetime (*see* Letter 30 to Henri Oldenburg). It was judged that his God "is only an imaginary God, who is anything but God," as his biographer, Pastor Johannes Colerus, wrote in 1704. If, by any method whatever, God may be identified with created things, he ceases to be God. An atheist is one who, while affirming in words the existence of a being called God, denies the existence of the true God, that is, the personal, transcendent, Creator God known through revelation*. In this case, atheism means rejection of revelation or of the law*, as the unique or primordial source of the knowledge* of God. Theism derived from revelation, on the other hand, is compatible with a skeptical position on the capacity of reason to know God. Hence this paradox: Spinoza was called an atheist precisely because he asserted that he could know God a priori; and the accusation came from the very people who "openly profess to have no idea of God" (*A Theologico-Political Treatise* chap. 2).

4. Atheism As the Fate of Modernity

a) Atheism in the Face of Revealed Theology. Religion based on revelation is not satisfied with basing the duty to believe on the political argument, but wishes to be recognized as true. It does not dissociate knowledge of the true God from the practice of pious actions. Obedience takes the form of a total adhesion of the person*, both intellectual and moral. The way in which the truth that God exists is recognized determines the attitude toward atheism. Really to believe in God is to believe in the true God, as he has manifested himself to humankind. Conversely, to know God only through reason is to forge an idol. The first step toward atheism is taken when humankind gives up basing its knowledge of God on obedience in faith*. Because faith demands more than simply prudent, politically proper adhesion to a superior normative principle, it opens up at the same time the possibility of rejection.

The atheist, who risks damnation, becomes a bold spirit, a libertine. He is defined not so much by denial of the existence of God as by his liberation from revealed dogmas*. One who relies entirely on reason in all things and who, out of principle, challenges not the political but the spiritual authority* of the community of believers, is an atheist. This situation, which requires all people to situate themselves with respect to revelation, gives rise to a new form of atheism: not one defined negatively by an accusation, but one that the libertine assumes positively as a profession of faith. In the face of revelation, atheism becomes at least thinkable, if not actually acceptable, as its other. Modern civilization, based on the rationality of the natural sciences*, even makes of atheism a kind of common sense. It is belief that has become absurd and dangerous.

b) Atheism of the Enlightenment. Atheism can be extended to denote the affirmation of the primacy of reason in the discovery of truth. To cultivate reason and modern natural science is to reject dogma and therefore deny the revealed God. The denial (of the existence of God) is then the secondary consequence of a position that could be set out in a credo, the one that Molière puts in the mouth of the great libertine lord: "I believe that two and two are four" (*Dom Juan* III, 1). Confidence in the powers of reason and mathematical science is indeed atheism, for it implicitly excludes any transcendence. Atheism is the negative version of the same rationalist credo: "I believe only that two and two are four." During the period running from the 16th to the 18th century, atheism gradually lost its taint of criminality. Enlightened thinkers led the way in this change, and their judgment was subsequently confirmed by legislation. Pierre Bayle (1697) challenged the final argument that maintained atheism in the realm of the illicit, and the identification of libertinism with dissolute morals. Not only could an atheist be an honorable man, but reason was a surer guide to good conduct than blind obedience to a retributive power or servile submission to clerical authority. Montesquieu rejected the penal character of crimes of opinion: "Where there is no public action, there is no element of crime" (*The Spirit of Laws* XII, 4). Along with the deism* of natural religion atheism became a militant form of humanism. The essential thing was not to carry on theoretical discussions about the existence of God but to fulfill a morality that, rather than enslaving humankind, guaranteed it dignity and responsibility. With modernity, atheism, which can be defined neither by the affirmation that God does not exist nor by indifference in matters of religion, derives its consistency from the critique of revealed religion. This is why, in relation to revelation, atheism and rationalist theism, although formally opposed, come together. Atheism belongs to the movement of the Enlightenment because its object is to liberate humankind from enslavement to dogmatic authority.

c) Humanism and Nihilism. Modernity thus reverses the direction of the traditional theologico-political argument: it is no longer atheism that is dangerous for truly human morality, but religion. Feuerbach's position radicalizes Bayle's: not only can an atheist be an honorable man, but only an atheist is an honorable man. To be an atheist becomes a duty of humanism, which consists in renouncing the illusion of an eternal* life, and so to concern oneself with the things of this world, seeking a happiness that is limited but remains within the scope of what humankind can attain.

Marx*'s critique of Feuerbach and, by extension, of Enlightenment humanism, claims that this humanism is derived, in its very anticlericalism, from a theological (that is to say, an ideological) problematic that misconstrues the reality of the material forces that make up its infrastructure. The humanist critique of religion in fact secretes a new form of religiosity: with reference to Bauer, Marx speaks of "atheism" as the "last stage of theism, the negative recognition of God" (*The Holy Family* chap. VI). If we want religion to cease dominating consciousness, it is useless to struggle against it with the weapons of rational argument. It is necessary to change the material conditions of existence: "Empty in itself, religion is not fed by heaven but by the earth, and it collapses by itself with the dissolution of the absurd reality of which it is the theory" (Letter to Ruge, 13 March 1843). Atheism, a "development of theoretical humanism," must give way to communism, a "development of practical humanism" (*Outlines of a Critique of Political Economy).*

When Nietzsche* develops the notion of the "death of God" (*The Gay Science* §125), he is not describing the happy event of human liberation but the abolition of the meaning of existence. Atheism is the work of modernity, the most contorted face of nihilism, the disenchantment of the world. It has ceased to be a demand and a struggle, and has become a fate. The madman reveals to humankind the murder that they themselves have already committed: modern civilization, based on natural science* and technology, makes obsolete both any metaphysical resort to the idea of God and any faith in revelation. At the same time, Nietzsche opens the way to reflection on the religious meaning of atheism, for he provokes the question of which god it is that is dead.

B. Theological Problematics

The theological question of atheism is a recent one. Atheism was in fact almost nonexistent in the cultural world in which the earliest Christian theology was organized. The principal debates that accompanied and influenced that organization were those between Christianity and Judaism*, on the one hand, and Christianity and paganism, on the other, and atheism played no role in either. Considered within the category of idolatry*, paganism clearly seemed to be devoted to the cult* of false gods, whom the Church Fathers* easily saw as demons*. The idol—the god that is "the work of men's hands" (Ps 115: 4–7), the god that is essentially available to humankind and reveals of the divine only what humankind needs—indicates perhaps that in some sense the religious life of paganism was possessed by evil numinous forces. But pagan cults were not the whole of paganism. When Christian theology came to conceptualize its relation to classical antiquity, it resorted to an interpretation of ancient philosophy to assert that the gospel of Christianity was its guardian; this was intelligible to the pagans because they had been "prepared" by the same Logos whose full manifestation in Jesus* of Nazareth Christianity itself proclaimed.

The Christian reading of the classical philosophers was certainly a tendentious one. The bias of Christian interpreters, however, should not conceal the principal fact: even if classical antiquity had not established a unified philosophical theism, the denial of God (of the god, of the divine) was almost entirely foreign to it. Whoever lived in the company of idols surely lived with no God and with no hope* in the world (Eph 2:12). And yet, the language that the pagans spoke allowed them to name God. Measured against the knowledge to which theology lay claim, that naming may have appeared meager. But theology always devoted its apologetics to this weak discourse and never to a denial of God.

It was only in modern times (*see* A 4 above) that the stakes and conditions of the naming of God were changed. When the denier of God appeared—very rarely—in patristic and medieval theology, it was in the guise of a madman. The desire to establish foundations was certainly vigorous enough in medieval thought to give rise to a language of rational demonstration, but the foundations were those given to itself by a faith in search of "intelligence." Neither Anselm's argument, nor the "ways" of Thomas* Aquinas, nor Duns* Scotus's search for a first principle derived in any way from an apologetic intention. Patristic and medieval apologetics defended "Christian truth" against pagans, Jews, and heretics (a category that included dualists and Muslims). By contrast, the theological task of defending "religious truth" in the face of irreligious objectors is very much a modern one.

This complex task led to two theoretical strategies, neither of which can yet be regarded as obsolete.

1) By taking as its first goal the demonstration of the truth of the "religious," the new apologetics—for which P. Charron suggested the sequence of treatises *(De veritate religiosa, De veritate christiana, De veritate catholica)*—clearly stated that the first words of theology are not uttered in the name of Christianity alone, but in the name of all practices (in ritual or in language) that rest on an affirmation of God, whether or not that affirmation has anything specifically Christian about it. On the theoretical stage of modernity, the atheist appears not as one who denies the reasons of Christianity, but as one who challenges the general framework of "religious" references within which Christian discourse seemed to take its place with ease. To confront this challenge there then arose a procedure of defense and illustration of the religious phenomenon, something which found its perfected form in the *Discourses* of Schleiermacher*. The procedure consisted essentially in answering the denial of God with an affirmation about humanity. Atheism is thus interpreted as a tragic gesture of self-mutilation brought about by denial of the most precious realm of human experience (*see* Lubac* 1944).
2) Because atheism, which is probably more than a philosophical opinion, is not less than such an opinion, it was no doubt legitimate that theology should want to confront it on its own terms by convicting it of irrationality. Superficially identical, the language of demonstration then reappears in the service of entirely different interests. The arguments used by medieval theology to confirm the rational basis of faith become only preliminaries to faith. The atheist frequently claims to be the true philosopher, and this is exactly what the modern form of the proof of the existence of God calls into question. Theology wants to say more about God than does metaphysical theism. But it does not want to say less, and it wants to say as much. So the fate of theism cannot be a matter of indifference to theology. A theology for which God was also the "prime unmoved mover" or "self-sufficient being" is thus succeeded by a theology for which the existence of the prime mover or of the *causa sui* must first be proved before these concepts can take on a specifically Christian character. It is also necessary that the Christian specifics be provided on the basis of a language sufficiently rational to be common to all.

If classic atheism thus provokes the response of a theology that says little about it, since it does not claim to possess more than the affirmative force of a reason that Catholic tradition* calls "natural," it seems that this is because atheism itself says rather little on the subject. In a certain sense, atheism cannot help but provoke frustration in the theologian, for the very good reason that atheism is rarely interested in God, and because the denial of God is for atheism the opening move that allows it to gain access to what it regards as the real questions. Since atheists are people who want to stop talking about God altogether, it is not surprising that their denials are brief. Indeed, atheists are sometimes satisfied with the presumption of being right, leaving to theists the concern with longer arguments (Flew 1984; an inverse formulation in the "reformed epistemology" derived from A. Plantinga, in which the existence of God is an elementary, basic fact, which one may attempt to deny but which does not call for demonstration). The idea that the cause of God may not be quite what is called the "god of the philosophers" is in the end foreign to atheists.

There was thus a shuffling of the cards in the 19th century when atheism added a critique of theological reasoning to its classic procedure of denial. The new atheism derived from Feuerbach and reaching its paroxysm in Nietzsche certainly had no criticism to make of the small stock of materialist or determinist axioms that supplied classic atheism. But somewhere between La Mettrie or Holbach and Feuerbach, the God to be philosophically denied had changed faces. In the interim, indeed, the God of Jesus Christ had carried out what was perhaps his first entry into philosophy. After Hegel*, Schelling*, and Kierkegaard*, the task of atheism became for the first time that of an a-theology. If denial were necessary, it would have to go as far as they had carried their position. It would thus be necessary to deny an Absolute that had passed into history and of which history had preserved the trace (Schelling), to deny that the Absolute was life and that its life was the "play of love* with itself" (Hegel), to deny the paradoxical hypothesis of the Most High who draws near to humanity in the "form of the slave" (Kierkegaard). Atheism, therefore, took on its modern form by challenging arguments that, in its classic form, it had philosophical (and theological) license to ignore: that is, christological, soteriological, kenotic, and Trinitarian arguments.

It was precisely at this point that atheism became a theological problem, in the richest sense. The God whose death was proclaimed by Nietzsche's madman in §125 of *The Gay Science* was in fact the one who had tied his fate to that of the Crucified One. The atheist presented himself as the "Antichrist." And even though there has been no lack of chronologically post-Nietzschean philosophies that deny a pre-Christian God (logical positivism is the most brilliant example), recent theology has had to meet the challenge of the greatest denial, not of the supreme Being, but of creative and redemptive love. It did so and continues to do so in many ways, with answers that probably do no more than identify the terms of the problem.

1) Against the anthropological dissolution of Christian realities carried out by Feuerbach, one might argue (Barth*) that this was a pure and simple epistemological error. The aporia of atheist reason arises, in fact, precisely because it is carrying out the work of reason. Reason is defined by lack of faith, and so, faced with God, it adopts a theoretical posture that is existentially the most inadequate possible. It leaves itself the means only to construct its own god (which will thus be an idol), or to deny what it has not known, a denial that will thus have no impact, even if it takes on concepts of God with strong theological determinants. In a sense, Feuerbach was right, insofar as he proposed a critique of religion, seeing it as an act of piety to deny the god with which humanity maintains a "religious" relationship that excuses it from believing.
2) The brutalities of "dialectical theology" could not be accepted unmodified by a Catholic theology whose supreme teaching authorities had made specific allowance for a rational knowledge of God (*see* especially Vatican* I, DS 3004, 3026). Its influence was nevertheless felt, in conjunction with a critique of which the Barth of the *Römerbrief* was unaware: that of Heidegger*. Of what god can it be said that he is dead? By transposing the concept of idol from the ethical-religious to the theoretical realm, J.-L. Marion (1976) set out a challenge to "conceptual idols." Just as an idol of stone or wood places the god at the disposal of humanity, so a concept may be said to function in an idolatrous way by restricting God to the services he performs for a particular metaphysics. To the extent that one then adopts the Heideggerian reading of the history of "metaphysics," it will be possible to say that the God who is dead is the God who has been at the service of ontology, the God of onto-theology And the reply to a "conceptual" atheism is to speak of the "truly divine" God, the God who himself breaks all the idols when his paternal goodness is revealed in the face of Jesus Christ.
3) Thenceforth, theology would be able to carry out a critique of atheism only by also issuing a challenge to theism. The atheist may sometimes recognize that Christians are themselves atheists of many gods (the best example is Bloch 1968), and Christians often specify that they speak otherwise about God because they are speaking of a different God. Between theism and atheism, Protestant theology reacted in classic (or neo-classic) fashion by organizing itself as meticulously as possible as *theologia crucis* (Jüngel 1977; Moltmann 1972). In the age of the "death of God," the God of whom it is possible to speak is precisely the God who has taken up the cause of one condemned to death. The *veritas christiana* is thus articulated in the absence of any *veritas religiosa.* Atheism, then, is not important by reason of its antimetaphysical burden, which it seems to share with Christianity. If it is really

necessary to reply to atheism, it is in order to show (e.g., Piret 1994) that the Christian God confronts humanity as the giver of a future (in an age of the "eternal return of the same"); to show that he confronts humanity by instituting an economy of forgiveness that forces the dismissal of any *ressentiment* (the reference is to Nietzsche); or (referring again to Nietzsche) in order to counter an ontology of the will to power with a dialectic of crucified and conquering love. It was fitting that theology reply to the a-theological intentions of modern atheism by purifying what it says of God of any nontheological element.

4) The "death of God" is finally not only an event occurring in theory, it is the master event of an age and the presupposition of an experience of the world. The distinctive note of this age (an age of "secularization*," an age of "nihilism") is no longer that the existence of God is denied but that it is forgotten. Classic atheism weighed the proposition "God exists" and declared it false. In an age of nihilism, this proposition is no longer false, but devoid of meaning. Whoever speaks of God is not even in error, he is simply using words without meaning. And this atheism (already held by logical positivism) takes on what could be called its "postmodern" form under the influence of Jacques Derrida, finding its fulfillment in extremist demolitions of everything ("logocentrism," "phonocentrism," etc.) that seems tied to metaphysics. The reaffirmation of God in an age of nihilism thus stands alongside other reaffirmations, without which it would have only incantatory power: the reaffirmation of meaning, for example, of truth, of the humanity of humankind, among others. This work of reaffirmation is being carried out in various places and in diverse ways. Theologies of a "hermeneutic" type (Bultmann*, etc.) devote themselves to bringing to light the unforgettable questions to which the affirmation of God provides an answer. With H. U. von Balthasar*, the background of a doctrine of creation* requires that Christianity also answer for the "meaning of being*"; and if the case arises, it must answer by taking the place of those philosophical discourses that no longer do so (*Herrlichkeit* III). And, in the wake of the late works of Wittgenstein, theologians bring out the global reality of the "forms of life" and the "language games" within which one may speak of God without sinning against "grammar," whether the grammar of concepts or the grammar of experience.

A problem that has been resolved is no longer a problem, and atheism remains a theological problem despite the attempts that have been mentioned. Some tasks remain.

1) If the God who is dead is only the God of metaphysics, the hypothesis advanced by Heidegger (*Identity and Difference,* Pfullingen 1957) must be subjected to the test of a detailed reading of the intellectual history of the West, of which we now possess only fragments. The God of the *Disputationes Metaphysicae* of Suarez* is unquestionably the God of onto-theology; the God of Anselm* or of Bernard* is unquestionably not; while the God of Thomas Aquinas may or may not be. But in order for theology to be able to maintain a fertile relationship with its past, we will have to know much more about that past and about the two logics that seem to have been operative in it: contamination of the theological by the metaphysical, as well as subversion of the metaphysical by the theological.
2) To an a-theological atheism, theology will reply with a theological position on the question of God in which christological and Trinitarian arguments play the role not of specifying an already formed concept, but of indicating what kind of God remains thinkable. The elimination of any "natural knowledge" in favor of "positive" thought (Schelling), or of a "more natural" theology (Jüngel) for which only "God speaks well of God" (Pascal*), nevertheless comes up against the utopian character of a strictly theological conception devoid of preexisting understandings. Taken in its kerygmatic dimension, theology aims its message at the Jews and the pagans. Insofar as its audience is pagan, it at least owes it the obligation of giving a meaning to words, beginning with the word *God,* before formulating for their benefit the complex statements in which *God* will attain its full meaning. This is so even if it involves criticizing in return the preliminary definition.
3) It may be conceded to Heidegger and to the heirs of Wittgenstein that it is important to praise God more than to think about him (Heidegger), or that the true place of "God" is in the language of prayer* and ritual rather than the language of a theory (e.g., D. Z. Phillips). The old question of the *demonstratio religiosa* ought then to reappear in a new guise.

For Hellenism, the interest in God or the divine was part of the *bios theoretikos,* the way of life fitting above all for the philosopher. But in late modernity, of what "life" can the interest in God be a part, and of what form of life can it be said that it is essentially atheist? These queries indicate that the question of God is inseparable from a question about humanity, and that the affirmation of God cannot be isolated from affirmations about humanity. There are several ways of answering them. It can be considered that the description of the world proposed by Heidegger in *Being and Time* is accurate enough for it to be necessary to grant atheism an existential status. In that case, the affirmation of God must be seen as a work of distancing (distance taken in relation to the innate conditions of experience—Lacoste 1994). One might also refer to Husserl's descriptions of the "life-world" in order to bring out the original character of belief and to grasp it as an innate recourse against the reduction of reality to fact, something that plays a large role in the genesis of atheism. One might also borrow from the Augustinian tradition a hermeneutics of desire and of anxiety, attributing to humanity an eschatological and a priori openness that cannot be lost, and which prohibits reducing the question of meaning to an analytics of *Dasein* and of existence as being-for-death. Whatever the outcome of a debate that puts in play irreducible perspectives not necessarily implying a contradiction, one point at least must be set out forcefully. There can be no consistent theological answer to atheist denials, whether those of a classic, a modern, or a postmodern atheism, unless that answer is integrated into a broader logic than that of discursive-conceptual assertions. In short, they must be met with a distinctive logic of spiritual experience*.

• A. Harnack (1905), *Der Vorwurf des Atheismus in den drei ersten Jahrhunderten,* Leipzig.
F. Le Dantec (1906), *L'athéisme,* Paris.
P. Hazard (1935), *La crise de la conscience européenne,* Part 2: *Contre les croyances traditionnelles,* Paris.
H. de Lubac (1944), *Le drame de l'humanisme athée,* Paris.
J. Maritain (1949), *La signification de l'athéisme contemporain,* Paris-Bruges.
W. Nestle (1950), "Atheismus," *RAC* 1, 866–70.
J. Lacroix (1958), *Le sens de l'athéisme moderne,* Paris.
G. Vahanian (1962), *La mort de Dieu: La culture de notre ère postchrétienne,* Paris.
R. Vernaux (1964), *Leçons sur l'athéisme contemporain,* Paris.
W. Pannenberg (1967), "Typen des Atheismus und ihre theologische Bedeutung," *Grundfr. syst. Th.,* 347–60.
K. Rahner (1967), "Atheismus," *SM(D)* 1, 372–83.
E. Bloch (1968), *Atheismus im Christentum,* Frankfurt.
J. Lacroix (1968), *Athéisme et sens de l'homme,* Paris.
G.M.-M. Cottier (1969), *Horizons de l'athéisme,* Paris.
A. McIntyre, P. Ricœur (1969), *The Religious Significance of Atheism,* New York.
H.M. Barth (1971), *Atheismus und Orthodoxie,* Göttingen.
J. Moltmann (1972), *Der gekreuzigte Gott,* Munich.
C. Tresmontant (1972), *Le problème de l'athéisme,* Paris.
F. Padinger (1973), *Das Verhältnis des kirchlichen Lehramtes zum Atheismus,* Vienna-Salzburg.
F. Dezinger, et al. (1976), "Atheismus," *TRE* 4, 349–436.
J.-L. Marion (1976), *L'idole et la distance,* Paris.
J. Natanson (1976), *La mort de Dieu, essai sur l'athéisme,* Paris.
J. Figl (1977), *Atheismus als theologisches Problem,* TTS 9.
E. Jüngel (1977), *Gott als Geheimnis der Welt,* Tübingen.
É. Gilson (1979), *L'athéisme difficile,* Paris.
J.B. Lotz (1981), *In jedem Menschen steckt ein Atheist,* Frankfurt.
L. Kolakowski (1982), *Religion: If There Is No God...,* London.
A. Flew (1984), *God, Freedom and Immortality,* Buffalo-New York, 13–68 (1st Ed., *The Presumption of Atheism,* 1976).
W. Winiarcyk (1984), "Wer galt im Altertum als Atheist?" *Ph.* 128, 2, 157–83.
M.J. Buckley (1987), *At the Origins of Modern Atheism,* New Haven.
G.A. James (1987), "Atheism," *EncRel(E)* 1, 479–90.
W. Bauer, K. and B. Aland (1988), "Atheos," *Wörterbuch zum NT,* Berlin.
G. Almeras, S. Auroux (1990), "Dieu (critique de l'idée de)," *LNPh* I, 653–55.
J. Deschamps (1990), "Nihilisme," *LNPh* 2, 1748–50.
D. Folscheid (1991), *L'esprit de l'athéisme et son destin,* Paris.
Catéchisme de l'Église catholique (1992), Paris, §2123–26.
J.-Y. Lacoste (1994), *Expérience et Absolu,* Paris.
P. Piret (1994), *Les athéismes et la théologie trinitaire,* Brussels.
G. Minois (1998), *Histoire de l'athéisme,* Paris.

Jean-Yves Lacoste

See also **Agnosticism; Existence of God, Proofs of; Faith; Knowledge of God**

Attributes, Divine

I. Religious Knowledge of the Divine Names and Attributes

Believers of every religion have meditated on the divine attributes and have invoked a god or the gods using a variety of names. In the Bible*, God* himself reveals his perfections in the experience* that human beings have of him and that they express in their prayers*. It is in fact impossible to pray to God without recalling his goodness, his power, his mercy*, and his justice*. And in that other "book," which is nature or the creation*, the human spirit discovers a whole series of perfections (beauty, order, light, and so on) that come from God.

1. Judaism

a) The Hebraic Notion of Name. In the Hebraic notion of *shèm,* "name*," Procksch (*Theologie des AT* 1950) discerns two elements: the noetic and the dynamic. One is its meaning or its etymology, the other implies an archaic conception of the name, which includes a property that might have magical uses.

The name designates the secret nature of a being, without giving a logical definition or symbolic representation of it, and it contains the active presence or power of that being. The name of God*, therefore, contains his mysterious power, and by invoking his name we enter the sphere of mystery* or magic.

b) The Name of Exodus. The just men of the Old Testament wished to know the name of God. "*What is your name?*" ask Jacob (Gn 32:30) and Manoah (Jgs 13:17) of the angel* of YHWH. But the real meaning of the divine name is given only to Moses. In the theophany* of the burning bush, Moses says to God: "Suppose I go to the Israelites and say to them: 'The God of your fathers has sent me to you,' and they ask me: 'What is his name?' Then what shall I tell them?" God says to Moses: "I am who I am" (Ex 3:13–14) (*see* B.N. Wanback, Bib 59 [1978]). On Mount Sinai God reveals himself to Moses as "the compassionate and gracious God, slow to anger, abounding in love and faithfulness, maintaining love to thousands" (Ex 34:6). God is praised in the Psalms* as the "saint" (Ps 33:21), "true" (Ps 57), "just" (Ps 89), "powerful" (Ps 89), and "merciful" (Ps 136) God. The divine names or attributes are thus revealed.

In Judaism* the name of God is not to be spoken *(shèm ha-meforèsh),* and God is called "the Place" *(maqqom)* or "the Name" *(Shèm)* (*see ThWNT,* vol. 5, 251 ff.). In his letter to Marcella (Ep. 25), Jerome mentions ten biblical names that the Jews used to invoke their Lord.

2. Christianity

a) New Testament. John calls God "Spirit" (Jn 4:24), "Light" (1 Jn 1:5), "Love*" (1 Jn 4:8, 16), But where his Gospel is original is in the revelation* of the three personal divine names: Father*, Son, and Holy* Spirit. Jesus* revealed that "Father" is the true name of God (Jn 17:6; Rom 8:15; Gal 4:6).

b) The Fathers* of the Church* had a threefold motivation in their study of the divine attributes. They wished to teach Christian perfection as the imitation of God (this was the work of Athanasius* and the Cappadocians, Clement of Alexandria, and Origen*); to affirm Christian monotheism* against paganism*; and (in the controversies against Arius and Eunomius) to show the equality of the divine Persons* in the unity of the divine essence. Thus, divine names like "Light" are both names that characterize the divine essence and are common to the three Persons of the Trinity*, and the proper names of the divine Persons that express their relations among themselves and to humankind. Basil*, for example, shows in his *Treatise on the Holy Spirit* that "God is light," the Son is the "Light born of the Light" (Nicene Creed*), and the Spirit is the "Light in which we see the Light" (Ps 35:4).

3. Islam

In Islam a celebrated hadit (the authenticity of which has been questioned) says that God has 99 names (100 minus one) and that "whoever keeps them in mind will enter paradise." From this derives the use of the string of 99 beads *(subha, misbaha),* each one corresponding to a divine name: God is Existing, Eternal, Unique, Perfect, Living, Omnipotent, Omniscient, Creator, Sovereign, Master of Fates, Just, Certain, Guide,

Beneficent, Generous, Indulgent, Friend of Believers, and so on. The one-hundredth name is the supreme Name, the hidden name that God reserves for himself.

Exegesis of the divine names has given rise in Islam to an extensive literature on the meaning of the names, their theological explanation in the framework of the *sifat Allah,* and their spiritual meditation as practiced by the followers of the *tasawwuf.* In his *Maqsad,* Gazali (†505/1111) presents an exegesis of the divine names characterized by "moderate Sufism," based on the list of Walid (†468/1075), but he points out that both the Koran and the tradition attest to a certain number of other names.

II. Theological Reflection on the Divine Attributes

Philosophers and theologians have sought to ascend from the created perfections to the uncreated perfections of God. Nevertheless, treatises that proposed the divine attributes as objects of contemplation* were late in appearing.

1. The Divine Names *by Dionysius the Areopagite*

a) Title. In the late fifth or early sixth century the author who wrote under the pseudonym of Dionysius the Areopagite—known now as the Pseudo-Dionysius*—composed a treatise titled *Divine Names (Peri theion onomaton)* (*see DN* I, 585 B; XIII, 984 A and *MT* III, 1033A), in which he explains the names God gives to himself in Scripture*. The title locates this treatise in a whole Neoplatonic tradition. Porphyry had written the treatises, now lost, "On Divine Names" and "On Statues," and a commentary on *Cratylus.* The treatise by Jamblicus "On the Gods," and the one by Theodore of Asinus, "On Names," have also been lost. The *De Mysteriis* of Jamblicus, which contains an explanation of divine names (I, 4), has survived.

b) Classification of Divine Names. In chapter III of *Mystical Theology,* Pseudo-Dionysius situates his *Divine Names* in relation to lost works (such as the *Theological Sketches* and *Symbolic Theology*) and to *Mystical Theology,* and he characterizes these treatises on the basis of the distinction between affirmative and negative theology*.

Affirmative theology deals with three categories of divine names: 1) Names concerning the single and triune divine nature, the Trinity and the Incarnation* of the Son, that Dionysius had set out in the *Theological Sketches* (*MT* 1033 A-B). 2) Intelligible divine names, such as Good* (chap. IV), Being* (chap. V), Life (chap. VI), Wisdom* (chap. VII), Power (chap. VIII), and finally the One (chap. XIII), all explained in *Divine Names.* 3) Symbolic divine names, that had been treated in *Symbolic Theology:* "In *Symbolic Theology* we dealt with the metonymies relating the tangible to the divine, we said what is the meaning in God of forms, figures, parts, and organs; the meaning in God of places and ornaments; the meaning of anger, sorrow, and resentment; the meaning of enthusiasm and intoxication; the meaning of oaths, curses, sleep, and waking, and all the forms with which divine sanctity is clothed to give it a face" (*MT* 1033 A-B).

Divine names thus have to do with the divine nature, its intelligible attributes, and the metonymies or metaphors that attribute to God human actions or passions*. God is both anonymous (*DN* 593 D) and polyonymous (*DN* 596 A), following the first two hypotheses of Parmenides: anonymous and ineffable in his absolute transcendence, polyonomous insofar as he may be glorified through the multiplicity of beings that proceed from and participate in him. God is known through both affirmative and negative theology. One follows the order of divine procession *(proodos)* which descends from the Principle to the lowest ranks of created things, the other follows the order of conversion* *(epistrophè)* of everything toward the Principle and ascends from what is "the furthest" from God to God himself. At the conclusion of this ascent we penetrate into the Darkness which is beyond the intelligible, and there is no longer merely concision but an absence of language, a total cessation of speech and of thought. God is the ineffable, like the One of Parmenides: "It is not named or spoken of, not an object of opinion or of knowledge, not perceived by any creature" *(Parmenides).*

c) Structure of the Divine Names. In the treatise divine names are organized following the fundamental distinction between 1) "the names suitable for divine realities" (*DN* 596 D); and 2) "the names derived from the operations of his providence*" (596 D). Dionysius gives the name "causative qualities" to "the Good, the Beautiful, Being, the Life-Giving, the Wise, and all those denominations that the Cause receives from the gifts that are fitting to his goodness" (640 B). With reference to the pairs of opposed categories in Parmenides, he makes it clear that these are "effigies" or "simulacra" (909 B) and, at the beginning of chapter X, that the "Omnipotent" and the "Ancient of Days" are "names that concern the procession *(proodos)* from the principle to the end" (937 B), which is also true of Peace*.

The divine names are the Good, Goodness, Beauty, and Love (chap. IV), Being (chap. V), Life (chap. VI), Wisdom, Intellect (chap. VII), Power, Justice*, Salvation*, Inequality (chap. VIII), Greatness, Smallness, Identity, Diversity, Resemblance, Difference, Rest, Movement, Equality (chap. IX), Time* and Eternity* (chap. X), Peace (chap. XI), Holy of Holies, King of Kings, Lord of Lords, God of Gods (chap. XII), the One (chap. XIII).

2. Thomas Aquinas

a) Commentary on Divine Names. Thomas* Aquinas wrote *Expositiones super Dionysium de divinibus Nominibus* (Pera) around 1260–61 (according to Walz) or 1265–66 (according to Pera). His commentary is the last of the major Western commentaries on *Divine Names,* after those of Jean Sarrazin, Robert Grosseteste, and Albert* the Great. He transposed Dionysius into the Scholastic* world, while Dionysius became, through quotations from his works, one of the three most important writers in the Thomist synthesis.

b) Treatise of Divine Names in the Summa Theologica. Thomas Aquinas takes up the question of divine names in *Summa Theologica* Ia, q. 13, where he studies the relationship between divine names and divine essence and sets out his theory of analogy* with reference to the knowledge* of God. Indeed, all of questions 3 through 13 (q. 3: simplicity*, q. 4: the perfection of God, q. 5: the Good, q. 6: Goodness, q. 7: infinity, q. 8: the existence of God in things, q. 9: immutability*, q. 10: eternity, q. 11: unity, q. 12: knowledge of God, and q. 13: the divine names) in which he discusses divine perfections, make up a treatise on divine names within the *Summa Theologica.*

The question of divine names poses two problems with reference to the relationship between divine attributes and the divine essence. On the one hand there is the problem of the mode of attribution of divine attributes to the divine essence, on the other the problem of the multiplicity of divine attributes and the unity or simplicity of the essence. For Thomas, divine attributes on the one hand characterize *(substantialiter)* (Ia, q. 13, a. 2, resp.) the divine essence. But on the other, the distinction between the multiplicity of divine names and the simplicity of the essence is only a distinction of reason*. Thus, the Thomist doctrine of the predication of divine attributes and of analogy undermines agnosticism* and lays a foundation for the knowledge of God.

c) The Three Ways. Following Dionysius, Thomas distinguishes three ways of knowing God: the affirmative way, the negative way, and the way of eminence. The affirmative way names God on the basis of created perfections, the negative way excludes any limit to created perfections when it affirms them of God, and the way of eminence affirms that God eminently possesses in himself all the qualities or perfections of created beings. The resemblance between created beings and Creator makes it possible to attribute the perfections of the created to the Creator by analogy, but these qualities fit him so imperfectly that, when they are applied to God, their limitations must be denied. This is knowledge of God through negation. And because the divine essence cannot be known in itself, God remains ineffable.

An anonymous opuscule attributed to Thomas, *De Divinis Moribus,* which deals principally with divine attributes in relation to created beings, asks the Christian to imitate divine perfections.

III. Spiritual Contemplation of Divine Attributes

Along with theological reflection on divine names, there has also been extensive reflection of a more properly spiritual kind on the attributes of God, or the divine perfections. In the *De perfectione* Gregory* of Nyssa defines Christian perfection on the basis of the "names of Christ*." Augustine* remarks that, according to Plato, the wise man is he who knows and imitates God and whose happiness is participation in divine qualities (*City of God* I. VII. chap. V), and he opens the first book both of the *Soliloquies* (I. c.1. 2–6) and the *Confessions* with an elevation on the names of God: "Who then are you, my God? What, I ask, but God who is Lord?" (*Confessions* I. iv. 4).

In his *De Consideratione* (I. V) Bernard* of Clairvaux implies a method for the "consideration" of the divine perfections. The *Monologion* of Anselm* is a speculative and emotional meditation on the divine attributes and the divine persons. God is the Sovereign Being; from this principle Anselm deduces all the perfections that are fitting to his divinity. Finally, in the *De triplici via,* Bonaventure* establishes a relationship between the divine names and the three ways, purgative, illuminative, and unitive. He locates the meditation on the divine attributes in the unitive way, as was also done by Garcia de Cisneros, in his *Exercitatorium spirituale,* and by Ignatius Loyola, in the fourth week of his *Spiritual Exercises.*

In the 16th century Teresa of Avila recommended to her nuns that they think of the attributes of God at the moment of beginning their prayers: "Oh Supreme Dominator... Bottomless Abyss of wonders! Beauty that enfolds all beauties! Strength that is strength itself! Oh God! Why do I not have all the eloquence, all the wisdom of mortals, to be able to set forth... a single one of those many attributes that reveal to us some little bit of that supreme Master, our supreme Good! (*The Path of Perfection* chap. 22). And, in the third stanza of the "Living Flame," John* of the Cross compares the divine names to "lamps of fire" *(lámparas de fuego),* which give to the soul* a "warmth of love." In the *Contemplatio ad amorem* Ignatius Loyola meditates on the divine names, which are like "rays coming down from the sun," or like "waters flowing from the spring" (*Exercises* no. 237).

Turning to the 17th century, in 1620 the Jesuit Leonard Lessius published a treatise in Antwerp, *De perfectionibus moribusque divinis,* and then in 1640, and in Brussels, a treatise entitled *Divine Names.* He distinguishes between absolute attributes, which belong to God alone, and relative attributes, which concern created beings as well (e.g., providence and justice). He provides a logical division of the 14 divine attributes (infinity, immensity, immutability, eternity, omnipotence, wisdom, goodness of the divine being, sanctity, kindness, sovereign rule, providence, mercy, justice, last things) to which all the others are connected. This is why his treatise is divided into 14 books. His method of meditation is both speculative and emotional.

Jean-Jacques Olier composed an unpublished treatise on the divine attributes, in which he distinguishes 19 divine attributes, almost all unrelated to created beings: the existence of God, his necessity, his independence, his sufficiency, his unity, his truth, his perfection, his infinity, his simplicity, his sanctity, his greatness, his immensity, his eternity, his knowledge, his love, his will, his goodness, his justice, and his strength. He sets forth a method "for praying about the divine attributes." In prayer, the soul "communes" with these divine attributes: "This contemplation [of the divine attributes] sets the soul in perfection. For, as these attributes are the perfections of God, the soul coming to commune with God and with his divine perfections, enters at the same time into sublime perfection" (vol. I).

Jean Eudes sets out this same doctrine in his *Entretiens intérieurs de l'âme chrétienne avec son Dieu:* "O my God, I give myself entirely to you: inscribe in me a perfect image of your sanctity and your divine perfections" (*Entretien* V).

It was probably Cardinal Bérulle's "devotion" to the divine attributes, as expressed in his *Grandeurs de Jésus,* that prompted Bossuet to write his *Élévations sur Dieu, sur son unité et ses perfections.* Fénelon also wrote a *Traité de l'existence et des attributs de Dieu.* In it he establishes the existence of all the divine attributes by the fact that God is Being: "When I say of the infinite being that he is simply Being, and nothing more, I have said everything.... Being is his essential name, glorious, incommunicable, ineffable" (chap. V).

• C. Toussaint (1903), "Attributs divins," *DThC* 1, 2223–35.
P. Pourrat (1937), "Attributs divins," *DSp* 1, Paris, 1078–98.
R. Criado (1950), *El valor dinámico del Nombre divino en el Antiguo Testamento,* Granada.
A.-M. Besnard (1962), *Le mystère du Nom,* LeDiv 35.
J. Auer (1978), *Gott der Eine und Dreieine, KKD* 2, 356–580.
G. Scholem (1983), *Le Nom et les symboles de Dieu dans la mystique juive,* Paris.
D. Gimaret (1988), *Les noms divins en Islam,* Paris.
E.R. Wierenga (1989), *The Nature of God: An Inquiry into Divine Attributes,* Ithaca-London.
J. Werbick (1995), "Eigenschaften Gottes," *LThK3* 3, 528–29.

Ysabel de Andia

See also **Dionysius the Pseudo-Areopagite; Eternity of God; Jealousy, Divine; Justice, Divine; Knowledge, Divine; Negative Theology; Omnipresence, Divine; Simplicity, Divine**

Augustine of Hippo

Among the Fathers* of the Church, Augustine (354–430) left the largest body of work (more than 800 sermons, some 300 letters, and 100 treatises), in which he deals with all the fundamental problems of theology*. His life is also the best known. Not only did he write the *Confessions,* which, although not an autobiography, contains autobiographical elements, but he also had a biographer in the person of his friend Possidius, bishop* of Calama. To this may be added the information he himself provides in the *Philosophical Dialogues,* the *Retractations,* sermons, and letters.

1. Life

From all these documents it is evident that the whole of his subsequent life was marked by his experience* of conversion*. This did not take place on a single occasion but lasted for 14 years, and it represented a clear dividing line in his existence. Before his conversion Augustine led a life that was quite conventional for his period, and in particular had a brilliant career as a teacher of rhetoric. Born in the small town of Thagaste (present-day Souk-Ahras in Algeria) on 13 November 354 to a middle-class family, Augustine soon distinguished himself by his intellectual qualities. From 365 he was a student of rhetoric in Madauros, but for lack of resources he returned to Thagaste for a year. In 370 his father, Patricius, sent him to Carthage to continue his education, thanks to the support of Romanianus, a family friend. He became an outstanding rhetorician, seeking honors and pleasure. He soon chose to cohabit with a woman of an inferior class, whom he consequently did not marry, although she bore him a son, Adeodatus.

At the conclusion of his studies, before beginning to teach in Thagaste in 372, he read the *Hortensius* "by a certain Cicero." The book provoked such turmoil in him that it marked a turning point in his life (*Confessions* III. iv. 7–8). This was the first step toward the discovery of God*, *interior intimo meo et superior summo meo,* the first moment of his conversion. Not only did Augustine move from rhetoric to philosophy*, but more deeply, he discovered Wisdom* and was led to read the Bible*. He was disappointed, however, to find that it did not display the stylistic qualities of Cicero.

Yet his thirst for truth* persisted, which explains why he became an adherent of Manicheanism* and remained one for 10 years. An auditor, he hoped to be initiated into the mysteries as one of the Elect, and in doing so to replace faith* with reason*. But his encounter with Faustus of Mileu (in 382–83), who was reputed to be a most learned Manichean, made him realize that Manicheanism was far from providing the key to all mysteries and that it was in fact contrary to rationalism* (*Confessions* V. vi. 10–vii. 13). Augustine therefore gradually distanced himself from it. In 384 his appointment as a teacher of rhetoric in Milan, although supported by the Manicheans, allowed him to break definitively with the group.

It was then that he met Ambrose*, whom he appreciated for his human qualities and his preaching*. Introduced by Simplicianus, friend and successor of Ambrose, to the reading of the *Libri Platonicorum,* he experienced a genuine intellectual conversion (*Confessions* VII. x. 16–xxi. 27). It cannot be determined with certainty whether these books were those of Plotinus or of Porphyry, or both. In any event, they oriented Augustine toward inwardness and led him to recognize the creative role of God. But by themselves they were not enough, and Augustine explains: "Unless I had sought your way in Christ* our Savior, I would not have been expert but expunged" (*Confessions* VII. xx. 26).

However, his reading of the Epistles of Paul in July 386 (*Confessions* VII. xxi. 27) still did not bring about his decision to ask for baptism*. To overcome his hesitations he required the example of the conversion of the rhetor Marius Victorinus (*Confessions* VII. ii. 3–iv. 9), the evocation of the life of the hermits of Trier (*Confessions* VIII. vi. 13–vii. 18), and above all the episode of the garden in Milan (*Confessions* VIII. xii. 28–30), where the conversion of his will was accomplished. He gave up his position as teacher of rhetoric and withdrew with a few friends to Cassiciacum, near Milan, to devote himself to prayer* and philosophical dialogue. On Easter night 387 he was baptized by Ambrose in Milan, along with his son Adeodatus and his friend Alypius. He stayed a while in Cassiciacum and then decided to return to Africa. Before embarking and after his celebrated ecstatic experience in Ostia (*Confessions* IX. x. 23–25), his mother Monica departed this life.

On his return to Thagaste in 388 Augustine organized a more structured community known as "the servants of God," and avoided all cities that had vacant bishoprics. However, after the death of Adeodatus, he agreed to go to Hippo "to see a friend whom [he] hoped to turn toward God… . [He] was not worried, because there was a bishop. But [he] was seized, made a priest*, and that led [him] finally to become a bishop" (Sermon 355. 1).

In fact, Bishop Valerius, who was aged and knew little Latin, asked during a liturgical service for assistance from a priest. Augustine, who was unexpectedly present, was literally overcome by the crowd and led to the bishop. More than reticent because of his monastic commitment and what he considered his lack of preparation, he secured a delay, but was ordained in 391. Better educated than most of his colleagues, he pursued his conversion and devoted himself to the study of Scripture*. He was soon called upon to defend the faith against Donatism* and Manicheanism, from which came his celebrated debate with the Manichean, Fortunatus, on 28 September 392. Valerius also helped him to establish a monastery in Hippo. Recognizing his abilities, Valerius almost immediately asked him to take on quasi-episcopal functions and had him preach on faith and the creed at the Council* of Hippo on 8 October 393.

In 395 he was consecrated coadjutor of Hippo, so that he might remain in that church. Then, on the death of Valerius in 395 or 396, he became titular bishop. Although Augustine was a contemplative, a renewal of conversion led him to agree to assume pastoral duties, including service and preaching*. He devoted himself wholeheartedly to these tasks, following the well-known maxim, "For you, I am a bishop; with you, I am a Christian" (Sermon 340). He was solicitous toward everyone, and particularly concerned for the cohesion of his community, threatened as this was by various heresies*, among which Pelagianism was noteworthy from 412 on. On this account he was reluctant to leave Hippo, but was brought to do so in order to participate in various councils, where he often played a decisive role. He thus traveled throughout North Africa.

In addition to the many works he wrote in this period, the Letters, discovered in 1975 by Johannes Divjak, and the Sermons, found in the Mainz library in 1990 by François Dolbeau, provide a better idea of his activity during these years. As a bishop who was also a monk, Augustine felt sorrow at his distance from the men with whom he had led a life in common in the monastery of Hippo: Alypius, Possidius, Evodius, and Profuturus, all of whom had become bishops. He nevertheless maintained a firm friendship with them, which contributed to the unity* of the African Church in a context made difficult by many heresies and by the fall of Rome*. It was in these circumstances that Augustine wrote *The City of God* and the *Retractations.* The latter represents a unique book in the history of thought. In it, Augustine takes up all his works one by one, providing correctives and additions. This was on the eve of his death, which occurred on 28 August 430, in a Hippo besieged by the Vandals.

2. Anthropology

Whereas Books I to IX of the *Confessions* constitute an important biographical source, Books X to XIII lay out the broad outlines of Augustine's anthropology. The *Confessions* (from the Latin verb *confiteor*) designate in fact a threefold confession: avowal of past sins, confession of faith, and thanksgiving for creation*, in which his anthropology is articulated.

In focusing solely on his writings concerning the Pelagian controversy and taking these out of context, or on the Jansenist* reinterpretation of his work, commentators have often criticized Augustine for propounding a pessimistic anthropology. This component exists, but it comes late in his work, dating from the years around 415. It derives from the requirements of a particular polemic, and therefore calls for a nuanced reading. In fact, Augustinian anthropology is resolutely optimistic and is defined on the basis of the schema: *creatio, conversio, formatio.* Furthermore, this schema is constant, even though it was masked by other questions in the course of the Pelagian polemic.

a) The Schema: Creatio, Conversio, Formatio. Augustine was made aware very early of the need to develop a solid anthropology. Having discovered through Ambrose's preaching the spiritual dimension of the image of God in the human person, he was thereby able to refute the Manicheans on this point *(De Genesi contra manicheos)* and to deepen the notion of the relationship between Creator and created being. But Augustine did not stop with a simple reflection on the image of God. He situated it at its point of emergence in the text of Genesis and, in the course of exercising his duties as bishop, he commented five times on the first chapters of that book (*De Genesi contra manicheos, De Genesi ad litteram liber imperfectus, Confessions* XI-XIII, *De Genesi ad litteram, City of God* XI). In doing so he proposed a theological ontology and a spiritual anthropology, and dealt with fundamental questions: "Who made created beings? How and why?" (*City of God* XI. 21).

Creation holds a central place in his commentary. In opposition to the Manicheans, he emphasizes its goodness and interprets it as the gift of being*. But, whereas all other beings are perfect according to their kind, man has an intermediate position (Letter XVIII): according to the inclination of his heart, he fulfills or destroys himself, and from this comes the decisive role of conversion.

As one who was strongly influenced by the Neoplatonic notion of conversion, and who went through the experience of conversion throughout his life, Augustine frequently emphasizes its necessity for the fulfillment of being (*Confessions* XIII. ii. 3). It is through conversion that "the created being takes form and becomes a perfect being" (*De Genesi ad litteram* I. iv. 9). Angels*, which for Augustine represent perfect creation, give an idea of this: "Turned from his unformed nature toward God who formed him, the angelic creature is created and formed" (*De Genesi ad litteram* III. xx. 31). Conversion and *formatio* are simultaneous for angels, while for human beings there is a gap between the two.

By the term *formatio,* a variant of *forma* difficult to translate, Augustine designates the fulfillment of being, which he expresses chiefly with the metaphors of illumination and rest in God, which goes some way toward evoking deification, in which freedom* and grace* act in concert.

b) Freedom and Grace, or the Echo of the Pelagian Polemic. The problem of the relationship between freedom and grace took on its full importance during the course of the Pelagian polemic. But from the moment of his conversion, as he was reiterating: "You converted me to yourself" (*Confessions* VIII. xii. 30), Augustine was aware of the synergy between freedom and grace. Although he stressed grace during the controversy, he nevertheless did not underestimate the role of freedom, as he explains in the *Retractationes* II. 37): "In my book *The Spirit and the Letter,* I violently combated the enemies of the grace of God," that is, the Pelagians. He goes on (II. 42): "The book in which I answered Pelagius to defend grace and not to attack nature*, which is bestowed and governed by grace, is called *Nature and Grace.*" In fact he had no intention of calling nature into question. He simply wanted to show that, in itself, nature is nothing, and that the role of God is central. One particular form of Augustinianism, by radicalizing his positions, was to distort them.

Analogously, due to an erroneous exegesis of Paul (Rom 5:12) that he based on the inaccurate translation of the *Vetus Latina,* as well as to his polemical intentions, Augustine came to an excessively rigid position on the question of original sin* and infant baptism. If the context of all this is ignored, there is a danger of misinterpreting Augustine's thought. It is important to see, as he explains in the *Enchiridion,* that he understands everything in the light of the new creation.

Moreover, Augustine simultaneously emphasizes the place of freedom and states that "he who has created you without you does not justify you without you: he has created someone who was not conscious, he does not justify someone without that person's consent" (Sermon 169. 11).

Through grace, "free will is not removed but helped" (Letter 157. 2). Finally, Augustine comes to a very balanced vision of the relationship between freedom and grace, as evinced, for example, in his book *The Spirit and the Letter* (III. 5) and in Sermon 26. Polemic leads him into certain excesses, but his intention is to foreground the role of the Holy Spirit, as he does much more serenely in *De Trinitate.*

3. Trinitarian Theology

De Trinitate is an account of his meditation on the Trinity*. Augustine did not wish to publish it, but resigned himself to doing so around 426, after the first 12 books had been stolen from him and published without his knowledge. He did not purport to present a systematic exposition of the Trinity but an expression of his thinking, which he might continue to develop and deepen, as he had already done in Sermon 52. The book had an influence that he did not foresee and lastingly marked Western Trinitarian theology. Having read all the works on the Trinity that were extant at the time, Augustine in fact broached all basic questions pertaining to the subject: the relationship between the unity of essence and the Trinity of Persons*, circumincession*, the creative Trinity, and Trinitarian analogies*.

a) The Trinity: A Mystery of Love. From the moment of his conversion, Augustine attempted to understand the mystery* of God. He was soon absorbed by its dynamics, which is nothing other than Trinitarian love* (*De Trinitate* XV. ii. 3). His thinking, therefore, was not merely speculative, but also spiritual and mystical*. Some of his works—*De Trinitate, On John's Gospel, On John's Epistle,* and the *Regulus*—bring together themes that he was the first to treat in terms of their interrelationship. In all these books Augustine points out that charity is the basis of intellectual, spiritual, and community life, and he advocates a welcoming attitude in order to penetrate the mystery of love that God is. As he explains in the *On John's Gospel* (76. 4): "The Father*, the Son*, and the Holy Spirit come to us when we go toward them; they come to offer us their help, and we offer them our obedience. They come to illuminate us as we contemplate, they come to fill us as we welcome them." An exchange, a constantly renewed gift on the part of the Trinity is then accomplished, and we are introduced into the life of the Trinity.

Augustine also repeats an image, that of the *cor unum* of the first community of Jerusalem*, in order to express the life of the Trinity (*On John's Gospel* 14. 9). Therein lies the entire mystery of the unity of the Trinity, a theme he develops extensively in *De Trinitate.* The creator of this unity is none other than the Holy Spirit. "When this Spirit, God of God, gives Himself to man, He inflames him with the love of God and of his neighbor, because He is Love. Man can love God only through God" (*De Trinitate* XV. xvii. 31). He thereby enters into this mystery of love and can love as the Father loves the Son, or as the Son loves the Father, or be love as the Holy Spirit is love, and live the life that is given to him by the Trinity. *De Trinitate* attempts to give an account of this very dynamism, which accounts for the structure of the work.

b) Two Books. Augustine begins with two books: Scripture and creation. In a first stage, corresponding to the first seven books of *De Trinitate,* he tries to define the nature of the Trinity as it appears in Scripture. Against the Sabellians, he first affirms the unity and equality of the Trinity, then he studies the distinctive mission of each Person of the Trinity in order to show that there is not subordination but equality among them. Thereafter, he rereads the theophanies* of the Old Testament to determine whether they evoke the

Trinity. Having to engage in polemics with resurgent Arianism*, he recalls the divinity of Christ* and emphasizes Christology* and the mystery of the Incarnation*. In Books V and VII he proposes a specifically Trinitarian vocabulary. However, he soon sees that words are inadequate to speak of the Trinity. "What are these three?" To be sure, we do speak of three persons, but the term is only approximate, because the divine Persons are infinitely more than human persons (*De Trinitate* VII. iv. 7). Augustine does not go beyond a formal definition of person, but he prepares the way for further developments by Boethius*, Richard of Saint*-Victor, and Thomas* Aquinas.

Augustine gradually realizes, however, that the study of Scripture and a rational procedure do not allow him to go any further in his investigation. He therefore adopts a different perspective in Books VIII through XV. He no longer considers the Trinity in itself, but envisions it from the viewpoint of the human being, created in its image. He is then led to introduce what may be called Trinitarian analogies, which establish a link between anthropology and Trinitarian theology. The principal analogy, of the lover, the beloved, and the love, derives from his meditation on the Trinity. In Augustine's view it characterizes the Trinity in itself, which is conceived as a circulation of love among the divine Persons, each Person being established in its being by the loving gaze of the other. The other analogies—the soul*, knowledge, and love (IX); memory, intelligence, and will (X); memory, inner vision, and will (XI)—refer only to the human being and have sometimes been defined as psychological. They are influenced by Neoplatonism, particularly by Porphyry, but Augustine proposes them merely as hypotheses and never as trinities in themselves. He applies them to the soul, insofar as it is created in the image of the Trinity (which Porphyry did not say), and attempts thereby to show that, although the Trinity may be inaccessible in itself, it is on the other hand accessible by taking as a point of departure its expression in the human person. Moreover, in Books XIV and XV he studies an important point: the renewal of he who is created in the image, a renewal that is accomplished in the image of the Trinity and which constitutes the human being as a subject. "We will then be transformed," he writes, "that is, we will pass from one form to another, from the obscure to the luminous form. For the obscure form is already an image of God and thereby of His glory*.... This nature, the noblest of created things, once purified of its impiety by its creator, leaves its deformed form to become a beautiful form" (*De Trinitate* XV. viii. 14).

Here he reiterates the reflections he had developed in his commentaries on Genesis. In Book XV he also considers the procession of the Spirit and sets out the preliminary elements for a theology of the *Filioque**. But when he comes to say that the Spirit proceeds from the Father* and from the Son, it is the result of his investigation and not simply a dogmatic assertion.

4. The Two Cities

Another work by Augustine, published in the same period (c. 427), although it was begun in 412, had a great influence on later thought: *The City of God.* As in *De vera religione,* Augustine propounds an apologia for the true faith, the faith that leads to beatitude*. "Two loves have made two cities: love of self going as far as contempt for God has engendered the earthly city, love of God driven as far as contempt for the self has engendered the heavenly city" (XIV. 28). Augustine had long reflected on the theme of the two cities. It is found as early as *De vera religione, De catechizandis rudibus,* and *De Genesi ad litteram,* before being theorized in *The City of God* on the basis of a refutation of paganism* (I-X) and an affirmation of Christianity (XI-XXII). But the interpretation of the theme is difficult and has given rise to many controversies. One can no doubt see an opposition between Rome and the heavenly Jerusalem in the choice of *civitas* for the title of the work: it was written shortly after the fall of Rome and, while strongly marked by that event, intended to show that it was not the end of history*.

However, we should not be too hasty in assimilating the City of God to the Church*, as writers in the 19th century tended to do. Augustine begins rather with the parable* of the wheat and the chaff in order to situate these two realities. The Church has a central place in the thought of Augustine the pastor* of souls. He defines it as the mystical body of Christ, or even as Christ in his entirety, whose soul is the Holy Spirit (Sermon 267. 4). He develops his ecclesiology* principally in response to Donatism*, and in the light of the mystery of the Incarnation. He also points out that the Church presupposes communion* in faith, the sacraments*, and love, and that outside the Church there is no salvation*. This last point, however, needs some qualification, because Augustine is not referring here to the hierarchical church but to the Church understood as the community of the just, of both the Old and the New Covenant*. His perspective is thus much less restrictive than might have appeared at first sight. In fact, the City of God that he evokes is in some sense the city of which Scripture speaks. Its goal is beatitude, the eternal Sabbath* in which "we will rest and we will see; we will see and we will love; we will love and we will praise," and in this we can see a link between the City of God and Augustinian eschatology*.

Moreover, Books XIX through XXII of *The City of*

God are concerned with the final ends of the two cities and thus develop essential themes of Augustine's work, present from the earliest *Dialogues:* friendship, happiness, and peace*. These themes are supplemented, as in the works of the other Fathers of the Church, with a long reflection on the Resurrection* and salvation, interpreted in terms of the accomplishment of the six ages of the world*, which are understood as repeating the six days of Genesis and procuring beatitude and eternal rest.

Influenced by Porphyry, Augustine also presents in the work a theology of history, which to some degree reiterates and develops the celebrated reflection on time* that he had presented in Book XI of the *Confessions.*

Genius of the West, "doctor* of grace," Augustine left a considerable body of work, fragments of which are still being discovered, which strongly influenced the Latin Middle Ages. He was also the "doctor of charity," not only because of his famous maxim, "Love and do what you will," but also and especially because of the place he gives to charity, both in friendship, which was the very heart of his life, and in his pastoral duties and his spiritual* and communal life, of which it was the wellspring.

• Complete works: Mauristes, Paris, 1679–1700.
PL 32–46.
In addition: G. Morin (1930), *Sermones post Maurinos reperti,* Rome.
Letters 1–29, found by J. Divjak, BAug 46B.
A. d'Hippone: Vingt-six sermons au peuple d'Afrique, Ed. F. Dolbeau, Paris, 1996.
Partial works: CSEL, CChr.SL, BAug (with translation).
Possidius, *Vita Augustini,* text and Italian trans. by M. Pellegrino, Rome, 1955.
♦ L. S. Le Nain de Tillemont (1710), *Mémoires pour servir à l'histoire ecclésiastique des six premiers siècles,* vol. 13, Paris.
J. Mausbach (1906), *Die Ethik des heiligen Augustinus,* Fribourg.
M. Heidegger (1921), *Augustinus und der Neuplatonismus,* in GA 60, *Phänomenologie des religiösen Lebens,* 1995, 160–300.
B. Roland-Gosselin (1925), *La morale de saint Augustin,* Paris.
H. Arendt (1929), *Der Liebesbegriff bei Augustinus: Versuch einer philosophischen Interpretation,* Berlin.
É. Gilson (1929), *Introduction à l'étude de saint Augustin,* Paris.
H.-I. Marrou (1938), *Saint Augustin et la fin de la culture antique,* Paris.
"Bulletin augustinien," *Ath* (1940–51), *AthA* (1951–54) and *REAug* (1955–).
P. Courcelle (1950), *Recherches sur les* Confessions *de saint Augustin,* Paris.
F. Masai (1961), "Les conversions de saint Augustin et les débuts du spiritualisme en Occident," *RMAL* 67, 1–40.
T. J. van Bavel (1963), *Répertoire bibliographique de saint Augustin, 1950–1960,* Steenbrugge.
G. Bonner (1963), *St. Augustine of Hippo: Life and Controversies,* London (repr. 1986).
A.-M. La Bonnardière (1965), *Recherches de chronologie augustinienne,* Paris.
P. Brown (1967), *Augustine of Hippo, a Biography,* London.
L. Verheijen (1967), *La règle de saint A., I-II,* Paris.
A. Mandouze (1968), *L'aventure de la raison et de la grâce,* Paris.
O. Perler (1969), *Les voyages de saint Augustin,* Paris.
R. A. Markus (1970), *Saeculum: History and Society in the Theology of St. Augustine,* Cambridge.
G. K. Hall, et al. (1972), *Augustine Bibliography,* Boston (repr. 1981).
A. Trapé (1976), *San Agostino: L'uomo, il pastore, il mistico* (2nd Ed. 1988).
P. P. Verbraken (1976), *Études critiques sur les sermons authentiques de saint Augustin,* Steenbrugge.
A. Schindler (1979), "Augustin/Augustinismus I," *TRE* 4, 646–98.
K. Flasch (1980, 1994), *Augustin: Einführung in sein Denken,* Stuttgart.
O. O'Donovan (1980), *The Problem of Self-Love in St. Augustine,* New Haven-London.
L. Verheijen (1980–88), *Nouvelles approches de la* Règle *de saint Augustin,* Paris.
H. Chadwick (1986), *Augustine,* Oxford.
C. Mayer (Ed.) (1986–94), *Aug(L),* vol. I.
G. Madec (1989), *La patrie et la voie,* Paris.
C. Mayer, K. H. Celius (Ed.) (1989), *Internationales Symposion über den Stand der Augustinus Forschung,* Würzburg.
M.-A. Vannier (1991), Creatio, conversio, formatio *chez saint A.,* Fribourg (2nd Ed. 1996).
J. Wetzel (1992), *Augustine and the Limits of Virtue,* Cambridge.
B. Studer (1993), *Gratia Christi: Gratia Dei bei Augustinus von Hippo,* Rome.
G. Madec (1994), *Petites études augustiniennes,* Paris.
J. Rist (1995), *Augustine: Ancient Thought Baptized,* 2nd Ed., Cambridge.
R. A. Markus (1996), "A.," *DEPhM,* 101–8.
B. Stock (1996), *Augustine the Reader: Meditation, Self-Knowledge, and the Ethics of Interpretation,* Cambridge, Mass.-London (2nd Ed. 1998).
G. Madec (1998), *Le Dieu d'Augustin,* Paris.

Marie-Anne Vannier

See also **Augustianism; Catechesis; Monasticism; Platonism, Christian; Political Theology**

Augustinianism

"It was not always the best part of Saint Augustine* that in fact exercised the deepest or at least the most visible influence; the task set for us is thus easy to define: constantly to appeal from Augustinianism in all its forms to Saint Augustine himself" (Marrou 1955).

It is much more difficult to analyze the notion of Augustinianism, which covers a long history and is extremely complex. It is vague and, like many other "-isms," easily carries a pejorative connotation, all the more so because there is only one noun to designate both *Augustinian* quality and *Augustinist* defect. E. Portalié (1903) distinguishes between: 1) *Augustinianism,* the doctrine of the Order of Hermits of Saint Augustine on grace* (2485); and 2) *Augustinism,* which "either designates in a general manner the totality of Augustine's doctrines, or even the particular philosophical spirit which animates them; *or,* more particularly, his system of thought insofar as it considers the action of God*, grace, and liberty*" (2501). F. Cayré (1951) makes a number of subdistinctions: 1) *historical Augustinianism,* which is "the entirety of the doctrine of Saint Augustine as it appears in his work"; 2) *contemporary, official Augustinianism,* which is "the entirety of doctrines on grace which have since antiquity stamped the action of Saint Augustine and have entered into the common teaching of the church*"; 3) *partial Augustinianisms,* "particular aspects of the thought of Saint Augustine, emphasized at various times" (about 10); 4) *great Augustinianism,* an "ordered synthesis of the thought of Saint Augustine, not only on grace, but on the totality of Christian doctrine and on the principles that insure its vitality as evidenced by the persistence of its action; and 5) *false Augustinianisms:* predestinationism, Protestantism*, Jansenism*, and ontologism* (317–24). We will confine ourselves here to a brief and inevitably incomplete attempt at discernment: first, of the *Augustinian* spirit during Augustine's own lifetime and then during a period of calm acceptance; and second, of the *Augustinist* crises that have occurred over the course of 15 centuries on the question of grace and predestination* and on the theory of knowledge.

I. The Augustinian Spirit

1. During Augustine's Lifetime

a) Augustine's doctrinal activity was in no way aimed at establishing a personal system. It was directed toward an understanding of faith* (following the principle, *Crede ut intelligas,* that was adopted by Anselm*), in and for the African Christian communities, through interpretation of the Holy* Scriptures, which contain Christian doctrine (the theme of *De doctrina christiana*).

b) But this interpretation was strongly influenced by the event of Augustine's conversion* and the ensuing spiritual experience*. Three fundamental values can be discerned:

1) Interiority, the *Deus interior intimo meo et superior summo meo* (*Confessions* III. vi. 10), the discovery of the purely spiritual nature of God and of the soul*, thanks to the books of the Platonists; a theme deepened in the meditation on memory (*Confessions* X) and on Trinitarian spirituality (*De Trinitate* VIII-XV).
2) Community, incorporation into the Church through baptism*, but also the common life of brothers and then of the clergy*, based on the ideal of the apostolic community of Jerusalem* (Acts 4:32–35: *cor unum et anima una*), ideal form of the Church and prefiguration of the *City of God.* This practice of common life, following the *Rule* of Augustine, was continued in two families, the regular Canons and the Order (of Hermits) of Saint Augustine (O.[H.] S.A.)
3) The absolute primacy of God's grace: the merciful kindness of God toward Augustine, experienced in his conversion. In 396–97, Simplicianus (Ambrose*'s successor as bishop of Milan) provoked Augustine to a profound meditation on chapters 7 and 9 of The Epistle to the Romans, after which he understood that the grace of God anticipates any human initiative, including belief and desire. Composed shortly thereafter and marked by this discovery, the *Confessions* contain the germ of the Pelagian controversy. Pelagius was scandalized by Augustine's prayer: "Grant what you command, and command what you will" (*Confessions* X. xxix. 40).

c) At the same time, in concert with Aurelius (†432), bishop of Carthage and primate of Africa, Augustine played the role of theological expert in the Catholic episcopate of Africa, an honor that his colleagues obviously did not contest. To the many requests that were made of him he responded with thousands of sermons, hundreds of letters, and about a hundred books.

d) The controversies he provoked (Manicheanism*, Donatism*, Pelagianism*) themselves arose from his pastoral activity and were made necessary because of the various religious antagonisms with which African Christendom was afflicted. The controversial works are peremptory retorts that mercilessly refute the opposing argument point by point, using the techniques of legal dispute. They should not be and should not have been exploited (sometimes in a simplistic way) in any process of dogmatization (dogma*) of Christianity. In contrast, the great works of reflection *(Confessions, De Genesi ad litteram, De Trinitate)* are meditative and questioning, not at all inclining toward dogmatism.

e) In fact, after 40 years of service, Augustine had covered the entire field of Christian doctrine: God, the Trinity*, Christ* and salvation, the Church as *Christus totus,* the sacraments*, sin*, grace and predestination, personal and community spiritual life*—all without the slightest trace of a system. He certainly did not wish to establish *an* or *the* Augustinianism, but rather to pursue the defense and illustration of Christian truth*.

2. Calm Acceptance

a) Latin Christendom was to find in this body of occasional if not disparate works what might well be called its theological common property, incorporating in coherent form all the elements of Christian culture: philosophy*, theology*, law*, spirituality, mysticism*. And this was quickly recognized, as witnessed by the legend of the "portrait" of the old Lateran library dating from the sixth century: *Diuersi diuersa patres, sed hic omnia dixit, romano eloquio mystica sensa tonans* (Marrou 1955: "The various Fathers* of the Church have explained various things, but he alone has said all in Latin, explaining the mysteries* in the thunder of his great voice").

b) In the sixth century, Caesar of Arles († c. 532) was still making frequent use of Augustine's sermons and assured their diffusion through the collections he made of them. He did this not because he was some kind of plagiarist, as scholars too often conclude, but for the good of souls. In this he was merely conforming with Augustine's own practice, since Augustine would habitually prepare sermons that would then be delivered by colleagues who were less gifted at preaching* than he was.

c) With copy after copy pouring forth from monastic scriptoria, the works of Augustine were extraordinarily widely distributed and exercised an incalculable influence on medieval, and especially monastic, spirituality. Homilaries, collections of sermons that were read during the night office and later in the dining hall, had become widespread by the seventh century. Augustine's theme of the restoration of the soul* in the image of God exercised a powerful influence, notably in the 12th century (Javelet 1967). The reception of the works of the Pseudo-Dionysius* did not eclipse that of Augustine by Meister Eckhart (†1327; Courcelle 1963) and among the Rhineland*-Flemish mystics generally. J. Ruusbroec (†1381) was an Augustinian canon in Groenendaal. He was responsible for the conversion of G. Groot (†1384), founder of the Brothers of Common Life and initiator of *devotio* moderna,* to which Gerson (Jean Charlier †1429) gave theological status. The *Confessions* was bedside reading for many contemplatives. Teresa of Avila, to cite only one example, saw herself in it as in a mirror (Courcelle 1963).

d) In the ninth century Augustine was considered as "the master, after the apostles*, of all the churches," according to the testimony of Gottschalk of Orbais (Chatillon 1949), who considered himself an Augustinian in his (disastrous) preaching concerning dual predestination (*see* II 1 f above). Aside from being condemned by church councils, he was refuted by Duns* Scotus (Madec 1978), who contrasted the Augustinianism of predestination with that of the absolute simplicity* of God, indicating that everything can be found in Augustine. The refutation is worth what it is worth, but it certainly shows that Duns Scotus had a good Augustinian library at his disposal. He later found better arguments in the Greek fathers* of the church and was the first to apply the "law of communicating Platonisms," in the phrase of E. Gilson (1972), that is, to combine Augustinianism and Dionysianism (Koch 1969).

e) During the "renaissance" of the 11th and 12th centuries, powerful doctrinal personalities such as Anselm of Canterbury, Bernard* of Clairvaux, but also Peter Abelard*, Hugh of Saint*-Victor, and many others, maintained their Augustinian inspiration, each according to his own inclinations and for his own benefit and that of his colleagues. Also in the 12th century, the librarian of the Abbey of Clairvaux gathered a large part of Augustine's works into a Corpus of 12 volumes. But we can only speculate about the potential readership he had in mind, for there are no superstars in the quiet reading of the works of Augustine.

f) However, Peter Lombard freely mined those works for quotations, which he then put in "theological" order in the four books of the *Sentences.* They contain 1,423 mentions of Augustine, 4 of Pseudo-Dionysius, 193 of Ambrose, 150 of Jerome, and 139 of Gregory* the Great. Because of this manual, upon which it was obligatory to comment in all schools, basic theology during the major period of Scholasticism* came to be composed of 80 to 90 percent of Augustinian elements, even if these were passed through a Scholastic* filter. There are more than 2,000 quotations of Augustine in the *Summa Theologica* alone (Elders 1987). "Albert* the Great and Saint Thomas, far from presenting themselves as adversaries of Saint Augustine, as they were reproached for doing, set themselves to learn from him and, while modifying certain theories, introduced and absorbed the entire theology of the Doctor of Hippo.... Thus, there was no strictly Augustinian school ... because all schools were.... What disappeared was Augustinianism in too narrow and limited a form, bestowed on it by particular questions then much debated, an Augustinianism that was too Platonic. But *great Augustinianism,* with its views on God, on divine ideas, on the Trinity, on revelation*, not to mention grace, still holds sway over our minds" (Portalié 1903).

g) The decadence of Scholasticism brought about serious crises, which will be considered in part II. Suffice it to say that these crises were at a point of no return, and it is perhaps useful to recall the judgment of Harnack (1907): "All the major personalities who recreated a new life in the Western church or who purified and deepened piety came, directly or indirectly, from Saint Augustine and were trained in his school." This is to assert that the "heretics" themselves—Luther*, Calvin*, Baius, Jansenius, and the rest—before becoming "misdirected Augustinians" (Lubac 1931), wished to be and believed they were good disciples of Augustine.

h) During the period of Christian humanism* there appeared the first editions of the *Opera omnia,* that of Amebach in Basel in 1506, and that of Erasmus* in 1528–29, also published in Basel and reprinted several times. The edition prepared by the theologians of Louvain, published by Plantin in Antwerp in 1577, also reprinted many times, was in use throughout most of the 17th century (Ceyssens 1982), before there appeared the edition of the Benedictines of Saint-Maur (Paris, 1679–90). This was also the time of the first translations: *The City of God* by Raoul de Presles, appearing as early as 1486. All of this is evidence of Augustinian vitality.

i) The Great Century in France has also been called "the century of Saint Augustine" (Sellier 1982). If this was the case, it was not only because of the Jansenist controversy. The spirituality of Bérulle, for example, is of Augustinian inspiration. Mersenne, Meslan, and Antoine Arnauld pointed out to Descartes* his affinities with Augustine (Lewis 1954). Pascal* was Augustinian in the *Pensées* as well as in the *Provinciales* (Sellier 1970). Father André Martin of the Oratorians (under the pseudonym of Ambrosius Victor), compiled a *Philosophia christiana,* a clever compilation of extracts from Augustine, which was of much use to another Oratorian, Malebranche. Bossuet was an Augustinian, as was Fénelon in another way, along with so many others that it would be tedious to list them all. Arnauld d'Andilly translated the *Confessions;* and his brother Antoine Arnauld translated not only the anti-Pelagian writings, but also various short works and the *Sermons of Saint Augustine on the Psalms,* in seven volumes.

j) After an eclipse, which was perhaps not total, during the Enlightenment and the French Revolution, Augustine gradually regained visibility in the difficult restoration of Christian thought, filtered through the work of Descartes and Malebranche. His presence is real, although ill defined, in traditionalism* (Lammenais, Bautain), in Christian rationalism* (Maine de Biran, Bordas-Dumoulin, Lequier), and in ontologism (Brancereau and Hugonin in France, Ubaghs in Belgium, Rosmini in Italy). It gained force in the work of Father Gratry. (On all these movements, *see* Foucher 1955.) The *Annales de philosophie chrétienne,* founded by A. Bonnety in 1830, also belong to this movement.

In the Oxford Movement, Newman *(Apologia pro vita sua)* considered Augustine as "the great light of the Western world, who, though not an infallible teacher, shaped the mind of Europe." Pusey published his own translation of the *Confessions* as the first volume of the *Oxford Library of the Fathers.* In Germany we must at least mention the school of Tübingen, the work of J. A. Möhler, as well as the *Summa* of J. Kleutgen, S.J., *Theologie*... and *Philosophie der Vorzeit.*

k) From 1841 to 1862 J.-P. Migne reprinted the Saint-Maur edition of the works of Augustine in Volumes 32–47 of his *Patrologie latine.* And by the end of the 19th century France could pride itself on being the only country to have two complete translations of the works of Augustine (Poujoulat and Raulx, Bar-le-Duc, 1864–73, in 17 volumes; Péronne et al., Paris, Librairie Vivès, 1869–78, in 34 volumes).

l) When he assumed the editorship of the *Annales de philosophie chrétienne* in 1905, L. Laberthonnière adopted the motto: "Let us seek as though we must find, let us find as though we must seek" (*De Trinitate* IX. i. 1). M. Blondel* (1930) celebrated "the constantly renewed richness of Augustinian thought." As early as 1933 Father F. Cayré (1884–1971), concerned with balancing neo-Thomism with a kind of neo-Augustinianism, launched the *Bibliothèque augustinienne* and in 1943 created the *Centre d'Études augustiniennes,* where Augustinian studies experienced a rapid expansion in the context of a movement of return to the Fathers of the Church. It has even been written that it was Augustine who was the great theologian of Vatican* II (Morán 1966). On this point, we should simply note that J. Ratzinger (1954), an expert on the council*, had written his thesis on the Augustinian doctrine of the church as people* and house of God. The thesis was published in the 16th centenary of the death of Augustine, something which was also celebrated by an important international congress that prepared a survey of Augustinian studies and so helped to ensure their revival. The proceedings of the congress were published in three volumes: *Augustinus Magister.* Even today, the Augustinian spirit flourishes where it will.

II. Augustinist Crises

1. Grace and Predestination

a) In order to attempt to achieve clarity, it is first appropriate to set out a strict and narrow definition of Augustinianism as a particular interpretation of the mystery* of salvation, an interpretation that can be and has been challenged. According to Dom O. Rottmanner (1908), it is "the doctrine of unconditioned predestination and particular salvific will as Saint Augustine developed it in the last period of his life... surrendering no part of it until his death." Subsequent history then becomes a series of doctrinal crises and provocations.

b) An Augustinian Crisis? We noted above (I 1 b) that in reflecting on Romans in order to reply to Simplicianus, Augustine had had the revelation of an absolute primacy of grace over any human initiative. This has been interpreted as a doctrinal crisis, an upheaval that transformed Augustinian doctrine into a "nest of contradictions" (Flasch 1980). But in the mind of Augustine it represented progress. It has also been thought (Hombert 1966) that the work caused a falling out: the silence of Simplicianus and of Aurelius himself is thought to have been reproving. If this were the case, it would also have been reprehensible, for the result was that Augustine was later to become entangled alone in the excesses of his *intellectus fidei* (Solignac 1988).

c) The Pelagian controversy was essentially an affair of the church and the councils (Wermelinger 1975). Certainly, Augustine led the battle with his many writings against Celestius, Pelagius, and Julian of Eclanum, but the African bishops were behind him. However, it cannot be denied that his interpretation of the consequences of original sin* aroused protests. As early as 413, some went so far as to treat Augustine as a heretic (ibid.). In the heat of controversy, Augustine's thought hardened, or rather his interpretation of Holy Scripture, especially Romans (*see* Solignac 1988), for it must be remembered that Augustine had no intention of constructing a personal system. The African bishops did not adopt his thought wholesale. The canons of the Council of Carthage (418; *DH* 222–30) make no mention of the limitation of saving grace or of predestination, and nor do pontifical documents (Innocent I, Zosima; *DH* 217–21).

d) Since the late 16th century, the monks of Provence, Cassian and his disciples, have inappropriately been characterized as "semi-Pelagians." On the contrary, they in no way relied on Pelagius, but admired the works of Augustine. They merely challenged his theory of grace and predestination, which they deemed "contrary to the opinion of the Fathers of the Church and to the sense of the church" (Letter from Prosper to Augustine). In other words, they saw Augustine's thinking in these areas as innovative and tending toward heresy*. It might be said that they were the first critical Augustinians. Augustine answered that although they had taken the trouble to read his books, they had not taken the trouble to make progress with him while reading them: that is, progress in the understanding of faith, which is the comprehension of Holy Scripture. Prosper of Aquitaine (†463) has been called the "first representative of medieval Augustinianism" (Cappuyns 1929), and he certainly did much work in defense of Augustine. By 431, a few months after Augustine's death, he secured from Pope* Celestine a letter in praise of the great bishop* of Hippo and generally (that is, prudently) approving his doctrine, while recalling that his predecessors had always considered Augustine among the best teachers (*DH* 237). Prosper did much for the adoption of a moderate Augustinianism, opposed to the criticisms of the monks of Provence, while recognizing along with them that we must not discuss the mystery of predestination formulated by Paul in Romans 8:28 ff. (*DH* 238–49).

e) In fact there was a risk that the idea might logically degenerate into predestinationism: if God predestines the elect to eternal bliss, logically he also predestines the others, the reprobates, to eternal damnation. Perhaps this is "a fearsome weapon" forged in some anti-Augustinian circle (Orcibal 1989). But the priest* Lucidus had to issue a retraction on this question at the Council of Arles in 473 (*DH* 330–42). Around 520 Fulgentius of Ruspe also attempted to dissuade Monimus from this position. The Council of Orange (529; *DH* 379–97), under the impetus of Caesar of Arles, gave official status to a "softened," "moderate" Augustinianism, and in the opinion of Portalié (1903, 2526), this was "the most important event in the history of Augustinianism": "Already... all of Jansenism is condemned by the very council that most exalted Augustinian doctrine. It will remain definitively established that, in *legitimate and Catholic* Augustinianism, there is not, in the proper sense of the word, a predestination to death and further that God really wills the salvation of all men" (1527).

f) Nevertheless, there were serious resurgences. The first was provoked in the ninth century by Gottschalk, a renegade monk from Orbais, who began to preach on dual predestination, following a formulation of Isidore of Seville: "There is a dual predestination, that of the elect at rest, that of the reprobates in death" (*Sentences* II. 6. 1). Such an argument could have only disastrous consequences for pastoral activity. Gottschalk was condemned by several synods, including the Synod of Quierzy (*DH* 621–24). His refuter, Duns Scotus, was also condemned (*see* I 2 d above) at the synod of Valence (*DH* 625–33).

g) The great Scholastics, Thomas, Bonaventure*, Gilles of Rome (O.H.S.A., †1316), and the others, explained and developed the (Augustinian) doctrine of grace and liberty in their schools, variously in relative tranquility. But predestinationism returned in the form of the absolute determinism of Thomas Bradwardine (†1348) and was transmitted to John Wycliffe (1384). It was, however, condemned at the Council of Constance* (*DH* 1151–95). There were further resurgences with Luther* and especially Calvin*. On their Augustinianism, *see* L. Cristiani (1954) and J. Cadier (1954).

h) At the Council of Trent*, Jerome Seripando, prior general of the Order of Saint Augustine and later archbishop of Salerno (†1563), insisted that Augustine could be relied on as a faithful interpreter of Paul, rather than the schemas of the controversialist theologians. Although the council Fathers did take some note of his views, this was not true of the theologians, who continued to follow Scholastic methods of discussion.

In Louvain there was the affair of Baius (Michel de Bay †1589) (Bañezianism*-Molinism-Baianism), an avid reader of Augustine's works but confused in his system of the natural and the supernatural*, as well as on the question of original sin and grace (Lubac 1965). Condemned at the Sorbonne and later in Rome* (*DH* 1901–80), Baius always submitted humbly. But the matter was not finished (*see* Orcibal 1989: "Rome, Louvain et l'autorité de Saint Augustin"). The controversy known as "De auxiliis" (on the different modalities of the assistance of grace) was provoked by the work of Father Luis Molina (†1600) entitled *Concordia: The Harmony of Free Will with the Gifts of Grace, the Prescience of God, Providence, Predestination, and Reprobation* (Lisbon, 1588; Antwerp, 1595). It opposed Dominicans and Jesuits, the former defending, with Bañez, physical predetermination (that is, efficient causality), the latter God's "average science." Pope Clement VIII created a commission that met more than 120 times between 1598 and 1611, though without reaching a conclusion. His successor, Paul V, thought it necessary to put an end to the debate and begged the adversaries to refrain from mutual censure (*DH* 1997).

But soon thereafter came Jansenius (Cornelis Janssen, 1585–1638), fellow student of Jean Duvergier de Hauranne, the future abbé de Saint-Cyran. In 1619 Jansenius discovered the central principle of Augustine's doctrine in the distinction between two kinds of grace: the grace of Adam* and the grace of Christ, and he devoted twenty years to the preparation of *Augustinus; or, the Doctrine of Saint Augustine on Health, Illness, and the Curing of Human Nature against the Pelagians and the Marseillais* (condemned for five propositions by Innocent X; *DH* 2001–7). The posthumous publication of this work, in Louvain in 1640, in Paris in 1641, and in Rouen in 1643, would transform the intellectual and spiritual life of Christendom into an Augustinist battlefield.

i) Rather than the "century of Saint Augustine," the 17th century might be called that of the failure of Augustinianism, if we accept the severe and striking verdict of L. Brunschvicg (1927): "It is a matter of determining who this Augustine is whom all parties agree in making the infallible arbiter of orthodoxy. Is he the theoretician of Ideas whom Neoplatonic speculations returned to the religion of the Word*? Is he the theoretician of grace, fired by zeal against the freedom of Pelagius as was the apostle Paul against the wisdom of the philosophers? Both, it will be said. Jansenius and Ambrosius Victor gave contradictory interpretations of Augustinianism; they do not, however, contradict one another as historians. But the century of clear and distinct ideas no longer resigned to simply recording a chaotic collection of heterogeneous texts.... It was thus inevitable that the contributions of Neoplatonism and of the Gospels to the work of Augustine be separated like two rivers on parallel courses, whose waters have never really mixed. And hence arose the conflict of two perfectly organic systems, both Augustinian, whose antagonism and incompatibility it is impossible to mask, once it is admitted that a synthesis, even if it were to take place above the level of reason*, nevertheless requires that it be defined for itself in its internal ordering.... In the end, although there has probably never been, in any period of religious history, a flowering of geniuses superior to the one that occurred in France with Pascal and Malebranche, Fénelon and Bossuet himself, it seems that this wealth had no effect but to make more dangerous the imaginary obsession with heresy—Jansenism or rationalism*, quietism* or Gallicanism*—which made each one suspect the others, and finally rarefied the atmosphere of French Catholicism to the point of making it unbreathable."

The Jansenist drama of conscience (Ceyssens 1954), as well as the misfortune of all the Augustinians of the period, lay in absolutizing the Augustinian doctrine of grace and predestination, in the "dogmatic monopoly" (Neveu 1990) against which Richard Simon (1693; *see* Ranson 1990) reacted healthily: "I only wish that those who pride themselves on being his disciples would not pass off all their master's feelings as articles of faith." This was not to Bossuet's liking (Rouméliote 1988), but it was exactly the point of view of Augustine himself (*Letters* 148, 5).

2. Theory of Knowledge

a) For Augustine, all intellectual knowledge is participation in the Word, which is Truth* and Wisdom*. If the Platonists were able to know God, the true God, one in three, this was thanks to the Word, which illuminates anyone who comes into this world. The Christian, reading the prologue of the Gospel of John through to the end, adheres to Christ, the illuminating Word of God and the savior Word incarnate. This is the principle of Christian rationalism that can be found in various forms in Duns Scotus (Madec 1977), Anselm (Madec 1994), Peter Abelard (Gregory 1973), Hugh of Saint-Victor (Simonis 1972), Bonaventure (Madec 1990), and later Malebranche (Gouhier 1926).

b) With the establishment of the university in the 13th century, a clear distinction between philosophy and theology became essential. This brought in its wake new conceptions of the relationships between faith and reason and between nature* and grace, and new debates that lasted for centuries. Albert the Great advised Thomas Aquinas to follow Augustine in theology and Aristotle in philosophy. He followed the advice and discerned in Augustinian doctrine a different philosophical component. According to him, Augustine had followed Plato as far as Catholic faith allowed (*De spir. creaturis* X. 8). This perception was of capital importance, because it accredited the idea that Augustinian doctrine was a synthesis of Platonism and Christianity—it was a Christian Platonism*—an idea that has governed doctrinal studies on Augustine down to the present. It is, however, a false idea, for although Augustine did not hide his debt to the Platonists, he did not have the sense of being obliged to *follow* them, for the simple reason that he believed he had found in their books a doctrine that could be at least partly identified with that of the prologue of the Gospel of John.

c) Taking up the Thomist perception, P. Mandonnet (1911) offered a negative definition of philosophical Augustinianism as a state of doctrinal confusion: "Lacking formal distinction between the realms of philosophy and theology, that is, between the order of rational truths and the order of revealed truths.... A similar tendency, moreover, to erase the formal separation between nature and grace." This notion is inconsistent (Madec 1988). It derives from a Scholastic discrimination whose rigidity constrains the inherent mobility of Augustinian doctrine. If the distinction between philosophy and theology is still compelling or pertinent, then all Augustinianism must be classified as theology.

d) Commentators have nevertheless striven to label an abstraction. É. Gilson (1926–27) created "the deplorably pedantic but clear expression 'Avicennan Augustinianism'" to define "the position of Guillaume d'Auvergne, Roger Bacon, Roger Marston, and perhaps John Peckam," and "Aristotelian Augustinianism" for the position of Alexander of Hales, Jean de la Rochelle, and Bonaventure. F. Van Steenberghen (1966) later dismissed the illusion of a "philosophical Augustinianism": "Only in the realm of theology can there be any question of Augustinianism for the theologians of today; all the distinctive traits which have been used in an attempt to characterize 'pre-Thomist Augustinianism' or the 'Platonic-Augustinian movement' belong in reality to the theological movement formally considered and find their grounding in this fact."

The fact remains, however, that the happily ineffectual condemnation of certain Thomist theses by É. Tempier in 1277 (Thomism*) was, according to Portalié (1903), "the last victory of the Augustinians."

e) The definition of *political Augustinianism* is modeled on the definition by Mandonnet: "It is the tendency to absorb the natural law of the state into supernatural justice* and ecclesiastical law. But what was only a tendency of mind for the African thinker became a doctrine for the heirs of his political thought, and a particularly vigorous doctrine, because it led to the theocratic conceptions of the Middle Ages" (Arquillière 1954). This formulation is as inept as the preceding one and the thesis was severely criticized by H. de Lubac (1984). It remains true that medieval theocratic theories are based on a radical misunderstanding in the interpretation of *De civitate Dei* (political theology*). In that work Augustine developed not a philosophy but a theology of history* (Marrou 1954), of the history of salvation completed with the Coming of Christ in the sixth age of humanity, one that cannot therefore be set out in detail through the history of the Church, contradictory to the theory of Joachim de Flore, as revised and corrected by Bonaventure (Ratzinger 1959).

f) According to F. Van Steenberghen (1966), "the doctrinal mission of Saint Bonaventure seems to have been to bring out the unity of Christian knowledge, at a time when growing emancipation was creating a serious threat of a break between reason and faith." In order to accomplish this mission, he repeated the doctrine of the Word, God and man, who guarantees the unity of faith and understanding, science and wisdom, because he is the only Teacher (Madec 1990), "the environment of all sciences, in which are hidden all the treasures of the wisdom and the knowledge of God" (*In Hex. coll.* I. 11).

g) According to L. Brunschvicg (1927), Malebranche (1638–1715) was the promoter of "Catholic rationalism." This was owed to Descartes, but especially to Augustine, who taught him that Christ is the internal teacher, the eternal Wisdom who presides over all minds in all their acts of thought: it is a question here not so much of any vision of God as such, but of vision *in* God. Christ is simultaneously the "eternal Word, [the] universal Reason of minds" and the "incarnate Word, Author and finisher of our faith." The work of the incarnate Word is related to contemplation* of the eternal Word as faith is to understanding. The way in which Malebranche had the Word speak in his *Méditations chrétiennes* provoked sharp responses from Antoine Arnauld and Pastor Jurieu, but their intention was simply to malign Malebranche's meditations and prayers (Madec 1969).

h) In the 19th century the theme of the vision of God inspired several Christian thinkers (*see* I 2 j above) in the movements known as Christian rationalism and ontologism. But there was a certain degree of confusion engendered, probably because these thinkers had no means of freeing themselves from the philosophy-theology grid. The condemnations from Rome that some of them suffered certainly derived from a Scholastic conception of the relationships between faith and reason and between nature* and the supernatural. It will suffice to mention the cases of A. Rosmini Serbati (†1855) (*DH* 3201–40), A. Günther (†1863) (*DH* 8228–31; Simonis 1972), and J. Froschammer (1821–93) (*DH* 2850–61; Simonis 1972).

i) The expression "Christian philosophy" has been generally and peacefully used for a long time. It is contained in the title of the oldest French journal of philosophy (*see* I 2 j above). It was only in the heyday of Neoscholasticism that it became the object of a vigorous debate (Henry 1955), in which historians argued like philosophers attached to the definition of philosophy through the autonomy of reason. The debate barely touched on the Fathers of the Church or Augustinianism. H. de Lubac (1979), however, notes that the problem was mentioned at the session of the Thomist society in Juvisy in 1933 by Father A.-D.Sertillanges, who immediately dismissed it: "The new sense of the word 'philosophy' symbolizes a conquest to which we cannot submit. Since Saint Thomas Aquinas, the two realms of reason and faith have in principle been clearly distinct. . . . Replacing in any way philosophy under the dependence of faith would be 'to retreat to before Saint Thomas,' *to return to the confusionism of medieval Augustinianism,* and by the same token to put ourselves 'in a very bad position, isolating us from the thinking world that means to think freely.'"

L. Laberthonnière (†1932), the troublesome friend of Blondel, cut off by ecclesiastical prohibitions, did not participate in the argument, but he alluded to it. According to him, "we can only speak of 'Christian philosophy' if what we call by this name *is Christianity itself.* This is what was done in the beginning. And it was only after the invasion of Aristotelianism* that, in separating on the pretext of distinguishing, we created the mortal conflict between philosophy and theology, the natural and the supernatural, within which we struggle so miserably" (1942). The question should remain open, peacefully.

• A. Harnack (1900), *Das Wesen des Christentums,* Leipzig.
E. Portalié (1903), "Augustinianisme (École et système des augustiniens)," *DThC* 1, 2485-2501; "Augustinianisme (Développement historique de l'—)," *DThC* 1, 2501–61.
O. Rottmanner (1908), *Geistes Früchte aus der Klosterzelle,* Munich, 11–32.
P. Mandonnet (1911), *Siger de Brabant et l'averroïsme,* Louvain.

É. Gilson (1926–27), "Pourquoi saint Thomas a critiqué saint Augustin," *AHDL* 1, 5–127.
H. Gouhier (1926 *a*), *La philosophie de Malebranche et son expérience religieuse,* Paris; (1926 *b*), *La vocation de Malebranche,* Paris.
L. Brunschvicg (1927), *Le progrès de la conscience dans la philosophie occidentale,* Paris.
M. Cappuyns (1929), "Le premier représentant de l'augustianisme médiéval: Prosper d'Aquitaine," *RThAM* I, 309–37.
M. Blondel (1930), "La fécondité toujours renouvelée de la pensée augustinienne," *Cahiers de la Nouvelle Journée* 17, 1–20.
H. de Lubac (1931), "Deux augustiniens fourvoyés: Baius et Jansénius," *RSR* 21, 422–43; 513–40.
L. Laberthonnière (1942), *Esquisse d'une philosophie personnaliste,* Paris.
F. Chatillon (1949), "Le plus bel éloge de saint Augustin," *RMAL* 5, 234–37.
F. Cayré (1951), "Aug., Note complémentaire," *DThC,* Tables I, 317–24.
H.-X. Arquillière (1954), "Réflexions sur l'essence de l'augustianisme politique," *AugM* II, 991–1001.
J. Cadier (1954), "Calvin et saint Augustin," ibid., 1039–56.
L. Ceyssens (1954), "Le drame de conscience augustinien des premiers jansénistes," ibid., 1069–76.
L. Cristiani (1954), "Luther et saint Augustin," ibid., 1029–38.
G. Lewis (1954), "Augustianisme et cartésianisme," ibid., 1087–1104.
H.-I. Marrou (1954), "La théologie de l'histoire," *AugM* III, 193–212; (1955), *Saint Augustin et l'augustianisme,* Paris.
J. Ratzinger (1954), *Volk und Haus Gottes in Augustins Lehre von der Kirche,* Munich.
L. Foucher (1955), *La philosophie catholique en France au XIXe siècle avant la renaissance thomiste et dans son rapport avec elle,* Paris.
A. Henry (1955), "La querelle de la philosophie chrétienne, Histoire et bilan d'un débat," in *Philosophies chrétiennes,* RDCCIF 10, 35–68.
J. Ratzinger (1959), *Die Geschichtstheologie des heiligen Bonaventura,* Munich-Zurich.
P. Courcelle (1963), *Les Confessions dans la tradition littéraire,* Paris.
H. de Lubac (1965), *Aug. et théologie moderne,* Paris.
J. Morán (1966), "La presenza di San Agostino nel Concilio Vaticano II," *Aug.* 6, 460–88.
F. Van Steenberghen (1966), *La philosophie au XIIIe siècle,* Louvain-Paris.
R. Javelet (1967), *Image et ressemblance au XIIe siècle,* Paris.
J. Koch (1969), "Augustinischer und Dionysicher Neuplatonismus und das Mittelalter," in W. Beierwaltes (Ed.), *Platonismus in der Philosophie des Mittelalters,* Darmstadt, 317–42.
P. Sellier (1970), *Pascal et saint Augustin,* Paris.
W. Simonis (1972), *Trinität und Vernunft: Untersuchungen zur Möglichkeit einer rationalen Trinitätslehre bei Anselm, Abelard, den Viktorinern, A. Günther und J. Froschammer,* Frankfurt.
É. Gilson (1972), *Le thomisme,* 6th Ed., Paris.
T. Gregory (1973), "Considerazioni su *ratio* e *natura* in Abelardo," *StMed* 14, 287–300.
O. Wermelinger (1975), *Rom und Pelagius,* Stuttgart.
G. Madec (1977), "L'a. de Jean Scot dans le *De praedestinatione,*" in R. Roques (Ed.), *Jean Scot Érigène et l'histoire de la philosophie,* Paris, 183–90; id. (1978), *Iohannis Scotti De diuina praedestinatione,* CChr.CM 50, Turnhout.
H. Gouhier (1978), *Cartésianisme et augustinisme au XVIIe s.,* Paris.
H. de Lubac (1979), "Sur la philosophie chrétienne: Réflexions à la suite d'un débat," in *Recherches dans la foi,* Paris, 127–52.
K. Flasch (1980), *Augustinus: Einführung in sein Denken,* Mayence.
L. Ceyssens (1982), "Le 'saint Augustin' du XVIIe siècle: l'édition de Louvain (1577)," *XVIIe siècle* 34, 103–20.
P. Sellier (1982), "Le siècle de saint Augustin," *XVIIe siècle* 34, 99–102.
H. de Lubac (1984), "Augustianisme politique?" *Théologies d'occasion,* Paris, 255–308.
L. Elders (1987), "Les citations de saint Augustin dans la *Somme théologique* de saint Thomas d'Aquin," *DoC* 40, 115–67.
G. Madec (1988), "La notion d'augustianisme philosophique," in *Jean Scot et ses auteurs,* Paris, 147–61.
A. Rouméliote (1988), "Bossuet gendarme de l'augustianisme face à R. Simon et J. de Launoy," in P. Ranson (Ed.), *Saint A.,* Dossiers "H," 399–405.
A. Solignac (1988), "Les excès de l'*intellectus fidei* dans la doctrine d'Augustin sur la grâce," *NRTh* 110, 825–49.
J. Orcibal (1989), *Jansénius d'Ypres (1585–1638),* Paris.
G. Madec (1990), *Saint Bonaventure: Le Christ Maître,* Paris.
B. Neveu (1990), "Le statut théologique de saint Augustin au XVIIe s.," in coll., *Troisième centenaire de l'édition mauriste de saint Augustin,* Paris, 15–28.
P. Ranson (1990), *Richard Simon ou du caractère illégitime de l'augustianisme en théologie,* Lausanne.
V. Carraud (1992), *Pascal et la philosophie,* Paris.
G. Madec (1994), *Petites études augustiniennes,* Paris.
P.-M. Hombert (1996), *Gloria gratiae,* Paris.

Goulven Madec

See also **Augustine of Hippo; Bañezianism-Molinism-Baianism; Grace; Jansenism; Pelagianism; Political Theology; Predestination; Sin, Original**

Authority

A. In the Church

a) New Testament and the Fathers. In the ancient Roman Empire, *auctoritas* indicated power endowed with prestige, an indirect social power that was superior to immediate, coercive power *(potestas).* Since Augustus, supreme authority had been represented by the emperor, from whom magistrates and jurists in turn derived their authority.

The New Testament contains no direct equivalent of this Roman concept, and the Vulgate itself does not use the word. However, the terms *dunamis* (e.g., in 2 Cor 8:3 and Eph 3:16) and *exousia* (e.g., in Mt 21:23–27) are of interest in this regard. While *dunamis* means power and the means of executing it, in a general sense, *exousia* more specifically indicates a mandate legitimized by God*. As a relational concept, with reference to the origin of legitimization (emperor, God), *exousia* has certain features in common with *auctoritas.*

The Latin Fathers* from Tertullian* onward speak of *auctoritas Dei* or *Christi.* This authority could be extended to witnesses and disciples: there are references, in this sense, to the authority of the apostles* and of the ancients, but also to the authority of the canonical books* of the Bible*. This usage took as its model the authority of the emperor, from which legitimate representatives derived their own power. Thus, authority was assimilated to the notion of tradition* and the doctrine of apostolic* succession.

In the writings of Tertullian and, for example, Cyprian*, authority remained a derivative from Roman legal terminology. Augustine*, however, used the notion in a less institutional perspective, giving it a place in his theory of knowledge: divine authority, and the authority of Holy* Scripture, form the basis for authentic knowledge. Although he allotted first place to the authority of the Catholic Church*, as the ultimate criterion of truth*, Augustine did not mean by this any specific legal institution, but rather the authenticity of the universal Church. Nevertheless, by subordinating the individual reason* of Christians to the authority of the church, Augustine helped to create the basic problems that were to disrupt Christianity at a later stage.

b) Middle Ages and the Reformation. The principle of the authority of Holy Scripture was never called into question during the Middle Ages. However, in practice authority was directly linked to the people who governed the church. Just as the philosophers of antiquity and the Fathers of the Church were considered in the universities as *auctoritates,* so popes*, bishops*, and other holders of church offices were considered to have a natural authority, which was conflated with that of the church and the apostles. This implied a broadening of the range of written sources of authority within the church: Scripture in the strict sense was supplemented by the decisions of councils*, papal decrees, canon* law, and the texts of the Fathers*. As a result, members of the church hierarchy could cite a multitude of established authority, external to Scripture but all theologically justified.

The Reformers denounced this development. Luther* in particular gave Holy Scripture an absolute priority over all other authority, human or institutional: "We do not accord to the church any authority that goes beyond Scripture" (*WA* 40 3, 434, 13). This idea was clear enough in itself, but it did not resolve the concrete problems of church government, nor did it provide any hermeneutic* rules for the correct interpretation of Scripture. Most of the churches born out of the Reformation were quick to recognize the need for a church magisterium* endowed with authority, despite the divergent evolution of their respective structures*. The principle of authority was also applied in the interpretation of Scripture, for which the readings of ordained ministers and trained theologians came to be valued as standard. Nevertheless, it may be concluded that, because of the emphasis that they placed on the primordial authority of Scripture, the churches that developed out of the Reformation always retained a certain critical potential in this domain.

c) Modern Times. Ever since antiquity, philosophy* has regarded the critical use of individual reason and obedience to traditional authority as two antithetical attitudes. This tendency was especially reinforced during the Enlightenment and found its political expression in the French Revolution.

The systematization of modern thought on the basis of opposition to the concept of authority was principally the work of Kant*. In his view, the philosophy that preceded his was a "dogmatism" linked to authority, because it did not examine the conditions for the possible exercise of reason from a critical point of view. In the domain of moral philosophy, Kant taught that ethical authority must depend upon an internal principle, that is, on a good will determined by duty. In the final analysis, external authority always remained unjustified; only the autonomous person*, taking reason as his guide, could give a credible form to his own convictions. Drawing out the consequences of this principle of individual autonomy, modern philosophy adopted a critical attitude to all external authority from the outset. To the extent that it largely corresponded to the view that modern man took of himself in an individualist society*, modern philosophy could not help but enter into conflict with the Christian churches, which traditionally grounded their authority in the "external" jurisdiction of Holy Scripture and the church magisterium.

The authority of a religious text presents a complex hermeneutic problem, which may be clarified, on the one hand, by the theory of the divine inspiration of the text itself and, on the other, by the idea of a magisterium authorized to provide an interpretation of the text. While the Christian churches teach that the clarity (Luther, *WA* 18, 609, 4) and the obviousness of Scripture are enough to attest their authority, and that the Bible should be accessible to all believers (*DH* 4229), they also emphasize the necessity of the magisterium and of the theory of inspiration. Thus, Vatican* II assigns to the magisterium—"whose authority is exercised in the name of Jesus Christ" (*DH* 4214)—the task of authentically interpreting the word* of God.

d) Different Types of Authority. The philosophical critique of authority does not, of course, mean that the real organizations of the modern world have no dependence on relations of authority. In particular, Max Weber's distinction among three types of authority has been of great interest in sociology. Weber conceives authority within an organization as a relation of "domination," and distinguishes among "traditional" authority, "legal" (rational, bureaucratic) authority, and "charismatic" authority. The church represents an ideal type of traditional domination or authority; its power is organized hierarchically and is legitimized by a relation with the past. Legal authority is vested in the holder of an office by reference to his position within a system, independent of any personal quality; charismatic authority, by contrast, is legitimized by purely individual characteristics. Although Weber's classification is only one of numerous modern typologies of authority, it has dominated theoretical developments in the sociology of religion, as well as the empirical study of existing churches. A fourth type of authority has often been proposed, that of the specialist who has acquired a certain prestige through his competence but who does not enjoy any charismatic power in Weber's sense.

e) Authority in Discussions among the Churches. The Catholic and Anglican Churches have issued a document entitled *Authority in the Church,* in which Holy Scripture is defined as "the normative statement of the authentic foundations of faith.... It is through these written words that the authority of the word of God is transmitted" (op. cit., 2). The authority of the church is here placed first, yet it is Jesus Christ who constitutes "the authentic foundation," not Scripture itself. Dialogue arises, not from individual interpretations, but from "common faith," the yardstick by which each person tests the truth of his own belief. This common faith presupposes a community, a *koinonia* (op. cit., 4). Thus, the *koinonia* becomes a guarantee for the authority of Scripture. Within this community, people can also exercise authority. Certain persons, "by the internal quality of their lives," inspire a respect "that permits them to speak with authority in the name of Christ." Other people receive their authority from the ordained ministry*, which is "intrinsic to the structure of the church" and constitutes "another form of authority." Thus, "the perception of God's will for his church does not belong to the ordained ministry alone; it is shared by all its members" (op. cit., 4–6).

Rome did not approve this document, but this dialogue illustrates the way in which the question of authority has been addressed in numerous contemporary churches: it has been given traits that are simultaneously charismatic (the interior quality of life), traditional, and legal (the ordained ministry). The authority of Scripture, as well as that of persons, is rooted in a community that maintains the "common faith" as a criterion of truth. The modern notion of individual autonomy is taken into consideration in the form of the idea that each person, through the interior quality of his life, can have a share in authority.

It is the question of the authority of the pope over the bishops and the whole of the *koinonia* that presents the most difficult problem for the concrete reality of *oikoumene.* On this question, the dialogues have not produced any definitive results. In his encyclical *Ut unum sint* (1995), Pope John Paul II starts from the notion that the bishop of Rome must secure the communion* of all the churches "by the power and the authority without which this function would be illusory." In this sense, the function of the papacy still presupposes real power and authority, and cannot be purely symbolic.

Despite the difficulties that have been encountered, important convergences have become evident in recent times with regard to the way in which the churches understand the authority of the ordained ministry. The depth of this agreement is attested in the document *Baptism, Eucharist, Ministry,* published by the Commission on Faith and Constitution of the World Council of Churches. According to this text, the authority of the ministry is founded upon Jesus Christ: "authority has the character of a responsibility before God and is exercised with the participation of the whole community" (15). Although this authority comes from Christ, the authority of Christ remains unique. Yet it provides a normative model for the church: "authority in the church can be authentic only if it seeks to conform itself to this model" (16).

• H. Meyer, L. Vischer (Ed.), *Growth in Agreement: Reports and Agreed Statements of Ecumenical Conversations on a World Level,* Geneva, COE, 1984.

Jean-Paul II, *Ut unum sint: Encyclical Letter on Ecumenical Engagement,* Vatican, 1995.

♦ J. M. Todd (Ed.) (1962), *Problèmes de l'autorité,* Paris.

W. Veit, H. Rabe, K. Röttgers (1971), "Autorität," *HWP* 1, 724–34.

J. Miethke (1979), "Autorität I: Alte Kirche und Mittelalter," *TRE* 5, 17–32.

O. O'Donovan (1986), *Resurrection and Moral Order,* Leicester.

P. Avis (1992), *Authority, Leadership and Conflict in the Church,* London.

G.R. Evans (1992), *Problems of Authority in the Reformation Debates,* Cambridge.

Risto Saarinen

See also **Council; Holy Scripture; Indefectibility of the Church; Infallibility; Magisterium; Ministry**

B. Political Authority

Every theory of political authority must give an account of its purpose, the source of this authority, and the structure and limits of its actions. A *theological* account takes its bearings from Christian faith* in God's work of creation*, providence*, and salvation*. The diversity of theological accounts, past and present, is traceable to differing interpretations of the moments or phases of this divine work, and of the relationship of political authority to them.

a) Theological Positions and Their Historical Transformations. The main theological issue concerns the nature and extent of the involvement of political authority in the divine work of salvation. On this issue, there are broadly two positions. One presents political authority as belonging to God's preservation of his creation in the present conditions of humanity after the Fall. This preservation is the condition of his salvific action, but does not define it. Following the "two cities" schema of Augustine* and Luther*, this position stresses the unnatural, volitional basis of political authority, its entanglement with sinful strivings for power, the limited scope of its power, and the merely external (only indirectly moral) character of the social order upheld by it. The other position presents political authority as participating in the redemption of communal life, as both the object and the instrument of God's redeeming love*. In line with classical political thought, and authoritatively systematized by Thomas* Aquinas, this position stresses the naturalness and legitimity of political authority that creates an order with moral and spiritual power, and strengthens social bonds.

However, the opposition between these ideas has not always been maintained with all desirable clarity over the historical course of Christian political thought. For example, the "political Augustinianism" (to use Arquillière's phrase) of the medieval Latin church* strictly subjected secular rule to ecclesiastical rule, converting morally ambiguous and nonsalvific political activity into a function of the church, the community of salvation. Luther's Augustinian revival, by contrast, placed the community of salvation beyond the political reach, thus facilitating the absorption of the visible church into the state. On the Thomist side, the 19th century saw the Catholic Aristotelian vision of a harmonious society* united by political authority turn into the sociological vision of a functionally unified society that could do without political authority.

Such paradoxical transformations were due in part to the interaction between ecclesial and civil political concepts. These notions are linked to the established relationship between the law of the gospel and the law of creation, between love and justice, supernatural and natural virtues*, reason and revelation*. Generally speaking, the greater the opposition between these notions, the more church and state have divergent political theories. The weaker the opposition, the closer are the church and state political theories. Historically, the pressures for theoretical and practical parallelism have predominated: the Latin church and the Western empire, for example, engaged in ceaseless mutual plundering of each other's political ideology, organization, and political operations. Although religion became a private matter in the modern era, the trend toward institutional homogeneity still dominates: today, church and state alike must conform to the prevailing liberal and democratic political ethos. The more radical theological dualisms, with their antithetical constructions of ecclesial and civil community, have tended to be historical undercurrents that periodically erupt into challenges to the status quo.

b) Purposes of Political Authority. The New Testament portrays rulers as appointed by God to judge, punish, and reward (Rom 13:2–4; 1 Pt 2:13–14). It was to such texts that theologians up to the 13th century, and the Protestants of the 16th and 17th centuries, constantly referred in order to consider political authority in a theological manner. Thus, the Latin Fathers*, under Stoic influence (e.g., Ambrosiaster [fourth century], Ambrose*, Augustine) saw political authority as a postlapsarian divine ordinance that simultaneously expresses God's wrath against sinful humanity and his merciful will to protect the fragility of the social bond from wayward human passions*: it is a means of limiting inevitable punishment*. Accordingly, political action presupposes a common conscience of good and evil, of order and disorder, of individual good and the common good, according to which justice may be rendered. There is thus an objectivity of justice, law, and common good, recognized but not created by the ruler. Until the 17th century, it was commonly thought that the authoritative articulation of what was good and fair was found in Scripture*, preeminently in the two great commandments (Mt 22:36–40; Mk 12:28–31) and in the Decalogue, which specifies in more detail what is owed to God and to our neighbor. This forms the substance of justice or natural law *(lex naturae, ius naturale).* One should not, however, understand this notion too simply, for there are at least four "natures"—human nature as it was created, fallen nature, redeemed nature, and nature in the state of perfection—each of which has a distinct legal determination.

In the Augustinian tradition, society before the Fall was based on natural law: sexual union, procreation, education of children, common possession of material goods, equality, and unrestrained freedom. After the Fall, however, society was based on *ius gentium* (law of people) and *ius civile* (civil law), which, as inferior expressions of the natural law, establish private property*, the inequality of master and slave, of ruler and ruled, and the positive legal curtailment of individual freedom. The redeemed society is based on the gospel law of faith, hope*, and love. However, in an eschatological perspective, the penitential laws referring to purgatorial punishment played an increasing role over time. Traditionally, the secular jurisdiction* was modeled after, without being coterminous with, the institutions and laws of fallen nature, preoccupied with the protection of the property* and privileges of all and guaranteeing the safety and satisfaction of all needs. Ecclesiastical jurisdiction, for its part, extended to those institutions and societies based on natural and divine law: marriage* and family*, monastic communities, religious fraternities, churches, and charitable and educational institutions. This division was not always clear, for it was constantly challenged from the temporal side by the theocratic aspirations of kings and emperors. Inspired by Israelite monarchy and the Roman Empire, they claimed a universal jurisdiction that encompassed all matters of common interest *(communis utilitas),* including the entire visible organization of the church (doctrinal, administrative, and disciplinary).

Such claims were not imposed until the late 13th and early 14th centuries, when the consolidation of territorial polities was expedited by the appearance of a number of favorable factors: the revival of Roman law, the reception of Aristotelian political philosophy, and the resurgence of classical patriotism and republicanism. The outcome of these movements was a vision of the city founded within nature and reason, autonomous and unified by a single political and legal authority. This political authority, whether hereditary or elected, was thus conceived increasingly in terms of broader legislative and administrative functions, rather than as a simple juridical power. This conceptual change both reflected and reinforced the increasing importance of the nation on every level (economic, financial, legal, religious); and this was to produce modern European states. The unwitting contribution of the church to this development was formidable. By 1300, a succession of jurist-popes (e.g., Alexander III, Innocent III, Gregory IX) had welded the visible church into an organized hierarchy, integrated by a systematized body of canon law and by obedience to the supremacy of the pope, therein furnishing a relatively efficient model of the unitary state. Further, the ecclesiastical synthesis of corporational, imperial, feudal, and theocratic principles laid the foundations of the absolutist states of the 16th and 17th centuries.

Despite the Machiavellian tendency of the 16th and 17th centuries to make the stability and aggrandizement of the state the chief purpose of political authority, they were, nevertheless, the seedbeds of modern liberal conceptions. It was the social fact of religious divisions, together with the individualist and voluntarist strains in the Reformation, that offered fertile soil for the growth of ideas of personal rights and freedoms, voluntary community, active citizenship, representation, and self-government. The seeds were supplied by earlier generations: the Aristotelian ideal of a free and autonomous city, Christianized by Aquinas; the concepts of natural, ideas of natural law prior to the creation of states, and the notion of compact between individuals developed by Duns* Scotus, William of Ockham (c. 1285–1387), the Parisian nominalists, Pierre D'Ailly (1352–1420), Gerson (1363–1429), and, later, Almain (c. 1480–1515) and Mair (c. 1468–1550); and, finally, the principle of the jurisdictional supremacy of the community, supported by the conciliarists against papal absolutism, which entailed its rights to elect rulers, to consent to laws, and to be represented by an assembly. For these ideas, the rise of Protestant and, later, Catholic dissent supplied an urgent use; but, more importantly, it supplied the different theological underpinnings that gave them new directions. Most notably, the central Reformation (especially Lutheran) doctrine of the individual's faith as the unifying principle of the believing community gave to the concept of subjective right (both individual and collective) a foundation in radical spiritual freedom. Similarly, the Calvinist emphasis on the dependence of the political community on the Covenant* between God and humanity, on the model of God's successive covenants with Israel*, gave a religious and moral substance to the concepts of social contract, collective jurisdiction, political consent, and political participation. On the other hand, the revitalized Augustinian association of government with restraint, the coercive settling of conflicts, and the ordering of merely material benefits underscored the unnatural basis of political authority in the contractual agreement of calculating wills.

The 18th and 19th centuries witnessed a reaction against this conception of the external, unnatural, and coercive character of political authority, which had been perfectly expressed by Hobbes (1588–1679) and Spinoza (1632–77), with their concept of a formal legal mechanism of concentration of power. There was an interest in replacing the principle of outward conformity to a divinely ordained sovereign will with an organic and independent principle of social order. However, society was no longer defined in the classical Christian manner by a common theological and ethical rationality. In the deistic theodicy of the liberal economists and English utilitarians (e.g., Adam Smith [1723–90], David Hume [1711–76], J. S. Mill [1806–73], and Jeremy Bentham [1748–1832]), it is the spontaneous operation of market forces that best serves the natural end of society, namely, economic security. In a system in which the operation of these forces is acceptable because it is impersonal, democratic, and nonviolent, the role of political authority is restricted to the enforcement of property rights. Liberalism may have glorified the pursuit of happiness, but it had to acknowledge that the individual conscience needs to take society into account for fear of anarchy (Wolin 1960). By contrast, the sociological reaction against the formalism of political power began with the socialized conscience, which makes individuals susceptible of scientific study and social manipulation. According to the theocratic Catholicism of counterrevolutionary French writers (Joseph de Maistre [1753–1821] and Louis de Bonald [1754–1840]), society owes its unity to a mysterious divine *mythos* whose cultural and institutional forms are revealed before being unified by a conscious political and economic effort. It is not political authority alone, but the whole social hierarchy culminating in king and pope that embodies the unified common will. Later, Saint-Simon (1760–1825), Comte (1798–1857), Durkheim (1858–1917), and Marx* converted this theological socializing of the divine into a profane and scientific socializing of what transcends individuals. Thus the active principle of social cohesion is found, according to Durkheim, in "collective representations" or, according to Saint-Simon, in industrial organization. From this viewpoint, political authority has little purpose other than setting up a harmonious, self-functioning social system, or occasionally helping the administration of experts.

Contemporary theological conceptualizations of the purpose of political authority continue to reflect the somewhat tense interactions of the Thomistic-Aristotelian and Augustinian traditions bequeathed by the Reformation and the Counter-Reformation. At the core of both Catholic and Protestant thought is the notion of human rights, transpolitically rooted in subjectivity. For Protestant thought, heir to the liberalism of Locke (1632–1704) and the economists, political authority has the restricted mandate of securing the fundamental rights to life, liberty, and property. In the tradition of Augustinian realism, refined by post-Kantian pluralism (of which Reinhold Niebuhr [1892–1971] is representative), the competence of the state is limited to the securing of the rights of every person and to the arbitration of conflicts of interest, even though it also needs to create the moral consensus required for justice in the city. However, modern technological development, with all the ensuing possibilities, leads even the most classical liberals to sanction increased intervention by political authority to ensure equality of rights. Thus, there has been a partial rapprochement between contractarian liberalism and the Catholic tradition, which has always accorded to political authority a more comprehensive mandate to define, create, and sustain both the spiritual and material common good of society. Modern Catholic philosophers such as Etienne Gilson (1884–1978) or Jacques Maritain (1883–1973), along with Protestant natural-law thinkers such as Emil Brunner (1889–1966), have no difficulty in extending human rights to include certain social rights. Maritain and Gilson have more difficulty in sustaining the attribution of independent rights to collectivities, whether natural or supernatural, as was characteristic of earlier Catholic thought (*see* Leo XIII's *Rerum Novarum* or Pius XI's *Quadragesimo Anno*). Today, it is not so much the rights of families, churches, or guilds that political authority is responsible for safeguarding as the rights of persons*, by means of a plurality of institutional involvements. Hence, the complex governmental apparatus for administering the provision of goods and services does little to advance the integrity and harmonization of the community so central to the Thomist vision. Current theological emphasis on the church's prophetic and critical role, as in both liberal and Marxist versions of liberation* theology, is accompanied by a deemphasizing of her political structure* of authority and discipline, and of her role as public educator.

c) Sources of Political Authority. For the most part, the Christian political tradition has presented a dual-source theory of political authority: divine election and human election. Until the late 13th century, the Pauline premise of God's ordination of rule and rulers held sway. God's continuing sovereignty in the human community requires that rulers be considered as delegates or representatives of God, "images" of "the divine majesty," "earthly substitutes for his hand," exhibiting universally "his justice and his mercy" (John of Salisbury, *Policraticus* 4, 1). From Carolingian times onward, the designation of both temporal and spiritual rulers as "vicars" of God or of Christ was intended to convey the strict feudal subordination of vassal to lord, and the divine liege-lord's power to remove the title to rule from a rebellious vassal. As medieval coronation ceremonies reveal, communal consent in the institution of monarchs largely amounted to recognition of God's appointment of the ruler, albeit the divine election operated through legal traditions of royal lineage or hereditary succession. Not until the absorption of Aristotle, and the revival of Roman law and a republican culture, was the people's essential role in the election of political authority widely acknowledged.

The theory of popular election, as developed in the late Middle Ages, was that God, from whom all political authority originates, invests all self-sufficient and independent, or "perfect," human associations with the right to establish a political authority to serve the common good. Scotist and Ockhamist voluntarism* introduced an individualist leaning into the idea of natural community by basing it on a pact *(pactum)* of individuals endowed with natural rights anterior to the creation of the state. Common to both Thomistic and nominalist thought, especially as mediated to the 16th and 17th centuries by the Parisian conciliarist tradition, was the notion that political authority owes its legitimacy to God, who uses the human institutions. Introducing the biblical theme of the Covenant into the question of choosing a government reinforced the prominence of divine institution. In the most celebrated of these theories, found in a Huguenot pamphlet entitled *Vindiciae contra tyrannos,* God grants equal authority to both contractual parties, in return for promises of obedience to God's law, each having responsibility for its own and the other's compliance with the terms. However, while the more theocratic (Protestant and later Catholic) conceptions of the Covenant thus gave way to the divine will, rival secular conceptions derived the "fundamental law" of the political covenant exclusively from the communal will, identifying it with the ancient custom of the realm. The 17th century was dominated by the polarization of two absolutized political wills: the unlimited divine right of hereditary monarchs and the parliamentary repositories of popular sovereignty. Nevertheless, despite the extreme voluntarism of Hobbes, Spinoza, and Pufendorf (1632–94), the Scholastic natural-law tradition was revitalized in both Catholic circles, by Vitoria (c. 1483–1546), de Soto (1495–1560), Molina (1535–1600), and Suarez* (1548–1627), and Protestant circles, by Grotius (1583–1645) and Althusius (1557–1638). Although indebted to individualist and voluntarist currents, these theorists thought that governmental or popular political will had to take into account certain constraints, such as man's social and reasonable nature, the objectivity of God's commandments, or the existence of a universal moral community and immutable justice.

One momentous contribution of this Scholastic revival was the basis it provided for international law by avoiding systems of thought in which there is no political right beyond the state. Drawing on the concept of universality developed by Roman civil and canon law—the universality of empire, of reason, of papal jurisdiction—these theorists articulated the idea of an international activity of lawmaking and law-abiding infused with intimations of a natural community of divine law. Throughout the era of sovereign nation-states, this idea of the foundation of international relations has been the only one that has permitted opposition to the more pervasive view of an international moral vacuum in which relations of force are qualified only by treaties and agreements. It is not coincidental that in our own time the Catholic natural-law tradition has supported both the idea of just war and the enterprise of international political authority, whether the United Nations or the European Union. True to its Thomistic and Aristotelian inspiration (in, e.g., Gilson, Maritain, John XXIII), Catholic thought has generally entertained high expectations of the competence of free and equal states to construct and administer the international common good.

d) Structure and Limits of Political Authority. The older view of political authority, with its biblical, Stoic, and patristic roots, emphasized the ruler's judicial role and assimilated his legislative and administrative role into it. Until the late 12th century, even the promulgation of a new law had a judicial character, being presented always as the interpretation, clarification, restoration, or reduction to writing of ancient custom. The proliferation of statute law, together with the extension of royal administration to new domains, provoked a concern with the problem of limiting governmental powers. The idea of the separation of powers, or of their division among numerous centers, came to the fore. This federalist idea was based on the Aristotelian description of political society as a composite whole made up of smaller units, defined by the experience of corporations. Such a pluralistic vision had two unsurpassed exponents in Nicholas* of Cusa and Althusius. A conciliarist steeped in Christian Platonism*, Nicholas of Cusa depicted the church, and analogously the empire, as a mystical hierarchy of corporate bodies and representative authorities, each constituted by and acting through divine will and human collective will. Two centuries later, Althusius conceived political society as an association of lesser associations, both private and public, each a political community formed by contract according to natural, divine, and positive laws. The German tradition of political, legal, and social pluralism, descending through Hegel* and the historical school of philosophical jurisprudence, has left its mark on all subsequent Christian pluralist theories. Common to Dutch neo-Calvinist, Swiss Reformed, and Catholic social philosophies, and their applications by Christian political parties throughout Europe, has been the endeavor to combine traditional Christian social and political principles (whether articulated as laws of nature or as divine ordinances) with a concept of historical dynamics. They all envisage the historical unfolding of differentiated structures and institutions of society according to divinely given interior norms, the state being only one structure among many, limited by the rights of the others. Today, Dutch neo-Calvinism (represented by Herman Dooyeweerd [1894–1977] and his followers) and Catholicism (represented by postwar Thomism) are the most optimistic about the harmonious integration of society on Christian principles. By contrast, the Swiss Reformed tradition (represented by Brunner) retains more Lutheran pessimism about the politically and socially achievable good. Brunner's stronger emphasis on the irreducible disordered state of fallen community, and the gulf between earthly justice and divine charity, distances him from the hopes for the spiritual transformation of society entertained by the Calvinist and Thomist approaches. These latter, however, differ in their conceptions of social structure and the state in relation to it. From the Dutch viewpoint, society comprises a set of intersecting spheres on the same plane, the state sphere being sharply defined by its public and legal aspect; from the Catholic viewpoint, society comprises a hierarchy of natural and voluntary communities, the state being the most inclusive, powerful, and broadly competent. Thus, despite the extensive development by Catholic social philosophy of the principle of "subsidiarity," requiring that greater communities respect the integrity and competence of the lesser communities embraced by them, Catholic thinkers still exhibit more willingness than their Calvinist contemporaries to endow the most universal authority with a broader, integrative social role.

Traditionally, however, Catholic social teaching has rigorously qualified state authority by the church's magisterium*. Until its concessions to democracy in the wake of World War II, the Catholic hierarchy upheld medieval Gelasian dualism, modified to accommodate the reality of modern states. This doctrine no longer distinguished, as had Pope Gelasius (492–96), between two orders of authority—spiritual and temporal—within the single ecclesial community, but rather distinguished two separate, self-sufficient, and self-governing communities of church and commonwealth. Protestant thought has, by contrast, tended to cement the church's link to the state, either by subjecting the church to the secular power (as in Lutheran and Anglican established churches), or by merging the civil and ecclesiastical aspects of political authority (as in Swiss, Dutch, or Scottish Calvinism). Lutheranism*, by virtue of its radically spiritual conception of the church as constituted by God's free word* of grace*, is theoretically more disposed toward political subversion and opposition. In the Dutch Reformed tradition, the church benefits from the self-regulation accorded to all institutional "spheres" but imposes no special limitations on the action of political authority.

The contemporary political creed of liberal democratic pluralism that has become the civil religion of most developed polities since the end of World War II seriously challenges the traditional theological circumscriptions of political authority. Its central tenet is that the political common good consists in an indefinitely extendable set of individual rights and freedoms, the securing of which is the purpose and justification of political authority. These rights and freedoms, required for the self-determination of persons, do not permit the public expression or legal protection of institutions and prerogatives that operate to limit them. Hence, it seems that no effective theoretical limitations of political authority can now proceed from Catholic or Protestant circles—not from the Catholic concept of the church as a superior *societas perfecta,* nor from the Calvinist principle of the sovereignty of each in his own "sphere," nor from the Lutheran ideal of radical Christian freedom, at least without critical reappraisal of political individualism and the dominant discourse of human rights.

• J. Althusius, *Politica methodice digesta,* Ed. C.J. Friedrich, Cambridge, Mass., 1932.

Augustine, *De civitate Dei,* BAug 33–37.

E. Brunner, *Gerechtigkeit,* Zurich, 1943.

J. Calvin, *Institution de la religion chrétienne,* Ed. J.D. Benoît, vol. 5, Paris, 1957–63.

H. Dooyeweerd, *De Wisbegeerte der Wetsidee,* Amsterdam, 1935–36.

[P. Duplessis-Mornay], *Vindiciae contra tyrannos,* Ed. H. Weber, et al., Geneva, 1979.

J. Gerson, *De potestate ecclesiastica,* in *Œuvres complètes,* Ed. P. Glorieux, vol. 6, Paris, 1965, 210–50..

H. Grotius, *De jure belli ac pacis libri tres,* Amsterdam, 1646 (repr. Oxford, 1925).

John of Salisbury, *Policraticus,* Ed. C.C.J. Webb, Oxford, 1909.

John XXIII, *Pacem in terris, AAS* 55 (1963), 257–304.

Leo XIII, *Rerum novarum,* in *Acta Leonis XIII,* vol. 4, 1894, 177–209.

M. Luther, *Von weltlicher Obrigkeit, wie weit Man ihr Gehorsam schuldig sei, WA* 11, 245–80.

J. Maritain, *Man and the State,* Chicago, 1951.

F. Suarez, *Tractatus de legibus ac Deo legislatore,* Ed. L. Perena, V. Abril, P. Suner, 8 vols., Madrid, 1971–81.

Thomas Aquinas, *ST* Ia, q. 96, a. 4; IIa IIae, q. 42, a. 2, ad 3; *De regimine principum ad regem Cypri.*

♦ R. Scholz (1944), *Wilhelm von Ockham als politischer Denker und sein Breviloquium de principatu tyrannico,* Stuttgart.

R. Folz (1953), *L'idée d'Empire en Occident du Ve au XIVe siècle,* Paris.

H.X. Arquillière (1955), *L'augustinisme politique,* Paris.

J.W. Gough (1957), *The Social Contract: A Critical Study of Its Development,* Oxford.

E.H. Kantorowicz (1957), *The King's Two Bodies: A Study in Medieval Political Theology,* Princeton.

S.S. Wolin (1960), *Politics and Vision: Continuity and Innovation in Western Political Thought,* Boston.

B. Hamilton (1963), *Political Thought in Sixteenth Century Spain: A Study of the Political Ideas of Vitoria, De Soto, Suarez and Molina,* Oxford.

M. Reydellet (1981), *La royauté dans la littérature latine de Sidoine Apollinaire à Isidore de Séville,* École française de Rome.

J.H. Burns (Ed.) (1988), *The Cambridge History of Medieval Political Thought c. 350–c. 1450,* Cambridge; (1991), *The Cambridge History of Political Thought, 1450–1700,* Cambridge.

J. Milbank (1990), *Theology and Social Theory: Beyond Secular Reason,* Oxford.

E. Herms (1994), "Obrigkeit," *TRE* 24, 723–59 (bibl.).

JOAN LOCKWOOD O'DONOVAN

See also **Aristotelianism, Christian; Augustinianism; Church and State; City; Conciliarism; Political Theology; Rome; Sin, Original; Stoicism, Christian; Traditionalism**

Average Science. *See* **Bañezianism-Molinism-Baianism; Knowledge, Divine**

Averroism. *See* **Naturalism; Truth**

Awakening. *See* **Edwards, Jonathan; Methodism**

B

Baianism. *See* **Bañezianism-Molinism-Baianism**

Balthasar, Hans Urs von

1905–88

More than any other contemporary theologian, Hans Urs von Balthasar encouraged theology* to rediscover the vital essence of its strictly scientific thinking. No one has been more insistent about the need to recover the long-lost unity of theology and holiness*, in the sense of a full and total opening of the spirit to God*'s revelation*. Guided by Anselm*, Balthasar understood how important to an authentic theology was the *adoratio* of one who understands with all his powers of reason* that the mystery* is beyond understanding. The invitation of *Dei Verbum* to make "Scripture*...the soul of theology" (*DV* 24) is applicable to little 20th-century theology. Even though Balthasar often preferred to take account of the four senses of Scripture rather than following the strict rules of historical and critical exegesis*, the reader of his work is nonetheless offered an intimate engagement with the Bible*.

A large part of his childhood was devoted to music*, for which he had real talent and which was to play an important part in his theological output. At the same time, he undertook research in philosophy* and literature (German doctoral thesis: *Apokalypse der deutschen Seele*). He entered the Society of Jesus and studied philosophy and theology at Pullach, then at Lyons. These years of deep friendship with E. Przywara (1889–1972), Lubac*, H. Bouillard, J. Danièlou (1905–74), and D. Mollat gave him the opportunity to immerse himself not only in the Church Fathers* and the masters of the Middle Ages, but also in the work of modern thinkers such as G. Bernanos and C. Péguy. In 1940 he met Adrienne von Speyr, whom he received into the Catholic Church: she was to influence the most decisive stages of his life (such as his leaving the Society of Jesus in 1950). Balthasar wrote of her: "Her work and mine cannot be separated, either on psychological or on philological grounds: they are two halves of a whole that, at its center, has a single foundation." Through her agency he made contact with Barth*. The deep influence of his dialogue with the Calvinist theologian would be seen in the texts collected in a volume of theological essays, *Verbum Caro,* in *Theologie der Geschichte,* and in *Glaubhaft ist nur Liebe,* introduction to *The Glory of the Lord.*

Balthasar was not called to participate directly in the work of Vatican* II, an exclusion mitigated by his appointment by Paul VI to the International Commission on Theology. A profoundly open man and a stubborn defender of tradition*, Balthasar was made a cardinal in 1988. Averse to public celebration, he had an intuition that he would never don the cardinal's vestments: he died two days before his public elevation to the College of Cardinals, on 26 June 1988.

With the *Epilog* of 1987, Balthasar concluded his 15-volume synthesis of theology. Few, least of all the author, believed that it could be brought to completion. Taking the form of a trilogy, it is based on the theological use of two transcendentals (beauty* 2, c), the True *(verum)* and the Good *(bonum),* and of a third concept to which he also accorded the status of transcendental, the Beautiful *(pulchrum).* The order of these concepts is reversed to give first place to the *pulchrum,* and they form the basis, respectively, of a theological esthetics, a theo-dramatics and a theo-logic. Two works offer a guide to the logical construction of the trilogy: the first being *Rechenschaft* (1965), with the later addition of *Noch ein Jahrzehnt* (1978), and the second being *Epilog.* While in *Rechenschaft* Balthasar sets out the key points of his theological output, *Epilog* offers more of a testament that links in retrospect the fundamental ideas found in the triptych. The trilogy sets out to show that the center of revelation is still today the one wholly meaningful reality. Paradoxical as it may seem, given the complexity of the subject matter and the difficulties it offers the reader, Balthasar sets out to present his contemporaries simply with the "reasons for hope*" in Christianity (*see* 1 P 3, 15) and can be seen as one of the long line of apologists who, over the centuries, have presented the center of the Christian faith*.

a) Theological Esthetics. For too long, Balthasar has been regarded as an esthete, and he is in danger of being remembered for even longer only as the author of *Herrlichkeit.* Such a partial reading is unjustified and threatens to get in the way of an understanding of his theology. *Herrlichkeit: Eine theologische Ästhetik* must be considered as the first part of the system, complete and organic in itself, but also and simultaneously as a first step toward the overall presentation of the mystery. Revelation, in Balthasar's scheme, does not arrive solely by way of the *pulchrum,* which presents the first act by which it may be discerned; it must be continued and integrated into the *bonum* and the *verum.*

This part of the work is therefore entitled *Herrlichkeit* (glory*): the philosophical *pulchrum* is studied in the context of the Biblical *kabod* and the Johannine *doxa.* Glory is the irradiation of being* itself, which presents itself thus, *sic et simpliciter,* with no outward covering. In its free revelation, glory is gratuitous and transcendent; it is the first expression of God's opening toward the world*. The theological esthetic can be understood with the help of several keys to interpretation.

One may first distinguish between the perception of glory and the rapture or ecstasy that follows it. The "perception" is the object of fundamental* theology; dogmatics*, meanwhile, deals with the "ecstasy". The *Erblickungslehre,* as a doctrine of perception, studies the double movement that constitutes the evidence of revelation. The objective movement consists of the manifestation of the phenomenon, which carries within itself the reasons for its essence and existence, while the subjective movement relates to knowledge* by faith. According to Balthasar, perception is possible insofar as God reveals his *Gestalt.* This is the expression of the absolute, the revelation that begins from itself but "refers back" to its constituent essence and depth. And in this revelation, the content *(Gehalt)* is identical to the figure that expresses it *(Gestalt).* With these assertions Balthasar anticipates the closing pages of *Herrlichkeit,* where he will in fact emphasize that the New Testament gives the *Gestalt* its whole meaning: the mystery of God's incarnation* visually perceived by the believer in Jesus*' self-presentation. The stage of perception is followed by that of subjective evidence, by which a fitting knowledge of the *Gestalt* is obtained. The subject still moves toward the object; but in this case God offers both an object to be perceived and the means to receive this object properly. To the richness of the *Gestalt*—to the objective evidence that fully expresses the divine *doxa*—there must therefore be added a corresponding faith, in other words, the simplicity of a cognitive act whose capacity for receiving truth *(Wahr-nehmung)* enables it to give full expression to the meaning of the perception. What is given in theological terms, in short, is the primacy of a *fides quae* that enables the *fides qua* to be understood as an act whose content is already, in itself, rich in the fullness of the mystery. So, in its self-presentation, the manifestation of glory reveals at the same time its form and its content (envisaged as a constant referral beyond the form itself), on the one hand; and on the other hand faith, as an adequate and coherent understanding of the content as much as of the form.

A second stage gives content to the *pulchrum:* this is the rapture or ecstasy engendered by receptiveness to an ever growing sense of wonder (a receptiveness that itself results from man's first astonishment when confronted with the mystery). In this case the ego goes beyond itself, breaks with its individuality and allows itself to be absorbed by the *Gestalt;* and the demands of the glory that appears and promises personal participation in the mystery of the divine life, then lead to a behavior approaching *Gelassenheit,* in other words, to a complete and total relinquishment of the self to the mystery. This philosophical perspective is clearly dependent on Eckhart (1260–1328) and Heidegger*, although to understand its full significance it must be considered in the context of Ignatius Loyola (Ignatian spirituality*). Balthasar was always influenced by Loyola's viewpoint, and in his writing *Gelassenheit* initially implies total obedience, a laissez-faire attitude toward the actions of others, a renunciation that results from the believer's radical receptiveness and openness toward God's will. Whoever wishes to enter into God's revelation *(Selbsausslegung Gottes)* thus has no other path to take but that of the overall figure *(Gesamtgestalt)* revealed by God's incarnation. Balthasar is thus able to forge an unbreakable link between the historical revelation of Jesus* of Nazareth, the true heart of revelation, and its mediation or historical continuation through the presence of the church*, the context for every authentic act of faith.

The particular nature of Balthasar's Christology* may be seen here, as expressed in the category of obedience, and culminating in kenosis*, interpreted in the Johannine* sense of glory and love. Indeed Balthasar continually emphasizes that love is a necessary condition for any action of the Trinity. For him this love, the essence of the divine nature itself, keeps nothing back; it is not measured by the standard of human love, but is determined only by the free initiative of God. This analysis allows Balthasar to avoid christological representations predetermined by anthropology*. The act of loving, of which the Son's kenosis offers the only full realization, is on the one hand the condition that allows God to retain his freedom*, and, on the other hand, the one "transcendental" condition needed in order to participate in the mystery of his revelation.

The church is analyzed in the same manner in several of Balthasar's writings *(see Sponsa Verbi, Der antirömische Affekt or Schleifung der Bastionem).* Considered as the "body" of Christ, and above all as his "bride," the church contains in essence the complexity of the mystery: it is both a reality dependent on its "head" and a free agent capable of choice. The church expresses the logic of mediation, revealed principally in Christ, that invites us to understand faith simultaneously as a human and a divine act. It is indeed the church of Mary, and thus a pure *fiat* of obedience toward its Lord; but it is also the church of Peter*, and so a ministry* with the aim of developing the community. Balthasar is thus able to set out an ecclesiology* based, on the one hand, on the act of welcoming the gift of grace*—whose theological paradigm is provided by Mary*'s "passivity"—and on the other hand, on concrete decisiveness and action, as exemplified by Peter's ministry. This ecclesiology, moreover, exposes a rather independent tone, especially in its insistence on the theological interpretation of womanhood (woman*) or of the ministry.

b) Theological Dramatics. Theological dramatics establishes and ensures a coherent progress from the *pulchrum* to the *verum.* Between "seeing" and "speaking" there must be placed a *bonum,* which reveals on the one hand God's pure and freely given gift to the world, and, on the other hand, mankind's free and responsible reply. The term *dramatics* here has a meaning close to the theatrical sense: it concerns that dynamic by which the public and the actor encounter one another, by which the spectator can be aware of himself as a participant inasmuch as he is immersed in the heart of the logic of representation, and by means of which, finally, we find ourselves fundamentally engaged in questions that involve not one moment of life, but existence itself. Thus the very nature of theology demands that it contain a dramatic narrative—its object, indeed, is the drama that is played out in the relationship between God and humanity. The special characteristic of drama is to "transform an event into a visual image," and to force a consideration of personal existence in the light of a "role" and a "mission*" that shatters the image of the self as the outcome of pure chance. So, in the face of the evidence of earthly being, the framework of existence is constructed with an awareness of this *mission* and this *role;* and it is by understanding them with reference to the existence of the man Jesus, which can itself be interpreted in terms of pure mission and pure obedience to the Father, that one can allow this mission and this role to unfold fully.

The volume entitled *Prolegomena* sketches in the axes along which Balthasar's anthropology* is to develop—an anthropology that takes shape and evolves in the light of, and along the trajectory of, the self-expression of the *Gestalt Christi.* Balthasar's anthropology, indeed, is not based on any self-unfolding of human subjectivity, but is composed solely on the basis of the objectivity of the *Gestalt Christi,* since this contains the true reasons that can account for the subject who receives it. The drama is therefore formed of God's engagement with humanity, and from the basis of God's very power of action.

The starting point of Balthasar's thinking here is the theology of the Incarnation, inasmuch as it presents in concrete form a relationship between mankind and God *(Mit-Einander)* by which man becomes essentially a participant *(Mitspieler).* The question of mankind is thus expressed in terms of two fundamental themes: the formulation of the role and the mission, and the relationship between finite and infinite* liberty. With the definition of the first, the subject discovers that he can be God's partner in a dramatic action. The second allows him to glimpse, on a formal level, the development of the drama. The latter enacts the fundamental question that constitutes personal existence—"Who am I?"—and no one can answer this question without identifying himself, at least implicitly, with a "role." Scripture, for its part, obliges us to see ourselves each as receiving a "mission," summoned and sent forth by the Father* in the image of Jesus Christ. Inevitably, the question of personal liberty then arises: only an *analogia libertatis* (analogy*) is capable of setting down and explaining the relationship between mankind's finite liberty and the region of infinite liberty to which he is summoned.

Because it is created, personal liberty gives rise to a dramatic existence: according to our decisions, the "being-toward-another" *(Zu-Einander)* may become a "being-for-another" *(Für-Einander)* or equally a "being-against-another" *(Gegen-Einander).* The liberty of the subject, in consequence, does not begin by confronting another finite liberty, but rather by opening immediately onto an absolute liberty—and even, in the light of revelation, onto a "triune" liberty. In the "experience of liberty," the subject understands himself to be constantly approaching this liberty, and is perhaps even aware that he is only free insofar as he is traveling toward it. This discovery further reveals to the human subject the absolutely unshareable nature of his "very being" *(Ichsein)* and the unlimited extent to which being* may be shared.

The essential problem remains, however: "Who is man?" The answer is clear: *imago Dei.* This Biblically modeled anthropology sees in the theme of God's image the fullest expression of what man is, because it is directly linked to the act of the Creator God (creation*). Man is the reflection *(Abbild)* of an archetype *(Urbild),* and is enveloped by the mystery that grants him, as an essential dimension, the ability to attain full self-realization in freedom. Balthasar's debt to Irenaeus* is very clear at this point.

The *Theodramatik* also studies the problem of the meaning of the death on the cross as a sign of the love of the Trinity. God reveals himself here in his intimate nature: he is a God who approaches death as a loving God. The quotation from Kierkegaard that appears as an epigraph to the final volume of the *Theodramatik* makes all the clearer the project and the aim underlying the whole second part of the trilogy: the cross and the death of the innocent are "the pure expression of the Trinity's eternal vitality." Pain, suffering, the cross, and death are the ultimate expressions of God's love: they constitute a unique sign that allows us to see how far God can go when he expresses himself in the essence of his being, which is love. The absolute uniqueness and singularity of Jesus of Nazareth are therefore crucial: indeed, they reveal not only the soteriological value (salvation*) of this death, but also the fact that this event alone is a concrete demonstration of God's action. "One of the Trinity* has suffered" (*DS* 401, 432) is the leitmotiv running through this set of themes. The event of the Crucifixion can already be discerned in the event of the Incarnation: Jesus, in a constant and "progressive" kenosis, breaks with the glory of divinity, assumes human flesh*, and finally encounters death and the experience of the tomb. These pages betray the great fascination that, consciously or otherwise, Adrienne von Speyr held for the theologian of Basel.

Kenosis in Balthasar's work is to be taken as the last word*, expressed in human language, that makes credible God's manifestation to humanity. The hymn to the Philippians (Phil 2:6–11) undoubtedly offers a basis for this theology. In this christological hymn, indeed, it is the intertrinitarian origin of kenosis that is highlighted: it is always seen as a constant, eternal movement of renunciation based on obedience. It can, moreover, be said of the Father that he performs a first, original "kenosis" when he begets the Son: freely but totally, he empties himself of his divinity and passes it in its entirety to the Son. Thus is clarified by the meaning of the words by which Jesus expresses his awareness of his relationship with the Father: "All that is mine is yours" (Jn 17:10). The same free and total giving, by which the Father becomes a "father" and the Son a "son," is also manifest in the Holy* Spirit, which guarantees that this act of dispossession is indeed based on love. Balthasar attempts, by way of this divine self-dispossession, to situate in the immanent Trinity each of the further possible "separations" that can be seen in the economic Trinity. The Son's abandonment on the cross—the extreme expression of separation—is possible only because it is already implicit in the first, insurmountable separation that produces the Trinitarian impulse. In this way the cross expresses in human terms (with an analogy whose correspondence is imparted exclusively by Jesus himself) what is confirmed within the Trinity—the act of total and absolute giving in love. The Trinity is thus defined as a "Person*" in the act by which God gives himself utterly as the Father, and receives himself utterly as the Son. Such a definition implies that the total separation of Father and Son, in Jesus' death, could be achieved only in a total intimacy between one and the other (engendering). The unity experienced by the divine Persons in their relations within the Trinity is thus the basis of the unity and singularity achieved by death when it separates the Son from the Father. Obedience to the Father's will and obedience to the Holy Spirit henceforth constitute the hermeneutic* keys that allow the Crucifixion to be read as a death by love and in the name of love. On this depends love for the Father, understood as a fulfillment of his will that is received in a pure and simple acceptance that goes as far as death. So this viewpoint transforms the event of death into a Trinitarian event: the whole Trinity is engaged and involved in Jesus Christ. In the light of Christology, the "death of God" becomes for Balthasar the fundamental point toward which revelation itself leads—as the Bible* itself testifies. This death, moreover, is also the moment at which the soteriological meaning of the sufferings endured for us by the innocent man is revealed. The Christ who becomes "sin*" and on whom God wreaks his "anger" at the sins of the world is none other than the Son who freely accepts the "pain" felt by God at mankind's refusal of love. The traditional theme of vicarious substitution must then arise; and from Balthasar's standpoint its appearance only serves to highlight "the omnipotent impotence of God's love" (divine omnipotence*). The Son refused and forsaken by the Father is actually a Son forever welcome, since his life is bound up with that of his Father. This Son therefore bears the sins of the world (Rom 9:22f.), and dies on the cross so that nobody after him may die with God's approval. In this way, nothing that occurs is brought to pass by the world, and everything displays the constant and fundamental difference that exists between this action of God's and every possible human realization.

God's Trinitarian love upon the cross is therefore not, as it would be in a Plotinian reading, an impoverishment of all love. On the contrary, this moment reveals precisely the very essence of God and indeed allows us to understand truly what it means to love "until the end" (Jn 13:1). While death represents the limit beyond which man cannot go, and while the suffering of the innocent man may make us empathize with Dostoyevsky's doubt and may lead us to cry scandal* at the mention of God's love, still it must equally be maintained that God has not remained immune to this scandal and this limit. On the contrary, he has accepted them into himself: it is only in this way that they can be decisively conquered and seen to have a meaning. When death becomes the expression of infinite love, one can still speak of a mystery, but only through the paradox of the cross, the last real victory in a drama that does not end in tragedy.

c) Theological Logic. The *Gestalt Christi,* which has been encountered in the context of "glory," where it was offered to a faithful contemplation, and then in the "drama," to make mankind capable of involving himself in the divine action and thus experiencing his own liberty to the full, now reaches the last act: the definitive form of truth*. The *Theologik* is largely concerned with analyzing the relationship between divine truth and created truth: can the Truth of revelation be expressed within the structure of created reality? The key questions that take shape over the three volumes of the *Theologik* attempt to express the "fundamental mystery" *(Grundgeheimnis)* of the Christian faith: how is it ontologically possible for a human logos to possess the divine Logos within itself? The logos is therefore at the heart of the *Theologik*—not in its transcendental precomprehension as *verum,* but rather in what goes beyond this, as *alètheia,* in the sense of John's Gospel*. Indeed, John's vision determines Balthasar's understanding of truth: John 1:18 opens his christological considerations (in *Wahrheit Gottes*), and John 16:13 concludes his interpretation of truth (in *Der Geist der Wahrheit*) in pneumatological terms. Jesus of Nazareth is the Father's exegete, but it is the Holy Spirit that opens the eyes of believers so that they can see the truth in its entirety.

The understanding of the concept of truth and of its links with the *bonum* and the *pulchrum* serves here as a preamble to strictly theological analysis. The first volume of the *Theologik, Wahrheit der Welt,* reuses unaltered a work that first appeared in 1947. There was good reason for placing this text at the start of the *Theologik,* since it clearly points up latent intuitions that slowly took shape later on, leaving their mark on *Herrlichkeit* as much as the *Theodramatik.* It is in this volume that the relationship between the *Gestalt* and the *Grund* is analyzed in depth; and one can recognize in it with hindsight the origin of the remarkable developments of the first volume of *Herrlichkeit.*

What is truth? A simple answer in terms of metaphysical thought would immediately fall short, for while the *verum* is certainly "a property of being in its manifestation," such a definition must nonetheless be supplemented by the many connotations of the Biblical term *'emet.* For Balthasar, truth is a disclosure of being, and this disclosure is by its nature an offering. It could be argued that the *Theologik*'s original intuition lies in its recognition of the *mystery of being.* Not only absolute being, but all being, partakes of the mysterious, and it is the mystery of liberty and knowledge themselves that force us constantly to go beyond each finite form of liberty and knowledge. For Balthasar, however, the mystery is not something incomprehensible: on the contrary, it is a reality that one may experience, and which becomes manifest through images and words. Images, because they refer constantly to the root of the manifestation and mark the beginning of an encounter between subject and object; words, because they give a stable form to the dialogue between the *I* and the *Thou* and facilitate an understanding of the self and the world.

The interpretation of the mystery allows other characteristics of truth to be defined, first and foremost freedom. Truth, indeed, is given in a dynamic movement that refers appearance back to the fundamental essence of which it is the expression; thus one can only arrive at truth to the extent that the essence is revealed in its mystical nature. This implies that the truth of being will always be determined by a dialectic of "disclosure and dissimulation" *(Enthüllung-Verhüllung);* this relationship allows the identity of being to be discovered, not merely as "being-in-self" *(An-Sich-sein)* but also and above all as "being-for-self" *(Für-Sich-sein).*

Existence is the mode of being of truth, and it is up to this essential freedom, which is unconditional and therefore supreme, to choose to reveal its own foundation. So, while the act of knowing gives truth its final connotation, nevertheless knowledge does not derive from the subject, but rather from being, which freely decides to open itself and reveal the foundation of its own existence. Thus truth acquires the full sense of *alètheia:* it is simple revelation, the pure manifestation of being, which "eludes all meanings and systematizations" and which expresses itself ultimately as love. It is therefore the responsibility of truth to be believable and shared.

Just as in the case of Beauty and Goodness, the content of Truth, which Balthasar identifies with its foundation, cannot be "defined" by human reason. Its nature is such that its essence transcends historical existence. And if one must then have recourse to another logic, it can only be that of love, since it allows us to apprehend the true dimensions of the eternal mystery.

Balthasar was certainly not gifted with concision: his output over half a century consists of more than a thousand items (monographs, articles, commentaries, translations, introductions to various works, critical editions, etc.). However, one short phrase, written almost on the spur of the moment, may be taken as the kernel of his whole theological oeuvre: "To make the Christian message credible and acceptable to the world." These words summarize Balthasar's theological project, which finds its best and most audacious expression in *Glaubhaft ist nur Liebe (Love Alone),* the essential starting point for anyone wishing to come to grips with his work.

It is impossible to approach without a certain sadness the image in the *Epilog* with which Balthasar describes his work: a bottle thrown into the sea, which floats on until, perhaps, somebody may find it. Contemporary theology has not yet had the courage to face up to Balthasar or to plunge into his enormous output. For all its fascination and appeal, this is difficult theology. Poetry, theater, music, art, and philosophy take their places beside a reading of Scripture in the tradition of the Fathers, the master theologians and the saints, to make up a unique whole that offers an assurance of hope*—a hope that consists of a certainty of God's free and merciful love. In this context, Balthasar was able to express his conviction that hell* might be empty. This viewpoint does not imply a hereafter without a hell; rather it involves a responsible conception of a believer's present, offered to his contemporaries in the true light of revelation—to show God's face in a crucified man brought back to life.

• H. U. von Balthasar (1948), "Theologie und Heiligkeit," WuW 3, 881–96, New Ed. in *Verbum Caro,* Einsiedeln, 1960, 195–225.

H. U. von Balthasar (1950), *Theologie des Geschichte,* Einsiedeln.

H. U. von Balthasar (1952), *Schleifung der Bastionem,* Einsiedeln.

H. U. von Balthasar (1960–86), *Skizzen zur Theologie,* 5 vols., Einsiedeln [vol. 1 (1960), *Verbum Caro*; vol. 2 (1961), *Sponsa Verbi*; vol. 3 (1967), *Spiritus Creator*; vol. 4 (1974), *Pneuma und Institution*; vol. 5 (1986), *Homo Creatus Est*].

H. U. von Balthasar (1961–69), *Herrlichkeit: Eine theologische Ästhetik,* 7 vols., Einsiedeln.

H. U. von Balthasar (1963), *Das Ganze im Fragment,* Einsiedeln.

H. U. von Balthasar (1963), *Glaubhalft ist nur Liebe.*

H. U. von Balthasar (1965), *Rechenschaft 1965.*

H. U. von Balthasar (1973–83), *Theodramatik,* 5 vols.

H. U. von Balthasar (1974), *Der antirömische Affekt,* Einsiedeln.

H. U. von Balthasar (1985–87), *Theologik,* 3 vols., Einsiedeln.

C. Capol (1990), *H. U. von B.: Bibliographie 1925–1990,* Einsiedeln.

♦ M. Albus (1976), *Die Wahrheit ist Liebe,* Freiburg.

W. Löser (1976), *Im Geiste des Origenes: H. U. von B. als Interpret der Theologie der Kirchenväter,* Frankfurt.

G. Marchesi (1977), *La cristologia di H. U. von B.,* Rome.

R. Fisichella (1981), *H. U. von B.: Amore e credibilità cristiana,* Rome.

M. Lochbrunner (1981), *Analogia caritatis,* Freiburg.

A. Vignolo (1982), *H. U. von B.: Estetica e singularità,* Milan.

G. de Schrijver (1983), *Le merveilleux accord de l'homme et de Dieu: Étude de l'analogie de l'être chez H. U. von B.,* Louvain.

E. Babini (1987), *L'antropologia teologica di H. U. von B.,* Milan.

L. Roberts (1987), *The Theological Aesthetics of H. U. von B.,* Washington.

A. Scola (1991), *Hans Urs von B.: Uno stile teologico,* Milan.

K. Lehmann, W. Kasper (Ed.) (1991), *Hans Urs von B.: Gestalt und Werk,* Einsiedeln.

R. Fisichella (1993), "Rileggendo Hans Urs von B.," *Gr* 71, 511–46.

G. Marchesi (1997), *La cristologia trinitaria di H. U. von B.: Gésu Cristo pienezza della rivelazione e della salvezza*, Brescia.
R. Nandkisore (1997), *Hoffnung auf Erlösung: Die Eschatologie im Werk Hans Urs von B.*, Rome.

RINO FISICHELLA

See also **Analogy; Barth, Karl; Beauty; Bultmann, Rudolph; Descent into Hell; Glory of God; Johannine Theology; Kenosis; Lubac, Henri Sonier de; Mystery; Rahner, Karl; Revelation; Theology; Truth**

Bañezianism–Molinism–Baianism

a) Definitions. These terms designate three theological systems and trends that came to light in the 16th century and were inspired respectively by the writings of Domingo Bañez (1528–1604), Luis de Molina (1535–1600) and Baius (Michel de Bay, 1519–89). Each of these theologians claimed he was able to give a rational basis to the relations between grace and freedom, as well as to questions related to divine science* and to God*'s determination of future contingents. These attempts took place in a particular context: on one side there was the fight against the Lutheran and Calvinist negation of free will; on the other side, the effort to avoid the pitfall of Pelagianism*. The reaction provoked within Catholic theology* by Protestant notions stirred one of the liveliest debates it had ever experienced on the role of freedom in supernatural* acts.

The Society of Jesus found itself at the center of these controversies, since Molina himself was a Jesuit and since his colleagues were determined to defend Molinism against its various adversaries. In any case, the Jesuits were not as faithful to the ideas defended by Molina as to the fundamental inspiration of Molinism, which consisted in asserting the role of freedom in supernatural acts in a manner that was in full agreement with the instructions of Ignatius of Loyola (17th orthodoxy rule in the *Constitutions;* Ignatian spirituality*); and also, most probably, with the humanistic pedagogy brought into play in Jesuit colleges. This inspiration of Molinism placed it in opposition both to Baianism and to Bañezianism, whose theories stated that free will could not refuse grace as long as it is an effective grace. Bañezianism quickly became the official doctrine of the Dominicans. As for Baianism, it was initially the theory of a handful of Lovanist theologians but took on a new lease of life in the 17th century, when it was paradoxically revived by the *Augustinus* (1640) and the Jansenist movement.

b) History of the Controversies. The background to these debates is the Council of Trent*'s decree on justification*, dated 13 January 1547 (session VI, chap. V, *COD* 671–81, *DS* 1525–80). According to this decree, justification goes beyond the unaided forces of man and requires prevenient grace, through which God helps man to convert without any merit on man's own part. But according to that same decree, man does not receive that grace passively, without any cooperation on his part, and this means he is given a chance to refuse it rather than accept it.

The first conflict on the question of the agreement between grace and freedom occurred in January 1582. It was, therefore, a good deal earlier than the publication of Molina's *Concordia.* Bañez, a Spanish Dominican, was confessor to Teresa of Avila (Carmel*). From 1581 he occupied the first chair in theology at the University of Salamanca, where he opposed what has been called a "pre-Molinist" tendency. This happened on the occasion of a dispute defended in Salamanca by the Jesuit Prudencio de Montemayor, who held that Jesus Christ* would not have died freely, and would have procured no merit, if he had received from his Father* the command to die. Discussions followed, on both predestination* and justification: these discussions pitted Bañez, on the one side, against the Augustinian Luis de León, a defender of the Jesuit, on the other. The tribunal of the Spanish Inquisition in Valladolid refused to condemn Luis de León's theses, but it did decide, on 5 February 1584, to forbid him to teach them in public or in private.

On the other hand, starting in 1585 the Jesuit Leonard Lessius (1554–1623) inaugurated his professorate in Louvain by combating the theses of Chancellor Michel de Bay, whom he accused of getting dangerously close to Pelagianism in his refutation of "Calvin*'s Manicheanism*." When Lessius intervened, Baius had already been engaged (since 1567) in a long exchange with the pontifical authorities, on account of his notion of original gifts. He thought that, although these gifts were not natural, they were due to the integrity of nature*, so that "God could not, in the beginning, have created man as he is born today": that is, willing to do good*, but incapable of this without divine help (*DS* 1901 *Sq*). This has been called the thesis of the impossibility of the state of pure nature. In 1586 Lessius published his *Theses theologicae,* which denounced Baius's doctrine. They were censored in 1587 by the Faculty of Louvain *(censura lovaniensis),* which accused them of semi-Pelagianism. Lessius appealed to Pope* Sixtus V, who cancelled the censorship in 1588 with the reassurance that Lessius's doctrine was sound.

The theses that set Lessius and the Faculty of Theology in opposition to each other were as follows. According to Baius and his defenders, it is God* who determines the will, so that effective grace is a grace that cannot be rejected, with Providence* and predestination not taking into account either the determination of secondary causes or each individual's merit. For his part, Lessius defends the notion that in the determination of will, the role of divine grace is only one of cooperation, because will is determined on its own, even in the supernatural order. Grace is therefore not effective on its own but only insofar as the will accepts it and cooperates with it. Providence and predestination take into account the secondary causes as well as the merit of each individual, which means that they bring into play divine prescience of conditional futures.

The controversy took a new meaning again in 1588 with the publication of Molina's *Concordia* in Lisbon. Molina was a Spanish Jesuit who was teaching theology in Evora during that time. His *Concordia* dealt with divine science and will, with Providence and with predestination (*see* Thomas* Aquinas, *ST* Ia, q. 14, 19, 22 and 23), and it endeavored above all to reconcile these with human freedom (which explains the title), by means of a theory fairly close to that of Lessius. The Portuguese Dominicans were disturbed to recognize in the book some of the theses defended in 1581 by Montemayor. Cardinal Albert of Austria, the Inquisitor General in Portugal, suspended the sale of the book and consulted Bañez, who uncovered in the *Concordia* some 10 propositions, the teaching of which had already been forbidden to Luis de León. He condensed his criticism in three objections, but Molina refuted these and as a consequence the suspension of the book was reversed in July 1589. In an appendix of a new edition of the *Concordia,* Molina wrote his answer to Bañez's objections.

However, the controversies surrounding the *Concordia* did not then cease. They pursued their course in Rome*, at the time of the "congregations *de auxiliis,*" which were consultative theological debates for the study of Molina's book. Initiated by Clement VIII, these explored the problem of the infallibility of effective grace (is it irresistible? Does it produce its effect as a matter of necessity?). The Dominicans Diego Alvarez, P. Beccaria, and Thomas de Lemos distinguished themselves in these debates, as did the Jesuits Robert Bellarmine*, Claudio Aquaviva, Michel Vasquez, Pierre Arrubal, and Gregory of Valencia. The two great Jesuit theologians Francisco Suarez* and Gabriel Vasquez did not participate in any of these congregations, but their influence on them was considerable. The congregations were spaced out between 1598 and 1607, and Paul V brought them to a close on 28 August 1607. In accordance with the opinion of the bishop* of Geneva, Francis de Sales (1567–1622), whom he had consulted, Paul declared that the "physical premotion" of the Dominicans was not Calvinist, and that the "simultaneous help" and "average science" of the Jesuits did not fall under the accusation of Pelagianism. He also forbade anyone from censoring either opinion as long as the Holy See did not find it opportune to make a definitive decision regarding the controversy (*DS* 1997)—something he never did. The quarrel went on in spite of this ban, so that in 1611 Paul V forbade the publication of any work on the subject of grace that had not received the authorization of the Inquisition. The ban was reiterated by Urban VIII.

The controversy was revived later with Cornelius Jansen, or Jansenius (1585–1638), a former student of Jacques Jansson, himself a former student of Baius, and one who had been entrusted in Louvain with the investigation into Lessius. Jansenius obtained his doctor's degree at Louvain in 1619. His *Augustinus* (published posthumously in 1640) was intended to oppose the position defended by the Jesuits in the congregations *de auxiliis,* a position that fell, according to him, under the accusation of semi-Pelagianism. His doctrine on grace was later defended against the Molinists by Antoine Arnauld and Blaise Pascal*, in particular in the second of the latter's *Provinciales* (1656), which was devoted to the subject of sufficient grace and effective grace. (For the controversy that brought the Molinists and Jansenists into opposition, *see* Jansenism*.)

c) Average Science, Physical Premotion, and Predetermination. The core of the debate between Dominicans and Jesuits is an alternative between two concepts, that of physical premotion and predetermination and that of average science. The major stakes are the relations between freedom and grace and the relations between primary cause and secondary causes; the role of the knowledge of future contingencies (notably the forecasting of merits) in divine preordination (involving questions about Providence and predestination); the definition of effective grace and sufficient grace; the foundation of the infallibility of divine grace and science; and finally, the nature of freedom.

Molinism is a theory of the simultaneous participation of grace and free will: once human will is elevated through grace to the capability of accomplishing supernatural acts, it freely produces those supernatural acts. In this regard, Molinism is opposed to the Dominicans' majority thesis, according to which grace not only cooperates with will but, on top of the influx that makes the will capable of supernatural acts, also exerts upon it a motion that causes it to perform these acts. So it is not so much a question of a cooperation between grace and free will as of a subordination of free will to divine causality. This "premotion" is called "physical" in order to express the fact that the motion of grace is not merely moral, and to show that in this case, free will does not possess the power to thwart it. A physical determination, in fact, is a determination *ad unum.* In the theory of simultaneous participation, on the other hand, the motion exerted by grace upon the will is of a moral nature only and is such that its effect depends on the cooperation of the will, which could very well choose not to cooperate. The question raised by both doctrines is therefore that of the principle that causes the will to produce supernatural acts. Does this determination come totally under grace? In other words, is the will able or unable to withhold its consent to grace? And how can one establish the difference between sufficient grace and effective grace, on the one hand, and between prevenient grace and cooperating grace, on the other? Does one designate that the intrinsic characteristics of graces that have different natures (as the Dominicans would like), or rather the determinations that manifest the relationship between grace and a will which is free to consent to it or not (as the Jesuits want)? For the Molinists, it is the cooperation of the will that renders divine help efficient, and this divine help is not of a different nature when the will does not consent to it. Whether it gives its assent or not, the will is at the source of what characterizes the same grace as effective or sufficient, prevenient or cooperating.

As for the theory of physical premotion and effective grace, it allowed the Dominicans to establish the infallibility of divine science on a simple principle: God determines reality in accordance with his decrees. For Molina, this meant annihilating the freedom of creatures. That was why he took up a theory of the Jesuit Pierre Fonseca (1528–99), who had already influenced Lessius. According to Fonseca's theory, besides the natural science (of the possible) and the free science (of the real, a science that takes into account the divine decrees through which God has decided on such state of things rather than another), one should see in God a third science, through which he knows what the free will would do in all the circumstances in which it might find itself. And since this average science *(scientia media),* as Molina calls it, distinguishes itself from free science and thus anticipates the determination of divine will, it allows the determination of created wills to have some independence with regard to the divine decrees, while maintaining the infallibility of the divine prescience. Indeed, it is sufficient for God to know the real circumstances where created wills are (which falls under free science) in order to know what they will in fact do. In this way the theory of average science allows for a bringing together of divine prescience and the self-determination of created wills. It refuses an infallibility founded on a grace acting *ab intrinseco,* subscribing instead to the idea of an infallibility that rests on a grace acting *ab extrinsico.* The Dominican view, therefore, opposed to this a divine knowledge of conditional futures through free science; the view on predetermination thus served to show the anteriority of the divine decrees over the divine knowledge of future contingencies. The alternative, average science or free science, thus had as its principal theological stake the role held by the forecasting of merits in predestination: it was therefore a matter of solving a question left undecided by the cautious formulation of the Tridentine decree of 1547.

d) Historical Impact of These Debates. The controversy was so far-reaching that no one was able to avoid it altogether, and most of the great thinkers of the 17th century had to confront it one way or another. This was the case for Arnauld and Pascal, of course, but also for Descartes*—whose concept of human freedom has been shown by Gilson to owe, on the purely philosophical level, a debt to the theological controversies of his time. Even Malebranche addressed it, in his *Réflexions sur la prémotion physique* of 1715. There he intended to criticize the Thomist understanding of the connection between freedom and grace, a misconception which could, he claimed, be solved with recourse to his own system. The quarrel did not completely fade away during the 18th century and the French Revolution. Indeed it was revived in the course of the 19th century, after the encyclical *Aeterni Patris* of Leo XIII (4 August 1879) made a call to reestablish Catholic teaching on the basis of Thomas Aquinas's thought. The Thomists saw in this an implicit approval of the doctrine of Bañez. As for the Jesuits, who had always identified with Thomas Aquinas, they applied themselves to showing the agreement between Molinism and Thomism*, and to distinguishing Bañezianism from Thomism. At the forefront of the polemic were T. de Régnon, defender of Molinism, and H. Gayraud, who championed Bañezianism. The debate continued into the early 20th century, placing on opposing sides the Molinist A. d'Alès and the Bañezian R. Garrigou-Lagrange. As a matter of fact, it was only at the beginning of the 20th century that the two religious orders involved in these controversies ceased to demand of their respective members that they conform to their official position on these questions (*see* letter no. 1 by P.G. Smith, S. J., to Father de Lubac*, and no. 3, in *Lettres de monsieur Étienne Gilson au Père de Lubac,* Paris, 1986). However, these doctrines did not disappear, a fact attested to by J.-H. Nicolas's polemic against J. Maritain, who had proposed to introduce into the problematics of evil* the concept of *breakable divine motion,* and who thus came up against the opposition of what he himself called a "neo-Bañezianism."

• Baius (1563), *De libero hominis arbitrio et ejus potestate,* Louvain; (1563), *De justitia et justificatione,* Louvain; (1565), *De meritis operum,* Louvain; (1696), *Michaelis Baii celeberrimi in Lovaniensi Academia Theologie opera: Cum bullis Pontificum...,* Köln.

Bañez (1584), *Commentarium in Iam partem summae theologicae*; *Commentarium in IIam IIae... ,* Salamanca.

Molina (1588), *Concordia liberi arbitrii cum gratiae donis, divina præscientia, providentia, prædestinatione et reprobatione ad nonullos partis divi Thomae articulos,* Lisbon; (1589), *Appendix ad concordam liberi arbitrii,* Lisbon; (1595), *Liberi arbitrii cum gratiae donis... concordia, altera sui parte auctior,* Antwerp.

Lessius (1610), *De gratia efficaci, decretis divinis, libertate arbitrii et praescientia Dei conditionata,* Antwerp; (1641), *Censura Lovaniensis,* Paris.

J.-H. Nicolas (1960), "La permission du péché," *RThom* 60, 5–37, 185–206, 509–46.

J. Maritain (1963), *Dieu et la permission du mal,* Paris.

♦ A. Serry (1700), *Historia congregationum de auxiliis...,* Louvain.

L. de Meyer (1709), *Historiae controversiarum de auxiliis divinae gratiae...,* Antwerp.

Du Chesne (1731), *Histoire du baianisme,* Douai.

F.H. Reusch (1873), *Luis de León und die spanische Inquisition,* Bonn.

G. Schneemann (1881), *Controversiarum de divinae gratiae liberique arbitrii concordia initia et progressus,* Freiburg.

T. de Régnon (1883), *Bañez et Molina,* Paris.

H. Gayraud (1889), *Thomisme et molinisme,* Paris.

X. Le Bachelet (1903), "Baius," *DThC* 2/1, 31–111.

P. Mandonnet (1903), "Bañez," ibid., 140–45.

H. Quilliet (1907), "Congruisme," *DThC* 3/1, 1120–38.

A. Astrain (1913), *Historia de la Compania de Jesus en la Asistencia de España,* Madrid.

É. Gilson (1913), *La liberté chez Descartes et la théologie,* Paris.

X. Le Bachelet (1913), *Auctarium Bellarminianum,* Paris.

R. Garrigou-Lagrange (1915), *Dieu, son existence, sa nature,* Paris.

X. Le Bachelet, et al. (1924), "Jésuites," *DThC* 8/1, 1012–1108.

A. d'Alès (1927), *Providence et libre arbitre.*

F.-X. Jansen (1927), *Baius et le baianisme,* Louvain.

E. Vansteenberghe (1929), "Molina," *DThC* 10/2, 2090–92 and 2094–2187.

H. de Lubac (1946), *Surnaturel: Études historiques,* Paris (2nd Ed. 1991).

H. Rondet (1948), *Gratia Christi,* Paris.

J. Orcibal (1962), "De Baius à Jansénius: le *comma pianum,*" *RevSR* 36, 115–39.

H. de Lubac (1965), *Augustinisme et théologie moderne,* Paris; *Le mystère du surnaturel,* Paris.

J. Orcibal (1985), *Jansénius d'Ypres (1585–1638),* Paris.

W. Hasker (1989), *God, Time and Knowledge,* Ithaca-London, 19–52.

W. Hübener (1989), *"Praedeterminatio physica," HWP* 7, 1216–25.

T.P. Flint (1998), *Divine Providence: The Molinist Account,* 2nd Ed., Ithaca-London.

Laurence Renault

See also **Bellarmine, Robert; Calvinism; Conversion; Grace; Jansenism; Justification; Knowledge, Divine; Liberty; Pascal, Blaise; Pelagianism; Predestination; Providence; Spirituality, Ignatian; Supernatural; Trent, Council of**

Baptism

I. In Scripture

1. Terminology

The verb *baptizein,* from *baptein,* which had only secular usage, means "to submerse, to baptize." It is used in this general sense in the Septuagint (2 Kgs 5:14). The New Testament also contains this usage (Mk 10:38), but uses the word principally to designate Christian baptism. Hence came the nouns *baptismos* (the act of immersion, which from the third century came more frequently to designate baptism) and *baptisma,* baptism.

2. Jewish World

The Old Testament mentions the use of water for ritual purification (Lv 14–15; *see* Mk 7:1–5). The members of the Qumran community advocated daily ablutions in their intense desire to purify themselves (1QSIII, 3–11). Toward the first century, in addition to circumcision, the baptism of converts developed, as something designed for the purification of pagans who wished to become Jews. Extant sources do not permit a precise dating of its appearance, and current scholarship tends to the view that it had no influence on Christian baptism (Légasse 1993).

3. New Testament

The presentation of baptism in the New Testament is not uniform. It underwent an evolution and has reached us via differing traditions.

a) Baptism of John the Baptist. What was usually called the Baptist movement (Thomas 1935) is now seen as an array of different trends, and there is a tendency to situate John the Baptist's action within its singularity. The Gospels* and the Acts take pains to harmonize their respective traditions concerning John and Jesus*. They make the former the precursor of the latter, regardless of the conflicts between the two groups, and distinguish their respective baptisms by means of the opposition between water and spirit (Mt 3:11 and parallel passages). John "proclaimed a baptism of repentance for the forgiveness of sins" (Mk 1:4; *see* Lk 3:3). Matthew, who restricts the remission of sins to the person of Jesus (1:21, 26:28), speaks with respect to John only of a "baptism of repentance" (3:11) and thereby indicates the efficacy attributed by other witnesses to the baptism of John. The latter had several characteristics. First was the active role of the baptizer: unlike ablutions, when one washes oneself, baptism was administered by another person. Second, it was a unique act, open to all willing to convert. It was finally an eschatological task, carried out by the prophet* of the last days, and a way to "flee from the wrath to come" (Mt 3:7). The ritual is not precisely described: water was used, but nothing indicates total immersion.

b) Baptism of Jesus by John. The fact is attested to, even though it has seemed shocking that Jesus received a baptism for the remission of sins. Matthew explains that he had in this way to "fulfill all righteousness" (3:15). The texts hardly describe the baptism itself. Rather, they tell of the prophetic investiture (Perrot 1979) of Jesus, on whom the Holy* Spirit descends like a dove, and the inauguration of his ministry*. The scene is Christianized to the point that it later served as a model for the baptism of Christians. By the same token, the characteristics of the baptism of John were transferred onto Christian baptism—with the essential difference, however, that the latter involved a relationship with Jesus.

c) Jesus the Baptist. The current tendency is to accept the testimony of John 3:22f., even though a gloss specifies that "Jesus himself did not baptize, but only his disciples" (Jn 4:2). There is no later mention of these early days of Jesus as a Baptist, perhaps for theological motives. On the one hand, John specifies that the Holy Spirit had not yet been given (Jn 7:39), while on the other hand, all the actions of Jesus tend to show that salvation* comes less from a ritual gesture than from his very person.

d) Baptism of Christians and Its Meanings. The New Testament writings give evidence of theological work on the meaning of baptism (lists of pericopes, or brief passages, in Guillet 1985). The earliest information is provided by Paul, who already speaks of baptism as a received tradition* (1 Cor 1:11–17). But we lack information for the period separating the baptism of John

(c. 30) and the earliest writings of Paul (c. 55). We therefore do not know whether the first Christians abandoned circumcision, which Pauline circles were already placing in opposition to baptism (Col 2:11ff.), nor why they adopted baptism as a rite of adherence (Acts 2:41) to Christ and to his body. The baptism received by Jesus himself probably had nothing to do with it.

Paul developed the theology* of baptism in a very original way by deepening the relationship between the baptized and Jesus, going so far as to assert that "all of us who have been baptized into Christ Jesus were baptized into his death" (Rom 6:3). The pneumatological and ecclesiastical meaning of baptism is nonetheless affirmed, because "in one Spirit we were all baptized into one body" (1 Cor 12:13). Colossians, which constitutes an admirable baptismal catechesis*, elaborated still further the relationship to the Resurrection at a later stage of the tradition (2:12).

In the synoptic Gospels, baptism is presented as a rite of water that Jesus himself received, with the Holy Spirit, at the beginning of his mission.

As for Acts, this book poses in particular the problem of the relationship of baptism to the Holy Spirit. According to Acts 2:38 and 10:47, baptism is accompanied by the gift of the Holy Spirit (after or before). According to Acts 8:15 f. and 19:2–6, the laying* on of hands is added to the baptismal rite with a view to the gift of the Holy Spirit. Attempts have been made to distinguish these two traditions by the formulations used: baptism in (or on) the name of Jesus Christ (Lucan tradition, with the gift of the Holy Spirit); baptism for the name of the Lord Jesus (Pauline tradition, with the laying on of hands; *see* Quesnel 1985). According to Légasse (1993), the second expression is the older one. Initially indicating only the relationship to Jesus, it acquired a stronger theological sense by following the evolution of Christology*. As for the relationship between baptism and the Holy Spirit, the tradition is ambivalent.

John 3:5 reaffirms this relationship and sets out the necessity of baptism in order to enter into the kingdom* of God*, an affirmation that later took on great significance. 1 John 5:6ff. leads toward a synthesis in attesting that Jesus Christ came not with water alone (John), nor blood (Paul), nor by the Holy Spirit of pneumatology, but that these three move toward the One, the Christ*, the wound in whose side let flow blood and water before he gave up the spirit (Jn 19:30–34).

The most complete presentations of baptism are found in the conclusions of Matthew and Mark, which belong to later textual strata. In both, the risen Christ solemnly sends his apostles on a mission. Mark 16:16 establishes a link between baptism and faith*, whereas Matthew 28:19 presents a Trinitarian formulation whose success was later evident in baptismal liturgies.

Beyond the diversity of its traditions, the New Testament thus ends by presenting baptism as a unique act with water (Eph 4:5), carried out by the church* in the name of the Trinity* to join the baptized to the community. As for the rite, it is nowhere described precisely. Acts 8:38 indicates that Philip and the eunuch go down "into the water," while verse 37 (Western tradition) points to a christological profession of faith.

II. In History

1. First Four Centuries

The diversity of traditions encountered in the New Testament continued, since Christian baptism did not refer back to an originating biblical text, as the Eucharist* did to the Last Supper. And although the baptismal ritual expanded during Christian antiquity, there was only a single celebration of Christian initiation*. Unity came more from a general understanding of baptism as a Trinitarian celebration of entry into the Church than from a (nonexistent) ritual uniformity.

Evidence from the second century is scant (Benoît 1953). Chapter seven of the *Didache* presents baptism after the instruction of the first six chapters. It mentions baptism in the name of the three divine Persons*, but also in the name of the Lord (9, 5). It provides details on the use of water, possibly only by sprinkling, and on the fasting that was counseled for all those who were able. Justin added in the middle of the century that the meaning of baptism is an illumination *(phôtismos),* and he noted that the celebration leads to the Eucharist (*I Apol.* 61, 65).

The third century saw significant expansion of ritual (exorcisms, holy* oils, laying on of hands) which basically derived from Scripture*, even though this expansion found support in practices of the ancient world. Tertullian* was the first to provide a treatise on baptism (early third century). The *Apostolic Tradition* (in Rome c. 215) offers the first ritual worthy of the name. It begins with a catechesis (numbers 15–20), which might last for three years, and is presented as an ordeal with many exorcisms. Baptism takes place after a vigil (probably at Easter). After the renunciation of Satan and a first anointing by the presbyter* with the oil of exorcism, the naked candidates go down into the pool with a deacon*, for a threefold profession of faith by means of questions and answers and a threefold submersion in the water. There follows a christological anointing by the presbyter with chrism, reclothing, and entry into the church. There the bishop* lays his hands on each person while making a prayer for the gift of the Holy Spirit. Then he performs a third, Trinitarian, anointing, and gives each person the kiss of peace. There follows a general prayer and the bringing of gifts for the Eucharist. This very ample ritual influenced the entire Western tradition. Its ecclesiastical sense should be emphasized: having become Christians on their entry into the catechumenate, and chosen *(electi)* in the final phase, the baptized become worshipers by receiving the sacrament of faith and thereby truly enter into the Christian community. The celebration is carried out by the bishop, accompanied by deacons and presbyters, and it is crowned by the Eucharist.

One cannot generalize on the basis of this information, however, particularly with respect to the Eastern Church, in which various traditions were present. In Syria, for example, the Acts of Thomas (Syriac, early third century) linked the gift of the Holy Spirit to a prebaptismal anointing (the seal), and this was still the case with John Chrysostom*: they contained neither a profession of faith nor an act of renunciation. In Alexandria baptism took place at the Epiphany, the feast of the baptism of Christ and hence of Christians. The Coptic liturgy developed a baptismal theology along the lines of the synoptic Gospels. Like Jesus, the Christian was baptized at the outset of his existence, thus receiving the Holy Spirit in view of his mission. Forty days later there took place a presentation at the temple*.

The second half of the fourth century saw a flowering of major baptismal and mystagogical catechesis* that reflected the importance attributed to Christian initiation by the bishops of the time: Cyril (or John) of Jerusalem, John Chrysostom, Theodore of Mopsuestia, and Ambrose. They provide plentiful information on baptismal theology and rites (Camelot 1963), which at the time tended to be communicated from one church to another. They indicate the greater importance attached to the Pauline* theology of baptism, as a passing through the death and Resurrection of Christ. This notion, infrequently represented before this time, helped to give the gift of the Holy Spirit a more prominent place, in parallel with the Council of Constantinople* of 381. Postbaptismal rites also appeared where they had not existed earlier.

Baptism of infants is mentioned explicitly for the first time by Tertullian in the early third century, in order to express his opposition ("Yes, let them come, but when they are older, old enough to be taught," *De baptismo* 18, 4. The *Apostolic Tradition* indicates clearly, moreover, that there was no question, as in later practice, of baptizing children alone. They were baptized with their parents (a probable continuation of the "household" baptism mentioned in Acts 16:15). Thereafter, in the fourth century, we can observe a wave of delay in baptism. The Cappadocians, John Chrysostom, Jerome, Augustine*, and others, born of Christian parents, were baptized as adults, perhaps for reasons relating to penitential discipline (Jeremias 1967), but once they had become bishops, they declared themselves in favor of infant baptism.

Theological difficulties arose with the appearance of Novatianism*. The disciples of Novatian rebaptized Christians wishing to join their movement. In the church as a whole there were two traditions on this point: Africa and Asia Minor also rebaptized, whereas Rome* and Egypt were satisfied with a laying on of hands. There was a vigorous controversy between Africa and Rome in the mid-third century. Several African councils met to consider the question, and Cyprian wrote his letters 69 through 74 on the subject. Pope* Stephen held to the principle: *Nihil innovetur nisi quod traditum est, ut manus illis imponatur in paenitentiam* (Ep. 74. 2. 2–3): "Let there be no innovation, but let us merely follow the tradition by a laying on of hands as a sign of penance*." Cyprian, for his part, argued that there was only one baptism, the one conferred by the central church, for there was only one Church and only one Holy Spirit, and no one could have God as a Father* if he did not have the Church as a mother (Ep. 74. 7. 2). Moreover, "outside the Church, there is no salvation" (Ep. 73. 21. 2). In baptism, the church transmitted what belonged to it. The so-called baptism of heretics was nothing but an aquatic rite.

This position was not maintained. The Council of Arles in 314 adopted the Roman idea and affirmed that the value of baptism depended on the content of the faith professed (can. 8). The Council of Nicaea* in 325 ratified these views (cans. 8 and 19).

The controversy continued against Donatism*, in the form of a conflict that Augustine succeeded in resolving by moving from Cyprian's ecclesiological concept of baptism to a christological one. Baptism did not belong in the first instance to the church, but to God and to Christ. Whoever the minister, it was always Christ who baptized (Jn 1:33), hence the celebrated sentence: "If Peter baptizes, he [Christ] baptizes; if Paul baptizes, he baptizes; if Judas baptizes, he baptizes" (*Commentary on John* VI. 5–8, CChr.SL 36. 56–57). In this context arose the technical notion of minister of a sacrament. Augustine distinguished the *potestas* of baptism (which belonged only to Christ) from the *ministerium* of the minister. The latter did not give of himself (Cyprian), he was only the servant of Christ. From that point on, it has been accepted in the West that, in case of emergency, anyone can baptize, even someone who has not been baptized, provided he intends to do what the Church does (*DS* 1315, 1617).

The critique of Pelagianism* provided the occasion for further refinements. The Pelagians did baptize infants, but on account of the innocence of infants, the Pelagians denied that they received baptism for the remission of sins. Augustine made the objection that their baptism itself indicated that they had to be saved. "From what, if not from death, from vices, from the bonds, the slavery, the darkness of sin? As their age prevents them from having committed any personally, there remains original sin" (*On the Merits of Sins and Their Remissions, and on the Baptism of Little Children* 412, I. 26. 39, PL 44, 131).

We can thus see the development of the doctrine of original sin in Augustine, under the dual presupposition of the personal innocence of children (presupposed by the argument) and the already accepted baptism of infants that was bestowed "for the remission of sin." Once asserted, the doctrine in turn became a motive for baptizing children. Infant baptism later prevailed in the West, to the point of obscuring the positive values of baptism asserted, for example, by John Chrysostom (*Baptismal Catecheses* III. 5–6).

In the Donatist controversy Augustine further developed the features of what was to become the doctrine of the character of baptism (*DS* 1609). Wishing in fact to emphasize the definitive aspect of the sacrament, he spoke of *sacramentum manens.* Among the images used to explain its reality was that of the sheep marked with its owner's brand.

From the second half of the fourth century on, the majority of the Mediterranean population became Christian. This success brought about changes in the sociological composition of the Church, as witnessed by the letter of Innocent I to Decentius of Gubbio, showing the consequences of this new situation for baptism and confirmation, the Eucharist, and the ministries*. As for Christian initiation, East and West took separate paths. The former gave pride of place to the unity of initiation and granted to presbyters the right to confer it in its entirety. The West maintained for confirmation* a link to the bishop, which led to a gradual dissociation between baptism and confirmation.

2. High Middle Ages in the West

In the fifth century infant baptism became more frequent than baptism of adults. In episcopal cities baptism was still administered at Easter by the bishop, who performed confirmation and gave the Eucharist in the same ceremony. In rural areas priests increasingly baptized children at birth and gave them Communion with the sacred blood. On rare occasions Communion was delayed until a visit by the bishop.

Liturgical books of the eighth century, after providing questions and answers on faith, added a baptismal formula modeled on Matthew 28:19, which, it may be assumed, was already known in the West two centuries earlier (De Clerck 1990). The relationship between faith and baptism was thereby modified. One was no longer baptized by professing one's faith, and the pattern of questions and answers can be seen as a kind of preliminary condition for baptism, which was itself performed by the minister with the help of a formula designating precisely him as subject of the action ("I baptize you"). This formula became the pattern for other sacraments*.

3. Middle Ages in the West

It can be said that from the 12th century the West practiced baptism *quam primum:* that is, administered it as soon as possible after birth. This represented a complete break with paschal baptism, and also with First Communion*, which was postponed around this time until the age of reason. Thus, each of the three sacraments of Christian initiation, once parts of a single celebration, became autonomous. In the list of the sacramental septenary established in 1150, baptism, confirmation, and the Eucharist are listed separately. For their part, the Scholastic theologians systematized the teaching received, as can be seen, for example, in the *Summa Theologica* of Thomas* Aquinas, IIIa. q. 66–71.

The question also arose of children who died without baptism, a pressing question in a society with high infant mortality and where the theology of baptism was dominated by the consideration of original sin. There was a refinement of the theory of the "limbo* (intermediate place) of children." Not having been baptized, they could not enter the kingdom of God, according to John 3:5. On the other hand, their innocence made it repugnant to think of them as damned. According to Thomas (*Sent.* II. d. 33, q. 2), these children were deprived of the beatific* vision, but because nature was not in itself turned toward the supernatural*, they did not suffer from this loss: "There is no sadness in being deprived of a good to which one is not suited" (Boissard 1974). This theology, softer than Augustinian views, was never adopted as a doctrine of the church. It nevertheless had a great deal of influence and did not dispel all fears. In this connection there were "sanctuaries of respite," places of pilgrimage* where children who had died without baptism were carried and placed on the altar, where some of them seemed to recover a brief moment of life, which was taken as an opportunity to baptize them.

4. Reformation and Modern Times

The major figures of the Reformation challenged neither baptism as such nor infant baptism in particular. Criticism came from the Anabaptists*, who opposed infant baptism on the biblical premise that the New Testament requires faith for baptism; as well as on the ecclesiological premise that the Church can be made up only of those who confess their faith. The Anabaptists were the precursors of the 17th-century Baptists*, who professed the same theology of baptism and administered it through immersion.

5. 20th Century

This century is marked by two major events, the ecumenical movement and the Second Vatican* Council*.

a) The constitution *Sacrosanctum Concilium* of Vatican II devotes numbers 64 to 70 to baptism. Number 64 decides on the restoration of the adult catechumenate, to be accomplished in stages. Number 66 calls for the revision of the rite of infant baptism in order "to adapt it to the real situation of the very young." Number 69 proposes, for a child baptized in an emergency, the composition of a rite of welcome into the community (*see* chap. VI of the Rite of the Baptism of Little Children) and, for people baptized in other faiths, a rite of admission into full communion with the Church (in the Ritual of the Christian Initiation of Adults).

These proposals were carried out by the Consilium for the realization of the constitution. The Ritual of the Baptism of Little Children was published in Latin in 1969, and the same year in a provisional French translation. The French text was finally approved in 1984. It contains important "doctrinal and pastoral Notes" that provide a key for the ritual part. The principal modifications are of two kinds. On the one hand, baptism has again become a liturgy of the Word*. On the other, this was the first time in the history of the church that it published a ritual "adapted to the real situation of the very young," a fact that permits the assertion that in the consciousness of the church the theological model of baptism is indeed that of adults. This adaptation also means that parents, and not godparents, are now in the forefront. They "exercise a true ministry*" (Notes, no. 40) when they request baptism for their child and themselves profess the faith of the church. The Ritual for the Christian Initiation of Adults was published in Latin in 1972, in a provisional French edition in 1974, and an approved edition in 1997. The notion of Christian initiation, rediscovered by L. Duchesne in the late 19th century, was adopted by Vatican II and heads all rituals. The Ritual for the Christian Initiation of Adults is a large book that, in addition to "doctrinal and pastoral Notes," contains the ritual of catechesis, which may last as long as three years, and the ritual of the sacraments of initiation. It is structured in four periods (first evangelization, catechesis, final fast, and mystagogy), and three celebrations (entry into catechesis, decisive call and inscription of the name, and the sacraments themselves). The sacraments are customarily celebrated during the Easter vigil by the bishop, or else by the priest, who in this case may himself confirm the newly baptized (no. 228; *see LG* no. 26, stipulating that the bishop is the originating minister of confirmation). This prescription is the exact opposite of that of the High Middle Ages, and thus does away with the principal cause of the dispersal of Christian initiation through several rituals.

b) The ecumenical movement has obviously been concerned with baptism. From its first conference in Lausanne in 1927, "Faith and Constitution" placed on the agenda the question of a document of doctrinal convergence on baptism. It went through various versions before being published in Lima in 1982 under the title of *Baptism, Eucharist, Ministry (BEM),* so that it might be examined by various churches, whose responses led to a report published in 1991.

These advances have allowed for mutual recognition by churches of baptisms celebrated within each one, in particular in Belgium (1971), France (1972), and Germany (Concord of Leuenberg, 1973) (Sicard 1991). The CIC now favors the validity of non-Catholic baptism; it stipulates: "People baptized in a non-Catholic church community must not be baptized conditionally, unless there is a serious reason to doubt the validity of the baptism, considering both the matter and the formula used for its administration, as well as the intention of the adult who has been baptized and the minister who has done the baptizing" (can. 869 §2).

III. Theology of Baptism

The Christian initiation of adults constitutes the model of baptism. It best realizes its ritual expression and offers the best basis for theological reflection. Indeed, it is on the basis of the initiation of adults that an understanding of the particular case of infant baptism can be attained.

1. Baptism and Personal Fate

Baptism, whether of children or adults, constitutes the basis of the personal identity of the Christian. In the case of infant baptism, its principal sign is the bestowal of the name, which begins the ritual procedure. For the adult, this identity is received in the midst of the tragic course of his existence. It is a deliberate choice, on the one hand against the evil* that he has experienced in his former life (renunciation), and on the other, in favor of God, his Christ, and the Holy Spirit, whose love is stronger than any form of death (profession of faith).

2. Meaning of the Baptism of Adults

All baptisms are carried out through the mediation of a Christian community, but this is not the ultimate purpose of the ritual. The questions asked immediately before the administration of the water concern faith in the Trinitarian God. This expresses the sacramental value of the event as an act of God, carried out by his Church, and not merely a rite of belonging. This sacramental logic leads naturally to a consideration first of the ecclesiastical relations established by baptism, followed by a contemplation of the Trinitarian relations in which baptismal grace* resides.

a) Baptism as the Establishment of a Relation to the Church. According to Acts 2:41, "there were added that day about three thousand souls"; and since the verb has no object, it can be understood that the newly baptized were added to Christ, in whose name they were baptized, as well as to the community. Verse 47 supports this interpretation: certain variants name the Church. Every baptism is carried out by the Church and one of its ministers (bishop, priest, or deacon) in the Church (for "no one can have God as a Father if he does not have the Church as a Mother" Cyprian, Ep. 74. 7), with a view toward establishing the Church. What church does the baptized person join? Not only the local community, because moving to another community does not involve rebaptism. The sacramental dimension of baptism and the recent agreements for interchurch recognition of baptism encourage the assertion that the baptized are joined to the Church of God. But this is necessarily accomplished through the mediation of a particular church. And because all churches are not in communion with one another, it must be recognized that although the baptized are joined to the Church of God, at the same time they become members of a denominational church, although the Catholic Church, for one, considers that there "subsists" in it the fullness of "churchness." Under the heading of Incorporation into the Body of Christ, the *BEM* writes: "Celebrated in obedience to our Lord, baptism is a sign and a seal of our engagement as disciples. Through their own baptism, Christians are led to union with Christ, with every other Christian, and with the Church of all times and places. Our common baptism, which unites us to Christ in faith, is thus a fundamental bond of unity*. We are one people and we are called to confess and to serve one Lord, in every place and throughout the world. The union with Christ that we share through baptism has important implications for Christian unity: 'There is...one baptism, one God and Father of all' (Eph 4:4–6). When baptismal unity is realized in the one holy, Catholic, and apostolic Church, an authentic Christian witness may be rendered to the love of God that cures and reconciles. This is why our single baptism in Christ constitutes an appeal to the churches for them to overcome their divisions and to visibly manifest their communion" (no. 6). Baptism indeed constitutes the foundation of the unity of Christians, within a Church of which one becomes a member by an act of Christ (and not by the cooptation of other members), as well as among churches that find in that unity the reason for their ecumenical efforts.

Baptism establishes a relationship to God through the mediation of a church, but it does not exclude other paths to salvation by Christ, for "all things were created through him and for him" (Col 1:16), and "God our Savior...desires all people to be saved" (1 Tm 2:4). For although it is correct to say that baptism in faith does save, it is more accurate to assert that it is God who saves through baptism, or through other means of his mercy*. According to classical theology, the necessity of baptism is as a precept*, and not as a means, for "God has not tied his power to the sacraments" (Thomas Aquinas, *ST* IIIa, q. 64, a. 7). The necessity for baptism is felt by anyone who perceives in the sacrament the realization of a covenant* with God.

b) Baptism as the Establishment of Trinitarian Relationships. The relationship to Christ, chronologically the first (Acts 2:38; 1 Cor 1:13), also turns out to be the most fundamental (Rom 6:3–11). This is corroborated by the first gesture of the celebration, the making of the sign of the cross, and by the Western tradition of celebrating baptism at Easter. From the point of view of the baptized, in fact, baptism consists of passing into the death of Christ in order to rise with him and "walk in newness of life" (Rom 6:4). From the point of view of Christ, baptism is the act through which he commits his faithfulness to those who have given him their faith, and this is affirmed in other terms by the doctrine of baptismal character (*DS* 1609). We can thus see a structure of reciprocity governing the logic of the sacramental act. The intention of God in Christ is received by people who answer him in the Holy Spirit, with a view to building the Church. In baptism Christians receive their vocation. As the prayer accompanying the anointing with chrism states: "Henceforth, you are one of His people, you are members of the body of Christ, and you participate in his dignity as priest, prophet, and king." This vocation is elaborated in *Lumen Gentium* 34–36. Read in this way, the Christian life is from beginning to end a baptismal life.

The relationship to the Holy Spirit is affirmed in the New Testament. For Luke it is the strength of God received for mission*, while for Paul the emphasis is on inward transformation and sanctification. Even though there is a specific gift of the Holy Spirit at confirmation, its absence at baptism does not follow, since baptism is given in the name of the Father, the Son, and the Holy Spirit. The gift of the Holy Spirit is the remission of sins (Jn 20:22f.). To be baptized is thus to receive a Spirit different from one's own and to be called to bear its fruits (Gal 5:22) in a "spiritual" life*.

"All who are led by the Spirit of God are sons of God" (Rom 8:14). The outcome of the baptismal process is the relationship to God, recognized as Father and Creator, with the confident existence that this relationship provides, for "If God is for us, who can be against us?" (Rom 8:31–39).

3. Particular Meaning of Infant Baptism

a) Justification for Infant Baptism. Since baptism is a sacrament of faith, how can we accept the validity of a true baptism celebrated at an age that in principle excludes any personal expression of faith? The answer consists in asserting the need for a substitution, a vicarious faith that the tradition of the Church locates at two levels. On the one hand, there is the faith of the Church, in which every sacrament (and not only infant baptism) is celebrated. This compels the recognition that the expression "baptism, a sacrament of faith" has not only a subjective meaning (the baptized must give their answer of faith), but also an objective meaning: by baptizing, the Church establishes the sacramental figure of its faith in the salvation of God. This permits us to understand that the subject of faith is not primarily an individual, but the Church, the people of God. In other words, the existence of infant baptism also brings to the fore the dimensions of faith itself.

On the other hand, the faith of others *(fides aliena)* is required, in the sense that the faith of the Church must be transmitted by concrete individuals. In the view of theologians who accept it, infant baptism is justified when it is requested by believers (Thomas Aquinas, *ST* IIIa, q. 68), and these do not necessarily have to be the child's own parents.

b) Reasons for Infant Baptism. Among the theological reasons for infant baptism, first place must be given to God's will for universal salvation, which is also applied to little children. The very existence of infant baptism demonstrates that they matter in the eyes of God. Another reason is original sin. Even though no current sin is clearly imputable to infants, they are nevertheless born into a world in which human beings have immemorially needed to be saved by God (*DS* 1514). Moreover, infant baptism is a perfect image of the gratuitous nature of salvation: even before children can possibly respond, God's initiative is celebrated for their benefit. This is the reason for the prevenient grace that is of such importance to Lutherans. It can be elaborated along more existential lines by showing how infant baptism comes together with the very mystery of human existence. Humankind in fact has little mastery over its own life. In any event, no individual initiates his own coming into existence. Infant baptism represents a symbolic reduplication of this fact, which probably explains its persistence through history, despite constant criticism. Finally, infant baptism offers a paradigm of ecclesiastical solidarity, because it would have no meaning if salvation were only individual. Here too, then, it brings to the fore various dimensions of faith.

c) Objections to Infant Baptism. These have often been expressed and are summed up in the Instruction on the Baptism of Little Children promulgated by the Congregation for the Doctrine of the Faith in October 1980. In addition to the impossibility of a profession of faith already mentioned, the two principal objections concern the kind of Church to which infant baptism leads, and the question of liberty*.

The critique of the multitudinist Church to which the practice of infant baptism leads has often been voiced during the second half of the 20th century. This voice has also been heard, and many churches have taken measures in the face of "generalized infant baptism" (J.-J. von Allmen 1967), in particular regarding the preparation of parents. Social and ecclesiastical changes in the West have brought about a more open position with respect to infant baptism (Gisel 1994).

The most frequently heard objection concerns the liberty of children and a sectarian conception of the baptism of little children. Whatever may have been true in the past, the new Catholic rite is addressed to the parents, and it is they who are invited to profess their own faith at the baptism of their child. The child is of course the one who is baptized, but a possible later withdrawal by the child cannot be considered an apostasy, insofar as the child has not yet personally adhered to the faith of the baptism. Moreover, the objection can be refuted by a philosophical reflection on liberty, which is not, in fact, to be confused with perpetual caprice, but represents the power to make choices and to register them throughout life. One might equally ask if this objection does not also reveal some uncertainty on the part of the parents regarding their own practices of faith.

d) Particularities of the Baptism of Adults and Children. We can hold to the traditional assertion according to which there is only one baptism (Eph 4:4) if we clearly bring out the different logical bases of infant baptism and adult baptism. The differences between the two forms of baptism are obvious. They concern the subjects (adults—little children), the minister (bishop—priest or deacon), and the ritual sequence (three years—a single celebration). Beyond these differences, there are two distinct models. In the Christian initiation of adults, numerous elements of the approach to faith precede baptism. Baptism is celebrated on Easter night along with confirmation and the Eucharist (*see* RCIA, no. 34), which initiate the time of mystagogy. When it comes to infant baptism, the model is exactly the reverse: everything that precedes baptism for adults comes after it for children. We are thus confronted with two different logical bases for the same baptism, a logic of conversion* for adults, and a logic of ongoing education for children (De Clerck 1991).

• 1. General Works

A. Hamman (1969), *Baptême et confirmation,* Paris.

H. Bourgeois (1982), *L'Initiation chrétienne et ses sacrements,* Paris.

2. Scripture

J. Thomas (1935), *Le mouvement baptiste en Palestine et en Syrie (150 av. J.-C.–300 ap. J.-C.),* Gembloux.

J. D. G. Dunn (1970), *Baptism in the Holy Spirit: A Re-examination of the New Testament Teaching on the Gift of the Spirit in Relation to Pentecostalism Today,* London.

C. Perrot (1979), *Jésus et l'histoire,* Paris (2nd Ed. 1993), 95–136.

J. Guillet (1985), *Entre Jésus et l'Église,* Paris.

M. Quesnel (1985), *Baptisés dans l'Esprit B. et Esprit Saint dans les Actes des Apôtres,* LeDiv 120.

S. Légasse (1993), *Naissance du baptême,* LeDiv 153.

3. History

J. Daniélou (1951), *Bible et liturgie: La théologie biblique des sacrements d'après les Pères de l'Église,* Paris.

A. Benoît (1953), *Le baptême chrétien au IIe siècle: La théologie des Pères,* Paris.

L. Villette (1959–64), *Foi et sacrement,* vol. 1: *Du Nouveau Testament à saint Augustin,* Paris; vol. 2: *De saint Thomas à Karl Barth,* ibid.

M. Dujarier (1962), *Le parrainage des adultes aux trois premiers siècles de l'Église,* Paris.

J. Ysebaert (1962), *Greek Baptismal Terminology: Its Origin and Early Development,* Nimègue.

P. T. Camelot (1963), *Spiritualité du baptême,* Paris (2nd Ed. 1993).

J. C. Didier (1967), *Faut-il baptiser les petits enfants? La réponse de la tradition,* Paris.

J. Jeremias (1967), *Le baptême des petits enfants pendant les quatre premiers siècles,* Le Puy.

G. Kretschmar (1970), "Die Geschichte des Taufgottesdienstes in der alten Kirche," in K.F. Müller, W. Blankenburg (Ed.), *Leiturgia: Handbuch des evangelischen Gottesdienstes,* vol. 5, Cassel, 1–348.

E. Boissard (1974), *Réflexions sur le sort des enfants morts sans baptême,* Paris.

G. Kretschmar (1977), "Nouvelles recherches sur l'initiation chrétienne," *MD* 132, 7–32.

A. Jilek (1979), *Initiationsfeier und Amt: Ein Beitrag zur Struktur und Theologie der Ämter und des Taufgottesdienstes in der frühen Kirche (Tr. ap., Tertullian, Cyprian),* Frankfurt.

P. De Clerck (1986), "La dissociation du baptême et de la confirmation au haut Moyen Age," *MD* 168, 47–75.

V. Saxer (1988), *Les rites de l'initiation chrétienne du IIe au VIe siècle: Esquisse historique et signification d'après les principaux témoins,* Spoleto.

A. Benoit, C. Munier (1994), *Le baptême dans l'Église ancienne (I-IIIe siècles),* Berne.

4. Liturgy

a) Contemporary Rites

Ordo baptismi parvulorum, Rome, 1969 (2nd Ed. 1973).

Ordo initiationis christianae adultorum (OICA), Rome, 1972.

"Ordo initiationis puerorum qui aetatem catecheticam adepti sunt," chap. V, *OICA.*

b) Studies

A. Stenzel (1958), *Die Taufe: Eine genetische Erklärung der Taufliturgie,* Innsbruck.

A. Kavanagh (1978), *The Shape of Baptism: The Rite of Christian Initiation,* New York.

R. Cabié (1984), "L'Initiation chrétienne," in A.-G. Martimort (Ed.), *L'Église en prière,* New Ed., Paris, 21–114.

B. Kleinheyer (1989), *Die Feiern der Eingliederung in der Kirche,* Regensburg.

P. De Clerck (1990), "Les origines de la formule baptismale," in P. De Clerck, E. Palazzo (Ed.), *Rituels: Mélanges offerts à P.-M. Gy* O.P., Paris, 199–213.

O. Sarda (1991), "Baptême des enfants en âge de scolarité: La situation en France," *MD* 185, 61–83.

N. Duval, J. Guyon (1993), "Le baptistère en Occident," *MD* 193, 53–70.

5. Ecumenism

A. Houssiau (1970), "Implications théologiques de la reconnaissance interecclésiale du baptême," *RTL* 1, 393–410.

A. de Halleux (1980), "Orthodoxie et catholicisme: Un seul baptême?" *RTL* 11, 416–52.

COE, Foi et Constitution (1982), *B., Eucharistie, Ministère: Convergence de la foi* (Lima, January 1982), Paris.

Presses de Taizé (1991), *Rapport sur le processus "BEM" et les réactions des Églises, 1982–1990* (repr. Paris, 1993).

D. Sicard (1991), "Reconnaissance du baptême: Perspectives œcuméniques," *MD* 185, 117–30.

G. Sava-Popa (1994), *Le baptême dans la tradition orthodoxe et ses implications œcuméniques,* Fribourg.

6. Theology

J.-J. von Allmen (1967), "Réflexions d'un protestant sur le pédobaptisme généralisé," *MD* 89, 66–86.

K. Barth (1967), *KD* IV/4 (*Dogmatique,* Geneva, 1969, vol. 26).

J.-J. von Allmen (1978), *Pastorale du baptême,* Fribourg.

Congrégation [romaine] pour la doctrine de la foi (1980), *Instruction sur le baptême des petits enfants, DC* 77, vol. 1797, 1107–13.

A. Houssiau, et al. (1983), *Le baptême, entrée dans l'existence chrétienne,* Brussels.

H. Bourgeois (1991), *Théologie catéchuménale: A propos de la "nouvelle" évangélisation,* Paris.

P. De Clerck (1991), "Un seul baptême? Le baptême des adultes et celui des petits enfants," *MD* 185, 7–33.

P. Gisel (1994), *Pourquoi baptiser: Mystère chrétien et rite de passage,* Geneva.

Paul De Clerck

See also **Anointing of the Sick; Confirmation; Eucharist; Marriage; Ordination/Order; Sacrament**

Baptists

Baptists believe that only those who make a personal profession of faith* in Jesus Christ should be baptized, and that baptism* should be by immersion. They believe, furthermore, that every member of a local church should participate in the government of that church, and that no external authority, ecclesiastical or political, should interfere in its affairs.

a) Origins. There were two kinds of Baptism in England in the 17th century: these were known as General Baptism and Particular Baptism. The former group carried the conviction, inspired by Arminianism (Calvinism*), that redemption was "general" and that all men could be saved. It was at first an extreme form of Puritanism*. Some of the members of this group sought refuge in Amsterdam where, under the influence of the Anabaptist* movement, they became convinced that baptism should be reserved for believers. In 1609 their spiritual leader, John Smyth (c. 1554–1612), baptized himself before baptizing his companions. In a treatise written the same year *(Parallels, Censures, Observations)* he defended the idea that each "federal community," or community of covenant*, constituted a church in which ecclesiastical authority* fully inhered.

In 1612 Thomas Helwis (c. 1550–c. 1616) took part of the group back to England and published an appeal for complete religious toleration, *The Mistery of Iniquity.* From this group sprang others that would, in time, baptize only by immersion. Particular Baptism, on the other hand, held to the strict Calvinist doctrine that Christ* had died only for the "particular" group of the elect. This current formed in London in the 1630s by separating from Congregationalism*. Its 1644 creed* holds that baptism is only for those who have faith, relying in part on Matthew 28:18 f. (McBeth 1990). Another confession, published in 1689, long remained the touchstone of orthodoxy in this group.

b) 18th Century. The rationalism* of the 18th century led most Baptists of the first group to adopt a Christology* that was more or less close to Arianism*. By 1719 a majority of them refused to reaffirm their belief in the Trinity*, and at the end of the century some of them were very close to Unitarianism*. The second group, in contrast, adopted a strengthened Calvinism. Its best theologian, John Gill, was a resolute defender of the doctrine of election* (*The Cause of God and Truth,* 1735–38). In the second half of the century, under the influence of the Great Awakening, a more moderate version of Calvinism gradually came to predominate, placing on believers the obligation to proclaim the gospel. Expounded by Andrew Fuller (1754–1815) in *The Gospel Worthy of All Acceptation* (1785), this more moderate Calvinism gave impetus to the creation of the Baptist Missionary Society (1792). In North America the "Separate" Baptists, products of the Great Awakening, swelled the ranks of the Particular (also called "Regular") Baptists. There were also General Baptists (known as "Freewill" Baptists) in England and the United States. Some of their North American leaders, including Isaac Backus and John Leland, helped to impose the idea of a separation between church* and state.

c) 19th Century. The number of Baptists increased in the 19th century, and theological precision came to count for less than the expansion of the church. In 1833 the New Hampshire Confession, widely adopted in the United States, was deliberately silent on the points of disagreement between the Regular and Freewill Baptists (who had opposing views on predestination*). In England Robert Hall (1764–1831) succeeded in persuading his coreligionists to admit to Communion Christians who had not been given the baptism of believers. The Baptists who did not agree with this development formed separate groups: the "Anti-Mission" Baptists in the United States, the "Strict and Particular" Baptists in England. In the southern United States, which had formed a separate convention since 1845, the "Landmark" movement became distinctly sectarian by deciding in the 1850s that baptism was valid only when it was administered by Baptists. In 1887–88 in England, the beginnings of a certain theological liberalism came under attack from Charles Haddon Spurgeon (1834–92), the greatest English-language preacher of the time. The Baptist Union, which absorbed the General Baptists in 1891, maintained a very conservative Protestantism*. During this time, Baptism had established a foothold in Europe, largely due to J.G. Oncken (1800–84), and in other parts of the world due to foreign missions.

d) 20th Century. In the early 20th century North American Baptism produced an eminent representative of social Christianity, Walter Rauschenbusch (1861–1918), and a modernist* theologian, Shailer Mathews. Fundamentalism* nevertheless predominated between the wars, with such writers as W.B. Riley, J. Frank Norris, and T.T. Shields, for whom orthodoxy consisted in believing in the imminence of the Second Coming of Christ (Parousia*). The resulting debate provoked the secession of a large number of Baptists and the formation of new groups, who still called themselves Baptists but had a visceral distrust of biblical criticism and any other symptom of liberalism. This debate had repercussions outside North America, but theological polarization was generally less pronounced. Later, the ecumenical movement (although supported by the English historian Ernest Payne) was regarded with suspicion, especially out of fear of a compromise with Catholicism*. Since 1979 the Southern Baptist Convention, the largest Protestant denomination in the United States, has been torn by quarrels over the inerrancy of the Bible*. Undoubtedly, the most well-known Baptists of the modern era have been Billy Graham (1918–) and Martin Luther King (1929–68).

• W.L. Lumpkin, *Baptist Confessions of Faith,* Valley Forge, 1959 (Rev. Ed., 1969).
H.L. McBeth, *A Sourcebook for Baptist Heritage,* Nashville, Tenn., 1990.
♦ E.C. Starr (1947–76), *A Baptist Bibliography,* 25 vols., Philadelphia.
G. Rousseau (1951), *Histoire des Églises baptistes dans le monde,* Paris.
R.G. Torbet (1955), *Ventures of Faith,* Philadelphia.
B.R. White (1983), *The English Baptists of the XVIIth Century,* London.
M. Thobois (1986–91), "Histoire des baptistes de France," *Croire et Servir,* Paris.
H.L. McBeth (1987), *The Baptist Heritage,* Nashville, Tenn.
W.H. Brackney (1988), *The Baptists,* New York.
T. George, D.S. Dockery (Ed.) (1990), *Baptist Theologians,* Nashville, Tenn.
B. Stanley (1992), *The History of the Baptist Missionary Society, 1792–1992,* Edinburgh.
J.C. Fletcher (1994), *The Southern Baptist Convention,* Nashville, Tenn.
A.W. Wardin (Ed.) (1995), *Baptists around the World,* Nashville, Tenn.

David W. Bebbington

See also **Anabaptists; Calvinism; Congregationalism; Fundamentalism; Protestantism; Puritanism**

Barth, Karl

1886–1968

Karl Barth was certainly the most influential Protestant theologian (Protestantism*) since Schleiermacher*, leaving a body of writing that has been the subject of constant debate. His major work, *Die Kirchliche Dogmatik (Church Dogmatics),* could be compared to a cathedral of theological thought.

I. Life and Work

Barth was born in Basel in 1886, to a family of theologians. In turn he studied theology with the leading representatives of 19th-century liberal theology*: A. von Harnack (1851–1930), H. Gunkel (1862–1932), and W. Herrmann (1846–1922). In Geneva he became familiar with Calvin*'s work. Then he was appointed pastor at Safenwill parish in Aargau, where the social structure led him to join the movement for social Christianity and encouraged him to join the battle for social justice geared toward the coming of the kingdom of God*.

The war of 1914–18 had a profound and decisive impact on Barth: the conformist stance taken by many of his teachers brought him to question the very foundations of their thought. He therefore focused on the Epistle to the Romans in order to try to find an answer to the questions that weighed on him. As a result he wrote *Commentary,* of which both editions (1919, 1922) acted as a sign of contradiction in the German theological heaven, and, along with a few lectures, marked the emergence of what is known as "crisis" or "dialectical" theology.

Barth was appointed to teach in Germany, at Göttingen, Münster, and then Bonn. With several young colleagues (F. Gogarten, E. Thurneysen, E. Brunner, G. Merz, and R. Bultmann*), he traced the fundamental features of dialectical theology, which found its main organ of expression in the magazine *Zwischen den Zeiten.* After a first unfinished essay (1927) he began writing his brilliant work *Die Kirchliche Dogmatik.* This work took almost 30 years to complete and finally consisted of no fewer than 26 volumes.

Adamantly opposed to the rise of Nazism, Barth was one of the main actors in Kirchenkampf, in the founding of the church, and the primary writer of the *Barmen Theological Declaration* in 1934. This last contrasts the service of Christ* alone to that of secular ideologies and powers. He was subsequently denied his chair in Bonn and took refuge in Basel, where he taught until 1962, and worked tirelessly on the construction of the theological edifice that would bring him worldwide fame. In the meantime he continued to formalize his vision of the relationship between church and state (church* and state) in *Christian Community, Civil Community* (1935), and produced a magisterial commentary on the Credo. He also gave a more "human" dimension to his project by offering the *Humanity of God* (1956) as a starting point for all theological thought, and during his last semester of teaching he summarized what seemed to him to be essential for all theological approaches in *Introduction to Evangelist Theology.* Once again, Barth played a decisive role in the formation of the Ecumenical Council* of Churches (Amsterdam, 1948). He was never willing to accept that Nazi totalitarianism and communist totalitarianism were basically equivalent, and after the Second World War he continued to sympathize with socialism. Solicited during Vatican* II, he related his reflections in *Ad Limina Apostolorum* (1966). A great music lover and admirer of Mozart, Barth died in Basel on 10 December 1968.

II. Theological Work

Marked by tremendous scholarship (the excursuses extracted from *Dogmatics* can at times be like small monographs), Barth's thinking did not develop in a strictly systematic way. Rather, in its presence, one feels as if it is the free course of a huge river, swelling as it merges with all the bodies of water it meets. Nevertheless, what unifies the whole is its tremendous capacity always to start from the point of view of God in order to properly speak of men and to promote the idea that this God is never so much God as in the revelation* of God: Jesus Christ. Three periods can be distinguished in the expression of this impressive thought: early stages (until 1919), the period of Barth's dialectical theology (1920–1932), and after 1932, the mature thinking of *Dogmatics.*

1. Early Stages

The early stages of Barthian theology are marked by his liberal training—according to which it was appropriate to find the paths to the best possible "adaptation" of the spirit of Christianity to the realities of modern culture. Moreover, moved by the difficulties of working-class life, the young pastor at Safenwill was influenced by the thinkers of social Christianity (H. Kutter and L. Ragaz) and by the social eschatology of Blumhardt, father and son, which led him to join the Swiss Social-Democratic party in 1915.

Moreover, all his life he remained convinced that preaching was the fundamental loci theologici; he did not hesitate to preach regularly, would qualify his great word as "ecclesial" (*Kirchliche Dogmatik*), and could admit that: "I was always more inclined . . . to concern myself with the pastoral problem par excellence, the problem of preaching. I sought to pave my way between the problem of human life and the contents of the Bible*. As a pastor*, I had to speak to men faced with the contradictions of life, and speak to them about the incredible message of the Bible. . . . Often these two splendors, life and the Bible, gave me the impression—and still, no?—of being Scylla and Charybdis. If this was it, the origin and goal of Christian preaching, I said to myself, who then can be, who then must be, pastor and preacher? . . . It is this critical situation that made me discover the essence of all theology" *(Word of God and the Word of Man).*

With the First World War striking Barth as the failure and collapse of liberal theology, he returned to the Word* of God; the first commentary on *The Epistle to the Romans* (1919) launched a way of reading Biblical texts that would reveal "God as God." God escapes all human speculation but, in Jesus Christ, offers to pronounce a formal and definitive *yes* over the sinful world. Thus, in the Gospel, there is the "revolution* of God," which "breaks all the dependent ties to this world" and which, because it comes from God, is "even the revolution of everything that the world can call revolution."

2. Dialectical Theology

At the same time the school of theology known as dialectical emerged. Its major themes were especially expressed through the magazine *Zwischen den Zeiten,* the second edition of *Römerbrief* (1922), and the studies that appeared in French in *Word of God and Word of Man.* Here, God is essentially presented as the "wholly Other"; God alone is God, infinitely different from his creature, who cannot, alone, have access to God. But what man cannot attain by himself, God will give him through his Word, through which God can be revealed, and put within human reach. However, the word thus pronounced in Jesus Christ on humanity is none other than an unshakeable "yes," overcoming all the "no's" that nevertheless call, as if by the essence, nature, and sin of men. The theology that tries to recognize this God and this "yes" can only be dialectical; it develops in the never resolved tension that lies between the might and the truth of God and the human weakness and error, which the former—in Jesus Christ—nevertheless never ceases to invest and subvert: "During the Resurrection*, the new world of the Holy Spirit* touches the old world of the flesh*. Nevertheless, it touches it—like the tangent of a circle—without touching it; and while it doesn't touch it, it touches it like the new world" *(Epistle to the Romans)*. This is why dialectical theology also appears like a theology of crisis, for the investing and subversion of the revelation puts the humanity of humans in permanent "crisis" (etymologically, "in judgment"). The eschatology* thus invests the present through the Word of God pronounced on it and makes it into a time "between time"; "the destiny of our generation is to find itself between two eras. Perhaps one day we will belong to time coming?... We find ourselves in the very middle. In this empty space.... The space has opened for the question of God" (Gogarten).

The group of theologians who recognized each other in this movement were soon to disband under the pressure of centrifugal force and their magazine ceased to be published in 1933. But Barth had already begun *Dogmatics.*

3. Dogmatic Theology

The first volume of *Dogmatics* was published in 1932, a year that marked the beginning of an intense period of literary production that lasted almost until Barth's death*. It was marked by the appearance of 26 volumes of this large work (almost 10,000 densely packed pages), which nevertheless was not finished, as well as by several independent books. *Dogmatics* systematizes and deepens the major notions of dialectical theology: God is God, and only God can make it known who God is; the objective truth about the world and humans (created, reconciled and saved by God) is not grasped through the subjective perception that they may have but through the revelation that God gives. *Dogmatics* therefore is divided into five major parts: 1) the prolegomena, which presents the Word of God, through which the only access to God is possible; 2) the doctrine of God, in which we see the God of Jesus Christ revealed as Trinity*; 3) the doctrine of creation* (corresponding to the work of the Father*); 4) the doctrine of reconciliation *(Versöhnung)*, indicating the work of the Son—incomplete; 5) the doctrine of the final redemption *(Erlösung)*, which more specifically bears on the work of the Holy Spirit—and which Barth did not have a chance to start.

a) Divine Revelation and Analogia Fidei. Two methodological principles dominate the huge structure of *Dogmatics:* on one hand, the challenge, at the base of all theological undertaking, of the play of *analogia entis* (analogy of being*) in favor of an *analogia fidei* (analogy of faith); and on the other hand, a pronounced christological focus. The first of these principles corresponds to Barth's constantly reiterated point concerning the qualitative difference separating God from the world and humans and the fact that, because only God is able to speak about God, we cannot have access to God except through his revelation. The idea of founding theology on some kind of continuity of being between the world and humanity on the one hand, and God, on the other, is dismissed; the Thomist theologies (Thomas* Aquinas, Thomism*) and Scholastics* are blamed for doing so in the name of the principle of *analogia entis.* This is what Barth begins to show in his commentary on Anselm* of Canterbury's *Proslogion*—on the proofs of the existence* of God—published in 1931 under the title *Fides Quaerens Intellectum* (Faith in Search of Its Intelligence): theology cannot be understood as a philosophical (philosophy*) kind of undertaking, developing "natural" knowledge of God, starting from an analysis of the world or the human condition to get to being; it only counts in terms of the self-comprehension of faith in search of it own intelligence. Of course, theology cannot speak of God except through analogy, even if analogy can only stem from the domain of faith *(analogia fidei)* and not being. Hence, the famous declaration from the prolegomena of *Dogmatics:* "I regard *analogia entis* as an invention of the Antichrist and I believe that it is because of this that one cannot become Catholic. To this I will add that all the other reasons that one may have for not becoming Catholic seem childish and not very substantial" (*KD* I, 1, p. XII).

From this perspective, theology was to develop as a kind of commentary on the Word of God, the prolegomena of which ("doctrine on the Word of God") shows that it evolves and pronounces itself in three forms: 1) the preaching* of the Church; 2) itself, submitted and subjected to the written work of biblical accounts; 3) Jesus Christ in person, the Word of the true God, heart of the Gospel and measure of all interpretation (hermeneutic*) of the Scriptures* and thereby also of all preaching. Moreover, from the same drive that rejected *analogia entis,* Barth—combining critiques of religion, especially those of Marx*, Nietzsche*, and Freud*—denied that there was any theological value in religion as religion, which was understood as a human attempt to appropriate God, and contrasted the "descending" movement of faith to it.

b) Trinitarian God and Christological Focus. The second characteristic trait of Barth's theology involves the christological focus that it carries out: "An ecclesiastical dogmatic* theology must be christological in its fundamental structure as in all of its parts, if it is true that its only criterion is the revealed Word of God, evidenced by the Scriptures and preached by the Church, and if it is true that this revealed Word of God is identical to Jesus Christ. A dogmatic theology that does not, from the beginning, seek to be a Christology* is under a foreign yoke and very nearly no longer serves the Church.... Christology must be everywhere in theology.... Christology is everything or nothing" (*KD* I/2, p. 114 §15.1). This christological emphasis led Barth to solve several fundamental theological questions in a specific way: the Trinitarian notion of God that marks his entire oeuvre does not come from any particular metaphysical speculation, but from the revelation of God who is only unveiled through the work of Christ and his Spirit; the Creation doctrine is not understood as an objective presentation of the "natural" fact, but as the very place of God's Covenant* with the world and humans (*KD* III,1–4); the notion of predestination* is perceived only as the extension of the doctrine on choice*, the heart of which is Christ.

Through the years and pages, the radical thoughts of the early period gradually gave way to an approach that was more attentive to the depth of the human condition. This is what the 1956 programmatic lecture on the *Humanity of God* translated in condensed fashion: "With Jesus Christ, as the Bible shows, we are not dealing with man in an abstract manner: this is not a man who thinks he is self-sufficient with a little religion and religious morality, thus becoming God himself; at the same time, this is not an abstract God, that is, separated from man by his divinity, distant and foreign and therefore not human, but in some way, inhuman.... In his person, Jesus Christ is precisely the true God to man, and as true man, the faithful partner of God; He is both the Lord who lowers himself to communicate with man, and the Servant*, raised to the point of communion* with God.... Thus he announces and assures man of the free grace of God, as he also attests and assures God about man, and, at the same time, the right of man before God.... What God is in truth, as what is man, is something we don't have to search blindly for or invent; it is to be discovered where the truth about one and the other reside: in Jesus Christ, where, the fullness of their coexistence and their Covenant* is presented to us" (*Humanity of God,* 1956).

The various points thus referred to are particularly developed in the last, only partially written part of *Dogmatics.* The outline of this part, in relation to the work of reconciliation carried out by Christ, was to include three stages: the Lord as servant *(vere Deus),* the servant as Lord *(vere homo),* the veritable witness. The last two volumes concern baptism*—understood as the human act* of receiving grace, and excluding from this fact the baptism of small children—and the ethic presented as prayer* and as invocation.

c) Ethics: The Law, Form of the Gospel. For Barth, Christian ethics depend completely on the revelation of God to which those ethics respond. Each part of *Dogmatics* thus leads to a series of ethical questions. In the doctrine of God (*KD* II/1 and 2, v. 6–9), the essay on choice and grace is followed by a presentation of the "commandment of God*." The law is presented in an original way, not as separate from the announcement of the gospel, but as its "form." Barth thus distances himself from Luther*. He asserts that his doctrine of the "two reigns," separating the religious domain from the political one and connected to an overly radical distinction between law and gospel, may have led to the blindness of the German protestant Churches before the rise of Nazism. However, to obey God's commandment is to attest that one lives well from and under the grace of God; to conform to the commandments of the law is to concretely translate the reality of the "yes" pronounced on this world by the gospel. In the same way, the questions connected to sexual ethics* or to life—biological, social, or professional—are discussed at the end of the part devoted to the doctrine of creation and influenced by liberty* (*KD* III). Lastly, in analyses that are more strictly christological (*KD* IV), ethics take the form of commentary on Our Father: to obey the commandment of God therefore means invoking God in a practical and concrete manner and to be ever more influenced by God's paternity.

Barth's Influence

Barth's influence was as immense as his oeuvre, and his disciples came from all parts of the theological scene: some developed the almost sacred transcendence of God, while others insisted that faith needed to make a political commitment. In fact, Barth's remarkable success favored the conjunction of two a priori independent movements that are nevertheless convergent: his rigorous defense of the autonomy of God and of the "scientific nature" of theology, on the one hand, and his opposition to Hitler and his defense of the underdog, on the other. In fact, it was as a herald of extreme causes and contested and threatened dignities, nevertheless demanded and defended with vigor, that Barth perhaps, without really knowing, most marked his era. This being the case, he combined, in a most dialectical way, the "no" and the "yes": God's "no" to the sinning world, condemned and rejected, and yet at the same time irrevocably accepted in Jesus Christ; "no" to Nazism, but also—on another level entirely—to E. Brunner's natural* theology, nevertheless accompanied and subverted by the "yes" of this prolific author, who considered the simple acquiescence of God's commitment to the world the height of faith and theology. It is expressed by the sigh, *"Ach, ja!"*—"Well, yes!"

Barth's posterity comes in many shapes: "on the right," it includes certain forms of orthodoxy that insist on the need to return to the Scriptures, on referring to reformers and the urgency of organizing theological thought in systematic fashion. But there are also various kinds of "leftist Barthianism" (F. Marquardt, G. Casalis), which promote theology's essential commitment and are interpreted in many ways (P. Maury, J. L. Leuba, R. Mehl, H. J. Iwand, H. Vogel, O. Weber, W. Kreck). Barth's Catholic audience was large and did manage to renew several problems (Balthasar*, H. Bouillard, H. Küng). However, generally speaking Barth did not have any real successors. Perhaps he was too big; although anyone studying theology today must study his thought, his very radical character and his rejection of certain problems, which sometimes goes as far as denying the existence of these problems—notably that which touches on the particular substance of the world and the humanity of humans—make it difficult for it to confront the challenges that constantly lie before theology in the present and future.

• K. Barth (1932–67), *Die Kirchliche Dogmatik,* Zollikon-Zurich, vols. I–IV and Index 1970.

K. Barth (1935), *Communauté chrétienne, communauté civile,* Geneva.

K. Barth (1950), *Esquisse d'une dogmatique,* Neuchâtel.

K. Barth (1956), *The Humanity of God.*

K. Barth (1958), *Word of God and the Word of Man,* Tr. Douglas Horton, Mangolia, Mass.

K. Barth (1966), *Ad limina apostolorum,* Zurich.

K. Barth (1971–), *Gesamtausgabe,* Zurich.

M. Kwiran (1977), *Index to Literature on Barth, Bonhoeffer and Bultmann,* Basel.

H. A. Drewes (Ed.) (1984), *Karl Barth Bibliographie,* Zurich.

♦ H. U. von Balthasar (1951), *Karl Barth, Darstellung und Deutung seiner Theologie,* Einsiedeln.

G.C. Berkouwer (1957), *Der Triumph der Gnade in der Theologie Karl Barths,* Neukirchen.

H. Bouillard (1957), *Karl Barth,* 3 vols., Paris.

H. Küng (1957), *Rechtfertigung: Die Lehre Karl Barths und eine katholische Besinnung,* Einsiedeln (2nd Ed., Munich, 1987).

G. Casalis (1960), *Portrait de Karl Barth,* Geneva.

O. Weber (1964), *La dogmatique de K. Barth,* Geneva.

H. Zahrnt (1969), *Aux prises avec Dieu: La théologie protestante au XXe siècle,* Paris, 11–66, 107–60.

H.J. Adriaanse (1974), *Zu den Sachen selbst: Versuch einer Konfrontation der Theologie Karl Barths mit der phänomenologischen Philosophie Edmund Husserls,* The Hague.

W. Härle (1975), *Sein und Gnade: Die Ontologie in Karl Barths Kirchlicher Dogmatik,* Berlin.

E. Busch (1978), *Karl Barths Lebenslauf,* Munich.

E. Jüngel (1982), *Barth-Studien,* Gütersloh-Zurich-Köln.

K. Hafstad (1985), *Wort und Geschichte: Das Geschichtverständnis Karl Barths,* Munich.

M. Beintker (1987), *Die Dialektik in der "dialektischen" Theologie Karl Barths,* Munich.

K. Blaser (1987), *K. Barth 1886–1986: Combats—idées—reprises,* Bern.

P. Gisel (Ed.) (1987), *Karl Barth: Genèse et réception de sa théologie,* Geneva.

C. Frey (1988), *Die Theologie Karl Barths,* Frankfurt.

H. Köckert, W. Krötke (Ed.) (1988), *Theologie als Christologie: Zum Leben und Werke Karl Barths,* Berlin.

R. Gibellini (1994), *Panorama de la théologie au XXe s.,* Paris, 11–32.

A.J. Torrance (1996), *Persons in Communion: An Essay on Trinitarian Description and Human Participation, with Special Reference to Volume One of Karl Barth's* Church Dogmatics, Edinburgh.

J. Webster (1998), *Barth's Moral Theology: Human Action in Barth's Thought,* Edinburgh.

Jean-François Collange

See also **Balthasar, Hans Urs von; Bonhoeffer, Dietrich; Bultmann, Rudolf; Lonergan, Bernard John Francis; Lubac, Henri Sonier de; Tillich, Paul**

Basel-Ferrara-Florence, Council of

1431–45

The Council* of Basel-Ferrara-Florence was the 17th ecumenical council of the Catholic Church*. It brought together two councils that differed in context, orientations, and to some extent in participants: Basel represented the continuation of Constance* and of conciliarism* (and is considered ecumenical by Catholics only with regard to its first 25 sessions, before the breaking off of relations with the pope*); Ferrara-Florence was led by the pope and devoted to union with the Greeks.

1. Council of Basel (1431–49)

a) Convening and Chronology. The *Frequens* decree of Constance had provided for the regular convening of a council. In conformity with the decisions taken at Pavia-Siena (1423–24), Martin V convened a general council in Basel at the beginning of 1431 and appointed Cardinal Cesarini as president (Mansi 29, 11–12; Cardinal Aleman succeeded him in 1438).

That council held 45 sessions in Basel (1431–48) and five in Lausanne (1448–49). Eugenius IV, who succeeded Martin V in March 1431, dissolved it in December 1431 in order to transfer it to Bologna (Mansi 29, 564–67). He then revoked his decision in 1433 when faced with the council's resistance (Mansi 29, 78–79), dissolved the council again in September 1437, with its transferral to Ferrara (*Concilium Florentinum*... I-1, 91–99) confirmed at the end of December (ibid., 111–12). In spite of the opening of the new council in Ferrara, Basel continued to consider itself as the sole legitimate council and as superior in power to the pope. Indeed, it deposed him in June 1439 (Mansi 29, 179–81), replacing him in November with the antipope Felix V. The latter resigned in April 1449, thus dealing its death blow to the assembly of Basel-Lausanne.

b) Activity of the Council. During its first session, in December 1431 (*COD* 456, 14–22), the council decided to adopt three objectives: rooting out heresy*, establishing peace* among all Christians, and reform of the church. The Hussite heresy was not eradicated (Hus*), but the diplomatic action taken by the council was certainly important. As for the attempts made to reform the church, these did produce some results (which a number of national concordats ratified), but such attempts were transformed into a fight to impose upon Eugenius IV the authority* of the council. That authority, however, did gradually weaken, (political support, for it was in decline, but it should also be mentioned that there were fewer bishops* than clerics* in the assembly and that each of its members had a vote). Not only did the council fail in its attempt to reform the church, but it also failed to bring about a successful union with the Greeks, although some contacts were established. Its final theological result was slim, despite the historical importance of what was an important gathering place for the climate of a newly burgeoning humanism.

2. Council of Ferrara-Florence (1438–45)

a) Chronology. The council opened in Ferrara on 8 January 1438 under the chairmanship of Cardinal Albergati (*COD* 513–17). The Greeks arrived in March, but although the solemn inauguration of the council took place on 9 April, they did not want to broach the essential point (that of adding the *Filioque** to the creed) for several months. The first question to be raised was that of purgatory*, in June-July, while the eight sessions devoted to the *Filioque* took place from October to December. Because of the plague, the council was transferred to Florence by Eugenius IV on 10 January 1439, with the agreement of the Greeks and the Latin synod (*COD* 523). Eight dogmatic sessions were held there in March. After this there were some partial meetings and a few other sessions until 6 July, when a solemn session marked the celebration of union with the Greeks. The council continued its meetings after the departure of the Greeks, and on 14 October 1443 was transferred to Rome* (*COD* 583–586), where it closed some time in 1445 (Hofmann 1949).

b) Activity of the Council. Conducted by Eugenius IV in the presence of the patriarch of Constantinople, Joseph II, and of the Byzantine emperor, John VIII, this council made it its task to achieve union with the Greeks by discussing, in sequence, all the contentious points: the procession of the Holy Spirit and the principle of its addition to the creed, purgatory, the primacy of the pope, the Eucharist* (which part of the anaphora accomplishes the consecration?), the liturgical use of unleavened versus leavened bread, and the vision of God* in beatitude*. Once union was achieved with the Greeks, Eugenius IV endeavored to extend it to other Eastern churches.

Ferrara devoted its discussions of the summer of 1438 to the question of purgatory, although without achieving any results (Greek doctrine was very vague on this point, but the Greeks rejected the Latin idea of a purifying fire). Discussions in the autumn of 1438 dealt with the addition of the *Filioque* to the Creed of Nicaea-Constantinople and with the meaning of the interdicts that Ephesus* and Chalcedon* had imposed on any addition. The Latins claimed that the *Filioque* was not an addition but an explanation required by the circumstances. On this occasion, the Greeks encountered considerable dialectical artfulness of the Latins. But for their own part—notably through their principal spokesman, Mark Eugenikos—they insisted on traditional argument. This put them in an inferior position during the discussions, which they were tempted several times to break off. It was in Florence in March 1439 that the important dogmatic sessions on the procession of the Holy Spirit took place. Mark Eugenikos, for the Greek side, confronted the Dominican Jean de Montenero, for the Latin side.

In these exchanges there was a very generous use of biblical and patristic florilegia (often prepared in advance, florilegia dealing with the *Filioque* represented a literary genre in their own right). The Church Fathers* most in demand were Basil* of Caesarea, Cyril* of Alexandria, Epiphanius, Didymaea, and, on the Latin side, Augustine*. The Greeks preferred this patristic approach to dialectics, even if the quotations were subsequently exploited by Montenero in a Scholastic* manner. Montenero relied on a humanist of the first order, Ambrose Traversari, general of the Camaldolese order, to find and translate the Greek texts.

This method, which was intended to shed light on the harmony between the Greek and Latin Fathers, won over some important Greek delegates (Bessarion, Isidore of Kiev, George Scholarios), who were able to influence their own camp (except for a few irreducible followers who grouped around Mark Eugenikos) in favor of union. Several months, however, were required in order to get to that point. The Latin dialectics was not to the liking of the Greeks, and the patristic texts were not sufficiently precise on the contentious points (does the Spirit proceed *from* the Son or *through* the Son?). An agreement was reached, however, on 8 June. The decree of union, *Laetentur caeli* (6 July 1439), stipulates that both expressions concern the same faith*, which is the following: "the Holy Spirit is eternally from the Father* and the Son, it gets its essence and its living being from both Father and Son, and it proceeds eternally from the former and the latter as if from one sole principle and from a single inspiration" (*COD* 526, 39–45). The definition makes room for the two languages, Greek and Latin, by naming the Son "cause" or "principle" of the Spirit with the Father (ibid., 527, 6–10), and it makes it clear that it is from the Father that the Son receives all, including the fact that the Spirit proceeds from him (ibid., 11–16).

Following this agreement, which brought a solution to the most difficult point, the other matters were dealt with in less than a month (continuation of the decree on union, *COD* 527, 17–528, 43). The addition of the *Filioque* to the creed was declared legitimate; the use of unleavened bread and that of risen bread were declared equally valid, according to the tradition* of each church; the soul* could be purified after death* by punishment in purgatory, and souls were assisted by the prayers of the living; the blessed contemplated God as he is in himself (but in varying degrees according to merit: the Greeks were insistent on having this clarification; on the Greek position, *see* Alberigo 1991); finally, the Roman pontiff, successor of Peter*, held preeminence over the whole universe, with all the other patriarchs keeping their privileges and rights (patriarchate*, jurisdiction*). (As far as the Eucharist was concerned, the question of the "form" of the sacrament* (the consecrating words) had been reserved for an oral agreement.) On all these points, the procedure that was followed involved the use of *cedulae,* or written texts put forward in advance by the Latins, who therefore had an advantage. The problem of the primacy of the pope was one of the most difficult to settle, in particular because it put at stake the power to convene a council*, which the emperor did not want to give away to the pope. As a result, this issue did not figure in the text of the decree.

Encouraged by the success of the union and by the decree stating the primacy of the pope, Eugenius IV launched another attack against the council of Basel (*Moyses vir Dei,* 4 September 1439, *COD* 529–34). He then sent all the Eastern churches the text of the decree confirming union and asked for their support. They answered favorably, and other unions were thus concluded. First, union with the Armenians, who had been invited to the council and who had arrived there in August 1439 (*COD* 534–59); the definition of Chalcedon*, which they had never received, was passed on to them, as was, in addition, the Latin teaching on the sacraments. Union with the Copts came on 4 February

1442. The Copts were called "Jacobites" because they were monophysitic (monophysitism*) (*COD* 567–83): the decree contained a Trinitarian account, the canon* both of the Old and New Testaments, and a christological account, as well as an explanation of salvation*, and of rites and sacraments. On 30 November 1444 there followed union with the Syrians (*COD* 586–89); they were supplied with details on the procession of the Holy Spirit, the two natures of Christ* and the two expressions of his will (with quotation from Chalcedon and Constantinople* II; *see* monothelism*). Finally, on 7 August 1445, a union with the Chaldeans, Nestorian obedience, and the Maronites of Cyprus, who had a reputation for being monothelites (*COD* 589–91), completed Eugenius IV's unifying work.

c) How the Council Was Received. There is still an explanation to be given regarding "the failure of this success," to use Gill's expression. The Orthodox people never accepted the union, and accused their bishops of having betrayed their faith. These very bishops, once they were back home, had the impression they had been operating under duress in Florence: the precariousness of their situation, their isolation from home, the emperor's eagerness to conclude the union in order to obtain the pope's help against the Turks and save Constantinople, all these considerations contributed to a strengthening of that feeling (even though, in the course of the discussions, the emperor had exercised no pressure and the pope no blackmail). The circumstances were ambiguous, and the union was concluded too quickly (for an example of misunderstanding, with the Copts, on the matters of primacy and dogma, *see* P. Luisier, *OCP* 60, 1994). Furthermore, Popes Martin V and Eugenius IV, in contradistinction to the council of Basel (Alberigo, 1991), considered union above all as a return to the Roman Church. As a result, instead of leading to the communion* of churches that others desired, their approach ended up more often than not as a uniatism, denounced as representing the annexationist ambitions of Rome.

It can be added that the Latin theological methods had not succeeded in convincing the Greeks (except Bessarion or Isidore, who became cardinals of the Roman Church), and that the council, kept much too busy with the objective of quickly finding an acceptable text for the union, had neglected other factors that were essential for the lasting success of the agreement: for example, the question of liturgical communion between the two parties (Alberigo 1991).

• Acts: Mansi 29–31.

Decrees, *COD* 435–591 (*DCO* II/1, 931–1210).

Concilium Basiliense, Studien und Quellen zur Geschichte des Conzils von Basel, Ed. J. Haller, 8 vols., Basel, 1896–1936.

Concilium Florentinum, Documenta et Scriptores, 11 vols. in 14 vols., Rome, 1940–77.

Monumenta conciliorum generalium saeculi XV, vols. I-III (Basel), Ed. F. Palacky, E. Birk, R. Beer, Vienna, 1857–92 (one index vol., Vienna, 1935).

♦ G. Hofmann (1949), "Das Konzil von Florenz in Rom," *OrChrP* 15, 71–84.

J. Gill (1959), *The Council of Florence,* Oxford; (1964), *Personalities of the Council of Florence,* Oxford; (1965), *Constance et Bâle-Florence* (*HCO* 9), Paris.

J. Decarraux (1970), *Les Grecs au c. de l'union, Ferrare-Florence 1438–1439,* Paris.

J.W. Stieber (1978), *Pope Eugenius IV, the Council of Basel and the Secular and Ecclesiastical Authorities in the Empire,* Leyden.

J. Helmrath (1987), *Das Basler-Konzil 1431–1449: Forschungstand und Probleme,*Köln.

J. Gill (1989), *Church Union: Rome and Byzantium (1204–1453),* London.

Coll. (1989 and 1990), *AHC* 21 and 22 (colloquia on Ferrara-Florence).

M. Mollat du Jourdin, A. Vauchez (Ed.) (1990), *Histoire du christianisme,* VI: *Un temps d'épreuves (1274–1449).*

G. Alberigo (Ed.) (1991), *Christian Unity: The Council of Ferrara-Florence 1438/1439–1989,* BEThL 97.

Bernard Meunier

See also **Conciliarism; Constance, Council of; *Filioque;* Humanism, Christian; Pope; Schism; Structures, Ecclesial; Unity of the Church**

Basil (The Great) of Caesarea

c. A.D. 329–79

a) Life. Basil of Caesarea was the oldest of many children in a patrician Christian family in Cappadocia. Among his brothers and sisters were two bishops (Gregory* of Nyssa and Peter of Sebastea), an ascetic, and a virgin. Basil was a good student in Caesarea and later in Constantinople and Athens, where he studied with famous rhetoricians. He made the acquaintance of Gregory* of Nazianzus who became his dearest friend. Gregory's education took place at the confluence of Christian faith* and the finest Hellenistic culture. Charmed by the gospel, he gave up the profession of rhetorician, had himself baptized, and decided to enter the monastic life. But he soon became concerned with the affairs of the church* at Caesarea. He helped his bishop*, was ordained as a priest* in 362 or 364, and was elected bishop of Caesarea in 370. Over the course of a few years, Basil carried out intense doctrinal and ecclesiastical activity. He died while still young—in 379, according to tradition, or perhaps in 378.

Basil was a man of the church and a man of action, a key figure of his age and an organizer and leader of men, but he was also a man of the heart, fragile, and sensitive. Even though he was afflicted with ill health, Basil was active in many domains, including theology*, monastic life, preaching*, politics, social action, the defense of justice*, and the liturgy*.

b) The Theologian. Confronted with the second generation of Arians, represented by Aetius and Eunomius, Basil concerned himself with three major doctrinal questions touching mystery of the Trinity*.

Divinity of the Son. Basil's first theological work, *Contra Eunomium (Against Eunomius),* dismantles the calm rational argument with which his adversary wished to establish, on the basis of an analysis of language, the created nature of the Son. Eunomius called the Son "offspring," and used the unique and incommunicable term "unengendered" to express the substance of God*. The essential point of Basil's speculative analysis is to establish the distinction between essential and relative attributes* in God and to show that the latter imply no proliferation of a single and identical substance. The names Father* and Son, then, are relative names *(Contra Eunomium).* With this work, Basil inaugurated the shift that allowed the term *hypostasis* to move from its original meaning of "substance" to that of "act of persisting in substance" or "subsistence."

Development of Trinitarian Doctrine Throughout his life, Basil sought to reconcile the churches of the East. This reconciliation depended on the reconciliation of Trinitarian formulations used by the various churches: The Nicenes, who upheld that the Persons of the Trinity* were consubstantial*, sometimes with an ambiguity as to its mode, had to resolve this ambiguity by clearly affirming the three divine hypostases. For their part, those who upheld the three hypostases had to wholeheartedly accept the consubstantial in order to avoid being suspected of believing in three hypostases that were unequal in substance. The unilateral formulations of both camps would thus complete and balance one another. The result of this work was to settle the dogma* of the Trinity, which was affirmed in the East following the First Council of Constantinople*.

Divinity of the Holy Spirit Basil's major doctrinal work was the treatise *De Spiritu Sancto,* in which he attacked both the radical Arianism* of Aetius and Eunomius and the position of the Macedonians at the First Council of Constantinople. The occasion for the treatise was a challenge concerning the liturgical doxology used by Basil: "Glory to the Father, with the Son and the Holy Spirit," his adversaries preferring the doxology "through the Son and in the Holy Spirit." Behind these nuances among prepositions lay hidden the question of the equality or dissimilarity of the three divine Persons*. Against the adage of his adversaries, who argued from the difference of language that there was a difference in nature, Basil showed that Scripture uses all these prepositions for all three Persons, and he asserted that this lexical resemblance expresses the identity of their common nature. Then, relying on the Trinitarian baptismal formula, the author set forth a long doctrinal argument on the basis of the biblical names of the Holy* Spirit, the Spirit's activities, and the Spirit's gifts for our salvation* in order to show that the Holy Spirit must be "co-numbered" with the Father and the Son and receive the same honor *(homotimie)* as they.

c) Basil's Other Fields of Action. Basil was not the inventor of Eastern monasticism*, but he was a major maker of rules for it. His *Moral Rules* classify 1,542 verses of the New Testament under 80 headings and present a practical exegesis* of biblical teachings for those who wish to live the gospel in a community. The author addresses not only monks but also lay* persons belonging to a movement of Christian reform that was attempting to impose itself on the faithful as a whole. The *Large* and *Small Rules* are a gathering of questions raised by disciples on the different aspects of religious life, and Basil always seeks to give answers taken from Scripture. Basil was also a major liturgical reformer. The Eastern tradition* attributes to him a *Liturgy* that is still being used in the churches of the East.

Removed early from monastic life in order to concern himself with the church and the problems of his time, Basil was primarily an eloquent and effective preacher. His homilies on wealth were as radical as the later ones of John Chrysostom*. Basil severely condemned lending at interest (understood as lending for consumption). He took initiatives in favor of the poor, "opening the granary of the rich," struggling against the "black market" during a famine, and organizing soup kitchens from which pagans and Jews also benefited. Finally, he was an innovator in creating in his city an immense hospital, the Basiliad.

Basil left a large correspondence (around 360 letters) in which can be found his strategy for the government* of churches, his doctrinal struggles in the East, the contradictions he encountered, his attitude toward Rome, his courageous opposition to the Arian emperor Valens, and, finally, a network of deep and moving friendships.

- Paul Jonathan Fedwick, *Bibliotheca Basiliana Universalis: A Study of the Manuscript Tradition, Translations and Editions of the Works of Basil of Caesarea,* IV: *Testimonia, Liturgical and Canonical Compositions, Florilegia, Catenae, Iconography;* IV, 2: *Manuscripts—Libraries* (Corpus Christianorum), Turnhout, 1999.

Basil of Caesarea, *Against Eunomius the Heretic.*

Basil of Caesarea, *Hexaemeron.*

Basil of Caesarea: *Letters,* Defferrari, R.J. (Ed. and Tr.), Loeb Classical Library 1926–34.

Les règles monastiques and *Les règles morales et portrait du chrétien* (1969), Maredsous.

♦ P. Humbertclaude (1932), *La doctrine ascétique de Basile de Césarée,* Paris.

S. Giet (1941), *Les idées et l'action sociale de saint Basile,* Paris.

D. Amand (1949), *L'ascèse monastique de saint Basile: Essai historique,* Maredsous.

H. Dörries (1956), *De Spiritu Sancto: Der Beitrag des Basilius zum Abschluss des trinitarischen Dogmas,* Göttingen.

T. Spidlik (1961), *La sophiologie de saint Basile,* Rome.

J. Bernardi (1968), *La prédication des Pères cappadociens: Le prédicateur et son auditoire,* Paris.

R. Courtonne (1973), *Un témoin du IVe siècle oriental: Saint B. et son temps d'après sa correspondance,* Paris.

P.J. Fedwick (1979), *The Church and the Charisma of Leadership in Basil of Caesarea,* Toronto; id. (Ed.) (1981), *Basil of Caesarea: Christian, Humanist, Ascetic,* 2 vols., Toronto.

J. Gribomont (1984), *Saint Basile Évangile et Église: Mélanges,* 2 vols., Bégrolles-en-Mauges.

B. Gain (1985), *L'Église de Cappadoce au IVe s. d'après la correspondance de Basile de Césarée,* Rome.

R. Pouchet (1992), *Basile le Grand et son univers d'amis d'après sa correspondance,* Rome.

B. Sesboüé (1998), *Saint Basile et la Trinité: Un acte théologique du IVe s.: Le rôle de Basile de C. dans l'élaboration de la doctrine et des langages trinitaires,* Paris.

BERNARD SESBOÜÉ

See also **Arianism; Constantinople I, Council of; Liturgy; Modalism**

Beatification. *See* **Holiness**

Beatitude

A. Historical Theology

The concept of beatitude is limited to the ancient and medieval world; it was definitively replaced by the concept of happiness in the 18th century. The shift from the ancient philosophical to the medieval theological concept of beatitude is, however, subject to discussion, and to some degree it raises the question of the nature of the relationship between Christian theology* and ancient philosophy*. Finally, the shift from beatitude to happiness has yet to be examined. This discussion will be confined to these two points, providing for the latter only a brief outline.

The concept of beatitude is central for a theological determination of the aim of human action. To the extent that the revelation given to Abraham prescribes for humankind, in the three monotheistic religions, a renunciation of any purely earthly happiness ("Go from your country and your kindred and your father's house to the land that I will show you"; Gn 12:1), beatitude designates in part the state of the soul after death. The concept of beatitude can be broken down into three categories: earthly beatitude (the existence of which is questionable), the aim of human action; the heavenly beatitude of the blessed; and the intermediate beatitude obtained by the fulfillment of salvation, which is neither purely earthly (on this earth but not of this earth), nor yet fully heavenly, because it is experienced by an earthly being. It is this problematic status of beatitude, worked out in developments based on the ancient philosophical concept, that is worth considering.

The concept of beatitude has three principal sources: a) biblical, b) philosophical (largely Aristotelian and Stoic), and c) Augustinian. The Augustinian concept is a revision of the philosophical concept on the basis of biblical revelation*.

1. Sources

a) Biblical Sources. The happiness promised by God* in the Pentateuch is tied to the grant of a country to his people and to the prolongation of earthly life (*see* Deuteronomy): It is a *good* land that our Lord gave us. Israel* ought to find *happiness*... the two words are related in Hebrew (Ecumenical Translation of the Bible). This happiness is linked to obedience to the Law* (Dt 5:16); it is an earthly beatitude summed up by the possession of a family, a house, and a vineyard, in an ideal of security and prosperity (Dt 28:30). The Book of Job would show the limits of this Deuteronomic conception of beatitude but not radically challenge it. The failure of the conception is such that the hypothesis of divine sadism is seriously considered (Jb 10:13–17, 16:14, 30:21), and is contradicted only by the hope of resurrection* (Jb 19:26; *see* Ez 37:1–14). The choice seems clear: either life is limited to this earth and it is impossible to speak of beatitude (impurity of man, universal iniquity, absence of God), or else a resurrection* is possible, and the beatitude that is bound to it with the promise of a contemplation of God is of an eschatological order. Everything concerning beatitude is summed up in these words: "But when I hoped for good, evil came; and when I waited for light, darkness came" (Jb 30:26). The two speeches of YHWH and the two answers of Job contain nothing, on either earthly beatitude or beatitude after death, that can attenuate this recognition.

Eschatological beatitude, which takes the form of a messianic joy in the prophetic literature (Is 9:2, 35:10, 55:12, 65:18), is realized in the New Testament in the form of a participation in the joy of the resurrection manifested in Christ: "that my joy may be in you, and that your joy may be full" (Jn 15:11). In the Epistle to the Romans Paul uses the term *makarismos,* often translated as "blessing," to express beatitude in a context in which happiness is linked to the forgiveness of sin: "So also David pronounces a blessing *[makarismos]* upon the man to whom God reckons righteousness apart from works" (Rom 4:6). *Makarios* is frequently used in the Gospels*, particularly (13 times) in the text of the Beatitudes (Mt 5:3–11; Lk 6:20–26). This text articulates nothing about the character of beatitude; it is a sequence of declarations of thanksgiving setting out the paradoxical conditions for an entry into the kingdom* of God.

b) Philosophical Sources. According to Democritus, the noun *eudaimonia* expresses the fact that beatitude has its seat in the soul*, which is also the location of the *daimôn* (Dem. B 171). Euripides defines beatitude as the government of the soul by a good *daimôn* (*Orestes,* line 677). With Plato and Aristotle, beatitude is connected to philosophy, which observes that all men seek beatitude, but only philosophy can obtain it. For Plato, happy is the man who is just and good, unhappy the man who is unjust and wicked (*Republic* 353e–354a). Only the philosopher succeeds in seeing through every good the source of all of them, the Good* itself. Beatitude is the fruit of a conversion* toward the Good; it belongs to whoever flees the multiplicity of goods to move toward the One, toward the Good beyond essence. Socrates is the image of the wise man, of whom Xenophon asserts that he is the "happiest" (*Memoirs* IV. 8) and whom Plato considers "the most just of all men" (*Phaedo*).

Aristotle states an axiological axiom: "Everyone acts for a good that represents the supreme Good" (*Politics* 1252a 2–3). Beatitude is thus health for the sick or subsistence for the poor. For Aristotle, the prefix *eu* of *eudaimonia* means "to live well and to act well" (*"to eu zèn kai to eu praktein,"* *Nicomachean Ethics* 1095a 19–20). Beatitude is sought as a good, and a good that is an end in itself, a *teleion agathon* (ibid. 1097b 8). Beatitude is further an autarchic state; there can be no beatitude without self-sufficiency: "a complete and autarchic state, beatitude is the end of all activity"—*ton prakton* (ibid. 1097b 20–21); *prakton* was later interpreted as "active life." It is appropriate to make a distinction between this beatitude, which is at least the implicit aim of any practical activity, and the beatitude specific to the theoretical life, the beatitude of the philosopher, a beatitude that is possible only because something divine, the intellect, is contained in man (ibid. 1177b 26–28).

The beatitude of the philosopher is distinguished from that of the common man only by the reflexive element that it borrows from divine intelligence. Therefore, we cannot really speak of "philosophical beatitude" but, at most, of "intellectual beatitude," meaning the reflexive beatitude of the man who discovers in the theoretical life the greatest beatitude. Intellectual beatitude is thus not superimposed on beatitude in general; their relations are more complex. Intellectual beatitude presupposes beatitude in general, but cannot be reduced to it. More precisely, intellectual beatitude comes as an addition to beatitude in general. Christianity was to break this relationship of supplement by setting out an ideal of eschatological beatitude that presupposes the correctness of Job's recognition of the impossibility of earthly happiness defined in terms of security and prosperity. This ideal of beatitude took shape in various forms of asceticism and hermitic life, providing anticipatory confirmation for Nietzsche's notion of "hatred of life."

The Aristotelian doctrine nevertheless leads to an aporia, insofar as the articulation between the two types of beatitude leaves open the question of the exact connection between intellectual beatitude and contemplation *(theoria).* At least two paths opened up to overcome this aporia. The Christian path and the emanationist interpretation derived from the 11th-century Islamic philosopher-scientist as Avicenna. Avicenna made intellectual beatitude into a divinization of the *pars melior nostri* (Spinoza), the intellect. The physicalist and naturalist interpretation derived from the 12th-century Islamic philosopher Averroes left this ideal of intellectual beatitude intact while emptying it of any mystical* and visionary element. The church* fought against this ideal in the name of the personal character of salvation*, for to conceive of intellectual beatitude as the exercise of an intellect as a common agent leads to a kind of suprapersonal incorporation, or indeed to a pantheist absorption into pure intellectuality.

c) The Augustinian Source. Augustine* accomplished a synthesis of the two preceding sources from the beginning of his intellectual career (386–91), and this synthesis, which remained unchanged, makes up a kind of foundation for his Trinitarian and historical-political speculation. even though, particularly under the influence of his theology of grace*, he later corrected its voluntarist intellectualism. Augustine translates *eudaimonia* by *felicitas* and blends the two conceptions of beatitude, the ancient and the Christian, into a synthesis of *eudaimonia* and *makarismos.* He identifies as *esse cum Deo* life according to reason* and *vita beata,* the happy life (*De ord.* II. 2. 4–10). He establishes a hierarchy of goods at the summit of which stands the supreme Good *(summum bonum),* definable as supreme Truth* and supreme Beauty. This hierarchy is constructed on the basis of two principles. The first is "Everything that is is good," or in another form, "Nature as nature is good," *omnis natura in quantum natura est, bona est* (*De Lib. Arb.* III. 13. 36). The second principle holds that life and the search for truth are distinguishing criteria, which means that a horse is better than a stone and a man better than a horse, even if his will is perverted. Beatitude thus consists of the knowledge of truth: "Because the supreme Good is known and preserved in the truth, and because that truth is wisdom*, let us discern in it and let us preserve the supreme Good, and let us take joy in it.... For this truth reveals to us all the goods that are true" (ibid. II. 13. 36).

The best commentary on these passages from Augustine is provided by Pascal*: "The soul* goes forth in search of the true Good. It understands that the good must have these two qualities: that it lasts as long as the soul and can only be taken away from the soul with the soul's consent, and that there is nothing more worthy of love.... The soul traverses all created beings and cannot cease its journey until it has reached the throne of God, in which it begins to find its rest" *(On the Conversion of the Sinner).* Pascal is also Augustinian in his contempt for philosophy. The Platonist philosophers are the closest to the truth insofar as they emphasize the contemplative search for the supreme Good by the soul, closer in particular than the Stoics, who count only on their own resources, while the Platonists count on participation in the supreme Good, but they lack the virtue of humility (which is all the more lacking in the Stoics).

2. Medieval Development of Beatitude

The development of the notion of beatitude in the Middle Ages was extremely complex and remains largely uninvestigated. The part that has been most studied concerns Thomas* Aquinas. The interpretation of thinkers like Dante* or Meister Eckhart remains extremely open and is still problematic.

a) Before the Translation of the Nicomachean Ethics *(1246–47).* In the *Cur Deus Homo,* Anselm* proceeds along Augustinian lines, and makes beatitude the center of his ethical reflection. Similarly, for Abelard*, in the *Dialogus inter Philosophum, Judaeum et Christanum,* the true ethics is the one that discovers the beatitudes, an ethics in conformity with the Beatitudes of the Gospels, which is thus not an earthly ethics. The *Sentences* (c. 1155–58) of Peter Lombard (†1160) present a discussion of ethics that remains in part centered on the nature of beatitude, particularly in relation to the *desiderium naturale* (op. cit. IV. d. 49, 1). Lombard wrote shortly before the translation of the *Nicomachean Ethics,* which was to change the manner in which the problem was considered.

b) Albert the Great and Aquinas as Readers of the Nicomachean Ethics. The translation of the *Nicomachean Ethics* by Robert Grosseteste, because it made commentary on the text possible, brought about a profound change in the understanding of Aristotle. The first attempt at a synthesis of the ancient and Christian doctrines of beatitude, that of Augustine, then came into rivalry with a second attempt, carried out chiefly in two stages within the Dominican school by Albert* the Great and Thomas Aquinas, while the first continued to inspire in part the debate on ethics in the Franciscan school. The debate between Augustinians and Thomists was thus a debate between Franciscans and Dominicans—that is, between mendicants and preachers. It is customary to contrast the voluntarism of the Augustinian Franciscans (through Duns* Scotus up to Luther*) to the intellectualism* of the Aristotelian Thomists. But this schematization is superficial. Franciscan teachers such as Alexander of Hales (1165–1245) used Aristotle positively, and German Dominicans were very strongly influenced by the Neoplatonism of Dionysius the Pseudo-Areopagite in a way that substantially changed their reception of Aristotle and introduced significant nuances into their intellectualism (in the end, voluntarism does not necessarily imply anti-intellectualism). Albert the Great wrote two commentaries on the *Nicomachean Ethics*—the first in Köln in 1248–52, immediately after the complete translation of the text, and the second in 1268–70. However, it was Thomas Aquinas who drew from the text all the resources that it offered for a Christian theological deepening of the notion of beatitude.

Thomas came up against a whole series of difficulties. The most immediate were that, on the one hand, Aristotle defines only one beatitude for this life, and even though he mentions beatitude as linked to the theoretical life, it is not certain that he accepts the possibility of a continuation of this state of intellectual beatitude in a hypothetical survival of the divine element of man. On the other hand, Thomas does not raise the question of divine beatitude (in Aristotelian theology, the Prime Mover does not experience beatitude). With respect to the latter point, the solemn doxology of 1 Timothy 6:15 mentions "the blessed and only Sovereign" (*see* 1 Tm 1:11: "the blessed God") and thus places on the same level the oneness, transcendence, and beatitude of God. Thomas shows both that beatitude, in the Aristotelian sense, is in fact humanly inaccessible and that being-with-God, in which beatitude after this life consists, is the fruit of grace. Beatitude is nothing other than possession of the supreme Good, and this can only be anticipated in this life.

Dante systematized this separation by distinguishing, within this first distinction between the beatitude of mortal life and the beatitude of eternal life*, three types of beatitude: 1) beatitude of active mortal life, 2) beatitude linked with the contemplative life, and 3) beatitude of eternal life. There is a hierarchy: the third is at the summit, as it is the supreme beatitude, the fruition of the supreme Good *(fruitio Dei);* the second is almost perfect; and the first is almost imperfect (*Convivio* II. iv. 10; IV. xvii. 9): "Our beatitude... we may find in some imperfect way in active life—that is, in the operations of the moral virtues*—and then in an almost perfect way in the exercise of the intellectual virtues" (ibid. IV. xxii. 18). Dante thus does two things: he confines truly human beatitude to beatitude in the first sense, which is the fruit of the practical intellect, and simultaneously accepts a supreme felicity *(somma felicitate)* linked to speculation. He was anticipated on this point by Thomas Aquinas, who strongly emphasized the absolute superiority of "speculative felicity" *(felicitas speculativa)* (*Exp. EN* X. lect. XII, s116 ff., *see CG* III, 37).

3. Later Times: The Concept of Happiness and the Critique of Theology

While the medieval development is complex, the shift from the concept of beatitude to the modern concept of happiness is even more obscure. A first cause of a break appeared in the 13th century, among nontheological thinkers (e.g., in the Faculty of Arts in Paris, Siger de Brabant and Boethius of Dacia). These men reappropriated the Aristotelian concepts of beatitude and the philosophical life by bracketing the Christian bond between beatitude and eschatological hope; but philosophical felicity did not yet exclude the existence of a theological beatitude. Some Renaissance texts, on the other hand, provide a vivid sense of the moment of passage from the thought of beatitude to the thought of happiness, with surprising forms of compromise. For example, Valla writes, "Who can doubt that beatitude is identical to and can be given no better name than pleasure?" (*De Voluptate* III. ix, fol. 977). Cassirer comments: "Christianity, according to Valla's argument, is not hostile to Epicureanism; it is itself nothing but an elevated and so to speak sublime Epicureanism" (1927).

Thomas Aquinas had emphasized the fact that delectation *(delectatio)* is necessary for contemplative beatitude, but only in a concomitant fashion (*ST* Ia IIae, q. 180, a.7). The critique of theology and the development of hedonism challenged this subjection of delectation and allowed for a revaluation of pleasure and even of sensuality. The concept of happiness, from this point of view, can be considered as resulting from a secularization of the concept of beatitude, or at least of that part of the concept that has to do with "natural beatitude," as distinct from "supernatural* beatitude" (a distinction contrary to the ancient and medieval spirit). The relation (whether teleological or dependent) between these two types of beatitude was thus deeply compromised. For example, Spinoza identified one with the other and even reversed the Thomist relationship: "We delight *(delectamur)* in whatever we understand by the third kind of knowledge, and our delight is accompanied with the idea of God as its cause" (*Ethics* V, prop. XXXII). The claim for autonomy of natural beatitude was thus linked to a critique of theology. Natural beatitude underwent a mutation and was transformed into a happiness that contained pleasure as a component. Supernatural beatitude, detached from natural beatitude, thereby became an autonomous object, whose reason for being lay in the brutal certainty of the impossibility of human happiness (demonstrated by Kant*). This provided weapons for the critics of theology. The concept of happiness could then take on not only a critical, but a subversive meaning: "Happiness is a new idea in Europe" (Saint-Just).

• H. Sidgwick (1886), *Outlines of the History of Ethics,* London.

É. Halevy (1901–4), *La formation du radicalisme philosophique,* 3 vols. (repr. 1995).

E. Cassirer (1927), *Individuum und Kosmos in der Philosophie der Renaissance,* Leipzig-Berlin, (7th Ed. Darmstadt, 1994).

K.E. Kirk (1931), *The Vision of God: The Christian Doctrine of the Summum Bonum,* New York.

E. Cassirer (1932), *Die Philosophie der Aufklärung,* Tübingen.

A.J. Festugière (1936), *Contemplation et vie contemplative selon Platon,* Paris.

J. Maritain (1950), *Philosophie morale,* Paris.

R.A. Gauthier (1951), *Magnanimité,* Paris; (1958), *La morale d'Aristote,* Paris.

J. Dupont (1958, 1969, 1973), *Les Béatitudes,* 3 vols., Paris.

R. Mauzi (1960), *L'idée de bonheur au XVIIIe siècle,* Paris (2nd Ed. 1995).

G.H. von Wright (1963), *The Varieties of Goodness,* London.

D. Roloff (1970), *Gottähnlichkeit, Vergöttlichung und Erhöhung zu seligem Leben,* Berlin.

J. Ritter, O.H. Pesch, R. Spaemann (1974), "Glück, Glückseligkeit," *HWP* 3, 679–707.

A. de Libera (1992), *Penser au Moyen Age,* Paris.

D. Bradley (1996), *Aquinas on the Twofold Human Good,* Washington.

Frédéric Nef

B. Systematic Theology

Secularized and transmuted into happiness, beatitude thus seems to need to be rethought in new terms and to be hoped for again. The question of happiness, moreover, seems to require being given theological coordinates. In any event, the historical and theoretical facts are relatively clear.

There can be no doubt that the eclipse of beatitude is the index of a certain death of hope. The systems of thought through which the metaphysical fate of the West has been carried out have been numerous, but they all have in common at least either the realization of the *eschaton* in history (Hegel), or a rigorous discrediting of the eschatological problem (Nietzsche*). And they implicitly consent to a reign of death over man (and over the access to meaning), of which Heidegger* has provided two expositions, in the period of *Being and Time* through a meditation on being-for-death, and in the "late" texts through a meditation on "serenity" that provides "mortals" with their proper existential relationship to being*. Philosophical references, on the other hand, should not conceal the fact that the crisis of hope is also an intratheological crisis. The return to prominence of the eschatological problem has certainly (since J. Weiss) been the principal distinctive characteristic of theology*. This return to prominence is, however, ambivalent. In the more traditional theologies, it may point to the reunion of man with the beyond. But it may also be expressed in the form of eschatologies* carried out during the course of history (Bultmann*), or in the form of a neomillenarianism for which the future provides "a new paradigm of transcendence" (J. Moltmann). A world for which it was essential that its form "is passing away" (1 Cor 7:31) seems to have been replaced, in more than one field of theological research, by a world in which it would be required (in the very name of eschatological critiques) to build a dwelling for man (J.B. Metz, et al.). And the existence of Christians who profess the creed in its entirety with the exception of the last article is not a case of theological teratology, but demonstrates that the shadow of nihilism can cover even a part of the Church*.

Beatitude, as distinguished from happiness, might therefore provide a major conceptual tool for a theological critique of nihilism. This critique would require the performance of a work of genealogy. Did the appearance of the concept of "pure nature*" and the repression of the "natural desire for the beatific* vision" lay the groundwork, from within theology, for the secularizing work of modernity (Lacoste 1995 *b*)? Was what came to light in Hegel, Nietzsche, and Heidegger a certain real fulfillment of what theologians had previously accomplished in the realm of the hypothetical, the reduction of man to the present conditions of the exercise of his humanity? Is God* "dead" because men wished to satisfy themselves with their *present* experience* of God? These questions describe in brief the distance that has to be traveled in order to deconstruct the despairing concepts of the humanity of man.

An eschatological reality, beatitude is not on the scale of Heidegger's *Dasein* or "mortals," nor on the scale of the Nietzschean superman, nor that of Hegel's wise man who has reached the fruition of absolute knowledge. In order to be thought and desired, it therefore requires the dissolution of the relationships of representation according to which *Dasein,* or the "mortals," and similar notions, stand for a true manifestation of the humanity of man. The task is thus to establish an eschatological position on the question of man, permitting the destruction of any equation between being and being-in-the-world, or being and being-in-history. And the paradoxical concept of the "natural" desire for the "supernatural*" clearly authorizes this destruction by forcing us to think of man on the basis of his absolute future, and to measure according to that absolute future any present experience that we have of ourselves and of God. Happiness, in this way, would be worthy of man only by being simultaneously incapable of fulfilling man, in the recognition that it is not beatitude. The critical authority for any form of happiness, beatitude would thus allow granting to human finitude the only horizon—infinite*—on the basis of which man exists in the theological truth of his being; it would allow us to think of what we are *in fact* on the basis of what we are *by vocation.*

Criticizing happiness does not amount to denying it, but would well and truly permit the establishment of the conditions for a Christian eudaemonism. The experience of the world, taken in the strict sense, is perhaps the pathetic experience of precarious joys lived under the rule of death. But if the world is not the Creation* and nothing more, it is not the opposite of Creation either, and it maintains enough of its created reality for the desire for happiness not to be contemptible (or impious). The Old Testament representations of the happy life lived in the land given by God must therefore maintain a certain validity after the work of undermining to which they were subjected by the New Testament promises* of beatitude. The experience of happiness must involve an element of discomfort, for happiness is only happiness. This experience, however, must be able to take place without the hoped-for beatitude giving a taste of ashes to the happiness possessed. Happiness has its theological secret, which is to stand as a memory of Creation in the history of the world. This memory cannot claim to erase the world-becoming of the Creation, or put in parentheses the eschatological challenge of happiness by beatitude, but its right to exist is incontestable. The world is not man's homeland, and any logic of dwelling stumbles against the more primordial quality of nondwelling, *Unzuhause* (Heidegger). It is possible, however, in the world or at least at its edges, without shame, and without the suspicion of a touch of any kind of "inauthenticity," to have the experience of a well-being there (Lacoste 1995 *b*). Thus defined, happiness no longer stands in opposition to beatitude as a secular reality to a theological reality; the tension between happiness and beatitude is in fact an intratheological tension. Happiness, therefore, no longer appears as a denial of hope; it is a sabbatical experience, in which man lives from the blessings* pronounced by God in the first days on the work of his hands.

The subversive force of the promises of beatitude cannot, however, be obfuscated, nor can the fact that beatitude is an eschatological experience that can be anticipated in the time of history. The words of beatitude addressed to the poor, the meek, and the persecuted in Matthew and Luke are not words of happiness, and are intelligible only when cast against the background of the anthropological displacement that sees a humiliated and crucified Messiah* become the most exact witness of the humanity of man. "Perfect joy" is not found where a theory of happiness would locate it, but is, in fact, bound up intrinsically with modes of being properly kenosised (kenosis*). The time before the end, the preeschatological time of the Church*, is under the sign of "tribulation" *(thlipsis).* This time is devoid of neither the joys of contemplation* nor the joys of the liturgy*, and can thus shelter experiences that must be interpreted as icons of eternal beatitude. But it is inseparably a time lived under the sign of the cross, in which the blessed life lies in the paradoxical acts of the *imitatio Christi.* This time is indeed pre-*eschatological,* and the joy of being saved must be its dominant tone. This time is, however, *pre*-eschatological, and cannot bestow the fruition of the goods of the kingdom*, but puts them at man's disposal only in a paradoxical mode, which requires us to keep our distance with respect to any logic of happiness while not entering into possession of a beatitude that remains an object of hope. Dominated and criticized by beatitude, happiness is also dominated by the kenotic activities of the one who prepares himself to welcome beatitude by welcoming the biblical word of the Beatitudes. The humanity of man, in a world that is saved but remains worldly, would thus be to inhabit the space between happiness and beatitude.

• J. Pieper (1967), *Hoffnung und Geschichte,* Munich.
J. Greisch (1980), "La contrée de la sérénité et l'horizon de l'espérance," in R. Kearney, J. S. O'Leary (Ed.), *Heidegger et la question de Dieu,* Paris, 168–93.
G. Greshake (1983), *Gottes Heil–Glück des Menschen,* Freiburg.
D. Mieth (1983), "Das 'christliche Menschenbild'—eine unzeitgemäße Betrachtung?" *ThQ* 163, 1–15.
R. Spaemann (1990), *Glück und Wohlwollen: Versuch über Ethik,* Stuttgart.
O. Boulnois (1995), "Les deux fins de l'homme: L'impossible anthropologie et le repli de la théologie," *EPh* 2, 205–22.
J.-Y. Lacoste (1995 *a*), "Le désir et l'inexigible: Préambules à une lecture," *EPh* 2, 223–46; (1995 *b*), "En marge du monde et de la terre: L'aise," *RMM* 100, 185–200.

JEAN-YVES LACOSTE

See also **Aristotelianism, Christian; Contemplation; Ethics; Life, Eternal; Naturalism; Secularization; Vision, Beatific**

Beauty

1. Antiquity and the Middle Ages

a) Divine Beauty. There is no biblical theology* of beauty, and yet the Fathers of the Church, Augustine* and the Dionysius* the Pseudo-Areopagite in particular, speak of divine beauty. Of course, the Platonic, or Neoplatonic, climate in which Christianity developed does play a role, but it cannot explain everything, for Plato had put his finger on an essential element of human experience that must have made complete sense to Christians. In describing the revelation of ideal Beauty in perceptible beauty, "the most obvious *(ekphanestaton)* and attractive" of all the images of Ideas of this world (*Phaedrus* 250 d), and the elevation of the soul* of beauties to Beauty, Plato, and afterwards Plotinus, did indeed introduce, with unprecedented strength, the theme of the supremely desirable nature of the Absolute.

The Beauty of which Plato speaks is far from being, like Kantian beauty, the object of "disinterested" pleasure—that is, without desire (AA V, 203–210). Rather, it gives rise to Eros by definition (*Symposium* 203 c,

204 b). The experience of beauties "mixed" with this world, says .in *Enneads* (I. 6. 7; V. 8. 7), wakens love* of "Beauty in itself in all its purity" (I, 6, 7) and sets the soul* in motion toward its "home" (I. 6. 8). It is still necessary to go to the end. If the particular feature of beauty is indeed a "call to oneself" *(vocare ad se),* as Albert* the Great repeats in *De pulchro et bono* (Of the Beautiful and the Good, q. 6, a. 1; *see* Pseudo-Dionysius, *Divine Names* IV, 7), all finite and moral beauty (Jüngel 1984, citing Schiller) nevertheless runs the risk, if one is deaf to the call of supreme Beauty, of becoming that "bitter" beauty that Rimbaud cursed.

It is undoubtedly easier to hear this call than to follow it, as Augustine* shows when he tells how he found himself enchanted by divine beauty and taken from himself, "ravished" in the literal sense—"ravished to you by your beauty" (*rapiebar ad te decore tuo; Confessions* VII. xvii)—yet was still a prisoner of earthly beauties: "I loved you very late, beauty so old and so new" (*sero te amavi pulchritudo tam antiqua et tam nova,* ibid. X. xxvii). Pseudo-Dionysius, on the other hand, describes the end, or goal, of ascension. By identifying the Beautiful with the Good*, he pronounces a hymn to the beauty of God* (*Divine Names* IV, especially 7 and 10, but also 14, 18) in genuine "liturgical rapture." The Platonic erotic element is then adopted again, but in a subversive manner, with help from a completely different but closely related theme—that of hope*. It is in connection to promises of eschatological beatitude* (the "life of the world to come") that desire is determined.

To speak of divine beauty, as is done in ancient theology, is not to say that Beauty is God and thus make it absolute. "God is not God because he is beautiful, he is beautiful because he is God," says Karl Barth* transposing Augustine's suggestion on the objectivity of beauty in *Kirchliche Dogmatik* (1932; vol. II). Nor is it to define something in God that we would know exactly; it is rather to express a fervor, as can be seen in the language of the mystics*. There are many examples. John* of the Cross writes, "I know there could not be a more beautiful thing" ("I Know the Source," v. 4; *see Spiritual Canticle* 5, 7, 24, 35). The English poet George Herbert (1593–1633), expresses it in "Dulnes," a poem from *The Temple,* by stating: "Thou art my lovelines, my light, my life/ Beautie alone to mee."

b) Beauty in the World and Concept of Beauty. Nevertheless, inasmuch as the ancient and medieval theologians give content to the idea of beauty, they extract it from the experience of beauty in the cosmos* and from everything that it contains, rather than from the experience of art. In their eyes, art is not the source of beauty. A beautiful piece of art does not belong to the scale of beauties referred to in the *Symposium,* and Plato is able to condemn art without contradicting himself (e.g., in *Republic* X). Of course, Christian antiquity and the Middle Ages created major art, but undoubtedly not for itself, and without any clear consciousness of the specificity of the fine arts (Eco 1987). Love of the beauty of God's house (*see* Ps 26:8) fills church builders, but it is not a love of "pure" beauty. When Suger (c. 1081–1151) had the abbey church of Saint Denis built and decorated, he was more spellbound by the sparkle of the gold and gems, and especially by the light streaming into the church, symbol of divine light, than conscious of a specific beauty of Gothic architecture (Erwin Panofsky, *Gothic Architecture and Scholasticism,* 1957). Suger was not the only one to perceive above all the beauty of the world, created reality that allows one to imagine the Beauty of the Creator and to which not one single human creation can compare. The Fathers had already reinterpreted the Stoic and Neoplatonic themes of cosmic beauty in light of Genesis and saw in this beauty a gift from God. For Augustine, God spreads beauty over the world abundantly, for he "is not jealous of any beauty," as he states in *De musica* (On Music, VI, §56). For the Pseudo-Dionysius, "the superessential Beauty" makes the outpouring of this radiant source that springs up from itself shine forth upon all things to adorn them in beauty (*Divine Names* IV, 7). And the perception of these two beauties is linked, as is shown by the formula with which Thomas* Aquinas sums up the Pseudo-Dionysius on this subject: Dionysius "says that God is beautiful inasmuch as he is the cause of the clarity *(claritatis)* and harmony *(consonantiae)* of the world" (*ST* IIa IIae, q. 145,a. 2).

Claritas, clarity or light, and *consonantia,* harmony or proportion, are the elements that classically entered into the definition of beauty during the Middle Ages. (*See De musica* VI, §58, in which Augustine writes that the beauty of the world is due to the harmony of the four elements; and *De divisione naturae* III, PL 122, 638A, in which John the Scot Eriugena [c. 805–77] describes this beauty as stemming from the harmony between the different natures that compose the world. For examples of the "esthetics of light," *see* Eco 1987, chaps. 3 and 4.) These elements can also be found in the criteria of beauty—*claritatis, consonantia,* and *integritas*—specified by Aquinas (*ST* Ia, q. 39, a. 8), who is therefore not original on this point (the *integritas,* or perfection, which appears in this passage only, is not explained). Moreover, Aquinas never examined the esthetic question for itself, and one cannot ramble on about these criteria by isolating them from their context (Eco 1970), inasmuch as it does not involve a general theory of beauty, but a theory of Beauty of the Son, *consonantia* in terms of image of the Father* and *claritas* in terms of the Word*, *lux* and *splendor intellectus.*

Even when Aquinas takes a more direct look at beauty, it is again through a question on another subject that he introduces his famous definition, *pulchra enim dicuntur quae visa placent,* or "beautiful things are those that are pleasing to look at" (*ST* Ia, q. 5, a. 4, ad 1). This should not imply naïve indulgence in the pleasure of seeing or hearing, but rather the idea that beauty results from a judgment and even a "disinterested" judgment. This formula does explain a principle that has just been introduced: "The beautiful concerns knowledge" *(respicit vim cognoscitivam).* For Aquinas, the beautiful does not give rise to desire directly, like the Good; it is even through this relationship to knowledge that the idea of the beautiful distinguishes itself from that of the Good (*ST* Ia IIae, q. 27, a. 1, ad 3). The beautiful is what is pleasing about simple knowledge—*cuius ipsa apprehensio placet* (ibid.; *see* Eco 1970; 1987).

2. Modern Times

a) Reformation. Criticizing Roman statuary, Bernard* of Clairvaux said that he admired its beauty rather than respected its sacred character (*mirantur pulchra quam venerantur sacra,* PL, 182, 915). Aquinas thought that musical instruments should not be used in divine ceremony, for they gave pleasure rather than encouraged good interior disposition (*ST* IIA IIae, q. 91, a. 3, ad 4). The reformers felt the same way, but in much more systematic fashion. For Hegel, "religious representation retreated from the perceptive element and entered into the interiority of the soul and thought" *(Aesthetics, ThWA* 13, 142). Furthermore, the reformers' rejection of the Catholic use of images*, which they considered idolatrous, led them to doubt "religious" beauty, and even, in the case of Reformed churches, the use of music* in worship (*see* Söhngen 1967).

The Calvinist and Zwinglian liturgies, therefore, excluded all music except for the singing of psalms*. Some iconoclasts even destroyed organs along with statues (Cottin 1995). Luther*, on the contrary, had theological reasons for considering music "ranked right behind theology" (*WA* 30/2, 696). For him, music was not invented by man. Rather, it was God's creation that filled the whole world—*invenies musicam inditam seu concreatam creaturis universis* (ibid.). It was a precious gift that soothed the soul and chased away the demon* (ibid.; *see WA.B* 5, 639). It therefore had an entirely natural place in worship (Söhngen 1967) in all its forms and not only in the form of singing in unison.

Even today, although some theologians hope that Protestantism* will steer away from its excessive "liturgical fast" (Cottin 1995), others don't want to forget "that beauty, especially the religious kind... can be a trap" (Gagnebin 1995). The Catholic Reform movement, on the other hand, was in full support of the object of baroque beauty, glorifying the glory* of God.

b) Philosophy. Beauty rejected or accepted in this way does not belong to the world, but to art, and this is the beauty that will be the goal of modern esthetics, or esthetics in general. (The term *esthetics* appeared for the first time in 1750, in A.G. Baumgarten's *Aesthetica.*) Kant* even preferred nature's beauty to the beauty of art (*Critique of Judgment,* §42, AA V, 298–303), but Hegel began his *Aesthetics* by "excluding" "natural beauty" because it was foreign to the spirit (Introduction, *ThWA* 13, 13). Just as the spirit is above nature, artistic beauty is above natural beauty (*ThWA* 13, 14; *see* 27). This change in perspective is not different from the theological point of view, for the focus of attention is thus shifted from God to man. The idea of a nature foreign to the spirit is no longer the idea of creation*, in which the preceding centuries saw the work of divine art; the only work in which one can recognize the spirit is human art. In the perceptible form, of course, the spirit is still alienated, and art is but the first stage in its self-blooming—a stage that is skipped today (ibid., 25), since spiritual beauty cannot be represented by beautiful form (*ThWA* 14, 128–29) and the Christian God can only be expressed in all the depth of the concept through exterior form (*ThWA* 13, 103). But inasmuch as art belongs to the same sphere as religion and philosophy*, in terms of the perceptible presentation of truth* (*ThWA* 13, 21–22) and the "manner... of expressing the divine" (ibid. 21), it thus acquires a dignity that it never had and that it retains in our culture, no matter how we consider it. Even in Nietzsche*'s work, where the anti-Platonic stance divides truth from beauty, there are "ugly" truths—*Zur Genealogie der Morale* (1887). Even "truth" itself "is ugly," Nietzsche holds in *Kritische Studienausgabe* (XIII), and while the contrast between a "real world" and a world of appearances is an illusion, he writes in *Götzendämmerung* (1889; "Twilight of the Idols," *KSA* VI), it is art, the extolling of vital power, that shatters this illusion. Beauty is the sign of this power (ibid.); Socrates's ugliness, a sign of "decadence," refutes the value of his thought, Nietzsche holds in "The Problem of Socrates" (§3, ibid.). And although Heidegger* neither contemplates beauty nor forms an esthetic, all viewers are indeed absent from the essay, "The Origin of the Work of Art." Nevertheless, Heidegger grants a power to art, that of calling forth and expressing "truth." This pushes the major trends in the philosophies of art to an extreme.

c) Theology. This absolute approach to art and beauty was reluctantly received by theologians, who only acknowledged one veritable expression of Truth, divine revelation* (Jüngel 1984). Thus, Kierkegaard* radically separated the esthetic domain from the domain of faith*. The esthetic relationship to Christianity in no way involves the fact of living. The Christian, "apostle," or "martyr of truth," is not a poet of the religious.

This point of view could perhaps be useful when considering the problem of beauty in the liturgy*. In the liturgy the beauty of the music, objects, and architecture "are oriented toward the infinite* beauty of God" in certain ways (Vatican* II, *SC,* Constitution on the Sacred Liturgy, chap. 7, art. 122). Objects used in worship must be beautiful, "so as to signify and symbolize celestial realities" (ibid.); exterior forms are made to "arouse contemplation" of the heart of things (Council of Trent*, session 22, chap. 5). It is therefore appropriate for the liturgy to be beautiful—or at least not ugly, so as not to distract attention. The focus should not be on the forms of the ceremony, but, obviously, it does not involve procuring an esthetic experience. It is not beauty in itself that gives access to God, and the liturgy is prepared in the midst of a sacramental presence that is in no way immediately perceptible or immediately desirable. C.S. Lewis writes: "This bread, this wine: no beauty we could desire" (*Poems,* 124). And in the poem "Consécration," Claudel writes: "*Cet objet entre les fleurs de papier sec, c'est cela qui est la suprême beauté*"—that is, "This object between the dried-paper flowers—this is what supreme beauty is" *(La messe là-bas).*

The passages that Barth devoted to divine beauty and included in the definition of the glory of God provide a good example of this reluctance to apply the idea of beauty to God. Barth holds that beauty is not a "major notion" or a divine attribute* to be placed on the same level as the others, and that, above all, one must not fall into "estheticism" (*Kirchliche Dogmatik,* II). A theology that is loyal to what God reveals of himself must nevertheless acknowledge that "God is beautiful" *(Gott... auch schön ist),* source of joy and object of desire. In fact, Barth uses very strong expressions in this sense. Therefore, three aspects of divine beauty can be distinguished: the beauty of the fullness of divine essence, the beauty of the Trinity* of God, which is "the mystery* of his beauty," and the paradoxical beauty of Jesus Christ, who "had no form or comeliness that we should look at him, and no beauty that we should desire him" (Is 53:2), but who nevertheless reveals all the beauty and all the glory of God.

The Swiss theologian Hans Urs von Balthasar* (1905–88) formally acknowledges Barth for recognizing divine beauty (*Herrlichkeit,* I), but he wants to go much further and "develop" this notion, as he already says in the first sentence of *Herrlichkeit,* "Christian theology in the light of the third transcendental"—that is, Beauty.

By thus naming Beauty "the third transcendental," Balthasar also carries out a genuine "theoretical coup" (Lacoste 1986), already initiated by E. Przywara. The Beautiful does not, indeed, belong to the classic list of those general properties of Being* that "transcend" the limits of categories and that the Scholastics* called transcendental. Nor is there a fixed number of them. When there are only three, these involve Being, Truth, and Good, and not beauty. The thing *(res)* and the something *(aliquid)* can also be cited. Nevertheless, the identity of the Beautiful and the Good, which differ only in notion (*ST* Ia IIae, q. 27, a. 1, ad 3), allowed some to think that the Beautiful should be added to the list. Jacques Maritain (1935) firmly supported this position. Not only is the Beautiful transcendental, but it is "the splendor of a total of all that is transcendental" (*see also* Coreth, *Metaphysik,* Innsbruck, 1963). Eco (1987) only acknowledges "an implicit integration of the beautiful into the transcendental." He thinks it happened progressively and discretely in medieval thought.

Be that as it may, the reason for this decision is obvious. It clearly calls for distinguishing the work of founding a theological esthetics, from all that would be considered a theology of esthetics (*H* I) and, therefore, not confusing "the transcendental Beauty of revelation" with "secular beauty"—for example, as Chateaubriand does. The task of this theology of esthetics (a theological doctrine of perception) is precise. It is to decipher the "configuration" *(Gestalt)* of God, that is revealed in the story of salvation*, and eminently in Christ*, "center of the configuration of revelation" (*H* III, C). Although the nonsecular esthetic experience in which he perceives the appearance of divine glory in the finite configuration, the unique and absolutely privileged figure of Jesus, must be analogous* to all experience of beauty, it is also in the "unconfiguration" *(Ungestalt)* of the Crucified One that God allows himself to be known, and this recognition does not have a secular analogue. And although the nonsecular esthetic experience through which one perceives the appearance of divine glory—in the finite, unique, and absolutely privileged figure of Jesus—must be analogous (analogy) to all experience of Beauty, it is also in the *Ungestalt* of the Crucified One that God allows himself to be known, and this recognition does not have a secular analogue.

• Albert the Great, *De pulchro et bono,* in Thomas Aquinas, *Opera omnia,* Ed. Busa, Stuttgart, 1980, VII, 43–47.
Augustine, *De musica,* BAug 7.
H. U. von Balthasar, *Herrlichkeit,* Einsiedeln, 1961–69.
K. Barth, *KD* II/1, §31, 733–51 (*Dogmatique,* Geneva, vol. 7).
G. W. F. Hegel, *Vorlesungen über die Ästhetik, ThWA* 13–15.
M. Heidegger, "Der Ursprung des Kunstwerkes" (1936), in *Holzwege,* Frankfurt, 1949, 7–68.
E. Kant, *Kritik der Urteilskraft,* AA V, 167–485.
S. Kierkegaard, *Ou bien…ou bien* (Either-Or), *OC* III and IV, Paris, 1970; *Étapes sur le chemin de la vie* (Stages on Life's Way), *OC* IX, 1978; *Post-scriptum aux Miettes philosophiques* (Concluding Unscientific Postcript to Philosophical Fragments), *OC* X and XI, 1977.
Plato, *Banquet, Phaedo, Hippias Major.*
Plotinus *Enneads* I, 6 and V, 8.
Pseudo-Dionysius, *Divine Names* IV, 7 and 10.
Thomas Aquinas, *Commentary on the Divine Names* IV; *ST* Ia, q. 5, a. 4, ad 1; q. 39, a. 8; Ia IIae, q. 27, a. 1, ad 3.
♦ J. Maritain (1935), *Art et scolastique,* Paris.
E. de Bruyne (1946), *Études d'esthétique médiévale,* Bruges.
E. von Ivánka (1964), *Plato Christianus,* Einsiedeln.
O. Söhngen (1967), *Theologie der Musik,* Cassel.
I. Murdoch (1970), *The Sovereignty of Good,* London.
U. Eco (1970), *Il problema estetico in Tommaso d'Aquino,* 2nd Ed., Milan (bibl.).
P. Evdokimov (1972), *L'art de l'icône: Théologie de la beauté,* Paris.
A. Grabar (1979), *Les voies de la création en iconographie chrétienne: Antiquité et Moyen Age,* Paris (2nd Ed. 1994).
A. Nichols (1980), *The Art of God Incarnate,* London.
E. Jüngel (1984), "Auch das Schöne muß sterben, Schönheit im Lichte der Wahrheit," *ZThK* 81, 106–26.
W. Jens, H. Küng (1985), *Dichtung und Religion,* Munich.
J.-Y. Lacoste (1985), "Visages: Paradoxe et gloire," *RThom* 85, 561–606; (1986), "Du phénomène à la figure," in "Minima Balthasariana," *RThom* 86, 606–16.
J. Riches (Ed.) (1986), *The Analogy of Beauty: The Theology of Hans Urs von Balthasar,* Edinburgh.
U. Eco (1987), *Arte e bellezza nell'estetica medievale,* Milan.
F. Burch Brown (1990), *Religious Aesthetics,* London.
C. Harrison (1992), *Beauty and Revelation in the Thought of St. Augustine,* Oxford.
M. Sherringham (1992), *Introduction à la philosophie esthétique,* Paris.
P. Sherry (1992), *Spirit and Beauty: An Introduction to Theological Esthetics,* Oxford.
M. Zeindler (1993), *Gott und das Schöne: Studien zur Theologie der Schönheit,* Göttingen.
W. Lesch (Ed.) (1994), *Theologie und ästhetische Erfahrung,* Darmstadt.
J. Cottin, L. Gagnebin (1995), "Art," *Encyclopédie du protestantisme,* Paris, 48–62 (bibl.).
P. Évrard (1995), "Esthétique," ibid., 521–27 (bibl.).
F. Samuel (1996), "La question de l'économie divine et la pensée de Hans Urs von Balthasar," *Aletheia* 10, 59–77.
J.-L. Chrétien (1997), "Du Dieu artiste à l'homme créateur," in *Corps à corps: A l'écoute de l'œuvre d'art,* Paris, 91–121.
L. Karfíková (1998), De esse ad pulchrum esse: *Schönheit in der Theologie Hugos von St. Viktor,* Turnhout (bibl.).

IRÈNE FERNANDEZ

See also **Glory of God; Idolatry; Images; Liturgy; Love; Platonism, Christian**

Beghards. *See* **Beguines; Rhineland-Flemish Mysticism**

Beguines

The diversity of forms of life considered by historians as "Beguinal" and the variety of terms that designated such experiences in the late Middle Ages make any definition of the phenomenon difficult. The Beguine movement can at least be placed in a precise context. Beginning in the late 12th century, throughout the West, new religious experiences developed that associated the laity with a life made up of penitence and contemplation*. Women (woman*) were particularly likely to adopt this way of life; they entered upon the service of God* without taking monastic vows or accepting the constraints of communal living or a rule approved by the ecclesiastical hierarchy*. Living as nuns, they remained secular. These "semi-nuns," as many historians now characterize them, were at first designated by the term *mulieres religiosae* (religious women). But in the northern half of Europe, they were soon given the name *beguinae.* Elsewhere, the same experiences received other names. According to Jacques de Vitry (†1240), one of the first to write about the movement, "they are called *béguines* in Flanders and Brabant, *papelardes* in France, *humiliées* in Lombardy, *bizokes* in Italy, and *coquenunnes* in Germany."

It was in urban settings that the Beguine experience proliferated. Some Beguines lived alone, leading an itinerant existence or living under the family roof; others gathered together in a house; still others resided in "courts," called "Beguinages." Veritable villages within the city, these Beguinages were made up of several houses or convents, which were provided with a chapel, a hospital, and other common buildings. The Beguines lived on charity and the work* of their hands. By the 13th century, numerous cities sheltered several dozen Beguine communities, but it is impossible to give precise numbers or to provide a map for the Beguine movement. Many Beguines lived in solitude and, in contrast to traditional convents, many communities left no documentary traces. The phenomenon was nonetheless widespread and substantial. A demographic imbalance characterized by an excess of women, very high among populations emigrating to cities, and a certain resistance of traditional religious orders to new spiritual tendencies go some way toward explaining its magnitude.

In the beginning, *Beguine* was a deprecatory term, a synonym for *heretic,* for the movement had many detractors. To be sure, the pope had approved the Beguine communities in 1216, "not only in the diocese of Liège, but in the kingdom of France and in the empire" (according to a letter by Jacques de Vitry). In addition, a bull of 1233 had granted them pontifical protection. However, many churchmen had difficulty in accepting the intermediate situation *(Zwischenstand)* of the Beguines, which implicitly called into question the distinction between clergy* and laity that had been reaffirmed by the Gregorian reform, as well as all the social and legal classifications familiar to the church*. Because they did not know where to locate them, the laity reproached the Beguines for their "hypocrisy," whereas the secular clergy were hostile to the privileged relations that often bound them to the mendicants (Franciscan spirituality*) and removed them from the jurisdiction of the clergy. In addition, the networks of informal social relations in which the Beguines participated could only trouble the institution of the church.

Even outside their communities, the Beguines met, prayed together, and discussed their experiences. Above all they read, used writing, and appropriated the sacred texts and translated them into the vernacular languages. Some of them composed treatises, as evidenced by the mystical works of Beatrice of Nazareth (†1268), Hadewijch of Antwerp (c. 1240), and Margaret Porette (†1310). The immediate relationship that some maintained with God in contemplation* and ecstasy left no role for priestly mediation. Moreover, several English historians consider the mystical adventures of the Beguines as a kind of refuge for women who felt excluded from a church controlled by men. It would, however, be inappropriate to reduce the Beguine movement purely and simply to the mystical* element, which engaged probably only a small number of Beguines. Similarly, there was never a spirituality (and still less a theology*) particular to the Beguine movement.

In dealing with the Beguines, the institutional church adopted two different attitudes. Sometimes it rejected the Beguines; at other times it tried to assimilate them.

In rejecting the Beguines, the church identified them as heretics*. This was particularly true in the Rhineland, where the Beguines were persecuted as early as the 13th century. Then, at the Council of Vienna* of 1311–12, a major condemnation was delivered against some Beguines in the decrees *Cum de quibusdam mulieribus* and *Ad nostrum.* These decrees were promulgated in 1317–18 by John XXII, who in a new decree, *Sancta Romana,* grouped the Beguines together with the Fraticeli. First mentioned in 1311 in a pontifical brief, "The Sect of the Free Spirit," to which Beguines and Beghards were accused of belonging, never had any substance except in the mind of inquisitors (and for some uncritical historians). The heresy of the "Free Spirit" denounced in Vienna was, in fact, essentially the result of a compilation produced on the basis of quotations extracted from *The Mirror of Simple Souls,* the banned treatise of the Beguine Margaret Porette, who was declared a heretic and burned in Paris in 1310.

Conversely, in attempting to assimilate the Beguines, the church forced some Beguines to adopt the rule of Saint Augustine* or to join a third order. In the diocese of Liège and in Flanders, the church authorities and the civil government carried out a kind of enclosure of the Beguines. Those who were isolated were assembled in particular places, called "Beguinages," which from then on were the only authorized form of association for the Beguines. Adherents were given rules and regularly visited by priests* who were specifically assigned to them. While the Beguine movement faded elsewhere, the large Beguinages in the north survived the crisis of the first quarter of the 14th century.

• A. Mens (1941), *Oorsprong en betekenis van de Nederlandse Begijnenbewegen,* Louvain.
S. Axters (1950), *Geschiedenis van de vroomheid in de Nederlanden I,* Antwerp.
E.W. McDonnell (1954), *The Beguines and Beghards in Medieval Culture,* New Brunswick, N.J.
R. Manselli (1959), *Spirituali e Beghini,* Rome.
H. Grundmann (1961), *Religiöse Bewegungen im Mittelalter,* 2nd Ed., Darmstadt.
R. Guarnieri (1965), *Il movimento del Libero Spirito,* Rome.
R.E. Lerner (1972), *The Heresy of the Free Spirit in the Later Middle Ages,* Berkeley-Los Angeles-London.
J. Tarrant (1974), "The Clementine Decrees on the Beguines: Conciliar and Papal Versions," *AHP* 12, 300–308.
J.-C. Schmitt (1978), *Mort d'une hérésie: L'Église et les clercs face aux béguines et aux béghards du Rhin supérieur du XIVe au XVe siècle,* Paris.
R.E. Lerner (1983), "Beguines and Beghards," *DMA* 2, 157–62.
W. Simons (1989), "The Beguine Movement in the Southern Low Countries: A Reassessment," *BIHBR* 59, 63–105.
G. Epiney-Burgard, E. Zum Brunn (1992), *Femmes troubadours de Dieu,* Paris.

Michel Lauwers

See also **Priesthood; Rhineland-Flemish Mysticism; Woman**

Being

Ontology is a term that appeared late (in Goclenius's 1613 *Lexicon philosophicum*); and the philosophical tradition from Plato to Meinong and beyond speaks of objects said to be located beyond being (the Good* or the One in Platonism and Neoplatonism), or beyond being and nonbeing (Meinong's "nonexistent objects"). Notwithstanding these two reservations, the term *ontological* may be applied to any ordered inventory of those things to which a reality is attributed. Theology deals with objects whose reality it is not alone in asserting (God*, evil*), and with objects whose reality it alone asserts (intradivine relations), but it always claims to name those objects in an order that corresponds to their reality. As a result, theological discourse is impossible without articulated ontological decisions, and that discourse must necessarily situate itself in relation to ontological decisions that are made within nontheological frames of reference.

a) Divine Substance, Logos, and Metaphysics. Choosing the God of the philosophers against the gods of paganism was one of the major decisions of the early church* (Ratzinger 1968; *see also* Pannenberg 1967, Stead 1986). The choice of *logos* over *muthos,* the conception of Christianity as "true philosophy*" and of pagan philosophy as a "preparation for the gospel," and the development of a Christology* that linked the Johannine Word/Logos to the Hellenistic Logos/Reason are all factors showing how Christianity developed its doctrines (its canonical interpretation of the foundational texts, whose authority* it based on the authority of God) by making use of the conceptual resources offered by Greece. On the other hand the intellectual climate of late antiquity, characterized by an eclectic practice of philosophy, a frequently religious conception of the philosophical life, and the dissemination of doctrines in a "popular" form (*see* Nock 1964, e.g.), explains the style of the Christian use of Greek words and ideas. This took the form of isolated borrowings rather than the adoption of theories, and the theological appropriateness of these borrowings sometimes concealed spectacular philosophical blunders and imprecisions.

The entry of Greek concepts into Christian language was solemnly ratified when the Council* of Nicaea* inserted into its confession of faith* a nonbiblical word, *homoousios,* "consubstantial*" (from *ousia,* "essence" or "substance*"), in order to affirm the divinity of Jesus Christ, while simultaneously denying, against Arius, that he was *an* (intermediate) god born from the supreme God. Because the Nicene formulation made it possible to name what God the Father* and Jesus Christ are in common (what Aristotle calls "primary substance," *Cat.* 5, 2a 11–19), but not to name what each one possesses uniquely, the future would belong to new conceptualizations that originated in both Greek and Latin: the introduction of the concepts of *hupostasis* and *prosôpon/persona* (respectively, "hypostasis" and "persons"). But the orthodoxy that was thus constituted, with the dual goal of evangelizing the empire and replying to formulations that were considered inadequate, set itself up as the correct reading of the founding events of Christianity only by partially substituting the language of *being* for the language of history* and narrative*. This assertion must, of course, be qualified. On the one hand, any question about the identity of God or of Jesus* could be answered by reference to the many names and titles contained in the biblical text. On the other, the establishment of a theology interested primarily in the being of God and Christ* (this interest defined in the strict sense what Greek patristics called *theologia* from the fourth century; *see* Eusebius of Caesarca, *HE* I. 1. 7) would never be an obstacle to the proclamation of the great deeds of God and of everything called in Greek the "economy" *(oikonomia)* of the Covenant* and of salvation*. A complex system of cross-references, lastly, would always unite "theological" and "economic" concerns, with the latter never being fully absorbed by the former. But a displacement had in fact taken place.

In saying of the *homoousios* of Nicaea that it made it possible to "grasp the coherence of the intrinsic ontology of the gospel," Torrance's argument in favor of the patristic theology of the first four centuries (1988, 144; cautious discussion in Lehmann 1973) expressed an idea held by the patristic era and by medieval theology. But there is another characteristically modern idea according to which there was an inherently corrupting element in the Greek *logos.* The idea was developed starting with Luther*'s polemic against Scholasticism*, which he considered a modern counterpart to Augustine*'s struggle against Pelagianism*. Against a theology based on the belief that one could not become a theologian without studying Aristotle, Luther proposed a theology born from experience* (*WA* 1. 226. §43 f.; *WA* 5. 163. 28: *Vivendo, immo moriendo et damnando fit theologus, non intelligendo, legendo aut speculando;* "one becomes a theologian by living, or rather by dying and being condemned, not by understanding, reading, or speculating"). Against the classic concepts of Christology (dogmatic interest in the *being* of Christ), he set up the primacy of soteriology and the believer's living relation to Jesus as his savior: "Christ is not called Christ because he has two natures. What difference does that make to me? But he bears the magnificent and consoling name of Christ because of the ministry* and the burden that he took up; that is what gives him his name*. That he is by nature man and God is a matter that concerns him. But the fact that he devoted his ministry and poured forth his love* to become my savior and redeemer is where I find my consolation and my good" (*Commentary on Exodus, WA* 16. 217–18). The polemic was ritually repeated and amplified in Protestantism* after the Reformation (*see Le platonisme des Pères dévoilé* by M. Souverain [1700], a French Huguenot who converted to Anglicanism*), and Luther's tone reappears in the rejection of "metaphysics" in favor of ethics formulated by Ritschl in his magnum opus on justification* (1870–74). The sharpest form of objection, however, derived from theoretical developments occurring outside theology. 1) The linguistic theory of W. von Humboldt (1767–1835) was the first of these developments. By saying that every language carried out a prismatic decomposition of the world and then conducted a sui generis organization of reality, Humboldt (On the Kawi Language of the Island of Java," *GS* VII/1) in fact laid out the bases for a linguistic critique of ontological categories (*see,* e.g., Benveniste, *Problèmes de linguistique générale* 1, Paris, 1966; *see* C.H. Kahn, *The Verb "Be" in Ancient Greek,* Dordrecht-Boston, 1973). It then became possible to ask each language to reveal its vision of the world, and thereby its philosophy. A discipline, "ethnophilosophy," was created with the work of P. Tempels S.J. (1906–77) on the implicit ontology of the Bantu language (*La philosophie bantoue,* 2nd Ed., Paris, 1948; *see also* A. Kagame, *La philosophie bantu-rwandaise de l'être,* Brussels, 1956). And it also became possible to identify a new object, "Hebrew thought," and methodically to distinguish it from another object that was called "Greek thought." In its fully developed form (T. Boman, *Das hebräische Denken im Vergleich mit dem Griechischen,* 2nd Ed., Göttingen, 1954), this led to the identification of a dynamic kind of thought as opposed to a static one. In the dynamic kind of thought (Hebrew), appearance is reality, as opposed to a thought concerned with what lies beneath appearances; it is a thought concerned with history, not ignorant of it; a thought of concrete totality as opposed to an abstracting and individualizing thought. The philological merit of J. Barr was in showing (*Semantics of Biblical Language,* Oxford, 1961) that this involved an unjustified identification. What had been attributed to a language was not rooted in the structure of that language but in what the biblical writers using it had wanted to say. But even after such a refutation, the question of a biblical *experience* of the world, unquestionably different from that of Hellenism, remains open. 2) The second theoretical development was the appearance of a philosophical critique of Hellenism, from Nietzsche* to

Heidegger* and beyond. In Nietzsche the attack on Christianity is carried out as an adjunct to the attack on Platonism*: for the use of the "people," Christianity had doctrinally adopted a Platonic rejection of movement, time*, and the reality of things as they are in the here and now. In Heidegger a new object was identified under the name of *metaphysics,* by which must be understood a finite manner of thinking ("closure of metaphysics"), one born (in Greece) and mortal, governed by presuppositions that it cannot itself criticize (e.g., a certain rule of *presence,* a certain *forgetting of being* in favor of the existent), and living thought has the task of "overcoming" *(überwinden)* it ("Das Ende der Philosophie und die Aufgabe des Denkens," in *Zur Sache des Denkens,* Tübingen, 1969). And because any discourse linked to the Greek *logos* was metaphysical during the time of metaphysics, it goes without saying that the task assigned to "thought" in general by Heidegger is also assigned ipso facto to any theology that wishes to survive metaphysics.

Recent scholarship has thus seen a replacement of the theological polemic against the Hellenization* of Christianity by a theological critique of metaphysics, often intensified under the influence of objections formulated by E. Levinas, in the name of the "question of the other," against any thought of being (including Heidegger's). In a realm characterized more by projects than actual realizations, several directions are open. If the terms of metaphysics are all obsolete, what texts can be found to enable theology to perform its role? 1) As an initial response we can assert the urgency of a rigorous *reading* of the biblical text. And in a cultural climate marked by the development of *sciences of the text,* the desire to preserve intact the exigencies of theological method might lead to attributing to those sciences (because they are dignified by the name sciences) the capacity to provide theology with conceptual tools free of metaphysical contamination. Structural linguistics thus appears (G. Lafon, CFi 96; A. Delzant, CFi 92; *see also* M. Costantini *Com(F)* I/7, 40–54) as a new *organon* for theology. 2) In response to the presumed exhaustion of the key words of metaphysics, it was necessary to call on that which metaphysics had left unthought. A theology asserting the death of the concept of substance would thus attempt to respect the signifying intention that guided the adoption of *consubstantial* at Nicaea by moving from the language of substance to the language of love—the agape of Jesus is one with the agape of the Father, *homoagape* (Hick 1966; but *see* Mackinnon 1972). A theology concerned with maintaining its distance from a representation of God on the Greek model of *noûs* (adopted by Philo), or on the modern model of subjectivity, would find in the biblical lexicon of *spirit (ruach-pneuma)* the basis for attempting a new language (Lampe 1977 [but one that leads to a unitarian theology]; Pannenberg, 1980, *Syst. Theol.* I, Göttingen, 1988; *see* Stead 1995).

3) Beyond fragmentary conceptual rearrangements, the idea of a theological overtaking of metaphysics (Marion 1977; Milbank 1997) is congruent with the hypothetical assertion that metaphysics had already been overtaken in the time of metaphysics ("a nonchronological exit from metaphysics," Carraud 1992), or that certain forms of thought ("spirituality" according to Martineau 1980) have, by their essence, a capacity for avoiding metaphysics. What is left unthought by Heideggerian "destruction" is, therefore, just as important as what is left unthought by metaphysics. And if it is true that the history of metaphysics still remains to be written after the fragmentary indications supplied by Heidegger (for an outline, *see* H. Boeder *Topologie der Metaphysik,* Freiburg, 1980), a history of the nonmetaphysical moments or tendencies of Christian discourse has also yet to be written. 4) Assuming that the late 20th century has experienced "the end of philosophy," theology is not alone in confronting the "task of thought," and a theology with postmetaphysical intentions cannot be indifferent to other forms of discourse with similar intentions. Substituting a thought of the gift for a thought of the object in order to reject the naming of the human person as a *subject* (J.-L. Marion, *Étant donné,* Paris, 1997); conceiving of an "ontology with a human face" (Chapelle 1982 or C. Bruaire); rooting the meaning of human experiences in a "metahistory" (M. Müller)—these ways of talking about human beings are close enough to discourse about God for the interest of theology in such approaches to be obvious. And when theology also recognizes that its mission includes a universalizing contemplation of the meaning of being (Balthasar*, *Herrlichkeit* III/1, 974–83), this involves in addition a theological contribution to the task of thought and to the survival of thought in an age of nihilism.

During the same period, more than one historical issue has been subject to a reexamination that has led to significant conclusions (*see* E.P. Meijering, *ThR* 36 [1971], 303–20; A.M. Ritter, *ThR* 49 [1984], 31–56). Studied on the basis of Greek theories of substance, and then with reference to the theological struggles that led to its adoption, the *homoousios* of Nicaea appears in fact as the product of a desire for meaning surpassing any philosophical conditioning, so that its use, and the confession of belief in it, remain possible regardless of the fate of Greek concepts of *ousia* when they are considered with philosophical rigor (Stead 1977, 1985; Grillmeier 1978; Hanson 1988; Barnes and Williams 1993).

Patristic studies have produced a good deal of evidence that the Christian restructuring of Platonism* (Ivanka 1964; *see* Waszing 1955; E.P. Meijering, *VigChr* 28 [1974], 15–28) produced more than merely a new Platonism. In this regard we can cite Gregory* of Nyssa's construction of a concept of the infinite that owes nothing to Greek metaphysics (Mühlenberg 1967); the development from Pseudo-Dionysius* through Gregory* Palamas of theories of participation in God that subvert the entire Greek ontology of participation (survey in Karayiannis 1993); and Augustine's insertion of relation at the heart of substance (*see* d below). Christian dogma* and its language no longer appear as "a work of the Greek spirit on the ground of the Gospel" (Harnack, *Lehrbuch,* 4th Ed., 1909; repr. Darmstadt, 1983) but as the fruit of a kerygmatic effort carried out with the help of Greek words whose conceptual charge was changed in the process as a general rule (e.g., with reference to the definition of Chalcedon, A. Grillmeier, *Jesus der Christus im Glauben der Kirche* I, Freiburg-Basel-Vienna, 1979).

Hence, whatever the relevance of an interrogation of the meaning of being in the dimensions of universal history (Heidegger), and whatever usefulness its theological reception might have, it should perhaps become apparent that the question of the links to be established between Christianity and Hellenism/metaphysics is primarily a hermeneutical* question.

The technical language of theology is an interpretive language, and its interpretation is carried out with reference to the biblical text. The words chosen for the process of interpretation are available words, selected because they are endowed with a meaning that permits inserting them into true propositions. Because words with meanings do not exist in isolation but within languages and, in the case of concepts, within theories (whether established in rigid form, as in the case of the Aristotelian theory of *ousia,* or more flexibly, as with the general ideas about *ousia* in the philosophical *koinè* of late antiquity), no terminology can of course enter theological usage without carrying traces of its pretheological usage, with the latter perhaps having some influence on the former. But because theological usage itself is established by reference to the biblical text, the first question must concern the elementary logical or ontological requirements of the Christian faith as these emerge from the reading of the Bible. Thus, the *homoousios* of Nicaea articulates in a rigorous form what is already said in John 10:30—"I and the Father are one."

Theology speaks of its particular objects in a language that has been used for naming other objects. The biblical text itself is not written in a sacred language that has been created for the naming only of theologically significant realities. It is therefore a work of piety—of theological critique—to analyze the nontheological implications carried by theological words and concepts. The deep symbolism of the Pentecost narrative (Acts 2:1–13), however, shows that the "wonders of God" can be expressed in, or translated into, any language. In the hermeneutic terms derived from Gadamer and Ricœur, fusion is always possible between the perspectives of the biblical text and the perspectives of any present moment, and the "world of the text" of the Bible is always accessible to any individual, no matter which "world" his own language and *epistèmè* make him an inhabitant of.

The history of theology should be read as a history of meaning—of a will to interpret—bound up with a *capacity to speak.* Meaning exceeds what is said, in this domain more than any other (on this excess as a general law of hermeneutics, *see* J. Grondin, *L'universalité de l'herméneutique,* Paris, 1993), and the idea of the final word is foreign to the forms of logic that should preside over the work of theology, which are forms of logic of present interpretation (J.-Y. Lacoste *RPL* 92, 1994, 254–80). Present interpretation obviously cannot find its conceptual tools in just any pretheological or theologically neutral ontology. But in order to name rigorously the realities it has the task of discussing, theology may draw on the resources provided by more than one philosophical inventory of reality. And of the three principal procedures adopted by the philosophy of the present time to question the reality of reality—first the "question of being" and the "destruction of metaphysics," second ontology as hermeneutics, and finally analytic philosophy and the "theory of objects"—it seems clear that each one can contribute to the precise formulation of a Christian discourse that wishes to express the "excess of God" in relation to any metaphysical sense (Marion 1977; Corbin 1997); or to the continuity of a provision of meaning within the discontinuity of the ages of thought; or, finally, can provide the basic grammar that must govern any use of Christian words that seeks an exact reference to the objects of faith (e.g., Mackinnon 1972).

• J.H. Waszink (1955), "Der Platonismus und die altchristliche Gedankenwelt," *Entretiens sur l'Antiquité classique* III, Vandœuvres-Geneva, 139–74.

E. von Ivánka (1964), *Plato christianus,* Einsiedeln.

A. D. Nock (1964), *Early Gentile Christianity and Its Hellenistic Background,* New York.

J. Hick (1966), "Christology at the Cross Roads," in F.G. Healey (Ed.), *Prospect for Theology,* London, 137–66.

E. Mühlenberg (1967), *Die Unendlichkeit Gottes bei Gregor von Nyssa,* Göttingen.

W. Pannenberg (1967), "Die Aufnahme des philosophischen Gottesbegriffs als dogmatisches Problem der frühchristlichen Theologie," *Grundfr. syst. Th.,* 276–346.

J. Ratzinger (1968), "Der Gott des Glaubens und der Gott der Philosophen," *Einführung in das Christentum,* Munich, 103–44.
F. Ricken (1969), "Nikaia als Krisis des altchristlichen Platonismus," *ThPh* 44, 321–41.
D.M. Mackinnon (1972), "'Substance' in Christology—A Cross-Bench View," in S.W. Sykes, J.P. Clayton (Ed.), *Christ, Faith and History,* Cambridge, 279–300.
K. Lehmann (1973), "Kirchliche Dogmatik und biblisches Gottesbild," in J. Ratzinger (Ed.), *Die Frage nach Gott,* QD 56, 116–40.
G. Lampe (1977), *God As Spirit,* London.
J.-L. Marion (1977), *L'idole et la distance,* Paris.
C. Stead (1977), *Divine Substance,* Oxford.
C. Andresen (1978), "Antike und Christentum," *TRE* 3, 50–99 (bibl.).
A. Grillmeier (1978), "Piscatorie-Aristotelice," in *Mit Ihm und in Ihm,* 2nd Rev. Ed., Freiburg-Basel-Vienna, 283–300.
E. Martineau (1980), "Gilson et le problème de la théologie," in M. Couratier (Ed.), *Étienne Gilson et nous,* Paris, 61–71.
W. Pannenberg (1980), "Die Subjecktivität Gottes und die Trinitätslehre: Ein Beitrag zur Beziehung zwischen Karl Barth und der Philosophie Hegels," *Grundfr. syst. Th.* 2, 96–111.
A. Chapelle (1982), "Ontologie," course notes, Institut d'études théologiques, Brussels.
C. Stead (1985), *Substance and Illusion in the Christian Fathers,* London; (1986), "Die Aufnahme des philosophischen Gottesbegriffes in der frühchristlichen Theologie: W. Pannenbergs These neu bedacht," *ThR* 51, 349–71.
R.P.C. Hanson (1988), *The Search for the Christian Doctrine of God: The Arian Controversy 318–381,* Edinburgh.
T.F. Torrance (1988), *The Trinitarian Faith,* Edinburgh.
V. Carraud (1992), *Pascal et la ph.,* Paris.
M.R. Barnes, D.N. Williams (Ed.) (1993), *Arianism after Arius,* Edinburgh.
V. Karayiannis (1993), *Maxime le Confesseur: Essence et énergies de Dieu,* ThH 93, 31–276.
B. Pottier (1994), *Dieu et le Christ selon Grégoire de Nysse,* Turnhout, 83–142.
C. Stead (1995), *Philosophy in Christian Antiquity,* Cambridge.
M. Corbin (1997), *La Trinité ou l'Excès de Dieu,* Paris.
J. Milbank (1997), "Only Theology Overcomes Metaphysics," in *The Word Made Strange,* Oxford, 36–52.

b) God and Being. It was in the very text of its Scriptures* that Christianity found the suggestion of a thought of God as being. Exodus 3:14, in the Septuagint, says in effect "I am the existent" *(egô eimi ho ôn).* The translation is hardly defensible philologically (*see* Caquot in Coll. 1978, 17–26); Aquila and Theodotion translated it closer to the Hebrew, "I will be who I will be" *(esomai hos esomai),* and so did the Vulgate "I am the one that I am," "I am the one that I am" *(Ego sum qui sum).* But as soon as a theological language with conceptual characteristics began to take shape alongside biblical language, and in order to provide biblical language with added precision, the Septuagint version of Exodus 3:14 unfailingly provided a major biblical anchor for the idea of a God who, before all, *is*—an idea it had already supplied to Philo. (Other biblical references were adduced: the claims of authority by the Christ of John ["I am"]; Rom 4:17: God "calls into existence the things that do not exist"; Rev 1:8: "[God] who is.")

It has been said of Latin patristics that, from the first use of Exodus 3:14 (by Novatian), "the ontological meaning of the name* revealed to Moses caused no difficulty for anyone" (G. Madec in Coll. 1978, 139). In this tradition* Augustine provided a classic interpretation of the theological primacy of being (but he also referred to Ps 4:9 and 121:3, in order to express the *sum qui sum,* an expression that he used in a technical sense and that does not articulate being: the *idipsum* [*see Conf.* IX. iv. 11; *De Trin.* III. iii. 8; *En. Ps.* 121]). The God of Augustine reveals himself under two names, his "substantial name" *(nomen substantiae: sum qui sum)* and his "name of mercy*" (*nomen misericordiae:* God of Abraham and Isaac). If God *is,* however, then man, inhabitant of the "region of unlikeness" (*Conf.* VII. x. 16, himself seems to be one who is not. Contemplated in God, being is immutability* and eternity*. In that case, being can be attributed to man only with reservations. Defined as the one who changes and passes, man is also the one of whom it can be said that he "is" not. He is defined by his sin* as "the one who goes far away from being [and] travels toward nonbeing" (*En. Ps.* 38. 22; CChr.SL 38, 422). He is also the one who truly is only at the conclusion of a conversion*. Augustine's contemporary, Jerome, also affirmed that God alone truly *is,* and further believed that the name given in Exodus 3:14 revealed the divine essence (*Ep.* 15. 4. 2, CSEL 54. 65. 12–18).

Greek theology also affirmed the being of God. Despite his knowledge of Hebrew, Origen* continually quoted the Septuagint version of Exodus 3:14; and this was the text he relied on to develop the notion of God's relationship to created beings as a relationship between the one who "truly is" to something that is by participation. In Gregory* of Nazianzus, God is an "infinite and undetermined ocean of essence" (*Or.* 38. 7, *ousia*), and John of Damascus quoted this blend of a concept and an image, with reference to the name revealed to Moses, by saying that God had "totally gathered *ousia* into himself, like an ocean" (*Fid. Orth.* I. 9). However, the influence of Platonism on the Greek Fathers* qualified these assertions. The Good, according, to Plato "transcends essence," *epekeina tès ousias* (*Republic* VI, 509b), and the One of Plotinus transcends intellect and being (e.g., *Enneads* VI. 9. 3; on the history of this theory before Plotinus, *see* J. Whittaker, *VigChr* 23, 1969). The idea of a God who is not, or who does more than be, was an idea that could be, and was in fact, formulated in a radical way by the Gnostic Basilides: "The God who is not," *ho ouk ôn* *theos* (Hippolytus, *Ref.* VII. 20). And although the Fathers did not formulate it in a radical way, there was enough Neoplatonism in Pseudo-Dionysius that his God was not being but the "demiurge of being" (*Divine Names* V. 817 C), and that *anonymity* was seen to be better suited to God than any name, including the name of being, and that everything belonging to the realm of being issued from God as *absolute goodness* (ibid., 820 C). Another Platonist, Marius Victorinus, was also the only Latin Father to assert that God—the Father—transcends being.

It was left to Byzantine theology, and especially to Gregory* Palamas, to specify the terms of a theory of participation in God. If the absolute future of man must be thought of under the figure of "divinization," *theôsis,* in accordance with 2 Peter 1:4, then God (or at least his "nature," *phusis*) must be open to participation. To indicate that a doctrine of divinization does not undermine the doctrine of divine transcendence, Pseudo-Dionysius had proposed a paradoxical formulation: God is "the unshareable shared," *ametekhtôs metekhetai.* In Gregory Palamas the already classic distinction (e.g., Basil, PG 32, 869 AB) between divine energies (open to participation, the *dunameis* of Pseudo-Dionysius) and essence (not open to participation, the *henôseis* of Pseudo-Dionysius) provides a coherent solution to the problem. The prerogatives of apophasis are preserved, because the divine essence (or "superessence," *huperosiotès*) remains strictly incomprehensible. But the prerogatives of an ontology of the divine are also preserved. By forcing the development of an eschatological doctrine of the humanity of man, the concept of divinization also makes it necessary to speak of a God who is—with the qualification, of course, that "if it was necessary to distinguish in God between essence and what is not essence, this is precisely because God is not limited by his essence" (V. Lossky, *A l'image et à la ressemblance de Dieu,* Paris, 1967).

Two theories were thus bequeathed to the Latin Middle Ages: the Dionysian primacy of the Good and the Augustinian primacy of Being. Although there was no lack of nuances and intermediate positions, several distinct positions can be identified. 1) His teacher, Albert* the Great, had passed on to Thomas* Aquinas a thought of the anteriority of being in respect to goodness which simultaneously preserved the unknowability and anonymity of the divine being. The two directions were preserved by Thomas within an impressive orchestration. On the one hand, the primacy of being is the keystone of the entire theological-philosophical edifice. God is "pure act of being," *actus purus essendi* (hence nothing in him exists in the mode of the possible), and he is "subsistent being itself," *ipsum esse subsistens.* Hence the Absolute does not appear as an *existent* but as being in the infinitive sense (the distinction between *esse* and *existens* was probably transmitted to the Latin Middle Ages by Boethius*; *see* Hadot in Coll. 1978). The epistemology of Thomas Aquinas is not, however, governed by the exegesis* of Exodus 3:14, but by that of Romans 1:20 ("his [God's] invisible attributes, namely, his eternal power and divine nature, have been clearly perceived, ever since the creation of the world, in the things that have been made"). And since God is knowable through creation, the omnimodal perfection of the divine *esse* is set forth only at the conclusion of a conceptual ascent for which the existents given to perceptual experience provide both a point of departure and a direction. On the other hand, in order to preserve divine unknowability within the very conceptual structure that binds the Creator to creation, Thomas attributes to the concept of being the modality of analogy: being is not understood of God in the way it is understood of creation. And by postulating that the real difference between essence and *esse,* which applies to all created beings, does not apply to the Creator, he preserves the transcendence of God by affirming his *simplicity**. 2) Bonaventure* responded to the Augustinianism* of Thomas by a reaffirmation of Dionysian theology. The *Itinerarium* records the movement from a metaphysics of divine being to a thought of the Good that locates its scriptural basis in Luke 18:19 ("No one is good except God alone") and Matthew 19:17. And to an inductive ontology for which created beings provide the first steps in the reasoning process, Bonaventure responds with an ontology that attempts to apprehend all existents in the light of the Trinitarian mystery* (*see* d below). 3) Another ontology was constructed by another Franciscan, Duns* Scotus, and based on a univocal concept of being that led him to see in the *infinite* the sign of the divinity of God. Recalled in the prayer* that opens the *De primo principio,* the revelation* of the divine name in Exodus 3:14 is taken as an invitation to seek God through reason in the historical present of experience. Scotist theology aims, however, to be a *practical* science oriented toward charity: the speculative primacy of being is therefore limited. 4) The attempt to reconcile the Dionysian and Augustinian viewpoints was the distinctive characteristic of the Rhineland-Flemish theology derived from Albert the Great (*see* Libera 1984). "Purity of being," *puritas essendi,* divine life understood as "bubbling," *bullitio,* are the words Eckhart used to create a mystical* ontology of divine being. This mystical ontology achieved its pure form in the work of Ulrich of Strasbourg. It has God alone as object, and because it speaks of being in a sense that belongs only to God, it can see being as a specific name of God. Later spiritual tradition frequently followed a similar approach. For example, God showed himself to Catherine of Siena while saying to her that he is the one who is, and she is the one who is not (Martène and Durand, *Amplissima collectio,* vol. 6, col. 1354, Paris, 1729). We might also mention the representative of another school, the Dionysian Thomas Gallus (Thomas of Verceil, †1246), a theologian of Saint-Victor, author of a mystical reading of Exodus 3:14. Instead of appearing as an "intelligible name," intended to open the path to rational inquiry, the name given to Moses is a "unitive name," a name whose meaning is reached only in the *unitio* of the soul* with God.

If *ontology* is a modern word, this is because modernity unquestionably strove to think of God only within the context of being, as the first thinkable entity, and it did so by subverting the Augustinian point of view. For example, Suarez* replaced a God of whom it must be admitted that he is because he says that that is his name, with a God about whom, before asking what he is, metaphysics sets out beforehand all the logic of what being means. The *primus ens, seu Deus,* does not appear until the 30th of the *Disputationes metaphysicae,* and neither his infinity, nor his status as first cause call into question the meaning of being. There was thus established in the 17th century (*see* Wundt 1939), and fully developed in the 18th by C. Wolff (1679–1754) and his students, a general science of the *ens in latitudine sumptum* which made of *theologikè epistèmè* a *special science,* "dealing with a particular region of the existent as a whole, while the primacy of that singular existent... neither enclosed nor any longer contained within itself any possibility of a correlative universalization of its field" (Courtine 1990).

The reaction against the God of Suarez and Wolff came first from Hegel*, for whom God is not an existent but the existent itself—*Gott ist das Seyende selbst.* This thesis, the preeminent speculative thesis, makes it possible to make the unveiling of the meaning of being dependent on the unveiling of divine life. Reaction also came from Schelling*, who says that God is not an existent but the "Lord of being," the "superexistent" *(das Überseiende),* defined first by his liberty* (Ex 3:14 translated as "I will be whom I will"). He is not the God of an ontology but of a "meta-ontology" (Courtine in Libera and Zum Brunn 1986; *see also* Hemmerle 1968). Lastly, Kierkegaard*'s reaction: separated from all created beings by an "infinite qualitative difference," revealed to man in the form of an "absolute paradox" (the *morphè doulou* of Jesus Christ), God ceases to be an object of thought and the confession of his mercy makes any discourse on his being unnecessary. Of these currents, Kierkegaard was the first to be accepted by contemporary theology, in which he presided over "dialectical" thought, the thought "of the crisis," organized by Barth* and his followers. Probably derived from R. Otto (*Das Heilige,* 1917; but already in the *valde, valde aliud* of Augustine, *Confessions* VII. x), the idea of a God "wholly other" (*das ganz Andere; see Römerbrief,* 1921) recapitulates an old hyperbolic affirmation of divine transcendence, that of God as "nothingness*." Barth later modified it (as early as the studies of Anselm* published in 1931) with more positive statements. A constant remained, however, which was the concern to prohibit theology from containing a discourse on God made up of philosophical or ontological elements; and Exodus 3:14 was therefore subjected to a disontological exegesis that read it as a revelation of God's faithfulness.

But the strongest critiques of ontological language were to come from within philosophy. Devoted to raising a question—the question of the "meaning of being"—that the metaphysical tradition was said to have forgotten, Heidegger's enterprise led him to postulate: 1) that metaphysics had neglected being to interest itself in the idea of supreme existent (and had granted to God this status of supreme existent); and 2) that the God who had come into philosophy, as guarantor of the "onto-theological constitution of metaphysics," was ipso facto a God sentenced to death. Even though he says why the "God of the philosophers" is dead, Heidegger nevertheless does not suggest another way of speaking of God, and limits himself to asserting the absolute heterogeneity of language about being versus language about God: "Being and God are not identical, and I would never attempt to think of the essence of God by means of being.... If I were still obliged to set out a theology in writing—which I am sometimes inclined to do—then the term *being* could not possibly ever enter into it. Faith has no need of the thought of being. When faith relies on it, it is no longer faith" (*Poésie* 13, 60–61). Theological consequences inevitably followed. A theological interest in God, for example, led to the assertion (Marion in Bourg, et al. 1986) that making being the first name of God condemned God, "in every form of metaphysics, to submit himself to the new demands imposed on him by philosophy." And if it is thus necessary to think of God "without being," or (Levinas 1982) of a God "not contaminated by being," the critique of onto-theological idols can then assume its positive face in a theory of divine names for which the Good (charity, agape) possesses absolute primacy (Marion 1982). Exodus 3:14 must then be given an apophatic reading, and the naming of God finds its canon in 1 John 4:7 and parallel passages, the duty to think of God as *actus parus amandi or caritas ipsa subsistens.*

Other tendencies exist. The Neoplatonic conception of a Principle of existents which itself does not have to be is not dead, whether it leaves open the possibility of an affirmation of God (e.g., I. Leclerc, *RelSt* 20, 63–78; *see* S. Breton, *Du principe,* Paris, 1971) or combines the influence of Plotinus with that of Meinong to think of an Absolute that perhaps does not exist (Findley 1982). It is just in regard to divine being that, defended by the thesis "Being that is only spirit is being that is only being" (Bruaire 1983), the recent posterity of Hegel inquires about the meaning of being. Having learned from Heidegger that God is not an existent, but wishing to maintain a theological usage of the lexicon of being, we may also speak of God as "sanctity of being," *holy Being* (J. Macquarrie, *Principles of Christian Theology,* London, 1977). For Tillich, God appears as *Being-itself* (*Systematic Theology* 1, 264–65), and this is so in order to provide theology with its only nonsymbolic assertion. It is finally a characteristic of recent scholarship that Protestant theology has begun to exorcise its fear of being and to acknowledge the ontological implications of Christian discourse (Dalferth 1984).

The 20th century has also witnessed a notable renewal of the Thomist metaphysics of *esse.* Indeed, it was Gilson who coined the expression "metaphysics of Exodus" to designate the ontological interpretation of Exodus 3:14. In response to Heidegger's hypothesis of a metaphysical "forgetting" of being, German interpreters of Thomas (Siewerth 1959; Lotz 1975; et al.) have asserted that the God of Aquinas is not the sovereign existent of onto-theology (a point conceded also finally by J.-L. Marion, *RThom* 95, 31–66), and that the onto-theological constitution of metaphysics perhaps also grew out of a forgetting of *esse.* At the same time, interpretation attempted to grasp once again the Thomist doctrine of analogy*, which had long been obscured by the distortions of Cajetan (Montagnes 1963). Despite the repercussions of Barth's protestations (*KD* I/1, VIII, 40, 138, 178–80), in which he attacks *analogia entis* as the pure and simple invention of the Antichrist, asserting rather that Creator and created being can enter into a relationship of analogy only in the eyes of faith *(analogia fidei),* the Przywara's meditation on analogy has certainly provided conceptual tools for thinking about the transcendence of God (*see* the canon of Lateran* IV that Przywara has set at the center of his investigation: "Between Creator and created being, we may not make note of a likeness without at the same time noting an even greater unlikeness" [*DS* 806]).

Let us lastly mention that the recent Jewish translations and readings of Exodus 3:14 (H. Cohen, the revelation of "the being who is an I"; F. Rosenzweig, revelation of the name as promise* to be there with the people*; M. Buber, a God who promises his presence and whom it is not necessary to evoke as one evokes the gods of Egypt) have had some effect on Christian writers who no longer read the Old Testament in the Septuagint and one of whose principal concerns is to substitute historical for metaphysical categories. Although the *nomen substantiae* has recently been vigorously debated—and the debate remains open—it is certainly the *nomen misericordiae* that has received the most attention.

• M. Wundt (1939), *Die deutsche Schulmetaphysik des 17. Jahrhunderts,* Tübingen.

M. Heidegger (1957), "Die onto-theo-logische Verfassung der Metaphysik," in *Identität und Differenz,* Pfullingen, 31–67.

G. Siewerth (1959), *Das Schicksal der Metaphysik von Thomas zu Heidegger,* Einsiedeln.

B. Montagnes (1963), *La doctrine de l'analogie de l'être d'après saint Thomas d'Aquin,* Louvain-Paris.

K. Hemmerle (1968), *Gott und das Denken nach Schellings Spätphilosophie,* Freiburg-Basel-Vienna.

É. zum Brunn (1969), "La ph. chrétienne et l'exégèse d'Ex 3, 14 selon É. Gilson", *RThPh* 94–105.

J. Whittaker (1971), *God Time Being,* Oslo.

W. Beierwaltes (1972), "*Deus est esse—Esse est Deus:* Die onto-theologische Grundfrage als aristotelisch-neuplatonische Denkstruktur," in *Platonismus und Idealismus,* Frankfurt, 4–82.

J.B. Lotz (1975), *Martin Heidegger und Thomas von Aquin,* Pfullingen.

Coll. (1978), *Dieu et l'être: Exégèses d'Exode 3, 14 et de Coran 20, 11–24,* Paris.

A. Chapelle (1979–80), "Dieu dans l'histoire," course notes; School Saint-Jean-Berchmans, Namur.

M. Couratier (Ed.) (1980), *Étienne Gilson et nous,* Paris, 80–92 (P. Aubenque), 103–16 (J.-F. Courtine), 117–22 (P. Hadot).

J.N. Findlay (1982), "The Impersonality of God," in F. Sontag, M.D. Bryant (Ed.), *God: The Contemporary Discussion,* New York, 181–96.

E. Levinas (1982), *De Dieu qui vient à l'idée,* Paris.

J.-L. Marion (1982), *Dieu sans l'être,* Paris.

C. Bruaire (1983), *L'être et l'esprit,* Paris.

É. Gilson (1983), "L'être et Dieu" (169–230) and "Yahweh et les grammairiens" (231–53), *Constantes phil. de l'être,* Paris.

I.U. Dalferth (1984), *Existenz Gottes und christlicher Glaube: Skizzen zu einer eschatologischen Ontologie,* BEvTh 93.

A. de Libera (1984), *Introduction à la mystique rhénane,* Paris.

U.G. Leinsle (1985), *Das Ding und die Methode: Methodische Konstitution und Gegenstand der frühen protestantischen Metaphysik,* Augsburg.

A. de Libera, É. zum Brunn (Ed.) (1986), *Celui qui est: Interprétations juives et chrétiennes d'Exode 3, 14,* Paris.

D. Bourg, et al. (1986), *L'être et Dieu,* CFi 138.

J.-F. Courtine (1990), *Suarez et le système de la mét.,* Paris.

L. Honnefelder (1990), Scientia transcendens: *Die formale Bestimmung der Seiendheit und Realität in der Metaphysik des Mittelalters und der Neuzeit (Duns Scotus–Suarez–Wolff–Peirce),* Hamburg.

S. T. Bonino, et al. (1995), *RThom* 95, 5–192 (articles on Thomas Aquinas, Heidegger, and metaphysics).

c) Eucharistic Conversion. "This is my body, this is my blood": The theology of the words of the Eucharist spoken over the bread and wine necessarily called upon concepts charged with naming the process during which what was bread and wine becomes the body and blood of Christ. After long being satisfied with saying that bread and wine "become" the body and blood of Christ (Irenaeus*, *Adv. Haer.* V. 2. 3), Greek patristics proposed a long list of verbs, all of which expressed the notion of change without presenting any real conceptual differences between them (Betz 1957): *metaballein* (Clement of Alexandria, *Exc. ex Theod.* 82 [GCS III, 132, 12]; Pseudo-Cyril of Jerusalem, *Cat. myst.* 4, 2; 5, 7 [SC 126, 136, and 154]; Theodore of Mopsuestia, *Fragment on Matthew 26:26* [PG 66: 713]; Theodoret, *Eranistes* dial. I [PG 83: 53, 57]; liturgy of Saint John Chrysostom*); *metapoiein* (Gregory of Nyssa, *Or. cat.* 37, 3 [Strawley, 143, 149]; Theodore of Mopsuestia, *Fragment on 1 Corinthians 10:3 f.* [Staab, 186]; Cyril* of Alexandria, *Fragment on Matthew 26:26* [TU 61: 255]); John of Damascus, *De fide orth.* 4, 13, [PG 94, 114]; *methistanai* (Gregory of Nyssa, *Or. cat.* 37, 2 [Strawley, 147], Cyril of Alexandria, *Fragment on Matthew 26:26* [TU 61: 255]); *metarrhuthmizein* (John Chrysostom, *Hom. de prod. Judae* 1, 6 [PG 49: 380]); *metaskeuazein* (John Chrysostom, *In Matthias Hom.* 82, 5 [PG 55:744]; John of Damascus, *Vita Barlaam* [PG 96: 1032]); *metastoikheioun* (Gregory of Nyssa, *Or. cat.* 37. 3 [Strawley, 152]); and *metaplassein* (Cyril of Alexandria, *Fragment on Matthew 26:26* [TU 61: 255]). Ambrose*, the principal Latin exponent of a theology of eucharistic conversion, used a fairly rich vocabulary, in which *mutare, convertere,* and *transfigurare* named the event of the Eucharist (*mutare: Sacr.* 5. 4. 15, 16, 17; 6. 1. 3; *Myst.* 9. 50, 52; *convertere: Sacr.* 4. 5. 23; 6. 1. 3; *transfigurare: De Fide* IV. 10. 124; *De incarn.* 4. 23). To name the eucharistic conversion is not to theorize it, and the terms employed bear little conceptual weight. And when they wanted to integrate the Eucharist into a larger theological framework, the Fathers frequently set up an analogy between the Eucharist and the Incarnation* (already in Justin, *Apol.* I. 66. 2 and in Irenaeus), the birth of what would become the doctrine of *impanation* (Betz: "sacramental incarnation").

As they were seeking to name the event of the Eucharist, the Fathers were simultaneously seeking to name the relationship that the bread and wine of the Eucharist maintained with the glorified Christ sitting at the right hand of the Father. In the *Eucologue* of Serapion, the bread and wine are the *homoiôma* of the body and blood of Christ (Funk II, 174, 10–24); in the *Dialogus de recta in Deum fide* (c. 300), Adamantius speaks of *eikones;* in Theodore of Mopsuestia, the categories are those of "image" and "symbol" (*Hom. cat* 16. 30; Tonneau-Devreesse 581–83); while in Pseudo-Dionysius, the mystical participation in Christ in the Eucharist takes place in the order of meaning (*sèmainetai kai metekhetai,* PG 3: 447C). *Tupos* and *antitupos* were frequently used. From Tertullian* on, the Latin Fathers frequently relied on the vocabulary of *figura* to deal with the question: Gaudencius of Brescia saw in the Eucharist an "image," *imago,* of the Passion* of Christ; and in Augustine, *signum* and *similitudo* are the most frequent terms. But this lexicon is intelligible only if it is interpreted within the framework of an *epistemè* in which the symbol really participates in what is symbolized and the image participates in the reality of what it represents. The language of conversion ("metabolic" language) and "symbolic" language do not at all challenge one another.

However, once Ratramne (†868) decided to contrast *in figura* and *in veritate,* the balance between symbolism and metabolism was destroyed; and in the two debates on the Eucharist in the Latin Middle Ages, from the refutation of Ratramne to that of Bérenger (†1088) and beyond, a new lexicon was to appear and become predominant, that of *substance.* The concepts later used by Scholasticism were already present in Lanfranc, probably the first theologian to investigate the Eucharist using a primarily ontological approach: substance, essence, conversion (PL 150: 430B). Guitmond of Aversa spoke of "substantial transmutation," *substantialiter transmutari* (PL 149: 1467B, 1481B). In 1140–42, the author of the *Sentences of Roland* coined the neologism *transubstantiation,* which was accepted by the Church in 1215 at the Fourth Lateran Council (*COD* 230, 35–37).

It was during the unionist debates of the 13th century that *metousiôsis* got the technical meaning of a Greek equivalent for *transsubstantiatio.* It was not until the confession of faith of Dositheus of Jerusalem (1672) that it became commonly used in an Orthodox theology that was then broadly Latinized (modern and contemporary Orthodoxy*). But it played only a marginal role (reactions provoked by the confession of faith of Cyril Lukaris) in discussions of the Eucharist arising out of the Reformation.

It was before the appearance of Aristotle's *Physics* and *Metaphysics* on the Western intellectual stage that Latin theology gave prominent status to the concepts of "substantial conversion" and "transubstantiation." And although it is true that Aristotle's philosophy of nature provided a pair of terms *(substance/accident)* to express the mystery of the bread and wine that remain phenomenally bread and wine while their deepest "being" has become the body and blood of the risen Christ, the concept of transubstantiation clearly appeared as something unthinkable within Aristotelianism. Proof that the concept of transubstantiation was not a contradiction in terms, that the thing was metaphysically possible, thus required that Thomas

Aquinas redefine accidents so that they might exist without a subject, only to be accused by the Averroist philosophers of using a monstrous notion (*see* R. Imbach, *RSPhTh* 77, 1993, 175–94). From its appearance to its development by Thomas, a term that probably at the outset said nothing more than the compounds with *meta-* of Greek patristics was thus encumbered with a large burden of description and explanation. Thomas Aquinas's theorization was not universally accepted, and the status of "eucharistic accidents" (*see* F. Jansen, *DThC* 5/2, 1368–1452, still indispensable) was a preoccupation of (Western and Catholic) theology until the 20th century, during the course of many debates in which there regularly reappeared (as with Wycliffe and Hus*, among others) an empiricist conception of the "nature" or "substance" of things that necessarily led to a eucharistic theology of *consubstantiation* (*impanation,* the substance of the bread and wine remain, after the consecration, united to the body and blood of Christ). Nor was acceptance of an ontology of nature at two levels, substantial and accidental, sufficient to impose the idea of substantial *conversion.* Hence, Duns Scotus held to a description that postulated an *adduction* of the body and blood of Christ that does not produce a new substance but a new *presence.*

In the meantime a term already used by Ambrose (*Myst.* 3. 8, CSEL 73: 91 ff.) and Gaudentius of Brescia (*Tractatus* 2. 30, CSEL 68: 31), *praesentia,* was taken up by the theologians of Saint-Victor (*see* Hugh of Saint-Victor, *De sacramentis* 11. 8. 13, PL 176:470–71, on the distinction between "corporal presence" and "spiritual presence"). Bonaventure (*In Sent. IV,* d. 12, a. 1, q. 1), and William of Auvergne (*De Sacramento Eucharistiae,* Venice, 1591), frequently used the notion of *praesentia corporalis* with reference to the Eucharist. Thomas Aquinas, on the other hand, showed some reluctance, because the idea of presence seemed to him linked to that of localization. For this reason the *praesentia in terris* of the Eucharist was not a dominant element in the Office of Corpus Christi promulgated in 1264 by the bull *Transiturus,* and was Thomas's work (Gy 1990). *Praesentia* appeared in one of the errors of Wycliffe, the condemnation of which was ratified by the Council of Constance* in 1415 (*DS* 1153).

From the 13th to the 15th century the identity of words could not conceal the shift in meanings, and the metaphysical concept of substance tended more and more to become a physical concept—a concept for which nominalist thinkers had no need. A fear of annexing the gift of the Eucharist to the sphere of worldly realities, the refusal to use superfluous entities, and the rejection of any takeover by philosophy of theology, all help to explain Luther's rejection of transubstantiation (after a first stage in which he saw it as a mere academic hypothesis, *WA*6: 456, 508; *WA* B10: 331). The *Formula of Concord* provided the official explanation of this rejection (*BSLK* 801: 5–11). Confession of belief in presence, on the other hand, remained complete (*vere et substantialiter, CA* 10, *Apol CA* 10), and Luther supplied a theory for it that had two aspects. On the one hand, he postulated that the risen Jesus can be present in the bread and wine insofar as he takes part in the ubiquity of the Word by virtue of the communication of idioms ("ubiquism"). On the other hand, recourse to the patristic model of the "eucharistic theology of incarnation" and to the Stoic model of the complete interpenetration of bodies, *velut ferrum ignitum* (*WA*6: 510), allowed him to affirm the combined gift in the sacrament* of the substance of the bread and the substance of the body and blood of Christ (*BSLK* 983: 37–44). Hence, there is both *impanation* and *consubstantiation,* although it appears that Luther never used the second term (the concept does not necessarily imply a formal negation of Catholic transubstantiation, since "substance" is not understood univocally in the two cases; *see* J. Ratzinger, *ThQ* 147 [1967], 129–58, especially p. 153).

Calvin*'s understanding is not as clear. On the one hand, he frequently used the notions of *figura, signum* (distinguished from its *res*), *imago,* and *symbolum.* But on the other hand, he saw the sign as "linked to the mysteries," *mysteriis... quodammodo annexa* (*Inst.* Iv. 17. 30), and rejected all strictly symbolic interpretation (*see* his *Petit Traicté de la Saincte Cene de Nostre Seigneur Iesus Christ* of 1541). The idea of corporal, somatic presence is rejected. But against Lutheran ubiquism is set a pneumatological hypothesis that makes it possible not to conclude from this rejection that the risen Christ is absent: "Given that the body of Jesus Christ is in heaven, and we are on this earthly pilgrimage," how can the body of Christ possibly be given in Communion? "It is through the incomprehensible virtue of his Spirit, which joins well together things separated by distance" (*Geneva Catechism* of 1542, §354). It would thence be possible to confess that, "by the secret and incomprehensible virtue of his Spirit, [Christ] nourishes us and gives us life with the substance of his body and his blood" (*Confession de foy* of 1559, §36).

Zwingli*, on the other hand, held to a strict symbolism: "believing is eating" (*SW* 3: 441), and the bread and wine perform a labor of meaning just as an inn's sign announces the wine on sale (*see* G.H. Potter, *Zwingli,* Cambridge, 1976). Anglicanism rejects the notion of transubstantiation. It confesses that "the body of Christ is given, received, and eaten at Communion, but in a celestial and spiritual manner," and its *lex orandi* prohibits the worship of the consecrated bread and wine (Article XXVIII; *see* the "Black Rubric" that concludes the "Order for the Administration of the Lord's Supper" in the Book of Common Prayer: "The bread and wine of the sacrament remain still in their very natural substances and thus may not be worshipped").

Reaffirmed at the Council of Trent* (which also used the language of presence, *DS* 1636) and considered at the time "very apt" for naming the eucharistic conversion (*DS* 1652; *see also* 1642), the concept of transubstantiation was not called into question within Catholicism* before the 20th century. Protestant doctrines experienced no significant developments during the same period, which saw above all a considerable marginalization of the practice of the Eucharist in the churches born of the Reformation (except for the Anglican Church). On the other hand, the post-Tridentine period saw sustained philosophical interest in the problem of the eucharistic conversion, in two ways: 1) With new ontologies of the thing, there were new ways of saying that the nature of things (physics) did not make the Eucharist absurd. Thus, Descartes, Malebranche, and Leibniz attempted to prove that the expression of faith in the Eucharist was not compromised by philosophies of nature in which the substance of bodies was reduced to extension (Descartes), in which only metaphysical atoms possessed reality in the last instance (Leibniz), and so on (*see* Armogathe 1977; Tilliette 1983). 2) At the very time that philosophy was supposedly separate from theology, the questions raised by the eucharistic conversion also provoked thought among philosophers. From Leibniz to Blondel*, taking in F. von Baader and Rosmini (three of whose theses were challenged after his death by the Roman magisterium* in 1887, *DS* 3229–31) along the way, the eucharistic misadventures of substance have shown that they were not limited to defying logic and metaphysics but that they had a genuine capacity to enrich thought.

Hegel (*Encyclopedia* §552) is important here for having incidentally inserted a critique of the Catholic theory of the Eucharist in the framework of a general critique of Catholicism, which he accuses of revealing its lack of inwardness when, in the host, it offers God up for worship with the external aspect of the thing *(als äußerliches Ding)*. This foreshadowed the way in which classic conceptualizations would be called into question by recent speculation, in the last debate devoted to the Eucharistic conversion. In a time when there were hardly any theologians who asserted that the eucharistic conversion was a *physical* process (but *see* F. Selvaggi, *Greg.* 30 [1949], 7–45 and 37 [1956], 16–33), after the ground-breaking work of J. de Baciocchi (1955, 1959) and in the sphere of influence of Dutch theologians (P. Schoonenberg [e.g., *Verbum* 26 (1959), 148–57, 314–27; 31 (1964), 395–415]; E. Schillebeeckx 1967), as well as of the member of the Swiss Reformed Church Leenhardt (1955), it was against any philosophy of nature and not simply Aristotelian-Thomist hylemorphism, that objections were commonly raised in the 1960s. Philosophy of nature was held to be incapable of giving a true account of the eucharistic conversion. An ontology of the thing was said to be inadequate, or to have become inadequate (Gerken 1973, bibl.; *see* W. Beinert, *ThPh,* 1971, 342–63). And in the programmatic framework of an existential ontology, a relational ontology, or an ontology of the sign, new names were proposed—"transignification," "transfinalization"—to express the newness that comes about when the bread and wine are consecrated (to complete the concept of transubstantiation, J. Monchanin had already coined the words "transituation" and "transtemporalization").

We can summarize what has been accomplished by this discussion, now finished. 1) Having made its appearance before the establishment of Scholastic Aristotelianism, the concept of transubstantiation is not necessarily destined to disappear simply because Scholastic Aristotelianism is dead. Thus it has been said that the concept contained nothing more than a "logical" explanation of the words of the sacrament taken literally (Rahner 1960); and Anscombe, a disciple of Wittgenstein, proposed her own defense of the concept (1981; *see* Cassidy 1994). 2) The fate of the concept of being is not tied to that of substance (Welte 1965; on contemporary questions linked to substance, *see* Loux 1978 and *HMO* 871–73), which was the reason Schillebeeckx proposed replacing transubstantiation with the neologism *transentatio.* Each particular ontology, on the other hand, is not equally capable of expressing the eucharistic conversion. There are realities whose being is identical to the meaning they have for human beings (money, according to Anscombe, the flag, according to Welte), but it is not certain that an ontology of the sign or an ontology of finalization, whatever their good intentions, can fully express the eucharistic conversion (*see,* e.g., the critiques of C.J. de Vogel *ZKTh* 97, 1975, 389–414; reply by Gerken, ibid., 415–29; summing up by J. Wohlmuth, ibid., 430–40). *Bread* and *wine* designate more than physical-chemical objects, but they do not designate less (*see* E. Pousset, *RSR* 54 [1966], 177–212). 3) Not very determinate when it began to be commonly used in eucharistic theology, the concept of "presence" in recent philosophy and theology has acquired determinations that have enriched its use and have preserved the idea of *real* presence from any danger of connoting a reification. In its enriched contemporary sense, presence is a mode of being of the person* in relation. (But it should perhaps be recalled that Durand de Saint-Pourçain was already speaking of the "relational presence" of Christ in the Eucharist, and that in the 19th century G. Peronne and A. Knoll gave privileged status to relation in their interpretation of the Eucharist.) Within the sphere of influence of the *Mysterienlehre,* on the other hand, the eucharistic conversion probably requires integration into a broader economy of the presence of Christ: *current* presence of salvation* in the liturgical celebration and *real* presence of the body and blood of Christ cannot be dissociated from one another (*see* Betz, *MySal* 4/2, 263–311; broad agreement in Pannenberg 1993; *see also* Lies 1997). Lastly, the clearer understanding of the link between memory and anamnesis (e.g., A. Darlap *ZKTh* 97 [1975], 80–86) makes it possible to organize a fully theological concept of presence and its specific temporality (e.g., R. Lachenschmidt, *ThPh* 44 [1966], 211–25; J.-Y. Lacoste, *Note sur le temps,* Paris, 1990), and thus to present arguments that leave no openings for Heideggerian critiques of "metaphysics" (Marion 1982).

• J. de Baciocchi (1955), "Le mystère euchar. dans les perspectives de la Bible," *NRTh* 77, 561–80.

F. J. Leenhardt (1955), *Ceci est mon corps,* Neuchâtel-Paris.

J. Betz (1957), *Die Eucharistie in der Zeit der griechischen Väter I/1: Die Aktualpräsenz der Person und des Heilswerkes Jesu im Abendmahl nach der vorephesinischen griechischen Patristik,* Freiburg.

J. de Baciocchi (1959), "Présence euchar. et transsubstantiation," *Irén.* 33, 139–64.

G. Ghysen (1959), "Présence réelle et transsubstantiation dans les définitions de l'Église catholique," *Irén.* 33, 420–35.

K. Rahner (1960), "Die Gegenwart Christi im Sakrament des Herrenmahls," *Schr. zur Th.* 4, 357–86.

M. Schmaus (Ed.) (1960), *Aktuelle Fragen zur Eucharistie,* Munich.

B. Neunhauser (1963), *Eucharistie in Mittelalter und Neuzeit, HDG* IV/4 *b.*

J. Betz (1964), *Die Eucharistie in der Zeit der griechischen Väter II/1: Die Realpräsenz des Leibes und Blutes Jesu im Abendmahl nach dem Neuen Testament,* 2nd Ed., Freiburg.

B. Welte (1965), "Zum Verständnis der Eucharistie," in *Auf der Spur des Ewigen,* Freiburg-Basel-Vienna, 459–67.

E. Schillebeeckx (1967), *Die eucharistische Gegenwart,* Düsseldorf.

A. Gerken (1973), *Theologie der Eucharistie,* Munich.

J.-R. Armogathe (1977), "Theologia Cartesiana," *L'explication physique de l'euch. chez Descartes et dom Desgabets,* The Hague.

M. J. Loux (1978), *Substance and Attributes,* Dordrecht.

G. E. M. Anscombe (1981), "On Transubstantiation," in *Collected Philosophical Papers* 3, Oxford, 107–12.

J.-L. Marion (1982), "Le présent et le don," in *Dieu sans l'être,* Paris, 225–58.

X. Tilliette (1983), "Eucharistie et philosophie," course notes, Institut catholique de Paris.

P.-M. Gy (1990), *La liturgie dans l'histoire,* Paris, studies 11 and 12, 223–83.

W. Pannenberg (1993), *Systematische Theologie* 3, Göttingen, 325–56.

N. Slencza (1993), *Realpräsenz und Ontologie: Untersuchung der ontologischen Grunlagen der Transsignifikationslehre,* Göttingen.

D. C. Cassidy (1994), "Is Transubstantiation without Substance?" *RelSt* 30, 193–99.

L. Lies (1997), "Realpräsenz bei Luther und die Lutheranern heute," *ZKTh* 119, 1–26, 181–219.

d) Being, Relation, and Communion. The reasons for theological interest in the being of relation are obvious. In fact, theology's first task was, and remains, to elucidate a relation, that between Jesus of Nazareth and the God of Israel*. The one who is called "Lord," and who thereby participates in the sphere of existence of YHWH, is also "Son" and "Servant." And when Nicaea* I defined the consubstantiality of God the Father and the Son, Christianity thereby recognized an intradivine reality in relation. Against Arianism* it was said that the engendering of the Son was not an opening of the divine onto the nondivine, but an eternal event coming to pass in God alone. And against any form of modalism* it was thus said that Father, Son, and Holy* Spirit were not only *names* designating *ways* in which God had made himself knowable, but that the divine monad contained in fact an eternal triplicity. The development of Trinitarian and later of christological dogma thus occurred through the articulation of paradoxes. To affirm the irreducibility in God of the being-Father, the being-Son, and the being-Spirit, the Cappadocian Fathers coined a formulation that was to be accepted by the entire church: the unity of essence *(ousia)* in God contains a triplicity of hypostases *(hupostaseis)* or persons *(prosôpa).* And when it was necessary to affirm the radical unity of the human and the divine in Jesus, another formulation was created, it was not as widely accepted: in the single hypostasis/Person of the Son, divine nature *(phusis)* and human nature are united. Some conclusions followed from this: 1) If, on the one hand, nothing exists in God in the mode of *accident,* and if, on the other, the being-God (the divine *substance*) is common to the Father, the Son, and the Holy Spirit, and finally, if nothing else is specific to each one but the mode in which he possesses divinity, then relation *(ad aliquid)* is indeed internal to God (Augustine, *De Trin.* IV. V. 5–6; IX. xii. 17). This led Thomas Aquinas to formulate the unprecedented concept of *subsistent relations* (*ST* Ia, q. 30, a. 2; q. 41, a. 6; *CG* IV. c. 24. 3606, 3612). The detailed construction of the paradox according to which relation is in God a *res subsistens* was the major contribution of the Latin Middle Ages to Trinitarian theology (*see* Krempel 1952, *DThC* 15, 1810 ff.; Henninger 1989). 2) And if the christological mystery is not that a divine hypostasis is united in Jesus to a human hypostasis, but that a human nature is united to divine nature in the single hypostasis of the Son, or Word, then the humanity of Christ is paradoxically an an-hypostatic, a-personal humanity, a lexicon worked out in detail by "neo-Chalcedonian" theology in the sixth century.

Decisions made by theologians and councils did not bear on the being of relation in general, but on the being of certain relations. The Latin Middle Ages, which carried out a Trinitarian glorification of the *esse ad,* also used a general ontology in which the *esse ad* was qualified only as an *esse minimum* (*see* Breton 1951). And it was in fact a definition of the person, the letter of which did not take into account the most remarkable thing that theology had to say concerning what "person" means in regard to God—namely, Boethius's definition (the person is an "individual substance with a rational nature")—which carried the most weight in what the Christian West thought concerning the person (but *see* Dussel 1967 on the theological context that shows the full meaning of the definition, and C.J. de Vogel, *ZKTh* 97 [1975], 400–414, on the real implications of a metaphysics of rational substance). What was developed under the pressure of the internal necessities of Trinitarian theology and Christology was nevertheless destined to find a broader application. Stoicism* saw in man a being of communion, *zôon koinônikon* (Chrysippus), but when patristics meditated on the bond of communion* that should prevail in the Church, it formulated the explanation in reference to Trinitarian unity (Cyprian*, CSEL 3: 285; see the eighth preface for Sundays per annum of the Roman Missal of 1969). Divine transcendence is unceasingly affirmed in Christian discourse (going as far as the extreme forms taken by the proclamation of a God who is "entirely other"), but Christian discourse also proclaims the absolute future of the human person in terms of a participation in the divine nature (divinization, *theôsis; see* 2 Pt 1:4). The Protestant tradition is alone in raising objections to this, suspecting a desire to be God in the place of God, a refusal that God be God, something that Luther sees as the secret of sinful man (*see* the *Disputatio contra scholasticam theologiam* of 1517, *WA* 1: 225, §17, and Jüngel 1980). Between God/Christ and human beings, moreover, a relation of imitation, *mimèsis,* is presented as necessary and possible as early as the writings of Paul. However modest a place is held in the Scripture by the theologumen of the creation in the *image* and *likeness* of God (*see DBS* 10: 365–403; *TRE* 6: 491–98), it is nonetheless omnipresent in patristic and later literature.

That the human modalities of being maintain a relationship of image to model with the divine and christological modalities of being, and that being-in-relation is in this connection a decisive factor, have only been clearly set out in recent theory. Certainly, from Augustine onward theological descriptions have had ternary rhythms (e.g., in Augustine, the triad of memory, intelligence, and will) that set them in a relation to the Trinitarian rhythm of divine life. The theologians of the 12th century made frequent use of this convention, and the interpretation of the creation by reference to *vestiges* of the Trinity* was impressively developed by Bonaventure and gave off its final glimmers in Nicholas* of Cusa ("every created thing...is a bearer of an image of the Trinity," *De pace fidei* VIII). Equally, since the patristic era the central place of a logic of love in Christianity conferred a key position on the interpretation of the relation to others (e.g., Gregory* the Great, PL 76: 1139), to the point that Richard of Saint-Victor attempted a construction of the Trinity following the human model of loving interpersonality. But if the human person exists as an image of God, the great majority of patristic writings, as well as the medieval theologians, saw the best evidence for this elsewhere: in the being of spirit that is specific to human beings in the midst of creation or in an incomprehensibility that human beings share with God. Neither Trinitarian relations nor the mystery of the humanity of Christ was dealt with by the different theories and practices of analogy developed from the 13th century onward. For example, Suarez had a theology of divine relations but conceived of "real created relations" (*Disp. Met.* 27) in a way that owed nothing to theology. Neoscholasticism hardened the terms, but it was certainly faithful to a general orientation. "No doubt...the cause imprints its likeness on what it produces, but if this effect is inadequate, the likeness as well is deficient; thus the created being and God do not fit univocally in any perfection; and those perfections that are analogically common to them are entirely general properties of being, among which—barring the assertion of a more or less generic resemblance between the first cause and its effect—it is not possible to include the vital exchanges that faith sees within the divine" (M.T.-L. Penido, *Le rôle de l'analogie en théologie dogmatique,* Paris, 1931). Between human person and divine Person "a minimum of (proportional) unity of meaning" is of course guaranteed. On either side the being-person is substantiality and incommunicability (ibid.). But one thesis admits of no restriction: "There is no analogy between the created personality and the 'subsistent relation' that theology discovers in God" (ibid.).

In order for this thesis to cease being self-evident, two conditions had to be fulfilled: a philosophical acceptance of Trinitarian and christological reasoning, and the appearance of an ontological vulgate in which the *esse ad* was no longer the most tenuous of entities but the fulfillment of being. 1) Hegel was certainly the first thinker to methodically allow Christology and the logic of divine life to carry out a labor of reorganization on the *logos* of ontology. *The Phenomenology of Mind* is placed under the protection of an Absolute that is conceived both in Trinitarian terms ("interplay of love with itself") and christological terms (an interplay that experiences "seriousness, patience, pain, and the work of the negative"). The system assembled in the *Encyclopedia* includes a Christology (*see* Brito 1983), and finally an anonymous Christology and triadology preside over the unfolding of the *Science of Logic.* The theological ambitions of the system were obscured by the Hegelian Left's production of a partial Hegelianism* that retained the dialectic while dismissing Absolute Spirit. Another philosophy that chose to know the absolute only by thinking of the "positive" content of its revelation, the later philosophy of Schelling, had no real influence on the theology of its time. By refusing to dissociate discourse on the One God from discourse on the Triune God, both philosophies, in any event, sounded the knell for any separation between theology and ontology. 2) The philosophical glorification of relation (which, in the end, meant barely more than interpersonal relation) took several forms. In the popular form that it assumed in philosophies of dialogue (M. Buber, F. Ebner; *see* Theunissen 1965; Böckenhoff 1970) it consisted in denying the possibility of giving an account of the human ego in terms of a substantial identity with itself ("adseity") and to situate the concrete advent of the *I* in the encounter with the *Thou.* In the cautious form it assumed in Heidegger, the determination of being-in-the-world as "being-with," *Mitsein* (*Sein und Zeit,* §25–27), is an existential determination, an a priori element of existence. In G. Marcel it was in the guise of the priority of the *we* and of communion that *Mitsein* assumed a preeminent place in Francophone philosophy. And there is a long list—the project of a "metaphysics of charity" in Laberthonnière, the *Ordo amoris* of Scheler (*GW* 10: 345–76), G. Madinier (*Conscience et amour,* Paris, 1938), D. von Hildebrand, among others—of contemporary thinkers who could have taken as their own the words of C. Secrétan describing a reign of love that would produce "the most perfect conceivable unity, the living unity of converging, intertwined wills which, reciprocally penetrating one another, mutually affirm one another and come together in a single will" (*Le principe de la morale,* Paris, 1884).

Taken on by theology, such themes could not fail to receive an exuberant welcome. 1) An ontology in which the meaning of *esse* remains unperceived as long as the *esse ad* is not thematized necessarily had an influence on ecclesiology*. As early as the *Catholicisme* of Lubac* (1938), reliance was placed on an existential ontology to think of the "social aspects of the dogma." On the one hand, the Church appeared to be the location of fully "personal" existence; on the other, "the supreme flourishing of the personality... in the Being of which every being is a reflection" (op. cit., 256) was called on to illuminate the "personal" meaning of belonging to the Church. The *newness* out of which Christian experience claims to live could then be thought of as the gift of an ecclesial mode of existence (or "ecclesial hypostasis") that a phenomenology of the eucharistic celebration had the task of describing (Zizioulas 1985). The pairing "visible" and "invisible," or "empirical Church" and "essential Church" (Bonhoeffer*), thereby ceased to govern interpretation. The essential in fact (the definitive, the eschatological) is really given within the empirical Church in the liturgical acts where its total identity is manifested, but the essential (a fully ecclesial and a fully personal existence) has a presence in the mode of anticipation, in the mode of a meaning that takes possession of the present on the basis of an absolute future (Zizioulas). Being thus ceases to manifest its meaning only in the order of the factual; the being of fact is determined by the being of vocation (Lacoste 1994). 2) A redistribution of reasons then occurred, in which the concept of person has presided over a back-and-forth between anthropology and Trinitarian theology. On the one hand, a concept of person refined by intersubjective experience has served to project onto the mystery of God an insight acquired by the work of philosophical anthropology (e.g., Brunner 1976), and this has restored currency to the question of anthropomorphism* (*see* Jüngel 1990). On the other hand, notions developed to express divine life have been called on to serve (half descriptively, half prescriptively) to express the being of man. In hyperbolic formulations, J. Monchanin (1895–1957; fragmentary work scattered in *De l'esthétique à la mystique,* Paris, 1957; *Mystique de l'Inde, Mystère chrétien,* Paris, 1974; *Théologie et spiritualité missionnaire,* Paris 1985), for example, writes that "we have to live in circumincession with our brothers" (*TSM,* 37). Indeed: "There is...a profound analogy between human person and divine Person, *subsistent* relations.... Both are *esse alterius....* Is this analogy not required by the creation of man *ad imaginem Dei?* What is deepest in him, the personality, cannot be *essentially* other in him than in God" (*TSM,* 55). 3) This intellectual climate thus made possible the program of a "Trinitarian ontology." To the observation that "never in the history of Christianity did Christian specificity *(das unterscheidend Christ-*

liche) determine newly in a durable way the precomprehension of the meaning of being and the point of departure of ontology" (Hemmerle 1976), the reply was given that "if love is what remains, then the emphasis shifts from the same to the other, then it is movement... then it is relation that occupy the center" (ibid., 38). It has also been asserted that "communion constitutes life. Existence is an event of communion. The 'cause' of existence and the 'source' of life are not being in itself... it is the divine Trinitarian communion that personalizes being as an event of life" (C. Yannaras, *La liberté de la morale,* Geneva, 1982). The ecclesiology of communion is also fulfilled here: "If by nature the being of God is relational... should we not then conclude, almost inevitably, that given the final character of the being of God for every ontology, substance, insofar as it indicates the final character of being, can be conceived only as communion?" (Zizioulas 1985; *see* Lossky already in 1967).

The *imago Trinitatis* is consequently not only the secret of the human person, but purely and simply the secret of being, an argument defended in investigations begun by T. Haecker, followed by C. Kaliba (1952) (a student of Heidegger influenced by Siewerth), and including H.E. Hengstenberg (1940) (to whom we owe the formulation "Trinitarian metaphysics"). With Balthasar (1983) the theme is integrated into the general history of Christian concepts (summary in Oeing-Hanhoff 1984). H. Beck has provided the leitmotif for these investigations: "If every finite existent is a divine creation, and if this creation necessarily bears a resemblance to and a participation in its creator, then every existent is an image of the Trinity: *analogia entis ultimatim est analogia trinitatis*" (*SJP* 25, 1980). It was also in the divine life—the Trinitarian life of absolute spirit—that C. Bruaire (1983), on the basis of a new reading of Hegel, saw the unfolding of a logic of the gift that revealed all the secrets of being ("ontodology"). 4) While remaining at a distance from these discussions and programs, Protestant theology has not, however, been entirely absent from them. Long suspicious of the lexicon of being, it has recently learned again how to use it. In the work of Ebeling (1979), it is indeed in the framework of an ontology of relation, and in order to provide a theological contribution to ontology, that theological anthropology thinks of the being-before-God, the "*coram* relation." In Jüngel, the eschatological existence that the new man lives in faith is a mode of *being,* in the strict sense, and man is *ontologically* determined by the relation that makes him "hearer of a word* that essentially constitutes him" (1980). With entirely different philosophical tools, Dalferth works toward the same juncture of the reasons of being and the reasons of the *eschaton* (1984). Much less dominated by the pathos of absolute otherness than were his early works, Barth's *Dogmatik* already proposed more than one link between Trinitarian theology, Christology, and theological anthropology (*see,* e.g., Jüngel, *Barth-Studien,* ÖTh 9, 127–79, 210–45; *see also* Torrance 1996). And despite all its vagueness, the theory of the *new Being* proposed by Tillich (*Systematic Theology* 2: 78–96, 118–36, 165–80; 3: 138–60) in its way performed a similar service. A Catholicism that conceives of the relations between theology and philosophy more subtly, a Protestantism that is no longer afraid of philosophy, and an Orthodoxy* working toward the marriage of patristic thought with some modern themes—the three branches of Christianity now seem to be treating as a common task the development of a theological ontology.

• T. Haecker (1934), *Schöpfer und Schöpfung,* Leipzig.

H.E. Hengstenberg (1940), *Das Band zwischen Gott und Schöpfung,* Regensburg.

S. Breton (1951), *L'esse* in *et l'esse* ad *dans la mét. de la rel.,* Rome.

C. Kaliba (1952), *Die Welt als Gleichnis des dreieinigen Gottes,* Salzburg (2nd Ed., Frankfurt, 1991).

P. Hünermann (1962), *Trinitarische Anthropologie bei F.A. Staudenmaier,* Freiburg.

A. Krempel (1962), *La doctrine de la rel. chez saint Thomas d'Aquin,* Paris.

M. Theunissen (1965), *Der Andere: Studien zur Sozialontologie der Gegenwart,* Berlin-New York (2nd Ed. 1977).

E. Dussel (1967), "La doctrina de la persona en Boecio: Solución cristológica," *Sapientia* 22, 101–26.

V. Lossky (1967), "La notion théol. de personne humaine," in *A l'image et à la ressemblance de Dieu,* Paris, 109–21.

J. Böckenhoff (1970), *Die Begegnungsphilosophie,* Freiburg.

G. Siewerth (1975), "Das Sein als Gleichnis Gottes," in *Sein und Wahrheit,* Düsseldorf, 651–85.

A. Brunner (1976), *Dreifaltigkeit: Personale Zugänge zum Geheimnis,* Einsiedeln.

K. Hemmerle (1976), *Thesen zu einer trinitarischen Ontologie,* Einsiedeln.

G. Ebeling (1979), *Dogmatik des christlichen Glaubens* 1, 334–55, 376–414.

E. Jüngel (1980), "Der Gott entsprechende Mensch: Bemerkungen zur Gottebenbildlichkeit des Menschen als Grundfigur theologischer Anthropologie," in *Entsprechungen,* BevTh 88, 290–317.

H.U. von Balthasar (1983), "Welt aus Trinität," *Theodramatik* IV, 53–95.

E. Brito (1983), *La christologie de Hegel,* Paris.

C. Bruaire (1983), *L'être et l'esprit,* Paris.

I.U. Dalferth (1984), *Existenz Gottes und christlicher Glaube,* BevTh 93.

L. Oeing-Hanhoff (1984), "Trinitarische Ontologie und Metaphysik der Person," in W. Breuning (Ed.), *Trinität: Aktuelle Perspektiven der Theologie,* Freiburg-Basel-Vienna, 143–82.

J.D. Zizioulas (1985), *Being As Communion,* Crestwood, N.Y.

E. Salmann (1986), *Neuzeit und Offenbarung: Studien zur trinitarischer Analogik des Christentums,* Rome.

M. Henninger (1989), *Relations: Medieval Theories 1250–1325,* Oxford.

E. Jüngel (1990), "Anthropomorphismus als Grundproblem

neuzeitlicher Hermeneutik," in *Wertlose Wahrheit,* BevTh 107, 110–31.
J. Splett (1990), *Leben als Mit-sein: Vom trinitarisch Menschlichen,* Frankfurt.
P. Schulthess (1991), "Relation," I, "History," *HMO,* 776–79.
M. Erler, et al. (1992), "Relation," *HWP* 8, 578–611.
J.-Y. Lacoste (1994), *Expérience et Absolu,* Paris.
J. Splett (1996), "Ich und Wir-Philosophisches zu Person und Beziehung," *Katholische Bildung,* 97, 444–55.
A. J. Torrance (1996), *Persons in Communion: Trinitarian Description and Human Participation,* Edinburgh.

JEAN-YVES LACOSTE

See also **Aristotelianism, Christian; Communion; Eucharist; Nothingness; Philosophy; Platonism, Christian; Theology**

Bellarmine, Robert

1542–1621

a) Life. Francesco Roberto Bellarmino was born in Montepulciano, and was the nephew of Cardinal Cervini, who chaired the Council* of Trent* during several sessions and reigned as pope, under the name of Marcellus II, for a few weeks in 1555. The young Bellarmine joined the Society of Jesus in 1560, and after his studies at the Roman College he was entrusted with the charge of various commissions in Italy, where he revealed his talents as a poet and a preacher. Delegated to Louvain in the spring of 1569 in order to preach against the Protestants, he started there with the teaching of theology*.

It was the beginning of a long teaching career, with an inclination toward controversy. In fact, it was for teaching controversial matters to the English and German students that the fourth general of the Jesuits, Everard Mercurian, called him back to the Roman College in 1576. These controversial courses were published under the title *Disputationes de controversiis christianae fidei* in Ingolstadt in 1586–93 and in Venice in 1596. In 1589–90 Bellarmine accompanied Cardinal Henri Cajetan in France as theological counselor. He was appointed rector of the Roman College in 1592, and became the theologian of Clement VIII (1592–1605), who made him cardinal in 1599.

After a brief interval as archbishop of Capua (1602–5), Bellarmine came back for good to Rome*, where he was asked to conduct some complex and dangerous affairs for the papacy. They included an "Interdict" ruled by Paul V in 1606 against Venice, following some detrimental measures it had just taken against the church and the clergy; affairs regarding England in 1607–9 because of the oath imposed by King James I on all Catholics; the Gallican controversies of 1610–12, including the anonymous publication in 1609 of the *De potestate papae* by William Barclay; and Bellarmine's reply, in 1610, with the *De potestate summi pontificis in rebus temporalibus* (*see* Gallicanism*). Bellarmine's functions at the Holy Office and his intellectual curiosity made him the privileged discussion partner of Galileo, who dedicated to him his discourse on floating objects (August 1612) and to whom he had to announce the condemnation of 1616.

In his late years, Bellarmine devoted himself to commentary on the Psalms*, *In omnes psalmos dilucida expositio* (Rome, 1611), and to the composition of treatises on piety, among which the most famous is the *De ascensione mentis in Deum* (Rome, 1615). He died almost an octogenarian in 1621. His posthumous fortunes are linked to the history of the Society of Jesus. The matter of his beatification, which started as early as 1627, was stopped and relaunched several times and did not come to a successful end until the 20th century (1923; canonization, 1930).

b) Works. The works of Bellarmine are surrounded by controversy, and so are closely associated to the circumstances of his life and to the needs of the church* at that time: among other things, Bellarmine was connected to the condemnation of Giordano Bruno in 1600 and to the trial of Thomas Campanella in 1603. Bellarmine's works revolve around two main areas: biblical criticism and ecclesiology*—along with the political philosophy* that is closely related to it. In the internal quarrels on grace* Bellarmine's attitude was always moderate, both in Louvain with Baius and his disciples and in Rome, where in 1602 he dissuaded Clement VIII from engaging his authority in this matter (Bañezianism*). While the Society of Jesus endeavored to support the middle-course position of Luis de Molina's *Concordia* (1588), Bellarmine remained in the background, and he even had to intervene in 1614 to moderate the positions of his former student Leonard Lessius (1554–1623). The particular nature of Bellarmine's task often allowed him to propose compromises, when facing Protestant theologians, and a middle-of-the-road approach concerning the questions being disputed.

Regarding the sources of revelation*, in his *Controversia* (1590), Bellarmine underscores that the Word* of God* may be written or nonwritten. The first three of the work's four volumes are on *The Written Word of God.* Volume I covers the list of the canonical books, volume II examines the different versions and translations, and volume III is concerned with the elements of interpretation. With regard to biblical inspiration, Bellarmine opts for a position in favor of a simple *assistance* from the Holy* Spirit, and not for a direct and permanent *inspiration* of the Scriptures*. Bellarmine holds that God did not reveal himself in the Scriptures only, but also in traditions*. He then proceeds to carefully sort out divine, apostolic, and ecclesiastical traditions and those traditions touching on faith* and customs. Making distinctions among the traditions allows a better understanding of the criteria of validity and the degrees of authority* that come into play. Borrowing certain points from Augustine*'s treaty *De Doctrina Christiana,* Bellarmine establishes rules for a better distinction between the false traditions, which are to be discarded, and traditions that are really necessary for Revelation (*Controversia,* vol. IV, *The Unwritten Word of God*). As for the meanings of passages, Bellarmine asserts quite strongly that the judge of the Scriptures is the church.

The other point discussed is that of political power and of its relation to ecclesiastical power, in particular with the pope*'s (3a *Controversia, De summo pontifice*). Facing the Venetian, Anglican, and Gallican theologians, Bellarmine resorts to a fundamental political analysis: no civil authority can rightly claim a divine right. Rather, political power is dependent on the right of the people, and public officials should be chosen by the majority of the people, who can therefore modify the shape of the government. Things are different, however, in the ecclesiastical regime, which is divinely established like a monarchy tempered by the aristocracy (the bishops are real ministers* and princes in the particular churches*). The relationship between the two authorities rests on their respective orders. Bellarmine borrows from tradition the thesis of an indirect authority held by the Roman pontiff (which is to be understood from its object, not from its mode), that allows him to intervene in temporal affairs, not directly in their quality as temporal, but when it is relevant to save or protect spiritual interests.

Bellarmine's doctrine on the relationship between political and ecclesiastical authority is based on an ecclesiology that revealed itself to be a determining factor in two ways. He defined the church as a *societas juridice perfecta,* a juridically complete society* (Congar), since it possesses indeed its own aims, members capable of reaching those aims, and an authority* that ensures the relationship that makes them into a society. The lengthy and strong analyses made by Bellarmine were not merely of capital importance to post-Tridentine ecclesiology, but they also largely influenced modern political thought, mainly with those who, opposed to Bellarmine on the question of the relation between church* and state, have attempted to transfer Bellarmine's definition of the church onto the state itself (Hobbes, primarily).

A learned exegete aware of the intellectual responsibilities that fall on the shoulders of a Roman pontiff whose authority he exalted, Bellarmine showed the cautious side of his character at the beginning of Galileo's difficulties. Although in the anti-Protestant controversies he was anxious to protect the literal interpretation of the Bible, he was not an adversary of the new physics. In his letters to Federico Cesi, founder of the Academy of Lynxes, and to the Carmelite Foscarini (1615), a defender of Copernicus, he recommended proposing heliocentrism as a hypothesis *(ex suppositione)* and not in an absolute manner. The importance of his works and the positions he held make him the initiator of choice presented by the Society of Jesus, between Scholastics and "innovators," in the different realms of ecclesiology*, political philosophy*, exegesis*, and the new science.

• *Opera omnia* (1721), Venice; (1856–62), Naples; (1870–74), Paris.

Ed. and trans. until 1890; *see Sommervogel* vol. 1, col. 1151–1254; vol. 8, col. 1797–1807 then S. Tromp (1930), *De operibus S. R. B.,* Rome.

X.-M. Le Bachelet (Ed.) (1911), *Bellarmin avant son cardinalat, 1542–1598: Correspondance et documents,* Paris; (1913), *Auctarium Bellarminianum: Complément aux Œuvres du cardinal B.,* Paris.

De laicis or the Treatise on Civil Government, Tr. K.E. Murphy, New York, 1928 (New Ed., Westport, Conn., 1979).

♦ X. Le Bachelet (1903), "B.," *DThC* 2/1, 560–99.

J. de La Servière (1909), *La théologie de B.,* Paris.

J. Brodrick (1928), *The Life and Works of Blessed Robert Cardinal B.,* 2 vols., London.

X. Le Bachelet (1931), *Prédestination et grâce efficace. Con-*

troverse dans la Compagnie de Jésus au temps d'Aquaviva (1610–1613),* 2 vols., Louvain.
Y. Congar (1952), "Église et État," *Cath* 3, 1430–41 (repr. with other articles in *Sainte Église: Études et approches ecclésiologiques,* Paris, 1963).
G. Galeota (1966), *B. contro Baio a Lovanio,* Rome; (1988), "Robert B.," *DSp* 13, 713–20.
M. Biersack (1989), *Initia Bellarminiana: Die Prädestinationslehre bei Robert B. S. J. bis zu seinen Löwener Vorlesungen, 1570–1576,* Stuttgart.
L. Ceyssens (1994), "B. et Louvain (1569–1576)," in M. Lamberigts (Ed.) *L'augustinisme à Louvain,* Louvain, 179–205.

JEAN-ROBERT ARMOGATHE

See also **Augustianism; Bañezianism-Molinism-Baianism; Church and State; Ecclesiology; Gallicanism; Pope; Society**

Benedict of Nursia. *See* **Monasticism**

Berengarius of Tours. *See* **Eucharist**

Bernard of Chartres. *See* **Chartres, School of**

Bernard of Clairvaux

1090–1153

1. Life

Born at Fontaine-lès-Dijon, Bernard was a member of the Burgundian nobility. He received his first instruction from the canons of Saint-Vorles de Châtillon. In 1113, accompanied by his brothers and a number of his friends whom he had persuaded to accompany him, he entered Cîteaux, the new monastery founded in 1098, to follow the Rule of Saint Benedict more strictly than was the case under traditional monasticism*. In 1115 he was sent out to found Clairvaux, of which he would be abbot until his death. The monastery developed very rapidly under his energetic leadership, and from

1118 on, other monastic foundations began to proliferate from it. During the first years of his abbacy Bernard enjoyed the friendship and teaching of William of Champeaux, founder of the Abbey of Saint*-Victor and latterly bishop* of Châlons-sur-Marne, and was thus able to complete his intellectual training. He also befriended another William, the Benedictine abbot of Saint-Thierry, near Reims, with whom he studied the Song of Songs and the commentary on it by Origen*. Bernard rapidly made a name for himself as a spiritual master. His written work, which he began around 1124 with the treatise *On the Degrees of Humility and Pride* and the homilies *Super missus est*, revealed from the outset a remarkable literary talent. He was to maintain this all his life with a variety of treatises, numerous liturgical sermons, the series of 86 *Sermons on the Song of Songs* (generally recognized as his masterpiece), and a correspondence of which more than 500 letters survive.

The extraordinary rise of the Cistercian order during the first half of the 12th century brought conflict with the monks of Cluny, and Bernard was forced to justify himself in the *Apology.* His desire for reform was not limited to monasticism, but extended to the life of the clergy* and the bishops, and to the church* as a whole. Bernard therefore found himself rapidly caught up in matters which were then troubling the church—in the affair of the schism* of Anacletus, he took Innocent II's side and had him recognized as the rightful pope* (1130–38)—and he was obliged to travel throughout Western Europe. In 1140, urged on by William of Saint-Thierry, he opposed Abelard* and obtained his condemnation at the Council of Sens. He intervened again in 1148 at Reims against Gilbert de la Porrée (c. 1075–1154), though the latter was not condemned. In 1145 one of his disciples was elected pope under the name Eugenius III, and Bernard continued to advise him, in particular addressing to him the five letters which compose the treatise *De consideratione* (1148–52). Eugenius III sent him to the Languedoc to preach against the Cathars. It was again at Eugenius's behest that he preached the Second Crusade, for the failure of which he was held partly to blame.

Bernard died at Clairvaux on 20 August 1153. A controversial and much-criticized figure, though highly influential, he was widely considered a saint while he was still alive (it was in such terms that William of Saint-Thierry began to write his biography between 1145 and 1148), and was canonized in 1174. The 12th century was the golden age of the Cistercians, a monastic order distinguished by numerous writers of great literary, theological, and spiritual worth, all of whom had come under Bernard's influence. We will mention here only those who, along with Bernard, have been called "the four evangelists of Cîteaux": William of Saint-Thierry (c. 1075–1148), who forsook his abbacy and the Benedictine order in 1135 to become an ordinary Cistercian monk at Signy, Guerric d'Igny (1070?–1157), and Aelred of Rievaulx (1110–67). While they had a common doctrine, each presented it with an individual style and nuance, helping to make this century an exceptionally fruitful period.

2. A Monastic Theology

"Chimera of his age," as he called himself (*Letter* 250, 4), adviser to popes, spiritual master—Bernard was all these, but was he a theologian? Since the appearance of Gilson's study (1934) this question seems to have been settled. Yet Bernard would probably have rejected the term for himself, since he uses the words *theologus* and *theologia* only with reference to Abelard and his work. While a few of his own writings, such as *Grace and Free Will, Letter* 77 on baptism, or Book V of *De consideratione* do have a clear theological content, many are devoted to monastic and spiritual instruction. It is this dual aspect of Bernard's work, however, which allows us to understand the special status of his thought. He never sets out to deal with theological questions for their own sake, but is always seeking how a meeting between humankind and God* may take place. It is very much in this context that he comes to consider the relations within the Trinity or the Word*'s union with humanity in Christ*. So in *De consideratione,* after asking himself five times in succession what God is, and replying in a variety of ways, he repeats the question and answers it thus: "What he is to himself, he alone knows" (V. 24). While he shows himself to be not insensitive to this kind of questioning, and even demonstrates some virtuosity in his handling of it, it is not his habitual register and he prefers to leave it alone. The final formula referred to above is more a nonanswer than an evocation of God's transcendence, since what interests Bernard is not the definition of the divine essence but the fact that God reveals himself as both an interlocutor with humanity and its final goal.

This fundamental tendency in Bernard's thought makes it impossible to distinguish the "theological" (speculative) element in his work from the spiritual or ascetic part. The *pro nobis* that is God's special characteristic keeps Bernard from becoming mired in speculation, and focuses his thoughts on mankind's turning—or turning back—toward God, a process that culminates in mystical and beatific union. Bernard's habitual concern is with the history* of salvation* in all its aspects. In this context he plays constantly on the twin identities of the "bride" spoken of in the Song of Songs—she is at once the Church and the individual soul*—and hence comes to see the history of salvation as the history of all humanity. Knowing is an activity of tasting for oneself what one has discovered from God. Understood in these terms, theology* involves not only anthropology* and the liturgy*, but also asceticism*, obedience, and so on. It is only authentic when put into practice, and in such a way as to bring about an increase in charity. The theologian is not, therefore, one who has studied under eminent teachers, but the one who allows himself to be taught by the Holy* Spirit itself in the course of his daily work, as Bernard wrote to Aelred of Rievaulx—in other words, he who has experienced God's goodness and can thus evoke that experience in his readers or listeners (*Letter* 523). In this way a return is possible to the early sense of *theologian,* which is to be encountered especially in monastic literature and in particular in the work of Evagrius Ponticus (c. 345–99). In order to distinguish it from the academic variety, theology of this kind is referred to as "monastic theology," by which is meant a theology based on experience* (Leclerq 1957; Gastaldelli in *Aci,* 1990, 25–63)—a practical theology encompassing the whole of existence (Hardelin 1987).

3. Teachings

a) Humility. In his first work, *The Degrees of Humility and Pride,* Bernard defines three degrees of truth*: humility, charity, and contemplation*. The primary impetus of that theology which strives after union with God is anthropological. It consists of self-knowledge: in other words, knowledge of one's own nothingness*. Man is only a creature. While he is superior to the animals, who lack reason*, he is inferior to the angels*. Above all, he has failed to maintain his original state, and that failure has estranged him both from God and from himself, placing him in a "region of difference." It is through humility that he may return to himself and achieve self-knowledge, stripping himself of everything with which pride has covered him. Humility is therefore the first degree of truth because it allows one to know what one is: nothing. "When I did not yet know the truth, I believed that I was something, while in fact I was nothing" (*Humility* IV, 15). Elsewhere Bernard emphasizes the "miracle" that is man, this being in whom opposites meet: reason* and death, nothing and something—or better, nothing and something great, since God magnifies this nothing. But even as it leads man back to himself, humility is already leading him back to God, too. Indeed, the humble man, who is only himself, renounces the possession of something unique to himself that would define him; and by abandoning all *proprium,* he opens in himself the space in which God can act. Humility leads back to the pure form in which man was created. Man is nothing (in his own right) because his being* is to be the image and likeness of God. He fulfills himself in this openness to God.

From here it can be seen what direction Bernard's Christology* will take. The Word is both that which gave man his form, in the beginning, and that which now re-forms him in the image of Jesus Christ. The Word is a constant mediator between God and man, both as an image of the divine substance and as an example of perfect humility. Bernard firmly insists upon the exemplary nature of Christ's humanity. But he points out that Christ did not come solely to offer an example to be followed (as he criticizes Abelard for saying): he is in himself the Savior. He is not merely the way and the truth, he is also the life: "Great indeed, and most necessary, is the example of humility, great and deserving of welcome is the example of charity, but neither one nor the other has any foundation, nor in consequence any solidity, if redemption is lacking. With all my strength I wish to follow the humble Jesus*; I wish to kiss him, to render love* for love to him who has loved me and given himself for me, but I must also eat the Paschal lamb" (*Against the Errors of Abelard* 25). Much has been said (admittedly largely on the basis of ill-attributed texts) of the devotion of Bernard and the Cistercians to Christ's humanity. But it has not always been noticed what lies at the root of this devotion: the restoration of the image and likeness, understood as a reformation—in other words, as a conformation to him who is the true Image. Man's salvation, from this point, proceeds by way of participation in Christ's Passion* and the cross. Following the Epistle to the Romans, Bernard sees this participation as fulfilled in baptism*, and then in monastic profession understood as a second baptism (*On Precept and Dispensation* XVII, 54).

Liturgy* plays an essential role here in that it represents the various moments of the life of Christ by means of monstration and actualization ("Just as in a sense he is sacrificed again each day when we proclaim his death, so he seems to be born again when we have visualized [*repraesentavimus*] his birth with faith"; *Sermon* 6 for the Christmas Vigil, 6); and this act of making present in turn implies imitation*. Aelred of Rievaulx would develop this theme at more length.

b) Charity. "Our Savior wished to suffer so as to be able to sympathize, to become unfortunate so as to learn to be merciful, in order that, just as it is written of him" (Heb 5:8). "So might he also learn mercy*. Not that he did not know beforehand how to be merciful, but what he had known by nature through all eternity*, he now learned within time* through experience" (*Humility* III, 6). Because it is the divine act which truly takes account of human suffering and death, the Incarnation* therefore exemplifies a charity that is the second degree of truth. Charity can be attained only under the influence of the Spirit, which purifies the will and enables mankind to persevere in its conversion*. The pinnacle of charity is the fusion of man's will with that of God—a fusion in which the reality of love is clearly manifest. The theme of the prescription of charity is central to Bernard and the other Cistercians. This is especially so for Aelred, who approaches it in his *Mirror of Charity* with the image of the "three Sabbaths*," which stand for three progressive loves: love of self, love of one's neighbor, and love of God. In his *Spiritual Friendship,* Aelred further describes the progress from friendship with one's neighbor to friendship with God.

c) Contemplation. The third degree of truth represents humanity's realization of its destiny: union with God. But is this *unitas spiritus* equivalent to the union of Father* and Son in the Trinity*? Bernard refuses to make this identification (*On the Song* 71), but William of Saint-Thierry and Aelred maintain it, and in doing so propose a daring theology of deification (sanctity, in Bernard's terms). Such an identification is possible when the Spirit "becomes in its own way, for man's relationship with God, exactly what it is, in consubstantial* unity, for the Son's relationship with the Father or for the Father's with the Son;... when in an ineffable, inconceivable manner the man of God deserves to become, not God, but what God is: man becomes by grace what God is by nature*" (William, *Letter* 263). Mystical phenomena such as ecstasy anticipate the eternal union of God and man. But the latter is already encountered in much more frequent experiences—daily even, according to Bernard—in which the individual person is visited by the Word or the Spirit. This leads Bernard (followed by Guerric d'Igny and Aelred) to posit an intermediate advent of Christ between his coming in the flesh and his coming in glory*. This second advent consists of the indwelling of the Trinity* in man, and is more beneficial than the first advent since, according to Bernard, Christians should not restrict themselves to contemplating Christ's humanity, but go beyond knowledge* "according to the flesh*," which is normally the preserve of the novice. This striving toward something beyond Christ's flesh is expressed by the recurring quotation in Lamentations 4:20, "Under his shadow we shall live among the nations," where "shadow" denotes the incarnation. Christ's flesh thus has a didactic value to those who are still "carnal" or children (*On the Song* 20, 6–7; William, *Oration* X), who recognize in it the nearness of God and who rely on it to convert their desire. So Bernard and William, but above all Aelred, do not hesitate to put imagination into the service of meditation.

It should be added that the three degrees of truth are implicated in one, and in particular that the exercise of charity is already a union with God and may be presented as an anticipation of eschatology. This would at least be so in the case of William and Aelred, although rather than anticipation, for them, it is more a matter of a temporality governed by what Gregory* of Nyssa termed *epektasis,* an infinite progression toward union with God. Moreover, the practical and the contemplative life are intimately connected, and for this reason the principle of union is man's conformation to Christ ("I am united when I am conformed"; *On the Song* 71). Bernard's mysticism* is inseparably sponsal and communitarian.

d) A Theological Esthetic. The idea of form is central to Bernard, and by extension it is able to express the central tenets of Cistercian thought: humanity being alienated from God in the land of unlikeness (deformation), redemption (reformation), and the life of conversion (conformation) that leads to union with God. At the heart of this process is the notion of Christ as the creating and re-creating Form. The same category, furthermore, serves to express the truth of everything that is, in other words the appropriateness of each thing to its form, and hence the beauty* *(formositas, species)* of each thing. Bernard rails against "the deformed beauty and beautiful deformity" *(deformis formositas ac formosa deformitas)* of the sculptures in some cloisters (*Apology* XII, 29); and the austerity of Cistercian architecture* was an attempt to convey only the purity of form. Everything that obscures form distances us from truth and similarly from beauty. In general terms, "he is wise for whom things have the taste of what they are" (*Miscellaneous Sermons* 18, 1). The concept of form also guides the whole quest for simplicity characteristic of the monastic and Cistercian ideal, and leads Bernard and his disciples to talk of the beauty of the saints. Only humility transforms the individual being into a theophany*.

e) Mariology. While Bernard has the reputation of being a "Marian doctor," he owes this largely to texts that have been wrongly attributed to him. He is in any case against the doctrine of the Immaculate Conception of the Virgin (*Letter* 174), and says nothing on the subject of her bodily assumption (Amadeus of Lausanne [c. 1110–59] and Aelred were the first two Cistercians to maintain the latter doctrine). But while he talks less about Mary* than others do, he remains nonetheless one of her most inspired eulogists.

f) Sources. Bernard's main source, and that of his disciples, is Scripture*. All their works are steeped in it. To Scripture are added the Latin Fathers*, especially Augustine* and Gregory* the Great. The influence of the Greek Fathers remains controversial except for that of Origen, which is undisputed. Ancient monastic literature, such as Cassian, the *Vitae Patrum* and so on, represents another important source.

• Aelred de Rievaulx, *Opera ascetica,* Ed. A. Hoste, C.H. Talbot, CChr.CM I, 1971 (*Le "Aelred de Rievaulx," Miroir de la charité,* Bégrolles-en-Mauges, 1992; *L'Amitié spirituelle,* Bégrolles-en-Mauges, 1994; *Sermones I-XLVI,* Ed. G. Raciti, CChr.CM IIA, 1989; *Sermones inediti,* Ed. C.H. Talbot, Rome, 1952.
Bernard of Clairvaux, *Sancti Bernardi Opera,* Ed. J. Leclercq, H. Rochais, C.H. Talbot, Rome, 1957–77 (complete works in publication, SC).
Guerric d'Igny, *Sermons,* SC 166 and 202.
Guillaume de Saint-Thierry, *La contemplation de Dieu,* SC 61; *Lettre aux Frères du Mont-Dieu,* SC 223; Guillaume de Saint-Thierry, *Le miroir de la foi,* SC 301; *Oraisons méditatives,* SC 324.
♦ É. Gilson (1934), *La Théologie mystique de saint Bernard,* Paris; (1953), *Saint Bernard théologien, ASOC* 9.
J. Leclercq (1957), *L'Amour des lettres et le désir de Dieu,* Paris; (1963–92), *Recueil d'études sur saint Bernard et le textes de ses écrits,* 5 vols., Rome.
A. Altermatt (1977), "*Christus pro nobis:* Die Christologie Bernhards von Clairvaux in den 'sermones per annum,'" *Aci* 33, 3–176.
A. Härdelin (1987), "Monastische Theologie: Eine 'praktische' Theologie vor der Scholastik," *ZKTh* 109, 400–415.
Coll. (1990), *La dottrina della vita spirituale nelle opere di San Bernardo di Clairvaux, Aci* 46.
P. Verdeyen (1990), *La Théologie mystique de Guillaume de Saint-Thierry,* Paris.
J.R. Sommerfeldt (Ed.) (1991), *Bernardus magister,* Kalamazoo-Cîteaux, SD 42.
Coll. (1992), *Bernard de Clairvaux: Histoire, mentalités et spiritualité,* SC 380.
R. Brague (Ed.) (1993), *Saint Bernard et la philosophie,* Paris.
Coll. (1993), *S. Aelred de Rievaulx: Le Miroir de la charité, CCist 55,* 1–256.
C. Stergal (1998), *Bernard de Clairvaux: Intelligence et amour,* Paris.

PHILIPPE NOUZILLE

See also **Abelard, Peter; Beauty; Love; Mary; Monasticism; Mysticism**

Bernard Sylvester. *See* **Chartres, School of**

Bérulle, Pierre de

1575–1629

a) Life. Pierre de Bérulle was born on 4 February 1575 at the castle of Sérilly, in the province of Champagne, to a family that belonged to the *noblesse de robe* owing to its role in the magistracy. He received his early schooling at the *collège* of Boncourt, then at the *collège* of Bourgogne, and finally, from 1590 on, with the Jesuits at the *collège* of Clermont. When he returned to his mother's home he came into contact with the circle of devout individuals around his cousin Marie Acarie (1566–1618), Benet of Canfield (1562–1610), Father Coton (1564–1626), Michel de Marillac (1563–1632) and Pacifique de Souzy. The following year Bérulle he gave up his law* studies and turned instead to the study of theology* at the *collège* of Clermont, then at the Sorbonne, since the Jesuits had been expelled from the kingdom. He was ordained priest* in 1599 and appointed king's chaplain. In that capacity he assisted Du Perron (1556–1618), bishop* of Évreux and future cardinal, at the Conference of Fontainebleau (4 May 1600), against the protestant Du Plessis Mornay (1549–1623), author of the *Traité sur l'Eucharistie* (1598) in which he attacked the doctrine of the real presence and identified the pope* as the Antichrist. The broad culture of the young Pierre de Bérulle made him, on that occasion, a polemicist of great value. In 1602, after showing some hesitation about joining the Society of Jesus, he devoted his energies to the reform of Catholic institutions in France. Bérulle was active in the coming to France of the Carmelites, recently reformed by Teresa of Avila (1515–82). He remained, until his death, their Father Superior and their Perpetual Visitor. By imposing on the Carmelites of Châlons (1615) a vow of servitude to Mary*, Bérulle started a violent conflict with the Carmelites, who attempted in vain to take over the government of the nuns. The spiritual renewal of France required also a profound reform of the clergy. In 1611, at the request of the bishop of Paris, Bérulle founded the Oratory of Jesus, a society of priests following the model of the Oratory of Philippe Néri (1515–95). The Oratorians put themselves at the disposal of the ordinaries (local bishops) while remaining exempt juridically. They did not take religious vows. Like the Jesuits, they took on the management of colleges more often than parishes or seminaries. Bérulle was also a diplomat. In 1619 he forced the queen mother, who had fled to Angoulême, to make peace with Louis XIII, and in 1624 he obtained from Urban VIII (1623–44) the required dispensations for the marriage* of Henrietta of France, the king's sister, to the future king of England, Charles I. Being pro-Spanish, Bérulle came into conflict with Richelieu's policy, which favored an alliance with England, and he thus fell from grace. Urban VIII made him cardinal in 1627. He died on 1 October 1629.

b) Writings. *Bref discours sur l'abnégation intérieure* (1597); *Traité des énergumènes* (1599); *Trois discours de controverses (sur la mission des pasteurs*, le sacrifice* et la présence réelle)* (1609); *Discours de l'état et de la grandeur de Jésus* (1623); *Vie de Jésus* (1629); *Élévation à Jésus-Christ Notre-Seigneur sur la conduite de son esprit et de sa grâce vers Madeleine* (1627); *Opuscules de* piété (*OP*); *Lettres.* These works were published by Bourgoing in 1644.

c) Theological Ideas. The path followed by Bérulle's thought took him from a theology of the insignificance of creatures to a christological anthropology*, via a meditation on the humanity of Jesus*. Bérulle's first work was the *Bref discours de l'abnégation intérieure.* He took inspiration from the *Breve compendio intorno a la perfezione cristiana* composed by Isabelle Bellinzaga, most probably under the guidance of the Jesuit Father Gagliardi (1538–1607). Already discernible here is one of Bérulle's fundamental notions: Christian perfection consists in driving away by means of *abnegation* the self-love that forms an obstacle to the love* of God*; and the double foundation of that abnegation is the inseparable knowledge* of God and of oneself. Consciousness of the greatness of God, a consciousness of having no existence by oneself but only according to the manner of a created being, and finally, a consciousness that the creature cannot concern itself with its Creator without admitting hyperbolically that this creature himself exists according to the manner nothingness* rather than on that of being*: all this produces abnegation and makes it the gate through which spiritual experience* must find its way. One must indeed "consent to one's origin," and human beings cannot have recollection of their creation, cannot accept what they are before God, without denying or renouncing whatever gives them the appearance of being: that is, without rooting themselves in an essential nothingness.

The theme of annihilation thus brings Bérulle close to Benet of Canfield, an Englishman converted from Anglicanism*, who had already suggested that it was by means of annihilation that human beings pass from natural to supernatural* existence. There is, undoubtedly, a difference of emphasis: with Canfield, the annihilation is effected through meditation on the suffering Christ* and through exterior actions*, whereas in Bérulle we do not as yet find the explicit reference to Christ. In any case, however, it is via Canfeld that Bérulle found a language and overtones close to the *Théologie mystique* by Harphius (1400–1477), to Ruusbroec (1393–1481), and to Alphonse de Madrid (†1535).

Proceeding from a thoroughly Augustinian acknowledgment of the nothingness of man, Bérulle next concentrated on a second annihilation, the divine kenosis* of Philippians 2:6–11. Then came the major discovery, brought about by the *Audi filia* (1574) of John of Avila (1499–1569): if the humanity of Jesus has its "subsistence" in God's Word*, this means that it does not have its subsistence in a human being*. The anhypostasis* of the humanity of Christ thus gives the example of the most radical type of abnegation, a self-denial lodged in the very core of the human being. The aim of spiritual life became then, for Bérulle, a matter of living one's "servitude" in the image of Christ the "slave," taking part in the *morphè doulou.* Received as a grace*, while at the same time being integrated into a logic of choice, servitude is both ontologically revealing and offers a pattern for actual living. Man is nothingness striving toward nothingness (Duns* Scotus). "We have nothing, if not our nothingness and our sin" (*Collationes,* Sept. 1615), and sin is "a second nothingness that is worse than the first" (*OP,* 228). Ratifying in servitude, however, what makes the creature (and a fortiori the sinning creature) a nothingness rather than a being is paradoxically the experience that allows man to remain a being; and that experience speaks the double language of a theology of Creation* and a theology of Incarnation*.

Bérulle does not approach the Incarnation by the path of imagination, but rather via the divine idea, closer to the Platonic thought of the Rhineland*-Flemish mystics. Following Gabriel Biel (1425–95), Benet of Canfield's *Rule of Perfection* (1593) defined the spiritual* life with a maxim: the will of God is God himself. Bérulle was consistent with this tradition. According to him, in fact, the possession of God happens through knowledge of his will, and knowledge of the divine will is carried out in the renunciation of self-will. Henceforth, the Incarnation, that "divine invention" whereby God has mysteriously joined the created and the uncreated, reveals the ultimate meaning of such a renunciation. The secret of this "new mystery" is, in fact, "the destitution that the humanity of Jesus* feels in renouncing its own and ordinary subsistence in order to be clad in a foreign and extraordinary subsistence... what is renounced is the divine subsistence, the actual Person of the Son" (*Grandeurs* II, X). So the logic of nothingness and abnegation is not nihilistic. On the contrary, it is the logic of a greater real intimacy between Creator and creature.

On the *motive* of Incarnation, Bérulle's Christology* fluctuates between the views of Duns Scotus and Thomas* Aquinas. The Scotist thesis stated that Incarnation would have taken place even if man had not sinned; Bérulle's early writings did in fact frequently present Christ as completion; the idea was also the underlying theme of Christ as the "true worshipper" (*OP,* 190). At the time of *Grandeurs* (1620), however, Bérulle's emphasis was on the theme "for our salvation*" (the *propter nos homines et propter nostram salutem* of the Creed of Nicaea-Constantinople), and he thus aligned himself with the Thomist position: the Incarnation is first of all considered a work of salvation*. From the Trinitarian decree of the Incarnation ("the will of God to send his Son on earth"), Bérulle's contemplation* of the mystery* of Christ went next to the "being of Jesus... who offered himself": the Christology of the Incarnation then opened out into a Christology of sacrifice*, all the more necessary since the sacrifice of the cross was already entirely present at the moment of the Incarnation (Heb 10:5). And because the sacrifice offered by Christ was indicative, to the highest degree, of him being the "monk of God," Bérulle's Christology led to a real sacerdotal anthropology, allowing the creation of a theology of priesthood that sustained for a long time the post-Tridentine clergy.

The "mysteries of Jesus" developed as a new theme. After the solemnity of Jesus (1615), Bérulle initiated a feast celebrating "Jesus among men" (1625), in which a sacred court gravitated around Christ, composed of the saints who were closest to him during his "itinerant" life: the Virgin Mary*, the Apostles*, Mary Magdalene, John the Baptist. In 1615 Bérulle drew all the possible spiritual consequences from a Chalcedonian and post-Chalcedonian Christology of the nonsubsistence of the humanity of Christ, whereas in 1625 he was primarily contemplating God made man in all the concrete relations he had entered into with humanity. From the substance of mystery, Bérulle went on to its economy. This shift gives the clearest indication of his change from a Scotist perspective to a Thomist one.

The Incarnation, therefore, inaugurates a new type of relationship with God, expressed through the servitude of Christ himself, and expressed also in an exemplary manner by Mary, who supplied Bérulle with a model. Servitude is "essential" for Bérulle because it achieves a just relationship between God and creature, between "being and nothingness"; and that is why the upholding of being can be truly real in human beings only in the "substance in Jesus" (*OP,* 226). The man Jesus, in perfect abnegation, does not subsist in himself but in the Word. Likewise, human beings must subsist in God with Jesus: "Man is sanctified outside of himself" (*OP,* 244). Bérulle said also, in Johannine* terms, that one must subsist in Jesus as Jesus subsists in the Father*. And in terms closer to Thomas Aquinas he also spoke of relation, of "relation toward" Jesus (*OP,* 249). The notion of "cohesion" means, in this context, voluntary adhesion to the Son, subsistence in him.

Bérulle's influence was considerable, first of all on the Oratorians: on Charles de Condren (1588–1641), for example, who developed the Berullian notion of the sacrifice and abnegation of Christ in the Eucharist*; and on Guillaume Gibieuf (1580–1650), who continued with the Marian devotion of the founder of the Oratory. Carmelites such as Madeleine de Saint-Joseph (1578–1637) also felt Bérulle's influence, as did important figures such as Vincent de Paul (1581–1660), who learned from him the role of the priest as being at the service of all, and Jean Duvergier de Hauranne (1581–1643) (Jansenism*). Bérulle's theology of the priesthood* had an impact on seminaries run by the Eudists, the Lazarists, and the priests of Saint-Sulpice, which had been founded by Monsieur Olier (1608–57). At the beginning of the century, Henri Bremond, referring to Bérulle, spoke of a "French school" of spirituality. Today, the notion of a Berullian school is preferred.

• Pierre de Bérulle (1644), *Œuvres de l'Éminentissime et Révérendissime Pierre Cardinal de Bérulle,* Ed. R.P.F. Bourgoing, 2nd Ed., 1657, Paris; photographic by l'Oratoire, 2 vols. (Montsoult, 1960); (1856), *Œuvres complètes de Bérulle, cardinal de l'Église romaine, fondateur et premier supérieur de l'Oratoire,* Ed. Migne, Paris; (1937–39), *Correspondance,* Ed. J. Dagens, 3 vols., Paris-Louvain; (1995–), *OC,* Paris.

C. de Condren (1943), *Lettres du Père C. de Condren (1588–1641),* pub. P. Auvray, A. Jouffrey, Paris.

♦ H. Bremond (1921), *Histoire littéraire du sentiment religieux en France,* vol. III: *La conquête mystique,* Paris.

C. Taveau (1933), *Le cardinal de Bérulle, maître de vie spirituelle,* Paris.

J. Orcibal (1947 and 1948), *Les origines du jansénisme,* II et III: *Jean Duvergier de Hauranne, abbé de Saint-Cyran et son temps (1581–1638),* Paris-Louvain.

J. Dagens (1952), *Bérulle et les origines de la restauration catholique (1575–1611),* Paris.

P. Cochois (1963), *Bérulle et l'École française,* Paris.

M. Dupuy (1964), *Bérulle, une spiritualité de l'adoration,* Paris.

J. Orcibal (1965), *Le cardinal de Bérulle: Évolution d'une spiritualité,* Paris.

M. Dupuy (1969), *Bérulle et le sacerdoce: Étude historique et doctrinale: Unpublished Texts,* Paris.

F. Guillèn Preckler (1974), *"État" chez le cardinal de Bérulle: Théologie et spiritualité des "états" bérulliens,* Rome.

S.-M. Morgain (1995), *Pierre de Bérulle et les Carmélites de France,* Paris.

M. Vetö (1997), "La christo-logique de Bérulle," in *Opuscules de piété,* Paris, 7–136.

Y. Krumenacker (1998), *L'école française de spiritualité: Des mystiques, des fondateurs, des courants et leurs interprètes,* Paris.

Stéphane-Marie Morgain and Jean-Yves Lacoste

See also **Anhypostasy; Carmel; Descartes, René; Devotio moderna; Nothingness; Platonism, Christian; Priesthood**

Bible

Jews and Christians give the whole of their sacred writings the name of Bible, from the Greek *biblia,* meaning "books*." The Jews traditionally give their 24 holy books the name of *Tanakh,* which is an acronym of *Torah* (Law*), *Nevi'im* (Prophets*), *Ketuvim* (Writings). The Christian Bible consists of the Old Testament—39 books in the Protestant canon* (the same books as in the Jewish Scriptures, though differently divided) plus seven deuterocanonical books in the Catholic canon—and the 27 books of the New Testament. At the beginning of our era, despite their common origin, Samaritans, Jews, and Christians did not have the same collections of books for their Holy* Scriptures. The present notion of the Bible, a fixed list of books, with the codex showing them in a well-determined order, did not really appear until the third or fourth century. What the New Testament calls "the Scriptures" is the Old Testament. The term *New Testament* (*testament* or covenant*, Greek *diathèkè*) comes from the prediction by Jeremiah of a "new covenant" (Jer 31:31–34). The pair Old Testament/New Testament has its origin in the fact the Christians repeated Jeremiah's prophecy* (*see* 1 Cor 11:25; Lk 22:20; 2 Cor 3:5–14; Heb 8:7–13, 9:15, and 12:24).

1. Old Testament

At the beginning of our era, the order of the biblical books was, as follows, for the rabbis: Pentateuch, Prophets (Former and Latter), Writings; for the Christians, following the Septuagint and Vulgate translations: Pentateuch, Historical Books, Books of Wisdom*, Prophets. The final spot thus assigned to the Prophets was due to the belief in the fulfillment, by Christ*, of their oracles (Scripture*, fulfillment of).

The composition of the Old Testament is spread out over the first millennium B.C. The main Hebrew manuscripts that served as sources for the modern translations go back to the 10th and 11th centuries. Some earlier translations (essentially the Septuagint, a work done by Jews whose language was Greek, second century B.C.), as well as the Hebrew and Aramean biblical texts from Qumran (first century B.C.) and other sites, have confirmed the essential fidelity of the Hebrew textual tradition.

A large part of the Old Testament is made up of works of great length, in which the main periods of the history* of Israel* are reflected, and in which it is possible to distinguish the following periods: the period of the Twelve Tribes (or the period of the Judges, or the Pre-Monarchical period, c. 1220 B.C.–1020 B.C.); the United Monarchy (Saul, David, and Solomon); the Divided Monarchy (c. 922 B.C.–587 B.C.), with the Northern Kingdom of Israel (c. 922 B.C.–721 B.C.) and the Southern Kingdom of Judah (c. 922 B.C.–587 B.C.); the Babylonian Exile (587 B.C.–539 B.C.); the postexilic period, or period of the Second Temple*, also called Persian period (539 B.C.–333 B.C.); the Hellenistic period (333 B.C.–63 B.C.); and, finally, the Roman period, starting in 63 B.C.

The last edition of the major literary series is now generally believed to date from the period of the Second Temple, but the core of these works is older; it grew as a response to historical events.

a) Pentateuch. The history proper of Israel started with the conquest of Canaan, c. 1220 B.C. National identity started then, with the help of an oral narrative: the God of nations and of Israel (universalism*) created the world (creation*), called the patriarchs, and made their descendants, the Hebrews, go from slavery in Egypt to his service in Canaan. The anomalies that do not allow attributing authorship of the Pentateuch to Moses were accounted for, starting in the 18th century, but it was not until the 19th century, above all in Germany, that there appeared the hypotheses that classified the sources according to their period. The most famous of their proponents was Julius Wellhausen (1844–1918). More recent scholarship has not invalidated his reconstruction of the Bible's history, which still serves as a basis for numerous research endeavors. Wellhausen presented his findings as follows:

A first narrative was written in prose at the time of the United Monarchy, from a monarchical point of view. It is known as the J, or Yahwist, source because it singles out YHWH, or Yahweh (*Jahweh* in German), as a divine name*. One century later, there was another version in the Northern Kingdom, the E (Elohist) source, which favors the divine name of Elohim. That source is now often considered to be a mere supplement of J. Finally, J and E were combined and gradually completed. The Pentateuch reached its present state during the exile, thanks most probably to a third source, the P, or priestly, source, which added some material made up of laws and archives while reorganizing the previous traditions.

The conclusion of the five books of the Torah, leaving the Israelites in the plains of Moab, at the doorstep of Canaan, of which they had not yet taken possession, was adapted particularly for people living in exile. However, in spite of all the additions brought about during four centuries, the basic pattern of the Pentateuch was still faithful to the first narrative: Creation of the world, election of Israel, liberation from Egypt, serving God in the Promised Land.

b) Historical Books. The fifth book of the Pentateuch, Deuteronomy or "Second Law," is independent from sources J, E, and P, and stands out somehow from the narrative rhythm of the first four, which it concludes, for it is connected to the Book of Numbers (Dt 1–3). In its latest form, it presents four speeches addressed by Moses to Israel as the people are getting ready to cross the Jordan River and enter Canaan. The core of the book is said to be, according to many critics, Deuteronomy 5–26, in other words the "Book of Law" discovered in 622 B.C. by King Josiah, who made it the basis of his reform (2 Kgs 22–23). While concluding the Pentateuch, Deuteronomy connects it to the part of history that came later. That "Deuteronomist" part of history (Deuteronomy, Joshua, Judges, 1 and 2 Samuel, and 1 and 2 Kings) stretches from the time of Moses (13th century B.C.) to the death of King Josiah (609 B.C.); it emphasizes the Sinai Covenant (Mount Sinai is called "Horeb" in this version) and the Davidic Covenant. Obeying the word of YHWH brings about the blessings* promised by the Covenant, whereas disobedience brings about curses, in particular the loss of the Promised Land.

A resumption of older traditions thus ended up with a unified whole, most likely in two steps. There was first a narrative dating back to the seventh century to support Josiah's reform. That narrative presents Josiah as the worthy successor of Moses and David. A revision (at the latest in 561 B.C., the date when Joachin was given a reprieve by the king of Babylon) adapted the text for the somber reality of the exile (2 Kgs 21:10–15 and 23:25b–25:30). The Book of Chronicles is more recent; it covers approximately the same span of time as the earlier books, but the dominant point of view is the reconstruction of the Second Temple, after the exile. Esdras and Nehemiah, which also date back to the fifth or fourth century B.C., although most probably from another author, extend the Book of Chronicles to the Persian period. Facing Hellenization, 1 and 2 Maccabees (deuterocanonical books) tell the story of the successes of the Jews' resistance and of the unforeseen turn of events in the seizure of power. The First

Book of the Maccabees uses again the narrative patterns of Joshua's conquests; the Second Book thematizes the theological interpretation of the conflict. All these works, dating back to the period of the Second Temple, often resort to the process of systematically rereading and reusing expressions, images, and patterns borrowed from earlier narrations.

c) The Wisdom Literature. The Song of Solomon, a collection of love* poems, is part of this literature and is attributed to Solomon, the sage par excellence (*see* Song 1:1, 3:7, 3:9, 3:11, and 8:11). These works represent literary* genres that are well known in Middle-Eastern court literature—instructions given by a father to his sons, dialogues on justice* and suffering, royal autobiographies, essays in verse—but they all bear the mark of faith in YHWH, the God of Israel. Except for the Wisdom of Sirach (written c. 200 B.C.–175 B.C.), it is possible only to speculate about the dates of the Books of Wisdom*, since they do not make reference to history. A great part of the Book of Proverbs is from a preexilic period; Job, with the trauma of exile as its background text, is from the sixth century; Ecclesiastes corresponds well to the crisis caused by the Hellenistic ideas of the third century B.C.; finally, the Wisdom of Solomon dates from the first century B.C.

It is usual to classify the 150 Psalms* in the same category of works. Through the conventions of their form (corresponding to their liturgical use) the depth of human sensitivity expresses itself. A good third of the Psalms are individual laments; the remaining psalms fall into the categories of community laments, hymns, expressions of thanksgiving, royal psalms, and canticles from Zion.

d) The Prophets. The prophets, who were said to be active "writers" under the Divided Monarchy, during the Exile, and during the Restoration (c. 750–450 B.C.) are Isaiah, Jeremiah, Ezekiel, and Daniel (the four "major" prophets), and Hosea, Joel, Amos, Obadiah, Jonah, Micah, Nahum, Habakkuk, Zephaniah, Haggai, Zechariah, and Malachi (the "minor" Prophets, this adjective being used on account of the brevity of their surviving texts). The Lamentations, traditionally attributed to Jeremiah, are a collection of liturgical pieces devoted to the ruin of the Temple. These books contain the constant themes present from the eighth century on in prophetic predication: the apostasy of Israel brought about the breaking off of the first relation that united God and his people; the judgment* of God, which will be executed by human agents (pagan nations); and, finally, the reestablishment of the Jewish people on its land——this last theme becoming more marked and definitely clearer after the destruction of Jerusalem and the exile of 587.

The words and actions of the prophets were recorded in books, sometimes with narratives, that were developed in such a way that they would be applicable to Israel at all times. As a consequence, the books were often revised and augmented with prophecies from a time subsequent to that of the prophet whose name they bear. The deuterocanonical Baruch is a reflection on the meaning of exile and of the restoration of Israel.

e) Other Writings. Some books can hardly be considered to belong to one of the preceding four categories. They are brief narrations composed with art (Ruth, Esther, and the deuterocanonical Tobit and Judith), whose heroes are exemplary individuals, rather than rulers, and are often women (woman*). With the possible exception of Ruth (which is significant for David's genealogy), these narratives date from the Second Temple.

The last impetus of literary fertility in the Old Testament arose from the Jewish resistance to the Seleucid tyrant Antiochus Epiphanes (175 B.C.–164 B.C.). The book of Daniel bears the name of its hero, whom it places during the Babylonian Exile (to be decoded as "Seleucid domination"). The visions of Daniel 7–12 constitute the first upsurge, in the Old Testament, of an apocalypse in the full sense of the word. These texts give the people of the Almighty and Daniel's party the assurance of victory and of eternal* life. This literary genre, already announced in Ezekiel, Isaiah 24–27 and 40–66, and Zechariah, reaches its peak with the first Judaism* and the New Testament.

2. New Testament

The four Gospels*, the Acts of the Apostles*, the 13 Pauline Letters, the Letter to the Hebrews, the seven so-called catholic, or universal, letters, and the Revelation to John—these are the 27 Books of the New Testament. They were all written in Greek (the Greek of the *koinè*), around the Mediterranean, between A.D. 50 and the beginning of the second century. The oldest written documents are fragments of papyrus from the second and third centuries. The oldest of the documents that are complete are written on parchment, and are spread out from the fourth to the ninth centuries.

a) Letters of Paul. The seven "authentic" letters of Paul (in other words, those whose attribution is not contested) are the oldest documents of the New Testament, even though they do mention earlier Christian traditions (e.g., Rom 1:3–4, 3:25–26; 1 Cor 15: 3–4; Phil 2:6–11; and Gal 3:28). Paul wrote these letters when he was performing his duties as pastor* and theologian, and so they fit the situations in the communities that he had founded or knew.

In the First Letter to the Thessalonians (A.D. 51–52), Paul reestablishes friendly relations with the community and speaks up on various subjects, above all on the "second coming" of Christ. In the Epistle to the Galatians, Paul says that Christians who have converted from paganism* do not have to conform to such Jewish observances as circumcision. The First Letter to the Corinthians gives the apostle's opinion on the divisions in the community, on a case of incest, on trials, on marriage* and virginity, on the food offered to idols, on the assembly of the community, and on resurrection*. The Letter to the Philippians and the Second Letter to the Corinthians have as their themes the attacks endured by Paul in the course of his ministry*, financial problems, life after death*, and the obstacles brought against Gentile Christians by the Judeo-Christian missionaries. The Letter to Philemon is a petition addressed to the head of a Christian family to have him greet, once more, in his home, Onesimus, his runaway slave. The Letter to the Romans (A.D. 58), the last and longest of Paul's letters, teaches that both Jews and Gentiles have equal need for the justice* of God to be revealed to them in Christ; it teaches that faith* is what gives access to the benefits of this revelation*, that the death and Resurrection of Jesus have brought freedom* (liberation from sin*, from death, and from law*) and make life possible according to the Spirit, that the rejection of the gospel by Israel is neither total nor definitive, that the tensions between "strong" and "weak" in the community may find a resolution inspired by the pattern of the future reconciliation of Jews and Gentiles.

b) Gospels and Acts of the Apostles. The first three Gospels are called "synoptic" because it is possible to draw parallels among their respective versions on the life, death, and Resurrection of Jesus. The patristic tradition's claims that the four Evangelists were eyewitnesses to the events they were relating are not, in all likelihood, very plausible. The Evangelists most probably worked on the basis of written traditions and perhaps oral ones. Writing shortly before or shortly after the destruction of the Second Temple (A.D. 70), and within a climate of imminent or present persecution, Mark was the first one to make use of the traditions that reported on the teaching of Jesus (including parables*, controversies, and proverbs), on his healing* powers, and on his Passion*. Mark gives his writings the form of an unbroken narrative, in which Jesus appears as a master, a healer, and a suffering Messiah*. The narrative stops suddenly at 16:8. In 16:9–20, the Gospel of Mark is an abstract of some accounts of apparitions borrowed from the other Gospels (second century). In about A.D. 90 Matthew and Luke seem to have made use (independently of each another) of the Gospel of Mark, a collection of *logia* or "pronouncements" by Jesus called the Q Source (from the German *Quelle,* or "source"), and some other traditions.

Matthew tries to show to his community, where the Judeo-Christian element was dominant, that God's promises to Israel have been realized with the coming of Jesus, and that it is the permanent presence of Christ that henceforth must found the existence of the people of God.

Luke addresses his Gospel (and the Acts of the Apostles) to Theophilus (meaning "friend of God"), who may have been either a real person or a typical reader. For the use of Gentile Christians, Luke presents the ministry* of Jesus (prophet, martyr, and role model) as a new era in the history of salvation*, and the Twelve Apostles as the link between Jesus and the Church* led by the Spirit.

John brings in a chronology and different characters; he puts long speeches in Jesus' mouth. This fourth Gospel is the outcome of a whole process in the Johannine "school," bearing the traces of independent sources, including the hymn of John 1:1–18, a series of seven "signs," the farewell speech, and the Passion narrative. The moment when the Christian Jews were expelled from the synagogues was perhaps the opportunity to write it up in its final version (*see* Jn 9:22, 12:42, and 16:2). The essential mission* of the Johannine Jesus is to reveal his divine Father*. Far from being a defeat, the cross represents the exaltation of Jesus, the "hour" toward which all his life and all his teaching were aiming, the beginning of eternal life for the believers.

The Acts of the Apostles is a continuation of the Gospel of Luke and is by the same author. Acts is devoted to the activities of Peter* and Paul, and relates the spreading of the gospel from Jerusalem* to Rome* under the guidance of the Holy Spirit. Luke has a tendency to idealize the life of the Christian community and presents a portrait of Paul that is different from the one found in Paul's own letters. Luke wants to show that, in spite of the opposition to which they are subjected by the Jews and the pagans, the Christians do not represent a political threat for the Romans, and they never ceased to be guided by the Spirit.

c) Deutero-Pauline Letters. There are six letters that are traditionally attributed to Paul, but whose attribution is contested to varying degrees. The historical context of these letters is from around the year 100. Their authors—admirers, or perhaps disciples, of Paul—wished to keep his spirit alive and to respond to new situations in the way he would have done so himself, or in the way he ought to have responded, according to them. Pseudepigraphy was, at the time, a common and accepted practice.

The Second Letter to the Thessalonians recommends caution regarding the speculations on the Parousia* and their consequences on the evaluation of human activity. The Letter to the Colossians stresses the unique fulfillment of the new life that only Christ can bring to us. The Letter to the Ephesians, which assimilated the substance of the Letter to the Colossians, develops the main Pauline themes and sets forth the designs of God: the Gentiles are now part of the people of God, in equal terms with the Judeo-Christians, in a quasi-preexistent Church. The Pastoral Epistles (1 and 2 Timothy and Titus) give instructions on ecclesiastical life and discipline, and exhort the Christians to practice the virtues* that are appropriate for good citizens of the Roman Empire.

d) Other Letters. Intended for the Judeo-Christians who lose their courage, the Letter to the Hebrews has as its main themes Christ as grand priest, the perfect effectiveness of his sacrificial death, and the celestial cult* thus established. Strangers and travelers on earth, Christians have in Jesus a chief and a guide for their pilgrimage*.

The universal, or catholic, letters have titles that associate them with apostles' names, but in all likelihood these are borrowed pseudonyms. Of these, James's Epistle gives practical instructions for everyday life and warns against a radical interpretation of the Pauline doctrine, which would enhance faith to the detriment of good works. The First Letter of Peter is concerned with the social alienation of the Christians of Asia Minor, who have come from paganism*, and reminds them of their dignity as chosen people. Jude stigmatizes the perversion that turns the gift of God's grace* into license to such an extent as renouncing Christ. The Second Letter of Peter declares that the Parousia will come in due time, and implies that the faithful were misled by a wrong interpretation of the Pauline doctrine.

The three Letters of John reflect the history of the Johannine community, which a split over the matter of the humanity of Jesus seems to have torn apart.

e) Revelation to John. This book is simultaneously epistle, prophecy, and apocalypse; it is intended for the Christians of Asia Minor at the time when the authorities wanted to force them to take part in the cult of the deified emperor, toward the end of Domitian's reign (A.D. 95–96). An author by the name of John (who does not claim to be the apostle or the evangelist) conveys a message to the seven churches of Asia. The clairvoyant uses images from Ezekiel, Daniel, and the Jewish apocalypses to urge these churches to hold out, because the victory already won by the Resurrection of Jesus will soon manifest itself to the whole world. The faithful will then live in beatitude* with Christ, the Lamb* of God, in the New Jerusalem.

The author's hostile attitude toward Rome and its representatives is totally different from the cooperative attitude recommended by Paul, the Pastoral Letters, and 1 Peter. One may wonder about the Book of Revelation's general movement: does it describe a linear process directed toward a peak, or does it keep coming back to the same events under slightly different guises? That debate is an old one; whatever the interpretation, a fundamentalist, or literal, reading does not do justice either to the historical design or to the literary strength of the work.

3. Two Testaments

The Old Testament focuses on narrating the stories of the Creation, the election of Israel, and the Exodus and conquest and on relating the service of God. The New Testament's core is Jesus' kerygma. It announces his death and his Resurrection "in conformity with the Scriptures" (1 Cor 15:3–4).

a) Fulfillment. The authors of the New Testament all had in common the certainty that the promises of the Jewish Scriptures had been fulfilled in Jesus Christ (Scripture*, fulfillment of). Speaking of "fulfillment" does not imply in the least the end or the revocation of the Old Testament. The early Christians, including those who came from paganism, considered the Old Testament to be still valid in its scope as God's Word*.

Considered this way, Jesus is the new Moses, the mediator of the New Covenant, the long-awaited Davidic king. With his coming, the Holy Spirit has finally spread.

There is no book in the New Testament that is not saturated with references to or borrowings from the Scriptures (e.g., Is 61:1–2 is cited in Lk 4:18–19), that does not reuse Old Testament metaphors (the Royal Pastor in Jer 23 and Ez 34 is used in Jn 10), that does not use Old Testament stylistic devices, such as Christ a spurting rock (1 Cor 10:4) or a new Adam* (Rom 5:14). Jesus appears as the new Elijah (1 Kgs 17:17–24; Lk 7:11–17; 2 Kgs 4:42–44; and Mt 14:13–21), as Wisdom dispensing life (Prv 8:22, 9:1–6 and Jn 6), as the Creator (Gn 1:1–5 and Jn 1:1–18), and as the just one condemned and rehabilitated, according to the pattern of the plaintive Psalms, in the Passion narratives (notably, the use of Ps 22 in Mt 26–27).

New contents are assigned to such venerable Old Testament terms as *law, justice,* and *life* because "at many times and in many ways, God spoke to our fathers by the prophets, but in these last days he has spoken to us by his Son" (Heb 1:1–2).

The structure of fulfillment is well attested within the Old Testament proper. In it God is seen fully involved in human history*, being faithful to his Word, which is in command of this history. The New Testament has merely radicalized what the Old Testament had always done. To that effect, a key period of the Old Testament has served as a model to the New Testament. The sixth-century exile and the return from exile were indeed interpreted as a new exodus, a repeat of that founding moment when the people of Israel, liberated from Egypt, entered the Promised Land. The first Christians lived their experience as a renewal of the same type, even though there was no common measure between their circumstances and the preceding ones.

Some of the aspects of the Jewish Scriptures were, however, considered unsuitable for the novelty of proclaiming Our Lord Jesus as sole authority. The Law started to be reinterpreted (Mt 5–7, Gal, and Rom). A contrast was emphasized, through which the new prevailed over the old (Heb 8:8–13, 9:15, and 12:24). Designating the Jewish Scriptures under the name of Old Testament, or Old Covenant (2 Cor 3:14; *see also* 2 Cor 3:6), became common toward the end of the second century (Melito of Sardis in Eusebius, *HE,* 4, 26, 14). The Christian interpretation thereafter oscillated between two poles: continuity and discontinuity.

b) Interaction. A certain consciousness of problems of terminology raised by the expressions *Old Testament* and *New Testament* becomes manifest today. The pejorative connotation of the word *old,* when it tends to mean "outdated," is being felt. As for the word *testament,* it no longer has any connection, as far as we are concerned, with the notion of the Covenant. To talk about "Jewish Scriptures," as has been suggested, runs the risk of neglecting the Deuterocanonicals, which, though completely Jewish, even when written first in Greek, are absent from the Jewish Bible. Other designations have been tried, such as "First Testament" (an ancient solution was *prius Testamentum,* but this has never been adopted for good). However, neither *second* in relation to *first,* nor *new* in relation to *old* has any chance of being accepted. In any case, the usage has not changed much.

It is at a deeper level that the question of the Christian attitude toward the revelation transmitted by Old Israel arises. In the second century, Marcion proposed the elimination of the Old Testament. It has always been maintained, however, in the Christian Bible. How is it to be understood? Is it a collection of religious writings to be read for their own sake? Is it there in preparation for learning the gospel, or is it merely a necessary prerequisite for understanding the New Testament?

Christians, of course, have to read the Old Testament by piecing together, with the help of history, the author's communication with his contemporaries, which amounts, at least as a first step, to not referring him immediately to the New Testament or to the Christian faith. Other readers will be sensitive to the human and religious values of the texts, as well as to the literary genius of the authors. But since, to a lesser degree, the Christian Bible is not exactly the same whether the Deuterocanonical books are included in it or not, the presence, beside the Old Testament, of the New Testament, cannot be without impact on our reading of the former.

• P. Beauchamp (1976), *L'un et l'autre Testament,* vol. 1: *Essai de lecture,* Paris.
P. Grelot (Ed.) (1976), *Introduction à la Bible,* vol. 3: *Introduction critique au Nouveau Testament,* Tournai-Paris.
J. D. G. Dunn (1977), *Unity and Diversity in the New Testament,* London (2nd Ed., 1990).
R.N. Soulen (1981), *Handbook of Biblical Criticism,* 2nd Ed., Atlanta.
J. A. Fitzmeyer (1982), *A Christological Catechism: New Testament Answers,* Ramsey (2nd Ed. 1991).
N. Frye (1982), *The Great Code: The Bible and Literature,* New York-London.
H. Koester (1982), *Introduction to the New Testament,* Philadelphia.
R. Rendtorff (1983), *Das Alte Testament: Eine Einführung,* Neukirchen-Vluyn.
P. Beauchamp (1987), *Parler d'Écritures saintes,* Paris.
G. Josipovici (1988), *The Book of God: A Response to the Bible,* New Haven-London.
N. Lohfink (1989), *Der niemals gekündigte Bund,* Freiburg-Basel-Vienna.
P. Beauchamp (1990), *L'un et l'autre Testament,* vol 2: *Accomplir les Écritures,* Paris.
R.E. Brown (1990), *Responses to 101 Questions on the Bible,* Mahwah, N.J.
R.E. Brown, J.A. Fitzmyer, R.E. Murphy (Ed.) (1990), *The New Jerome Biblical Commentary,* Englewood Cliffs, N.J.
J. Reumann (1991), *Variety and Unity in New Testament Thought,* Oxford-New York.
B.S. Childs (1992), *Biblical Theology of the Old and New Testaments,* Minneapolis.
R.E. Brown (1994), *Introduction to the New Testament Christology,* London.
C.-B. Amphoux, J. Margain (Ed.) (1996), *Les premières traditions de la Bible* (coll. "Histoire du texte biblique," no. 2), Lausanne.
R. Dupont-Roc, P. Mercier (1997), *Les manuscrits de la Bible et la critique textuelle,* Paris.

RICHARD J. CLIFFORD AND DANIEL J. HARRINGTON

See also **Apocalyptic Literature; Apocrypha; Book; Canon of Scriptures; Exegesis; History; Intertestament; Jesus, Historical; Johannine Theology; Judaism; Law and Christianity; Literary Genres in Scripture; Myth; Narrative; Pauline Theology; Scripture, Fulfillment of; Scripture, Senses of; Tradition; Translations of the Bible, Ancient**

Biblical Theology

Introduction

Biblical theology: this expression might seem like a pleonasm in Christianity; and yet, biblical theology does have its own mission to fulfill: to give a rational account of the outward way Christian faith* is expressed today, to evaluate how faithful it is to biblical writings, and to rejuvenate this fidelity. Exegesis* and theology* are not reducible to one another: biblical theology's function is to articulate them with each other. The problem is an old one: "Will we reach the point of being unable to do anything without you?" *(ut tu solus necessarius videaris),* wrote the bishop*-theologian Augustine* (PL 22, letter 104) to the exegete Jerome. Biblical theology does not have its own definite boundaries in academia. The majority of endeavors in biblical theology do not show under that field's label. The most recognizable form, with a didactic end, is called either "theology of the Old Testament," or "theology of the New Testament." A theology of the two Testaments is called upon to show what kind of connection unites them. We will adopt here the latter perspective. A farthermost goal, yet an old one.

In 1956, R. de Vaux wrote that a biblical theology "founded on both Testaments" is "the final outcome of our studies" (*ZAW* 68, 225). In 1960, G. von Rad considered that a biblical theology that "will overcome the dualism" between a treatment of the "arbitrarily separated" Old Testament and New Testament is "the still more distant aim of our efforts." In 1962, P. Grelot presented his *Sens chrétien de l'Ancien Testament* as an "outline" (*see* P. Beauchamp, *L'un et l'autre Testament: Essai de Lecture,* 1976).

No one underestimates the difficulties. The final aim, which gives value to partial attempts and unites scholars, relies on a fact. The first bearers of the biblical books* are the communities of observant Jews for the Old Testament, and Christians for both Testaments. From the beginning, these communities bring together both knowledge* and faith*, on account of the fact they are assembled for celebration (liturgy*) around the Book. This reading is articulated with preaching*, instruction, and prayer*. If it works well, then biblical theology will also. At the same time, the Bible not being the exclusive property of any group, the language the believers use about it must be intelligible to all. Biblical theology teaches how to abandon *prejudice,* verifies whether the *presuppositions* given by doctrine bear fruit or not: there is nothing there to isolate the discipline.

1. Problem of the Unity of the Bible

The project of a biblical theology, thus conceived, presupposes that the notion of a unity of the Bible is acceptable; but then, that notion is not purely and simply imposed from the outside by the limits of the canon*: rather, it is a notion that has presided over the phases of its composition, and it has even left some traces. The Bible is often called a "library rather than a book." This pedagogical formula should not replace one kind of naivety with another. Commentators discover in the Old Testament a "library" where certain books communicate with each other because writers and editors have attempted to harmonize them.

If we detect these transversal interventions, it is thanks to the commentators: "deuteronomic revisions" (e.g., prophecy*-fulfillment), "sacerdotal resumptions" (covenants of Noah and Abraham), repetition of the kings' story by the Chronicler (the lineage Adam-Moses-David), narrative thread of the Gospels* linking units previously independent of one another, and so forth. Other processes are less artificial: narrative surveys, summaries such as those that von Rad called "Credos"; globalizations: "all the prophets*" (Jer 7:25, 28:8; Ez 38:17; 2 Chr 6:15); repetition of Isaiah and of all the revelations* of the past in the "Deutero-Isaiah" (Is 41:22, 43:8–13, 44:7); or summaries in the latest Wisdom* literature: Wisdom 10:1–11:4; Sirach 44–49. It was necessary, when going from age to age, that the heavy mass bequeathed by previous generations should be made "portable" and readily remembered. The sustained series of resumptions is indicative of the fact diversity was welcome. Finally, and above all, there is the same function in the New Testament, which is "also a theology of the Old Testament" (E. Jacob 1968): a claim to fulfill "law and prophets" (Mt 5:17), a recourse to "all the Scriptures*" (Lk 18:31; *see also* Lk 24:44; Acts 3:18; Jn 19:28, etc.).

One learns thus that there is no appropriation of the Bible by one community without those risky shortcuts that have recurred at every stage and continue to do so today. The phase of deconstruction is not invalidated for that. It contributed to the discovery of multiple meanings (Clavier 1976) by using instruments that lose their effectiveness in one particular direction: why, then, should one be surprised that they do not lead toward it? In matters of faithfulness to a certain heritage (here, a cultural and spiritual genealogy), faith is not the only approach in which interpreting is equivalent to making a choice.

It has been said that the Bible, as a literary work, has no center. That is no longer valid if it is considered the basic book for all communities. Celebrations of Easter or of Atonement, catechesis*, and preaching order ways of interpreting. Biblical theology is not free, for instance, to turn away from the account of Christ's Passover* to Israel*'s Passover, nor is it free to elude the confrontation between Paul and the law* of Moses. Granted that Christ's cross is the center of both Testaments, the paths that are opened are numerous.

The concept of unity (one of the names of transcendence) crumbles if unity is accomplished by smoothing over the outlines of what is being assembled. This applies to all levels, but above all to the line (union and separation) that goes in between the two testaments. Within each one, the tensions are not all loaded with equal meaning.

The pair Law/Prophets is signaled by the canonical form of the book, said to be at once unified and divided. The multiple transversal interventions show what is done between these two areas (Deuteronomy between Law and Prophets). A third one (Writings, Psalms, and Wisdoms) bears the words of man (unrevealed experience, questions, requests) whereas Law and Prophets bear the Word* of God.

The poles are there only to help toward an exchange in movement. Let us note here that the Old Testament can and must be considered first within its own perimeter, whereas the New Testament can in no case be understood without the former.

2. Biblical Theology and the Sciences

The critical requirements concern the state of the text, its circumstances, and the conditions of its production. Efforts expended in these areas open up, in terms of the search for meaning, a space that is not always occupied; but biblical theology cannot rush immediately into it. Criteria must be found in a reflection of a philosophical nature. Assuming, said Augustine, that I can get to Moses, "how would I know that he is saying the truth?" (*Confessions* XI. iii. 5). The Bible, wrote M-J. Lagrange in 1904, "depends no more exclusively on history* than it does on philosophy*" (*La Méthode historique,* xv); this is a way of saying that, separated from one another, neither history (taken as encompassing all the sciences of man), nor philosophy can sustain theology. In that very same year, Maurice Blondel published his essay "Histoire et dogme: Les lacunes philosophiques de l'exégèse moderne," in *La Quinzaine,* 1904 (repr. in Blondel's *OC* 2, Paris, 1997).

Given below is only a brief outline of the principal itineraries possible.

a) Language. "The grammatical is the theological" *(Primo grammatica videamus, verum ea theologica),* declares Luther* at the opening of the 1519 *Operationes in Psalmos* (Jena Ed., 1600). The very first step of biblical theology consists in going to concepts through the paths of words, those of the biblical Hebrew and Greek, an indispensable path to the feeling of cultural unfamiliarity and the reclassifying of ideas. G. Kittel (Tübingen) is the author of the best-known work on the Greek words of the New Testament; these words are preceded by the treatment of their usage in their environment and in the Old Testament (*ThWNT:* 1933–73).

Invited to write a few pages in Kittel's work (1964), Cardinal A. Bea hailed it as "the most important achievement of contemporary Protestant exegesis in the entire world," and he also expressed the wish that some day a single author would do the same thing, "in the same spirit" for both Testaments. He remarked, in passing, on the "undeniable inconvenience" of separating them in their teaching. From another viewpoint, J. Barr had already expressed some scathing criticisms of this work, among which the following: "The nonreligious language of the Bible has as much *theological* importance [emphasis added] as its religious language" (*The Semantics of Biblical Language,* Oxford, 1961).

Since then, Kittel's work has been followed by other glossaries (for the Old Testament, Botterweck and Ringgren, *ThWAT,* 1973–). There are innumerable studies on "themes" (with a more or less complex lexical content) that supply us with the components of a biblical theology.

b) Literary Form. The study of literary form has asserted its rights since Richard Simon, who blamed the theologians, in 1678, for "not having done sufficient thinking on the different manners of speaking about the Scripture" (*Critical History* III, 21). He recognized that setting this point straight is a way of sparing theology from making errors, but it does not sustain it: the grammarians "do explain the history of the Old Testament, but they do not contribute to a better knowledge of religion" (III, 8). This "way" of talking comes from society* (the "Republic of the Hebrews"). The mid-18th-century book by Bishop R. Lowth (1710–87), *De Sacra Poesi Hebraeorum Prelectiones* (Oxford, 1753), is an achievement that stands out in history: it suggests a purely stylistic study of the Bible and expresses reservations regarding *theologiae sacraria* (*Praelectio* II). That particular work influenced J.G. Herder (1744–1803), a humanist, philosopher, and preacher who attached importance to the value of esthetics in enhancing knowledge, and who refused to put poetry and truth* in opposition to each other. H. Gunkel (1862–1932), founder of the *Gattungsgeschichte* (history of literary* genres, also called *Formgeschichte*), inherited the same spirit. He aimed at selecting the most archaic spots of enunciation (preliterary), but also at recognizing, with the *Sitz Im Leben* (life-situation) of textual units, the communicative contracts to which their forms (preliterary or literary) belonged. Already "the work's intention" tends to supplant "the author's intention." This method occupies an intermediate position between linguistics and the social sciences. Today exegesis more distinctly perceives that the message of faith is entrusted also to the sensitivity of the addressee, thanks to images, rhythms, and symbols, and thanks as well to the power of representation radiated by a narrative*. An esthetic theology (beauty*) was thus launched.

c) Social Sciences. The *Formgeschichte* scarcely inquired into the social body: progress in this direction is a challenge of present research, triangulated around the individual body, the social body, and words. Formerly dominated by history, the position of the social sciences has gradually been reversed, and from there, these sciences can be raised to a higher level through an exploration of the "mystery of society" (G. Fessard), enlightened by the Bible and enlightening it in return.

1) The theme of covenant* comes not only under the comparatist's domain (political treaties in the ancient Near East), but also under the theory of contracts in a philosophy* of law that contributes to the intelligibility of history. 2) The internal and external relations of Israel went through successive phases leading to the phase of the first church*, whose social model concerns the Bible (political theology*). 3) History is interested not only in change, but also in long periods. The history of Israel is that of a culture. The Word* could not become flesh in man unless it existed in a culture: therefore, biblical theology records the significance of that concept.

3. Shifts in Biblical Theology

a) Beginnings. "Far from being a novelty, biblical theology was the original form of theology" (F. Prat 1907). The allocution form (sermons, apologias, cateches) is dominant. The nascent biblical theology was relaying the dialogue between the gospel and the Old Testament. It was not only a matter of legitimizing the social status of a religion, nor was it merely a strategy or an expedient to convince or to defend oneself. It was meant to renew in oneself "the constant passage, thanks to Christ, from the Old Testament to the New Testament," in which Origen* (†253–54) saw, with reason, "a fundamental characteristic of Christianity, and somehow its birth certificate forever being renewed in people's minds" (H. de Lubac*, *Histoire et Esprit,* 1950). This passage is renewed because the depth of its origins signifies its constant presence.

Passage: this word allows a choice among several meanings: continuity, progress, leap, and at the limit, rupture. The fact that this passage is "constant" means, in any case, that the point of arrival never exhausts the resources of the point of departure. Irenaeus* (†195), facing the awe-inspiring arguments of Marcionism*, had honored the notion of pedagogy, in continuity. When Trinitarian (Trinity*) theology assumed its full importance, it needed the space of both Testaments to present itself according to the economy of revelation: "The Old Testament manifested the Father*, the Son (filiation*) *more obscurely.* The New Testament manifested the Son and allowed a *glimpse* of the divinity of the Holy* Spirit. Today, the Spirit is among us and it lets itself be known *more clearly*" (Gregory* of Nazianzus, PG 36, 161).

Being a determining factor for the theological use of the Bible, this relationship between obscurity and clarity gets various treatments. It is the simple relationship of the visible to the invisible, of the terrestrial to the celestial; or it is the disclosure of the meaning of a first obscure event, thanks to the impact of a subsequent event. That later event is the coming of Christ, to whom the eyes owe their healing*: the range of meanings in the Scriptures (Scripture*, senses of) fluctuates among these orientations. A point of capital importance, the theme of obscurity is rooted in the gospel itself: the parables* are obscure; the eyes and the heart* are blind, even to the life of Jesus*, and finally to the whole Scripture (Mt 13:15, 13:34 f.).

b) Theology As Science. When the Middle Ages made it their task to have a theology that would be a real discipline, there was an obstacle; it was brought about by the *poetic* writing of the Bible, which constituted an obstacle to the systematic expression of truth. Thomas* Aquinas's *Summa Theologica* faced that obstacle; and it was eventually overcome with the help of Dionysius* the Pseudo-Areopagite. Precisely because they are the "lowest" *(infima)* forms of knowledge, images and representations are the best suited to lead to such a high level of knowledge that it is above our understanding (*ST* Ia, q. 1, a. 9, ad 3). The esthetics that cares for figures of style is therefore welcome right away, but it is a secondary principle that passes on its style to the doctrine: the Bible formulates in the literal sense all the truths that are necessary to faith (Ia, q. 1, a. 10, ad 1). By this, Aquinas refers to that which is "necessary to exhibit it without error" *(fides quae).*

c) Turning Point of the Reformation. The Renaissance introduced an entirely new form of obscurity, first with more requirements in philology, and gradually with less credulity in matters of history. Tradition* no longer being received in the same capacity as the Bible as a source of revelation, the clarity of the Scriptures *(perspicuitas),* which tradition had obscured, was asserted. Out of this came simultaneously: an unprecedented new energy allowing for a maximum of critical certainty, and a strong intensity of theological investment in exegesis. As a theologian, Luther maintained that the opposition of Law and gospel *(Gesetz und Evangelium),* already present in the Old Testament, did not disappear from the New. His method was not typological: faith opens directly the words of the Old Testament to their Christic meaning. Distrusting allegories as Luther had done, Calvin* gave more importance to typology, a mode of reading that recognizes in the realities of the Old Testament a veiled presence of the Christian mystery*. A new crisis eventually occurred, with the questioning of the credibility* of the Scriptures as historical document.

d) Richard Simon and Pascal. With the *Histoire critique du Vieux Testament* (1678, 5th Ed. 1685), Richard Simon (*see* 2 b above) opened debates with the Protestants. He denied that the Scriptures were clear, and he was pleased to see that tradition was trying to find a cure for their obscurity. Pascal* (†1662) had placed the discussion on a different field. The *Pensées* are what Pascal left of a project centered on biblical theology: he used, in writing them, the style of an allocution, which had been used in very early works of theology; he assembled notations on the biblical "manners" of speaking, deductive reasoning leading to decision making, a Christian anthropology*, and hermeneutics* inspired by the gospel. The obscurity of the prophecies, of rhetorical figures, and of Jesus' miracles*, can be clarified only with a change occurring in the heart* that they had previously disturbed: everything takes a meaning in the "order of charity." Inclined to take too much advantage of the miseries of man, with a view to convincing him, Pascal was indifferent to the historical problems raised by Richard Simon; he nonetheless succeeded in bringing about a revival of the old hermeneutics for use in the modern age.

e) Liberal Exegesis and Theologies. In fact, the gap between the scholars' interests within Protestantism* was increasing. Scholars studying history and science would be the first to show a greater creativity, which would emancipate them to varying degrees from a theology less than sensitive to biblical modality (it had become closer to it, e.g., with J. Cocceius; *see* covenant*). J.-P. Gabler (1787, in Strecker 1975) stands out for assigning separate titles to two theologies, the biblical and the dogmatic*. The object of the latter is to "philosophize on divine matters," but as far as biblical theology is concerned, there is no suggestion that it should philosophize: it belongs to the realm of history, and is supposed to teach "the thoughts of holy writers of the past on matters of a divine character" (ibid., p. 35). The tendency of this type of biblical theology made it impossible to distinguish it from the history of religions. In a university where theology never lost its place, it appealed to some philosophers (such as Schleiermacher*, then Hegel*), detached from dogma*, but more open to religious matters than the philosophers of the Enlightenment. From the 19th to the 20th century, the task to be accomplished involved recognizing the stalemates of liberalism and collecting the benefits associated with it. J. Wellhausen (1844–1918), a writer and researcher of exceptional brilliance, extremely productive in history but increasingly unfamiliar with theology, went far in his separation of the two Testaments. The Old Testament is, in his opinion, the account of decadence, starting from beginnings that had been brilliant, and the gospel serves above all as an internal norm for human beings. For A. Harnack (1851–1930), a prominent figure in erudite liberal circles, the churches show their paralysis by delaying their separation from the Old Testament: the very same reasons that had led the church, when it faced Marcionism*, to accept the Old Testament, should lead the church of today to dissociate itself from it. The propensity (which had its political implications) to see in the variety of cultures separate essences lends further weight to the "Athens versus Jerusalem*" stereotype. Because of the specialization of disciplines, focus is on the respective environments of the Old and of the New Testaments rather than on what connects them. A. Schweitzer (1875–1965), musicologist, physician, exegete, and writer, celebrated 150 years of "The Lives of Jesus" by concluding: "We have the right to detach Jesus from his period" (*Das Messianitäts- und Leidensge-*

heimnis: Eine Skizze des Lebens Jesu, 1901, 3rd Ed. 1956, Tübingen), because his expectation of an end to the world, the key to his biography, cannot be repeated. The secret of his life is his heroic fidelity to the oracles of the Servant*. We have to join him through a decision "of will to will." Elaborated away from dogma*, in a sort of semi-rupture with liberalism, Schweitzer's contribution counts.

f) Renaissance of Protestant Theology. His contribution counts for Bultmann* (1884–1976). With the Lutheran Bultmann and the Calvinist K. Barth* (1886–1968), we witness a Renaissance of the founders' theology. Kierkegaard* (1813–55) had already prepared that revival. Both Bultmann and Barth agree to break away from a biblical theology, which would be reduced to mere scientific description. Bultmann, however, values it greatly. He "demythologizes" (myth*) in order to suppress this "false scandal*" that hurts the sciences* of nature, but he considers this approach of science to be merely the condition allowing it to better hold to "the true scandal of faith" (P. Ricœur). He understands this faith according to Luther, in a doctrine of a vigorous economy. His concept of the connection between decision and knowledge lies within the framework that he finds in Heidegger*. His theology of the New Testament explores Paul and John in particular: "He does not take sufficiently into account the synoptic tradition" (Conzelmann). Correlatively, the function of the narration (narrative* theology) is severely reduced in his works. The Old Testament is necessary only to show that since man is accountable to the Law, he is also in a position to be accountable to the gospel. The synoptic narrative fades away in favor of the kerygma. Even Kant* gives more importance to factors affecting sensibility and to esthetics. The primacy of charity receives its rightful place, but its ecclesial forms are not theologically relevant. Bultmann's itinerary as a theologian starts with exegesis. As for Barth, he is an exegete only when it comes to theology. His commentary on Romans aims to bring out "the concepts' internal tension" present in the text (*Römerbrief,* 2nd Ed. 1922), and even if it means "being severely blamed," it also means striving to go to the "very core of the enigma rather than merely be content with the document.... I am absolutely overwhelmed by the desire to do so!" (ibid.). At a considerable remove from Bultmann, his reading of the Old Testament is truly christological. He dismisses allegory, but he occasionally practices an audacious typology (*KD* III/1: *Christ and the Church Read in Genesis 2*). This work, rich and vigorous, involved in the tragedies of that time, has been given dimensions that are in proportion to the Bible itself. Always under the authority of the absolute alternatives, its perspective is not hermeneutic.

g) Old Testament As Opening Point. Instead of revealing the "truths" of the Old Testament, G. von Rad (1957, 1960) prefers to classify its "traditions," which are superimposed and combined versions of history. Their relevance for biblical theology is not their objective content, but the beliefs (the Credos) they encourage on the gracious gift; he orders each version around his declaration or kerygma, in sequence, and he infers the ritual setting *(Sitz im Leben).* That is how the capacity for "creative reinterpretation" of the narrative is measured in the Old Testament, and how much appeal the book will have in the future. Von Rad can conclude: the reinterpretation of the Old Testament by the New is radical, but interdependent with a series, which invites the theologian to rethink the problem of the unity of the Testaments. This work, which is in Bultmann's sphere of influence, has been judged hardly sensitive to the radical discontinuities (Conzelmann 1964). Its repeated defense of typology, even if it gives few examples of it, has met with reservations. On the other hand this work, for not having highlighted wisdom and apocalyptic* writings, has drawn the criticism (Pannenberg) of giving too narrow a basis to a Christology* that wants to be coextensive to the duration of the universe, a basis that the Old Testament should have supplied. Any biblical theology reopens questions on the connection between the carnal fact and the Word*.

h) Catholic Exegesis Today. It often presents, in its task, the deficit and the advantage of a smaller theological investment. "The study of the Holy Scripture must be like the soul of theology": this maxim from Vatican* II (*DV* 6, 24) reinforces a wish expressed by Benedict XV (1920, *EnchB* 483), who quoted Leo XIII (1893, ibid., 114). In spite of the obvious character of this maxim, practicing it is not easy. The norms of the magisterium* that were most noticed in modern times have more than once restrained the fruitfulness of exegesis, but their bearing was exercised more often on the narrative than directly on biblical theology. Present-day biblical theology gets its material in several ways. First of all, through living tradition, including through the spiritual writers, old and recent, that are closest to the biblical source. The renewal of interest for patristic literature (SC 1942–) will sooner or later benefit exegesis, inasmuch as the exercise of hermeneutics teaches us to find inspiration in ancient writers without actually reproducing them. The Catholic exegetes of today are becoming more sensitive to the theological implications of the studies carried out by Protestant exegetes. Catholic exegetes have often evaluated the works of their Protestant counterparts only from the point of view of the historian. Protestant exegetes have obtained results that the Catholics could not obtain for themselves, the reason being that they did not have the freedom to push their research very far; but things having settled down for a century and a half, today's Catholic exegetes are indebted to the Protestants for their good work. Historical-critical exegesis is now incorporated for good in the norms and in the history of Catholic tradition*, and it is not fair to blame it for its limits. If those limits were better recognized, they could lead to articulate exegesis to other practices. In 1943, Pius XII *(Divino Afflante Spiritu)* gave biblical exegesis a place of honor that he certainly would not grant to "spiritual meaning" (Scripture*, senses of). By way of compensation, this major document contained provisions that gave it its balance: it assigned as first objective *(potissimum)* to exegesis the elucidation of the "theological doctrine" of the texts (*EnchB* 551). This directive was not what attracted the greatest attention. The object of the constitution *Dei Verbum* of Vatican* II (1965) was wider. It asserted the parity and the tight union between Scripture and tradition*. It further stated that "it was not only from the Scripture that the Church took its certainty on all the points of the revelation*" (*DV* II, 9): with this point concerning "certainty" according to faith, junction of Scripture and tradition, the field of biblical theology is defined, as well as the risks it entails. This same document enhances without fuss a typological reading (*DV* IV); but, on the other hand, inasmuch as "theological studies and fraternal dialogues" bring Christians and Jews closer to each other, as recommended by *Nostra Aetate* (1965, no. 4), biblical theology is encouraged to respect the specificity of the Old Testament and to find the spiritual scope of its "literal meaning."

• Reference Works with Extensive Bibliographies

Dictionnaire de la Bible. Supplement, 1928–, Paris.

G. Strecker (Ed.) (1975), *Das Problem der Theologie des Neuen Testaments,* Darmstadt (collection of articles 1787–1974).

H. Graf Reventlow (1982), *Hauptprobleme der altestamentlichen Theologie im 20. Jahrhundert,* WdF 367. (English trans., London, 1985.)

H. Graf (1983), *Hauptprobleme der biblischen Theologie im 20. Jahrhundert,* Darmstadt. (English trans., London, 1987.)

R.J. Coggins, J.L. Houlden (Ed.) (1990), A *Dictionary of Biblical Interpretation,* London.

Modern Problematics

Interpretation: Biblical Theology Bulletin (trimestrial), Grand Rapids (1946–).

Interpretation: A Journal of Bible and Theology (trimestrial), South Orange, 1971–.

Biblical Theology: Problems and Propositions

R. Simon (1678), *Histoire critique du Vieux Testament,* Paris, Rotterdam (5th Ed., 1685).

F. Prat, "La théologie biblique et son enseignement dans les séminaires," *Recrutement sacerdotal,* December 1907, 1–15.

P. Grelot (1962), *Sens chrétien de l'Ancien Testament: Esquisse d'un Traité dogmatique,* 2nd Ed., Paris.

B.S. Childs (1970), *Biblical Theology in Crisis,* Philadelphia.

H.J. Kraus (1970), *Die biblische Theologie: Ihre Geschichte und Problematik,* Neukirchen-Vluyn.

X. Léon-Dufour (1970), *Vocabulaire de théologie biblique,* 2nd Ed. Paris.

P. Beauchamp (1976), *L'un et l'autre Testament: Essai de lecture,* Paris.

H. Clavier (1976), *Les variétés de la pensée biblique et le problème de son unité,* Leyden.

P. Beauchamp (1982), "Théologie biblique," in B. Lauret, F. Refoulé (Ed.), *Initiation à la pratique de la théologie,* vol. 1: *Introduction,* 185–232, Paris; (1990), *L'un et l'autre Testament,* vol. 2: *Accomplir les Écritures,* Paris; (1992), "Accomplir les Écritures. Un chemin de théologie biblique," *RB* 99, 132–62.

N. Lohfink (1993), *Studien zur biblischen Theologie,* Stuttgart.

P. Ricœur, A. Lacocque (1998), *Penser la Bible,* Paris.

Old Testament Theologies

W. Eichrodt (vol. 1, 1933; vol. 2, 1935; vol. 3, 1939), *Theologie des Alten Testaments,* Leipzig.

G. von Rad (1957), *Theologie des Alten Testaments,* vol. 1: *Die Th. der geschichtlichen Überlieferungen Israels;* (1960), vol. 2: *Die Th. der prophetischen Überlieferungen Israels,* Munich.

E. Jacob (1968), *Théologie de l'Ancien Testament,* 2nd Ed., Neuchâtel.

G. Botterweck, H. Ringgren (Ed.) *Theologisches Wörterbuch zum Alten Testament (ThWAT),* (1973–, 8 vols. published in 1997) (English trans., Grand Rapids, 1974–.)

R. Rendtorff (1983), *Vorarbeiten zu einer Theologie des Alten Testaments,* Neukirchen-Vluyn. (English trans., 1994.)

C. R. Seitz (1997), *The Old Testament As Abiding Theological Witness,* Grand Rapids-Cambridge.

New Testament Theologies

M. Meinertz (1950), *Theologie des Neuen Testaments,* Bonn.

H. Conzelmann (1967), *Grundriss der Theologie des Neuen Testaments,* Munich.

R. Bultmann (1968), *Theologie des Neuen Testaments,* 5th Ed., Tübingen. (English trans., London, 1965.)

J. Jeremias (1971), *Neutestamentliche Theologie,* vol. 1: *Die Verkündigung Jesu,* Gütersloh.

L. Goppelt (1975, 1976), *Theologie des Neuen Testaments,* 2 vols.

For additional bibliographic references *see* ***Scriptures, Senses of.***

PAUL BEAUCHAMP

See also **Bible; Canon of Scriptures; Exegesis; Hermeneutics; History; Holy Scripture; Jesus, Historical; Johannine Theology; Literary Genres in Scripture; Narrative; Narrative Theology; Pauline Theology; Scripture, Fulfillment of; Scripture, Senses of**

Biel, Gabriel. *See* **Nominalism**

Bishop

1. New Testament

a) Definitions. There are five different usages of the word *episkopos* in the New Testament. It is the title of Jesus Christ* in 1 Peter 2:25, and it designates Christians in charge of a ministry* of vigilance in Acts 20:28; Philippians 1:1; 1 Timothy 3:2; and Titus 1:7. In Ephesus, the expression is used for elders designated by the Holy* Spirit as pastors* of the Church* of God* (Acts 20:28).

This term, which was already secular in the Septuagint, was borrowed from the profane Greek, and that does not exclude the influence of the synagogal model, which sees the *arkhisunagôgos* being assisted by the *huperetès,* like the episcopate being assisted by the deacons*. The influence of the *mebaqqer* of Qumran on the origins of the episcopate does not seem plausible.

b) Episcopate. In charge of a local church*, the bishops are distinct from the apostles*, prophets* and doctors*—itinerant and charismatic—and also from the deacons, their collaborators. On the other hand, it is not possible to distinguish them in any other way than through the vocabulary of the *presbyterium* who occupy the same functions in communities that are more Judeo-Christian (Acts 20:17 and 28 place them in the same category). They are always mentioned in the plural (the singular of 1 Tm 3:2 and Ti 1:7 is generic, like *presbuteros* in 1 Tm 5:1). They are also presidents (Rom 12:8; 1 Thes 5:12; 1 Tm 5:17) and pastors (Eph 4:11).

In the Pastorals, the episcopate is being entrusted with the teaching ministry regarding prophets and doctors (1 Tm 3:2: *didaktikos*, 4:11, 6:2; Ti 1:9), which is what *Didache* 15, 1–2. says explicitly. Faith is left in their custody (1 Tm 6:20; 2 Tm 1:12, 14, and 4:2; Ti 1:13). They are required (1 Tm 3:1–7) to have solid Christian qualities, a good family life ("the husband of one wife... with all dignity keeping his children submissive") and good standing in society ("he must be well thought of by outsiders, a statement of good character from people in the community").

2. Classical Profile of the Bishop

a) Monoepiscopate. In the *Didache* (98) and the writings of Clement (96?), which reflect the context of Corinth and of Rome* (and it was probably the same in Alexandria), the *épiskopè* is exercised collegially (1 Clem. 44, 1. 4–5). The letters of Ignatius of Antioch (110–150?) are the first clear evidence of the monoepiscopate (for Syria) and of a subordinate articulation of priests* and deacons. Monoepiscopate and tripartition of the ordained ministry are not therefore scriptural: Vatican* II mentioned tripartition as being *ab antiquo* (*LG* 28). In any event, the uniqueness of the bishop and the territoriality of his jurisdiction represent signs and safeguards regarding the actual catholicity of the eucharistic and ecclesial assembly ("Wherever the bishop appears... the Catholic Church is present," Ignatius, *Sm.* 8, 2; *see also* Nicaea*, can. 8, *COD* 9–10); bishops without a well-determined seat and territory and auxiliary bishops are unknown (coadjutors are extremely rare). As for chorebishops in charge of rural districts, they would be downgraded and called *presbyterium* after the Peace* of the Church.

Monoepiscopate does not mean monarchical episcopate: the bishop must be elected with the support of his church; he must have the benefit of reception*, in his church as well as from his colleagues, in order to keep his office. As attested by Cyprian*, he deals with his colleagues, but also with his people* (*Ep* 14, 4; 34, 4).

b) Election. Election is necessary, but it is not sufficient for obtaining the office: also needed is the laying* on of hands of all the bishops of the region (at least three, Nicaea, can. 4, *COD* 7), which is accompanied, for the ordained, by the gift of the Holy* Spirit.

c) Apostolic Succession. Clement (1 Clem. 44, 2–4) invokes already the rule of the apostolic* succession. Irenaeus* (180) reproduces the Roman list, which comes from Hegesippus (150?). Peter* is not mentioned at the top of the list, because bishops do not take the place of the apostles* and they only in part succeed them; the succession is not established according to the uninterrupted chain of the laying on of hands, but according to the presidency of a local* church, which expresses the link uniting the apostolic faith* of all and the apostolic ministry of a few.

Succession lists—which later on would start with the mention of the founding apostle—were established everywhere (Antioch, Alexandria, etc.) according to the same principles.

d) President of the Local Church and Link with the Catholic Communion. Established symbolically by the whole group of his colleagues, the local bishop represents, in his church, the faith and the communion of all the Church. He is thus ordained to preside over the service of the word* and of the sacraments* (baptism*, Eucharist*, reconciliation). Both elected and received, simultaneously, by his church, he can represent it in its relationship with all the others. He is the link par excellence of the ecclesial communion*. This provides the basis for the ecclesiological weight of the regional and ecumenical councils*.

e) The Metropolitan. Established in the regional capitals, the Metropolitan also presides over the councils under his jurisdiction. Canons 4 and 6 of Nicaea (*COD* 7, 8–9) back his customary role (future patriarchate*), to the point that an episcopal ordination* is null and void without his consent: the sacramental power of the ordained bishop is regulated by the higher power of the ecclesial communion.

In the preceding stipulations, the Catholic bishop (or the present-day Orthodox bishop) sees the classical role of his ministry as pastor and celebrant, with the major responsibility of announcing the apostolic faith as well as the communion in his church and among the churches. Without corresponding literally to the absolute will of Jesus Christ*, this role appears, however, to be a faithful transcription of it, for which there is no prescription in spite of numerous historical vicissitudes.

3. Subsequent Evolution

In the East, Justinian imposed celibacy on the bishops (*CIC (B). C* 2, 25–26), who until recent times were recruited among the monks or widowers. Popular participation in the election of the bishops has survived only in Cyprus and in Antioch: the Byzantine emperors, then the czars, eliminated it elsewhere. Finally, for want of an effective primate, among other factors, the Orthodox bishops have not met in ecumenical council* since A.D. 787.

In the West, despite numerous holy bishops, and attempts at reform *in capite et in membris,* the vicissitudes of the episcopate were much more serious following its integration into feudal structures, then later into those of the ancien régime. In spite of the general law, political authorities quite often controlled the election of bishops; they were even able to get the right to do so by obtaining a concordat from Francis I. The Germanic principalities and the Italian peninsula during the Renaissance witnessed the gravest kinds of abuses: holding more than one bishopric, failing to reside in the diocese, nonordained bishops (because of the split between order and jurisdiction*), monopoly exercised by the nobility, lack of reaction against the Reformation. In spite of the Council of Trent*, it was only the fall of the ancien régime that brought an end to such abuses, which were still being practiced at the time.

While frequently keeping an *episkopè* that was larger than the local pastorate and was endowed with a different kind of base, the Reformation often had to reject an episcopate that was hardly credible evangelically. The German Lutherans transferred that function to the temporal authority of the prince, on the basis of *praecipuum membrum ecclesiae.*

4. Theology of the Episcopate after Vatican II

Completing the work of Vatican* I, which had remained unfinished, Vatican* II presented the episcopate against the background of the communion of the local churches, by establishing its foundation on its sacramentality and to a degree renewing its relationship with the Roman primacy. Four orientations are notable:

a) Pastoral service is again at the forefront (*LG* 18, 1; *LG* 24, “the task has been entrusted to the pastors . . . a true service following the Scripture*”; *LG* 27, “to be of service”). As a consequence, the benefice system is abolished for good.

b) Sacramentally Based. Based on Jerome’s opinion (*Ep.* 146), the medieval thesis (P. Lombard, *IV Sent.* 24, PL 192, 904) according to which the episcopate distinguishes itself from the presbyterate only for a matter of jurisdiction has been corrected: “the episcopal ordination confers fulfillment of the sacrament of the order*"; furthermore, "as it confers the task of sanctifying, it also bestows that of teaching and governing" (*LG* 21). As matters of principle, order and jurisdiction are reunited, with orthodox theology* are rekindled, and the episcopate becomes again a full-fledged ministry: "the pastoral charge... is fully entrusted to the bishops; they should not be considered as the vicars of the Roman pontiffs, because they do exercise their own power, a power that is theirs... and that is not at all obliterated by the superior and universal authority; on the contrary, it is strengthened, reinforced, and defended by it" (*LG* 27).

c) Exercising the Triple Ministry of the Word, the Sacraments, and the Pastorate. Vatican II (*LG* 25–27) specifically states the mutual inclusion, in the episcopate, of the pastorate (organizing concept), the ministry of sacraments, and the ministry of the word*, by granting the latter a privilege: "preaching* the gospel is the first responsibility of the bishops" (*LG* 23).

d) Forming a College with Peter's Successor at Their Head, the Bishops Have in Their Charge the Whole Church. "The order of the bishops that succeeds the apostolic college in the magisterium* and in the pastoral government*... constitutes, in union with the Roman pontiff, its head, and never without its head, the subject of a supreme and plenary authority over the whole church" (*LG* 22). The institution of the episcopal conferences is strengthened by this, as well as the existence of the regional churches within the whole church. But the college as such is not empowered to act without the pope's authorization (authority*).

5. Ecumenical Requests

a) Growing Consensus Regarding the Episkopè. For the Orthodox Christians, who have only a regional primate, the relationship between bishop and pope remains a problem. The Anglican Church has kept the episcopate along with the presbyterate and the diaconate, but it hesitates to see in this a condition of the church's *esse.* The Lutherans officially accept entering into communion with the "historical" episcopate, but they enhance that according to their tradition*. The Reformed are more reticent. The Lima document *(BEM)* recommends in any case that all churches accept the episcopate, on the condition that it be linked together with collegial and synodal responsibility.

In 1982, this document, emanating from the ecumenical Faith and Constitution Commission of the Church of England (a commission of which the Catholic Church is a member), took up again a suggestion that had already been made in Lausanne in 1927: "In the constitution of the early church one finds the episcopal commission as well as the council of elders and the community of believers. Each of the three systems of church organization (episcopalism, presbyterianism, and congregationalism*) has been accepted in the past for centuries, and is still accepted by important portions of Christendom. Each of them is considered by its supporters as being essential to the church's good working order. Consequently, we consider that, under certain conditions, to be stated more clearly, the three systems will have to take their respective places simultaneously in the organization of the reunited Church" (*BEM,* no. 26).

b) Possible Contributions of Catholic Ecclesiology. Certain kinds of progress are possible here, as long as the divine right of the episcopate is better circumscribed and episcopocentrism is toned down by showing that the episcopate is at the service of realities that are more decisive than itself—the Holy Spirit, the gospel, the Eucharist, the people* of God (*CD* 11)—and by linking it in a better way with local synodality (synods* and councils). Collegiality* can become acceptable to other churches insofar as it shows that the bishops do not so much constitute "the higher governing body of the universal Church" (K. Rahner*) as the organs of communion among the local diocesan churches that make up the whole Church. Finally, the historical determinations contingent on the present relationship between primacy and episcopate (for example the direct nomination of almost all the bishops by the pope) should be recognized as such.

• H.W. Beyer, H. Karpp (1954), "Bischof," *RAC* 2, 394–407.

L. Koep (1954), "Bischofsliste," ibid., 407–15.

Y. Congar (Ed.) (1962), *L'épiscopat et l'Église universelle,* UnSa 39 (contributions by Y. Congar, H. Marot, C. Vogel).

H. Legrand (1969), "Nature de l'église particulière et rôle de l'évêque," in coll., *La charge pastorale des évêques,* UnSa 74, 103–223.

J. Neumann (1980), "Bischof I," *TRE* 6, 653–82 (bibl.).

H. Legrand, J. Manzanares, A. Garcia (Ed.) (1988), *Les conférences épiscopales: Théologie, statut canonique, avenir,* CFi 149.

R. Brown (1989–91), "Brief survey of New Testament evidence on *episkopè* and *episkopos,*" in *Episkopè and Episkopos in Ecumenical Perspective,* FOP 102.

The Porvoo Common Statement with Essays on Church and Ministry in Northern Europe (1992), London.

H. Legrand (1993), "Les ministères dans l'Église locale," in B. Lauret, F. Refoulé (Ed.), *Initiation à la pratique de la théologie,* 3rd Ed., vol. 3, 181–285.

J.B. d'Onorio (1994), "Nomination des évêques," in P. Levillain (Ed.), *Dictionnaire historique de la papauté,* Paris, 1178–83.

H.J. Pottmeyer (1994), "Bischof," *LThK3* 2, 484–7.

Hervé Legrand

See also **Apostolic Succession; Collegiality; Communion; Deacon; Local Church; Pope; Presbyter/Priest; Regional Church; Vatican II, Council of**

Blessing

A. Biblical Theology

Blessing is speech endowed with power that communicates the benefits of salvation* and life. It is also a prayer* of praise and thanksgiving for benefits received.

a) Vocabulary of Blessings. Hebrew lexicons identify two groups of words with the root *brk.* One group is related to kneeling (from *bèrèk,* "knee"); the second, which is used nearly 400 times in the Old Testament, has the sense of blessing. It is found most frequently in Genesis (88 times), particularly in the story of the patriarchs, and in Psalms* (83 times), in connection with the praise of God*. The language of praise is also well represented in Deuteronomy (51 times) and to a lesser degree in the Wisdom* books, but it plays only a minor role in the books of the Prophets.

The root *brk* has the basic meaning of the power of life and of salvation. Associated to a very great degree with speech, it has a similar efficacy. Hence, blessing accomplishes what it expresses. Although not equivalent to them, it has strong affinities with the words *peace* (shâlôm), happiness (tûb),* and *life (chaîim).* It frequently appears in contexts involving the vocabulary of *love* ('ahab), grace** and *benevolence (chén), fidelity and loyalty (chèsèd),* and *success (çâlach).* Another term meaning "happiness" *('èshèr)* is practically synonymous with blessing, and is sometimes translated as such. Not as rich in nuances as the root *brk,* it has a clearly declarative sense: happy/blessed *('ashrè)* "is the man who walks not in the counsel of the wicked... but his delight is in the law of the Lord" (Ps 1:1–2). The word *'ashrè,* translated as *makarios* in Greek, introduces the literary form of the Beatitudes (*see* Mt 5:3–11).

The vocabulary of the curse, on the other hand, is very diversified. The curses of the Covenant* (Dt 27:11–26) contrast the blessed *(bârûk)* to the cursed *('ârûr).* The verb in the intensive means: "to make a curse effective." There is also the root *'âlâh,* "curse," *qâlal,* which adds the nuance of being small or contemptible, *qâbab,* which expresses execration in a somewhat magical sense, and *zâ'am,* which communicates the idea of anger. The interjection *hôi* can be either an exclamatory curse (Is 1:4) or an expression of mourning: "Alas!" (1 Kgs 13:30).

b) Diverse Expressions. In its simple active form, the verb is used only as a passive participle, *bârûk,* in various formulations: "Blessed be the LORD, who has delivered you" (Ex 18:10); "Blessed be Abram by God Most High" (Gn 14:19); and "May he be blessed by the Lord, whose kindness has not forsaken the living or the dead!" (Ru 2:20). The participle designates the state of the one who possesses the blessing and who, as such, deserves appreciation, homage, or praise.

The intensive conjugation is by far the most frequently attested (233 times in the active voice). To bless someone is to grant him or wish for him the power needed to accomplish a particular task in a particular situation. The verb takes on various nuances depending on whether the person being blessed is a superior, an inferior, or someone of equal rank. It is not necessary to articulate the contents of the blessing; the verb has intrinsic power. When a person blesses God, the blessing is akin to praise. The noun *berâkâh* appears 71 times (16 in Genesis and 12 in Deuteronomy) with the many nuances of the verb.

c) Meaning of Blessing. In the Bible*, the blessing has lost the magical quality that it may have had in the Semitic world. Its efficacy derives from the Word* of God, a God who wills the happiness of man, but who does not bring it about outside the bounds of his liberty*. By promoting the good of the other and by recognizing his merits, the blessing first of all expresses a bond of solidarity and communion among beings, even in those circumstances in which it is the equivalent of a greeting. People who bless one another are bound together. The curse that excludes a person from the group makes life impossible for the rejected individual. God blesses his Chosen People* and its members. He communicates his blessing directly or through authorized mediators, such as the head of the family, the king, the priest*, or the prophet. The blessing God grants to Abraham is a pledge that all the families of the earth are called upon to benefit from it by reference to Abraham (Gn 12:1–3). The blessing that God gives to man when he creates him includes all living things in the universe (Gn 1:28–30). It is to be transmitted from generation to generation. The family is the first site of this transmission, as the history* of the patriarchs shows (Gn 27). The blessing is tied to the Covenant, and observance of the law is the condition enabling the people to enjoy happiness and prosperity on the land that God has given them (Dt 30:15–20). The blessing is an integral part of worship, as can be seen in Solomon's prayer at the dedication of the Temple (1 Kgs 8:54–61).

When man blesses God, he responds by praise and thanksgiving to the work of God. The blessing is a major element in the prayer of Israel*. Thus the root *brk* is often found in the Psalms, linked with such other terms as *hâlal* (to praise) and *yâdâh* (to confess). Indeed, the blessing bursts through the bounds of ritual, because it is a spontaneous expression of the soul of Israel.

d) Blessing in the New Testament. The Septuagint translates *brk* most often with the verb *eulogeô* and its derivatives, *eulogètos* and *eulogia.* The Semitic background prevents the interpretation of these terms as merely "speaking well." In the New Testament the verb is found 41 times, the adjective 8 times, and the noun 16 times. It is most frequent in the synoptic Gospels (particularly Luke), Paul's letters, and Hebrews.

Following the lines of the doxologies of the Old Testament and Jewish tradition*, God is the first to be blessed (Lk 1:68). He is blessed as Creator (Rom 1:25) and as "Father* of the Lord Jesus" (2 Cor 11:31). Several blessings provide elaborations of God's work in the history of salvation, culminating in Jesus Christ (2 Cor 1:3–7; Eph 1:3–14; and 1 Pt 1:3–9). Jesus* is the quintessentially blessed (Lk 1:42 and 13:35). It is in Christ that the Father blesses his faithful with all spiritual blessings (Eph 1:3). It is through him that the blessing given to Abraham may reach all humanity (Acts 3:25–26). Mary* is the first blessed among all women (Lk 1:42), and the elect are blessed of the Father (Mt 25:34). At the Last Supper, Jesus pronounced the blessing on the bread (Mt 26:26; Mk 14:22). Far from being a magical formula, this blessing is a prayer of thanksgiving for the work of salvation accomplished by God, as suggested by Jewish ritual. The accounts establish a connection between the verbs *eulogeô* and *eukharisteô,* "to give thanks." In the doxologies of the Book of Revelation, the association of *eulogia* with the terms *glory** and *honor* support the meaning of praise.

• H. W. Beyer (1935), "Eulogeô," *ThWNT* 2, 751–3.
J.-P. Audet (1958), "Esquisse historique du genre littéraire de la 'bénédiction' juive et de l'Eucharistie chrétienne," *RB* 65, 371–99.
W. Schenk (1967), *Der Segen im NT,* Berlin.
C. Westermann (1968), *Der Segen in der Bibel und im Handeln der Kirche,* Gütersloh.
J. Guillet (1969), "Le langage spontané de la bénédiction dans l'AT," *RSR* 57, 163–204.
J. Scharbert (1973 *a*), "Krb hkrb," *ThWAT* 1, 808–41; (1973 *b*), "Die Geschichte der *bârûk* Formel," *BZ* 17, 1–28.
C. A. Keller, G. Wehmeier (1978), "*Brk* pi. segnen," *THAT* 1, 353–76.
H. Patsch (1981), *Eulogeô, EWNT* 2, 198–201.
C. T. Mitchell (1987), *The Meaning of* brk *"to bless" in the Old Testament,* Atlanta.

Joseph Auneau

See also **Covenant; Creation; Cult; Eucharist; Father; Filiation; Praise; Prayer; Psalms**

B. In the Liturgy

a) Overview. Christian liturgies* in both East and West bring together under the heading "blessings" very diverse prayers, at least some of which are continuous with prayer* practices previously used in Judaism*. Some of these prayers—such as those for blessing or consecrating oils for liturgical use or for blessing a spouse at a wedding—are integrated with the celebration of the sacraments*. Others have a place within the celebration of the Eucharist or among the prayers of the divine office. Still others are related to all the various circumstances of the life of families, societies, and religious communities.

The importance of these blessings has varied a great deal according to times and places. In addition, their religious tone has also varied to a certain degree, depending on whether the particular blessing emphasized thanksgiving for divine benefits, with a tone close to that of the ancient Eucharist, or involved, as in the Middle Ages in Germany, an aspect of exorcism*. In any event, it is essential for every blessing that it be an invocation of divine goodness.

Blessings are important in the life of the church*, the family*, and society*. As a result, various blessings, depending on their field of importance, have always been under the auspices of the particular ministry* of the bishop*. For example, as a general rule, the consecration of churches—or, in another domain, royal coronations—are reserved for bishops. Most other blessings, in the Catholic Church, have been assigned to priests*, with no sharp demarcation between a blessing given by a priest and one pronounced by the father in a family setting.

b) Main Collections of Blessings in the Liturgical Tradition.

- *Apostolic Tradition* (probably Rome, first third of the third century) preserves two examples of blessing: the blessing at the end of the eucharistic prayer and the blessings of the milk and honey in the celebration of baptism*. The latter followed a practice of the very early church, before the separation between the Eucharist and a meal took place. At that time milk and honey were given to the newly baptized between the Communion* of bread and the Communion of wine, in a sort of ritual of the Promised Land, in antithesis to the bitter herbs of the Jewish Passover ritual (which recalled the exodus from Egypt).
- *Sacramentary of Serapion* (bishop of Thmuis), a collection of Greek prayers from Egypt (probably from the fourth or fifth century).
- Byzantine *Euchologe,* body of liturgical prayers from around the ninth century.
- In the West, various formulations of the blessing of the Easter candle by the deacon*, which had remained rather close to the Jewish blessing of light (there are examples beginning in the fourth century, of which the best known is the *Exultet* of the Roman liturgy).
- Episcopal blessings given at the end of the Mass. These blessings are of Gallican origin, and their form was restored for festivals in the Roman Missal of 1970.
- *Sacramentary of Gellone,* a Carolingian manuscript that gives the earliest evidence of the body of rural blessings used in the Middle Ages.
- *Rituale Romanum* (1614), with a limited number of blessings, considerably expanded in 1874 and 1895.
- After Vatican* II, the *De Benedictionibus* (1984), which eliminates the element of exorcism and presents a proclamation of the Word* of God* as a preamble to any blessing. In addition, the ministry of blessing is carried out in certain cases by a deacon or a member of the laity*.

• J. Goar (1730), *Euchologion sive Rituale Graecorum,* 2nd Ed., Venice.

A. Franz (1909), *Die kirchlichen Benediktionen des Mittelalters,* Freiburg.

P.-M. Gy (1959), "Die Segnung von Milch und Honig in der Osternacht," in B. Fischer, J. Wagner (Ed.), *Paschatis Sollemnia: Festschrift J. A. Jungmann,* Freiburg, 206–12.

B. Botte (1963), *La Tradition apostolique de S. Hippolyte: Essai de reconstitution,* Münster.

A. Stuiber (1966), "Eulogia," *RAC 6,* 900–928.

E. Moeller (1971–79), *Corpus benedictionum pontificalium,* CChr.CM 162–162 c.

A. Heinz, H. Rennings (Ed.) (1987), *Heute Segnen: Werkbuch zum Benediktionale,* Freiburg.

A.-M. Triacca, A. Pistoia (Ed.) (1988), *Les bénédictions et les sacramentaux dans la liturgie,* Rome.

S. Parenti, E. Velkovska (1995), *L'Eucologio Barberini gr. 336,* Rome.

Pierre-Marie Gy

See also **Cult; Liturgy; Praise; Prayer; Sacrament**

Blondel, Maurice

1861–1949

1. Renewal of Philosophical Perspectives

a) Early Writings. From his work *L'Action* (1893) to "Principe élémentaire d'une logique de la vie morale" (1903), Blondel uses the "method of immanence" that appeared in the *Lettre sur l'apologétique* (1896). The perspective is centered on the inherent content of human action, and its full application leads to the necessary presence of transcendence within the heart of our acting. This phenomenological analysis is an attempt to solve the problem set forth in the short thesis *De Vinculo substantiali* (1893), the action being identified with the substantial link that is sought. However, Blondel tends more toward a Pascalian than a Leibnitzian perspective: reason* should acknowledge its own insufficiency and openness to the hypothesis of the supernatural, which could be verified only by the faithful action.

b) Prospecting and Reflection. In "Le point de départ de la recherche philosophique" (1906), Blondel distinguishes two complementary directions of thought: that of "prospecting," oriented toward synthetic and concrete action, and the analytical and derived "reflection" or "retrospection" by which thought reflects upon its action to analyze its conditions and components. Philosophical knowledge only emerges by taking into account both of these dimensions. Thus it can either be a reflection on the integrity of the prospective synthesis, as was *L'Action* in 1893, or a prospective grasping of the reflection itself, eliciting this "metaphysics to the second power" used in the trilogy.

c) Later Works. The achievement period begins with *L'itinéraire philosophique de Maurice Blondel* (1928), in which he rereads his own history and announces the main themes to come; it ends with *Exigences philosophiques du christianisme* (1950), which gives precious insights about his methodology. At the center, there is his great work: the trilogy (*La Pensée* I and II, 1934; *L'Être et les êtres,* 1935; *L'Action* I and II, 1936–37) and *La philosophie et l'esprit chrétien* (I and II, 1944–46). Blondel thus tried to solve the problem posed in 1930 in *Une énigme historique: Le "Vinculum Substantiale" d'après Leibniz**—a deeply modified continuation of his Latin thesis. Blondel now uses a "method of *implication*" with metaphysical reach. The fundamental relation is the tension between the *noetic* and the *pneumatic,* inseparable and unconfusable. The noetic, "concrete universal," remains only in the pneumatic, "singular concrete," an original point of view on the universal, the "ontological breath" in a center of perception. The irreducibility of the noetic to the pneumatic in any finite being, a sign of its finitude, such is matter, of which only God* is exempt. Consequently, Blondel builds an integral realism that overrides the impasses of both dogmatic realism and critical idealism. He thus opens philosophy* to a dialogue with "the Christian spirit," the enigmas of reason and the revealed mysteries elucidating each other.

2. Blondel and Catholic Theology

a) Historicism and Extrinsicism: History and Dogma (1904). Applying the philosophy of action to the biblical question, at the heart of the modernist crisis, Blondel first denounces the historicism that substitutes the "science" of history* for its reality and the extrinsicism that only establishes an extrinsic relationship of the facts with dogma*. These two "incomplete and incompatible solutions" miss the mediation between history and the dogma constituted by tradition*, the faithful action of Christian people* that ties us to the founding action and from which is "extracted what enters little by little in writings and formulas." In this way he resolves the modernist crisis, in right if not in fact.

b) "Efference" and "Afference": The Social Week of Bordeaux and Monophorism (1910). Under the pseudonym Testis, Blondel set forth to untangle the "fundamentalist crisis," which is symmetrical to modernism. He defends social Catholicism* against the attacks of those who assimilate it to "sociological modernism." He establishes that the thesis of the purely extrinsic afference of Christian truths* "is no less inexact than the thesis according to which everything derives from within, by efference": two varieties of the same type, which he would call "monophorism." On the contrary, Christianity thrives on the intimate conjunction of a double afference, internal and external. This was already shown in the "Méthode de la Providence" by Cardinal Dechamps, which Blondel studied in 1905–7, and also in *Le problème de la philosophie catholique* in 1932.

c) Blondel's Impact on Contemporary Theology. It is difficult to measure Blondel's impact on theology, which is more often implicit. It does seem considerable, however, particularly with regard to the fundamental developments of Vatican* II. To mention only two central figures, Blondel's influence on Lubac was key, not only on the supernatural or the sense of active tradition, but also on the entire philosophical substructure of his "organic work." Balthasar*'s theology was also influenced by Blondel, even though Balthasar initially distanced himself from Blondel. Still, his last works acknowledge Blondel's capital importance.

- R. Virgoulay, C. Troisfontaines (1975–76), *M. Blondel: Bibliographie analytique et critique*: I. *Œuvres de M. Blondel* (1880–1973); II. *Études sur M. Blondel* (1893–1975), Louvain.

C. Troisfontaines (Ed.), *OC,* Paris, 1995.

♦ A. and A. Valensin (1911), "Immanence (méthode d')," *Dictionnaire apologétique de la foi catholique* 2, 579–612.

R. Virgoulay (1980), *Blondel et le modernisme: La philosophie de l'action et les sciences religieuses, 1896–1943,* Paris.

P. Favraux (1987), *Une philosophie du Médiateur: M. Blondel,* Paris-Namur.

P. Gauthier (1988) *Newman et Blondel: Tradition et développement du dogme,* Paris.

C. Theobald (1988), *M. Blondel und das Problem der Modernität,* FTS 35.

M. Leclerc (1991), *L'union substantielle: M. Blondel et Leibniz,* Namur.

R. Virgoulay (1992), L'Action *de M. Blondel (1893): Relecture pour un centenaire,* Paris.
H. Wilmer (1992), *Mystik zwischen Tun und Denken: Ein neuer Zugang zur Philosophie M. Blondels,* Freiburg.

MARC LECLERC

See also **Balthasar, Hans Urs von; Catholicism; Experience; Lubac, Henri Sonier de; Modernism; Newman, John Henry; Pascal, Blaise; Philosophy; Rationalism; Relativism; Religion, Philosophy of; Revelation**

Body. *See* **Soul-Heart-Body**

Boethius

c. 480–524

Anicius Manlius Torquatus Severinus Boethius was the son of Flavius Manlius Boethius, consul in 487. Boethius was treated as friend and adviser by the Arian emperor Theodoric, and was himself consul in 510. An undeserved charge of treason kept him under house arrest until his execution. Dante* placed this "last of the Romans and first of the Scholastics" among the doctors* in his Paradise.

1. Works

a) Boethius perceived the danger that the increasing linguistic separation of the eastern and western halves of the Roman Empire, and the encroachments of the barbarians, would put access to Greek philosophical culture at risk in the West. He therefore set about translating Plato and Aristotle into Latin, but only a small part of the logic corpus was completed before his death, together with commentaries on Porphyry's Isagoge and Cicero's Topics, and some logical monographs of his own. With these should be grouped the treatises *De arithmetica* and *De musica,* both heavily dependent upon Greek sources.

b) Boethius also wrote five short theological tractates: *On the Catholic Faith; Against Eutyches and Nestorius; On the Trinity; Whether Father, Son, and Holy Spirit are Substantially Predicated of the Trinity;* and *De Hebdomadibus.* The influence of Augustine* is clear, but Boethius goes further and develops arguments of his own. The first tractate is a confession of faith*, without detailed philosophical analysis. The second was prompted by the debate invoked by a letter from an Eastern bishop* to the pope* on points of Christology. Present at the debate, Boethius learned of the Nestorian view that Christ* is both *of* and *in* two natures, and the Monophysite, "Eutychian" view that Christ is *of* two natures, but not *in* two natures. He therefore addresses the underlying questions about "nature" and "person*" and their relationship, and created a definition of the person which would have the most influence (a person is "an individual substance of a rational nature," *naturae rationabilis individua substantia, Contra Eut. et Nest.* 3). The christological controversy had been going on in Greek: Boethius was the first to attempt a comprehensive treatment in Latin. He was thus led to complete the philosophical terminology of Cicero and, with Marius Victorinus, determined the Latin equivalents of the Greek terms for the whole of the Middle Ages. In the two tractates on the Trinity*, of which the first is by far the more developed, Boethius explores concepts of form, unity, plurality, identity, and difference. He makes the point that the Aristotelian categories apply differently to God*. In the Godhead all accidents are substantive. Only relation exists absolutely between the Persons of the Trinity. The *De Hebdomadibus,* on "How substances are good in virtue of their existence without being substantial goods," takes the form of a series of axioms that can be applied by those wise enough to the resolution of the problem that is the subject of the treatise.

c) The Consolation of Philosophy depicts Boethius in prison awaiting execution, discoursing with a personified Philosophy about how to come to terms with the problems of evil*, liberty*, and providence*. Boethius begins from a Stoic viewpoint, but moves with Philosophy's help to a position in tune with Christian Platonism*. The duty of the soul* is to seek its Creator, the One who is above all change and who has nothing to do with evil. All goods are one, and the pursuit of happiness is the pursuit of unity with the One who is the Good*. Eternity he sees as the complete, simultaneous and perfect possession of endless life (*interminabilis vitae tota simul et perfecta possessio, Cons.* V, 6), another definition that was to have a major influence. Boethius owes a substantial debt here to the first part of *Timaeus* (all that was then accessible in the West). Providence now begins to look different: it permits things that we do not perceive as good at the time but that prove to be right for us. Boethius thus comes to a different kind of acceptance from the Stoic, and to hope. *The Consolation of Philosophy* led its medieval readers to wonder whether Boethius was a Christian, for there is no question in it of Christ or of salvation* by the cross. Nevertheless, everything in it is *theology**, in Augustine's sense, and there is nothing in Boethius's Platonism that is incompatible with Christian faith.

2. Posterity

a) Boethius's logic texts shaped the study of logic in the West until the 12th century, when the remainder of Aristotle's texts on logic were rendered into Latin. Boethius's contribution encouraged the early medieval emphasis on problems of epistemology and signification.

b) Boethius's theological tractates were taken up with enthusiasm by scholars of the early 12th century (such as Gilbert de la Porrée), and they had an important influence on the development of the use of logic in theology. The *De Hebdomadibus* prompted an interest in demonstrative method that was to grow with the translation of Euclid and the reintroduction of Aristotle's *Posterior Analytics* into the West, also during the 12th century. The *De Trinitate* contains a version of the Platonic division of knowledge that places mathematics between theology and the sciences* of nature. This encouraged 12th-century attempts to classify the sciences and, importantly, implicitly stressed the division between those aspects of theology that can be attempted by philosophical methods and those that are historical, depending on revelation* (a division taken up by Hugh of Saint*-Victor and others). Use was also made in the Middle Ages of what Boethius has to say about which of the Aristotelian categories apply to God, and the ways in which they do so.

c) Boethius's most influential work throughout the Middle Ages was *The Consolation of Philosophy.* This work was much imitated, notably by Gerson in his *De Consolatione Theologiae.*

• Boethius: PL 63–4 (complete works).

Commentarii in librum Aristotelis De Interpretatione, Ed. C. Meiser, Leipzig, Teubner, 1877–80.

De arithmetica and *De musica,* Ed. G. Friedlein, Leipzig, Teubner, 1867 (repr. Frankfurt, 1966).

De Consolatione Philosophiae, Ed. L. Bieler, CChr.SL 94.

De syllogismis hypotheticis, Ed. L. Obertello, Brescia, University of Parma, 1969.

In Isagogen Porphyrii Commenta, Ed. S. Brandt, CSEL 48.

Theological Tractates and *De Consolatione Philosophiae,* Ed. H. Stewart, E. K. Rand, S. J. Tester, LCL.

♦ M. Nédoncelle (1955), "Les variations de Boèce sur la personne," *RevSR* 29, 201–38.

P. Hadot (1963), "La distinction de l'être et de l'étant dans le *De Hebdomadibus* de Boèce," MM II, 147–53.

P. Courcelle (1967), *La consolation de Philosophie dans la tradition littéraire: Antécédents et postérité de Boèce,* Paris.

L. Obertello (1974), *Severino Boezio,* 2 vols., Geneva.

H. Chadwick (1981), *Boethius: The Consolations of Music, Logic, Theology and Philosophy,* Oxford (repr. 1990).

M. Gibson (1981) (Ed.), *Boethius: His Life, Thought and Influence,* Oxford.

M. Masi (1981), *Boethius and the Liberal Arts,* Berne.

L. Pozzi (1981), "Boethius," *TRE* 7, 18–28 (bibl.).

A. J. Minnis (1987) (Ed.), *The Medieval Boethius: Studies in the Vernacular Translations of the De Consolatione Philosophiae,* Cambridge.

C. Micaelli (1988), *Studi sui trattati teologici di Boezio,* Naples.

Gillian R. Evans

See also **Arianism; Aristotelianism, Christian; Attributes, Divine; Monophysitism; Nestorianism; Stoicism, Christian**

Boethius of Dacia. *See* **Naturalism; Truth**

Bogomiles. *See* **Catharism**

Bonaventure

1217–74

I. The Franciscan

1. Life

Giovanni Fidanza, the future Bonaventure, was born about 1217 in Bagnoregio, a little town near Orvieto. His father was a physician. At about the age of 12 Giovanni recovered from a serious illness through the intercession of Saint Francis of Assisi. After his studying at the Faculty of Arts in Paris from 1235 to 1243, he entered the Franciscan Order, taking the name of Bonaventure. He studied in the Faculty of Theology under Alexander of Hales, John of La Rochelle, Eudes Rigauld, and William of Middleton. He was licensed as a bachelor of Scripture in 1248, produced a commentary of the *Sentences* of Peter Lombard in 1250, received a master's degree in 1252, and was granted his *licentia docendi* (teaching license) at the end of 1253 or the beginning of 1254. Forthwith he became a teaching master in the friars' schools. Then, on 2 February 1857 he was elected minister-general of the Franciscan Order.

In October 1259 at Mount La Verna Bonaventure conceived the idea of his *Itinerarium mentis in Deum (The Soul's Journey into God).* He visited Italy, then France, and in Paris he preached the *Collationes de Decem Praeceptis* (Collations on the Ten Commandments) from 6 March to 17 April 1267, *De Septem Donis Spiritus Sancti* (On the Seven Gifts of the Holy Spirit) from 25 February to 7 April 1268, and *In Hexaemeron* (In the Six Days: The Hexameron) from 9 April to 28 May 1873. The last of this series of lectures was interrupted when Pope Gregory X made him cardinal-bishop of Albano. Consecrated bishop* in Lyons on 11 November 1273, Bonaventure prepared the Second Ecumenical Council* of Lyons*, which opened on 7 May 1274, and he preached a sermon at the council on 29 June 1274.

On 15 July 1274 Bonaventure was dead. He was buried in the Church of the Franciscan Friars in Lyons. Brother Peter of Tarantasia, a Dominican and cardinal-bishop of Ostia, celebrated the mass, preaching on the text of 2 Samuel 1:26, *Doleo super te, frater mi Ionatha* ("I am distressed for you, my brother Jonathan"). He said: "There were many tears and lamentations. God, indeed, had given him such grace that whosoever met him, their heart was instantly won over with love for him" *(Ordinatii Concilii).* Canonized on 14 April 1482, Bonaventure was declared a doctor* of the church on 14 March 1588.

2. Franciscan Roots

a) Franciscan Vocation. Saint Francis of Assisi's influence manifested itself several times in Bonaventure's life. The first of these interventions constitutes a kind of miracle*. Seriously ill, Bonaventure was vowed to Saint Francis by his mother. He would always feel fervent gratitude for the healing* thus brought about. This is why in 1260 he agreed to the Narbonne chapter's request and began to compose *The Life of Saint Francis,* which is known under the title of the *Legenda Maior* (The Major Life). For Francis, the friars' fundamental virtues* were simplicity, a prayerful mind (prayer*), and poverty. Knowledge as such, or study, had nothing to do with this. But, although Francis was not an intellectual, his thought and experience* had not made him an enemy of learning. Francis merely judged scholars in light of their relations with God*. He forbade neither study nor learning, on condition that the friars abandoned all attachment to possessions and were theologians "on their knees."

In Francis's various writings, which were known by Bonaventure, certain themes appear, which have contributed to the development of his theological thought. In Francis's "Letter to All the Faithful" (*Writings and Early Biographies: English Omnibus of Sources for the Life of St. Francis,* 4th Rev. Ed., 93), the address is revealing: "I decided to send you a letter bringing a message with the words of our Lord Jesus Christ, who is the Word of the Father*." In chapter 23 of the *Rule of 1221* he writes: "Almighty, most high and supreme God, Father, holy and just, Lord, King of heaven and earth, we give you thanks for yourself. Of your own holy will you created all things spiritual and physical, made us in your own image and likeness." In the same chapter of the *Rule,* Francis's first rule, he continues: "We are all poor sinners and unworthy to even to mention your name, and so we beg our Lord Jesus Christ, your beloved Son, *in whom* you are *well pleased* (Mt 17:5), and the Holy Spirit to give you thanks for everything, as it pleases you and them; there is never anything lacking in him to accomplish your will, and it is through him that you have done so much for us."

The theme of God's humility may have been suggested to Bonaventure by the Letter to a General Chapter *(Omnibus),* where Francis wrote: "What wonderful majesty! What stupendous condescension! O sublime humility! O humble sublimity! That the Lord of the whole universe, God and Son of God, should humble himself like this and hide under the form of a little bread, for our salvation. Look at God's condescension, my brothers, and *pour out your hearts before him.*" (Ps 61:9).

b) The School in Paris. The friars arrived in Paris in 1219 and set up their school in 1239 at the Monastery of the Cordeliers under the headship of Alexander of Hales. Bonaventure entered this monastery in 1243. There he increased his knowledge* of the mystery* of God by familiarizing himself with the works of Alexander, including his *Glossa* (Glosses), his *Disputed Questions (antequam esset frater),* or Questions Discussed (Before Becoming a Friar), and his *Questions (postquam esset frater),* or Questions (After Becoming a Friar). Alexander borrowed from the Greek Fathers* a theology* of the Trinity* that tackles this mystery* from the standpoint of the distinction among the divine Persons*, a view that Bonaventure adopted, while remaining Augustinian in the bulk of his thought. Thus, as he discusses in *On the Mystery of the Trinity* (q. 8, Quaracchi, vol. V, 115), the highest knowledge of the Trinity is found at the level of the *primitas* (primacy/prime person): "The Father produces the Son, and by means of the Son and with the Son, he produces the Holy Spirit: God the Father is, therefore, by means of the Son and with the Holy Spirit, the principle of all creation. For if he did not produce them eternally, he could not, through them, continue to produce through the span of time*. On account of this production, as is right, he is therefore called the source of life. For, since in this way he possesses life within himself, by means of himself, he empowers the Son to possess life. Eternal life* is therefore the only life, with the result that the reasonable mind, which emanates from the blessed Trinity and which is its image, returns in a sort of intelligible circle by means of memory, intelligence, and will, as well as by means of the deiformity of glory*, to the blessed Trinity."

It is clear that Bonaventure assimilated the teaching of Alexander, whom he called his "father and master"; and he profited from Alexander's sources, the Greek Fathers, especially from John of Damascus, Dionysius* the Pseudo-Areopagite, and the theologians who wrote in Latin, including Hilary* of Poitiers, Anselm*, Bernard*, and Richard of Saint*-Victor.

II. The Theologian

1. Writing and Theology

For Bonaventure, Scripture* was an absolute, the Word* of God. In the prologue to his *Breviloquium* (Summary) commenting on the text of Ephesians 3:14–19, Bonaventure writes: "One must begin at the beginning—that is to say, accede with pure faith* to the Father of light—by kneeling in our hearts*, so that through his Son, in his Holy Spirit, he gives us the true knowledge about Jesus Christ and, together with his knowledge, his love*. Knowing him and loving him, and as it were buttressed by faith and rooted in charity, it will then be possible for us to know the breadth, the length, the height, and the depth of the Holy Scripture, and, through this knowledge, to reach the total knowledge and inordinate love of the blessed Trinity. The saints' desires bend toward it: therein lies the end and aim of all truth and of all good*."

Knowledge of the cosmic Christ* is thus the source of an understanding of Scripture. Here on earth, we cannot possess this knowledge except through faith, for which God grants us the necessary wisdom*, for only wisdom allows us to penetrate the development of the Word of God and, in its light, to grasp the contents of the universe in its true dimensions. Scripture was made for man. Man is therefore capable of acquiring this knowledge and, through this knowledge, of discovering God's plenitude, in knowledge and love. Bonaventure describes the start, the revelation* that one receives through faith, progress, which covers the contents of the history*, and the end, which is the plenitude of God. Theology thus makes it possible to embrace at a glance the breadth of Scripture and to draw spiritual nourishment from it in an effective way. It is the epignosis of revelation: "Theology is the pious knowledge of truth* understood through faith" (*De Septem Donis,* col. 4, n. 5, Quaracchi, vol. V, 474). As Yves Congar says of Bonaventure in his "Théologie" (*DThC* XV, 394–97): "Rather than being an expression of faith in reason*, the light revealed in the human intellect is a gradual reintegration into the unity of God, through love and for love, of the intelligent man and of all the universe known by him."

2. Science and Wisdom

Scripture, therefore, is not a branch of learning; it is the Word of God, who seeks to make us better. Theology, on the other hand, is a branch of learning, unified and perfect. And what is more, it is a form of wisdom, for it does not merely exercise our faculty of reason. It is a living knowledge, in which intellectual meditation is constantly renewed and awakened through religious experience*.

Bonaventure's overall work is immense. It comprises 10 volumes of a critical edition, under the general editorship of Fidelis a Fanna, in Quaracchi (1882–1902). Bonaventure commented on Ecclesiastics and on the Gospels* according to Luke and John. He "read"—that is, he explained and commented on—the four books of Peter Lombard's *Sentences.* He discussed the Trinity, knowledge* about Christ, and evangelical perfection. As minister-general, and because of his teaching duties, he gave *Collations* (Lectures) on the Ten Commandments, on the seven gifts of the Holy Spirit, and on the six days of Creation* (*In Hexaemeron*). We know his 50 model sermons for Sundays*, 395 sermons destined for special Holy Days, and 62 sermons *de diversis.* But Bonaventure's two capital works are his *Breviloquium* and his *Itinerarium mentis in Deum.*

According to H. de Lubac* in his *Exégèse médiévale* (Medieval Exegesis, Paris 1961), *Breviloquium,* which will be discussed later, "shows a capacity for total synthesis never perhaps equaled." The *Itinerarium mentis in Deum* is, as it were, a discourse on the best method of reaching God through contemplation*. Bonaventure's Franciscan experience made God present in his heart and readable by him in Creation. Moreover, his philosophical viewpoint led him to follow back in time toward God himself the traces* *(vestigium)* and images of God. But the theologian takes precedence over the metaphysician in guiding the mind to the heart of the religious mystery and to contemplating God, no longer as the Creator but as God the Trinity, living infinitely and causing to live he who abandons himself to the effusions of his Holy Spirit, God All-Being and All-Good. Thus he succeeded in creating a synthesis of the Pseudo-Dionysian schemas and Augustine*'s authentic thought, an achievement that is all the more remarkable in that Bonaventure had to overturn the fundamental orientation of the Pseudo-Dionysius, which was totally alien to his Christocentrism.

What separated Bonaventure's conceptions from those of Thomas Aquinas could be described as a fundamental difference over the interpretation of given reality. Thomas stands firmly within the notional category, Bonaventure refuses to abandon the historic category, in which Jesus Christ is the intermediary in all methods, in all knowledge, and in all activity, being the way, the truth, and the life, the unique and universal center. As E. Gilson says: "As the two most universal interpretations of Christianity, Saint Thomas's and Saint Bonaventure's philosophies complete each other, and it is because they complete each other that they can neither exclude each other nor coincide" (1943, 396).

III. Bonaventure's Exemplarism

1. Vision of the World

M.-D. Chenu thought the *Breviloquium* "the most satisfactory embodiment—after the *Itinerarium mentis in Deum*—in a theological compendium of knowledge, of Franciscan inspiration." Indeed, Bonaventure developed his theological knowledge there according to a clear and limpid plan. After a prologue in which comments on the text of Ephesians 3:14–19 and discovers in it the foundation of theology as scriptural teaching—*sacra Scriptura quae Theologia dicitur* ("Holy Scripture as recounted by theology")—Bonaventure develops a very spare exposition, organized so as to be meditated on rather than to be taught. The general structure of the *Breviloquium* is very simple: Part one (9 chapters) deals with the Holy Trinity; part two (12 chapters) with the world, the Creation of God; part three (11 chapters) with corruption due to Original Sin*; part four (10 chapters) with the incarnation* of the Word*; part five (10 chapters) with the grace* of the Holy Spirit; part six (13 chapters) with sacramental remedies (sacrament*); and part seven (7 chapters) with the Last Judgment*. Bonaventure describes his goal as the following (*Breviloquium,* Prologue, 6, Quaracchi, vol. V, 208). "Since theology speaks of God, who is the first principle; since, as the highest branch of knowledge and doctrine it resolves everything in God as the first principle and sovereign, in the allocation of reasons, in everything that is contained in this short treatise, I have striven to seek the explanation in the first principle, in order to show thus that the truth of the Holy Scriptures comes from God, deals with God, is in conformity with God, has God as its end, in such a way that indeed this branch of knowledge seems unified, ordered, and, with good reason, is named theology."

a) The Trinity as Creator. Bonaventure as theologian does not describe God. Rather, he recounts him, and he always recounts him as God the Trinity. As the *Breviloquium* (p. 1, c. 2; vol. V, 211a) reads: "Faith, because it is the principle of the cult* of God and the foundation of the doctrine in accordance with piety, requires us to hold a very high and very pious opinion about God. We would not hold a very high opinion about God if we did not believe that God can reveal himself totally. We would not have a very pious opinion about him if we believed that he could do it, but did not want to. Thus, having a very high and very pious opinion about God, we will say that he reveals himself completely while possessing eternally a loved one and another-one-loved-mutually. Thus God is one and threefold."

In a Christmas sermon preached in 1257, Bonaventure expressed himself thus: "When the fullness of time decreed in the divine presence came to pass, the Word, formerly concealed within God, came into the bosom of the very chaste Mother. Thus Christ came into the flesh without, as it were, leaving the fountainhead, as John says in chapter 14, verse 10." In the capital question through which Bonaventure explores whether the divine nature* was capable of uniting itself with human nature (*In III Sent.*, d.1, a.1., q.4; III, 8; *see* Christ* and Christology), he gives his definitive answer in the form of a meditation on the history of salvation, or rather, on the history of creation. In this case his theology is based on arguments about what is appropriate rather than on what is necessary. Among the divine Persons, the one who is the most capable of being incarnated is the Son, because if the form of man is assumable because of man's status as the image of God, the Son is the image of the Father. Man therefore assumes, outside of God, the role assumed within God, in the full sense, by the Son, who is "the image of the invisible God" (Col 1:15). On earth man continues to fulfil the vital and original function that the Son fills in the inner life of God. Now the Son is the Word of the Father. The Father shows himself through him. Therefore, in the same way that in order to show the idea the sense of the Word is joined to the tangible word, in order to reveal God it was proper that the Word of the Father should unite himself with flesh. Moreover, the Son is a Son engendered eternally. It was proper then that God incarnate should be of the race of men, therefore Son* of man (filiation*). At the heart of creation, the Son-Being is therefore a pale reflection of what the Son-Being in himself represents exemplarily in God himself. The creature, a copy of God, of exemplary origin at the start, cannot be known in his structure except if the original is known, since the structure lives in its entirety only by means of the original and reflects that original in attenuated form. The world is a mirror of God in which the threefold structure is reflected. And in the primitive structure of the creation, the Son possesses a special relationship with the world, on the grounds of exemplary causality.

Bonaventure always links the fact that Christ is a model or exemplar of man to the fact that the eternal Word is himself the exemplar of every creature: "Christ's generation was the exemplary reason for every emanation, because God had placed everything in the Word that he had engendered. For the same reason, his predestination* was the exemplary reason for every predestination" (*In III Sent.*, d.11, a. 1, q. 2). Bonaventure bases himself here on a metaphysical principle that guides his thoughts: *Posterius per illud habet reduci, quod est prius in eodem genere* ("The posterior must turn back to what is anterior of the same kind"). The density of being of this exemplary cause, of this *prius* (anterior) ontology, is so great that the return, the *reducio,* of the creature to the Creator, can only be managed through him, the ontological *prius,* the original model.

It can be said that the threefold appropriations* are the foundation of Bonaventure's exemplarity. In fact Bonaventure explains that the Father is the fountain of plenitude, "a spring of water gushing up to eternal life" (Jn 4:14) that is manifested in the Son and empowers him to manifest it in creation. If creation is the work of the three Persons, each Person expresses himself in it according to his attributes—the Father with his all-powerfulness, the Son with his wisdom, the Holy Spirit with his goodness.

b) Creation, Contemplation. For Bonaventure, every creature is a vestige of God, not in an accidental way but in a real way. Man is naturally and substantially an image of God because he receives continually from God—who is present within him—a creative influence, which makes him capable of taking him for subject. As L. Mathieu says (1992, 99): "The Father, at the heart of the divinity, utters speech eternally, his Word, in whom he tells his whole being* and his whole power, and who contains the eternal reasons of beings; it is the eternal Word or the Word uncreated. And in the same way that the Father expresses himself and declares himself through his Word, the Persons of the divinity express themselves and declare themselves through a temporal word, which is the creature or *verbum creatum,* a reflection or echo of wisdom expressed eternally by the Father in the Word uncreated." "Every creature is a word of God," writes Bonaventure himself when commenting on Sirach 42:15 (c.1, q. 2, resp., Quaracchi., vol. VI, 16).

c) Path to God. When he discovers himself to be the image of God, man recognizes himself to be the subject of a quasi-original relationship between God and himself. As soon as God draws the world toward himself and thus introduces it into his inner being, the circle of the Trinity, which until that time was closed on itself in spite of all the exemplary relations, reveals itself to the world through a transcendence of the exemplary relationship. Bonaventure sees this transcendence in the Incarnation* of the Son and in the sending of the Holy Spirit.

Bonaventure defined the different stages of the return to God in his *Itinerarium mentis in Deum.* The first stage leads us toward the traces* of God, the physical world in which we contemplate the power of God, his wisdom, and his goodness: God is present in the center of things. Then starting with the physical, the study of the microcosm makes us scale the ladder of created beings as far as the world of the spirit, which is free from any physical limits. Further still, the study of the powers of the soul grants us access directly to God, since our soul is his image and our soul receives the light of his eternal reasons: we discover in ourselves the personal action of God, recreating our supernatural* being and inaugurating thus a new relationship, the presence of grace. Thenceforth, we find ourselves ready to contemplate God in the unity of his essence and the plurality of his person. First of all, we discover the idea of being in our smallest pieces of knowledge, for it is implied in every concept. The idea of Good, of the Being that reaches outside itself and gives itself, raises us ever higher until we contemplate the Trinity, whose fruitfulness is the supreme explanation. At the end of the ascent, silence falls. Let us pass, once Jesus* is crucified, "from this world* to the Father. After having seen the Father, we can declare along with Philip: 'that is enough for us'" *(Itin.* c.7, n.6, Quaracchi, vol. V, 313).

2. Theology of the Poor

For Bonaventure the presence of God is both a simple and a complex process. We must go outside ourselves by accepting the idea that we cannot exist by our own means and by asking for the help of the divine light, because reading, which ends with words, is not enough. The inner gaze, which goes beyond the words and reaches the reality that they express, is also required. Withdrawing into oneself again constitutes a haphazard groping for that source in whom we have motion, life, and being. It is rising above our condition while trying to reach the inaccessible. It constitutes an abandonment of all sustenance required for being, because nothing can assuage us except what exceeds our capacity (*De scientia Christi,* q. 6, resp., Quaracchi, vol. V, 35).

The notion of God implies all that, but also the idea of realizing that God himself has taken our poverty in hand in a real plan for salvation (*Breviloquium,* p.5, c.2, n.3, Quaracchi, vol. 5, 253–54). For we would like to be happy and we chase after happiness, but happiness is like the shore, which seems very close to the sailor but always remains very far away (*In II Sent.,* d. 19, a 1, 1, resp. Quaracchi, vol. II, 460). We want to be happy and we only know how to create our own misery. But God, in his abundant mercy*, becomes man for us. He does not do so because we are worthy, but he makes us worthy by the very fact that he makes himself man. God created the world in order to make himself manifest, according to Bonaventure. Taking to extremes his meditation of a poor man following in the footsteps of Saint Francis, he concludes: "Everything is made manifest on the cross" (*De triplici via,* c.3, n.5, Quaracchi., vol. VIII, 14). Christ—in fact, God made man—won at that moment, in an incomprehensible poverty, the right to be our partner in a dialogue where it is no longer clear who is the poorer. In the history of the world, always in the process of making itself, God abandoned himself thus, without defense, by placing man in the position of being the wealthier, of being the one who was in a position to give. God made himself indigent. It is up to us to give ourselves by giving something to the poor man. Thus, in God, closes the circle of love that Bonaventure had spread in his work *(Apologia pauperum,* c.2, n.12, Quaracchi., vol. VIII, 242–3).

- Sancti Bonaventurae, *Opera omnia,* 11 vols., Quaracchi, 1882–1902.

Sancti Bonaventurae, *Opera theologica selecta, ed. minor,* 5 vols., Grottaferrata, 1934–35. *Works of St. Bonaventure.* St. Bonaventure, New York: Franciscan Institute, 1955–
Ewert Cousins (Tr.), *The Soul's Journey into God, The Tree of Life, The Life of St. Francis.* New York, 1978.
Lawrence Cunningham (Tr.) *The Mind's Journey to God,* Chicago, 1979.
E. E. Nemmers (Tr.), *Breviloquium.* St. Louis, 1946.
Les six lumières de la connaissance humaine, Tr. P. Michaud-Quantin, Paris, 1971.
Sermones dominicales, Ed. J.-G. Bougerol, Grottaferrata, 1977.
Questions disputées sur le savoir du Christ, Ed., Tr. and Intro., E.-H. Weber, Paris, 1985.
Le Christ Maître, Ed., Tr. and Comm. of the sermon "Unus est magister noster Christus," G. Madec, Paris, 1990.
Sermones de tempore, Ed. J.-G. Bougerol, Paris, 1990.
Les six jours de la création, Tr. M. Ozilou, Paris, 1991.
Sermones de diversis, Ed. J.-G. Bougerol, Paris, 1993.
Les dix commandements, Tr. M. Ozilou, Paris, 1994.
J.-G. Bougerol, *Bibliographia Bonaventuriana (1850–1973),* Grottaferrata, 1974.
♦ É. Gilson (1929), *La philosophie de saint B.,* 2nd Ed., Paris, 1943.
F. Stegmüller (1947 *Sq*), *Repertorium Commentariorum in Sententias Petri Lombardi,* Würzburg.
J. Ratzinger (1959), *Die Geschichtstheologie des Heiligen Bonaventuras,* Munich.
H. U. von Balthasar (1962), *Herrlichkeit* II/1, Einsiedeln, 267–361.
A. Gerken (1963), *Theologie des Wortes,* Düsseldorf.
J. B. Schneyer (1969–90), *Repertorium der lateinischen Sermones des Mittelalters,* BGPhMA 43.
J.-G. Bougerol (1973), "Une théologie biblique de la Révélation," in coll., *La Sacra Scrittura e i Francescani,* Rome-Jerusalem, 95–104.
E. H. Cousins (1978), *Bonaventure and the Coincidence of Opposites,* Chicago.
J.-G. Bougerol (1988), *Introduction à saint B.,* Paris; (1989), *Saint B.: Études sur les sources de sa pensée,* London.
L. Mathieu (1992), *La Trinité créatrice d'après saint B.,* Paris.
A. Murphy (1993), "Bonaventure's Synthesis of Augustinian and Dionysian Mysticism: A New Look at the Problem of the One and the Many," CFr 63, 385–98.
A. Nguyen Van Si (1993), "Les symboles de l'itinéraire dans l'"Itinerarium mentis in Deum' de B.," *Anton.* 68, 327–47.
O. Todisco (1993), "Verbum divinum omnis creatura: La Filosofia del Linguaggio di S. Bonaventura," *MF* 93, 149–98.

IV. In the Tradition of Bonaventure

Bonaventure's genius inspired an abundant line of disciples, who engaged in numerous controversies concerning Franciscan spirituality*, poverty, and eschatology*, but also concerning the classic problems of metaphysics and theology. Among them can be cited the headmasters who succeeded Bonaventure: Guibert of Tournai, Eustache, Guglielmo di Baglione, Walter von Brügge, John Pecham, William de la Mare, Matthew of Aquasparta, Bartholomaeus of Bologna, John of Wales, Arlotto di Prato, Richard Middleton, Raymond Rigauld, John of Murres, Gonsalvo of Spain, and Alexander of Alexandria.

Guibert of Tournai, who immediately succeeded Bonaventure in the chair of the school of the friars (headmaster 1257–60), is known for his sermons and his treatise *Eruditio regum et principum* (The Study of Rules and Principles). Eustache (headmaster 1263–66) is the author of *Quodlibets, Disputed Questions,* and a few sermons. Guglielmo di Baglioni (headmaster 1266–67) left several *Disputed Questions* and *Quodlibets.* Walter of Bruges (headmaster 1267–69), author of a *Commentary on the Sentences,* became bishop of Poitiers in 1279. John Pecham (headmaster 1269–71), archbishop of Canterbury in 1279, is the author of the *Tractatus pauperis contra insipientem* (1270; Treatise on the Poor Man Compared to the Foolish Man) and of several quodlibets. William de la Mare is known above all for his authorship of the *Correctorium fratris Thomae* (Of the Correctors of Brother Thomas), in which he criticizes the work of Thomas Aquinas.

Matthew of Aquasparta is the most famous of the disciples of Bonaventure, whose Augustinianism* he brought to perfection. Father Victorin Doucet wrote as an introduction to the critical edition of Matthew's *Quaestiones disputatae de gratia* (Quaracchi, 1935; A Discussion of Questions about Grace), an exhaustive study of the life, writings, and doctrinal authority* of this man who was named cardinal in 1288 and was entrusted with political missions for the pope. Bartholomaeus of Bologna (headmaster 1276–77) left behind sermons and *Disputed Questions.* Richard Middleton (headmaster 1284–87) is known above all for his *Commentary on the Sentences,* his *Disputed Questions,* and his *Quodlibets.* Although he refused to sit for his degree and therefore for his masters degree, Petrus Joannis Olivi is edited and studied more and more, for he represents one of Bonaventure's most remarkable disciples (Council of Vienna*). Lastly must be cited Alexander of Alexandria (headmaster 1307–8) who wanted to deliver an *Abbreviato Commentarii Santi Bonaventurae* (Digest of Saint Bonaventure's Commentaries).

In the 14th century the Franciscan School neglected Bonaventure to rally around John Duns* Scotus, who had managed to create a synthesis between Bonaventure's thought and that of recent developments in logic and metaphysics—despite the efforts of Chancellor Jean Gerson (nominalism*). In 1482 Sixtus IV canonized Bonaventure. In 1588 Sixtus V raised him to the ranks of the doctors of the church. Between 1588 and 1596, the Vatican edition of Bonaventure's writings was published at the pope's urging. It contains 94 works and short treatises whose authenticity is not always well established. Nonetheless, it has the merit of having collected Bonaventure's works. The editions of Mainz (1609), Lyons (1678), Venice (1751), and Paris

(1864–71) simply reproduce the Vatican edition. The Conventual Franciscans founded the College of Saint Bonaventure in Rome, but they did not pursue the study of Bonaventure's work and thought. The Irish Franciscan Luke Wadding tried to sift out the doubtful short treatises, but his death prevented him from finishing this work. In 1722, Casimir Oudin published a *Dissertatio* on Bonaventure's writings.

In 1772–74 Benedetto Bonelli turned again to the work of the Venetian Franciscans and, after his *Prodromus ad opera omnia Santi Bonaventurae,* published three volumes entitled *Santi Bonaventurae operum supplementum.* But all these efforts did not succeed in reinvigorating the study of Bonaventure's thought. It could be said that from the 14th to the 15th century—apart from the Capuchin friar, Bartholomaeo de Barberiis, who proved to be their best interpreter—the school of Bonaventure no longer existed, even if numerous quotations from Bonaventure can be found in the works of Bernardino of Siena (1380–1444).

Then, in 1874, thanks to the activity of Father Bernardino da Portogruaro, Franciscan minister-general, as well as that of Fathers Fidelis a Fanna and Ignatius Jeiler, the Saint Bonaventure College was created in Quaracchi and entrusted with taking up again the critical edition of Bonaventure's work. As E. Longpré says, "This monumental edition has brought about the renaissance of Bonaventure's works, of which, in France, the important book by Étienne Gilson has given the signal. This return to Saint Bonaventure in Christian thought must be considered as one of the most important events in contemporary religious history" (Longpré 1949).

- Gilberti de Tornaco, *Tractatus de pace,* Ed. E. Longpré, Quaracchi, 1925.

Gonsalvi Hispani, *Quaestiones disputatae et de Quodlibet,* Ed. L. Amoros, Quaracchi, 1935.

Guillelmi de Militona, *Quaestiones de Sacramentis,* Ed. C. Piana, G. Gàl, Quaracchi, 1961.

Ioannis Pecham, *Quodlibet quatuor,* nunc primum edidit Girardus J. Etzkorn, Grottaferrata, 1989.

Matthaei ab Aquasparta, *Quaestiones disputatae de gratia,* cum introductione critica de magisterio et scriptis eiusdem doctoris, Ed. V. Doucet, Quaracchi, 1935.

Matthaei ab Aquasparta, *Quaestiones disputatae de productione rerum et de providentia,* Ed. G. Gàl, Quaracchi, 1956.

Matthaei ab Aquasparta, *Quaestiones disputatae de fide et cognitione,* Quaracchi, 1957.

Matthaei ab Aquasparta, *Quaestiones disputatae de Incarnatione et de lapsu,* Quaracchi, 1957.

Matthaei ab Aquasparta, *Quaestiones disputatae de anima separata, de anima beata, de ieiunio et de legibus,* Quaracchi, 1959.

Matthaei ab Aquasparta, *Sermones de B.M. Virgine,* Ed. C. Piana, Quaracchi, 1962.

Matthaei ab Aquasparta, *Sermones de S. Francisco, de S. Antonio, de S. Clara.* Appendix: *Sermo de potestate papae,* Ed. G. Gàl, Quaracchi, 1962.

Petri Ioannis Olivi, *In II Sent.*, 3 vols., Quaracchi, 1922–26.

Petri Ioannis Olivi, *Quaestiones quatuor de Domina,* Ed. D. Pacetti, Quaracchi, 1954.

Petri Ioannis Olivi, *Quaestiones disputatae de Incarnatione et Redemptione. Quaestiones de virtutibus,* Ed. A. Emmen, E. Stadter, Grottaferrata, 1981.

- E. Longpré (1928), "Matthieu d'Aquasparta," *DThC* 10, 375–89.

L. Veuthey (1931), "Alexandre d'Alexandrie, maître de l'université de Paris," *EtFr* 43, 145–76, 319–44.

A. Teetaert (1932), "Pecham," *DThC* 12, 100–140.

P. Glorieux (1933), *Répertoire des maîtres en théologie de Paris au XIIIe s.,* II, Paris.

L. Jarreaux (1933), "Pierre Jean Olivi," *EtFr* 45, 129–53.

V. Doucet (1934), *Maîtres franciscains de Paris,* in *AFH* 27, 531–64.

E. Longpré (1949), "Bonaventure," *Cath.* 2, 122–28.

R. Manselli (1955), *La* Lectura super Apocalipsim *di Pietro di Giovanni Olivi. Ricerche sull'escatologismo medioevale,* Rome.

E. Stadter (1961), *Psychologie und Metaphysik der menschlichen Freiheit: Die ideengeschchtliche Entwicklung zwischen Bonaventura und Duns Scotus,* Munich-Paderborn-Vienna.

P. Mazzarella (1969), *La doctrina dell'anima e della conoscenza in Matteo d'Acquasparta,* Padua.

D. Burr (1976), *The Persecution of Peter Olivi,* Philadelphia.

C. Bérubé (1983), *De l'homme à Dieu selon Duns Scot, Henri de Gand et Olivi,* Rome.

D. Burr (1989), *Olivi and Franciscan Poverty,* Philadelphia.

F.-X. Putallaz (1991), *La connaissance de soi au XIIIe s.: De Matthieu d'Acquasparta à Thierry de Freiberg,* Paris.

F.-X. Putallaz (1995), *Insolente liberté: Controverses et condamnations au XIIIe s.,* Fribourg-Paris.

F.-X. Putallaz (1997), *Figures franciscaines, de Bonaventure à Duns Scot,* Paris (bibl.).

Jacques-Guy Bougerol†

See also **Augustinianism; Beatitude; Cosmos; Duns Scotus, John; Life, Spiritual; Millenarianism; Mysticism; Scholasticism; Spirituality, Franciscan; Spiritual Theology; Vienna, Council of; Voluntarism**

Bonhoeffer, Dietrich

1906–45

a) Life. A Lutheran theologian from the cultured German middle class, Bonhoeffer was appointed in 1931 to the posts of private lecturer and university chaplain in Berlin. In the debates sparked within the Protestant churches by Hitler's accession to power in 1933, he emphatically dissociated himself from the "German Christian movement" and the National Socialist regime. In 1935, after briefly serving as a pastor* to the German communities in London, he became head of the Confessing Church seminary at Finkenwalde (Pomerania). His literary output from this period comprises *The Cost of Discipleship* (1937) and *Life Together* (1939). His participation in the resistance to Hitler subsequently brought him new experiences within the secular sphere, and these would find expression in his unfinished *Ethics.* He was arrested in 1943 and at first interned in the military prison of Berlin-Tegel. Thanks to the leniency of some of the guards, he was able to carry on an uncensored theological correspondence with his friend E. Bethge, who was to publish these letters in 1951 under the title *Letters and Papers from Prison (Resistance and Submission).* Shortly before the end of the war, on 9 April 1945, Bonhoeffer was hanged at the concentration camp of Flossenbürg, along with other conspirators. The day before, he had taken his leave of an English fellow-prisoner with the words, "It is the end—and, for me, the beginning of a new life."

b) The Church. In his thesis, *Sanctorum Communio,* Bonhoeffer set himself the task of carrying out a "dogmatic investigation toward a sociology of the church*," which was nonetheless to lead him to a "theological transcendence of sociology" (Soosten 1992, 263). "We do not believe in an invisible Church . . . we believe that God* has made the concrete and empirical church, in which the Word* and the Sacraments* are administered, into his community" (SC 191). With this assertion Bonhoeffer distanced himself on the one hand from E. Troeltsch, who concerned himself with the religious nature of the Christian personality rather than with the church, and on the other hand from K. Barth*, whose idea of revelation* implied a critical questioning of the empirical church.

Bonhoeffer saw the "recognition of the revealed reality of God's community" as the starting point of theology*, and as a faithful disciple of his Lutheran teacher R. Seeberg, acknowledged the possibility of "positive theological knowledge" (SC 81). His expression, derived from Hegel*, of "Christ existing as a community" (SC 128 and *passim*) takes up some of Saint Paul's pronouncements (the typology of Adam* and Christ, the community as the body of Christ). Ecclesiology* is here rooted in a Christology* and a soteriology of substitution. Bonhoeffer never lost sight of the irreversible relationship of priority that exists between Christ as head and the body of his community. He saw in Christ "the measure and the norm of our actions" (SC 120). Consequently, there could be no doubt in 1933 as to the *status confessionis* of the "Jewish question," and Bonhoeffer demanded that his church take up the cause of the persecuted. In the event that this protest should prove ineffective to dissuade the state (church* and state) from its policy, he urged that an "evangelical council" should publicly denounce the regime's iniquity. The Confessing Church, however, never entirely shook off its cautious reticence regarding the anti-Semitic policy of the Nazi state. It was for this reason that in 1944 Bonhoeffer wrote, in *Widerstand und Ergebung,* that "it has fought during these years only for its own preservation" (*WEN* 328), whereas "the church is only a church when it exists for others" (*WEN* 415). This new church would be characterized by voluntary poverty and by the capacity to proclaim Christ, the Lord of the world, to an emancipated and secularized humanity. From this viewpoint, it was up to theology to interpret Christianity in secular or nonreligious terms. Bonhoeffer, however, did not get the opportunity to carry out this task himself in a developed and systematic form.

c) Ethics. At the beginning of the 1930s Bonhoeffer put into perspective the Lutheran doctrine of the orders (which persisted, in a modified form, in his *Ethics*) with reference to Jesus Christ. The orders were no longer to be seen as inviolable "orders of creation," but simply as "orders of conservation." The individual's love* of his own race* was subordinated to the Christian commandment of peace*. This idea (encouraged by the friendship he had formed with the French pacifist Jean Lasserre in 1930 at the Union Theological Seminary) led him to join the World Alliance for Promoting International Friendship through the Churches. This activity culminated in 1934 in his address to the assembly of church representatives at Fanö in Denmark, in which he urged them to present themselves as an "ecumenical council" and forbid all Christians to take part in war*. In *Nachfolge* Bonhoeffer rejects the "cheap grace*" proclaimed by the evangelical church, as well as the notion that the personal journey of Luther*, who left the cloister to return to worldly life, could be taken as justification for an exclusive devotion to the performance of professional duties. He reiterates and clarifies the Lutheran tradition* with this principle: "Only the believer obeys, only the obedient believes" (*N* 52).

In his *Ethics,* which he worked on from 1940, Bonhoeffer extends the domain of Christian activity. While he had originally intended an *Ethics* aimed at the radical wing of the Confessing Church (those known as "Dahlemites"), he now asks in a more general sense how Christians, by their way of life, offer a response to Jesus Christ. It is in this spirit that he introduces the concept of responsibility into theological ethics. By taking up the christological category of "substitution," he is able to derive a fundamental anthropological structure, that of "existence for others." "All responsibility to God and for God, to mankind and for mankind, is always the responsibility of the cause of Christ, and in this way only of my personal life" (*E* 255). Thus Bonhoeffer dissociates himself from the modern notion of individual autonomy and goes beyond the idea (always conducive to political compromise) of a Christian life devoted to the performance of professional duties.

d) Christology. Several of Bonhoeffer's works take ecclesiology and ethics directly as their themes, but he offered only one development specific to Christology. However, this development is central to his theology. It is to be found in the lectures he gave under this title at Berlin in 1933 and which were preserved in the form of the notes taken or copied by students. In considering the doctrine of the Person* of Jesus Christ, Bonhoeffer begins with the presence of the Lord crucified and raised up to heaven. He discusses at length the dogmatic constructions of the early church and the Reformation, and approaches the christological controversies of the Reformation period as a disciple of Luther. He agrees with K. Barth and E. Brunner in considering the Council of Chalcedon* to be the touchstone of dogmatics*. In the *Ethics,* too, Christology plays a fundamental role in the understanding of reality. Since in Jesus Christ "the reality of God passed into the reality of this world," it is for Christians to "participate through Jesus Christ in the reality of God and of the world" (*E* 39 *Sq*). The positive link between Christ and the world is further emphasized in *Widerstand und Ergebung*. To live a life of "self-responsibility," to wish to "assume an existence without God," is not therefore to live impiously, because "God allows himself to be expelled from the world and nailed to the cross," and because it is "only in this way that he can be with us and help us" (*WEN* 394).

e) Legacy. Certain of Bonhoeffer's writings, such as *Widerstand und Ergebung* (translated into 16 languages) have been read the world over. On the level of academic theology, however, his work has had few repercussions, even in German-speaking countries. Some individual theologians have drawn inspiration from him (in particular his *Widerstand und Ergebung*) in the working out of their own agendas: for example, G. Ebeling in his hermeneutic* theology, W. Hamilton in his "theology of the death of God," and H. Müller in his attempt to reconcile Protestant theology with the ideological dominance of the Communist party in the GDR. Through the work of A. Schönherr, a pupil of Bonhoeffer, the phrase "the church for others" played a key role for an evangelical church seeking a path between compromise and refusal in the socialist society of the GDR. Beyond Europe, in Latin America, South Africa and East Asia, Bonhoeffer's voice has echoed as an encouragement in the ears of Christians fighting for greater social justice.

• D. Bonhoeffer, *Widerstand und Ergebung,* Munich, 1951 (Rev. Ed. 1970).

D. Bonhoeffer, *Werke,* Ed. E. Bethge, et al., 16 vols., Munich, 1986–98.

D. Bonhoeffer, *Sanctorum Communio: Eine dogmatische Untersuchung zur Soziologie der Kirche, W* 1, 1986.

D. Bonhoeffer, *Nachfolge, W* 4, 1989 (*Le prix de la grâce,* Neuchâtel-Paris, 1962).

D. Bonhoeffer, *Ethik, W* 6, 1992.

♦ H. Müller (1961), *Von der Kirche zur Welt: Ein Beitrag zu der Beziehung des Wortes Gottes auf die societas in Dietrich Bonhoeffers theologischer Entwicklung,* Leipzig (2nd Ed. 1966).

E. Bethge (1967), *Dietrich Bonhoeffer: Theologie, Christ, Zeitgenosse,* Munich (6th Ed. 1986).

A. Dumas (1968), *Une théologie de la réalité: Dietrich Bonhoeffer,* Geneva.

E. Feil (1971), *Die Theologie Dietrich Bonhoeffers: Hermeneutik, Christologie, Weltverständnis,* Munich (4th Ed. 1991).

C. Gremmels, I. Tödt (Ed.) (1987), *Die Präsenz des verdrängten Gottes: Glaube, Religionslosigkeit und Weltverantwortung nach Dietrich Bonhoeffer,* Munich.

G. Carter, et al. (Ed.) (1991), *Bonhoeffer's Ethics: Old Europe and New Frontiers,* Kampen (From the Fifth Conference of the International Bonhoeffer Society, Amsterdam, 1988).

J. von Soosten (1992), *Die Sozialität der Kirche: Theologie und*

Theorie in Dietrich Bonhoeffers, Sanctorum Communio, Munich.
E. Feil (Ed.) (1993), *Glauben lernen in einer Kirche für andere: Der Beitrag Dietrich Bonhoeffers zum Christsein in der Deutschen Demokratischen Republik,* Gütersloh.
Coll. (1995), *Dietrich Bonhoeffer heute, EvTh* 55.
E. Feil (Ed.) (1997), *Internationale Biographie zu Dietrich Bonhoeffer,* Gütersloh.

ERNST-ALBERT SCHARFFENORTH

See also **Balthasar, Hans Urs von; Barth, Karl; Bultmann, Rudolf; Secularization; Tillich, Paul**

Bonnetty, Augustine. *See* **Fideism**

Book

The Hebrew *séfèr,* which appears approximately 190 times in the Bible*, probably comes from the Akkadian *sipru* (meaning "letter" or "written document"), which also yielded *saparu* ("decree" or "legal document"). In the Septuagint it is most often translated by the Greek *biblion,* and sometimes *biblos* (feminine). The same terms appear in the New Testament (*biblion* appears 34 times and *biblos,* with a similar meaning, 10 times). The transposition of the Greek plural (1 Macc 1:56), which in Latin became *biblia,* produced the French feminine form *la Bible.* Translation by the word *book* covers very diverse meanings, to be evaluated case by case. In the Bible, a book is a document written in any of several different media—stone (the "tablets" of Ex 24:12, 31:18, and 32:15), clay, wood, papyrus, leather (parchment), and copper—of very variable length. These writings were endowed with a particular authority* and intended to be read by a defined human group.

Because of the materials used, and especially because of the difficulties of writing, written documents were long the reserved domain of specialized scribes. Their activity took place in five privileged areas. First came everything that touched on the founding myths*, including the epic *Gilgamesh* and the creation* poem *Enuma Elish,* both of which took on their classic forms in Babylon under Nebuchadnezzar I. Texts of laws were also inscribed, such as the code of Hammurabi, ruler of Babylon in the 18th century B.C. (The diorite stele enscribed with Hammurabi's code is now in the Louvre Museum.) Documents were often kept in temples (*see* Dt 31:24–26). Diplomatic or commercial treaties were also committed to writing. Scribes also kept in writing the annals of the kings, such as those of Sennacherib and Assurbanipal (eighth century B.C.). We no longer have the sources cited by the compilers of the Bible, such as the "Book of the Acts of Solomon" (1 Kgs 11:41), the "Book of the Annals of the Kings" of Israel and Judah (1 Kgs 14:19, 29; 2 Kgs 23:28, 24:5). Finally, the scribes took the trouble to preserve accounts of wisdom*, often very ancient—for example, the Egyptian "The Instruction of Amenemope," which has parallels in Proverbs 22:17–23:14. Deuteronomy 6:9 and 11:20 presuppose a democratization of the practice of writing, as it instructs the father of the family* is to write excerpts from the law* for his household.

Around the beginning of the first millennium B.C., the alphabet supplanted the cumbersome pictographic systems of Egypt and Mesopotamia, and insured a more rapid spread of writing, as attested by archeology. As a result, at the time of the first kings of Israel a substantial body of oral traditions came to be transcribed in writing. Transcription became necessary to enable all the tribes to possess a common history*. We no longer have the "Book of the Wars* of the Lord," cited in Numbers 21:14, nor the "Book of Jashar" (*see* Jos 10:13 and 2 Sm 1:18), which was probably related to the entry into Canaan. The book form would also become the instrument for a common law. A great place was given to the discovery of the book in the Temple* in 622 B.C. (2 Kgs 22 and 23). The identification of this book with a part of Deuteronomy (De Wette 1817) is now generally accepted. But the book that was preserved in the Temple lacked readers. With the reform of Josiah, the "book of the law," in the words of Deuteronomy (28:58 and 61, 29:20, and 31:26), Joshua (1:8, 8:34, and 24:26), and Nehemiah (8:3 and 9:3) became a reference for the people*. What was written was normative, even for the king (Dt 17:18). This was "the Book of the Covenant*" (2 Kgs 23:2, 21)—that is, it contained what had to be done to remain within that Covenant. The loss and the forgetting of the book brought about the loss and the forgetting of the Covenant.

The word of the prophet* dies at the very moment that it is spoken. But, in order to keep these words alive and ensure the survival of some witness to the pronouncements made against an Israel* that was unfaithful to the law, the prophets set them down in writing (Is 30:8; Jer 30:2; Hb 2:2) or, more often, their disciples did so (Jer 36:2 and 36:18). This writing was often carried out over the course of several centuries, before concluding in a completed book containing oracles from which "nothing will be taken away." The documentation that was assembled by Nehemiah (according to 2 Macc 2:13–14) deals essentially with kings and prophets. Far from being devalued speech, writing became an enduring reality, making sense for times and situations other than those in which the word was originally proclaimed, and supporting repetitions for readers still to come.

Gradually, the "book" was able to bear a strong symbolic charge. Whereas God had put his words directly into Jeremiah's mouth (Jer 1:9), Ezekiel is given a "book" to eat (Ez 3:1). The prophet incorporates a divine will that takes the form of a universal project covering all of history. The author of Ecclesiasticus identifies personified Wisdom with the "Book of the Covenant" (Sir 24:23), in which he discovers the work of God since the Creation*. There came a time of apocalypses, which gave prominence to the theme of the sealed book, the ultimate revelation* (Dn 7:10; Rev 5:1–10 and 20:12). The New Testament (especially the Gospel according to Luke) presents Jesus* with the book (Lk 4:16–21) and sees Jesus as a hermeneutic interpreter of all the Scriptures* (Lk 24:27, 44 f.).

• L. Alonso-Schoeckel (1965), *La Palabra inspirada,* Barcelona.

L. Febvre (1971), *L'apparition du livre,* Paris.

S. Breton (1979), *Écriture et Révélation,* Paris.

A. Lemaire (1981), *Les écoles et la formation de la Bible dans l'ancien Israël,* OBO 39.

B. Gabel, C. B. Wheeler (1986), *The Bible as Literature,* Oxford.

W. Kelber (1991), *Tradition orale et écriture,* Paris.

J. Goody (1993), *The Interface between the Written and the Oral,* Cambridge.

A. Paul (1995), "Les diverses dénominations de la Bible," *RSR* 83, 373–402.

J.-P. Sonnet (1997), *The Book within the Book: Writing in Deuteronomy,* Leyden.

ALAIN MARCHADOUR

See also **Apocalyptic Literature; Bible; Canon of Scriptures; Holy Scripture; Law and Christianity; Word of God**

Brethren of the Common Life. *See* ***Devotio moderna***

Bruno, Giordano. *See* **Naturalism**

Bucer, Martin

1491–1551

Martin Bucer, son and grandson of coopers, was born in Sélestat and died in Cambridge. His life as a reformer reflected a turbulent time, was laden with theological and ecclesiastical plans, and was filled with success and failure. After joining the Dominican order in Sélestat in 1506–7, he was restless for more than 10 years—"need makes the monk," he would say later. Fate would have it that he would join the friars of the Heidelberg order, where, in 1518, he met Martin Luther*, who was then at the beginning of his pubic career as reformer. The Heidelberg debate converted* Bucer to "Martinian" ideas. Luther's theology*, in its basic assertions, was thenceforth part of Bucer's own thinking. They included the priority of the Scriptures over tradition*, justification through faith* alone, and the primacy of academic theology over traditional ecclesiastic institutions.

In 1521 Bucer withdrew from his order, left the priesthood, and was officially relieved of his monastic vows. He spent some time with the knights Franz Von Sickingen and Ulrich Von Hutten, the last defenders of a form of feudalism that had been momentarily revived by humanism*. He married Élisabeth Silbereisen, a cloistered nun, who had also been recently defrocked. Because authorities wanted to excommunicate him, Bucer took refuge with his pregnant wife in Strasbourg, where his father was citizen. He then launched a 23-year-long career as pastor* and reformer in that Alsatian city. From there, he traveled through a large part of Europe, on horse or by mail coach, turning his city into one of the centers of the Reformation. For Bucer, Strasbourg was an ideal platform for the reform movement, not only inside his own pastorate but outside it as well. The ministry* of the reformer would go out and bring his reforms into the Strasbourg commune. Moreover, this partnership between a man and his city was characteristic of the Reformation, finding echoes in Luther, Zwingli*, Farel, Calvin*, and many others.

From the beginning of his ministry, Bucer had a fundamental insight: the church is thrust into the center of a society* and must always continue evangelizing. The church and Christendom are inextricably linked together, including all of humanity. Both have a continual missionary task.

Both in his thinking and destiny, Bucer had a kind of stigmata, a chronic wound from his century, that never healed, but was constantly being reopened. It resulted from the conflict between seeing the church as responsible for all of human society and seeing it as an inward-looking entity on the margin of the "other" humanity—an inclusive or exclusive church. Bucer himself would never undo this Gordian knot, preferring to defend the idea of a church that is both at the same time, like the mission* that Christ* himself seemed to have entrusted to his disciples (Mt 28).

In 1524, in his capacity as secular priest*, Bucer was appointed preacher of one of seven parishes of the Alsatian city of Sainte-Aurélie, the community of the guild of market farmers. The people there were unhappy with their parish priest's lack of theological education. In the parish ministry, Bucer suggested that in order for the Reformation to be genuine, it had to constantly have practical repercussions. Consequently, he became pragmatic and remained so from then on, never hesitating to change opinion or direction when required to do so as the pastor of his flock. Historians have often commented on Bucer's changing quality. He never became a theoretician and didn't want to. This partly explains why he was not understood in his lifetime—in particular, among his theologian colleagues. He never liked overly resolved positions. For

Bucer, the meaning of all human existence was living otherwise by living for others as they are in their everyday life. Service in love*—charity—is the only goal worthy of saved man; it is the antidote for egotism, real life that has become possible again. All of Bucer's theological thought stems from this standpoint, and the church was to be the place to establish this "living in Christ."

As early as 1530, at the imperial Diet of Augsburg, Bucer specified the principal points that were particular to his ecclesiastical plan: 1) The multitudinous aspect of the church (open to society, in accordance with a maximalist definition) should coexist with the professing aspect (intense personal commitment and claimed as such) as experienced in the parish and in "small Christian communities" (*ecclésioles,* in French) that are created within them; 2) plurality of the ministries; 3) collaboration between ministry and civil authority*; 4) ecclesiastic* discipline based on ordinances expressed by the magistrate; 5) restructuring of the parishes; 6) regular synods* composed of secular* delegates and "pastors"; 7) catechetical education for both children and adults; (8) baptism* of children, followed by a reformulated confirmation*; and 9) attempts to reconcile ecumenical bodies with the dissidents of the magisterial Reformation as well with the traditional church.

All of Bucer's work—theological, pastoral, literary, and diplomatic—was devoted to these nine major points. And yet, his standards seem to have been set too high. As early as 1540–41, his undertakings, which were formerly successful, began to deteriorate. Although he struggled, traveled relentlessly through Europe, and wrote more incisively and extensively, nothing developed. His ecclesiastic plan, symbolized by the final attempt at "Christian communities," those small local churches among large parishes, crumbled. Ostracized from Strasbourg in April 1549, he lived in exile in Cambridge. Disappointed but headstrong, Bucer tried one more time, in England, to launch his plan. Time had taken its toll. He still had the heart, but no longer the strength. He died two years after his arrival in Cambridge, complaining of English fog and "bad" times. Forgotten by his peers, his vision for the church would take root in Protestantism* like a rhizome, cropping up in different forms, especially in 17th- and 18th-century Pietism*, and in the 19th century's Great Awakening.

• Bucer, Martin. *Consilium theologicum privatim conscriptum.* (Martini Buceri Opera omnia. Series II, Opera Latina; vol. 4) (Studies in Medieval and Reformation Thought; vol. 42), Leyden-New York, 1988.

Bucer, Martin. *Enarratio in Evangelion Iohannis.* (Martini Buceri Opera Omnia. Series II, Opera Latina; vol. 2) (Studies in Medieval and Reformation Thought; vol. 40) Leyden-New York, 1988.

♦ C. Hopf (1946), *Martin B. and the English Reformation,* Oxford.

K. Koch (1962), *Studium pietatis: Martin B. als Ethiker,* Neukirchen.

J. Müller (1965), *Martin B. Hermeneutik,* Gütersloh.

P. Stephens (1970), *The Holy Spirit in the Theology of Martin B.,* Cambridge.

M. de Kroon, F. Krüger (Ed.) (1976), *B. und seine Zeit,* Wiesbaden.

G. Hammann (1984), *Entre la secte et la cité: Le projet d'Église de Martin B.,* Geneva.

J. V. Pollet (1985), *Martin B.,* vol. I: *Études;* vol. II: *Documents,* Leyden.

M. Greschat (1990), *Martin B.: Ein Reformator und seine Zeit, 1491–1551,* Munich.

Coll. (1993), *Martin B. in Sixteenth-Century Europe: Actes du Colloque de Strasbourg (28–31 août 1991),* vols. I and II, Leyden-New York-Köln.

D.F. Wright (Ed.) (1994), *Martin B. Reforming Church and Community,* Cambridge.

Gottfried Hammann

See also **Calvin, John; Calvinism; Gospels; Luther, Martin; Lutheranism; Methodism; Protestantism**

Bultmann, Rudolf

1884–1976

I. Life and Works

Between 1921 and 1951, after completing studies in theology, Rudolf Bultmann taught the New Testament in Marburg, West Germany. In 1923 he met Heidegger*, who greatly influenced his thought. Most of Bultmann's writing focuses on exegesis of the New

Testament. His thought has a threefold mission: to attest to the radical exigency of God* calling man; to read texts expressing this exigency, using all the resources of modern literary criticism; and to understand that this calling plays an essential role in recording the human condition, which is seen as existential.

II. Theology

1. Reading and Understanding the New Testament

As a teacher of the New Testament, Bultmann first and foremost had remarkable knowledge about the world and Greek culture, and he was an unparalleled exegete. To the end, his work revolved around questions relative to the New Testament. Bultmann's theological genius lies in the fact that he is far from being purely erudite; he questions the significance of ancient texts for today's world and raises the question of modes of interpretation.

a) History of the Synoptic Tradition. In 1921 Bultmann was one of the first to show the "mechanism" behind the literary formation of the synoptic Gospels*. By comparing the three synoptic Gospels, in his *History of the Synoptic Tradition,* he shows that the current gospel framework is not formed by a single story, but by relatively small units that, to start, were more or less independent. Therefore, he retraces the "history of forms" *(Formgeschichte).* Analyzing each of these "forms," or basic units, Bultmann is led to determine the life situation—or *Sitz im Leben*—in which they may have been written. He then reconstitutes the stages of writing that, ever since the first texts were collected, may have led to the present text of the Gospels. It is from this history that Bultmann is able to tackle the question of the historical Jesus.

b) Jesus. According to Bultmann, in *Jesus* (1926; translated into English as *Jesus and the World,* 1934), there is almost nothing to say about the historical Jesus insomuch as the texts of the New Testament are more testaments of the faith* of the early Christians than historical documents. As a result, in terms of faith, what is important is not so much the content as the radical event to which it attests, essentially indicated by the message brought by Jesus. Indeed, even though only some historically questionable facts are known of Jesus' life, the Nazarene's message is not beyond reach. In essence, Jesus announced the approaching kingdom* of God—that is to say, God himself—and called for a decision. Jesus' call to faith is thus like an invitation to "take the omnipotence of God (divine power) seriously, at precise moments in life.... It is the conviction that the faraway God is, in reality, the nearby God, under the condition that man decides to let go of his normal attitude and that he is really ready to see the nearby God before him" *(Jesus).*

c) Existential Interpretation and Hermeneutics. Bultmann saw the New Testament as fundamentally revealing the existential reality of the human condition. His reading of the Bible* strives to be resolutely modern or contemporary in at least two ways: "scientific," in that it retraces the evolutionary stages of the faith of the early Christians and reveals truly fundamental elements of the mythical elements that propel them, and "existential," in the sense of the existential philosophy* that was then emerging—the message in the Bible shows elements of the authentic coming of the human subject before his humanity, which is *ek-sistence,* stemming from the self to access the self, through the event of grace* and the decision of faith. This method of interpretation, which Bultmann took from the New Testament itself, especially allows us to better understand the "genius" of his commentary on the Gospel According to John (1941) and it opens the way for his *Theology of the New Testament* (1953).

d) Kerygma and Mythos. In 1941 Bultmann gave a lecture titled "New Testament and Mythology" (*see L'interpretation du Nouveau Testament,* Paris, 1955) that, once the war ended, caused a great uproar that lasted until the mid-1960s. The lecture shows that the language of early Christianity is prescientific and essentially influenced by myth*. The same is true for early Christian representations of the world in general and the more or less "miraculous" ways of describing things, particularly the interventions of God. Nevertheless, although the forms of this language seem irretrievably outdated and incomprehensible to modern man, the message, or kerygma, within the text remains relevant and contemporary.

It belongs to the theology that is forever extracting the message—kerygma or Word* of God—from the mythic layers in which it is both couched and imprisoned, thus making the message available to readers of this day and age. This is the goal of "demythologizing" the New Testament. This idea caused a great uproar and was widely debated; it was both enthusiastically supported and vehemently condemned. Most of the components of the controversy appear in the five volumes of *Kerygma und Mythos* (1948–55).

2. Man before the Calling of God

a) Faith and Understanding. *Glauben und Verstehen* (Faith and Understanding) is the title of the four volumes that collect the essential aspects of Bultmann's strictly theological thought. It indicates that the two realities of faith and reason* do not contradict each other, but rather echo each other, while being on different levels. Indeed, faith is strictly existential. It does not consist in understanding something, but in understanding itself in a radical, authentic way. To believe is to understand oneself before God. However, sinners "want to live on their own, by their own means, instead of living from radical abandonment to God, which God grants and sends. The grace of God liberates them from this sin*, they open themselves to it through radical abandon—that is, into faith" (*Glauben und Verstehen,* II, p. 60). As for "understanding," the essential goal is to allow human reason to play its part autonomously. It is not existential, but it sheds light on the existential, reveals the forms of its language, and allows us to return to the event of the decision of which it is made and to its consequences. To "understand" is to have a foretaste—a "precomprehension" *(ein Vorverständnis)*—of authentic existence. It does not, however, bring it about. Only the *daß* can reach it, the pure kerygma event that tears man from his inauthentic torpor.

b) History and Eschatology. Led by the decision of faith, to be made again and again at every moment in order to *exist* authentically, the believer reaches authentic humanity, stamped with the seal of historicity. To exist is to tear oneself away from anonymous destiny; it is to enter into one's own historicity, discovering one's ability to decide. The eschatological dimension that fills the entire New Testament is henceforth understood as the horizon of the "final" call that, from God himself, rings out to summon us to the authentic decision and to bring about genuine historicity.

In Jesus' preaching, the "end" of history, about which eschatology* speaks in general terms, is understood as the end of the individual it addresses, and the individual confronts the "final" responsibilities that are his own. Thus, the New Testament both individualizes and historicizes eschatology. Eschatology no longer only belongs to the end of history, but penetrates it in order to transform it. Playing off semantic meanings that do not work in other languages, Bultmann says that eschatology brings history from the pure occurrence of facts *(Historie)* to *Geschichte* (from the verb *geschehen,* meaning "to arise," "to come to pass," or "to happen"). At this point, man finds himself formed in his very historicity (*History and Eschatology,* 1957).

c) Ethics. The sign of kerygma renders a decision on ethics necessary. This is, however, but another form of the decision of faith itself. The fundamental ethical decision only implements the opening that the decision of faith creates because of its very nature. This opening then takes on the form of neighborly love*. As radical exigency, open to all neighbors without restriction or discrimination, love is certainly called to take on concrete forms every day. However, love is not exhausted in these forms, and what characterizes it above all involves the infinite exigency that it fundamentally carries.

III. Posterity

We have especially discussed the Bultmannian school from the 1950s and 1960s, in relation to his proposal for demythologizing the New Testament and the consequences it could have both in terms of the faith of the believer and in terms of possible investigations into the "historical Jesus." Following E. Käsemann's lead, some have indeed shown that the "historical Jesus" is perhaps not as unattainable as our Marburg professor had thought. Moreover, theologians like Oscar Cullmann have attempted to react to this way of dissolving history by developing a theology of "the history of salvation." Nevertheless, despite some exaggerations, Bultmann was able to develop a proposal that strongly marked his era and he did so with rare coherence.

• A bibliography of Bultmann's works (1908–67) appears in Bultmann (1967), *Exegetica,* Ed. E. Dinkler, Tübingen. For 1967–74, *see ThR* (1974) 39, 91–93. *See also* M. Kwiran (1977), *Index to Literature on Barth, Bonhoeffer und Bultmann,* Basel.

R. Bultmann (1921), *Geschichte des synoptischen Tradition,* Göttingen.

R. Bultmann (1926), *Jesus,* Berlin.

R. Bultmann (1949), *Das Urchristentum im Rahmen des antiken Religionen,* Zurich.

R. Bultmann (1953), *Theologie des Neuen Testaments,* Tübingen.

R. Bultmann (1955), *L'interprétation du Nouveau Testament,* Ed. and Tr. O. Laffoucrière, Paris.

R. Bultmann (1933–65), *Glauben und Verstehen,* 4 vols., Tübingen.

R. Bultmann (1958), *Geschichte und Eschatologie,* Tübingen.

♦ K. Barth (1952), *Rudolf B.: Ein Versuch, ihn zu verstehen,* ThSt(B) 34.

G. Ebeling (1962), *Theologie und Verkündigung: Ein Gespräch mit Rudolf B.,* Tübingen.

R. Marlé (1962), *Mythos et Logos: La pensée de Rudolf B.,* Geneva.

G. Hasenhüttl (1963), *Der Glaubensvollzug: Eine Begegnung mit Rudolf B. aus katholichem Glaubensverständnis,* Essen.

R. Marlé (1966), *B. et l'interprétation du Nouveau Testament,* Paris.

W. Schmithals (1967), *Die Theologie Rudolf Bultmanns,* 2nd Ed., Tübingen.

A. Malet (1968), *B.,* Paris.

J. Florkowski (1971), *La théologie de la foi chez B.,* Paris.

A. Malet (1971), *La pensée de Rudolf B.,* Geneva.

M. Boutin (1974), *Relationalität als Verstehensprinzip bei Rudolf B.,* Munich.
G. Ebeling (1977), *Gedenken an Rudolf B.,* Tübingen.
W. Schmithals (1980), "Bultmann, R.," *TRE* 7, 387–96.
A.C. Thiselton (1980), *The Two Horizons: New Testament Hermeneutics and Philosophical Description with Special Reference to Heidegger, Bultmann, Gadamer and Wittgenstein,* Exeter.
M. Evang (1988), *Rudolf B. in seiner Frühzeit,* Tübingen.
E. Hausschildt (1989), *Rudolf Bultmanns Predigten: Existentiale Interpretation und Lutherische Erbe,* Marburg.
E. Jüngel (1990), "Glauben und Verstehen, Zum Theologiebegriff Rudolf Bultmanns," in *Wertlose Wahrheit,* Munich, 16–77.
E. Baasland (1992), *Theologie und Methode: Eine historiographische Analyse der Frühschriften Rudolf Bultmanns,* Wuppertal.
F.J. Gagey (1993), *Jésus dans la théologie de B.,* Paris.
R. Gibellini (1994), *Panorama de la théologie au XXe s.,* Paris, p. 33–62.

JEAN-FRANÇOIS COLLANGE

See also **Barth, Karl; Bonhoeffer, Dietrich; Canon of Scriptures; Heidegger, Martin; Hermeneutics; Literary Genres in Scripture; Myth**

C

Cajetan, Thomas de Vio. *See* **Thomism**

Calvin, John

1509–64

The most important figure in the Protestant Reformation after Luther*, Calvin was born in Noyon in 1509. His father was a notary and secretary of the episcopal court and planned a career in the Church for his son. Calvin had a thorough education and solid humanistic training. We know that he spent a year (1522–23 or 1523–24) at the Collège de la Marche in Paris and then four years at the Collège Montaigu, where he earned a master of arts. He should then have begun theological studies, but contrary to his original intention his father had him study law*. Calvin says that this was because law was more lucrative, but it was probably not by chance that at the same time his father was in conflict with the cathedral chapter (he died excommunicate a few years later). Calvin studied law for four years in Orléans and Bourges and during this time began to study Greek with Melchior Wolmar. He then began a career as a humanist, as evidenced by the publication in Paris in 1532 of his commentary on Seneca's *De clementia.* It is not known whether Calvin was already consciously a Protestant at this time; the date of what he was to call his sudden conversion* *(subita conversio)* remains unknown. But in 1533 his friend Nicolas Cop, rector of the University of Paris, delivered an inaugural lecture that owed a good deal to Luther. Cop had to leave Paris as a consequence, and Calvin did the same. There followed three years of wandering in and out of France, during which Calvin went as far as Ferrara. In 1534 he abandoned the church livings that had allowed him to finance his studies, and in 1535, in Basel, he finished the first edition of *Christianae Religionis Institutio,* adorned with a dedication to François I that was at the same time a passionate defense of the persecuted French Protestants. The work was published in Basel in early 1536. At around the same time, Calvin returned to France for the last time and left with the intention of making a literary or scholarly career in Strasbourg or Basel, both of which were centers of Protestant humanism*. But his journey took him to Geneva, and this was the decisive moment of his life.

Geneva had just become independent from Savoy and joined the Reformation, largely impelled by the fiery preaching* of Guillaume Farel (1489–1565). When Farel learned of the presence of the young Calvin in Geneva, he came to ask him to stay and help him construct a Protestant Church and a Protestant society. Nothing was further from Calvin's intentions. He had no experience of organization or administration and wished for only one thing: to lead the quiet life of a scholar. But Farel solemnly cursed Calvin's future studies if he did not stay in Geneva. Calvin recognized the voice of God* and stayed.

He was first named a simple reader at Saint-Peter, but he soon became the leading minister. By 1537 he had already sketched plans for the organization of the life of the Church of Geneva, a confession of faith, and a catechism. But the population did not look kindly on the Church that had now been reformed at the hands of the French. The crisis came to a head at Easter 1538, when the three ministers, Calvin, Farel, and Coraud, refused to celebrate communion* because of the tensions existing in the city. They were immediately expelled. Calvin accepted an invitation from Martin Bucer (1491–1551) to Strasbourg, where he was minister of the French community in exile from 1538 to 1541. However, the political climate of Geneva changed, and he returned there in the autumn of 1541 and stayed until his death in 1564.

His second stay in Geneva was marked by a certain number of conflicts, many of which have left traces in the image we have of him. The best-known episode is the condemnation of Michel Servet (1511–53), who died at the stake because of his heretical views on the Trinity*. It is still spoken of as though it were the act of Calvin alone and as though it were an exceptional case in the 16th century. Other cases (such as that of Bolsec [?–1584] in 1551, tried for having opposed the Calvinist doctrine of predestination*, and the execution of Gruet in 1547 for blasphemy and pornography) and the generally negative image that we have of the way in which the consistory imposed the discipline of the Church point in the same direction. However, Calvin was never a dictator. Until at least 1555 his position in the city was precarious; and as for the decisions of the consistory (including those of Calvin), they were not always as harsh as certain extreme cases might lead one to believe. Recent historical work presents a more balanced picture, but the caricature of Calvin, as repeated, for example, by Stefan Zweig in *Castellio gegen Calvin,* will no doubt be difficult to change.

When Calvin arrived on the theological stage, the Protestant movement was already strongly divided by disagreements about the Eucharist between supporters of Luther and supporters of Zwingli*. Calvin felt closer to Luther, although he did not accept his more extreme views, in particular the conception ("ubiquism") that accorded omnipresence to the risen humanity of Christ*. But his principal concern was to reconcile the opponents. In this he was in agreement with Bucer, although he did not appreciate Bucer's tendency to rely on the ambiguity of formulations to conceal real doctrinal differences. He was persuaded that the reasons for the conflict would disappear if a serious study of the question were made from biblical and theological perspectives, and he at first thought—as seen, for example, in his *Short Treatise on the Lord's Supper* (1541)—that this was possible. But although he was able to reach a doctrinal agreement with Heinrich Bullinger (1504–75), what is now known as the *Consensus Tigurinus* of 1549, and to come to a common view with Ph. Melanchthon (1497–1560), the controversy revived in his final years, particularly with the most rigid Lutherans, such as Westphal and Heshusius. Their disagreement on the Eucharist, on some points of Christology*, and on predestination thus separated the Lutheran and Reformed Churches until the Concord of Leuenberg in 1973. But the dispute had political or ecclesiastical significance only in places where large numbers of the two communities lived side by side, that is, especially in Germany. In Geneva, Calvin was the principal planner, organizer, and leader of the Reformed Church. He was the one who gave the Church its structure, its liturgy*, its religious music*, and its discipline. As early as his proposals of 1537, he intended to organize the spiritual life* of the community around the regular celebration of Communion, but he never managed to persuade the Genevans to make it as frequent as he wished.

He did accomplish two of his plans: the introduction of the singing of the Psalms* in the liturgy and the establishment of a system of supervision by the elders. In the *Ecclesiastical Ordinances* of 1541 Calvin proposed a fourfold division of functions in the Church (pastor*, doctor, elder, and deacon*), as well as the establishment of a consistory, a group of ministers and elders that was to supervise the life of the Church and examine cases worthy of censure (from reprimand to excommunication). He thereby established the presbyterian-synodal system of church government* that is still, broadly speaking, in operation in Reformed Churches throughout the world.

From the liturgical and homiletic point of view, Calvin's Geneva followed the Swiss tradition inaugurated by Zwingli. The structure of the service was founded on that of the medieval sermon rather than that of the Mass, and preaching followed the method of *lectio continua* of the Bible* rather than the division into pericopes used in the Middle Ages. Calvin himself preached in an improvisatory style several times a week. From 1549 his sermons were transcribed and corrected for distribution. We have several hundred of them (189 on Acts and 342 on Isaiah). He also frequently made commentaries on the Old and New Testaments in his capacity as doctor of the school of Geneva, which was to become an academy in 1559 when Théodore de Bèze (1519–1605) was called to Geneva to assume leadership of it.

We may classify the very numerous works of Calvin under five rubrics:

1) *The Institution of Christian Religion,* "in which is included a summary of piety, and almost everything that it is necessary to know in the doctrine of salvation." In the first edition (1536), written in Latin, the *Institutio* contained six chapters and followed the outline of Luther's catechisms: law*, faith*, prayer*, the sacraments*, the false sacraments, and Christian liberty*. In 1539 Calvin reworked and augmented the text, abandoning this outline but not replacing it with a different coherent structure. The third edition in 1543, modified again in 1545 and 1550, was even longer and still without a satisfactory form. Finally, the fourth edition of 1559, longer than all the earlier ones, organized the material into four books following the pattern of the earlier creeds: knowledge of the Creator, knowledge of the Redeemer, participation in the grace* of Christ (broad terms, the themes of sanctification, justification*, and predestination), and visible mediations (particularly the Church and the sacraments but also political organization in the final chapter). This edition of the *Institutio* is the most thorough and complete exposition of Calvin's theology. It well deserves its status as a classic of Christian dogmatics*, even though a substantial number of the additions made between 1536 and 1559 are strongly polemical and reflect all the controversies in which Calvin had been involved over the quarter century separating the first from the final version. It is a systematic work: that is, it presents only one aspect of Calvin's thought, although it is an essential aspect. Other works show the operation of this constantly probing intelligence from other angles, and the *Institutio* alone cannot provide an accurate idea of its author. The French translation of the *Institutio* by Calvin himself, published in 1541, also played a decisive role in the evolution of the French language and French literature.
2) *The exegetical work.* Alongside the hundreds of sermons already mentioned, there are a series of *Commentaries* on the entire New Testament, with the exception of 1 and 2 John and Revelation. The latter he admitted barely understanding. These commentaries appeared at irregular intervals between 1540 *(Romans)* and 1555 *(Harmony of the Gospels).* Calvin did not write commentaries on all of the Old Testament, and only some of the works that he published on the subject, from 1551 on, can be considered commentaries in the modern sense of the word *(Isaiah, Genesis, Pentateuch,* and *Joshua).* The others are the fruit of sermons or exegetical lectures.
3) *The polemical work.* Calvin also wrote a large number of apologetic works defending the Reformation and polemical works on controversial theological subjects. A good example of the former is the *Reply to Sadolet* that Calvin wrote during his stay in Strasbourg in 1539. The best known of the latter is the treatise *De aeterna praedestinatione Dei* of 1552, which repeats and develops arguments on free will and predestination already used against Albert Pighi (c. 1490–1542) in his *Defensio sanae et orthodoxae doctrinae* (1543).
4) The catechisms and confessions. Along with the Ecclesiastical Ordinances should be mentioned the Geneva Catechism and Form of Prayers and Ecclesiastical Chants (both 1542). It was also Calvin who prepared the first sketch of the *Confessio gallica* in 1559, one of the major texts of this kind in the 16th century.
5) *The correspondence.* This was very large, and extended from England in the west to Poland and Hungary in the east. Like Bullinger in Zurich, Calvin was in constant contact not only with friends or other reformers but also with entire communities, refugees, former students in prison and sometimes martyred for their faith, members of the petty or high nobility, princes, and monarchs. His letters shed extraordinary light on his life, his interests, and his activities but also on the tumultuous history of the Reformation and the beginnings of the Counter-Reformation.

The principal characteristics of Calvin's theology are as follows. Like Luther, Calvin belongs to the Augustinian tradition, which explains his insistence on the corruption of human nature, the ineffectiveness of works for salvation, and justification *sola gratia* and *sola fide.* It is in this context that we must situate his concept of dual predestination. However, Calvin goes much further in this area than the Augustinian tradition, as represented, for example, by Thomas* Aquinas, for he holds not only that some are predestined for salvation while others are cast aside (the "outcast") but also that predestination to damnation is a deliberate act of divine sovereignty. Such an idea of God obviously poses a problem, from which have arisen many conflicts in Reformed theology up to and including the recapitulation of the entire question by Barth* (*KD* II/2). But it is not really the confessional specificity of Calvinism*, which is limited to making explicit ideas that were indeed bequeathed by Augustine*.

There are also differences between Calvin and Luther, some of which are due to Calvin's humanistic education. Alongside justification, Calvin laid emphasis on sanctification, the continuous work of the Holy* Spirit, on the *tertius usus legis* (ethical practice) as the principal function of the law as opposed to Luther's preference for the *usus elenchticus* (law made to convict man of sin*), and on the continuity between the Old and New Testaments. The importance of the role of the Holy Spirit is particularly apparent in the Calvinist doctrine of the Eucharist: it is the Spirit that "abolishes distance" and unites us in the sacrament with the risen Christ who has ascended to heaven. This last point brings to the fore what Lutherans were to call the "*extra calvinisticum,*" the idea that the divine nature of Christ transcends the confines of his humanity. One might say that on this point Calvin is close to the school of Antioch*, while Luther has more affinities with the school of Alexandria.* But Calvin also went further than Luther on another point in restoring force to the second commandment* (the prohibition of images*) and by strictly imposing it in the architecture* and decoration of churches.

In contrast to medieval theology—about which he generally spoke ill, although he certainly owed more to it than he thought—Calvin, like other reformers, criticized speculation and allegory. Allegory finds in texts meanings that are not there, and speculation seeks a knowledge of God that is abstract and therefore sterile. Calvin thus begins the *Institutio* by clearly indicating the link between knowledge* of God and self-knowledge, asserts that all true knowledge of God comes from obedience—that it serves the honor of God and our interests and is inseparable from piety—and asks what God is in relation to us rather than what he is in himself (*Institutio* I. 1–2). In his exegesis* of the Old Testament in particular, Calvin is careful not to give a prematurely christological interpretation of texts, and he pays much more attention to the traditions of Jewish exegesis than many other commentators.

Calvin did not believe himself called on to do original work, rather that he had been given the task of restoring the "true face of the Church," something that had been more visible in the early centuries, according to him, than in the thousand years preceding the Reformation. The *Institutio* was in his view a manual of *Christian philosophy**: once it existed, he would be able to devote himself to exegesis of and commentary on the Bible without the need to undertake investigation as each new theological problem arose. Calvin's commentaries and his correspondence broadened the audience for his work in Geneva without changing its nature. It was always a matter of reforming the Church for the glory* of God and the good of the people of God. There can be no doubt that Calvin was a major figure in the history of the Church.

•Joannis Calvini, *Opera omnia,* vols. 1–59, Brunswick (1869–95).
Joannis Calvini, *Opera selecta,* vols. 1–5, Stuttgart, 1926–36.
Joannis Calvini, *Institution de la religion chrestienne,* repr. of the 1541 Edition (J. Pannier, Ed.), 4 vols., Paris, (2nd Ed. 1961); repr. of the 1560 edition (J.-D. Benoît, Ed.), 5 vols., Paris, 1957–63.
Joannis Calvini, *Supplementa calviniana,* vols. 1–8, Neukirchen, 1961–94.
Registres de la Compagnie des Pasteurs de Genève au temps de Calvin, Ed. R.M. Kingdon, vols. 1–2, Geneva, 1962–64.
A. Erichson (1900), *Bibliographia calviniana,* Berlin (Repr. Nieuwkoop, 1960).
W. Niesel (1961), *C.-Bibliographie, 1901–1959,* Munich.
D. Kempff (1975), *A Bibliography of Calviniana, 1959–1974,* Leiden.
See *Calvin Bibliography* published yearly in *Calvin Theological Journal* since vol. 6 (1971).
♦J. Doumergue (1899–1927), *Jean Calvin: Les hommes et les choses de son temps,* 7 vols., Lausanne.
F. Wendel (1950), *Calvin: Sources et évolution de sa pensée religieuse,* Paris (bibl.); 2nd Rev. Ed., Geneva, 1985.
P. van Buren (1957), *Christ in Our Place: The Substitutionary Character of Calvin's Doctrine of Reconciliation,* Edinburgh.
A. Biéler (1959), *La pensée économique et sociale de Calvin,* Geneva.
A. Ganoczy (1964), *Calvin théologien de l'Église et du ministère,* Paris.
R. Stauffer (1964), *L'humanité de Calvin,* Neuchâtel.
A. Ganoczy (1966), *Le jeune Calvin,* Wiesbaden.
T.H.L. Parker (1986), *Calvin's Old Testament Commentaries,* Edinburgh.
T.H.L. Parker (1987), *John Calvin: A Biography,* London.
E.A. McKee (1988), *Elders and the Plural Ministry. The Role of Exegetical History in Illuminating John Calvin's Theology,* Geneva.
T.F. Torrance (1988), *The Hermeneutics of John Calvin,* Edinburgh.
R. Gamble (Ed.) (1992), *Articles on Calvin and Calvinism,* 14 vols., London.
O. Millet (1992), *Calvin et la dynamique de la parole,* Paris.
W. de Greef (1993), *The Writings of John Calvin: An Introductory Guide,* Grand Rapids, Mich.
T.H.L. Parker (1993), *Calvin's New Testament Commentaries,* Edinburgh.
B. Cottret (1995), *Calvin: Biographie,* Paris.
J.-F. Gilmont (1997), *Jean Calvin et le livre imprimé,* Geneva.
O. Millet (Ed.) (1998), *Calvin et ses contemporains,* Geneva.

Alasdair Heron

See also **Bucer, Martin; Calvinism; Humanism, Christian; Luther, Martin; Lutheranism; Protestantism**

Calvinism

Calvinism is not understood as a precise doctrine. Very broadly, the term designates everything that is closely or distantly related to the history and culture of the Reformed Churches*, although John Calvin* (1509–64) was neither the first nor the only leader of the Reformation, and although after Calvin's death, Calvinism was not always faithful to its namesake's way of thinking.

The terms *calvinien* and *Calvinist* seem to have appeared in France and England in the second half of the 16th century, which shows the extent to which Calvin was already seen as the principal figure of the Reformation. But the Reformation had begun with Zwingli* in Zurich, and many Reformation leaders, both French and German speaking, were older than Calvin and had become involved in the movement much earlier than he. The Germans included Martin Bucer* (1491–1551), Wolfgang Capiton (1478–1541), Leo Jud (1482–1542), Oswald Geishüsler—also known as Oswald Myconius—(1488–1552), Johannes Huszgen (1482–1531), and Heinrich Bullinger (1504–75). Among the French reformers were Guillaume Farel (1489–1565) and Pierre Viret (1511–71). In the succeeding generation, however, Calvin and Geneva dominated the scene, and his personal influence was considerable throughout Europe, from Hungary to Scotland. Because Calvin's influence was decisive in the Reformed Churches, they can be called Calvinist, even if the title is not entirely accurate. In France, the pejorative synonym "Huguenots" was used, perhaps first applied to the Genevans and then to all Calvinists, derived from the German *Eidgenossen,* meaning "confederates."

A sketch of the history of Calvinism in general is essential before being able to provide details of its theological, intellectual, and cultural history. Most of Germany and Scandinavia supported Luther*, whereas the Reformation narrowly defined spread to eastern and western Europe. In the Holy Roman Empire, it took root particularly in the western part of what is now Germany as well as in Bohemia and Hungary. Unlike Lutheranism, the Reformed Church was not officially recognized in the empire until the Treaty of Westphalia in 1648. In France the Huguenots made up a significant minority within a fundamentally hostile state, as attested by the wars of religion in France, the Edict of Nantes, and the consequences of its revocation. Calvinism triumphed in Holland and Scotland, and its widespread influence in England was among the causes of that nation's religious and political crises in the 17th century. Then Calvinism spread to North America with the Puritan emigration. The intellectual history of Calvinism is thus linked to the history of western Europe and North America, particularly in the late 16th and the 17th centuries, when it dominated the scene. The gradual decline of Calvinist orthodoxy, on the other hand, did not bring an end to the influence of Calvinism in general. In eastern Europe, the outcome of the Thirty Years' War did not completely destroy the Calvinist Churches but reduced them to silence. It was only with the Edict of Toleration of Holy Roman Emperor Joseph II in 1781 that they recovered some degree of freedom of expression.

Different forms of Calvinism can be distinguished in the 16th and 17th centuries. In Switzerland the memory of Zwingli remained alive, and Bullinger seemed as important as Calvin to his contemporaries. When the Reformation spread into Germany, Zurich did not play a lesser role than Geneva. And when a particular form of Calvinist theology was developed in Heidelberg around 1560, with Kasper Olevian (1536–87) and Zacharias Ursinus (1534–83), who together drew up the Heidelberg Catechism of 1563, Calvin, Bullinger, and Melanchthon (1497–1560) all contributed to it; but this theology, the first form of "federal" theology, was nonetheless a new synthesis.

The influence of Calvin was most notable in France, Holland, and Scotland, although the theologies of resistance to "impious monarchs" that were to be developed in those three countries were entirely contrary to his convictions and recommendations. The indirect consequence of this development was that the second entry of the Reformation onto German territory, around 1600, was more distinctly Calvinist but in a form developed well after the death of Calvin. The political ambitions of the Reformation princes, which were to lead to the disaster of the Thirty Years' War, played a significant role in this outcome. It can nevertheless be said that one of the strengths of Calvinism in general was its capacity to survive even in hostile surroundings, thanks to a rather typically Calvinist sense of the independence of the church* from the state and thanks to specifically ecclesiastical institutions (consistory, synod*, and so on) that had been created in a form that made them impervious to political authorities.

What may be called classical Calvinism was established after the death of Calvin and combined elements taken from Zurich as well as from Geneva. It reached its full development with the Theology of the Covenant (or federal theology) of the mid-17th century. This was a synthesis of the particularly Calvinist notion of predestination* and of a conception of the covenant* that owed more to Zwingli and especially to Bullinger than to Calvin. Bullinger had developed the theme of the single covenant of the Old and New Testaments to defend the practice of the baptism* of children against the Anabaptists*. A distinction was later added between the "covenant of works" (the original Covenant) and the "covenant of grace" (after the Fall), which is in some sense equivalent to the Lutheran dialectic of law and gospel. In Scotland, the concept of covenant took on a markedly social and political connotation, and the idea of the covenant of works was used as a framework for thinking about the political order and natural law, a task to which a number of Reformation writers devoted themselves in the 17th century in Scotland, England, France, Holland, and Germany. Along with the thought of the Puritans, which was decisive in North America, that of the French and English adversaries of absolute monarchy was one of the essential sources of the modern conception of democracy*, the separation of powers, and the social contract.

Federalism reached its full theological development in the middle of the 17th century as evinced by the Westminster Confession (1647) and the *Summa Doctrinae de Testamento et Fœdere Dei* (1648) of Johannes Koch (1603–69). Meanwhile, the importance of predestination in Reformation doctrine had been brought to the fore by the Arminian controversy. On this question, Jacob Harmensen (1560–1609) defended a more moderate view than Calvin's and deemed that God decides that some will be saved because he foresees that they will have faith (to a certain extent, they might even "merit" their salvation). In 1618–19, the Synod of Dort rejected five theses presented by the Arminians in their *Remonstrance* of 1610. The name *Remonstrants* was later used to designate the Arminians, and the term *counter-Remonstrants*—or sometimes *Gomarists*—was used for the victorious supporters of Franciscus Gomarus (1563–1641).

In place of the rejected Arminian theses, the Synod of Dort formulated what are known as the five essential points of Calvinism. They are the following: 1) Human nature is totally corrupted by sin*, (2) divine election is unconditional, (3) the reconciliation bestowed by God* in Jesus Christ is in fact confined to the circle of the elect, (4) grace is irresistible, and (5) the elect will persevere until final salvation*. Thereafter, this unambiguous doctrine of "dual predestination" was to be a source of constant conflict in the Reformation tradition, and only a minority of Churches and theologians would subscribe to it today.

The most remarkable attempt at a reformulation is no doubt that of Karl Barth* (1886–1968) in *Die kirchliche Dogmatik* ("Church Dogmatics," II/2, 1–563), although this type of theology is not a Calvinist invention but belongs to the Augustinian tradition (*see*, e.g., Thomas* Aquinas's *Summa Theologica* Ia, question 23). As these examples demonstrate, Calvinist thought is greatly concerned with being systematic, rational, and coherent. This concern with clarity and method is in part the legacy of humanism*, which played a cardinal role in the Reformation. It can also be seen at work in Calvinist circles in the interaction between theology and other disciplines, such as jurisprudence, philosophy*, and the sciences. And in the generations that followed the apogee of federal theology, Reformation thinkers were indeed more creative in these areas than in theology itself, with the remarkable exception of Jonathan Edwards*.

Calvinism generally remained in contact with the movement of ideas. For example, Pierre de la Ramée (1515–72), a professor at the Collège de France who was assassinated in the Saint Bartholomew's Day Massacre, became a Calvinist at the Colloque de Poissy in 1561, and his logic, linked to Melanchthon's theology, exercised a profound influence on Protestant thought of the late 16th and the 17th centuries. As another example, the theological and scientific ideas of England's Francis Bacon (1561–1626) probably owed a good deal to Calvinist influence. We should also note that the Calvinists of the 17th century were generally open to Cartesian ideas—with the exception of the Dutch counter-Remonstrants, who were dominated by the imposing Dutch theologian Gijsbert Voet (1589–1676). And John Locke (1632–1704), although hardly orthodox, was a typical product of the Calvinist intellectual tradition in England. Of primary importance, however, was the Académie réformée of Saumur, founded in 1593. An intellectual center for all of western France, it was particularly remarkable for its professors of Oriental languages and its jurists, who formed what has been called the "critical school," whose members included John Cameron (1579–1625), Louis Cappel (1585–1658), and Moïse Amyraut (1596–1664). Also important was the Academy of Sedan, among whose teachers was Pierre Bayle (1647–1706), compiler of the celebrated *Nouvelles de* *la République des Lettres* (from 1684) and author of the monumental *Dictionnaire historique et critique* (Rotterdam, 1697). Bayle's influence on the Enlightenment cannot be overestimated. It can thus be said that Calvinism in its way fostered both the Enlightenment (because of its intellectual and systematic aspect) and Pietism*, which was directly derived from the Puritan systematization of the *ordo salutis* in terms of stages of Christian experience (*see* the Westminster Confession, X–XX).

Calvinist theology underwent considerable renewal in the 19th century. The father of liberal theology, Friedrich Daniel Ernst Schleiermacher* (1768–1834), belonged to the Reformed tradition, as did more conservative theologians such as the leader of Dutch neo-Calvinism, Abraham Kuyper (1837–1920), Charles Hodge (1797–1878) and Archibald Hodge (1823–86), and Benjamin Warfield of Princeton (1851–1921), not to mention those who inspired the liturgical renewal in the United States and Scotland. In addition, 19th-century Calvinists tried to remedy the fragmentation of their Churches, and the first steps were taken toward federation. The World Alliance of Reformed Churches, created in 1875, is today the largest existing Protestant confessional family and includes more members than the families of Lutherans, Anglicans, Methodists, or Baptists.

The greatest Reformed theologian of the 20th century—although he cannot be confined to narrow confessional limits—is Karl Barth*. One of his most remarkable students, the Scottish theologian T. F. Torrance (1913–), has undertaken an extension of the domain of theological reflection beyond its traditional boundaries by taking into account the problems posed by the natural sciences*. In North America an important role was played by a more conservative and confessional Calvinism of Dutch origin (Cornelius van Til, 1895–1987), but the influence of Reinhold Niebuhr (1892–1971), who came from a German Reformed background, was probably more significant in the long run. In the years following World War II, along with the Scotsman John Baillie, he was the only Protestant theologian who could really be set against Barth.

• H. Heppe (Ed.), E. Bizer (Rev.) (1958), *Die Dogmatik der evangelisch-reformierten Kirche,* Neukirchen.

E. F.K. Müller (Ed.) (1903), *Die Bekenntnisschriften der reformierten Kirche,* Leipzig, Repr. Zurich, 1987.

W. Niesel (Ed.) (1938), *Bekenntnisschriften und Kirchenordnungen der nach Gottes Wort reformierten Kirche,* Zurich.

G. Thompson (Ed.) (1950), *Reformed Dogmatics Set Out and Illustrated from Sources,* London, repr. Grand Rapids, Mich., 1978.

L. Vischer (Ed.) (1982), *Reformed Witness Today: A Collection of Confessions and Statements of Faith Issued by Reformed Churches,* Bern.

O. Fatio (Ed.) (1986), *Confessions et catéchismes de la foi réformée,* Geneva.

♦A. A. van Schelven (1943, 1951), *Calvinisme Gedurende Zijn Bloeeitijd,* vols. 1–2, Amsterdam.

J. T. McNeill (1954), *The History and Character of Calvinism,* Oxford.

K. Halaski (Ed.) (1977), *Die reformierten Kirchen,* Stuttgart.

J. H. Leith (1977), *Introduction to the Reformed Tradition,* Atlanta.

W. Neuser (1980), "Dogma und Bekenntnis in der Reformation: Von Zwingli und C. bis zur Synode von Westminster," *HDThG* 2, 165–352.

H. Hart (Ed.) (1983), *Rationality in the Calvinian Tradition,* Lanham, Md.

M. Prestwich (Ed.) (1985), *International Calvinism 1541–1715,* Oxford.

R. V. Schnucker (Ed.) (1988), *Calviniana: Ideas and Influence of John C.,* Kirksville, Mo.

E. A. McKee, B. G. Armstrong (Ed.) (1989), *Probing the Reformed Tradition: Historical Studies in Honor of E. A. Dowey,* Louisville, Ky.

H. A. Obermann (Ed.) (1991–92), *Reformiertes Erbe: FS für Gottfried W. Locher zu seinem 80. Geburtstag,* vols. 1–2 (*Zwingliana* 19/1–2), Zurich.

Coll. (1992), *Encyclopaedia of the Reformed Faith,* Louisville, Ky.

R. Gamble (Ed.) (1992), *Articles on Calvin and Calvinism,* London.

D. C. McKim (Ed.) (1992), *Major Themes in the Reformed Tradition,* Grand Rapids, Mich.

W. F. Graham (Ed.) (1994), *Later Calvinism: International Perspectives,* Kirksville, Mo.

H. Blocher (1995), "Néo-calvinisme," *Encyclopédie du protestantisme,* Paris, 174–75.

P. Gisel, F. Higmar (1995), "Calvin," *Encyclopédie du protestantisme,* Paris, 172–73.

W. McCornish (1995), "Calvinisme," *Encyclopédie du protestantisme,* Paris, 173–74.

Alasdair Heron

See also **Anglicanism; Calvin, John; Congregationalism; Family, Confessional; Lutheranism; Methodism; Protestantism; Puritanism**

Cano, Melchior. *See* **Loci theologici**

Canon Law

The term *canon law* is used to designate the body of law that organizes the activity of the Catholic and Orthodox Churches*. The Churches that came out of the Reformation tend to speak of "discipline" instead. The term is a translation of the traditional Latin expression *ius canonicum.*

a) The Law of the Catholic Church. The law of the Church is contained in two codes. The first, called *Codex Iuris Canonici* ("Code of Canon Law"), is concerned with the Roman Church. It was promulgated in 1983 by Pope John Paul II following a revision of the first code promulgated by Benedict XV in 1917. The second code, called the *Codex Canonum Ecclesiarum Orientalum* ("Code of Canons of the Eastern Churches"), is concerned with the Eastern Catholic Churches and was promulgated in 1990. It took up the uncompleted work of codification begun in 1927 under the pontificate of Pius XI, which was halted in 1958 because, on 25 January 1957, John XXIII had announced the convening of the Second Vatican Council* as well as the revision of the Code of Canon Law of the Catholic Church. It was thus already clear that the future canon law would make reference to the declarations of Vatican* II. It took 20 years to complete the revision of the Roman code, following work by committees in which canonists from around the world participated. In a similar way, the code of canons of the Eastern Catholic Churches was prepared by a long effort lasting 16 years.

The law of the Catholic Church is not confined to the codes, although between the two of them they make up the most important part of the *universal law* of the Church—that is, the law applicable throughout the Church and promulgated by the pope*. Canon law is also contained in scattered official texts, rarely brought together, either of universal law or making up the body of the *particular law* of the Church. The latter category of law is important because it emanates from institutions capable of creating their own law or has to do with groups able to be endowed with a particular law. This is true of particular Churches or local* Churches and their associations (ecclesiastical regions and provinces and conferences of bishops). It is also true of all associations, whether or not they fall under the jurisdiction of sacred institutions. Taken as a direct application of universal law when that law so provides or, more broadly, promulgated in conformity with universal law, particular law has the capacity to be more flexible and closer to local or specific conditions. Communities of the Church count on it to provide a framework for their activity and to demonstrate their identity.

In addition, there are other sources of law, for canon law is a legal system developed in the way that major modern legal systems have developed. These sources include general principles of law and authentic interpretations provided by the legislative body itself. To these sources is added the jurisprudence produced by ecclesiastical courts, either in matrimonial matters—when the courts have ruled on requests for annulment of marriage*—or on administrative questions following disputes brought before the jurisdiction authorized to hear complaints against decisions made by people in power. Closely related to canon law itself, there are two important bodies of law. First is the *concordat law,* made up of documents of all kinds, defining the relations between the Catholic Church* and states or political societies*. There is also what is called in the Catholic Church *ecclesiastical civil law,* covering all the branches of national law encompassing religious life, the law of physical and legal persons, and the law of property. For example, for France, this law includes the rule of separation applied to religious denominations, the rule of recognized and nonrecognized denominations in Alsace-Moselle, and the statutes in force in the overseas departments and territories.

b) Codification. The use of codification in order to present the basic sources of canon law is recent. It dates from the late 19th century, a period in which the Napoleonic Code served as a model. In fact, at the time there was a problem of accessibility of the law. This problem was due to the increase in the volume of legal texts in the period following the Council of Trent*, when the popes were very active in legislative matters, in particular through the dicasteries (bureaucratic subdivisions) of the Roman Curia that were created as early as the mid-16th century. The process of codification provided a clear presentation of the law in short articles. However, this required an effort of logical construction, which accomplished a break with the preceding method. Until this break occurred, the principle of *corpus iuris canonici* had been followed, consisting in providing to the jurist the whole body of law that had previously been promulgated. The jurisconsult, before codification, could resolve questions posed to him by going through previous law as far back as Roman law, relying on the authority of published texts. It should be recalled that, as early as the fourth century, canon law was assembled in collections, at first chronological and later systematic, bringing together various sources, conciliary decisions, pontifical decretals, and even Roman civil law.

In 1140, Gratian, a monk of Bologna, began, on his own, to attempt a unification of previous law by publishing a compilation of texts under the title *Concordia Discordantium Canonum* ("Concordance of Discordant Canons"). After presenting texts on a single subject from various authorities, Gratian provided an opinion. Collectively, these opinions were known as the *dicta Gratiani.* The work had great success and gave rise to the work of the men known as *decretists,* or commentators on the decrees of Gratian. A century later, Pope Gregory IX decided to have Raymond de Pennafort carry out work similar to Gratian's, with a view to provide knowledge not only of law before Gratian but also of law that had been promulgated after him. Once the work had been completed, it was promulgated in the famous bull *Decretals of Gregory IX.* Thus augmented and commented on by the decretists, all these laws were once again assembled in 1500 in a single volume called the *Corpus Iuris Canonici* ("Body of Canon Law") so as to refer to the *Corpus iuris civilis* of Justinian.

In 1917 jurists found themselves facing a legal text that was novel in relation to those they had known earlier. They had to transform their method of working. Trained to reason as jurisconsults, they had to start relying on the text of the code in their reasoning. There followed a period in which the activity of the canonist was confined to a labor of exegesis. This goes a long way toward explaining the disaffection toward canon law that was particularly noticeable in the years following World War II—in France, for example, where the Catholic Church went through the experience of a missionary pastoral movement. Canon law seemed unable to provide a framework for this movement. Limited by its method, it was even more limited by its categories, based on an ecclesiology* that defined the Church alone as *societas juridice perfecta.*

A new interest in canon law made itself felt after the promulgation of the second Code of Canon Law in 1983. The question arose as to whether the procedure of codification would be repeated or whether there would be a return to a more traditional method of presentation of the law. But, even though it was vigorously debated, this was not an essential question. It was considered more important that the new code had incorporated the ecclesiological categories of Vatican II. The council thus appeared as the originator of many new institutions and legislative materials that a jurist could use as a basis for his interpretations.

c) Content of the Two Codes of Canon Law. In 30 headings for the Code of Eastern Churches and in seven books for the Roman Code, canonic legislation is presented in several key groups: the organization of the Church and its canonical offices of government*, law concerning forms of worship, and law dealing with the teaching function. There is—explicitly in the Roman code and implicitly in the Eastern code—a presentation organized around the three functions that Christ—who is priest, prophet, and king—had entrusted to the Church: teaching, sanctification, and government. The baptized or the faithful participate in the exercise of these functions, either individually (following the law of physical persons) or grouped in communities (following the law of associative communities). Their participation takes on a particular character within the communities erected by the Church itself—that is, dioceses and parishes. The ecclesiological reality of particular Churches "in which and through which the Catholic Church exists" (Canon 368) is fundamental. It allows us to understand and to situate in another way the legislation concerning the institutions that exercise a hierarchical power over the entire Church (or the patriarchates* in the case of the Eastern Churches). There are also legislative sections devoted to institutions specific to the Catholic Church, such as laws governing the consecrated life and a law of sanctions (or, following the old terminology, penal law).

d) Canonic Doctrine. Because of the place given to the teaching of canon law in the Catholic Church, particularly in the many university faculties, a doctrine does exist that is large and vigorous and available in several dozen specialized journals. All questions related to canon law and its legal institutes can be treated there. At the same time, it should be noted that, by the end of Vatican II, several theories on the bases of canon law had come to light, sometimes going so far as to be organized into schools. Among the most well known, those classified under the broad designation "theology of canon law" attempt to give an essentially different character to canon law as compared to national law. This is true for the German Mörsdorf, whose approach dismisses a preexisting general notion of law but provides a supernatural* basis for canon law on the grounds of the theological notions of Word* and sacrament*. It is also the case for the Swiss Corecco, who structures law as *ordo fidei* and not as *ordo rationis.*

This enterprise of a new foundation for canon law is generally presented as a renewal within the Catholic Church of a movement inaugurated among German Protestants in the middle of the 20th century, when the Evangelical Churches organized themselves in a specific way in the face of the state. On the other hand, other schools are attached to the autonomy of canonic science in relation to theology*—for example, the editorial board of the journal *Concilium* and the school of Navarre, which gives canon law the role of establishing the proper relation between the constitution of the Church and its reality as a sacrament of salvation*. In addition to these schools, there are methods in which the practice and the application of the law provide a status for its development and interpretation.

e) Orthodox Canon Law. For the Orthodox, canon law is a theological and legal discipline. The body of ecumenical conciliary canonical legislation, which is known by the common title *Nomocanon* or *Syngtama Canonum,* was officially confirmed by the synod* of Constantinople in 920. It makes up the *ratio materiae* of that law and consists of 85 canons attributed to the Apostles*, canons decreed by the first seven ecumenical councils of the first millennium, canons decreed by 11 local councils (third to ninth centuries), and canons of 13 Fathers. All this makes up the *Corpus iuris canonici* of the Orthodox Church. This conciliary legislation is an integral part of the canonical tradition. The fundamental canonical principles expressed by this legislation are fully affirmed in our day in the text of all the constitutional *status,* or *charters,* of the Orthodox Churches and govern their organization and functioning.

• (1984) *Code de droit canonique, Texte officiel et traduction française,* Paris.

E. Corecco (1985), “La réception de Vatican II dans le Code de droit canonique,” in G. Alberigo, J.-P. Jossua (Ed.), *La réception de Vatican II,* Paris, 327–91.

D. Le Tourneau (1988), “Dix ans d’application de code en France,” *ACan* 34, 11–116.

P. Valdrini (Ed.) (1989), *Droit canonique,* Paris (2nd Ed. 1999).

PATRICK VALDRINI

See also **Ecclesiastical Discipline; Gratian; Jurisdiction; Law and Legislation**

Canon of Scriptures

1. History

a) The Jewish Bible. The Hebrew Bible was assembled gradually. The Torah (Genesis through Deuteronomy) was the first to be completed; its establishment is attributed to Esdras (*see* Neh 8:2), which places it in the middle of the fifth century B.C. or perhaps at the beginning of the fourth. In the course of the third century B.C., It was translated into Greek by a group of Jews at Alexandria by royal request and for cultural (indeed, political reasons, as recounted in the *Letter of Aristeas*) as well as for liturgical reading. This was the beginning of the Septuagint (also known as the LXX).

The prophetic corpus was assembled at the latest during the third century B.C. since at the beginning of the second century, Jesus ben Sirach was familiar with Isaiah, Jeremiah, Ezekiel, and the twelve Minor Prophets* (as can be seen in Sir 48:22–25 and 49:6–10); indeed, toward 164 B.C., Jeremiah was numbered among the “books*.” Around 116, the Greek translator of Sirach shows in his prologue to the book that he knew the two groupings of the Law* and the Prophets, which appear by then to have become closed, while a third group consisted of an indeterminate number of writings and apparently remained open to new additions.

By Prophets must be understood the earlier prophets, that is to say our historical books from Joshua to 2 Kings, and the later prophets, from Isaiah to Malachai; the other books consisted at least of Psalms, Job, Proverbs, 1 and 2 Chronicles, Ezra-Nehemiah, and even Daniel. At the time of ben Sirach’s translator, most of these books had been translated into Greek, but “what was originally expressed in Hebrew does not have exactly the same sense when translated into another language. Not only this work, but also the law itself, the prophecies, and the rest of books differ not a little as originally expressed" (Sirach prologue). At the turn of the first century, 2 Maccabees 2:13 attributes to Nehemiah the gathering together of the "the books about the kings and prophets, and the writings of David [that is, the Psalms]," an undertaking continued by Judas Maccabeus around 160 B.C. The Law and the Prophets are mentioned in 2 Maccabees 15:9, and 1 Maccabees 12:9 speaks of the encouragement given by "the holy books which are in our hands." In addition, there is a quotation from Psalm 79 in 1 Maccabees 7:17.

While Judaism* was thus enlarging its scriptural corpus little by little, the Samaritans, who had been hostile to the Jews since the fourth century, restricted themselves to the Pentateuch. Their refusal of the Prophets and the other books may have been absolute by the time their schism was consummated in 128, with the destruction of their sanctuary at Gerizim by John Hyrcanus I. In the first centuries B.C. and A.D., opinions within Judaism diverged. The Sadducees recognized the authority* of the Torah alone, though this does not preclude their having known the other books (*see* TJ, Megillah 7, 70 d). The inhabitants of Qumran seem to have accepted all the books that would be accepted after their time in the Hebrew canon (except possibly Esther), but they found room in addition for Sirach and for Enoch and other apocalyptic writings.

The Jewish translators at Alexandria had used a Hebrew text in its premodern state; in this respect, 1 Qumran Isaiah[a] resembles the Septuagint, while 1 Qumran Isaiah[b] foreshadows the Hebrew text that would become canonical. At the beginning of our era, Judaism had a standard Hebrew text, on the basis of which a partial revision of the Greek translation was apparently undertaken in Judea, as evidenced by the manuscript of the Minor Prophets found in a cave at Nahal Hever. The first Greek translation of Ezra-Nehemiah, the 1 Esdras of the LXX, had already been supplanted in the previous century by a new translation, the 2 Esdras of the LXX. Song of Solomon, Ruth, and Lamentations were translated for the first time, in Judea, perhaps for use among the Diaspora at major festivals. In the case of Esther and Tobit, there is no trace of a Judaean revision of the original Greek translations, although the latter has been found at Qumran in both Hebrew and Aramaic. Ecclesiastes would not be translated into Greek until the end of the first century A.D.

For the Pharisees, the basis on which a book was accepted seems to have been its composition prior to the cessation of prophecy (*see* 1 Macc 9:27) during the Persian period and its transmission to the Great Synagogue (*Mishnah, Abôt* 1, 1; *see* Neh 8?). Taken literally, even Ezra-Nehemiah, 1 and 2 Chronicles, Daniel (considered as prophetic, as seen in Mt 24:15) and Song of Solomon were accepted, but Esther, Ecclesiastes, and Sirach posed a problem. After the destruction of Jerusalem in A.D. 70, the Pharisean assembly of Jamnia around the year 90 seems to have taken a stand on only two points relating to the canon: the Song of Solomon "stained the hands" (i.e., it was sacred and canonical) and thus could not be used at secular festivals, while Ecclesiastes, already accepted by the school of Hillel, continued to be accepted, though some would keep questioning its canonicity until the end of the second century. On the other hand, Sirach, which may have been accepted at Qumran, was not discussed, and it remained outside the canon. Greatly appreciated among Jewish families (*see* 2 Macc 15:36), but lacking at Qumran, Esther seems to have been accepted only after the assembly of Jamnia.

Soon afterward, Josephus, in *Flavius Josephus against Apion,* asserted that the Pharisaic canon was fixed and consisted of 22 books, including Esther and Ecclesiastes but combining Ruth with Judges and Lamentations with Jeremiah. At the end of the second century, the Hebrew canon (*TB, Baba Bathra,* 14 b) consisted (and would henceforth consist) of 24 books, Ruth and Lamentations being by that time distinct from Judges and Jeremiah. The closure of the Hebrew canon was imposed on Pharisaism, the only current form of Judaism that had survived after the destruction of Jerusalem in A.D. 70. Before or during the second Jewish revolt (A.D. 131–135), Akiba excluded the "outer books" (Mishnah, Sanhedrin 10, 1), these being "the *gilyônîm* and the books of the *minim*" (*Tosefta, Yadaim* 2, 13). This has often been interpreted as an allusion to the Gospels* and other Christian writings, but some scholars take it to refer to books originating with the Jewish sects of the period. Was Christianity the principal motive? This seems unlikely since the process of the formation of the Hebrew corpus led it to become closed at the moment when Judaism was aiming to ensure its survival by means of what remained to it—its sacred books along with its God*.

The list of 22 books given by Flavius Josephus (*Against Apion,* 38–41) contains the five books of the Law, 13 books of the "prophets who were after Moses" (probably Joshua, Judges-Ruth, Samuel, Kings, Isaiah, Jeremiah-Lamentations, Ezekiel, the Twelve, Job, Daniel, Ezra-Nehemiah, Chronicles, and Esther), and four "Writings" (Psalms, Proverbs, Ecclesiastes, and the Song of Solomon). Probably a century later, the list of *TB Baba Bathra,* 14b, gives a different composition: the Prophets now consist only of Joshua, Judges, Samuel, Kings, Isaiah, Jeremiah, Ezekiel, and the Twelve, while to the group of Writings have been added all those other books previously considered as prophetic, with Ruth preceding Psalms, Job, Proverbs, and Ecclesiastes; Daniel is no longer regarded as prophetic. This new division into 24 books would change no further, except for the order of the Writings; the five "scrolls" (Song of Solomon, Ruth, Lamentations, Ecclesiastes, and Esther) would not be grouped together until the Middle Ages.

b) The Christian Old Testament. At the time of Jesus*, Hellenistic Jews had a collection of books in Greek more extensive than the list fixed by the Pharisees at the end of the first century.

This larger Greek collection may have been assembled on principles similar to those advocated by the Pharisees. Besides Proverbs, they read two books attributed to Solomon—Ecclesiastes and the Song of Solomon. The LXX added the Wisdom of Solomon (composed in Greek). They combined Lamentations and Jeremiah. The LXX further added Baruch and the Letter of Jeremiah to Jeremiah. They retained Ezra-Nehemiah and Chronicles as history and supplemented the LXX with 1 and 2 Maccabees and even 3 and 4 Maccabees. Fictionalized stories (Ruth, Jonah, and Esther) were accepted. The LXX also admitted Tobit and Judith. Finally, Sirach, which had remained outside the Pharisees' canon, although frequently cited by them, was retained in the LXX. From this time on, there is a noticeable tendency on the part of both the Pharisees and the LXX to be wary of the apocalyptic writings (other than Daniel) that were so valued at Qumran.

With the exception of Jude, the New Testament displays the same reservations toward Jewish apocalyptic* literature and is restricted largely to the books retained by the Pharisaic canon. Christianity subsequent to the New Testament found itself faced with two collections of books, the Hebrew corpus and the LXX.

While used by the early Christians, the LXX was little by little rejected by Jews in favor of the Greek translations by Theodotion and Aquila. The Christians, largely ignorant of Hebrew, read the LXX. Justin Martyr, for example, did so around A.D. 160 in his disputes with the Jews, though he was aware of the differences between the Greek text and the Hebrew one used by Trypho (*Dialogue,* 73; 89). In any case, Justin made no use of books that were absent from the Hebrew canon. Even before 150, Marcion rejected the entire Old Testament and retained only Paul and Luke from the New Testament: Justin, Tertullian*, and Irenaeus would refute this anti-Judaism (Marcionism*).

Around 170, Melito of Sardis (Sc 31, 21 *Sq*) brought back from Palestine a list of books recognized by the Jews; these books, also accepted by the Christians, included neither Esther nor the books peculiar to the LXX, although Melito drew inspiration from Wisdom of Solomon for his Easter homily. On the other hand, at the same period, Christians in Africa translated the LXX into Latin (the *Vetus Latina*), including Wisdom of Solomon, Sirach, and so on. At the end of the second century and the beginning of the third, Tertullian and, more explicitly, Cyprian* drew on these books that were not in the Hebrew Bible, as did Clement of Alexandria, who made much use of Wisdom of Solomon and Sirach and even cited apocalyptic writings on occasion.

Origen*, who in his *Hexapla* would compare the LXX and the other Greek translations to the Hebrew text, was aware of the difference between the Hebrew Bible and the LXX. His contacts with Judaism initially made him cautious regarding the books and additions specific to the LXX, and he did not comment on any of them. It may be that the texts peculiar to the LXX were not read in Christian liturgical assemblies, but Origen continued to cite them from time to time, even as scriptural text (*see* SC 71, 352f). Around 240, in his *Letter to Africanus* (SC 302, 532–535), he declared that even though he had not, in his dialogues with the Jews, made use of the books refused by them, there is no reason for Christians to feel obliged to reject the books derived from the LXX, which they currently used. At the end of his life, Origen excluded the "Apocrypha*," which he opposed to the "testamentary" books, in other words, those of the Hebrew Bible (*Endiathêkoi: Commentary on John* II, 188). It is unclear whether he reserved the books specific to the LXX for the use of novices (*see* SC 29, 512 *Sq*) or even of initiates.

The fourth and early fifth centuries were a time of contrasts. Around 350, Cyril of Jerusalem knew the 22 books of the Hebrew canon (PG 33, 497 c-500 b). Reacting to those who rejected the Old Testament and those who were attached to the Apocrypha, he asked, "What is the point of wasting one's efforts discriminating between the controversial books, if one is ignorant of those that are recognized by all Jews and Christians?" (PG 33, 496 a). The 22 books were, however, read in the text of the LXX, including Baruch and the Letter of Jeremiah with Esther. Cyril also sometimes cites Wisdom of Solomon and Sirach.

In his Easter letter of 367 (PG 26, 1 436–1 440), the more open-minded bishop of Alexandria, Athanasius*, distinguished the "Apocrypha" from the 22 Hebrew books (except for Esther), read in the text of the LXX, but he added a group of "uncanonical" books intended for novices: Wisdom of Solomon, Sirach, Esther, Judith, and Tobit, to which he appended the *Didache* and *The Shepherd* of Hermas. The canon of Athanasius's

Old Testament prefigured that of the Council* of Laodicea in 360, which included Esther (canon 59). It was at this period that the biblical corpus began to be referred to as a "canon" (from the Hebrew *qânêh,* a stick or cane, hence a rule or norm).

The contrasts grew even more marked in the Latin Church. Jerome, working in Bethlehem, at least between 391 and 404, retained only the books of the Hebrew Bible. He regarded Sirach, Wisdom of Solomon, Judith, Tobit, and 1 and 2 Maccabees as doubtful (PL 29, 404 c) and "apocryphal" (PL 28, 556) books. They could be read in order to edify the people but not to confirm the dogma* of the Church (PL 28, 1243 a), an ambiguous position that confused Athanasius's distinctions. Around 400, Rufinus referred to the books that were read in church, but that were not the basis of the faith, as "ecclesiastical" (CChr.SL 20, 170 *Sq*).

Astonished by the Latin translations of Jerome, who advocated *veritas hebraica,* Augustine remained strongly attached to the LXX's traditional place within the Church, which included books to which Christians in Africa had been attached since the second century. Augustine* took part in the Council of Hippo in 393 and, as a bishop, in the Councils of Carthage in 397 (CChr.SL 149, p. 340) and 418. These councils fixed the Old Testament canon, which included without any distinction the books considered controversial in the East, or Rufinus's "ecclesiastical" books. Augustine restricted himself to this list (*Docrina Christiana,* II, 8, 13). In 405, Innocent I did likewise in his letter to Exuperius, bishop of Toulouse. The Vulgate, probably assembled as early as the fifth century, would include the books that the Hebrew canon had excluded.

In the 12th and 13th centuries, doubts resurfaced as to the canonical status of these books. Hugues de Saint-Cher excluded them, and Thomas Aquinas accepted them. In 1441 the Council of Florence admitted them, but the influence of Jerome was still felt. Luther* disallowed them, as did Cardinal Cajetan (1532). In 1546 the Council of Trent* included them officially in the canon of the Roman Catholic Church. However, in 1566, Sixtus of Siena proposed the term *deuterocanonical* for the books that Rufinus had called *ecclesiastical*—Esther, Tobit, Judith, Baruch, the Letter of Jeremiah, the Wisdom of Solomon, Sirach, the Greek additions to Daniel, and 1 and 2 Maccabees. The Protestants would term them "apocryphal."

c) The New Testament. For the Christians of the first two centuries, mention of the Scripture* or Scriptures (Mt 26:54) implied the Old Testament. The earliest use of the words *Old Testament* in the sense of a collection of books is found in 2 Colossians 3:14. On the other hand, the expression *New Testament* appeared only around 200 in the writings of Clement of Alexandria (*Stromata* 5, 85, 1) and Origen (*De Principiis* 4, 1, 1) to designate the corpus that had itself only gradually been formed. The Second Letter of Peter (written around 125?) seems intended to complete the New Testament corpus, which collects the letters of Paul (referred to in 2 Pt 3:16) and also contains Matthew, Luke-Acts, 1 Peter, and Jude. All these writings are referred to in 2 Peter, but the letter mentions neither John, the three letters of John, nor James.

The Apostolic* Fathers and the apologists* still had no New Testament corpus and only rarely cited New Testament texts as Scripture. Justin was the first to refer to the Gospels* as "Memoirs of the Apostles" (*Apology* 1, 66, 3), and may have been dependent on an early "evangelical harmony," composed around 140 (*see* Boismard-Lamouille). The best-known such work was the *Diatesseron,* which combined the four Gospels. It was produced around 170 by Tatian, who had to know all four Gospels in order to do the work. Several factors would lead the Christians to fix the New Testament canon. From the first half of the second century, the Judeo-Christians had their own (apocryphal*) gospels, some of which had disturbing features. Other texts of a suspect pietism appeared. Then came Gnosticism* (already mentioned by the Apostles but resurgent), the sectarian spiritualism of Montanus, Marcionism*, which accepted only ten of Paul's letters and a mutilated Luke (*see* Irenaeus, *Against Heresies,* 1, 27, 2–3). Finally, there was the danger that the *Diatesseron* might supplant the four Gospels.

The earliest list of the New Testament writings that has come down to us may be the Muratorian Canon, which was discovered and published it in 1740 (*see DACL* 12, 1935, 543–60). The original may have dated from the end of the second century, although A. C. Sundberg (1973, *HTh* 66, 1–41) dates it from the middle of the fourth century. This fragmentary annotated list, perhaps Roman in origin, omits Hebrews, James, 1 and 2 Peter, and 3 John but adds the Wisdom of Solomon and expresses reservations about the Apocalypse of Peter and *The Shepherd* of Hermas; finally, it challenges the texts of Marcion and other heretics.

Before 200, Irenaeus was the first to draw on the New Testament more than on the Old Testament; he distinguished the time of the prophets (the Old Testament), the life of Jesus* (the Gospels), and the testimony of the Apostles* (the remainder of the New Testament). Thus, because it was apostolic and traditional, almost the whole of the New Testament (except for Philemon, Hebrews, James, 2 Peter, and Jude) was one with the Old Testament. In Irenaeus's view, there were only four Gospels. This "tetramorphic gospel" was closed and was to be regarded as Scripture, as were the letters of Paul and Acts (*Against Heresies,* 3, 12, 9, 12).

The list given by Origen in the *Homily on Joshua 7:1* was already complete but, except for the Gospels, remained open. Cyprian cited almost all the New Testament writings as Scripture, though he, like Tertullian, may have excluded Hebrews.

The sixth-century *Codex Claromontanus* (D) includes a Latin list of the books of Old and New Testaments, which is based on a Greek original that may go back to around 300. The few omissions are probably due to scribal error, and Barnabas, *The Shepherd* of Hermas, the Acts of Paul, and the Apocalypse of Peter are marked off with a line. Around 350, Cyril of Jerusalem (*Catechesis* 4, 36) had a fixed canon, but it did not include Revelation. The same omission was made in the canon of the Council of Laodicea, about 360. Soon afterward, Athanasius, in his Easter Letter of 367, gave what would become the definitive list, though this did not stop Gregory* of Nazianzus from omitting Revelation again a short while later. In 397, on the other hand, the third Council of Carthage declared the complete New Testament canon closed, with the same 27 texts as Augustine's (*Doctrina Christiana,* II, 8, 13).

In Syria, the *Diatesseron* was abandoned in favor of the four Gospels only during the fifth century, while the Peshitta still lacked 2 Peter, 2 and 3 John, Jude, and Revelation. The Councils of Florence (1441) and Trent (1546) officially proclaimed the canon of 27 New Testament books. Erasmus*, while accepting this complete canon, expressed doubts about the apostolic origin of Hebrews, James, 2 Peter, 2 and 3 John, and Revelation. And Luther, too, found Hebrew, James, Jude, and Revelation less valuable—an echo of the ancient uncertainties. Today the New Testament canon, for all the Western Churches, includes the 27 books fixed on in the fourth century.

2. Theology

According to Luke 24:27, the Old Testament foretells the coming of Jesus Christ*, to whom the New Testament bears witness. Relying on this principle, the Fathers and the councils who enumerated the books of the canon produced lists for both Testaments.

a) The Christian Canon. In establishing a list of books, the Christian canon, unlike the Jewish one, specified neither language nor edition. History records and exegesis* demonstrate the multiplicity of accepted texts. Christians in more direct contact with Judaism—in particular Jerome—tended to restrict themselves to the canon recognized by Jewish tradition, but this was not the position of the entire Church, which read the LXX and the translations derived from it. The LXX, of course, presented a text that often differed from the Masoretic texts and added further books. The canonical status of the added books, which has been debated right up until the present day, divides Catholics and Protestants. Catholics incorporate these books into the body of the Old Testament. Protestants generally place these "deuterocanonical" or "apocryphal" writings between the Old Testament and the New while recognizing their importance to an increasing extent.

The very diversity of the textual traditions, for example, between the LXX and the Masoretic texts, of which the early Christians were aware but which is more fully studied today, does not alter the necessity of consulting the texts in their original languages. However, the study of these Greek and Hebrew texts reveals more clearly the polymorphous aspect of the ancient textual traditions (going back before Christianity in the case of the Old Testament), without making it possible to exclude any particular form of the text. Adopted by the ancient Church, the LXX, itself subject to occasional variation (e.g., by the inclusion of Sirach and Tobit, not to mention the translation of Daniel by Theodotion), was often spoken of as divinely inspired. In the New Testament, passages of unknown origin and transmission that were sometimes disputed are generally recognized as canonical today (e.g., Mk 16:9–20; Lk 22:43–44; Jn 7:53–8:11).

b) Criteria for Canonicity. The criteria for canonicity are few but strict. Literary authenticity—the fact that the Torah, for example, is attributed to Moses and James, 2 Peter, and Jude to one Apostle or another—no longer figures among the criteria. Modern exegesis has achieved a clearer picture of the origins and literary history of the texts without casting doubt on their canonical status. Within Judaism, the doctrinal criterion of coherence to the Torah was already added to the historical criterion of transmission to the Great Synagogue.

Within Christianity, the first criterion is that of apostolicity, the testimony of the primitive Church. This is also the basis for the acceptance of the Old Testament, as Jesus and the Apostles knew it, as well as for the inclusion of the apostolic writings.

The ancient uncertainties concerning the "catholic" epistles and Revelation were resolved by other criteria, one of which was the traditional reception* of these various writings within the early Christian communities and in particular their liturgical use. Augustine (*Doctrina Christiana,* II, 8, 12) favored the testimony of the most important Churches, in particular those whose origins were linked to an Apostle.

Orthodoxy* was another criterion that, from the second century, led to the exclusion of pseudepigrapha, apocalypses, gnostic writings, and so on. A canonical writing was one that bore witness to the "rule of faith*" (Irenaeus, *Demonstration of the Apostolic Preaching,* 3).

c) A Canon Within the Canon? Within the Jewish canon, the Torah holds a preeminent position. The other books comment on its reception, present rereadings of it, or derive prayers from it. Within the New Testament, Vatican* II *(Dei Verbum,* 18) recognized the superiority of the Gospels, which bear witness to the life and the words of Jesus. But these questions of precedence do not affect the canonicity of the other accepted writings.

In the case of the New Testament, the debate took another turn with A. Käsemann's continuation of the Lutheran principle. Käsemann studied the internal contradictions in the New Testament (e.g., the ones between Romans and James) and in particular those that exhibit *Frühkatholizismus,* or "protocatholicism*," and seem to point to typically Catholic doctrine—such as sacramentalism, hierarchy, and the dogma of Acts, 1 and 2 Timothy, Titus, and 2 Peter. The problems of internal criteria he found there led him to consider Romans and Galatians, along with their treatment of justification* by faith, as the heart of the New Testament. Catholic theology refers to the principle of the development, of the Church, even in the time of the Apostles, under the guidance of the Holy* Spirit.

• E. Käsemann (1951), "Begründet der neutestamentliche Kanon die Einheit der Kirche?," *EvTh* 11, 13–21.
H. von Campenhausen (1967), *Die Entstehung der christlichen Bibel,* Tübingen.
J. A. Sanders (1972), *Torah and Canon,* Philadelphia.
J.-D. Kaestli, O. Wermelinger (Ed.) (1984), *Le canon de l'Ancien Testament: Sa formation et son histoire,* Geneva.
J. A. Sanders (1984), *Torah and Community,* Philadelphia.
B. S. Childs (1985), *Old Testament in a Canonical Context,* Philadelphia.
B. M. Metzger (1987), *The Canon of the New Testament: Its Origin, Development, and Significance,* Oxford.
Ch. Theobald (Ed.) (1990), *Le canon des Écritures: Études historiques, exégétiques et systématiques,* LeDiv 140.
J. A. Sanders, H. Y. Gamble, G. T. Sheppard (1992), "Canon," *AncBD* 1, 837–66.
Y.-M. Blanchard (1993), *Aux sources du canon, le témoignage d'Irénée,* CFi 175.
L. M. McDonald (1995), *The Formation of the Christian Biblical Canon,* 2nd Ed., Peabody, Mass.

Maurice Gilbert

See also **Apocrypha; Bible; Book; Exegesis; Hermeneutics; Holy Scripture; Intertestament; Magisterium; Marcionism; Tradition; Translations of the Bible, Ancient**

Canonization. *See* **Holiness**

Cantor, Georg. *See* **Infinite**

Cappadocian Fathers. *See* **Basil (The Great) of Caesarea; Gregory of Nazianzus; Gregory of Nyssa**

Capreolus, John. *See* **Thomism**

Carmel

Rooted in the founding experience of the desert, established under the patronage of the prophet Elijah ("gather all Israel to me at Mount Carmel," 1 Kgs 18:19), Carmel owes its mystical vocation to strictly theological tasks: realizing the experience* of a living God and, at the same time, exploring the human soul seized by contemplative grace. Although very much in evidence in the thinking of Thomas Aquinas, these preoccupations were more or less completely absent from the Scholastic theology of the following generation. And precisely because it persevered in its primary intention, the Carmelite theological tradition was generally underestimated. However, teachers like John* of the Cross (1542–91) or Anthony of the Mother of God (†1641) brought to it all the power of their own biblical and patristic learning, as well as their Scholastic training, putting these at the service of a spiritual pedagogy that more official theological approaches of the time lacked.

1. Until Teresian Reform

The Carmelite Rule (produced in the Holy Land around 1210) called on members of that order to "meditate day and night on the law of the Lord." Carmelite theology was born from this prayerful contact with the biblical text. It adopted the monastic tradition of *lectio divina:* through allegory and tropology, the literal meaning of the Scriptures leads the reader to an anagogical understanding—the only strictly mystical one—of the mystery that it expresses. The interaction between prayer (which was not formalized as a separate religious exercise until the Renaissance, something that can be seen in the timetables and methods for it) and theology in the modern sense of the word is permanent here. Having this purely contemplative aim, it was between 1250 and 1260 that Carmel had progressively to leave the Holy Land because of pressure from the Muslims and came to establish itself in the major Western university centers of Cambridge, Oxford, Paris, and Bologna. While it triumphed in the top Scholastic circles, it prolonged the monastic exegesis* and helped channel it toward what would henceforth be artificially known as "spirituality." In any case, the balance between reading, study, and theological work here corresponds to that of the ancient *otium,* being an outer complement to the inner *quies.* This state entails engaging in a minimum of outward activities and is far from "earthly uses, even apostolic," pure from all intention to seek earthly recompense. However, this distancing from pastoral service was continuously debated within Carmel from the moment it came to Europe.

The first Western Carmelite text that has come down to us is *Ignea Sagitta* (1271) by Nicholas of France. It is an apologia for a way of life that still fundamentally considers itself to be eremitical, its themes being the *fuga mundi* (escape from the world*), silence, and *quies: fuge, tace, quiesce* ("distance yourself, be silent, keep quiet"). At a time when Europe was in the throes of urbanization, it involved rediscovering the desert, that place where Jesus* speaks to his friends in their heart and reveals his mysteries to them. Henceforth, this desert would become that of the cell, outside and inside, of the "cellar" of the Song of Songs, where the Holy* Spirit strengthens, nourishes, and fills the inner person. "Purity of heart" allows the contemplative to become intoxicated from the "Lord's cup" rather than from the "chalice of Babylon." The radical choice between these two "cups" determines the spiritual path, which is represented as an ascent of Mount Carmel, at the summit of which there is the genuinely Christian mystical experience. Here one can recognize the outline of what would become, three centuries later, the *Ascent of Mount Carmel* of John of the Cross. There are also the seeds of Teresa of Avila's major themes, such as, for example, her description of prayer as "the exchange of friendship." We might also note the emphasis placed on the emotional life of the spirit, something drawn very much from the Cistercian tradition of Saint Bernard of Clairvaux and William of Saint Thierry, a tradition that would subsequently permeate the entire Carmelite tradition. Within university circles, Gerard of Bologna (head from 1296 to 1318), was the first Carmelite university teacher in Paris. The Aristotelianism he used was derived from Averroes. Otherwise, he followed the intellectualism of Godefroy of Fontaines and asserted the radical passivity of the will as well of the intellect. Generally, the Carmelites were known to be inclined toward nominalism*. Such was the case, for example, with Guido Terreni (†1342), Baconthorpe's teacher, and, with Jean de Pouilly, the main representative of the derivative Aristotelianism* of the period. With the emergence of John Baconthorpe (†1348), who was, by contrast, a hyperrealist, Carmel entered the top rank of university life. Known as the quasi-official theologian and philosopher of the order, the *doctor resolutus* should be considered in the first place for what he brought to the tradition of *lectio divina.* His distinctive contribution in this area involved his perception of the unity of the two Testaments. According to Baconthorpe, the revelation* of the mystery of God, perceived by Elijah only in "a low whisper" (1 Kgs 19:12) of the desert breeze, is fully realized in Jesus and offered to the Christian contemplative soul.

On a more academic level, Baconthorpe's critical spirit was compared to that of Duns* Scotus. His method places him between Thomas Aquinas and Pierre d'Auriol. Although Baconthorpe cannot be regarded as a disciple of Thomas, the latter is ranked high among the doctors he cites, and he often refers to Thomas's doctrine to confirm his own. Nevertheless, he distinctly criticizes the *Aquinate,* especially those of its arguments favoring the thesis that "the intellective soul is the substantial form of the body" (*CG* II, 68). Even if he claims to acknowledge the thesis, Baconthorpe underlines its weak points and holds that none of the proposed arguments is entirely convincing. Although he acknowledges that the union of body and soul is "natural," it is only in the sense in which that union is not self-contradictory, which is all that is needed for God to have been able to carry it out through his *potentia absoluta.* This critique must be read in the context of a rather weak notion of "demonstration" and "certitude:" for Baconthorpe, truth results more from the absence of any objection than from a clear affirmation.

In terms of the philosophy of nature, Baconthorpe championed physical atomism, which continued to form part of the Carmelite *ratio studiorum* until the 17th century. It was this Christian atomism that would be the primary source for the philosophy* of Pierre Gassendi (1592–1655).

Shortly after Baconthorpe, Philippe Ribot (†1391) —his *Tractatus de quattuor sensibus sacrae scripturae* (manuscript Vat. Ottob. Lat 396) has just been found—offered *Liber de Institutione primorum monachorum,* a fundamental text in the development of Carmelite spirituality. Considered for a long time to be the "primitive rule," in the 15th century it was translated into English, French, and Spanish. Teresa of Avila annotated this last translation, which helped her learn about the primitive life of Carmel. Ribot's work is a commentary—indeed, a rather bare allegory—on Elijah leaving for the banks of the Kerith (1 Kgs 17:2–6). Ribot proposes two objectives of Carmelite monastic life: one that is within human power, the other remaining in God's power alone: "We will acquire the first through our work and virtuous effort, with help from divine grace. It consists in offering God a holy heart, unsullied by all immediate stains of sin*. We reach this goal when we are perfect and in *Kerith,* which means buried in charity. The other goal of this life is sent to us through a pure gift of God…: to taste, to a certain extent, in one's heart, and to experience in one's mind the forces of divine presence and gentle glory* from above. This is called 'drinking from the stream of God's delight'" (I, c. 2)

Here we can recognize the two aspects of all Christian life, that of nature* and that of grace, which have become the two aspects of Mount Carmel insofar as they involve the contemplative experience. Genuinely typical of Carmelite theology (*see* H. de Lubac*, *Exégèse Médiévale,* 1964), this commentary has a striking Christocentrism, with Jesus offering his disciple the perfect realization of this double faithfulness to the Creator and the creature.

From the end of this first period, we must also cite Michele Aiguani (or Nicolas of Bologna, † around 1400), lecturer on Holy Scripture in Paris in 1360 and the author of an important commentary on the Psalms* in which he follows Rabbi Salomon ("great doctor of Jews") and Nicolas de Lyre for the literal meaning. At around the same time (1364, to be precise) another Carmelite, Saint Peter Thomas, founded the Faculty of Theology in Bologna , while yet another, Mathurin Courtoys, did the same in Bourges. In England, the academic vitality of the Carmelites placed them at the forefront in the battle against Wyclif's heresy* (John Wyclif, 1328?–84). John Cunningham, in particular, won fame.

With the reformer Jean Soreth (1394–1471), under whose leadership the female branch of the order was born and grew rapidly, Carmel's biblical tradition was reoriented in an emphatically modern direction: *meditatio et oratio,* in his work, take on an autonomy that relates them to the *devotio* moderna,* paving the way for the spiritual growth of Teresian Carmel. Along with this evolution and within the same tradition of a devout humanism*, Battista Spagnoli (1447–1516, the "Christian Virgil," according to Erasmus*) found a way to reconcile classical culture and Christianity by showing how Christians had historically received pagan literature (*De Vita beata* and *De Patientia*). As a final representative of this pre-Renaissance period, we should note Nicolas Calciuri (†1466) and his description of the spiritual life as a threefold "desire for celestial things:" desirous love*, delectable love, and gracious love.

This period opened the way for the era of the great modern doctrinal debates. Theologians such as Everard Billick in Köln (†1557) and the Prior General Nicolas Audet (1481–1562), who took part in the Council of Trent*, would play significant roles. A century later, Giovanni Antonio Bovio (1566–1622) would take part in the controversy over grace (bañezianism*) by defending the Jesuit stance.

2. Around the Teresian Reform

Teresa of Jesus (of Avila) (1515–82) and John of the Cross (1542–91) did not, therefore, emerge miraculously within a Carmel that is too often characterized in modern times as an intellectual desert. The themes that these Doctors* of the Church would make particularly their own were already present in their heritage. Indeed, their brilliance must not make us forget other significant representatives of the same tradition. There is also Jaime Montanes (1520–78), for example, whose christological overtones can be related to Teresa's requirement of exclusive love, or John of the Cross's "todo y nada": "To not look for something, to not look at anything, to listen to nothing, desire nothing, and finally, to love nothing other than the only Jesus Christ, for he alone is the life of our soul." In the same vein, we might also cite Miguel Alfonso de Carranza (1527–1606), Diego Velasquez, Juan Sanz (1557–1608), Francesco Amerly (†1552), Miguel de la Fuente (1573–1625).

a) The Doctrine of the Reformers. Teresa defines prayer as an affective discourse sustained by a simple gaze upon Christ. The fundamental role of the humanity of Christ is evident in his prayer that is closest to his experience, in contrast to a theological framework of which Teresa knows more than her protestations of ignorance imply. Faithful to the *devotio moderna,* she binds herself to Christ's humanity for the whole length of the spiritual journey, right up to the highest state of union. The two Carmelite masters present infused contemplation*—grace freely given—as the end of contemplative life. Nevertheless, it is an end for which the soul prepares itself through practicing the virtues, in a phase of the spiritual life when it apparently retains more initiative*. A certain imprecision of terminology, in Carmelite writers as well as in the work of authors such as Molinos, allows for an intermediate form of prayer that occurs between meditation and contemplation, that is, "acquired contemplation": John of the Cross does not entirely abandon the concept, which we can see clearly represented, for example, in Thomas of Jesus, who discusses a "mixed contemplation" that corresponds to the kind John of the Cross himself describes in *The Ascent of Mount Carmel.* Similarly, Joseph of Jesus-Mary *(Quiroga)* distinguishes infused contemplation from the form of contemplation that is obtained through the help of faith* and the ordinary assistance of grace. The notion of God's presence put forward by the Frenchman Laurent de la Résurrection (1614–91) can be compared to that proposed by Thomas of Jesus: acquired contemplation unifies the action of grace with the simplified activity of the will, while in infused contemplation it is God alone who supports the soul.

Teresa distinguishes three forms of God's taking control of the faculties of the unified soul: the will is appeased, the intellect is simplified, and the memory is suspended. This mystical union is transient and is usually accompanied by moments of ecstasy during the "spiritual betrothals" (V *Demeures*), but it becomes permanent in the "spiritual marriage" (VI and VII *Demeures*) (this is the founding terminology of Teresian mystical literature). The soul, at that time, is in a state of spiritual perfection, which is not, however, to be identified with the perfection of charity, even if the two states are normally connected. The rule is that "God only gives himself entirely to us when we give ourselves entirely to him" (*Chemin de Perfection,* 28, 12).

b) Legacy. Among the immediate disciples of the two Carmelite doctors, we should note John of Jesus and Mary (Aravalles) (1549–1609, author of *Tratado de Oración* and *Instrucción de Novicios*); Innocent of Saint-André (1553–1620), who wrote *Teologia Mistica* (1615) under the name Andrès Locara; Gratien of the Mother of God (1545–1614), who wrote a *Dilucidario* and *De la Oración Mental;* and Mary of Saint Joseph (†1603), author of *Libro de la Recreaciones.* In the Congregation of Italy (canonically autonomous since the reform of 1600), John of Jesus and Mary, known as the Calagurritain (1564–1615), was the theologian who most echoed Thomas Aquinas, writing *Theologia Mystica* (1607) and *Schola de Oratione et Contemplatione* (1610). In his *Suma y Compendio de los Grados de Oración* (Rome, 1610), Thomas of Jesus (1564–1627) studied the problems of mystical theology from a Scholastic perspective, reversing the approach of his teachers. He wrote *De Contemplatione* (Anvers, 1620) on the forms of infused contemplation, *De Oratione Divina* (Anvers, 1623) on contemplative supernatural life, and *De Perceptionibus Mentalibus,* which was not completed. An unconditional advocate of John of the Cross and who fell out of favor among reformers when John died, Joseph of Jesus and Mary Quiroga (†1628) aimed to show that there were parallels between his teacher's doctrine and the doctrines of Dennis and Thomas Aquinas. Finally, Philip of the Trinity, with his *Summa Teologiae Misticae* (Lyon, 1656), completed the Scholastic summary of mystical theology that Thomas of Jesus had started.

Strictly mystical theology lost its popularity in the 18th century in Carmel and other movements. It was not until 1874 that the Teresian tradition would be reignited: Berthold-Ignacious of Saint Anne's republishing, in Brussels, of the *Summa* by Philip of the Trinity and by publication of *Instruction des Novices* by John of Jesus and Mary. This was the eve of a new spiritual birth of Carmel, that of Thérèse of the Child Jesus (spiritual childhood*) and Elizabeth of the Trinity*. Under the auspices of Father Bruno of Jesus-Marie and maintaining itself very much in the Teresian tradition from 1931 on, Carmelite studies would prove to be a veritable laboratory of mystical psychology and theology laboratory, paralleled by Teresians such as Father Marie-Eugène de l'Enfant-Jésus among the French Carmelites.

c) Theological Reverberations. The great mystics Teresa of Avila and John of the Cross were theologically valuable in that they triggered considerable developments in the study of the human soul. But this birth of modern religious psychology in no way contradicts a strictly doctrinal rigor: both Teresa and John saw the good spiritual director as first of all a *letrado,* an expert in the tradition*. The search for such theological competence, combined with the anxiety evoked by the misbehavior in student life outside convents and monasteries, led rapidly to the foundation of discalced colleges in the university centers of Spain: Alcalá de Henares in 1570, Baeza in 1597, and Salamanca in 1581. As early as 1592, when Teresian Carmel was canonically separated from the rest of the order, the *Constitutions* of the reform required students to follow "the doctrine of Thomas Aquinas, both in terms of philosophy and theology": the fundamentally contemplative nature of Thomism* was valuably recognized here.

The intellectual life of the reformed Carmel henceforth saw a flourishing at the philosophical level, first of all in the *Commentarii cum Disputationibus in Universam Aristotelis Stagiritae Logicam* (Madrid, 1608) by Diego of Jesus (†1621), which opened the way for the *Cursus Complutensis* (Alcalá, 1624–28), published by Michael of the Trinity (1588–1661), Anthony of the Mother of God (1583–1637), and John of the Saints (1583–1654), which was then further complemented in 1640 by *Metaphysica de Biagio de la Conception* (1603–94). The determination to be absolutely loyal to Thomas Aquinas, combined with a desire for intellectual unanimity within the Alcalá school, meant that only propositions accepted by all these religious figures (or at least by a majority vote) came to light. As a result, the work that did get through was extremely scholarly and polished.

On the theological level, the famous *Cursus Theologicus de Salmenticenses* obeys the same rules. Its definitive form is that of 14 volumes of literal commentary on the *Summa Theologica* of Aquinas. The first volume was published in Salamanca in 1631 and the final one in Madrid in 1712 (final edition, in 20 vols., in Paris, from 1870 to 1883). The first of its authors, Anthony of the Mother of God (1583–1637), comments on the *De Deo Uno,* the *De Trinitatis,* and the *De Angelis;* Dominic of Saint Teresa (1604–59) comments on beatitude, human acts, and the virtues; and John of the Annunciation (1633–1701) comments on grace, justification, charity, the religious state, the Incarnation, the sacraments in general, and the Eucharist and penance. Anthony of Saint John the Baptist (1641–99) published the first part of volume 12, and Ildephonsus of the Angels (1663–1737) finished the work. Later, and in the same tradition of a theology that was principally academic, teachers such as Anastasius of the Cross (1706–61) and Paul of the Conception (1666–1734) followed the *Salmenticenses.* However, a certain Philip of the Trinity (*Cursus Theologicus,* 5. vols., Lyon, 1633–63) and Gabriel of Saint Vincent chose instead to comment directly on the *Summa.*

3. After the Teresian Reform

The rest of the order did not, however, remain unproductive while the theology of the reformed Carmel theology was flourishing. In Italy the prolix revelations* of Marie-Madeleine de Pazzi (1556–1607) point to a complete inner experience that gave rise to authentically theological thought despite what she herself claimed. The depth and precision of her intuitions, like the biblical structure of her texts, provide the elements of some very rich doctrinal thinking on grace, the humanity of Christ, the relationship between the Church and the Trinity*, and even on the role of the Holy Spirit in the work of salvation*. In France, at the beginning of the 17th century, the entire Carmelite family participated in a decisive manner in the "mystical invasion" brilliantly described by H. Bremond. On one hand, the introduction of Teresian Carmel under the influence of Pierre de Bérulle* and of Bernières de Louvigny and Madame Acarie's circle would enrich the doctrine of the French school as well as that of authors as eminent as Francis de Sales. On the other hand, the non-Teresian branch of the order discovered a new vitality, notably around the figure of the humble blind friar Jean of Saint Samson (1571–1636), the "Saint John of the French Cross," according to Bremond. Having entered the Carmelite order after visiting the Paris monastery on the Place Maubert, it was in Brittany (in the monasteries of Dol and Rennes) that he would become the soul of what was known as the Touraine reformation, in particular through his disciples Dominique of Saint-Albert (1595–1634) and Léon of Saint John (1600–1671).

Jean of Saint Samson's brilliant spiritual discourse has a rare mystical power, and although the structure is often chaotic, it fills more than four thousand pages. These were more or less put together by his friends (edited by Donatien of Saint Nicholas in 1651 and 1656). A critical version is still to be published. In these writings can be detected the influence of a wide spiritual reading. Rhineland-Flemish mysticism can be discerned and was very influential in France at the time. But there are also traces of the writings of Constantin de Barbançon, Pierre Guérin, and Thomas Deschamps and even of Catherine of Genoa and Achille Gagliardi. Indeed, the writing reflects a theological renaissance that owed less to Scholasticism than to prayer itself and to a love of literature. Notably, themes inherited from Ruusbroec and Harphius are developed in the account of the most intense states of union. This experience is reflected in a Trinitarian and eucharistic doctrine that very boldly describes the journey between the soul and God that leads to "pure love." In the Bonaventurian tradition, the favored path is that of "aspiring" prayer*, "the loving and passionate impulse of the heart and mind through which the soul goes beyond itself and all created things," intimately joining with God in the ardor of a love that is in itself knowledge and thus near to theology.

In Flanders, the Touraine reform would influence Michel of Saint Augustine (1621–84). His *Institutionum Mysticarum Libri Quatuor* (Anvers, 1671), published in Latin and Flemish, showed him to be an important theorist on mystical life, which, according to him, is "nothing other than the practice of God and the science of divine things. Therefore, it involves both speculation and practice, modeling man after God in intellect and will." Even after the direct influence of the major reformers had waned, Carmelite thinkers of the 18th and 19th centuries continued to produce important works. Among the discalced monks, let us simply mention Theodore of the Holy Spirit (†1764) and his *De Indulgentiis* and *Jubilaeo* by a reference work in its area and also the huge exegetical work of Cherubim of Saint Joseph (†1716). Finally, apart from dogmatic theology, the *Cursus Theologiae Moralis* from Salamanca (7 vols., 1665–1753) is one of the most sizable works on morality ever published, and it would be appreciated as such by Alphonsus* of Liguori and the 18th-century moralists. As for the old observance, one should note Spain's continuous return to Baconthorpe's doctrine, thanks to Cornejo de Pedrosa (†1618) in the 17th century and to Emmanuel Coutinho (†1760) in the 18th century.

4. The Contemporary Period

As regards the traditional observance, we ought to note in particular the role played by Titus Brandsma, a Dachau martyr (1942), in the study and publication of traditional Carmel. This role was furthered by the institute, within the university of Nijmegen, that bore his name, and by the works of the *Institutum Carmelitanum,* founded in Rome in 1951. Mention must also be made of the dogmatic theologian Bartolomeo M. Xiberta (1897–1967), expert at Vatican* II. His christological and sacramental studies foreshadowed the works of B. Poschmann and Karl Rahner*. At the same time, among the discalced Carmelites, the *Térésianum* in Rome, founded in 1935, has become an international center for the study of mystical literature and theology.

5. Carmel and Marian Theology

From the moment it appeared in the West, the white cloak of Carmel has represented devotion to the one who has always been "Our Lady of Mount Carmel." We ought not to be surprised, therefore, to learn of an omnipresent Marian theology. Baconthorpe or Ribot, for example, strongly promoted the doctrine of the Immaculate Conception, the liturgical celebration of which was introduced as early as the 14th century into the order's calendar. At the same time, Saint Simon Stock's supposed vision—he was prior general of the order from 1254 to 1264—stressed devotion to the scapular, which was associated with "Sabbath privilege," which involved release from purgatory* for Carmelite scapular wearers as early as the Saturday after death. This devotion grew rapidly. During the 15th century, the Carmelite confraternities achieved great popularity, to the point where donning the scapular became one of the principal Marian devotions of Christendom.

It was at the end of the 15th century that Arnoldo Bostio developed the Carmelite outline of Marian devotion by collecting scattered elements. Friars were to offer everything to God through the hands of Mary* and be in a constant relationship with her in order to acquire an intelligence and heart that is entirely devoted to inspiring all good work.

Standing at the crossroads between mysticism and Mariology, Michel of Saint Augustine and Mary of Saint Teresa (Maria Petyt, 1623–77), whom Michel guided, would receive the gift of mystical union with Mary. Maria Petyt's accounts, published by her spiritual director in her *Life* (in Dutch) and in *De Vita Mariaeformi,* distinguish three stages of mystical union. In the first, the soul perceives the presence and help of the Virgin. Mystical contemplation occurs in the second, where God is perceived in Mary or Mary is perceived in her union with God. In the third stage, "there is such an intimate and stable connection to God and Mary that, because of dissolving love, God, Mary, and the soul seem to form one, as if dissolved, absorbed, submerged, and transformed into a single thing. This is the final and supreme end that the soul can reach in the Marian life."

Beyond works of devotion, this Marian piety would result in a strong theology, represented, for example, in the meditations of Jean de Saint-Samson on the role of Mary during the Passion* of her Son. It would have great pastoral importance in modern times, where it especially served as antidote to a widespread Jansenism* and went far beyond Carmel, propagated especially by Jesuit preachers.

• Teresa of Jesus, *Obras,* 1st Ed. by Luis de León, Salamanca, 1588.

Teresa of Jesus, *Obras completas,* 1st critical Ed. by S. de Santa Teresa, 9 vols., Burgos, 1915–24.

Teresa of Jesus, *Obras completas,* critical Ed. by E. de la Madre de Dios and O. del Niño Jesús, 3 vols., Madrid, 1951–59 (1 vol., 1962).

Luis de León, *Opera,* vols. I–VII (1891–1896), vols. VIII–IX (1992, 1996), vol. X, Escorial.

Martial de S. Paul, *Bibliotheca scriptorum... c. discalceatorum,* 1730.

Bartholomæus a S. Angelo-Henricus a SS Sacr. (1884), *Collectio scriptorum Ord. c. excal,* Savone, 1884.

♦ H. Bremond (1921), *Histoire littéraire du sentiment religieux en France...,* vol. 2: *L'invasion mystique,* Paris.

G. Etchegoyen (1923), *L'amour divin, essai sur les sources de sainte Thérèse,* Bordeaux-Paris.

B. Xiberta (1931), *De scriptoribus scholasticis saeculi XIV ex Ordine Carmelitarum,* Louvain.

Élisée de la Nativité (1935), "La vie intellectuelle des Carmes," *EtCarm* 20, 93–157.

J. Brenninger (1940), *Directorium carmelitanum vitae spiritualis,* Rome.

J. Dagens (1952), *Bibliographie chronologique de la littérature de spiritualité et de ses sources (1501–1610),* Paris.

Enrique del Sagrado Corazón (1953), *Los Salmenticenses,* Madrid.

T. Brandsma, G. de Sainte-Marie-Madeleine (1953), "Carmes," *DSp* 2/1, 156–209.

B. Xiberta (1956), *Carmelus, Commentarii ab Instituto Carmelitano editi,* Rome.

J. Orcibal (1959), *La rencontre du C. thérésien avec les mystiques du Nord,* Paris.

M. Jiménez Salas (1962), *Sta Teresa de Jesús, Bibliografia fundamental,* Madrid.

L. Cognet (1966), *La spiritualité moderne,* vol. 1: *L'essor: 1500–1650,* Paris.

O. Steggink (1970), "L'enracinement de saint Jean de la Croix dans le tronc de l'Ordre carmélitain," in *Actualité de saint Jean de la Croix,* Bruges, 51–78.

O. Steggink (1972), "Carmelitani," *Dizionario degli Istituti di Perfezione* 2, 460–507.

Simeone della Sagrada Famiglia (1972), *Panorama storico-bibliografico degli autori spirituali carmelitani,* Rome.

M. Andrés (1976), *La teología española en el siglo XVI,* Madrid.

P. Garrido (1982), *Santa Teresa de Jesús, San Juan de la Cruz, y los Carmelitas españoles,* Madrid.

J. Smet (1985), *The Carmelites: A History of the Brothers of Our Lady of Mount Carmel,* 4 vols., Darien.

CARLO CICONETTI AND STÉPHANE-MARIE MORGAIN

See also **Bérulle, Pierre de; Contemplation; John of the Cross; Life, Spiritual; Mysticism; Prayer; Spiritual Theology**

Carmelites of Salamanca. *See* **Carmel; Thomism**

Casel, Odo. *See* **Mystery**

Cassian, John. *See* **Prayer**

Casuistry

Casuistry is the art of judging particular cases (*casus* in Latin) in the light of moral rules. Most of the time we know immediately that a given action is, for example, a murder or a robbery. Conscience* makes the judgment at once (*conscientia* in Latin, literally "the fact of knowing at the same time" the abstract principle and the concrete case). But the situation is not always so simple. Conscience can be confused by an unusual case and not know what to think of it. Casuistry then becomes necessary. The principle of casuistry is that it is necessary to decide difficult cases by reasoning in the light of moral principles and not, for example, by obeying a concrete commandment of God immediately perceived. This is to say that there is an important place for deliberation in the moral realm.

a) Judaism. It is logical that in Judaism, where the Law is so important, there is a very rich jurisprudence and casuistry, collected in the tradition* of the scribes and rabbis and found both in Scripture* (e.g., Ex 20:1–23:19) and in the Midrash (especially the Halakha).

b) The New Testament. It can be said that Jesus* and Paul belong to some degree to this tradition. On several occasions in the Gospels*, Jesus is seen making an interpretation of the requirements of the Law, for example, with respect to divorce (Mk 10:2–12; Mt 19:1–12) or the sabbath* (Mk 2:23–28). As for Paul, in 1 Corinthians 8, he discusses the question of whether it is legitimate to eat the meat offered in sacrifice to idols. Paul and Jesus, however, criticized certain aspects of the casuistry of their time, either because it lost sight of the true intent of the law (Mk 2:27), because it was obsessed with the letter (1 Cor 8), or because it invented ingenious ways of avoiding true moral requirements (Mk 7:9–13).

c) Patristic and Medieval Periods. Casuistry could not degenerate into legalism or sophistry in the patristic period because it was firmly situated in the larger context of moral and spiritual education. Developing moral rules and studying their application to particular cases was subordinate to the requirement to foster virtues* and conquer vices.

In the Middle Ages casuistry was essentially an adjunct to private confession. Beginning in the sixth century in the West, first in Celtic regions then throughout the Church*, there were manuals for confessors—"penitentials"—that analyzed and classified sins* and indicated the corresponding penances*.

d) Greatness and Decline of Protestant Casuistry. The Reformation was at first hostile to casuistry. Luther* considered the late medieval penitential system to be moralizing and reproached it for concentrating on acts of sin and penance and for failing to see that sin and repentance are above all spiritual directions. Further, in reaction against Scholasticism*, Luther thought reasoning was a hanging offense.

At the end of the 16th century and in the beginning of the 17th, English Puritans such as William Perkins (1558–1602) and William Ames (1576–1633) considered it indispensable to provide the faithful with subtle moral guidance, on the model of the *summae* of Catholic casuistry (*Summae casuum conscientiae*), but based on the principles of Protestantism*. They were the pioneers of the Anglican tradition of casuistry that flourished with theologians such as Jeremy Taylor (1613–67) and that Kenneth Kirk (1886–1954) attempted to revive in the 1920s. Unlike its Catholic counterpart, Anglican casuistry is not linked to the confessional and does not seek to judge the gravity of sins already committed. It seeks, rather, to shed light on the line of conduct to be adopted in a particular situation.

Before the end of the 17th century, the Lutherans themselves had taken up casuistry (e.g., J.H. Alsted [1588–1638], F. Balduin, C. Dannhauer [1603–66], J.A. Osiander [1622–97]), but the tradition of Protestant casuistry came to a sudden end shortly thereafter. The reasons for this are various. We can note the influence of Lutheran pietism* and its reaction against the theological and ethical rationalism* of Protestant Scholasticism. Pascal*'s *Provinciales* (1656–57), which denounced the permissiveness of the probabilist casuistry of the Jesuits, was also greatly influential. Then there was the apparent growth of a certain complacency regarding the individual's capacities of judgment, emanating from a newly minted confidence in the autonomy of the moral sense, reason, and conscience. Finally, there was the almost exclusive interest of the moralists of the late 17th and 18th centuries in metaethical controversies, dealing either with the nature or with the foundations of morality.

e) Catholic Moral Theology. During this time the place of casuistry in Catholicism remained stable. In reaction against what it saw as the moral laxity of Protestantism, the Catholicism of the Counter-Reformation placed even greater emphasis on moral law. From that period until World War II, its moral theology took the form of manuals of casuistry, the model for which had been provided by Jean Azor (1536–1603) in his *Institutiones morales* of 1600–1601. The most influential of these manuals was the *Theologia moralis* (1748) of Alphonsus* Liguori, who has been the patron saint of confessors and moral theologians since 1950, which clearly indicates the permanence of his authority. Alphonsus Liguori managed to put an end to the debate, which had raged in the 17th century and continued in the 18th, on the possibility of legitimately straying from the moral law. In the middle of the 17th century, probabilism, a theory formulated by Bartolomeo de Medina (1527–80), was widespread in the Catholic Church. According to this theory, conduct not in conformity with the law but that can with reason be morally defended (i.e., conduct that is "probable") is morally acceptable, even if there are stronger arguments in favor of different conduct. "Probability" can be "intrinsic" and consist of the strength of the argument or "extrinsic" and consist of the prestige of the authority that can be invoked in its favor. The Jansenists were horrified by a doctrine that could justify the loosest conduct, sometimes on the basis of a single authority. They were on the contrary advocates of an austere form of "tutiorism." This holds that in case of doubt one must make the surest (Latin *tutior*) decision, and in its austere form it considers that the safest course is to act in conformity with the law. On three occasions (1665, 1666, 1679), the Church condemned the laxity of the conclusions of certain probabilist arguments, and by the late 17th century, laxism had practically disappeared. But in 1690, Rome* also condemned the extreme forms of tutiorism. The continuing debate between the more moderate forms of these positions was resolved by the "equiprobabilism" of Alphonsus Ligouri. According to this, one may prefer a probable opinion over the law, but only in cases in which opinions for and against have the same force. Since the 1950s there has been a preference, over the legalist concerns of the manuals, for a moral theology more sensitive to the spiritual context of moral deliberation. The significant work of Bernard Häring (1954), for example, sees in moral life a response to the grace of God, and conversion and the growth of virtue are essential themes.

The role of law in moral life has also been relativized because it has been shown that law is not enough to make a decision. Between a law and its application there must be a deliberation, which is more than a logical operation. Discernment and prudence* are required: discernment of the intent of the law and of the moral character of the situation and prudence in order to understand them through one another. Conscience is a matter not only of conformity but also of creativity.

For the advocates of proportionalism* (e.g., R.A. McCormick), casuistry cannot consist of conforming oneself to the requirements of the law. Its role is to discern and to choose, in a given situation, the conduct in which there is the greatest proportion of good in relation to evil. On the contrary, for the "absolutists" or "deontologists" (e.g., Germain Grisez and John Finnis), the casuist must have certain absolute moral rules as guides. In particular, any intent to harm is strictly forbidden.

f) Contemporary Protestantism. Similar debates have recently taken place in Protestant moral theology, although there is a strong prejudice against law and rational deliberation and a preference for focusing on spiritual context and moral intuition. Barth* saw casuistry as an abstract and rationalistic method for arriving at moral judgments through deduction: this point of view was shared by Bonhoeffer*, Emil Brunner (1889–1966), and Helmut Thielicke (1908–86). Following Barth, Richard Niebuhr (1894–1962) and Paul Lehmann (1906–94) prefer vague formulations: a good action is a "response" or a "correspondence" to divine activity. The ethic* of Joseph Fletcher's situation (1905–91) manifests the usual Protestant suspicion toward law and casuistry but opens the door to a certain rationality in accepting that it is legitimate to calculate the conduct most likely to maximize well-being (utilitarianism*). The most remarkable of those who have opposed this Protestant depreciation of the role of rules is Paul Ramsey (1913–88). He produces convincing arguments in favor of the necessity for clear and definite rules of conduct. For him, certain moral rules for him are "without exception." He is finally an advocate for a form of casuistry in which the rules and their relationships would be revisable in the light of what is taught by morally novel cases.

• J.H. Alsted (1621), *Theologia casuum...*, Hanover.

W. Ames (1639), *Conscience with the Power and Cases Thereof,* repr. Amsterdam and Norwood, N.J., 1975.

J. Caramuel y Lobkowitz (1651–1653), *Theologia moralis fondamentalis,* Frankfurt.

B. Pascal (1656–57), *Les Provinciales.*

H. Busenbaum (1657), *Medulla theologiae moralis,* Paris.

A. de Liguori (1748), *Theologia moralis,* repr. P. Leonardi Gaude, Graz, 1953.

K.E. Kirk (1927), *Conscience and Its Problems: An Introduction to Casuistry,* London.

B. Häring (1954), *Das Gesetz Christi,* Fribourg.

J. Fletcher (1966), *Situation Ethics,* Philadelphia.

P. Ramsey (1967), *Deeds and Rules in Christian Ethics,* Lanham, Md.; "The Case of the Curious Exception," in G.H. Outka and P. Ramsey (Ed.), *Norm and Context in Christian Ethics,* New York, 1968, 67–135.

♦ É. Baudin (1947), *La philosophie de Pascal,* vol. III ("Pascal et la casuistique"), Neuchâtel.

R. Brouillard (1949), "Casuistique," *Cath.* 2, 630–38.

J.T. McNeill (1951), *A History of the Cure of Souls,* New York.

Thomas Wood (1952), *English Casuistical Divinity: With Special Reference to Jeremy Taylor,* London.

A.R. Jonsen, S. Toulmin (1988), *The Abuse of Casuistry in Early Modern Europe,* Cambridge.

N. Biggar (1989), "A Case for Casuistry in the Church," in *Modern Theology* 6/1, Oxford, 29–51.

P. Cariou (1993), *Pascal et la casuistique,* Paris.

J. Keenan, Th. Shannon (Ed.) (1995), *The Context of Casuistry,* Washington, D.C.

V. Carraud, O. Chaline (1996), "Casuistique," *DEPhM* 213–22.

J. Mahoney (1997), "Probabilismus," *TRE* 27, 465–68.

NIGEL BIGGAR

See also **Alphonsus Liguori; Ethics; Intention; Jansenism; Proportionalism; Spiritual Direction**

Cataphrygians. *See* **Montanism**

Catechesis

The word "catechesis" and its cognates ("catechism," "catechumen," "catechist," and so on) are connected with the Greek verb *katekheo* ("to resound") and first meant "oral teaching." This meaning is found both in the New Testament and in Hellenistic writings (e.g., Cicero, *Ad Atticus* 15, 12, 2; Flavius Josephus, *Vita,* 65; Lucian, *Asinus,* 48). Since Christian initiation* (and thus baptism*) required knowing both Christian dogma and moral, the history of catechesis is also that of teaching lay Christians, especially children, the essential elements of Christianity.

a) Old Testament Background, the New Testament, and the Apostolic Fathers.* In the few cases of conversion found in the Old Testament, such as Ruth, no prior instruction is required (Ru 1:16). The texts, however, stress the duty of teaching the commandments of God* to children (e.g., Dt 6:7 and 20). Moreover, religious reforms required a catechesis of the whole nation, such as is described in 2 Kings 22 and in Nehemiah 8. Judaism*, which practiced proselytism, had certainly found the means to teach newcomers, but little is known in this regard. One can infer they served as models for the catechesis of the new religion: Christians were made, not born, since all Christians were converts. Instruction about Jesus and his teaching, the "gospel," therefore formed part of what was handed on. Instruction about the relation of the new religion to the law of Judaism was of special importance at the stage when conversion was principally from Jewish communities (*see* Heb 6:3). The earliest catechesis of which we have details is given in the *Didache,* in which a text called "The Two Ways" (cc. 1–6), repeated in the *Epistle of Barnabas* and elsewhere, was probably based on a Jewish model. This text presents the duties of the convert to the "Way of Life" (honesty, chastity, humility, and charity), which separates him from the world and from the "Way of Death." The *Shepherd of Hermas* (Book 2) hints at a similar prebaptismal catechesis in Rome.

b) From the Apologists to the Council of Nicaea.* There is no reliable information on the catechesis of the early second-century Christian gnostics*, such as Valentinus or Basilides. We know a little more about the adherents of the "great Church." Justin (†165) alludes to catechesis in his *First Apology* (65), describing the baptism and first Eucharist* of new Christians. We do not know who taught them since the catechist was not a separate office. Irenaeus* addresses his *Proof of the Apostolic Preaching* to Marcian, presumably a layman, "setting forth the preaching of the truth to confirm his faith." The method of catechesis in Rome in the early third century is disclosed in the *Apostolic Tradition,* ascribed to Hippolytus of Rome. This set of rules specifies who can be admitted to baptismal catechesis (cc. 15f.), the length of their preparation (three years, but it could be less) by a lay or clerical teacher, and their status in the assembly (cc. 17–19). As for the *didaskaleion* of Alexandria*, mentioned by Eusebius (v. 260–340) in his *Church History* (Books 5, cc. 10f.; 6, c. 63), it had nothing to do with elementary instruction.

c) The Imperial Church. With the end of persecution and the official promotion of Christianity came widespread conversions and a new Christian literature. Much of this literature is related to catechesis inasmuch as it promotes transmitting the knowledge of what makes up Christianity, but it is aimed at instructors (now almost universally the clergy) rather than at the laity they taught. Numerous prebaptismal catecheses have also survived, for example, by either Cyril (or John) of Jerusalem (v. 315–86), John Chrysostom*, Ambrose* of Milan, or Theodore of Mopsuestia (v. 350–428). Two treatises dealing with method and content of catechesis, for the use of catechists, deserve special mention: the *Catechetical Oration* of Gregory* of Nyssa and *Catechizing the Uninstructed* by Augustine*. Gregory adopted a dogmatic* presentation of the content of the faith, privileging the affirmation of the Trinity* and the doctrine of salvation*; the theology* of baptism and of the Eucharist formed the final part of his work. In contrast, Augustine, in his treatise addressed to a deacon named Deogratias, who had questioned him on several points, adopted a narrative that followed the order of the Bible, from the creation* to the beginnings of the church. Neither Augustine nor Gregory, however, explicitly mentioned the Creed or the Lord's Prayer as bases of catechesis.

d) From the Patristic Period to the Reformation. Following the conversion of Germanic peoples to Christianity and the generalization of infant baptism, prebaptismal catechesis ceased in the Christian world. It was replaced in the West by the instruction of children and young people. Numerous injunctions from local councils and bishops* in the period 800–1500 show the efforts made to ensure that the Creed, the Lord's Prayer, and the *Ave Maria* were known and understood by all. Summaries of what needed to be taught were written, such as the *Elucidarium* by Honorius of Autun (early 12th century; PL 172, 1109–76), in a question and answer format. In the next century, Thomas Aquinas also wrote such texts (*Opuscula* 4, 5, 7f., and 16), which were widely diffused. Jean Gerson (1363–1429) owns a special place in the history of catechesis. Concerned with education (he wrote several pedagogical works), he wrote a short catechism for children, the *ABC des simples gens.* He thus prepared the grounds for the publication of Luther*'s two *Catechisms* in 1529. Luther may not have invented a new literary genre, but he helped the spread of such works throughout Europe. His *Catechisms,* which were thought to hold the substance of his doctrine, came to be seen as authoritative works in Lutheranism*. The catechism was key in the propagation and strengthening of Protestantism*, in parallel to the multiplying reformed confessions. Calvin*'s *Geneva Catechism* (1541), which followed his *Instruction in Faith* (1537), was a great success and came to be used, for example, by churches in Scotland and England. The *Heidelberg Catechism* (1563) brought together Lutheran and Calvinist elements in 129 questions and answers divided into three sections (man's misery, man's redemption, and the action of grace). One may also cite the Anglican catechism in the *Book of Common Prayer* of 1662 (with material taken from the *Prayer Books* of 1549, 1552, and 1604), which was widely used until the mid-20th century.

The Catholic Church's response to the Reform catechisms came with the *Roman Catechism,* developed by the Council of Trent*. Unlike the important question-and-answer catechism (1555) of Peter Canisius (1521–97), it was made to be used by pastors* (hence its title *Catechismus... ad parochos*). Surprisingly free from the polemics of its time, it seemed a synthesis of Catholic doctrine.

e) From the Reformation to the Present Day. The 17th and 18th centuries saw the production in many churches of manuals to teach children, as well as catechisms, often in the form of questions and answers.

In France, there was the catechism of Bossuet (1627–1704), the *Catéchisme du diocèse de Meaux. Par le commandement de Mgr. l'illustrissime et révérendissime Jacques Bénigne Bossuet Evesque de Meaux, Conseiller du Roy en ses Conseils, cy-devant Précepteur de Monseigneur le Dauphin, premier Aumônier de Madame la Dauphine* (1687). It consists of three catechisms (questions and answers): one for beginners and those to be confirmed, one for the more advanced and those preparing for first communion, and, finally, for the even more advanced, a catechism on the feasts and observances of the church. In a warning (Avertissement) to the priests, curates, fathers, mothers, and all the faithfuls of the diocese, Bossuet wrote that parents were the first catechists and ought therefore to know the catechism. He approved of the *Grand Catéchisme historique* (1683) of Claude Fleury (1640–1723), the church historian, a work that was also popular. An interesting, if ephemeral, attempt to impose a single catechism throughout France was made with Napoleon's *Catéchisme à l'usage de toutes les églises de l'Empire français* (1806), also known as the *Catéchisme impérial.* Based on Bossuet's second catechism, it was produced during a troubled time in the history of the French church. Its advocating devotion to the Napoleonic dynasty ensured its obsolescence after 1814. Dupanloup's *Catéchisme chrétien* (1865) is also interesting. The full title is *Le catéchisme chrétien ou un exposé de la doctrine de Jésus-Christ, offert aux hommes du monde par Mgr. l'évêque d'Orléans de l'Académie française, suivi d'un Abrégé et sommaire de toute la doctrine du Symbole par Bossuet.* Intended for adults as a summary of the Christian faith, it follows a dialogue format that owes much to Bossuet.

One of the most significant publications in the late 20th century has been the *Catechism of the Catholic Church,* which was approved by Pope John Paul II in 1992 (text revised in 1997, standard Latin edition). An extraordinary assembly of the Synod* of Bishops, held in 1985 for the 20th anniversary of the end of Vatican* II, had voiced the desire for "a catechism or compendium of all Catholic doctrine, both on faith and on morals," that could serve as "a reference" for the catechisms written in various countries. The presentation of the doctrine had to be biblical and liturgical, and a sound doctrine was to be suited to Christians' life in today's world. The format of the *Catechism* owes to the *Catechism* of the Council of Trent, with its division into four parts: "The Profession of Faith" (the Creed), "The Celebration of the Christian Mystery" (the sacraments*), "Life in Christ" (the Commandments), and "Christian Prayer" (The Lord's Prayer). It takes into account the dogmas of Mary* (1854, 1950) and papal infallibility as defined by Vatican* I. Its content reflects the teachings of Vatican II but also addresses somewhat the issues of the liberation* and feminist theology and even animal rights. Its most striking feature, however, is the constant recourse to the Bible* and to liturgy. In this, it is faithful to what was initially requested. It is too early still to say whether it has succeeded in the second task (being adapted for modern life). If postmodernism* has undermined the authority* of Bible and liturgy, it may not be relevant to refer to them. On the other hand, the prudence* of the *Catechism,* its approach to controversial issues, and the willingness to explain and to listen allow an effective presentation of Catholic convictions. It has been widely diffused, and there is no doubt that it will constitute a reference for catechesis for some years to come, both inside and outside the Catholic Church.

- Mgr Hézard (1900), *Histoire du catéchisme depuis la naissance de l'Église jusqu'à nos jours,* Paris.

G. Bareille (1923), "Catéchèse" and "Catéchuménat," *DThC* 2/2, 1877–95 and 1968–87.
E. Mangenot (1923), "Catéchisme," *DThC* 2/2, 1895–1968.
J.-C. Dhotel (1967), *Les origines du catéchisme moderne, d'après les premiers manuels imprimés en France,* Paris.
A. Lapple (1981), *Kleine Geschichte der Katechesen,* Munich.
G.J. Bellinger (1983), *Bibliographie des Catechismus Romanus ex decreto concilii Tridentini ad Parochos: 1566–1978,* Baden-Baden.
E. Germain (1983), *Deux mille ans d'éducation de la foi,* Paris.
G.J. Bellinger (1988), "Katechismus," *TRE* 17, 710–44.
Ch. Bizer (1988), "Katechetik," *TRE* 17, 687–710.
W. Jetter (1988), "Katechismuspredigt," *TRE* 17, 744–86.
K. Hauschildt (1989), "Katechumenat/Katechumen," *TRE* 19, 1–14.

Lionel R. Wickham

See also **Baptism; Initiation, Christian**

Catechism of the Catholic Church. *See* **Catechesis**

Catharism

a) History. It was thanks to commerce and to the Second Crusade (1147) that Catharism, a dualist heresy*, spread from Constantinople through the Balkans, Germany, Italy, and the south of France.

The genealogy and history of dualist doctrines has not yet been written, and it would be risky to specify the doctrinal link that led from early Manicheanism* to the Western Cathars of the 12th century. It is nevertheless known that the Byzantine Empire in the 10th century experienced movements of opposition to the political and religious capital. In Bulgaria, where Christianization was recent and where Paulicianism (a dualist sect that appeared in the seventh century) had maintained some influence, a protest movement crystallized around the priest Bogomil. In the refutation produced by Cosmas in the late 10th century (Puech 1945), Bogomilism appears as a heresy with strong ascetic tendencies closely connected to local monasticism*. The patriarch of Constantinople, Theophylact, defined Bogomilism as "Manicheanism mixed with Paulicianism" (Obolensky 1948). The Bogomils' influence reached as far as Constantinople itself. The link between national claims and dualist tendencies was found during the same period in the dualist sects of Asia Minor, the Phoundagiagites.

Between 1167 and 1172 (or around 1176; Thouzellier 1984), during a Cathar council held near Toulouse, Nicetas, the "pope" of Constantinople, converted to an absolute dualism the heretical bishops of Carcassonne, Albi, Agen, and Toulouse, along with the Lombards, who had been moderate dualists until then. The doctrine prospered in Languedoc and maintained a certain cohesion there. Its representatives taught in public and were willing to debate. They traveled from place to place in pairs and had as many women as men in their ranks—the women conducted schools and had their own houses in villages. They found help, hospitality, and protection from many nobles. In Italy, by contrast, dissensions arose rather early and gave rise to several Cathar factions.

The Albigensian Crusade was launched against protectors of the heretics after the murder of a papal legate in 1208. Many nobles of the south of France were dispossessed of their estates, which became royal lands. The tribunal of the Inquisition was established in 1233 to fight heresy and to prosecute the heretics and their followers. Deep discontent ensued, and the action of the inquisitors provoked movements of rebellion, such as the unsuccessful revolt of Trencavel in the jurisdiction of Carcassonne in 1240. Some who escaped from war* and prosecution took refuge in Lombardy and Aragon, and others followed the last bishops and *parfaits* into regions in which the king as yet had no hold. These last bastions of resistance fell in turn in 1244 (Montségur) and 1255 (Quéribus). From then on, Catharism was maintained in secret.

Differences had long existed between the kings of France and Spain over the sovereignty each one claimed in the regions of the south of France. The Treaty of Corbeil (1258) had officially put an end to the dispute. However, when the domain of Toulouse was directly subjected to French authority because of the death of Alphonse de Poitiers and of Countess Jeanne (1271), the Comte de Foix formed an alliance with the infante of Aragon, whom some Toulousains wished to have as ruler of the region. Philip the Bold came in person to take possession of his uncle's legacy and took the Comte de Foix prisoner (1272). For their part, the inquisitors obtained confessions from nobles who had been vassals of the king of Aragon and allies of the Comte de Foix. These accused men maintained relations with former compatriots who had been judged and released and had established communities in and around Toulouse.

A few years later, inhabitants of the jurisdiction of Carcasonne, who had not obtained the protection they expected from Philippe le Bel against the activities of the inquisitors, turned to the son of the king of Mallorca (a relative of the king of Aragon and the Comte de Foix) and asked for his help. There were riots in Carcassonne and Limoux, a royal city. They were followed by massive arrests and hangings. Among the people captured in Limoux in September 1303 was the *parfait* Jacques Autier. His father Pierre, former notary of the counts of Foix, had become a Cathar minister. He had traveled through Languedoc with his son and reorganized their church. Many communities, disseminated over a wide territory, lived there in religious autarchy, and family connections played a significant role in the transmission of Catharism. These believers were for the most part descendants of former landowners or even of *faidits* (banished) nobles. United by their belief in a religious doctrine, they formed an active minority in opposition to French settlement. They shared neither the language nor the culture of the men of the north of France.

Appointed by the pope to the head of the tribunal of the Inquisition in Toulouse in 1307, the Dominican Bernard Gui began to track down the last of the *parfaits,* their accomplices, and their followers, some of whom had been questioned by his predecessors and by the inquisitor Geoffroy d'Ablis in Carcassonne. The arrest of Jacques Autier in 1303 and that of his father probably in the following year tolled the knell for Catharism. In the course of the 17 years of his mandate, the inquisitor Bernard Gui passed sentence on 650 people.

Without the support of Philip the Bold in 1274 and Philippe le Bel in 1304, the Inquisition would have been unable definitively to halt the rise of Catharism in Languedoc. This religious movement was an important cause of political instability.

b) Doctrine. Catholics gave these heretics various names, including Cathars—from the Greek *katharos,* meaning "pure." Other names either followed the classifications of patristic heresiology, such as Albigensians and Manicheans, or referred to their geographic origin, their occupations, or their leaders. They called themselves "good men," "good Christians," or friends of God*.

The members of the sect based their teaching on the Bible*, from which they excluded almost all the Old Testament and which they interpreted in their own way, paying particular attention to the Gospel* According to John. The doctrine was built on the belief in the existence of two gods, one good and the other evil, who were hostile to one another from all eternity*. These gods created two worlds, one material and the other spiritual and invisible. Satan, the evil god, left his kingdom and invaded the court of heaven to seduce the angels*. The good Father God drove him out along with his troops and the fallen angels. (In Italy there was a less radical variant that preserved a monotheist theology: although omnipotent, God allowed Satan to organize chaos.) Fallen souls* had fallen to earth and were imprisoned there in bodies created by the devil. In order for the soul seeking the lost paradise to recover its spiritual body, abandoned inert in the world of the good God, the individual had to join the Cathar sect. During a particular ceremony called *consolamentum,* the officiant (or *parfait*) freed the soul. This sacrament*, the only one that the Cathars recognized, was performed by the imposition of hands and of the évangéliaire. It was the baptism* of the Spirit, "spiritual baptism of Jesus Christ, and baptism of the Holy Spirit" (Cathar Ritual, SC 236 §9, 227). It came "as a supplement" to "the other baptism," the baptism of water, "which was insufficient for your salvation" (ibid., §13, 253–55). The *parfait* then revealed to the new member the Our Father of which he was the guardian and which he alone had the right and the duty to pronounce. An ordinary believer would be authorized to recite it only at the hour of his death*.

The consolamentum was both a rite of ordination* for the *parfaits* and the supreme sacrament for the ordinary believer, received at the moment of his death. To receive the consolamentum and enter into the Cathar brotherhood, the future *parfait* had to commit himself to strict asceticism*, marked by long periods of fasting. He refused to lie, to swear, or to kill. From then on, he no longer feared death, for he knew that it enabled the soul to return to the spiritual world. Finally, his diet excluded (except for fish) any food that was of animal origin or that was the result of sexual intercourse. Because sexuality was considered diabolical by nature, he took a vow of chastity. Believers waited for the hour of death to ask for this sacrament. It was granted to them without confession of their sins, if they had not lost the power of speech and could recite the Our Father that the *parfait* then taught them. They then had to maintain a total fast until their death. Most of the time, believers had previously made a pact with a *parfait* in order to be sure of being received into the sect, a custom that was established during the siege of Montségur (1244) under the name of *convenenza*. If the believer could not be "consoled" or "hereticized," his soul would then wander from body to body until it encountered the body of a believer purified by this sacrament before his death. This belief in metempsychosis seems to have been brought to Languedoc in the late 13th century by ministers of the sect who had spent time in Lombardy.

In known Cathar rituals—whether in Provençal, late vulgar Latin, or Latin—the Lord's Prayer is always quoted in Latin, sometimes with a commentary. There are two minor variants from the version of the Latin Church. The first is in the fourth petition ("Give us this day our daily bread"), where *epiousios* is translated *supersubstantialem* ("supersubstantial"), as in the Vulgate, and not "daily." The Cathar interpretation here follows a Greek patristic tradition that sees it as an allusion to the Law* and to the teaching of Christ and not to the Eucharist. The prayer concludes with a doxology ("For thine is the kingdom, the power, and the glory for ever and ever. Amen!"), which was then unknown in the Latin liturgy* but used by the Eastern Church. As for the rest, it is plausible that the Cathar *traditio orationis* derives from the Gelasian heresy and "is rooted in the Christian subsoil of the primitive churches of Africa and Northern Italy" (ibid., intro., 56). Other rites performed among *parfaits* or among believers and *parfaits,* such as the adoration, signified both respect and recognition among followers of Catharism.

Both heresy and non-Christian religion, Cathar dualism represented a real danger for orthodoxy, for it was preached within the framework of well-organized ecclesial structures*, with its dioceses, bishops, and clergy*, the hierarchy of which was modeled on that of the Roman Church. The refutation of Cathar dualism (and of dualism in general) was a major theological task that permitted a reaffirmation of Christian monotheism* confronted with the problem of evil*.

• H.-Ch. Puech, A. Vaillant, *Le traité contre les Bogomiles de Cosmas le prêtre,* Paris, 1945.

Chr. Thouzellier, intro., Ed., trans. and notes, *Rituel cathare,* 1977, SC 236.

Anselme d'Alexandrie, *Tractatus de hereticis,* Ed. A. Dondaine, "La hiérarchie cathare en Italie," II, *AFP* XX, 1950, 308–24.

Bernard Gui, *Liber Sententiarum inquisitionis Tholosanae,* Ed. Ph. van Limborch, Amsterdam, 1692; *Manuel de l'Inquisiteur,* vol. I, Ed. G. Mollat, CHFMA, 8, 1926.

Bonacursus, *Manifestatio haeresis Catharorum,* PL 204, 775–92.

De heresi catharorum in Lombardia, Ed. A. Dondaine, *AFP* XIX, 1949, 306–12.

Disputationes Photini Manichaei cum Paulo Christiano, Propositiones adversus manicheos, PG 88, 529–78.

Durand de Huesca, *Liber antiheresis,* Ed. K. Selge, *Die ersten Waldenser,* II, *AKuG* 37, 2, 1967; *Liber contra Manicheos,* Ed. Ch. Thouzellier, *Une somme anticathare. Le* Liber contra Manicheos *de D. de Huesca,* SSL Études et documents, 32, 1964.

Eckbert de Schönau, *Sermones contra Catharos,* PL 195, 11–102.

Ermengaud de Béziers, *Contra haereticos,* PL 204, 1235–72.

Euthyme Zigabène, *De Haeresi bogomilorum narratio,* Ed. A. Ficker, *Die Phundagiagiten,* Leipzig, 1908, 87–111; *Panoplia dogmatica,* XXVII, 19, PG 130, 1290–1332.

Jacques de Capellis, *Summa contra hereticos,* Ed. D. Bazzochi, *L'eresia catara,* t. II, Bologne, 1920.

Livre des deux principes, Ed. Ch. Thouzellier, SC 198, 1973.

Moneta de Crémone, *Adversus catharos et Valdenses,* Ed. Th.-A. Ricchini, Rome, 1743, New Ed., Ridgewood, N.J., 1964.

Raynier Sacconi, *Summa de Catharis,* Ed. A. Dondaine, *Un traité néomanichéen du XIIIe s.,* Rome, 1939, 64–78; Ed. F. Sanjek, *AFP* 44, 1974, 31–60.

♦ C. Douais (1900), *Documents pour servir à l'histoire de l'Inquisition dans le Languedoc au XIIIe et au XIVe siècle,* 2 vols., Paris.

D. Obolensky (1948), *The Bogomils: A Study in Balkan Neo-Manichaeism,* Cambridge.

A. Dondaine (1949, 1950), *La hiérarchie cathare en Italie, AFP* XIX and XX.

Y. Dossat (1959), *Les crises de l'Inquisition toulousaine au XIIIe siècle (1233–1273),* Bordeaux.

A. Borst (1953), *Die Katharer,* Stuttgart.

M. Loos (1974), *Dualist Heresy in the Middle Ages,* Prague.
J. Duvernoy (1979), *Le catharisme: L'histoire des cathares,* Toulouse.
G. Rottenwohrer (1982–93), *Der Katharismus,* 4 vols. (8 vols.), Bad Honnef.
Chr. Thouzellier (1984), "Cathares," *EU* 4, 379–85.
A. Pales-Gobilliard (1991), "La Prière des cathares," in *Prier au Moyen Age,* Paris.
A. Pales-Gobilliard (1994), *Poursuites et déplacements de population après la croisade albigeoise,* CTh HS, Amiens.
A. de la Presle-Evesque (1994), *Le conflit franco-aragonais de la fin du XIIIe siècle et ses conséquences religieuses et politiques,* CTh HS, Amiens.

Annette Pales-Gobilliard
and Galahad Threepwood

See also **Evil; Gnosis; Manicheanism; Marcionism; Waldensian**

Catholic Church. *See* **Catholicism**

Catholicism

While there are some concepts that denote very broad groupings encompassing several Churches or Christian communities (e.g., the "genus" of Protestantism or its "species" Calvinism), Catholicism is, strictly speaking, a useless category. Its original usage, faithful to its etymological meaning, has declined, giving rise to the doctrinal or geographical doublet "Catholicity"; and the Catholic Church, according to its own ecclesiology, is the sole constituent of Catholicism. Inasmuch as the word's contemporary usage includes social and cultural aspects, however, it would be impossible to limit Catholicism to its place in doctrinal history. Hence, three principal definitions of Catholicism are offered.

1. Catholicism as a Denomination

The Catholic Church is the largest and, geographically speaking, the most widely distributed of all the Christian Churches. With over a billion members, it includes a good half of all who belong to a Christian Church worldwide. Although its heartland is in Europe, it is not restricted to a single ethnic or geographical milieu (Kaufmann 1994). The Second Vatican* Council, using models developed by the two previous councils (those of Trent* and Vatican I*), set out its official definition of itself at length, notably in its dogmatic constitutions *Dei Verbum* and *Lumen Gentium.*

A doctrinal and cultural whole, known for convenience as *Catholicism,* can be extracted from these texts, making possible a sociocultural approach to the Church (the word "Catholicism" itself appears neither in *Dei Verbum* nor in *Lumen Gentium*). According to these texts, one of the distinctive features of Catholicism is the universal government of the Church (*LG* 23) exercised by the pope as bishop of Rome, in communion with the college of bishops. The ordained ministry in the Catholic Church has the role not only of ecclesiastical government but also the official proclamation of dogma (the teaching role) and the celebration of the sacraments (the sanctifying role); on a local level it is structured according to three degrees: bishop, priest, and deacon (*see LG* 27–29) and restricted to men. Ministerial and baptismal priesthoods cooperate in different ways in the celebration of the sacraments (*LG* 11). Each believer is a bearer of the Christian message by word and example (*LG* 12), but only an explicit ecclesiastical mission can confer authoritative character on that message. The right of determining the content of the Christian faith and of excluding unorthodox interpretations (heresy* and infallibility*), is the preserve of councils, bishops in communion with the pope, or the latter alone (*LG* 25). The exercise of the magisterium* concerns not only the expression of faith (dogma) but also Church structures* (including law), customs (in other words, the various forms of divine worship), and even some fundamental points of ethics*.

The doctrinal basis of Catholicism comprises Holy* Scripture (canon* of Scriptures) and the more or less normative interpretations of it given by the ecclesiastical magisterium and the authorized witnesses of the Church past and present (tradition*; Theological Places*) (*DV* 10). The development of Church structures and of their mode of operation is regulated by universal or local decisions having legal status (canon law; jurisdiction).

Despite the strikingly unified nature of its structure and teachings, Catholicism in its various forms exhibits an irreducible diversity, including theological schools, local churches, inculturation, and distinctive traditions (*see LG* 13). Moreover, its history has always been characterized by internal movements of opposition to the prevailing doctrine—for example, Jansenism*, Gallicanism*, and Modernism*—whose formulations were sometimes condemned and sometimes not. Certainly the Catholic Church no longer claims in the face of the other Christian Churches to hold a monopoly on ecclesiality and the authentic conditions of the Christian experience. It does, however, maintain that it is a visible manifestation of the Church of Christ, with all its necessary components (*LG* 8).

Catholicism condemns the Orthodox and Protestant churches, above all, in the Orthodox and Protestant churches for their refusal to recognize the pope's universal episcopate and, in the latter case only, the lack of a ministry legitimized by apostolic* succession. To these points should be added doctrinal differences that, even though numerous ecumenical initiatives have enabled them to be somewhat reduced, still remain unresolved. These concern the Eucharist, the procession of the Holy Spirit, Mary, the cult of saints, and the theology of ministries.

2. Catholicism as a Vision of the World

If there exists a "Catholic" experience of the world, it is not to be confused with the manifestations of the Christian Church that bears that name, though it is at least historically linked to it. It is based on attitudes, movements of thought, and modes of behavior in part determined by the life and doctrine of the Roman Church, though not directly deducible from these (Gabriel and Kaufmann 1980). So, for example, in the view of C. Schmitt (1923), Catholicism is linked to a political conception grounded in "the rigorous application of the principle of representation."

3. Normative Definitions of the Catholic Phenomenon

While the epithets "Roman and "Catholic" have a long history (Congar 1987), the noun "Catholicism" appeared only during the modern era (Imbs 1977). And it was even more recently—during the 19th century—that it took on the connotation of a qualitative definition. Three principal varieties of this are met with.

a) The Complementary Nature of Catholicism and Protestantism. Schelling* (1841–42), in his *Philosophie der Offenbarung,* saw Catholicism as a necessary but one-sided impulse that Christianity was destined to transcend as its historical course unfolded (*see also* Heiler 1923). For Schleiermacher* (1830), it was a legitimate form of the Christian faith, but one to which Protestantism was destined to remain irredeemably alien.

b) Catholicism as an Aberrant Development. From this standpoint, Catholicism is perceived as a judicial and dogmatic distortion of Christianity. This development is seen as having originated far in the past (Protocatholicism*) but as reaching its fullest manifestation in the modern period (e.g., Sohm 1892; Harnack 1931–32).

c) Catholicism as a Positive Definition of the Essence of Christianity. Since the start of the 19th century, theologians (especially Catholic ones) have tried to define the "essence" of Christianity. The most striking formulations in this regard are to be found in the work of J.A. Möhler (1825), who holds that "only everybody can compose the whole, and the unity of the whole cannot but be a totality"; in K. Adam (1924), who writes of "the integral assertion of values, an opening to the world in the most comprehensive and most noble sense, the marriage of nature with grace, of art with religion, and of science with faith, so that 'God may be all in all'"; in Henri Sonier de Lubac* (1938): "To see Catholicism as one religion among others…is to mistake its essence…Catholicism is Religion. It is the form that humanity must put on so as to at last be itself. It is the one reality which has no need of conflict in order to exist, and is thus the opposite of a "closed society," though here Catholicism denotes less a "content" than a "spirit"; and finally in Hans Urs von Balthasar* (1975), who employs the adjective while as far as possible avoiding the noun, writes of "a revelation and communication of the divine Totality."

Today, however, this set of themes is rarely approached under the heading of "Catholicism" but rather from the standpoint of a catholicity that goes beyond the confessional boundaries of Catholicism in its fulfillment of the Church's vocation (Congar 1949; Seckler 1972, 1988).

• J.A. Möhler (1825), *Die Einheit in der Kirche und das Prinzip des Katholizismus,* Darmstadt, 1957.

F.D.E. Schleiermacher (1830), *Der christliche Glaube,* 2nd Ed., vol. I, Berlin.

F.W.J. Schelling (1841–42), *Philosophie der Offenbarung* (copy Paulus), Frankfurt, 1977.

R. Sohm (1892), *Kirchenrecht,* vol. I, Leipzig.

F. Heiler (1923), *Der Katholizismus,* Munich-Basel.

C. Schmitt (1923), *Römischer Katholizismus und politische Form,* Hellerau.

K. Adam (1924), *Das Wesen des Katholizismus,* Augsburg.

A. von Harnack (1931–32), *Lehrbuch der Dogmengeschichte,* 5th Ed., 3 vols., Tübingen (repr. Darmstadt, 1983).

H. de Lubac (1938), *Catholicisme: Les aspects sociaux du dogme,* Paris.

Y. Congar (1949), "Catholicité," *Cath* 2, 720–25.

W. Beinert (1964), *Um das dritte Kirchenattribut,* Essen.

M. Seckler (1972), *Hoffnungsversuche,* Fribourg, 128–40.

H.U. von Balthasar (1975), *Katholisch,* Einsiedeln.

P. Imbs (Ed.) (1977), *Trésor de la langue française,* vol. V, Paris, *s.v.*

K. Gabriel, F.-X. Kaufmann (Ed.) (1980), *Zur Soziologie des Katholizismus,* Mayence.

Y. Congar (1987), "Romanité et catholicité," *RSPhTh* 71, 161–90.

A. Dulles (1988), *The Reshaping of Catholicism,* San Francisco.

M. Seckler (1988), *Die schiefen Wänden des Lehrhauses,* Fribourg, 178–97.

F.-X. Kaufmann (1994), "Christentum VI," *LThK* 3 2, 1 122–1 126.

Leonhard Hell

See also **Anglicanism; Calvinism; Church; Infallibility; Lubac, Henri Sonier de; Lutheranism; Orthodoxy; Pope; Protestantism; Universalism**

Causa Sui. *See* **Aseitas**

Cause. *See* **Being; Creation**

Censorship, Doctrinal. *See* **Notes, Theological**

Chalcedon, Council of

451

The Council of Chalcedon* made a major contribution to christological dogma. It must initially be viewed in the context of the progress of debate since the time of the Council of Ephesus*.

1. From Ephesus to Chalcedon

a) The Repercussions of Ephesus. The Council of Ephesus (431) had reached its conclusion with the "act of union" of 433. John of Antioch, representing the theology of the school* that had trained Nestorius, had accepted that Mary should be known as "Mother of God" *(Theotokos)* and, while distinguishing the human and the divine natures of Christ, acknowledged in him a single "person" *(prosôpon).* Cyril* of Alexandria had acquiesced, renouncing his own formula, "the unique nature of the incarnate Word*." Soon afterward, in 435, Bishop Proclus had substituted for this phrase the expression "a single hypostasis of the incarnate Word," and the introduction of the term "hypostasis" (in the sense of "physical act of existence" or "existing person") foreshadowed the future definition of Chalcedon.

However, the "act of union" of 433 had not put an end to the divisions. Some Eastern Christians continued to regard Cyril as a heretic, either because they misunderstood his earlier pronouncements or because they were still followers of the Nestorianism* condemned at Ephesus. On the other hand, some of Cyril's supporters criticized him for having approved in 433 a form of words that spoke of "two natures." Some believed that this formula implied a separation of human and divine nature, while others were already tempted by what would become the heresy* of the monk Eutyches.

The latter, indeed, would adopt a position totally opposed to the doctrine of Nestorius. Professing a radical Monophysitism*, Eutyches was summoned before a synod by Flavian, patriarch of Constantinople, and excommunicated (448). But the emperor Theodosius II, convinced of Eutyches's doctrine, in turn convoked a council that met at Ephesus on 1 August 449.

b) Leo the Great and the "Tome of Leo". A native of Tuscany, Leo had become bishop of Rome in 440. He was to play a major political role at a time when barbarian invasions threatened the western part of the empire. He also proved to be a remarkable pastoral priest, working at the organization of the liturgy and of monastic life in the Roman community and giving sermons striking for their doctrinal solidity and purity of style. His concern for orthodoxy and for the peace of the Church would lead him to intervene decisively in the christological controversies of his time. It was in this context that on 13 June 449 he addressed a long dogmatic letter, the "Tome of Leo," to the patriarch of Constantinople. Refuting the heresy of Eutyches, in which he saw a new form of Docetism*, Leo emphasized that the properties of Christ's human nature and of his divine nature must be preserved. Such a distinction did not, however, entail separation since, as he pointed out, the two natures were themselves joined in "a single person": "Each form accomplishes its own task in communion with the other." This unity of the person made it permissible to say that the Son of man descended from heaven or that the Son of God was crucified (one can recognize here what later theology would term the "communication of idioms*"). By its insistence on the two natures, Leo's doctrine was of course nearer to Antioch's position than to that of Cyril. Nonetheless, it attained a balance in its formulations that directly foreshadowed the theological synthesis of Chalcedon.

c) From the "Robber Council of Ephesus" to the Council of Chalcedon. The "Tome of Leo" was aimed at the bishops who were to meet at Ephesus in August 449. But this council took place in the worst of circumstances: a majority in favor of Eutyches had been arranged in advance. Despite the presence of the Roman delegates, Eutyches was rehabilitated, while Flavian was to be barred from the episcopate and sent into exile. Pope Leo was told of this tumultuous assembly, which he labeled a "robber council." Challenging everything that had occurred, he asked Theodosius to convene a general synod* in Italy, but the emperor did not reply and let it be known that he entirely approved of the council of 449.

It was only after the death of Theodosius (450) that the situation could progress. The new emperor, Marcian, suggested to the pope that a new council should be held in the East. Then, despite Leo's misgivings, he announced his decision to call one at Nicaea. Leo did not oppose this but requested that agreement be reached on the faith set out in the "Tome" and indicated that he would preside over the assembly himself through the intermediary of his legates. Marcian finally transferred the council to Chalcedon, opposite Constantinople, where the bishops, some 500 or 600, began their work on 8 October 451.

2. The Work of Chalcedon

a) The Dogmatic Decree. At first the bishops were unwilling to add a new definition to that of Nicaea* I. Then, after the teachings of Cyril and of Pope Leo had been approved, the imperial commissioners announced that a formulation of the faith would be worked out by the council. It was solemnly proclaimed in the emperor's presence at the sixth session (25 October 451).

After a long preamble, exhorting the preservation of the faith formerly defined by Nicaea and Constantinople* I, the document restates the two opposing errors of Nestorius and Eutyches and sets against them, respectively, the letters of Cyril and Leo. Next follows the definition proper: a broad, majestic statement, blending formulae from various sources and, above all, showing the influence of the theology set out in the "Tome."

This definition begins by confirming the doctrine promulgated in 431 by the Council of Ephesus. It is punctuated, indeed, by the expressions "a single and same Son" (at the beginning and end) and "a single and same Christ" (about halfway through, where the description of Mary as *Theotokos* also appears). The progression of the statement is thus revealing, beginning as it does from a consideration of unity, with which it also culminates.

Against this background, however, the text's original feature resides in its affirmation of duality. This first stands out in the first part: "our Saviour Jesus Christ, equally perfect in divinity, and equally perfect in humanity, at once truly God and truly man, of a rational soul and body, consubstantial with the Father* by his divinity and at the same time consubstantial with us by his humanity." Most notably, the second part of the statement introduces the terminology of the two natures: "recognized in two natures, without confusion, without change, without division, and without separation (*asugkhutôs, atreptôs, adiairetôs, akhôristôs*), the difference in these natures being in no way annulled as a result of union, the particularity of one and the other nature being on the contrary preserved, and convergent in a single person and a single hypostasis, a Christ neither splitting up nor dividing into two persons, but a single and same Son." Certainly the standpoint of unity remains clearly present even in these formulations, as witnessed in the two adverbs translated by "without division" and "without separation" and the attribution to Christ of a single "person" or "hypostasis." But the first two adverbs ("without confusion, without change"), the affirmation of a single hypostasis "in two natures" (and not merely "of two natures"), and the insistence on the respective properties of either nature all attest to the particular thrust of Chalcedon, which, while confirming the contribution made by Ephesus, was opposed as a matter of priority to the errors of Eutyches and his supporters.

b) The Conciliar Canons. The work of Chalcedon was not confined to its definition of dogma. The council also had the task of ruling on matters regarding individuals (so, e.g., Theodoret, suspected of Nestorianism, was rehabilitated), and it produced 28 canons concerning clerical and monastic discipline as well as problems of ecclesiastical administration.

Canon 28, however, was to be the cause of some serious incidents. Not only did it accord "primacy of honor" to the bishop of Constantinople, the "new Rome" (as the first Council of Constantinople had done). It also gave him a power of jurisdiction* over a large part of the East, and, while admitting the preeminence of the Apostolic See (the old Rome), it linked this preeminence to the imperial city's prestige and not to the authority conferred by Jesus on Peter*. Canon 28 was challenged by the Roman legates. The conciliar Fathers*, followed by Marcian and the patriarch Anatolius, wrote to Leo asking him to approve the council in its entirety. But the pope would give his assent only on matters of faith. He therefore ratified the doctrinal decrees of Chalcedon while rejecting canon 28.

3. The Legacy of Chalcedon

a) The Reception of the Council. The dogmatic definition of Chalcedon gave rise to violent conflicts during the following century. While the West received it without difficulty, the East was split into three factions: the Chalcedonians, the upholders of Nestorianism, and the proponents of Monophysitism. In the sixth century, the emperor Justinian, who advocated a form of "Neochalcedonism," aimed to reconcile the Monophysites and the Chalcedonians. He exerted a considerable influence on the second Council of Constantinople (553), whose dogmatic canons constitute an Ephesian interpretation of Chalcedon. Despite this effort at clarification, however, the Church* would remain split until the present day between "Chalcedonian churches" and "pre-Chalcedonian churches."

b) Chalcedon Today. In spite of some criticisms directed by Luther* at the terminology of the two natures, the definition of Chalcedon was generally accepted in the modern West as the major expression of christological dogma. The anniversary of the council in 1951 stimulated an attempt at a contemporary reinterpretation: "Chalcedon, end or beginning?" Subsequently, the dogmatic definition was subjected to harsh criticisms: its conceptual language was inadequate, the term "nature" was ambiguous, there was a risk of dualism, and there was an ignorance of the historical dimension and an ineffectiveness in resolving the christological problem. However, some of these objections have been removed because of a hermeneutics* that takes account of the context of Chalcedon as well as the scope of its definition. It may certainly be admitted that the image of the two natures expresses the identity of Christ in too static a way and that the concepts employed bear the mark of the culture of the time. The contribution of Chalcedon was nonetheless to establish a norm for Christology*, which must attempt to consider the union of humanity and divinity in Jesus Christ "without confusion, without change, without division and without separation."

• Acts: *ACO* II.

A.-J. Festugière (1982), *Éphèse et Chalcédoine: Actes des conciles,* Paris.

A.-J. Festugière (1983), *Actes du concile de Chalcédoine: Sessions III–VI,* Geneva.

Decrees: *COD* 75–103 (*DCO* II/1, 175–234).

♦ J. Lebon (1936), "Les anciens symboles dans la définition de Chalcédoine," *RHE* 32, 809–76.

A. Grillmeier, H. Bacht (Ed.) (1951–54), *Das Konzil von Chalcedon: Geschichte und Gegenwart,* 3 vols., Würzburg.

H. M. Diepen (1953), *Les Trois Chapitres au concile de Chalcédoine,* Oosterhout.

R. V. Sellers (1953), *The Council of Chalcedon,* London.

A. Grillmeier (1958), "Der Neu-Chalcedonismus," *HJ* 77, 151–66.

P.-Th. Camelot (1961), *Éphèse et Chalcédoine,* Paris.

J. Liébaert (1966), *L'Incarnation,* I: *Des origines au concile de Chalcédoine,* Paris, 209–22.

J. Pelikan (1971), *The Christian Tradition. A History of the Development of Doctrine,* I: *The Emergence of the Catholic Tradition (100–600),* Chicago, chap. 5.

W. de Vries (1974), *Orient et Occident: Les structures ecclésiales vues dans l'histoire des sept premiers conciles œcuméniques,* Paris, 101–60.

A. de Halleux (1976), "La Définition christologique de Chalcédoine," *RTL* 7, 3–23 and 155–70.

B. Sesboüé (1977), "Le Procès contemporain de Chalcédoine," *RSR* 65, 45–80.

A. Grillmeier (1979), *Jesus der Christus im Glauben der Kirche,* I: *Von der apostolischen Zeit bis zum Konzil von Chalcedon (451),* Fribourg-Basel-Vienna, 751–75 (2nd Ed. 1990).

J.-M. Carrière (1979), "Le mystère de Jésus-Christ transmis par Chalcédoine", *NRTh* 101, 338–57.

L. R. Wickham (1981), "Chalkedon," *TRE* 7, 668–75.

B. Sesboüé (1982), *Jésus-Christ dans la tradition de l'Église: Pour une actualisation de la christologie de Chalcédoine,* Paris.

A. Grillmeier (1986), *Jesus der Christus im Glauben der Kirche* II/1, *Das Konzil von Chalcedon: Rezeption und Widerspruch (451–518),* Fribourg-Basel-Vienna (2nd Ed. 1991).

B. Sesboüé (Ed.) (1994), *Histoire des dogmes,* t. I: *Le Dieu du salut,* Paris, 393–428.

Michel Fédou

See also **Christ/Christology; Cyril of Alexandria; Ephesus, Council of; Hypostatic Union; Monophysitism; Nestorianism; Person**

Character

"Character" comes from the Greek *kharakter* ("imprint"), which itself comes from the verb *kharattein* ("to engrave"). It usually refers to the distinctive features of a person or thing. Two particular meanings should be noted: 1) within the Catholic theology of the sacraments*, character refers to the lasting spiritual impression through baptism*, confirmation*, and ordination*, and 2) in contemporary ethics*, philosophy*, psychology, and theology, character is the set of particularities of one person as distinct from another. We shall concentrate on the significance of character for Christian anthropology and ethics and on the philosophical resources that inspire contemporary discourses.

Philosophers such as Martha Nussbaum and Alasdair MacIntyre are reflecting, however differently, on the constructive potential of an ethics based on notions of virtue and moral character. Paul Ricoeur deals with character in the context of personal identity within the larger framework of his ethical project: "character... indicates the set of durable dispositions by which one recognizes a person" (Ricoeur 1990).

Among contemporary theologians, Stanley Hauerwas (1944–) has been most prominent in attempting to construct an ethics in terms of the idea of character: "The language of character cannot be avoided in Christian ethics if we are to do justice to the significance of the continuing determination of the self necessary for moral growth" (Hauerwas 1985 [1975]).

For MacIntyre, Hauerwas, and others, the failure of the Enlightenment project of justifying morality obliges us to search for more tenable ethical theories: hence the retrieval of classical theories of virtue and character, especially those of Aristotle and Thomas Aquinas, and analyses of the role of communal traditions in the formation of moral character.

Aristotle treats what today we call "moral character" in the *Ethica Nicomachea* (*Nicomachean Ethics*), where he stresses the agent's good or bad formation through his actions. Thus, an action cannot be deemed good or bad in itself but has to be considered together with the agent's intention. Only when the agent knows what he is doing, when he has made a conscious choice on behalf of a certain action for its own sake, and when he acts in accordance with a firm and reliable character can his action be deemed just and reasonable (*EN* 1105a, 28–32). "Character" here translates the Greek word *ethos,* while *ethike arete* can be translated as "excellence of character" or "moral excellence." The excellences of character are distinguished from the excellences of intellect but also related to them because intellect and character complement each other. According to Aristotle, character is closely linked to appropriate action. An action is appropriate, according to the famous definition, if it is in a mean between excess and deficiency. The mean is concerned not only with actions but also with passions. The choice of the mean is the result of reasoning (*EN* 1106b, 36–1107a, 5), which depends on practical reason (prudence), an indispensable notion if one wishes to understand what character is. Indeed, the truth that practical wisdom seeks is that which coincides with right intention (*EN* 1139a, 26–30), without which moral character does not exist.

Moral character includes not only excellences such as courage, truthfulness, justice, and moderation but also aspects considered in terms of good social behavior, such as generosity, mildness of temper, humor, modesty, and a broad sense of hospitality and friendship. But how is this character formed? According to Aristotle, one becomes virtuous by doing virtuous things. First, we are engaged in such acts because we have been taught to do so; later, we understand that our virtuous actions are right. Moral maturity is achieved through both education and habituation, within a favorable social environment. This is why Aristotle stresses the importance of the role that parents, teachers, and the *polis* play in this formation and the ensuing danger when they fail.

Thomas Aquinas generally agrees with Aristotle about character but adds some clarifications, especially with regard to the concepts of will and intention. Moreover, he considers the character-forming virtues from a Christian theological perspective, stating that charity (love*) is the form of all the virtues. For Aquinas, choosing between different possibilities is dependent on both reason and desire, but choice is in itself an act of determination and will. Choice is, then, the result of intention, and this intention is morally significant because by it we are formed as agents of the act (*STh* Ia IIae, q. 19, a. 7). Both Aristotle and Thomas underline the need to will to do good, not just to do good.

"For Aristotle and Aquinas, therefore, to say that a man has character seems to mean at least that he has acquired certain kinds of *habitus* called virtues" (Hauerwas 1985 [1975]). These "*habitus*" are not habits in the ordinary sense of the term; they are "readiness for action" that is not momentary but lasting (ibid.). Thus, character is formed "from repeated acts of deliberate decision and, when formed, issues forth in deliberative decision" (ibid.). The difference between teleological action and intentional action is crucial for Hauerwas. Intention is distinct from mere purposive behavior. "We are profoundly what we do, for, once action is understood in its essential connection with our agency, it is apparent that by acting we form not merely the act but ourselves in the process" (ibid.). Hauerwas explores both the private and the public aspects of character and its possibilities of change and growth, but, notwithstanding how our character is formed, "it must be nonetheless *our* character if...men are self-agents" (ibid.). Hauerwas frequently developed a theological thesis: that "the idea of character can provide a way of explicating the kind of determination of the believer in Christ without necessarily destroying the tension between the 'already but not yet' quality of the Christian life" (ibid.). Hauerwas, together with many other theologians, demands in this respect a new appraisal of the function of narrative* in the moral development both of an individual and of the Christian community in which the individual is formed (Hauerwas 1981). The importance of others must be acknowledged in any Christian ethics of character: it is, indeed, others who transmit founding narratives and examples of the Christian life (Hauerwas 1983).

A Christian ethics of character, however, is only one among the different approaches to Christian life advocated today. Its particular emphases on the individual person, on his or her formation as a responsible agent, on the role of narrative, and on the church as the milieu for the formation of character provide essential aspects, but an ethics of character also includes the potential of conflict. The best Christian might at times be forced to make painful decisions and to violate his or her own Christian character. When it is necessary to make a moral decision and neither the Christian tradition nor the Christian community is able to offer enough help, when the plurality of aspects of an individual character is shocking because of its contradictions, and when, finally, all kinds of Christian and non-Christian narratives call for attention, then recourse to some understanding of natural law or obligation, to teleological ethics, and to discourse ethics may be of help. A Christian ethics that ignores character is as insufficient as an ethics of character that takes no account of any other element of the moral life.

• Thomas Aquinas, *ST* Ia IIae, q. 19 and 49–67.
S. Hauerwas (1975, new Ed., 1985), *Character and the Christian Life: A Study in Theological Ethics,* Notre Dame, Ind., and London.
S. Hauerwas (1981), *A Community of Character: Toward a Constructive Christian Social Ethics,* Notre Dame, Indiana, and London.
S. Hauerwas (1983), *The Peaceable Kingdom: A Primer in Christian Ethics,* Notre Dame, Indiana, and London.
A. MacIntyre (1985), *After Virtue: A Study in Moral Theory,* London.
J. Stout (1988), *Ethics after Babel: The Languages of Morals and Their Discontents,* Boston.
P. Ricoeur (1990), *Soi-même comme un autre,* Paris.
M. Nussbaum (1993), "Non-Relative Virtues: An Aristotelian Approach," in M. Nussbaum and A. Sen (Ed.), *The Quality of Life,* Oxford, 242–69.
M. Canto-Sperber, A. Fagot-Largeault (1996), "Caractère," *DEPhM,* 200–209.

Werner G. Jeanrond

See also **Ethics; Virtues; Wisdom**

Character, Sacramental. *See* **Sacrament**

Charisma

In the New Testament, "charisma," from the Greek *kharis* ("grace*"), designates the exceptional gifts given to some of the faithful for the good of the community. In 1 Corinthians 12:8–11, Paul offers of list of charismata: wisdom, knowledge, faith, the gift of healing, the working of miracles, prophecy, the discernment of spirits, speaking in tongues ("glossolalia"), and its interpretation; in verse 28, he adds the charismata given to the apostles, the prophets, teachers, and leaders of the community. In medieval terminology, charismata are elements of grace given for the edification of the community *(gratia gratis data)* and not for the sanctification of individuals *(gratia gratum faciens).* The term "charisma" achieved prominence in the sociology of religion and political sociology thanks to the influence of Max Weber. Pentecostalism*, both Protestant and Catholic ("Charismatic Revival"), has given a prominent place to the Pauline emphasis on charismata. The emphasis given by Vatican* II to the multiplicity of charismata in the one Church, the recipient of the gifts of the Holy* Spirit, has provided the basis for a renewal of the theology of charismata.

• W. E. Mühlmann et al. (1971), "Charisma," *HWP* 1, 893–999.
K. H. Ratschow et al. (1981), "Charisma," *TRE* 7, 681–98.
G. Dautzenberg et al. (1994), "Charisma," *LThK3* 2, 1014–18.

Jean-Yves Lacoste

See also **Grace; Pentecostalism**

Charity. *See* **Love**

Chartres, School of

a) To give even just a general view of the school of Chartres, it is impossible to dispense with a detour through historiography. Its fame began at the end of the 19th century. According to R. L. Poole and A. Clerval, it had been one of the most prestigious centers of studies and teaching in the 11th and 12th centuries. Good and excellent works, devoted to authors more or less attached to this school, have consolidated its reputation since that time. But in 1970, R. W. Southern expressed an iconoclastic opinion. He stated that we possess very few reliable documents on this school, and he concluded from this that Chartres was nothing more than an episcopal school like so many others. Indeed, it was much less important than the ones in Paris and in Laon, and its teaching was outdated. However, the well-argued responses of P. Dronke, N. M. Haring, and E. Jeauneau, among others, have led to a general agreement that the school of Chartres certainly existed as an organized institutional body, although not a well-known one and no doubt less exceptional than first assessments had claimed. In addition, the quality of its masters (more numerous than Southern had thought), as well as the propagation of its teachings and of what can be called the spirit of Chartres, ensured its important place in the intellectual history of the 12th century.

Bishop Fulbert (1006–28) gave the school an early brilliance. At the beginning of the 12th century, this bishop, together with the great canonist Ivo of Chartres (1090–1115) and the first of the school's great masters, Bernard of Chartres, made their mark. From the latter's time, complex networks extending both inside and outside the school can be seen to emerge, and the best way of presenting them is to follow them.

b) A subdeacon in Chartres from the beginning of the century until his death (c. 1126, no doubt), Bernard was a master at the cathedral school in 1112 and chancellor in 1124. These are the only facts we possess about him. As for his thought, until the 1980s it was known only through a few doxographic elements, the most detailed of which came from John of Salisbury, himself a student of the pupils of Bernard. In particular, John relates that the latter was a *grammaticus*—a master of grammar and literature—of high quality but also "the most perfect Platonist of his times." He cites especially Bernard's way of drawing a parallel between the grammatical fact of the paronymy and the cosmography of the *Timaeus* (which, nonetheless, John himself does not cite). Another comparison was that of the three states of the idea: first of all isolated in its purity, then tending toward the material, and finally imbued with its subject. Lastly, John drew attention to Bernard's comparison of the series of noun/verb/adjective: *albedo* (whiteness), *albet* (whitens), and *album* (white).

In 1984, P. E. Dutton announced his discovery of Bernard's glosses on the *Timaeus.* The glosses were on only the first half of the *Timaeus* since that was all that was known of it in the Middle Ages (it appeared in Calcidius's translation and with his commentary). Dutton published Bernard's glosses in 1991. This important text increases considerably our knowledge of Bernard's philosophy* and of certain aspects of his influence. Several allusions in this commentary reveal an interest in morality that did not emerge from the doxography. Above all, his commentary makes his Platonism clear. The data supplied by John of Salisbury gave a static image of it: there is the idea, the matter and the composite of the two, unstable and without real existence. As for the glosses, they very often emphasize the *formae nativae,* "the forms which come into the world*," images of the ideas that enter into matter to produce the world of the senses. Of course, that concept was already indicated in the *Timaeus* (50c), but Calcidius did not stress it, while Bernard makes it a principal element of his cosmology. In addition, there can be discerned in these glosses an effort to attribute to matter a specific role in the constitution of the tangible, but the idea is suggested several times without any development. Bernard was not a theologian; he was a Platonist. It is true that Plato, along with Macrobius and Boethius*, pervades everything in the 12th century and even in theology, where the reading of the *Timaeus* is a parallel to the meditation on the first lines of Genesis. The practice of linking these philosophical and literary studies is in any case characteristic of the school of Chartres.

Two of Bernard's pupils were among the greatest minds of the century: William of Conches and Gilbert de la Porrée (Gilbert of Poitiers).

c) Not much is known about the life of William of Conches. He began to teach in 1120. Various clues lead to the supposition that it was in Chartres, but no formal proof of this exists. Around the year 1140, he left his place of teaching for the court of the duke of Normandy, Geoffroy le Bel Plantagenêt. William died soon afterward, in 1154. His work is composed of fairly numerous commentaries on different authors; of a *Philosophia,* which is a work of his youth; and of a *Dragmaticon,* which takes the form of an erudite dialogue with Geoffroy le Bel. According to John of Salisbury, William was "the most learned *grammaticus* after Bernard of Chartres," and he is known to have commented on the *Institutiones Grammaticae* of Priscian, on Virgil, on Juvenal, and on the *Marriage of Philology and Mercury* by Martianus Capella. He himself said he was a *physicus,* interested in nature. Specifically, he knew the Arab works of medicine translated in the 11th century by Constantine the African. A theologian, William analytically traced the route from the creature as far as God: the effective cause of the world is divine power, its formal cause is wisdom, and its final cause is goodness. We next discover the three persons of the Trinity* that Abelard* had presented in this way as early as 1120 (divine attributes; appropriation). In his glosses on *The Consolation of Philosophy* by Boethius* and on the *Timaeus* and in his *Philosophia mundi,* William, like Abelard, ventured to identify the Holy Spirit as the Soul of Plato's world; and again like Abelard, he retracted in the face of criticism. His annotated readings of Boethius and of the *Timaeus,* as well as his reading of Macrobius's *Commentary on the Dream of Scipio,* were grist for his Platonism. As with his interest in the poets, the interest William took in this philosophy is no doubt the result of Bernard's teaching.

But William's most original trait is certainly that he constructed the concept of nature*. He definitely did not know Aristotle's *Physics,* but the *Timaeus* taught him that forms, images of the "ideas that really exist in the archetypal world," "enter" the primordial matter of the world. In this way are formed the elements. According to Constantine the African (c. 1020–87), these are minimal particles, each made up of two compatible qualities of which each element got one from itself and the second from another (fire is hot in itself, dry because of motion; air is humid in itself, hot because of fire; and so on). As an image of its archetype, the world is "the ordered set of all creatures." Following Calcidius, William discerned in the world the work of the Creator, the work of nature, and the work of the artisan. He thus diverged from an Augustinian view, scriptural and ultratheological, according to which everything is a divine miracle*, the ripening of the grape just as much as the changing of the water into wine in Cana. For William, "the Creator's work consists of having created at the beginning all the elements, or of having done something against nature; nature's work consists in the fact that like engenders like: men engender men; donkeys engender donkeys"; or again, "from the trunk of a tree God can make a calf, but has he ever done so?" William of Saint-Thierry accused William of Conches of having "followed the insane philosophers for whom nothing exists except bodies and bodily things, without any other god in nature than the aid of the elements and natural regulation." But William of Conches stated that he "took nothing away from God" since nature was God's work. We therefore find in his ideas a form of physics and naturalism* that is compatible with a Christian theology and the novelty of which was rooted in Platonist soil.

d) Gilbert de la Porrée was born about 1075. After studies at the schools of Chartres and Laon, he taught in Paris and at Chartres, where he was chancellor from 1126 to 1137. In 1142 he became bishop of Poitiers, his native town. He died in 1154.

In the main, his work consists of commentaries on books of the Bible (Psalms, Epistles of Paul) and of Boethius's theological opuscules. In the latter, Gilbert put forward a philosophy that has to be reconstructed, for it is presented there in fragments according to the requirements of a text glossed phrase by phrase. Gilbert constructs in this way a deep and original ontology whose pivot is the Boethian distinction between "what is" *(id quod est)* and being* *(esse).* He rewords this conceptual pairing by using the respective terms "what is" and "that whereby it is" *(id quo est).* Or else he uses another pairing, that of "subsisting" and "subsistence." The individual being is what it is on account of a group of subsistences stacked up as are the universals on Porphyry's tree, moving from the species to the most general kind. These are its specific subsistence and its generic subsistences. The subsistences have no existence since they constitute the "being," which, according to Boethius's own words, "is not yet" *(non dum est);* and as for the *quod est,* it does exist "once it has received its form of being." For Gilbert, then, only the individual exists *(individuum),* while the universal, which he calls the *dividuum,* results from a "similarity" among individuals of the same genus, of the same kind, which are united only by a "conformity" and which do not possess the sort of ontological identity postulated by the various realisms. Each individual *(id quod est)* is something *(est aliquid)* through *one* set of subsistences, of which each subsistence is an individual only insofar as it belongs to that composite of all of them together, which is identical to no other. In this way, "the *platonitas,* constituted by the whole of everything which, in deed or by nature, has belonged, or belongs, or will belong to Plato." This agglomeration *(concretio)* "does not produce, but exhibits" *(non fecit sed probat)* individuality, which is therefore a unifying subsistence.

So in Gilbert we encounter a Platonist who welcomes nominalist ontology (nominalism*). In fact, Gilbert remains a Platonist: the "concrete" forms *(in concretione in abstractae)* that constitute the substance of a subsistant are for him "the image of ideas" *(idearum icones).* From Bernard's teaching he retains the *formae nativae* (but not the phrase, which does not occur in Gilbert's work).

A theology that can be called philosophical developed on the base of this ontology. Following Boethius, who himself followed Aristotle, Gilbert made theology the third and highest of the "speculative sciences," the other two being physics and mathematics. According to Gilbert, of the nine "rules" Boethius formulated in his short treatise called *hebdomades,* only the seventh is really theological. It states that "for all that is simple, its being and what it does are one and the same" *(omne simplex esse suum et id quod est unum habet).* There is in God, therefore, an identity of the *quod est* and of the *quo est:* for this reason, his power, his wisdom, and so on do not differ from "the essence by which we claim he is" and which is "a single form." "God is just for the very reason for which he is God"; or again, "God is essence, he is not something" *(aliquid).*

According to Gilbert, to say that "God is by reason of his essence" does not mean that the essence is other than him and that the same idea is true when one considers the Trinity. The persons of the Trinity are God "by reason of the divine essence," and since this essence is single and one, each person is one for that reason, and all of them together are one. Bernard* of Clairvaux wanted to have Gilbert condemned at a council* held in Rheims (1148), accusing him of having taught that "the divine nature, or *divinitas,* is not God but the form by means of which he is God, just as humanity is not man but the form by which he is man" (deity*). Gilbert was not condemned. He had not taught what Bernard was claiming he had taught, and his stunning theological erudition had given him the means of shoring up his doctrine with solid guarantees. It is clear that if the *esse* and the *id quod est* do not equal one in God, it is not possible to say that the "divinity" is in himself the same way that humanity is in man.

Apart from this philosophical theology, we find in Gilbert, who was educated at Laon as well as at Chartres, a theology of the glossator, something that is seen in his scriptural commentaries. This theology is also a "science," but one with a specific status: "The face of God is reflected in the mind *(in mente)* as in a mirror; when under the influence of the Lord the power of the mind which is called the intellect is brought to bear, that is called a science" (unpublished, cited by Nilsen). Gilbert distinguishes two sorts of truths: that of grammar, of dialectics, and so on and that of the Law, the prophets, of the Gospels. The second is "according to piety," but not the first.

e) Thierry was the third great chancellor of Our Lady of Chartres, where he succeeded Gilbert in 1141. It was probably he who had spoken in defense of Abelard at the Council of Soissons (1121), and he attended the Council of 1148 in Rheims, when Bernard of Clairvaux failed to have Gilbert condemned. He is the one to whom Bernard Silvestris dedicated his *Cosmographia* and Hermann of Carinthia dedicated his translation of Ptolemy's *Planisphere.* Thierry annotated Cicero's *On Rhetorical Invention* and compiled and commented on the texts that make up the *Heptameron*—a manual of liberal arts, which proves in particular that he knew Aristotle's treatises on logic, barely glimpsed by Abelard. He wrote a treatise on the six days of creation* *(De sex dierum operibus)* and composed a commentary on Boethius's *De Trinitate,* apparently on several occasions, if we can believe the editor who attributed three commentaries to him. Even though such repetition seems unlikely, these three commentaries attributed to Thierry allow the inference of the existence of a tradition homogeneous enough that it can be called the tradition of Chartres.

The above bibliography reveals Thierry's to be a mind that ranged over different areas of knowledge, and his polymathy inspired in him differing ways of treating fundamental theological themes. For instance, he proposed a mathematical formula of the Trinity. If one considers in the first place that God is a unity, one will conceive that the unity applying itself to itself engenders "the equivalent of the unity": thus, the Father engenders the Son, "a perfect image of unity." In the second place, the principle of cohesion according to which everything attaches to its own unity is illustrated in God in the form of a love between the unity that engenders and the unity engendered—this is the Holy* Spirit, the "connection" from one to the other, which is not unequal to them and is not different. Besides, "the divine form is every form" since all forms share in him and therefore share in the unity. They therefore derive from him just as numbers derive from the mathematical unity, in such a way that "the creation of the numbers is the creation of things"; and these things are affected by the initial multiplicity, which is duality.

All the above reveals to us a pythagorism that is inherent in Platonism. In the same way, Bernard's and Gilbert's *formae nativae* appear again when Thierry says that the forms of things are the images of the true forms and that certain phrases by classical philosophers, "understanding of the divinity, wisdom of the Creator," prove that they glimpsed something of the subsistence of forms in the Son*. Although Thierry borrowed the double schema of the threefold relationship and of creation from Platonizing arithmetic, he also superimposed on grammar a theological interpretation of the meaning of names: "Names are joined eternally in the divine mind *(in mente divina)* even before men impose them on things; therefore men imposed them on the things to which they were joined in the divine mind—and it seems to us that men did that under the influence *(instinctu)* of the Holy Spirit. As for "physics," an area alien to the liberal arts, it gave him the means to explain by means of the nature of the elements the order of the six days of creation." Light, the first thing created, is the light of fire, naturally placed first among the elements. Its heat produces vapors that settle above the air and therefore makes the surface of the water fall. Thus, land appears, and once warmed, it produces plants. From the vapors, stars are formed, and their motion increases the warmth to the point of causing animals to appear, fish, birds, land animals, and man among them. The first six verses of Genesis can be recognized in this process, and springing from them, the "seminal reasons," placed by God in the elements, develop into later productions.

f) Clarembaud of Arras, who died after 1170, had Hugh of Saint*-Victor and Thierry of Chartres as his teachers. He annotated Boethius's *Hebdomades* and *De Trinitate* and was the author of a short unfinished treatise on creation that he had intended as a complement to Thierry's. In any event, he remained close to the latter. He took up again the arithmetical speculation on the Trinity and the concept of God as *forma essendi* (a form coming into being), which in any case is a Boethian theme, and he interpreted the forms in material shape as images of divine ideas. He kept his distance from Gilbert, whose nominalist conception of the universal he particularly rejected: "Although renowned doctors have propagated the idea that singular men are men by dint of singular humanities, we have tried to show that there exists a single and same humanity through which singular men are men."

g) Bernard Silvestris, who was born about 1100 and died about 1160, taught at Tours. He is linked to Chartres only because of his dedication of his *Cosmographia* to Thierry, but one could add that he is also linked to Chartres by his culture and cast of mind—the "Spirit of Chartres," which is recognizable by intuition but cannot be localized. Bernard annotated Martianus Capella and the first six chants of the *Aeneid,* considered as the metaphorical account of "what a human mind suffers when lodged for some time in a human body." He wrote a *Mathematicus,* a poem where astrology is challenged; an *Experimentus,* a treatise on divination of Arab origin; and, above all, a *Cosmosgraphia,* which was written in alternating prose and verse and treats, in two parts (*Megacosmos* and *Microcosmos*), the genesis of the world and of man while dealing along the way with an abundance of encyclopedic material. Its style is beautiful in both verse and prose. As for the content, three aspects are noteworthy. First, his Platonism: as in the *Timaeus,* matter is in a state of disorder but remains a source of inexhaustible fecundity. It receives "forms," the first of which are those of the elements, before one sees the whole of the cosmos* unfold. But in Bernard Silvestris's work, the myth expands far beyond Plato's into a real metaphysical epic. At the beginning, matter, called *Silva,* implores *Noys,* who is divine thought, to rescue her from the "confusion" of her situation. Apart from *Noys,* a host of characters *(Natura, Endelichia, Physis)* will intervene to save the world from chaos. They are all female, and the character that dominates it all receives names from all three genders: *Deus, Usia Prima,* and *Tugaton.* Second, the feminism: in addition to the primacy of feminine personifications of cosmological events, a superimposing of images identifies Eden, the first garden where humanity came into being, with a pregnant belly. The masculine sex is not mentioned until the end of Book II. Finally, the paganism*: a few allusions to Christian beliefs, very rare and without links among them, do not counterbalance a fable that is entirely philosophical and, more specifically, Greek.

h) Can John of Salisbury (born between 1115 and 1120) be considered as belonging to the school of

Chartres? The fact that he was bishop in this town from 1176 to his death in 1180 has nothing to do with it. However, he provides information on several members of the school of Chartres and its teachings. His own masters were William of Conches, Thierry of Chartres, and Gilbert de la Porrée. Moreover, he had also heard Abelard, the logician Alberic of Paris, and the grammarian Pierre Hélie. From 1148 he spent his life involved in the affairs of two archbishops (Thomas à Becket was one of them) and of one pope. He was the author of the *Policratus,* a political work ("on the frivolity of courtiers"), of the *Pontifical History,* but also of the *Metalogicon,* where, in elegant Latin and amid many scholarly digressions, he dealt with the content of Aristotle's *Organum,* about knowledge and reason*. It is the work of a somewhat disillusioned great man of letters who recommends a tempered skepticism in matters "doubtful for the wise." If one holds, perhaps arbitrarily, the characteristics of the school of Chartres to be a taste for "grammar," Platonism, and the invention of nature, John can lay claim only to the first of these characteristics. From the philosophy he learned at the school of Chartres, he retained only a few facts, quite precise ones, but also fragmentary and even anecdotal.

• Bernard de Chartres, *The* "Glosae super Platonem" *of Bernard of Chartres,* Ed. P. Dutton, Toronto, 1991.

Bernard Silvestre, *Bernardus Silvestris. Cosmographia,* Ed. P. Dronke, Leiden, 1978.

Bernard Silvestre, *The Cosmographia of Bernardus Silvestris,* trans. W. Wetherbee, New York, 1973.

Clarembaud d'Arras, N.M. Haring, *Life and Works of Clarembald of Arras,* Toronto, 1965.

Gilbert de la Porrée, N.M. Haring, *The Commentaries on Boethius by Gilbert of Poitiers,* Toronto, 1966.

William of Conches, *Philosophia,* PL 90, 1127–78; 172, 39–102.

William of Conches, *Dragmaticon;* it. trans. E. Maccagnolo, *Il divino e il megacosmo,* Milan, 1980, 251–453.

William of Conches, *Glosae super Platonem,* Ed. E. Jeauneau, Paris, 1965.

John of Salisbury, PL 199; *Policraticus,* Ed. C.C.J. Webb, Oxford, 1909.

John of Salisbury, *Metalogicon,* Ed. J.B. Hall, Turnhout, 1991.

Thierry de Chartres, N.M. Haring, *Commentaries on Boethius by Thierry of Chartres and His School,* Toronto, 1971.

♦ Notes on Bernard de Chartres, Bernard Silvestre, School of Chartres, Clarembaud d'Arras, Gilbert de la Porrée, William of Conches, John of Salisbury, Thierry de Chartres, with bibl. (Ed., studies) in *Dictionnaire des lettres françaises: Le Moyen Age,* Paris, 1992. Also: L.O. Nielsen (1982), *Theology and Philosophy in the Twelfth Century,* Leiden (on Gilbert).

P. Dronke (1984), "Bernardo Silvestre," *Enciclopedia Virgiliana,* I, 497–500.

J. Jolivet (1995), "Les principes féminins selon la 'Cosmographie' de Bernard Silvestre," in *Philosophie médiévale arabe et latine,* Paris, 269–78.

JEAN JOLIVET

See also **Humanism, Christian; Intellectualism; Natural Theology; Nature; Philosophy; Platonism, Christian; Theological Schools**

Chenu, Marie-Dominique. *See* **Thomism**

Childhood, Spiritual

The expression "spiritual childhood" is today inseparable from the "way of childhood" of Theresa of Lisieux (also known as Sister Teresa of the Child Jesus, 1873–97), who gave shape to a basic attitude that was first biblical and then Christian.

a) Biblical Roots. There is no child without a father. The increasingly vivid experience of the fatherhood of God, for Israel first ("Thus says the Lord, Israel is my firstborn son"; Ex 4:22) and then for everyone on the basis of the choice of Israel ("And of Zion it shall be said, 'This one and that one were born in her'"; Ps 87:5), runs through the entire Judeo-Christian revelation*. As the ultimate expression of this, Jesus* presents himself as the only Son, "the firstborn among many brothers" (Rom 8:29), making the father–son relation the one from which all others proceed (Eph 3:15).

In this perspective the theme of spiritual childhood crystallizes around the concern of YHWH for his people*, whom he bears "as a man carries his son" (Dt 1:31), so that the faithful are invited to discover themselves in a total dependence on God ("Is not he your father, who created you, who made you and established you?"; Dt 32:6), outside of which their fragility is absolute ("Ah, Lord God! Behold, I do not know how to speak, for I am only a youth"; Jer 1:6). The proper attitude is thus one of total confidence (God replies to Jeremiah, "Do not say, 'I am only a youth'"; Jer 1:7), bringing about a tranquillity and passivity that define the normal interior state of the human person before God: "I do not occupy myself with things too great and too marvelous for me. But I have calmed and quieted my soul, like a weaned child with its mother" (Ps 131:2). We should note that in all this, although there is tenderness ("Can a woman forget her nursing child...?"; Is 49:15), there is above all humility, and biblical civilization hardly sees in childhood the ideal state of positive innocence that characterizes the modern view of it.

In the New Testament and the tradition*, it is under the sign of this humility that childhood expresses the spiritual attitude appropriate to the new birth (Jn 6:1–6): "Whoever does not receive the kingdom of God like a child shall not enter it" (Lk 18:17). In the background there will always be the example of Jesus himself. who, "born of woman" (Gal 4:4), has joined us in our essential fragility, while teaching us to live it as sons of Mary* and Joseph.

b) Before Theresa. Over the centuries, the fact that Christian life was understood as the birth and growth of divine life meant that spiritual childhood became a central theological theme. It was developed by the mystics* in the direction of the necessary passivity of the human person in the hands of God. Countless writers developed one or another of the theme's aspects before it was treated as a specific inner way by French writers of the 17th century. Bérulle* and the Oratorians, as well as the reformed Carmelites* (particularly that of Beaune), associated this way of childhood with the contemplation* of the infant Jesus, that is, with "adherence" to the God hidden beneath the infirmities of his incarnation, making us divine to the extent of our own spiritual childhood.

c) Theresa de Lisieux. It was with Theresa, proclaimed a doctor* of the Church in 1997, that spiritual childhood became a distinct spiritual school. Following in the tradition of Bérulle, on the decisive Christmas night of 1886 she perceived her apostolic vocation as an appropriation of the childhood of Jesus: "On this night when he made himself weak and suffering for my love*, he made me strong and courageous, he clothed me with his armor" (*Manuscript A,* 44 v). There had just taken place in her the Copernican revolution that characterizes spiritual childhood: totally powerless before the ordeals of life, both great and small, she made of this very powerlessness the wellspring of a total abandonment in God, observing the promise of Saint Paul, "I will not boast, except of my weaknesses" (2 Cor 12:5), and determining never to attempt to overcome them by herself. From that time forward her own weaknesses became an additional capacity for allowing Jesus to manifest his strength in her weakness, right up to the death* she experienced in the most extreme pain as well as the most extreme jubilation. Two months earlier she had explained to her sister what she understood by "remaining a little child before the good Lord."

It is recognizing one's nothingness*, awaiting everything from the good Lord, as a "little child expects everything from his father; it is not worrying about anything, not making a fortune. Even the poor give a child what he needs, but as soon as he grows up his father no longer wants to feed him and tells him: 'Work now, you can take care of yourself.' It's so I wouldn't hear that that I did not want to grow up, feeling unable to earn my livelihood, the eternal life* of Heaven" (*Conversation,* 6 August 1897).

Her "little way" overwhelmed later spirituality, making of Theresa the most popular mystic of modern times and making spiritual childhood the almost obligatory form of all inner life. It remained for philosophy* belatedly to bring forth a way of thinking about childhood, for example, in F. Ulrich, *Der Mensch als Anfang,* and G. Siewerth, *Metaphysik der Kindheit.*

• H. Bremond (1921), *Histoire littéraire du sentiment religieux en France,* III, 2, Paris, 202–49.

A. Combes (1948), *Introduction à la spiritualité de sainte Thérèse de l'Enfant-Jésus,* Paris.

H. Paissac (1951), "Enfant de Dieu," *VS* 85, 256–72.

M.F. Berrouard et al. (1959), "Enfance spirituelle," *DSp* 4, 682–714.

H.U. von Balthasar (1970), *Schwestern im Geist,* Ensiedeln, 14–349 (*Thérèse de Lisieux: Histoire d'une mission,* 1973).

P. Descouvemont (1990), "Thérèse de l'Enfant-Jésus," *DSp* 15, 576–611.

Thérèse de l'Enfant-Jésus (1992), *OC,* Paris.

Max Huot De Longchamp

See also **Life, Spiritual; Mysticism**

Choice

1. Old Testament

God's initiative toward Israel* is described as "choice," especially in Deuteronomy, where its gratuitous nature is strongly emphasized. Whereas with human beings choice is always motivated, God's choice of Israel is a case of pure predilection. It is incomprehensible, unmotivated, filling one with amazement and gratitude (Dt 4:37; 7:6ff; 9:4ff, 10:14f; *see* Ps 33:12; 135:4). The commitment to service and fidelity that this gratitude entails is only a response to this predilection (Dt 14:1).

a) Terminology. The term "to choose" (*bâchar* 164 times, Greek *eklegesthai*) belongs to everyday life. One chooses people or things appropriate for a particular purpose: men for a military operation (Ex 17:9), stones for a sling (1 Sm 17:40), and so on. Choice is also expressed by other terms—to take (*lâquach:* Jos 24:3), to love (*'âhab:* Hos 11:1; Mal 1–3), and to know (*yâda*?: Am 3:2; Gn 18:19)—or it is implied by expressions such as "people* of the Lord" (Ex 19:5f.; Dt 26:18f.; Ps 28:9).

b) Beneficiaries of Choice. The category of choice is employed in interpreting the past: Abraham (Neh 9:7), Jacob (Ps 105:6), Moses (Ps 106:23; Sir 45:4), and the Exodus (Ez 20:5). It is applied to the heart of a people, to kings (Dt 17:15; 2 Sm 6:21, 16:18), to priests (Nm 16:4–7; Dt 18:5, 21:5; 1 Sm 2:28), and especially to Jerusalem* (Dt 12:18; Jos 9:27; Ps 78:68, 132:13f.) and the dynasty of David (2 Sm 7:14ff.; 1 Kgs 8:16; Ps 78, 89; *see* messianism*).

c) The Dramatic Aspect of Choice. The prophets* do no like to speak of "choice" with regard to themselves (*see* "take": Am 7:15; "send": Is 6:8; "establish": Jer 1:10). They fear that this idea may be wrongly understood as implying an automatic guarantee of salvation. The more ancient of the prophets do not even speak of a unique choice of Israel or Zion; rather, they seem to make it purely and simply relative (Am 9:7: "Are you not like the Cushites to me, O people of Israel? [...] Did I not bring up Israel from the land of Egypt, and the Philistines from Caphtor and the Syrians from Kir?") or to see in it a mark of greater responsibility (Am 3:2: "You only have I known of all the families of the earth; therefore I will punish you for all your iniquities").

Thus, the theological aporias that lie in the idea of choice come to the surface. The opposite concept, "reject" (*mâ'as*), emerges. One finds "to not choose," "to pass over," as with the brothers of David (1 Sm 16:6–10), but also the stronger sense of "reject," "annul the choice already made," as in the case of Saul (1 Sm 16:1) or of the ancient cult sites (Ps 78:67). Faced with the infidelity of a people, one is impelled to ask God, "Have you utterly rejected Judah? Does your soul loathe Zion?" (Jer 14:19; *see* 6:30, 7:29; Ps 89:39–46). The historical book of Deuteronomy does not offer a clear answer. It notes the infidelity of the two kingdoms and their "rejection" (2 Kgs 17:20, 23:27, 24:20). If hope does survive, it is not explicitly expressed (2 Kgs 25:27–30).

Conversely, during the exile and after, according to the prophets, the possibility of rejection is decisively excluded, in such a way that a new choice of Israel is spoken of (Zec 1:17, 2:16; Is 14:1) or in such a way that the irrevocability of the first choice is emphasized (Jer 31:37, 33:23–26; Is 41:8f., 44:1–5; Ez 20:32ff.), on grounds of its gratuitous nature (Is 43:10, 20f.; 45:4). The perfect fusion between divine choice and man's response is outlined in the mysterious figure of the "Servant," the "Chosen One" (Is 42:1, 49:7).

Once the idea is established that the people of God have been irrevocably chosen, there remains the problem of individuals: who, after all, really belongs to the chosen people? The expression "chosen ones," first used to name an entire people (Ps 105:43, 106:5; Is 65:9, 15, 22; 1 Chr 16:13), comes to have an eschatological connotation. In contradistinction to the "impious," it denotes "the just," "the humble," or "the saints" (Is 65:9, 15; Wis 3:9; 1 Hen 1:1, 5:7s, 25:4f., 38:2,ff., 39:6f.) and no longer simply coincides with the empirical Israel. In Qumran, the expression "the chosen ones" becomes a term of self-designation for the community, but always within an eschatological perspective (1QSVIII, 3; 1QSXI, 16; 1QHII, 13; 4QflorI, 19).

2. The New Testament

While still referring to the choice of Israel (Acts 13:17), the irreversibility of which Paul reaffirms (Rom 11:28f.), in the New Testament the term is applied to Jesus*, the Church*, and the individual believer.

a) Jesus, God's Chosen. Used in very few but nevertheless important texts to express the intimate relationship between Jesus and the Father*, as part of the Servant figure (Jn 1:34; Lk 9:35, 23:35), the theme never developed. The title "Son" proved to be more suitable to express Jesus' uniqueness.

b) The Church, the Chosen. Divine choice is at the root of the calling not only of the Twelve (Lk 6:13; Acts 1:2; Jn 15:16, 19; *see* Mk 3:13f.) and of Paul (Acts 9:15) but of all Christians (1 Thes 1:4; Acts 15:7). It connotes an entirely altruistic nature and a preference for the poor (1 Cor 1:26ff.; Jas 2:5). The term "kingdom of priests, holy nation, chosen people" (Ex 19:6; Is 43:20) is given to the Church in 1 Peter 2:9. Local communities can be symbolically designated by the name "chosen" (2 Jn 1, 13; 1 Pt 5:13). Christians are called "chosen" (Col 3:12; 1 Pt 1:1; 2 Tm 2:10), but only in Romans 16:13 is the term used in the singular: "Greet Rufus, chosen in the Lord." Is this a softened meaning of "eminent Christian"?

The Pauline writings in particular, by using apocalyptic* categories, understand election as being part of God's eternal intention. It is interpreted christologically: through pure grace*, the Father loved us and chose us in Christ, through Christ and in consideration of Christ, from time* immemorial (Rom 8:28ff.; Eph 1:3–14).

c) The Choice of the Christian. Nevertheless, the Christian is subject to the final Judgment Day. The Divine choice offers grounds for trust: "Who shall bring any charge against God's elect?" (Rom 8:33), but believers must commit themselves "with fear and trembling" (Phil 2:12): "Therefore, brethren, be all the more diligent to make your calling and election sure" (2 Pt 1:10). In John, the tragic proximity of Judas the betrayer casts a shadow of uncertainty: was he chosen as well (Jn 6:65, 10:29, 17:2), or was he not (Jn 6:70, 13:18)? In some texts, the accent falls on caution: "For many are called, but few are chosen" (Mt 22:14), and the term retains all its eschatological value (Mk 13:20, 22, 27; parallel passage in Mt 24:22, 24, 31; Lk 18:7; Rev 17:14).

• G. Schrenk, G. Quel (1942), "*eklegomai/eklogè/eklektos,*" *ThWNT* 4, 147–97.

H.H. Rowley (1950), *The Biblical Doctrine of Election,* London.

P.J. Daumoser (1954), *Berufung und Erwählung bei den Synoptikern,* Eichstatt.

K. Koch (1955), "Zur Geschichte der Erwählungsvorstellung in Israel," *ZAW* 67, 205–26.

P. Altmann (1964), *Erwählungstheologie und Universalismus im AT,* BZAW 92.

H. Wildberger (1970), "Die Neuinterpretation des Erwählungsglaubens Israels in der Krise der Exilzeit," in H.J. Stoebe (Ed.), *Wort-Gebot-Glaube: Beiträge zur Theologie des AT. W. Eichrodt zum 80. Geburtstag,* AThANT 59, 307–24.

J. Bergmann, H. Ringgren, and H. Seebaß (1973), "*bär,*" *ThWAT* 1, 592–608.

J. Coppens (1981), "L'Élu et les élus dans les Écritures saintes et les Écrits de Qoumrân," *EthL* 57, 120–24.

P. Beauchamp (1995), "Élection et Universel dans la Bible," *Études* 382, 373–84.

Vittorio Fusco

See also **Covenant; Israel; Messianism/Messiah; People of God; Predestination; Universalism**

Christ/Christology

The term *Christ* (Hebrew *mâshîach,* messiah*; Greek *christos,* anointed) recapitulates the confession of *Christian* faith. The whole body of titles attributed to Jesus of Nazareth are summed up in this word, which has semantically subsumed all other titles that indicate the identity of Jesus (Lord, Son of God*, and so on) and has imposed itself in the designation of the one called Jesus Christ. This is so true that in Antioch, the "disciples of the way" of Christ were called Christians (Acts 11:26). Later, Ignatius of Antioch invented the neologism "Christianity (*Ad Magn.* 10. 3, SC 10 *bis,* 105).

For this obvious reason, many other articles in this encyclopedia take up in one way or another the subject of Jesus in history* and in Christian dogma*: the Son of the Father* in the Trinity, the Son* of man, the Servant, the Lamb* of God. They deal with his "mysteries" (Incarnation*, Passion*, Resurrection*) as well as with the development of Christology (particularly on the basis of the first seven ecumenical councils*). On the other hand, the primary motivation for Christology lies in the doctrine of salvation. This article, devoted principally to the human-divine identity of Christ, sets out a synthesis and refers throughout to relevant specialized articles.

1. Genesis and Development of the Christology of the New Testament

Between Jesus and Christ lies the space of the confession of faith, "Jesus is the Christ," in which the verb was soon replaced by the juxtaposition of subject and attribute. For the disciples of Jesus, this confession is the fruit of the Easter mystery*: "This Jesus God raised up, and of that we all are witnesses... God has made him both Lord and Christ, this Jesus whom you crucified" (Acts 2:32–36). The proclamation of the Resurrection has been called the "cradle of Christology" (Schnackenburg). But for the disciples it came at the conclusion of a period of companionship with Jesus and inaugurated a broad movement of reflection that made his identity explicit.

a) From Jesus to the Confession of Christ. The Gospels retrace for us the development of the faith* of the disciples through the pre-Easter ministry* of Jesus. Although the Gospels clearly have a theological purpose, they nevertheless allow us to grasp some of the concrete experiences of history (the historical Jesus*) that do not depend on that crystallization of faith provoked by the Resurrection. Jesus met men whom he called to follow him and to live with him. Everything took place within the framework of a life lived in common. The human identity of Jesus is an evident fact that leaves no room for doubt. He is a being of flesh and blood, who eats and drinks, who is capable of joy and sadness, of tenderness and anger. It was on the basis of the speech and behavior of this man that the disciples were invited to recognize that there was more in him than in Jonah or Solomon (Lk 11:31), that he was more than just a man. Indeed, this man speaks with a unique authority and not like the scribes (Mk 1:21–27). He proclaims that the kingdom* of God is at hand, as his own presence indicates. He speaks in parables* that are figurative expressions of the event inaugurated by his presence.

His behavior is in total harmony with his speech: he says what he does, and he does what he says. He proclaims the mercy* of God for sinners, and he shares their table. He gives concrete expression to the salvation he brings by performing miracles* that are an anticipatory sign of the salvation of the body. His speech is inhabited by an unprecedented claim: to forgive sins* (Mt 9:1–9; Lk 7:36–50), to fulfill and even to correct the law* of Moses through his own teaching (Mt 5:21–48, 19:8). He calls on people to leave everything to follow him (Mt 10:37). He lays claim to a unique relationship to God (Mt 11:27; Lk 10:22; Mk 13:32), whom he calls his own Father (*Abba;* Mk 14:36) with words that no Jew before him had dared use. In the pivotal scene at Caesarea, Jesus questions his disciples about his own identity: "But who do you say that I am?" (Mt 16:15). Peter*, on behalf of the other disciples, answers by expressing his dawning faith: "You are the Christ." Matthew completes this first confession by adding "the Son of the living God," so that the primitive Church*'s confession of paschal faith* makes explicit Peter's act of messianic faith. Jesus authenticates this word of faith as a word of revelation* (Guillet 1971).

In the exercise of his ministry, Jesus attracts opposition and threats. He goes up to Jerusalem*, where he knows that death awaits him, just as it awaited many prophets*. The danger and the final ordeal do not cause him to deviate from his mission*. His life has been an existence for his Father and for His brothers, a "pro-existence" (Schürmann). The same will be true of his death, the meaning of which he himself provides by instituting the meal of the Eucharist*. His death on the cross (Passion*) is the preeminent scandal, one that disperses the group of Twelve. Apparently, everything is against Jesus: the Jews and the Romans (the pagans) have joined together to defeat him. His friends desert him, and even God does not answer his cry of abandonment (Mt 27:46). What, then, is left of his claim to be the "Son"? However, the centurion overseeing the execution confesses, "Truly this man was the Son of God!" (Mk 15:39) or "Certainly this man was innocent" (Lk 23:47). In his manner of dying, Jesus gave a sign of his true identity. But it will take the Resurrection and all the reflection to which it gives rise for the scandal to be overcome and changed into an emblem of glory.

It is generally agreed today that it is inappropriate to look to the lifetime of Jesus for the use of titles explicitly expressing his identity. The pre-Easter ministry of Jesus was a period of *implicit* Christology. His identity was already revealed at that time through his speech and behavior. The disciples groped for ways of expressing that identity by using various terms from the Old Testament that they adjusted to Jesus' in order to articulate the excess of meaning that they saw in him. At first, they probably understood him as the "eschatological prophet" (Schillebeekx), that is, not only the last of the prophets but a prophet unlike the others, the "definitive" or "absolute" prophet. The term *Messiah* (Christ) and the title "Son of David" were used for him, as evidenced by the inscription on the cross. But the Gospels never put this term in the Jesus' own mouth. He maintained a certain reticence on the subject because of the political and temporal ambiguity to which it might give rise. Jesus truly accepted it only in the scene of his trial before Caiaphas (Mk 14:61), when the ambiguity is definitively resolved. On the other hand, "by always placing the expression Son of Man on the lips of Jesus to identify himself, the Aramaic-speaking Christian community surprisingly recalls the *I* of Jesus, and with such frequency that it can only be explained by the shock produced on Jesus' own disciples" (Ch. Perrot). As for the title "Son of God," to the extent that its use goes back to a pre-Easter practice, it is closely united with the prophecies of the Old Testament because it had been applied to the people of Israel* (Ex 4:23ff.). Paradoxically, in the light of future developments, in these early times it is employed less than the expression Son of Man. The claim to call oneself "the Son" is more important than the specific title (Kasper).

b) From the Christology of the Resurrection to the Christology of the Incarnation. The point of departure for the explicit Christology of the New Testament is the Resurrection of Jesus, which sets the divine "seal" on his pre-Easter journey and confirms all his claims. From now on, the scandal of the cross will assume meaning. The disciples can proudly proclaim the Resurrection of the Crucified One: "Christ died for our sins in accordance with the Scriptures... he was buried,... he was raised on the third day in accordance with the Scriptures" (1 Cor 15:3f.). This event is immediately given a threefold interpretation: 1) Jesus has been exalted (Acts 2:33) and now sits in his humanity at the right hand of God in his glory*, which means on an equal footing with him. 2) The Resurrection confirms Jesus' claim to divine filiation (Ps 2:7, quoted in this context by Acts 13:33 and Heb 1:5). God has definitively revealed himself in Jesus (Pannenberg). The term Son of God thenceforth takes on the strong meaning that Christian dogma will always recognize. 3) Finally, the Resurrection inaugurates the time of eschatology*: "If Jesus is risen, it is already the end of the world" (Pannenberg). The soteriological dimension of the Resurrection is also emphasized: Jesus died "for all" (2 Cor 5:15), and raised "for our justification" (Rom 4:25), and risen, he has bestowed the Holy* Spirit. The Ascension scene recapitulates in its own symbolism these ever more lofty assertions: of Jesus of Nazareth it is said that he has been "declared to be the Son of God in power according to the Spirit of holiness by his resurrection" (Rom 1:4). The subject is Jesus considered in his humanity; the divine titles are presented as complementary attributes. The "lofty titles" conferred on Jesus are, in effect, interpretations of his identity. The Christian community confesses as the Son of God one who called himself "the Son" in an absolute sense and who behaved in a filial manner to the point of death. This is what contemporary theology* has vulgarized with the expression "Christology from below," or primitive Christology, an already complete Christology that could not be repressed by subsequent developments. It is not a Christology of "adoption" of the man Jesus as Son of God because the one who was thus declared with power was already "his Son" (Rom 1:3).

On this foundation, which contains within itself all future developments of Christology, the reflection of the faith of the disciples, as it is set forth in the New Testament, was to effectuate a movement going from the end of Jesus' journey to its beginning. "Son" is itself a term of origin. Who was this risen one, exalted on the right hand of the Father, in the eyes of God "before" his manifestation in our history? What meaning ought to be given to the title "Son" that he so strongly claimed for himself? This led to two kinds of reflection.

1) On one hand, there was a rereading of the ministry and death of Jesus in the definitive light of his resurrection. In compositional terms, the writers of the Gospels intended to testify that the Jesus with whom they had lived was already the one whom he claimed to be and that his resurrection fully revealed the Son of God: "The beginning of the gospel of Jesus Christ, the Son of God" (Mk 1:1). Many Gospel scenes are therefore constructed as proclamations (kerygma) that invite an explicit confession of faith. The scenes of revelation, such as the Baptism* of Jesus and the Transfiguration, play an important role in this respect. The manifestations of the power of Jesus are also emphasized, creating a tension with his condition as "Servant." In the same perspective, the accounts of Jesus' childhood in Matthew and Luke, which are really prefaces added to narratives that began with his public life, give a sign of his divine origin by converging in the same affirmation of his virginal conception (Mary*).
2) On the other hand, the vision of faith seeks to fathom the origin of Jesus before his manifestation in the world. Pauline* Christology, for its part, describes this vast movement, which begins with the experience of the Risen One on the road to Damascus, then focuses on the mystery of the cross and opens out into a Christology of mission: "God sent forth his Son" (Gal 4:4); "sending his own Son in the likeness of sinful

flesh" (Rom 8:3). Then, in a series of hymns, some of which may have had a liturgical origin, Paul inscribes the event of Jesus in a great parabola that comes from God and returns to God. The hymn of Philippians 2:6–11 thus describes the journey of abasement (kenosis*) and glorification of the one who at the outset "was in the form of God." The preexistence of Christ is thereby assumed. The hymn of Colossians 1:15–20 broadens the theme by showing that the primacy of Christ in the order of redemption and reconciliation corresponds to and has its basis in his primacy in the order of creation*: "all things were created through him and for him" (Col 1:16). Paul applies to the person of Christ what the Old Testament said of the Wisdom* that was present alongside God at the creation of the world and that is mysteriously personified in certain biblical passages (Prv 8:22–31; Jb 28; Bar 3:9–4:6; Eccl 24; Wis 7). But the identification is not complete because the divine reality present in Christ goes beyond that of Wisdom. The hymn of Ephesians 1:3–14 goes back to describe the purpose that God foresaw in Christ from before the creation of the world. Christ, in whom the entire universe is to be "united" (Eph 1:10), is already the heart of the Father's plan in the original mystery of the divine life. The same epistle contains a passage that shows the inversion between the movement of discovery and that of exposition, an inversion that accomplishes the passage from a Christology from below to a Christology from above: "In saying 'He ascended,' what does it mean but that he had also descended into the lower parts of the earth? He who descended is the one who also ascended far above all the heavens, that he might fill all things" (Eph 4:9f.).

The Ascension, which was first in the order of manifestation, turns out in fact to be second in the complete order of realization. It was with the Ascension that the quest of faith began to ask itself about the descent; the normal exposition of the mystery begins with the origin and goes on to the end. The Epistle to the Hebrews—taking account of its particular status in the Pauline corpus—presents the Son, in whom God has spoken to us in these last days and "whom he appointed the heir of all things" and also as the one "through whom also he created the world," "the radiance of the glory of God, and the exact imprint of his nature" (1:2–3). Here too, "his glorification reveals the profound being of Jesus; it leads to a recognition of His preexisting filiation" (A. Vanhoye).

The Gospel of John is shot through with the question of the identity of Jesus: "Who are you?" (4:10, 5:12f., 8:25, 12:34), "Whence have you come?" (3:8, 7:27f.), and "Where are you going?" (8:14–22, 13:26, 14:5, 16:5). Jesus himself knows "where I came from and where I am going" (Jn 8:14). But it is the movement of his existence that accomplishes this revelation, for "no one has ascended into heaven except he who descended from heaven, the Son of Man" (Jn 3:13); and again, "Then what if you were to see the Son of Man ascending to where he was before?" (6:62); "And now, Father, glorify me in your own presence with the glory that I had with you before the world existed" (17:5). "The return reveals the origin, the ascent the descent, the glory the Son of man and the foundation of the Kingdom*, the return home the original home" (Van den Bussche). The prologue of John is the last word of the Christology of the New Testament. It brings us back up in God to that absolute beginning of the one who *was* both with God and God himself, the divine and creating Word* that was made flesh. This definitive formulation sums up the movement of a Christology descending from above.

This movement has been discussed as a "projection" of the end onto the beginning (Thüsing). This projection is not psychological but rather "logical" and "intrinsically necessary" (Jüngel) and even "ontological" by virtue of the biblical principle, "What is true of the end must also already determine the beginning" (Pannenberg, Thüsing). What concerns God is from always to always. Rigorously speaking, one does "not become" God: Jesus was manifested according to what he had always been. The idea of preexistence was drawn from the eschatological assertions themselves: the Omega and the Alpha coincide (Hengel, Perrot). This idea had many attestations in the Bible (Is 41:4, 44:6; Rev 1:8, 21:6, 22:13); we meet it again in the Epistle of Barnabas (6, 13; SC 172, p. 125).

2. Development of Christological Dogma

The New Testament's identification of Jesus as Christ, Lord, and Son of God was strongly affirmed in the earliest confessions of faith during the period of the Apostolic Fathers. Differing formulas coexisted—first those of the authors and then those of the churches. The ecclesiastical symbols resulted from the encounter between two types of confession of faith: the Trinitarian confession and the strictly christological confession that reflected the kerygmatic discourse of Acts (*see* Acts 2). On one hand, the second Trinitarian article came to include the christological titulary of Jesus; on the other, the christological sequence became attached to the second article.

In these early days, from Clement of Rome to Justin,

the Christology of the Church Fathers recapitulated the development of New Testament Christology. Very quickly, however, the "descendant" point of view came to dominate the "ascendant" view, though both remained present. In one sense, the last word of New Testament Christology—"The Word is made flesh"—became the first word of patristic Christology, linked with another text, Philippians 2:6–11.

a) Pre-Nicaean Christology. The confession of Christ was equally provocative for the Jewish world and the pagan world of the time in three ways: it proclaimed the divinity of a man, which seemed to call monotheism* into question; it claimed that salvation came through a man who had suffered the most degrading corporal punishment; and it spoke of immaculate conception, which reminded both cultures of mythological stories of a dubiously sexual kind. Thus, it was soon attacked by both Jews and pagans (Justin). The first conflict in Christian circles questioned, for various reasons, the humanity of Christ; it arose in particular from the Gnostics* and their Docetism*. The glorification of the resurrected Christ in the divine realm made it seem unbelievable that the Word of God had been present in a human form afflicted with so many humiliations. Docetism raised again the idea that the earthly manifestation of Jesus was simply an apparition, his flesh was illusory, he had received nothing from the Virgin, and it was not he who suffered on the cross.

In the face of this serious conflict concerning the humanity of Jesus, the ecclesiastical reaction was quite clear. On the first stirrings of docetism, Ignatius of Antioch stressed the confession of "Jesus Christ of the lineage of David, [son] of Mary, who was *truly* born, who ate and drank, who was *truly* persecuted by Pontius Pilate, who was *truly* crucified and died [...] who was also *truly* resurrected from among the dead" (*Aux Trall.* 9, 1; SC 10 *bis,* p. 119). The battle against gnosticism and docetism would continue to be waged tirelessly by Irenaeus*, Tertullian*, Clement of Alexandria, and Origen*. Against these tendencies, Irenaeus was the first to articulate, with great realism, a Christology in which a true God becomes a true man (*Adv. Haer.* III, 21, 4), "recapitulating" in this act the entire history of salvation, from beginning to end, in order to bring it to fruition (III, 23, 1, etc.). He emphasized in particular the symbolic parallel between the creation of Adam*, drawn from virgin earth by the hands of God, and the generation of Jesus, formed in the womb of a virgin by an act of God (III, 21, 10). Tertullian, in his turn, would be a vehement defender of the reality of the flesh of Christ, flesh that is "the joint of salvation" (*Res.* 6; PL 2, 802). This argument for the generation of Jesus was intended to conserve the human truth of his earthly journey, in particular the reality of his death and resurrection. However, there was an inverse temptation to reduce the mystery of Christ by making Jesus an "adopted" man, a divinity dwelling temporarily among humans. It was for this view, known as adoptionism*, that Paul of Samosata was condemned.

b) The Christology of the Great Councils. In the early fourth century, Christology entered a new phase, which we may term the conciliary phase, between the first and second Nicaean* councils. (Each of the seven councils* is discussed in its own entry in this work, so it will suffice here to summarize the dialectical movement that continued through them.) Arius questioned the divinity of the person of Jesus of Nazareth on the ground that a God who is one could not undergo change and suffering. The Council of Nicaea affirmed the divine, eternal, and consubstantial* filiation of the man Jesus. The movement in response, matching that of the question, goes from the human to the divine, in an ascendant perspective. At Nicaea the confession of the divinity of Christ was the object of a distinction that on the one hand translated it into the terms of Greek thought and on the other reinforced its radicality. This definition, connected to the innovations drawn from the conceptual vocabulary of Greek philosophy into the text of the Creed, provoked numerous troubles in the East that were not really resolved until the First Council of Constantinople*. But in the interim, Apollinarius, a Nicaean convinced of the divinity of Christ, rejected the idea that he had a real human soul. His thinking was rooted in the schema Word-flesh *(Logos-sarx),* which arose in Alexandria, but in a sense that excluded the soul: the Word occupied in Christ the place of the human spirit, will, and liberty*. The motivation was both religious (the divine Word cannot coexist with a truly responsible and free human spirit) and speculative (two "complete" realities, divinity and humanity, cannot form a real unity). But Christ then became a kind of theological monster, for human flesh separated from a human spirit does not constitute a human being. The scriptural and rational arguments of the Fathers* of the Church stated the objection that the unique mediator must be as completely a man as he is perfectly God. Up to that point, the temptation to reduce the mystery of Christ had elicited significant clarifications concerning the completeness of his humanity (flesh, soul, and spirit) and the full truth of his divinity. With these points thenceforth beyond challenge, debate shifted to the manner of the union between the Word of God and his humanity.

In the fifth century, as part of a backlash following

the definition of Nicaea, the problem took its point of departure not from the man Jesus but from the Word of God. The question became one about the modality of the incarnation or humanization of the eternal Son insofar as it conditioned the constant ontological constitution of his simultaneously divine and human being. In the way he understood the "conjunction" between the divinity and the humanity of Christ, Nestorius established a distance between the two, to the point of rejecting the traditional communication between idioms*. If the Word underwent a second generation in the flesh, Mary is in a sense the true "mother of God"; the Word was the subject of the Passion, and Christ died in a true sense. Hence, the Council of Ephesus* (431), giving canonical status to a letter that Cyril* of Alexandria had addressed to Nestorius, affirmed, in light of the rule of faith of Nicaea, that the eternal Son of God himself conformed to generation in the flesh by reason of His action of persisting *according to the hypostasis,* that is, not as a reality external to him but as something affecting His very person. What occurred at that moment implicated the concrete unity of the Word and His humanity for His entire existence. Underlying the debate on dogma at Ephesus, there was a persistent tension between the two schools of Alexandria* and Antioch, the first thinking according to the schema Word-flesh and the second supported by the schema Word-man *(logos-anthrôpos).* It was not until the act of union of 433 that the two schools were reconciled in the text of a christological confession that leaned more toward Antioch and became the matrix for the definition of Chalcedon.

But, although the Council of Ephesus clearly brought out the *unity* of Christ, it remained vague on the distinction remaining in him between divinity and humanity. The monk Eutyches, trapped by what was not yet clarified in the language of Cyril, intended to confess only a single nature after the union; but he understood the matter in a superficial way and asserted a fusion or confusion between humanity and divinity, as though the former had been lost in the latter like a drop of water in the ocean. After the vicissitudes of the robbery at Ephesus (449), the Council of Chalcedon* (451) received the dogmatic letter of Pope Leo to Flavian and composed a new confession of christological faith that clearly affirmed the unity of the person of Christ "in two natures." It thus emphasized *distinction.*

Unity and *distinction* remained the two poles of the debate on the interpretation of Chalcedon. This council, seen by some in the East as a return to Nestorianism, provoked the schism* of some churches attached to the Monophysitic language of Cyril. The emperors sought to restore the religious unity of their subjects by intervening with a series of dogmatic edicts. Summoned by Emperor Justinian in an atmosphere of violent conflict with Pope* Vigilius, the Second Council of Constantinople* (553) attempted to win over the Severian Monophysites to the letter of Chalcedon by proposing an interpretation of Chalcedon in the light of the doctrine proclaimed at Ephesus, that is, by emphasizing the *unity* of Christ. "In two natures" had to be understood "solely from a conceptual standpoint" *(tè theôria monè)* and not as positing the two natures existing separately. The communication between idioms was illustrated by an extreme formulation: "He who was crucified in the flesh . . . is true God, Lord of glory, and one of the Holy Trinity*" (can. 10).

In the seventh century, the controversy over the interpretation of Chalcedon sprang up again. Intending to emphasize the unity of Christ, two Eastern patriarchs, after proposing the ambiguous doctrine of a single "theandric" operation of Christ, won Pope Honorius over to the doctrine of a single will in Christ. The difficulty raised earlier by Apollinarius resurfaced: how could two wills not oppose one another? At the heart of the debate was the interpretation of the scene of Christ's agony. The First Lateran Council of 649, in formulations composed by Maximus* the Confessor, asserted that there were two wills in Christ, as a very function of His two natures, because the will is a faculty of nature. The Third Council of Constantinople*, in a new interpretation of Chalcedon emphasizing *distinction* this time, confirmed these assertions. The last council with a clearly christological program was Nicaea* II. After the iconoclastic crisis that raged in the East in the eighth century, it affirmed the legitimacy of the cult of images* on the foundation of the incarnation because the Word of God, the perfect image of the Father, had made himself visible in the Christ, who could say, "Whoever has seen me has seen the Father" (Jn 14:9). With this council, the strictly dogmatic development of Christology can be considered complete. Subsequent councils made only brief allusions to christological dogma, most frequently to repeat past affirmations. The latest council, Vatican* II, established its anthropology (GS) on the mystery of Christ with the intent of showing that this mystery is the truth of man.

3. Medieval Christology

The Middle Ages thus inherited as a given the christological dogma developed in the patristic period. The contribution of the scholastic theologians, whose intention was to shift theological discussion from *authorities* to *reasons,* was to turn the results of previous work into speculative questions. Thus, from the Council of Frankfurt in 794 to Thomas* Aquinas, three opinions presented by Peter Lombard vied for support among writers on the question of the mode of union of the divine person to the humanity of Christ (adoptionism*). Thomas held the opinion that the man Jesus Christ is made up of two natures and that he is a single person, simple before the incarnation and "compound" thereafter, an opinion that became something more than an opinion because he considered that the other two had been condemned (*ST* IIIa, q. 2, a. 6).

Another question was posed along the same metaphysical lines: does the humanity of Christ possess an existence distinct from that of the Word (its own *esse*)? The condemned opinions said yes. But is it possible in light of the only valid opinion? Does the unity of *subsistence* recognized in the two natures of Christ necessarily imply their unity of *existence (esse)?* Thomas opted for the numerical unity of the act of existing in Christ. But later, considering that the humanity of Christ must not be deprived of an act that seemed to belong to the completeness of nature, Scholastic* theology tended to maintain the thesis of two *esse* in Christ, sometimes recognizing its opposition to Thomas, sometimes trying to reconcile the two theses. The documents, recently reconsidered (Patfoort), show that the angelic doctor constantly professed the unity of existence in Christ, with the exception of one passage indicating a moment of hesitation.

Another major medieval debate concerned the motives for the incarnation. Early on, Anselm* of Canterbury wrote a work titled *Why did God become man?* The question was later posed in these terms: Was the incarnation exclusively the consequence of man's sin (the Thomist position), or did it belong to the creative plan of God (the Scotist position; *see* incarnation*). Nor did Thomas neglect to treat at length the mysteries of the life of Christ with a concrete perspective.

The Middle Ages was also involved in thorough reflection about the knowledge of Christ, which was not called into question in Catholic theology until about a century ago (Christ's* Consciousness). Throughout the medieval period, popular spirituality and piety developed great devotion to the humanity of Christ, as illustrated in the hymn attributed to Bernard* of Clairvaux, *Jesu, dulcis memoria.*

4. Modern Period

The Christology of Luther* remained basically that of the ancient tradition*, even though he criticized its excessively speculative orientation. Taking its inspiration from Alexandria, it strongly emphasized the divinity of the Mediator who had taken on as a man the path of kenosis. For Luther, Christ is above all the Savior, and the *solus Christus* is inseparable from the *sola fide.* In his interpretation of salvation, did he overemphasize the role of the divinity of Christ at the expense of His humanity (Congar)? Although certain passages point in this direction, the humanity of Christ, in Luther's view, plays its full role for our salvation (Lienhard).

The Christology of Calvin derives more from Antioch, is sometimes close to the formulations of Saint Leo I, and emphasizes the humanity of Jesus: The incarnation is the place of mediation in which God and man are both different and in dynamic relationship (Gisel). The principle of the *extra calvinisticum,* whereby the incarnate Lord never ceased to have his existence and his truth "also outside the flesh," was at the origin of a polemic with Lutheran theologians, particularly with reference to the sacraments*. This thesis seemed to call into question the unity of the two natures of Christ. According to Calvin, this unity is dynamic but is not a fusion; he rejected any deification of the humanity of Jesus and all "Christolatry" (Gisel).

One of the strong points of early modern Protestant scholasticism was the development of the doctrine of the three offices *(officia)* or functions of Christ—prophet, priest, and king—which originated, it seems, with A. Osiander (1498–1552). By reason of his human-divine person, Christ is in fact our only doctor and master (Mt 23:8ff.), he is an eternal priest of the order of Melchizedek (Ps 110:1), and he is the king who reigns eternally over the house of Jacob (Lk 1:32ff.). These three functions develop the idea of anointment present in the term Christ. In the Old Testament the king and the priest were anointed with oil, while anointment by the Spirit established the ministry of the prophets. Calvin made this a central theme of the Reformation by developing the doctrine in *The Christian Institutes* and had it introduced into catechisms. The schema of the three offices of Christ served to systematize the doctrine of salvation. It is noteworthy that it was adopted by Catholic theology in the course of the 19th century and used in ecclesiology*. It is found again in Vatican* II to express the three functions of the people of God (by reason of the royal and universal priesthood*) and also the three truly ministerial functions of the ordained ministry (*LG* 25–27).

5. The Christology of the East

The Orthodox East (Orthodoxy*) has always remained faithful to the Christology of the fathers of the church and of the ancient councils, which it rereads in the light of the teachings of the synthesizers John of Damascus, Maximus the Confessor, Pseudo-Dionysius*, and later Gregory* Palamas. This Christology has remained "from above": it is the Christology of the incarnate Word, God made man. But it remains wary of certain imbalances because of Monophysite tendencies that leave little room for the human. It likes to place to the fore the human-divine *theandric energy* of Christ as well as the *synergy* of His two natures. Without neglecting the kenosis of Christ or the mystery of the cross, the East emphasizes the resurrection. The Jerusalem church that the West calls the Church of the Holy Sepulchre is for the East the Church of the Resurrection *(anastasis);* in soteriology, it emphasizes the divinization of man by the humanity of the Son of God. Orthodoxy respects the depth of the mystery and does not question the how of it. Christ is above all the very icon of God among men: "The humanity of Christ is the human image of His divinity, the icon of Christ reveals the mystery of unity, and depicts the theandric image" (Evdokimov).

Thus, the Orthodox East is very reticent toward the developments of Christology in the West, criticizing them for falling into a human Monophysitism: "The balance of Christological theandrism is broken" (Evdokimov). This perplexity is also felt toward the contemporary procedures of interpretation of the Scriptures in the West.

6. Philosophical Christology in the West

The Enlightenment of the 18th century produced a major rationalist critique of the dogmatic image of Christ presented by the churches. Philosophy* opposed to this image an interpretation of Jesus in the light of reason*, which exalts the exemplary quality of His humanity. Jesus is thus the "Wise Man of Nazareth," the "master of the human race," the preeminent philosopher," who goes to His death "more nobly than Socrates," a "martyr of truth* and virtue*" (F.X. Arnold). This is the Jesus of Herder. Kant*, in *Religion within the Limits of Reason Alone* (1793), presents the first "philosophical Christology": Jesus is the exemplary divine man, the idea and the image of whom Kant deduces from the ideal embedded in our reason. The role that philosophy then gave to itself was to translate the meaning of revealed representations into the language of reason. Even though, in the view of Christian faith, this enterprise is reductive, the image of Jesus that it offers is not without grandeur.

Today, philosophers and theologians are conscious of a major phenomenon: for three centuries the philosophy of Western Europe has made the person of Christ a central matter of its concern. This is obvious in Hegel* but is also found in many others: in Europe, Spinoza, Leibniz*, Fichte, Hölderlin and Schelling*, Schleiermacher*, Kierkegaard*, Nietzsche*, and in France alone, Pascal*, Maine de Biran, Rousseau, Bergson, Blondel*, Simone Weil, and many others. With diversified approaches, philosophical Christology is an investigation of the *Idea Christi,* that is, of the manifestation of the Absolute in the contingency of history*. Christology sheds light on the cardinal notions of philosophy: "subjectivity and intersubjectivity, the transcendental, temporality, corporeality, consciousness, death, and so on, all realities that Christ made his own by being incarnate" (Tilliette).

The 19th century approached the problem of Christ not from the point of view of reason but from a historical perspective. It saw the beginning of the opposition between the "historical Jesus" and the "Christ of faith," which still influenced the first half of the 20th century (Jesus*, Historical).

7. The Christological Movement of the Second Half of the 20th Century

It is generally agreed that the contemporary christological movement began in 1951, that is, on the 15th centenary of the definition of Chalcedon. At the origin of this movement lies the work of Rudolf Bultmann* on the Protestant side and of Karl Rahner* on the Catholic. Adopting a view opposite to that of the liberal theology of the 19th century, for both exegetical and theological reasons, Bultmann deems that we can know almost nothing about Jesus. What counts is not Christ according to the flesh but the preached Christ, who is the Lord and whose word "calls out" to me today. The dogmatic problem posed by Bultmann lies in the distance he sets between *fact* and *meaning.* For his part, in 1954, Rahner proposed a program for the renewal of Christology: to rethink the relationship between classic Christology and biblical evidence; to complete ontological Christology with an existential Christology; to question the definition of Chalcedon, considered more as a beginning than an end; and to develop a transcendental Christology, that is, to deduce the conditions of possibility in man for the credibility* of Christ. Since then, a number of Protestant (Tillich*, Pannenberg, Moltmann, Jüngel) and Catholic (von Balthasar*, Rahner, Kasper, Schoonenberg, Schillebeeckx, Forte, Gonzalez de Cardedal, Moingt, Hünermann) theologians have produced works of Christology.

Let us simply mention a few dominant characteristics. A primary concern is that of verification: Christology can no longer be built on the basis of the confession of faith and conciliar definitions without in turn grounding that confession in the history and the fate of Jesus (Pannenberg, Kasper). In other words, the questions of fundamental* theology must be integrated into the exposition of dogmatic theology. The second concern, related to the first, has to do with the movement of Christology. Whereas classic Christology took its immediate point of departure from the incarnation, contemporary theology, faithful in this respect to the New Testament, generally gives priority to Christology "from below" or ascending Christology, that is, consideration of the man Jesus confessed as Lord, Christ, and Son of God (Pannenberg, Küng). "Christology from above" or descending Christology, then, takes over in a second stage, in the light of the writings of Paul and John. For the same reason, the contemporary christological movement has carried out a massive return to Scripture (in particular with Schillebeeckx) while respecting the difference between implicit and explicit Christology and the originality of the different traditions about Christ. Christology has thus displaced its traditional center of gravity from the incarnation to the Easter mystery. It takes into consideration the history of Jesus and articulates the relationship between history and faith in light of the correspondence between the earthly Jesus and the glorified Christ (Thüsing, Kasper). The most recent essays give their full weight to the narratives themselves, with the effects of meaning that are particular to them. From the preoccupation with history, there is thus a movement toward a Christology of narrative*. Many writers read the revelation of the Trinitarian mystery in the cross of Jesus (Balthasar, Moltmann, Jüngel).

In this context, the difficult question of the consciousness and the knowledge of Jesus, for long stymied as a result of the modernist crisis, could be taken up again, particularly in the contributions of Rahner, who at first suggested a distinction between "immediate vision," expressing the immediate relationship of Jesus to His Father, and strictly "beatific*" vision, the latter being in no way a prerequisite for the former. Then he provided an account of the way in which the phenomenon of hypostatic union could become in Jesus a lived experience by placing it at the primordial, "transcendental" pole of His consciousness and not at the categorizing, thematic, and objective pole (Christ's* Consciousness).

Let us finally mention the originality of the Christology of liberation (liberation* theology) in Latin America. It is characterized by the interest shown in a historical Jesus who shared human suffering and contradiction in order to proclaim a kingdom of justice* and of "liberation." Faith in Jesus requires not only orthodoxy but also "orthopraxis," that is, "correctness of action in the light of Christ" (Boff). This Christology has been suspected of revolutionary and Marxist deviation because of its manner of promoting the struggle of the poor for their liberation. Justice nevertheless requires that we recognize that the divinity of the Risen One is in no way obscured.

8. Christology and Cosmos; Christ and Other Religions

By the middle of the century, a reaction against a Christology that was too exclusively redemptive raised again the question of the cosmic dimension of Christ (Teilhard de Chardin). This perspective was supported by the patristic movement, which rediscovered the ancient Christologies of Irenaeus and Tertullian, in which Christ appears both as the creator of the cosmos* and as its center and its goal. The Christocentrism of the creation has become a common assumption, present in the documents of Vatican II.

The question raised most recently with great intensity is that of the universality of Christ with respect to the salvation of all humankind. There is more and more awareness that Christianity is a religious tradition among many others. In the perspective of interreligious dialogue, can we consider these other religions as "ways of salvation," and in what sense can we do so without calling into question the uniqueness of Christ Mediator, who presents himself as "the way"? Three positions have been taken on this question (J. Dupuis): exclusivism (there is no salvation outside the Church* that professes Jesus Christ), inclusivism (the uniqueness of the person of Christ is the constituent and universal element of salvation), and "pluralism" (a theocentrism in which the person of Christ is considered either normative or not normative). The last position, which speaks of a "Copernican revolution," constitutes a radical challenge to Christian convictions. The meaning of these debates is still open.

• **a) General Works**

J. Feiner, M. Löhrer (Ed.) (1969–70), *MySal* III/1 and 2: *Das Christus Ereignis* (*Mysterium Salutis: Dogmatique de l'histoire du salut,* vols. 9–13, 1972–74), especially R. Schnackenburg, "Christologie des NT" (III/1) and H. Urs von Balthasar, "Mysterium Paschale" (III/2).

B. Lauret, F. Refoulé (Ed.) (1982), *Initiation à la pratique de la théologie,* II: *Dogmatique* 1, Paris (3rd Ed. 1988).

b) Christology of the New Testament

L. Cerfaux (1951), *Le Christ dans la théologie de saint Paul,* Paris.

V. Taylor (1953), *The Names of Jesus,* London.

O. Cullmann (1957), *Die Christologie des Neuen Testaments,* Tübingen.

F. Hahn (1963), *Christologische Hoheitstitel,* Göttingen.

P. Bonnard (1966), *La Sagesse en personne annoncée et venue: Jésus-Christ,* Paris.

A. Feuillet (1966), *Le Christ, Sagesse de Dieu d'après les épîtres pauliniennes,* Paris.

P. Lamarche (1966), *Christ vivant,* Paris.

A. Vanhoye (1969), *Situation du Christ. Hébreux 1–2,* Paris.

J. Guillet (1971), *Jésus devant sa vie et sa mort,* Paris (2nd Ed. 1991).

J. Dupont (Ed.) (1975), *Jésus aux origines de la christologie,* Louvain (2nd Ed. 1989).

M. Hengel (1975), *Der Sohn Gottes,* Tübingen (*Jésus, Fils de Dieu,* 1977).

H. Schürmann (1977), *Comment Jésus a-t-il vécu sa mort?,* Paris.

Commission biblique pontificale (1984), *Bible et christologie,* Cité du Vatican.

J.A. Fitzmyer (1986), *Scripture and Christology: A Statement of the Biblical Commission with a Commentary,* New York.
B. Sesboüé (1994), *Pédagogie du Christ,* Paris.

c) Dogmatic Development

M. Schmaus et al. (Ed.) (1965–80), *HDG* III: *Christologie-Soteriologie-Mariologie.*
A. Grillmeier (1975), *Mit ihm und in ihm: Christologische Forschungen und Prospektiven,* Fribourg-Basel-Vienna.
A. Grillmeier (1979, 1986, 1989, 1990), *Jesus der Christus im Glauben der Kirche* I, (2nd Ed. 1990), II/1 (2nd Ed. 1991), II/2, II/4, Fribourg-Basel-Vienna (*Le Christ dans la tradition chrétienne,* CFi 72 (I), 154 (II/1), 172 (II/2), 192 (II/4).

d) Scolasticism

P. Kaiser (1968), *Die Gott-Menschliche Einigung in Christus als Problem der spekulativen Theologie seit der Scholastik,* Munich.
F. Ruello (1987), *La christologie de Thomas d'Aquin,* Paris.
E.-H. Wéber (1988), *Le Christ selon saint Thomas d'Aquin,* Paris.

e) Reformation Christology

M. Lienhard (1973), *Luther témoin de Jésus-Christ,* Paris.
N. Blough (1984), *Christologie anabaptiste: Pilgram Marpeck et l'humanité du Christ,* Geneva.
P. Gisel (1990), *Le Christ de Calvin,* Paris.
M. Lienhard (1991), *Au cœur de la foi de Luther: Jésus-Christ,* Paris.
N. Blough et al. (1992), *Jésus-Christ aux marges de la Réforme,* Paris.
P. Gisel (1995), "Jésus (images de)," *Encyclopédie du protestantisme,* Geneva-Paris, 750–85.

f) Orthodox Christology

P. Evdokimov (1959), *L'Orthodoxie,* Neuchâtel-Paris.
P.N. Trembelas (1959), *Dogmatique de l'Église orthodoxe catholique,* vol. 2, Chèvetogne.
J. Meyendorff (1969), *Le Christ dans la théologie byzantine,* Paris.

g) Philosophical Christology

W. Schönfelder (1949), *Die Philosophen und Jesus Christus,* Hamburg.
S. Breton (1954), *La passion du Christ et les philosophes,* Teramo.
H. Küng (1970), *Menschwerdung Gottes: Eine Einführung in Hegels theologiches Denken als Prolegomena zu einer künftigen Christologie,* Fribourg.
Th. Pröpper (1975), *Der Jesus der Philosophen und der Jesus des Glaubens,* Mayence.
E. Brito (1979), *Hegel et la tâche actuelle de la christologie,* Paris-Namur.
X. Tilliette (1986), *La christologie idéaliste,* Paris.
X. Tilliette (1990), *Le Christ de la philosophie: Prolégomènes à une christologie philosophique,* Paris.
X. Tilliette (1992), *La semaine sainte des philosophes,* Paris.
M. Henry (1996), *C'est moi la vérité,* Paris.

h) Modern Christological Movement (Systematic Essays)

P. Tillich (1957), *Systematic Theology,* vol. 2, London.
K. Rahner (1954), "Probleme der Christologie von heute," *Schr. zur Th.* 1, Einsiedeln, 169–222.
R. Bultmann (1958), *Jesus,* Tübingen.
K. Rahner (1960), "Zur Theologie der Menschwerdung," *Schr. zur Th.* IV, 137–56.
R. Bultmann (1961), *Theologie des Neuen Testaments,* Tübingen.
W. Pannenberg (1964), *Grundzüge der Christologie,* Gütersloh.
C. Duquoc (1968, 1972), *Christologie,* vol. I: *L'homme Jésus;* vol. II: *Le Messie,* Paris.
P. Schoonenberg (1969), *Hij is een God van Mensen,* Malmberg, Nev.
H. Urs von Balthasar (1969), *Herrlichkeit: Eine theologische Aesthetik,* III/2: *Neuer Bund,* Einsiedeln.
J. Moltmann (1972), *Der gekreuzigte Gott,* Munich.
K. Rahner and W. Thüsing (1972), *Christologie: Systematisch und Exegetisch,* Fribourg-Basel-Vienna.
C. Duquoc (1973), *Jésus, homme libre: Esquisse d'une christologie,* Paris.
L. Bouyer (1974), *Le Fils éternel,* Paris.
W. Kasper (1974), *Jesus der Christus,* Mayence.
H. Küng (1974), *Christ sein,* Munich.
E. Schillebeeckx (1974), *Jezus, het verhaal van een levende,* Bloemendaal.
A. Schilson, W. Kasper (1974), *Christologie im Präsens,* Fribourg.
O. Gonzalez de Cardedal (1975), *Jesus de Nazaret,* Madrid.
H. Urs von Balthasar (1976), *Theodramatik,* II/1: *Die Personen des Spiels* (1978), II/2: *Die Personen in Christus,* Einsiedeln.
Bloemendaal (German trans.), *Christus und die Christen: Die Geschichte einer neuen Lebenspraxis,* Fribourg, 1977.
E. Jüngel (1977), *Gott als Geheimnis der Welt,* Tübingen (trad. fr. 1983, 2 vols.).
K. Rahner (1977), *Grundkurs des Glaubens,* Fribourg-Basel-Vienna (trad. fr. 1983).
E. Schillebeeckx (1977), *Gerechtigheid en liefde: Genade en bevrijding.*
E. Schillebeeckx (1977), "Jésus de Nazareth: Le récit d'un vivant" *LV(L)* 134, 5–45.
F.J. Van Beeck (1979), *Christ Proclaimed: Christology as Rhetoric,* New York.
B. Forte (1981), *Gesù di Nazaret, storia di Dio, Dio della storia,* Rome (trad. fr. 1984).
B. Sesboüé (1982), *Jésus-Christ dans la tradition de l'Église,* Paris.
J.C. Dwyer (1983), *Son of Man and Son of God: A New Language for Faith,* New York.
H. Urs von Balthasar (1985), *Theologik,* II: *Wahrheit Gottes.*
J. Moltmann (1989), *Der Weg Jesu Christi: Christologie in messianischen Dimensionen,* Munich.
J. Moingt (1993), *L'homme qui venait de Dieu,* Paris.
J. Dupuis (1993), *Introduzione alla cristologia,* Casale Monferrato.
P. Hünermann (1994), *Jesus Christus Gottes Wort in der Zeit,* Münster.
I.U. Dalferth (1994), *Der auferweckte Gekreuzigte: Zur Grammatik der Christologie,* Tübingen.

i) Liberation Christology (Latin America)

L. Boff (1972), *Jesus-Cristo libertador,* Petropolis.
J. Sobrino (1977), *Cristologia desde America latina,* Mexico.
J.L. Segundo (1982), *El hombre de hoy ante Jesus de Nazaret,* 3 vols., Madrid.
J. Sobrino (1982), *Jesus en America latina,* Santander.
J. Sobrino (1991) *Jesucristo liberador,* Madrid.

j) Christology and Cosmos; Christ and Other Religions
R. Pannikar (1964), *The Unknown Christ of Hinduism,* London, New Ed., 1981.
P. Teilhard de Chardin (1965), *Œuvres,* vol. 9: *Science et Christ,* Paris.
G. Maloney (1968), *The Cosmic Christ: From Paul to Teilhard,* New York.
D. Flusser (1970), *Jésus,* Paris.
G. Vermes (1973), *Jesus the Jew,* Londres.
P. Lapide (1976), *Ist das nicht Josephs Sohn? Jesus im heutigen Judentum,* Stuttgart-Munich (*Fils de Joseph?,* 1978).
R. Arnaldez (1980), *Jésus, Fils de Marie, prophète de l'islam,* Paris.
E. P. Sanders (1985), *Jesus and Judaism,* London.
R. Arnaldez (1988), *Jésus dans la pensée musulmane,* Paris.
J. Dupuis (1989), *Jésus-Christ à la rencontre des religions,* Paris.
S. J. Samartha (1991), *One Christ-Many Religions: Toward a Revised Christology,* New York.

k) Images of Christ in Culture
F. P. Bowman (1973), *Le Christ romantique,* Geneva.
D. Menozzi (1979), *Letture politiche di Gesù,* Brescia.
A. Dabezies et al. (1987), *Jésus-Christ dans la littérature française: Textes du Moyen Age au XXe siècle,* Paris.
B. Cottret (1990), *Le Christ des Lumières: Jésus de Newton à Voltaire (1680–1760),* Paris.

BERNARD SESBOÜÉ

Christ's Consciousness

Great reserve is required when treating a question as intimate and as delicate as Christ's consciousness. And yet it is Jesus* himself who invites the question with the insistent call he addresses to whoever takes an interest in him: "But who do you say that I am?" (Mt 16:15). Traditional faith and theology have not lacked for positions on the matter over the centuries. Contemporary thought has been able to produce a number of invaluable clarifications.

1. The Ancient Tradition

The earliest Christian centuries did not consider problematic what later centuries were to treat under the name of the "knowledge" (more "objective") and then the "consciousness" ("subjective") of Christ. The apostolic witness, its New Testament crystallization, and finally the resulting faith* in the truth of the humanity of Christ led the early Fathers* of the Church to accept, without prejudice to his divine identity, that Christ's human intelligence had been exercised according to the common human condition, ignorance included.

However, two approaches to the mystery* of Christ, broadly distinguishable in the patristic period, had an influence in this area. More intent on emphasizing the conditions of the concrete historicity of the life of Jesus, the school of Antioch*—Eustathius early on, probably Diodorus of Tarsus, but especially his pupil Theodore of Mopsuestia and certainly Theodoret of Cyrrhus—placed maximum emphasis on the humanity assumed by the Word*. Along with the capacity of Jesus to work autonomously, they emphasized the correlative limitations affecting him, in the order of knowledge as in the order of will. The tendency was reversed in the school of Alexandria*. Origen*, for example, assimilated the condition of the soul* assumed by the Word to that of iron plunged into the fire: "As iron is in the fire, so the human soul [of Christ] is always in the Word, in Wisdom*, always in God*; and everything that it does, everything that it thinks, everything that it understands, is God" (*De Principiis* II. 6. 6). In order to avoid the risk of later providing support for Arianism*, there were ingenious "economic" explanations of an "ignorance" that the New Testament makes it necessary, in spite of everything, to recognize in Christ (Athanasius*, *Contra Arianos* III. 43f.; Cyril* of Alexandria, *Thes.* XXII; Basil*, *letter* 236; Gregory of Nazianzus, *Discourses* 30. 15f.). But this ignorance also allowed for a contrasting emphasis on the "perfection in divinity" of the Word. It was specified that the ignorance was compensated for by that direct communication between the divine and the human that was guaranteed by the hypostatic* union. A particularly suggestive passage of Cyril, principal representative of the school of Alexandria, says, however, "The Word of God, by virtue of economy, has allowed this flesh that is his to follow the laws of its own nature. For it is human to progress in age and wisdom, and I would add, even in grace.... By virtue of this plan [of economy], he thus allows human limitations to govern him" (*Christ is one,* 74).

Although their positions bore on the being* of Christ, the great christological councils* did not directly address his psychology, and it was only in the sixth century that this was explicitly considered. Around that time, one notes in Severian circles the affirmation of Christ's omniscience. But then a movement derived from the school of Antioch, attached to the Anomoean Eunomius (Sozomen, *Ecclesiastical History* VII. 17), replied with the affirmation of Christ's ignorance, in support of which it referred to Mark 13:32 and John 11:34. This was the crisis of the "Agnoetes" (or of the "Themistians," from the name of Themistios, deacon of Alexandria c. 536–40). They were fought by Theodosius of Alexandria (536–67), then by Eulogius of Alexandria (580–607). The latter even corresponded about them with Gregory* the Great, who condemned them in 600, as did the Lateran Council in 649 (*DS* 474–76 and 419). The movement had little influence in the West because of the analysis articulated by Augustine* (*Letter* 219) with reference to a comparable position of Leporius. In his *Letter XIV* to the deacon Ferrand, Fulgencius of Ruspina wrote for his part, "We may clearly affirm that the soul of Christ has the full consciousness of its divinity. However, I do not know whether we should say that it knows divinity as God knows himself, or rather that it knows divinity to be divinity but not *as* divinity." The theory of omniscience (from the mother's womb) thus prevailed thereafter, by reason of the hypostatic union and the communication of qualities that it induced (idioms*) (*see* John of Damascus, *Orthodox faith* III. 21f., and the compilation called *Doctrine of the Fathers,* chap. 16, second half of the seventh century). The extreme development of this tendency was reached in the ninth century with Candidus, "a little-known theologian of the beatific* vision of Christ" (H. de Lavalette).

2. From the Medieval Period to the Threshold of the Current Age

Medieval theology developed a systematic reflection on the knowledge or, rather, on "the knowledges" of Christ and even went so far as to distinguish six of them. Abelard*, for his part, still represented those positions that belonged to the end of the patristic period: "Christ saw God with the greatest perfection" (*Epitome of Christian Theology* c. XXVII).

As for Thomas* Aquinas, in distinguishing in Christ a threefold human knowledge, he staked out a position that established a school. The three forms of this knowledge were the knowledge of the blessed (*comprehensorum, ST* IIIa, q. 10, a. 1–4), innate knowledge (*indita* or *infusa, ST* IIIa, q. 11, a. 1–6), and experiential knowledge (*acquisita, ST* IIIa, q. 12, a. 1–4). Rooted in concrete experience, the third was by definition limited and incremental, and Thomas in fact gave it more and more consideration, with Scripture* forcing its recognition. The second was communicated to human intelligence "directly from above," but by means of the mediation of "*impressed species.*" In that lay its difference from the first form of knowledge, that immediate and perfect participation in the vision of God himself, which was the prerogative of the blessed in heaven. There was, however, a strict relationship and a close correspondence between the knowledge of vision and innate knowledge, the former constituting the foundation and the content of the latter, which in turn provided the former the means for its human manifestation.

In the Renaissance, Erasmus* (on the basis of reference to Scripture, especially Lk 2:52) and then, in the framework of the Reformation, Luther* and Calvin* (on the basis of a strong attachment to the truth of the Incarnation*) called for circumspection with respect to the "communication of properties" (*see Institutes* XIV. 1). There were in Jesus real limitations and an actual development in the order of knowledge*.

It was not until the late 19th century that medieval positions were once again questioned by Catholic theologians. This was done not for theoretical or ideological reasons but out of a concern to take into account the results achieved by the application of the historical and critical method to the texts of the Gospels. This was the case with the theologian H. Schell (1850–1906), who denied to Christ not only the beatific vision but any form of omniscience and, for this reason, saw his *Katholische Dogmatik* put on the Index of forbidden works in 1898. But it was especially true for the modernist* camp and for Loisy first of all. His radical positions provoked reactions that the magisterium saw fit to bring to an end with two severe interventions.

In 1907 the decree *Lamentabili,* 32, condemned the proposition according to which "one cannot reconcile the natural meaning of the gospel texts with what our theologians teach about the consciousness and the infallible knowledge of Christ" (*DS* 3422). The same Holy Office answered in 1918 that one could not teach without danger that it was "not evident that the soul of Christ, during his life among men, possessed the knowledge enjoyed by the blessed" or that "the soul of Christ had been ignorant of anything" (*DS* 3645–47). Again, in his encyclical *Mystici corporis* (1943), Pius XII thought it necessary to repeat the classic opinions on the perfection of the "knowledge of vision" realized "from the very first instant of his incarnation" (*DS* 3812).

3. A Transformation of the Problem

These positions taken by the hierarchy were directly aimed only at avoiding misconstructions in the common teaching of the early part of the century. They were not intended to settle debates still in progress or not yet open. Proof of this can be found in the fact that two recent documents (Commis. bibl. pontif., *Bible and Christology,* 1984; Commis. theol. intern., *The Consciousness That Jesus Had of His Mission,* 1985) refrain from mentioning any beatific vision in the pre-Easter Jesus.

a) Mention should be made here of the discussion, particularly vigorous after World War II and in a context arising out of modernism, on the existence in Christ, alongside his divine "I," of a human "I" that was the subject of his human thoughts and actions and that is manifested in the gospel narrative*. Another proposition distinguished two "selves" within the single "I" of the divine person*, two distinct centers of consciousness, one divine, the other human. On the basis of this discussion, in which P. Galtier and P. Parente were the notable participants, it became clear that if (as Pius XII suggested again in *Sempiternus rex* in 1951, *DS* 3905) Chalcedon* was to be respected, it had to be judged that, as a single person and hypostasis, the incarnate Word is also a single subject conscious of itself, hence a single "I," a single personal consciousness. This made it necessary to leave the problematics of an (objectifying) "knowledge" tied to the perspective of a rational and metaphysical psychology and resolutely adopt the problematics of consciousness, something particularly emphasized by M. Nédoncelle.

b) A decisive stage was reached with the "Dogmatic Considerations on the Psychology of Christ" by Karl Rahner* (1962), which followed a 1954 article on Chalcedon. In any spiritual being, the theologian pointed out, being and being present to oneself go together. Thus, the hypostatic union of human nature with the person of the Word brought about in itself, for that nature, a consequence in the order of consciousness. Christ's consciousness of himself is the consciousness that he is the Son of God. We may continue to designate as "vision" that immediate relationship with God, but it is then to be understood as not beatific. It is a fundamental condition of existence, a primordial ontological determination, of a transcendental and not a categorizing or thematic order.

Giving a "quasi-mythological" cast to the idea of a beatific vision realized from the very first moment of conception, such a consciousness is called on to actualize itself, to grow and develop throughout the historical course of an existence in fact set under the sign of human temporality. By the same token, the "principle of perfection" that had so broadly predominated until then was subject to fundamental revision. The patristic formulation of Chalcedon, "perfect in humanity," then appeared to be understood as stating that Christ is a "complete" man, "fully" a man. He is not a being who enjoys all the perfections ideally possible for a man, including those of the realm of consciousness, since this would indeed be contrary to the truth of the Incarnation.

c) In all these developments, closer attention to the evidence of the Gospels on the historicity of the human condition of Jesus played a major role. On the gradual nature of his coming to consciousness of the danger that weighed on him and on the questions of his ignorance of the Day of Judgment* or of the expansion of the fruit of his mission beyond Israel*, the work of exegetes such as R. Schnackenburg and A. Vögtle required the revision of medieval and classic opinions. For, whatever may be true of the claims of transcendence actually manifested by Jesus, it is nevertheless necessary to accept the truth of those facts that only persistent a priori positions had prevented us from seeing clearly set out in the gospel narrative. Jesus experienced wonder, disappointment, and surprise. He developed both in the discovery of beings and situations and in the knowledge of his own fate. He was even lacking in knowledge, and he had to learn and practice obedience day by day.

It is essential here to avoid projecting into the psychology of the pre-Easter Jesus what is true only of the preexisting Word or the glorified Christ. This is so even if Jesus of Nazareth is never presented as being unaware of the unique character of the relationship he had always maintained with the one he did not fear to designate as his own Father* (*see* the episode of the Temple*, Lk 2:49).

4. The Faith of the Son of God Incarnate

In the end it is the question of the identity of Christ that is at stake in the question posed about his knowledge and his consciousness. Jesus is an authentic man. As Hans Urs von Balthasar*, among others, notes, "the inalienable nobility of man lies in his being both able, and obliged to freely project the plan of his existence into a future that he does not know." But Jesus is also the Son of God, in the unity of a single concrete being. He has agreed to bring everything that he is as Word and Son of God to that choice that he has made, according to the will of the Father but in full harmony with him, to make himself truly a man. The result is that, in his incarnate state, the Word has agreed to receive and to know according to the pattern of human knowledge even what God gives him to be and to know according to his relationship of intra-Trinitarian immanence with him. In this way, in Jesus Christ, incarnate Word, there is not on one side an omniscient Word and on the other a man limited in knowledge in every direction but rather "one and the same Son and Word of God" who, having truly taken on the human condition, knows himself, wills himself, and lives himself according to the truth appropriate to that condition.

Jesus always perceived his relationship of filiation to his Father as one of absolute intimacy, well conveyed in human words by the term "Abba" ("papa"). This relationship always appeared to him as constitutive of his being and of all his conditions of existence, including his existence as a man. This relationship set the whole of his life under the dual sign of growth and obedience. It allowed the Epistle to the Hebrews to hail in him "the founder and perfecter of our faith" (Heb 12:2; *see* Balthasar, J. Guillet, A. Vanhoye). In the final analysis it explains his abandonment and his total surrender of self on the cross as it explains his resurgence from among the dead. It was in this relationship that he knew himself humanly as God/Son of God.

• P. Galtier (1939), *Vérité du Christ,* Paris.

A. Michel (1941), "Science de Jésus-Christ," *DThC* 14, 1628–65 (+ Tables 2583–86 and 2650–55).

P. Parente (1951, 1955), *L'Io di Cristo,* Brescia.

E. Gutwenger (1960), *Bewußtsein und Wissen Christi,* Innsbruck.

H. de Lavalette (1961), "Candide, théologien inconnu de la vision béatifique du Christ," *RSR* 49, 426–29.

H. Urs von Balthasar (1961), *Fides Christi,* in *Sponsa Verbi,* Ensiedeln, 45–79.

K. Rahner (1962), "Dogmatische Erwägungen über das Wissen und Selbstbewußtsein Christi," *Schr. zur Th.* 5, 222–45 (2nd Ed. 1964).

A. Vögtle (1964), "Exegetische Erwägungen über das Wissen und Selbstbewußtsein Christi," in *Gott in Welt: Festgabe für K. Rahner,* Fribourg-Bâle-Vienne, I, 608–67.

M. Nédoncelle (1965), "Le Moi du Christ et le moi des hommes à la lumière de la réciprocité des consciences," in Coll., *Problèmes actuels de christologie,* Paris, 215 *Sq.*

A. Feuillet (1966), "Les *Ego eïmi* christologiques du quatrième évangile," *RSR* 54, 5–22 and 213–40.

H. Riedlinger (1966), *Geschichtlichkeit und Vollendung des Wissens Christi,* Fribourg-Basel-Vienna.

H. Urs von Balthasar (1966), *Zuerst Gottes Reich,* Ensiedeln.

A. Grillmeier (1979 and 1989), *Jesus der Christus im Glauben der Kirche* I (2nd Ed. 1990) and II/2, Fribourg-Basel-Vienna.

J. Guillet (1980), *La foi de Jésus-Christ,* Paris.

J. Moingt (1993), *L'homme qui venait de Dieu,* Paris, 561–90.

E. Poulat (1996), *Histoire, dogme et critique dans la crise moderniste,* Paris.

JOSEPH DORÉ

See also **Beatitude; Christ/Christology; Hypostatic Union; Incarnation; Jesus, Historical; Kenosis; Monophysitism**

Christmas. *See* **Liturgical Year**

Chrysostom, John

c. 350–407

Born into the aristocracy in Antioch, John Chrysostom belonged to a Christian family and from his youth would be in contact with monastic circles. After being ordained a priest* in 386, he was soon entrusted by the bishop* Flavian with preaching* in the church* of Antioch, and his reputation as a preacher explains his epithet of "chrysostom," or "golden-mouthed." In 398 he succeeded Nestor, bishop of Constantinople. Having quickly come into conflict with the imperial family and particularly with the empress Eudoxia, he was twice sentenced to exile and died of exhaustion in 407. He is held in great honor in the Orthodox world, where he is viewed as a martyr.

a) The Christian Life Defined. At the end of the fourth century, John Chrysostom reflected on the early history* of the Church. His homilies on the Acts of the Apostles, the only integral commentary on the Acts to have come down to us from the patristic period, show that he saw in the first Christian community a model for his contemporaries, a model, moreover, that had been renewed in the angelic life of the first monks. Since Pentecost, which he called "the metropolis of Christian feasts," the Holy* Spirit has spread everywhere, calling the baptized to lead that perfect life of which the apostle* Peter provides the example. Chrysostom was aware that henceforth it was a matter of rooting Christian usages in a *popular* church ("multitudinist"). The rite of baptism* gave entry to a new life (*Baptismal Catecheses* SC 50 and 366), and the preacher developed a spirituality of Christian virtues* (Wenger 1974). His praise of virginity and the predominant place that he gave to monastic life was counterbalanced by his lauding of marriage* and of the parental role in the teaching of the faith*.

b) The Priesthood. His treatise on the priesthood* (SC 272) was widely circulated in the early Church. Including both bishop and priest under the term *hiereus,* John Chrysostom stated the unique character of the episcopal ministry* and defined its three distinctive traits: the bishop was the leader of the faithful and guided the Church, he celebrated the Eucharist, and, as the guarantor of the integrity of the faith, he had to ensure its transmission. The very profusion of John Chrysostom's homiletic works bears witness to the importance he attached to preaching activities. Himself a target of violent attacks, he rose up against the political maneuvers that prevailed at certain ecclesiastical elections (*On Priesthood* III, 11).

c) Reflections on Society. Following Basil* the Great of Caesarea and Gregory* of Nyssa, John Chrysostom viewed slavery in the same way that he viewed private ownership. That is to say, he saw both as resulting from original sin*. Going so far as to envisage a society* in which slavery would no longer exist, particularly in his homilies on the Acts of the Apostles, he made a proposal for social reform that included the common ownership of goods, based on the example of the first Christian community (*In Acta* ii, 3; PG 60, 93). The bishop must be entrusted with the management of the ecclesiastical patrimony and with the organization of the various charitable works—on this point John Chrysostom stood for a centralizing notion of clerical functions. But the novelty of Chrysostom's thought resided in the prominence given to education ("On Vain Glory and Childhood Education"). He emphasized that in the first instance the responsibility for forming the new generations of a Christian society fell to the parents.

d) His Polemic against the Judaizing Christians and the Jews. Modern readers are bound to be repulsed by Chrysostom's homilies *Adversus Judaeos* and the amount of space allotted in the body of his works to the polemic against the Judaizing Christians and against the Jews. The historical role of his works in the development of Christian anti-Judaism and anti-Semitism must be acknowledged. However, historians such as Wilken (1983) suggest that this condemnation should be tempered by a few observations. In Antioch, where the *Adversus Judaeos* homilies were delivered, the Jewish community was not a repressed minority but a large and powerful group that, moreover, exerted a strong attraction on very many Christians. John Chrysostom could also remember the favors from which the Jews had benefited under Julian's reign, particularly from the plan for rebuilding the Temple* of Jerusalem*. Educated in the school of Libanius, John Chrysostom resorted to defamatory rhetoric that he used virulently and in bad faith, employing a whole sheaf of hackneyed arguments, including the Old Testament prophecies* against Israel*. But his words consisted of a polemic and not a call to violence* and persecution, and this polemic could not be defined as anti-Semitic since racial references do not occur in it at all. He even occasionally held up Jewish piety as an example to his followers. But he was certainly incapable of conceiving of Judaism's survival after the advent of Christ, particularly when the capture of Jerusalem and the destruction of the second temple marked the fulfillment of the prophecies.

In addition to these historical considerations, it should be mentioned that the late 19th-century French translations of John Chrysostom's works are also not exempt from anti-Semitism and must be used with caution. Moreover, it would be wise to take another look at the whole manuscript tradition in order to eliminate from them the Byzantine interpolations, which are likely to have reinforced the polemic against the Jews.

• PG 47–64; over 20 volumes published in SC, some edited by A.-M. Malingrey.

Palladius, *Dialogue sur la vie de Jean Chrysostome* (SC 341–42).

♦ Ch. Baur (1920–30), *JnChr. und seine Zeit,* Munich.

A.-J. Festugière (1959), *Antioche païenne et chrétienne: Libanius, Chr. et les moines de Syrie,* Paris.

D. C. Burger (1964), *A Complete Bibliography of the Scholarship on the Life and Works of Saint JnChr.*, Evanston, Illinois.
E. Nowak (1972), *Le chrétien devant la souffrance: Étude sur la pensée de JnChr.*, ThH 19.
A. M. Ritter (1972), *Charisma im Verständnis des JnChr. und seiner Zeit*, Göttingen.
G. Dagron (1974), *Naissance d'une capitale: Constantinople et ses institutions de 330 à 451*, Paris.
A. Wenger (1974), "JnChr.," *DSp* 8, 331–55.
Coll. (1975), *JnChr. et Augustin (Actes du Colloque de Chantilly, 22–24 septembre 1974)*, Paris.
R.L. Wilken (1983), *JnChr. and the Jews*, Berkeley.
M.A. Schatkin (1987), *JnChr. as Apologist*, Analekta Vlatadon 50, Thessalonique.

JEAN-MARIE SALAMITO

See also **Baptism; Bishop; Judaism; Presbyter/Priest; Property; Virtues**

Church

1. Biblical Roots

a) The Old Testament. In the context of Christian theology*, the term "Old Testament ecclesiology*" can be used only in an indirect sense. The Church in the Christian understanding does not make its appearance until New Testament times and presupposes the coming of Jesus Christ. The idea that Christians have of themselves as a Church is nonetheless influenced by certain elements drawn from the Old Testament. This is indicated in the first place by the concept of "*ekklèsia,*" the principal term used to designate the Church in the New Testament and the term that most frequently translated the Hebrew "*kahal*" (assembly of the political and ritual community) in the Septuagint. The link can also be seen in images designating Christianity as "a royal priesthood" (1 Pt 2:9), a "temple" (e.g., 1 Cor 3:16), the "people* of God*" (Heb 4:9), and in the way in which Paul uses the image of the olive tree to connect the community of Christians to the promises* of the Old Testament (Rom 11:18). Much more than the repetition of old ideas, this represents the expression of a material continuity between the old covenant* and the new.

The concept of the "people of God" represents the principal Old Testament "prefiguration" of what would later be called the "Church." Used originally to designate the patrilineal family group, the term increasingly came to be used to mean the whole of Israel*, as opposed to other peoples. According to Deuteronomy 4:7 and 7:7, Israel is a people to whom God is particularly close, smaller than others, but distinguished from them by virtue of its having been adopted and chosen by God. It received its identity from God, in his act of bringing it out of Egypt and making with it the covenant of Sinai. It thereby became both a political and a religious entity. The evolution of the idea of choice* in early Judaism* nevertheless shows the gradual growth within Israel itself of a separation between the chosen and sinners. This is confirmed by the two other basic concepts of Old Testament "ecclesiology," *kahal* and *edah.* The former designates the assembly of those who receive the law* of YHWH and practice the divine cult*. Although this assembly is not identical to "the people established as a state" (Berger 1988), the link with political reality is stronger here than in the parallel concept of *edah,* which denotes only the ritual community. These notions and representations took on particular significance as the political identity of Israel was called into question, and they were further developed in Hellenistic Jewish thought. Old Testament ecclesiology thus gradually moved away from the founding political choices in an attempt to define the true Jew, who, as such, would be able to triumph in the final battles (Apocalyptic* Literature). This can be seen as a precursor of the idea of the New Testament community, which was not made up of one nation alone but brought together "Jews and pagans," stamped by their belonging to Christ,* of which baptism* was the seal.

b) Jesus and the Church. Jesus* of Nazareth makes no more mention of an explicit ecclesiology than does the Old Testament. To be sure, the New Testament puts the word *ekklèsia* in his mouth, but this should probably be attributed to the primitive Christian community

(Mt 16:18, 18:18). Did the post-Easter community, by developing the Church and its institution, thereby distort the message of Jesus (Loisy: "Jesus proclaimed the kingdom* of God, but it was the Church that came")? Once again, it is more accurate to speak of a fundamental continuity, and it even seems possible to attribute to Jesus something like an "implicit ecclesiology" (Trilling). What is meant by this is that, in proclaiming the reign of God, Jesus was not, so to speak, launching his message into the void. He also called disciples and determined the manner in which they should commit themselves to following him. The disciples who were called were those who accepted the three essential signs of the "kingship of God": a fundamental openness to a God of goodness and mercy*, the only source of life and of a future; the radical practice of the new justice* and of the commandment of love*, including reconciliation with and love of enemies; and the willingness to sacrifice* oneself even to the point of death*. If it is possible to see in these tendencies the concrete basis from which the "Church" was to arise, then there was a deep reason for the primitive community to attribute to Jesus explicit ecclesiological statements (whatever may be said in addition about the use made of these statements in the history* of the Church).

c) The Church as Ritual Assembly. New Testament accounts show that those who believed in Jesus began to meet in assemblies immediately after Easter. In Acts this movement is linked to the outpouring of the Holy* Spirit and to Peter*'s Pentecost speech, which brought about the conversion of a large number of people. Acts 2:42 sets out the ideal model of the primitive Christian community, whose essential characteristics are the teaching of the apostles*, the breaking of bread, and prayer*, as well as certain forms of common life of a charitable nature. These elements are also found in other places in the New Testament, particularly in Paul, as distinctive signs of the Church. This organization—particularly in the primitive community of Jerusalem*—raised some questions of articulation with and demarcation from Judaism, as evidenced by the Johannine corpus and by the reported fact of the Christians of Jerusalem assembling in the Temple* to pray (Acts 2:46). The image of these assemblies or meetings most particularly suggests the use of the term *ekklèsia.*

d) Paul: The Church as the Body of Christ. Theological reflection on the Church as the community of Christ has followed various models. The most fully developed concept of it is certainly found in Paul and his disciples. A fundamental characteristic of Pauline ecclesiology is its christological underpinning. Christians form a community through their existence "in Christ." Baptism is a participation in the death* and resurrection* of Christ (Rom 6), and this belonging to Christ renders the differences among people (according to sex, nationality, social position) free of any power to separate them (1 Cor 12:12f.; Gal 3:26ff.). In the same way the Communion of the Lord gives us a share *(koinônia)* in the body and blood of Christ, so that those who in this way participate in Christ form a single body: the "body of Christ" (1 Cor 12:27), the "body in Christ" (Rom 12:5), or even Christ himself (1 Cor 12:12). In Paul this idea is associated with the image, drawn from Greek political philosophy*, that assimilates the city* to a body made up of several members, each one of which carries out its own task. The description of communitarian reality in terms of a diversity of duties and ministries*, in Romans 12:4–8 and 1 Corinthians 12:12ff., follows this model. This does not hold for the deutero-Pauline epistles to the Ephesians and the Colossians, where Christ is presented as the head of the body (Eph 1:22, 5:23; Col 1:18), and the difference between Christ and his members is emphasized. Paul also on occasion describes the community from the point of view of the power of the Holy* Spirit. The spirit of the new life is the "Spirit of Christ" (Rom 8:9). The Lord himself is the Holy Spirit (2 Cor 3:17). In the Holy Spirit we have been baptized into a single body ,and we have been given one Spirit to drink (1 Cor 12:13; *see* 10:4), and the variety of ministries represents a single gift *(charisma)* of the one Spirit (1 Cor 12:11). It can be seen that the difference between the spiritual reality of the Church and its concrete manifestation was not yet the fundamental problem it would become in the context of a later ecclesiology.

e) The Church and Israel. In addition to the central schemata of the Pauline corpus, the New Testament provides other ways in which to interpret the theological reality of the Church. Matthew, for example, proposes an image of the Church that has been described as centered on "the true Israel" (Trilling). It is sketched in particular in the passages dealing with a mission of Jesus directed especially toward Israel (Mt 10:5f., 15:24). The Twelve Apostles represented the 12 tribes of the Israel to come (Mt 10:1f., 19:28), while the Sermon on the Mount (Mt 5–7) offered a summary of the "Torah of the true Israel," something that was concretized in the order of the Christian community (Mt 18). This vision of Matthew's, however, makes room on the one hand for an awareness of the sin of an Israel that did not recognize the hour of Christ's visitation (Mt 21:33ff., 23) and on the other for the idea of a universal salvation*, by which Christ's mission* was extended to the entire world, so as to include all peoples in the Church (Mt 28:19ff., 5:15; *see also* Acts 28:26–28). The theme of "Israel and the Church" appears again, under different guises, in other New Testament passages. There is, for example, the image of the bridegroom and the bride, the latter representing both Israel, to which the Messiah* has come (Lk 12:36: the disciples belong to the bridegroom; Mt 25:1–13), and the community of Christians (2 Cor 11:2). The image of the heavenly Jerusalem (Gal 4:26f.; Heb 12:22f.; Rev 21:10–27) inscribes the Church among the future events awaited by the Jews, thereby dissociating it from the present reality of Israel. On the other hand, the New Testament also puts forward the idea of a permanent and continuous link, for example, in the chapters on Israel in Romans 9 through 11, where the Church of the pagans is included in the promise made to Abraham (11:17ff.), while at the same time there is expressed the hope that all of Israel will finally be saved. The passages on the Temple, which is the community (1 Cor 3:16), or on the people of God, to whom rest is promised (Heb 4:9), show a similar continuity between Israel and the Church.

f) Services and Ministries. From the time of the New Testament, the Church developed ministerial structures that took on a multiplicity of forms, and these are not of a nature to provide a direct model for the Church of today. Jesus himself "instituted" no ministry, but the choice of the Twelve Apostles, which must probably be attributed to Jesus himself, shows that even before Easter the movement did not lack a certain internal articulation. Later we can distinguish in the earliest communities at least two kinds of structure. On the one hand, there were ministries based on the gifts enumerated in the Epistles of Paul (1 Cor 12; Rom 12); among them in particular was apostleship, which shows that the charismatic character of these ministries did not necessarily exclude the exercise of doctrinal and pastoral authority*. It was also up to the apostle to bear direct witness to the Resurrection, a function that could not of course be perpetuated by any permanent structure. We can also recognize on the other hand a form of organization—clearly based on Jewish models—centered on the role of the elders (*see* Acts 19), in which various duties (particularly the doctrinal and pastoral functions linked to apostleship) might also be transmitted by ordination* (1 Tm 4:1–4, 5:22; 2 Tm 1:6). We can see here the outlines of the problem of "proto-Catholicism*," though it is unclear to what extent this problem simply reflected the demands weighing on the community as the life, death, and resurrection of Jesus became more distant in time (e.g., the requirement of preserving Christian identity in the face of the growing danger of doctrinal error) and to what extent it was related to the Christian community's break with Judaism (*see* Berger 1988). The problem, in any event, could not be ignored, and it continued to hold the Church in a state of uncertainty. There is no doubt that the Church is *not* the kingdom of God. But in the variety of its forms as an empirical social entity, it is nevertheless composed of the people of that kingdom, who attest to its coming and await its fulfillment. In every age, the social reality of the Church must in any case be evaluated and critiqued in relation to its testimony and to its hope.

2. Representations and Concept of the Church in the Course of Its History

a) The Early Church. The Church of the earliest days developed ecclesiastical structures* that were already contained in embryo in the New Testament. The problem of the internal and external unity* of the Church, and hence of its capacity to remain in the truth*, became ever more pressing. As characteristic points of this development, we should mention the growing role played by the bishop*. He was responsible for each particular Church, guaranteeing its truth in Christ, and presiding over the celebration of the Eucharist* (*see* Ignatius of Antioch, *Ad. Smyrn.* VIII). In addition, certain Episcopal sees gained considerable influence because of the growth of urban communities that were established as regional ecclesiastical centers (they would later become archbishoprics and patriarchates*). Irenaeus* of Lyon was the first to introduce a significant ecclesiastical emphasis into ancient theology. For him the Church was the place of the Spirit of God, the house of truth and salvation. It was founded on the Holy* Scriptures, which it preserved in faithfulness to the preaching* of the apostles. The Church's ministers, having their place in the apostolic* succession, guaranteed the complete transmission of apostolic truth. Hippolytus of Rome went further than Irenaeus in asserting that sinners did not truly belong to the Church, a thesis that brought him into conflict with Callistus I of Rome. This disagreement already reflected the tension that existed between the true Church and its material institutional reality.

In Eastern theology of the third century, Clement of Alexandria emphasized the coincidence of the earthly with the heavenly Church, while Origen* insisted on the necessary spiritual and moral sanctity of the members of the Church, in particular of its ministers. In the West, around the same time, leaving Tertullian aside, it is especially important to mention the importance of Cyprian* of Carthage, whose ecclesiology granted a central place to the episcopal function. Cyprian was convinced that the unity of the Church had to be guaranteed by the unity of its bishops; it was to this Church, structured and represented by the bishops, that devolved the role of being the sole path to salvation ("no salvation outside the Church").

b) Augustine. The theology of the early Church developed no ecclesiological program more significant than that of Augustine*. It reflected, more than any others did, the new situation that had been created and the new questions that had been raised since the Church (through the act of Constantine) had formally entered the political realm. Opposing the tendency that, particularly in the East, aimed at establishing a positive relationship between Church* and state, a relationship that might signify in the very history of salvation, in the *City of God* Augustine emphasizes the differences between the two orders. He distinguishes between two great "cities": the city of God, the communion* of those who are moving toward the divine goal, and the city of the devil, bringing together human beings and angels* who have chosen the way of evil*. Knowledge of who belongs to which group is the privilege of divine predestination*. As for the Church, it is manifestly a compound of good and evil, elect and outcast. The call that comes through baptism is not identical to the eternal election of God. Augustinian ecclesiology thus recognizes a tension between the true Church of the elect and the external visible institution that prefigures many later developments in theological thought. The visible institution of the Church, under the leadership of the bishops, nonetheless remains the salvific body to which it is necessary to belong in order to enter into beatitude*. In this sense (as *conditio sine qua non*), the ancient principle of "no salvation outside the Church" still holds for Augustine. The state, on the other hand, that "great gang of bandits," has no other function but that of integrating and moderating all the egotistical motives of mankind in such a way as to preserve external peace* as much as possible. In this respect at least, it supports the work of the Church.

c) The Middle Ages. The question of the primacy of the pope* played an important and constant role in medieval Latin ecclesiology. This can be explained by the growing political ambitions of the bishop of Rome* and by the conflicts that set him in opposition both to the representatives of temporal power (emperor, princes) and to church authorities (bishops, councils*). Although the teaching of early scholasticism* favored a relative independence of temporal power from the pope (Rupert of Deutz), other voices arose that gave to the Church (i.e., the pope) supremacy over temporal power (Gerhoh of Reichersberg) by virtue of the universal sovereignty of Christ. This line of argument, which was to prevail over the one that favored the independence of temporal rulers, is clearly visible in the ambitions of Innocent III, who laid claim to complete spiritual and temporal power over the Christian people. It found its supreme expression in 1302 in the bull *Unam Sanctam* of Boniface VIII. According to this document, Christ entrusted to the pope the two swords, temporal and spiritual, and total submission of the person to the pope is a necessary condition for salvation. The crisis of the papacy in the 14th and 15th centuries later provoked a quarrel over the relations between the pope and the council of bishops. The "conciliar" option, which subjected the pope to the authority of the Church and its councils (decree "*Haec sancta synodus*" of the Council of Basel* in 1415), conflicted with the "papalist" option, which granted absolute primacy to pontifical power and authority (bull "*Laetentur caeli*" of the Council of Florence* in 1439) and condemned conciliarism*.

Until the 14th century, Latin theology possessed no dogmatic* treatises that dealt specifically with ecclesiology. It tended instead to examine the nature of the Church within the framework of sacramental theology or Christology*. We are touching here on the second focus, more strictly theological, of medieval ecclesiology. Baptism and the Eucharist are the two sacraments* to which early Scholasticism (Hugh of Saint-Victor) attributed the power of integrating the believer into Christ and into his mystical body the Church. The Eucharist is not only the symbol (as a sign of the abundance of wheat and grapes) but also the efficient cause and the vital principle of the mystical body of the Church. By receiving the Eucharist in a worthy manner, believers come together as one in the peace of the Church. At the same time, the offering of the eucharistic sacrifice* by the priest is understood as an act in which the entire Church participates, as a kind of mysterious sacrificial communion (Peter Damien, Eudes of Cambrai). Major Scholastic theology (Bonaventure*, Thomas* Aquinas) added christological depth to this idea, affirming that it is the *gratia capitis* of Christ, which, in its superabundance, overflows onto the members of the body of the Church. According to Thomas, the humanity of Christ is the *instrumentum coniunctum* (joint instrument) of this operation, and the sacrament is its *instrumentum separatum* (separate instrument) (*ST* IIIa. q. 62. a. 5). The members of the Church are the saints in heaven (including those of the old covenant) and the just on the earth—those, that is, who possess faith* and love—whereas sinners, who are not in a state of grace*, are often considered dead or imperfect members. From this, late Scholasticism derived the idea that only the predestined are truly members of the Church (Wycliffe, Hus*). The opposing argument (anticipating the position of Bellarmine*) defined the Church as the communion* of those who observe and outwardly confess the true faith, participate in the sacraments, and submit themselves to the pope (John of Ragusa, Juan de Torquemada). The universal Church was thus identified with the Church of Rome.

d) The Reformation. Luther* forged his conception of the Church in opposition to the claim of the "papal Church" that it was the only true Church. For his part, Luther understood the Church as the people of God gathered in the Holy Spirit and receiving its existence and its sanctity from the divine Word (the Church as "creature of the Word*"; *WA* 6. 650). The preaching of the Word is therefore the essential characteristic of the true Church, even if other elements may be added to it (Baptism, Communion, ministries, prayer, the cross, respect for authority). For Luther, the Church of Rome was not the "true old Church," for it had falsified the gospel. The ecclesiastical theses of Lutheran confessional writings—most of them composed by Philipp Melanchthon—define the Church as "the assembly of the saints, in which the gospel is taught in its purity and the sacraments administered according to the rule" (*CA* VII). The Church represents the ritual assembly of all those who are living in justifying faith and so have received new birth by the Holy Spirit. The signs and distinctive marks of this assembly are the preaching* of the gospel and the administration of the sacraments (by ordained ministers: *CA* XIV).These two activities alone make of it a Church because they transmit and continually retransmit the Holy Spirit, who brings forth faith (*CA* V). In order to preserve the true unity of the Church, it is enough if it preaches the gospel and administers the sacraments in conformity with Scripture. The ceremony of worship may vary, and even less is it necessary to adopt a specific hierarchical structure (bishops, pope), even though Lutherans explicitly accept the episcopacy as a regional authority of an essentially doctrinal character, without temporal power (*CA* XXVIII). Opposing the Catholic position, Lutherans make a distinction between the Church understood as a visible assembly, brought together through participation in the sacraments, and the true Church, understood as a communion of hearts* in the Holy Spirit. The latter is nevertheless recognizable by the external signs of the Word and the sacraments (dual sense of Church in *Apol.* VII). Melanchthon later placed more and more emphasis on the visible Church, which he saw as an assembly of the chosen, or *coetus vocatorum,* sometimes also called *coetus scholasticus.* Out of the plurality of ministries that Luther still accepted, Melanchthon gradually eliminated all but one, the primary duty of which was public preaching of the Word. He showed little interest in the specific meaning of the sacraments for the essence of the Church.

Calvin*'s ecclesiology, which played a decisive role for the Reformed Churches, was based on the idea of predestination*, that is, on the idea of the Church as the communion of the elect in Christ, as *electorum turba* (*Inst.* IV. 1. 2). On the other hand, Calvin speaks above all of the visible Church, which he describes as the mother of all pious souls*. The true Church, the Church of pure preaching and the administration of the sacraments, is opposed to the false, papal Church. Christ instituted four kinds of ministers: pastors*, doctors*, elders, and deacons*, among whom the first (who have the duty of preaching the Word) occupy the most important position. The elders have chiefly to watch over the good conduct of the members of the community and hence also over disciplinary measures in the Church (in concert, if necessary, with civil authorities). In this respect, the Reformed tradition approaches the Church from a totally different angle than that of Lutheranism*.

e) Later Protestantism. Later Protestantism, in contrast to the Reformation and to Protestant orthodoxy, developed its idea of the Church on the basis of particular orientations of the believers who adhered to it. Pietism*, for example, emphasized personal faith and sanctification and relegated the pure preaching of doctrine to second place (Spener, von Zinzendorf). In the Enlightenment, it was moral sentiment that was understood to unite individuals in a "Republic governed by the laws of virtue," whereas the institutional Church, with its "statutory" rites and dogmas*, was seen at best as fulfilling only a propaedeutic function for those who did not have the moral force to do without it (Kant*). These two tendencies came together in the thought of Schleiermacher*, who defined religion as a "feeling of absolute dependence." This feeling, with which no one was as "powerfully" inspired as Jesus of Nazareth, represents the "total life" in which all who believe in this same Jesus commune; ultimately—and here Schleiermacher departs from Kant—it finds its necessary form in the visible Church, which is a part of society* insofar as it introduces the religiosity attached to Jesus into social and cultural reality (we can see here the beginnings of the "cultural" approach of liberal Protestantism*). Despite certain divergences in the area of the philosophy of religion*, this cultural concept of the Church continued to guide Protestant theologians of Hegelian inspiration, down through

R. Rothe, according to whom the ecclesiastical form of Christianity tends to become dissolved in the whole of the social body and its political organization. Theologians such as A. Ritschl—for whom Jesus, in proclaiming the kingdom of God, was aiming at a "moral organization of humanity"—and E. Troeltsch—for whom Christianity represented the most important historical expression that had ever appeared of the a priori religiosity of man—were also, in a different way, dependent on this neo-Protestant approach.

In the 19th century, there came from confessional Lutheranism (Löhe, Vilmar, Klieforth, and, to a lesser extent, von Harless and Harnack) the strongest reaction against this vision of a Church reduced to the level of a mere religious or moral consciousness. For these writers, the Church is above all the institution of salvation founded by Christ. It must administer the Word and—most particularly—the sacraments through the intermediary of an ordained minister who stands before the community in the name of Christ. The confession of faith—that is, the confession of Lutheran faith, the only true faith—plays a decisive role here. In relation to that confession, moral consciousness, religion, and piety appear as subjective factors of secondary importance.

f) The 20th Century. It fell above all to Barth* to take a position against neo-Protestantism and its notion of the Church. For Barth the central task of the Church is to proclaim the word of God revealed in Christ. Hence, there is a long discussion in his *Dogmatik* of the gathering together, the building up, and the mission of the Christian community, as these were carried out by Christ in the Holy Spirit. This missionary Church of Barth played a decisive role in the image that the German Confessional Church formed of itself in the National Socialist period and in its fight against the false doctrines that claimed to accommodate the unique word of Christ by attaching to it other slogans, such as "people," "race*," and "history*." With Bonhoeffer*'s maxim calling for a "Church for the others," this image also marked the consciousness of the evangelical Church under Communist domination (Alliance of Evangelical Churches of the DDR), as attested by the proposal for a Church that would be a "communion of witness and ministry," the idea of which was taken up in the *oikoumenè* as a whole.

Apart from this vision of the Church, and apart from the renewal of the Lutheran confessional idea (Elert, Althaus), other approaches remained more faithful to the legacy of the 19th century. We should mention here the late thinking of E. Brunner, who essentially wished to see in the Church a simple meeting of persons*, devoid of any institutional character. In this he repeated the argument of the canonist R. Sohm concerning the fundamental contradiction between the Church and the law*. We should also recall Tillich's concept of the Church in which the notion of "spiritual communion" played a central role. This spiritual communion, to be sure, finds in the "manifest" Church (characterized by preaching, the sacraments, and the confession of faith) its decisive and—by its explicit reference to Christ—exemplary expression, but it also takes place in many other movements and groups, even outside the Christian religious and philosophical framework. Tillich also endeavored to study the influence of the Christian spirit on culture and to denounce the contradictions that were supposed to exist between Christian preaching and the world* of today.

This line of thought has recently been taken up in the discussion of the multitudinist Church. In opposition to a vision of the Church understood as a communion of confession and service, some theologians have adopted the perspectives of the sociology of religion and argued for a churchliness, which would also take into account people who are distant from the Church, in their concrete Christianity. As an "institution of liberty*" (Rentdorff), the Church offers the gospel but prescribes no particular social form, no communitarian commitment. It simply wishes to encourage the development of a religious and ethical* consciousness, Christian in the broadest sense, thereby endowing itself with the internal openness necessary for it to have a presence in culture and society.

g) Catholic Ecclesiology since the 16th Century. The development of the Catholic Church since the 16th century has been first of all marked by an anti-Reformation emphasis. Against a vision based on justifying faith and preaching of the Word, Bellarmine, taking up pre-Reformation principles, described the Church as an assembly of persons* who possess three characteristics: they confess the same faith, they participate in the same sacraments, and they recognize the authority of the Roman pontiff. The Church thus defined is, according to Bellarmine, as visible as the Republic of Venice. Gallicanism* in the 17th century and Febronianism in the 18th sought (without ultimate success) to limit the sovereignty of the pope by means of the general council. In the Enlightenment period the Church was described as a spiritual society whose members pursue happiness through shared religious practices, a happiness that leads them toward humanity in the spirit of that religion; this is precisely the goal toward which the hierarchy established by Christ is aiming. In the 19th century it fell especially to the Catholic school of Tübingen (Drey, Möhler, Döllinger) to develop a deeper analysis of the spiritual essence of the Church. For these writers the Church is an organism imbued with the Holy Spirit, which at different levels creates the hierarchical articulations—duties and ministries—necessary for the preservation of its unity. By contrast the so-called school of Rome (Scheeben*), which prepared the ecclesiological theses of Vatican* I, focused exclusively on the Church's legal structure. In the dogmatic constitution *Pastor aeternus* promulgated by that council (dated 18 July 1870), nothing is in fact discussed but the pope. It dogmatically establishes his jurisdictional supremacy in the Church and, as a corollary, his doctrinal infallibility* when he speaks ex cathedra. The council, which initially intended to prepare a general ecclesiological program, did not succeed in dealing with other subjects, so that consequently the idea of the Church was effectively reduced to its legal-hierarchical dimension. This conception was later broadened in different directions, thanks to a new approach to divine worship (liturgical movement, encyclical *Mediator Dei* of Pius XII [1947]) and to a deeper christological analysis that, on the basis of Scripture, understood and described the Church as an institution both of law and of love (encyclical *Mystici Corporis* of Pius XII [1943]). A new movement of secular apostleship would also be influential, as would, finally, the ecclesiology of Vatican* II (in particular the dogmatic constitution *Lumen Gentium* [1964]). Indeed, on more than one point Vatican II went well beyond the official ecclesiology that had been established until then. The council broke new ground by using different biblical images, particularly that of the pilgrim people of God. It took a positive attitude toward non-Catholic Christian confessions (and the non-Christian world), which it integrated into an ecumenical vision of the Church. The council also developed the doctrine of the episcopal college, which—when it meets in council and in communion with the pope—holds supreme authority in the Church. In addition, Vatican II came to a new understanding of the ministry of the bishop in relation to his consecration and his functions, and it reintroduced the diaconate as a specific ministry in the Church. The development of the Catholic notion of the Church since Vatican II has been particularly concerned with the concept of "*communio.*" This, however, presents a profound ambivalence since it can denote the coming together of Christianity, in all its diversity, around the altar or an ecclesial unity founded on the pope and given legitimacy by him alone.

3. The Different Approaches of the Church in the Current Ecumenical Dialogue

We can briefly distinguish three ecclesiological approaches in the contemporary ecumenical movement, depending on whether the Church is understood from the Orthodox perspective, the Catholic perspective, or the point of view of the heirs of the Reformation. But Orthodox ecclesiology did not go through a historical evolution comparable to that of the two major Western traditions* as just outlined; and the Churches descending from the Reformation provide a large spectrum of ecclesiological conceptions that diverge from one another in details.

a) Eastern Churches. The ecclesiological thought of the Eastern Churches is characterized by conscious recourse to the Trinitarian model. They seek a middle way between "christological sacramentalism," which leads to institutionalism and clericalism, and "pneumatological propheticism," threatened by the specter of subjective spiritualism (Kallis). To this end and by reference to the image of the body of Christ, they understand the Church as a living organism, one that finds its center and its everlasting source in the celebration of the Eucharist (the "eucharistic ecclesiology" of Afanassieff, Schmemann, Zizioulas) and that the Spirit of God transforms into a new creation (divinization, *theôsis*). On the organizational level this ecclesiology focused on the local* Church uses on the one hand the autocephalic principle, according to which the local or national Church does not constitute a *part* of a whole but the *concretization* of the whole. On the other hand this very principle obliges local churches to come together in synods* and thus to be governed by a consensus that guarantees the unity of the body of Christ. The ministry of the bishop, placed in the apostolic* succession, constitutes the link that maintains that unity in time* and in space. As bearer of the truth spoken by the Holy Spirit, the Orthodox Church takes note of the existence of other Christian Churches, but it can enter into full eucharistic communion with them only if there is a consensus on the fundamental questions of ecclesiology.

b) The Catholic Church. In the 20th century the ecclesiology of the Catholic Church was formulated in the decrees of Vatican II. The principal difference from the Eastern approach lies in the legal form inherited from the Latin tradition and particularly from Vatican I. The Catholic Church appears here as a legal entity governed by the bishop of Rome, who holds supreme jurisdictional power and absolute doctrinal authority (in the final analysis he is infallible). In parallel and jointly with the pope, the episcopal college (placed in the apostolic succession) represents the pastoral and doctrinal organ of the universal Church, an organ that has taken on new importance since Vatican II, particularly in the extraordinary form of the council. This legal framework constitutes the bond by which the

Church, as the spiritual people of God, is gathered together and governed. As in Eastern ecclesiology, the center of spiritual life is the celebration of the Eucharist, with which the other sacraments, in particular Baptism, are coordinated. The preaching of the word of God contributes to the edification of hearts, to the education of minds, and to the proclamation of the will of God for the world. In and with the Church, all its members—particularly those known as the laity—are called to serve one another and to serve the world in love. It is in these basic ecclesiastical perspectives, to which all members of the Church are subject, that the different ministries are rooted: that of the bishop (endowed with the fullness of the sacrament of ordination*) and that of the priest—both of whom possess sacerdotal, doctrinal, and pastoral functions—as well as that of the deacon*. The Church in this complex sense is designated in its entirety as a "sacrament," that is, as "a sign and an instrument through which is achieved intimate union with God, as well as the unity of the entire human race" (*LG* 1). In spite of the many spiritual bonds that have been tied with other Christian Churches, first of all with the Eastern Churches—but also with believers of other religions and all nonbelievers of goodwill—the goal of ecumenical effort remains the unity of all Christians and of all Churches in communion with the bishop of Rome.

c) The Churches Descended from the Reformation. The Churches laying claim to the legacy of the Reformation are to be differentiated on three principal points from the Eastern Churches and the Roman Church. They are characterized in the first place by the ecclesiological primacy granted to the word of God transmitted through Scripture and preaching. Faithful to the formulation of Luther, defining the Church as a "creature of the divine Word," they have in many respects given the Word a privileged position over the sacraments, to the point of seeing in the latter only specific forms of the Word. The second distinctive element of this ecclesiological tradition consists in its granting to the question of ministry and ecclesiastical structures only a secondary role. To be sure, all the evangelical Churches have ministries, among which, as a general rule, there is a special ministry, conferred by ordination, for the public preaching of the Word and the administration of the sacraments. Many Churches that sprang from the Reformation also accept the episcopacy, or at least the functions of a regional *episkopè*. But in no case does the episcopal structure represent a necessary condition for churchliness or for church unity. This explains why the (forced) break in the apostolic succession of the bishops in the evangelical Churches in Central Europe in the 16th century does not constitute, in their view, an essential ecclesiastical deficiency despite objections from the Orthodox and Catholic Churches. This naturally implies an alternative concept of the conditions for church unity. According to *CA* VII, in order for there to be true unity, all that is needed is agreement in the preaching of the gospel and in an administration of the sacraments (Baptism, Communion) in conformity with their original institution, and this thesis—which is found in the current ecumenical canon of the Protestant Churches—constitutes one of the most serious difficulties for ecumenical dialogue. Their specific approach to the question of the ministry has led the Churches descended from the Reformation—this is their third major characteristic—to involve the laity in the administrative and doctrinal responsibilities of the Church. This is clearly evidenced in the evangelical synod, made up of both lay members and ordained clergy. The synod is to a great extent charged with establishing church regulations, which also quite often involves doctrinal decisions.

On the basis of these specific orientations, there is nevertheless a large variety of possible options and forms of organization. For example, the Anglican Church, the North American Episcopal Church, and the Lutheran Churches of Scandinavia grant particular importance to the office of bishop and to the apostolic succession, although that does not constitute an insurmountable obstacle to their eucharistic communion with other Churches founded on different principles. There are also some Churches of the congregationalist type (congregationalism*, disciples of Christ), in which universal structures are little developed or even nonexistent. Finally, there are Churches (Baptists*, Quakers) in which the sacraments are understood and administered in an entirely different way from that in other Churches. Positions also diverge as to the normative doctrinal value of confessions of faith. These differences are the subject of interconfessional discussions that have often opened up possibilities for ecclesiastical communion (on the basis of the criteria of *CA* VII) inconceivable in other traditions. We may add that the Old Catholic Church, within the sphere of influence of the Catholic tradition, and certain particular Churches (notably in India) in the Orthodox sphere have shown themselves to be more flexible toward the conditions of church unity than the principal currents of their respective traditions.

4. Principles of an Ecumenical Ecclesiology

The Church is, in the first instance, the *communion* of all whom God has called in the Holy Spirit by Jesus Christ, whether this communion is seen on a local or a world level. If it is impossible to speak of an explicit institution of the Church by Jesus before Easter, it is on the other hand possible to see its "implicit" origin in the kingdom of God whose coming Jesus proclaimed as well as in the group of men that he called to him and whom he bound to his message. The Church is the work of the Holy Spirit through the Word, through faith, and through Baptism. In the Holy Spirit, the crucified and risen Jesus Christ is present as the real and constant foundation of the Church. In its earliest form the Church was a ritual assembly where the gospel was preached and Communion was celebrated in memory of the Lord, where participants prayed to God in recognizing their sins, giving thanks, and begging for his help (*see* Acts 2:42). In this ritual practice and especially in the sharing in the body and blood of the Eucharist, the Church established itself and continually renewed itself as the "body of Christ" (1 Cor 10:16f.). Through the Spirit of God, it was able to confess the Lord Jesus (1 Cor 12:3). It was the "temple" in which dwelled the Holy Spirit (1 Cor 3:16). It expressed itself as a communion of love and established itself as a community through the variety of gifts and ministries bestowed by the Holy Spirit (1 Cor 12:12ff.), among which also appears the ministry conferred by ordination. At the same time, it was sent to proclaim the gospel throughout the world (Mt 28:19ff.) and to serve all humankind. As the "people of God" (Heb 4:9), it knew that it could rely on the promises* made to the Fathers of the old covenant (*see* Rom 11:18) and understood itself as traversing the ages toward the eschatological goal that had been assigned to it (*see* Heb 13:14).

According to the creed of Nicaea-Constantinople, the marks ("notes") of the Church are these: *unity,* conferred on it by the will of God who calls it through Christ in the Holy Spirit, as people of God over the ages, despite all sectarian divergences and cultural disparities, but also as a communion of the living and the dead; *sanctity,* which God grants it, despite its sins*, by daily forgiving and renewing it; *catholicity,* as the qualitative fullness of salvation that is offered to it and to all creation* and that confers on it, in a more quantitative sense, its saving meaning for all mankind; and it is *apostolic* because it is founded on the testimony and the ministry of the apostles and because it is sent into the world as messenger of the kingdom of God. The distinctive signs of the Church, which are simultaneously its constituent elements, are the preaching of the gospel in faithfulness to Christ and the celebration of the sacraments—particularly the Communion of the Lord (the Eucharist) and Baptism—in accordance with their original institution. The Church as eucharistic communion is first of all a local community, but it also exists at a regional and a universal level. It is the place and the very communication of salvation in Christ, which does not by any means exclude the possibility of salvation outside the Church.

This Church of the confession of faith, the "idea" of which we have just described, existed de facto in a concrete and empirical form and was therefore *stamped with the rupture of sin.* The Church, as communion of all the baptized, is a mixture ("*corpus permixtum*") made up of those who, in their heart* and in their life, follow the call addressed to them in Baptism and of those who do not live that calling. The numerous intermediate degrees between these two choices make any division that claims to be definitive impossible (Mt 13:24ff.) and pose the real problem of the multitudinist Church. The imperfection of the empirical Church is also expressed in sectarian divisions that reflect not only a legitimate diversity but also a deformation of the single Christian truth and the inevitable resulting quarrels. The ecumenical movement has shown, however, that the predicates "true" or "false" cannot unequivocally be attributed to one sectarian Church or another.

As the original witness of the apostles grew more distant in time and the Church was confronted with new cultural, existential, and political situations, the problem of a possible historical deviation in relation to the single truth was posed ever more acutely. At the same time, the growth of the Church made its unity a question of survival. From the time of the primitive Church, these two factors brought about the creation of *institutions* designed to make it possible for Christianity to remain in the truth and to continue to live in communion. It was this concern that gave rise to the canon* of Scripture, the confession of faith (along with the dogmatic decisions made by the later Church), and church structures (particularly the episcopacy and synods or councils). Added to this is the fact that institutions are, generally speaking, indispensable for the establishment of rules of common conduct and the definition of laws that a living community might accept in order to forestall dissensions that might threaten its existence. The traditional distinction between institutions of divine law (the sacraments, the ministry) and institutions of human law holds in this respect only relative value, insofar as we must also deal with the question of their respective justifications and their concrete limits.

This problem is expressed in a particularly acute form in the question, also under debate in the ecumenical movement, of the *ministry* of the Church. The ministry now conferred by ordination is not attested in that form in the New Testament, and even less may it be said that it was instituted by Jesus of Nazareth. This is true for the ministry of the preaching of the Word and the administration of the sacraments, which the Lutheran tradition considers to have been instituted by God (*CA* V), as well as for the episcopal structure of Orthodox and Catholic conceptions. Prefigurations of the pastoral ministry can of course be found in the New Testament, with the apostles and their successors responsible for teaching and practical life within their community, but this duty was not yet linked to any power to administer the sacraments. On the other hand, at least in Pauline communities, we encounter a multiplicity of services and titles that already suggest a certain degree of structural differentiation. But if theology is justified in relating to Christ himself the later institution of a church ministry conferred by ordination, this is because it judges that there took place in history a development in accordance with Christ's intentions, a development that the Lord of the Church placed at His service. This is precisely what makes it impossible to distinguish, in the analysis, between a "divine" law and a "human" law. But this means, above all, that the reality of the ministry, as it has developed in the course of history, does not have the fundamental importance for the Church that must be recognized in the preaching of the gospel and the administration of the sacraments. The same observation applies to the apostolic succession of bishops—which certainly represents an appropriate sign but can be neither a guarantee nor a condition of validity* for ministries (Lima, Porvoo)—and to the historical form of the papacy—whose role, dogmatically established by the two Vatican councils, still constitutes an obstacle among Churches. What can be said on this subject is that there must necessarily be a specific ministry on the local level, endowed with particular competence in matters of doctrine, the administration of the sacraments, and church unity, thereby guaranteeing the common exercise of gifts and duties. And if it is appropriate for such a body to exist regionally and universally, it is nonetheless necessary that this ministry, insofar as it is responsible for problems of doctrine and discipline, be bound on the local, regional, and universal levels to synods and councils that are also open (in accordance with the Protestant approach) to members of the Church who are not ordained. This is why one or another historical form the ministry may have assumed cannot be erected into a sine qua non for church unity and true churchliness. It is of course necessary, particularly on the universal level, to find forms of common decision making for the different Churches, and the question of a universal ministry for church unity must be taken into consideration, even in the Protestant perspective. But the ecumenical model, which views church unity as a conciliar communion bringing together Churches that are different both confessionally and culturally, starts in any event from the principle that differences in structure are not an obstacle to such a communion, as long as the duty of a regional *episkopè* is properly exercised in these Churches, in one way or another. It is also necessary to arrive at a fundamental consensus on matters of faith and doctrine as well as on the understanding of the sacraments. This, however, does not preclude possible divergences in dogmatic formulations. Finally, it is necessary that the perfect communion of Churches, as realized at the table of the Lord, also be confirmed in the face of the problems of the world today, in a common responsibility of service and love.

5. Ethical and Sociological Aspects

If an understanding of the Church involves ethical aspects, this is not only in the sense that its members are regenerated in the Holy Spirit and called to a new life in love and responsibility. The Church itself should also be seen as the (collective) subject of ethically responsible action. This aspect of its reality is revealed, both internally and externally, in the manner in which it determines and manages its structures as well as in the way in which, by the positions it takes and its collective conduct, it assumes or evades its responsibilities. The oft-raised topics of "democracy*" and "bureaucracy" in the Church raise questions about large areas of church reality where the mode of operation, as set in place by human beings, may or may not be faithful to the essence lying behind that reality. The truth assigned to the Church is of course, in itself, inviolable and thus cannot depend on a democratic decision. But the search for relevant and current forms of expression, as well as the manner of assuming its responsibilities in preaching and particularly of choosing its leaders in one area or another (e.g., bishops)—all these together, for a Church that understands itself as the people of God, call for democratic procedures and structures (synod).

It is also by an ethical choice that the Church decides how it will assume its task in society and what structures should be chosen for that purpose. In the course of its history the Church gradually came to exercise a share of responsibility over the social body as a whole, in particular with the Constantinian turn, which played a fundamental role, especially for the medieval order. In modern times the process of secularization* has brought about a retreat of the Church in public life, and in some European countries Church members now make up only a minority of the population. Any theocratic pretensions of the Church toward society would therefore not only be subject to challenge on dogmatic and ethical grounds but also anachronistic. Freedom of opinion and conscience must remain guaranteed to citizens. According to the functionalist-pluralist theory of society (Luhmann), religion and the Church that "administers" are there to respond to a limited number of needs that still exist in modern society ("control over contingency"). The Church is not, however, ready to confine itself to that role. Rather, it sees its prophetic and diaconal mission to be that of affirming God's goodwill toward all people: by giving an orientation to human endeavor, by drawing attention to error, and by offering charitable assistance. The Church cannot give up this mandate, even when official society wishes to challenge it, as might be the case, for example, in modern dictatorships. It is in just this perspective that the relation between Church* and state must also be considered. Starting from the principle of separation between these two orders, a principle in accordance both with the understanding the Church has of itself and with the modern idea of a state free of any credo, one might consider a structure that would facilitate an encounter between the Church and those in secular society without however subjecting the Church to legal supervision. In this respect the legal model of the "corporate person subject to public law" would, from the Church's standpoint, provide a better basis than that of an institution governed by private law. For a modern society that is confronted with many dangers, this would also be an opportunity to take into account, through a certain number of structural adjustments and contractual rules, the contribution of the Church to the preparation of a future worthy of humankind.

• *Lumen Gentium,* Vatican II, Dogmatic Constitution on the Church, 21 November 1964.
Baptême, eucharistie, ministère (texte de convergence de *Foi et Constitution*), Paris, 1982.
♦ Y. Congar (1941), *Esquisse du mystère de l'Église,* Paris (2nd Ed. 1966).
L. Cerfaux (1942), *La théologie de l'Église suivant saint Paul,* Paris.
H. de Lubac (1953), *Méditation sur l'Église,* Paris.
O. Semmelroth (1953), *Die Kirche als Ursakrament,* Frankfurt (2nd Ed. 1963).
T. F. Torrance (1955), *Royal Priesthood,* Edinburgh.
K. Barth (1964), *L'Église,* Geneva.
H. Mühlen (1964), Una Mystica Persona: *Die Kirche als das Mysterium der Identität des heiligen Geistes in Christus und den Christen—eine Person in vielen Personen,* Munich-Paderborn-Vienna (Rev. Ed. 1967).
H. Rahner (1964), *Symbole der Kirche: Die Ekklesiologie der Väter,* Salzburg.
H. Küng (1967), *Die Kirche,* Fribourg.
N. Nissiotis (1968), *Die Theologie der Ostkirchen im oekumenischen Dialog: Kirche und Welt in orthodoxer Sicht,* Stuttgart.
L. Bouyer (1970), *L'Église de Dieu, Corps du Christ et temple de l'Esprit,* Paris.
MySal (1972), IV/1 (contributions by N. Füglister, H. Schlier, W. Beinert, H. Fries, O. Semmelroth and Y. Congar).
MySal (1973), IV/2 (contributions by P. Huizing and B. Dupuy).
Y. Congar (1975), *Un peuple messianique, salut et libération,* Paris.
J. Moltmann (1975), *Die Kirche in der Kraft des Geistes,* Munich.
W. Pannenberg (1977), *Ethik und Ekklesiologie,* Göttingen.
U. Kühn (1980), *Kirche, HST* 10, Gütersloh (2nd Ed. 1990).
J. Zizioulas (1981), *L'être ecclésial,* Geneva.
F. Refoulé and B. Lauret (Ed.) (1983), *Initiation à la pratique de la théologie,* vol. III, Dogmatique 2 (2nd Ed. 1993) (contributions by J. Hoffmann, H. Legrand, and J.-M. Tillard), Paris.
A. Houtepen (1984), *People of God,* London.
G. Martelet (1984–90), *Deux mille ans d'Église en question,* 3 vols., Paris.
H. Döring (1986), *Grundriss der Ekklesiologie,* Darmstadt.
J.-M. Tillard (1987), *Église d'Églises,* CFi 143.
K. Berger et al. (1988), "Kirche," *TRE* 18, 198–344 (bibl.).
E. Herms (1990), *Erfahrbare Kirche: Beiträge zur Ekklesiologie,* Tübingen.
W. Pannenberg (1993), *Systematische Theologie* 3, Göttingen, 13–567.
A. Birmelé (1995), "Église," in P. Gisel (Ed.), *Encyclopédie du protestantisme,* Geneva-Paris, 483–99.
A. Birmelé, J. Terme (Ed.) (1995), *Accords et dialogues œcuméniques,* Paris, 81–117 ("L'Église de Jésus-Christ: La contribution des Églises issues de la Réforme").
B. Forte (1995), *La Chiesa della Trinità,* Rome.
K. Rahner (1995), *Selbstvollzug der Kirche, SW* 19, Düsseldorf-Fribourg.
J.-M. Tillard (1995), *L'Église locale,* CFi 191.
O. González de Cardedal (1997), *La entraña del cristianismo,* Salamanca, 247–300, 683–811, and passim.

Ulrich Kühn

See also **Authority; Baptism; Being; Church and State; Communion; Council; Ecclesiastical Discipline; Eucharist; Gospels; Government, Church; Hierarchy; Indefectibility of the Church; Infallibility; Local Church; Magisterium; Ministry; Priesthood; Regional Church; Sacrament; Schism; Structures, Ecclesial; Synod; Unity of the Church; Word of God**

Church and State

According to the Bible*, God* alone is the sovereign master of humanity, of its peoples and history*. All power proceeds from him (Jn 19:11; Rom 13:1), to be placed at the service of justice* and peace*. Such is Caesar's limited field of action, by comparison to God's, which is virtually limitless (Mt 22:21). Conscience*, truth*, and meaning are a matter for God alone. The power that punishes crime and inclines to good* is "the servant of God" (Rom 13:4), and 1 Pt 2:13–15 exhorts us to obey "every human institution" in all conscience. But when power forsakes the order established by God and declares itself divine, "We must obey God rather than men" (Acts 5:29). When power deifies itself, it must be met with resistance and condemnation (*see* Rev 13:7–18). The issue of the relations between Church and state is raised by the way in which the Christian community understands its role in society and by the degree of control which the state attempts to exert over religious life. These relations may take the form of distinction or interpenetration, of hostile separation or of cooperation.

1. From Persecution to Interpenetration

a) Antiquity. Until 313 Christianity was a *religio illicita.* The apologists of the second and third centuries pleaded that Christians should have the mere right to exist. Tertullian demanded *libertas religionis* (*see Apologeticum* 24, 6; *Ad Scapulam* 2, 2) for Christians within the pagan state, declaring their loyalty toward the empire. The persecutions of Decius (250), Valerian (257), Diocletian (303–4), and Galerius (305–11) attempted, on a huge scale but without success, to put a halt to the Christian phenomenon. Constantine and Licinius (Milan, 313) gave Christians the freedom to honor the supreme deity in accordance with their rites, individually and as a collective body. Constantine entrusted the bishops* with civil and judicial responsibilities and took initiatives to resolve the Donatist and Arian crises by calling the councils* of Arles (314) and Nicaea* (325). He exiled the bishops who were deposed and so was born the confusion between the political and ecclesiastical spheres. At the same time, Eusebius of Caesarea developed a political* theology* according to which the emperor had received from God the mission of governing the Church* as a "common bishop" or "external bishop." Henceforward the interpenetration of political and ecclesiastical power got under way. Theodosius I would soon impose the Nicene faith* on the whole empire (380).

The Byzantine "monist" model persisted until 1453, kept up in the state Orthodox churches. The autocephalous churches tended to identify themselves with one nation ("phyletism"). The monarch led the church, which was inseparable from the political establishment, leaving the bishops to administer the sacraments* and preach* dogma*.

In the West there was from the fourth century an emphasis on the distinction between the different spheres of activity. Ambrose* of Milan made it clear to Theodosius that he was "in the Church and not above the Church" (*Ep.* 20, 36). Pope* Gelasius I summarized in a celebrated phrase the necessary distinction between *auctoritas sacerdotale* and *potestas imperiale (Ep. ad Anastasium),* both having their origins in God. There were now two centers in what had become a Christian society. Thus arose the "dualist" model—the dialectic between temporal power and spiritual power—characteristic of the West.

b) The Middle Ages. The Germanic kingdoms held that the Church's property and its ministers were at the disposal of the sovereign. In the case of the Franks and the Visigoths in Spain, the king, consecrated by unction, appointed the bishops, who were thus instruments of government.

Alcuin suggested to Charlemagne that he was the new David. He himself wrote to the pope telling him that he should confine himself to prayer*. The supervision of *christianitas* was the king's affair. Under the successors of Louis the Pious, however, the divided imperial power began to crumble, and the Frankish bishops assumed the role of the nation's conscience (council of Metz, 859).

During the age of feudalism, bishops and abbots were chosen by their overlords, who conferred on them pastoral responsibility *(officium)* along with temporal remuneration *(beneficium).* This "secularization*" of the hierarchy* resulted in a corrupt attitude to ecclesiastical office (simony) and a decline in the morals of the clergy (Nicolaitanism). In the wake of the monastic reforms of Cluny and Gorze, the forces of renewal became centered on the papacy from Leo IX (1073–54) onward, culminating in the initiatives of Gregory VII. The "Gregorian reform" marked the turning point of the Middle Ages. In the name of *libertas Ecclesiae,* it fought for the freedom* of investiture, a right obtained with the empire in the concordat of Worms (1122) and with the major Western monarchies in similar agreements. Elections were to be free, and the temporal powers would now confer only the *beneficium.* The hierarchical Church once again presented itself as independent of political power and frequently in opposition to it. From the eighth century, the papacy headed a state (the Patrimony of Saint Peter) that was intended to guarantee its independence.

With its two recognized heads, Western Christianity threw itself between 1150 and 1300 into a power struggle between *Sacerdotium* and *Regnum* that concluded in the papacy's favor. From Innocent III (1198–1216) to Boniface VIII (1294–1303), the papacy was at the height of its temporal influence. It upheld the right of the spiritual power to have control over the temporal power and to intervene as required *(occasionaliter)* when the latter failed in its responsibilities *(ratione peccati).* The theory of "direct power," which would come to the fore in the texts of Boniface VIII (*see* the bull *Unam Sanctam,* 1302), asserted that the pope, as vicar of Christ*, was the agent of his power in both the temporal and the spiritual orders.

The "exile in Avignon" (1305–76) and the ruptures of the Great Schism* (1378–1417) resulted in a strengthening of the power of Christian monarchs. Some theorists, inspired by William of Ockham, handed over to temporal power the task of ensuring Christian unity. In England, Wycliffe proposed the king as the head of the national church. In the 15th century, "nation" states wrung increasingly extensive concessions from the papacy regarding the nomination of bishops, such as the Pragmatic Sanction of Bourges in 1438 and, later, the Concordat of Bologna (1516).

c) Reformations and Confessionalism. In this context, the Lutheran, Calvinist, and Anglican Reformations offered new conceptions of the relations between Church and state. Luther* envisaged a total separation between the "temporal kingdom," devoted to maintaining society within the law*, but without significance in terms of redemption, and the "spiritual kingdom" governed solely by the Word* of God and the gifts of the Holy* Spirit, but with no bearing on the temporal order. The prince was responsible for calling synods* and for ensuring the purity of the faith. The Church, which was "spiritual," existed in seclusion in the midst of a political community, under the orders of the prince. A secularization of the ecclesiastical institution is visible here, associated with a new sacralization of temporal power. Protestant law, as represented by Samuel Pufendorf, would state that the Church had legal existence only by virtue of the rights that the prince graciously conceded to it. In the Holy Roman Empire the system of the denominational state (Lutheran, Reformed, or Catholic) held sway from 1555 to 1806, according to the principle of *cuius regio eius religio* ("of which region, of that religion"). The Anglican Reformation placed the national Church under the dominance of the king.

Catholic rulers had obtained ecclesiastical rights by means of papal concessions. From the 16th century, Spain and Portugal enjoyed a right of patronage—in other words, of complete control over ecclesiastical life—in their colonies in Latin America, the Indies, and the Philippines. In Europe rulers had the right of veto *(placet)* over documents from Rome and heard all appeals against ecclesiastical jurisdiction* on "appeal *ab abusu.*" In the Germanic countries Febronianism (a movement with episcopalian tendencies, comparable to Gallicanism*) intensified the desire for withdrawal into national churches. In Austria, Joseph II suppressed the convents and confraternities and imposed scrupulous regulation of worship* and religious teaching. During the Enlightenment period, ecclesiastical institutions were tolerated as long as they contributed to cohesion and social control, in other words, to the aims of political power.

In this context a new canonical discipline evolved: "ecclesiastical public law." Fostered by the school of Würzburg, it drew on a category already employed by Bellarmine* in the 16th century to the effect that the Church was a society governed by its own law that did not derive from that of the state. Its sphere of competence was distinct and autonomous from the state's. In joint matters, however, the two powers, in the service of the same people, were required to cooperate.

2. Between State Neutrality and Hostility

a) The American and French Revolutions. The American and French Revolutions brought to an end the age-old interpenetration between the two powers of Church and state. In the United States a new model came into being. The First Amendment to the U.S. Constitution (1791) prohibited the making of any law concerning the establishment of religion or forbidding its free exercise. America advocated the liberty of citizens and the absolute neutrality of the state in matters of religion. In France the Declaration of the Rights of Man of 1789 granted freedom for all "opinions, even in religion" (art. 10). The Convention nonetheless attempted to nationalize the Church by imposing on it the unilateral legislation of the Civil Constitution of the Clergy (1790). The philosophy of Napoleon Bonaparte's Concordat (1801) and of the Organic Articles relating to the "recognized religions" (Catholic, Protestant, and Jewish) was that religion, being useful for social control, should be regulated and remunerated by the state.

b) 19th-Century Nostalgia for the Confessional State. Under the aegis of ultramontanism, the papacy again became the emotive center of the Catholic world, while the regalism of previous centuries lived on in the Catholic states, both in Europe and in Latin America.

Gregory XVI and Pius IX condemned liberal thinking on religious freedom*, rationalism*, indifferentism, and the separation of Church and state (*see Syllabus,* 1864). Leo XIII regarded Church and state as distinct but called to peaceful cooperation. From 1860, Church public law conceptualized the relationship between Church and state as one between "two legally perfect societies." The Church hoped to preserve its independence by presenting itself, like the state, as a society in possession of all the elements necessary to its mission,* and it insisted on its freedom as an institution. Some authors have taken this model as the basis for a theory of the "indirect power of the Church *in temporalibus.*"

In the 20th century no further right of episcopal presentation or nomination was to be granted to civil authorities, with the exception of Spain in 1941. The concordats signed by Pius IX approved the dual principle of the Church's autonomy in its own field and of collaboration with states in matters referred to as mixed, such as marriage* legislation, religious education in state schools, and religious assistance to armies, prisons, and hospitals. The creation of the Vatican City state by the Lateran Accords (1929) was intended to ensure the temporal independence of the Holy See.

c) Hostile Divisions. A violent anticlerical backlash brought about a unilateral breaking off of the traditional links between Church and state in Catholic countries such as France (1905), Portugal (1910), Mexico (1910), and republican Spain (1931). The concordats with fascist Italy (1929) and Nazi Germany (1933) did not prevent Pius XI from condemning these two ideologies, with *Redemptor hominis* and *Mit brennender Sorge* (1937), respectively.

From 1917 in the Soviet Union and then after 1945 in its European satellites and in Asian and African Communist countries, the Churches were faced with a new type of state characterized by an antireligious ideology. These countries set out in their constitutions the principle of a dual separation between Church and state and between the Church and education, established on 23 January 1918 by the Decree of the Soviet of the Commissars of the People. They maintained the freedom of conscience and worship at the same time as that of antireligious propaganda. The state imposed dialectical materialism as its official philosophy and discriminated against professed believers. China stipulated further that no religious community should receive any order from abroad (1949), leading to the creation in 1957 of the Patriotic Catholic Association, with no links to Rome*. Communist Albania claimed the distinction of being the first entirely atheist state in the world. The fall of Communism in Central and Eastern Europe in 1989 and 1990 led these countries to adopt liberal principles concerning religious freedom.

d) The Right to Religious Freedom. Since 1945 the principle of religious freedom has come to the fore in the constitutions of democratic states and international agreements. In 1948 and again in 1961, the Ecumenical Council of Churches* adopted a declaration on religious freedom that envisaged it as a right deriving from the dignity of the person*, a right whose effective exercise should be guaranteed by the state. At Vatican II (1962–65), the Catholic Church in turn, with the declaration *Dignitatis humanae,* moved from a moral to a legal conception of this right and acknowledged that the state must guarantee citizens and their religious communities the freedom necessary for the exercise of the various personal, family, educational, cultural, and associative aspects of religious faith, within the limits implied by the maintenance of order, health, public morality, and the rights of third parties (*DH* 7). *DH* 13 asserted that the freedom of the Church as a social group was sufficiently guaranteed when the common right to religious freedom was ensured. It further reiterated that the Church's innate divine right to liberty was the "fundamental principle of the Church's relations with public authority and the whole civil order." The constitution *Gaudium et spes* (76, 2–3) reaffirmed the reciprocal autonomy and cooperation necessary between Church and state.

3. Current Models

These remain marked by the tensions of the past.

a) Persecution. There are still in existence religious regimes that prohibit the exercise of other religions (such as Saudi Arabia) or that discriminate against their adherents. Similarly, some officially atheist states limit religious freedom.

b) State Churches. The "established churches," such as the Church of England or the Lutheran Churches in

Scandinavia, are administered by the civil legislature and executive. Their status does not, however, imply any limiting of the religious freedom of other denominations. The Greek Orthodox Church and the Reformed Churches in some cantons of Switzerland enjoy the status of churches protected and supervised by the state.

c) Institutional Separation. In the United States, France (since the law of separation of 1905), and the Netherlands (since 1982), the Churches now have a status only in private law.

d) Institutional Separation and Cooperation. In Ireland the Church runs the education system. In the Latin countries, cooperation is defined by concordat: in Portugal (since 1940), in Spain (1976–78), and in Italy (1984). Germany, Austria, and most of the cantons of Switzerland exhibit the most developed form of institutional cooperation, guaranteed by the constitution and augmented by concordats or bilateral agreements with the various denominations. The churches are recognized as corporations under public law, with the power to levy taxes on their members.

e) Recognized Religions. The French system of 1801 survives in the legislation concerning religions in Belgium and Luxembourg, and also in Alsace and Moselle in France, where the Concordat of Napoleon is still current.

f) The International Character of the Holy See. The Holy See—rather than the Vatican state—is active as either a member or an observer in the international organizations of the United Nations system. It also takes part in international conferences and is a signatory to numerous international conventions while emphasizing its unique character. The Catholic Church participates in relations with the international community by virtue of its own constitution as a transnational body with supreme power in its own domain and maintains relations with states on a basis of judicial parity. The international position of the Holy See, a product of history and of the Church's definition of itself as a society *sui iuris,* autonomous and independent of any temporal power, is consistent with the model of relations between Church and state that the Catholic Church has defended over the centuries.

• J.B. Lo Grasso (1940), *Ecclesia et Status: Fontes selecti,* Rome (2nd Ed., 1952).

♦ A. Ottaviani (1925), *Institutiones Iuris Publici ecclesiastici,* 2 vols., Vatican (4th Ed., 1958, 1960).

H. Rahner (1964), *L'Église et l'État dans le christianisme primitif,* Paris.

G. Barberini (1973), *Stati socialisti e confessioni religiose,* Milan.

E.R. Huber, W. Huber (I 1973, II 1976, III 1983, IV 1988), *Staat und Kirche im 19. und 20. Jahrhundert,* Berlin.

J. Listl (1978), *Kirche und Staat in der neueren katholischen Kirchenrechtswissenschaft,* Berlin.

L. Spinelli (1979), *Libertas Ecclesiae,* Milan.

J. Téran-Dutari (Ed.) (1980), *Simposio sudamericano-alemán sobre Iglesia y Estado,* Quito.

R. Minnerath (1982a), *Le droit de l'Église à la liberté. Du* Syllabus *à Vatican II,* Paris; (1982b), *L'Église et les États concordataires (1846–1981),* Paris.

R. Minnerath (1986), "Église et État dans l'Europe des Douze," *ConscLib* 32, 11–143.

M. Pacaut (1988), *La théocratie: L'Église et le pouvoir au Moyen Age,* Paris.

L. Bressan (1989), *La libertà religiosa nel diritto internazionale,* Padua.

R.M. Grant et al. (1989), "Kirche und Staat," *TRE* 18, 354–405.

J.-B. d'Onorio (Ed.) (1989), *Le Saint-Siège dans les relations internationales,* Paris.

J.-B. d'Onorio (Ed.) (1991), *La liberté religieuse dans le monde,* Paris.

Coll. (1991a), "La liberté religieuse dans les pays musulmans," *ConscLib* 41, 7–109.

Coll. (1991b), "La liberté religieuse en Europe de l'Est," *ConscLib* 42, 36–127.

Coll. (1992), "La liberté religieuse en Afrique," *ConscLib* 43, 17–107.

Coll. (1993), "La liberté religieuse en Amérique latine," *ConscLib* 45, 21–113.

Coll. (1994), "La liberté religieuse dans le Pacifique Sud," *ConscLib* 47, 36–119.

Revue européenne des relations Églises-État (1994–), Louvain.

ROLAND MINNERATH

See also **Authority; Church; Government, Church; Secularization; Society**

Circumincession

In Trinitarian theology*, circumincession expresses the dwelling of the persons* of the Trinity* in one another as well as their mutual gift. In Christology, it means the interpenetration of divine and human natures in the person of Christ* Jesus*.

a) Biblical Basis and Early Patristic Development. It is essentially in the Johannine* writings that the ideas of dwelling and mutual gift are found, for example, "Believe me that I am in the Father and the Father is in me" (Jn 14:11). Christian soteriology is presented as entry into the relation that unites the Father, the Son, and the Holy* Spirit: "In that day you will know that I am in my Father, and you in me, and I in you" (Jn 14:20) or "By this we know that we abide in him and he in us, because he has given us of his Spirit" (1 Jn 4:13).

These passages are of course focused on the unity of Father, Son, and Holy Spirit in action. But this unity implicitly refers to the unity of being*, and it is in this sense that the Fathers* of the Church* understood it. The point of departure for thinking in this area was the relation between Father and Son:

The Father is in the Son because the Son proceeds from him. The Son is in the Father, because he derives from no other his being as Son (Hilary*, *Trin.* 3. 4; CChr.SL 62. 25). Hence, the Father and the Son dwell in one another and give themselves to one another because they are consubstantial* (Cyril* of Alexandria; PG 74. 244c). With the development of Trinitarian theology, assertions concerning the Father and the Son were extended to the Three Persons: The true God* is a Trinity by persons, One by nature. Through this natural unity, the Father is entirely in the Son and the Holy Spirit, and the Son is entirely in the Father and the Holy Spirit, just as the Holy Spirit is entirely in the Father and the Son. No one among them is external to the others (Fulgencius of Ruspina, *De fide ad Petrum* 4, CChr.SL 91A. 714).

b) Greek Theology. Until the seventh century, the fathers of the church had no special term for the mutual indwelling and the gift of the Three Persons. In the Greek world, christological controversies fostered the introduction of a specific vocabulary with the verb *perikhôréô* and the noun *perikhôrèsis.* Gregory* of Nazianzus introduced the verb to explain that the unity of the two natures in Christ has the effect that what is particular to God can be attributed to human beings and vice versa: this is known as the communication of idioms* (*Ep.* 101. 31; SC 208. 48). The interpenetration of the two natures establishes the exchange of properties. Maximus* the Confessor used this notion and introduced the noun. *Perikhôrèsis* thus designates in the person of Christ the movement of penetration of divine nature into *(eis)* or toward *(pros)* human nature. With pseudo-Cyril in the late seventh century, the notion entered into the domain of being. So, *Perikhôrèsis* designated the penetration of human nature by divine nature within the hypostatic* union. The unity of the person established the coinherence or *perikhôrèsis* of the two natures (*Trin* 24; PG 77. 1165*cd*).

The same writer introduced the vocabulary into Trinitarian theology: Other words related to Christ concern the *perikhôrèsis* of the persons one in the other, as, "I am in the Father and the Father is in me" (Jn 15:16) (*Trin* 23; PG 77. 1164*b*).

Perikhôrèsis thus expresses the union of the three persons in a single essence (*Trin* 10). They are a single God, for each is in the two others and each gives himself to the two others. This doctrine was taken up by John of Damascus (*Fid.* 1. 8; Kotter) and by later Greek theology. It made it possible to avoid the two pitfalls of all Trinitarian theology: the separation of the three persons (Arianism*, tritheism*) or their confusion (modalism*). Moreover, the *perikhôrèsis* of the two natures in Christ is based on that of the three persons of the Trinity (John of Damascus, *Fid.* 3. 7; Kotter 2. 126).

c) Latin Theology. In the 12th century, the notion of indwelling was taken up again in Trinitarian theology on the basis of the Scriptures* and the Latin Fathers, without recourse to a technical term. The term *circumincessio* was, however, introduced into theological vocabulary with the translation of *De fide* of John of Damascus by Burgundio of Pisa in 1153–54, although Peter Lombard, who cited it, did not adopt the word (*Sentences* 1. 19. 4). It did not appear until the following century, in Alexander of Halès (†1245), in reference to works by Peter Lombard and John of Damascus (*In Sent.* 1. 19. q. 2).

After Alexander of Hales, the term "circumincession" became common, first in the Franciscan school, then among other theologians, although it did not gain universal currency. Writers also continued to present the notion of indwelling without using the term, for example, Thomas* Aquinas (*ST* Ia, q. 42, a. 5) and the Council of Florence* (Decree of Union with the Jacobites, 1442; bull *Cantate domino, DS* 1330).

Independently of Trinitarian theology, the concept of circumincession appeared in Christology in Albert* the Great (*In Dyon. ep.* 4; Simon 489, 492). It underwent little development. The spelling *circuminsessio* is found from the late 13th century both in Trinitarian theology (Durand de Saint-Pourçain, *In Sent.* 1. 19) and in Christology (Henry of Ghent, *Quodlibet* 13). This is due to the "French" pronunciation of Latin, in which *ce* and *se* are identical.

The notion of circumincession has also made some mark in the 20th century in the Trinitarian anthropology* of J. Monchanin (1895–1957), according to whom "we must live in circumincession with our brothers." (*See* in particular *Théologie et spiritualité missionaires;* Paris, 1985.)

• A. Deneffe (1923), "*Perichoresis, circumincessio, circuminsessio:* Eine terminologische Untersuchung," *ZKTh* 47, 497–532.

G. L. Prestige (1936), *God in Patristic Thought,* London.

M. Schmaus (1963), "Perichorese," *LThK2* 8, 274–76.

P. Stemmer (1983), "Perichorese: Zur Geschichte eines Begriffs," *ABG* 27, 9–55.

V. Harisson (1991), "Perichoresis in the Greek Fathers," *SVTQ* 35, 53–65.

JACQUES FANTINO

See also **Consubstantial; Salvation**

City

I. Old Testament

The word "city" in the biblical context does not have the resonance given to it by Greco-Roman civilization. It refers solely to the urban phenomenon. It designates the political and social representation of a people* through the form of authority that is exercised in a visible way (institutions, monuments, symbols) in the socioeconomic form of a city. The Hebrew word *'îr,* the one most frequently used (1,087 times), has generally been translated into Greek by *polis,* but it simply means "town." We also find *qireyâh* (from *qîr,* "wall," with place-names using *qireyat*) and the metonymic use of *she'arîm* ("doors": Ex 20:10; Dt 5:14), which imply the existence of walls. These walls, and the towns they protected, existed in Canaan long before the history* of Israel* began.

1. Before the Monarchy

Unlike many civilizations, Israel did not attribute its existence as a people to the "foundation" of a city. It was a "wandering Aramean" and not a founding hero whom it recognized as "father" (Dt 26:5). The narratives* of origin and the patriarchal cycles give the impression of an identity acquired at the price of a negative view of the world of cities. The first city to appear in the Bible* is the city of Enoch built by Cain the murderer (Gn 4:17); and the Babel episode (Gn 11) denounces humankind's attempt to "make a name for ourselves" against God by building "a city and a tower." In this perspective, no city can claim to be the center or the model of the world*. The division of land between Abram and his nephew Lot (Gn 13:11ff.) clearly illustrates a fundamental choice: Lot chooses to live "among the cities" and Abram "in the land of Canaan" (Gn 13:12). The good choice is made by the one who remains apart from the cities and their dangers (as evidenced by Sodom and Gomorrah). From the outset the history of Israel is founded on an experience of displacement—a displacement, nevertheless, that looks toward the fulfillment of a promise* and is marked by attempts to settle in a land.

The history of the conquest, as narrated in Joshua, preserves this negative vision. The tales of the capture of cities such as Jericho and Ai involve the total destruction of the city in question (Jos 6:20f., 8:28). This signifies a great suspicion of these rich and idolatrous city-states of Canaan (Ez 16:49). Deuteronomy expresses another point of view in recognizing that Israel has found a "land that he swore to your fathers . . . with great and good cities that you [Israel] did not build" (Dt 6:10), and it formulates a set of laws adapted to urban communities. It is possible to conclude, particularly on the basis of Judges, that the Israelites gradually settled into the urban system of Canaan while neither creating new cities nor reestablishing old ones. Later, the view taken of very large pagan cities (Ez 27–28: Tyre; Jon 3:3, 4:11: Niniveh) did not always lack elements of admiration.

2. The Cities of Israel

a) The Power of the Kings. It was in fact on the basis of an already established city—Jerusalem*, capital of the Canaanite Jebusites—that David brought the city into the history of Israel (2 Sm 5:6–12). He seized a fortified city, and by installing the "house of the king" there he made of it "the city of David" (mentioned 22 times in Samuel and Kings: *see also* ark of the covenant*; royal sepulchres). He and his successors also provided the kingdom with a network of border cities (e.g., Beersheba). From then on the city became an indispensable element for the people under the monarchy. King Omri even replaced the first capital of the kingdom of the North, Tirzah, by the only genuinely new city, Samaria (1 Kgs 16:24). The Israelite city experienced the ambiguities of the institution of royalty: power and justice* rarely went together. Force ruled: the city was surrounded with solid ramparts (Is 22:9ff.)—according to Leviticus 25:31, this is the difference between a "city" and a "village"—and possibly with a citadel. It was thus able to shelter the inhabitants of the countryside in case of an invasion. It concentrated political power since it contained the palace of the king or of a governor and religious power since the Deuteronomic reform, in principle, limited this to a single sanctuary, the Temple* of Jerusalem alone. It held military (1 Kgs 9:22), administrative (scribes), and ritual (priests) personnel and fostered the growth of crafts and commercial activities (1 Kgs 10:15). Justice was put to the test in the city: the abuse of power and wealth created new conflicts that the Israel of the desert could not have imagined, and these can be seen in the survival of idolatrous cults* and conflicts between rich and poor. The religious and social order depended on the authority of the king. After the exile this authority was taken over by the priests of the Temple and groups of "elders" who dispensed justice at the "gates" of the city in the name of "Wisdom" (Prv 8:3, 31:23). It is difficult to tell to what extent the law* establishing "cities of refuge" (Nm 35:9ff.; Dt 19:1–13) was applied.

b) Dangers and the Promise. The prophets* perceived the painful ambiguity of the world of cities. Often of rural origin, devoted to the salvation* of the people, they denounced the perversion that led to ruin: the nadir of this perversion was represented by inequality (Am 3:9–15), arrogance (Is 9:8f.), and religious faithlessness (Hos 10:1–5). Transgression by a city was punished by its destruction by an enemy through starvation, massacre, and razing of its walls. The prophets proclaimed this in Samaria as in Jerusalem* and in the great capitals of the East. For them, there was only one city, Jerusalem. It could never be destroyed without one day being rebuilt (Ez 40; Zec 14). This current of belief in a sure and certain restoration (Is 1:26, 24:23, 48:35) was also reflected in poems, psalms*, and prophetic texts that exalted the "holy city" (Is 52:1).

II. New Testament

1. The Scene of the Proclamation

The synoptic Gospels* present Jesus* preaching in cities as well as villages. When he preached outside towns, it was to a public that had come from those towns to seek him out. He was not seen in Caesarea. In fact, he avoided cities (Mk 1:45) in order to forestall public demonstrations. Luke uses the word *polis* for cities such as Nazareth and Bethlehem (Lk 2:3f.), which were not "cities" in the political sense like the cities of the Decapolis, and Mark uses it for Capernaum (Mk 1:33). Jesus inveighed against the cities of Israel (Mt 11:20–24 and parallel passages) as well as Jerusalem (Mt 23:37 and parallel passages) as collective entities, in the manner of the prophets.

Integration into an urban world determined the early development of the apostolic mission* (Lk 10:1). In obtaining hospitality, as in preaching in the synagogue or the public square, the apostles found the city an essential component in the acceptance or rejection of the Good News (Acts 13–16). The routes of Paul's missionary journey's passed among the great cities of the "diaspora," out of which Paul himself had come, enjoying the rights of a Roman citizen as a native of Tarsus. It was in cities that "churches" were organized by "elders" (Acts 15:23; Ti 1:5). This universe of Greco-Roman cities had a broad influence on the way of life and the institutions of the emerging Church, particularly on their combination of communitarian and hierarchical aspects.

2. The Image of the City

Several lines of interpretation take shape on the basis of the always ambiguous image of the city: 1) a traditional line of hostility to the "city" as a place that is closed off to God and that fosters human pride. Jesus laments over the cities of the lake: Bethsaida, Chorazin, and Capernaum (Lk 10:12–15). The "great city" of Revelation 16:19 is doomed to destruction with all the other "cities of the nations," whereas the "holy city, the new Jerusalem" (Rev 21:1) is not a human work* but comes from God. 2) A new line of interpretation appears in the letter to the Ephesians. Israel is represented there as a city that has the power to grant citizenship to new inhabitants. Excluded from citizenship of Israel (i.e., because they lack circumcision), Gentiles can become instead "fellow citizens" of the "saints" (Eph 2:11f.) of the new community saved by Christ*. "Legal" status takes precedence over ethnic or geographical situation and makes possible the beginnings of thinking about universality. 3) The richest line of interpretation for ecclesial tradition* is set out in the letter to the Hebrews, which speaks of the journey of the people of God toward the heavenly city. The Christian has no "permanent city" but seeks a "city to come" (Heb 13:14), which Abraham had already hoped for (Heb 11:10). Christians can also play a role in history* without subordinating themselves to the authorities, as was proved by the attitude of Christians loyal to the structures of the Roman world. The city of which God is the architect (Heb 11:10) and the "constitution" *(politeuma)* that Philippians 3:20 sets in heaven ("our citizenship is in heaven") make possible a radical challenge to all secular appetites and powers as well as to theocratic pretensions. This theology* of the "two cities" was to have a long-lasting legacy.

• R. de Vaux (1967), *Institutions de l'Ancien Testament I et II,* Paris.
Colloque de Cartigny (1983), *La ville dans le Proche-Orient ancien. Cahiers du CEPOA* 1, Louvain.
G. A. London (1992), "Tells: City Center or Home?," *Eretz Israel* 23, 71–79.
C. H. J. de Geus (1993), "Of Tribes and Towns: The Historical Development of the Israelite City," *ErIs* 24, 70–76.
M. Beaudry (1994), "L'urbanisation à l'époque du Fer," in J.-C. Petit (Ed.), *Où demeures-tu? La maison depuis le monde biblique: En hommage au* Pr *G. Couturier,* Montreal, 31–51.

XAVIER DURAND

See also **Authority; Jerusalem; Kingdom of God; People of God; Political Theology; Prophet and Prophecy; Temple**

Clarembald of Arras. *See* **Chartres, School of**

Clement of Alexandria. *See* **Alexandria, School of**

Clement of Rome. *See* **Apostolic Fathers**

Cleric

Klèros, which in biblical Greek means "share," "legacy," took on a religious nuance in Philo: God* is the "share" of his people* and the people is the "share" of God. The idea was adopted by Christians and became for them a permanent tradition*. In the second and third centuries, a distinction between clergy and laity* appeared, the clergy being those in the Christian community who were especially attached to the service of God. The expression was to retain a broader and somewhat vague sense, designating more than the principal ordained ministries*. In the Roman-Frankish liturgy, the *Supplement* to the *Gregorian Sacramentary* contains a rite of tonsure to "make a cleric," distinct from ordination* to any ministry (Deshusses ed. I, 417).

As the canonists and theologians of the Middle Ages saw it, all the baptized benefited from the Christian cult*, and their participation consisted of joining in without being its performers in the strict sense. The public ritual of the Church* was carried out only by public persons, the clergy, in a division of labor that broadly corresponded to the existing levels of culture and to the medieval idea of the division of roles among the major social categories, the "orders," that is, the "prayers" *(oratores),* the "fighters," and the "workers."

In the Roman Church the evolution of culture and, simultaneously, a more positive perception of the place of the baptized in the Church have together strengthened the idea of active participation and a diversity of roles in the church assembly (*see* Vatican* II, *SC* no. 26). On the other hand, by abolishing orders* below the diaconate in the Latin Church, Paul VI (*Ministeria Quaedam,* 1972) and the Code of Canon* Law of 1983 (c. 217, §1) have now established an identity between clergy and ordained ministers (except that an ordained minister can lose clerical status but not the ordination he has received [can. 290]). A point has thus been clarified that the Council* of Trent* had left imprecise when it asserted that there was a distinction between clergy and laity according to divine law (*DS* 1776). Paul VI's decision limits clerical status to bishops, priests*, and deacons* and abolishes lower ranks of the clergy.

The orders below the diaconate (subdeacon, lector) survive in the Eastern Church.

• Y. Congar (1954), *Jalons pour une théologie du laïcat,* Paris.
H. Müllejans (1961), *Publicus und Privatus im Römischen Recht und im älteren Kanonischen Recht,* Munich.

PIERRE-MARIE GY

See also **Hierarchy; Lay/Laity; Orders, Minor; Ordination/Order**

Code. *See* **Canon Law**

Collegiality

The debate on collegiality—a term in fact not used in Vatican* II—was the most vigorous of the council* (along with the debate on Mary*). It led to §§19–27 of *LG,* in which "college" is understood as the body *(collegium, corpus, ordo)* made up of all the bishops*, including the bishop of Rome*, by reason of their identical ordination* and their hierarchical communion* with the pope* and among themselves: "Hence, one is constituted a member of the episcopal body in virtue of sacramental consecration and hierarchical communion with the head and members of the body.... The order of bishops, which succeeds to the college of apostles and gives this apostolic body continued existence, is also the subject of supreme and full power over the universal Church, provided we understand this body together with its head the Roman Pontiff" (*LG* 22). Considered by some as the backbone of Vatican II, the importance and the limits of this doctrine can be more clearly seen today.

1. Importance

It is in ordination, in a unified fashion, that the doctrine locates the origin of the power of order and jurisdiction* of the bishops. Three consequences follow from this.

a) Until then (restatements of this opinion had come from Pius XII and John XXIII), many thought that bishops received their jurisdiction from the pope. For Vatican II, on the other hand, that jurisdiction comes to them directly from Christ* through their ordination. "Every legitimate celebration of the Eucharist is regulated by the bishop, to whom is committed the office of offering the worship of Christian religion to the Divine Majesty and of administering it in accordance with the Lord's commandments and the Church's laws, as further defined by his particular judgment for his diocese" (*LG* 26). Any split between order and jurisdiction is overcome, and bishops must therefore be seen as "vicars and ambassadors of Christ" and not to be "regarded as vicars of the Roman Pontiffs" (*LG* 27).

b) In the area of canonical principles, there follows a new organization of powers between the pope and the bishops. The former no longer grants powers to the latter, but he keeps for himself, because of his primacy and for the common good of the Church, certain prerogatives that the bishops could, by right, exercise.

c) Institutions are thus beginning to make possible a more vital expression of the communion of churches, in particular the epicospal bodies, which "are in a position to render a manifold and fruitful assistance, so that this collegiate feeling may be put into practical application" (*LG* 23). According to the synod* of 1985, no one can doubt their pastoral usefulness and even less their necessity in the current situation. Inspired by the ancient patriarchal churches, are they prefigurations of new forms of those churches?

2. Limits

The assertion according to which the college holds in solidarity all ecclesiastical power has probably not allowed the realization of all the hopes that many Fathers placed in it. Collegiality in fact suffers from practical inefficacy and theoretical ambiguity, both of these being due to its definition on the basis of pontifical power.

a) In the first place, the college of individual bishops was insufficiently understood in terms of the communion among the churches over which they preside. Ordination is, to be sure, presented as the basis for communion, but *LG* 22 (quoted above) speaks only in terms of its relation to the universal Church. From this comes the inability to correctly articulate collegiality and the communion of churches. If this is so, it is probably because empirically 44 percent of the members of the college (according to the *Annuario Pontificio* of 1995) either do not preside over a Church or no longer do so; and this is verified in the chain of reasoning of the *CIC* of 1983, which believes it possible to establish what is meant by clergy* and laity*, the pope, the college of bishops, the Roman Curia, and the nuncios, *before* any consideration of the local Church. Such a modern conception, which understands collegiality on the basis of universal primacy, could not possibly be ratified by the Orthodox Church or form a basis for the requests of particular churches for more responsibility.

b) The college, in addition, remains dependent on its head, but the latter does not have a canonical obligation to act in collaboration with the college. Thus, if the college is understood on the basis of its head, who personally has the same power as the entire membership, and simultaneously the college can never act without its head (which is called hierarchical communion [*LG* 21 and 22]), whereas by virtue of his office the pope has "full, supreme and universal power over the Church. And he is always free to exercise this power" (*LG* 22), then collegiality does not necessarily change the centralized image of the Church based on Vatican* I, which the majority of the fathers of Vatican II precisely wished to attenuate by means of this doctrine. This interpretation can be based on the magisterium by John-Paul II (motu proprio *Apostolos suos,* 1998).

The weakness of the doctrine of collegiality also derives from a lack of correlation between the college of bishops and the communion of diocesan churches because Vatican II generally places the bishop *facing* his Church and almost never *in* it (exceptions: two quotations, one from Cyprian* [*LG* 26, no. 31], and the other from Augustine*: "For you I am a bishop; but with you I am a Christian" [*LG* 32]). The silence on the Episcopal ministry* of the pope in Rome, mentioned only in a historical aside (*LG* 22), is a symptom of the same lack.

3. The Possible Development of Collegiality

The fruitfulness of the doctrine of collegiality, within the Catholic Church as in the ecumenical area, is dependent on the doctrinal integration of the most novel (but traditional; *see* Cyprian, *Ep.* 36 and 55) axiom of Vatican II, "particular churches (31), fashioned after the model of the universal Church, in and from which churches comes into being the one and only Catholic Church" (*LG* 23). This axiom is incompatible with the guiding image of a college that brings together, in the same way, bishops who are bishops only by ordination and those who preside over a church. Moreover, the idea that the bishops are all equal and interchangeable in the college of which the pope is the head has to be supplemented by the traditional perspective according to which the bishops have always assembled (metropolitan and patriarchal jurisdictions, of considerable weight in relation to simple dioceses) to take charge of the encounter of the gospel with each specific culture, thus giving rise to the providential multifariousness (*LG* 23) of regional Churches in matters of liturgy*, theology*, spirituality, and canon* law. In this respect, the link established by *LG* 23 between the reality of the patriarchates* and that of bishops' conferences should still prove fruitful.

• Congar (Ed.) (1965), *La collégialité épiscopale: Histoire et théologie,* UnSa 52.

J. Grootaers (1986), *Primauté et collégialité: Le dossier Gérard Philips sur la* Nota Explicativa Praevia, Louvain.

H. Legrand, J. Manzanares, A. Garcia (Ed.) (1988), *Les Conférences épiscopales: Théologie, statut canonique, avenir,* CFi 149.

H. Legrand (1991), "Collégialité des évêques et communion des Églises dans la réception de Vatican II," *RSPhTh* 75, 545–68.

A. de Halleux (1993), "La collégialité dans l'Église ancienne," *RTL* 24, 433–54.

Hervé Legrand

See also **Apostolic Succession; Bishop; Communion; Jurisdiction; Local Church; Ordination/ Order; Regional Church; Vatican II, Council of**

Commandments. *See* **Decalogue**

Communion

It is not fortuitous that the ecumenical movement and the implementation of the major orientations of the Second Vatican* Council* have provoked new interest in what is known in the West as *communion* and in the East as *koinônia.* In fact these two traditional terms—which are not entirely synonymous—designate a range of realities that are closely related and are all at the heart of the Christian experience*: the new relationships that the Easter of Christ brings into being in a humanity "recapitulated" *in Christ,* the nature of the Church* of God*; the bond between the divine persons* in life the Trinity, and the *oikonomia.* But it is impossible to approach this subject without first having clarified the question of vocabulary. *Communio* and *koinônia* do not cover precisely the same range of meanings. In addition, the root *koinon* has no exact equivalent in Hebrew or Aramaic, and the biblical words translated by terms formed on its basis are many. Furthermore, they often have extremely varied uses (as in the case of *habûrah*).

I. The Terms and Their Origin

1. Communio-Communicatio

a) Communio. Contrary to belief and appearances, *communio* does not come from *cum* (with) and *unio.* It comes from *cum* and *munis,* an adjective derived from *munus* (office, duty) meaning "that fulfills its office." Something is *com-munis* that "shares the office" and, in a derivative sense, what is "shared among all," hence in common. This relationship of the term to the idea of a large number had the effect that sometimes it came to evoke banality, vulgarity, or even impurity*. In classical Latin the noun *communio* means sharing, shared ownership, common characteristics, and sometimes community (Ernout-Meillet 1951). It is a rather rare term, although it is used by Cicero.

In patristic Latin, when the term was applied to Church matters, this classical meaning took on particularly Christian overtones. These were derived from the fact that the community in question had its source in what God himself continually *communicates* to the Church (Word*, ministry*, sacraments*, the most important of which is the Eucharist*) and what believers are called on to *communicate* to one another, particularly through mutual material assistance. There was *communio* in the goods *communicated* by God, and it embraced all the members of the body of Christ (*see,* e.g., Tertullian*, *De Virg. vel.* 2. PL 2. 891). In this communion, *societas, congregatio, fraternitas, concordia,* and *pax,* all fruits of the Eucharist, attained their fulfillment.

In the Latin Middle Ages the noun *communio* was used almost exclusively to designate the receiving of the Eucharist. The other elements of the communal experience of the Church were then evoked especially by the term *communicatio.*

b) Communicatio. Like the verb *communicare,* the noun *communicatio* comes from an adjective, *municus,* derived from *munis* (in the way that *civicus* is derived from *civis*). *Communicare* has several meanings, including "to tell" and "to share or participate." The effect of this is *communio.* This is why the nouns *communicatio* and *communio* are close and sometimes used interchangeably, although they are not strictly synonymous.

The Christian Latin of the early centuries seems to have preferred *communicatio* to *communio,* probably because it added a dynamic element. It also evokes, at least implicitly, the active presence of Christ in his Holy* Spirit and the mutual dependence of the disciples. Christ is the *communicator* of salvation*, the Holy Spirit the *communicator* of the gifts of the Father* that give concrete form to that salvation in a *communio* of grace*; and in the community, each one is a *communicator* of the benefits of divine generosity. In prayer*, particularly in the synaxis of the Eucharist, Christians know that they are *communicantes* with all the saints throughout the ages (Roman canon). For typical uses of the vocabulary of *communicatio,* among countless examples, see especially, in addition to Tertullian (*De praescr.* 43. 5, PL 2. 58–59; *De virg. vel.* 2, PL 2. 891; *De pud.* 22. 2, PL 2), the Vulgate of Jerome (Acts 2:42; Rom 12:13; 1 Cor 10:16; 2 Cor 8:4, 9:13, 13:13; Gal 6:6; Eph 5:11; Phil 4:14–15; 1 Tm 5:22, 6:18; Phil 6; Heb 2:14; 1 Pt 4:13, 5:1; 2 Jn 11), which uses *communio* only once (Heb 13:16). The new edition of 1986, however, has frequently corrected the old editions by favoring the word *communio.* A glance at the *Tabula aurea* (by Peter of Bergamo) and the *Index* *thomisticus* shows the frequent use by Thomas Aquinas of *communicatio* and *communicare.*

Antonyms to *altari communicare,* meaning "to take part together at the altar" where the sacrament of *communio* is celebrated, are the verb *ex-communicare* and the noun *excommunicatio.* To exclude from the (eucharistic) *communio* is above all to deprive one of the *communicatio* of those benefits of which the celebration of the Eucharist is the sacrament, particularly the fraternal *communicatio* that binds the community together. The sign of exclusion is precisely this barring from church life. Local councils wanted it to be radical (e.g., Toledo I in 400, can. 15, Mansi 3. 1000; Second Council of Arles in 443, can. 49, Mansi 7. 884, etc.). But from the 12th century a distinction was established between the *excommunicatio* that "*a communione fidelium separat*" (separates from the communion of the faithful) and the *excommunicatio* that simply deprives one of the sacramental *communicatio* (Decr. I. v. tit. 39. c. 49). The latter cuts one off from the *communicatio in sacris* (communion in the sacraments), but not necessarily from everything implied by the belonging to Christ for which the baptismal character remains the sign. In the wake of Vatican II we speak therefore of a *communicatio in spiritualibus* (spiritual communion, which in the Middle Ages was the equivalent of *communicatio in sacris: see* Thomas Aquinas, *ST* IIIa, suppl. q. 21, a. 4), which is the foundation of a true *communio etsi non perfecta* that remains (*UR* 3). It is on this imperfect *communio* of all the baptized, the source of which is the Holy Spirit who continually *communicates* the benefits of Christ even beyond the visible borders of that *communio,* that the Catholic Church has grafted its ecumenical commitment.

2. Koinônia

a) From One Language to Another. The passages of the Vulgate that we mentioned to show the New Testament basis of the Western theology* of *communicatio* and *communio* are passages in which the Greek terms translated come from the root *koinos (koinônia, koinônein, koinônos, koinônikos).* This root also has for its semantic field (in contrast to *idios,* what is particular to each one, private) ideas of common participation, association, and common sharing of a single reality. We are thus close to the Latin *communio;* in this case too there is a suggestion of the idea of vulgarity or impurity, even in the New Testament (Mk 7:2–5; Acts 10:14–15, 11:8f.; Rom 14:14; Rev 21:27). However, in biblical Latin, the Greek words formed on the basis of *koinos* are also translated by terms other than those derived from *munis* (or *munus*). These terms are principally *participatio* and *particeps* (1 Cor 9:23, 10:16, 18, 20; Rom 15:27; Rev 1:9; 18:4), *consors* (2 Pt 1:4), and *societas* and *socius* (Mt 23:30; Rom 11:17; 1 Cor 1:9; 2 Cor 1:7, 6:14, 8:23; Gal 2:9; Phil 1:7, 2:1, 3:10; Phlm 17; Heb 10:33; 1 Jn 1:3, 6, 7). On the other hand, the Latin term used to translate a word from the *koinos* group can also translate other Greek terms, such as *metokhos* and its cognates. Thus, *koinônia* is translated once as *communio,* eight times as *societas,* six times as *communicatio,* once as *collatio,* and once as *participatio.* But in 2 Corinthians 6:14, *participatio* also translates *metokhè.* It is clear, then, that *koinônia* and *communio* and *communicatio* are not entirely synonymous. Generally, *koinônia* emphasizes participation in a common reality, *communicatio* the dynamism of the gift, and *communio* the resulting situation. But the meanings are rarely very sharply distinguished.

In addition, in the Septuagint and the New Testament, the *koinos* group is used to define several Hebrew terms, although it is not the only way in which they are translated. In fact, the root *koinos* has no exact equivalent in Hebrew. In addition, some of its implications did not apply in Israel*. The closest root is *hbr,* but few (13) of its instances are translated by words from the *koinos* group. It is used to describe the unifying bond of the people* (as in Ez 37:16ff.) and avoiding evocation of community with YHWH, to condemn association with the pagan gods (Hos 4:17). The most important derivative of *hbr* for our purposes is *habûrah.* This refers, especially in Pharisee circles, to a community generally united around a teacher, in which the desire to follow the Law in a strict fashion creates particular bonds of fraternity and solidarity. The Qumran community, however, rarely used terms derived from *hbr* to express its ideal, which was also stamped by a radicalizing reading of the precept of love* of one's neighbor. Rather, it gave itself the name *yachad,* which emphasizes cohesion, unity, solidarity and which the Septuagint sometimes translates as *homothumadon* or *epi to auto* (which is found in Acts 1:14, 2:44ff.) (Fabry 1982). In the context of Hellenistic Judaism, Philo and Josephus used terms derived from *koinos,* particularly *koinônia,* to present the ideal and the way of life of the Essenes and the Therapeutics (e.g., *Quod omnis probus liber sit,* 80–84: *Spec. Leg.* I, 131–221). But this brought new overtones, inherited from Greek culture, to the Old Testament vision of the community. These then passed into Christian tradition, even as early as the New Testament.

b) Koinônia *in the Greek World.* In classical Greek, words derived from *koinos* were generally used to designate matters concerning various groupings or associations of citizens (e.g., state*, family*, sexual encounter, trade association, union with the gods). It was always a matter of indicating a community that was created in virtue of its sharing in the same realities (*koina pasi panta,* said Pythagoras: Jamblique, *Vie de P.*, 30, 168), of participating together in a common good, and, as a corollary, to bring about that participation. Association and participation were inseparable in this context. Hence, *koinônia* was the form of life corresponding to the social nature of human beings. It reached its apex in friendship *(philia):* "Among friends, everything is in common." Plato has no hesitation in associating the gods themselves with the perfect *koinônia* he aspires to (*Gorgias* 508 a). Aristotle gives a prominent place to the dimension of friendship that imbues any *koinônia* (*Nicomachean Ethics* VIII. 11. 1159; IX. 12. 1171). In the *Politics* he uses the word almost as a synonym of community (Gauthier-Jolif 1959). We should especially recall the ideal of the *adelphoi* assembled by Pythagoras of Samos (c. 580 B.C.): the certainty of belonging to the same God led them to mutual devotion concretized by the common ownership and sharing of goods that was emphasized in neo-Pythgoreanism. We might also point to the way in which the Stoics saw the human being as a *koinônikon zôon,* a communal being. It is certain that these ideals, particularly those of small groups or fraternities hungry for authentic *koinônia,* remained very much alive in those Greek cities where the gospel was proclaimed (Popkès 1976).

In the New Testament, terms derived from *koinos* are used rather infrequently. There are 73 occurrences, among which 19 are of *koinônia* (13 of these are in the Pauline corpus, where words derived from *koinos* appear 33 times). Again, they do not appear at all in Clement of Rome, only infrequently in the writings of the Apostolic* Fathers*, though more frequently in Justin. Thereafter their use burgeoned. Such terms sprang spontaneously from the pens of the Cappadocian Fathers, where they expressed various elements of church life, often in relation to the Eucharist (Lampe 1968). But here too, other Greek terms that had been Christianized expressed the same ecclesial reality, such as *ekklesia* and *sunagôgè*. The depth of fraternal *koinônia* is often expressed by *sumphonèsis;* by the verb *metekhein* (already in 1 Cor 10:17–21, in parallel with *koinônia*), which emphasizes participation; and by the nouns *metokhè, eirenè, agapè,* and generally by all expressions concerning unity (*sun-*), fraternity (*adelphotès,* already in 1 Pt 2:17, 5:9, which the Vulgate translates as *fraternitas*), unanimity (already in Phil 2:2), cohesion, association, and community. It is therefore clear that theological reflection cannot confine itself to a narrowly focused study of the uses of the term *koinônia* in the Scriptures*.

In the New Testament, the Greek term, which had a multiplicity of meanings, came to indicate those values that, belonging to Christ, contributed to the life of the community. These values included participation of all in the same gift of God actualized by the body and blood of the Lord (1 Cor 10:16, 1:9), association with the life of God that this gift provides (2 Pt 1:4; 1 Jn 1:3; *see* 2 Cor 13:13), the resulting union with Christ (Phil 3:10; 1 Pt 4:13), consequent fraternal bonds (1 Jn 1:7; 1 Cor 10:18ff.; 2 Cor 1:7; 8:23; Gal 2:9; Phil 1:5ff.; Phlm 6:17), the form of community life that actualizes those bonds (Acts 2:42), the disinterested spirit of sharing (Rom 15:27; 2 Cor 9:13; Heb 13:16) manifested in material assistance to poor churches (2 Cor 8:4) and to the missionaries of the gospel (Gal 6:6; Phil 4:14), and association with the suffering and the promises of the gospel (Rom 11:17; 1 Cor 9:23; Heb 10:33). *Koinônia* is never given as a definition of the Church, but it is understood that everything expressed by the term or its cognates belongs to the essence of the Church. This is why—without it being burdened with overtones foreign to its use in Scripture—the term *koinônia* gradually came to be seen, along with *communio,* as the equivalent of a definition of the Church considered in its being of grace (that which the hierarchical ministry* is called on to serve). Bilateral ecumenical dialogues and the declaration of Faith and Constitution "received" at the Seventh Assembly of the COE (Canberra 1991) helped this development.

We will adhere to what is now the generally current usage and will avoid any distinction between *communio (communicatio)* and *koinônia.* We will therefore speak of *communio-koinônia,* presupposing all the nuances we have just presented.

II. Salvation of the Human Person in Communion

1. The Person

The Christian tradition asserts that the human beings are fulfilled and saved in *communio-koinônia.* It thus makes of *communio-koinônia*—with God and among human beings—the essence of salvation.

a) For the Scriptures, in fact, the human being is by nature a relational being, turned toward the other, because he has been created in the image and likeness of God. On the one hand, he has his being* only from God, in a constant relation of dependence on divine generosity, actualizing himself in an individual relationship as one who speaks with God or indeed as a responsible partner with him. The human being can exist only *from* God and *before* God. On the other hand, for the two traditions of the first chapters of Genesis, the human being is created both as singular and plural: "in the image of God he created him; male and female he created them" (Gn 1:27); "It is not good that the man should be alone; I will make him a helper fit for him" (2:18). The woman* *('ishâh)* is for the man *('ish)* the equal that allows him to be himself, precisely through her difference. Each of them is thus created *toward the other* (2:18–24). Each fully possesses human nature. They exist as fully independent subjects, neither being a part of the other. But they are subjects open to the other, in a relationship that belongs to their nature. Hence, they are an "image of God" only in this mutual openness. Their identity is inseparable from the otherness that makes each of them fully a subject, either of whom may, however, attain realization without a communion of the *I* and a *you* in a *we*. They are persons in communion.

b) On this basis the Christian tradition established a distinction between individual and person that was deepened by its reflection on the mystery* of the divine Trinity*. There is a single human nature, but it exists only in a diversity of persons. Each person is unique, irreplaceable, not interchangeable. Each one is different, *hapax.* Now this otherness opens out onto communion. In Greek, "person" is *prosôpon,* a word made up of *pros* and a derivative of *ôps* (eye, look), hence "what is in front of the eyes of others," as "the person opposite someone" (Chantraine 1974). The understanding implied here points to a recapitulation of the totality of human nature in a mode that, going beyond the various determinisms that human nature involves, renders it singular "in the eyes" of God and others, something that exists in freedom and otherness. The concept of the individual disregards the otherness of the concrete human being because it designates him as bearer of the objective properties of common human nature. It perceives him in his belonging to what is the lot of all human beings, the possession of what constitutes universal humanity, the definition of *homo.* The concept of person, on the other hand, distinguishes him by seeing him as an *I* set in a face-to-face encounter with other persons. To this encounter he brings that which he alone is, whatever makes him different from others. And it is precisely on the strength of this irreducible particularity that, far from blending into the identity of a common human nature, he can enter into a communion of giving and receiving. The person is revealed only in the operation of mutual relations and communion. As individual, the human being is defined by the integrity and perfection of nature in him; as person, he is defined by the singularity that allows him to go beyond himself in communion with others. When it came to an understanding of how God himself is a communion of three persons, the tradition specified that every human being is an image of the creator God precisely because he is called on to realize himself by establishing with others a flourishing community on the basis of a single and indivisible human nature. In this he realizes his vocation (Lossky 1944). The person fulfills himself only in his relation with others by making his own originality and difference not the source of an asphyxiating self-enclosure but rather the source of a gift in which the very attributes of nature are directed toward communion.

2. The Restoration of Communio-Koinônia

For the Scriptures, the tragedy of humanity comes from the breaking of the communion with God and among human persons. Already in the Yahwist stratum of Genesis, after the break with God (3:6), the man dissociates himself from the woman (3:12). From Cain onward, the rest of history* is stamped by the transformation of what should be communion into rivalry. This is the origin of human misfortune. And the salvation offered by God has as its object the "recapitulation" (*anakephalaôsis*) of communion (Irenaeus*).

a) The Old Testament already points in this direction. The covenant (especially Hos 2:21f.; Is 54:1–17; Jer 31:2–34; Ez 16:59–63), illustrated by the relation of bride and bridegroom (Jer 2:2, 3:6–12), establishes between God and the people a bond of fidelity that is salvific for the people. But according to the law of the covenant, it is also necessary to restore fraternal bonds (*see* Lv 19:1–37; Dt 15:1–18), "you shall love your neighbor as yourself" (Lv 19:18). God wishes to reassemble (roots *hbr, koinos*) the people that has been split into two kingdoms (Ez 37:15–28; Mi 4:6; Is 43:5ff., 49:5, 56:8; etc.), and all the nations are drawn into this assembly (Is 2:2; Ps 87; etc.). Thus, the promise to Abraham—that all nations would be blessed in him (Gn 12:1–3, 17:4–8, etc.)—will be fulfilled in a communion according to the grace that is his as father of the faith*.

b) For John the Baptist the moral ideal that goes inseparably with conversion* is essentially marked by a relation to one's neighbor and to the community (Lk 3:10f.), in a way that radicalizes the Torah. Christ deepens this message not only in the encounter with a rich man (Lk 18:18–30; Mt 19:16–30; Mk 10:17–31) but also in the totality of his words and signs. He desires to transform human relations by giving them a communitarian meaning of sharing and of attentiveness to the needs of others. This is what the Kingdom* requires. Alms and concern for little children and the suffering belong to the Good News. The dual commandment to love God and one's neighbor here reveals its deepest meaning (Mt 22:36–40; Mk 12:28–34; Lk 10:25–28). It implies a challenge to any rigid separation between the just and sinners (Lk 15:1f.; Mt 9:11, 11:19; Mk 2:16; Lk 5:30, 7:34, 19:7), Jews and Gentiles (Lk 10:29–37; Mt 15:21–28). Although Jesus* states that he was sent only to the lost sheep of Israel (Mt 15:24) and before his resurrection* sends his disciples only to the Jews (Mt 10:5f.), the gathering of all humanity is proclaimed in the eschatological promise of a feast to be shared with Abraham, Isaac, and Jacob (Mt 8:11). Jesus' commissioning of the disciples in Matthew 28:16–19 (*see* also 24:14) strikes a corresponding note. Never evoked explicitly, *communio-koinônia* does nevertheless find expression through the ministry of Jesus.

c) The Letter to the Hebrews understands the coming of the Son of God in human flesh as a *communio-koinônia:* "Since therefore the children share in flesh and blood, he himself likewise partook of the same things.... Therefore he had to be made like his brothers in every respect" (Heb 2:14–17). The reality of what the tradition calls "incarnation*" comes from the realism of this *communio-koinônia,* which makes Christians in turn "sharers" *(metokhoi)* in that which is Christ (3:14). This unites them among themselves and commits them to the *koinônia* of sharing. The mutual communion implied by the Incarnation is expressed here more explicitly than in Romans 1:3, Galatians 4:4, Philippians 2:7, 1 John 4:2, and even John 1:14. On this Son-humanity *communio-koinônia,* in our view, is grafted the *communio-koinônia* humanity-Christ. Paul sees it above all as the participation of adopted children in the inheritance of the Son (Rom 8:17; Gal 4:4–7) and in his glory* (Rom 8:17; 2 Cor 4:14–17) but also as *koinônia* in his suffering (Phil 3:10; Rom 8:17). There, everything is lived with him (*sun-*) in the Holy Spirit. The Johannine* tradition emphasizes this association differently but just as strongly (Jn 12:26, 14:3, 17:24). The church fathers (e.g., Athanasius*, *Incarn.* 5. 11. 54) say that the *koinônia* of the Son and humanity is so deep and intimate that the knowledge* of God and even incorruptibility become possessions of a divinized humanity. The communion that is the Incarnation governs the divine purpose.

d) Without using the word *koinônia* in this context, the Pauline corpus (Rom 10:12; 1 Cor 12:13; Gal 3:28; Col 3:11) sees realized *en Christô* and *en pneumati* the coming together of all human, religious, and social categories. But Paul (1 Cor 12:12–31) inserts that unity into the operation of mutual relations by which the body of Christ, the Church, lives (1 Cor 12:27f.). The author of Ephesians (who uses a verb derived from *koinos* only at 5:4) explicitly links the unity of reconciliation brought about by the cross (2:13–17) and the new relations between Jews and Gentiles that follow: near-far (2:13), division-peace* (2:14f.), enmity-union in a single spirit (2:11–18), foreigner-fellow citizen (2:19). He regards this as the state of salvation (2:4–10), called on to blossom into a new life in which mutual relations are transformed into the single body of reconciliation (1:23, 4:16, 5:30), the single temple constructed by all, the single family of God (2:19, 3:6). Salvation comes through communion.

The Gospel* of John, which also presents the cross as the event that brings together *(sun-agô)* in unity the dispersed children of God (Jn 11:52), is fond of images that evoke the unity of communion, for example, the one flock (led by a single shepherd; 10:11–18), but especially the vine that is Christ (15:1–17). Individuals remain as living branches of this vine only by persevering in a mutual love that leads them to give themselves up *(tithèmi)* for others (15:13; *see* 10:15, 17:18, 13:37f.). The title of disciple requires mutual love (13:34f.) and the unity that is inseparable from it (17:20–26, where *agapè* and unity are woven together). Even though the word *koinônia* is not used, we are here at the heart of the communion with the Father that the eating of the bread of life (which signifies both faith and the body and blood of Christ; 6:47f., 53–56, 63) makes possible and maintains. For their dwelling (*menein en*) in Christ associates the disciples with his dwelling in the Father (14:20, 17:21). That dwelling then includes them in the mutual relations between Father and Son. They do not thereby lose their personal identity. Just as the Son is not dissolved in the Father but faces him as a free subject of action and of life, so the disciples are not dissolved in the Son but remain free subjects. In fact, they become not Sons *(huios)* but children of God (*tekna theou;* 1:12, 11:52), associated as such in intradivine relations. They are not understood as children of God in a purely individualized and isolated way but in virtue of their reality and being as a group (17:1–26; *see* 10:14, 26–30, 15:15). This is the source of their mutual love.

e) The first letter of John explicitly defines in terms of *koinônia* (without saying that it is a question of the Church) this dual relation of which the knot is Christ, with his blood: "so that you too may have fellowship *(koinônia)* with us; and indeed our fellowship is with the Father and with his Son Jesus Christ" (1 Jn 1:3); "If we say we have fellowship with him while we walk in darkness, we lie and do not practice the truth; but if we walk in the light, as he is in the light, we have fellowship with one another, and the blood of Jesus his Son cleanses us from all sin" (1 Jn 1:6–7). Note the place of the Father and the expression "to have fellowship" *(koinônia).*

The author dwells on the demands of a fraternal *koinônia* (2:10, 3:10–20, 4:11ff.) to the extent of sharing (3:17). In this is actualized the surrender of oneself (3:16), inspired by the action of the Son and the Father (4:9ff.), who dwell in the disciples (3:24, 4:12–16) through their anointing by the Holy Spirit (2:20, 27, 3:24, 4:13), and in whom those who have true knowledge dwell (2:24–27, 3:24, 4:16, 5:20). Christian life is life in communion.

In a more static perspective, 2 Peter says that the vocation of Christians is to be *koinônoi* of the divine nature *(phusis).* For that purpose they are called to fraternal friendship and the *agape* (2 Pt 1:4, 7) while waiting for the Day of the Lord (3:1–13).

Patristic thought, followed Western medieval theology, established the doctrine of grace primarily on the affirmations of the Johannine tradition and of 2 Peter, correlated with passages from Paul. Despite different perspectives, Greeks and Latins conceived of it as the gift that leads one into the entirely free *communio-koinônia* of God and his image. The East spoke primarily of divinization, the West of invisible mission, divine indwelling, the supernatural; the East of uncreated grace (the divine energies), the West of created grace. For all, grace was the work of the Holy Spirit as *communicator.* Thomas* Aquinas (*ST* Ia, IIae, q. 112, a. 1) defines it as the *communicatio* of a communion with the divine nature through assimilative participation.

III. The Divine Communio-Koinônia Trinity of Persons

1. From Oikonomia *to the Trinity (Theologia)*

a) It was on the basis of the divinization of believers that Athanasius, Basil*, and the Cappadocians, as well as Didymus, after having defended the divinity of the Son and then of the Holy Spirit, developed a theology of the Trinity*. In the West, Augustine* echoed them but in a different perspective. Although Scripture never states that God is *communio-koinônia* of three persons, the Johannine tradition (Jn 14:16, 16:7–15), Matthew 28:19, and particularly 2 Corinthians 13:14 ("The grace of the Lord Jesus Christ and the love of God and the fellowship *[koinônia]* of the Holy Spirit be with you all") encouraged a conception of the divine mystery that saw it as the *communio-koinônia* that was the origin and model of any human communion. For example, Basil (*Letter* 38, PG 32, 332a–333): "a united differentiation, a differentiated unity," " a kind of continual and indivisible *koinônia.*" The being of God is *koinônia.* This is so both *in se* and in his activity *pro nobis (oikonomia).*

b) For the East, everything in God is relational. There is not first a Father, then a Son who would then enter into relations with one another. They are Father and Son through the relation that makes one of them Father and the other Son. The single divine nature exists only in the communion that comes from the fact that the Father causes to be born from him a Son who is as much God as He is and a Holy Spirit who is as much God as He. And yet the Son and the Holy Spirit possess the entire divine nature in a unique manner that the Father could not possibly imitate without destroying himself as Father and source of Trinitarian life. The eternal generosity of the Father comes from the fact that there originate in him not copies of himself but "others than himself," without whom he would not be. There is no more a Father without a Son than a Son without a Father. Each divine person exists only in the relation of *koinônia* with the other who gives him being. Each is neither more nor less God than the two others. They are the one God in the *koinônia* of relations that distinguishes them.

In the West the Eleventh Council of Toledo (675) declared, "What the Father is, he is for the Son, not for himself. What the Son is, he is for the Father, not for himself" (*DS* 528). The eternal act of granting to the Son everything that he is, not *a same being* as his but his *being itself,* makes the Father the Father. God is the *koinônia* of three relational beings each one of whom exists only in relation to the others. The West, which, following Augustine, emphasized above all the unity of *ousia*—whereas the East emphasized the *hypostases*—speaks in this context of subsisting relations (Thomas Aquinas, *ST* Ia, q. 29, a. 4), but it is still a matter of communion, considered here on the basis of a single nature. Neither three gods nor three modes of a single person, God is *communio-koinônia* of three persons who are one God indivisible in his unity.

2. From Trinitarian Communion to Oikonomia

a) Enlightened by this Trinitarian doctrine revealed to it by *oikonomia,* the tradition reread the latter with new eyes. It understood why in the New Testament none of the three divine persons bears witness of himself: the Father bears witness of the Son (Mt 3:17; 17:5), the Son of the Father (Jn 4:34, 5:30, 6:38, etc.), the Holy Spirit of the Father and of the Son (Jn 14:26, 15:26). The ministry of Jesus is enveloped by this *perikhôrèsis* (circumincession*) of mutual relations. We can also understand why one cannot enter into the communion of Christ without participating in the Trinitarian communion of the Son and God's communion with human distress.

b) In this light we can look again at the creation "in the image and likeness of God." Because God is "persons in communion," the human person cannot be perceived otherwise than in a relation of *communio-koinônia* with God, with the other, with others, a relation that is directed toward those others who are in turn directed toward him. Through this reciprocity, he participates, in his very being, in the personal life of the creative Trinity. His need of others is therefore not a lack but a dignity that finds its source in participation in the being of the Triune God. His communion with the "wicked" (2 Cor 6:14), for that reason, wounds him in himself.

IV. The Church of God Is a *Communio-Koinônia*

Although Scripture never makes *communio-koinônia* the definition of the Church, it is nevertheless in the Church of God, as Scripture reveals it, that is brought together everything it says of *communio-koinônia,* including the relations among Father, Son, and Holy Spirit. Augustine (*Homilies on the Gospel of John,* tract. 14. 9, 18. 4, 39. 5; *Sermon* 47.21 and *Guelf.* 11. 5,6; *De symb. ad cat.* 2. 4; *Ep* 170. 5, 238. 2, 13. 16; *Coll. cum Maxim.* 12) has no hesitation in making the Pentecostal community of Acts into an image of the Trinitarian communion (Berrouard 1987). The totality of church traditions affirms that the unity accomplished by the Word, the bread, and the cup of the Eucharist is the ecclesial *communio-koinônia* (Tillard 1992). The patristic tradition recognizes that the fabric of the Church is made of the bonds of communion rooted in the fraternity of the body of Christ. The church fathers teach unanimously that the communion of sharing with communities in need is a concrete form of the *agape* that is the life of the Church. The oldest canon law rules on sharing among Churches and particularly between preachers and communities. Finally, the right hand of *koinônia* that Cephas (Peter*), James, and John extend to Paul and Barnabas is understood as a sign of the real communion of all local* churches in the diversity of their practices. *Communio-koinônia* is not absent from any of the elements that make up the Church.

1) The idealized description of the primitive community of the Acts of the Apostles (2:42–47, 4:32–35, 5:12ff.) shows a fraternity conceived in the fire of the Holy Spirit (Dujarier 1991) based on the hearing of the apostolic word, *koinônia* (2:42); the breaking of bread, prayer, and common property (*apanta koina;* 2:44, 4:32); and the sharing of possessions. The tradition reads this as the self-description of the emerging Church, which was not yet organized. There are questions about the meaning of *koinônia* (Dupont 1972; Panikulam 1979). Everything encourages us to recognize it as the specific form of friendship provoked by shared faith, which makes of all "one heart and soul*" (Acts 4:32) in solidarity (*homothumadon;* 2:46, 5:12) and equality (*epi te auto;* 2:44, 47). This primitive community is indeed the initial cell of the Church.
2) For 1 Corinthians (10:16–22), the bread and wine of the table of the Lord are *koinônia* with the body and blood of Christ. By sharing this one bread (*metekhome;* 10:17), all become a single body (10:17) of which it is said (12:12–31) that it is the Church. This common participation (*metekhein;* 10:21) makes Christians *koinônoi* (10:18, 20) of the Lord, who creates their unity. It is not said that only participation in the Lord's Supper makes the Church since (1 Cor 12:12f.; Eph 4:5) Paul attributes this function also to Baptism and the New Testament as a whole to the Word*. Nevertheless, *koinônia* with Christ (1 Cor 1:9) takes on reality here because there is a common sharing of his body and blood. The church fathers (especially John Chrysostom*, Cyril* of Alexandria, and Augustine) say that the ecclesial body of Christ *(Christus totus)* comes from the seizure of all its diverse members by the power of the body of reconciliation, the "pneumatic" body of the Risen One received in the Eucharist, which has been the same on every altar ever since the first Easter (Tillard 1992). The Church manifests itself in its full truth as body of Christ only in the Eucharist.
3) According to 1 Corinthians 12:25ff., among the members of the ecclesial body there must be no division *(skhisma)* but rather mutual concern *(merimna).* This is the case first of all within each local church. There one "has *koinônia*" in faith and mission* (2 Cor 8:23; Phil 1:5; Phlm 6:17; Ti 1:4), in suffering (2 Cor 1:7; Phil 4:14ff.), and in hope* (1 Cor 9:23). There we live as members of the body by being *sug-koinônoi* (Phil 1:7). This requires mutual aid to the extent of the *koinônia* of sharing (Rom 12:13; Gal 6:6; Heb 13:16), with all the enthusiasm of the community of Pentecost. But this sharing also extends to Christians of other churches. Paul relies on the *koinônia* of spiritual

and material goods (Rom 15:26f.) to promote collections for the poor of Jerusalem (2 Cor 8:4, 9:13). Ecclesial communion concerns the human being in solidarity called for by the very nature of the person who is saved *en Christô*.

4) The diversity of local Churches and their particular ways of living the one faith cannot call into question their mutual communion. The right hand of *koinônia* that, after a sharp conflict, the "pillars" of the Church of Jerusalem* extended to Paul and Barnabas (Gal 2:9) is seen as the sign of that catholic *koinônia* in the same gospel, the same faith, and the same ministry for the same mission, in a multiplicity of customs and traditions. This places the emphasis on the truth* of the gospel as the bond of *koinônia* (2:5–14), not on the fabric of fraternity or legal requirements (Reumann 1994).

Beyond mutual material aid, bonds of fraternity are tied among local Churches since they "recognize" in one another the same faith, the same hope, the same baptism—and soon the same ministry and the same Eucharist. They are sister churches (2 Jn 13), *communing* in the same divine choice (2 Jn 13; 1 Pt 5:13f.). Tertullian, enumerating goods possessed in common, concludes, "We are a single Church, everything that belongs to one of us is ours" (*De Virg. vel.* 2, 2 PL 2. 891). Around 1150, Anselm of Havelberg, relating his discussions with Archbishop Nicetas of Nicomedia (PL 188, esp. 1217–20), testifies to the importance of the theology* of sister churches for the East (Congar 1982). The Church is a communion of local churches, themselves grouped into patriarchates of equal apostolic roots and equal dignity, for which the Roman Church is neither the mother nor the *magistra* but the elder sister and the "president" (PL 188. 1217). After Vatican* I the decree of Vatican II on ecumenism*, and the dialogue between Paul VI and the Patriarch Athenagoras, the expression has resumed its place in Catholic ecclesiology* (*UR* 1 4; *Tomos Agapès* 388–91; *DC* 87, 1990. 951–52; 88, 1991. 689–90; 91, 1994. 1069–70). Within this communion the function of the first-founded see and its bishop* is above all to "watch" over the communion while respecting the dignity and responsibility of sister churches. This role has been challenged since the schisms of the Reformation, but the Orthodox churches do not deny it.

5) The Apostles' Creed includes among the truths of faith the "communion of saints." The expression comes neither from the New Testament nor from the ancient creeds. The Nicene-Constantinople Creed does not mention it, nor do Eastern creeds. It is found in Jerome, in a rescript of Theodosius of 388 (uncertain meaning), in a mutilated text of the *Acts* of a council of Nîmes of 394, and in the Latin translation of a letter of Theophilus of Antioch of 401, the Greek original of which is lost. The *Credo* of Nicetas of Remesiana (between 381 and 408) is the first solid evidence of it and provides the earliest commentary. Nicetas (a friend of Paulinus of Nola) seems to have taken it from southern Gaul, where creeds proliferated. He understands it as the "communion of believers *(sancti)* with one another." Others (Faustus of Rieti, c. 452, pseudo-Augustinian sermon 242) think only of a communion with martyrs and saints or with the departed faithful (Badcock 1920; Benko 1964). But it might mean, in the Apostles' Creed, communion with holy *(sancta)* things, hence the Eucharist and probably Baptism, explaining its place between the Church and the remission of sins for resurrection and eternal life*. It would thus correspond in the Latin Credo to the mention of Baptism in the Eastern creeds.

It is clear that the living faith has gradually brought the two meanings together (Tillard 1965). They actually suggest one another, for one is *sanctus* in the communion of the faithful and by communion with holy things. The richest vision is perhaps that of Theodore of Mopsuestia in the East: "Since by a new birth they have become perfect in a single body, they are now also strengthened as in a single body by communion with the body of the Lord; and, in concord, peace, and the devotion to good, they all come to be one.... Thus we will unite in communion with the holy mysteries, and by that communion we will be joined to our head, Christ our Lord, of whom we believe we are the body and through whom we attain communion with the divine nature" (*Hom. cat.* 16. 13, ed. Tonneau-Devreesse, 555).

6) This passage appears to be the very definition of the Church in its being of grace. The Church is communion with the Father, flowering in fraternal communion, communicated in Baptism, and especially in the Eucharist, by the Holy Spirit of the one who, having fully communed with our humanity in his Incarnation, has been raised to bring us into communion with his Trinitarian life.

• F.J. Badcock (1920), "Sanctorum communio as an Article of the Creed," *JThS*, 106–26; (1930), *The History of the Creeds*, London.

J. Y. Campbell (1932), "*K.* and Its Cognates in the New Testament," *JBL* 51, 352–82.
Vl. Lossky (1944), *Théologie mystique de l'Église d'Orient,* Paris, 116–17.
J. Gaudemet (1949), "Notes sur les formules anciennes de l'excommunication," *RSR* 22, 64–77.
J. N. D. Kelly (1950), *Early Christian Creeds,* London (3rd Ed. 1972).
A. Ernout, A. Meillet (1951), *Dictionnaire étymologique de la langue latine,* Paris.
A. Piolanti (1957), *Il mistero della communione dei Santi,* Rome.
R. A. Gauthier, J. Y. Jolif (1959), *L'éthique à Nicomaque,* intro., trans., and comm., vol. II, comm. 2.
J. Schmitt (1959), "L'organisation de l'Église primitive et Qoumrân," RechBib 4, 217–31.
S. Benko (1964), *The Meaning of* sanctorum communio, London.
J.-M. R. Tillard (1965), "La communion des saints," *VS* 113, 249–74.
G. W. H. Lampe (Ed.) (1968), *PGL,* Oxford.
L. M. Dewailly (1970), "*Communio-Communicatio:* Brèves notes sur l'histoire d'un sémantème," *RSPhTh* 44, 46–63.
Tomos Agapès (1971), Rome-Istanbul.
J. Dupont (1972), "La *k.* des premiers chrétiens dans les Actes des apôtres," in G. D'Ercole, A. M. Stickler (Ed.), *Communione interecclesiale, collegialita, primato, ecumenismo,* Rome, 41–61.
P. Chantraine (1974), *Dictionnaire étymologique de la langue grecque,* vol. 3, Paris.
W. Popkes (1976), "Gemeinschaft," *RAC* 9, 1100–45.
G. Panikulam (1979), *K. in the New Testament,* Rome.
J. Hainz (1981), "*K., Koinôneo, Koinônos,*" *EWNT.*
J. Fabry (1982), "*Yâchad, yâchîd, yachdâw,*" *ThWAT,* 3, 595–603.
Y. Congar (1982), *Diversités et communion,* Paris, 126–34.
J. D. Zizioulas (1985), *Being as Communion,* Crestwood and New York.
M. F. Berrouard (1987), "La première communauté de Jérusalem comme image de la Trinité," dans *Homo spiritalis, Festgabe für Luc Verheijen,* Würzburg, 207–24.
J.-M. R. Tillard (1987), *Église d'Églises, l'ecclésiologie de communion,* Paris.
M. Dujarier (1991), *L'Église-Fraternité,* Paris.
C. M. La Cugna (1991), *God for Us,* San Francisco.
J.-M. R. Tillard (1992), *Chair de l'Église, chair du Christ,* Paris.
R. W. Wall (1992), "Community, New Testament *K.,*" *AncBD* 1, New York.
X. Lacroix (1993), *Homme et femme, l'insaisissable différence,* Paris.
J. Reumann (1994), "The Biblical Witness of *k.,*" in *On the Way to Fuller K. Official Report of the Fifth World Conference of Faith and Order,* Geneva.
J.-M. R. Tillard (1995), *L'Église locale: Ecclésiologie de communion et catholicité,* Paris.

JEAN-MARIE R. TILLARD

See also **Anthropology; Baptism; Being; Christ/Christology; Circumincession; Holiness; Love; Person; Trinity; Unity of the Church**

Conceptualism. *See* **Nominalism**

Conciliarism

a) Conciliarism, also known as conciliary theory, is a doctrine that places the general council* above the pope* and accords it supreme power in the Church*: the power to determine the principles of faith* and to maintain unity*. The answer that it contributes in the debate about the nature of supreme power and the place in which that power is found is the product of a reflection on the Church, its nature, and the presence of the Holy* Spirit. This is why conciliarism is not primarily a political doctrine but belongs to the history* of theology*. Although there are points of convergence among different conciliary theories, there is no common doctrine, and the theory varies from one theoretician to another. The 15th century is considered the century of conciliarism, by reason of the decrees passed at the Council of Constance* to put an end to the division of the Church and of the radicalization of conciliary ideas that took place at the Council of Basel*. Religious Gallicanism* is considered to be a French form of conciliarism.

b) All the forms of conciliarism in the 15th century were consequences of the pontifical schism* (1378–1418). They extended and radicalized what Conrad Gelnhausen and Henry of Langenstein had timidly proposed, restoring unity to the Church by convoking a general council *(via concilii).* The sources of conciliarism are, however, much older. In addition to the recognized authority of the ecumenical councils of the early Church, we must mention, on the one hand, legal and theological documents and, on the other, practices peculiar to the medieval Church, such as the deposition of the pope and the possibility of appealing to the future general council against a pope's decision. We can cite as examples of the latter, Philippe IV the Beautiful's appeal against Boniface VIII, and the appeal of Louis of Bavaria, together with the Franciscans around him , against John XXII. Renewed at Constance on the closing day of the council, this particular practice ran into strong opposition from Martin V.

Of primary importance among the legal sources are the decree of Gratian (D. 40 c. 6) and the various commentaries on it, among which is that of Huguccio (†1210), as well as various glosses. These 12th-century documents pose the question of power in the Church and the limits of that power and the possibility of judging and deposing the pope, among others. Jurists of the time generally accepted the possibility of trying the pope for the crime of heresy*, whether open or private, without having beforehand determined who would be the judge. They established rules that would be an invaluable help to the conciliarists of Constance. For example, they determined that, "where faith is in question, the synod* is greater than the Pope" *(Ubi de fide agitur... tunc synodus est maior papa)* and that "what is of concern to everyone should be discussed by everyone" *(Quod omnes tangit, ab omnibus iudicatur).* In the period of the quarrel over Boniface, various jurists and theologians repeated and reinforced the same ideas: among these, for example, were Guillaume Durand the Younger (†1331), author of the treatise *De modo concilii generalis celebrandi,* and the Dominican Jean of Paris (†1306), author of *De potestate regia et papali.* The latter argued, among other things, that the pope had limited power since full power resided in the Church as a whole; that the council could try and depose the pope in the case of heresy, scandal, or incompetence; and that both his authority and his primacy were conferred on him by the Church. The treatise of Jean of Paris is the direct though unacknowledged source for Pierre d'Ailly and Jean Gerson, who both participated in the work of Constance, as well as for Jacques of Heaven (of Jüterborg), who was present at Basel, and for many others. In the late 14th and early 15th centuries it was generally accepted that Christ* alone was the head of the Church, that the pope held power in the Church because the Church granted it to him, that without the Church the pope was nothing, and that the Church could try and depose him for acts of heresy, simony, and other serious crimes. These were the principal points of ecclesiology* that Matthew of Krakow, for example, set out in his *De praxi Romanae curiae,* one of the sources for the conciliarism of Thierry de Niem.

The influential role played by Marsilius of Padua and William of Ockham in the development of conciliary doctrines is well known. However, the conciliarists belonging to the period before the Council of Pisa (1409)—that is, Conrad Gelnhausen, Henry of Langenstein, Pierre d'Ailly, and Matthew of Krakow—seem to have been unaware of Marsilius. After Pisa and before the Council of Basel, only Thierry de Niem made extensive use of *Defensor pacis.* The opinions of these early conciliarists owed much more to William of Ockham, although he never attributed a significant role to the general council and never accepted its infallibility. (William did, however, frequently stress the superiority of the Church over the pope.) In the early 15th century William's *Dialogue* influenced both Francesco Zabarella in Italy and a group of Parisian theologians: Pierre d'Ailly, Gerson, and Jean de Courtecuisse.

c) At the opening of the Council of Constance, the principal conciliarists—Gerson, d'Ailly, Zabarella, and Niem—jointly affirmed that the promise of infallibility* and indefectibility* had been made to the whole Church and not to any individual person. As a consequence it was the Church that was the supreme body and the locus of power. So while they accepted the primacy of the pope, the conciliarists did not see him as the head of the Church. They reserved this title for Christ alone. They envisaged the pope as a constitutional monarch or prime minister, subject to the power of the council and removable. Since he was neither faultless nor infallible, the pope could be tried, deposed, and replaced. The argument, which came from Zabarella, that made the general council the representation of the universal Church *(universalis ecclesia, id est concilium)* was fundamentally important in this already structured set of doctrines. In fact it legitimated a displacement of the center of interest from the Church to the council.

The decree *Haec sancta synodus* of 6 April 1415, accepted by the Council of Constance shortly after the flight of the anti-Pope John XXIII, is the most important of the "conciliarist decrees." In its preamble and first paragraph the council asserted its legitimacy and defined its three goals: eradication of the schism, union, and reform of the Church. Legitimately reunited, it defined itself as a general council. As such, it claimed to represent the universal Church, to derive its power directly from Christ, and to require obedience from any person, including the pope, in matters concerning faith and union (Mansi 27 590 D). On 9 October 1417, shortly before the election of Martin V and not unrelated to that election, the council adopted the decree *Frequens* (Mansi 27 1159 BE) in order to organize the convocation of future councils. By virtue of this decree, Martin V first convened the Council of Siena (1423) and then the Council of Basel (1431–49), which was dissolved by Eugene IV in the very year that it opened. The policies of Eugene on the one hand and the attachment of the Fathers of Basel to the spirit of Constance on the other at first led the Council of Basel to forbid both the dissolution of the council and its transfer to another location (decree *Cogitanti;* Mansi 29 24 D-26 A)—after Eugene IV had ordered the transfer of the council to Ferrara—to try the pope, to remove him, and to replace him with Amédée VIII, duke of Savoy, who took the name Felix V. It was, therefore, in the circumstances of a struggle against the pope that the council claimed its own infallibility. And having become an instrument of battle, the conciliarism of the Basel gathering provoked a new division of the Church and a new pontifical schism. After the experience of Basel, the papacy, followed by many theologians, would always engage itself more openly on the quest for pontifical monarchy.

d) The effects of the sudden radicalization that conciliarism underwent in Basel show, on a practical level, that no balance of power between the pope and the council was established there and that no rule was decreed either on the government* of the Church between two councils or on its government in the case of a vacancy in the Seat of Peter. On the theoretical level, they show that there was at the time no common conciliary theology. The numerous ecclesiological treatises of the time that expound conciliary ideas express only the opinions of individual theologians, and the reconstruction of a common fund of opinions and arguments is the work of historians. And even these are not agreed on the character and value of the principal documents passed at Constance and Basel. The most controversial is the decree *Haec sancta.* Some grant this the dogmatic weight of an article of faith recognized de facto by the two councils, by Martin V, by Eugene IV (at first), and by the principal theologians of the 15th century. Others, however, emphasize that it was only because of specific historical circumstances that brought the council to decree its superiority over the pope, in order to put an end to the schism. It was thus an urgent measure provoked by the flight of John XXIII and a decision with only a limited scope, which the Council of Basel nevertheless worked very hard to change into a dogma* (Mansi 29 187).

• The main sources comprise the texts of the councils of Constance and Basel: see Mansi 27–29, Venice, 1784.

♦ B. Tierney (1955), *Foundations of the Conciliar Theory,* Cambridge.

O. de La Brosse (1965), *Le pape et le concile: La comparaison de leurs pouvoirs à la veille de la Réforme,* Paris.

P. de Vooght (1965), *Les pouvoirs du concile et l'autorité du pape au concile de Constance,* Paris.

Fr. Oakley (1969), *Council over Pope? Towards a Provisional Ecclesiology,* New York.

A. Black (1970), *Monarchy and Community: Political Ideas in the Later Conciliar Controversy 1430–1450,* Cambridge.

R. Bäumer (Ed.) (1976), *Die Entwicklung des Konziliarismus,* Darmstadt.

G. Alberigo (1981), *Chiesa conciliare: Identità e significazione del conciliarismo,* Brescia.

Fr. Oakley (1983), "Conciliar Theory," *DMA* 3, 510–23 (bibl.).

H.-J. Sieben (1983), *Traktate und Theorien zum Konzil,* Frankfurt.

H. Smolinsky (1990), "Konziliarismus," *TRE* 19, 579–86 (bibl.).

A. Frenken (1993), *Die Erforschung des Konstanzer Konzils (1414–1418) in den letzten 100 Jahren, AHC* 25, 1–2.

S. Swiezawski (1997), *Les tribulations de l'ecclésiologie à la fin du Moyen Age,* Paris.

Zénon Kaluza

See also **Authority; Basel-Ferrara-Florence, Council of; Constance, Council of; Council; Gallicanism; Indefectibility of the Church; Infallibility; Pope; Structures, Ecclesial**

Condonation. *See* **Indulgences**

Confession. *See* **Penance**

Confirmation

1. The First Four Centuries

The relationships between baptism* and confirmation have been very frequently discussed, particularly by Anglican theologians since the 19th century. In the line of A. J. Mason, Dom Gr. Dix (1946) minimized the importance of baptism in favor of the gift of the Holy* Spirit received at confirmation. In reaction, G. Lampe (1951) stressed the gift of the Holy Spirit accomplished at baptism. These debates can now be overcome on the condition of recognizing the existence, from the New Testament on, of different traditions and diverse emphases placed on the rites of Christian initiation carried out in the course of a single celebration. It is essential to take this ritual unity into account in order to understand the sacramental life of the early centuries, which had no technical term to designate the postbaptismal rites or what we now call confirmation—*baptism* at the time designated the process as a whole and thus had a broader meaning than it does today.

The difficulty of articulating the function of water and the role of the Holy Spirit appeared in the New Testament itself. There is often an opposition between the baptism with water of John the Baptist and the baptism with the Holy Spirit of Jesus* (Mt 3:11 and parallel passages; Acts 1:5, 11:16, 19:1–7). Sometimes the gift of the Holy Spirit precedes and leads to baptism (Acts 10:44–48). Most frequently, water and the Holy Spirit are mentioned together in succession (Acts 2:38; Jn 3:5; 1 Jn 5:6ff.). The Pauline writings several times omit mention of the Holy Spirit (Rom 6:3–11; Gal 3:26ff.; Col 3:9ff.) and sometimes of Christ* (1 Cor 12:13).

This diversity continued in the ancient Church*, where three traditions* can be distinguished. The tradition of Antioch (*Acts of Thomas, Baptismal Catecheses* by John Chrysostom*) had only an anointment with *muron* (holy* oils) on the forehead, the *sphragis* ("seal"), then three immersions, and the Eucharist*. In Jerusalem* (*Mystagogic catecheses* by Cyril), the three immersions were followed by the anointment with *muron,* to which was attributed the gift of the Holy Spirit, and by the Eucharist. The West had prebaptismal rites (exorcisms*), followed by three immersions and postbaptismal rites for the gift of the Holy Spirit, carried out by the bishop*: the laying* on of hands, anointment, and sometimes the sign of the cross; everything came to a conclusion with the Eucharist. Thus, the gift of the Holy Spirit, always considered in the initiation* as a whole, was sometimes attributed to prebaptismal rites, sometimes to postbaptismal rites. The East gave a privileged place to anointment (which the New Testament seems to conceive of as a literary symbol), and the blessing* of the oil by the bishop (later by the patriarch) assumed major importance there. The East also had laying on of hands. Under the influence of the pneumatological discussions of the late fourth century (Council of Constantinople*, 381), of the greater importance accorded to the

Paulinian corpus (particularly Rom 6), and also probably of the reconciliation of heretics carried out by rites similar to postbaptismal rites (B. Botte; *see* Saint-Palais d'Aussac 1943), in the late fourth century, the East adopted postbaptismal anointment with pneumatological implications. The three rituals preserved in the *Apostolic Constitutions* (III. 16; VII. 22; VII. 39) give evidence of these modifications.

We can thus observe in Christian antiquity that initiation was accomplished through a variety of rites but in the unity of a single celebration. This diversified unity is attested in the West in both liturgical practice and theological reflection. The *Apostolic Tradition* (Rome, early third century) describes catechumenate and initiation in the framework of a vigil (probably at Easter); baptism took place in a baptistry and concluded with a christological anointment done by a presbyter*; the baptized then went into the church, where the bishop gave them a Trinitarian anointment, a pneumatological laying on of hands, and the sign of the cross. Also, speaking of Novatian—the validity of whose ordinations he questioned—Pope* Cornelius wrote to Fabius of Antioch (251), "However, after having escaped from illness, he did not even obtain the others (ceremonies; *ton loipôn*), in which it is necessary to participate according to the rule of the Church, and he did not receive the seal (*sphragisthènai*) of the bishop; not having obtained all that, how could he have obtained the Holy Spirit?" (Eusebius of Caesarea, *HE* VI. 43. 15; SC 41.157).

For his part, Cyprian* wrote that Christians are born from either sacrament* (*sacramento utroque nascantur: Ep.* 72. I. 2 and 73. XXI. 3); in each case he relied on John 3:5 and thus was most probably thinking of water and the Holy Spirit. And even if these passages are not to be interpreted in the (posterior) framework of doctrine of a sacramental septenary, they evidence an awareness in the West that the Holy Spirit is given most especially to Christians, in the course of their initiation, by postbaptismal rites carried out by the bishop.

In the late fourth century (baptism* II, 1 end), the increase in the number of Christians gave rise to different practices. The East favored the unity of initiation, for which the presbyter became the usual minister; the relationship to the bishop was maintained by the use of oil that he had blessed (Spain also had this discipline for a time). The West permitted presbyters to celebrate baptism and the Eucharist, but confirmation retained its link with the bishop. This Western discipline was established by the time of Innocent I, who in his letter to Decentius, bishop of Gubbio, in 416 recognized that presbyters had the right to baptize, but bishops alone could confirm ("record"). "From the point of view of the history* of the liturgy*, this is the origin of confirmation or, more precisely, the framework in which confirmation came to be understood as a particular sacrament" (Kretschmar 1983).

2. The Middle Ages

a) Terminology. The vocabulary of *confirmatio,* to designate the intervention of the bishop after the rite of water, appeared in Gaul in the mid-fifth century; the first mention is found in canons 3 and 4 of the Council of Riez (439; CChr.SL 148, 67). "The terms *preficere, perfectio, confirmare, confirmatio* express the conviction that the rite of confirmation adds to baptism a kind of perfection.... All that the word expresses is the feeling that confirmation is a complement to baptism" (Botte 1958; *see* Fischer 1965). The relationship to the eucharistic meaning of *confirmare* is eloquent (De Clerck 1986). From there, the terms passed into liturgical books from the eighth century on.

b) Growing Dissociation of Baptism from Confirmation. The new situation created in late antiquity was well expressed in the Pentecost homily delivered by a bishop in southern Gaul, probably Faustus of Riez (formerly attributed to Gallican Eusebius [between 460 and 470], CChr.SL 101, 331–41; *see* Van Buchem 1967). He presents the question in these terms to his listeners: "After the mystery* of baptism, what good can be done for me by the ministry* of the one who is going to confirm me?" His answer relies on a military comparison: the soldier, after having enlisted in the army, has to be armed for combat. Hence, "The Holy Spirit... in baptism gives fully as to innocence, and at confirmation grants an increase as to grace* (*augmentum... ad gratiam*).... In baptism we are washed, after baptism we are strengthened" (Van Buchem 1967). This homily points then in the direction of a theological justification for the recently established practice; it tends to recognize the distinction between baptism and confirmation by attributing specific effects to them. It had unexpected success in history since the False Decretals of the ninth century attributed it to a fourth-century pope (Melchiades or Miltiades; PL 130. 240–41); it later passed into the *Decretal* of Gratian (III. V. 1–2; Friedberg I, 1413). The Scholastic* theologians accepted it as a papal authority* of the fourth century. During the High Middle Ages, in episcopal cities, Christian initiation continued to be celebrated by the bishop at Easter; confirmation often took place a week later (R. Maur, *De clericorum institutione* II. 39, PL 107. 353). In rural areas, the priest baptized and gave the Eucharist (in the species of wine); the relationship to Easter gave way to a relationship to birth. It was stressed that parents should not fail to present their child to the bishop for confirmation on his next visit, if it were to take place. The ritual of confirmation was barely developed; there was no pastoral role (Gy 1959). At the time there was no attempt to justify the delay in confirmation; one has the feeling that what began as an exception had slowly become the rule. For example, Alcuin, a great scholar educated by the reading of the fathers* of the church, listed the sacraments blithely in the order baptism, Eucharist, and confirmation (*Ep.* 134 and 137; PL 101. 613–14; MGH. Ep. 4. 202 and 211).

In the 12th century, the practice of baptism *quam primum* had been established; confirmation took place during the bishop's visit, and the Eucharist was delayed until the Age of Reason. We thus find again the sequence of Christian antiquity, but the rites, considered as three of the sacraments of the septenary (1150), had become autonomous. It was on these grounds that Scholastic theologians were to create the theology* of confirmation. With formulations that go back to Faustus *(augmentum gratiae—robur ad pugnam),* they stated that the specific grace of confirmation is the gift of the Holy Spirit; like baptism, it confers a character, that delegates to the spiritual combat; its material is the oil blessed by the bishop and its form the formula *Consigno te* (Thomas* Aquinas, *ST* IIIa, q. 72).

3. The Reformation and Modern Times

The fundamental critique by the Reformation of confirmation was its lack of a biblical basis; Reformation Churches thus did not see it as having sacramental value, although they maintained it as an ecclesiastical ceremony. Bucer*, however, considered it as a sacrament, although he noted that its meaning was that of a profession of faith at the conclusion of the teaching of the catechism (Bornert 1989); this novel view, accepted by Lutheranism* and Anglicanism*, had considerable influence. As for Calvin*, he abolished confirmation. The Council of Trent* reasserted the sacramental value of confirmation, for which the bishop was the usual minister (*DS* 1628–30). The *Catechism* of Trent stipulates, "It is not fitting to administer this sacrament to those who do not yet have the use of reason*; and although we do not think it necessary to wait for the age of twelve, it is at least appropriate not to administer it before the age of seven" (chap. 17, §4).

In the 18th century, the Reformed Churches, under the influence of the Swiss pastor J.F. Ostervald, reintroduced a confirmation, understood as the personal adhesion of the baptized to what his parents had asked for him; the Geneva liturgy* of 1945 calls it "the normal complement (and as it were the second half) of the baptism of children" (von Allmen 1978). This appears to be a clear indication of modernity; after the Renaissance, in a world ruled by subjectivity, the baptism of little children seemed culturally inconceivable without the possibility of a later personal repetition. This role has often been played by confirmation.

In the Catholicism* of this period north of the Alps, there was a constant delay in the age of confirmation (Levet 1958). This explains why in those countries the decree of Pius X on the first communion of children by the age of six or seven (1910) officially reversed the order of succession of sacraments, while that order remained intact in the Mediterranean countries.

4. Vatican II and the New "Ritual"

The council* documents do not contain a renewed presentation of confirmation; only *LG* 26 specifies that the bishop is the *originating* minister. This slight terminological change has wide bearing; it legitimates the practices of the Eastern Churches since late antiquity and allows bishops to delegate priests to confer confirmation, and it thereby removes the principal historical cause of the separation between baptism and confirmation.

Still more important was the publication of the new *Ritual* (1971), which opens with the apostolic constitution *Divinae consortium naturae.* This asserts for the first time in an official document "the unity [of the three sacraments] of Christian initiation"; it is thereby explicitly linked to the ancient tradition, passing over the historical development of the West since the High Middle Ages (a vision that the *CEC* [1992] faithfully reproduced). The apostolic constitution defines the effect of the sacrament as being the gift of the Holy Spirit itself (*donum ineffabile, ipsum Spiritum Sanctum*). An essential change, "as a profession of the unity of a single sacrament" (Gy 1986), it replaces the medieval sacramental formula with that of the Byzantine liturgy (Ligier 1973): "N. be marked by the Holy Spirit, the gift of God." And in a convoluted expression, it finally specifies the essential rite of the sacrament: "The sacrament of confirmation is conferred by the anointment of the holy chrism on the forehead, done by laying on of hands, and by these words: '*Accipe signaculum Doni Spiritus Sancti.*'"

In the ecumenical area, the relationship between baptism and confirmation continues to raise difficulties. For example, in the *Report on the process of 'BEM' and Reactions of the Churches* of 1991 (*Clarification Notes* 10), one reads, "*a)* The reactions to the BEM...reveal...disagreements about the manner in which the anointment and the seal of the Holy Spirit should be expressed in the baptismal rite, and on their relationship to communion and participation in the Eucharist. *b)* In fact, an evolution is coming to light in the attitude and the practice of Churches as to confirmation, while they are at the same time increasingly rediscovering that in the beginning there was only a single complex rite of Christian initiation. They continue to consider confirmation from two different perspectives. For some, confirmation is the special sign of the gift of the Holy Spirit, a sign which takes its place in the entire process of initiation; for others, confirmation is especially the opportunity for a personal profession of faith on the part of those who have been baptized at a younger age. All agree that the first sign of the process of initiation into the body of Christ is the rite of baptism with water; all agree that the objective of initiation is to be fed by the Eucharist."

5. Theology and Pastoral Expression of Confirmation

The theology* of confirmation is most clearly expressed in the relationships it has with baptism, the Eucharist, the Holy Spirit, and the Church.

a) Relationship to Baptism. In contrast to Scholastic attempts, it now seems futile to attempt to find in baptism and confirmation specific effects that can be properly distinguished. It is more fruitful to view them as two poles in the dynamic continuity of Christian initiation. Any theology of confirmation that does not closely associate it with baptism turns out to be ill founded from the point of view of the tradition*. The relationship between the two sacraments is often expressed by the relationship between Easter and Pentecost, between the mission of the Son and the mission of the Holy Spirit.

b) Relationship to the Holy Spirit. This is the common denominator of what can be said about confirmation. This relationship, however, is not exclusive, as though the Holy Spirit were not at work in the other sacraments. But it takes on a particular force. Following many other documents, the apostolic constitution *Divine consortium nature* asserts that through confirmation the baptized receive, as an ineffable gift, the Holy Spirit itself. Just as Christ is at work in all the sacraments, but the Eucharist provides to communicants His body and His blood themselves, so through confirmation the Holy Spirit communicates itself in an entirely special manner to Christians, as the breath of their personal life and the strength necessary for the evangelical mission*. The new sacramental formulation makes it possible to unfold these meanings while not denying that the Spirit blows where it wishes.

c) Relationship to the Bishop and the Church. This relationship, which was strictly maintained in the Western tradition until Vatican II, is also affirmed by the East, which attributes a great deal of importance to the blessing of the oil by the bishop or by the patriarch. Although it has often been explained by a difference in power between the bishop and the presbyter, it is more meaningful to see it against the background of the relationship between the third and fourth articles of the Credo, between pneumatology and ecclesiology*. It is in fact the Holy Spirit who gives body to the Church (second epiclesis* of the Eucharist prayers), as it gave His human body to Jesus ("conceived by the Holy Spirit, born of the Virgin Mary*") and as it gives Him His eucharistic body (first epiclesis). The presence of the bishop (or of his delegate) as minister of confirmation thereby indicates that to become a Christian means opening oneself to a communion* with the entire Church for which the bishop is responsible (Bouhot 1968).

Confirmation thus clearly appears as a sacrament, an ecclesiastical act mediating an action of God*, a sacrament of initiation, intended for all Christians in order to communicate to them the supreme gift of God, and not only for the most committed among them to a particular responsibility in the Church (Moingt 1973). As for the order of succession of the three sacraments of initiation, it is far from a matter of indifference despite the avatars of Western history. It is in any event important that Western theology never attempted to justify confirmation conferred after the Eucharist (Bourgeois 1993).

d) Pastoral Problems. The pastoral realization of confirmation poses many problems, for its most usual practice is set in opposition to its *Ritual* and its theology. The two currents noted above in the report of the WWC are also found within Catholicism*. As a function of the current conditions of Christian witness, the second tendency is leading to a delay of confirmation to a later age, in light of a deeper Christian commitment. It takes its place in the line of the Western tradition (Bourgeois 1993). However, it risks confusing confirmation, a sacrament of initiation, the pneumatological seal of baptism, and commitment. The latter, which represents a fundamental dimension of Christian life, is, however, coextensive with the whole existence of Christians, without being particularly linked to a specific sacrament. We should avoid thinking a priori that confirmation provides the pastoral answer to all questions posed by the Christian development of the young.

• **a) Ritual**
Ordo confirmationis, Rome, 1971.

b) Bibliography
L. Leijssen (1989), "Selected Bibliography on Confirmation," *QuLi* 70, 23–28.

c) Studies

Fr. de Saint-Palais d'Aussac (1943), *La réconciliation des hérétiques dans l'Église latine: Contribution à la théologie de l'initiation chrétienne,* Paris.

G. Dix (1946), *The Theology of Confirmation in Relation to Baptism,* London.

G. Lampe (1951), *The Seal of the Spirit: A Study in the Doctrine of Baptism and Confirmation in the New Testament and the Fathers,* London.

B. Botte (1958), "Le vocabulaire ancien de la confirmation," *MD* 54, 5–22.

R. Levet (1958), "L'âge de la confirmation dans la législation des diocèses de France depuis le concile de Trente," *MD* 54, 118–42.

P.-M. Gy (1959), "Histoire liturgique du sacrement de confirmation," *MD* 58, 135–45.

J. D. C. Fisher (1965), "The Use of the Words '*confirmare*' and '*confirmatio*,'" in *Christian Initiation: Baptism in the Medieval West,* London, 141–48.

L. A. Van Buchem (1967), *L'homélie pseudo-eusébienne de Pentecôte: L'origine de la* confirmatio *en Gaule méridionale et l'interprétation de ce rite par Fauste de Riez,* Nimègue.

J.-P. Bouhot (1969), *La confirmation, sacrement de la communion ecclésiale,* Lyon.

L. Ligier (1973), *La confirmation Sens et conjoncture œcuménique hier et aujourd'hui,* ThH 23 (see M. Arranz [1991], *OCP* 57, 207–11).

J. Moingt (1973), *Le devenir chrétien: Initiation chrétienne des jeunes,* Paris.

G. Kretschmar (1983), "Firmung," *TRE* 11, 192–204.

M. Maccarone (1985), "L'unità del battesimo e della cresima nelle testimonianze della liturgia romana dal III al XVI secolo," Lat 51, 88–152.

P. De Clerck (1986), "La dissociation du baptême et de la confirmation au haut Moyen Age," *MD* 168, 47–75.

J. Zerndl (1986), *Die Theologie der Firmung in der Vorbereitung und in den Akten des Zweiten Vatikanischen Konzils,* Paderborn.

R. Bornert (1989), "La confirmation dans les Églises de la réforme: Tradition luthérienne, calvinienne et anglicane," *QuLi* 70, 51–68.

P. De Clerck (1989), "La confirmation, moyen de catéchèse?," *QuLi* 70, 89–100.

A. Nocent (1991), "La confirmation, questions posées aux théologiens et aux pasteurs," *Gr* 72, 689–704.

H. Bourgeois (1993), "La place de la confirmation dans l'initiation chrétienne," *NRTh* 115, 516–42.

PAUL DE CLERCK

See also **Baptism; Eucharist; Initiation, Christian; Sacrament**

Congar, Yves. *See* **Thomism**

Congregationalism

Congregationalism is a radical form of Protestant ecclesiology* in which every local community (congregation) gathered around its ministers fully embodies the universal Church*. Its chief characteristics are the independence and strict autonomy of each community, the democratic government of the communities, and the logical application of the theology* of the universal priesthood* of the baptized.

The story of Congregationalism is centered on the English-speaking world and begins with the realization that the ecclesiastical policy of Elizabeth I (1533–1603) was not tending toward the establishment of a rigorously Protestant* Church of England but rather to the choice of a middle way between Rome* and Geneva (the Elizabethan Settlement). As early as 1550, groups ("Separatists") had broken away to form purely protestant cells. This movement gathered momentum after the promulgation of the Act of Uniformity of 1559; and in 1582, when R. Browne (c. 1550–1633) published two works championing a Congregationalist theology of the Church, his stand found enough answering expectation for these tendencies to become an organized movement, known initially as "Brownists." Congregationalist parishes were created at Southwark, Norwich, and elsewhere. Browne himself fled to the Netherlands after being imprisoned for schism, then broke with his community and returned to the bosom of the Church of England, but his successors at the head of the movement completed the split.

Congregationalism was then faced with immediate persecution, and the Congregationalist leaders J. Greenwood, H. Barrow, and J. Penry were executed in 1593. Congregationalism went underground in England, and an emigration ensued, chiefly to America. The conflict between Charles I and Parliament permitted the Congregationalists to make an official reappearance, henceforward under the name of "Independents," and Cromwell's policy allowed them (as it did the Puritans, with whom their early history is closely intertwined) to conceive the dream of an English Christianity with a Presbyterian or Congregationalist structure. The Restoration put an end to this dream, and in 1662 a new Act of Uniformity made the Congregationalists and their allies into "nonconformists." The Toleration Act of 1689 nonetheless granted them the right to exist.

Despite the status imposed on it, Congregationalism was to exercise a real influence on English intellectual and religious life over the following two centuries. Excluded from the universities, the Congregationalists founded academies of a high caliber and would later play a part in the foundation of the University of London. And while there was no Congregationalist theology strictly speaking—rather, Congregationalists practiced a moderated Calvinism*—Congregationalism still numbered among its ranks some theologians of high standing, such as J. Owen (1616–83), T. Hooker (1586–1647), I. Watts (1674–1748), and P. Doddridge (1702–51) and (in America) J. Cotton (1584–1652), J. Edwards*, and H. Bushnell (1802–76).

The governing principle of Congregationalism never condemned the Congregationalist communities to isolation. From the 17th century it was clearly accepted that the absolute independence of the communities did not preclude a degree of interdependence, the first goal of which was to organize evangelical activity, then external mission*. In 1790 "county unions" were set up. The year 1831 saw the creation of the Congregational Union of England and Wales. In 1920 the former districts were regrouped into provinces, each having a "provincial moderator" responsible for coordinating the appointment of ministers*. In 1970 the Congregationalist communities founded the Congregational Church in England and Wales, and then in 1972 the largest part of the new Church merged with the Presbyterian Church of England to form the United Reformed Church. Similar processes of federation and union took place in America and in the mission countries. A significant minority of the English communities refused this development, however, and these still maintain the principle of the total independence of the local cells within the body of the (liberal) Congregational Federation and the (evangelical) Evangelical Fellowship of Congregational Churches.

Although Congregationalism has always refused to equip itself with confessional texts that would set a norm, circumstances have led to the drafting of a number of professions of faith. In the Declaration of Savoy (1658), a text closely faithful to the 1643 Confession of Westminster, 120 communities declared themselves in favor of an ecclesiastical constitution of the Congregationalist type and not of the presbyterian-synodal model. The Declaration of Faith, which followed the establishment of the Congregational Union in 1832, is notable for the way it distances itself somewhat from Congregationalism's original Calvinism. The Declaration of Faith of 1967 is original in presenting the positions of other Christian Churches alongside the confessed theology of Congregationalism. The most representative Congregationalist texts are, however, the "contracts of alliance," ratified by the communities, in which they express in a consistent and stereotyped manner the ecclesiological ideas that have impelled Congregationalism since its inception. Lastly, the Congregationalists celebrate the Eucharist* and baptism* and practice infant baptism.

• B. Hanbury (1839–44), *Historical Memorials Relating to Independents or Congregationalists,* 3 vols., London.

W. Willistom Walker (Ed.) (1893), *Creeds and Platforms of Congregationalism,* New York, repr. 1960.

H.W. Clark (1911–13), *History of English Nonconformity, from Wyclif to the Close of the Nineteenth Century,* 2 vols., London.

G.G. Atkins, F.L. Fagley (1942), *History of American Congregationalism,* Boston and Chicago.

H.M. Davies (1952), *The English Free Churches,* Oxford.

D. Horton (1952), *Congregationalism: A Study in Church Polity,* London.

H. Escott (1960), *A History of Congregationalism in Scotland,* Glasgow.

Congregational Journal, Hollywood, Calif., 1975–76.

R.B. Knox (Ed.) (1977), *Reformation, Conformity and Dissent,* London.

M. Deacon (1980), *Philipp Doddridge of Northampton,* Northampton.

J.-P. Willaime (1982), "Du problème de l'autorité dans les Églises protestantes pluralistes," *RHPhR* 62, 385–400.

Galahad Threepwood

See also **Anglicanism; Calvinism; Local Church; Puritanism**

Conscience

Narrowly defined, conscience refers to the painful awareness of wrongdoing and to the seat of such feelings. A broader definition speaks of conscience as an inner source of moral authority that judges and guides us. The history of the idea of conscience is extraordinarily complex, touching most aspects of the history of morality. The concept cannot simply be explained through the history of terms (conscience, *Gewissen, conscientia, synt*[*d*]*eresis, suneidesis*) because their meanings vary depending on their contexts. One must look at what determine conscience in each case and especially at the concept of personality and the type of society that are involved. In Christian theology*, the concept of conscience varies according to given anthropological and soteriological concepts as well as the understandings of moral life in relation to God*, Christ*, and Spirit.

1. Antiquity

The first instance of the word *suneidèsis* is found in Democritus (*VS* B 297); the corresponding verb can be found, for example, in Xenophon (*Memorabilia* II) or Sophocles *(Antigone)* and means a "sharing of knowledge." The activity of conscience was unknown in primitive Greek culture. Homer's heroic characters, lacking in reflective moral awareness, locate the goodness of an action* not in intention* but in the consequences that it entails, especially with respect to reputation or dishonor. Moral identity is a function not of conscience but of the approval or disapproval from the group, which bestows honor or shame depending on whether one respects the conventions linked to traditional social roles. The tragedians are more interested in moral conflicts because tragic figures are less completely identified with convention. Aeschylus *(Agamemnon)* and especially Euripides *(Orestes)* describe the torment of the guilty person conscious or his fault by interiorizing the myth* of the Furies pursuing the criminal. This is still remote from later notions of conscience: the tragic hero suffers not only from internal conflict but also from the defilement imposed by destiny. Neither Plato nor Aristotle systematically discusses conscience. Later Platonists seemed to recognize conscience in Socrates' demon*, who warned him against wrongdoing *(Phaedrus),* although it was probably divinatory in character. In Aristotle, ethical knowing and judging are attributed to *phronèsis.*

The crucible for Western views of conscience was Roman Stoicism, for which conscience is an internal moral guide that approves or disapproves a conduct. The highest element in the human being is the presence of natural law* (Cicero, *De legibus;* Seneca, *Epistulae*), which can morally guide behavior and is known as such by reason. This is why Cicero identifies "right conscience" *(recta conscientia)* and "right reason" *(recta ratio)* in *De finibus.* This view of conscience as "a sacred spirit within us that observes and controls our good and bad actions" (*sacer intra nos spiritus malorum bonorumque nostrorum observator et custos;* Seneca, *Epistulae*), also found in Tacitus, Livy, and Quintillian, drifted into popular usage and formed part of the background to the New Testament.

2. Scripture

a) Old Testament. There is no term for conscience in the Old Testament, which nevertheless describes the troubles caused by remorse (1 Sm 24:5f.; 2 Sm 24:10; Ps 32:3f.; Is 57:21) and the peace* brought on by a clean conscience (Ps 26; Jb 27). "Heart" (1 Kgs 2:44, 83:38; Eccl 7:22; Jb 7:6) is the seat of self-knowledge, which depends on God's omniscience and omnipresence as lawgiver and judge (Is 139; Prv 16:2, 20, 27). The concept that conscience would play a deliberative or guiding role does not appear, however. In the Old Testament, reflective distance from God may be covert disobedience (Gn 3:1–7), and knowledge of God's law must be affective and practical rather than a cause for thought. The Septuagint (ancient translations* of the Bible) rarely uses *suneidèsis* (Eccl 10:20; Wis 17:11; Sir 6:26, 42:18).

b) The New Testament. Conscience is not an essential concept in the New Testament. The term is absent from the Gospels*, where the "heart" is still the center of moral knowledge and will (Mt 5:8, 5:28, 15:10–20; Mk 7:18–23; Lk 6:45). Conscience appears a number of times in the Paul's letters but without the connotations that it has today. Conscience is not the central theme of Pauline theology. Paul appeals to his good "conscience" to justify of his ministry* (Rom 9:1; 1 Cor 4:4; 2 Cor 1:12; compare Acts 23:1, 24:16) and waits for a similar judgment from others (2 Cor 4:2,

5:11). Romans 13:5 contains an anticipatory idea of conscience: Christians must obey the state to avoid a later condemnation. When Paul speaks of conscience when discussing the issue of flesh sacrificed to idols (1 Cor 8:1–13, 10:18–31; Rom 14)—passages that would be key in later theological developments—conscience is the capacity not of moral direction but of self-condemnation. The "strong" conscience, who knows the nothingness of idols, is free from self-accusation about consuming meat sacrificed to them, but this strong freedom should not scandalize the "weak" conscience, which, not possessing the same knowledge, may be wounded by such action. Here, conscience is not a source of absolute moral certainty (it is knowledge, not conscience, that liberates from scruple); nor does conscience act autonomously (the strong act out of love* for the weak). A further crucial passage for later thinkers is Romans 2:14–16; although the text is often thought to furnish exegetical warrant for the idea of a "natural law" written in the heart and guarded by conscience, it may be that Paul referred only to those pagans who "by nature do what the law requires" and not to humanity in general. Moreover, the center of gravity in Paul's thinking lies elsewhere: it is Christ*, not nature, conscience, or law, that is ultimate (Gal 3:24). The pastorals refer to "good conscience" (1 Tm 1:5, 19), "clear conscience" (1 Tm 3:9; 2 Tm 1:3; compare 1 Pt 3:16, 21), and its opposite (1 Tm 4:2; Ti 1, 15), to speak of honesty. Although the usage here is less immediately soteriological (and closer to post-apostolic usage; *see* 1 Clem 1, 3, 24 and 41, 4), the connection between conscience, understood in this sense and faith* (1 Tm 1, 5, 19 and 3, 9) is important. In Hebrews, conscience is the locus of guilt, which is cleansed by Christ's priestly sacrifice* (Heb 9:9, 14, 10:22; compare Ignatius, *Trall.* 7).

In the New Testament, therefore, conscience is a secondary notion. Introspective concerns are generally absent from the New Testament, which does not explain or justify behavior in terms of an "inner voice" attributed to God. Partly this is because of the weight accorded to public conventions and roles in a culture oriented to honor and shame. Further, the language and perspectives used are not that of later theologies or philosophies. What would be later associated with the notion of conscience, such as moral experience, control, and approval, is expressed in the New Testament in terms of Spirit, justification*, faith, and the return of the Lord to judge human beings *(parousia*).* In this light, the New Testament differs both from Stoicism and from Philo's notion of conscience as the organ of reproof *(elegkhos)* and inner judge *(dikastes)* presiding over and evaluating actions (*De fuga et inventione,* §118; *De decalogo,* §87).

3. Patristic and Medieval Period

a) The Fathers. Although systematic treatment of the subject is rare in the Fathers*, the notion of conscience gained importance during the patristic period. Drawing on Stoic sources (Christian Stoicism*), Origen develops the notion of moral principles universally known (*Contra Celsum* 1, 4, SC 132), and, in an important commentary of 1 Corinthians 2:11, he identifies conscience and the Spirit of God within us (*In Psalmos* 30, 6, PG 12, 1300 b), an idea that would be taken up again later. John Chrysostom* turns conscience into a key factor of morality: the voice of conscience reveals the moral law, which is the general or natural context in which Christian morality shows its specificity (*De statuis, Opera omnia,* 1834). Augustine*'s view is significantly different: natural law theory is chastened by its repudiation of the moral optimism of Pelagianism*, and, although he can speak of the golden rule (Mt 7:12) as "inscribed in the conscience" (*scripta [in] conscientia; Confessions* 1, 18), conscience is essentially knowing that God knows us (10, 2) and a confirmation of divine judgments (*Enarrationes in psalmos* 7, 9, CChr.SL 38) rather than in relative detachment from divine presence.

b) The Medieval Period. Medieval discussions of conscience generally focus on two terms: *synteresis* (a corrupt translation of *suneidèsis*) and *conscientia.* In general, the discussion emerges from the passage in Pierre Lombard's *Sentences* (c. 1100–60), in which he wonders about Romans 7:15 if there are two wills within the sinner in conflict with himself and in which he briefly refers to Jerome's commentary of Ezekial 1:4–14. Jerome identifies the eagle in Ezekiel's vision with what he calls *synteresis;* if this capacity was retained after the Fall, Jerome asserts that some wicked persons did not retain what he calls *conscientia.* Commentators solved the contradiction by distinguishing *synteresis* as the ultimate ground of moral knowledge from *conscientia* as the application of principles. The distinction receives sophisticated treatment from Bonaventure* and Thomas* Aquinas. For Bonaventure, *conscientia* belongs to affectivity; as such, it is a *habitus,* a disposition, not a deduction. Aquinas, by contrast, views *conscientia* as an act of bringing moral principles to the actual situation (*De veritate* 17, 1), whereas *synteresis* is the *habitus* that contains the basic principles of natural law (*ST* Ia IIae, q. 94, a. 1, ad. 2). Unlike what would be done later, however, Aquinas views these principles more as a formal framework than as a set of rules whose application is to be determined with the help of a casuistry*.

The distinction between *synderesis* and *conscience*

explains how the issue of knowing whether conscience is always an obligation is dealt with. *Synderesis* cannot err; conscience, however, may err by not applying the principles correctly, but it must always be obeyed since obedience to God's law is a basic principle of *synderesis.* To disobey even a mistaken conscience is therefore to act against *synderesis.*

In all these debates, conscience is increasingly viewed as a guide in the moral realm rather than the seat of guilt. Although it operates in relative independence and not under God's direct impulse, conscience should not be construed subjectively. Aquinas's insistence on practical reason's reference to an objective moral order distinguishes him sharply from Abelard*'s intention-oriented and quasi-absolute conscience: "There is no sin that is not against conscience" (*non est peccatum nisi contra conscientiam; Ethica* 13).

4. Reformation

A decisive shift occurs with the Reformers, especially Luther*. Conscience no longer is associated with vows, asceticism*, and penance* (association strengthened at the Fourth Lateran* Council, which had made confession obligatory). Henceforth, faith rather than practical reason becomes key with regard to ethics. Conscience is no longer treated as part of the metaphysics of created personhood* but is integrated into the soteriological notion of sin* and grace*. For Luther, conscience is the site of a struggle between hopeless ethical and religious justification through law on the one hand and faith in the justifying word* of God on the other. When conscience is "terrified of the Law... rely only on grace and the word of comfort" (*WA* 40/1, 204). No longer naturally oriented toward God, but set in the context of Christ's liberating work, conscience really is a matter of faith: "faith born of this word will bring peace of conscience" (*WA* 1, 541). Conscience is not the center of moral judgment since faith acknowledges God's judgment about the person rather than conscience's judgments about the person's acts. Good conscience thus comes before doing good deeds and not the reverse. Moral and pastoral theology must thus move away from the formation of conscience or its instruction in religious observances to deal first and foremost with conversion* and trust. Calvin*, similarly, emphasizes that conscience is best understood in relation to salvation*; freed by Christ's gift (*Inst.* III, 19, 15), conscience need not heed anyone, even though externally it is due to civil obedience.

5. Modern Times

a) Philosophy Modern thinkers often read the Reformation as asserting the rights of individual conscience over Church authority*. It is mistaking faith for subjectivity, as well as underestimating the objective character of classical Protestantism*. To turn Christianity into a religion of conscience (Holl), one needs a certain philosophy of modernity, in which authority is accorded to conscience as an autonomous faculty of self-governance, increasingly detached from rational consideration of moral reality. Montaigne describes it as a mean of self-knowledge ("I have my laws and my court to judge myself"; *Essais* III). Descartes* conceives conscience as affective rather than rational *(Passions de l'âme).* Spinoza understands it within the perspective of his ethics of self-preservation (*Ethica* IV). Conscience thus becomes the nucleus of personal decision around which orbit other realities (authoritative doctrines, public conventions) that furnish material for debate. Conscience is close to moral freedom seen as autonomy, whose concept entails that the essential condition of moral existence is the absence of determination by nature or society. Such affirmations find their political expression in the principle that "it is nothing but tyranny to wish to predominate over conscience" (Bayle), a principle that lies at the heart of liberal pluralism.

The English school of "moral sense" (the Earl of Shaftesbury [1671–1713], Francis Hutcheson [1694–1746], and Joseph Butler [1692–1752]) turns conscience into "a principle of reflection in men, by which they distinguish between, approve and disapprove, their own actions" (Butler). Against this, Hume (1711–76) argues that conscience is a matter of feeling and not reason *(A Treatise of Human Nature),* thereby distancing conscience from nature and giving his theory a distinctive voluntarist twist. In the German idealist tradition, Kant* and Hegel* bring conscience closer to subjectivity. For Kant, conscience, self-sufficient and subject to no guidance, is "moral judgment passing judgment upon itself" *(Die Religion innerhalb der Grenzen der blossen Vernunft);* that is, moral reason is judging itself. Rather differently, Hegel considers conscience as "formal subjectivity" *(Philosophie des Rechts),* a view that would deeply affect later philosophers, notably Heidegger* *(Sein und Zeit)* and Ricoeur *(Soi-même comme un autre),* for whom conscience is to accuse but a call to authenticity.

The influence of theories of the pathological genesis of conscience should also be noted. According to Nietzsche* *(Zur Genealogie der Moral)* and Freud*, conscience arises in the struggle between desire and external constraints and is no more than an arbitrary mechanism confronting the self. The conventional character of conscience has also been underlined by sociology, which views conscience as an internalization of social representations.

b) Theology. Post-Reformation Protestantism shifts the issue of conscience to subjectivity. Calvinists such as Perkins (1558–1602) or Ames (1576–1633) look for subjective certainty of salvation in conscience. It means a rigorous examination of one's behavior in light of the commandments casuistically interpreted. This moralism, quite different from the Reformers' insistence on the priority of divine acquittal, can also be found elsewhere, for example, in the writings of Jeremy Taylor (1613–67), who understands conscience as well as Christian living in a way that, although not quite Pelagian, emphasizes the role of will. These developments helped reinforce the individualist conception of conscience: since it had but a distant relation to the doctrine of salvation, conscience had to become a concern for the conformity of the person to him- or herself. This concern for personal authenticity had other roots also: idealist philosophy of consciousness, pietism*, and the rise of a religious notion of subjectivity, in which the moral self is the seat of divine presence. Thus, Schleiermacher* defines conscience out of God-consciousness of the community *(Der christlicher Glaub)* followed by liberal Protestantism (Biedermann, Gass, Schenkels). In the first half of the 20th century, a quite antithetical position was espoused by Bonhoeffer* *(Ethik)* and especially in Barth*'s protest *(Ethik)* against "the ethics of naturalist or idealist subjectivism" and his trust in the evidence of conscience. For Barth, conscience depends on our adoption by God; it is not a reality that we have because conscience is participation in God's knowledge of the redeemed, and its primary activity is not self-examination but prayer*, which corresponds to the almost miraculous rarity of its apparition.

Recent Catholic work on conscience has often abandoned the juridical tone of manual traditions of moral and pastoral theology in favor of personalist understandings of conscience. Vatican* II even gave official encouragement in its emphasis on freedom: "the gospel has a sacred reverence for the dignity of conscience and its freedom of choice" (*Gaudium et spes* 41). Post–Vatican II theologians, such as Auer, Fuchs, or Böckle, make conscience the center of moral existence, which is characterized by responsibility.

6. Systematic Issues

Formal and material issues are closely tied in theories of conscience. At the formal level, we may distinguish those accounts that begin with analysis of the agent from those that begin with consideration of the field within which the agent exists. The former seldom refer to the theological categories, and philosophy or the social sciences are a favored ground for Christian anthropology. In the latter, by contrast, the process is essentially theology, and there is little concern with finding harmony between Christian and non-Christian anthropologies. On a material level, one can start with the experience of obligation and define personal existence in terms of constitutional human decisions and acts: conscience is then seen as freedom, will, or personal commitment, only secondarily related to authority, tradition*, or revelation*, which are construed heteronomously. By contrast, one can deem essential the instances external to the person and think that moral existence is determined by something other than itself: the others, society* and its organization, and, above all, God's creative and redemptive acts. Then it is faith, not consciousness, that prevails; moral reason is not introspection but discerning an objective order; tradition and authority shape rather than inhibit authenticity. On all these issues, the debate remains open.

• P. Abelard, *Ethica,* Ed. D. Luscombe, Oxford, 1971.
K. Barth, *Ethik,* Ed. D. Braun, 2 vols., Zurich, 1973, 1978.
D. Bonhoeffer, *Ethik, DBW,* vol. 6, 1992.
J. Butler, *Fifteen Sermons,* in *The Works of Joseph Butler,* Ed. W.E. Gladstone, vol. 2, Oxford, 1896.
M. Luther, *Resolutiones disputationum de indulgentiarum virtute,* 1518, *WA* 1; *In epistolam S. Pauli ad Galatas Commentarius,* 1535, *WA* 40/1.
F. Nietzsche, *Zur Genealogie der Moral, Werke: Kritische Gesamtausgabe,* Ed. G. Colli, M. Montinari, vol. 6, 2, Berlin, 1968.
Thomas d'Aquin, *De veritate* 15–17; *ST,* Ia, q. 79, a. 12 et 13; Ia IIae, q. 19, a. 5 et 6; IIa IIae, q. 47, a. 6, ad 1 and ad 3.
Vatican II, *Constitutions, décrets, déclarations, messages,* Paris, 1967.
♦ M. Kähler (1878), *Das Gewissen,* Halle.
L. Brunschvicg (1927), *Le progrès de la conscience dans la philosophie occidentale,* Paris.
W. Jaeger (1934–47), *Paideia: Die Formung des grieschichen Menschen,* 3 vols., Berlin.
O. Lottin (1942–60), *Psychologie et morale aux XIIe et XIIIe siècles,* 6 vols., Louvain.
C.A. Pierce (1955), *Conscience in the New Testament,* London.
E. Wolf (1962), "Vom Problem des Gewissens in reformatorischer Sicht," *Peregrinatio,* vol. 1, Munich, 81–112.
H. Reiner (1974), "Gewissen," *HWP* 3, 574–92.
M.G. Baylor (1977), *Action and Person: Conscience in Late Scholasticism and the Young Luther,* Leiden.
H. Chadwick (1978), "Gewissen," *RAC* 10, 1025–1107.
T.C. Potts (Ed.) (1980), *Conscience in Medieval Philosophy,* Cambridge.
J.G. Blüdhorn et al. (1984), "Gewissen," *TRE* 13, 192–241.
B. Baertschi (1996), "Sens moral," *DEPhM,* 1371–79.

JOHN WEBSTER

See also **Casuistry; Ethics; Ethics, Autonomy of**

Consequentalism. *See* **Utilitarianism**

Constance, Council of

1414–18

Forced to close the Council of Rome almost as soon as it had opened and to flee the Papal States, Antipope John XXIII had to seek the support of Sigismund, King of the Romans (Church* and State). A new council was announced and convoked by the latter, but it was to take place within the territory of the empire, at Constance. Gregory XII, the pope* of Rome* who lived in Rimini, would be represented; but Benedict XIII, the antipope of Avignon, would forbid his supporters to attend. The council opened on 1 November 1414 by John XXIII.

For decision-making purposes, the council was organized, on the model of the universities, into "nations," each of which held one vote. The Italian, French, Germanic, and English nations were established at the outset, and the Iberian delegations subsequently combined to form the Spanish nation. The other countries represented at Constance were attached to one or another of these five nations. The cardinals made up a separate college, holding a single vote. These divisions were the cause of endless discussions, numerous violent arguments, and the domination of the debates by the academic clergy. They echoed both the geographical and the sociological composition of the council. The five nations grouped together delegations from all the states and ecclesiastical provinces of Latin Europe, and these delegations contained a high number of professors and university-educated prelates. The ecumenical nature of the Council of Constance is still debated.

The council had three goals: the return to union (Church unity*), the reform of the Church and of the Curia, and the defense of the faith*.

a) The flight of the antipope in March 1415 helped the council, which was opposed to him. Apprehended and brought back to Constance, John XXIII was tried and deposed. As a result of this decision, Gregory XII spontaneously abdicated. The council then sent a delegation, led by Sigismund, to obtain Benedict XIII's abdication. Benedict refused to yield and was therefore tried and deposed in July 1417. The delegation did, however, obtain agreements from several countries in the region that they would switch their allegiance.

Now acephalous, the Church found itself governed by a council for the first time. The question then arose of whether to elect a new pope without delay or to carry out reforms before the election and force the pope, once elected, to abide by them. Sigismund favored the second solution, which would ensure his domination of the council. The cardinals, on the other hand, afraid of being subjected to the reforms carried out by the radicals, wanted the election to be brought forward. The council, modifying slightly a proposal by Pierre d'Ailly, then decided that the electoral college should be made up of all the cardinals and six representatives from each nation. On 11 November 1417, the electors chose Cardinal Oddo Colonna, who took the name of Martin V. This election reestablished union and marked the end of the pontifical schism*.

b) Although a commission of "reform of the Church in its head and in its members" was created in 1415, the difficulty of the undertaking and the multiplicity and range of the proposals, along with the conflicting machinations of different parties, made it impossible. The council did not attend to the matter until the summer of 1417. However, on 6 April 1415 it published the decree *Haec sancta synodus,* which asserted the General Council's precedence over the pope in matters of faith, Church union, and reform; and then, on 9 October 1417, it published the decree *Frequens,* which laid down regulations for the convocation of future councils and the handling of any future schism. Together, these represent the key acts of 15th-century conciliarism*. Christendom hoped for the reform of Church structures* and financial affairs—which included the encouraging and perpetuating of simony, the accumulation of profits, and pontifical collations, that sorry legacy of the Avignon papacy—wishes that remained unfulfilled. Before the closing of the council on 22 April 1418, however, the Fathers and Martin V did draw up a list of the reforms that the pope would have to undertake with the help of the Curia.

c) As for the eradication of heresy*, condemnations fell principally on John Wycliffe and his supporters. The council condemned Wycliffe (who had died in 1384) as a heretic. It declared Jan Hus* and Jerome of Prague to be heretics and condemned them to death. They were burned alive at Constance. It also decided that communion* of the laity in both kinds, which had recently become the practice in Bohemia, was heretical. The French and the Poles joined forces to call for the condemnation of John Parvus and John Falkenberg, the apologists for tyrannicide, but were unsuccessful. This last endeavor, moreover, revealed a major point of disagreement between these two delegations and Martin V on the right of appeal to a future council, which the new pope immediately decided to prohibit.

• H. Finke, *Forschungen und Quellen zur Geschichte des Konstanzer Konzils,* Paderborn, 1889.

H. Finke, *Acta concilii Constantiensis,* 4 vols., Paderborn, 1896–1928.

A. Frenken, *Die Erforschung des Konstanzer Konzils (1414–1418) in den letzten 100 Jahren,* Paderborn (*AHC* 25, Heft 1–2), 1993.

H. von der Hardt, *Magnum œcumenicum Constantiense concilium,* 6 vols., Frankfurt-Leipzig, 1696–1700.

COD 403–41.

♦ E. Delaruelle, E.-R. Labande, P. Ourliac (1962), *L'Église au temps du Grand Schisme et de la crise conciliaire* (1378–1449).

A. Franzen, W. Müller (Ed.) (1964), *Das Konzil von Konstanz: Beiträge zu seiner Geschichte und Theologie,* Fribourg-Basel-Vienna.

J. Gill (1965), *Constance et Bâle-Florence.*

R. Bäumer (Ed.) (1977), *Das Konstanzer Konzil,* Darmstadt.

G. Alberigo (1981), *Chiesa conciliare: Identità e significato del conciliarismo,* Brescia.

W. Brandmüller (1990), "Konstanz (Konzil von)," *TRE* 19, 529–35.

J. Wohlmuth (1994), "Le concile de Constance (1414–1418) et le concile de Bâle (1431–1449)," in G. Alberigo, *Les conciles œcuméniques,* vol. I, Paris, 203–55 (bibl.).

ZÉNON KALUZA

See also **Church and State; Conciliarism; Ecclesiology; Eucharist; Government, Church; Pope**

Constantinople I, Council of

381

a) History. The First Council* of Constantinople, which met in May 381, was at the outset a council of the East, convened by Theodosius. It was chaired first by Meletius of Antioch until his death, then by Gregory* of Nazianzus until he tendered his resignation, and finally by Nectarius, the new archbishop of Constantinople. The council brought together approximately 150 bishops*; its best-known members were part of the Cappadocian group of the friends of Basil*, who had died prematurely: his brothers Gregory* of Nyssa and Peter of Sebaste, his close friend Gregory of Nazianzus, his correspondent Amphilochius of Iconium, and Meletius, the controversial bishop* of Antioch, whom Basil never stopped supporting. Cyril of Jerusalem and Diodorus of Tarsus were also present. The proceedings of the council are lost, and the historical documentation at our disposal is very incomplete. It was not an "ecumenical" council in the same sense that this adjective had when it was conferred on Nicaea* because this time there was no participation by the West. The synodal letter of 382 sent by the Fathers* to Rome* does refer to the "ecumenical synod* of Constantinople"—but this assembly remained in fact shrouded in almost total silence for three-quarters of a century. The debates between Cyril of Alexandria and Nestorius, at the time of Ephesus*, always refer to the text of the symbol of Nicaea and seem to be unaware of that of Constantinople. The latter's ecumenical authority would not be recognized until this symbol was read and acclaimed at the Council of Chalcedon*; this was to lead, in consequence, to a recognition of ecumenical authority* and of the ecumenical authority of the council itself. Since then, the Council of Constantinople has been universally regarded as the Second Ecumenical Council.

b) The Doctrinal Work of Constantinople I. The work of Constantinople I consisted chiefly in putting an end in the East to the Arian heresy*, confirming the decision of Nicaea and proclaiming the divinity of the Holy* Spirit, which had been challenged since 360 by three distinct currents. The radical Arianism* (Anomean) of Aetius and Eunomius saw the Holy Spirit as a creature of the Son and the Son as a creature of the Father*. The Egyptian "tropics" (who reasoned on the basis of "expressions" *[tropoi]* from Scripture*) were orthodox as far as the Son* was concerned but saw the Holy Spirit as a created angel*. Athanasius* had replied to them in his *Letters to Serapion Concerning the Holy Spirit.* Finally, in the East, the "combatants against the Holy Spirit" *(pneumatomachians),* who were also called the Macedonians, after Macedonius, the deposed archbishop of Constantinople, pointed to the natural inferiority of the Holy Spirit due to the inferiority of its creative role. It was the pneumatomachians who mainly preoccupied Constantinople I. The council attempted to reconcile them, but in vain.

c) The Symbol of Constantinople. The decisions of Constantinople I were expressed in a symbol received since then in all the Churches* as a liturgical symbol and often called the symbol of "Nicaea-Constantinople."

The Council of Chalcedon attributes the paternity of that symbol to the Fathers of Constantinople. Its obscure origin, however, has prompted a number of hypotheses (Kelly, Ritter, Abramowski). It does not take up the text of the symbol of Nicaea or that of Jerusalem* (Harnack), and the hypothesis that Epiphanius of Salamina was its first author in 374 is no longer accepted. The Fathers probably used an Eastern symbol that had integrated the typical additions of Nicaea (Ritter). The part written by the Fathers of Constantinople is uncertain, except for the third article, dealing with the Holy Spirit, for which the influence of the Cappadocian Fathers, Basil's friends, appears to have been instrumental. This article offers in fact a recapitulation of Basilian pneumatology.

The second article takes up again the *consubstantial** of Nicaea, but it renounces the formula "of the Father's substance," probably considered ambiguous because it is partitive.

The third article comprises the new sequence on the Holy Spirit, made up of five formulas: 1) The first formula states the divine character of the Holy Spirit, by emphasizing that it is "Holy" in nature, like God*, sanctifying, and not sanctified the way creatures are. 2) The second does not proclaim that the Holy Spirit is God, as Basilian reserve, in a spirit of reconciliation, had always refused to do, but it calls it "Lord," a specifically divine name given it by Scripture (2 Cor 3:17). 3) The function of the Holy Spirit is divine since it "gives new life" (Jn 6:63; 1 Cor 15:45) thanks to its creative and deifying role. 4) "It proceeds from the Father": this formula calls on the only New Testament regarding the origin of the Spirit (Jn 15:26). But to a sentence that had an "economic" meaning (the going forth of the Holy Spirit toward the world), the council gives the meaning of an eternal procession* of the Spirit within the Trinity*. The Spirit "proceeds," in the same way that the Son is begotten. Therefore, it is not a creature. The procession expresses its hypostatic property; it is a way of expressing the Spirit's consubstantiality with the Father and the Son without actually using the word. The Spirit's link to the Son is left undetermined, and thus it opens the way to the future controversy about the *Filioque**. 5) "With the Father and the Son, he is jointly worshipped and glorified": this formula, which takes up a famous argument by Basil, is based on the link between *lex credendi* and *lex orandi* so as to express in a different way the Holy Spirit's affiliation to the Trinity. Constantinople I performed that work of reconciliation and of peace*.

The council had another important by-product. In a synodal letter sent to Rome* in 382, the same Fathers delivered the first Greek version of what was to become the Trinitarian formula common to East and West: "One sole divinity, power, and substance of the Father, the Son, and the Holy Spirit, all equal in honor and in coeternal royalty, in three perfect hypostases, or still in three perfect Persons*" (*DCO* II/1, 81). This formula was used again by the Second Council of Constantinople*.

d) The Disciplinary Canons. The council also promulgated four canons, the third of which remained the most famous. It was intended to affirm the authority of the bishop of Constantinople, the new Rome: his seat had assumed considerable importance since the city had become the capital of the Eastern Empire; he was given "the preeminence of honor after the bishop of Rome." This canon was never to be accepted by the popes* of ancient Rome and similarly with canon 28 of Chalcedon.

• *COD* 21–35 (*DCO* II/1, 67–95).

♦ J.N.D. Kelly (1950), *Early Christian Creeds,* London (3rd Ed. 1972).

I. Ortiz de Urbina (1963), *Nicée et Constantinople,* Paris.

A. M. Ritter (1965), *Das Konzil von Konstantinopel und sein Symbol,* Göttingen.

Coll. (1982), *La signification et l'actualité du IIe concile œcuménique pour le monde chrétien d'aujourd'hui,* Geneva.

G. Alberigo (Ed.) (1990), *Storia dei concili ecumenici,* Brescia (*Les conciles œcuméniques,* vol. I, L'histoire, 1994, 59–70).

A. de Halleux (1990), *Patrologie et œcuménisme,* Louvain, 303–442.

L. Abramowski (1992), "Was hat das Nicaeno-Constantinopolitanum mit dem Konzil von K. zu tun?," *ThPh* 67, 481–513.

BERNARD SESBOÜÉ

See also **Creation; Creeds; Fathers of the Church; Filioque; Nestorianism**

Constantinople II, Council of

553

The Second Council* of Constantinople, the fifth of the ecumenical councils, was convoked by Justinian to provide a definitive orthodox interpretation of the Council of Chalcedon*. The main tasks that the emperor put to the council were to reformulate the teaching of Chalcedon in terms that would be more universally acceptable and to declare nonorthodox three "chapters" or elements representative of the christological tradition of Antioch* that the Council of Chalcedon had not condemned: the person and works of Theodore of Mopsuestia, the first of the great theologians of Antioch; the polemical works of Theodoret of Cyrrhus, directed against Cyril* of Alexandria; and Ibas of Edessa's *Letter to Maris,* in which Ibas also had strongly attacked Cyril. Theodore of Mopsuestia had not been explicitly named at Chalcedon, while Theodoret and Ibas, who had condemned the heresy* of Nestorius, had been recognized as orthodox.

a) Aftermath of Chalcedon. For the great majority of Eastern Christians, scandalized by the affirmation at Chalcedon of the equality and relative autonomy of the human nature of Christ*, these "three chapters" from Antioch were the very symbol of the Chalcedonian spirit of compromise with the century. Only a more divine notion of Christ, such as formulated by the Alexandrian doctors* Athanasius* and Cyril, could be the norm for Christian faith* and worship. As for the Latin West, it saw in the formulas of Chalcedon both a Christology* that better suited its more practical conception of salvation and a tribute to the doctrinal authority* of Leo, bishop* of Rome*. Therefore, to abandon Chalcedon would be an offense against both orthodoxy* and papal primacy. Episcopal hierarchies opposed to Chalcedon had been in place in Egypt and Syria since the 480s, and there were many of them by the end of the 530s; on the other hand, the "Acacian schism" (484–519) between Rome and Constantinople had been provoked by the pope's disquiet over the attempts of the patriarchs of Constantinople to formulate a Christology not based on Chalcedon.

b) The Role of Justinian. As soon as he became emperor in 527, Justinian understood the political and religious necessity for an official formulation of Christology and an interpretation of Chalcedon that would rally the empire. After a fruitless attempt at dialogue with the bishops opposed to Chalcedon (533), Justinian had the local synod* of Constantinople condemn those who clung to an exclusively pre-Chalcedonian terminology (536). The emperor, who was himself a highly original theologian, took the initiative in orienting theological study toward a new conception of Christ's person*. His goal was to reach a synthesis between the Chalcedonian formulas, which were opened to a variety of interpretations, and the explicitly theocentric Christology of Cyril, which 20th-century historians have called "neo-Chalcedonianism" or "neo-Cyrilianism." The rejection of the "three chapters" from Antioch was the essential negative element in this new synthesis.

Between 543 and 545, Justinian published his first edict condemning the "three chapters," most of which has since been lost. On 13 July 551, he issued a second edict, *De recta fide,* which was accompanied by a long treatise setting out the reasons for condemning the chapters *(Epistula contra tria capitula).* Pope Vigilius (537–555), who had arrived in Constantinople, either voluntarily or under compulsion, at the end of 546, seems to have agreed with Justinian, and he condemned the "three chapters," in April 548, in his *Judicatum.* There was a storm of protest in the West over this apparent abandonment of Chalcedon, which forced Vigilius to renege his position. After a period of open conflict with the emperor, he retracted his "judgment."

c) A Turbulent Council. Only a council officially assembled by the emperor could reestablish unity. Convoked by Justinian, 152 accredited bishops, among whom perhaps 11 were from the Latin West, sat between 5 May and 2 June 553. The emperor could be certain of the docility of this gathering, which was dominated by Greeks and under the authority of his influential adviser, Theodore Asquidas. He therefore left the direction of the council to the bishops alone. On 24 May, Vigilius, who did not attend any of the meetings out of fear of negative reactions from the West, sent a letter to the emperor *(Constitutum)* stating his position: the theological errors of the three doctors of Antioch needed to be condemned, but their persons and their works had to be spared out of respect for Chalcedon and for the dead. On 26 May, Justinian responded by sending two letters to the council reflecting the changes in Vigilius's position and telling the bishops that they should cease to be in communion* with him as long as he would not accept their collective judgment.

At its eighth and final session, on 2 June, the council approved a document comprising an introduction and 40 canons. The last four canons condemned the "three chapters" as well as a classic list of heretics, including Origen*—whose "school" seems to have been condemned for various reasons, and at Justinian's request, even before the council opened. By contrast, the first 10 canons form a systematic Christology, combining the terminology of Chalcedon with that of Cyril and affirming clearly that the Divine Word* is the sole subject of Christ's actions, the only hypostasis that exists in his two natures (canons 2–3, 5, 9). This declaration excludes any conception that might separate the natures within Christ and limits the distinction between them, however irreducible they may be, to "a merely conceptual consideration" (canon 7). It also recognizes the legitimacy of some of Cyril's expressions, which the Council of Chalcedon had not accepted (canon 8), and makes his conception of the uniqueness of Christ's person normative. This is based on a "hypostatic or composite union" (canon 4; hypostatic* union), which wholly excludes any interpretation that might imply a "confusion" of Christ's two natures into one (canon 8). Finally, the document forcefully reaffirms the principle of "communication of idioms*": it is literally accurate to apply the title "Mother of God" to Mary* (canon 6), and the council also ratifies the confession of the "theopaschites," that "he who was crucified in the flesh, Our Lord Jesus Christ, is truly God and Lord of Glory, and one in the Holy Trinity" (canon 10).

Six months later, the pope declared that he was ready to accept the canons of the council, and he made his agreement public in a declaration, *Constitutum II,* dated 23 February 554, which completely contradicts his earlier position. The reaction of the Western bishops was extremely negative, especially in Africa, where there had been a whole body of literature hostile to the council and its decrees, as well as in northern Italy and Gaul. Under Vigilius's successor, Pelagius I (556–61), the church of Aquileia seceded from Rome over the question of the "three chapters," starting a schism* that lasted until the late seventh century. Gregory* the Great indicated that he accepted Constantinople II, along with the other ecumenical councils, but he also felt a need to insist that the condemnation of the theologians of Antioch did not in any sense contradict the teachings of Chalcedon (*Epistulae,* 1, 24; 3, 10; 9, 148). Apart from these popes, Western writers took time to include Constantinople II among the ecumenical councils, and many Greek sources from the seventh century and later seem to have only a vague notion of its work.

Nowadays, historians tend to minimize the doctrinal importance of Constantinople II, seeing it as no more than an instrument for Justinian's clumsy policy toward the Church. Some 20th-century Catholic writers (Amann, Moeller, Devreesse), seeking to weaken the very powerful affirmation of Christ's divinity formulated at Constantinople II, have argued that the council's decisions were not canonically valid because it was not in communion with Rome when it promulgated them and that it was merely the condemnation of the "three chapters"—which in itself has no doctrinal significance—that was accepted later by Vigilius and his successors. More recently, however, Orthodox and Protestant historians (Chrysos, Meyendorff, Frank) have shown that there was substantial continuity in procedure and doctrine between the first four councils and Constantinople II and have recognized the dogmatic declaration of this, the fifth council, as both a genuine clarification of the teaching of Chalcedon and an authentically ecumenical attempt to take account of the value of rival theological formulas.

• Acts: *ACO* IV/1 and IV/2.
Text of the dogmatic declaration, *ACO* IV/1, 239–45.
Decrees: *COD* 107–22 (*DCO* II/1, 240–71); *DS* 421–38 (can. only).
Justinian's Edicts in *Drei dogmatische Schriften Justinians,* ABAW. PH NS 18.
Vigilius, *Constitutum I,* CSEL 35, 230–320.
Vigilius, *Constitutum II, ACO* IV/2, 138–68.
Facundus d'Hermiane, *Pro defensione trium capitulorum,* CChr.SL 90 A, 4–398.
Liberatus, *Breviarium, ACO* II/5, 98–141.
Evagrius Scholasticus, *Historia ecclesiastica* IV, 10–38, Ed. J. Bidez, L. Parmentier, London, 1898, 160–89.
♦ J. Bois (1908), "Constantinople (IIe concile de)," *DThC* 3/1, 1231–59.
E. Schwartz (1940), "Zur Kirchenpolitik Justinians," ABAW. PH NS, 2, 32–81.
R. Devreesse (1946), "Le Ve concile et l'œcuménicité byzantine," *Miscellanea Giovanni Mercati* 3, StT 123.
E. Amann (1950), "Trois chapitres," *DThC* 15/2, 1868–1924.
C. Moeller (1951), "Le Ve concile œcuménique et le magistère ordinaire au VIe s.," *RSPhTh* 35, 412–23.
E. Chrysos (1969), *Hè ekklesiastikè politikè tou Ioustinianou kata tèn erin peri ta Tria Kephalaia kai tèn Pemptèn Oikoumenikèn Sunodon,* Thessalonica.
F.X. Murphy (1974), "Constantinople II," in F.X. Murphy, P. Sherwood, *Constantinople II et Constantinople III,* 9–130, Paris.
P.T.R. Gray (1979), *The Defence of Chalcedon in the East 451–553,* Leiden.
G.L.C. Frank (1991), "The Council of Constantinople II as a Model Reconciliation Council," *TS* 52, 636–50.

Brian E. Daley

See also **Anhypostasy; Chalcedon, Council of; Christ/Christology; Ephesus, Council of; Hypostatic Union; Idioms, Communication of**

Constantinople III, Council of

680–81

The Third Council of Constantinople, also known as the Fourth Ecumenical Council, affirmed the reality of the two wills and the two activities, divine and human, within Christ*, by condemning the doctrines of monothelitism* and monoenergism*. This dogmatic definition, preceded by that of the Lateran Council of 649, was the final outcome of the long labor of theological clarification accomplished by Maximus* the Confessor.

a) The Role of Maximus the Confessor. Like Pope Honorius, Maximus had approved the *Psèphos* (decree) of Patriarch Sergius of Constantinople (patriarchate*) and had first been disarmed in front of the novelty of the problem posed by the prayer* of Jesus* at Gethsemane: his human will appeared to be contrary to the divine will, and Sergius had concluded in favor of the negation of that will. Maximus subsequently highlighted the reality of that human will and showed its soteriological importance.

In the first place, between 634 and 640, Maximus affirms that Christ really does have a human will by applying to the particular case of the will his own *logos/tropos* distinction. It thus becomes possible to distinguish between the notions of *otherness* and of *opposition,* which had been confused up until that time. The contrariousness of the human will in relation to the divine will is not due to its *logos,* in other words, to its essential reality, but to a certain *tropos,* that is, a personal mode, a "tendency" of the sinner's human will. But the fact that this human will is other than the divine will is due to its essential reality, to its *logos.* Hence, the opposition is not necessary in the hypothesis of the two wills. Since Christ is perfectly holy and without sin*, any opposition of his human will to his divine will is excluded a priori (*see Op* 4, between 634 and 640, PG 91, 60 A-61 D; *Op* 20, before 640, 236 A-237 C).

Then, between 641 and 646, Maximus interprets Jesus' Gethsemane prayer in a new way by considering his human will no longer in the apparent refusal but in the act* of free acceptance of the cup (Mt 26:42). To answer fully the problem of the opposition of the human will to the divine will, Maximus highlights this free consent of Jesus' will, which reveals his perfect agreement with the divine will (*see Op* 6, c. 641, PG

91, 65 A-68 D; *Op* 7, c. 642, 80 C-81 B; *Op* 16, after 643, 196 C-197 A; *Op* 3, c. 645–46, 48 BD). The will being the principle of activity, the problem of monoenergism was solved at its root.

In doing this, Maximus was enhancing in Christology* the active role of the humanity of Christ in its historical reality. The agreement between human will and divine will is part of Jesus' earthly life, in his perfect obedience to the Father*, which takes him to his death on the cross (*see Phil* 2:8). At Gethsemane, the union of the two wills reveals itself in the interpersonal relation between Son and Father, as this relation has unfolded humanly, according to the dynamic of a free will. Obedience is the exact word to describe this fully human attitude of the Son toward his Father, in the order of freedom* (*see* PG 91, 68 D).

b) The Local Council of the Lateran. Maximus became the principal adversary of monothelitism, and he victoriously confronted Pyrrhus, the former patriarch of Constantinople, in a public dispute in Carthage in July 645 (PG 91, 288–353). In 646 he started living in Rome*, which had become the center of resistance to monothelitism. While Emperor Constans II, in his *Tupos* of 647, strictly forbade talk of one or two wills or operations, Pope* Martin I summoned a council in the Lateran, in October 649, in order to affirm dogmatically the two wills and operations and to condemn monothelitism and monoenergism. Maximus was the theologian of that council, and he certainly wrote the main texts, in which it is possible to recognize his expressions (*Op* 6, PG 91, 68 D). Faced with the hypothesis of the two contrary wills, the council affirmed that the two wills of Christ, divine and human, are united in full agreement; and faced with the hypothesis of two subjects desiring opposing things, the council affirmed one sole subject, Christ, who divinely and humanely desires one single thing: our salvation* through his Passion*. The two operations were affirmed in the same manner (*see DS* 500, 510, 511). What was new in these affirmations concerned the human will and its soteriological role through the activity that ensues. To express the meaning of Jesus' free consent at Gethsemane, it had to be said that our salvation had been desired and realized humanly by a divine being*.

Constans II reacted by arresting Martin and Maximus, who would both seal with their martyrdom* the affirmation of Christ's human freedom in his agony; the death of the pope in 655 and that of the theologian in 662 also expressed the freedom of the Church* against political power.

c) The Third Council of Constantinople. This dispute ended up at the council, which took place in Constantinople from November 680 to September 681, during the reign of Emperor Constantine IV. Against monothelitism and monoenergism, that council clearly affirmed the reality of the two wills and of the two operations of Christ, in the perspective of Chalcedon*'s definition, whose expressions were reused word for word (as well as Leo's expressions from his *Tome à Flavien*), the wills and the operations being considered properties of the two natures of Christ: "We proclaim in him, according to the teaching of the Holy Fathers*, two natural wills and two natural operations, without any division, any change, any partition, and any confusion. The two natural wills are not at all, as the impious heretics have said, opposed to one another. But Christ's human will follows his divine and all-powerful will; it does not resist it and does not oppose it; it rather submits to it [. . .]. The natural difference in this unique hypostasis can be seen in the fact that each of these two wills desires and acts in its own domain, in communion with the other. For that reason, we glorify two wills and two natural operations participating together in mankind's salvation" (*DCO* II-1, 287–91).

By the same token, the council condemned all those who had professed monothelitism and monoenergism, among whom was counted Pope Honorius (*DS* 550–52). That unique case—a bishop* of Rome condemned as a heretic by an ecumenical council—gave rise later to great discussions (in particular with regard to infallibility*). In reality Honorius was never formally a heretic, having died in 640, long before the solution of the problem. He therefore did not have the time to retract his unfortunate monothelite formula of 634. Maximus always defended his memory, and the council of 649 did not condemn him. The dogmatic assertion of the free human will of Christ and of the resulting operation guaranteed the full humanity of Christ, considered from his center, from his heart*.

• Acts: *ACO, Series secunda* II/1 and 2.

Decrees: *COD* 124–30 (*DCO* II/1, 273–93).

♦ P. Sherwood (1952), *An annotated date-list of the works of Maximus the Confessor,* Rome.

H. Rahner (1964), *L'Église et l'État dans le christianisme primitif,* Paris.

M. Doucet (1972), *La Dispute de Maxime le Confesseur avec Pyrrhus,* Montreal.

Ch. von Schönborn (1972), *Sophrone de Jérusalem,* Paris.

F.X. Murphy, P. Sherwood (1973), *Constantinople II et III,* Paris.

J.M. Garrigues (1976), "Le martyre de saint Maxime le Confesseur," *RThom* 76, 410–52.

F.-M. Léthel (1979), *Théologie de l'Agonie du Christ: La liberté humaine du Fils de Dieu et son importance sotériologique mises en lumière par saint Maxime le Confesseur,* Paris.

FRANÇOIS-MARIE LÉTHEL

See also **Chalcedon, Council of; Christ/Christology; Maximus the Confessor; Monothelitism/Monoenergism**

Constantinople IV, Council of

869–70

a) Prehistory. In 858, Ignatius, patriarch of Constantinople, was deposed for political reasons and replaced by Photius, a layman. Pope* Nicholas I challenged that election on two grounds: the patriarch of Constantinople could not be deposed without the agreement of Rome*, and the election of Photius did not conform to the canons in any way whatsoever. At the same time, Nicholas demanded the reintegration, under Roman jurisdiction*, of Illyricum, Calabria, and Sicily, which had been annexed to the patriarchate of Constantinople by the iconoclastic emperors.

A synod* that met in Constantinople in 861 confirmed the deposition of Ignatius, with the agreement of the Roman legates, who were to be subsequently disavowed by the pope.

In 863 a synod at the Lateran deposed Photius and those he had ordained. Nicholas I invoked the primacy of Rome (which gave it the right to intervene in the affairs of the other patriarchates*), contested the doctrine of the pentarchy (equal dignity of the five patriarchates: Alexandria, Antioch, Constantinople, Jerusalem*, and Rome), and recognized only three "apostolic" patriarchates: Rome, Alexandria and Antioch.

In response to this, Photius sent an encyclical letter to the Eastern patriarchs in which he stated that the rank of the bishops* depended on the political importance of their city and also condemned Rome's addition of the *Filioque** to the symbol of Nicaea*. In 867 he organized the meeting of a council in Constantinople (known as the "Photian council"), which anathematized Nicholas I (this was the "Photian schism*").

A political upheaval in Byzantium caused the departure of Photius and the return of Ignatius. In June 869 a Roman synod, presided over by Pope Hadrian II, anathematized Photius and burned the acts of the Photian council. In October of the same year, and at the request of the Byzantine emperor, the Fourth Council of Constantinople was opened.

b) History and Issues. This council lasted 10 sessions. What was at issue was Rome's intervention in the internal affairs of another patriarchate and its role as a source of orthodox faith*. The subject of the *Filioque,* raised for the first time in Photius's encyclical letter to the Oriental patriarchs, was not broached.

The final decree *(horos)* of the council recognized the first seven ecumenical councils and condemned Photius.

The council's 27 canons deal with tradition*, Roman primacy, the patriarchates, images*, the heretical doctrine of the two souls*, and disciplinary questions (election of a layman* to the patriarchate, intrusion of political power in the affairs of the Church*, etc.)

c) Reception. The council's decisions pertaining to Photius were abrogated in 879 by Pope John VIII and by a synod held in Constantinople under the chairmanship of Photius himself (who had been reconciled with Ignatius and had again been made a patriarch) in the presence of the pope's legates and of the Eastern patriarchs.

Constantinople IV is acknowledged as ecumenical by the Latin Church but not by the Greek Church, which holds to the "seven ecumenical councils." Some Orthodox theologians consider the 879 synod to be ecumenical.

• *COD,* 157–86 (*DCO* 1, 354–407).
Acts, Mansi 17, 373–725.
♦ D. Stiernon (1967), *Constantinople IV, HCO* 5, Paris.
P.-Th. Camelot, P. Maraval (1988), *Les conciles œcuméniques,* I: *Le premier millénaire,* Bibliothèque d'histoire du christianisme 15, Paris.
G. Alberigo (Ed.) (1990), *Storia dei Concili Ecumenici,* Brescia.
G. Dagron, P. Riché, A. Vauchez (Ed.) (1993), *Évêques, moines et empereurs (610–1054)* (*Histoire du christianisme,* vol. IV), Paris, 169–86.

Marie-Hélène Congourdeau

See also **Church and State; Council; Creeds; Heresy; Pope**

Consubstantial

a) Traditional Foundations. Although the word "consubstantial" did not begin to circulate before the beginning of our era, its semantic roots join the most ancient usages of words such as "essence" *(ousia),* "substance" *(hupostasis),* or "nature" *(phusis).* In this respect, three main and independent authorities played a constant role as sources of inspiration and of language throughout the genesis of patristic thought: Plato, Aristotle, and the Stoics. Plotinus, however, was the first to use *homoousios* in philosophical language. In his *Enneads* (IV, 7 [2], 10), he states that the human soul*, in its intrinsic goodness, has something divine "because of the kinship and the consubstantial" with "divines things," *dia suggeneian kai to homoousion* (Bréhier). Porphyry uses *homooousios* five times; Jamblic, once, to pick up on Plotinus's idea: the soul is mixed with divinity (*Mysteries of Egypt* 3, 21). In the fifth and sixth centuries, an isolated use of *homoousios* would be seen again among each of the two last great masters of neo-Platonism, Syrianus and Simplicius. Meanwhile, the Christian authors of the same period would have used this term more than 200 times, according to G. W. H. Lampe, *A Patristic Greek Lexicon.* One can see from which side the term "consubstantial" triggered a truly intellectual creation, judging by its literary vogue.

b) Pre-Nicene Christian Usage. Beginning with Irenaeus* and Tertullian*, the Fathers* denounced the Gnostic usage, declaring the consubstantiality of spiritual beings with divine Plerome. The first Trinitarian usage of *homoousios,* foreign to the Gnostic context, appeared in the correspondence between the two Dionysius, the homonymic bishops* of Rome* and Alexandria, only around 265, although neither one made personal use of it. Not long afterward, in 286, a synod* condemned Paul of Samosata at Antioch; a homousian *Letter of Sirmium* stated in 358 that this synod had censured *homoousios;* but this was a mere supposition, easily understood in the tumult of ideas after Nicaea*.

c) The Nicene "Consubstantial." "The exact signification of *homoousios* in the Nicene Creed is not only difficult to elucidate, it is useless to pretend to search for it," observed C. Stead (1994) at the end of an excellent analysis of the non-Christian and Christian recourses to the concept or to the word before Nicaea. A relevant remark from a historian of classical thought but who forbids himself to grasp the *pastoral* nature of the choice of this term at the council* of 325. Let us try, then, to define precisely the original signification of Nicene "consubstantiality." In the *Exposition (of faith) of the 318 Fathers* (*DCO,* II-1, 1994), this word first refers to monogenesis, "unique engendered" (*see* Jn 1:18; 3:16, 18) which the creators of the symbol detached from "Son of God," to which it is always adjoined in analogous formulations of faith* of the period, and which they joined to "born of the Father*" in lieu of the traditional formula "before all centuries" (Skarsaune 1987). The design of the origin of the Son (filiation*), understood as divine "generation," is thus detached from the reference to cosmology according to a shift in perspective that started with Alexander of Alexandria, *Letter to Alexander of Thessalonica.* Thus, both words, *monogenesis* and *homoousios,* or rather the two expressions that carry these words, one made of traditional elements, *ek tou patros monogenès* and one that constitutes a polemical addition that is not scriptuary and is completely unknown to tradition, *homoousios tô patri,* explain each other. Consequently, this "consubstantiality" refers back to the unique generation of the Son by the Father.

Indeed, the two parallel expressions ensure, along the same line, the inclusion of other polemic additions introduced in the formula of baptismal faith that serves as a basis for the drafting of the Nicene Creed:

1) *toutestin ek tes ousias tou patros,* "that is to say of the Father's essence," a logical precision formulated according to Theognostos, bishop of Alexandria between 250 and 280, who served to reinforce "born of the Father, unique engendered"
2) *theon alethinon ek theou alethinou,* "the true God of true God," scriptuary allusion (Jn 17:3) corroborating the metaphor that is both Johannine (1 Jn 1:5, 8:12) and eminently Origenian (Boularand 1972) and that precedes *phôs ek photos,* "light born of light," a metaphor absent from other classical creeds and thus still an Alexandrian sign characteristic of the Nicene Creed

3) *gennethenta ou poiethenta,* "engendered, not created" ("made"), a reference to the Scripture* (at least for "engendered": Ps 110:3; Prv 8:25), serving to immediately introduce *homoousios*

In short, here *homoousios* takes on meaning focusing on the origin of the Son. Such a focus, imposed by the Arian contestation, is the distinctive particularity of Nicean *homoousios.* The identity of the nature between the Father and Son is not defined in itself, but it is affirmed as far as the origin of Monogenesis, as was required by the common faith. If the Nicene Fathers could have accepted such recourse, it is precisely because in the immediate context of their creed, *homoousios* was no longer situated, at least in their eyes, on the level of philosophy* or of the gnosis* of the past, where it would remain burdened by ambiguities. The signifying value of the term, in harmony with the pastoral need of the hour, consisted of expressing the still radically mysterious origin of the Son.

The reception* of *homoousios* in its proper theological dimension would impose a strong effort of original invention for generations of thinkers, beginning from the pioneering work of Athanasius of Alexandria*, *Against the Arians* (c. 340), up until the clear distinction between the three hypostasis and the divine essence in the Cappadocian synthesis, in particular among Gregory* of Nazianzus (*Theological Orations,* c. 380). During this debate of ideas, Christian thought determined how Nicene "consubstantiality" signified a union of numeric nature without imposing a Trinitarian modalism* and how it suggested a specific union of hypostasis without shattering the essential identity and simplicity* of the divine Trinity*. For the first time, in 382, a synodal letter explicitly extended the consubstantiality of Christ* to the entire Trinity. At the Council of Chalcedon* (451), the same concept would be used to clarify the double consubstantiality of Christ: it designates in the order of divinity the unity of the first substance and in the order of humanity, the specific identity of the second substance.

• *Conciliorum oecumenicorum Decreta* II-1 (1994), 34–35.

♦ I. Ortiz de Urbina (1942), "L'*homousios* preniceno," *Orientalia christiana periodica* 8, 194–209.

J. N. D. Kelly (1950), *Early Christian Creeds,* London (3rd Ed., 1972).

L. M. Mendizabal (1956), "El Homoousios Preniceno Extraecclesiastico," *Estudios ecclesiásticos* 30, 147–96.

I. Ortiz de Urbina (1963), *Nicée et Constantinople,* Paris.

E. Boularand (1972), *L'hérésie d'Arius et la "foi" de Nicée,* II, Paris.

O. Skarsaune (1987), "A Neglected Detail in the Creed of Nicaea (325)," *Vigiliae Christianae* 41, 34–54.

B. Sesboüé, B. Meunier (1993), *Dieu peut-il avoir un Fils? Le débat trinitaire au IVe siècle,* Paris.

G. C. Stead (1994), "Homoousios," *Reallexikon für Antike und Christentum* XVI, 364–433.

Charles Kannengiesser

See also **Arianism; Athanasius of Alexandria; Nicaea I, Council of; Trinity**

Consubstantiation

A term unknown to the Scholastics and to the early Reformation, "consubstantiation" appeared around 1560 in Calvinist polemics to characterize Lutheran eucharistic theology (which asserted the presence of Christ* "in, with, and under" the bread and wine of the Eucharist*. Theories of consubstantiation go back to the patristic use of christological concepts in eucharistic theology (Betz 1979): just as Christ is truly man and truly God*, so the body of Christ is truly ("substantially") present, while the bread and the wine themselves remain truly present. The current eclipse of the Greek and medieval concept of substance and the disappearance of physical explanations of the Eucharist have in this instance done away with any real difference between Catholic and Lutheran theories or demonstrated that there never was any such difference in the first place. Consubstantiation has also been spoken of as an "impanation"; they are synonymous.

• J. Schaedtke (1977), "Abendmahl III/3," *TRE* 1, 106–22.

J. Betz (1979), *HDG* IV.4.a.

The Editors

See also **Being; Eucharist**

Contemplation

The concept of *contemplation* has a double history—that of Greek *(theoria)* and Latin *(contemplatio).* The passage from *theoria* to *contemplatio,* like all translations of Greek theological vocabulary into Latin, was accompanied by a mutation of the content. Here is how this mutation can be roughly characterized: While *theoria* is a concept of philosophical origin, keeping a certain ambiguous ground between theology* and philosophy*, *contemplatio* is a concept bound to Latin Christian theology and, more specifically, to one of its subdivisions, spiritual* theology. From Augustine* to Teresa of Avila, by way of Bernard* of Clairvaux and the Carthusian Spiritual School, the concept of *contemplatio* historically underwent a gradual deviation toward psychology, drawing on Augustinianism*, where it had already come to designate a "spiritual state of mind."

1. Philosophical and Scriptural Elements in the Origin of the Concept

We should distinguish two different kinds of elements constituting the concept of *contemplatio:* on the one hand, Platonic and Aristotelian definitions, on the other, a biblical element from the Old Testament (essentially in the figures of Moses and Elijah), as well as from the New Testament—Martha and Mary (Lk 10:38–42) and Paul's ecstasy (Acts 9:3–9, 22:6–11; 26:12–18; *see* Stolz 1947).

The Platonic and Aristotelian definitions of contemplation—*theoria*—do not coincide. For Plato, *theoria* was the high point of knowledge delivering the best of the human being (*Rep.* VII 532 *c.*) It is exercised by the *nous* (*Phaedrus* 247*c*) and relates to love* (*Symposium* 192 *c*) by being part of the Good*, a good that is beyond being* (*The Republic* 509 *b*). This definition opens for the Greek Fathers the possibility of deification through *theoria.* In Aristotle, on the other hand, *theoria* is defined as the high point of virtuous life, "life by the intellect" (*Nicomachean Ethics* X, 7), which opens the way for "divinization of the intellect" along the lines of *De Anima* III:5: "If the intellect is something divine as opposed to human, then life by the intellect is also divine, as opposed to human life." For Plato, *theoria* is something mysterious (*Symposium* 209 *e*), a revelation of the Beautiful that is inaccessible to any conception (*Symposium* 211 *a*), an ecstatic science of the Beautiful itself (*Symposium* 211 *c*)—in a word, an intuitive knowledge of the absolute. In Aristotle, on the other hand, *theoria* is unrelated to the regressive knowledge of pure Action, a disjunction thus opening between *De Anima* III:5 and *Nicomachean Ethics* X:7 on the one hand and *Metaphysics* I, 9 on the other, a problematic space of articulation that engulfs Avicenna (who synthesized divinization through the agency of the intellect in conjunction with the Primary Driving Force) and then Christian Aristotelianism*, especially radical Aristotelianism of the 13th century. The Aristotelian and Platonic ideas of *theoria* underwent an attempt at unification on the one hand within pagan and possibly anti-Christian Neoplatonism (Plotinus, Proclus, and Damascius) and on the other within the Christian Platonism* of the Greek Fathers (Origen*, Gregory* of Nyssa, and Maximus* the Confessor), including and above all in its most radical attempts at negative* theology (Pseudo-Dionysius*).

We cannot emphasize enough the importance of Plotinus's doctrine of *theoria* (*see* Arnou 1921), which is definitely the first coherent synthesis of contemplation in the West. As a continuation of Plato's *Letter VII,* Plotinus developed an ineffable view of the subject of *theoria,* expanding its sphere into the whole *phusis*—in his system, the *phusis* contemplates, it has a contemplative nature *(phusis philotheamon):* "Nature . . . is capable of a kind of contemplation and it produces all its works in accordance with contemplation, which, however, literally speaking it does not possess" (III, 8, 1), all this in opposition to Aristotle (*Nicomachean Ethics* 10, 8, 8), where *theoria* is restricted to the gods and humans. Plotinus also accomplished a change in relation to Plato that influenced a whole series of contemplative doctrines. He insisted that the soul* should withdraw within itself in order to be divested of all form (*Enneads* VI, 9, 7) and arrive at viewing the One, a principle of forms having no form itself (*Enneads* I, 6, 9.) The ascensional dialectics of the soul toward Good (Plato) is replaced by a conversion* of the self into the One by means of voluntary deprivation and progressive interiorizing. On this basis, Plotinus prepared the essence of the Augustinian *contemplatio.*

Sources in Scripture are limited in number. In the Old Testament we can name the parable* of Leah and Rachel, the episode of Moses and the burning bush, and Elijah's vision of God*. The Song of Songs has a special status. While it served to support the development of the nuptial mystique* of contemplation and, therefore, played a major role in the history of the doctrines of contemplation, it contains no descriptive canonical text of contemplation or contemplative life. In the New Testament we must distinguish between the crude materials on contemplation or contemplative life—the parable of Martha and Mary, the episode of the Transfiguration (Mt 17:1–9 and parallels), and Paul's elevation to the seventh heaven—and secondary theological elaborations, mostly in Paul's epistles.

Strictly speaking, contemplation is not a biblical concept. But the event of transfiguration can be interpreted as a passage from Elijah's and Moses' fear-dominated contemplation to a contemplation of the Son guided by love* (Mt 17:7–8.). These sources point to the following traits of contemplation. In the Old Testament it is accompanied by a theophany* (the bush and the cloud). It is an unbearable face-to-face meeting with God, appeasing the nostalgia for his appearance, a nostalgia experienced by all creatures. It is a face-to-face meeting revealing the intolerable "otherness" of God. Therefore, contemplation appears as the experience* of a radical otherness (one would not be able to see God without dying). In the New Testament the episode of the Transfiguration corresponds to a theophany* in the person* of Christ*; what is contemplated there is the glory* of Christ's divinity through his humanity. This element of mediation transforms the act of contemplation from a terrifying face-to-face meeting into the very condition of deification. (God became man so that I can contemplate him and be able to become God myself.) Paul's experience marked the act of contemplation with an ecstatic touch that became an inherent part of it. We should emphasize that the two parables of the two different kinds of life (Leah/Rachel in the Old Testament and Martha/Mary in the New) make contemplative life superior to active life. Thomas* Aquinas thus distinguished a form of beatitude* that was peculiar to active life from another that was peculiar to contemplative life, so that contemplation became confused with this bliss, which anticipated the bliss of the blessed ones, or supreme bliss.

Hugh of Saint Victor (*Myst. Theol. Quest. Diff.* 23–26) distinguishes between contemplation (Rachel; *see* Gregory* the Great, *Moralia* VI, 18, *Hom sup. Ez.* XIV) and ardent love (Mary). On the one hand there is "the intellect or the capacity of knowing" and on the other "affection or the capacity to love." Two different "paths to excellence" correspond to these two capacities. One is contemplation, and the other is the intuitive wisdom of love, which is its superior and above all knowledge, "knowing through ignorance that is uniting above the mind" (Pseudo-Dionysius; *see* Ruello, Intr. to Hugh of Saint Victor, SC 408, 47 *Sq.*). This typology linking the parables of contemplative life in the Old Testament with those of the New Testament draws a dividing line between intellectual contemplation and affective contemplation, thus leading to questions about the subordination of the latter to the former and the nature of knowledge achieved through love.

The scriptural element was reinterpreted from the standpoint of philosophical *theôria.* For example, in Gregory of Nyssa's *Life of Moses,* the face-to-face meeting between Moses and God is subject to exegesis* by means of the Platonic conception of *theoria* (SC 1 *bis,* 117 *Sq,* the burning bush, 211 *Sq,* darkness).

2. From the Philosophers' **Theoria** *to the* **Theoria** *of the Greek Fathers*

The transformation of pagan *theoria* into Christian *theoria* was accomplished within the critical acceptance of Platonism by the fathers* of the church,* especially the Greek Fathers (Ivanka 1964). The concepts of *theoria* and theology pre-dated the Fathers. These were Greek concepts that had evolved prior to the Christian dogma*. But they were reworked in dogmatic Christianity in a way that changed them profoundly (and maybe betrayed them). Their transformation has never been studied systematically in its totality, but we can at least outline some traits of the Fathers' concept of contemplation.

In addition to by the term *theoria,* borrowed from the philosophers, the Greek Fathers explain contemplation by *gnosis* (see *DSp* 2/2, 1765–66). This term is more specific to religion and more widely accepted than *theoria*—"it is the light that penetrates the soul as a result of one's obedience to the commandments" (Clement of Alexandria, *Stromateis* III, 5, 44). In a sense, *gnosis* prepares *theoria. Theoria* is the goal of life, the goal of the wise man, one of the characteristics of (Christian) gnostics, a pure prayer* (Clement of Alexandria). Origen distinguishes three levels: one moral (Abraham), one natural (Isaac), and one of *inspection,* or contemplation (*inspectivus,* Jacob). Clement sees a *theoria* through the person of Christ and a direct *theoria* of God, subdivided into a beatifying, angelic, and human *theoria.* Gregory of Nyssa distinguishes two stages, that of the cloud (intellectual *theoria*) and that of darkness (mystical *theoria*), corresponding to two stages in the life of Moses. He often uses the term *theognosia* to name mystical contemplation (e.g., in his *Life of Moses* PG 44, 372 d, SC 1 *bis,* 203).

Theognosia is to be distinguished from *theoria:* "Philosophies fail before arriving at the light of *theognosia*" (*Life of Moses* PG 44, 329 *b*, 113). The Song of Songs is simultaneously *theognosia* and *philosophia* (PG 44, 788 *c*). Evagrius Ponticus (†399) turns *theoria* into "the essential activity of the intellect, its life, its happiness" (*Centuries* 1, 24). The supreme *theoria* is the *theoria* of the Trinity*, "uniform gnosis" (*Centuries* I, 54), surpassing the *theoria* of the intelligible. It is supreme contemplation, a "state above all forms" (*Centuries* 7, 23) that Evagrius most often names *theologia.* Pseudo-Dionysius gives each level of the hierarchy (angelic or ecclesiastical) its own degree of *theoria,* as befitting. He does not equate *theoria* and negative theology (as John* of the Cross does). *Theoria* goes further than negative theology—the latter puts a limit on the intellect that *theoria* transgresses. *Theoria* is conceptualized as deification *(theosis)* and as ecstasy, by giving ecstasy a nonpsychological meaning. Ecstasy is a "departure from the human condition" (R. Roques, *DSp* 2/2, 1898).

For Pseudo-Dionysius and for a whole branch of the Dionysian tradition following him on this point, contemplative ecstasy is beyond intelligence and beyond reason (*De Div. Nom.* 872 *a-b*): "The most divine knowledge* of God is the one acquired through ignorance in a unification that is beyond intelligence (*huper noun*), at the moment where intelligence, having moved away from all beings and subsequently detached itself from the self, unites with the most radiant light."

For Aristotle, *theoria* is accomplishing what is peculiar to man—that is, living by intellect and virtue. For Plotinus, ecstasy is also an intellectual abandon of the self. Therefore, the pagan conception and the Dionysian conception are clearly opposites: contemplation is either surpassing humanity by leaving the human behind or accomplishment of humanity through the divinization of the intellect.

3. Contemplatio, *from Augustine to the End of the Middle Ages*

The term *contemplatio* originates with Cicero (*De Nat. Deorum* I, 14, 37) and Seneca (*Letters to Lucilius* 95, 10). Augustine*, in his doctrine of *contemplatio,* is indebted both to Latin Stoicism* and to Plotinus. He defines it as a face-to-face vision of God in eternal life*, as an end to all action and supreme bliss (*De trin.* 1, 8, 17; 1, 10, 20). Mary, as opposed to her sister Martha, epitomizes contemplative life (*Sermon* 169, 13 *Sq*). The philosophical distinction between *bios praktikos* and *bios theoretikos,* or between *otium* and *negotium,* is frequently used in the exegesis of Martha and Mary. In his *Summa Theologica,* Thomas* Aquinas devotes questions 179 to 182 of IIa IIae to this issue and declares that contemplative life is preferable for the following reasons: it is intellectual, more lasting, more delightful, and self-sufficient; leisure and rest; it is also preoccupied with things divine and peculiar to man. We must point out that Thomas attributes the contemplative/active division to life as transformed by the intellect. Taken on its own, life does not know this distinction (q. 179, a. 1).

Augustine starts from a theory of the soul in order to determine the nature of *contemplatio.* He does this, first, by making *contemplatio* the highest activity of the soul, the supreme level, just below apprehending true being (*De quant. An.* 33, 76). This activity consists in seeing the truth, in a celebration of Good *(fruitio, perfruitio).* And he continues further by reversing and shifting the analogy* of the *Republic.* Making the soul an *analogon* of the Trinity*, he introduces *contemplatio* inside Trinitarian life. In so doing, he achieves the interiorization Plotinus had begun. *Contemplatio* is accomplishing loving from inside; it is simultaneously a vision of Truth*, hearing and being in contact with the Word*, in a system of spiritual meanings that was not invented by Augustine (it goes back to Origen) but was endowed by him with a rich phenomenology of the sensibility and affectivity that evolved further throughout all the Middle Ages and was completed by Bernard.

This double definition of interiority, as love, and of *contemplatio,* as an intra-Trinitarian act, contains a risk. In fact, it contains even its own reversal, that of psychologizing *contemplatio* or reducing it to the sphere of the affective. From the time of Augustine, there have been two rival conceptions of *contemplatio*—one intellectualist and the other affective—and this rivalry would punctuate the history of *contemplatio* doctrines in the Middle Ages. Meister Eckhart and Dante* defended to a certain extent the intellectualist position, although with some important nuances. We must note, however, that Eckhart has no doctrine of *contemplatio* (unlike Dante, who exhibits an elaborate doctrine).

Yet things are not that simple, and there was a whole spiritual movement that developed a type of negative Augustinian theology in competition with or parallel to Dionysian negative theology. During the Middle Ages, almost all authors of treatises on the subject of *contemplatio* drew from these two sources, combining their elements in various ways.

Certainly, Augustinian negative theology of *contemplatio* has a more obvious affective character (e.g., in Thomas Gallus), but Dionysian negative theology has an affective dimension, too. This is a major point in determining the place of the concept of *contemplatio* in the economy of metaphysics. In fact, the affective conception of *contemplatio* prepared the change that saw on the one hand theology splitting into dogmatic theology and spiritual* theology and on the other philosophical knowledge breaking away from spiritual experience.

a) Place of Contemplatio. There is a text from the 13th century that has been constantly cited and pillaged as an authority. It is the *Scala Claustralium* by the Carthusian Guigues II, which was long attributed to Bernard of Clairvaux. This work allows one to place *contemplatio* at the top of a series of exercises—reading, meditation, prayer, *contemplatio*—that constitute the four ascending levels of spiritual* life. Bernard had already distinguished *contemplatio* and *consideration* (*De Consid.* II, 2): "Contemplation can be defined as the ability of the soul to have a true and infallible intuition about things *(verus intuitus)*...while consideration is...an intention of the mind in search of truth."

Hugh of Saint Victor distinguishes *cogitatio, meditatio,* and *contemplatio* (PL 175, 116), marking the difference between the last two in terms of *topos:* "what meditation seeks, contemplation finds." He also uses a quaternary schema distinguishing "four modes of contemplation": meditation, soliloquy, circumspection, and ascension (*De Cont. et eius speciebus* I–IV). If the first three levels are defined by Guigues II according to their function (*officium*), contemplation is defined according to its effect (*effectus*), which is that "man becomes almost entirely spiritual" (*De Cont. et eius speciebus* VII, 1. 174). Contemplation is "the pleasure of being gentle" (*Scala Cl.* III, 1. 48), "a gentleness which delights and revives" (*Scala Cl.* III, 1. 46). It has, therefore, a specific place in the regulated planning of spiritual exercises in monastic life, being conceived as an institutionalized form of contemplative life, and is described in terms of emotion and desire, not knowledge.

b) Structure of Contemplatio. Pseudo-Dionysius (*De Div. Nom.* 4, 8; *see also* Thomas Aquinas, *ST* IIa IIae, q. 180, a. 6) applies to the soul the Aristotelian distinction between the three types of movement (circular, oblique or helicoidal, and linear or longitudinal). Since contemplation unites the powers of intellection, he identifies it with the circular movement. This conceptual transference was to be utilized in at least two ways in the history of doctrines: first, in the opposition between meditation, which is linear, and contemplation, which is circular (Quiroga, *Apologia Mistica* 4, 1 *Sq* for an informed summary), and then, in the distinction that is inherent to contemplation, namely, between speculative contemplation, which is linear or helicoidal, and anagogic contemplation, which is circular or linear (*see,* e.g., Guigues du Pont, *Treatise on Contemplation*). Speculative contemplation is intellectual, and anagogic contemplation is affective: "There are two types of this contemplation, to test a small number: speculative and anagogic, or affirmative and negative, or even intellectual and affective" (*ibid.* III, 4.) The first one rises to God by affirmation and speculation; the second, by negation and affection. Anagogic linear contemplation is a direct and violent movement toward God, while anagogic circular contemplation is a movement bringing the soul back to itself to discover God there (introversion). Thus, the conceptual schemes are interwoven to the extreme: a physical classification serves as a basis to a mystical one that is dependent, in its turn, on the Plotino-Augustinian model of introversion, from turning back to oneself—toward God, or toward God through the self.

c) Theological Value and Object of Contemplatio. Thomas Aquinas systematized the philosophical and mystical elements we have outlined here in his theory of contemplation. According to Aquinas, contemplation furnishes true knowledge of the divine being, but this knowledge must be distinguished from that of the divine essence achieved through beatific* vision. In fact, theologians have hesitated on the issue of what the object of contemplation is (attributes*, glory*, God's being or essence). The current negative response was not unanimous in the Middle Ages. Augustine and Thomas himself hesitated and even maintained that contemplation provided a vision of God himself, particularly for Moses and Paul (*see ST, Summa Theologica,* IIa IIae, q. 175, a. 3 and q. 180, a. 5), while at the same time they affirmed that the vision of the divine essence was inaccessible even to those who were blessed (Thomas Aquinas, *In Ev. Sec. Ioh.* C. 1, lec. 11, n. 1). For example, Pseudo-Dionysius, who identifies the essence of God with "unlimited light," refers to the Platonic *topos* of the dazzling intellect and declares divine essence to be out of his reach. The goal is "to be united in ignorance with the one who is beyond all essence and all knowledge" (*On Myst. Theol.* 1, 1). How can we fit the contemplation of man on his journey with the contemplation of the blessed one, supreme terrestrial beatitude with supreme celestial beatitude?

Aquinas's solution is to reinterpret Aristotelian *theoria* in order to make it a preparatory stage of the contemplation (*ST* IIa IIae, q. 180): *Theoria* is a contemplation of God within Creation*. Thus, *theoria* is defined as knowledge through speculation (*cognitio specularis*) that is distinct from contemplation, which is plain intuition (*intuitus simplex,* III *Sententiarum,* d.

35, q. 1, a. 3, ad 2.). Contemplation is *unio* and *informatio,* a union with the Principle and acquisition of form (*ST* Ia IIae, q. 3, a. 5, ad 1); it contains the substance of human beatitude. Aristotelian *theoria,* a terrestrial and scientific aspiration, leads, in return, only to limited beatitude (*ST* Ia IIae, q. 3, a. 6 resp. et ad 1–3). And even if contemplation is an act of the speculative intellect (*intellectus speculativus, ST* Ia IIae, q. 3, a. 5), we must distinguish between contemplation and speculation. Contemplation is nondiscursive, as it possesses truth and enjoys it, while speculation is a discursive searching for the truth (*see In Eth.* 10, 10, no. 2092). Beatitude and life are susceptible to being contemplative, while it befits intellect, knowledge, and science to be speculative. Therefore, contemplative life, which leads to supreme beatitude, supposes exercising a speculative intellect and procures a speculative kind of knowledge. The Aristotelian divorce between practice and theory, which Plotinus tried to override by emphasizing the theoretical element of all praxis, thus finds a twofold expression in Aquinas. The speculative is opposed to practice, but the contemplative, which presupposes the speculative, is to overcome this opposition. And by making Aristotelian *theoria* an anticipation of contemplation, Aquinas implicitly reproaches Aristotle for remaining in a state of scission.

4. **Contemplatio** ***in Modern Times***

a) Mutations of Contemplation. The Renaissance marked a turning point in the history of mysticism (Certeau 1982). The introduction of an autobiographical system in the description of "superior states" (Musil), the massive invasion of hysteria as a figure of truth or of neurasthenia (Surin), and the promotion of femininity—all these constituted an irreversible evolution. From the perspective of historiography, this interpretation is very fragile. The ecstasy of Ostia contains all the required autobiographical elements; the feminine mystique is a major trait of medieval spirituality (Hildegarde of Bingen and Hadewijch of Antwerp) and so on. Yet it has some validity. Indeed, the Renaissance underwent a subjectivist turn in relation to the mystical doctrines of contemplation, but this turn must be described within these doctrines and not only within the categories of the psychoanalysis of history*.

From this immanent point of view, the transition can be characterized as the mutation of the very concept of contemplation that passed from a cognitive acceptance to a purely psychological acceptance. The question of the objective content of knowledge of the act of contemplating, which is a central question for any Thomistic dogmatic theology or the mystical theology of someone such as Hugh of Saint Victor but also equally important to Nicholas of Cusa (whose thought lies at the borderline between two worlds), loses its pertinence in the modern schools of spirituality, such as the Salesian* School, the French schools evolving from Pierre de Bérulle*, and the reformed Teresian school of Carmel*. Certainly, there are some great mystics in the baroque and classical ages (Benoît de Canfeld, Angelus Silesius, Jean de Saint-Samson, and Bérulle), but there are almost no contemplative theologians or philosophers. When Suarez* writes his *De oratione,* we have to do with a distinct work in terms of its metaphysics; when Spinoza speaks of contemplation, the latter is deprived of its primary meaning.

This drifting is typical of the Latin Church. The Eastern Church never experienced it, no doubt because its doctrines of contemplation have always had a mystic and practical character at the same time. Its theological tradition* has a more pronounced mystical orientation, and its *theoria* is always related to divinization *(theosis).* Ascetism is the common good of the Church.

On the other hand, the cultural phenomenon of the Renaissance had no effect on religious thought in the traditionally Orthodox countries (mostly Russia and Greece). The major event in the East was a complex transfer of Byzantine mystical theology into a Slavic context, marked, among other things, by the absence of autochthonous Scholastics*, which gave, for instance, the opportunity for a revival of Hesychasm* in the 19th century. But this transfer does not fit into the organizational model of Western history, which is that of a Renaissance break with the Middle Ages. Philosopher-theologians such as Solovyov*, Florensky, and even Berdyaev represent, from this point of view, cultural exceptions inasmuch as they continued to attribute a normative value to contemplation for metaphysical knowledge—something unthinkable in the post-Teresian and post-Kantian West.

b) From Contemplation to Prayer, the Reformed Carmelite Order. Although the writings of Teresa of Avila appear to be generally autobiographical, they contain a very traditional teaching of mystical theology. Teresa's originality lies elsewhere—namely, in creating a landmark in the movement to subjectivize mystical life (*see,* e.g., Certeau 1982). Some were only too happy that Teresa broke with Pseudo-Dionysius in order to lay the foundations of a psychological method in mystical matters.

Teresa does not speak of *contemplation* but of *orison,* a term she borrowed from the Spanish spiritual leaders Osuna, Peter of Alcantara, and John of Avila, who sympathized with the movement of the *recogidos.*

Prayer is the act of praying *(oratio).* Therefore, it designates, first of all, a specialized activity, an "interior occupation" (Jean-Baptiste de la Salle) of the psychological human subject (the angels* do not offer prayers, but they contemplate; nature does not pray, while, according to Plotinus, it does), a strictly religious activity (if there is a "philosophical contemplation," however disputable its status, there is no "philosophical prayer"). With prayer, contemplation is emptied of all metaphysical content. (And John* of the Cross, who has a true doctrine of contemplation, a heritage of the finest tradition, does not differ on this point from the Teresian conception.)

Teresa distinguishes five levels of prayer: 1) prayer of meditation, 2) prayer of peace, 3) prayer of dormant powers, 4) prayer in union with God, and 5) prayer of spiritual marriage (*Book of Life* and *The Interior Castle*). In *Abodes of the Soul,* Teresa distinguishes between the prayer of meditation (corresponding to the first three abodes) and the prayer of contemplation (the last four abodes), which parallels the classical distinction between meditation and contemplation, only here the distinction is made in the dynamic subject of the soul, moving from the more superficial to the more profound, reducing the introversive movement to an introspection of the states of the soul. The goal Teresa seems to set herself is providing readers with psychological criteria and allowing them to find their own place in this argument: "Peace of mind, union, ecstasy—these are all expressions that in the beginning had a theological meaning, without relating directly to any special psychological experience. Hence, this theological meaning has passed into the background" in Spanish mysticism (Stolz 1947).

These psychological states, finally, contain visions, ecstasies, and revelations* preparing one for spiritual marriage. Nuptial mystique, which has one of its sources in the metaphor of the Church as the spouse of Christ—"the marriage of the lamb is come, and his bride has made herself ready" (Rev 19:7)—and, earlier, in the metaphor of Israel* as the spouse of God—"Therefore, behold, I [God] will allure her [Israel], and bring her into the wilderness, and speak tenderly to her" (Hos 2:14)—draws its origin from the allegorical commentary of the Song of Solomon. The comments by Origen and Gregory of Nyssa fixed its framework of interpretation—namely, in terms of spiritual meanings and of the overall significance of the text, which is seen as describing simultaneously the union between God and the Church and that between the soul and God. The emotional theories of contemplation resorted on a massive scale to this type of allegory (*see,* e.g., the commentaries by the anti-intellectualist William of Saint-Thierry or those of Thomas Galluus, who is an affective Dionysian). Bernard of Clairvaux's *Sermons on the Song of Solomon* are, therefore, taken within the framework of the entire movement that they synthesize and, in fact, largely surpass. This nuptial mystique finds a complete literary expression in the *Poems* of Hadewijch of Antwerp and *The Spiritual Canticle* of John of the Cross. Ecstasy is an important element in the life of prayer that Teresa depicts in detail in her *Interior Castle.* It is a decisive characteristic for the psychologization and subjectivization of contemplation.

Taken by itself, ecstasy is only a superficial phenomenon that may accompany contemplation, but, in fact, it signals the weakness of human nature, which is why the ancient authors mistrusted it in the first place and warned the contemplatives against it. Ecstasy poses a conceptual problem—that of knowing if, in the act of contemplation, the intellect goes out of itself. Is ecstasy a movement of the soul going out toward the fine point of the intellect, or is it a radical movement of the intellect going out of its own self?

It was within the traditional framework of negative theology that John of the Cross developed his rich and complex doctrine of contemplation. He believed that contemplation was "mystical theology" (*Ascent of Mount Carmel* II, VIII): "This is why we call contemplation, which gives us understanding of the highest knowledge of God, 'mystical theology'—that is to say, the secret wisdom* of God, since it is hidden from the understanding that receives it." This contemplation is considered inborn: "Since contemplating is nothing but a secret, peaceful, and loving infusion of God" (*The Dark Night of the Soul* I, XI); "this secret, dark...contemplation is mystical theology...a hidden sense that according to Saint Thomas is communicated and injected into the soul by love" (*The Dark Night of the Soul* II, XVII). Defining contemplation as a "dark night," he thus revives the Dionysian tradition of caliginous contemplation: "This night that we name 'contemplation'" (*The Dark Night of the Soul* I, VIII). Contemplation is a beam of darkness, a shadowy light, an enlightened night, a "dark cloud making the night bright" (*Poems* IV).

The caliginous contemplation of medieval authors originates in the Dionysian doctrine of divine darkness. For Pseudo-Dionysius, God is found in a "superluminous darkness," "unbound light" that equals "darkness" (*see Letter to Caius, Letter V to Dorothea,* PG 3 1066 A and 1074 a). Gregory of Nyssa also developed a mystique of the cloud in his *Life of Moses* (PG 44, 360 D, SC 1 *bis* 177 *Sq*) and in his *Commentary on the Song of Songs* (PG 44, 1000 CD.) Contemplation is a "science of love" (*ibid.* II, XIX), a "mystical intelligence, confused and obscure" (*ibid.* II, XXIV). It is supernatural, peaceful, solitary, substantial. That is why John of the Cross could call it "an overall and obscure infusion" (*The Living Flame of Love* III, 3). Contemplation is a science but it is also delightful, which makes it close to "secret knowledge." It is a "knowledge in love with God" (*Dark Night* II, 5), a "secret science of God." In *The Spiritual Canticle* XIX, 5, he writes, "This delightful science . . . is mystical theology that is a secret science of God, that spiritual people call 'contemplation'; it is extremely delightful because it is a science by way of loving." Mystical theology or negative theology is a science "achieved through love, where one not only 'knows' but at the same time savors" (prologue to *The Spiritual Canticle*). John of the Cross insists on the fact that it is God who introduces the soul to contemplation and, in His grace*, operates in it. The soul just accepts and has nothing else to do but "pay attention to God lovingly, without wanting to feel or see anything . . . to receive the light supernaturally infused is to understand passively" (*Ascent to Mount Carmel* II, 15). The main difficulty of the contemplation doctrines—the ranking of intellect and affect—is resolved by equating contemplation with a science that is identical with love, a science that is knowledge. In a vocabulary that is still traditional, this solution consecrates the divorce between mystical contemplation and philosophical contemplation. Thus, mystical theology received a considerable existential autonomy, and contemplation, in solidarity with radical negative theology, became completely self-sufficient. The Thomistic problem of overcoming the opposition between the speculative and the practical—through contemplation—disappeared. Natural understanding is a prisoner of the senses and is even enlightened by supernatural intelligence, "which in the prison of the body has no disposition, nor capacity, to receive a clear notice of God" (*Ascent to Mount Carmel* II, 8).

Thus, the following axiom may be derived: "More or less everything the imagination can conceive and the mind can receive or understand in this life, is only, or can only be, a means for future union with God" (*Ascent to Mount Carmel* II, 8). It is not the natural character of understanding that impedes the intellectual apprehension of God, but it is "this state"—that is, the mortal condition of finitude—that does so. That which is of supernatural* order does not alter this limitation that is inherent in creation; it only opens Nature to a superior passivity, bending it to the demanding conditions of an obscure and arid contemplation. The double recognition, first, of Thomas* Aquinas as a magister of dogmatic theology (by Leo XIII in 1879) and, second, of John of the Cross as a magister of mystical theology (by Pius XI in 1926) would ratify the scission and shift of the well-appropriated roles in the 16th century.

c) Perspectives. From John of the Cross until the present day, the history of the concept of contemplation has evoked few commentaries. Contemplative minds have continued to experiment and theologians to systematize, but the concept of contemplation has remained overall unchanged. We must, however, distinguish clearly the history of Latin spirituality and that of the East.

Catholicism, after the Council of Trent* and after Teresa, experienced two complementary phenomena: on the one hand, a greater specification of congregations and religious orders in the various kinds of spirituality, adding various shades of meaning to the concept of contemplation, and, on the other, solid systematizing in describing the various states of contemplating, partly related to the controversy over "acquired contemplation," in which the Carmelites played a major role. This feud, which had its origins in the quarrel of quietism* (as well as in the Molinist background), revolved around the line to be drawn between what is natural (acquired contemplation) and what is supernatural (infused contemplation). Saint Joseph, a representative of the Salamanca School that contributed a systematic rereading of John of the Cross in the light of Thomas Aquinas, deals with it, for example, in his le *Cursus Theologiae Mysticae Scholasticae* (1736). The quarrel reached its climax in around 1900 in a debate between A. Saudreau (*La Vie d'union à Dieu,* 1900) and A.F. Poulain (*Des grâces d'oraison,* 1901), at the time when two great Carmelite contemplatives—Theresa of Lisieux (called Theresa of the Child Jesus, 1873–97) and Elizabeth of Dijon (called Elizabeth of the Trinity, 1880–1906)—picked up the Saint Johnsian concept of contemplation. We can say of Theresa that she caused contemplation to pass through a form of modern night, nihilism, whence it emerged restored to its original appearance. Theresa gave it a full ecclesiastic dimension (Balthasar 1970) and was probably the first person to describe the clash between contemplation and atheism*, which gave her writing an inimitable character as a result.

The Eastern Church, thanks to the publication of an anthology of ascetic texts titled *Philocalie* (compiled in 1782 by Nicodemus the Hagiorite), saw, in the 19th century, a revival of both monastic and lay spirituality and of the techniques of contemplation deriving from Byzantium, specifically Hesychasm*. By its sheer mass (2,500 pages) and its ability to put things in perspective (the collection starts with the Fathers of the desert and concludes with Gregory* Palamas and Palamism), this anthology contributed a great deal to the powerful identity of contemplation in the Orthodox Church, especially in Russia, which witnessed a true regeneration of the "prayer of the heart." This regeneration is called detachment, for example, in the teachings of the startzi or on Mount Athos, say, in the spirituality of someone such as Silouane (1866–1938), where contemplation relates, at the same time, to compassion.

We cannot say that contemplation was simply marginalized or omitted from the secular world. On the one hand, it certainly has not escaped the movement of secularization*, where esthetic contemplation came to replace mystique, since it is currently attributed the characteristics of immediacy, being above rational discourse, bringing intuitive knowledge of the universe and eventually knowledge* of God. On the other, the clinical devaluation of some states of mind related to contemplation has tarnished it with the discredit of a normative psychiatric science (*see* the works of Janet). It was only with Lacan's *Seminar* that female contemplative ecstasy has been rehabilitated as a "mystical relishing in things," which confirms the psychologized conception described previously, while at the same time opening a gap between it and this unambiguous attempt at psychological reduction. This fact seems to warrant a rethinking of contemplation for its own sake taking into consideration the critical contribution of philosophy*, namely, phenomenology.

Finally, multiple possibilities for a reevaluation of contemplation have been outlined by the "atheist mystique" of such writers as Wittgenstein and by the experience of boundaries as described by Blanchot, Klossowski, Bataille, and others. The state of mind these authors experienced and described escapes the traditional characterization of ecstasy and contemplation, but it borrows from both of these the desire for abandoning the self, giving up all control, breaking with immanence without creating a hierarchy between the here-and-now and the beyond, and without attaching these movements of the spirit to any theological framework. All this helps destroy the cosmological order in the realm of the psyche. If a theory of contemplation remains at all possible, it will be outlined henceforth against this background of disaster—but by agreeing to pay this price, it would be able to frustrate any reductionist endeavors.

• Angelus Silesius, *Cherubinischer Wandersmann,* Stuttgart, 1984.

Benoît de Canfeld, *La Règle de perfection/The Rule of Perfection,* Paris, 1982.

Denys le Chartreux, *De Contemplatione, OC,* Chartreuse de Montreuil-sur-Mer/Tournai, 1896–1913, vol. 41.

J.-P. de Caussade, *Traité sur l'oraison du cœur* et *Instructions spirituelles,* Paris, 1980.

Élizabeth de la Trinité, *J'ai trouvé Dieu, OC,* éd. du Centenaire, 3 vols., Paris, 1979–80.

Guigues du Pont, *Traité sur la contemplation,* Analecta Cartusiana 72, 2 vols., Salzburg, 1985.

Guigues II le Chartreux, *Lettre sur la vie contemplative (L'échelle des moines),* SC 163.

Guillaume de Saint-Thierry, *La contemplation de Dieu,* SC 61 *bis*; *Exposé sur le Cantique des Cantiques,* SC 82; *Lettre aux frères du Mont-Dieu (Lettre d'Or),* SC 223.

Hadewijch d'Anvers, *Mengeldichten,* Antwerp, 1952.

Henri Herp, *Spieghel der Volcomenheit,* 2 vols., Antwerp, 1931; *Theologia Mystica,* Köln, 1554, repr. Farnborough, 1966.

Hugues de Balma, *Théologie mystique,* SC 408 and 409.

Hugues de Saint-Victor, *La contemplation et ses espèces,* MCS II, Tournai-Paris, s.d. (v. 1955).

Hugues de Saint-Victor, *Six opuscules spirituels,* SC 155.

Jean de Saint-Samson, *Œuvres mystiques,* Paris, 1984.

Nicholas de Cusa, *Opera omnia iussu et auctoritate Academiae Litterarum Heidelbergensis ad codicum fidem edita,* Leipzig, 1932–45, Hamburg, 1950– , vol. 1, *De docta ignorantia,* 1932, vol. 4/1, *Opuscula,* 1959, vol. 5, *Idiota,* 1937, vol. 13/2, *De apice theoria,* 1974.

Anon., *The Cloud of Unknowing,* Oxford, 1944.

Anon. *(La) Perle évangélique,* 1602 (*see DSp* 12, 1159–69).

José de Jesús María Quiroga, *Apologie mystique en défense de la contemplation (Apologia Mística),* Paris, 1990.

Richard de Saint-Victor, *Benjamin Minor,* PL 196, 1–64; *Benjamin Major,* PL 196, 64–192.

J. van Ruusbroec, *Werken,* 2nd ed., Tielt, 1944–48 (*Écrits,* 2 vols. published, Bellefontaine, 1990, 1993).

Archimandrite Sophrony, *Starets Silouane moine du Mont Athos: Vie-doctrines-écrits,* Sisteron, 1973.

Thomas Gallus, *Comm. du Cantique des Cantiques,* Paris, 1967 (see *DSp* 15, 799–815).

♦ A.-F. Poulain (1901), *Des grâces d'oraison, traité de th. mystique,* Paris (10th Ed. 1922).

R. Arnou (1921), *Le désir de Dieu dans la philosophie de Plotin,* Paris (2nd Ed., Rome, 1967).

A. Gardeil (1925), "Les mouvements direct, en spirale et circulaire de l'âme et les oraisons mystiques," *RThom* 8, 321–40.

F. Cayré (1927), *La contemplation augustinienne,* Paris (2nd Ed., Bruges, 1954).

J. de Guibert (1930), *Études de th. mystique,* Toulouse.

J. Baruzi (1931), *Jean de la Croix et le problème de l'expérience mystique,* Paris.

R. Arnou (1932), *Le thème néoplatonicien de la contemplation créatrice chez Origène et chez saint Augustin,* Rome.

K. Rahner (1932), "Le début d'une doctrine des sens spirituels chez Origène," *RAM* 13, 113–45.

R. Arnou (1935), "Platonisme des Pères," *DThC* 12/2, 2258–392.

A.-J. Festugière (1936), *C. et vie cont. chez Platon,* Paris.

H.-C. Puech (1938), "La ténèbre mystique chez le Pseudo-Denys l'Aréopagite et dans la tradition patristique," *EtCarm* 23/2, 33–53.

V. Lossky (1944), *Th. mystique de l'Église d'Orient,* Paris.

A. Stolz (1947), *Th. de la mystique,* Chèvetogne.

R. Dalbiez (1949), "La controverse de la c. acquise," in *Technique et c., EtCarm* 28, 81–145.

Gabriel de Sainte-Marie (1949), *La c. acquise,* Paris.

J. Lebreton et al. (1953), "Contemplation," *DSp* 2/2, 1643–2193.

W. Völker (1958), *Kontemplation und Ekstase bei Pseudo-Dyonisius Areopagita,* Wiesbaden.

L. Kerstiens (1959), "Die Lehre von der theoretischen Erkenntnis in der lateinischen Tradition," *PhJ* 67, 375–424.

J. Leclercq (1961 *a*), *Études sur le vocabulaire monastique du Moyen Age latin,* StAns 48, Rome; (1961 *b*), "La vie contemplative dans saint Thomas et dans la tradition," *RThAM* 28, 251–68.

J. Pieper (1962), *Glück und Kontemplation,* Munich.
E. von Ivánka (1964), *Plato christianus,* Einsiedeln.
H. U. von Balthasar (1970), *Schwestern im Geist: Therese von Lisieux und Elizabeth von Dijon,* Einsiedeln.
F. Ruello (1981), "Statut et rôle de l'*intellectus* et de l'*affectus* dans la *Théologie mystique* de Hugues de Balma," in *Kartäusermystik und -mystiker,* ACar 55/1, 1–46.
M. de Certeau (1982), *La fable mystique,* Paris.
P. Hadot (1987), *Exercices spirituels et philosophie antique,* EAug, 2nd Ed.
F. Nef (1993), "*Caritas dat caritatem:* la métaphysique de la charité dans les sermons sur le Cantique des Cantiques et l'ontologie de la contemplation," in R. Brague (Ed.), *Saint Bernard et la philosophie,* Paris, 87–109.

Frédéric Nef

See also **Asceticism; Beatitude; Life, Spiritual; Mysticism; Prayer; Spiritual Theology; Vision, Beatific**

Conversion

1. Vocabulary

The biblical vocabulary of conversion is constituted of images, mostly images of return. The Hebrew verb *shoûv* means "to turn back," "to return to the point of departure." On the existential or ethical level (occurring more than 100 times), it connotes a change of direction, a modification of behavior. Rarely does this return consist in distancing oneself from God* (Nm 14: 43): it almost always involves coming back to him (prepositions *'el, le-, 'ad, 'al*) or to steer away from evil* (*min* and its compounds). The causative form "to make one return" gives God or his representative the initiative of return (Ps 80:4). The Greek equivalent is *strephô,* and its compounds are *apo-* or *epi-,* which most often conveys *shoûv* in the Septuagint. In the New Testament, *epistrephô* is often used to speak of conversion, especially in Acts.

In the Bible*, conversion also involves searching for God or the good* (Hebrew verbs *biqqésh* and *dârash:* Dt 4:29; Sol 1:6). It especially means to regret evil. The verb *niham* describes this aspect of conversion, which consists of changing one's mind if there is still time or of repenting if evil has been committed. Besides the human being experiencing repentance (Ex 13:17; Jer 31:19), God (*see* Jl 2, 13f.) is often the subject of this verb: he goes back on a decision (Ex 32:14) or regrets a past choice (Gn 6, 6f). Rarer than *shoûv, niham* is translated in the Septuagint as *metanoeô,* a mostly neutral verb in secular Greek ("to remark after the fact, to change one's mind, have regrets"). In the Bible it expresses religious and moral conversion, and in the New Testament specifically its lexical field associates it with faith (Mk 1:15), with baptism* (Acts 2:38), and with the forgiveness of sins (Lk 17:3). Conversion *(metanoia)* is also linked to return (Acts 3:19, with *epistrephô*).

2. Preaching: Sin, Conversion, Salvation

a) The Prophets. In prophetic preaching*, sin*, in whatever form (infidelity, Hos 2:7; rebellion, Is 1, 2ss; taking the Name* in vain, Am 2:7; abandonment of YHWH and idolatry*, Jer 2:13; etc.) is an evil that disturbs and corrupts the relationship between Israel* and God, to the misfortune of the former. Until the exile, the prophets* continuously denounce sinners and call them to return to God in order to restore a just relationship with him (Am 5:4, 14f.; Mi 6:6ff.), by rejecting idols (Hos 14:2ff.), and by a genuine change in their actual behavior (Is 1:16f.). Rituals and words are not enough (Hos 6:1–6). The reminder of God's mercy (Hos 2:16ff., 14:5–8) and the threat of judgment* (Is 6:9f.; Am 3:2) encourages Israel to return to God. There is not much hope since sin is deep rooted (Am 4:4–13; Jer 17:1), but "the rest will return" (Is 10:20–23).

From Jeremiah onward, the language of conversion begins to change: the prepositions that make of the return a step toward YHWH are replaced by those that make of it a refusal of evil. For Jeremiah, the misfortune that strikes a country constitutes a final call to listen and to convert (Jer 4:14, 25:5f., 26:2–5). Hardening* (18:11f.) leads to catastrophe (13:20–27). After this, God will return (12:15), he will make his people come back in order to enter into a new covenant* with him (31:18ff.). For Ezekiel, who insists on personal responsibility (Ez 18), conversion is a gift from God (36:25–32). The Deuteronomist Isaiah and Jonah considered the conversion of nations to the God of Israel (Is 45:14; Jn 1:3) (universalism*).

b) Deuteronomist School. Consciousness of a sin constantly threatening the covenant between Israel and its God is present in Deuteronomist theology, at least after the exile (Dt 9:24; Jos 24:19). Furthermore, the call to fidelity (Dt 6:4f.) is reinforced by an urgent invitation to conversion. (Dt 4:29). Stories illustrate its importance: salvation* is linked to the return to YHWH (Jgs 10:6–16; 1 Sm 7:2–12), and discourses throughout the Deuteronomist history* continuously remind us of this (1 Kgs 8:46–51; 2 Kgs 17:13). Moreover, conversion is a matter of urgency: a day will come when it will be too late (2 Kgs 23:25ff.). The Chronist works extend this message (Ezr 9:5–15; Neh 9) by insisting even more on the role of the Law* in the return to God (Neh 9:29). Thus, after the exile, repentance plays a key role in biblical spirituality (Dn 9:4–19). This is also seen in the Wisdom* theme found in the late writings (Wis 11:23f., 12:2; Sir 17:25f., 39:5).

c) Jesus in the Synoptic Gospels. The prophetic discourses reemerge right at the beginning of the Gospels*, where John the Baptist urgently calls people to conversion so that they will be saved from judgment (Lk 3, 7ff. par.). The baptism he administers signifies the will to return to God by turning away from sin (Mk 1:4f. par.). Jesus takes up this message but places it in a positive perspective as the Good News of the Kingdom* (Mk 1:15 par.). As signs that the kingdom has come, miracles* are also calls to conversion (Mt 11:20–24). To choose the will of God (Mt 7:21) and to renounce sin is essential to life, for hardening* is sterile (Mt 12:41s; Lk 13:1–9). But Jesus' attitude to sinners shows that, in his tenderness, God seeks those who are lost (Lk 5:32 par., 15).

d) The Church of the New Testament. The apostolic mission*, in which the announcement of the Resurrection* goes hand in hand with the invitation to confession (Acts 2:36ff,, 3:13–26), continues Jesus' mission* (Mk 6:12; Lk 24:47): a turning away from evil and toward the Lord, who has been raised from the dead to forgive sins (Acts 10:42f.), will allow one to escape judgment (17:30f.) and to obtain life (11:18). Baptism is a sign of conversion (2:38). This is also the case in Paul, who extensively develops the connection with the Resurrection. Conversion (1 Thes 1:9f.; Tm 2:4f.) consists of breaking from the old leaven to celebrate Easter with dignity (1 Cor 5:7f.), of assuming Christ* (Gal 3:27), of becoming a new creature in the image of the risen Lord, dead to sin but alive to God (Rom 6:1–14, 22ff.,12:2; Col 2:12f., 3:5–11). Paul also develops the ethical* consequences of this conversion (Col 3:12–17; Eph 4:17–32). John's Jesus speaks of a new birth (Jn 3:3, 5) and calls all people to the light (12:35f.) and to the source of living water (7:37ff.) by renouncing darkness (3:19ff.), lies (8:44), and vainglory (12:37–43) in order to become the child of God through faith (1:12). The child born blind (Jn 9) is the Johannine model of conversion.

3. Gestures and Words of Conversion

There are gestures, rituals, and words of conversion in the Bible. Thus, fasting, sackcloth and ashes (2 Sm 12, 16; Is 22:12; Jl 1:13; Jon 3:5f.; *see* Mt 11:21), lamentations, and cries and tears (Jl 2:12f.; Est 4:2f.) are signs of mourning but also penance*. There are penitential liturgies* (1 Sm 7:3–6, Hos 6:1–6), and, after the exile, a more or less standard kind of prayer* expresses the sense of sin (*see* Dn 9). In addition to the annual day of Expiations* (Lv 16), there are days of penitence (Jer 36:6; Zec 8:19). The prophets do not reject these rituals, but they do demand ethical truth* of those who practice them (Is 58: 3–7). Their preaching undoubtedly influenced the prayer of sinners that is echoed in the penitential psalms* (32, 38, 51).

• J. Behm, E. Würthwein (1942), "*metanoeô,*" *ThWNT* 4, 972–1001.
W. L. Holladay (1958), *The Root* shûb *in the OT,* Leiden.
Coll. (1960), *La conversion, LV(L)* 47, Lyon.
E. Lipinski (1969), *La liturgie pénitentielle dans la Bible,* Paris.
A. Tosato (1975), "Per una revisione degli studi sulla *metanoia* neotestamentaria," *RivBib* 33, 3–45.
J. A. Soggin (1979), "*shûb,* zurückkehren," *THAT* 2, 884–91.
B. R. Gaventa (1986), *From Darkness to Light: Aspects of Conversion in the NT,* Philadelphia.
H. Simian-Yofre (1986), "*nhm,*" *ThWAT* 5, 366–84.

André Wénin

See also **Baptism; Eschatology; Hardening; Heart of Christ; Judgment; Kingdom of God; Mission; Penitence; Preaching; Sin; Spiritual Theology**

Corpus Christi. *See* **Eucharist**

See **Eucharist**

Cosmos

A. Biblical Theology

1. Vocabulary

Kosmos (verb: *kosmein*) in Greek generally denotes "order" or "ornament (*taxis, tassein:* only "organization); it also designates the universe (space-time) and its harmony (see Origen*, *Princ.* 2, 3, 6). In the Septuagint, *kosmos* and *kosmein* are associated primarily with the Hebrew lexicon of ornament and sometimes with that of the cosmos created by God*, notably in The Wisdom of Solomon (16 times: "universe"). Biblical Hebrew has no equivalent for "universe"; *'ôlâm* means "indefinite time*" or "eternity" ("universe" in postbiblical Hebrew). The *chuqqôt* (decrees) establish the cosmic order according to a kind of covenant* *(berît). Çèdèq/çedâqâh* (frequent par. *mishepât*) may apply to the "good order" of creation* (Schmid 1968; Murray 1992).

2. Old Testament

The Old Testament preserves traces of ancient warrior (Ps 74:13f.; 89:9f.; Is 27:1; etc) or merely violent cosmogonies (Ps 104:7ff.; Jb 38:9ff.; Jer 5:22; Prv 22–31). The most demythologized text is Genesis 1:1–2:4: God creates order by speaking, by a series of acts of separation *(bdl),* by the division into species (*mîn:* Beauchamp 1969), by the establishment of the calendar (week, sabbath, celebrations). In the Torah, the blessing* that maintains the order of the cosmos and the curse that overthrows it (Lv 26; Dt 28) are articulated in the terms of a covenant to which heaven, earth (Ps 50:4), and mountains (Mi 6:1; *see* Dt 27:12f.; Ps 50:1f.) are witnesses. With the flood, God responds to human disorder by unleashing cosmic chaos (Gn 7–8), after which He promises to maintain the order of the seasons (8:22), regulates the use of violence* (animals*), and enters into an "eternal covenant" (*berît 'ôlâm:* 9:8–17) with humanity and all living things. The oldest occurrence of this theme is probably in Hosea 2:20–24 (Hebrew; 18–22ff. in translations), since Jeremiah 33:20 (day and night), Isaiah 54:9f. (reference to Gn 9), and Isaiah 24:5 date from the exile. Ezekiel 34:25–31 promises a "covenant of peace*" *(berît shâlôm)* that animals will observe. Noncanonical writings attribute cosmic order to a divine oath (*1 Hen* 69:16–25) or to the power of the Name* (Prayer of Manasseh 3; see magic texts).

The cosmic and social order is subject to the influence of God, of human sin*, and, in mythologies, chiefly of gods or devils. Traces of this remain in the Old Testament (Ps 82; Gn 6:1f.; Is 24). *1 Hen* 6–10 again gave them prominence, perhaps recalling the Greek theory of the conflict of cosmic elements. Where lesser importance is attributed to cosmic and supracosmic factors, human error comes to the fore. The cause of cosmic evil* is generally human error, punished by God (Hos 4:1ff.; Jl 1–2). It is God who "creates light and darkness, good and evil" (Is 45:7), who threatens a new flood (Zep 1:2f.), and promises a return to harmony (Is 45:9f.).

This return to cosmic *shâlôm* can be achieved by ethical* or liturgical means. Beginning with the Babylonian festival of Akitu, the ritual of which is known, scholars have found traces of an autumn new year celebration. Although not designated as ritual texts, the royal psalms* 72 and 89 illustrate the cosmic and royal import of the themes of *çèdèq, mishepât,* and their fruit, *shâlôm* (Ps 74, 82; Is 11:1–9, 24, 32–33). In most ancient societies, temples*, including the temple of Jerusalem*, were representations of the creation and of the divine realm: heaven and earth met in them (Patai 1967). In the course of social change, the myth* remained but was reinterpreted. Genesis 1, for example, demythologizes "the army of the heavens" and the monsters of the deep. Genesis 2 grants humanity (Adam*) royal status. Certain hymns (e.g., Ps 72) or oracles (Is 11:1–9) were transposed into eschatology* (Murray 1992). Apocalypses reread archetypes in order to decipher contemporary events. A similar cosmic breadth appears in writings that are simultaneously apocalyptic* and wisdom writings (Stone 1976), such as Job 38–39, Ecclesiastes 1:4–7, The Wisdom of Solomon 7:17–20, and *1 Hen.* Close to Stoic conceptions (regularity of the cosmos: *see* the hymn to Zeus of Cleanthes), Philo interprets the solemnity of the new year as a reconciliation of the *stoikheia* in conflict (Schweizer 1988; *see* Wis 16:17–22, 19:18–21).

3. New Testament

Jesus* was to disappoint and reject messianic expectations in the form that they had assumed. His disciples recognized in him the Lord of the cosmos through his charismatic power and his intimate connection to created things—expressed in hymnal form in Ephesians 1:3–10, Colossians 1:15–20, and John 1:1–4. In him, God has "recapitulated" all things. Paul (Gal 4:3, 9; *see* Col 2:8, 20) fights against the subjection of some to the *stoikheia tou kosmou,* "cosmic elements," or (with reference to Jewish observances considered obsolete) "rudiments," also called "angels*," "principalities," or "powers" (Schweizer 1988). Jesus has freed us from their ascetic or ritual requirements by his victory. Paul asserts both the filial condition of the Christian in Christ* and the present suffering of all creation (Rom 8:18–23; v. 19: *ktisis*) (Fitzmyer 1992), which cries out for deliverance. For him, "justification*" *(dikaiôsis, dikaiôma),* the central theme of Romans, preserved all the semantic breadth of the Hebrew *çèdèq (çedâqâh);* it included the cosmic order. There could not possibly be any salvation* outside the teleological perspective of the cosmos.

Revelation interprets present suffering and the coming manifestation of Christ as Lord of all. The cosmology of the book adopts the schema of the parallel between heaven and earth and adapts Jewish eschatology* to a millenarian Christian vision, which explains the reservations of a part of the ancient Church*. The history of Johannine theology later showed the relevance of those reservations.

• R. Patai (1967), *Man and Temple in Ancient Myth and Ritual,* New York.

H. Schmid (1968), *Gerechtigkeit als Weltordnung,* BHTh 40, Tübingen.

P. Beauchamp (1969), *Création et séparation,* Paris.

M. Stone (1976), "List of Revealed Things in the Apocalyptic Literature," in F. Cross (Ed.), *Magnalia Dei (Festschrift Wright),* New York, 413–62.

A. Broadie and J. Mac Donald (1978), "The Concept of Cosmic Order in Ancient Egypt in Dynastic and Roman Times," *AnCl* 47, 106–28.

E. Schweizer (1988), "Slaves of the Elements and Worshippers of Angels: Ga 4:3, 9 and Col 2:8, 18, 20," *JBL* 107, 455–68.

J. Fitzmyer (1992), *Romans: A New Translation with Introduction and Commentary,* New York.

R. Murray (1992), *The Cosmic Covenant,* London.

M. Douglas (1993), "The Forbidden Animals in Leviticus," *JSOT* 59, 3–23.

ROBERT MURRAY

See also **Adam; Animals; Covenant; Creation; Ecology; Eschatology; Liturgy; Pauline Theology; Temple; Time; World**

B. Historical and Systematic Theology

To the theologies* that meditated on it, the experience of Israel* bequeathed first of all a cosmos that was radically lacking in divinity or numinousness. For the Greek notion of an "order of the world" and a "friendship" among heaven, earth, gods, and men, as Plato describes it (*Gorgias* 507*e*–508*a*), the creation* narratives* substitute the perception of a created universe in which beings taken as objects of worship by pagan cults (sun, moon) are no longer anything but divine artifacts. Although desacralized, the cosmos nevertheless continues to call forth jubilation and praise* from the believer. It is the throne of YHWH (Ps 93[92]:2), it is established and strengthened by Him (Ps 1, 24[23]:1f., 65[64]:7, 74[73]:17, 89[88]:12, 136[135]:6). And even if the primeval experience of Israel was of a God* who saves, the song of the "wonders" of God describes Him as both author of the law* and creator of heaven (Ps 19[18]), and YHWH is praised for having created the "greater lights (Ps 136[137]:7) as well as for having brought Israel out of Egypt (Ps 11ff.).

Both Cosmic reference to the created order and historical reference to an economy of salvation* were preserved in Christian writings, Patristic and medieval, with no apparent tension between the two. To gnostic soteriology (Jonas 1974), for which man occupies in the cosmos only the position of the stranger—the "foreign"—and who must therefore be saved *from* the cosmos and from the "archons" who govern it, orthodox theology opposes the experience of believers perfectly at ease in "such a beautiful creation" (Irenaeus, *Adv. Haer.* II, 2, 1). And by asserting that the totality of things not only takes its origin in the creative benevolence of God but also has an eschatological destiny (Rev 21:5), Christianity seemed to be forearmed against any forgetfulness of the cosmic dimension of existence.

However, a factor of confusion entered into theological debates with the growing development of the physical sciences. Until the 12th century, the cosmos was only a theological object. But after the introduction of Aristotelian philosophy* of nature in the 13th century, and particularly after the first steps toward modern science in the 16th, the monopoly of theological discourse disappeared. Thereafter, cosmology became primarily a question for the physicist. But even though historians of science generally agree (Jaki 1980; *see also* Funkenstein 1986) that modern science would not have been possible if Judaism* and Christianity had not transmitted to it the concept of a created universe governed by its immanent laws, a theoretical misunderstanding ensued that saw theology first challenging the validity of scientific images of the cosmos (in the name of a biblical image that was supposed to possess a strictly descriptive value) and then ending up losing any interest in the cosmic dimension of Christian experience. The cosmos illustrated by the *Canticle of All Creatures* of Francis of Assisi was thus followed, in the early period of modern science, by a universe devoid of any theological significance whose "eternal silence" terrified Pascal*'s libertine. And a theology ill prepared to defend and illustrate its theological knowledge of the cosmos and unable to recognize that a theological hermeneutics cannot be contradicted by a physical description of the nature of things came, during the same period and for a long time thereafter, to favor an a-cosmic logic of Christian experience.

Already present in the withdrawal to inwardness known in the classic age—and then in pietism*, also present in any theology tempted to reduce man to his immortal soul* and to forget his body that is promised resurrection—theology lacking in the cosmic dimension no doubt reached its apotheosis in the 20th century under the theoretical aegis of the concept of "existence." Bultmann* (1940), for example, explains that "the idea of creation" is in no way a "cosmological theory"; when the New Testament uses the word *kosmos,* this is in a sense "incommensurable" (Bultmann 1940) with that of the Greeks: man is not part of the cosmos as of a reassuring totality, he is alone before God, and the theological coordinates of his experience can be elucidated without reference to his position in the midst of all the created universe. And while existential theologies reduced every relation to being-before-God, the theologies for which the "history of salvation" provided the governing concept were led to marginalize the doctrine of the creation and its corollaries in favor of a primordial experience (the experience of the covenant* and salvation given in history*), dismissing any other.

It is, however, noteworthy that interest in the cosmic order that cannot leave theology indifferent has resurfaced on the contemporary intellectual stage. It is not without significance that Heidegger* (1954; *see* Mattéi 1989) attempted in his late philosophy to describe with the enigmatic "quadripartite" *(Geviert)* a "world" made out of the "mutual belonging" and the "interplay" of four realities—earth, heaven, divine beings, and mortals—"communion" among which defined the Platonic cosmos. It is significant that in a much more sober enterprise, Maurice Merleau-Ponty (1908–61) attempted, starting from sensory experience, to rediscover a perceiving subject who would no longer be "an 'a-cosmic' thinking subject" (1945), but a subject whose "natural world," *omnitudo realitas,* would be "the horizon of all experiences" (1945). And it is not without importance that the scientific description of natural realities, by dint of emphasizing the ordered beauty* of the physical universe, which thereby genuinely deserves the name of cosmos, seems to have put an end in 20th century to the terror that arose in the classic period when the "closed world" of the Middle Ages disappeared.

To the muddled theism* or pantheism* sometimes suggested to the man of science by the beautiful order of reality and the elegance of the theories that account for it (*see,* e.g., d'Espagnat 1979 and Barreau, *RMM* 1981), theology should provide diverse responses. Everyone (no doubt since Teilhard de Chardin) is certainly convinced that, in principle and in their concrete organization, there is no contradiction between the language of science and the language of faith. The universe of the scientific cosmologist and the cosmos of the theologian are not a single theme. There is, however, no ambiguity: the adoption of divergent perspectives does not abolish the commonality of the object, and a theological doctrine of the cosmos speaks of the same realities as physics does. There are, however, major divergences sufficient to prevent complete concord. 1) In its theological reality, first of all, the cosmos is understood as the "visible and invisible universe"—as a whole of which only a part constitutes a physical object. Science says that nonphysical objects (angels*, "souls in purgatory*") are unknowable to it, that they do not exist for the rationality embodied by science. Theology, on the other hand, must be able to argue in favor of *invisibilia* whose existence is confessed by faith (*see,* e.g., Newman* 1838). 2) The cosmos, moreover, does not constitute the first among theological objects. The coordinates of biblical experience are primarily historical, and a theological logic of the cosmic order must take that priority into account. Creation and covenant (salvation) must be thought of together, something that Barth* (*KD* III/1) thoroughly demonstrated; and this can occur only in a theology to which the *ordo inventionis* supplies its order of reasons, in a theology that recognizes in the Lord of heaven and earth the Lord that it first knew in the form of the God of promises. 3) More than a question of origin, it is in fact an eschatological question that should give impetus to a theological discourse on the cosmos. Despite all the elegance of cosmic realities, man occupies in this cosmos the place of one who knows he is going to die and that death* is embedded in the order of things. Theology, of course, speaks on this side of death, but it does so in the name of eschatological promises* whose anticipatory realization it commemorates in the Resurrection* of Jesus*—and it is in fact the Resurrection that provides it with its best model for a rescue from nothingness* and for creation *ex nihilo* (Jüngel 1972). The present dwelling of man in the cosmos and the present theological meaning of the cosmic order are thus attached to the promise of a *new totality* (Rev 21:5). There is a physics only of spatial and temporal realities. These same realities that physics measures and describes nevertheless go beyond their scientific description, beforehand—as created realities—and afterward—by the absolute future that is promised for them and that they await "in a labor of childbirth" (Rom 8:18–23). It is centrally because it has at its disposal a doctrine that cannot be lost, of "new creation" (2 Cor 5:17) that Christianity owes it to itself to recognize the present theological meaning of the created world, as it is and in its entirety.

- J.H. Newman (1838), "The Invisible World," in *Parochial and Plain Sermons* IV, 13 (new edition in 1 volume, San Francisco, 1987).

E. Käsemann (1935), *Leib und Leib Christi,* Tübingen.

R. Bultmann (1940), "Das Verständnis von Welt und Mensch im Neuen Testament und im Griechentum," *GuV* 2, 59–78 (6th Ed. 1993).

M. Merleau-Ponty (1945), *Phénoménologie de la perception,* Paris.

M. Heidegger (1954), *Vorträge und Aufsätze,* Pfullingen, 157–79.

E. Jüngel (1972), "Die Welt als Mögligkeit und Wirklichkeit," in *Unterwegs zur Sache,* Munich, 206–31.

H. Jonas (1974), "The Gnostic Syndrome," in *Philosophical Essays,* Chicago, 263–76 (2nd Ed. 1980).

B. d'Espagnat (1979), *A la recherche du réel, le regard d'un physicien,* Paris.

S.L. Jaki (1980), *Cosmos and Creator,* Edinburgh.

L. Bouyer (1982), *Cosmos,* Paris.

A. Funkenstein (1986), *Theology and the Scientific Imagination from the Late Middle Ages to the XVIIth Century,* Princeton.

O. O'Donovan (1986), *Resurrection and Moral Order,* Oxford (*Résurrection et expérience morale,* 1992).

Coll. (1988), *Cosmos et création, Com(F)* XIII/3.

S.L. Jaki (1989), *God and the Cosmologists,* Edinburgh.

A. Gesché (1994), *Dieu pour penser,* vol. 4, *Le cosmos,* Paris.

Irène Fernandez and Jean-Yves Lacoste

See also **Creation; Ecology; Eschatology; Gnosis; History; Hope; Myth; World**

Council

The "council" is the assembly of legitimate representatives of the Church* meeting on a local or universal (ecumenical) level to deliberate and rule on Christian practices and ecclesiastical organization with a concern for unity* in matters of faith*. The Latin word *concilium* (also occurring as *consilium*) comes from *concalare,* "convene" (*see* Greek *ekklesia,* "church") and is synonymous with *synod, conventus, coetus.* It appears in its Christian meaning for the first time in Tertullian* (*De jejunio* 13.) It has been reserved for the assemblies of the universal Church since the Middle Ages, while regional ecclesiastical assemblies are usually called synods*.

1. The Birth of the Institution
The council has its precursors in the Greek popular assemblies, then in Rome in the colleges* of priests* and provincial assemblies. Since John Chrysostom* (*Hom.* 32 and 33), the institution of the council has largely been referred to the biblical model of the so-called council of the Apostles* (Acts 15). The latter episode exemplifies the defining characteristics of the council: the Church leaders (among whom Peter* plays an especially important role), faced with a conflict threatening the unity of the Church, assemble to exchange their views. They assume the responsibility of speaking for the entire Church with the help of the Holy* Spirit, and they take decisions that will be binding on the whole Church. In the second century A.D., the need to resolve certain local and regional conflicts, first in Asia Minor (against Montanism*), necessitated the holding of ecclesiastical assemblies. In the following century these became institutionalized, regularly gathering the Church representatives of one or more imperial provinces or of the entire western part of the empire (Arles, 314). After the conversion of Constantine, these gatherings came to rank as an official authority of the *oikoumene* (that is to say, of the Roman Empire) whose decisions acquired an obligatory character for the entire Church (ecumenicity.) In all their forms and at all levels, these invariably remained assemblies of bishops*; but there is also testimony to the presence of presbyters*, deacons*, and laypeople* (Cyprian*, *Ep.* 71, 1; Synods of Carthage [255] and Elvira [c. 302]). Subsequently we also find monks (mainly monastic superiors). All resolutions must be taken in "a spirit of unanimity" (by a two-thirds majority at Vatican* II).

2. Historical Evolution of the Ecumenical Councils
The councils, which were born of the will to preserve the unity of the Church in the face of theological and disciplinary crises, played a vital role in the area of ecclesiology and of canon law. This role, however, was differently defined, depending on the occasion, the context, and the image that the Church or the Churches involved had of themselves. Thus, different types of council appeared, and there were divergences between the denominations as to their number and ecumenicity. The following classification is based on unofficial Catholic historiography and has been adopted since Bellarmine*.

a) The Old Church. The first eight councils were convened and presided over by the emperor (be it directly or via his representatives) to confess the faith in Christ and the Trinity and to organize the Church. Their reception* by the universal Church was of crucial importance. Since the fifth century it had become indispensable that the bishop of Rome* approve them. The decisions of the councils had the value of imperial laws.

b) The Medieval Church. After the break with the Eastern Church in 1054, the eight General Councils of the Western Church were convened and conducted by the pope* as an extension of the reforming synods of the 11th century. They claimed an ecumenical character inasmuch as they rested on principles valid for all the Church.

c) The 15th-Century Church. There can be seen emerging, under conciliarism*, the pattern of the reforming council: in view of certain perils threatening the Church (Great Schism*, Eastern Schism), the bishops gathered (with the emperor's support in the case of the Council of Constance*) to reestablish unity and carry out Church reform. Nevertheless, the papacy successfully affirmed its primacy over the council.

d) The Modern Church. Henceforth, councils would be dominated by the papacy (convocation, agenda, direction, and the putting into effect of resolutions—Vatican* I: "*sacro approbante concilio*"—are all prerogatives of the Roman pontiff) and appear as a vehicle of the Church's renewal in the face of secular and inter-Christian attacks (the Reformation). Yet Vatican II established a council of a new type: if the council was still to be organized by the pope, the participants would at least be permitted to discuss freely and in line with their pastoral responsibility (even contrary to the propositions of the Curia), without excommunication. Nevertheless, all official public pronouncements are made by the pope "*una cum ss. Concilii Patribus.*"

3. The Theology of the Councils

a) General Points. The institution of the council finds its theological ground in the conciliarism of the Church of Christ, that is, of the people* who, "united by virtue of the unity of the Father* and the Son* and the Holy Spirit" (Cyprian, *De orat. dom.* 23, *plebs de unitate Trinitatis adunata*), must confess the gospel and convey it in its unchangeable purity to the whole inhabited universe *(oikoumene).* It is therefore a constitutive element of the Church, whose unity and catholicity it concretizes. There is fundamental agreement between the Christian denominations on this point despite those differences that, as we have said, issue from their specific ecclesiologies.

b) The Orthodox Churches. Only the first seven councils are recognized as ecumenical by the Orthodox Churches. Numerous local councils were later accepted by the whole of Orthodoxy, but none received the title "ecumenical." Since the beginning of the 20th century, there have been some attempts to convoke a pan-Orthodox council that might become the eighth ecumenical council (preliminary conference in 1930; pan-Orthodox conferences in 1961, 1963, 1965, and 1968; precouncil assemblies in 1976, 1982, and 1986). The theology* of *sobornost* (term introduced by the disciples of A. S. Khomiakov [1804–60]; *see* Orthodoxy* mod. and cont.) has played an important role. Defining the Church by its catholicity as the communion* of all its members (*catholica* corresponds to the Russian *sobornaya,* from the root *sbr,* "gather"), Orthodox theology implies that episcopal and conciliar resolutions are valid only if they are accepted of one accord.

c) The Roman Catholic Church. The current understanding of the council was defined by Vatican II (*LG* 22, 25; *CD* 4 *Sq,* 36–38) and by the *CIC* of 1983 (can. 337–41, where this topic is no longer treated in a specific section as in the *Codex* of 1917 [can. 222–29]) but is included in the article "*De Collegio Episcoporum.*" The episcopal college exercises its ecumenical power *(potestas)* through the council, with the prerogative of infallibility* if need be; only the pope can convene, conduct, adjourn, interrupt, or dissolve the council. It is also he who creates the agenda and who must accept, ratify, and promulgate the decisions before they become valid. All the bishops (including titular ones, i.e., those who do not effectively preside over any local Church) take part in the council, but other persons may also be invited by the pope.

d) The Churches of the Reformation. For the first reformers, the ecumenical councils were fallible institutions founded only by human law and having no authority* for the Church except if they interpreted Holy* Scripture correctly. This was mostly the case with the first four councils. The idea of conciliarity survived in the synodical structures of these churches (synod*).

e) The 20th-Century Ecumenical Movement. Since Vatican II the topic of the council has constituted an important subject in the bilateral ecumenical dialogues with the Catholic Church. The Anglican Communion pays special attention to this question (Venice 1976; Windsor 1981), which becomes all the more acute with the idea of *conciliary communion* or "counciliarity" (COE: Nairobi 1975) understood 1) as a joint process of deliberation and decision demonstrating the fundamental unity of churches and 2) as a disposition for mutual recognition on the basis of apostolic faith and an agreement on the sacraments* and the ministries* of eucharistic communion.

• J. D. Mansi, *Sacrorum Conciliorum nova et amplissima collectio,* 60 vols., Florence-Venice, 1757–98, Paris, 1899–1927.
E. Schwartz, *Acta Conciliorum Oecumenicorum,* Berlin, 1914– .
G. Alberigo et al., *Conciliorum oecumenicorum decreta,* 3rd Ed., Bologne, 1973.
Annuarium Historiae Conciliorum, Amsterdam, 1969– (bibl. continues).
♦ C. J. Hefele and H. Leclercq (1907–52), *Histoire des conciles,* 11 vols., Paris.
J. L. Murphy (1959), *The General Councils of the Church,* Milwaukee, Wis.
B. Planck (1960), *Katholizität und Sobornost,* Würzburg.
O. Rousseau (Ed.) (1960), *Le concile et les conciles,* Chèvetogne.
COE (1968), *Konzile und die ökumenische Bewegung* (COE study # 5), Geneva.
Pro Oriente (Ed.) (1975), *Konziliarität und Kollegialität als Strukturprinzipien der Kirche,* Innsbruck.
H. J. Sieben (1979), *Die Konzilsidee der Alten Kirche,* Paderborn.
W. Brandmüller (Ed.) (1980–), *Konziliensgeschichte,* Paderborn.
H. J. Sieben (1983), *Traktate und Theorien zum Konzil.*
H. J. Sieben (1984), *Die Konzilsidee des lateinischen Mittelalters,* Paderborn.
H. J. Sieben (1988), *Die katholische Konzilsidee von der Reformation bis zur Aufklärung,* Paderborn.
H. J. Sieben (1993), *Die katholische Konzilsidee im 19. und 20. Jahrhundert,* Paderborn.

Wolfgang Beinert

See also **Catholicism; Ecclesiastical Discipline; Ecumenism; Government, Church; Heresy; Hierarchy; Indefectibility of the Church; Local Church; Orthodoxy; Protestantism; Regional Church; Synod**

Counsels. *See* **Precepts**

Couple

Like other cultures, the Bible* frames very carefully the reality of the couple. Moreover, the Bible develops its identity and its symbolic impact in such a way that, while being removed from the domain of the sacred, it nevertheless becomes a central reference point of revelation* and of the history* of salvation*.

a) The Couple, Reality of Creation. The creation* stories of Genesis 1–3 immediately suggest a sexual humanity. On the sixth day, "God created man in his own image…male and female he created them" (Gn 1:27). In chapter 2 the story mentions an original Adam* whose solitude immediately calls for a counterpart, hence the creation of woman*. God, however, as creator of this couple, is carefully disassociated from sexuality. So, in this way, the Bible weakens the connection that is frequently made between Eros and the sacred, removing sexuality from the divine sphere. The couple is given autonomous status.

This human couple is described in strictly positive terms as the image of God, and the relationship between man and woman is evoked in a story filled with harmony and admiration (Gn 2:23ff.). The story of original sin (Gn 3) alters this relationship. The sin* described here is not sexual in nature, but its first effect involves the bond that unites man and woman. Henceforth, "seduction" and "domination" (3:16) is introduced into their experience as a couple. This new system, however, does not obliterate the positive vision offered in the first two chapters of Genesis.

The stories of the patriarchs illustrate the fact that a new era has been initiated, by touching both on Jacob's love* for Rachel (Gn 29:1–30) and the stories of violence* and rape (Gn 34:1–6). Positive depictions of couples (Hannah and Elkanah, 1 Sm 1:1–8; Tobias and Sara, Tb 7:13–8, 8, etc.) and negative ones (Samson and Delilah, Jgs 16:1–21; Job and his wife, Jb 2, 9, etc.) succeed one another in the Bible, and thus conjugal experience is represented in all its variety.

b) The Couple and the Covenant. Marked by sin, the reality of the couple is nonetheless maintained and confirmed within the biblical drama with the emergence of the covenant* theme. YHWH reveals himself as one who enters into a covenant with his people*. Derived from a political vocabulary, the word "covenant" had a connotation of conjugality as early as the eighth century in prophetic literature. Among the many names* used to designate YHWH in his relationship to Israel*, the word "bridegroom" occupies an eminent position. Hence the terms "prostitution" or "adulterous" are used to designate the infidelity and sin of Israel. The book of Hosea attests to this point of view: the prophet* receives the order to marry a prostitute, and in this symbolic couple the people will have to recognize its own unfaithfulness with regard to YHWH. Elsewhere, the relationship between a prophet and his wife acts as a sign and omen for Israel (see Isaiah and his family in Is 8:4–18; Ezekiel losing his wife in Ez 24:15–27). It is when receiving the order not to take a wife that Jeremiah (Jer 16:1–9) announces the imminent coming of days of judgment* and affliction. Nevertheless, the announcement of a new era, when the heart of Israel will be renewed and when the covenant will be protected from human infidelity, is also conveyed by means of nuptial references. Such references play a large role in the Zion oracles of the second Isaiah and in the texts that follow (49:21, 54:1–10, 61:10, 62:1–5, 66:7ff.).

This valorization of the couple culminates in the Song of Songs. In its most immediate literal sense, this dialogue praises the beauty and goodness of love between a man and a woman who are in a relationship of complete parity, one in which there is the original fullness referred to in Genesis 1 and 2. It should be noted that the entire tradition* of Jewish interpretation of the text sees it as celebrating the relationship between YHWH and Israel, while the Christian tradition sees it as the dialogue between Christ* and the Church*. The Song of Songs therefore serves to express in a supreme manner the full reality of that covenant between YHWH and Israel of which the prophets speak. But it is evidently highly significant that the perfection of this covenant finds expression in words that are charged with the richest human implication. Modern interpretation of the Song of Songs, in readily considering anthropological as well as spiritual aspects of the text clearly highlights how the Bible closely knits the human reality of the couple to that which guarantees it spiritually: the covenant.

Furthermore, it may be noted that the book of Proverbs (1–9) refers to divine Wisdom in the figure of a loving and loved wife; the sage is the spouse of this Wisdom*, of whom Solomon declares, "She is the one that I chose in my youth, I strove to have her as my spouse, and I became the lover of her beauty" (Wis 8:2).

c) The New Testament. In their opening chapters, the Gospels* according to Matthew and Luke mention the couple of Mary* and Joseph, parents of Jesus*. Beyond that, the question of the couple is not thoroughly explored. The nuptial theme nevertheless surfaces in Matthew 9:15 par., as well as in John 3:29, where Jesus is referred to as "the bridegroom," a title the prophets had given to YHWH. Another passage (Mt 19:1–12) deals explicitly with the man–woman relationship, when Jesus forbids any man to renounce his wife. Beyond its relevance in terms of moral discipline, the text in fact says something important about the person* of Jesus. Granted by Moses, divorce belongs to what is now an outmoded dispensation. But Jesus has inaugurated a new era, one in which humanity will find in itself the ability to transcend its weaknesses and so experience the original relationship of man and woman (*see* Gn 1–2).

On the other hand, the question of the couple is dealt with quite frequently in Saint Paul's Epistles. Galatians 3:28, by declaring, "There is neither Jew nor Greek, there is neither slave nor free, there is neither male nor female, for you are all one in Christ Jesus," seems to question sexual difference. The verse poses difficulties because it lists pairs that belong to separate orders of reality and discourse. Concerning the difference between the sexes, which Genesis 1 designates as a fundamental and good reality, it is rather unlikely that Paul simply wanted to announce the overcoming or the suppression of this difference. It seems, rather, that his words should be read as part of a text centered on the novelty of Christ: union with Christ allows the division and the violence designated by Genesis 3:16b to be overcome. This means that man and woman exist at last in accordance with God's original plan.

The letter to the Ephesians reflects the long development of a theory that helped shape ecclesiology that draws a parallel between the Christ–Church relationship and the conjugal relationship (Eph 5:21–33). This text is the final extension of the prophetic tradition and defines the greatness of the conjugal relationship. The woman is invited to submit to love, while the man is called to love, as Christ loves the Church. In this way the couple becomes a reflection of the relationship between Christ and the Church. Paul comments, "This mystery* is great"; in developing the theme further, the church fathers* would readily interpret the story of the creation of woman in Genesis 2 as a prophesy of the birth of the Church, the goal of creation, a goal revealed in the Incarnation* and made accessible in the sacramental life of the Church itself.

Running parallel to this and departing from ancient tradition, we witness in the New Testament the promotion of a celibacy that rests for its justification on the text of Matthew 19:12. This celibacy indicates a more fundamental relationship than the conjugal relationship, being both its source and its future. The Bible, in the Apocalypse, nevertheless closes with a nuptial image (the vision of the new Jerusalem* descending from the sky "prepared as a bride adorned for her husband" [Rev 21:2]). This is the last reference to the reality of the couple, recapitulating the figures of prophetic and wisdom texts at the point when the biblical revelation comes to an end.

• A. Neher (1954), "Le symbolisme conjugal: Expression de l'histoire dans l'Ancien Testament," *RHPhR* 34, 30–49.
P. Grelot (1964), *Le couple humain dans l'Écriture,* Paris.
D. Lys (1968), *Le plus beau chant de la création,* Paris.
M. Gilbert (1978), "Une seule chair" (Gn 2, 24)," *NRTh* 100, 66–89.
P. Beauchamp (1979), "Épouser la sagesse—ou n'épouser qu'elle? Une énigme du livre de la Sagesse," in M. Gilbert (Ed.), *La Sagesse de l'Ancien Testament,* Louvain, 347–69 (2nd Ed. 1990).
C. Yannaras (1982), *Person und Eros,* Göttingen.
J. Briend (1987), "Gn 2–3 et la création du couple humain," in (coll.), *La création dans l'Orient ancien,* Paris, 123–38.
A.-M. Pelletier (1989), *Le Cantique des Cantiques: De l'énigme du sens aux figures du lecteur,* Rome; (1993), *Le Cantique des Cantiques,* CEv 85.

Anne-Marie Pelletier

See also **Adam; Anthropology; Ethics, Sexual; Marriage; Messianism; Mysticism; Woman**

Covenant

The covenant, a central concept in the Bible* and in Christian theology*, designates the relationship between God* and his people* by analogy with privileged relations that men establish with each other by contract. This relationship, which is often described with the use of categories borrowed from nature or the fabrication of material objects, is projected into the field of individual and collective existence. Law, notably the law governing treaties and contracts, is part of the concept. Various different covenants between God and man are mentioned in the Bible and taken as articulations of the story of Salvation*. In modern times the covenant has also been used as a guiding theme in some global theological projects—known as "federal" theologies.

The idea of the covenant goes back to the Hebrew word *berît* and to its Greek equivalent, *diathèkè,* used in the Septuagint (LXX), the first Greek translation of the Hebrew Scriptures, begun in the third century B.C. However, it also covers other terms—*'édout,* for example, and other words meaning "oath." Exegetes and theologians rightfully speak of covenant with respect to literary forms or narratives* where the idea is found without explicit use of the term. In the Christian tradition* the Greek word *diathèkè* also introduced the use of the word "testament," notably in the division of the canon* into an "Old" and a "New" Testament.

I. The Old Testament

1. Human Covenants

a) Terminology. The etymology of *berît* is still disputed. The primitive meaning was undoubtedly that of a "bond," an "obligation." The word often designated a legal act or a contract and, at the same time, the obligations and commitments it entails. Parallel to *berît* there are words meaning "oath"; a contract of covenant was ritually sealed under oath, and this often took place inside a sanctuary. Thus, the divinity was the guarantor ("witness") of the operation. Steles were also erected as "witnesses." In that event, documents were drawn up (*sefer ha berit,* "document of covenant," often mistranslated as "book* of the covenant"), and symbolic acts were performed. The contracting parties exchanged gifts, traded clothing or arms, shook hands, partook of a meal (sacrificial meals including rites based on salt or blood), or called down malediction on themselves if they should break the treaty (this was, e.g., the meaning of the rite that consisted of passing between the two halves of a sacrificed animal).

The human relation sealed by the *berît* was first and foremost a bond of fidelity and peace, which was experienced as a familial attachment. A man was said to be the "brother, father, or son" of the person with whom he made a covenant, and "love* and fidelity" should be paid to him. This is why marriage* could also be considered a sort of *berît.* The particular services that the parties mutually imposed on themselves and guaranteed entered only in second place in the marital relationship. Strictly speaking, the laws* of Israel* should not be called "laws" but contractual obligations, as they were most often proclaimed in the form of covenant treaties.

Contracts could be concluded between peers or between partners of unequal power. The stipulated obligations might be reciprocal or unilateral. When the contract stated only the commitment of a powerful party to protect the weak or, conversely, only the obligations of a subordinate to his superior, the implicit counterpart was considered as self-evident, and therefore it was not necessarily stipulated in every case. The contracting parties could be individuals, small groups, or large political entities.

In all these forms Israel reproduced the social structure based on privileged contractual relations, which prevailed at that time in the Middle East and the preclassical Mediterranean region. Abundant comparative material on this subject is available (*see* D. J. McCarthy 1978), particularly in the field of relations between states and relations between sovereigns and their governing elite (including pacts between powerful sovereigns, oaths of civil servants, treaties of vassalage, diplomatic correspondence, royal inscriptions, charters granting fiefs, and royal donations). Despite numerous historical transformations, a surprising continuity in vocabulary, ritual, and literary forms can be recognized across regions and periods. In Hittite vassalage treaties of the second millennium B.C., the exposition of provisions is preceded by a recall of past relations between the parties, known as the "historical prologue" (which also played an important role in late

Old Testament texts treating the divine covenant). And this typical form is still found in a seventh-century treaty of Assurbanipal. The notion of a covenant with the divinity is also attested, though rarely, outside Israel; one example is found under the reign of Urukagina of Lagash (24th century B.C.), and two others are found in the Neo-Assyrian cultural area. However, such a transposition of the idea of the covenant is marginal outside Israel.

b) Forbidden Covenants. According to Exodus 23:32 and 34:12–16, in the earliest times Israel was forbidden to make covenants with non-Israelite groups living in the land. Although the dating of these two passages from Exodus is disputed, they are certainly anterior to the exile. The prohibition may not have been in effect everywhere, but where it did apply it was related notably to Israel, "a people dwelling alone, and not reckoning itself among the nations" (Nm 23:9). The foundation of the empire by David necessarily changed this state of affairs within the land as well as in international relations where Israel began to get a foothold. This aroused criticism from the prophets* against the policy of covenants between states. Later, in the period of exile and return, the prohibition was reinstated in Deuteronomic legislation (Dt 7:2). It ensued from the privileged contractual relationship established by the divine covenant between YHWH and Israel.

2. The Covenant between YHWH and Israel

a) The Prestate Period. A "theology of the covenant" that integrated all the traditions of Israel in a systematic concrete form did not appear until the time of the Deuteronomistic theologians. However, theologians of the time of Josiah (seventh century B.C.) seem to have adopted an antique conception of the privileged contractual relationship established between Israel and God.

There are frequent attempts to give a rather recent date to the passages related to this theme and to explain them as ulterior additions reflecting the Deuteronomistic conception. In fact, many points are unclear here. It is also true that not all the pre-Deuteronomistic indications necessarily go back to the origins of Israel. Nevertheless, the absence of any idea of covenant before the Deuteronomistic period is not the most credible hypothesis. The narrative recapitulations in Deuteronomy already presuppose the essential pattern on which the pericope of the Sinai is built in the book of Exodus, with its recall of the founding covenants contracted between YHWH and Israel. And this pericope itself contains elements that could come from a period preceding its literary composition. It is most likely a primitive core of Exodus 34:10–26 and the (more contested) primitive core of Exodus 24:1–11. Exodus 19:3–8, on the other hand, might belong to the stage of the final writing of the Pentateuch as well as the organization of the whole pericope on the model "conclusion of the covenant-renewal of the covenant."

The pre-Deutoronomic decalogue*, of uncertain dating, is designated in Deuteronomy by the term *haberît* and in the sacerdotal document by the term *ha-'édout* according to what seems to be already a traditionally accepted usage. It is not at all certain that the "terminological argument" can be alleged by eliminating the supposed Deuteronomic additions in Joshua 7:11–15 and Deuteronomy 33:9 and even less in Hosea 8:11 and Joshua 24:25. As for the Psalms*, there is no certainty about their dating (*see*, e.g., Ps 50:5 and related passages in Ps 81 and 95). Of course, the "formula of the covenant" (YHWH is the God of Israel; Israel is the people of YHWH) does not rightfully bear its name unless it is accompanied by the obligation of Israel to follow the divine laws. It expresses then the act by which YHWH establishes his relation with Israel, specifying the ensuing obligations for his people. In this form it is attested earlier in Deuteronomy, but in a brief form that would be more adequately designated as "formula of belonging," and is already presupposed in Hosea. The notion of Israel as the "people of God" goes back to the earliest times. It is already attested in the ninth century in a ceremony of covenant performed on the occasion of a coronation rite in Jerusalem* (2 Kgs 11:17) with expressions that do not have authentic Deuteronomic parallels. Again it is by a covenant that Josiah commits himself, along with the whole nation, to follow the book of the Torah found in the Temple* in 622 B.C. (2 Kgs 23:3), and it is difficult to imagine that in so doing he would introduce an entirely new style in the politicoreligious symbolism.

It may be that this royal ritual was revived only in Jerusalem and that the idea of a covenant with God no longer functioned outside Jerusalem. Before the foundation of the state, however, that bond with God had been the model of self-comprehension of this tribal society*, which, once liberated from Canaanite and Egyptian tutelage, refused to establish a central governing body within its own ranks, as seen in Gideon's declaration (Jgs 8:23). Power did not belong to a suzerain or even to a king brought forth from the heart of Israel but to God alone, who demanded exclusive submission. With the creation of the state, however, this privileged obligation to YHWH was concentrated on the king, who represented the people as a whole.

b) Covenant with the King. This was the starting point of the idea of the covenant of God with David (2 Sm 7:1–29, 23:5; Ps 89; Is 55:3; Jer 33:17–22), which undoubtedly suggests the covenant of God with Abraham (or other patriarchs). This appeared at the latest in the proto-Deuteronomistic revision of the Tetrateuch. Genesis 15:18 speaks of a covenant *(bérît)* between the Lord and Abraham, whereas these texts habitually spoke of the "oath" of God. The central contents of the commitment to Abraham is the granting of a territory; to David it is the duration of his dynasty. It is also a matter, in this context, of the vassal's fidelity and service. At the time of the exile, after the collapse of the Davidian dynasty, Deutero-Isaiah transferred the covenant with David to the whole people of Israel (Is 55:3–5).

c) Deuteronomist Theology. During and after the Neo-Assyrian domination of Judah, theologians of the Deuteronomistic school restored the ancient concept of the divine covenant. They rejected the Assyrian power structure, which was largely tributary to treaties and oaths of loyalty, but adopted its terminology and outer forms. The covenant was then founded on the oath of God to the Patriarchs. It had been concluded on the basis of the Decalogue on Mount Horeb (Mount Sinai) during the Exodus, and renewed in the land of Moab when the people came out of the desert, after the proclamation of the Deuteronomic Torah. The latter was considered to be the document of the covenant. This whole construction clearly finds its starting point in the free gracious act of God.

Deuteronomy 26:17–19, the central passage for understanding the Deuteronomic law as the "covenant of Moab" (Dt 29:1), is built on the model of a contract between peers, but the text itself rejects all notion of equality between the human and divine partners. Formal analogies with the model of the Hittite treaty of vassalage are found only in the late Deuteronomistic writings (e.g., in Dt 4:29–31; Jos 23; 1 Sm 2). Deuteronomy 5–31 gives a narrative account of the covenant concluded in the land of Moab. Presentation of the document of the covenant (Dt 5–26) is accompanied by a number of ritual-performative language acts. They include the constitution of the assembly that concludes the covenant (Dt 29:9–14, in the context of a narrative recapitulation), a protocolary formulation of the relationship established by the treaty (Dt 26:17–19), declaration of God's support pronounced by Moses and the priests (Dt 27:9–10), and expressions of blessings* and curses (Dt 28).

During the period of exile, the Deuteronomistic theory of the covenant was a means of accounting for the collapse of Israel by presenting it as the result of the rupture of the covenant with God. But no new hope* could flow from a covenant that had brought about curses. When the prophets who aroused such a hope appeared, in exile, it became necessary to reverse the poles of the Deuteronomist theory of the covenant. This is what occurred, more or less simultaneously, in different ways.

d) Deuteronomistic Revision of the Prophetic Books. The "Deuteronomistic" book of Jeremiah and a late layer of Ezekiel, which is dependent on it, countered the covenant of the exodus, thenceforth broken, with the future remission of sins*, the return and reassembling of Israel, and the establishment of a "new" and "eternal" covenant in which God—by the correlative gift of the "Spirit"—would renew the human heart* in such a way that men would never again break their commitments (Jer 30:3, 31:27–34; *see* 24:5ff., 32:37–41; Ez 11:17–20, 16:59–63, 36:22–32, 37:21–28; *see also* Ps 51:12ff.).

e) Sacerdotal Document. The narrative entity of the priestly school transforms the idea of the covenant. On God's side the commitment is eternal and will never be renounced. The generation that falls into sin is excluded from the covenant, but God reestablishes his former commitments in the next generation. This is why the sacerdotal document connects the covenant of God with Israel to the covenant concluded with Abraham (Gn 17) rather than its manifestation on Mount Sinai. The former, it is true, is not fully developed until Exodus 6:2–8 and particularly in Exodus 29:45–46. The covenant of Abraham was preceded by that with Noah, by which God bound himself to all of humanity and the animals* (Gn 9:8–17) in promising he would never again provoke a deluge. The law of saintliness, subsequently inserted into the Sinaitic pericope of the priestly document, attempts to integrate the Deuteronomistic conception of the covenant into this pure theology of the covenant of grace* (Lv 26:3–45). Still later, the sabbath* is introduced in the Pentateuch (Ex 31:12–17) as a new sign of the covenant (in addition to the circumcision imposed in Gn 17).

f) Deutero-Isaiah. Though the covenant is not given a central place in Deutero-Isaiah, as in the late layers of Jeremiah or Ezekiel, completely new actions of God are announced. The covenant with David—which legitimized the state and thus in the final instance brought about the ruin of Israel—had to be restored, but in the form of a covenant between God and the whole people who would assume collectively with regard to other peoples* the role of David (Is 55:3, a passage that also gives the key to 42:6 and 49:8; *see also*

61:8). This fits the idea of covenant into the vision of a pilgrimage* of peoples. The covenants of Israel and David are confounded, and even the covenant of Noah is included in the synthesis (Is 54:10).

g) Late Layers of Deuteronomy. All these new approaches are reflected and sometimes even anticipated in the late layers of Deuteronomy. A revised passage in Deuteronomy 7–9 develops a primitive form of the Pauline doctrine of the justification* of sinners (Dt 9:1–6) and introduces the priestly conception of the covenant with the patriarchs (Dt 7:12, 8:18, 9:6). Similarly, in Deuteronomy 4:1–40 (4:31) the universal perspective of the monotheism* of Deutero-Isaiah is profiled (Dt 4:6–8, 32–39). The extension of this layer in Deuteronomy 30:1–10, with the "circumcision of the heart," touches on the center of the "new covenant" theme (30:6).

h) Covenant as Encompassing Concept of the Hebraic Canon. The Pentateuch (i.e., the Torah, or the Law) is of a higher rank than the other parts of the biblical canon. The theme of the Law, in giving the motifs found at the beginning and end of the prophetic books of the Hebraic canon (Jos 1 and Mal 3), traces the literary framework within which they will appear as a sort of prophetic commentary on the Torah, the literary development of the promise* of Deuteronomic law concerning the prophets (Dt 18:15–18). And the book of Psalms opens with an evocation of the study of the Law, in a psalm that is attached by certain key words to the end of the Torah and to Malachi 3. In Deuteronomy 4, 6ff., it is "wisdom*" as a whole that is subordinated to the Torah.

The concept of the covenant is not as determinant. However, the Torah and the covenant are closely related, at least in the Deuteronomistic writings. In Deuteronomy, Israel receives the Torah in concluding the covenant with God. The law given with the covenant of the Exodus period remains the same in the new promised covenant (Jer 31:33). This also applies to the Pentateuch as a whole and, therefore, given its central role, to the whole of the Hebraic canon. Thereby the covenant itself becomes a central concept not only in its Deuteronomic acceptation but also as employed by other theologies and other literary entities.

This notion makes it possible to connect all the decisive themes of the Bible throughout a diversity of theologies. It is connected to the whole narrative history of Salvation by the covenants of Noah and Abraham and the other covenants concluded in the course of history. It is connected to the Law by the pericope of the Sinai and Deuteronomy. By Jeremiah 30–33 and parallel texts, it sums up all the prophetic promises. Inasmuch as it serves to designate the Decalogue and particularly the first commandment, it evokes the essence of the relation with God. The covenant is the site of the Torah where it unfolds in its multiple dimensions.

Naturally, at this level of the canon, widely varying theological systems do not combine into a new system. But they contribute, through the connection established between them by the common theme of the covenant, to establishing the unique situation of hearing the canonical text. The reading of the Torah in the synagogue is interrupted with the death of Moses on the threshold of the Promised Land and resumes with Genesis. The covenant is given, but its promises are not yet fulfilled. After the exile Israel will continue to live in dispersion or will return to Jerusalem, a Jerusalem that does not radiate with an eschatological light. This people has already experienced in its own body the effects of the rupture of the covenant and the ensuing malediction; it has faith in the fidelity of God and his pardon but still awaits concrete signs. Different theologies of the covenant can be attributed in this situation: 1) Deuteronomistic theology because it establishes the transgression and exposes the Torah that will be valid to the end, 2) the prophetic universalistic theology because it bears hope*, and 3) the priestly theology because it discovers the last reason of hope in the eternal fidelity of God that no human infidelity can discourage. Thus, the covenant, too, becomes an encompassing characteristic of the Hebraic canon.

There is no passage anywhere in the canon indicating that the new covenant promised for the end of time is not explicitly destined for Israel alone but extended to the peoples who come to Zion on pilgrimage. At the least, this idea appears in the use of the "formula of the covenant" with respect to other peoples besides Israel (e.g., in Is 19:25 and 25:8f.) and in the rereading of ancient texts of the Psalms, solely attested on the level of composition (e.g., Ps 25:14, 100:3).

i) Covenant in the Greek Canon. The structure is unchanged in the enlarged corpus of the Greek canon. Though the order of the books is modified under the influence of Greek models, the Pentateuch remains the base, and all the other books are only "commentaries." By evocation of motifs of the Law at the beginning (Jos 1) and end (Mal 3), they refer back to the prophetic entity. The books newly integrated into the canon contain, notably, the theory of the identity of Law and Wisdom (especially Sir 24 and Bar 4) as well as an initial systematization of the history of the foundation of Israel by seven covenants, in which the priestly element is given an important place (Sir 44–47). A similar approach is found—whatever the differences in details of arrangement—in certain Jewish authors of the period, whose writings, however, are not accepted in the canon but are considered apocryphal*—for example, the *Book of Jubilees* and the *Biblical Antiquities* of the Pseudo-Philo.

II. Judaism in the Time of Jesus

In the time of Jesus* the word *berît* had become so common that it could simply designate, as one of the various names of the "Law," traditional religion. It evoked above all the covenant of Sinai, that is, Israel's commitment to follow the Torah.

The Book of Jubilees organizes the biblical narrative around liturgy*; all the successive covenants are concluded on Shavuot (the Festival of Weeks or Pentecost), which is the "festival of the covenant."

It seems likely that this was the day on which the Essenes renewed by oath the covenant with God and the covenant between members of the community. Qumran's *Rules of the Community* describe a ritual of "entry into the covenant" (I QSI:16–II:18), a covenant that was renewed this way every year (I QDSII:19–23). In the *Damascus Document* the group is designated as the community "of the new covenant of the land of Damascus." They believed that the prophecy made in Jeremiah 31—as well as that of Ezechiel 36—had been fulfilled within the community (*see,* e.g., 1QHXVIII:25–28). But since the eschaton was still to come, the "new covenant" was not understood as a reality reserved for the end of time.

The same does not hold true for the Midrashic tradition, no doubt respected by the Pharisees of the time of Jesus. This tradition interpreted the "heart of stone" that must be replaced in the world to come by a "heart of flesh" (see Ez 36:26) as a figure of the "bad instinct" present in its own doctrine.

III. The New Testament

In the New Testament, as in Qumran, the promise of a new covenant is deemed to be already fulfilled—in Christ*, naturally—but unlike the Pharisees, the New Testament understands this covenant as simultaneously eschatological and terminal—that is, it cannot be gone beyond.

1. Tradition of the Last Supper

The tradition of the Last Supper is the heart of the theology of the new covenant. In an ancient layer of the text, Jesus, recalling Exodus 24:8, speaks of "my blood of the covenant, which is poured out for many" (Mk 14:24), or "my blood of the covenant, which is poured out for many for the forgiveness of sins" (Mt 26:28, with an allusion to Jer 31:34). A more recent layer, represented by Paul (1 Cor 11:25) and Luke (22:20), specifically designates the chalice as the "new covenant."

2. Paul

Paul presents himself as a "minister of a new covenant" (2 Cor 3:6). He knows that his ministry to the peoples (universal ministry) fulfills the promise of the coming of the Holy Spirit and the gift of a heart of flesh (2 Cor 3:3). Failure to understand this is to remain in the "old covenant" (2 Cor 3:14); the two covenants confront each other (Gal 4:24). But this terminology is the exception. The idea most often used by Paul to oppose the covenant, or "testament," as a promise made by God to Abraham is the Law (*see* Gal 3:15–18), meaning the law of Sinai. By its way of reasoning—for example, when Paul begins by asking whether it is God or man who is "in the right" *(diakaios)*—and by its way of citing the Old Testament—for example, the citation of Deuteronomy 30:12ff. in Romans 10:6–10, legitimized in the light of Deuteronomy 30:1–10—and also of forging ideas—for example, the notion of righteousness in Romans 10:3 (*see also* Dt 9:4)—Pauline* theology of the law is nourished principally by the theology of the covenant, such as it is developed in the late layers of Deuteronomy under the influence of the prophetic texts. However, Paul integrated not only Deuteronomy itself but also certain essential views of priestly theology. The commitments made in the framework of the covenant of Sinai being assimilated with the "law," the term *diathèkè* is then liberated to designate the promises made by God to the Patriarchs (Rom 9:4; Gal 3:15, 3:17; *see also* Eph 2:12). The justification of Abraham by faith* without law can be understood as an anticipation of the justification in Christ (Gal 3, 15–25; *see also* Rom 4).

Having adopted this linguistic usage and organized in that way his system of thought, Paul must necessarily ask himself if this Israel, which had rejected the message of Jesus, still took part in the covenant. He examines the question in Romans 9–11. He starts with the supposition that the covenants, *diathèkai* (Rom 9:4), belong by rights to Israel. He ends by affirming the certainty that when all other nations have been redeemed, Israel too will be admitted into the new covenant (Rom 11:25ff.), "for the gifts and the call of God are irrevocable" (Rom 11:29).

3. The Epistle to the Hebrews

The term *diathèkè* becomes a central concept in the Epistle to the Hebrews, where it appears particularly between Hebrews 7:22 and 10:16. In addition,

Jeremiah 31:31–34 is cited in Hebrews 8:8–12 and 10:16f. The epistle distinguishes between the "first" covenant and the "new" covenant, the imperfect covenant and the perfect covenant, the transitory covenant and the eternal covenant. This typology being on the level of cult, the "first covenant" may perhaps refer only to the rites established on Mount Sinai. Christ is the guarantor (Heb 7:22) and mediator (8:6, 9:14–18, 12:24) of the new covenant. By virtue of his sacrifice* (10:12–22), this covenant cancels the sins forever (9:11–15, 10:11–18), sanctifies (10:10, 10:29), and gives access to God (7:25, 10:19–22) and to "the promised eternal inheritance" (9:15ff.).

4. Nonterminological Development of the Vetero-Testimentary Theology of the Covenant

Without using the word *diathèkè,* the New Testament adopts in many other places the motifs grouped together in Jeremiah and Isaiah around the theme of the new covenant. This is true of the Johannine* writings, for example, in the first farewell speech of Jesus in John 14.

The interpretation of 1 Peter 3:21 would subsequently have a particular function. From this text—"Baptism, which corresponds to this, now saves you, not as a removal of dirt from the body but as an appeal to God for a clear conscience, through the resurrection of Jesus Christ"—it was understood that baptism* is a personal covenant with God. Luther*, for example, rendered it as, "Baptism is the covenant of a good conscience with God." This is not without verisimilitude. By taking the part for the whole, *eperôtèma* could mean the conclusion of a treaty (the ritual interrogation of the parties as to their respective obligations). The text would then refer to the vow that the baptized were asked to take in the ancient Church*. The notion of baptism as covenant was important in questions of personal piety and in the justification of the baptism of adults and Anabaptism.

IV. Christian Spirituality and Theology

1. Hermeneutics of Biblical Writings

At an early stage, the Christian canon made the distinction between the Holy* Scriptures of the "Old" and the "New" Testaments. This was based on 2 Corinthians 3:3–18, where, strictly speaking, it is only a matter of the Decalogue or, at the most, the Pentateuch. This distinction is fundamental for the hermeneutics* of a plurality of meanings in Scripture. Up to the beginnings of modern Bible science, it decisively marked the interpretation of the Bible and, moreover, theology and spirituality as a whole.

2. Spirituality and Mysticism

The expression "new covenant" used in the account of the Last Supper is central to the celebration of the Eucharist* and thus of the liturgy* as a whole; thereby the idea of the covenant could become an increasingly important factor in personal piety and the mystical experience*, particularly the nuptial mystique*. Intelligence of the primitive contents of the thought of the covenant could be maintained, at least in the Western Church, due to the fact that Saint Jerome translated the Old Testament *berît* as *foedus* and not as *testamentum.*

3. "Federal" Theology

The production of systems of theological thought centered on the idea of covenant can be attributed in particular to the Zurich reform movement. Huldrych Zwingli* early on came up against this radical wing of the new movement, which would give rise to the Anabaptist* current, prolonged in our day by the Mennonites and Huttites. The theoretical debate centered principally on the singularity or multiplicity of covenants. From there, the covenant became one of the master themes of reform theology, culminating in the "federal" theology influenced by the work of the Leyde theologian Johannes Coccejus (1603–69). With the expression "*foedus seu testamentum,*" the discussion turned around questions such as the distinction between the "*infralapsaire*" and the "*supralapsaire,*" and everything that had been treated by Scholasticism* under the heading "*lex naturae,*" "*lex vetus,*" "*lex nova.*" Broad systematic consequences followed from the number of covenants recognized and the way the different covenants mentioned in the Bible were interpreted and ranked.

Since then, this insistence on the idea of covenant has been particularly perpetuated in pietism* but also in Catholicism* by a "biblicist" vision of the story of Salvation, structured according to the various divine covenants.

It may well be that, again as a result of this "federal" theological approach, the word *covenant* has recently taken on greater importance in the dialogue between Jews and Christians. Since Pope* John Paul II spoke of the "never revoked covenant" of the Jews of our day, continuous debate has been under way to find out if Jews and Christians live under the same covenant or two distinct covenants and what the consequences on their mutual relations are.

V. Modern Bible Science

Undoubtedly modern Bible science rejects this "biblicist" theology of the covenant and contests the historical reality of most of the covenants on which it rests.

Wellhausen, for example, considers the covenant as a theological category that appeared, at the earliest, with the decline of Judaism* at the end of the royalty. A later generation of scholars thought they could bring to light an institution of covenant with traditional festivals, rituals, and texts belonging to the first times of Israel. But that construction is speculative and is now revealed to be untenable. Biblical theologies based on such hypotheses (such as those of Walter Eichrodt and Jean L'Hour) are no longer considered satisfactory.

Furthermore, scholars in Bible science realize that their vocation, above and beyond the study of historical realities, is the interpretation of texts. Consequently, the biblical theology of the covenant is subject to synchronic analysis based on canonical texts, using current methods of literary criticism. This approach, which is only at its beginnings, promises many fruitful surprises for theology. Because the covenant is a central element of biblical texts, the new perspectives will necessarily have an impact on hermeneutics as well.

• J. Coccejus (1689), "Summa doctrinae de foedere et testamento Dei," in *Opera omnia theologica, exegetica, didactica, polemica, philologica,* t. VI, Frankfurt, 49–132.

R. Kraetzschmar (1896), *Die Bundesvorstellung im Alten Testament in ihrer geschichtlichen Entwicklung,* Marburg.

P. Karge (1910), *Geschichte des Bundesgedankens im Alten Testament,* ATA 2, Munich.

W. Eichrodt (1933), *Theologie des Alten Testaments,* 3 vols., Stuttgart.

M. Noth (1940), *Die Gesetze im Pentateuch (Ihre Voraussetzungen und ihr Sinn),* SKG.G 17, 2, Halle.

G.E. Mendenhall (1955), *Law and Covenant in Israel and the Ancient Near East,* Pittsburgh.

K. Baltzer (1960), *Das Bundesformular,* Neukirchen.

W. Zimmerli (1960), "Sinaibund und Abrahamsbund," *ThZ* 16, 268–80.

A. Jaubert (1963), *La notion de l'alliance dans le judaïsme aux abords de l'ère chrétienne,* Paris.

J. L'Hour (1966), *La morale de l'alliance,* CRB 5.

U. Luz (1967), "Der alte und der neue Bund bei Paulus und im Hebräerbrief," *EvTh* 67, 318–37.

L. Perlitt (1969), *Bundestheologie im Alten Testament,* WMANT 36.

P. Beauchamp (1970), "Propositions sur l'alliance de l'Ancien Testament comme structure centrale," *RSR* 58, 161–93.

D.J. McCarthy (1972), *Old Testament Covenant: A Survey of Current Opinions,* Oxford.

M. Weinfeld (1972), *Deuteronomy and the Deuteronomic School,* Oxford, 59–157.

E. Kutsch (1973), *Verheißung und Gesetz: Untersuchungen zum sogenannten "Bund" im Alten Testament,* Berlin.

M. Weinfeld (1973), "*berît,*" *ThWAT* 1, 781–808.

P. Beauchamp (1976), *L'un et l'autre Testament: Essai de lecture,* Paris.

P. Buis (1976), *La notion d'alliance dans l'Ancien Testament,* Paris.

D.J. McCarthy (1978), *Treaty and Covenant: A Study in Form in the Ancient Oriental Documents and in the Old Testament* (New edition completely rewritten), Rome.

J.F.G. Goeters (1983), "Föderaltheologie," *TRE* 11, 246–52.

H. Frankemölle (1984), *Jahwe-Bund und Kirche Christi: Studien zu Form- und Traditionsgeschichte des "Evangeliums" nach Matthäus,* 2nd Ed., NTA 10.

E.W. Nicholson (1986), *God and His People: Covenant and Theology in the Old Testament,* Oxford.

H. Cazelles (1987), *Autour de l'Exode (Études),* SBi, 143–56, 299–309.

A.F. Segal (1987), *The Other Judaisms of Late Antiquity,* Brown Judaic Studies 127, Atlanta, 147–65.

G. Braulik (1989), "Die Entstehung der Rechtfertigungslehre in den Bearbeitungsschichten des Buches Deuteronomium: Ein Beitrag zur Klärung der Voraussetzungen paulinischer Theologie," *ThPh* 64, 321–33.

N. Lohfink (1989), *Der niemals gekündigte Bund: Exegetische Gedanken zum christlich-jüdischen Dialog,* Fribourg.

R. Rendtorff (1989), "'Covenant' as a Structuring Concept in Genesis and Exodus," *JBL* 108, 385–93.

N. Lohfink (1990), *Studien zum Deuteronomium und zur deuteronomistischen Literatur I,* SBAB 8, 53–82, 211–61, 325, 361.

E. Zenger (Ed.) (1993), *Der Neue Bund im Alten: Studien zur Bundestheologie der beiden Testamente,* QD 146.

N. Lohfink, E. Zenger (1994), *Der Gott Israels und die Völker: Untersuchungen zum Jesajabuch und zu den Psalmen,* SBS 154.

N. Lohfink (1995), "Bund als Vertrag im Deuteronomium," *ZAW* 107, 215–39.

R. Rendtorff (1995), *Die "Bundesformel": Eine exegetisch-theologische Untersuchung,* SBS 160.

NORBERT LOHFINK

See also **Bible; Canon of Scriptures; Couple; Creation; Decalogue; Grace; Israel; Law and Legislation; Liturgy; Promise; Universalism**

Creation

A. Biblical Theology

I. Vocabulary

In Hebrew, general terms—*'âsâh,* "to make"—or terms used metaphorically—*yâsad, koûn,* "to found"; *bânâh,* "to build"; *yâçâr,* "to mold"—may assume a sense close to "to create," especially when God* is the agent. But *bâra'* (48 occurrences, relatively late to appear) is the only verb specific to our concept of creation, never taking any subject other than God (suggested etymology: "to clear," "to make a clean sweep"; *see* Is 4:5 and context). Creation and conception are brought together in Isaiah 43:7 and 45:10 (*see* Ps 22:32, 102:19), favoring the polysemous *qânah* (to acquire, create, beget): Genesis 4:1, Psalms 139:13, Proverbs 8:22 (*see* 8:24f.), and Genesis 14:19. *Bâra'* is associated with "marvels" in Exodus 34:10; in Numbers 16:30, its derivative *berî'âh* (a unique occurrence) "something new" appears, and elsewhere it is juxtaposed with other words signifying "newness" (Is 48:6f., 65:17; Jer 31:22; Ps 51:12, 104:30; *see* 102:19). As early as the Septuagint and then in the New Testament, the idea of creation was expressed by *ktizein* and its derivatives (principal sense: "to found"), coupled in 2 Corinthians 5:17, Galatians 6:15, Ephesians 2:15 and 4:24, and Colossians 3:10 again with the theme of newness.

II. Location and Development of the Theme

1. Location

a) In the Old Testament. Biblical representations of creation abound, though they are too often reduced to just the one. In Genesis 1:1–2, 4 a, the action takes place within the rhythm of an inaugural time*, with the establishment of the calendar (Gn 1:14) and above all of the Sabbath. All parts of the cosmos* are made equal before the Creator. The word*, chief instrument of creation, separates, names, and blesses. The text, suggestive of a completely reworked warlike theophany* (1:2–3 a), attributes to the Creator the sentiment expressed in the hymnic formula. A synthesis (wrongly taken for a compilation) of several doctrines, the text belongs to a rhetorical genre employed in hymns of praise* in the sanctuary and in enforcing the rules of separation, particularly those concerning food (a source referred to as "priestly"). Made in the image of God, the human couple* is called on to "have dominion over...every living thing" (Gn 1:28) without eating their flesh. The reader will discover, in Genesis 9:2f., how this vegetarian diet was abolished after the Flood (see Gn 6:11ff.). These two passages come from the same source and are connected in terms of their ethical intention (violence*; animals).

Genesis 2:4b-3, 24, less pure than Genesis 1 and formally more archaic, is concerned not with the creation of the cosmos but with the harshness of the human condition. The Creator, referred to as "YHWH God," involves himself in the vicissitudes of his plan. Man is responsible. The theme of the "image of God" is dramatized: its ambiguity emerges with the voice of the serpent-tempter, who wins the struggle but not in perpetuity. The text resembles wisdom* literature and in particular the riddle genre (see 1 Kgs 10:1ff., 5:12f.).

Written during the period of exile, Deutero-Isaiah (Is 40–55) is the first document that combines the notion of creation with monotheism in a formal and didactic testimony. It sets out to hold together several different motifs in juxtaposition: creation and salvation*, cosmos and history*. In Jeremiah (10:11–16; *see* 23:23f., 27:5, 31:35, 32:17), the broadening of Israel*'s horizons (*see* Dt 4:32ff.) calls forth the theme of the creation. The Psalms* (above all the hymns) and the books of Wisdom are the classic locations of the theme. The words of praise enumerate the components of creation (Ps 104, 136, 148) or commemorate and evoke within the Temple*, center of the cosmos, its initial phase (Ps 19, 29, 93, 96–99). They culminate in the uttering of the Name* (Ps 8:2; *see* Am 4:13, 5:8). The Wisdom texts see in the permanent organization of the created order a principle that goes beyond it (Prv 3:19f., 8:22–31; Sir 1:4, 9, etc.). Ecclesiastes, for example, often takes its inspiration from Genesis 1–3 (Sir 16:26–17, 14; 33:7–15; 39:12–40, 11; 42:15–43, 33; 49:16). Job, faced with the misfortune of the just man, describes the creatures which surpass mankind. The Song of Songs contrasts the meaning of creation with idolatory* and illustrates the "end of the wise" through the perspective of a "renewed" creation, with a typological rereading of Exodus.

b) The New Testament. Romans 1:18–32 sets out four concepts: the refusal of the message of creation, idolatry, the corruption of sex and (1:31) of the heart, and the unity of human destiny. Classical pronouncements are restated, but the texts that associate Christ* with the act of creation are of later origin.

2. Development

The texts that integrate the most elements relating to the idea of creation do not pre-date the exile. Our knowledge of the chronology of the Psalms is particularly deficient. The core elements of Genesis 2–3 may go back well into the period of the monarchy. A distinction must be made between the dates of the texts themselves and those of the traditions* they incorporate. For example, the attribution to Melchizedek, the Canaanite priest-king of Salem, of a cult* of "God Most High, possessor of heaven and earth" *(qonéh)* (Gn 14:19; *see* Ps 124:8, 134:3) preserves vestiges of beliefs older than Israel (the *'l qn 'rs* ["God the creator," or "owner," of the "earth," or of the "land"?] of Karatepe in Phoenicia took the form *El-ku-ni-ir-sha* among the Hittites). In short, what is late to appear is not so much the belief in a creator God as the combination of this concept with the others.

III. Israel's Neighbors

Long before the existence of Israel, every variation of the creation theme was represented in the Near East, sometimes in magnificent works. Indeed, Israel itself was a people* of composite origin and therefore well placed to embrace a diversity of currents. Traces of cultural infiltration remain, as do those of a vigorous backlash. Considering only a few themes, we may note that creation often proceeds by means of a gesture that separates the intermingled elements or strikes the waters. In Mesopotamia the *Enuma elish* (11th century B.C.) told of the struggle of Marduk, sun god and godson, against Tiamat (Hebrew Tehôm: Gn 1:2), who was split in two, and Apsu. The origin of mankind was explained in various ways: man was created to do the gods' work for them and sustain them with offerings, or else he was molded from clay and the blood of a god. At Ugarit (a port in the north of Canaan), Baal, the sun god, struck the sea with a club made by the Kushar-wa-Hasis, the twin divine craftsmen. For the Canaanite world, however, creation was achieved above all through the vital energy (Cunchillos, *Creation in the Ancient Near East*) of sex, a view not unrelated to that of the Egyptians. In Egypt, Shu, or breath, was held to have separated the sky and the earth, but the theme of combat hardly appeared: the principal deity brought himself into existence and produced the earth from his own substance. Maât, the goddess of cosmic order, was present at the creation. In all the ancient cultures creation and providence* were seen in the same light.

IV. The Act of Creation

1. Its Objects

The created object is often partial: a mountain (Ps 78:54 [Dahood Bib 46, 1965]), a people (Ps 74:2; Is 43:1, 7, 15, etc.), a city* (Is 65:18), an institution, or living things (Gn 2:5–25). The origin of the human body is one of the points at which the idea of creation is associated with the experience of a manifestation without a proportionate cause (Ps 139:13f.; Jb 10:8f.; 2 Macc 7:22; *see* Prv 30:18f.). That which inspires praise is not merely the simultaneous creation of "heaven and earth" but the uniting of power and compassion in one act (Ps 147:32). The Creator himself feels love* and compassion for what he makes (Wis 11:23f.; Sir 18:13). The creative act even finds its consummation in the "creation" of a new (Ps 51:12) and converted (Jer 31:22) heart. It is no accident that a sense of the vastness of the cosmos and a penetration to the core of ethics* come together in writings of the same period. Israel's return to grace* is the heart of the creation: while it is compared to a resurrection* (Is 26:19; *see* 66:14), it is also represented as a scene of creation (Ez 37).

2. Its Forms

The image of creation as combat is to be found in Isaiah 27:1 and 51:9f. and Psalms 74:12–17, 89:10–13, 104:7, and so on, which call to mind the archaic cosmogonies. This motif, though resembling other mythologies, maintains its originality by reserving victory to a single God. What is more, it links the progress of salvation to the beginning of time. On the other hand, the artisanal conception is a peaceful one. The artisan, for example, is also a builder (Jb 38:4–7). In this context the solidity of the created work is perceived by the heart as a promise*: the earth "will not move" (Ps 93:1f., 96:10, 104:5). The making of idols is regarded as a parody of the creative act (Is 41:7; Sg 13:16). The idea of creation fits comfortably into the sphere of wisdom, which is celebrated in terms not only of skill but also of speech; and the nature of speech raises the question of origins. God, who creates with or "in" wisdom (Jer 10:12; Ps 104:24; Prv 3:19f.) or "by" wisdom (Wis 9:2), also creates while speaking (Ps 33:6–9, 147:4f., 15–18, 148:5f.) or even "by" speech (Wis 9:1). God's intimate relationship to his speech and his wisdom (Wis 8:3, 9:9f.) suggests the metaphor of conception (Prv 8:22), so opening the way for the New Testament texts that unite the Son of God and his speech in the creative act. A creation by means of speech comes close to a creation of everything out of nothing—an idea rarely expressed though presupposed in Proverbs 8:22–31 and clearly detectable in 2 Macc 7:28 (*see* Rom 4:17; but *see* Wis 11:17).

It is not surprising that, according to the Bible*, the concept of creation should be apprehended both by reason* (Rom 1:20) and by faith* (Heb 11:3). In the Old Testament, the choice* of a people by YHWH and the creation of the universe are gradually revealed as distinct but inseparable in the action of a single God. The action proceeds from his singularity, from his sanctity, and, paradoxically, from what is most incommunicable in him. The identity of God the creator with God the savior prepares the way for those texts—among the latest written of the New Testament—in which creation, the basis of a universal relationship with God, proceeds by way of the Unique: Christ (Col 1:16), the Son (Heb 1:2), or the Word* (Jn 1:3; *see* Rev 3:14). In him, creation is to be recognized as the first and last word of a God who takes up the narrative* of his acts under his Name.

• Edited works on biblical texts and their environment:
H. Gunkel (1895), *Schöpfung und Chaos in Urzeit und Endzeit: Eine religionsgeschichtliche Untersuchung über Genesis 1 und Ap Joh 12,* Göttingen (3rd Ed., 1910).
G. von Rad (1936), *Das theologische Problem des alttestamentlichen Schöpfungsglaubens,* in *Wesen und Werden des AT,* BZAW 66, Berlin, 138–47 (= [1971], *Gesammelte Studien zum AT,* t. 1, Munich, 136–47).
W.H. Schmidt (1964), *Die Schöpfungsgeschichte der Priesterschrift: zur Überlieferungsgeschichte von Genesis 1, 1–2, 4 a,* Neukirchen-Vluyn (3rd Ed., 1973).
P. Beauchamp (1969), *Création et séparation: Étude exégétique du ch. premier de la Genèse,* Paris.
Coll. (1970), *Les religions du Proche-Orient asiatique,* Paris.
C. Westermann (1974), *Genesis, Kapitel 111,* Neukirchen-Vluyn (English trans. Minneapolis, 1984).
L. Strauss (1981), "On the Interpretation of Genesis," *L'Homme, Revue française d'anthropologie,* 21, 5–20.
B.W. Anderson (Ed.) (1984), *Creation in the Old Testament,* Philadelphia.
L. Derousseaux (1987) (Ed.), *La Création dans l'Orient ancien: Congrès de l'ACFEB* (1985), Paris.
J. Bottéro, S.N. Kramer (1989), *Lorsque les dieux faisaient l'homme,* Paris (report: M.-J. Seux [1991], *Or* 60, 354–62).
H. Cazelles (1989), *La Bible et son Dieu,* Paris, 89–96.
S. Chandler (1992), "When the World Falls Apart: Methodology for Employing Chaos and Emptiness as Theological Constructs," *HThR* 95, 467–549.

PAUL BEAUCHAMP

See also **Adam; Animals; Cosmos; Couple; Ecology; Filiation; Monotheism; Myth; Temple; Verbe; Word; Word of God**

B. Historical and Systematic Theology

1. Antiquity

The primitive Church* inherited a faith* in God* the creator and so did not need to define the doctrine of the creation. Indeed, this was present from the first baptismal formulae, which profess faith in the "all-powerful Father*" *(pantôkrator).*

This phrase implicitly contains the idea of creation, both as noun and as adjective ("All-powerfulness ...signifies that by his power...God made the universe from nothing" [fifth or sixth century, BSGR, §227]; "the doctrine of creation expresses in the clearest manner...what the words 'All-powerful Father' already said" [Barth*, *Credo,* section IV]). The Father is inseparably creator of the world and Father of Jesus Christ, as the invocation of Polycarp (end of the first century/beginning of the second) emphasizes: "All-powerful Saviour..., Father of Jesus Christ..., God of the angels*, of the powers and of all creation" (*Martyrdom* of Polycarp* 14, 1, SC 10 *bis*). Polycarp's formula is notable for expressing directly the unity of divine action—the fact that it is at once creative and salvific—something that remains to this day a subject of theological comment.

a) Clarification of the Doctrine. However, this formula remained to be clarified. Its meaning could not be regarded as self-evident in a world where the cosmos* was generally represented either as derived from the One by a process of necessary emanation or as due to the organization of uncreated matter by a demiurge like that of the *Timaeus*—powerful no doubt, but not all-powerful, and not always good, as in the case of the

Demiurge of Gnosticism*. Nor was this a secondary matter but rather the "first and most fundamental point"—prior even to the notion of salvation*: "the Divine Creator who made the sky and the earth and all that they contain" (Irenaeus*, *Adv. Haer* II, 1, 1). So, as early as the second century, the church fathers*, in particular Irenaeus in his struggle against gnostic dualism, took up the task of defining the doctrine. The essential idea was that the "demiurge" of the universe—a title widely applied from the outset to God and/or Christ* (e.g., 1 Clem. 59, 2 [SC 167]; Justin, *Ap.* I, 13; Tatian [c. 160], *Ad Graecos* 45, PTS, 1995; Origen* in *Jo.* I, 19, §110 [SC 120]; formulae from baptismal or local rituals in BSGR, §26, 30, 131, 153, 204)—was the creator of the very matter that he organized, its "inventor," to summarize Irenaeus (*Adv. Haer.* II, 7, 5; 10, 4), and that he was not a lesser god but the trinitarian God himself (*see Haer* IV, 20, the first clear expression of the Trinity* as creator [Kern 1967]). The attribution to the Father was "natural" inasmuch as he was the origin (*ST* Ia, q. 45, a. 6, ad 2; see Balthasar*, Com[F] 1988, 16–17). This fundamental point of the creation of the very matter of the world would be upheld even by those theologians closest to emanationism, such as Pseudo-Dionysius*: "As every being proceeds from the Good*, so matter proceeds from it also" (*Divine Names* IV, 28), and even if it is "by an overflowing of his own essence that God produces all essences," he remains no less "transcendent" of all the beings which proceed from him (*Divine Names* V, 8).

b) Creation Ex Nihilo. This clarification culminated in the celebrated formulation of creation *ex nihilo* or *de nihilo,* which was already present in Scripture* (*see* above A IV 2), and remains widespread to this day in all denominations (*see,* e.g., Barth 1949; Tillich 1953; Lossky 1944; CEC 296–97). The phrase from Hermas's *Shepherd* (SC 53), "you made all things pass from nothingness* to being*" (*ek tou mè ontos,* Mand. I, 1), was often taken up by the fathers (from Irenaeus, *Adv. Haer* IV, 20, 2 to John of Damascus, eighth century, *De fide orthodoxa* II, 5, PG 94, 880), and the expression was generally adopted in the second century (Irenaeus, loc. cit.; Theophilus of Antioch, *A Autolycus* II, 4, SC 20), thus entering common and liturgical usage ("You have drawn all things from nothingness into existence, by your only Son...": *Apostolic constitutions,* VIII, 12, 7, SC 336). Augustine*, who produced five commentaries on Genesis, also used it (*de nihilo,* e.g., in *Gen. ad litt. imperf.* I, 2, PL 34, 221; *Conf.* XII, 7) against Manichaeism and Neoplatonist emanationism. Against Manichaeism he argues that since there exists only one creative principle, so matter comes from God and is therefore good, just like its maker. On a rather different front he opposes emanationism by stating that the being of the world does not derive necessarily from the being of God since no evolution can be allowed in God. Certainly, everything exists only because he exists—*quid enim est, nisi quia tu es?* (*Conf.* XI, 5)—but nothing exists other than by his free choice. By means of his Word*, God gives rise to the universe (*Conf.* XI, 6–7), including time*, that which defines the material, perhaps even the created, condition: "There was no time before God created time" (*Gen. contra man.* I, 2, 3, PL 34, 174; *Conf.* XI, 13), and neither was there space (*Conf.* XI, 5).

The expression was intended to present as the least objectionable a type of origin that had never before been conceived and that, more than any other, resisted representation. If God derived creation neither from some preexistent matter (which would imply dualism) or from his own substance (which would imply pantheism*), he must have created "from nothing." This "nothing" was not the mythical expression of a something, a name given to some formless matter or substrate of the world—an interpretation not excluded by the "earth without form and void" of Genesis 1, 2. Tertullian* writes of those who still believe that the world was made out of some matter and not *ex nihilo* (*Adv. Marc.* II, 5, 3, CChr.SL 1, 480)—and see Justin (creation "from formless matter," *Ap* I, 10) and possibly Clement of Alexandria (*Strom.* V, 14, 89; 6; 90, 1, SC 279). This point had constantly to be reiterated since it contradicted a fundamental conception (*see,* e.g., Anselm*, *Monologion* 8; Thomas* Aquinas, *De pot.* III, I, ad 7; *see ST* Ia, q. 45, a. 1, ad 3; Breton 1993, 144). Creation *ex nihilo* signified that being was God's free gift. It derived from an excess *(hyperbolè)* of goodness on his part (John of Damascus, *De fide orth.,* PG 94, 863) and not from some need in him. But the fact that creation was not necessary meant also that it was not a degradation of the divine. The world was not a "here below fallen from some unknown disaster" but a precious world because willed: a free and gracious gift. In Julian of Norwich's paradoxical vision (14th century), the world is tiny, like a hazelnut in the palm of the hand, but also solid and durable "because God loves it" (*Revelations of Divine Love* 5).

By the end of antiquity, *ex nihilo* had become a technical term to characterize accounts of creation (*see* Meginhard of Fulda's profession of faith, ninth century: the Holy* Spirit is not created because it is not *ex nihilo—neque factus, quia non ex nihilo, BSGR,* §245).

2. The Middle Ages Up until the 13th Century

a) Before the 12th Century. Before the 12th century, Latin theology* contributed nothing new that was of any significance to the idea of creation. Historians (Scheffzyck 1963; Grossi 1995) agree that, within the context of the Augustinian Platonism*, which served as a model before Aristotle (Christian Aristotelianism*) became current, there were two tendencies. One tendency understood the creation as the beginning of the history* of salvation (especially in the school of Saint*-Victor), while the other approached it more philosophically (above all in the school of Chartres*), though Anselm (*Mon.* 6–14) should also not be forgotten.

b) Peter Lombard and Lateran IV. Between the second half of the 12th century and the beginning of the 13th, the main elements of a clear doctrine of creation were established by Peter Lombard's (c. 1100–1160) account in his second book of *Sentences* and the dogmatic* definition of the creation by the Fourth Lateran* Council* (1215). According to Peter Lombard (*Sent.,* d. 1), there was a single creator of time* (contrary to Aristotle's notion of the eternity of the world, d. 2) and of all things visible and invisible, and he was the one Creator. He was the only one, indeed, who "makes something from nothing" (a clear distinction between *facere* and *creare*), as opposed to Plato's demiurge *(artifex)*—see also Bonaventure*'s formula: "Plato commended his soul* to its maker *(factori),* but Peter* commended his to its Creator *(creatori)*" (*Hexaemeron* IX, 24). God created freely, through goodwill and not from necessity, because he wished to communicate his beatitude* to others beside himself (*Sent.,* d. 3). And since this beatitude could be shared in only by means of intelligence, God created creatures possessed of reason (angels* and human beings), able to apprehend the sovereign good by intelligence, to love it as they apprehend it, to possess it as they love it, and to enjoy it as they possess it (d. 4).

As for Lateran IV, it reiterated, against the Cathars (Catharism*) that there was only "one single creative principle," God in three persons*, "who by his all-powerfulness created spiritual and corporeal creatures *de nihilo,* at the beginning of time" (*ab initio temporis utramque de nihilo,* the first use of the phrase by the magisterium*, *condidit creaturam, spiritualem et corporalem*). In this way, the council insisted on the goodness of creation.

3. From the 13th Century to the End of the Middle Ages

a) Exitus-Reditus. These ideas were so clear that the great theologians of the 13th century, Bonaventure and Thomas Aquinas in particular, were able to set their theology of creation firmly in the context of the "emergence" of beings from their principle and their "return" to this principle—*exitus-reditus* (Aquinas, I *Sent.,* d. 2 *divisio textus*) or *egressus-regressus* (Bonaventure, I *Sent.,* d. 37, p. 1, a. 3, q. 2, c.)—and to use the whole vocabulary of emanation (*emanatio, processio, diffusio, exitus, fluxus,* and so on) without the slightest equivocation. This had not been the case for John the Scot Eriugena (c. 810—c. 877). This Neoplatonic scheme, modified since antiquity by the concepts of divine liberty* and the economy of salvation (*see* Irenaeus), was developed still further by the attempt to consider creation as something embedded in the very life of the Trinity (Bonaventure, *Hex.* VIII, 12; *Breviloquium* II, 1, 2, e.g.; Aquinas, *ST* Ia, 45, 6). Creation was certainly a result of divine goodness—according to the Dionysian principle, taken up throughout the Middle Ages, that "goodness diffuses itself"—but of a goodness that decided to communicate itself and that would not be diminished if it did not communicate itself (Aquinas, *De pot.* III, a. 15, ad 1; a. 17, ad 1, ad 7). The sovereignty of the divine initiative with respect to the creation was absolutely safeguarded as a theological principle and therefore also its sovereignty with respect to the economy of salvation, of which the creation was at once the first moment and the abiding condition. In spite of the importance of the philosophical means employed, this was certainly a theological approach to creation. "The emanation of all that exists" from God, "that is what we call creation" (*ST* Ia, q. 45, a. 1). But this "emanation" was not some initial impulse in which the cause then lost interest. Rather, it set in motion what we might call a dynamic of return (*circulatio, regiratio,* Aquinas, I *Sent.*, d. 14, q. 2, a. 2), so strongly desired by God that he made himself flesh to enable it to come about.

God became incarnate to make this return possible since it had been rendered impossible by sin*: this at least Aquinas's opinion on the question of the motive for the Incarnation* (IIIa, q. 1, a. 3). Would the Word have made himself incarnate even if humankind had not sinned? Some theologians claimed as much, so as to endow the universe with a perfection worthy of the Creator's glory*. This opinion was generally characteristic of the "Franciscan school," but the first to formulate it was apparently Rupert of Deutz (c. 1075—c. 1130) (Scheffczyk 1963). It recurs in the work of Alexander of Hales (c. 1186—1245), *Summa halensis* IV, n. 23 a. Robert Grosseteste (c. 1175—1253) adverts to it with a characteristic formula: "There would have been no completion of the natural order if God had not made himself man" (*non esset... consummatio in rerum naturis nisi Deus esset homo, Hexaemeron,* ed. R.C. Dales, London 1982, 276). Duns* Scotus treats of it in a systematic way (*Lectio parisiensis in*

Sent. III, d. 7, q. 3 and 4). Bonaventure thought it possible, in qualified terms, though he preferred redemption as a motif for the Incarnation (III *Sent.,* d. 1, a. 2, q. 2). *See also* Nicholas* of Cusa, Suarez* (Scheffczyk), Malebranche (*Entretiens métaphysiques* 9), and Schleiermacher* (according to Barth, *Credo,* section IV, 37). Aquinas initially considered both assumptions tenable (III *Sent.,* d. 1, q. 1, a. 3) but finished by rejecting the "Franciscan" view, basing his opinion essentially on scriptural arguments while yet admitting that it was in itself possible (IIIa, q. 1, a. 3). But "it was sufficient for the perfection of the universe that creation should be naturally (*naturali modo*) ordered towards God as to its proper end" (ad. 2).

b) Bonaventure. Bonaventure departed from the classical position: "The whole machine of the world *(universitas machinae mundialis)* was brought into being by a single sovereign principle, in time and from nothing *(ex tempore et de nihilo)*" (*Brev.* II, 1, 1). *Ex tempore* since creation supposes a beginning in time: it is contradictory to speak of the eternity of a created world (ibid., q. 2; *Hex.* VI, 4). The creation is known only by means of revelation* (II Sent., d. 1, q. 1, a. 3) and is revealed only with salvation in mind. Scripture speaks of creation *(de opere conditionis)* only with a view to "reparation" (*propter opus reparationis, Brev.* II, 5, 8; see ibid., 2). It is made only to lead human beings to God: the world is like a book in which the creating Trinity shines forth (*Brev.* II, 12, 1). But one must know how to read this book, not taking it literally (*Hex.* II, 20) by attending merely to things since these are above all "vestiges" (traces*) of the Creator—*umbrae, resonantiae, picturae, vestigia, simulacra, spectacula,* and so on (*Itinerary.* II, 11)—in short, signs of God. What is important is to pass "from the sign to the signified" (ibid.).

c) Thomas Aquinas. Two points characterize Aquinas's concept of creation: the radical contingency of its creatures and the definition of creation as a relationship. The first point is made clear in the way in which he treats the problem of the eternity of the world. We know that Aquinas judged its noneternity impossible to prove (*ST* Ia, 46, 2). Creation in the strict sense of a beginning in time (*novitas mundi, see De pot.* III, 3, ad 6; Ia, 45, 3, ad 3) is known only through revelation (Ia, 46, 2) and thus by faith (a position for which Barth would be grateful to him, *KD* III/1, 2) even if the general dependence of things on the first Cause is accessible to reason* (Ia, q. 46, a. 2, 1). But to say, anyway, that an "eternal" world would be a created one (*nomen creationis potest accipi cum novitate, vel sine, De pot.* III, 3, ad 6) is a way of highlighting the contingency of every possible world. The duration of this world makes no difference, even if the fact of having a beginning expresses it better in the eyes of creatures who are themselves temporal (*De pot.* III, 17, ad. 8). In any case, an indefinite duration would have nothing in common with the eternity* of the Creator, which does not involve succession (Ia, q. 46, a. 2, ad 5), as Boethius* (cited by Aquinas) and Augustine (*Conf.* XI, 14) had already observed. This contingency stems from the fact that the created being is entirely relative, in the literal sense of existing only by its relationship to the Creator. Creation is defined by the relation of things to their source, is indeed no more than this relation (*ST* Ia, q. 45, a. 3; see q. 13), and without this relation the created being is nothing; *see* the emphatic wording of the *De aeternitate mundi:* the creature has no being other than that which is given to it *(nisi ab alio);* left to itself and considered in itself, it is nothing *(nihil est);* nothingness is more natural to it than being *(unde prius naturaliter est sibi nihilum quam esse)* (*see* Ia IIae, q. 109, a. 2, ad 2).

There is no continued creation (Ia, q. 45, a. 3, ad 3, e.g.): one and the same divine action creates and keeps in being a creature that exists only by its constant relationship to God (*semper refertur ad Deum, De pot.* III, 3, ad 6; *see* Ia, q. 104, a. 1, ad 4; *CG* III, 65; *De pot.* V, a. 1, ad 2). But by the same token, this creature exists fully since God gives being ceaselessly and in superabundance—so much so that paradoxically (and this is the very paradox of the analogy* of being, e.g., Przywara 1932), this vision of radical contingency is also a vision of the being of beings and of the richness of their existence in actuality. To deny the consistency, the autonomy, or the "perfection" of creatures is to insult the Creator (*detrahere perfectioni divinae virtutis, CG* III, 69). It was with good reason that Chesterton saw Aquinas as "Saint Thomas of the Creator."

d) The Later Middle Ages. Even though the later Middle Ages were far from being a period of intellectual decline, it must be admitted that they witnessed some "decline" (Scheffczyk 1963) in the theology of creation, inasmuch as the separation of faith and reason was emphasized and creation was seen as a matter of pure faith. It was dependent on God's incomprehensible omnipotence: as Duns Scotus saw it, there would have been no contingency in the world without contingency in divine causality itself (*nisi prima causa ponatur... contingenter causare, Opus oxoniense* I, d. 39, q. unica, no. 14). With Ockham's nominalism*, the link between God and the world was "loosened in the extreme" (Scheffczyk) since there was no longer any exemplary causality, and God, in an absolute freedom limited only by the principle of contradiction, brought into being entirely new creatures unrelated to any essence.

4. The Modern Era

a) The Reformation. The Reformation did not call into question the dogma* of creation, which had been reaffirmed at the end of the Middle Ages by the Council* of Florence*. Melanchthon is the most traditional of the reformers in the way he presents faith in the creation ("God, the Father of Our Saviour Jesus Christ, with the Son... and the Holy Spirit, created from nothing the sky and the earth, angels and men and all that is corporeal," *Loci praec. theologici*) and in his manner of finding the "traces of God" *(vestigia Dei)* everywhere in nature, which is made, "created," in order to "reveal God." According to Calvin* (*Inst.* 1, 14), what the Scriptures say about the creation is sufficient, and it is neither "permissible" nor "expedient" to speculate on the question. For Luther*, it is both important (e.g., *WA* 24, 18, 26–27) and difficult (ibid., 29–33; *see WA* 39/2, 340) to believe in the creation. He gives this faith an existential tone: it begins with the belief that we can do nothing by our own power, so dependent are we on God (*WA* 24, 18, 32–33; 43, 178, 42–179, 1). Moreover, it is a matter for all individuals on their own account—see the formula of the Catechism, "I believe that God created me, along with every creature" (*WA* 30/1, 183, 32–33 and 247, 20–21; 293, 15–16). In fact God draws each person ceaselessly from nothingness (e.g., *WA* 12, 441, 6) by the power* of a truly creative Word: "The words of God are realities, not mere words" (*res sunt, non nuda vocabula, WA* 42, 17, 24), and each person is a word or a syllable of the divine language (loc. cit., 19). *See* Bonaventure's "every creature is a word of God" (Bonaventure*, III, 1, b) and Aquinas, *ST* Ia, q. 37, a. 2: "the Father uttered by his Word... himself and his creatures" *(se et creaturam) //* Ia, q. 34, a. 3; *Quodl* IV, q. 4, a. 6. On the theme of creation and speech, *see* Kern (1967).

b) The 17th and 18th Centuries. The modern period saw the theme of creation slip from the hands of the theologians: they either lost interest in it—in the 18th century, for example, the Carmelites of Salamanca did not comment on the treatise on creation in *ST* "since this question is not generally dealt with in the schools" (*Cursus theologicus,* Proemium, §IV)—or, like Suarez, regarded it as a matter more philosophical than theological. In the 18th century the question of creation belonged to the field of philosophy*: Descartes*, Malebranche, and Leibniz* each had his own concept of it. One of the most interesting was undoubtedly that of Leibniz, who visualized the monads being born "from continual lightning-flashes of Divinity" (*Monadologie,* §47); but the idea of the best of worlds and the principle of sufficient reason would undergo a degeneration (by way of thc work of Wolff [1679–1754]) in Enlightenment theology, which combined an optimism often worthy of Pangloss with a rudimentary understanding of causality. This is evident, for example, in W. Paley's (1743–1805) *Natural* Theology* (1802): since there is no clock without a clockmaker (I), so nature, in which a universal adaptation of means to ends may be seen, especially among living things, cannot be without an "intelligent creator" (III, 75, and passim). Paley thus proposes a "cause" for the world "perfectly adequate" in its effect (XXVII, 408), without being aware that he is at best proving the existence of an "architect of the world" and "not a creator of the world" (Kant*, *KrV,* AA, III, 417). This "cause," uniquely efficient though of a purely constructive efficiency and fulfilling (albeit badly) the simple role of explaining the realities of nature, was the first in a long line of unequivocal statements of reality. Such a cause, which may doubtless also be discerned in the degenerate forms of the cosmological argument (proofs of the existence* of God), is practically worthless and theologically meaningless since the image of God the clockmaker has nothing to do with the Creator of which the Bible* speaks. This notion of causality, which became widespread at this period, reveals the impoverishment of ideas about the creation in the official theologies of the different denominations during the 18th century. The situation was scarcely to improve in the 19th century in spite of some timid efforts (*see* Scheffczyk).

We can see here a mistrust of the category of cause that remains strong to this day, with many theologians joining Heidegger* in bemoaning the "tendency" of "the Catholic theology of creation to rationalize" (unpublished text cited in coll., *Heidegger et la question de Dieu,* Paris, 1980). "A 'supreme cause' *(Weltgrund)* has nothing in common with the all-powerful Father confessed by the Christian faith" (Barth*, *KD* III/1, §40, 10; *see Grundriß* VIII, 59), especially when the relation of causality is actually conceived as existing within this world (Ratzinger 1964; Rahner 1976; Moltmann 1985). W. Kern (1967), on the other hand, advocates a reconsideration of causality.

5. The 19th Century

This impoverishment had two main effects. First, as in the 17th century, it left the field open to philosophy, which held sway over discussion of the creation in the 19th century. The concept underwent some remarkable developments in the great romantic idealist theories of Schelling* and Hegel*, whether in terms of a fall from or into the Absolute, of the advent of liberty in itself, of a creative fission in God, or of the dialectical unfolding of the Idea. For all their philosophical grandeur, these "detheologized theologies" (Przywara 1932) are hard to distinguish from pantheism*, particularly in view of their confusion between the Spirit of God and spirit pure and simple (in other words, really, the human spirit). Feuerbach (1804–72) clearly suspected as much: "The true meaning of theology is anthropology*" (preface to the second edition of *L'essence du christianisme*). And while "God is the essence of man," creation *ex nihilo* (I, 9, and Appendix, X–XI) is merely a projection of man's belief in his omnipotence and his desire to control nature, the means by which he sets himself up as "the goal and the savior of the world" (XI).

Next, theology found itself helpless before the new problems posed by biblical criticism (exegesis*) and the theory of evolution, with their questioning of the creation narratives* in Genesis 1–3. Certainly, faith in the creation was firmly upheld in the Catholic Church by the definitions of Vatican* I, but this was primarily in opposition to the philosophical currents of the period. The first chapter of the constitution *Dei Filius* actually repeats the definitions of Lateran IV, adding an explicit affirmation, in the face of the modern forms of monism and emanationism (can. 4, *DS* 3024), of the liberty of creation (*liberrimo consilio... de nihilo condidit creaturam, DS* 3002) and of the distinction between God and the world (*re et essentia a mundo distinctus;* ibid.). All this may have safeguarded the idea of the creation, but it said nothing of the relationship between myth* and history and left unsolved the question of how and to what extent the idea of creation can be distinguished from the images that transmit it. The world of faith was becoming parallel to that of the sciences*, bringing the danger either of a double truth* or of a continual alternation between materialist positivism and creationism (*see* Traducianism*) on the one hand and fundamentalism* on the other. And this problem persists today, at least in terms of public opinion, which does not clearly distinguish between faith in the creation and creationism.

It should be added that, from this point of view, the doctrine of creation was now only vaguely connected with the history of salvation. The creation was among the "preludes to faith," truths accessible in principle to human reason (this is implicit in the texts of Vatican I—explicitly, it is the existence of God as deduced from created things that is so considered, *DS* 3004 and 3026; *see DThC* III/3, 2192). It was not made explicitly part of the economy of salvation and so was in danger of being taken as that first moment with which one need no longer be concerned.

6. The 20th Century

a) Karl Barth. It is easy to understand Barth's protest against the idea that the first article of the Creed is a sort of "gentiles' lobby" where "natural theology can be given free rein" (*Grundriß* VIII, 55, 58). For him, on the contrary, the creation is known only through revelation (for which reason the "doctrine of creation" in *KD* III is presented as a commentary on Gn 1–3). Creation was essentially a divine act that initiated the history of salvation. It was the precondition of the covenant*, its "external foundation" (*KD* III/1, §41, 2), performed so as to render it possible; and the covenant in turn was the "internal foundation" of the creation (ibid., §41, 3) since it determined the nature of the creature desired by God's freely given love*. This reintegration of the creation into the history of salvation, this reunion of protology and eschatology*, gave the doctrine back its religious meaning, which explains Barth's enormous influence from this standpoint, even on Catholic theology (e.g., Ratzinger [1964] is very Barthian and acknowledges his formulation on the relationship between creation and covenant (*LThK2* 463; *see CEC* §288).

b) A Crisis in the Doctrine of Creation? The isolation of the doctrine of creation from all "natural theology," however, cut it off from all the speculative efforts of the centuries (which were also attempts to reach an understanding of faith), with the result that the theology of creation was once again impoverished. The overemphasis of the theme of salvation actually had the effect of devaluing that of the creation (a "contraction" already visible in the Roman liturgy* of antiquity, as Hamann [1968] points out), all the more so because it was often accompanied by an almost exclusive concern for an earthly salvation for humankind. A number of conventional discourses on "the God of the Exodus" as opposed to the God of the creation have revealed a lack of interest in the creation on the part of theologians. This is evidenced in essays that ask questions such as, "The creation, an outdated doctrine?" (*Études,* August–September 1981, 247–61) or "Should we be interested in the creation?" (*ETR* 1989, 64/1, 59–69). The apparent lack of interest is also evident in certain aspects of the reception* of Vatican* II. Without explicitly dealing with the subject, the council had developed in GS (chap. III) "a veritable theology of the creation" (Théobald 1993), implementing a very clear "anthropocentric bias" as compared with the ancient position (*see* GS, no. 12, §1) and defining mankind's activity as the "prolonging of the Creator's work" (no. 34, §2). This point of view, which allowed a positive conception of technology and more generally of mankind's role in history, as "a reflection of the creative act" (Breton 1993; Ratzinger 1964, qualified in Ratzinger 1968), certainly did not imply a contempt for the cosmos or an actual acosmism in the spirit of the council, though it appears that it has sometimes been interpreted in this way. It gave rise to an insistence on human creativity, as an image of a divine creativity that is, however, put in parentheses (Ganoczy 1976; on this subject, see the uneven but profound work of Berdiaev 1914). It also brought about a neglect or dwindling of the role of the creation in the catechetics* of the Churches: *see* S. Jaki (1980, 56; "the most neglected dogma in the Creed"), Ch. Schönborn (*Com(F)* XIII/3, 18–34), or Ratzinger (1986, English tr., appendix, 1995), who saw clearly that this led to a conception of God unrelated to matter, a negation of the fact that the true name of nature is creation, a neglect, indeed, of the world's horizon, which could not be without consequences for anthropology. The environmental movement, with all its excesses, has had the virtue of bringing back attention, however brutally, to the existence of the cosmos. The simplistic formulae that replace humankind's domination of the created world with "stewardship," or the standpoint of Moltmann (1985), who subordinates the "relevance" of faith in the creation to the solutions it offers to the ecological crisis, are hardly satisfactory; yet the critical function of environmentalism deserves to be taken seriously.

The pluralism of contemporary theological research makes it difficult to generalize, but a number of strands suggest that a better equilibrium is being reached: a better understanding of biblical narratives, a dying down of the controversies over evolution, a movement beyond the futile attempts to reconcile Scripture with science, the reasonable desire for a measure of intellectual unity that would take science seriously without turning it into a theological authority (Peacocke 1979; Pannenberg 1986; Polkinghorne 1988; *see* Fantino 1991, 1994), and above all a reintegration of the creation into the history of salvation, without its being absorbed therein (e.g., *Creation and Salvation,* 1989). After all, the creation has never been preached as mere knowledge but rather as a means of (re)introducing people to a relationship (Hamann 1968) that is the origin and end of the human individual: "Thou shalt love Him that created Thee" (*Epistle of Barnabas,* chap. XIX).

• Augustine, *De civitate dei* XI, BAug 35.

Augustine, *De genesi contra manicheos,* PL 34, 173–220.

Augustine, *De genesi ad litteram liber imperfectus,* PL 34, 220–46.

Augustine, *De genesi ad litteram,* BAug 48–49.

Augustine, *Confessions* XI–XIII, BAug 14.

K. Barth, *Credo,* Munich, 1935.

K. Barth, *KD* III/1–4, *Die Lehre der Schöpfung,* 1945–51.

K. Barth, *Dogmatik in Grundriß,* Munich, 1949, chap. VIII.

Bonaventure, *Breviloquium,* l. II; *Itinerarium mentis in Deum; In Hexaemeron.*

Conciles: Lateran IV (1215), *DS* 800; Florence (1442), *DS* 1333; Vatican I (1870), Constitution *Dei Filius,* cap. 1, *DS* 3001–3, et can. 1–5, *DS* 3021–25.

Hugues de Saint-Victor, *De sacramentis christianae fidei* I, 1 a, 2 a, 5 a, 6 a, PL 176, 187–216; 246 C—288 A.

Iraeneus, *Adversus haereses,* SC 100, 152–53, 210–11, 263–64, 293–94.

Jean Damascène, *Expositio fidei orthodoxa,* PG 94, 863–926.

P. Melanchthon, *Loci praecipue theologici* (1559), in *Ms Werke in Auswahl,* 9 vols. Gütersloh, 1952, vol. II, 1st part.

Pseudo-Dennis, *De divinis nominibus,* especially IV and V, PG 3, 693–826.

Thomas Aquinas, II *Sent.,* d. 1, 2, 12, 13.

Thomas Aquinas, *CG* II, chap. 15–30 et 31–38.

Thomas Aquinas, *De potentia,* q. III.

Thomas Aquinas, *De aeternitate mundi (contra murmurantes); ST* Ia, 44, 45, 46, 47.

♦ J.-B. Bossuet (1727), "Élévations sur la création de l'univers," in *Élévations à Dieu sur tous les mystères de la religion chrétienne.*

W. Paley (1802), *Natural Theology or, Evidences of the Existence and Attributes of the Deity Collected from the Appearances of Nature,* London.

L. Feuerbach (1841), *Das Wesen des Christentums* I, chaps. 7, 9, 10 and Appendix X and XI, *GW,* Ed. W. Schuffenhauer, Berlin, 1967–84, 5.

H. Pinard (1908), "Création," *DThC* 3/3, 2034–201.

N. Berdiaev (1914), *Le sens de la création: Un essai de justification de l'homme.*

E. Przywara (1932), *Analogia entis,* Munich, 1962, Einsiedeln.

D. Bonhœffer (1933), *Schöpfung und Fall, DBW* 3.

Vl. Lossky (1944), *Essai sur la théologie mystique de l'Église d'Orient,* Paris, chaps. 5–6 (2nd Ed. 1990).

A. D. Sertillanges (1945), *L'idée de création et ses retentissements en philosophie,* Paris.

P. Tillich (1951), *Systematic Theology,* Chicago-Londres, 163–210.

L. Scheffczyk (1963), *Schöpfung und Vorsehung, HDG* II. 2 a, Fribourg.

J. Ratzinger (1964), "Schöpfung," *LThK*2 9, 460–66 (bibl.).

W. Kern (1967), "Die Schöpfung als bleibender Ursprung des Heils," in *MySal* II, 440–544.

A. Hamann (1968), "L'enseignement sur la création dans l'Antiquité chrétienne," *RevSR* 42, 1–23 and 97–122.

J. Ratzinger (1968), *LThK, Das zweite vatikanische Konzil* III, 316–19.

Coll. (1976), *La création, Com(F)* I/3.

A. Ganoczy (1976), *Der schöpferische Mensch und die Schöpfung Gottes,* Mayence.

K. Rahner (1976), *Grundkurz des Glaubens: Einführung in den Begriff des Christentums,* Fribourg.

A.R. Peacocke (1979), *Creation and the World of Science,* Oxford.

P. Gisel (1980), *La création,* Geneva.

S. Jaki (1980), *Cosmos and Creator,* Edinburgh.

J. Moltmann (1985), *Gott in der Schöpfung: Ökologische Schöpfungslehre,* 2nd Rev. Ed., Munich.

W. Pannenberg (1986), "Schöpfungstheologie und moderne Naturwissenschaft," in *Gottes Zukunft-Zukunft der Welt,* Festchrift für J. Moltmann, Munich, 276–91 (English trans. *in* W. Pannenberg, *Toward a Theology of Nature,* Louisville, Kentucky, 1993).

J. Ratzinger (1986), *Im Anfang schuf Gott* (English trans. *In the Beginning: A Catholic Understanding of the Story of Creation and Fall,* avec un appendice, *The Consequences of Faith in Creation,* Edinburgh and Grand Rapids, 1995).
Coll. (1988), *Cosmos et création, Com(F)* XIII/3.
J. Polkinghorne (1988), *Science and Creation,* London.
Coll. (1989), *Création et salut,* Bruxelles.
S. Jaki (1989), *God and the Cosmologists,* Edinburgh.
J. Fantino et al. (1991, 1994, 1995), "Théologie de la création," *RSPhTh* 75, 651–65; ibid., 78, 95–124; ibid., 80, 143–67.
R. Albertz, J. Köhler, F.B. Stammkötter (1992), "Schöpfung," *HWP* 8, 1389–413 (bibl.).
S. Breton (1993), "Christianisme et concept de nature," in D. Bourg (Ed.), *Les sentiments de la nature,* Paris, 138–61.
G. Gunton (1993), *The One, the Three and the Many: God, Creation and the Culture of Modernity,* Cambridge.
C. Theobald (1993), "La théologie de la création en question, un état des lieux," *L'avenir de la création, RSR* 81/4, 613–41.
P. Davies (1993), *The Mind of God,* Harmondsworth.
A. Gesché (1994), *Dieu pour penser,* IV: *Le cosmos,* Paris.
V. Grossi (1995), "Création, salut, glorification," in B. Sesboüé (Ed.), *Histoire des dogmes* (bibl.), II, 15–24.
L. Ladaria (1995), "La création du ciel et de la terre," ibid., 25–88.
C. Elsas et al. (1996), "Schöpfung," *EKL* 4, 92–109 (bibl.).
K. Ward (1996), *Religion and Creation,* Oxford.

Irène Fernandez

See also **Being; Evolution; Father; Glory of God; God; Messianism/Messiah; Omnipotence, Divine; Providence; Secularization; Work**

Credendity. *See* **Credibility**

Credibility

Understood as a matter of the "natural" rational grounds that lead human beings to the threshold of "supernatural" faith*, the question of credibility is recent, although its treatment calls on the most classic motifs of Latin theology*.

a) From Patristics to Vatican I. In terms ritually repeated by all later analysts of faith, Augustine* defined it as the act of "thinking with assent," *cum assensione cogitare,* and explained that "no one believes anything if he has not first thought that it was necessary to believe" (PL 44. 963). The Council* of Orange (529), at which Augustinianism* was officially adopted by the Latin Church, defined the strictly supernatural character of faith: human beings do not bring themselves to believe, but God* himself leads them to believe through grace* (*DS* 375). Faith is an act of knowledge* and an act of the will, *cognitio* and *affectio* (e.g., Hugh of Saint-Victor, PL 176. 331), giving rise to the expression "voluntary certainty," *voluntaria certitudo.* The balance between the cognitive factor and the factor of will was maintained without difficulty by Scholasticism*. The content of faith is believable, something that Thomas* Aquinas expresses by relying simultaneously on objective reasons and on divine illumination: "Whoever believes has a sufficient motive to induce him to believe. He is in fact led to belief by the authority* of the divine teaching that miracles* have confirmed and, what is more, by the inner inspiration of God which encourages belief" (*ST* IIa IIae. q. 2. a. 9. ad 3).

External signs do exist that are capable of bringing about the intellectual attitude, situated between opinion and absolute certainty, that Thomas calls "vehement opinion," but he never proposes reliance on natural credibility as a normal precondition for the act of faith.

Bonaventure* uses very similar language. Because faith is not a form of knowledge, the will to believe is essential to it (*In Sent.* III. d. 23. a. 1. q. 2 resp.). Knowledge has its own certainty, "speculative certainty," just as faith has the "certainty of adhesion," and because the latter deals with primal truth*, faith is more certain than knowledge (ibid., q. 4 resp.). Finally, it is necessary that "the intellect be taught what is given to be believed *(credibilia)* so that it might think about it and that it have an inclination so as to be able to give its assent to what is to be believed" (ibid., a. 2. q. 2 resp.). There is a crucial point that should not be overlooked: the medieval theology* of faith had the goal of interpreting the *virtue** of faith, and its principal intention was not that of interpreting the reasons for belief offered to the unbeliever (although it recognized their existence); the idea of an apologetics of credibility was virtually unknown. And finally, although the idea of a "dead" faith devoid of all charity and the idea of the faith of demons* were always taken into consideration, these were aberrant cases; the faith that it was important to describe was living faith tied to hope* and charity.

It was probably because of contact with modern philosophy* that the theological analysis of faith was obliged to engage more vigorously with the believing subject and the rational grounds for credibility. After Descartes* it seems that Michel de Élizalde (in 1662) was the first to propose the hypothesis of a reasoning based on grounds of credibility, making it possible to attain infallible evidence of the fact of revelation*. But it was not really until the 19th century that its struggles against rationalism* and fideism* led Catholicism* to formulate an openly apologetic theory of credibility. Against rationalism, Vatican* I reaffirmed the doctrine of the fully supernatural character of the act of faith and the specificity of its grounds: faith does not believe by relying, as knowledge does, on *intrinsic evidence* but on *extrinsic evidence;* it believes "by reason of the authority of the God who reveals." But against fideism, the council asserted just as clearly the existence of a credibility intended for any form of reason* and endowed with evidence superior to that of simple probability. Among the factors of credibility offered to the unbeliever, the council (greatly influenced on this point by the apologetics of Cardinal V. Dechamps) gave a major place to the "fact" of the Church*, a privileged sign in favor of the revelation that it transmits.

b) From Vatican I to Rousselot. Vatican I was responding to internal theological debates, but it also established the status of credibility in an age of secularization*, and apologetic concerns were to dominate subsequent theological discussions. "Preambles to faith" then assumed a central position. To the unbeliever, said Father Pègues, apologetic reasoning may offer a certainty that is scientific and demonstrative, "a demonstration in the strictest sense of the term" (*RThom* 1912). Later, Father Harent said that in the view of reason, the act of faith "would appear as the conclusion of a series of propositions" (*DThC* 6/1), with reason in the end appearing no longer as a faculty of knowledge shared by all but as a speculative faculty at work in the mind of an intellectual to be converted.

Three stages in the critique of this discursive approach may be distinguished. 1) The diachronic schema according to which the intellect proceeds to a judgment of credibility and then deduces from that the duty to believe (the barbarism "credentity" frequently replaces the normal expression), before the will to believe opens the field of faith, was fully accepted by L. Billot, S.J. (1846–1931). The demonstration might be "unclear and slightly rudimentary.... It may also be perfect and scientific" (1905). The essential step is a break. By means of the critical and suspicious interpretation of evidence, reason may attain a "scientific faith." Faith in the strict sense (supernatural faith) is, however, a "faith of simple authority," or a "faith of homage": a faith that recognizes once and for all that it is dealing with a witness worthy of faith whose every word deserves belief. The theory does not require too much of reason: the vague idea of a supreme being*, a "spontaneous reasoning prior to any art of the syllogism" (ibid.), and one that includes veracity* among the perfections of that supreme being may provide sufficient rational preambles to faith. But it also expects too little from grace, which basically intervenes only to carry out in human beings the transmutation of a scientific faith into a "faith of homage." 2) The theory proposed by A. Gardeil, O.P. (1859–1931), is less unsatisfying. The diachronic schema is maintained and worked out in great detail. The analysis of faith discerns first "a phase of searching, of various consultations with the aim of determining in detail the truths that are to be believed," then "at the conclusion of this deliberation, the judgments of credibility and credentity, followed by a consent to the message and a choice of the faith proposed" (1912). But between the first and second editions of the book a preliminary step was introduced, that of a supernatural preparation. The entire procedure described in fact presupposes "an initial affection for God, the final end," and something like a "pre-existence of faith in... the intent to believe" (ibid.). Judgments of credibility and credentity are rational, but they are also the work of a reason that is made for the purpose of believing. The intellectualism* of the theory is also moderated by a concession: there are "psychological substitutes" for the purely rational perception of credibility, such as a "flair" or a "tact."

3) The analyses of P. Rousselot, S.J. (1878–1915), are broader in scope. Any linear schema in which grace would intervene to move the will after reason, perhaps operating on its own, had formulated its judgments of credibility and credentity is rejected in favor of a unifying interpretation of the "eyes" of faith. Here intellectual and affective factors occupy a position of reciprocal priority in which "love* gives rise to the faculty of knowledge and knowledge legitimates love" (1910). The objective visibility of signs of credibility (the "external fact") calls forth the capacity to see them (the "eyes of faith"), and this capacity (the "internal fact") is the sympathy of the subject with its object. The judgment of credibility is thereby replaced by an intellectual synthesis that has no need to be discursive; the analysis is explicitly aimed at granting no privilege to the faith of intellectuals over the faith of ordinary people. In the face of the realities that call forth faith, the subject responds by a certain use of the "illative sense" conceptualized by Newman*. In the final analysis the act of faith is supernatural from beginning to end; it cannot be thought of without reference to "an innate affective habit which, making us sympathize with the supernatural being…provokes in us a new faculty of sight" (ibid., 468). The abstract logic of arguments of credibility is thus replaced by a logic of attraction; and attraction operates, indistinguishably and simultaneously, on intelligence and on liberty*. A disciple of Rousselot, G. de Broglie, extended his intuitions in a theory of knowledge through signs and of the knowledge of value (knowledge of the "sign-value").

c) Contemporary Perspectives. Father Harent criticized Rousselot for reducing the perception of truth to the perception of beauty (*DThC* 6/1); this was at least a prediction of the direction in which H.U. von Balthasar* would continue Rousselot's analysis, the direction of a "theological aesthetics" that establishes congruence between "subjective evidence" and "objective evidence" in the perception of an articulated totality (of a "figure," *Gestalt*). But if for Rousselot faith, in the final analysis, had eyes only to see arguments, for Balthasar the attraction exercised by primal truth operates in a strictly Christocentric context; faith is no longer asked so much to give its assent to revealed doctrines "by reason of the authority of the God who reveals [them]," as to give its assent to the God who reveals *himself.*

These continuations presuppose some mediations. They presuppose the acceptance by theology of philosophies of the person*; for example, J. Mouroux says that "*search* by the person is what explains the understanding of credibility; *encounter* with the person is what explains the certainty of faith" (Mouroux 1939). They presuppose that the question of certainty and doubt is no longer posed in speculative but in existential terms; for example, Gabriel Marcel sought an "existential indubitable." They presuppose the reappropriation of a rich sense of ecclesial mediation, according to which the Church does not act primarily as magisterium* transmitting propositions to be believed but as a field of experience* and as a sign (already present in Dechamps, later in the "liturgical movement," and so on). They also presuppose that there has been a reappropriation of traditional thinking about the supernatural*, either through the philosophical influence of Blondel* or the later theological influence of Lubac*: not, to be sure, the notion of a "supernatural demanded by us" but a "supernatural demanding in us" (E. Le Roy).

In any event, perspectives seem to be fairly clearly established. Faith comes to human beings from the outside, from listening to a word* *(fides ex auditu):* the a priori possibility that this word is audible is a traditional teaching well reformulated by Rahner*. If faith is directed not toward propositions but toward "things" (Thomas Aquinas), and if the "thing" toward which it is centrally directed is a supreme good* revealed as love, then the problem of credibility cannot fail to become indissociable from the problem of divine "lovability." To Thomas's dictum that "nothing is loved unless it is first known," it may seem that contemporary Catholic theology tends to prefer a theory of the cognitive powers of love and a fortiori a theory in which divine love is knowable by man only by being the object of a love (*amor ipse intellectus,* said William of Saint Thierry). This tendency perhaps provides a point of convergence with Protestant theology. The latter has tended to be absent from debates about credibility because it has little interest in anything resembling a "scientific faith" and because it is suspicious of any theological enterprise that might seem to attribute an element of autonomous responsibility to reason in the act of faith.

- L. Laberthonnière (1903), *Essais de philosophie religieuse,* Paris.

L. Laberthonnière (1904), *Le réalisme chrétien et l'idéalisme grec,* Paris.

L. Billot (1905), *De virtutibus infusis,* 2nd Ed., Rome.

J. Martin (1905–06), *L'apologétique traditionnelle,* 3 vols., Paris.

F. Mallet (1907), *Qu'est-ce que la foi?,* 2nd Ed., Paris.

P. Rousselot (1910), "Les yeux de la foi," *RSR* 1, 241–59, 444–75.

Aug. and Alb. Valensin (1911), "Immanence (méthode d')," *DAFC* 2, 579–612.

A. Gardeil (1912), *La crédibilité et l'apologétique,* 2nd Ed., Paris.

P. Rousselot (1913), "Remarques sur l'histoire de la notion de foi naturelle," *RSR* 4, 1–36.

P. Rousselot (1914), "Réponse à deux attaques," *RSR* 5, 57–69.

V. Bainvel (1921), *La foi et l'acte de foi,* Paris.

A. Straub (1922), *De analysi fidei,* Innsbruck.

K. Adam (1923), *Glaube und Glaubenswissenschaft im Katholizismus,* Rottenburg.
S. Harent (1924), "Foi," *DThC* 6/1, 55–514.
E. Przywara (1924), *Religionsbegründung: M. Scheler, J.H. Newman,* Fribourg.
J. Mouroux (1939), "Structure "personnelle" de la foi," *RSR* 29, 59–107.
R. Aubert (1945), *Le problème de l'acte de foi,* Louvain.
H.U. von Balthasar (1961), *Herrlichkeit,* I: *Schau der Gestalt,* Einsiedeln.
K. Rahner (1963), *Hörer des Wortes,* neu bearbeitet von J.B. Metz, Munich.
G. de Broglie (1964), *Les signes de crédibilité de la Révélation chrétienne,* Paris.
E. Kunz (1969), *Glaube-Gnade-Geschichte: Die Glaubenstheologie des P. Rousselot,* Fribourg.
L. Malevez (1969), *Pour une théologie de la foi,* Paris-Bruges.
J.-L. Marion (1978), "De connaître à aimer: L'éblouissement," *Com(F)* III/4, 17–28.
R. Fisichella (1985), *La rivelazione: Evento e credibilità,* Bologna.
W. Kern, H.J. Pottmeyer, M. Seckler (Ed.) (1988), *Handbuch der Fundamentaltheologie* IV, Fribourg-Basel-Vienna.

JEAN-YVES LACOSTE

See also **Faith; Grace; Knowledge of God; Reason; Revelation; Supernatural**

Credo. *See* **Creeds**

Creeds

A. The Symbols of Faith

1. Definitions

Faith*, created by grace*, is an act* involving the whole person*, expressing commitment to God* as the one who reveals himself and saves the faithful. This act manifests itself in the totality of the Christian's life. But it appears more specifically in certain circumstances: when one confesses and proclaims in words the content of faith among believers (prayer*, praise*, sacramental liturgies*), when responding to heresy or opposing nonbelievers (this is the subject of the present article), or when bearing witness, to the point of martyrdom, to the firmness of one's commitment (martyr*). Verbal confessions of faith can take many forms, but they take a particular and privileged form in certain formularies called "symbols of faith," or "creeds" (from "Credo," "I believe"). These bring together—as the word "symbol" indicates—the three "articles of faith" concerning, respectively, the Father*, the Son, and the Holy* Spirit. Among the numerous creeds left to us by the first Christians (Hahn 1897), two are especially important: the Apostles' Creed, the Nicene Creed later developed by the Council of Constantinople and called the Creed of Nicaea-Constantinople.

2. History

The study of the creeds, promoted by Harnack and Kattenbusch, dates back to the 19th century. The declarative form of the symbols they showed is not the oldest form of creed. This distinction belonged to the liturgy of Baptism* and originally consisted of three questions posed to the catechumen at the moment of the triple baptismal immersion "in the name of the Father and of the Son and of the Holy Spirit" (see Mt 28:19). But the need to prepare catechumens led to the creation of a catechesis* that explained the "rule of faith" (second century). This was expressed at the time in affirmative texts rather than interrogative ones, which is the origin of declarative creeds. The initiated had to respect the rule of mysteries: creeds were part of the esoteric teachings of the Church* and could not be divulged to nonbelievers.

a) In the West. An ancient legend has it—a legend especially cited by Rufinus—that after Pentecost and before dispersing on their respective missionary paths, the Twelve, filled with the Holy Spirit, each specified one of the truths of faith. The sequence was to form the current "Apostles' Creed." This belief survived until the 15th century (Council of Basel*-Ferrara-Florence). It was meant to signify that this particular creed stemmed directly from the apostolic kerygma recorded in the discourse of Acts and the Epistles. But the story of the Apostles' Creed is more complex. This creed is a variation on the old Roman Credo, which combined two major affirmations: that of Trinitarian faith and of the redemptive death* and resurrection of Christ*. It insists on Jesus*' life on earth.

The Roman creed appeared in a more or less definitive and official form only at the end of the second century, in the Church* of Rome*, almost simultaneously in Greek and Latin. Kelly says that it emerged before the reign of Pope* Victor (189–197). The mention of the Descent* into Hell and the Communion* of Saints came later, appearing during the second half of the fourth century and apparently having Eastern origins. The dominance of the Church of Rome in the West caused local* Churches to agree on the Roman text. Among the various recensions, which vary infrequently from one another, and even then only in minor ways, the one that was ultimately adopted amplifies the Roman creed supposedly used in the south of France around the year 600. It was successful because of Charlemagne's attempt at make liturgy uniform (*see* below). The Apostles' Creed was never approved by an ecumenical council.

It is also important to mention the apocryphal creed known as the Athanasian or *Quicumque* (from its first word). An *expositio fidei* more than a symbol of faith, this text played a major role in the West during the Middle Ages and was even honored by reformers (Luther*, e.g., in *Die Drei Symbole Oder Bekenntnisse des Glaubens Christi,* gives it almost as much importance as the Roman and Constantinople creeds). This text was attributed to several ancient figures, Caesar of Arles and Fulgencius of Ruspina (Stylgmaier 1930), and the first mention of its existence can be found in a letter written by Augustine*. It is at least certain that its first version was in Latin. Even recently the *Quicumque* played a role in the liturgical life of the Christian West beyond the frontiers of Catholicism* (e.g., in Anglicanism*).

b) In the East. As in the West, the Eastern symbols emerged in the liturgical context of baptism, first in interrogative form and respecting the rule of mysteries. But because of the freedom and autonomy that the local churches had, there was a profusion of different creeds, and a single model did not evolve. Sharing essential elements, these creeds nevertheless vary in accordance with the theological emphasis (orthodox or heretical) of their authors. Their terms are often more speculative than the Western examples.

The Nicene Creed was written at the First Council of Nicaea* (323), the first ecumenical council*, called together by Constantine to put an end to Arianism*. The council was directed principally by Ossius of Córdoba, and the creed it produced consists of three articles (the one regarding the Holy Spirits was not developed) and a series of anathemata.

The First Council of Constantinople (381), convoked by Theodosius, slightly modified the second article of the Nicene Creed, while particularly developing the third, in opposition to pneumatomachian thought (Holy* Spirit). This new version of the Nicene Creed is called "Creed of Nicaea-Constantinople." Debate went on in the period between these two councils in response to the persistence of Arian heresy and the aversion of Eastern Christians, even the orthodox, to the nonbiblical term *homoousios* (the Son is *consubtantial* with the Father) that was included in the Nicene Creed. Moreover, the term was ambiguous because of the possible equivalence drawn between *ousia* and *hupostasis* at that time. The major protagonist in this controversy was Athanasius* of Alexandria, nevertheless accused by Eastern Christians of coming too close to Marcellus of Ancyra's modalism. It was the Cappadocian *mia ousia, treis hupostaseis* (Basil of Caesarea), finally accepted by Athanasius from 362 (Council of Alexandria), that resolved the problem.

The 1054 schism* between the East and West (Orthodoxy*) was partly due to the Western addition of "*filioque**" to the original writing of the Constantinople symbol, which had been drafted by an ecumenical council recognized by all.

3. Place and Moment of Creed

Up until the present time the rite of Baptism included one creed, presented in its oldest form as a threefold question and answer. The place of the Credo in the Eucharist* reminds Christians, more often than Baptism does, of the content of their faith. The inclusion of the Constantinople Creed in the eucharistic celebration was rapidly established in the East, following the Council of Chalcedon* (451). The initiative for this lay with the Monophysites, who wanted, in this way, to insist on the adequacy of a symbol that had been written prior to this council. In the West, the practice of chanting the Constantinople Creed was introduced progressively. This happened first of all in Spain, in opposition to Arianism (Third Council of Toledo, 589), and then in Ireland. Soon after this, Charlemagne imposed it in 795 as way of countering adoptionism*. Rome finally accepted it at the beginning of the 11th century. The role of the creed in the eucharistic liturgy varied: in the East it came just before the anaphor, after the Gospel or before the Communion in the West. Since this time, the Apostles' Creed and the Constantinople symbol have coexisted in Western tradition. The former is connected to the Eucharist and the latter with baptismal catechesis.

4. Role and Need for Such Expressions

Confessions of faith need to exist for the life of the Church and personal faith. In reciting a creed, each person gives content to his faith and acknowledges the unity* of the Church to which he belongs. Faith includes many other truths as well, but those set out in the symbols are central and irreplaceable. Karl Rahner* underlined the importance of these brief creeds while at the same time suggesting the possibility of reformulating faith today in a noncanonical way, in other possible texts, provided that such texts specify a faith in the historical Jesus*.

- A. Hahn, G.L. Hahn (1897), *Bibliothek der Symbole und Glaubensregeln der alten Kirche,* Breslau (repr. Hildesheim, 1962).

J. Stilgmayer (1930), "Athanase (le prétendu symbole d')," *DHGE* 4, 1341–48.

J. N. D. Kelly (1950), *Early Christian Creeds,* London (3rd Ed., 1972).

P. Benoit (1961), "Les origines du symbole des Apôtres dans le Nouveau Testament," in *Exégèse et Théologie,* vol. 2, CFi 2, 193–211.

O. Cullmann (1963), "Les premières confessions de foi chrétienne," in *La foi et le culte de l'Église primitive,* Neuchâtel-Paris, 47–87.

J. N. D. Kelly (1964), *The Athanasian Creed,* London.

A. M. Ritter (1965), *Das Konzil von Konstantinopel und sein Symbol,* Göttingen.

D. Stanley (1965), *The Apostolic Church in the NT,* Westminster.

H. de Lubac (1969), *La foi chrétienne: Essai sur la structure du Symbole des Apôtres,* New Ed., Paris, 1970.

H. von Campenhausen (1972), "Das Bekenntnis im Urchristentum," *ZNW* 63, 210–53.

P. Smulders (1975), "The "Sitz im Leben" of the Old Roman Creed," StPatr 13 (TU 116), 409–21.

K. Rahner (1976), *Grundkurs des Glaubens,* 430–40.

R. Staats (1999), *Das Glaubensbekenntnis von Nizäa, Konstantinopel: Historische und theologische Grundlagen,* 2nd Ed., Darmstadt.

BERNARD POTTIER

See also **Baptism; Constantinople I, Council of; Faith; Filioque; Heresy; Martyrdom; Nicaea I, Council of**

B. Protestant Tradition

"For one is not acting like a Christian if one fears affirmations: on the contrary, a Christian must take joy in affirming his faith*, or else he is not a Christian. And first and foremost [...], what does this expression mean: 'a theological assertion'? It means to strongly bond with one's conviction, to affirm it, confess it, and defend it to the end with perseverance" (Luther*, *Oeuvres 5,* Geneva, 1958).

This passage by the German reformer clearly illustrates the importance of creeds in the Protestant perspective and just how intertwined with the very essence of Christian faith is the act of confessing that faith. Of course, in this matter the Protestant tradition* understood itself to be following in the steps of the early Church*; and when it came time to collect the source texts in books of rites, the Protestant Churches did not hesitate to include the ancient creeds of the Apostles, Nicaea-Constantinople, and Athanasius. Therefore, it agrees with the ancient tradition that creeds are indispensable elements, for prayer* and praise* as well as preaching*, catechesis*, and teaching. In the context of the 16th century, creeds nevertheless took on new connotation, and these would mark Protestantism* up to the 20th century.

1. Insistence on the Doctrinal Element

To this day the Protestant tradition certainly uses creeds liturgically in the context of worship. But in the interconfessional confrontation of the 16th century, it was mostly as a clear definition of fundamental specifics that creeds doctrine played a decisive role. This doctrinal aspect can first be explained by the fact that the reformers debated the idea of a hierarchical and centralized Church authority*. Henceforth, the Church structures* that were established could be very diverse in terms of their place and time. The central reference of the Protestant faith was the doctrine, the coherent body of fundamental affirmations of that faith. The different creeds of the Protestant tradition aim to formulate this doctrine by giving it a visible, historical expression. They therefore play an essential role in the establishment and the life of Churches. Thus, when the pastor* is ordained, his admission to service in the Church depends not on his promise of obedience to a bishop* but on his acceptance of a creed.

At the same time, this doctrine is understood to play a role in the life of all believers and ought to enable them to assume, in full personal responsibility, a life before God*. In this case, the catechism acts as creed, and it is not by chance that the two are found side by side in Protestant confessional books.

2. The Principal Creeds: The Confessional Books

Creeds played an important part in the historic process of developing and strengthening different Protestant traditions. Regarded as the authorized expression of doctrine, they quickly gained force and appeared, beside the catechisms of various Reformations, in collections of reference texts called *Confessional Books.* Lutheranism*'s collection of confessional writings, the *Book of Concord* principally contains the creed known as the *Augsburg Confession* (1530) and its *Apology* but also the *Smalkadic Articles* (1537–38) and the *Formula of Concord* (1577). In the reformed work representative of Calvinism*, are the *Confession of La Rochelle* (1559), the *Later Swiss Confession* (1566), and the *Canons of the Synod of Dordrecht* (1619). In the case of Anglicanism* there are the *Thirty-nine Articles* (1571) in its *Book of Common Prayer.*

3. Theological Challenges

Because of their central place within the structures of Protestantism, creeds are of major theological importance.

a) Authority of Scripture and Authority of the Creed. Because the Reformation strongly emphasized recourse to Scripture *(sola scriptura),* it is advisable here to make a connection between creed and Scripture. In relation to the gospel, both Scripture and creed play the role of an authorized norm that aim to lead to the true living word* of God* that proclaims a Christ* to whom alone authority, strictly speaking, belongs. But at the same time there is a difference between them: the creed, in fact, is answerable to the Scriptures and only comments on it: it is, in other words, a "normed norm" *(norma normata),* whereas Scripture, in comparison, is a "normalizing norm" *(norma normans).*

b) Condemnation of Heresy and Concern over the Unity of the Church. A creed takes sides in both positive and negative senses. It reaffirms the essence of faith and counters threats against it. It therefore reveals abuses and condemns heresy*. Consequently, there is a divisive effect, and the Protestant Churches are today working on reinterpreting the divisions caused by 16th-century creeds. Indeed, in examining these divisions we can discover the true intention of creeds, which is unity* of the Church. In aiming to express what is essential, creeds call for a unity that strives to be universal. Particularity and universality constitute an irreducible tension in all creeds.

c) Confession of Faith and Witnessing. The preceding point emphasizes the importance of creeds in the Church. However, creeds also have a bearing on the life of the believer in a way that is expressed in witnessing. For the believer, a creed is the school in which individuals are apprenticed to the task of witnessing, of attesting to their faith before the world, by both word and deed and through their concrete commitments.

4. Recent Developments

a) Modern Debate. In modern times the act of confessing faith has often attracted criticism. Pietism*, for example, favored the living piety of the heart over dogmatic formulas, and during the Enlightenment, creeds were discredited, being seen as representing a servile and immature submission and as the source of fanaticism. As for historical criticism, it separated the traditional authority of ancient creeds by revealing the complexity of their history. And 19th-century liberal theology*, giving priority to religious feeling, denounced creeds as the obsessive objectification of this sentiment. This "liberal" rejection may have led to the emergence of national Churches (Reformed) that did not have creeds in their constitution.

b) Reaffirmation of Creeds in the 20th Century. In view of this debate, it was up to dialectical theology*, starting between the world wars, to reestablish the value of creeds. For Karl Barth*, for example, this resulted from the rediscovery of the word of God as something that demands a clear answer from its addressee. It was under the influence of this theology of the Word, emphasized by Dietrich Bonhoeffer* after Barth, that Protestant groups, in opposition to Nazism and its influence in the German Church, formed a Confessing Church as early as 1933–34. Its aim was to maintain the integrity of the Christian community during the crisis situation. In May 1934 a synod in Barmen adopted a declaration known as the "Declaration of Barmen," in which the status of creeds is discussed.

c) Status Confessionis. As early as the 16th century the distinction between those things that involve creeds and those that are indifferent in this respect *(adiaphora)* stirred up animated debate (the points at issue were things such as Catholic ceremonies and then, in the context of pietism, card games, dancing, and so on). This question was raised again by Bonhoeffer in the political context of the fight against Nazism when he declared that the Jewish question stemmed directly from faith and sin*. Throughout the 20th century the affirmation of *status confessionis* came to the forefront again in different sociopolitical debates (apartheid, nuclear arms, political asylum).

d) Multitudinist Churches and Creeds.—In accordance with concern over public space pronounced by the reformers, the Protestant churches considered themselves to be mostly multitudinist. The Churches born from the radical reform, however, asked for a much clearer commitment from members in terms of creeds and witnessing. And if this resolution may turn into a closing off, it remains true that the openness of multitudinist Churches does not necessarily entail the dissolution of creeds. Faith is not expressed once and for all. None of the creeds in history* would therefore be proposed as *the* creed par excellence. The unceasing confrontation with creeds inherited from the past does not mean that new ones cannot be written as part of the dialogue between the present situation and the Holy Scriptures.

• *The Book of Common Prayer and Administration of the Sacrements according to the use of the Church of England,* Cambridge and Oxford, s.d.

BSLK (1930), 1986[10] (FEL, 1991).

BSKORK (CCFR, 1986).

♦ R. Mehl (1971), "La place de la confession de foi dans l'élaboration dogmatique," *FV* 70, 214–25.

J. Wirsching (1980), "Bekenntnisschriften," *TRE* 5, 487–511.

L. Vischer (Ed.) (1982), *Reformed Witness Today,* Geneva.

E. Lorenz (Ed.) (1983), *Politik als Glaubenssache? Beiträge zur Klärung des Status Confessionis,* Erlangen.

A. Burgsmüller (Ed.) (1984), *Die Barmer theologische Erklärung: Einführung und Dokumentation,* Neukirchen.

G. Lanczkowski et al. (1984), "Glaubensbekenntnis(se)," *TRE* 13, 384–446.

A. Birmelé (1991), "Sens et autorité de la confession de foi dans les Églises luthériennes," FEL 13–21.

A. Gounelle (1995), "Statut et autorité des confessions de foi réformées," in M.-M. Fragonard, M. Peronnet (Ed.), *Catéchismes et confessions de foi,* Montpellier, 13–26.

Pierre Bühler

See also **Authority; Family, Confessional; Holy Scripture; Magisterium; Word of God**

Cross. *See* **Passion**

Crusades

In any theological dictionary the Crusades are of primordial importance both for relevance to the Christian Church's process of self-definition, particularly with regard to the relationship between sacerdotal and secular jurisdictions over matters that are not entirely spiritual and, second, on account of the development of the Western Church's penitential regime. They were also, outside any theological context, a major episode in the ongoing struggle between the Eastern and Western parts of the Christianized old Roman Empire.

Theologically, the Crusades were regarded by the participants, at least ostensibly, both as holy wars and as penitential pilgrimages for the purging of guilt, of greater atoning value than such alternatives as fasting and the self-infliction of physical pain. In fact they naturally also provided an outlet for territorial aggression in a way that allowed it to be regarded as spiritually enriching. In an era in which the unicity of a single sovereignty, both sacerdotal and secular, was being strongly reasserted in the form of papal overlordship of secular sovereigns, the extra spiritual benefit of visiting the places of Jesus' life and death, of standing on holy land, served to reaffirm what we can now see to have been a confusion between the temporal and the spiritual. The pilgrimage as penance seems to have arisen in the early eighth century. It gained its firm hold on the penitential practice of the West with the Cluniac revival, beginning in the 10th century.

The wars became possible, and perhaps inevitable, with the swelling in the numbers of pilgrims. In 1064, there were some 7,000 pilgrims to Jerusalem headed by the archbishop of Mainz. Later pilgrims joined together under armed guard for their own protection, gradually forming the view that the holy places belonged by right to the Christian Church and regarding their Turkish Muslim opponents as the aggressors. Crusading belligerence could then easily be transformed into a tool in the ecclesiastical and feudal diversion of purely aggressive martial instincts into righteous, holy, and spiritually beneficial warfare while also serving the apostolic ends of the Church, which aimed at the conversion and salvation of the infidel as well as the territorial extension of ecclesiastical power.

At the same time, the Crusades protected the West from the danger of being overwhelmed by the Islamic world, which existed almost constantly from the seventh century to the 17th. By keeping that danger at bay, the crusaders allowed the Church to develop its own practices and hierarchical structures, to have its legal system cloned in the secular world, and to elaborate its theology, relying heavily on antique concepts that had actually been mediated and modified as much by Arab theologians from Jerusalem as by those from northern Africa. The Crusades are therefore of importance in the Church's process of self-definition and in particular in forcing its ecclesiology to begin its retreat from claims to secular jurisdiction, whether direct or by means of a feudally conceived overlordship of secular sovereignties.

Relations between the Latin Church and Jerusalem at first remained good after the Hegira, or move of Muhammad to Medina in 623, and Muhammad's subsequent conquest of his native Mecca. They reached a peak of cordiality under Charlemagne. Only in the 11th century did they seriously deteriorate. The church of Christ's sepulchre was destroyed in A.D. 1010, and in 1071 the Seljukian Turks captured Jerusalem from the Arabs. The West was looking for new overland routes to the Far East, and the events of 1071 resulted in a Seljuk revival that temporarily crushed the Greeks and posed a serious commercial, military, and religious threat to the West.

In the ninth century, Leo IV had already promised spiritual profit to those who defended the Italian mainland against the Arabs, so assuming that spiritual sovereignty demanded temporal domination and could be used in its defense. In the late 11th century, Gregory VII, rallying to appeals from the East to protect Eastern Christendom from the incursions of the Islamic Turks, began to assemble an army. When Alexius Comnenus, the Byzantine emperor, appealed for reinforcements to recover Asia Minor for Eastern Christendom to Urban II, the pope gathered together in 1095 an army whose aims were not so much to recover Asia Minor for Alexius as to conquer Jerusalem for themselves. It was in Urban's pontificate that the term "Roman curia," with its overtones of pretensions to temporal power on the imperial model, appeared for the first time in a bull of 1089. The provision of military reinforcements to ensure the protection of Eastern Christianity had been turned into a holy war for the acquisition of sacred territory.

Furthermore, Urban granted a plenary indulgence* to all who took the Cross and either died on the crusade or won through to Jerusalem. This indulgence set a double precedent. It was apparently the first time a "plenary" indulgence, remitting all the vestigial punishment due to sin after absolution from guilt, had ever been issued, and it radically extended the pope's claim to be able not only to "bind and loose" in the sacrament of penance but also to usurp the divine prerogative of judgment after death.

Ways were invented in which the pope could be seen to be dispensing from an existing pool formed from the merits of Christ and the justified dead superfluous to what was necessary for the redemption and the justification of the righteous but that still further complicated the ecclesiology implied by the arrangement, introducing what could be mistaken for a system of weights and measures into the salvific work of Christ's redemption. The ability to grant plenary indulgences, later to become exploited widely and frequently, practically demanded a system that elevated the powers of Christ's vicar into those which were truly divine and were of their nature incapable of delegation.

There are many historical reasons, largely connected to the sociological consequences of plague and famine across northern Europe, for Urban's success at the March synod of Piacenza in 1095. They make understandable the wild enthusiasm generated by Urban's speech at Clermont later that year calling for the conquest of Jerusalem and promising members of the expedition the equivalent of full and complete penance. The crusade, preached in France on the basis of Urban's harangue, was essentially French. It established a French kingdom in the East, and the Crusades themselves quickly became both political, with French princes aspiring to establish principalities in the East, and mercantile, with predominantly Italian merchants seeking to establish profitable enterprises in the Middle East. What is important in the present context is the theological concept of papal dominion that underlay them and that had also underlain the investiture controversy of the 11th and 12th centuries.

When Jerusalem was finally taken after a month's siege in July 1099, there was some discussion about whether its government should be secular or theocratic. The matter seems to have been decided in favor of a lay ruler largely on grounds of available personalities, with a cleric to fill the vacant position of patriarch. The legal system adopted gave slightly more authority to ecclesiastical courts than was customary in the West, allowing them jurisdiction in all matters where Church property was concerned and also over all marital disputes, but this was not enough to imperil the principle adopted of independent lay sovereignty in temporal matters.

Although historians have given the Crusades numbers, they were in fact virtually continuous. After the second, which was preached by Bernard of Clairvaux but that failed, their religious nature was fortified by the launching of a successful counterwar by Saladin in 1187, an Islamic jihad that captured Jerusalem. The Third, Fifth, and Sixth Crusades were directed against the Islamic rulers of the holy places, but the word is also used of the Fourth Crusade against the schismatic Greeks, of the crusade against the Albigensian heretics of southern France, and against unsubservient Christian princes such as King John of England and the Hohenstaufen emperor Frederick II. "Crusade" came to denote virtually any military movement against insurrectionary, hostile, or heretical forces.

The Third Crusade to recapture the recently lost Jerusalem, while religious in conception and inspired by the idea of spiritual reform, was not papal but was organized in 1188 by the secular monarchs of Germany, England, and France. It was also much more conciliatory, finally ending with political union reinforced by marital arrangements and the foundation of the kingdom of Cyprus in 1195. The Fourth Crusade took place in the reign of Innocent III, who attempted to inspire the respect and power due to the vicar of Christ, his preferred title.

The Hohenstaufen emperor Henry VI, son the emperor Frederick Barbarossa, had died in 1197 preparing the Fourth Crusade after a reign of active hostility to Celestine III, who lived until 1198. Henry appointed his own bishops, spurned those nominated by the pope, and curtailed papal power in Sicily. However, he needed good relations with Celestine in order to have his son Frederick baptized by the pope with a view to becoming emperor and making the post hereditary. He offered to lead the Fourth Crusade but died before it was ready.

Innocent III attempted to adopt it and vainly sought to bring it back to its ecclesiastical objective and clerical direction. In the end, control was wrested from him by lay (mostly French) princes for their secular ends, forcing the papacy to retreat further from its aspirations to temporal sovereignty where that was possible and to feudal overlordship where it was not. The slow decline of an ecclesiology based on a theocratic ideal, vestiges of which would linger on into the 17th century, was forcing a major change in the way in which the Church was able to define its function. The crusading ideal, still much alive in the 17th century in France, where Père Joseph, Richelieu's gray eminence, was its staunch advocate, was by the early 13th century already declining into a political game. Even the crusade against the Cathars degenerated into a land-grabbing maneuver by the northern French barons.

ANTHONY LEVI

See also **Catharism; Nationalism**

Cult

a) The Experience of a New Cult. "Cult" and "cultish" designate a certain number of acts and practices for which early Christian communities did not have a common term, one that would have "embodied in its unity the diversity of new practices being formulated" (Perrot 1983). Conscious of the newness of the gospel and because they were participants in a thriving and rather agitated community life, the first Christians inherited a vision of cult that was mostly introverted and moralizing, drawing on the prophets* (Is 29:13), the Wisdom writings (Wis 3:6) or psalms (Ps 50, 51), and the preaching* of Jesus*. They were familiar with the terms that designated the ritual and ceremonial practices of the Temple*, but to a certain extent, they modified them. It was the life of Christ*, having become a salvaging destiny, the *opus salutis* of God*, for God and in God, that they henceforth considered in cultish terms: oblation, sacrifice*, priesthood* opening the way to God. A new word designated the "Lord's supper," that is, "Eucharist*." The new "service of God" led by the Holy* Spirit of Jesus thus was intertwined with the new life lived according to the Beatitudes* and the Ten Commandments and with the service of neighbor and the proclamation of the gospel (Lyonnet 1967). Inaugurated by Baptism*, this new life was marked by fervent prayer*, both individual and common, by the use of a christological hymnology (Phil 2:6–11; Col 1:15–20; Rev 15:3), by an attentive reading of the Scriptures*, and by listening to preaching and sharing the Lord's supper. All these practices fostered the status as an original, "new cult." To designate services and roles, general terms such as *leitourgia* or *diakonia* were used (Lengeling 1968) or terms that were as far as possible from the sacerdotal vocabulary of the Temple (and a fortiori from the vocabulary of pagan cults). The words that were retained—apostles*, elders *(presbuteroi), episkopoi*—seem to insist on the function of legitimate guides who could ensure the instruction, cohesion, and fervor of a group of believers (Lyonnet 1967). The development of Christian institutions, together with the establishment of forms of prayer, religious exercises (e.g., fasting), liturgical gatherings, and the calendar, would later cause new problems. Such problems were often inextricable from specific doctrinal developments: the need to give equal adoration to the three divine persons*, the understanding of the eucharistic action, the question of what degree of homage was due to the Mother of God and so on. As it extended into areas of mixed population, pastoral work had to face practical questions concerning familial cults, funeral customs, and the many superstitious practices of everyday life. The confrontation with state paganism* in times of persecution, the merging of various religious movements (Neoplatonism, gnosis*), the success of Cicero's and Seneca's Roman conceptions—all these may have led Christian theologians and leaders to consider the domain of "cult" in concert, even if discordant, with various religious movements to which Christianity was opposed.

b) Augustine on Cult. This is, in fact, what is boldly highlighted in book VI of *City of God,* where it seems Augustine* wants to settle definitively the debate that opposed the Church to the cultish beliefs and practices of Greek and Roman antiquity. The first problem was one of vocabulary. In terms of "cult," the language of Roman religious practice—even though it was adopted by authors as serious as Varro—could not properly express the uniqueness of Christian practice and thought. Latin translations* of the Bible*, on the other hand, tended to uses terms in the *colere/cultus* family (absent of psalter) to designate pagan or Jewish acts (Dn 3:17; Acts 17:23) and, more specifically, the cult of idols in passages where the Greek used *eidôlolatreia* (1 Pt 4:3; 1 Cor 10:14). Furthermore, its usage clearly showed that *colere* was never used in the first person (as an action) in private or public prayer, by contrast with verbs such as *laudare, benedicere, adorare,* and *glorificare.*

The theoretical problem is immediately raised in the preface of book VI. If cult is understood as a relationship of homage, recognition, and attachment, to be established with a divine being by means of ritual practice, a divine being to whom or to which this relationship is due as a form of service (*servitus,* Gr. *Latreia*), how can the truth of Christianity itself be expressed in terms of such a relationship, bearing in mind the failure of paganism? Augustine's argument consists of showing that the cult relationship can concern only a unique and true God, the creator of all corporal and spiritual beings and the one solely capable of giving eternal life. It does not involve a multitude of gods each with a specific function (*officium*) that relates to the beliefs and needs of the city* or the material help that an individual expects. After briefly acknowledging *Antiquities* by Varro, a universal scholar, Augustine criticizes him for basing cult on human needs and the demands of civic life ("as if the painter came before the painting," VI 4) and of thus degrading the figures of divinity. As for Christians, they certainly do have a "cult" (*Nos Deum colimus* VII), but the uniqueness of God the creator removes from cult any sense of a divinized intermediary to whom might be attributed a given element of the world or ownership of a given creature. On the other hand, this unique and true God needs neither our gifts nor our praises*, and our sinful condition makes us unable to harmonize with the liberality and gratuitousness of his gifts. It is therefore in Christ, the Word* of God and his light, that the *verus veri Dei cultus* announced by the *sacramenta* of the ancient covenant* can be established (VII). Therefore, in order to designate such a reality, the available words have to be readjusted. Too closely associated with Roman religion and capable of being used in profane and disrespectful ways, the terms from the *colere/cultus* family are discredited (X). The Greek term *latreia,* on the other hand, seems least inappropriate to express the absolute sovereignty of God and simultaneously opens up the opposite category of idolatry*. And because it also expresses the idea of a "cultish service" *(servitus)* susceptible of taking shape both in sacred signs *(sacramenta)* and within ourselves *(in nobis ipsis),* it can simultaneously consider cult as gesture and act and as interiorized attitude (X).

This interiorization can therefore be understood as God's indwelling of the temples that we are, and this is the idea behind all harmony. Augustine can therefore extend the "cordial" cult metaphor in which the heart is the altar *(ara cordis),* the Son the priest*, and the sacrifice a life exposed "to the point of blood" and in which the incense is the fragrance of a sanctified love*. Within this temple of the heart there is a circulation constituted of gifts given and returned. Within the heart's sanctuary, commemoration is made of divine gifts in a manner that recalls feasts and holy days. And in order for this commemoration to give rise to a sacrifice of fervent praise, the heart must purify itself of covetousness. In this way it certainly does imply a "consecration" *(ejus nomine consecramur),* a reorientation of the entire being away from desire *(appetitio).* The true cult, therefore, is a choice to be made over and over again since, in the end, it involves an exclusive love of God (*in toto corde, in tota anima,* and *in tota virtute*). Augustine later condensed his lyricism in a formula that won great success: *nec colitur nisi amando* (there is no other cult than love; *Ep.* 140, ad Honoratum 18, 45).

In a similar vein to Augustine, *cultus* also appears, something rare, in the text of a liturgical prayer. Indeed, in the Verona Sacramentary we read that in Christ "the fullness of the divine cult has come to us," *Divine cultus nobis est indita plenitudo.* The writers of Vatican II's constitution on the liturgy* would draw on this formula (c. 1, §5).

c) Cult and Virtue of Religion in Thomas Aquinas. Thomas Aquinas's *Summa Theologica* is most certainly influenced by Augustine in its approach to cult, yet its true originality emerges when Thomas links cult, the very and immediate act of virtue* of religion (*religio est quae Deo debitum cultum affert,* IIa IIae, q. 81, a. 5), with the cardinal virtue of justice*. The formal goal of religion is indeed to express reverence toward the unique God *(exhibere reverentiam)* in terms of his excellence and his sovereignty as creator and ruler of all things (q. 81, a. 3). Acknowledging divine excellence and his own submission, man shows the fundamental axis of cult, and this axis operates according to a double movement, either as a manifestation toward God *(exhibendo aliquid ei)* or as appropriation of what comes from God, in particular, the sacraments* and the divine names* (q. 89 prol.).

The exterior acts of cult, it goes without saying, are subject to an interior attitude, a spiritual activity that is directed toward God (*ordination mentis ad Deum* q. 81, a. 7) and is stable enough to form a virtuous habitus—the virtue of religion. The habitus can be enriched only by such acts. Moreover, with regard to the virtue of religion, these exterior acts do not only maintain a simple relationship of spontaneous manifestation or even of pleasure. The exterior cult in which body and sensibility are involved (q. 84, a. 2) is a cult rightly due *(cultus debitus):* created and in possession of creation*, man must return the creation to God, its creator, as a tribute of "glorification." Cult therefore pays homage to God's creative sovereignty; it is the reflection of a faith* that is revealed in the signs that sustain it in such a way that cult in fact surpasses the banal opposition between interior and exterior: gestures contain their own intentional and significant interiority.

The connection between cult and the virtue of religion, which itself stems from justice, led Thomas to develop some paradoxes that were not without consequence. Although, for example, one cannot measure charity, one can measure cult and religion: because they stem from a "moral" virtue, they fall under the discernment of "just measure" (q. 93, a. 2). Discernment should first focus on the status of those to whom cultic reverence is addressed and therefore on the particular cultic form this reverence is to take on each occasion: the cult of "latria," reserved for God alone, or the cult of "dulia," expressing reverence due to a created being according to various degrees of honorability (q. 94, a. 1, q. 103, a. 3). Any departure from the just measure will henceforth come from superstition, which is the excessive and undue transferral of the religious relationship to objects that do not call for it. Idolatry is its most serious form.

The connection between cult and virtue of religion also led Thomas to consider the fact that cultic realities stemmed first from natural reason*, even if a positive right would be the element to determine the precise rules and forms of rites (q. 81, a. 2). It seems there is room here for an anthropology of rites and cult that involves understanding man as a religious animal. However, the transition that leads the general function of the cult to its positive ends obliges one to consider the irreversible historicity of the Incarnation* and Passion* of Christ and therefore "the strictly Christian regime of religion" *(ritum christianae religionis)* (IIIa, q. 62, a. 6). The Thomist interpretation of cult goes from a theocentric explanation of the cultic relationship to a Christocentric interpretation, and the latter aims to redefine more than one concept in the first explanation.

At the heart of this interpretation a particular thesis is proposed and supported: God is not the object of the cult but its end. It is the nature of theological virtue to have God as its only object, as when one says that the believer gives faith to God *(credere Deo)* (q. 81, a. 5) or that charity truly "reaches" God (q. 24, a. 5). The divine cult, however, is the object (formal and material) of the virtue of religion, which organizes and arranges the means, attitudes, and acts and so appears as one of the signs of faith *(protestatio fidei per aliqua signa exteriora)* (q. 94, a. 1). Thus, despite the relative autonomy that it seems to have, the cult cannot be considered as a kind of sacred mechanism that will "reach" God independently of grace* and of divine communication, which is the realm of theological virtues. Thomas specifies his position by referring to the concept of *instrumental cause* (IIIa, q. 62, a. 4), as used in the theology* of the sacraments. The sacrament, which is part of the divine cult, is all the more involved in God's saving and sanctifying action (IIIa, q. 60, a. 5) in that it perfects the habitus on which the cult thrives in terms of the passion of Christ, founder of the new cult (IIIa, q. 62, a. 5). As an act that uses words, things, and people in a significant and palpable way, the sacrament cannot be reduced to a simple message. As an "instrumental cause," it refers—in its very manifestation and with a drive that strictly stems from practice—precisely to the domain in which unfolds the action of which it is the sensible figure. It also refers to the domain of God's good and sovereign will, which works to sanctify those with whom he has made a covenant.

Most important, in the end, is the specific refinement that Thomas contributed to the understanding of the cultic relationship in general and of the sacraments. The articulation of cultic life and the sacramental experience can be understood by reference to the Eucharist since it is in the Eucharist that "the divine cult is the main principle, in that it is the sacrifice of the Church, and the end and consummation of all the sacraments" (q. 63, a. 6). The Eucharist can be understood through the order*: for it is through order that the agents, legitimately qualified to transmit the sacraments, are born. It can be understood through Baptism and Confirmation since it is through these that emerge subjects who are capable of participating in the cultic and sacramental life of the Church*. The three sacraments (Baptism, Confirmation, Holy Orders), which grant a "character," entitle the believer to the legitimate and sacred practice of divine cult. More precisely, "each believer is delegated to receive or transmit to others that which concerns the cult of God" since each believer participates in the priesthood of Christ, "to which the faithful are configured" (q. 63, a. 3 and 5) and that constitutes the principle of the entire cult.

d) Reforms and Cultual Spirituality. To a great extent the crisis of the Reformation revolved around questions of theology and cultual practice. Within the diversity of theories and countertheories, one can acknowledge that all the various Reformation movements (one can include the artisans of Catholic reform) championed the same cult policy of opposition to the cult—a confrontation between established forms and interior attitudes meant to correspond to them. Luther* and Calvin* did not hesitate to question the whole logic of established cultual forms (critique of sacramental and ecclesiastical mediation, concept of sacrifice). The Council of Trent*, besides reaffirming the Church's sacramental and cultic practices, set itself the task of revalorizing them by restoring their "interior fullness" (Duvall 1985). It was hoped that this program would be through a renewal of Christian instruction—as well as by going back to the traditional form of cult and sacramental celebration—by providing the Church with ministers who could celebrate its cult and by favoring a genuine "participation" of the faithful. The *Catechismus ad Parachos* published in Rome* in 1566 (one of the first pastoral works to come out of Trent) offers a theory of this participation of the faithful, linking it, in the case of the Eucharist, to the central character of the sacrificial action (the only one that made full satisfaction, as was established in the council's session 22). Participating means "to participate in the fruits of sacrifice." However, the sacrifice of Jesus is both action and interior attitude: it is this attitude and this "mystery*" that pastors* have to carefully explain so that believers can develop an analogous attitude within themselves (can. 18, §7). Particularly revealing here is the distinction between the adverbs "sacramentaliter" and "spiritualiter." These were used to designate two dimensions that were intertwined in cultic practice (*see* session XIII of Trent, can. 8), and it justifies the practice of communion*, which would specifically be said to be "spiritual." This is a paradoxical conception, but it simultaneously leaves a vista open to a piety in which the Eucharist is the permanent horizon of thought and virtuous life, the horizon to which multiple forms of private and public devotions are connected (Duval 1985; Bremond 1932).

Pierre de Bérulle*'s disciples were to take the theological and ascetic notion of cult to its furthest extreme. As supreme act of adoration and reverence, cult is identified with the spirit of religion that allows the creature—once it recognizes the supreme sovereignty of God—to attain its highest dignity. This spirit of religion culminates in the person, the states and the sacrifice of Jesus, the incarnate Word, the "principle of grace and love in our nature" (Rotureau 1944). For this reason, any detachment from a noticeable good must be carried out and interpreted in terms of the religious states of Jesus Christ. It is sacrifice that is the key dynamic of these states and that sums up the entire work of Christ. Christians can participate in this through the Eucharist.

Such a vision of cult, beside its ascetic and moral weight, also involved ecclesiological theories since a central role was granted to the sacerdotal dimension of the ordained ministry, an idea that would be revived by the disciples and successors Bérulle, Condren, Jean Eudes, and J.-J. Olier. And it is finally notable that what appeared to be an entirely "spiritual" vision of cult and priesthood in fact revitalized the concrete forms of cultic action. Not only would the cult of the Church be the outside and formal facade of a religion that was experienced internally, but it was essentially meant to be an invitation to interiorize the "*exteriora,*" to existentially conform to what one does when celebrating the mysteries. Vincent de Paul and Olier would make this principle the key to training priests.

e) Impoverishment and Revaluation of the Cultic Experience. History* nevertheless seems to show that the way Tridentine reforms were imposed on often unwilling populations led to a kind of drying out of cult thought and practice (Certeau 1975). This fact clearly appeared in the division of ecclesiastic teaching subjects. According to an entirely non-Aquinas perspective, cult is linked to morality, which is itself directed back to one's duty to God and expressed in the Decalogue*. Cult is discussed in terms of comments on the first three commandments. The sacraments themselves are partly analyzed in this way and presented as supplementary to moral life or as prescribed or recommended observances ("commandments of the Church"). Thus, cult was brought back to unanimity of good example and the ceremonial to a mostly uninspired didacticism. The instrumentalization of public cult during the Enlightenment (precisely on this point, Schleiermacher* mocked the "pedagogical mania") was most certainly related to a particular conception of divinity. "Christians," wrote Y. Congar (1959), "had somewhat lost the feeling of the inclusion of God's 'philanthropy' in the theological. Henceforth, this very theology was no longer a perfect theology of the Absolute and Love. It tended to become a theology of cult, yes, a cult, a duty carried out for an Absolute that was thought to be enthroned very high, in a kind of celestial Versailles." Around the end of the 18th century and the beginning of the 19th, many religious thinkers shared the feeling that the cult experience was impoverished. The emergence of awakened movements serve as an example in the Protestant milieu. Within French-speaking Catholic circles it was perhaps in the work of a very close disciple of the first Lamennais, the Abbé Gerbet, that the tendency described by Congar was most obviously overturned; and it was in Dom Guéranger's work that the modern concept of cult most distinctly appeared. 1) In the *Considérations sur le Dogme Générateur de la Piété Catholique* (1829), Gerbet attacks rationalism* and deism*, but also, without naming it, he attacks the moral and disciplinary rigor that Guéranger would later denounce as having Jansenist origins. Before the spectacle of this "moral desert where the springs of love are drained, from where the living cult withdraws," he dismisses the solution proposed by pietism*. Instead he promotes a return to what he considers to be the "communion" dimension of cult, carried by a dogma* of which the content is precisely a "theandric" divine act. "Divine philanthropy" thus finds itself reestablished in its rights. "Rational charity" can give way to a "mystical charity" that finds "in every man's face the mark of a noble fraternity with the Man-God." The Catholic cult can therefore "banish the law of fear" and rediscover in itself its constituent dimension of "divine familiarity"; it can therefore reconcile dogma with the most experienced life. 2) Guéranger's *Institutions Liturgiques* (1840–51) adopt Gerbet's understanding of the fundamental link between cult and incarnation*, but the approach is more ecclesiological. The cult is an act, and fully an act as such: it cannot be reduced to its moral effects. This act is an act of the Church in the reality of society*. The Church exists as cult "in an act of religion," and its liturgies are the "social form" of its religion. It would be a mistake, therefore, to find a pretext for "seeking religion in one's own heart" since one would thus depart from "communion with this holy society," a communion that is the foundation of religion itself. "What makes Christianity perfect is that the eternal Word of God [...] *became flesh* in time*, and *lived among us* to found religion on the true cult, the *visible* symbols of which contain grace, and, at the same time, signify it." Thus, the social and tangible aspect of cult, henceforth considered "liturgy," contains both the principle and the means of its renewal and, for Guéranger, becomes the primary source for Christian regeneration, the way to transform the means of expression into a genuine work of civilization (Guéranger 1885).

The term "liturgy" would henceforth be considered more adequate for designating the essentially active dimension of cult. H. Clérissac found it to contain the "hieratic life of the Church" (Clérissac 1918). O. Casel, when reading the Fathers* again and granting liturgical requests' that continue to thrive in the Church of the East, aimed to reconsider the objectivity of the cultic action independent of the subjective feelings of its participants. Considered in terms of the category of "mystery*," cult is then seen as "divine action revealed with the intention that the celebrants participate in the very reality that is celebrated." Christianity, therefore, cannot be reduced to a dogma and morality and emphatically not to a ritual apparatus concerned with aestheticism and ceremonial: the "mystery of cult" is simultaneously the revelation* and the fulfillment, "in Christ," of what is revealed of Christ and by Christ (Casel 1922). In 1947 Pius XII (encyclical *Mediator Dei*) integrated the contributions of the liturgical movement with the official teaching of Catholicism*. Understood analogically in all its extended forms, the concept of cult here served as a means to think about the way all human existence was orientated toward God. Associated by Christ with the new cult of the new covenant, the Church, Christ's mystical body, best expresses this orientation through liturgy. "The sacred liturgy is therefore the public cult that our redeemer, as head of the Church, renders to the Father; it is also the cult rendered by the body of believers to their founder, and through him to the eternal Father. It is, in short, the integral cult of the mystical body of Jesus Christ, that is to say, of the Head of his members" (*La Liturgie,* Solesmes 1954). Vatican II's dogmatic constitution on the liturgy, *Sacrosanctum Concilium,* cites this definition in part. Nevertheless, it uses the vocabulary in an intentionally limited way. The overall concept here involves *opus,* the work of salvation*, considered in terms of its fulfillment in and by Jesus Christ. Carried out in the mystery of Easter, this work combines the salvation of human beings and the glorification of God. Derived from the very humanity of the Word, it introduces the "richness of the divine cult" to the human milieu. Henceforth the Church announces and exercises through its sacred liturgy "this work of salvation with which Christ associates it, and through which God is perfectly glorified, and men sanctified." Thus, one sees "cult" giving way to "liturgy," the latter concept seeming more able to realize the mystagogical impact of the officiating act and its "invitatory" character (Audet 1967). The terms "cult" or "spiritual cult" would then designate all that stems from an internal attitude of reverence and adoration experienced before God and, more generally, everything that a human existence includes that is "an agreeable offering to God" (Vatican II, GS 38, §1). And from this perspective, liturgical work would indeed include a cultic dimension, something that the *CIC* of 1983 clearly expresses (can. 834–40).

• Augustine (410–25), *De civitate dei,* BAug 33–37.
J.-J. Olier (1676), *Traité des Saints Ordres,* Ed. J. Gautier, Paris, 1953.
F. de Fénelon (†1715), *Lettres sur divers sujets de métaphysique et de religion,* New Ed., Paris, 1864, 265–310.
P. Gerbet (1829), *Considérations sur le Dogme générateur de la piété catholique,* Paris.
P. Guéranger (1840–51), *Institutions liturgiques,* 3 vols., Paris-Brusells (2nd Ed. [posthumous], 4 vols., Paris, 1878–85).
H. Clérissac (1918), *Le mystère de l'Église,* Paris.
O. Casel (1922), *Das christliche Kultmysterium,* Ratisbonne.
Pie XII (1947), *Mediator Dei,* Vatican City.
♦ L. Maury (1892), *Le réveil religieux dans l'Église réformée à Genève et en France, 1810–1850,* Paris.
H. Bremond (1932), *Histoire littéraire du sentiment religieux en France,* vol. 9: *La vie chrétienne sous l'Ancien Régime,* Paris.
G. Rotureau (1944), *Le Cardinal de Bérulle, Opuscules de piété,* Paris.
J. Galy (1951), *Le sacrifice dans l'École française de spiritualité,* Paris.
Y. Congar (1959), "Le Christ, image du Dieu invisible," *MD* 59, 132–61.
J.-P. Audet (1967), "Foi et expression cultuelle," in coll., *La liturgie après Vatican II,* Paris, 317–56.
S. Lyonnet (1967), "La nature du culte dans le NT," *La liturgie après Vatican II,* Paris, 357–84.
F. Lengeling (1968), "Liturgie," in L. Brunkhoff (Ed.), *Liturgisch Woordenbock,* vol. II, Ruremonde, 1573–96.
M. de Certeau (1975), *L'écriture de l'histoire,* Paris.
C. Perrot (1983), "Le culte de l'Église primitive," *Conc(F)* 182, 11–20.
J.J. von Allmen (1984), *Célébrer le salut, Doctrine et pratique du culte chrétien,* Geneva-Paris.
A. Duval (1985), *Des sacrements au concile de Trente,* Paris.

JEAN-YVES HAMELINE

See also **Liturgy; Mysticism; Religion, Philosophy of**

Cult of Saints

a) The Fundamental Idea. Very early in the history of Christianity, and even though Paul uses the term "saints" to mean the group of the baptized (Rom 1:7; 2; Cor 13:12), a division was created between two classes of the dead. This distinction influenced family practices at tombs, practices that in large measure the Christians held in common with the pagans. There were the dead for whom Christians prayed, and then there were those whose prayers* they invoked, notably the martyrs, and soon other saints along with them. This invocation of the saints had two aspects. On the one hand, there was the celebration of the anniversary of their birth into heaven, their *dies natalis.* On the other hand, and more generally, their prayers were sought. To the latter was spontaneously added the veneration of their tombs or their relics* and soon their veneration also in the liturgy* itself. Recourse to the prayer of the saints is one of the features of the "communion* of saints," which is at once a communion of holy people and a communion with those holy things that are the sacraments*.

b) Historical Development. Around the seventh century, in Rome as in Constantinople, the cult of the Virgin Mary* and of the saints in general had to some extent become delocalized—the universal celebration of a saint had earlier been an exception. From this time on, the cult was tied less strictly to the tombs of saints, even though these of course continued to be venerated. And in this way there would develop, within the Roman liturgy's sphere of influence and more specifically in the Frankish countries when the Carolingians decided to adopt this practice, a general calendar of the feast days of the saints supplementing that of the principal liturgical* feast days. This new calendar was itself completed by the inclusion of certain feasts of a more local character. In addition to the Virgin Mary (Annunciation of our Lady, Assumption, Nativity of the Virgin), of Saint John the Baptist, and of the apostles*, with, after Christmas, the feasts of Saint Stephen, Saint John Evangelist, and the Holy Innocents, this calendar included primarily the Roman martyrs. From Charlemagne's time, All Saints' Day, when all the saints are invoked together, was added to it. Of Irish origin, this feast seems to have been introduced to the European continent by the English scholar Alcuin.

c) The Place of the Cult of the Saints in the Liturgy. In the Roman liturgy, and subsequently in the Roman-Frankish liturgy, on feast days the cult of the saints affected principally the mass, the chief canonical hours of the divine office, and possibly processions. Similarly, in various circumstances the singing of the litany of the saints, the core of which first appeared in Rome in the seventh century, in Greek and later in Latin, introduced for the first time the direct invocation of the saints: "Saint Mary, Saint Peter, pray for us."

d) In the Mass and in the Divine Office. In the mass, at least since the time of Augustine, it is clear that the eucharistic* sacrifice is offered not to the saints but to God* in honor of the saints, who were commemorated on the day of their birth in heaven and mentioned every day in the Eucharistic Prayer. This practice followed the distinction made by Augustine (e.g., *The City of God,* X,1) between the worship rendered to God (in Greek *latreia,* latria) and the honor of a cult rendered to the saints (*douleia,* dulia). This distinction, which was to become classic in medieval theology (such as in Thomas Aquinas, *ST* IIa, IIae, q. 84–85 and 103), would be completed in the 13th century by the special category of the *hyperdulia* to the Virgin Mary (see Bonaventure*, *In Sent.* III, d 9, q. 3).

In the Roman liturgy the prayers, readings, and hymns of the old feast days have in many instances remained unchanged from the Carolingian period until the 20th century. In addition to the Eucharist*, the saints have been celebrated by the canonical hours of the divine office, particularly in nocturnal vigils, which held an important place among the pious practices of Christians. From the Carolingian period on, it was also during the divine office that the name day martyrology, a quotidian list of martyrs and other saints, was read.

e) The Calendar of Saints. The Middle Ages saw the number of feast days increase considerably, and the hierarchy of feasts came to be organized in a more complex way, with the latter even taking precedence over Sunday*. The new feast days concerned new saints or even newly honored aspects of sainthood—thus the Immaculate Conception of the Virgin Mary (8 December) celebrated Mary as one who, from her very conception, had been exempted from original sin*. From the 10th century, the task of the entering of the name of a saint (canonization) on the list of saints (martyrology) fell more and more to the pope. From the 12th and 13th centuries, popes reserved for themselves the exclusive right of canonization, and since the end of the Middle Ages, Catholic theologians have considered that canonizations involved papal infallibility*. Moreover, in the second half of the Middle Ages it became the general custom to give the name of a saint to a child at the time of its Baptism*. Following the Council* of Trent*, the calendar was pruned, and an official edition of the Roman martyrology was added to the liturgical books. All matters concerning canonization were entrusted to a new institution, the Sacred Congregation of Rites (1588). In the 17th century, a new distinction was made between the saints and the blessed, the second category enjoying only a local liturgical cult. It was also from this period that scholarly research was undertaken into the history of the saints and their cult (hagiography), particularly among a specialist group of Belgian Jesuits, named "Bollandists" after their founder.

The constitution of Vatican* II on the liturgy stressed the necessity of defining clearly the cult of the saints together with the Easter mystery* (SC, no. 104) and stated the timeliness of exempting certain feast days from general celebration by the Roman calendar (no. 111). In order to lessen the number of saints to be celebrated obligatorily, the new Roman calendar (1969) took into account the work of historians. It introduced a new balance between saints associated with Rome* itself and the saints of different continents. In the liturgical texts the spiritual originality of every saint is emphasized more clearly. A new Roman martyrology is still in preparation.

f) The Protestant Reformation and the Cult of Saints. While strongly asserting the primacy of Christ* and protesting against the abuse of the cult of saints, Luther* intended to purify the cult: he did not reject it. Article 21 of the Augsburg Confession states that the memory of saints should be preserved, but they should not be understood as mediators of grace. Calvin* rejected the cult of saints (*Inst.* I,12, I), but he attached great importance to the "host of the elect," understood as models of faith*. The Council of Trent proclaimed both the validity of the cult of saints (*DS* 1821–25) and the necessity of fighting against its possible abuses.

• H. Delehaye (1940), *Martyrologium Romanum ad formam editionis typicae scholis historicis instructum,* Brussels.

P. Jounel (1983), "Le culte des saints," in A.-G. Martimort (Ed.), *L'Église en prière,* New Ed., vol. 4, Paris, 124–45.

K. Hausberger, C. Hannick, F. Schulz (1985), "Heilige, Heiligenverehrung," *TRE* 14, 646–72.

Ph. Harnoncourt (1994), "Der Kalender," in *Gottesdienst der Kirche: Handbuch der Liturgiewissenschaft* 6/1, *Feiern im Rhythmus der Zeit* 2/1, Ratisbonne.

H. Auf der Maur (1994), "Feste und Gedenktage der Heiligen," in *Gottesdienst der Kirche: Handbuch der Liturgiewissenschaft* 6/1, *Feiern im Rhythmus der Zeit* 2/1, Ratisbonne.

P.-M. Gy (1995), "Le culte des saints dans la liturgie d'Occident entre le IXe et le XIIIe s.," in *Le culte des saints aux IXe-XIIIe s.,* Poitiers, 9–63.

Pierre-Marie Gy

See also **Holiness; Liturgical Year**

Culture. *See* **Inculturation**

Cyprian of Carthage

c. 200–58

Born into a wealthy pagan family, Cyprian converted to Christianity about the year 246. Having become bishop of Carthage in 249, he had to go into immediate exile to escape Emperor Decius's persecution, and he guided his community by correspondence for a year and half. On 14 September 258, he suffered martyrdom* under Valerian. We can lay aside his apologetic and moral theology, strongly influenced by Tertullian, in order to consider his theology of the Church* and its sacraments*, such as it emerges from his two most famous treatises and his bulky correspondence.

a) The Question of the Apostates. At the end of 249, Decius ordered his subjects to perform an act of piety toward the Roman gods, and many Christians obeyed. Later, these *lapsi* ("fallen ones") wanted to reenter the Church. Certain of the "confessors" (those who, for the faith, had endured prison and tortures) took on themselves the authority* to readmit them without conditions. Cyprian was opposed to this practice and in 251 published his *De lapsis* (on the Fallen Ones). He found extenuating circumstances for those who had yielded under torture (§13) but deplored that many had so easily chosen apostasy (§7–8) when they should, according to Matthew 10:23, have gone into exile (§10). He exhorted them not to demand an immediate pardon but to do penance and to give alms deducted from that wealth that, in order to escape persecution, they should have been capable of abandoning (§35).

On the other hand, and in the name of goodness and divine mercy*, Cyprian defended the reintegration of the apostates against the intransigence of Novatianism*. He rejected the view of the Church as a society of pure people: "When the apostle says 'In a great house there are not only vessels of gold and silver but also of wood and clay' (2 Tm 2:20) how can one dare to seem to choose the gold and silver vessels and [...] condemn the wooden and earthen ones?" (*Ep* 55, 25, 2).

b) A Certain Idea of the Church. Similarly, in his *De ecclesiae catholicae unitate* (On the Unity of the Catholic Church) of 251, Cyprian fought schisms* linked to the problems caused by the *lapsi* by preaching fidelity to the Church: "One cannot have God* as a father when one does not have the Church as a mother" (§6). He based the principle of Church unity on the cohesion of the Trinity* (§6, citing Jn 5, 8) and especially on concrete signs: Christ's tunic (§7), the family* gathered at Rahab's (§8, following Jos 2, 18 et seq.), the commandment to eat the paschal lamb* in a single house (§8, after Ex 12:46), and the dove that settled on Jesus* at his baptism* ("a simple and joyful bird, with no malice," whose pairings know "peace* and harmony") (§9). And to the unity* of the Church corresponds a single episcopate, "one and indivisible."

Scribal tradition gives two versions of the famous §4: one speaks of the "primacy" *(primatus)* given to Peter*; the other, although more developed, does not utter a word about this. Certain specialists think that the short text is a forgery from the fourth-century Roman Chancellery; many others attribute both drafts to Cyprian. It was said that, at the time of his quarrel with Pope Stephen I, Cyprian had corrected a passage that he thought would prove too favorable to Rome's claims. Whatever the result of the philological debate, it calls for two remarks. On the one hand, letters by Cyprian present the see of Rome as the "matrix and root of the Catholic Church" (*Ep.* 48, 3.1) or as "The principal Church, which engendered episcopal unity" (*Ep.* 59, 14.1). On the other hand, at the time the first publication of his *De unitate,* Cyprian was already saying—as he would when opposing Pope Stephen (*Ep.* 72, 3, 2)—that "every bishop himself directs his own actions and his administration, on condition that he renders an account of them to the Lord" (*Ep.* 55, 21, 2). In short, he saw in the choice of Peter by Jesus* a sign of unity for the whole Church and not the justification of third century Roman ambitions.

c) The Quarrel about the Baptism of Heretics and Schismatics. Pointing to tradition*, Stephen, bishop of Rome from 254 to 257, considered that whoever had received baptism from a heretic or schismatic bishop could rejoin the Great Church—the whole of the churches in communion with the Roman one—without a new baptism. Invoking an African Council held about 220, Cyprian refused to follow Rome on this point. According to him, "without exception, all heretics and schismatics are divested of all power and all authority" (*Ep,* 69, 1,1). Having no proper idea of the Trinity or of the Church, they could not confer a valid baptism (*Ep.* 73, 23,1). The conflict ended only with the martyrdom of the two adversaries. Cyprian's view continued to prevail in Africa in the fourth century, particularly in Donatism*. Augustine contributed to the victory of the Roman custom.

d) On the Eucharist. Cyprian's long Letter 63, sometimes titled *De sacramento calicis Domini* (On the Sacrament of the Lord's Chalice), is the first piece of writing entirely devoted to the Eucharist*. While certain people (the "Aquarians") celebrated this sacrament by pouring only water into the chalice, Cyprian thought that wine should be mixed with it in order to "do [...] what the Lord himself had done" (10, 1). In his opinion the Eucharist constituted "an oblation and a sacrifice*" that corresponded "to the Passion*" (9, 3). The union of the water and the wine "shows" the union of Christ and his people* (13, 3), while the bread "shows" the unity of the Church: "just as many grains gathered together, milled and mixed together, form a single loaf, in exactly the same way in Christ, who is the bread of heaven, there is [...] only one single body" (13, 4).

• CChr.SL 3–3 B (Preferred Ed.).
in SC: *A Donat. La vertu de patience* (291).
Correspondance, CUFr, 2 vols.
The Letters of St. Cyprian of Carthage, New York, 1984–89, 4 vols. with commentary by G. W. Clarke.
De l'unité de l'Église catholique, by P. de Labriolle, Paris, 1942.
♦ M. Bévenot (1981), "Cyprian von Carthago," *TRE* 8, 246–54.
J. D. Laurance (1984), *Priest as Type of Christ: The Leader of the Eucharist in Salvation History according to Cyprian of Carthage,* New York.
S. Cavallotto (1990), *Il magistero episcopale di Cipriano di Cartagine: Aspetti metodologici,* Plaisance.
V. Saxer (1990), "Cyprien de Carthage," *DECA,* 603–6.
P. A. Gramaglia (1992), "Cipriano e il primato romano," *RSLR,* 28, 185–213.
Ch. et L. Pietri (1995), *Naissance d'une chrétienté (250–430),* Paris, 155–69.
La *REAug* publie une *Chronica Tertullianea et Cyprianea.*

Jean-Marie Salamito

See also **Apologists; Baptism; Bishop; Church; Donatism; Eucharist; Martyrdom; Novatianism; Rome; Tertullian**

Cyril of Alexandria

c. 380–444

a) Life and Works. Cyril was born into a family that had migrated from Memphis to Alexandria*. It was no doubt under the supervision of his uncle Theophilus, archbishop of Alexandria (385–412), that he received the serious lay and religious education to which his later writings attest. Hagiographic sources recount in a very picturesque way his five-year stay in the cloister of Makarios in Nitria (PO I/1, chaps. 11–12). In 403 his uncle Theophilus took Cyril to Asia Minor to the rather grim Synod of the Oaktree (Chalcedon)*, where, on Theophilus's initiative, John Chrysostom*, archbishop of Constantinople, was deposed following false accusations (PG 103, 105–13). It was the first confrontation between Alexandria, Constantinople, and Antioch*, the town in which John Chrysostom had been educated. In 412, Cyril succeeded his uncle to the see of Alexandria. He was prominent from the outset through his very strong—and sometimes muddle-headed—concern for orthodoxy*, simultaneously opposing the Arians (Arianism)* and the Novatians, the Jews, and the pagans. The "hyperanimosity" for which Isidorus Pelusiota reproached him at the time of the struggle against Nestorius (Nestorianism*) had revealed itself well before this particular great quarrel (PG 78. 362).

Cyril's theological works are prolific. The year 429 is the watershed that divided them fairly clearly into two parts, with the start of the controversy with Nestorius. Two immense volumes on the *Pentateuch* (PG 68–69) constantly present Christ* as the prophetic truth* *(tupos)* of Mosaic law*. The Gloss on the *Psalms, Isaiah,* and the *12 Minor Prophets* (PG 73–74) reveals the same preoccupation. The commentary on the *Gospel according to John* (PG 73–74), on account of its size and its wealth of doctrine, is, however, the most remarkable of Cyril's exegetical writings. His interpretation is less prone to the kind of allegorizing associated with writers such as Origen or Didymus and through his concern for the literal meaning. He sometimes even borrows from the work of Jerome (Kerrigan 1952).

His specifically dogmatic works deal with the Trinity*: the *Thesaurus* (PG 75) and the *Seven Dialogues on the Holy Trinity* (SC 231, 237, 246). Cyril took his inspiration from Athanasius* and the great Cappadocians of the previous century, but he often rearranged the elements of the Christian views into an original synthesis. Man's kinship with the Word* incarnates him corporally and spiritually with God*. The Trinity, the Incarnation*, the Eucharist*, Baptism*, the indwelling of the Holy* Spirit, deification: all these major themes of his teaching Cyril constantly connected to each other, following the tradition of church fathers such as Athanasius and Gregory of Nyssa.

b) The Conflict with Nestorius. From 429 until his death* in 444, Cyril would focus his attention on the danger, to his mind, of the teachings of Nestorius, the priest from Antioch who, in 428, was chosen by Emperor Theodosius II to hold the see of Constantinople. Henceforth, letters, homilies, treatises (e.g., *Five Books against Nestorius;* PG 76–9-248) would have a single objective: the refutation of Nestorius's teachings on Christ. As early as 429, Cyril reacted against the new patriarch's sermons (Easter Homily, No. 17) (PG 77, 767–800, and his letter to the Egyptian Monks, *ACO* I, 1, 10–23). Cyril thought that Nestorius's objection to calling Mary* the Mother of God *(theotokos)* was a threat to the unity and even the divinity of Christ. Cyril wrote in an early letter to Nestorius that they have reached the point in certain circles "of no longer tolerating the admission that Christ is God; they prefer to say that he is the instrument or tool of the Deity; a theophoric man, or such like" (Ep 2: *ACO* I, 1, 23–25). A polemical exchange thus began in which Pope* Celestine was involved. Local synods were held in Rome* and Alexandria, which led to the emperor's convocation of an ecumenical council in Ephesus. Cyril hurriedly obtained the condemnation of Nestorius on 22 June 431.

c) Cyril's Christology. The Council of Ephesus thought that Cyril's second letter to Nestorius (*Ep.* 4; *DCO* II/1. 104–12) gave the authentic meaning of the Nicaean* symbol with regard to "the fact that the Word issued by God became flesh and became a Man": "The Word, having joined together by means of the hypostasis *(kath'hupostasin)* a living flesh and a rational soul*, became a man in an inexpressible and incomprehensible way and received the title of Son* of man, not by a simple wish or whim; neither, in addition, because he only took on the figure of a man *(prosôpon);* and we say that different are the natures gathered together in a true unity, and that from both together resulted a single Christ and a single Son, not that the difference in natures was eliminated by the union, but rather because the divinity and the humanity formed for us our unique Lord, Christ, and Son, by means of their ineffable and inexpressible coming together into the unity [...]. It was not an ordinary man who was first born of the Holy Virgin and on whom the Word descended later, but it is because, having been joined to his humanity from the very womb he is said to have suffered carnal generation, so much so that he appropriated generation through carnal means [...]. It is for this reason that the Holy Fathers have dared to name the Holy Virgin the Mother of God" (*DCO* II-1, 107–13). The unity of Christ required that the Word of God should himself be born of Mary. Were this not the case, we would be confronted by two subsistents, the Word and an ordinary man born of Mary. It is on account of the last-named attribute, the exercise of the concrete act of existing *(hupostasis),* that the Word claims as his own or assumes for himself generation through carnal means.

Cyril was perhaps the first to take up again in a christological context the distinction, first used to describe the Trinity, of the person* *(Kath'hupostasin)* and the nature *(phusis).* He also distinguished the *hupostasis,* the person that one is, from the *prosôpon,* the figure that one represents. The union realized here, which places the humanity of the Word made flesh in the category of the being* and not of the having*, is opposed to the union that would be created by "simple wish or whim."

Giving *phusis* a concrete meaning, Cyril would speak elsewhere, somewhat ambiguously, of a union *kataphusin* or *phusikè* (third letter to Nestorius, third Anathematism, *DCO* II/1, 142) and would also speak of "the unique, incarnated nature of the Word of God" *(mia phusis tou thesou logou sesarkômenè)* (*Contra Nestorius* I, PG 76, 60–93), an expression that he thought he was borrowing from Athanasius but that in fact came from Apollinarius (Apollinarianism*) (*Ep. ad Jov.* 250; *ACO* I/5, 65–66). These phrases would for a long time earn Cyril the title of the father of monophysitism*.

d) Reputation and Influence. Approved by the Council of Ephesus, integrated by those of Chalcedon* and Constantinople* II and III, the exegesis of Nicaea that Cyril had defended became a property of the Church*. Maximus* the Confessor, John of Damascus, Thomas* Aquinas, Denis Petau, and Scheeben*, among other theologians, would look back to Cyril. In

1882, Pope Leo XIII declared him a doctor* of the Church. In 1944, Pius XII devoted to him an encyclical letter, *Orientalis Ecclesiae* (AAS 36, 129–44).

• PG 68–77.
DCO II-1, 105–47.
Deux dialogues christologiques, SC 97.
Dialogues sur la Trinité, SC 231, 237, and 246.
Contre Julien, SC 322.
Lettres festales, SC 372 and 392.
♦ H. du Manoir (1944), *Dogme et spiritualité chez saint Cyrille d'Alexandrie,* Paris.
J. Liébaert (1951), *La doctrine christologique de saint Cyrille d'Alexandrie avant la querelle nestorienne,* Lille.
A. Kerrigan (1952), *St. Cyril of Alexandria, Interpreter of the Old Testament,* Rome.
J. Liébaert (1970), "L'évolution de la christologie de saint Cyrille d'Alexandrie à partir de la controverse nestorienne," *MSR* 27, 27–48.
A. Grillmeier (1979), *Jesus der Christus im Glauben der Kirche,* I, Fribourg-Basel-Vienna, 637–91 (*Le Christ dans la tradition chrétienne,* CFi 72) (2nd Ed. 1990).
A. de Halleux (1992), "Les douze chapitres cyrilliens au concile d'Éphèse (430–433)," *RTL* 23, 425–58.
M.-O. Boulnois (1994), *Le paradoxe trinitaire chez Cyrille d'Alexandrie,* EAug 143.

GILLES LANGEVIN

See also **Appropriation; Christ/Christology; Ephesus, Council of; Hypostatic Union; Monophysitism; Nestorianism; Trinity**

D

Daniel, Book of. *See* **Apocalyptic Literature**

Dante

1265–1321

Dante Alighieri cannot only be considered one of the greatest European poets but also a philosopher and a theologian of the highest rank. He knew how to use his poetic genius to express ideas that were often original and innovative.

1. Life

Dante was born in Florence in May or June 1265 in a noble but modest Guelph family. After elementary schooling in Latin grammar, his encounter with Brunetto Latini (politician, poet, and philosopher) and with the poetic and political milieus of Florence and of Bologna was decisive. It allowed Dante to deepen his knowledge of the Latin classics, rhetoric, philosophy*, and French poetry and to come into contact with contemporary Italian poetry. He completed his education, in all likelihood, auditing freely some courses at the Franciscan Studium of Santa Croce and at the Dominican Studium of Santa Maria Novella. This academic formation, received by Dante outside formal schooling, allowed him to make his own personal synthesis of the various elements of knowledge he had acquired.

At the age of 20 Dante married Gemma Donati, who bore him three or four children. In 1295 he embarked on a brief and disastrous political career: initially elected to various councils in Florence, he became prior in 1300 (15 June–15 August). Implicated in conflicts between the White Guelphs and the Black Guelphs, Dante sided with the former. Because of this he was condemned to exile at the beginning of 1302 and then to death. He lived for a while with other exiles on the outer edges of Tuscany, seeking a return to Florence, but around 1304 he started traveling in search of hospitable lords. He lived in various places, in Treviso, Lunigiana, Casentino, and Lucca, assuming some responsibilities in diplomacy or in chancellery. Profoundly marked by exile, he supported the expedition of Henry VII into Italy (1310), with the hope that this monarch would restore justice, peace, and freedom. But the premature death of the emperor (24 August

1313) brought an end to his dreams of ethico-political renewal. He spent his last years in Verona and Ravenna, where he never ceased hoping, until his death on 14 September 1321, that he would be allowed back to Florence because of his poetic merits (Paradise XXV).

2. Works

La Vita Nuova (c. 1294) marks the first step in Dante's career as a writer. The "libello" is made up of 31 poems interspersed in a text in prose (thus the name of *prosimetrum*) that is used as an autobiographical and self-interpreting framing device. Beatrice's presence acts as the fabric of this work—from the first encounter to a death that transforms Woman* into a "mediator of knowledge and of salvation*" (Contini)—in a path that will lead to the *Commedia.* Along with the *Vita Nuova* we should also mention the *Rime,* which bear witness to an "endless experimentation" (Contini), the *Fiore,* and the *Detto d'amore,* as well as two adaptations of the *Roman de la Rose* whose attribution to Dante rests on serious arguments. The Latin treatise *De vulgari eloquentia,* composed during the early years of exile (1303–5) and interrupted in book II (chap. XIV), presents itself, with good reason, as an original piece of work. Dante's goal is to offer a theoretical justification of the use, by writers in particular, of the so-called *vulgar language,* since this language enjoys priority and comes more naturally than Latin, which is fraught with artificiality. The treatise also includes original and important anthropological comment on the origin, the function, and the nature of language.

Composed during those same years and likewise unfinished (we have only 4 treatises instead of the projected 15), the *Convivio* was the first philosophical work to be written in Italian. A self-interpreting treatise, it owes much to Albert* the Great and Thomas* Aquinas. It presents itself as a collection of lessons given in the form of poems (the *Vivanda* of the *Banquet*) accompanied by a rich doctrinal commentary *(Il Pane).* In the first book Dante expounds the reasons for writing his commentary in Italian. His choice of language was made because the treatise was meant for a certain public: the people who have remained *nella umana fame* (in human hunger) for wisdom on account of family or civil obligations. In the second book, which relates the conflict between the old love (Beatrice) and the victorious love for *la donna gentile* (Philosophy), Dante expounds his views on the meanings of Scripture, which he then goes on to apply to his own work. He thus makes a distinction between the allegory of poets and the allegory of theologians. The former exposes a spiritual truth hidden under imaginary and untruthful facts; the latter exposes a spiritual truth hidden under historical facts (this difference will be eliminated in the *Commedia,* which uses allegory in both a poetic and a theological fashion). The third book is an opuscule that praises philosophy and is comparable to numerous contemporary opuscules written by masters of the Faculty of Arts. Finally, the fourth book is devoted to the study of the notion of nobility understood as *"perfezione di propria natura in ciascuna cosa."* In it, Dante tackles for the first time the political themes that are also central to the Latin treatise *Monarchia* (probably composed from 1316–17 onwards). Dante demonstrates with a remarkable syllogistic rigor the necessity of a universal monarchy; he makes of it the indispensable condition of peace* and of allowing the whole human race to realize its goal through the final actualization of the possible intellect (intellectualism*). Having stated the legitimacy of the Roman nature of the empire (book II), Dante goes on, in the last book, to establish its autonomy in relation to the Church*. He vigorously refutes the hierocratic interpretations of the pope's temporal authority and notably proves the illegitimate nature of Constantine's donation. Finally, he maintains that imperial authority has been delegated directly by God*: since human beings, who participate in corruptibility as well as incorruptibility, are ordained to two distinct ends, earthly beatitude and eternal beatitude*, God has delegated two distinct and independent guides, the emperor and the pope. That political doctrine, based on a clear distinction between theological and philosophical viewpoints, between the domain of faith and that of reason, was the result of some meditation, through which Dante—in spite of a constant presence of Thomist thinking—clearly broke away from Thomism*.

To these works should also be added a collection of 13 Latin epistles. Epistles V, VI, and VII were written on the occasion of Henry VII's expedition to Italy. Epistle XI was sent to the Italian cardinals assembled in a conclave to elect the successor of Clement V. Epistle XIII is a fundamental introduction to the *Commedia* and represents the third Dante commentary by himself. We should also mention two Latin eclogues (1319–20) and a lesson in natural philosophy entitled *Questio de aqua et terra* (1320).

3. The Divine Comedy

Composed in all likelihood between 1307 and 1321, not only is the *Commedia* Dante's major work, it also represents his theological synthesis. Rigorously structured around the numbers 3 and 10 for rhythm, the *Commedia* is made up of 100 cantos in *"terza rima,"* divided into three canticles (Hell, Purgatory, and Paradise), each consisting of 33 cantos. The *Commedia* is the narrative of a penitential journey to the three kingdoms beyond the grave. The poet accomplishes the journey during Holy Week in the jubilee year of 1300 and is guided by Virgil in the first two kingdoms and by Beatrice (replaced finally by Bernard* of Clairvaux) in the third. A real summa of knowledge mixes several literary genres, showing in particular an excellent grasp of travel literature. The poem is the multifaceted expression of an experience* that is simultaneously poetical, philosophical, and theological. It accomplishes, while transcending it, the *Convivio*'s doctrinal and pedagogical project. The narrative is governed by a practical and moral intention: the Dantesque journey is the journey of knowledge and at the same time one that is an ethical, political, and ecclesiastical renewal.

a) Hell. Located, according to Inf. XXXIV, at the center of the earth, which, in turn, is itself right in the center of the universe, hell* has the appearance of a crater divided into nine concentric circles. This place, where the damned suffer, is structured according to a strict ethical order, which is intelligible to the human mind. Virgil—whose explanations on hell's order (XI) are thought to be very clear because they explain "very well this abyss and those who are in it"—bases his classification of human misdemeanors on an Aristotelian distinction (EN VII, 1, 1145 a 15–17) between "incontinence, malice, and mad brutality." As a consequence the first circles of hell enclose those who have indulged excessively in the sin of the flesh, in gluttony, and in temporal pleasures (circles II–V). To establish a hierarchy of sins* related to malice and brutality, Dante makes use of a Ciceronian distinction (De off. I, 13, 41) between injustice *(iniuria)* by force and injustice by fraud. Violence* against one's fellow human being (seventh circle) includes tyranny and violence against oneself, which includes suicide (XIII). Among those human beings whom he considers violent against God, Dante includes the blasphemers (XIV), the sodomites (XV–XVI), and the usurers (XVII). He describes with particular meticulousness, in the 10 "bolgias" (or chasms) of the eighth circle, the manifold forms of injustice that human beings can inflict upon others through deception: these range from flattery (XVIII) to hypocrisy (XXIII) and simonists (XIX), thieves (XXIV), treacherous counselors (XXVI–XXVII), and forgers. The ninth circle represents the indescribable "bottom of the whole universe" (XXXII) where, in a lake of ice, those who have betrayed their parents, their benefactors, and—even worse—the empire (Brutus and Cassius) and the Church (Judas) suffer with Lucifer, "Emperor of the kingdom of grief" (XXXIV). Since free will constitutes the foundation of this ethical (ethics*) topography and of its corresponding punitive system, those who are indolent—among whom are to be found the neutral angels* (III) and the great minds of ancient times (IV Œ Paganism)—cannot find their place there. Heretics occupy a place apart in the sixth circle, between those who are incontinent and those who are violent.

b) Purgatory. According to Dante, purgatory* is a mountain located in the middle of the ocean. It was formed at the time of the fall of Lucifer and is divided into seven circular terraces where depraved tendencies are expiated through purgative sufferings whether of the physical or the moral order. Purgatory is preceded by the antepurgatory (for all those who were late repenting), and it is followed by the Garden of Eden, where the last acts of spiritual regeneration are accomplished. As with hell, the description of this kingdom is entrusted to Virgil, and it is to be found in the central canto of the *Purgatorio* (XVII), but it overflows, together with its doctrinal implications, into the adjoining cantos. In canto XVI the irascible Marco Lombardo, faithful to Thomas Aquinas (*ST* Ia, q. 115, a. 3–6), affirms in the face of astrological determinism the *"libero voler"* (76) of human beings, and he highlights the fact that "if mankind is perverted at present" (82), the ethico-political responsibility falls entirely on man's shoulders. The architecture of purgatory, described in canto XVII, follows precepts of a Scholastic (Scholasticism*) origin (they are partly at variance with the Aristotelian-Ciceronian criteria for hell). The distribution of souls (soul*-heart-body) on the seven terraces follows the order of the capital sins established by Gregory* the Great, and the doctrinal foundation borrowed fairly strictly from Thomas Aquinas is dependent on the Christian concept of love* as the cause of all actions (*ST* Ia IIae, q. 28, a. 6). Dante makes the distinction (*ST* Ia, q. 60, a. 1–3) between natural love (not culpable) and elective love (root of vices and virtues*). From this distinction follows a subdivision into three levels, as in hell, because love can be culpable in three different ways (95–96): "for the wrong object" (love of harming [evil*] others: pride, X–XII; envy, XIII–XIV; anger, XV–XVII), "for lack of vigor" (love for God expressed halfheartedly: laziness, XVII–XVIII), or "for too much vigor" (immoderate love for the material riches of this world: miserliness, XIX–XXI; greed, XXII–XXIV; lust, XXV–XXVII). Freedom and love are again analyzed in a synthetic fashion in canto XVIII, as factors in human action. Asked by Dante, Virgil explains what love is within the limits of reason and how man is free to follow an amorous impulse. Endowed with a natural disposition for love (identified with the desire to be joined with some exterior person or object), man possesses the freedom to evaluate—that is to welcome or to reject amorous passions*—while following his aspiration (which is also innate) for the real good*. The root of freedom is therefore in the intellective soul and more precisely in the faculty of making judgments, a faculty that is found between understanding (its prerequisite) and appetite.

c) Paradise. To present the climb toward God, Dante relies on the cosmology of his time. In this, the third part of the *Commedia,* the ascent initially follows the order of the seven planets; then the pilgrim rises to the crystalline heaven of the fixed stars; and he finally reaches the empyrean. The celestial topography is bound by a rigorous logic. Those who have practiced the four cardinal virtues* (temperance, prudence*, fortitude, and justice) are accommodated in the first six heavens. In the eighth heaven Dante undergoes an examination on the three theological virtues (faith*, hope*, charity, XXIV–XXVI) before acceding to the crystalline heaven, where Beatrice, who represents theology*, explains the angelic world to him (XXVIII). And when, at the completion of his purification, Dante gets to the empyrean heaven, the pure kingdom of light, he has reached "that goal of all longings" (XXXIII). At this point the ardor of desire dies out in the presence of a light, truth* itself, which dwells in itself alone, knows itself, and which by understanding itself, loves itself. The sight of God, principle of the love that moves the sun and the other stars, constitutes, therefore, both the completion of the sacred poem and the goal of human existence. But never at any point does the doctrine erase Dante's ethical and political concerns: we hear Saint Peter* heaping out invectives against papal abuses (XXVII), then Beatrice complaining that the human family is running wild for lack of rule and control (XXVII); canto VI celebrates the empire, and in canto XXX Beatrice shows Dante the Emperor Henry VII's seat, placed in the celestial rose. The examination to which the apostles (apostle*) Peter, James, and John subject Dante, under Beatrice's supervision, demonstrates the Comedy's deep theological convictions. This context does not only help Dante formulate his Credo (XXIV), it also allows him to remind us that love is the main driving force of existence.

It would be absolutely disastrous to consider the Comedy as the mere narrative of a journey to the hereafter or even the expression of an extraordinary mystical (mysticism*) experience. In fact it is a work that uses all the knowledge of its time in order to describe the transcendent world, and it does so with a view to accomplishing a political and ecclesiastical reform of that world. It depicts the fate of human beings in the hereafter to show what must be. It is therefore quite fair for Dante to claim, as he does in his Epistle XIII, that the *Commedia* is an ethical work.

• *Le opere di Dante,* testo critico della Società Dantesca Italiana, Florence, 1921 (2nd Ed. 1960); *La Commedia secondo l'antica vulgata,* Ed. G. Petrocchi, 4 vols., Verona, 1966–67.
Il Convivio, Ed. C. Vasoli and D. de Robertis, in *Opere Minori,* I, II, Milan-Naples, 1979.
Egloghe, Ed. E. Cecchini, ibid., II.
Epistole, Ed. A. Frugoni and G. Brugnoli, ibid., II.
Fiore and *Detto d'amore,* Ed. G. Contini, ibid., I, 1984.
Monarchia, Ed. B. Nardi, ibid., II.
Questio de aqua et terra, Ed. F. Mazzoni, ibid., II.
Rime, Ed. G. Contini, ibid., I, I, 1984.
Vita Nuova, Ed. D. de Robertis, ibid., I, I.
De vulgari eloquentia, Ed. P. V. Mengaldo, ibid., II.
♦ Coll. (1920–) *Studi danteschi,* Florence.
É. Gilson (1939), *Dante et la philosophie,* Paris (4th Ed. 1986).
B. Nardi (1942), *Dante e la cultura medievale: nuovi saggi di filosofia dantesca,* Bari (2nd Ed. 1949); id. (1960), *Dal "Convivio" alla "Commedia" (sei saggi danteschi),* Rome.
H. U. von Balthasar (1962), *Herrlichkeit* II/2, Einsiedeln, 365–462.
F. Mazzoni (1967), *Saggio di un nuovo commento alla "Divina Commedia": Inferno, canti I-III,* Florence.
G. Contini (1967), *Un'idea di Dante: saggi danteschi,* Turin.
G. Treccani (Ed.) (1970–78), *Enciclopedia dantesca,* 6 vols., Rome (2nd Ed. 1984).
G. Petrocchi (1983), *Vita di Dante,* Bari.

Ruedi Imbach and Silvia Maspoli

See also **Contemplation; Eschatology; Intellectualism; Naturalism; Political Theology; Scholasticism; Scripture, Senses of**

Day of YHWH. *See* **Parousia**

Deacon

a) New Testament. Usually connected to the episcopates (bishop*) (Phil 1:1; 1 Tm 3:2, 8, 12), the office of deacon is described in 1 Timothy 3:8–13. The Seven from Acts 6:1, 6 were not the first deacons, even though the tradition is often associated with them. The office of the Seven was different: preaching*, baptism*, evangelizing (mission*) (Acts 6:8ff., 8:5–13, 8:26–40, 21:8). They did not receive the title of deacon, although it was given to the Christian woman Phoebe (Rom 16:1).

b) Patristic Period. Rather vague on their functions, Ignatius of Antioch declared deacons to be messengers of the bishop (*Philad.* 10, 1; 11, 1). The *Apostolic Tradition* 8 underlines the direct link between the deacon and the bishop; the *Apostolic Constitution* (II, 29–32; SC 320, 248–50; III, 19; SC 329, 160–64) details his ministry* to the bishop: role in the liturgical assembly, tending to those in need (widows, orphans, sick, foreigners, etc.). There are deaconesses*, too, especially in the East.

In Rome* the seven deacons (for 42 priests), as everywhere, were in charge of finances and outside relations, which put them in a better position than priests for succeeding the bishop. Little by little, however, the deacons were entirely subordinated to the priests. And Jerome, by equating priests and bishops (*Ep.* 146), would arrive at a linear hierarchy of the three orders. Only the archdeacon was not included, while retaining a position of "vicar-general," responsible for temporal matters and for the clergy.

The success of this "*opinio Hieronymi*" fed the medieval thesis of sacramental equivalence between bishops and priests, and, in turn, this thesis partially explained why the Reformed churches only rarely kept the episcopate.

c) Waning of the Diaconate. From the sixth century onward, and even in the East, deacons were restricted to liturgical service, and the rest of their tasks—their deaconship—were given to others. In the 11th century the archdeacon became a priest, and the diaconate simply became an intermediary position, except for a few cardinals (as, for example, in the case of Antonelli, secretary of state of Pius IX. Antonelli died in 1902).

d) Reestablishment of the Diaconate as a Permanent Ministry. Drawing mainly on French and German pastoral and theological thought, and encouraged by Pius XII (who ascertained the sacramental value of the diaconate in his *Sacramentum Ordinis* of 1947), Vatican* II reestablished the diaconate as a permanent ministry (*LG 29; see AG* 15–16). The *Relatio* before the vote (*Acta Syn* III, III, I, 260–61) clarified the distinct character of this ministry. Priests and deacons are ministers of the word* and the liturgy*: the pastoral ministry defines the former, the deaconship and charity the latter. The long list of tasks assigned to deacons does not express the essence of the diaconate and has no empirical value. The *CIC* of 1983 certainly seems to talk about deacons as pastors (pastor*) and representatives of the Christ-head. Their participation in the three functions of Christ* differs only slightly from that of priests and bishops. But when it specifically discusses the subject of the pastoral in can. 517 §2, it places deacons and laity (lay/laity*) on the same footing.

In terms of this ministry, the expectations of Vatican II are complex: to revive the deaconship within a Church that is poor and sees itself in a serving role to create new resources for ministry; to modify the canonical status of the cleric*; and to rediscover the full diversity of the ministry within orthodoxy*.

e) Systematic Theology. The backbone of the diaconate is the deaconship. It is not the aim that the ordination of a particular few of these individuals should give an example of service. Rather ordination gives them grace* and requires them to stimulate and organize the Christian service for everybody and to take the necessary initiatives in this direction. This focal point of their ministry colors their service of the word and their liturgical responsibilities in a way that conforms with tradition. In fact, the deacons of antiquity did not preach. It was only in 1925 that they became extraordinary ministers of baptism* and funerals, and until Vatican II they did not perform nuptial blessings in either the East or the West.

The ministry of deacons makes those who hold it the born helper of bishops, because, in doctrinal terms, deacons are not auxiliaries to priests. They can perform extra-parish or diocesan responsibilities and thus receive a sector-based authority* vis-à-vis the priests. Thus, the relationship between bishop-priest-deacon is more triangular than vertical; and it is not an isosceles triangle, since according to Nicaea* (can. 18) the "deacons, servants of the bishop, are situated one degree below priests" (*COD* 14–15).

f) Pastoral Interests. Intended to revitalize service in poor and serving Churches, the diaconate mostly grew in rich churches: 62 percent of the world's deacons can be found in the United States and 40 percent of European deacons are in Germany. The ministry of deacons was meant first of all for young churches (*AG* 15–16), but 98 percent of deacons can be found in former Christendom.

The deacon promises a thorough evangelization: living in a family*, in a neighborhood, having a profession (able legally to participate in union activity and even in politics), deacons can bring social organizations and the Church closer together. Their experience can benefit preaching and decision making, and not only wedding (marriage*) celebrations, baptisms, funerals, and so forth.

Finally, Catholics can, thanks to deacons, be trained by a married, ordained minister and, moreover, can be called to the ministry*, a request that could be answered in the future. Most were called without volunteering, according to the needs of serving the gospel in the local church*, and on the basis of their known abilities rather than on the basis of candidature, something that is mandatory for priests (*see Instruction de la Congrégation des Sacrements,* AAS 23, 1930).

g) Ecumenical Perspective. The permanent diaconate draws a parallel between the Catholic and Orthodox Churches. Although the Reformation, focusing on the pastoral ministry, stressed the deaconship, the "document of Lima" (*BEM* n. 31) offers a significant opening by proposing to all that the threefold ministry be adopted and by describing the diaconate in terms acceptable to Catholics.

• A. Amanieu (1935), "Archidiacre", *DDC* 1, 948–1004.
Th. Klauser (1956), "Diakon," *RAC* 3, 808–903.
J.G. Plöger, H. Weber (1981), *Der Diakon: Wiederentdeckung und Erneuerung seines Dienstes,* Fribourg-Basel-Vienna.
H. Legrand (1985), "Le diaconat: renouveau et théologie," *RSPhTh* 69, 101–24.
J.N. Collins (1990), *Diakonia: Re-interpreting the Ancient Sources,* New York.
H. Renard (1990), *Diaconat et solidarité,* Mulhouse.

Hervé Legrand

See also **Bishop; Liturgy; Ministry; Presbyter/Priest; Vatican II, Council of**

Deaconesses

a) In the Ancient Tradition. The name deaconess *(Diakonissa)* appeared in the fourth century, in both Greek (First Council of Nicaea*, can. 19) and Latin *(Thesaurus Linguae Latinae, s.v).* In the New Testament, however, there is one instance (Rom 16:1f.) of a woman named Phoebe, *diakonos* of the church* of Cenchreae. Historians are not sure about the exact significance of Phoebe's role or of the role of deaconesses and widows in the Christian communities of the first centuries. Neither at that time, nor in the centuries that followed, was there a straightforward symmetry between the respective tasks of the deaconesses (mainly to help during the baptism* of adult women) and the deacons* (mainly the service of the Eucharist table and the proclamation of the Word*), nor between their respective liturgical and theological statuses. The deacons were greatly active in charitable service, but it is not clear whether deaconesses had a comparable role.

In the Byzantine liturgy* the rite of investiture or ordination* of deaconesses was particularly close to that of the ordination of deacons, but their role seems to have evaporated with the disappearance of adult baptism. In the 11th century the great Greek canonist Balsamon (PG 137, 441) noted this discontinuation. He considered the ordination of deaconesses of the abbesses of certain monastic communities to be "improper" *(katakhrèstikôs).* The possibility of restoring a female diaconate was discussed in the Catholic Church after Vatican II, taking into account on the one hand the differing witnesses of tradition on this question (Vagaggini, Martimort), and on the other hand the possible interpretations of the office of deacon and its relation to the Eucharist*.

b) In Protestantism Communities. In Protestantism communities, deaconesses developed from the 19th century onward. Their aim was to put into practice the New Testament notion of deaconship, not unlike certain Catholic communities that were committed to helping the poor.

• R. Gryson (1972), *Le ministère des femmes dans l'Église ancienne,* Gembloux.
C. Vagaggini (1974), "L'ordinazione delle diaconesse nelle tradizione greca e bizantina," *OCP* 40, 145–89.
A.-G. Martimort (1982), *Les diaconesses, essai historique,* Rome.
D. Ansorge (1990), "Der Diakonat der Frau," in T. Berger, A. Gerhards (Ed.), *Liturgie und Frauenfrage,* St. Ottilien, 31–65.

PIERRE-MARIE GY

See also **Deacon; Ordination/Order; Woman**

Death

A. Biblical and Systematic Theology

From the beginning, human beings have constantly sought to give meaning to the unthinkable thing that is death by inventing either immortality or a beyond. But in contrast to the eschatologies* attested in many religions, in Christianity there appears the idea of a God* who triumphs over death in and by death itself. However, before being able to speak of a Christian sense of death and elaborating a theology of death, it is necessary to reconstruct the biblical experience of death, in all its complexity and with all its hesitations, up to the threshold of the New Testament.

I. The Biblical Experience of Death

1. The Experience of Death in the Old Testament

The elements of biblical literature concerning the experience of death cannot easily be harmonized. This experience, in fact, appears to be deeply ambiguous. On the one hand, death is experienced as the natural culmination of life, and the people of the Old Testament may believe in God without believing in a beyond. On the other hand, death is felt to be an ordeal, an enigma, a non-salvation; and there appears, even if rather late, some hope* in a victory won by God over death.

a) Death as the Natural Culmination of Life. For the Israelite, earthly life is the quintessential gift of God and to live "old and full of days" (Gn 35:29) is the sign of God's blessing*: "Abraham breathed his last and died in a good old age, an old man and full of years" (Gn 25:8). According to the logic of Hebrew anthropology*, death affects not only the flesh *(bâsâr)* but also the soul (soul*-heart-body) *(nèfèsh).* Thus, man who is made from dust returns to dust (Gn 2:7; 3:19; Ps 90:3; Jb 34:15; Eccl 12:1–7). Human beings have received the earth as a legacy, and their vocation is to make it fruitful and themselves to multiply. Death is a natural inevitability that engenders no tragic feeling, and the absence of survival is compensated for by a large posterity (*see* 2 Sm 14:7).

But for the just man of the Old Testament, fullness of life is not reduced to prosperity; it is life lived with God. For this reason, Sheol*, or the dwelling of the dead, a place of darkness (Jb 10:21f.), is a fearsome place; there man is definitively cut off from God and can no longer praise him (Is 38:18). The dead live in a permanent sleep; their existence is so insubstantial that it is close to nothingness*. In addition, the many ritual prescriptions intended to protect against contact with death as against a fundamental impurity (purity*/impurity) indicate how difficult it was for Israel* to integrate the realm of death into its life of faith, and they constitute a major difference from the surrounding paganism, which maintained a thriving cult* of the dead.

b) Death as an Ordeal and a Curse. Death as the peaceful culmination of life is only one aspect of the believer's experience of death in the Old Testament. Another aspect is indeed the scandal of sudden death "in the middle of my days" (Is 38:10). The Psalms* in particular speak of the threat of a "bad death" whose harbingers are illness, poverty, solitude, and despair. We then see the appearance of a link between death and sin*, and the only recourse making it possible for the just to escape from a "bad death" is to turn toward God, the source of life: "For you will not abandon my soul to Sheol, or let your holy one see corruption" (Ps 16:10).

For the consciousness of Israel, the supreme enigma is nevertheless that the just man, too, experiences a "bad death." Not only may he die too soon, but he also faces the fearsome threat of death while he is living; death is as much a curse for the just as it is for the sinful. Thus in the Old Testament (particularly for the Yahwist) there is a foretaste of a consequence that only the New Testament affirms clearly: something in any case inherent in human finitude, death is also the wages of sin. The narrative* of Genesis thus presents death as the punishment of the sin committed by Adam* and Eve (Gn 2:17), and the same teaching is found in the Wisdom of Solomon (2:24). But one may "wonder whether it is biological death that is seen by Genesis as a consequence of sin and not rather the 'spiritual' death which consists of the prohibition of the tree of life (*see* Gn 3:22)" (Gesché 1995). By disobeying, Adam has chosen to live under the rule of death. There is, however, an alternative: a fullness of life with God, symbolized by the tree of life. "See, I have set before you today life and good, death and evil" (Dt 30:15).

YHWH is the master of life and death: "I kill and I make alive" (Dt 32:39). But the forces of death are always at work in creation*, and it was centuries before the biblical tradition* began to formulate the idea of a definitive victory over death. It was only from the second century B.C., in the Book of Daniel and in the Second Book of Maccabees, that there appeared the explicit affirmation of a resurrection* of the dead. This late belief—but one that was widespread (*see* Puech 1993)—pays tribute to the universal power (omnipotence*) of God, which reaches as far as Sheol, and to his justice*, which cannot possibly leave unrewarded those who have died as martyrs in the name of their faith in YHWH.

2. The Meaning of Death in the New Testament

Of the two faces of death represented in biblical experience, it seems that the New Testament does not exhibit the first, death as the natural culmination of life, but only the second, death as the power of sin, which makes of that culmination an absurd interruption. This is demonstrated in the attitude of Jesus in the face of death; and it is verified above all in the letters of Paul, which contain a veritable theology of death. In Johannine* theology death is a distinctive characteristic of the "world*," contrasted dualistically to the kingdom* of life that Christ* has come to bring. Whoever believes has already passed from death to life (Jn 5:24), but on condition that he love his brother; whoever does not love has remained in death (3:14).

a) It would obviously be presumptuous to claim to know the inner feeling with which Jesus* experienced the instant of his death. However, many signs indicate that he experienced the anguish, solitude, and sorrow that accompany human death. He experienced neither the "good death" of the just of the Old Testament nor the peaceful death of Socrates (e.g., Jüngel 1971). He took on the death of the sinner; and if he asked his Father* to take "this cup" from him, this is perhaps because he experienced his death as the failure of his mission. His cry "My God, my God, why have you forsaken me?" (Mt 27:46) can be interpreted as a cry of despair; but as the reference to Psalms 22 in Matthew and Luke suggests, it is at the same time a surrender to God, the source of life. In the death of Jesus, human death experienced under the sign of sin becomes an access to life. God thus remains faithful by raising Jesus into a new life. "Through the death of Jesus, the history* of the suffering and the death of the world is introduced into the history of God" (Greshake 1974).

b) Reflection on death is one of the keys of Pauline* theology, where death is directly linked to the apostle's teaching about sin, the flesh, the law, baptism, and the *pneuma.* All human existence is in fact understood as a field of tension between death and life. It is in Paul, furthermore, that the link between sin and death is affirmed in the most explicit manner (Rom 5:12; 6:23; 1 Cor 15:21), and in a way that was to be adopted by the entire subsequent Christian tradition. The old law was in the service of death (2 Cor 3:7ff.), and this death-dealing power of the law is conditioned by the flesh* *(sarx)* (Rom 8:3). Although the *sarx,* taken in itself, is not an active power of death, it is in it that the power of sin is manifested. What the law could not accomplish, God can; he thus sent his Son, who took on a flesh of sin to liberate us from the law of sin and death through the power of his spirit (Rom 8:2). Human beings are subject to biological death "because of sin"; but for whoever "dies with Christ," death is definitively conquered thanks to the Spirit that inhabits the Risen One.

For whoever is baptized in Christ, daily life is a death and a resurrection with him (Rom 6:2f.). Baptism* is a death mysteriously connected to the death and resurrection* of Christ; and for the baptized, all of Christian life, including physical death, is nothing but a permanent dying with Christ (Phil 3:21–23). By rejecting a life that wishes to be attached to itself and that is in reality only a death, the believer who lives in communion* with Christ has already conquered death. And this is why physical death, despite its somber and threatening character, is fundamentally relativized. "If we live, we live to the Lord, and if we die, we die to the Lord. So then, whether we live or whether we die, we are the Lord's" (Rom 14:8).

II. For a Theology of Death

1. The Official Teaching of the Churches

This teaching can be summarized in a few propositions.

a) Death Is a Consequence of Sin. This is a classic patristic affirmation (Origen, *Com. in Joh.* 13. 60, PG 14. 513B; Cyril of Alexandria, *De adoratione in spiritu et veritate* 16, J. Aubert I, 554). The Council of Trent* adopted it explicitly in the decree on original sin (*DS* 788ff.). The same assertion is found in the constitution *Gaudium et spes* of Vatican* II: "Christian faith teaches that this bodily death from which man would have been preserved had he not sinned will one day be conquered." (18). Similarly in the CCC of 1992: "Even though man's nature is mortal, God had destined him not to die" (1008). The magisterium* refers to several scriptural passages, in particular Genesis 2:17; Wisdom of Solomon 2:23f.; Romans 5:12; 6:23. But it should never be forgotten that this traditional teaching presupposes a doctrine of immortality that conceives it as a preternatural gift inherent in the state of original justice and not as a natural property of human beings before the Fall. The thesis is also present in Protestant confessions of faith, for example, the Apology of the Augsburg Confession (FEL §91) and the later Swiss Confession (CCFR 220ff.).

b) Death Is a Universal Fate. Even though the tradition prefers to speak of "dormition," Mary herself, who did not know sin, passed to God through death. And in 1 Corinthians 15:51 Paul asserts that those who are alive at the Parousia* will experience a radical transformation. The entire hymnography of the Byzantine Feast of the Dormition rings variations on this theme.

c) Death Is the End of Earthly Life. Catholicism*, and along with it the principal current of Christianity, rejects the idea of a universal salvation or a final restoration of all souls (apocatastasis*, anathematized by the Second Council of Constantinople; *see DS* 411), and it does not extend the concept of liberty* to its account of the afterlife. Death coincides with God's definitive judgment* (*DS* 464, 530ff.). The idea of a final restoration is also rejected by the Augsburg Confession (FEL §23) and by the Catechism of Heidelberg (CCFR 150). In the same perspective, Christianity has always rejected the idea of reincarnation, regardless of the way in which it is understood.

2. The Recent Orientation of Theology

Traditional treatises on the Last Things proposed an implicit theology of death, but one that was concerned principally with the fate of the dead after death, and they frequently indulged in a kind of cartography of the beyond. Under the influence of existentialist philosophies (Marcel, Sartre) and of phenomenology (Heidegger*, Fink), theological analysis has recently concentrated on the question of dying, that is, on the very instant of death.

a) The Inadequacy of a Definition. Death is a specifically human event that concerns the entire being, inseparably spirit and flesh. Death is a biological given common to all living beings. But strictly speaking, only humans are "mortal," insofar as they alone are capable of establishing a relationship with their own death. Following Heidegger, dying can be defined as the way of being by which *Dasein* relates to its death. We know death only through the death of others. But that is still death apprehended in a general sense, not death as the "inmost, absolute, uttermost possibility" of *Dasein* (*Sein und Zeit* 250). In defining existence as a being-toward-death, it is understood that human death is not an accident that comes from outside but a permanent possibility. Further, it is not only a sign of the innate finiteness of the human being; it can be the sign of an authentic existence. In contrast to Sartre, for whom death is an absurd interruption of temporality, for Heidegger it is precisely the daily confrontation with death that gives meaning to existence.

This ontological approach to dying brings out the inadequacy of the classic definition of death as the "separation of the soul from the body (soul-heart-body)." Indeed, this says nothing of the specificity of human death, insofar as it concerns the entire person as a spiritual and carnal entity. It designates death as the interruption of life but not death as a possibility immanent throughout existence and as a culmination of liberty. It is content with expressing in a descriptive way the traditional doctrine according to which, whereas the body decomposes after death, the soul of the just is introduced into communion with God. But in accordance with the unitary anthropology of the Bible*, the "soul" must be perceived "not as a part of man alongside the body, but as the vital principle of man considered in his unity and his totality, in other words, his 'ego,' the center of the person" (Katholischer Erwachsenen-Katechismus 1985). And it is possible to assert of the soul, understood in this way, that in death itself it experiences a greater proximity to the unity of this world of which the body is only a part. K. Rahner* (1958) goes so far as to think that "in death the soul does not become a-cosmic but, if one may say so, pan-cosmic."

b) The Interpretation of Death as the Wages of Sin. The scriptural passages on which the traditional theory of death as the consequence of sin is based call for a hermeneutics* that does not confuse the religious import of the biblical message with teaching of a scientific order. God does not will death. But that does not mean that human beings, had they not sinned, would have had an unlimited life on earth. The death that punishes the sin of the first man is not biological death but "spiritual death," that is, non-access to eternity, experienced in suffering and anguish as a fatal and absurd destiny; and the victory achieved by the risen Christ is not a victory over natural death but over the separation between man and the eternity* of God, of which it has become the most meaningful sign.

c) Death as Necessity and as Freedom. Human death is profoundly ambiguous. Just as man is spirit and matter, freedom and necessity, person and nature, so his death is a complex and dialectical reality. It is both the culmination of man as a spiritual person, that is, the fullness of his free spiritual reality, and the interruption of his biological life, that is, the most radical dispossession of the self (*see* Rahner 1985).

On the basis of this dialectic between necessity and freedom, between passivity and supreme accomplishment of the self, some theologians (Boros, Troisfontaines, Schoonenberg) thought it possible to develop the thesis of the final choice, according to which the instant of death coincides with an ultimate decision for or against God. But this hypothesis is by definition unverifiable, and the phenomenon of dying has all the appearances of a total dispossession of the self. Moreover, if we attempt in this context to think of a final act of freedom coinciding with the instant of passage, it has already escaped from temporality. The theory would therefore contradict the teaching of the Church on the irrevocable character of death as the definitive seal on our moral fate.

d) Death as a Paschal Mystery. If, finally, we leave the impenetrable instant of dying in order to take into account the death experienced by the dying person, that is, the passage, then, in a Christian perspective, we must speak of the two faces of death. Death indeed changes signs depending on whether it is the tragic manifestation of the power of sin (as a break with God) or the crucial site of the encounter with God. "Blessed are the dead who die in the Lord from now on" (Rev 14:13). Death can become a salvific event that brings to completion in man a sacramental encounter with Christ inaugurated by Baptism and the Eucharist*. Insofar as it is identified with the death of Christ, human death is the paschal sacrament of the passage from this world to the Father.

• M. Heidegger (1927), *Sein und Zeit,* GA 2, Frankfurt, 1976.
H.U. von Balthasar (1939), *Apokalypse der deutschen Seele,* III, Salzbourg-Leipzig, 84–230, "die Vergöttlichung des Todes"; id. (1980), *Theodramatik* III, *Die Handlung,* Einsiedeln, 88–124, "Die Zeit und der Tod."
K. Rahner (1958), *Zur Theologie des Todes,* Fribourg.
R. Troisfontaines (1960), *Je ne meurs pas,* Paris.
L. Boros (1962), *Mysterium mortis,* Olden-Fribourg.
E. Fink (1969), *Metaphysik und Tod,* Stuttgart; id. (1976), *Grundphänomene der menschlicher Daseins,* Freiberg-Munich.
G. Greshake (1969), *Auferstehung der Toten,* Essen; id. (1974), "Pour une théologie de la mort," *Conc (F)* 94, 79–93.
D.Z. Phillips (1970), *Death and Immortality,* London.
F. Wiplinger (1970), *Der personal verstandene Tod,* Freiberg.
P. Grelot (1971), *De la mort à la vie éternelle,* Paris.
E. Jüngel (1971), *Tod,* Stuttgart.
L.V. Thomas (1976), *Anthropologie de la mort,* Paris.
J. Ratzinger (1977), *Eschatologie: Tod und ewiges Leben,* Regensburg.
X. Léon-Dufour (1979), *Face à la mort: Jésus et Paul,* Paris.
E. Biser (1981), *Dasein auf Abruf: Der Tod als Schicksal, Versuchung und Aufgabe,* Düsseldorf.
H. Küng (1982), *Ewiges Leben?,* Munich.
G. Couturier (Ed.) (1985), *Essais sur la mort,* Montréal.
R. Martin-Achard (1988), *La mort en face selon la Bible hébraïque,* Geneva.
J.-Y. Lacoste (1990), *Note sur le temps,* Paris.
O. González de Cardedal (1993), *Madre y muerte,* Salamanca.
E. Lévinas (1993), "La mort et le temps," in *Dieu, la mort et le temps,* Paris, 13–134.
E. Puech (1993), *La croyance des Esséniens en la vie future,* 2 vols., Paris.
Fr. Dastur (1994), *La mort. Essai sur la finitude,* Paris.
A. Gesché (1995), *La destinée,* Paris.

Claude Geffre

See also **Adam; Life, Eternal; Resurrection of the Dead; Sin; Sin, Original**

B. Moral Theology

a) Thou Shalt Not Kill. God* alone is the master of life, from its beginning to its end (*Donum vitae,* intr. 5). Taking his place in deciding on the death of a human being, one's own or that of another, constitutes not only an injustice, because man is disposing of what does not belong to him, but above all an act of idolatry*. This explains the prohibition in the Ten Commandments (Decalogue*): "You shall not murder" (Ex 20:13). This prohibition is total: the commandments represent the absolutes of love. It therefore has no exception or dispensation; it is never permissible to kill one's neighbor. Only the realms of war (doctrine of the just war and of legitimate defense) and justice (application of the death penalty [punishment*]) require that it be subjected to qualification. In the Christian tradition*, life received at birth is not given over to the arbitrary will of man, for he is not himself his own beginning. He is therefore not the owner of his life but its steward; it is entrusted to his prudence*; he will be required to account for the way in which he has maintained it. This placing of life in the hands of the only created being that God willed for itself entails a series of moral duties, sometimes assuming a positive form (an obligation to act), sometimes a negative form (a prohibition against acting).

b) Duty to Protect One's Life. The first positive duty consists of preserving the life entrusted to the vigilance of the subject, thus of defending it from threats weighing upon it. This duty is expressed in two principles: legitimate defense and the moral obligation to preserve one's own health; only the second is analyzed here.

Contrary to what may have been said of it, the Christian tradition has never made of physical life a moral absolute. Of course, it has declared that "life is sacred," but this must be interpreted as follows: the human person* is sacred because he is created in the image of God and destined for Trinitarian life; this applies, by extension, to everything that makes up the person. Just as there is a "hierarchy* of truths" in dogmatics (dogmatic* theology), so there is a "hierarchy of duties" in morality, in which the preservation of physical life does not rank highest. On the contrary, man has the duty to expose his life to pay tribute to higher values such as charity, truth, and justice, or to accomplish the mission that providence has entrusted to him.

The martyr illustrates the first case: he confesses his faith* and offers his life as a token of homage to the one from whom "we hold life, growth, and being*." Martyrdom* has sometimes been likened to suicide. Of course, the witness knows that his act will cost him his life, but he does not seek death for itself. Circumstances force him to recognize that his witness can take on no form but a bloody one; but it is this witness that he seeks ("direct will") and not its consequence, death ("indirect will").

Every Christian has received a mission to bear witness, and he must place his health at the service of that mission and thus preserve it. This term presupposes a definition of health. In a century dominated by utilitarianism*, emphasis on mere good physical condition has become dangerous. The person risks being reduced to mere material actions and social contributions. But health implies the harmonious development of all human faculties, physical, psychological, intellectual, social, moral, and spiritual. "A complete view of human health assumes the greatest possible harmony between the forces and energies of man, the most fully developed spiritualization of the corporeal aspect of man, and the finest possible expression of the spiritual. True health manifests itself in the self-realization of the human person who has reached the freedom that mobilizes all energies to accomplish his complete human vocation" (Häring 1975).

Human beings thus have the moral duty to preserve their health with the means appropriate to their condition: rest, relaxation, and daily hygiene in normal circumstances; recourse to medicine and application of suitable therapies in case of illness. Premature aging due to the negligence of the subject constitutes a moral fault.

c) Prohibition of Suicide. The divine prohibition of murder and the obligation to preserve one's health suggest the reasons that led the Christian tradition to condemn suicide. Suicide in fact represents a threefold injustice. It runs counter to the natural love that every man should bear love toward himself: suicide is an injustice against oneself. It unilaterally breaks the bonds of solidarity with other human beings, in particular with the members of one's own family*: suicide is an injustice against others. Finally, it amounts to using one's life as though one were its owner: suicide is an injustice against the Creator. Only the final objection is determinative, and the two others flow from it.

Without reference to God, as is the case in a secularized society* (secularization*), the moral condemnation of suicide has difficulty in finding justification. One of two things is true, in fact. Either the individual draws his human dignity from his membership of the social body, which would then have the duty of dissuading the potential suicide from leaving it without its permission and if necessary of preventing this from happening. This is the usual practice today, but it amounts to placing society above the person and exposing the person to the totalitarian temptations inherent in every society. Or else, with the Christian tradition, one asserts that only the human person is destined for beatitude*, and thus that society is at his service to help him to realize his supernatural vocation. Even without any reference to God, society certainly has the duty to attempt to persuade someone whose attempted suicide represents a disguised call for help; but it should give way before the free and lucid will of someone who has decided to put an end to his days.

The Bible* mentions few suicides (Abimelek [Jgs 9:53–54], Saul and his rider [1 Sm 31:3–5], Zimri [1 Kgs 16, 18], Judas [Mt 27:5], etc.). Moreover, the Christian tradition is surprisingly silent on the subject up to the fourth century. The early attitude of the Fathers* of the Church was to not totally exclude suicide (Eusebius of Caesarea, *HE* VIII. 8; John Chrysostom*, *De consolatione mortis,* PG 56. 299; Ambrose*, *De virginibus,* PL 16. 241–43). Augustine*, however, established the doctrine (*City of God* I. 16–18, 20, 22, 27): whoever willfully kills himself commits a homicide. The Council of Orange (533) denied religious burial to anyone who died by suicide. Toledo XVI (693) excommunicated those who attempted suicide. Modern Churches, however, have learned to distinguish between the various psychological motivations that may lead to this act, and the 1983 Code of Canon Law has lifted almost all the sanctions that affected suicides; their remains can now receive religious burial.

d) Euthanasia and Medical Prolongation of Life. Euthanasia has sometimes been compared to suicide, and indeed, the two practices pose similar ethical problems. The word originally meant a "gentle and peaceful death"; today, "the term euthanasia designates the practices whose objective is to bring about the death of others so that they may avoid suffering" (Verspieren). These practices include acts that actually kill (active euthanasia) as well as omissions (passive euthanasia). In order for there to be euthanasia, two essential elements must come together: a relationship of cause and effect between the act of the agent and the death of the patient and the deliberate intention to seek that death.

Moral judgment concerning euthanasia may vary. Pope John Paul II (1995) has condemned it categorically: "I confirm that euthanasia is a serious violation of the law of God*, as a deliberate and morally unacceptable murder of a human person. This doctrine is based on natural law and on the written word of God" (§65). Conversely, certain Reformed theologians emphasize the "quality of life which is more important than its length" (Thevoz, Baertschi 1993).

On the other hand, euthanasia does not occur if the patient refuses the treatment indicated, against the advice of the doctor. The practitioner is in fact at the service of the patient and must give way before his freedom, even if he believes the patient to be wrong. "The rights and duties of the doctor are correlative with those of the patient. The doctor may act only if the patient explicitly or implicitly authorizes him to do so" (Pius XII). Nor does euthanasia occur if the doctor abstains from undertaking a treatment that he considers disproportionate with respect to the expected results or too burdensome for the patient and his family. Finally, the term *euthanasia* is totally unjustified when the doctor takes proportional risks (analgesic risks) to relieve the suffering of patients. What is known as the law of twofold effect is present in this context: the administration of "pharmaceutical cocktails" aims at reducing suffering (direct will), even if the practitioner knows that death may thereby be accelerated (indirect will); there is thus no moral objection to the practice. Accompanying the dying constitutes one of the highest forms of love of one's fellow beings. It sometimes takes the form of "palliative care," which makes suffering more bearable in the final phase of illness and provides an appropriate human companionship for the patient. "Those who have the courage and the love necessary to remain with a dying patient, in the silence that goes beyond words, know that that moment is neither frightening, nor painful, but the peaceful cessation of the functioning of the body" (Kübler-Ross 1975).

• P.L. Landsberg (1951, 2nd Ed. 1993), *Essai sur l'expérience de la mort* followed by *Problème moral du suicide,* Paris.
B. Häring (1975), *Perspective chrétienne pour une médecine humaine,* Paris.
E. Kübler-Ross (1975), *Les derniers instants de la vie,* Geneva.
P. Ramsey (1978), *Ethics at the Edges of Life,* New Haven.
H. Thielicke (1980), *Leben mit dem Tod,* Tübingen.
J.R. Nelson (1984), *Human Life: A Biblical Perspective for Bioethics,* Philadelphia.
K. Demmer (1987), *Leben im Menschenhand,* Fribourg.
Textes du Magistère (1987), *Biologie, médecine et éthique,* Paris.
B. Brody (1988), *Life and Death Decision-Making,* Oxford.
R. Veatch (1989), *Death, Dying and the Biological Revolution,* New Haven.
B. Baertschi (1993), "La vie humaine est-elle sacrée? Euthanasie et assistance au suicide," *RThPh* 125, 359–81.
Coll. (1994), "Est-il indigne de mourir? Autour de Paul Ramsey", *Éthique* 11, 6–99.
L. Gormally (Ed.) (1994), *Euthanasia, Clinical Practice and the Law,* London.

H. Ebeling (1995), "Selbstmord," *HWP* 9, 493–99.
Jean-Paul II (1995), *Evangelium Vitae,* Vatican City.
J. Keown (Ed.) (1995), *Euthanasia Examined,* Cambridge.
A. Fagot-Largeault (1996), "Vie et mort," *DEPhM,* 1583–90.
G. Meilander (1996), *Body, Soul and Bioethics,* Notre Dame, Ind.
Coll. (1998), "Euthanasia," *SCE* 11/1, 1–76.
B. Wannenwetsch (1998), "Intrinsically Evil Acts," in R. Hütter, T. Dieter (Ed.), *Ecumenical Ventures in Ethics,* Grand Rapids, Mich., 185–215.

JEAN-LOUIS BRUGUÈS

See also **Abortion; Ethics, Medical; Legitimate Defense; War**

Decalogue

The term *Decalogue* has its origin in three passages of the Old Testament that contain the expression "the Ten Words," or as more commonly and loosely translated, "the Ten Commandments" (Ex 34:28 and Dt 4:13 and 10:4). Although it is derived from Greek the term does not appear in the Greek translation (translations* of the Bible, ancient) of the Bible,* but it is found in Ptolemy's second-century *Letter to Flora,* in Irenaeus*'s (c. 130–200) Latin translation (*Adversus Haereses* [*Against Heresies*]), and in Clement of Alexandria (c. 150–c. 215) (*Paedagogus* [Pedagogy]). By the third century it had became common in the writings of Christians.

There are two versions of the Decalogue, one in Exodus 20:2–17, the other in Deuteronomy 5:6–21, differentiated by around 20 variations. Some of these are minor, but one of the most important concerns the motivation that accompanies the prescription of the Sabbath*. In addition to these two versions, the text of the Decalogue can be found in the Samaritan Pentateuch (*see* translations of the Bible, ancient), as well as on the phylacteries of Qumran (4Q128–29, 134, 137) and in the Hebrew Nash papyrus (first century B.C.), where it is followed by the beginning of the Shema Israel. These are indications of how important the Decalogue was.

a) Context. The text of Exodus 20:1–17 is inserted into a vast literary ensemble, the theophany* of Sinai, but it cuts the theophanic narrative in two: Exodus 19:1–25 is followed by 20:18–21. The Decalogue, a text that had already been composed and was inserted at a late stage, is thus connected to the covenant* between God* and Israel*. The version in Deuteronomy displays a very similar context. Indeed, the prescriptions of the Decalogue, given by God "at the mountain, out of the midst of the fire" (Dt 5:4), are written by him on two tables of stone given to Moses (Dt 5:22), which are called "the tablets of the covenant" in Deuteronomy 9:9–11. Following the episode of the golden calf, new tablets are given by God to Moses, who has broken the first tablets: he places them in the ark (Dt 10:4–5). The Decalogue is presented as a primordially independent text, distinct from the sets of laws that form the Code of the Covenant (Ex 20:22–23:33) or the Deuteronomic Code (Dt chap. 12–26), yet connected with the covenant, which gives the Decalogue its dimension of revelation*. Moses is ordinarily the one who transmits the divine law*, but by way of its opening formula, at least, God directly communicates the Decalogue to the people* of Israel: "I am the Lord your God, who brought you out of the land of Egypt" (Dt 5:6).

b) Genesis of the Decalogue. The existence of two versions of the Decalogue, with their differences, is a primary indication that its text is the outcome of a long literary history. The presence of prescriptions of different lengths, some formulated in a curt and negative style, others in a positive style (concerning the observance of the Sabbath and the honor due to parents), and a phraseology that is both similar to and different from that of Deuteronomy, have led commentators to suggest a primitive form of the Decalogue. The solution most often put forward has consisted in "uncovering" 10 short, negative words, although they are clearly hypothetical in nature. Certainly, the existence of such a text would allow us to understand the expression "the Ten Words," but that is not enough to prove that this expression goes very far back in time. We shall simply observe that it is possible to find sequences that are fairly comparable to the Decalogue in

Exodus 23:1–9; Leviticus 18:7–17, 19:3–4, and 19:11–12; and the series of curses in Deuteronomy 27:15–26. However, it is not easy to reach the number 10 in the texts just cited. On the other hand, it is possible that shorter sequences existed at an early stage, such as the triad of killing, stealing, and committing adultery, which is evidenced in Hosea 4:2, Jeremiah 7:9, and Job 24:14–15, although the order of the verbs is not always identical. Finally, it is also possible that worship played a role in the elaboration of certain positive or negative forms, as may be seen in Psalms 15:3–4 and 24:4. But there, too, there is nothing that would allow us to conclude that the Decalogue had an origin in worship. Its origin is lost to us, but the present condition of the text should be situated at the end of a long process that was not completed until the return from exile, when the observance of the weekly Sabbath was instituted. The motivation of the Sabbath in Exodus 20:11, which is no longer, as in Deuteronomy 5:15, the commemoration of the ending of bondage, suggests that it is based on Genesis 2:1–3, a text from the priestly redaction. God's resting on the seventh day then serves as the foundation for human beings' resting.

c) Structure of the Decalogue. Because the text of the Decalogue was written, according to the Bible, on two tables, the Ten Commandments have often been divided into two sets of five, the first concerned with God, the second with one's neighbor. This division into exact halves does not coincide with the literary structure of the text. Analysis permits us to discern three parts.

The first part (Dt 5:6–10) opens with the words: "I am the Lord your God who brought you out of the land of Egypt, out of the house of bondage." These find an echo in Deuteronomy 5:9: "I the Lord your God." The speaker is God; he first recalls the sign of his authority* and power (omnipotence*), the departure from Egypt, which for Israel was a departure from bondage. God sustains liberty*. However, the divine proclamation is not related only to the past; it is also turned toward the future of a covenant relationship, addressed to a people in which several generations coexist and which is faced with a choice between using its liberty to maintain the commandments of its God or not doing so. This God is presented as a jealous God, thus revealing a love* that is not indifferent to what the other is becoming, a love that punishes and shows mercy.

In the second part, God no longer speaks in the first person: instead, his name is pronounced in the third person (Dt 5:11–16). Here, the person being addressed is the male Israelite with responsibility for a household and for his parents. The observance of the Sabbath is based on the act of departing from Egypt, for which it serves as commemoration. Deuteronomy 5:15 refers back to the beginning of the Decalogue and structures the text around the theme of bondage and liberty.

In the third part (Dt 5:17–21), God is not named, but one's neighbor is mentioned four times. The male Israelite is invited to respect the life, wife, goods, and honor of his "neighbor."

Thus, the Decalogue lays down a way of life and liberty in a condensed style. The number of negative formulas—12 in all—shows that the role of the law is to be open to positive acts, to be developed unceasingly within the framework of the covenant.

d) Scope of the Decalogue. The second commandment states: " You shall not make for yourself a carved image" (Ex 20:4), but it is not directed against all figurative representation. It is only opposed to representations that are made into objects of idolatrous worship. Thus, Hezekiah uses it to justify destroying the bronze serpent made by Moses because the Jews burned incense before it (2 Kgs 18:4). The representations of animals* that could be seen in the Temple* at Jerusalem* had no more than an aesthetic value, whatever they may have signified originally (compare 1 Kgs 7:25, 29).

Respect for the name of YHWH (Ex 20:7) implies a ban on preaching false sermons while invoking this Name and, more generally, a ban on using it without a worthy motive.

"You shall not murder" (Ex 20:13) is aimed at illegal homicide and therefore at the murder of the innocent (the verb in Hebrew is *ratsakh*). This prohibition is located within the framework of a society* that did not regard the death penalty or war as transgressions of the Decalogue.

"You shall not steal" (Ex 20:15) concerns theft in general, not simply abduction, as may be supposed on the basis of Exodus 21:16 and Deuteronomy 24:7. The prescription has a universal application.

The "neighbor" mentioned in the final prescriptions of the Decalogue may have a limited range, being limited to members of the Israelite community (*see* Lv 19:16–18), but the term may be given a broader meaning.

Thus, the Decalogue establishes the law as a law of liberty, but it is not the whole of the law. It is addressed first and foremost to Israel, within the framework of the covenant, as is emphasized by the inclusion of the Sabbath, but also to every human conscience, called to recognize the creation as the work of a single God (Ex 20:11).

e) Decalogue and the New Testament. The Decalogue is quoted in the New Testament but never as a whole and never in the canonical sequence. The episode of the calling of the rich young man (Mk 10:17–22, Mt 19:16–22, and Lk 18:18–23) and the Sermon on the Mount (Mt 5:21–28) offer the best examples of this, for the quotations of the Decalogue concern only one's neighbor. In Romans 7:7, Paul also makes reference to the last part of the Decalogue. In Matthew 19:19, the prescriptions of the Decalogue on one's neighbor are reprised in a condensed manner with a quotation of Leviticus 19:18: "You shall love your neighbor as yourself" (Lk 10:27). This presentation can also be found in Romans 13:9–10, where love of neighbor is seen as the achievement of the whole of the law (as it is in Gal 5:14). James 2:8–11 also quotes the Decalogue and makes it a law of freedom in Christ*.

Perhaps the New Testament does not quote the whole of the Decalogue because knowledge* of the one God passes by way of Christ, who reveals God as the Father* and has all authority: "The Son of man is lord even of the Sabbath" (Mk 2:28). The first part of the Decalogue could not but be transformed by this revelation.

• J.J. Stamm (1959), *Le décalogue à la lumière des recherches contemporaines,* Neuchâtel-Paris.

P. Grelot (1982), *Problèmes de morale fondamentale,* Paris, 107–15.

F.L. Hossfeld (1982), *Der Dekalog: Seine späten Fassungen, die originale Komposition und seine Vorstufen,* OBO 45, Freiberg-Göttingen.

J. Loza (1989), *Las Palabras de Yahwe: Estudios del Decalogo,* Mexico.

G. Levi (1990) (Ed.), *The Ten Commandments in History and Tradition,* Jerusalem.

W.H. Schmidt, H. Delkurt, A. Graupner (1993), *Die Zehn Gebote im Rahmen alttestamentlicher Ethik,* EdF 281.

A. Wénin (1995), *L'homme biblique: Anthropologie et éthique dans le Premier Testament,* Paris, 105–29.

JACQUES BRIEND

See also **Covenant; Cult; Ethics; Idolatry; Law and Christianity; Obligation; Sabbath; Theophany; War**

Deification.

See **Holiness; Mysticism; Rhineland-Flemish Mysticism**

Deism and Theism

The term *déiste,* as P. Bayle noted, appeared in French in 1563 from the pen of the Protestant Pierre Viret *(Instruction chrétienne)* to denote those who believed in God* as creator, in divine Providence*, and in the immortality of the soul (soul-heart-body) but rejected revelation and in particular the dogma* of the Trinity. In English, *deist* appeared first in Burton's *Anatomy of Melancholy* (1621) and was subsequently used by Dryden in 1682. The libertine poem entitled *Les quatrains du déiste* has been dated to around 1620. Mersenne refuted it in 1624 in *L'impiété des déistes,* in which he presents the deist as a misanthrope damned by his own pride.

Deist was originally a polemical term denoting an anti-Trinitarian, a person suspicious of the supernatural*, of revelation and tradition*. Such a person demanded rational proofs for everything and relied on a foundation of ancient philosophical religion of a Stoic and Neoplatonic character to justify his beliefs by means of the theory of common notions (Cicero, *De natura deorum* II) and to insist on the possibility of a salvation* of the just in any religion, or indeed in none. The deist, an enemy of superstition, was afraid neither of death* nor of hell*, for which reason the soubriquet of Epicurean was sometimes applied to him. So as to be better able to attack the deists, their enemies attempted to classify them. G. Voetius (*Disputationes selectae,* Utrecht, 1648–60) counted them among the "practical atheists," alongside the libertines and Epicureans, but S. Clarke suggested some finer distinctions: 1) the "Epicureans," who believed in an infinite and intelligent eternal Being*, creator of the order of the world, but denied providence; 2) those who accepted providence but refused the idea of an absolute distinction between good* and evil* (erudite libertines); 3) those who accepted all the foregoing but denied the immortality of the soul and refused to consider human virtues* as identical to those of God*; and 4) those who had a sound and correct understanding of God and his attributes* but who rejected revelation. The glory of the pagan philosophers was that they had understood the duties of natural religion; the modern deists, by contrast, ridiculed all religion. Ultimately, Clarke made deism equivalent to atheism*.

a) Natural Religion. Herbert of Cherbury, considered the forefather of English deism, never used the term. He defended "lay religion," which corresponded to natural and truly universal religion. Confident in the power of human reason and suspicious of a revelation seen as corrupted by superstition and the priesthood's taste for power, he hoped to establish a kernel common to all religions, one that antedated all history* and therefore all revelation.

Natural religion comprised a small number of fundamental tenets: the existence of a supreme deity, intelligent, good, and provident, who was to be honored by the practice of virtue and who demanded the repentance of wrongs and promised reward or punishment after death. Christ* did not feature in it, though Jesus ("an Israelite theist," according to Voltaire) was held to be an exemplary human being and a model of upright living. The forms of outward religion* were regarded with indifference, after the example of the Stoic *adiaphora.* The characteristics of this primitive religion, the common basis of all religions, were simplicity, rationality, universality, invariableness, tolerance toward all beliefs and rituals (as long as they were compatible with morality), and the undisputed primacy both of ethics* over dogma* and of the spirit over the letter. One of the generally accepted consequences of this was the subordination of religious power to civil power. Its principal representatives, apart from Herbert of Cherbury, were Grotius (*De ver. rel. christ.*, I), Isaac d'Huisseau, and Spinoza (*Tract. theol. pol.,* chap. XIV).

Natural religion fulfilled various roles for its supporters. For Cherbury and d'Huisseau it was *conciliatory* and aimed at reuniting the divided Christian world. For Grotius and Abbadie it was *apologetic,* preparing infidels and recalcitrant spirits for Christianity. Or it was *polemical*—either against the established religions, considered as dogmatic and superstitious, or against erudite libertinism, which retained traditional religion so as to control the masses while keeping for itself a minimal religion with no strong obligations.

b) Deism/Theism. At the end of the 17th century, natural religion, from being a retreat in the face of religious conflict, became a war machine aimed at Christianity—particularly in England, where, after Herbert of Cherbury, deism was typified by its savage critiques of miracles* (Woolston) and the supernatural. Toland transformed deism into pantheism*; and with Hume and Voltaire the term, which had become a euphemism for "atheism," made way for theism, a purified religion befitting philosophers.

The word *theism* appeared in 1740 in Voltaire's *Métaphysique de Newton.* The deist, wrote Diderot (*Suite de l'apologie de M. l'abbé de Prades,* 1752), affirms the existence of God and the reality of evil but denies revelation and doubts the immortality of the soul and the retribution to come. The theist, on the other hand, concedes these points "and awaits a demonstration of revelation before admitting it." While the deist holds simple beliefs that make no practical difference to the demands of natural morality, the theist accepts the need for a form of worship, even if it is only a prayer* in adoration of the infinite* addressed to the rising sun, as in the case of Voltaire. Rousseau, Kant, and J. Simon returned to the concept of natural religion, although, in the "Savoyard curate's profession of faith" (*Émile,* IV), Rousseau expresses the belief that "the life and death of Jesus are those of a God."

Kant* identified the essence of religion with the ethical imperative "to recognize in our duties divine commandments (Decalogue*)." "Religion within the limits of simple reason," undogmatic (since faith* provides neither knowledge nor forms of worship) and comprising only practical and unconditional precepts*, was the culmination of an evolution that progressed, by way of the superstitious and ritualistic religions, to a pure religious faith, which joined the conscience* of the moral imperative to the idea of divinity. The universal Church* was the union of all just human beings; it was pure, egalitarian, and free.

In the 19th century, deism and natural religion would survive only as an inspiration for Masonic codes and to fulfill an aspiration toward the eternal and the infinite, which metamorphosed into a "school of religion" within French spiritualism, notably in the work of J. Simon. In the face of both the freethinkers and the Ultramontanists Simon insisted on the right to be at the same time rationalist and religious.

• *Les quatrains du déiste* (c. 1620), in F. Lachèvre, *Le libertinage au XVIIe siècle,* vol. 2, Paris (1909).
M. Mersenne (1624), *L'impiété des déistes,* Paris.
E. Herbert of Cherbury (1645), *De religione laici,* London.
A. Wissowaty (1676), *Religio rationalis,* Amsterdam.
E. Stillingfleet (1677), *A Letter to a Deist,* London.
J. Dryden (1682), *Religio laici or a layman's faith,* London.
C. Blount (1683), *Religio laici,* London.
J. Abbadie (1684), *Traité de la vérité de la religion chrétienne,* Paris.
J. Toland (1696), *Christianity Not Mysterious,* London.
Derham, William. *Physico-theology; or, A demonstration of the Being and Attributes of God, from His Works of Creation. Being the Substance of Sixteen Sermons, Preached in St. Mary-le-Bow-Church, London. At the Honourable Mr. Boyle's Lectures, in the Years 1711, and 1712.* London: W. Innys, 1742. (London, 1713) [selections].
A. Collins (1713), *Discourse of Freethinking,* London.
T. Halyburton (1714), *Natural Religion Insufficient and Reaveal'd necessary,* Edinburgh.
M. Tindal (1730), *Christianity as Old as the Creation,* London.
J. Leland (1754), *A View of the Principal Deistical Writers,* London.
D. Hume (1757), *The Natural History of Religion,* London; id. (1779), *Dialogues Concerning Natural Religion,* London.
Voltaire (1768), *La Profession de foi des théistes,* Geneva.
E. Kant (1793), *Die Religion innerhalb der Grenzen der blossen Vernunft,* Königsberg.
J. Simon (1856), *La religion naturelle,* Paris.
♦ C.M.D. di Accadia (1970), *Preilluminismo e deismo in Inghilterra,* Naples.
G. Gawlick (1973), *Der Deismus als Grundzug der Religionsphilosophie der Aufklärung,* Göttingen, 15–43.
Chr. Gestrich (1981), "Deismus," *TRE* 8, 392–406.
H. Gouhier (1984), *Les Méditations métaphysiques de Jean-Jacques Rousseau,* Paris.
Y. Belaval, D. Bourel (Ed.) (1986), *Le siècle des Lumières et la Bible,* Paris.
J. Lagrée (1989), *Le salut du laïc,* Paris; id. (1991), *La religion naturelle,* Paris.

Jacqueline Lagrée

See also **Atheism; Kant, Immanuel; Pantheism; Unitarianism; Virtues**

Deity

1. Sources

a) Bible. The Greek *theotes,* or *theiotes,* translated by the Latin *deitas,* "deity," but sometimes also by *divinitas,* "divinity," signifies God* considered in his essence. Deity therefore carries a double meaning: 1) the divine essence both in general and in the abstract, as distinct from its creation* but revealed by that creation (Rom 1:20); and 2) divine nature* as it has been united with humanity through Christ* and as the Christian is united with Christ through baptism* (Col 2:9). This second meaning has also been developed in Trinitarian theology* to include the divine essence as distinct from the three divine persons*.

b) Greek Patristics. *Theotes* played an important role during the major Trinitarian controversies (for example, Cyril of Alexandria, *Dialogues on the Trinity* III, 465d), and up until the 2nd Council of Constantinople* (*DS* 421). At that point it signified the unity of the divine substance, its unique and identical nature, its being* shared with the three persons (Trinity*). The term was often used by the church fathers*, the Pseudo-Dionysius* in particular (over 40 occurrences) and John the Damascene, to designate the divine essence in general. It refers thus to God in himself, in an abstract form that signifies the being-in-itself of the divine principle. It also connotes divine providence*, evoked by the various etymologies proposed for the word *theos* "God," deriving it from "to see" *(theoro),* or from "to run" or "to burn," according to Pseudo-Dionysius and John the Damascene. Deity sometimes refers to the divine nature of Christ, as distinct from his "humanity": that is, the divine essence as distinct and separate from any other essence. This can come about in two ways: 1) Deity can be envisaged as the source from which all creatures emanate, creatures that, according to their degree of perfection, are imitations of a supreme perfection that is peculiar to divine nature. The divine nature par excellence contains all creatures inherently (according to a Neoplatonic interpretation of Rom 1:20). 2) The divine essence can also be considered in its relation with divine persons. Pseudo-Dionysius does not elaborate on this point, except with reference to the person of the Father*, "source of the supersubstantial deity" (*DN* 2, 4, PG 3,

641 D), but without denying that the other persons also have deity: "the Trinity which is deity" (*DN* 13, 3, PG 3, 980 C). John the Scot Eriugena's Latin version of the Dionysian corpus transmitted to the Latin tradition this usage of the term *deity.*

2. Trinitarian Theology

a) In the 12th Century. In describing the origin of the Holy* Spirit, Saint Augustine wrote: "The Father is the principle of Divinity, better still, of Deity" (*The Trinity,* IV, 20, 29), so that the concept of deity would become the subject of bitter debate in Latin Trinitarian theology. Gilbert de la Porrée, bishop* of Poitiers (the school of Chartres*), made no clear distinction between the two meanings of *deity,* deity as a principle of creatures and deity as a principle of Trinitarian processions. For Gilbert de la Porée the pair God/deity corresponds to the *quod est* and the *quo est,* "that which is" and "that through which this is," inherited from Boethius*, for whom the pair expresses the composition peculiar to that which is being created (in contrast to divine simplicity*). If one disregards the persons, God is thus distinguished by his deity, defined as the principle *quo est:* there is therefore in God a principle by virtue of which and according to which God is God. But the rational distinction thus formulated, asserts Gilbert, cannot be posited as real in God, who in himself remains one and simple.

Gilbert's adversaries, led by Bernard* of Clairvaux, criticized him violently, in particular at the Council of Rheims (1148). They rejected any composition in God and asserted that "everything which is in God is God." They deemed the *quo est* principle to be like a cause on which God would depend, an anterior and superior principle. And to differentiate "God" and "deity," they would only accept the grammatical pairing of the concrete and the abstract. Henceforth they would have to postulate that the divine attributes* (eternal, good, wise, etc.) were pure synonyms. But this synonymy would risk depriving each attribute of its literal meaning, which would amount to denying the terms of Trinitarian theology. Accused of heresy in Rheims, Gilbert mounted his defense effectively and competently, but the opinion prevailed, wrongly, that his thesis had been censured. In any case the debate led future theologians to adopt as their motto: "all that which is in God is God himself." Once the problem was raised, however, it would remain unsolved until the next century.

b) 13th Century. The scholars of the 13th century took up the issue again: because of an improved knowledge of Greek and Arabic philosophy, they had at their disposal more refined logical and conceptual instruments. According to Albert* the Great, in God, essence *(quo est)* does not really differ from that which has the essence *(quod est),* but both truly express something of God: *quo est* does in fact play the role of formal cause. Albert returned to the work of John Damascene, for whom "deity is" signified that through which God is—*quo est (Deus)* (*In De Divinis Nominibus* 12, 3, Simon). According to Thomas* Aquinas, one can only form a true language of Trinitarian theology by simultaneously considering both the reality signified and the means of signification (*ST* Ia, q. 39, a. 4–5). He then introduces in God the notion of causal power and shows, with Augustine, that the generation of the Son must be understood as an intellective procession implying a presence unto itself. And he adds: "The power to engender signifies *id quo generans generat,* that by means of which the genitor engenders" (ibid., Ia, q. 41, a. 4). The generating principle engenders in compliance with the form according to which it is the producer and by means of self-assimilation, and the Son is therefore constituted as similar in nature to the Father. Thus, that by means of which the Father engenders is shared by the engenderer and the engendered (ibid., a. 5). And one can therefore say that the divine essence, as an object of divine thought, is the *quo* principle of generation, the principle of the unity of persons and of their distinction. Father and Son are united through their eternal co-relation in the same and unique divine essence, the principle and compass of the act of engendering for the Father, and the principle and compass of the act of being engendered for the Son. Thus, "the Father is the principle of all deity," and Thomas notes that in Trinitarian theology *deity*" is preferable to *divinity.* Although the two terms are frequently used indifferently, *divinity,* which derives from *divinum,* does indeed only express that which participates in deity and not that which is deity through its essence (that is, each of the divine persons: *Sent.* 1, dist. 15, expos. 2[ae] p. text.). And to explain the pair *quod est* and *quo est,* Thomas has recourse to the fundamental distinction between that which is "by participation" *(per participationem)* and that which is "by essence" *(per essentiam).*

c) Meister Eckhart. Taking advantage of the debate on the status of deity, the Rhineland scholar adopted the term in order to interpret grace* as communion* with the intra-Trinitarian life of God (Rhineland*-Flemish mysticism). In a *German Sermon,* he declares: "The Father is the beginning of deity, for in himself he understands himself, and from him emanates the Eternal Word* which resides within him. The Holy Spirit proceeds from these two, remaining in them all the while, he who is the result of the deity" (*S. all.* 15, *Deutsche Werke, [DW]* I, 252, 2–4).

> For this distinction without number, without multiplicity, one hundred is not more than one. If there had been one hundred persons in the Deity, it would be necessary to understand their distinction as being without number, without multiplicity, by recognizing One God therein. (*S. all.* 38, *DW* II, 234, 3–5)

In the Trinity, deity is anterior in nature (but of a timeless anteriority) to any emanation and to any knowledge that we can have of it. It is the divine essence as a measure and criterion of *ad intra* processions (*S. all* 21, *DW* I, 363, 10ff.). It is the "chamber of treasures of eternal paternity," there where the Son is (still) unexpressed and where, expressed, he will return, taking with him the soul in grace like the betrothed of the 45th psalm (*S. all* 22, *DW* I, 388, 1ff. and 10ff.).

Eckhart tells us: "I love to speak of the deity, for from the deity emanates all our happiness. It is where the Father says (to us): 'You are my Son, today I engender you in the splendor of sanctity (holiness*).' " (*S. all.* 79, *DW* III, 369, 2ff.). And to speak of it he returns to an analysis of Thomas, for whom the eternal procession of the Son is the formal and final cause of the temporal mission of that same Son in the soul (soul-heart-body) of the righteous person, who in this way becomes an adopted son. God would not be God if he did not communicate himself (*S. all* 73, *DW* III, 265, 7–9), and it is therefore by virtue of his deity that he communicates himself to the righteous who receive his deity. To be baptized in the Holy* Spirit is to be born in deity in its fullness, where the Father continually engenders the Son (*S. all* 29, *DW* II, 85, 4–86, 8). Numerous formulas of this kind thus followed from Thomasian thought on deity, as both the principle of intra-Trinitarian life and the source of grace.

Eckhart's interpretation also continued some of Gilbert de la Porrée's insights, and, through rigorous noetics, justified a complex Trinitarian theology, one that was compatible with the eminent unity peculiar to the triune God. But it was hardly understood, as is shown by a text from 1473 that describes the internal debates among theologians at the University of Paris: "The nominalists maintain that deity and wisdom are one unique and absolutely identical reality, for everything which is in God is God. The realists affirm that divine wisdom is distinct from deity" (E. Baluze, *Miscellanea,* Éditions J.-B. Mansi, Lucae, 1761).

• Eckhart, *Deutsche Werke* I–III, Ed. J. Quint, Stuttgart, 1936–.
N.M. Häring, *The Commentaries on Boethius by Gilbert of Poitiers,* Toronto, 1966.
Albert the Great, *In Dionysium De Divinis Nominibus,* Ed. P. Simon, *Op. Omn.* XXXVII/1, 1971; id., *In Dionysium De Caeleste Hierarchia,* Ed. Simon-Kübel, *Op. Omn.* XXXVI/1, Münster/W, 1993.
Thomas Aquinas, *ST* Ia, q. 3–42.
♦ A. Hayen (1935–36), "Le concile de Reims et l'erreur théologique de Gilbert de la Porrée," *AHDL* 10, 29–102.
M.E. Williams (1951), *The Teaching of Gilbert of Poitiers on the Trinity as Found in His Commentaries on Boethius,* Rome.
M.A. Schmitt (1956), *Gottheit und Trinität nach dem Kommentar des Gilbert Porreta zu Boethius, De Trinitate,* Basel.
H.C. van Elswijk (1966), *Gilbert Porreta. Sa vie, son œuvre, sa pensée,* Louvain.
J. Jolivet, A. de Libera (Ed.) (1987), *Gilbert de Poitiers et ses contemporains: Aux origines de la "Logica modernorum,"* Naples.

ÉDOUARD-HENRI WÉBER

See also **Asceticism; Deism and Theism; Incarnation; Modalism; Mystery; Simplicity, Divine; Tritheism**

Democracy

Democracy, from the Greek *dèmokratia,* "rule by the people," refers to a political system in which the people* is sovereign. Although often associated with liberalism or socialism, it does not necessarily imply the prevalence of individual rights of liberal democracy or the focus on social and economic justice inherent to social democracy.

During antiquity, drawing on Greek experience of democracy (Plato, Aristotle) and republican Roman institutions (Cicero), democracy was defined as the rule of the many, as opposed to the rule of the one (monarchy) or a few (aristocracy). The modern notion of democracy, however, goes back to the ecclesiology* and political theology* of the late Middle Ages. While a role for implicit consent to political authority* had long been recognized, the notion of government by the people began to emerge around 1250. The reappearance of Aristotelian thought gave credibility to the view that political society* and authority are autonomous and need not be instituted by God* and introduced the notion of participatory citizenship in the life of the city. This led Thomas* Aquinas, in contrast to the Augustinian tradition, to think that life within a political society was part of human nature (*De regimine* I c. 1). Authority may ultimately come from God, but Aquinas admitted that everyone's consent played a part in the establishment of a political society (*ST* Ia IIae, q. 90, a. 3; IIa IIae, q. 57, a. 2). Aquinas, however, rejected the theory of inalienable sovereignty of the people, although jurists went further: the Roman law maxim *quod omnes similiter tangit ab omnibus approbetur* ("that which concerns everyone should be approved by everyone") had been widely used to justify the consultative function of parliaments and to give a significant role to ecclesiastical elections in canon* law. Bartolo de Sassoferrato (c. 1313–57), for example, was bolder and developed the theory of the irrevocable supremacy of the people in the government of city-states. Marsilius of Padua (c. 1275/80–c. 1343) is, however, the best-known person in this regard. For Marsilius the authority comes from the people; it governs the church* as well as the temporal sovereign, who earns his position through elections and to whom the people delegate the power without alienating it (*Defensor pacis,* Dictio 1). William of Ockham (c. 1285–1347) was more moderate and conceded that the people's authority could be alienated; he thought, however, that the government was merely an instrument serving the needs of human beings originally created free. In general, conciliarism*, based on the theories of canon law, affirmed the supremacy of the church over the popes* and proved influential in the formation of modern political thought. Jean Gerson (1363–1429) and his followers used an analogy: as the general council* has legitimate authority in the church, the representative assembly has authority in secular society. Nicholas* of Cusa used the notions of original liberty* and equality, which are found in patristic and Roman law, to justify the existence of constitutional means of expressing consent (1433, II c. 14); for him, representation is not a symbolic personification, but delegation (ibid. c. 34).

The concept of democracy also owes a lot to the Reformation. The egalitarian potential of the Lutheran doctrine of the priesthood* of all believers was largely obscured by the invisibility attributed to the true church and its practical subordination to political authority. Calvinism*, on the other hand, played a major part in the development of the democratic thought because of the emphasis it placed on the idea of the covenant* as the foundation of ecclesial and political society. Particularly important contributions also came from the 16th-century Thomist revival among Dominicans, such as F. de Vitoria (c. 1485–1546) and D. de Soto (1494–1560), and Jesuits, such as Bellarmine* and Suarez*. These authors elucidated and systematized the Thomist doctrine of the naturalness of political society; that is, a doctrine implying that all men are originally social, free, and equal beings, which is essential to political consent. For Suarez, this meant that originally there had been a direct democracy (*si non mutaretur, democratica esset,* "if there had been no change, [society] would be democratic"; *Defensio fidei* III, 2, 9) but also complete alienation of power when choosing a prince (*non est delegatio sed quasi alienatio,* "it is not a delegation but almost an alienation"; *De leg.* III, 4, 1).

At the end of the 16th century, Huguenot writers thought that opposition to authority could be justified in some cases, which they proved by using Calvinist arguments to reconcile some resistance with the Paulinian notion of authority established by God (Rom 13:1–7). Some of them additionally used the analyses of the late Scholastics, especially the *Vindiciae contra tyrannos* (1579), which states that the prince is established both by God and constituted by the general consent of the people by means of a contract *(pactum)* between the people and him. Similar ideas can be found in Theodore de Beza (1519–1605). More revolutionary, the Scottish theorist George Buchanan (1506–82) rejected the Thomist notion of the irrevocable alienation of the people's authority as well as the Calvinist concept of covenant *(foedus)* between the people and God. Among the 17th-century English Levellers, who believed in the equality of all before God, an egalitarian theory of the sovereignty of the people finally appeared—a multitude of equal individuals to whom sovereignty is reverted if the prince were tyrannical. Locke (1632–1704) would formulate the classic expression of such ideas.

The Catholic Church's opposition to the rationalism* and anti-clericalism of the French Revolution* strengthened its misgivings about democracy. The popes rejected the attempts by "liberal Catholicism" (especially from Lamennais [1782–1854]) to renew Catholicism* with the separation of church and state, recognition of freedom of conscience*, and universal suffrage. They condemned all liberal and democratic ideas (*Mirari vos,* 1832, *Singulari nos,* 1834, *Quanta cura,* 1864, and the *Syllabus,* 1864). Under these circumstances, the concept of the authority of the prince coming from God was abandoned, and so were the potentially revolutionary notions of original freedom and equality, in favor of a "designation" theory in which authority is immediately granted by God while popular consent merely designates its bearer (Rommen 1945).

Democratic thought would be renewed in 20th-century Catholicism, especially thanks to Jacques Maritain (1882–1973), whose ideas inspired Christian Democratic political parties after World War II (Fogarty 1957). In its official teaching, the Catholic Church stated the right of citizens to "contribute to the common good" (*Pacem in terris,* 1963) and to "participate freely and actively in establishing the constitutional bases of a political community" (*Gaudium et spes,* 1965). It also warned against some of the dangers of democracy, especially the "risk of an alliance between democracy and ethical relativism" (*Veritatis splendor,* 1994). In Protestant thought, prominent theologians defended democracy against totalitarianism, including Karl Barth*, Emil Brunner (1889–1966), and Dietrich Bonhoeffer*, or in the United States Reinhold Niebuhr (1892–1971). Niebuhr thought that "Man's capacity for justice makes democracy possible; but man's inclination to injustice makes democracy necessary" (1944). At the end of the 20th century, the many forms of political theology seemed to find that democratic institutions, in any shape, were the best of all possibilities (Gruchy 1995).

• Marsile de Padoue, *Defensor pacis* (1324), Ed. R. Scholz, Hanover, 1932.

Nicholas of Cusa, *De concordantia catholica* (1433), in *Nicolai Cusani Opera omnia,* Ed. G. Kallen, vol. 14, Hamburg, 1959–68.

F. Suarez, *Tractatus de legibus ac Deo legislatore* (1612), Ed. L. Perena, V. Abril, P. Suner, Madrid-Coimbra, 1971–81.

J. Locke, *Two Treatises of Government* (1690), Ed. P. L. Laslett, Cambridge, 1960.

Thomas Aquinas, *De regimine principum ad regem Cypri.*

♦ J. Maritain (1936), *Humanisme intégral,* Paris; id. (1951), *Man and the State,* Chicago.

R. Niebuhr (1944), *The Children of Light and the Children of Darkness,* New York.

H. Rommen (1945), *The State in Catholic Thought,* Saint-Louis, Miss.

Y. Simon (1951), *Philosophy of Democratic Government,* Chicago.

M. Fogarty (1957), *Christian Democracy in Western Europe, 1820–1853,* London.

J. Quillet (1970), *La philosophie politique de Marsile de Padoue,* Paris.

Coll. (1974), *Les catholiques libéraux au XIXe siècle,* Collection du Centre d'histoire du catholicisme, Grenoble.

G. Mairet (1986), "Marsile de Padoue, *Le défenseur de la paix,*" Paris, *DOPol,* 525–28.

B. Roussel, G. Vincent (1986), "Th. de Bèze, *Du droit des magistrats,*" *DOPol,* 85–90 (bibl.).

J. de Gruchy (1995), *Christianity and Democracy,* Cambridge.

S. Veca (1996), "Démocratie," *DEPhM,* 367–73.

Robert Song

See also **Church and State; Freedom, Religious; Law and Christianity; Law and Legislation; Revolution; Society**

Demons

1. Bible

a) Old Testament and Postbiblical Literature. As with angels*, biblical demonology assumes the contribution of anterior civilizations but imposes on it three corrections: the reduction of the demons to the created status, the attribution of their perversity to their own liberty*, and the subordination of their action to divine permission.

In contrast with prebiblical times, the texts that take place before the Exile are rather austere. These offer allusions to the demons Azazel (Lv 16:8, 26), Lilith (Is 34:14), Rahab (Ps 89:11, Is 51:9), and Leviathan (Is 27:1), but the literary genre used does not encourage seeing these demons as real beings, no more than the "bad spirit" that agitates people (1 Kgs 22:22f.; 1 Sm 16:14–6, 16:23). Even Satan, the Accuser, the Adversary, the Slanderer (Septuagint: *diabolos,* Vulgate: *diabolus,* devil), qualified as "Son of God" in Job (1:6–12; 2:1–7), and the harmful and tempting serpent in Genesis (3:1–5), even though cursed by God* at the end of the narrative* (3:14f.), are not at first presented as demons. They are, however, after Exile (Zec 3:1f.; Wis 2:24; Tb 3:8, 17: the demon Asmodeus; 1 6:14). Isaiah 14:12ff. seems to adapt for the king of Babylon the tradition of a fabulous spirit named Lucifer, fallen because vanquished by God. Because of their malice, the demons are associated with infirmities and illnesses and are situated in the desert, the region of thirst and barren desolation. Postbiblical and Qumran writings, with their exacerbated apocalypticism (apocalyptic* literature), use obscure symbolism. In Qumran, the opposition is categorical between the Spirit of Light and the Spirit of Perversity or Darkness, and between God presiding over the army of the sons of God and the demons as the sons of Satan or Belial. Islam offers a demonology and suggests a crowd of evil spirits, such as Ifrit, Shaitan, Harut, and Marut, as well as the djinns, all ruled by Iblis, the main rebellious angel.

b) New Testament. The personification of Satan (37 occurrences), also called the devil (36 occurrences) or the enemy (Mk 1:13; 4:13–20; Mt 13:25, 28, 39; Lk 10:19; Acts 13:10; Rev 12:9, 20:2f.), is now clear. Satan is evil par excellence (Mt 13:19, 13:38; 1 Jn 2:13f.; Eph 6:16), he is the tempter (Mt 4:1–11; Lk 4:1–13; 1 Thes 3:5), the prince of this world (Jn 12:31, 14:30, 16:11) or the "god of this world" (2 Cor 4:4; Eph 2;2), and also Beelzebub "prince of demons" (Lk 11:15; Mk 3:22; Mt 10:25, 12:24–27; 2 Cor 11:14). Head of a group of followers (Mt 25:41), he tempts Jesus* himself (Mt 4:1–10) as well as Peter* and the disciples (Mt 16:23; Lk 22:31). As the liar and murderer (Jn 8:43f.), his most noxious influence is manifested in his obstinate refusal to receive Christ* the Revelator. But Christ vanquishes demons. He threatens them and gives them orders (Mk 5:9), and he reveals the proximity to the Kingdom* of God by chasing them and healing illnesses and infirmities (Mk 3:22–27; Mt 8:16f.; Lk 4:40f, 6:18f, 8:2, 27–13, 13:16) by virtue of the power he confides in his apostles* (Mk 16:17f.; Acts 5:16, 19:12).

2. Theology

a) Liturgy and Magisterium. To continue Christ's victory over the demon and the demons, the Church* practiced, from its inception, exorcism* during the liturgy of baptism* or, following a codified ritual, in the case of possession. In 543 a synod* of Constantinople declared, against the Origenism that postulated a demon's final repentance (apocatastasis*), that the free aversion to it was radical and definitive and that hell was therefore eternal for him (*DS* 409, 411). Against Manicheanism* and Priscillianism, the first Council of Braga (561) cautioned that the devil had been created by God in a state of excellence (*DS* 455, 457).

b) Fathers. Irenaeus*, like other Fathers*, fought the dualist and Gnostic positions on evil* and the devil. The *Sayings* of the desert fathers (monachism [monasticism*]) colorfully narrate their fight against the demons. Gregory* of Nazianzus viewed Satan's fault as a sin of pride, and this opinion won over the fable of a sexual sin committed by fallen angels with women (woman*). Augustine* recalls that the devil became hardened in evil and corrects in his *Revisions* (II, 30) his earlier account on the possibility of demons directly knowing human thoughts, which he had previously stated. He attributed to them only the possibility of inferring, based on hints, our inner lives.

c) Medieval Theology. In the Fathers' wake, Hugh of Saint Victor (school of Saint* Victor) claimed in the twelfth century that the demon's pride was based on his desire to be equal to God (*see* Gn 3:5). Peter Lombard (around 1100–1160) summarized the principal theses of patristic demonology, especially those of Augustine. Theologians of the following century, notably Bonaventure* and Albert the Great*, advanced the subject. Thomas* Aquinas eliminated all anthropomorphism* in order to hold on to the realm of the intellect and will. His positions can be summarized as such: God submits all created subjects to the test of temptation by assuring him the grace of being able to resist it so that, with man, the demon cannot do anything against the will, which remains free. One cannot attribute to the demon the desire to be equal to God, because, being of superior intelligence, he knows that such a pretension is outrageous for any creature. In the will of the spiritual essence of the angel there is no natural inclination toward evil, because only good* solicits it; the nature of the revolted angel, made only by the Creator, remains, as taught by Pseudo-Dionysius*, intact and admirable, it is his person that is perverted and cast into misfortune and spiritual sufferance by the refusal of that ultimate good, which is God's own beatitude* offered as a gift of grace. Lastly, concerning the problem of the moment of the fall of the supreme angels, Satan or Lucifer, argued by previous authors, Thomas studied the nature of intelligence and angelical will and the duration characteristic of the pure spirit. According to him, the angel first discovers the limits of his own perfection, which, even if eminent in the created register, does not include the absolute fullness of knowledge and love that pertains to God. The angel realizes that it is possible, by renouncing himself as rule and criteria, to receive this fullness through the divine offer to share by grace the infinite beatitude that belongs to the Trinitarian life (Trinity*). Faced with this invitation of grace, the evil angel did, in an ulterior moment, freely and definitively confine himself to his own noetic and volitive limits. Thus, he deprived himself of the coherence and radical unity that the communion* to the rule and ultimate measure of truth would have brought him. Thus deprived of what would have confirmed him in his own excellence, all that he is and all that he does turns in obscurity and hate. As such, the fire of hell is essentially a pain that cripples the person created by his own will and in his own darkened intelligence.

d) Modern Times. Thomas Aquinas's analysis, much like other "demonologies," depends on his doctrine of angels, which itself depends on anthropology*. It was accepted, nuanced, or rejected after him depending on the degree of agreement with his own fundamental principles. After Suarez*'s attempt at synthesis, there were few developments of the doctrine in Catholicism*, and from the 18th century the traditional conception recoiled in Protestantism* (*LThK* 3, III, 4). Modernity, which already had trouble considering seriously the idea of angel, most often dismissed the demon as a mythological superstition, and theologians preferred to remain silent on the subject. So much so that since Milton (1608–78), poets are the ones to have spoken about this matter in which the concept is voiceless. One need only think of Ivan Karamazov's temptation (Dostoyevsky, 1821–81), or that of Adrian Leverkühn, Thomas Mann's "Dr. Faustus" (1875–1955), or even of Eve in the *Voyage to Venus* by C. S. Lewis (1898–1963). Far from being picturesque scenes such as found in the *Temptation of Saint Anthony,* they show the abyss of the liberty created in the possible retreat over radical evil. It is important to note that in these very different works—and one can think also of Bernanos's *Monsieur Ouine* (1888–1948)—the demon appears as a character that is both fearsome and insignificant, truly a fallen angel, "an undone person" (Marion 1986). Whatever the psychological truth of such scenes, there is also without a doubt material there for the theologians' thought.

• Anselm, *De casu diaboli, Œuvre* II, Paris, 1986.

Thomas Aquinas, Summa Theologica Ia, q. 49; q. 63–64; q. 109; q. 114; *Summa Contra Gentiles* III, c. 4–15; c. 108–110; IV, c. 90; *De malo,* q. 1–3; q. 16.

♦ E. Mangenot, T. Ortolan (1911), "Démon," *DThC* 4, 321–409.
Coll. (1948), "Satan," *Etudes Carmélitaines,* Paris.
P. Auvray et al. (1952), "Démons," *Cath* 3, 595–603.
N. Corte (1956), *Satan, l'adversaire,* Paris.
A. Lyonnet et al. (1957), "Démon," *Dictionnaire de spiritualité ascétique et mystique* 3, 141–238.
L. Cristiani (1959), *Présence de Satan dans le monde moderne,* Paris.
K. Rahner (1959), "Dämonologie," *Lexicon für Theologie und Kirche* 2 3, 145–47.
W. Foerster and Schäferdiek (1964), "Satanâs," *Theologisches Worterbuch zum Neuen Testament* 7, 151–65.
H.A. Kelly (1968), *The Devil, Demonology and Witchcraft: Christian Beliefs in Evil Spirits,* New York.
A. di Nola (1970), "Demonologia," *Eenciclopedia dell religioni* II, 635–47.
D.R. Hillers, L.I. Rabinovicz (1971), "Demons. Demonology," *Encyclopedia Judaica* 5, 1521–33.
Coll. (1971), *Génies, anges et démons,* Sources orientales VIII.
A.J. Wensinck (1971), "Iblis," *EI(f)* 3, 690–91.
E.H. Wéber (1977), "Dynamisme du bien et statut historique du destin créé: Du traité *Sur la chute du diable* de saint Anselme aux *Questions sur le mal* de Thomas d'Aquin," in *Die Mächte des Guten und Bösen,* MM 11, edited by A. Zimmermann, Berlin-New York, 154–205.
O. Böcher et al. (1981), "Dämonen," *Theologische Realenzyklopadie* 8, 270–300 (bibl.).
O. Böcher, W. Nagel (1982), "Exorzismus," *Theologische Realenzyklopadie* 10, 747–61.
J.-L. Marion (1986), "Le mal en personne," in *Prolégomènes à la charité,* Paris, 13–42.
J. Ries, H. Limet (Ed.) (1989), *Anges et démons* (Homo religiosus 14), Louvain-la-Neuve.
Fac. Univ. St-Louis (1992), *Figures du démoniaque hier et aujourd'hui,* Bruxelles.
W. Kornfeld, W. Kirchläger (1992), "Satan (et démons)," *Dictionnaire de la Bible* 12, 1–47.
W. Kirchläger et al. (1995), "Dämon," *Lexicon für Theologie und Kirche* 3 3, 2–6; "Dämonologie," ibid., 6–7.

Édouard-Henri Wéber

See also **Angels; Apocatastasis; Hell; Sin**

Descartes, René

1596–1650

Descartes was not a theologian. He repeats on several occasions that he has "never made a profession of the study of theology*," that he has applied himself to it only for his "own instruction," and in particular that it can be learned only through divine "inspiration" or "assistance," that is, according to the authority conferred by the Church* (VIae *Responsiones*). This reservation itself is enough to indicate that Descartes understands by theology the explanation of "revealed truths that...are beyond our understanding" *(Discours de la Méthode)*. As for commentary on the Holy Scriptures*, he engaged in it infrequently and only when circumstances demanded it, but when he did so it was with a great assurance in his interpretive choices. These choices locate him in the tradition of Bellarminian exegesis*. This is evidenced, for example, by the direct political application of 1 Corinthians 13 and Matthew 18:15–18 as instances of the "laws of charity," made during his polemic in Holland with Voet (Calvinism*), the Calvinist critic of the Counter Reformation. Following Thomas* Aquinas (*ST* IIa IIae, q. 9, a. 2), Descartes made what would later become the subjects of so-called natural* theology (the demonstration of the existence of God* and of the immortality of the soul [soul-heart-body]) the matter of philosophy rather than of theology. Indeed, this is indicated by the very title of *Meditationes de prima philosophia in qua Dei existentia et animae immortalitatis demonstratur* (Paris, 1641; changed to *in quibus Dei existentia et animae humanae a corpore distinctio demonstrantur,* Amsterdam, 1642). Moreover, the dedicatory epistle of the *Meditations,* addressed to the faculty of theology of the Sorbonne, draws on the program prescribed by the Fifth Lateran* Council for "Christian philosophers." However, Descartes is of interest to theology not because of his proofs of the existence of God and of the real distinction between soul and body (soul-heart-body); nor because of his redefinition of the respective degrees of certainty reached by faith and by reason (*Regulae* III and XII; IIae *Responsiones*); nor even because of his theory of freedom, which allows man to see himself as the image of God (thesis of the unlimited nature of the will, *Meditations* IV). His theological interest lies in 1) the primacy he gives to omnipotence among the divine attributes*; 2) the advent of the concept of *causa sui,* which, on the one hand, derives from this; and 3) from the physical explanation of the Eucharist* imposed on him, on the other hand, by his new theory of corporal substance.

a) The Incomprehensible Omniscience of God. The celebrated *Letters to Mersenne,* of 15 April and 6 and 27 May 1630, set forth a fundamental and unchanging thesis of Cartesian metaphysics, that of the free disposal of truths, often called the creation* of eternal truths. These truths, whether it is a question of essences or existences, have the same status with respect to God, whose will is their efficient cause: that is, the status of created things. "You ask me by what kind of cause God has established the eternal truths. I answer you that it is by the same kind of cause that he has created all things, that is, as efficient and total cause. For it is certain that he is the author of both the essence and the existence of created things." It would be blasphemous to subject God to necessity, even logical necessity (the principle of contradiction), for that would be to conceive of him as finite; even his power (omnipotence*) is infinite and thereby incomprehensible. If God can do everything that we can conceive of, he is in no way limited by our rationality and can do what we cannot think of, particularly what appears to us as contradictory. Descartes thus repeats an Augustinian distinction: we can know God but not understand him. And he thereby opposes a vast movement of thought derived from Abelard*, in which the assertion that the wisdom* of God limits his freedom leads to the affirmation both that the divine will is determined by what his intellect represents to him and that divine and human rationality are analogous, indeed homogeneous. This current of thought culminates with Suarez*, who asserts the singleness of knowledge and, as something dependent on that, the singleness of being. Alone in his century, Descartes argued that "no essence can be attributed in the same way to God and to created things" (VIae *Responsiones*). In the face of this movement, which leads to the "emancipation" of philosophy from theology, we are compelled to locate Descartes on the side of a theological orthodoxy that maintains in its radicality the incomprehensible omniscience of God and stands firm on the refusal to distinguish faculties in God. "In God it is one thing to will, to understand, and to create, with none preceding any other, not even in reason." However, the three major post-Cartesians, Spinoza, Malebranche, and Leibniz*, were to reject the positions of Descartes and to complete the movement of emancipation by holding that possibilities are imposed on God: that is, that truths, identical for a finite or an infinite intellect, impose themselves on his will. The first consequence of this would be the abandonment, shared by all three, of the doctrine of the creation of truths.

b) God as Causa Sui. It is thus in order to "speak of God more worthily...than the vulgar do" (that is, late Scholasticism*) that the *Meditations* and the *Responsiones* (Iae and IVae in part) make of the infinite* through which God is attained in *Meditation* III (which concludes with his contemplation*) or of his inexhaustible omnipotence *(inexhausta potentia),* brought together in *infinita ou immensa potentia,* the supreme divine name. Moreover, because for every being, including God, it is possible to seek "the cause for which it exists" (principle of causality [Iae and IIae *Respon-*

siones]), Descartes goes so far as to attribute to God the concept of *causa (efficiens) sui* (considered unthinkable from Anselm* to Suarez) in order to think positively about his aseitas*. The immense power in God is "the cause or the reason" for which he needs no cause to exist, and because this cause is positive, God can be conceived as the cause of himself. To deal with the objections of the theologians Caterus (1590–1655) and Arnauld (1612–94), Descartes later proposed modifications in the *causa sui,* presenting it as a "concept common" to efficient and formal causes or as a simple analogy* to efficient cause, but he always maintained the principle of the submission of all existence to causality. He thus made possible, despite its difficulties, an a priori proof of the existence of God through causality, a causality on which is built the whole architectonics of demonstrations and divine attributes. The other divine perfections flow from this, insofar as they are all stamped with infinity: plenary and indeterminate substance, immensity, incomprehensibility, independence (aseitas), and omniscience.

Having become futile, caught as it was between positive theology and mystical (mysticism*) theology, speculative theology was in a severe crisis "when Descartes appeared" (Gouhier). Descartes, in fact, is less one who proposes the services of a new philosophy, the philosophy of clear and distinct ideas, to theologians who have learned to do without speculative theology in order to develop a "simple" (Burman 1648) and effective ("to reach heaven") theology, than the one who occupies the position of the last speculative theologian. At the very least, his discussion of the attributes of God in the *Meditations* and the *Responsiones* forms the last metaphysical repetition of the theological treatise on divine names (Marion), contemporary with the final *Quinquaginta nomina Dei* of Lessius (Brussels, 1640, posthumous). Bérulle had perhaps engaged the young Descartes in this matter in 1628; in any case it was approved by the Oratorians Condren and Gibieuf (*De libertate Dei et creaturae.* Paris, 1630). But it was also the tension prevailing in the architecture of divine names among infinity, perfection, and *causa sui,* as well as the primacy of the unconditioned omnipotence of God that the Cartesian theologians (Arnauld, Bossuet, and Fénelon) would have so much difficulty maintaining against the thesis that had become predominant (Spinoza, Malebranche, Leibniz*, Berkeley) of a rationality common to God and his creation, and against its corollary, the demand for a theodicy through which the 18th century would call on God to justify himself. And if Descartes wrote the last metaphysical treatise on divine names, this was probably because he was the first philosopher to be obliged to work at a time in which an established speculative theology using a philosophically convincing language was lacking.

c) Eucharist. From the moment when, (as early as the *Meteors* and the *Dioptrique* [1637]), and if considering real accidents as an unnecessary hypothesis, Descartes challenged the Aristotelian theory of the sensible world, he was obliged to formulate a theory of the Eucharist different from that of the Scotists or the Thomists. He develops it in the IVae *Responsiones* in replying to the Arnauld's objections about the mode of conversion from one substance to another in transubstantiation: our senses are never affected by the substance but only by its surface. It is therefore necessary to take into account the permanence of the surface, which, as an intermediary between bodies, is not a quality of bodies themselves (*Principia philosophiae* [1644] II, art. 10–15) and so can remain the same when bodies change. There is thus a change of substance beneath the formal permanence of the surface. Descartes relied on the Council of Trent*, which used the vocabulary of the sacred species—and not that of accidents (Council of Constance*)—to think of the eucharistic conversion of the bread and wine. The permanence of the movement of the corpuscles of the bread and wine, entirely explicable by the forms and movements of the particles of matter, before and after their conversion, assures the phenomenal invariance of the surface and hence of sensory perception. The letter to Mesland of 9 February 1645, which is more problematic, elaborated on what concerns the mode of presence of the body of Christ* in the Eucharist. The Cartesian physical explanation of the Eucharist was taken up and extended by Maignan (1601–76), Desgabets (1610–78), and Cally (1630–1709). With this doctrine, Descartes had been less concerned with doing theology than in rigorously developing his theory of substance. This is why the Eucharist—his explanation of which he submitted to the authority* of the Church (several faculties of theology censured it in the last third of the 17th century)—constituted nothing more, and nothing less, than a crucial experiment in the new theory of sensation.

• For the years 1800–1960, G. Sebba, *Bibliographia cartesiana: A Critical Guide to the Descartes Literature,* The Hague, 1964.

For the 1970s, le *Bulletin cartésien,* annual bibl. published in *ArPh,* 1972–.

Œuvres de Descartes, Eds. C. Adam, P. Tannery (A-T), Rev. by P. Costabel, B. Rochot, 11 vols., Paris, 1964–74.

♦ É. Gilson (1913), *La liberté chez Descartes et la théologie,* Paris.

A. Koyré (1922), *Essai sur l'idée de Dieu et les preuves de son existence chez Descartes,* Paris.

H. Gouhier (1924), *La pensée religieuse de Descartes,* Paris (2nd Ed., 1972); id. (1962), *La pensée métaphysique de Descartes,* Paris; id. (1978), *Cartésianisme et augustinisme au XVIIe siècle,* Paris.

J.-R. Armogathe (1977), *Theologia cartesiana: L'explication physique de l'Eucharistie chez Descartes et dom Desgabets,* The Hague.
J.-L. Marion (1981), *Sur la théologie blanche de Descartes,* Paris; id. (1986), *Sur le prisme métaphysique de Descartes,* Paris; id. (1996), *Questions cartésiennes* II, Paris, l. II.
G. Rodis-Lewis (1985), *Idées et vérités éternelles chez Descartes et ses successeurs,* Paris.
V. Carraud (1989), "Descartes et la Bible," in J.-R. Armogathe (Ed.), *Le Grand Siècle et la Bible,* Paris, 277–91; id. (1993), "Descartes: le droit de la charité," in G. Canziani, Y.C. Zarka (Ed.), *L'interpretazione nei secoli XVI e XVII,* Milan, 515–36; id. (1996), "Arnauld théologien cartésien? Toute-puissance, liberté d'indifférence et création des vérités éternelles," *XVIIe siècle,* 191, 259–73.
R. Ariew, M. Grene (Ed.) (1995), *Descartes and His Contemporaries,* Chicago.
J. Biard (Ed.) (1997), *Descartes et le MA,* Paris.

VINCENT CARRAUD

See also **Asceticism; Attributes, Divine; Bérulle, Pierre de; Conversion; Eucharist; Existence of God, Proofs of; Lateran V, Council; Mysticism; Natural Theology; Omnipotence, Divine; Soul-Heart-Body; Suarez, Francisco; Trent, Council of**

Descent into Hell

a) Biblical References. To elaborate on the theme of Christ's descent into hell*, two kinds of scriptural reference are generally put forward: 1) Certain passages seek to express the humiliation of the Son in all its reality, according to the descent/exaltation model outlined in Philippians 2:5–11, and assert that he spent "three days and three nights in the heart of the earth" (Mt 12:40), and that " 'He ascended' means that he had also descended into the lower parts of the earth" (Eph 4:9). Clearly these formulas refer to more than the entombment of Jesus*. The very word *Sheol* (hell*) is used to describe the final destination of this descent, but in a quotation of Psalms 16:10 used in Acts 2:27 (*see* also Rev 1:18, "I have the keys of Death and Hades," keys that Christ holds only because he went down that far). 2) Other texts speak of Christ's "visit," both a struggle and a foreshadowing, to the "dead" (1 Pt 4:6), of "spirits in prison" (1 Pt 3:19, "he went and proclaimed to the spirits in prison"), in order to tear them away from the "gates of hell" (Mt 16:18). The interpretation of 1 Peter 3:19 that sees therein an allusion to fallen angels (demons*) is not certain. Perhaps the description of tombs opening at the death of Christ in Matthew 27:51ff. is connected with this theme. 3) There is one last category, that is, texts that speak simply of a return from the place of the dead: "'Who will descend into the abyss?' (that is, to bring Christ up from the dead)" (Rom 10:7); or "the God of peace who brought again from the dead our Lord Jesus" (Heb 13:20).

These discreet affirmations would be elaborated in the early Judeo-Christian communities, to which intertestamentary literature (intertestament*) could provide an entire stock of speculations on the fate of people in Sheol (1 Hen., 4 Esd.). This is evident in the work *Shepherd* by Hermas (Sim. 9:16, 5), in certain apocryphal Gospels* (*The Gospel of Nicodemus, The Gospel of Peter*), and in Justin and Irenaeus of Lyons*, who mention an apocryphal text that they attribute at times to Isaiah, at times to Jeremiah: "The Lord God, the holy one of Israel, remembered his dead who slept in the earth of the tomb, and he came down to them to announce the good news of salvation*."

The imagery gained force, and writers claimed the presence at this event of John the Baptist and, counter to all chronology, that of the apostles*.

b) Patristic Theology. In the patristic literature devoted to the descent into hell from the time of Ignatius of Antioch, the central theme has been soteriological. Unlike the Gnostic hyper-spiritualization of Christianity, the stress is placed upon the reality of a death that leads to the knowledge of the *state of death* and the state of the dead. It was on this condition that Christ could hold the key "to death and to the afterlife." A theology* of the universality of salvation was soon added to this, according to which the descent into hell allowed Christ to meet with all of humanity who had died before the proclamation of the gospel and to offer them the remission of their sin* (Irenaeus of Lyons, *Adv. Haer.* 4, 27, 2).

The introduction of the formula *et descendit ad inferna* in the baptismal confession of faith* must be situated within this context. Absent from the Creed of Nicaea-Constantinople, it appeared in Semi-Arian formulations of faith of the mid-fourth century (Councils of Sirmium [PG 26, 693a] and of Nicaea [Theodoret, *HE,* 2, 21 4], 359), then more clearly at the end of the century in Aquila's version of the Apostles' Creed (*DH* 16) and gradually in various formulas of faith (*see DH* 23, 27s, 30, 76). From that time onward it would be part of the received text of the Apostles' Creed.

Debate then moved into the domain of Christology, raising the issue of Christ's human soul (soul-heart-body) (which enters hell alone, since his body [soul-heart-body] is in the tomb), and this some time before the Apollinarian dispute. Hippolyte, for example, speaks of the arrival of Christ in hell as of the presence of "a soul with souls" (Fr. *pasch.* 3, PG 10, 701A). Omitted by Athanasius of Alexandria* (*Ad Epct.* 5, PG 26, 1060), Hilary* of Poitiers, and Ambrose* of Milan, who attributed the descent into hell directly to the Word*, the mediation of the created soul of Christ later reappeared (Didymus, *In Ps.,* PG 39, 1233A–C).

In the East as well as in the West, sacred iconography has assured the theme of the descent into hell a wide distribution: Christ is represented as breaking down the portals of death, crushing Satan, and taking Adam*, Eve, and (more or less recognizable) the patriarchs by the hand.

c) Medieval Theology. Medieval systematicians were interested not so much in the identity of the dead liberated by Christ on Holy Saturday as in the precise terms of that liberation. From the time of Saint Augustine*, it has been more or less agreed that this liberation was granted to the just of the Old Testament. They suffered no punishment* for any personal failing, and were already justified by the faith that they had, in advance, in the one who was to come (according to Jn 8:56). Deprived of the vision of God by virtue of original sin, they were now to be liberated from that deprivation (Saint Thomas* of Aquinas, *ST* IIIa, q. 52, a. 5). As for the preaching* mentioned in 1 Peter 3:19, this could not be understood as a postmortem activity by Christ, but referred to the apostolic action that he exerted through the Church*.

In addition, the vocabulary increased in precision. Other words gradually came to replace the Hebrew terms *Gehenna* and *Sheol,* the former designating the lamentable fate of the outcast and the latter the waiting place of all the dead, just or unjust. Hell (which tended to be used in the singular by writers of French—*enfer* instead of *enfers*—and increasingly demonic in quality) became the place of the damned, while Limbo* came to refer most often to the waiting place (the "Limbo of the Fathers"), sometimes represented—as in Dante*'s *Divine Comedy*—by a circle on the periphery of hell proper.

d) Contemporary Reevaluation. The descent into hell has recently been the subject of a reevaluation in the work of Hans Urs von Balthasar*. Under the influence of the experiences of Adrienne von Speyr (mystically linked to the Passion* of Christ, on Good Friday she would experience a form of empathetic suffering that increased on Holy Saturday), Balthasar gives this theme a central place. In his treatment of the mystery of Easter he calls it the expression of the "display of the effects of the cross in the abyss of mortal perdition." He explicitly rejects the idea of any triumphant activity of Christ in hell and seeks on the contrary to discern in the *descensus* an ultimate passivity: "the dead being of the Son of God." His reflections upon the "final place" evoke motifs already present at the time of the Reformation in Anabaptist and mystico-spiritualist theologies, which considered this episode to be the lowest point of Christ's journey. The Calvinist catechism of Heidelberg, moreover, opposed such motifs to the traditional concept upheld by the Lutheran Formula of Concord. For Balthasar, however, the interpretation of the descent into hell is not merely one theological thesis among others. Rather, it is the structural axis of his entire theology, and it will not be possible to deliver a definitive judgment on it until the principles applied have been made the object of theological and ecclesiastical reception. In any case one can emphasize that this interpretation amounts less to a mediating of the opposition between the Origenist (universal salvation: *apocatastasis**) and the Augustinian concepts (salvation reserved for a small number) than to an almost total reevaluation of the traditional concept. This entails a reinterpretation, and an unprecedented expansion, of the notion of *kenosis**, as well as a new definition of sin as situated halfway between evil* committed (moral evil) and evil suffered (physical evil).

• J. Daniélou (1958), *Théologie du judéo-christianisme,* Paris (2nd Ed. 1991), 295–311.

Ch. Perrot (1968), "La descente du Christ aux enfers dans le Nouveau Testament," *LV(L)* 85, 5–29.

H. U. von Balthasar (1969), "Mysterium Paschale," *MySal* III/2, 227–55.

A. Grillmeier (1975), "Der Gottessohn im Totenreich," in *Mit ihm und in ihm,* Fribourg-Basel-Vienna, 76–174.

W. Maas (1979), *Gott und die Hölle,* Einsiedeln.

E. Koch (1986), "Hölle," *TRE* 15, 455–61 (bibl.).

M. Lochbrunner (1993), "Descensus ad inferos: Aspekte und Aporien eines vergessenen Glaubensartikels," in *FKTh* 9, 161–77.

Karl Heinz Neufeld

See also **Creeds; Death; Hell; Limbo; Resurrection of Christ; Salvation; Wrath of God**

Desire of God. *See* **Supernatural**

Deuterocanonical Books. *See* **Apocrypha**

Devil. *See* **Demons**

Devotio moderna

Conceived in the Netherlands at the end of the 14th century, *devotio moderna* was simultaneously a spiritual movement, a series of devotional practices, a certain concept of lay piety, and a particular form of communal life. Gerard Groote was its initiator (1340–84), and disciples soon took up his work through their deeds and their writings. During the 15th century the ideals and experiences characteristic of *devotio moderna* spread into a large part of northern Europe.

After university studies in Paris and a stay with the Carthusians (between 1374 and 1377), Groote, the son of a middle-class family, decided to lead a life devoted to reading, meditation, and prayer in his Deventer house. It was an austere life but quite moderate when compared with the asceticism* and penances that certain "religious laity" inflicted upon themselves during the same era. At the time of his "conversion*," Groote had written *Conclusa et proposita, non uota.* In this he wrote that the experience he intended to undergo was a "project," sealed by a "promise" and not by "vows" in the traditional sense. To "glorify, honor, and serve God*," Groote renounced a considerable number of activities, which he enumerated in his *Conclusa et proposita.* He set himself a program of spiritual reading (from the Gospels to Henry Suso's *Horologium*) and regulations designed to encourage "abstinence." In his "Moral Allocution" *(Zedelijke toespraak),* he defined a form of spirituality that might be taken up by lay people who remained in the world*. His experience and writings manifest his desire to return to an original Christianity and to create a lay version of the apostolic model.

Groote had turned over a part of his Deventer house to a few young women who did not belong to any religious order but who were "in need of a roof for the love* of God, in order better to serve God there in humility and penance" (statutes from 1379 for the "house of master Gerard"). Moreover, his activity as a preacher facilitated the formation of a first group of disciples, which his closest collaborator, Florent Radewijns (1350–1400) set up in Deventer in his residence. Other communities later sprang up, whose members, both laymen and clerics*, were called "Brethren of the Common Life." They shared a devout life, where their time was spent in copying manuscripts, in prayer, in works of charity, and, quite soon, in preaching.

Groote had already taken minor orders* so as to be able to recite the Gospels to the crowd and had requested a written authorization from the bishop* of Utrecht allowing him to preach in parishes. Within the houses of the Common Life, "conferences" *(collationes)* regularly brought together those brothers (sometimes designated by the term *collatie broeders*) and lay people who wished to hear their semipublic sermons. This type of mission*/evangelization facilitated the distribution of the ideals of *devotio moderna.* The brothers also shared the habit of taking personal notes while reading from the Holy* Scriptures and the great spiritual authors, and it was from this practice that the *rapiaria* originated. These were a sort of anthology or collection of quotations, serving as an aid to meditation. Most of the followers composed their own *rapiarium.* Some even compiled considerable works, like the *Rosetum* written by Jean Mombaer (vol. 1460–1501), which included texts drawn from his extensive reading. One version of the *Rosetum,* which would go through several editions, was preceded by an "invitatory to exercises of piety." Reading had no other purpose than to encourage piety.

It was subsequently Florent Radewijns who gave a concrete—and institutional—form to Groote's project. There is no doubt, however, that he impoverished his master's ideas. Indeed, his only concern was to determine a method capable of visibly arousing the devotion of the brothers he had brought together, to lead them to self-knowledge, and to help them to repress their passions*. The brother Gerard Zerboldt from Zutphen (1367–98), to whom is attributed the treatise *Super modo uiuendi hominum simul commorantium*—a point-by-point justification of the fundamental principles of the Common Life—later endeavored to systematize Groote's and Radewijns's ideas. Thus, in his *De reformatione uirium animae* and *De spiritualibus ascensionibus* he defined a series of exercises (examinations of conscience*, meditations on the last rights and on the Passion*), which would allow the "spiritual ascension" of the devout. Dirc van Herxen (circa 1381–1457), who administered several of the houses of the Common Life, was the author of texts devoted to exercises of piety, prayer, and meditation, as well as four pedagogical treatises that affirmed the necessity of educating the young in the service of God from the earliest age. Because they had spent less time in the world, children and adolescents were less tainted by sin* and more open to instruction than adults. Teaching was therefore one of the most important activities of the Brethren of the Common Life, who set up schools in several towns. The insistence on a close link between study and (Christian) life, as well as certain pedagogical innovations characteristic of the brothers' schools—for example the division into distinct classes according to the age and knowledge of the pupils—foreshadowed, at least for some historians, the ideals of humanist Christians and of Erasmus*.

In parallel to the houses of Common Life, Radewijns had opened in Windesheim, near Zwolle, a house of regular canons, which quickly found itself at the head of a sizable congregation. By the end of the 15th century this included a hundred or more houses throughout the Netherlands, the Rhineland, Westphalia, and the north of France. Jean Busch, a reformer of several religious houses, endeavored to disseminate the principles of piety characteristic of the Windesheim congregation (particularly in the *Liber de reformatione monasteriorum*). Unlike the Brethren of the Common Life, canons were clergy in the traditional sense, living according to a rule and devoted to contemplation. The environment in Windesheim seems to have been more sensitive to mystical experiences than that of the Common Life. Hendrick Mande (c. 1360–1431), who had the reputation of being blessed with frequent visions, wrote vernacular descriptions of contemplation* and of the soul's (soul-heart-body) union with God. Gerlac Peters (1378–1411), initially a brother of the Common Life, then a canon in Windesheim, took up the defense of mysticism*. He recorded his thoughts in a *Soliloquium* (which seems not to have been intended for circulation), often finding inspiration in Ruysbroeck, Tauler, and Eckhart.

There were many spiritual works in the 15th century, commending devotional practices and the exercise of virtues*, that historians connect with the *devotio moderna* movement: the long treatises of Wessel Gansfort (c. 1419–89), for example, on the different methods of prayer, on the sacrament* of the Eucharist* and on the Mass; or the celebrated *Imitation of Christ,* anonymously attributed to Thomas À Kempis (1380–1471), a disciple of Florent Radewijns and author of numerous treatises intended for meditation. The eight hundred manuscripts of the *Imitation* (between 1424 and 1500), the printed editions, as well as the reworkings and translations, all attest to the considerable success of this work devoted to the contemplation of Christ*'s humanity. The characteristic ideals of *devotio moderna* now had a wide distribution. It would seem that even certain Franciscan preachers, such as Pierre-aux-Boeufs (c. 1370–c. 1425/1430) or Jean Brugman (c. 1400–1473) had contributed to them.

The new devotion was "modern" in more ways than one. The importance of personal meditation and inner life, the idea of an "imitation of Christ" through meditation and charity—tendencies that were fairly common during the later centuries of the Middle Ages—were affirmed in *devotio moderna* as never before. Without doubt, the point worth noting is that the interiority cultivated by the disciples and successors of Gerard Groote was characterized by a great defiance with regard to any excessive or uncontrolled form of piety. The devout were to apply themselves to practices of cautious asceticism and devotion rather than to ecstasy or visions. Their devout life kept them at a distance, moreover, from any "vain science" (that is, knowledge detached from piety) and pure speculation. In this regard, *devotio moderna* marked a break, not completed in Groote's time, between theology* and spirituality (spiritual theology). And if we accept that such a break represented one of the characteristic traits of Catholicism* during this era, we must nevertheless strongly qualify the influence of "modern devotion" upon Protestantism*, and this despite certain shared features and despite the disappearance at the Reformation of most houses of the Common Life.

• P. Debongnie (1957), "Dévotion moderne," *DSp* 3, 727–47.
W. Lourdaux (1967), *Moderne Devotie en Christelijk Humanisme,* Louvain.
R.R. Post (1968), *The Modern Devotion: Confrontation with Reformation and Humanism,* Leyden.
G. Épiney-Burgard (1970), *Gérard Grote (1340–1384) et les débuts de la Dévotion moderne,* Wiesbaden.
St. G. Axters (1971), *De Imitatione Christi,* Kempen-Niedenheim.
A. Ampe (1973), *L'Imitation de Jésus-Christ et son auteur,* Rome.
W. Lourdaux (1977), "Frères de la vie commune," *DHGE* 18, 1438–54.
Coll. (1985), *Gert Grote en Moderne Devotie,* Antwerp.
K. Egger, W. Lourdaux, A. van Biezen (1988), *Studien zur Devotio Moderna,* Bonn.
H. Martin (1989), "Devotio moderna et prédication (début XVe–début XVIe s.)," *Publication du Centre européen d'Études bourguignonnes (XIVe-XVe s.),* 29, 97–110.
G. Épiney-Burgard (1992), "Les idées pédagogiques de Dirc van Herxen," in W. Verbeke et al. (Ed.), *Serta devota. Pars prior: Devotio Windeshemensis,* Louvain, 295–304.
F. O. Schuppisser (1993), "Schauen mit den Augen des Herzens: Zur Methodik der spätmittelalterlichen Passionsmeditation, besonders in der 'Devotio moderna,'" in W. Haug, B. Wachinger (Ed.), *Die Passion Christi in Literatur und Kunst des Spätmittelalters,* Tübingen, 169–210.
A. G. Weiler (1994), "Il significato della 'devotio moderna' per la cultura europea," *Cristianesimo nella storia,* 15, 51–69.

Michel Lauwers

See also **Beguines; Carmel; Imitation of Christ; John of the Cross; Rhineland-Flemish Mysticism; Spirituality, Franciscan**

Dialectical Theology. *See* **Barth, Karl; Lutheranism**

Didache. *See* **Apostolic Fathers**

Dilthey, Wilhem. *See* **Hermeneutics**

Diocese. *See* **Local Church; Regional Church**

Diodorus of Tarsus. *See* **Antioch, School of**

Dionysius the Pseudo-Areopagite

I. The Author and the Dionysian Question

The identity of the person who wrote the *Corpus dionysiacum* or *Areopagiticum* under the pseudonym Dionysius the Areopagite, the man who was converted by Paul after his speech on the Areopagus (Acts 17:34), is unknown. His writings were referred to at the meeting of the Chalcedonian bishops with the Monophysite Severian bishops, which took place at the synod* of Constantinople in 532. Hypatius of Ephesus expressed some doubts on the authenticity of these writings; and later, Thomas* Aquinas himself did the same (*see* Hausherr, *OCP* 2 [1936], 484–90). During the whole of the Middle Ages, the authority* of the *Corpus*'s author was founded on the fact that he was part of the apostolic age. The role of destroying that legend befell later to the humanists of the Renaissance, Erasmus* (*In novum Testamentum annotationes item ab ipso recognitae,* Basel, 1522) and Laurentius Valla (*In novum Testamentum annotationes apprime utiles,* Basel, 1526). The legend had, nonetheless, its defenders, even in modern times. Koch (*Philologus* 54 [1895], 238–454) and Stiglmayr (*HJ* 16 [1895], 253–73) ended up establishing definitively the dependence linking Dionysius to Proclus by showing that Dionysius had used, in his treaty on evil*, in chapter IV of the *Divine Names,* the *De malorum subsistentia* by Proclus.

J. Stiglmayr clarified the chronology of the *Corpus,* which came at a later date than the following events: after the Council of Chalcedon* (451); after the introduction of the credo, in mass, by patriarch Peter the Foulon (476); and after Emperor Zeno's *Henotikon* (482). It came, however, earlier than the authors of the beginning of the sixth century, who quoted from it: Andreas Caesariensis and Severus of Antioch's letter to abbot John.

Attempts have been made to identify the mysterious author of the *Corpus* with numerous figures: Ammonius Saccas, Dionysius bishop of Alexandria, a disciple of Basil*, Peter the Foulon, Peter the Iberian, Dionysius of Gaza, Severus of Antioch, Sergius of Resaina (the first translator of the *Corpus* into Syriac, a short time after it came out), a friend of John of Scythopolis (the author of the first scholia of the *Corpus*), Stephanus Bar Sudaili, or Heraiscus, a friend and disciple of Damascius (*see* Hathaway, *Hierarchy and the Definition of Order in the Letters of Pseudo-Dionysius,* The Hague, 1969, and S. Lilla, *Aug.* 22, 1982).

The author of the *Corpus* was probably, as is shown by his knowledge of the liturgy* of Antioch, a monk of Syrian origin who had a close relationship with Proclus's ideas (*see* Saffrey, StPatr IX, TU 94, 1966) and perhaps, according to S. Lilla, with those expressed by Damascius, whose courses he might have followed in Athens.

The meaning of the pseudonym under which he wrote is in itself a message: Dionysius the Areopagite was converted by Paul on the Areopagus, and likewise the Pseudo-Dionysius wanted to convert Greek thinking by introducing it in Christian theology (that is why the Sophist Apollophanes called him a "parricide" in Letter IV); he would thus get the benefit of the heritage represented by Athenian philosophy a short number of years before the closure of the academy by Emperor Justinian.

II. Works and Editions

1. Works

The *Corpus,* which has been transmitted to posterity, includes the *Celestial Hierarchy (CH),* the *Ecclesiastical Hierarchy (EH),* the *Divine Names (DN),* the *Mystical Theology (MT)* and a collection of ten Epistles *(Ep).*

a) Celestial Hierarchy. The treaty describes in 15 chapters the classes of angels* mentioned in the Old Testament and by Paul. The doctrine of Dionysius on the celestial hierarchy has Christian sources: Clement of Alexandria (*Strom.* VII), Gregory* of Nazianzus (*Discourses* 28 [theol. 2]), Cyril of Jerusalem (*Catecheses* 23 [myst. 5]), John Chrysostom* (*Homeliae in Genesim* and the eight baptismal homilies and the apostolic constitutions [VIII, 12, 7–8]). The ternary division of the hierarchical activity—an activity of purification, of illumination, of union—takes its inspiration, however, from Neoplatonic sources: one can see in Jamblique's *Book of Mysteries* and in Proclus's *Platonic Theology* the systematization of the notion of triad corresponds to a hierarchy of divine intelligences. For Proclus, any reality similar to the movement of intelligence—which is a movement from establishment, procession, and conversion *(monè, proodos, epistrophè)*—will be triadic. Dionysius reports on this doctrine to his master Hierotheus, whose writings he calls "second Writing" *(deutera logia)* (*DN* 681 B): "theology designates the totality of celestial essences with nine revealing names: our divine initiator divides them in three ternary dispositions" (*CH* 200 D). It is, however, the Bible above all that he invokes.

According to Dionysius, the ranks of the celestial hierarchy divide into three triads: 1) seraphim, 2) cherubim, and 3) thrones make up the first hierarchy or triad; 4) dominations, 5) virtues, and 6) powers make up the second; 7) principalities, 8) archangels, and 9) angels make up the third (*CH,* chapters VII–IX).

The first hierarchy receives directly the illuminations of the divine Thearchy (divining principle) and is united to it without intermediary. According to the Hebrew etymology invoked by Dionysius, the seraphim are the "burning ones"; the cherubim are those who are fulfilled with an outpouring of knowledge and of wisdom* (*CH* 205 B); and the thrones are those who receive and have God* in them (205 D).

The hierarchical order corresponds in decreasing degrees (starting from the summit) to the three activities that characterize any hierarchy, namely purification, illumination, and perfection or union. The second and third triads are united to God through the first one acting as an intermediary, and they receive a lesser illumination. As for the third hierarchy, it connects the celestial universe to the universe of human hierarchies. In that hierarchy, the angels are those who are nearest to human beings, and those who transmit to them the divine purification, illumination and perfection.

Regarding the exegesis* of the symbols used by the Holy* Scripture to mention the celestial dealings, Dionysius develops a whole theory of similar and dissimilar symbols, more appropriate than concepts to allude to spiritual realities that transcend the realities that can be felt. If the seraphim are represented by the image of fire, God himself is named at the same time "Sun of justice" and "Tenebrae better than luminous." The value of any symbol, on the other hand, is linked to the value of the intelligence using it: the more purified and illuminated the intelligence, the more united it is to God; the better it will know how to rise toward God, the better that anagogical act will be able to discover God in signs and symbols.

b) Ecclesiastical Hierarchy. The treaty first introduces a doctrine of ecclesial hierarchy, followed by a description and interpretation of the six main rites in Christian liturgy: baptism*, Eucharist*, consecration of the holy* oils (the *muron*), sacerdotal ordination, monastic profession, and funerary rites. Each rite is considered first in its liturgical unfolding *(mustèrion),* then in a contemplative or allegorical meaning *(theôria);* the intelligible content of that meaning is released from the symbol being felt, like a stone being released from its gangue, thanks to anagogical and apophatic activity of the intellect.

The ecclesiastical hierarchy, in the image of celestial hierarchy, includes different ranks: the initiators (bishops*, priests [priesthood*], deacons*) and the initiated (the purified, the illuminated, those who are in a state or in a process of perfection, or the monks). The bishops exercise the three functions of initiation, of illumination, and of perfection. Finally, Jesus* leads the celestial hierarchy as well as the ecclesiastical hierarchy.

c) Divine Names. This treaty is made up of 13 chapters: they show the procession *(proodos)* of the divine names*, starting with the distinction *(diakrisis)* and the union *(henôsis),* which rule in Trinity. Having considered God as superessential Cause, unknowable and unspeakable, as the One in the first hypothesis of *Parmenides,* as Cause connected to all that is, and thus, likely to be known and named, then as the One in the second hypothesis of the *Parmenides* (chap. I); having shown the union *(henôsis)* and the distinction *(diakrisis),* in God (the divine persons*) and outside of God (the processions and the names) (chap. II); having underscored the importance of the prayer* as introduction to the theology of divine names and having conjured up the teaching of his master Hierotheus, Dionysius proceeded to explain the divine names.

It is possible to distinguish: 1) the names that suit the divine realities (596 D), in God: Unity and Trinity (chap. II), and outside God: the procession; 2) the names stemming from the operations of his providence* (596 D), namely a) the etiological names (645 A–B): Goodness (good*), Beauty, Light, and Love (chap. III–IV, 1–17), the Being* (chap. V), Life (chap. VI), and Wisdom (chap. VII), Power (omnipotence) (chap. VIII); names opposed to each other, such as Big and Small (chap. IX), Ancient and Young (chap. X); b) the names that concern the process of principle to the end (937 B): the Almighty (chap. X), peace (chap. XI), that converts everything to integral unity (948 D); and c) the divine names of the Cause of everything (972 A): God (chap. XII) and the One (chap. XIII), "unity of all the positive attributes of the One who is Cause of everything" (977 B).

The great movement involving procession and conversion of the divine names starts with Goodness and ends with the One, which is perhaps another name for Goodness, since Dionysius says that the movement follows the path "from Goodness to Goodness through Goodness." However, if one notices that the procession of divine names is called "distinction" in opposition to the divine "union," it can be said equally that the order of divine names by Dionysius himself, starts with Union *(henôsis)* and ends with the conversion of all toward the One *(hen).* From Union *(henôsis)* to the One *(hen):* such is the framework of the *Divine Names.*

d) Mystical Theology. This treaty, a few pages long, is divided into five chapters. It starts with a prologue made up of a prayer to the Trinity and of an address to Timothy, to whom Dionysius recommends to raise his spirit toward the contemplation of divine matters. In the first chapter, on divine Tenebrae, he distinguishes negative (or apophatic) theology from affirmative (or cataphatic) theology, and he interprets the rise of Moses on the Sinai as the elevation of the intellect toward God. The darkness of Exodus 20, 21 represents then the absolute lack of knowledge in which the spirit is buried.

Seeing and knowing this "darkness more-than-luminous" is like "knowing that it is not possible to see or know the One who is beyond view and beyond knowledge." Like the sculptor who "carves" the blocks of marble to allow the shape of the statue to appear (Plotinus's example in *Enneads.* I, 6 [1]), it can similarly be said that "by the abstraction of the essence of things, we can praise superessentially Him who is superessential." Negative theology thus lets the superessential darkness appear by pushing aside what exists. It is necessary to "remove," "suppress," or "deny" all knowledge acquired in the contact of what is, in order to "know" the Unknown in the lack of knowledge and "see" the Darkness, which is usually concealed by the light present in what is. Negation, understood as removing or discarding *(remotio),* therefore has a role that is both ontological and liturgical, in the world of beings as well as in that of symbols: it must push light away from beings in order that divine darkness may appear in their hearts, and it must also lift the veil away from the symbols in order to show divine Beauty.

The negative way rises thus from negation to negation, starting with what is the farthest from the transcending Cause; that is contrary to affirmative theology, which starts with Principle to descend to the consequences that are farthest away. The movements of these two theologies, affirmative and negative, proceed therefore in opposite directions: they correspond respectively to a descending movement *(proodos)* by the intellect, and then to its ascending movement *(anagôgè, epistrophè)* (chap. II). The abundance or, on the contrary, the conciseness of the language correspond to these two movements: descent of what is intelligible toward the sensitive, or rise of the sensitive toward the intelligible and even beyond, all the way to the transcending Cause, for which speaking has to stop and only silence is appropriate. In this apophatic rise from outside to inside and from the lower to the upper, the *logos* diminishes and ends up in silence. Dionysius highlights the opposition between abundance *(polulogia)* of symbolic discourse on the one hand and both brevity of intellectual discourse *(brakhulogia)* as well as absence of words *(alogia),* characteristic of mystical union (chap. III), on the other hand.

This apophatic ascension toward the Cause via the sensible and the intelligible occurs in the last two chapters of the *Mystical Theology* (*see* chap. IV: "That he who is the pre-eminent Cause of all things sensibly perceived is not Himself any of those things"; chap. V: "That he who is the pre-eminent Cause of all things intelligibly perceived is not Himself any of those things"). Of that Cause, "there is no parole, no name, no knowledge" (we see once more, there, the affirmation of the first hypothesis of the *Parmenide,* 141*e*), and we therefore conclude to its transcendence and its unpredictability. Neither affirmative theology nor even negative theology can therefore characterize the Cause as such: they both remain in the realm of hypothesis, either before it or what comes "beyond it." The transcendence of the Cause, which is the source of everything, while being simultaneously detached from everything, is beyond reach, indeed inaccessible. God is "beyond everything."

e) Letters. There are 10 letters, which deal with the following: the 1st with the identification separating real knowledge and non-knowledge of God; the 2nd with Divinity beyond Goodness and beyond God (*see* beginning of the *MT*); the 3rd with the divine nature of Jesus, which remains hidden even after the Incarnation*; the 4th with Jesus and his "theandric" "activity" or "energy"; the 5th with divine darkness; the 6th with the refutation of errors to establish truth; the 7th with a polemic regarding Sophist Apollophanes, who accuses Dionysius of "parricide" and of the solar eclipse both of them watched in Heliopolis; the 8th with the monk Demophilus, who does not respect his hierarchical rank; the 9th with the symbolism of the Scriptures; and the 10th with the captivity of John the Evangelist at Patmos and his prompt liberation.

Dionysius mentions other works, lost or fictitious: 1) *On the Intelligibles and the Objects of the Senses,* 2) *Theological Sketches,* 3) *Symbolic Theology,* 4) *Divine Hymns,* 5) *On the Angelic Characteristics and Orders,* 6) *On the Just and Divine Tribunal*, and 7) *On the Soul.*

Finally, several other works have come to us under the name of Dionysius:

1) three letters: a letter to Apollophanes written in Greek between the sixth and the seventh centuries (CPG III, 6630); a letter to Timothy on the passion of apostles* Peter* and Paul, in different languages (Latin, Syriac, Armenian, Georgian, Ethiopian) (CPG III, 6631): and a letter to Titus kept in Armenian (CPG III, 6632);

2) an autobiography kept in Oriental versions (Syriac, Coptic, Arabic, Georgian, Armenian) (CPG III, 6633);

3) a treaty of astronomy in Syriac (CPG III, 6634);

4) a profession of faith in Arabic (CPG III, 6635);

5) a liturgical anaphora (Renaudot 2, 202–12, quoted by I. Ortiz de Urbina, *Patrologia syriaca,* Rome, 1965, 251).

2. Editions

The first edition of the *Corpus* was published in Florence in 1516. Two other editions were published in the 17th century: the first was prepared by P. Lanssel, in Paris in 1615, and the second by B. Cordier S.J., in Antwerp in 1634 and Paris in 1644. It was Cordier's edition that was re-edited in the *Patrologia Graeca* (PG III) in 1857. As for the 20th century, it gave us the first critical edition of the *Corpus:* it was prepared by B.R. Suchla (I, *DN*), G. Heil, and A. Ritter (II, *CH, EH, MT, Ep*). A third volume is being prepared: it will include the scholia in Greek, in Syriac, in Georgian, and in Armenian.

III. Translations and Medieval Commentaries

1. Translations

a) In Syriac. Dionysius's writings became known and spread very early in Syria thanks to Sergius of Resaina (†536), translator of the *Corpus,* and its preface writer, who was suspected of being its actual author. That opinion was put forward by I. Hausherr and H. Urs von Balthasar (*Schol.* 15, 1940). Phocas (end of seventh–beginning of eighth century) started a new translation of Dionysius enriched by personal notes (*see* Sherwood, *SE* 4, 1952; Duval, *La Littérature syriaque,* Paris, 1907; Baumstark, *Geschichte der syrischen Literatur,* Bonn, 1922).

b) In Armenian. A translation of Dionysius in Armenian was done as early as the eighth century by Étienne de Siounie.

c) In Latin. Dionysius became known in the West thanks to the manuscripts copied in the East and brought from there. Two studies on Dionysius's manuscripts are authoritative: G. Théry, in *NSchol* 3, 1929, 353–442, and H.F. Dondaine (1953).

In 758, Paul I sent to Pépin le Bref the whole collection of Dionysius's writings. In 827, at Compiègne, King Louis le Pieux received from the Eastern emperor a Greek codex of all of Dionysius's writings. He requested from the abbot of Saint-Denys, Hilduin, that a translation be prepared. Around 832, Hilduin offered it to him: it was quasi illegible. Charles le Chauve then kindly asked John the Scot Eriugena to start a translation that would be more understandable. It was completed in 852. Around 1140, the monk Joannes Sarracenus, as well as Hugh of Saint Victor, decided to work on Scotus's translation of the *Celestial Hierarchy* by making use of the notes left on the margins and between the lines by scholars John of Scythopolis, Saint Maximus* the Confessor, Anastasius Bibliothecarius, and a few others. Sarracenus's translation, very different from Hilduin's and from Eriugena's, is more faithful.

The *Corpus* was translated at the time of the Renaissance by Ambrosio Traversari and Marsilius Ficinus and during a period straddling the 16th and 17th centuries by Balthasar Cordier, Perionus, and Jerome Spert.

2. Medieval Commentaries

Hugh of Saint Victor (†1141) commented on two occasions the *Celestial Hierarchy,* his preferred text, on account of the importance that it gives to the notions of participation and of symbolism. Denys le Chartreux also gave his own commentary. The most important medieval commentary was delivered by Thomas Aquinas. Finally, during the Renaissance, Ambrosio Traversari (1431–37) and Marsilius Ficinus (1490–92) (*see DSp,* t. 3, 286–429) gave theirs.

• CPG III, 6600–35.

Dionysius Areopagita, Ed. B. Cordier, PG 3, 1857.

Denys l'Aréopagite, *La Hiérarchie Céleste,* Intr. by R. Roques, Study and critical text of G. Heil, Trans. and notes by M. de Gandillac, SC 58 *bis*; les *Noms divins* et la *Théologie mystique,* Critical edition by B.R. Suchla, A. Ritter, Intr., trans. and notes by Ysabel de Andia. (English translations: *Celestial Hierarchies* and *Mystical Theology* 2nd Ed. [London: Editors of the Shrine of Wisdom, 1965].)

Corpus dionysiacum I, *De divinis nominibus,* Ed. B.R. Suchla, PTS 33, 1990; II, *De coelesti hierarchia, De ecclesiastica hierarchia, De mystica theologia,* Ed. G. Heil, A.M. Ritter, PTS 36, 1991.

a) General Studies.

H. Koch (1900), *Pseudo-Dionysius Areopagita in seinen Beziehungen zum Neuplatonismus und Mysterienwesen, eine literarhistorische Untersuchung,* Mayence.

R. Roques (1954), *L'univers dionysien, Structure hiérarchique du monde selon le Pseudo-Denys,* Paris (2nd Ed. 1983); id. (1957), "Dionysius Areopagita," *RAC* 3, 1075–21.

R. Roques et al. (1957), "Denys l'Aréopagite (le Pseudo-)," *DSp* 3, 244–430.

W. Völker (1958), *Kontemplation und Ekstase bei Pseudo-Dionysios Areopagita,* Wiesbaden.

E. Corsini (1962), *Il trattato "de Divinis Nominibus" dello Pseudo-Dionigi e i commenti neoplatonici al Parmenide,* Turin.

E. von Ivánka (1964), *Plato Christianus, Übernahme und Umgestaltung des Platonismus durch die Väter,* Einsiedeln.

J.P. Sheldon-Williams (1967), "The Pseudo-Dionysius," in A.H. Armstrong (Ed.), *The Cambridge History of Later Greek and Early Medieval Philosophy,* Cambridge, 457–72.

B. Brons (1976), *Gott und die Seienden: Untersuchungen zum Verhältnis von neuplatonischer Metaphysik und christlicher Tradition bei Dionysius Areopagita,* Göttingen.

G.J.P. O'Daly (1981), "Dionysius," *TRE* 8, 772–80.

S. Lilla (1982), "Introduzione allo studio dello Ps. Dionigi l'Areopagita," *Aug.* 22, 568–77; id. (1984), "Dionigi," in E. Ancili, M. Paparozzi (Ed.), *La Mística. Fenomenologia e reflessione teologica,* Rome, 361–98; id. (1986 *a*), *Ps. Dionigi l'Areopagita,* Gerarchia celeste, Teologia mistica, Lettere, Rome; id. (1986 *b*), "Note sulla *Gerarchia Celeste* dello Ps. Dionigi l'Areopagita," *Aug.* 26, 519–73.

P. Rorem (1984), *Biblical and Liturgical Symbols Within the Pseudo-Dionysian Synthesis,* STPIMS 71.

Y. de Andia (1996), *Henosis: L'union à Dieu chez Denys l'Aréopagite,* Leyden.

b) Latin Text and Medieval Commentaries.

J. Durantel (1919), *Saint Thomas et le Pseudo-Denys,* Paris.

P.G. Théry (1931), *Scot Érigène traducteur de Denys,* Paris; (1932), *Études dionysiennes,* Paris (about Hilduin's translation).

Ph. Chevallier (1937/1950), *Dionysiaca, Recueil donnant l'ensemble des traductions latines des ouvrages attribués à Denys de l'Aréopage,* 2 vols., Paris.

C. Pera (1950), *Sancti Thomae Aquinatis in librum beati Dionysii De divinis nominibus expositio,* Turin-Rome.

H. Dondaine (1953), *Le corpus dionysien de l'université de Paris au XIIIe siècle,* Rome.

B. Faes de Mottoni (1977), *Il "Corpus Dionysiacum" nel medioevo: Rassegna di studi: 1900–1972,* Rome.

Ysabel De Andia

See also **Attributes, Divine; Negative Theology; Platonism, Christian**

Diphysitism

Dyphisitism is a doctrine defined at the Council of Chalcedon*, according to which Christ* has two natures *(duo phuseis),* human and divine. It is the opposite of monophysitism*.

See also **Monophysitism**

Ditheism. *See* **Tritheism**

Divine Names. *See* **Attributes, Divine**

Divinity. *See* **Deity**

Divinization. *See* **Holiness; Mysticism; Rhineland-Flemish Mysticism**

Docetism

The term *docetism* derives from *dokein* (to appear) and designates a theological concept shared by several gnostic heresies before it was also taken up by Manicheanism*. It consisted in granting to Christ* the Savior no more than a simple "appearance" *(dokesis)* of a human body. It represented the reaction of a Hellenistic thought, which bore the imprint of dualism and which sought to safeguard the transcendence and incorruptibility of the divine in the face of matter, considered a contrary principle. Christ, a spiritual being, could not have come in "the flesh*" but only as a spirit having taken on the appearance of "flesh."

1. Development

During the apostolic and post-apostolic eras, John's christological formulations, and some of his attacks (Jn 1:14; 1 Jn 4:2f.), or the clarifications of Ignatius of Antioch on the "complete" and "real" nature of the Incarnation* only afforded a glimpse of the poorly identifiable precursors of actual docetism. It was with the Gnosticism of the second century that Docetism would be established.

a) Among the Valentinians. Their system dissociates the Christ from above—an "aeon" issued from the "pleroma"—and the "psychic" Christ produced by the Demiurge. The historical Jesus* bore a body that contained no corruption. According to different schools, the nature of that body was either "pneumatic," or "psychic." He had passed through Mary* *(per Mariam)* like water through a tube: any generation of his body *ex Maria* was rejected. His "resurrection*" could only be understood in terms of his return to the pleroma.

b) In Marcionism. Docetism was even more radical in Marcionism because Marcion suppressed any idea of the birth and growth of Jesus Christ. According to Marcion, the Son of the superior god, a stranger to the material world, had appeared suddenly, in the 15th year of Tiberius, in an adult body. This body had had no earthly mother and presented only an appearance, an illusion of "flesh." Through a unique divine dispensation, this putative "flesh"—which was in itself neither passible nor mortal—had *truly* known the Passion* and death* on the cross. This rigorous Docetism would be somewhat attenuated by Apelles, a disciple of Marcion who departed from his teacher's thought and granted Christ a body that was real but exempt of birth, borrowed from the substance of the heavenly bodies.

All these christological concepts were accompanied by a same attitude of negation with regard to resurrection: the human body of flesh could be neither saved nor redeemed: salvation* and redemption concerned souls alone.

2. Reaction of the Church

Against these attempts at outrageous "spiritualization," Irenaeus* and, in his wake, Tertullian*, defended the "rule of faith" by placing the accent on the veritable incarnation of Jesus Christ and on the true historicity of his redeeming act. They strongly affirmed/asserted the unity of Christ, which derived from the conjunction of the divine Logos and the "flesh"—the flesh designating human substance. It is this "flesh" that, having partaken through Christ of the vivifying divine power, would be destined for salvation and resurrection. Tertullian, who vigorously maintained the permanent reality of divinity *(deus)* and of humanity *(homo)* in the sole "person*" of Jesus Christ (*Adu. Praxean* 27, 11), insisted also upon the authentic and complete nature of this human component, including soul (soul-heart-body) and material body, which the Word* received through his birth *of* the Virgin: it is by taking on a true "flesh" that Christ can save that of mankind and assure them of resurrection.

• P. Weigandt (1961), *Der Doketismus im Urchristentum und in der theologischen Entwicklung des 2. Jahrhunderts,* Heidelberg.

J.-P. Mahé (Ed.) (1975), *Tertullien, La chair du Christ* (SC 216), Introduction, pp. 11–180.

A. Orbe (1975), "La Pasión según los gnosticos," *Gr* 56, 5–43; id. (1976), *Cristología gnóstica: Introducción a la soteriología de los siglos II y III,* I-II, Madrid; id. (1990 *a*), "En torno al modalismo de Marción," *Gr* 71, 43–65; id. (1990 *b*), "Marcionitica," *Aug.* 31, 195–244; (1993), "Hacia la doctrina marcionítica de la redención," *Gr* 74, 45–74.

A. Grillmeier (1979), "Jesus der Christus im Glauben der Kirche," I, Fribourg-Basel-Vienna.

C. Munier (1993), "Où en est la question d'Ignace d'Antioche?," *ANRW* II, 27, 1 (especially 407–13).

René Braun

See also **Apostolic Fathers; Attributes, Divine; Christ and Christology; Gnosis; Incarnation; Marcionism; Resurrection of Christ**

Doctor of the Church

The term *doctor* originated in the New Testament title *didaskalos* (Acts 13:1, 1 Cor 12:28, etc.), a charismatic teacher in the service of the early Christian communities. It progressively took on a technical meaning, at any rate from the time of Pope* Leo the Great, to designate the ecclesiastic ministry of the major figures of theology. The doctoral ministry would later take on a university connotation, and there would be many professors of theology, and also medieval theologians, who would be known by a doctoral title. For example, Bernard* of Clairvaux was *doctor mellifluus;* Thomas* Aquinas, *doctor angelicus;* Alexander of

Hales, *doctor Irrefragabilis;* Bonaventure*, *doctor seraphicus;* Duns* Scotus, *doctor subtilis;* Ruusbroec, *doctor ecstaticus;* William of Ockham, *doctor invincibilis;* Gerson, *doctor christianissimus;* and Gregory of Rimini, *doctor acutus.*

In 1298, on the initiative of Pope Boniface VIII, the Roman magisterium* began to confer the title of Doctor of the Church* upon theologians who were considered to have been privileged witnesses of the Christian tradition* (*see* Vatican* II's *Presbyterorum Ordinis,* 19). The first declarations did no more than ratify what had already been an ancient choice under Latin Christianity, which commonly placed its theology under the protection of Ambrose* of Milan, Jerome, Augustine*, and Gregory* the Great. Similarly, since the ninth century, the Christian East had granted preeminence to Basil* the Great, Gregory* of Nazianzus, and John Chrysostom*.

There are 33 Doctors of the Church. Eight have been recognized as such by tradition. They are: Basil of Caesarea (4th century), Gregory of Nazianzus (4th century), John Chrysostom (4th century), Athanasius* of Alexandria (4th century), Ambrose of Milan (4th century), Gregory the Great (5th century), Augustine of Hippo (5th century), and Jerome (5th century). The rest were solemnly proclaimed (the date of the proclamation follows the century in which they flourished): Thomas Aquinas (13th century; 1567), Bonaventure (13th century; 1588), Anselm of Canterbury (11th century; 1720), Isidore of Seville (7th century; 1722), Peter Chrysologus (5th century; 1729), Leo the Great (5th century; 1754), Peter Damian (11th century; 1828), Bernard of Clairvaux (12th century; 1830), Hilary of Poitiers (5th century; 1851), Alphonsus Liguori (18th century; 1871), Francis de Sales (17th century; 1871), Cyril* of Alexandria (5th century, 1893), Cyril of Jerusalem (5th century, 1893), John of Damascus (8th century, 1893), the Venerable Bede (8th century; 1899), Ephraem the Syrian (4th century; 1920), Peter Canisius (16th century; 1925), John* of the Cross (16th century; 1926), Robert Bellarmine* (17th century; 1931), Albert* the Great (13th century; 1931), Anthony of Padua (13th century; 1946), Laurence of Brindisi (17th century; 1959), Teresa of Avila (16th century; 1970), Catherine of Siena (14th century; 1970), and Theresa of Lisieux (19th century, 1997).

The theological criteriology that preceded Vatican II held that the quality of a Doctor of the Church corresponded to four distinctive marks: 1) sanctity (holiness*) of life, 2) orthodoxy of doctrine, 3) quality and scope of theological work *(eminens eruditio),* and 4) formal recognition by the Church *(expressa ecclesiae declaratio).* The first three criteria were also applied to Fathers* of the Church, from whom the Doctors were distinguished by the fact that they can belong to a recent period of the Church and that they can receive a solemn approval (and not a rather vague *approbatio ecclesia*).

The fact that the more recently proclaimed Doctors, Teresa of Avila, Catherine of Siena, and Theresa of Lisieux, were the first women to be proclaimed Doctors, and the fact that they were women who possessed no technical competence in theology, incites one to review the traditional criteria. *Eminens eruditio,* quite obviously, no longer has any relevance here, and the fact that the title of Doctor has also been applied to Mary* in the capacity of "counselor of the Apostles*" also works against that criterion. Doctrinal orthodoxy and sanctity of life also took on a new and richer meaning when applied to those Doctors, in whom one could recognize—*cum grano salis*—a theoretical contribution (as in Theresa of Lisieux's "Little Way"), but for whom it seemed of prime importance that they incarnate figures of *Christian experience*—thus, an "orthopraxy" (Balthasar 1970).

The declarations of 1970 and 1997 (the Doctors recognized or declared before this time were all men belonging to the ecclesiastical hierarchy*) required, moreover, that a distinction be made between the charisma of the Doctors and the practice of a magisterium in the Church (Garrone 1971), while rendering null and void the distinction between the Church as *teacher* and the Church as *matter taught.*

The doctrinal role of the Doctors of the Church is distinct from the "unanimous consensus of the Fathers"—a notion that traditionally led one to consider the teaching of the Fathers as infallible insofar as they offered a converging interpretation of the Scriptures (Holy* Scripture)—but the attribution of the title of Doctor to authors who came after the era of the Fathers, whatever limits one might attribute to that era, probably conveyed the desire to allow the Middle Ages, then the modern age, to give their own Fathers (or Mothers) to the Church. But neither the works of the Fathers nor those of the Doctors were meant to be totally exempt of errors or theological imprecision. One should bear in mind simply that their main intention, the body of their doctrine, and the majority of their theses were in perfect communion with the orthodox teachings (Séjourné and Amman in *Dictionnaire de théologie catholique,* vol. XIV).

Thomas Aquinas was acknowledged as having a certain primacy among the Doctors of the Church during a period of Scholastic renaissance, which was above all a Thomist renaissance (*see* Leo XIII's encyclical *Aeterni Patris,* 1879, and also the Vatican II documents *Gravissimum Educationis,* 10, and *Optatam Totius* 16). However, the list of Doctors suffices to show that the intention of the Church was never to canonize one, or any, particular theological* school. The Doctors of the Church were privileged masters of doctrine and Christian experience. But the diversity of schools or tendencies within one and the same confessed faith has been a positive element, and one that has been encouraged, of the intellectual and spiritual life of the Church.

• E. Valton (1910), "Docteur de l'Église," *DThC* 4, 1509–10.
G. Marsot (1952), "Docteurs de l'Église," *Cath* 3, 936.
K. Rahner, H. Vorgrimler (1961), *Kleines theologisches Wörterbuch,* Freiberg.
H.U. von Balthasar (1970), *Schwestern im Geist,* Einsiedeln, 14–349.
G.-M. Garrone (1971), "Sainte Catherine de Sienne et sainte Thérèse, docteurs de l'Église," *DC* LXVIII, 25–29.

GILBERT NARCISSE AND GALAHAD THREEPWOOD

See also **Fathers of the Church; *Loci theologici;* Magisterium; Theology**

Dogma

1. Concept's History and Meanings

In current theological usage *dogma* refers to a truth that the Church* lays down as an obligatory belief. Although in the past, various concepts ("article of faith," "Catholic truth") were used in this sense, sometimes in an analogous way, since the Enlightenment era the idea of dogma has gradually superseded them. The term is also used in a wider sense to refer to the truths of faith that have not been raised formally to the status of a dogma (such as, for example, the profession of faith in the doctrine of the Trinity).

a) Secular, Jewish, and Christian Linguistic Usage in Antiquity. In its transitive form the Greek verb *dokein* means "to believe" or "to decide": it gives rise to the noun *dogma,* "opinion" or "decision." In its latter meaning, "dogma" appears as a technical term in legal language ("decree" or "law": as for instance in Plato's *Republic,* 414 b; *Laws,* 644 d, 926 d), while in its former we encounter it in the field of philosophy. In Plato, therefore, it can mean, "representation" (*Theaetetus,* 158 d), "opinion" (*Sophist* 265 c) or "principle, doctrine" (*Republic,* 538 c). It was the last meaning that the Stoa picked up and defined by postulating, in opposition to the suspension of judgment *(epokhè)* advocated by the Skeptics, the necessity of a *dogma* (Latin *decretum*), of an unequivocal intellectual understanding as a presupposition of moral action (*see* Cicero, *Academics* 2, 9, 27; Seneca, *Letters* 95; Epictetus, *Dialogues,* 4, 11, 8 passim; Marcus Aurelius, 2, 3; Sextus Empiricus, *Hypotyposes pyrrhon,* 1, 13–17). These principles differ according to the philosophical schools.

Although "dogma" is rarely mentioned in the Greek translations of the Old Testament, and when it is it occurs almost exclusively in the legal sense (*see 4 M* 4, 23s. 26 [LXX]; Dn 2, 13 passim [Theodotion]), Hellenistic Judaism actually used this term to refer to the Mosaic Tradition itself, which was thought to be superior to the philosophers' dogmas (*see 3M* 1, 3; Flavius Josephus, *Contra Appion* 1, 42; 2, 168 *Sq; Antiquities* 15, 126; Philo, *Legum all.*, 1, 54; 3, 1, 194 passim).

This Hellenistic usage turns up again in the New Testament (*see* Col 2:14; Eph 2:15), in parallel with the legal meaning (*see* Lk 2:1; Acts 17:7; Heb 11:23, variant). In Acts 16:4 the disciplinary decisions made by what is known as the "Council of the Apostles*" (*see* Acts 15:28) are called *dogmata.* Following the usage of Hellenistic Judaism, the Apostolic* Fathers spoke of "the dogma of the Lord" (*dogmata tou kuriou:* Ignatius of Antioch, *Epistles to the Magnesians* 13, 1; *Epistle of Barnabas* 1, 6) or they speak of the "dogma of the Gospels" (*dogmata tou euangeliou: Didache* 11, 3). The apologists* Justin, Tatianus, and Athenagoras—as well as the Alexandrians Clement and Origen*—applied the idea of "dogma" indiscriminately both to philosophical doctrines and Christian teachings, with the result that it seemed necessary to qualify the latter appropriately: Origen did this therefore by speaking of the "dogma of God*" (*dogmata theou* Comm. on Saint Matthew 12, 23), while Eusebius referred to "the dogma of the

Church" *(ekklesiastika dogmata)* with reference to their contents (*see HE* 3, 26, 4) as well as to the way in which they were laid down (for example, as a result of a synodal decision: *see* ibid. 5, 23, 2; 6, 43, 2). According to present-day criteria, the decisions about the faith made by the ancient Church councils* would be considered to be dogma, but the assemblies themselves did not choose this term. Emperor Justinian, on the other hand, did name them thus, thereby giving them the same status as the Scriptures (Holy* Scripture) (*Corp. Iur. Civ.*, nov. 131).

The term did not gain ground in the time of the Latin Fathers. Applied most often to philosophical doctrines or to Christian heresies*, they occasionally used the term to designate Christian doctrine. The situation stayed more or less the same throughout the Middle Ages. Only Vincent of Lerins's *Commonitorium* (v. 434) gave dogma a central theological position; for him, in the above work, dogma stood for the teaching of the Catholic Church (*dogma divinum, caeleste, ecclesiasticum, catholicum,* etc.), which provided the standard for scriptural interpretation and must thus be distinguished from the doctrine of the masters of error (*novum dogma,* etc.). For Lerins, the criterion of dogma is "what has been believed everywhere, always, by everyone." During the course of the centuries Church teaching might change in its form, but in its substance undergoes neither falsification nor dilution (*see Commonitorium* 23).

b) Medieval Concept: Article of Faith. In the Middle Ages the obligatory doctrines of the Church and the way in which they had been laid down were discussed, for the most part, under the term *articles of faith.* Tertullian* had already spoken of the Resurrection* as "the article which embodied the whole faith" (*De resurrectione mortuorum* 39: CChr. SL 2, 972). It was about the year 1150 that the term *articulus fidei* appeared in theological literature, replacing the expressions "*pars fidei*" and "*sententia symboli*" by which, until that time, the different propositions contained in the confession of faith had been designated. This notion, which at first only meant the smallest unit of a greater whole, received its first elucidation about the year 1230 (*see* the three "definitions" of the *Summa de Bono* by Philippe le Chancelier). This effort of conceptual clarification went hand in hand with a thorough study of the obligatory nature of the article of faith: in the first place, insofar as it was a necessity for salvation*, and in the second place, insofar as it actually pertained to divine truth. This double source of the obligation emerged clearly in the definition falsely attributed to Richard of Saint Victor: *Articulus est indivisibilis veritas de Deo artans [sic] nos ad credendum* (ibid.). By "article of faith," Thomas Aquinas understood truths that 1) are revealed directly by the Holy Scriptures; 2) have great importance for the faith and the life of the faith, to the extent that they are related to humanity's final end and to the Beatific Vision; and 3) are attached to a symbol (*see* especially *ST* IIa IIae, q. 1, a. 6–10). But the articles of faith do not only represent the standard of what the faithful are obliged to believe and the foundation of all Christian teaching. They also constitute the starting point for theology* as a whole.

When the great era of Scholasticism* turned again to the Aristotelian conception of knowledge it became necessary to establish what principles should be the starting points of theology, in order to reach by deductive methods a genuinely scientific knowledge. William of Auxerre deserves the credit for having been the first to have viewed the articles of faith as the principles of theological science (*see* the texts quoted by Lang 1964). Although the scientific nature of theology remained controversial, the idea that the articles of faith constituted the foundation of theology was not long in gaining acceptance. Even if all the truths of salvation are not stated explicitly in the articles of faith contained in the creed (as is the case of the Eucharist*, for example), to the schoolmen of that period they seemed to be particularly fruitful principles, from which could be extracted all the wealth of the faith. The late Scholasticism of the 14th century attributed not only to the articles of faith but to all the truths contained in the Scriptures the value of a first principle in the realm of theological science (*see* the evidence furnished by Lang 1964). At the same time, they questioned which truths should be considered to be "Catholic truths . . . necessary for salvation," and which authority could designate them as obligatory beliefs (William of Ockham, *Dialogus,* in Koser 1963). It seemed that the body of truths based on God's revealed authority* of God revealed (that is, divine faith, *fides divina,* corresponding to the explicit and implicit contents of the Scriptures) formed the nucleus of a more extensive field of truths, which also covered those revealed to the apostles* and transmitted orally, as well as the truths laid down by the first councils or those reserved for particular saints (as, for instance, the rules of the big monastic orders); these truths also possessed, in varying degrees, an obligatory nature. As for the authority to determine the faith of the Church, that was no longer attributed solely to the council, as the representative of the universal Church, but also, more and more, to the pope.

c) Rediscovery of "Dogma" in Modern Times. The Reformation had just revived the controversy about the obligatory doctrine of the Church when Vincent of Lerins's *Commonitorium* was rediscovered and edited by J. Sichard (Basel 1528). From then on, the term *dogma,* used in Vincent's work to mean the teaching perpetuated by the Church, gradually supplanted the medieval notion of "article of faith," whose meanings it appropriated. In opposition to the traditional Catholic understanding—adopted once again by the Council of Trent*—in which faith constitutes a harmonious whole encompassing various theological and disciplinary declarations guaranteed by the Church, there was an increasing insistence on the possibility of examining the validity of doctrine. Internal Church arguments about Jansenism*, Gallicanism*, and so forth and external criticisms of the Church from representatives of the Enlightenment reinforced this trend. The modern concept of dogma had its origin in an attempt to unite the different confessions around the central truths of the faith. In this connection, François Véron (1578–1649)—without employing the term *dogma* itself—spoke of declarations that, revealed by God, are proposed by the Church as truths that had to be believed: "part of the Catholic faith, and nothing but that, has been revealed in the word of God and proposed to all by the Catholic Church as obliged to be believed as coming from divine faith" (*Regula fidei catholica,* Latin translation Louvain, 1702, reproduced *in* Migne, *Theologiae cursus completus* I, Paris, 1839, 1037–112). His contemporary, Henry Holden (1596–1662), referred to such declarations using the traditional expression "articles of faith" but also as concepts of "dogma of the Catholic faith" or "divine" (*catholicae* or *divinae fidei dogma*). This usage was upheld particularly by theologians influenced by Enlightenment thinkers, theologians such as Felix Anton Blau (1754–98; *Regula fidei catholicae,* Mainz, 1780) and Philippe Neri Chrismann (c. 1751–1810; *Regula fidei catholicae et collectio dogmatum credendorum,* Kempten, 1792). For the latter, the dogma of the faith is "nothing else but...a doctrine and divinely revealed truth, and which has been proposed by the general opinion of the Church as obliged to be believed as divine faith, in such a way that the opposite doctrine is condemned by the Church as heretical" (ibid.).

While rejecting the reductive approach of these authors, neo-Scholasticism itself adopted the concept thus defined (*see* Joseph Kleutgen [1811–83], *Die Theologie der Vorzeit verteidigt,* vol. I, Münster, 2nd Ed. 1867: "The Christian Catholic Faith includes everything that the Church proclaims as being the truth which God has revealed to it, and it includes nothing other than that"). Without using the concept directly, Vatican* I defined *dogma* as a declaration contained in the Word* of God and laid down by the ordinary and universal magisterium* of the Church as an obligatory belief ("Let us add that one must believe by divine and Catholic faith everything which is contained in the Word of God, written or transmitted by Tradition, and which the Church proposes as a divinely revealed belief, either by means of a solemn proclamation, or through its ordinary and universal magisterium" [*DS* 3011]). The same council introduced papal infallibility*, claiming it as a "dogma revealed by God" (*DS* 3073). By this action the doctrine became definitive Church usage (*see* already *DS* 2629, 2879 s., 2909, 2922, 3017, 3020, 3041, 3043). Still, without using the concept itself (*see LG* 25; *DV* 7–10), Vatican II looked again at the fundamental problem before proposing a less doctrinal, more individual view of revelation and of the faith. In doing so it echoed the legitimate requests made at the turn of the century by the representatives of what is known as Modernism*.

Protestantism did not evolve along the same lines. Particularly in his dispute with Erasmus*, Luther*, who stressed the assertoric nature of faith, adhered to the medieval terminology, while disagreeing with the magisterium: "It is the word of God, and no one else, that must lay down the articles of faith" (*BSLK* 421, 24s.). He remained faithful, however, to the Trinitarian and christological confession of the first councils, not because he granted them any special competence regarding doctrine, but because he considered that their declarations were confirmed by the Scriptures and were therefore correct. The term *dogma* was then taken into the orthodoxy of early Protestantism in reference to the doctrine of the early Church, but when it came to the body of Protestant doctrine constituted in the 16th century, they talked of *Confessio* and of *doctrina* (*see* Ebeling 1964). After the Enlightenment, within Protestantism the term *dogma* became the object of a radical critique, the motives of which were partly of a spiritual kind and partly due to historical factors. But, while in the 19th century the Protestant call to subjectivity was in large part understood as the abolition of "dogma" (Baur; von Harnack), Barth* turned with renewed interest toward this concept. He himself defined dogma as "ecclesial preaching*, as long as it coincides with the word of God contained in the Bible*" (*KD* I/1, 283), while stressing the vast distance that separates this preaching from the word itself. Dogma, however, was widely challenged under the influence of Bultmann*, who demanded a modernized reinterpretation of the primitive Christian kerygma.

2. Dogma in Systematic Theology

Dogmas are for the Church the words that have an obligation. In this regard, despite their specificity, they must be viewed as the manifestation of a phenomenon of universal nature. All communities establish themselves and bind themselves together around certain fundamental convictions. Any challenge to these would threaten to destroy the whole. Even in the state governed by democratic law, where these convictions are based on the consensus of all the citizens and in this respect are considered to be open to revision, such beliefs express the "truth" according to which the community lives and acts. Now this truth, in the historic conditions contingent on its comprehension and wording, can only be grasped in particular and categorized declarations, which a transcendental meditation understands as so many signs and foreshadowings of absolute truth. It is also true of the dogmas of the Church, which want to express the divine truth in an obligatory way. Like all human definitions of truth, they take on an analogical form (*see DS* 806): that is, they translate only imperfectly that divine truth that, nonetheless, they do not disclaim that they express. In this way dogmas perform an indispensable role in the Church's community of communication, making possible agreement on truth and a coherent expression of Christian identity. That is what is already clearly affirmed in the New Testament, where for liturgical and catechetical ends it sometimes seemed necessary to sum up the primitive Christian kerygma in a striking phrase (*see,* for instance, Rom 10:9; 1 Cor 15:3ff.). It is also what the symbols of the ancient Church confirm, as do the doctrinal definitions of the ecumenical councils.

In the last resort this state of affairs is based on the Incarnation* as a structure of divine revelation. God, in Jesus Christ*, speaks in both the historical and the eschatological mode; in the Holy* Spirit he provides permanent witness and the continually renewed acknowledgment of his own communication. The transmission, throughout the fluctuations of history, of the permanent witness of a divine truth communicated once and for all: that is the task entrusted to the Church. It must, for that reason, always abide within the truth (indefectibility*) (*see LG* 12). The dogmas must not be understood as new revelations but as the unfolding—under the impetus of various forces—of the founding revelation to which the Scriptures attest and that are transmitted by the tradition of the Church (theological loci*). It is not enough to single out such and such a declaration from the Scriptures, for it is precisely over the correct interpretation of a particular statement that disagreement is often provoked. For this reason Nicaea* I had already found itself forced to have recourse to a nonscriptural term (*homoousios,* "consubstantial*") to put an end to the quarrel that certain theologians had started about the divinity of the Logos [Word], based on different biblical quotations. The Nicaean Creed, with its corresponding canons (*see DS* 125 *Sq*), can be regarded as a dogma before the fact. Over the course of history the Church can be seen to fix the truths of the faith in various forms: apart from the confessions of the early Church, pride of place should go to the decisions of the councils, which either present themselves as confessions of faith (as with the creeds of Nicaea I and Constantinople* I, in particular), or as doctrinal explanations, or as canonical decisions (by means of the traditional formula "*si quis dixerit...anathema sit,*" "if someone says...let him be anathema"). These decisions are not only related to questions of faith in the strict sense but also to Christian life and to the organization of the Church. With regard to the canons, since Vatican* I it has been thought that anathematization qualifies the incriminated thesis as heretical and therefore defines its opposite as "a divine and Catholic truth according to the faith." Nonetheless this is not absolutely true of the canons of the Council of Trent, nor even of those of Vatican I. In fact, until the Council of Trent inclusively, it was not only opinions deviating from the faith of the Church that were anathematized but also disciplinary deviations. And Vatican I insisted on condemning not only the heresies that had appeared in the domain of the faith itself but also the errors concerning "the preambles to the faith." Then Vatican* II abandoned the proclamation of anathematisms, as well as proclamations of dogmas in the strict sense, opting for a type of explanation of a pastoral nature.

Dealing with the doctrinal decisions of the Church, the magisterium assumed jointly by the bishops* and the pope performs a particular role as an authority that bears witness. According to the conception formulated by Vatican I and adopted again by Vatican II, the magisterium has the task of explaining in a definitive and obligatory form the truths of the faith contained in the Scriptures and in tradition. It can perform this task either by means of harmonized teaching by the pope and the bishops scattered over the whole world (ordinary teaching) or by a particular decision of a council or of the pope (universal teaching) (*see LG* 25; *CIC* 1983, can. 749). For believers, it is not only a question of accepting these dogmas obediently: in the present age, theology stresses the role of a more active reception of the doctrinal declarations (*see* Beinert 1991).

The idea of "dogma," in the form in which it emerged by means of the theologians of the Enlightenment era, aimed rather at setting aside topics of disagreement by restricting the body of obligatory doctrines. The magisterium* adopted this concept, while stressing that the adhesion of the faithful could not and should not limit itself to the dogmas officially proclaimed. According to the declaration of Vatican II about the order or the hierarchy* of the truths relative to their christological base (*see UR* 11), the faith of the Church constitutes a "differentiated global structure" (Kasper 1991), in the context of which the particular statements must be judged and interpreted.

3. Problem of Dogmatic Development

All knowledge of truth is part of history. This historicity can be understood in a positive sense as a quality of opening up and of unfinished business. It therefore falls to human reason* to constantly enlarge its perception of truth. But it can also mean that no truth exists, or that we grasp it only inadequately, or even that we cannot grasp it at all. Already in classical philosophy, the term *dogma* expressed the conviction that, despite all the challenges from Skeptics, there is indeed a true knowledge, which, however, cannot prevent the development of contrary opinions. With regard to the Christian faith, the perception of the historical character of its wording raises the question of the way in which it was constituted and of the degree of truth of particular declarations. If one seriously acknowledges that God, in Jesus Christ, communicated with us in the definitive reality of eschatology, that Jesus Christ in person is therefore the definitive truth of God (*see* Jn 14:6; Heb 1:1ff.), there are then no more revelations to expect. One should, however, see in Jesus Christ not only the end but also the fulfillment of a revelation that, under the guidance of the Holy Spirit, we have never finished understanding and assimilating (*see* Jn 14:26, 15:26, 16:13). Once they are set against this background, all the theories that interpret development unilaterally as tending either toward defection or toward progress are obviously inappropriate. According to the principles we have acknowledged, the development of dogma cannot be conceived except as "the explanation of what is implicitly contained in the original revelation" (Kasper 1991).

Such an explanation should not, however, be understood either according to a simple biological schema (*see* Vincent of Lerins, *Commonitorium* 23, cited by Vatican I [*see DS* 3020]) or in a purely logical sense (theology of the conclusion, neo-Scholasticism). The real process of the development of dogma is judged more fairly by viewing the tradition of the faith as a living event rather than as the transmission of particular theses (*see DV* 8). In the light of this, it is only of secondary importance to decide whether this event should be considered—citing only a few of the theories of dogmatic development—from the viewpoint of dialectics, as an auto-interpretation of the Christian idea (Möhler, Kuhn); or from the viewpoint of typology, as the continuous unfolding of new aspects of the faith in the fixed context of a global type (Newman*); or from a vitalist viewpoint, as the constantly renewed attempt to put the Word of God to the test through action (Blondel); or lastly, from the viewpoint of theological transcendentalism, as the historico-categorical expression of a knowledge that at its origin is of a transcendental nature (Rahner*). Until now it has too often been forgotten that by understanding dogmatic development as a process of progressive explanation there is an ultimate risk of merging it with the idea of "progress"; and that it must therefore be viewed also as a process of reduction and of concentration around an original truth, without nonetheless falling into the theory of defection. The revelation happened once and for all, and the witnessing of it is incorporated into the Scriptures. It is by returning constantly to the Scriptures that we assure ourselves of a critical resort against a concept of dogmatic development subordinated too exclusively to an idea of "progress." Even if the action of the Holy Spirit goes beyond the confines of a theory of dogmatic development, it is essentially this action that, according to Catholic belief, governs the evolution of doctrine and of religious life. The Holy Spirit acts within the Church, through the faith of the people of God *(sensus fidelium),* as well as through the preaching of doctrine, each depending on the other (*see LG* 12; *DV* 8). But the Spirit also intervenes in the work of the theologians, whose task is certainly not restricted to preparing the ground for the magisterium and to justifying its decisions after the event. That work also consists of studying the Word of God, such as it was pronounced once and for all, of examining the different interpretations to which it has given rise during the course of history, of reflecting on the internal coherence of the Christian message and of taking responsibility for it in face of contemporary questions. Although in the past it was particularly the existence of heretical movements within Christianity that inspired efforts to clarify and delimit dogma—except for the two Marian dogmas of 1854 and 1950, which reacted rather to religious requirements—Vatican II (particularly in the pastoral constitution *Gaudium et Spes*) considered the great challenges of the present age to be the "signs of the times" that had to be interpreted in the light of the gospel (*see GS* 4, passim). As history recedes from us the declarations of dogmas in no way seem like the end of a discussion but rather as pertinent and incidental contributions, which cannot be extended to other historical contexts without a good deal of interpretation (*see Mysterium Ecclesiae* 5 [AAS 65 (1973), 402–4]). Such interpretation need not, however, mean the destruction of dogma, as long as with the help of the historical knowledge acquired in this domain it takes as a guide the wording found by the Church and makes sure of expressing the idea in conformity with the realities of a new situation. Today, discussions center above all on the question of how the faith can preserve and express its identity not only through succeeding epochs with the same cultural climate (Western) but also from one culture to another. In order to finally achieve an ecumenical approach it is essential to know whether the condemnations pronounced in the evangelical confessions of the 16th century and in the canons of the Council of Trent remain valid today (*see* Lehmann and Pannenberg 1986, 1989).

♦ G. Kittel (1935), "Dogma-dogmatizò," *ThWNT* 2, 233–35.
A. Lang (1942–43), "Die Gliederung und die Reichweite des Glaubens nach Thomas von Aquin und den Thomisten: Ein Beitrag zur Klärung der scholastischen Begriffe: *fides, haeresis* und *conclusio theologica,*" *DT* 20, 207–36, 335–46; *DT* 21, 79–97; id. (1953), "Der Bedeutungswandel der Begriffe *fides* und *haeresis* und die dogmatische Wertung der Konzilsentscheidungen von Vienne und Trient," *MThZ* 4, 133–46.
J. Ranft (1957), "Dogma I," *RAC* 3, 1257–60.
E. Fascher (1959), "Dogma II," *RAC* 4, 1–24.
L. Hödl (1962), "*Articulus fidei:* Eine begriffsgeschichtliche Arbeit," in J. Ratzinger, H. Fries (Ed.), *Einsicht und Glaube,* Freiberg, 358–76.
C. Koser (1963), *De notis theologicis: Historia, notio, usus,* Petropolis.
G. Ebeling (1964), *Wort Gottes und Tradition,* Göttingen.
M. Elze (1964), "Der Begriff des Dogmas in der alten Kirche," *ZThK* 61, 421–38.
A. Lang (1964), *Die theologische Prinzipienlehre der mittelalterlichen Scholastik,* Fribourg.
H. Hammans (1965), *Die neueren katholischen Erklärungen der Dogmenentwicklung,* Essen.
W. Kasper (1965), *Dogma unter dem Wort Gottes,* Mayence.
K. Rahner, K. Lehmann (1965), "Kerygma und Dogma," *MySal* I, 622–707.
J. Ratzinger (1966), *Das Problem der Dogmengeschichte in der Sicht der katholischen Theologie,* Köln-Opladen.
W. Pannenberg (1967), "Was ist eine dogmatische Aussage?," *Grundfragen systematischer Theologie,* Göttingen, 159–80.
H.-J. Pottmeyer (1968), *Der Glaube vor dem Anspruch der Wissenschaft,* Fribourg, 300–304.
H. Küng (1970 *a*), *Unfehlbar? Eine Anfrage,* Zurich; id. (Ed.) (1970 *b*), *Fehlbar? Eine Bilanz,* Zurich.
J. Nolte (1971), *Dogma in Geschichte,* Fribourg.
K. Rahner (Ed.) (1971), *Zum Problem Unfehlbarkeit: Antworten auf die Anfrage von Hans Küng,* Fribourg.
G. Söll (1971), *Dogma und Dogmenentwicklung,* Fribourg.
M. Elze (1972), "Dogma," *HWP* 2, 275–77.
K.J. Becker (1973), "*Articulus fidei* (1150–1230). Von der Einführung des Wortes bis zu den drei Definitionen Philipps des Kanzlers," *Gr* 54, 517–69; id. (1976), "Dogma. Zur Bedeutungsgeschichte des lateinischen Wortes in der christlichen Literatur," *Gr* 57, 307–50, 658–701.
P. Schrodt (1978), *The Problem of the Beginning of Dogma in Recent Theology,* Frankfurt.
U. Wickert, C.H. Ratschow (1982), "Dogma," *TRE* 9, 26–41.
P.F. Fransen (1985), *Hermeneutics of the Councils and Other Studies,* Louvain.
W. Löser, K. Lehmann, M. Lutz-Bachmann (Ed.) (1985), *Dogmengeschichte und katholische Theologie,* Würzburg.
G. Mansini (1985), *"What Is a Dogma?" The Meaning and Truth of Dogma in Edouard Le Roy and His Scholastic Opponents,* Rome.
K. Lehmann, W. Pannenberg (Ed.) (1986), *Lehrverurteilungen-kirchentrennend?,* vol. I, Freiberg-Göttingen; id. (1989), ibid., vol. II, 15–170.
J.L. Segundo (1989), *El dogma que libera,* Santander.
W. Beinert (Ed.) (1991), *Glaube als Zustimmung,* Freiberg.
J. Drumm (1991), *Doxologie und Dogma,* Paderborn.
W. Kasper (1991), "Dogma/Dogmenentwicklung," *NHThG2* 1, 292–309.
N. Walter (1992), "Dogma," *EWNT2* 1, 819–22.
E. Schockenhoff, P. Walter (Ed.) (1993), *Dogma und Glaube,* Mayence.

PETER WALTER

See also **Dogmatic Theology; Faith; History; *Loci theologici;* Revelation; Theology; Word of God**

Dogmatic Theology

a) History. In antiquity, before the noun *dogmatics* was ever formulated, the adjective *dogmatic* was sometimes used—to qualify an intellectual activity, for example, and oppose it to "practical" or "ethical" activities. Medieval Latin does not seem to have been familiar with the word *dogmatic.* It resurfaced in the West with the humanists. But, according to O. Ritschl in *"Das Wort dogmaticus in der Geschichte des Sprachgebrauchs bis zum Augkommen des Ausdrucks theologia dogmatica"* (1920), it was only in 1634 that a Lutheran humanist, G. Calixt, first used the adjective in connection with theology*. In 1659, another Lutheran, L.F. Reinhart, used *dogmatic theology* in the title of a work, according to G. Sauter in *"Dogmatik I"*

(1982). From approximately 1680, the expression began showing up in the titles of numerous treatises of Catholic theology, and in the 18th-century courses and textbooks frequently included *dogmatico-Scholastic* in their titles. The use of the term *dogmatic theology* at that point indicated a double distinction—on the one hand, from moral theology, which had just gained its autonomy, and, on the other hand, from Scholastic (Scholasticism*) theology, which left no space for a historical research into Christian dogmatic material.

Understood at that time to be the construction of a theological "system" juxtaposed to the Scriptures (Holy* Scripture), as Protestant theology was very early on, and as Catholic theology would later be under the influence of the *methodus scientifica* of Wolff's school (Gazzaniga, for example, in 1768), dogmatic theology was an extension of much older forms of systematic theology.

Origen*'s *Peri Arkhon* or—perhaps more rightly so—Gregory of Nyssa's *Great Catechesis* (in *Patrologia Graeca)* are generally considered to be the first attempts at a systematic articulation of the content of Christian faith. In the eighth century John of Damascus's *Expositio de fide orthodoxa* (in *Patrologia Graeca*) is characterized even more clearly by fairly complete dogmatics. Even though he was undoubtedly more concerned with orthodoxy than with a deeper speculative examination, and even though his procedures in compiling somewhat offended the internal cohesion of the theological exposé, John of Damascus was a major witness to the evolution of theology. Latin theology received a first systematic summary with Augustine*'s *De doctrina christiana (see Patrologia Latina),* and the work's influence was great, since the great Augustinian categories *(res et signa, uti et frui)* were still at work in the 12th-century system of *Sentences* by Pierre Lombard, as pointed out by M.-D. Chenu in *La théologie au XIIe siècle* (1957). Systematization would finally be accomplished in the various surveys. They included the enigmatic *Summa sententiarum* (in *Patrologia Latina*), treated by R. Baron in *"Note sut l'enigmatique* Summa sententiarum," (1958); the *Summa aurea* by William of Auxerre (†1231), a true initiator in the theological use of philosophy; and the great constructions of the 13th century. These surveys saw theology as an organism built according to laws of Aristotelian science, and they believed that theology's connections to the Scriptures were beginning to loosen.

Protestantism* at first sought to tighten those links, but it should be noted that the elaboration of a systematic theology began very early on in Protestantism, with Melanchthon's *Loci communes* (1535) and Calvin's *Institution* (1539). Systematization grew still further under the Lutheran and Calvinist orthodoxy of the classical age, which did not hesitate to use even the conceptual methods of Aristotelianism* to grasp and present doctrinal content in the most systematic way possible—J. Gerhard, for example.

However, elaborated against the background of such a tradition, the first theologies to explicitly refer to themselves as *dogmatic* corresponded to a new climate. The project of a dogmatic thought expressed first of all the desire to move beyond the quarrels between schools to return to the official teachings of the Churches—the desire to teach a doctrine that was not subject to disputes, as noted by W. Kasper in *Die Methoden der Dogmatik* (1967). According to Karl Rahner's *Dogmatik* (1959) and Sauter's *Dogmatik I* (1982), dogmatic theology was thus understood to be a "science of the dogma* of the Church*," which it was obliged at the same time to justify, on the basis of the Scriptures and tradition, and to deploy by means of conclusion, as Yves Congar holds in *La foi et la théologie* (1962). The fate of this new discipline had, therefore, to be closely linked with that of another new discipline, the scientific history of dogma.

Because the new climate of ideas was marked by the "crisis of European consciousness" and by the struggle of the Enlightenment against traditional beliefs, it was also to resist the re-evaluation of the dogma that theological systematization eventually had to be redeployed under the modern form of dogmatics, W. Kasper holds in *Dogmatik* (1991). But because any apology of dogma was necessarily tied, in Catholic theology, to a defense and illustration of the Church as a teaching body, this evolution was not without risk. Catholic theology seemed, henceforth, to have found an immediate source in the magisterium—the *Theologia Wirceburgensis* (1771), for example, considers the Church to be a *regula fidei proxima* and situates it before the two *regulae fidei remotae*—Scripture and tradition—by a process that would have been equally incomprehensible to patristic and medieval theology.

Protestant theology in the 19th century, at Schleiermacher*'s urging, started off by taking its distances from systematic reasons, which were suspected of encouraging a confusion between theology and philosophy: It was as a "doctrine of the faith*" that Schleiermacher presented his synthetic summary. In his wake, influenced by his theory of feelings, the Erlangen school explained dogma on the basis of the experience* of faith, while the speculative theology of Hegel*'s disciples understood it as the self-explanation of absolute content, and Ritschl's school grasped it from an ethical perspective. "Dogmatic" did, however, find a renewed usage in 20th-century Protestantism—in particular, thanks to Karl Barth* and Emil

Brunner in *Dogmatik* (1946–60). During that century it was viewed from various perspectives. For example, Barth saw it as a "kerygmatic" intention; Paul Tillich*, as an opportunity to correlate human questions and theological answers; E. Jüngel, as a consequent exegesis; and Wolfhart Pannenberg, as a refounding of dogmatics within the framework of a theory of sciences.

Catholic theology in the first half of the 19th century saw the rise of a theology that conjugated strong ecclesiastical roots with a great openness to the intellectual currents of the era (the Tübingen* school was the best example of this). A hardening—"a change in the structure in Catholic theology" noted by B. Welte in *"Zum Strukturwundel der katolischen Theologie in 19 Jahrhundert"* (1965)—occurred, however, toward the middle of the century; and neo-Scholasticism then offered the spectacle of a systematism that tended to consider history as an element that could not be assimilated and modernity as a simple decline. It would be the task of Vatican* II, which reexamined and concluded numerous suggestions for renewal (patristic renewal, "new theology," etc.), to set forth a more dynamic concept (Kasper 1967, Sauter 1982). Dogmatics had come to be understood as the work of interpretation at the service of the present manifestation of the Word* pronounced once and for all (Geffré 1983). Exegesis* was received as a point of departure and missionary preaching as a goal. It was not, therefore, a case of a simple "apology of dogma." Several ways were open. The authors of *Mysterium salutis* adopted the perspective of the history of salvation*. Karl Rahner* was concerned with updating a deep ("transcendental") connivance between the word of revelation and the internal structure of the human spirit (1976). A similar concern motivated the work published by Bernard Lonergan* in 1972. And the theological esthetics of Hans Urs von Balthasar* (published in 1961–69) found their center of gravity in the sovereign self-manifestation of divine glory. To tell the truth, the different paths of contemporary Catholic dogmatics—historical, anthropological, or theological—complement each other, and each would be unilateral if it ignored the part of truth contained in the other points of view.

b) Object. Dogmatic theology did not have only dogma, strictly speaking, as its object. It also focused on the totality of Christian revelation, which it sought to perceive in an all-encompassing fashion, seeking a total reading, which demands one's attention to the results of Biblical theology*, which integrates in its understanding of God's Word* the interpretations established by tradition and the magisterium, and which constantly seeks to actualize the permanent meaning of the Word (Kasper 1991). Dogmatic theology, in this way, holds a discourse quite distinct from that held by the magisterium of the Church, toward which it functions in the manner of an introspective authority. There should be nothing surprising about this. The transmission of Christian doctrines through a hierarchical authority, on the one hand, never leads to the superfluity of theological intelligence. And because the Church, subject to that which is revealed to it, can at no time act in an arbitrary fashion, it is on the other hand incontestable that the dogmatic work of theology is never without meaning for the magisterium itself and for the evolution of its pronouncements (Congar 1980). The hermeneutic* location of dogmatics is the encounter between faith and reason. Dogmatics speaks neither the language of reason alone nor that of faith alone (Congar 1962). And taking into account the fact that there is a labor peculiar to the fundamental* theology, which is that of the *intellectus quaerens fidem,* it must be concluded that the work peculiar to the dogmatic is that of *fides quaerens intellectum.* The two, assuredly, cannot be dissociated, and it can be conceded that the critical and justifying procedures of fundamental theology must be established at all levels of dogmatic work and in all the treatises on dogmatics (Geffré 1972 and Kasper 1988). Both Rahner, reiterating that there is never an affirmation of God that does not imply an affirmation of man, and Balthasar, who showed that a theological doctrine of perception and a theory of rapture are inseparable, have insisted, each in his own way, upon the link between these two disciplines.

c) Method. The first obligation of dogmatics is without doubt that of not dissociating positive procedure and speculative procedure (J. Beumer 1954). Because Scholastic theology had shown only a tepid interest in historical questions and in the problem of history, it was inevitable that an indirect consequence would be the birth of a more or less autonomous and separate positive theology. During the growth of historical sciences there were authors, like Melchior Cano (1509–60), who viewed the positive procedure as a function of all theology. However, there were even more systematicians of baroque Scholasticism who, with Jean de Saint-Thomas (1589–1644), were able to view the positive work as a preliminary activity and properly exterior to theology per se—an activity that, in fact, began only when it was possible to at last syllogize. Dogmatic theology could only bring its work to fruition through a movement of perpetual return through which the *intellectus fidei* made a "positive" return to the contingent sources of faith while, reciprocally, the *auditus fidei* was reflected in the "speculative" intelligence of what one believed (Rahner 1959; Congar 1962; Geffré 1972). The theological usage of all the resources of historical criticism is, therefore, on the schedule of conditions of all dogmatics, on the same level as the theological usage of all the resources of philosophical rationality. Dogmatic reason cannot, for all that, be reduced to a form of historical reason or a form of philosophical reason. Dogmatics, on the contrary, is faithful to its own reason, when history and reason are assumed, connected, and accomplished all together in reason through a truth* that surpasses them (Rahner 1968; Kasper 1991).

A second duty of dogmatics would no doubt be to refrain from claiming to be a science of conclusions, as did baroque Scholasticism and neo-Scholasticism. The concept according to which dogmatics would have as its major goal the preparation of new definitions actually constitutes a "malady of theology" (Congar 1962). Rather than within heuristics it is within hermeneutics* that dogmatics can be organized in a healthy fashion, by endeavoring systematically to recover the truths of faith in their unity and their internal coherence *(nexus mysteriorum)* by simultaneously showing their correspondence with the quest for meaning of each generation of mankind.

A third duty would be to connect service of the Scriptures to service of the Church. Vatican II considered the Scriptures to be "the soul, as it were, of all theology" (*OptatamTotius,* 16). To be sure, from a Catholic point of view, the Scriptures must be read within the tradition of the Church; but, reciprocally, the doctrine of the Church can itself only be interpreted on the basis of Scriptures, *norma normans non normata.* And if the facts illuminate the Scriptures while the Scriptures, in return, allow their true perspectives to be perceived, one must also add that dogmatics is not truly ecclesiastical by virtue of its ongoing fidelity to orthodoxy alone, but also because its care for the Scriptures and for tradition is experienced within a Church constantly faced with the issues of an era, receiving them as questions addressed to its own faith (Kasper 1967).

d) Articulation. The history of dogmatics suggests several types of articulation of arguments and treatises (Grillmeier 1975; Kasper 1991). Major historical works include the following.

The *Peri Arkhon* by Origen, after a prologue detailing the author's intentions, is divided into two parts, the first of which (subdivided into three sections) outlines the doctrines of God, of rational creatures, and of the world, while the second discusses several difficult points. Because it does not venture to provide a complete theological synthesis, the work leaves out themes as important as the economy of salvation and the sacraments*.

The *Great Catechesis* by Gregory of Nyssa was composed as a triptych. The first part elaborates "theology" in the strictly patristic sense (the doctrine of one God in three persons*). The second treats the "economy" and is subdivided into a presentation of the historical effectuation of salvation (creation, sin, incarnation, and the cross) and a presentation of its appropriation (sacraments, faith, and spiritual life).

John Damascene's *De fide orthodoxa* is divided into four books due to his Latin translators, but the general framework of one hundred chapters, into which the work's content has been distributed, has a certain analogy with what later would be the syntheses of the 12th century (*see* E. Dublanchy's *"Dogmatique,"* 1910): the doctrine of the knowledge* of God and of the Trinity (book I, chap. 1–14), creation and Christian anthropology (book II, chap. 14–46), Christology (Christ/Christology) (book III, chap. 47–81, and the beginning of book IV), and sacraments, the problem of evil*, and eschatology* (book IV, chap. 82–100, and the rest of book IV).

Augustine's *De doctrina christiana* was organized according to one single, major articulation. The Trinitarian God *(res qua fruendum)* appears in it as the end of our *navigatio.* Christ and the Church are our means to arrive there.

In Augustine's wake, Peter Lombard's *Sentences* combine an exposition of the *res* (books I–III) and one of the *signa* (book IV, the sacraments). The *res* are, in turn, subdivided according to the Augustinian dichotomy of the *frui* (the Trinitarian God, book I) and the *uti* (creatures, book II). Christ's own role is that of leading the *utilia* to the *fruibilia* (book III).

Still faithful to the narrative order—*series narrationis*—of the Scriptures, Hugh of Saint Victor (†1141) divided his *De sacramentis christianae fidei* by following the *historia*—a term designating not only the content of the economy of salvation but also the method enabling one to grasp it. The first book, which outlines the "work of creation," covers "the beginning of the world to the incarnation." The second, which outlines "the work of reparation," covers "the incarnation of the Word* to the end and consummation of everything."

It was yet another Augustinian scheme that Abelard* used: *fides* (Trinty-Creation-Incarnation), *caritas* (charity-virtues-precepts), and *sacramentum.* Abelard is more important, however, in the history of theology for having been the first author to totally abandon the historical order of reasons and reduce all the facts of the economy of salvation to "scientific" categories, allowing the organization of everything within the light of general notions and synthetic principles.

Thomas* Aquinas, in quest of an *ordo disciplinae* for his *Somme,* resorted to neither Augustinian schemes nor even Aristotle's organizing scheme for the cosmos but rather to the Neoplatonic scheme of *emanation* and *return.* It was on this curve that he located the facts and the gestures of the economy of salvation. The first two parts speak, therefore, of the God as principle and the God as end, respectively, while the third is devoted to Christ, who is for us the path to God, *via est nobis tenendi in Deum* (Chenu 1950).

Two distinct currents emerged, and Thomas's strict theocentrism contrasted with a tendency mingling the ideas of Augustine, Bernard, and Bonaventure, in which theology is constructed according to a Christological and soteriological format attentive to existential ideas and the "wisdom of the cross." Theology, in these currents, can certainly not be reduced to an economy of *my* salvation. It can be seen, however, how much is owed them by the radical refusal of any sapiential theology as expressed by Luther* in the opposition of the *theologia gloriae* and the *theologia crucis.*

Between an essential theocentrism, constantly tempted to forget that the "glory of God is the living man," and an existential anthropocentrism, constantly tempted to dissolve the very substance of the theological, dogmatics has no choice; it is in a dilemma. It would be thus a new duty of dogmatics to connect the two approaches, for if the unifying theme of theology is God himself (Thomas Aquinas), this God is the God of mankind through Jesus Christ and in the Spirit (Holy* Spirit)—thus, theocentrism must include a well-understood anthropocentrism, which grasps all truth of faith as a truth of salvation (Rahner 1959; Kasper 1991).

• B. Keckerman (1602), *Systema SS. Theologiae,* Hanover.
G. Calixt (1634), *Epitome theologiae moralis,* Helmstadt.
L.F. Reinhart (1659), *Synopsis Theologiae Christianae Dogmaticae,* Noribergae.
M. Gazzaniga (1786), *Theologia dogmatica in systema,* Ingolstadt.
F.D.E. Schleiermacher (1821), *Der christliche Glaube,* Berlin.
M.J. Scheeben (1875–1903), *Handbuch der kath: Dogmatik,* Freiberg.
J. Pohle (1902–5), *Lehrbuch der Dogmatik,* Paderborn.
B. Bartmann (1911), *Lehrbuch der Dogmatik,* Freiberg.
K. Barth (1932–67), *KD,* Zurich (*Dogmatique,* Geneva, 1953–74).
M. Schmaus (1937–55), *Katholische Dogmatik,* Munich.
E. Brunner (1946–60), *Dogmatik,* 3 vols., Zurich.
P. Tillich (1951–63), *Systematic Theology,* 3 vols., Chicago.
H.U. von Balthasar (1961–69), *Herrlichkeit,* Einsiedeln.
B. Lonergan (1972), *Method in Theology,* New York.
K. Rahner (1976), *Grundkurs des Glaubens,* Fribourg-Basel-Vienna.
♦ H.-E. Weber (1908), *Der Einfluß der protestantischen Schulphilosophie auf die orthodoxe-lutherische Dogmatik,* Leipzig.
E. Dublanchy (1910), "Dogmatique," *DThC* 4, 1522–74.
O. Ritschl (1920), "Das Wort dogmaticus in der Geschichte des Sprachgebrauchs bis zum Aufkommen des Ausdrucks theologia dogmatica," in *Festgabe für J. Kaftan,* Tübingen, 260–72.
K. Barth (1928), *Die Theologie und die Kirche,* Munich.
M.-D. Chenu (1943), *La théologie comme science au XIIIe siècle,* Paris; id. (1950), *Introduction à l'étude de saint Thomas d'Aquin,* Paris; id. (1957), *La théologie au XIIe siècle,* Paris.
Y. Congar (1943–46), "Théologie," *DThC* 15, 341–502; id. (1952), "Dogmatique," *Cath* 3, 949–51; id. (1962), *La foi et la théologie,* Tournai; id. (1980), "Le théologien dans l'Église aujourd'hui," in *Les quatre fleuves* 12, 7–27.
J. de Ghellinck (1947), "Pagina et Sacra Pagina," in *Mélanges A. Pelze,* Louvain, 23–59.
J. Beumer (1954), "Positive und spekulative Theologie," *Schol.* 39, 53–72.
R. Baron (1958), "Note sur l'énigmatique *Summa sententiarum,*" *RThAM* 25, 26–41.
G. Gloege (1958), "Dogmatik," *RGG3* 2, 225–30.
K. Rahner (1959), "Dogmatik," *LThK2* 3, 446–59; id. (1968), "Dogmatik," *SM(D)* 1, 917–24.
W. Kasper (1962), *Die Lehre von der Tradition in der Römischen Schule,* Freiberg: id. (1967), *Die Methoden der Dogmatik,* Mayence; id. (1991), "Dogmatik," *NHThG2* 1, 310–20.
B. Welte (1965), "Zum Strukturwandel der katholischen Theologie in 19. Jahrhundert," in *Auf der Spur des Ewigen,* Freiberg, 380–409.
C. Geffré (1972), *Un nouvel âge de la théologie,* Paris; id. (1983), *Le christianisme au risque de l'interprétation,* Paris.
A. Grillmeier (1975), "Vom Symbolum zur Summa," in *Mit ihm und in ihm,* Freiberg-Basel-Vienna, 585–636.
W. Pannenberg (1977), *Wissenschaftstheorie und Theologie,* Frankfurt.
G. Sauter (1982), "Dogmatik I," *TRE* 9, 41–77.

EMILIO BRITO

See also **Canon of Scriptures; Dogma; Fundamental Theology; Gospels; *Loci theologici;* Notes, Theological; Theological Schools; Theology**

Donatism

Named after its initiator, Donatus, Donatism was a protest movement that shook the Church of Africa over a period of three and a half centuries (fourth–seventh centuries). The movement did not leave many texts except for a few acts of councils*, acts of martyrs, and the *Liber regularum* by Tyconius. In large measure, our knowledge of it comes via those who opposed it, namely Optatus of Milevis and Augustine*.

Social, economic, and religious divisions prevailing in North Africa at that time should be cited among the causes of the movement, but an even more precise cause is known, linked with the problem of the *lapsi,* a term referring to the fallen, that is those who had reneged their faith during the persecution at the time of Cyprian. The synod* of 251 had proposed reintegrating the *lapsi* in the Church after a period of penitence (penance*). The new persecution of 303–5 led many clergymen to surrender the books of Scripture (Holy* Scripture) *("traditors").* Donatists were absolutely intransigent toward them, banishing them indefinitely from the Church. To give full weight to their attitude, they began by casting doubt on the Episcopal consecration of Caecilian, celebrated rapidly after the death of his predecessor Mensurius, without waiting for the arrival of the bishops* of Numidia.

They deposed Caecilian—who would be rehabilitated by the Edict of Milan in 313 and the Council of Arles in August 314, before being reinstated in the see of Carthage on 10 November 316. Moreover, the Donatists questioned the presence at Caecilian's ordination* of another bishop, Felix of Aptunga, supposedly a *traditor.* (Felix would be absolved on 15 February 315.) The Donatists' attitude led Emperor Constantine to decree a harsh law against them. But that did not stop them. They organized their propaganda by multiplying acts of martyrdom and by 336 Donatus was already able to convoke at Carthage a council of 270 bishops who had been won over to his cause.

In calling for a church of the pure, in aspiring to martyrdom, proclaiming that there is only one single baptism and one single Church, and affirming that they were necessarily in the right, the Donatists defined themselves as the true heirs of the Church of Africa. They aspired to be the heirs of Cyprian. This assured them the sympathy of the people, and yet they reinterpreted his views broadly. The Donatists even provoked rebellious gangs called *circumcelliones* who terrorized the countryside; they were quickly condemned for this. The Emperor Constantine severely suppressed the Donatists and banished Donatus, who died in exile in 355. But the movement resumed and developed after Julian the Apostate brought the Donatist bishops back from exile between 361 and 363.

The schism* was consummated at the Council of Bagai on 24 April 394: 310 bishops were favorable to Donatus's successor, Primian. Augustine, after Optatus of Milevis, was one of the only bishops who could win out over the Donatists. After a conjunction of circumstances, the Catholics were able to call a conference in 403 with the purpose of defining the true representative of the Church in North Africa. Primian refused to take part. In 405 the emperor took a number of measures against the Donatists and in 411, when the balance was still fragile, the Conference of Carthage granted the victory to the Catholics. The Donatists gradually lost their influence, but continued to resist until the seventh century.

In their opposition to the *traditors* the Donatists were led to proclaim that the validity of the sacraments* depended on the sanctity of the ministers. Optatus of Milevis and Augustine argued against this thesis, advancing the catholicity of the Church, its universality that extended beyond the limits of Africa. And they countered an ecclesiology* that excluded sinners: they did so by arguing that baptism can be conferred by any Christian; the "ministers may change, but the sacraments are immutable" (*Against the Donatists* V, 4, 5) because their holiness comes from Christ* alone.

• Augustine, Works against the Donatists (BAug 28–32).

Optatus of Milevis, *Treatise against the Donatists* (SC 412–13).

♦ P. Monceaux (1912–23), *Histoire littéraire de l'Afrique chrétienne,* vols. 4–7, Paris.

Y. Congar (1963), "La théologie donatiste de l'Église et des sacrements," in *Introduction aux traités antidonatistes de saint Augustin,* BAug 28, Paris, 9–133.

R.A. Markus (1964), *Donatism, the Last Phase: Studies in Church History,* I, London.

R. Crespin (1965), *Ministère et sainteté pastorale du clergé et solution de la crise donatiste dans la vie et la doctrine de saint Augustin,* Paris.

S. Lancel (1979), "Les débuts du donatisme: la date du protocole de Cirta et de l'élection épiscopale de Silvanus," *REAug* 25, 217–29, Paris.

W. H. C. Frend (1971), *The Donatist Church, a Movement of Protest in Roman North Africa,* Oxford.
J.-L. Maier (1987–89), *Le dossier du donatisme,* 2 vols., Berlin.
C. Pietri (1995), "Les difficultés du nouveau système en Occident: la querelle donatiste (363–420)," in *Histoire du christianisme,* vol. 2: *Naissance d'une chrétienté (250–430),* Paris, 435–51.

Marie-Anne Vannier

See also **History of the Church; Ministry; Unity of the Church**

Double Truth. *See* **Naturalism; Truth**

Doxology. *See* **Glory of God; Praise**

Drey, Johann Sebastian von. *See* **Tübingen, Schools of**

Duns Scotus, John

c. 1265–1308

1. Biography

John Duns Scotus was born at Duns in Scotland. He became a Franciscan in 1280, studied in the colleges of his order, was ordained priest in 1291, and completed his training in Oxford around 1291–93. There, around 1300–1301, he produced a commentary on the *Sentences* of Peter Lombard. Called at the beginning of the academic year 1300 or 1302 to teach at the University of Paris as a bachelor under the tutelage of Gonzalvo of Spain, he probably took part in a dispute opposing his master and Eckhart (Rhineland-Flemish mysticism). In any event he set to work on a new *Commentary on the Sentences,* the *Reportatio Parisiensis.* However, his work on this was cut short in June 1303, when King Philip the Fair called for a council against Pope* Boniface VIII: Scotus refused to sign a petition to this effect and was forced into exile, presumably returning to Oxford. He later returned to Paris to teach, probably toward the end of 1304. Becoming a doctor in 1305, he was regent master (director of studies) of the Franciscan covenant in 1306–7. At the end of 1307 he left for Köln as a reader and died there on the 8 November 1308. Nicknamed the Subtle Doctor, accorded particular veneration within the Franciscan Order (above all for his defense of the Immaculate Conception) and in the diocese of Nola, his beatification was confirmed for the universal Church in 1993. He left numerous works, which form a critical dialogue with his contemporaries (Godfrey of Fontaines) and predecessors (Henry of Ghent at the University, Pierre de Jean Olieu among the Franciscans): commentaries on Porphyry and Aristotle, a thick *Quodlibet,* and three commentaries on the *Sentences*—a first version, the *Lectura,* representative of his Oxford teaching; a version consisting of notes taken from his teaching at Paris, the *Reportationes Parisienses;* and a final version, the *Ordinatio,* cut short in mid-revision.

2. Thought

a) Architecture of Theology. After the condemnations of 1277, which concerned 219 theses inspired by philosophy (naturalism*), Scotus, like many disciples of Bonaventure*, became convinced of the inadequacy of philosophy and the necessity of theology. "Philosophers maintain the perfection of nature and deny supernatural perfection," while "theologians understand the deficiency of nature* and the perfection of the supernatural" (*Ord.* Prologue = Prol., §5). Aristotle had rightly said that everyone desires beatitude*, but beatitude was understood only in general terms: philosophers could attain a merely abstract notion of God*, in an incomplete part of man (the soul [soul-heart-body]), and subject to the practical vagaries of thought. For this reason human beings needed a revelation in order to know their end distinctly and to know that they would attain it in the flesh and in perpetuity (§16). "God is the natural end of man, although this end cannot be realized through natural, but only through supernatural means" (§32; supernatural*). It was by revelation alone that humankind knew which actions were meritorious, in other words freely accepted by God as allowing us to be blessed (§18). Scripture* was thus necessary and sufficient to man in order to attain his end. In particular it presented that end (the beatitude of body [soul-heart-body] and soul) and the means necessary to attain it: the Ten Commandments (Decalogue*), which were epitomized by charity (Dt 6:5; Mt 22:37ff.).

The ideal of theology as the sole science was unattainable. Therefore there were several theologies: theology in itself (sufficient to its object) and theology for human beings (tailored to the human intellect). Their object was God, not as a common object (the subject of all theological propositions) but as a virtual object (capable of giving rise to all such propositions). In itself, theology was the intuition that God had of himself and of all things, and the blessed received a share in it. Human theology, in contrast, was abstractive: it applied by default to the concept of God the most perfect concept that we can conceive, that of infinite* being *(ens infinitum)* (§168). It was of him that the first necessary truths were uttered ("God is Trinity*"); as for the rest, they were spoken of him, but not because of him. Thus divine omnipotence* was not deduced from the concept of God but received by faith and attached to that concept, which gave a unity to all the divine attributes.

Any science must fulfill four criteria: certainty, the necessity of its object, the evidence of its premises, and syllogistic rigor (§208). The theology of the blessed fulfilled these four conditions. Divine theology in itself fulfilled the first three but was intuitive: more than a science, it was a form of wisdom. Human theology, however, which was concerned with a contingent revelation and history, did not fulfill the second condition—but this very fact led to a revision of the concept of science, to the effect that the formal rigor of a science was of more importance than the necessity of its object, which could be revealed contingently (§212). Thus human theology was not "subsidiary" (subordinate) to that of the blessed (a view that contrasts with that of Thomas* Aquinas). Finally, the end of revelation was charity; and consequently theology was a practical science (*Lect.,* Prol., §164). Everything that depended on practical reason—in other words, on the will—was practical. Morality, therefore, was the art of molding one's actions to charity by means of the will, and in this way to prepare oneself to receive the supreme recompense, beatitude. Thus, in theology, everything that was not metaphysics tended toward charity (*Ord.* Prol., §322; *see* Boulnois 1997).

b) Unity and Trinity of God. The first and necessary part of theology took as its object the divine being in its Trinitarian manifestation. The existence of God was known by way of the concept of "infinite being," which ensured the identity and uniqueness of the first principle reached by way of various metaphysical paths (*Ord.* I, d. 2; *De primo principio*): this was the beginning of a natural theology. God was known positively in the concept of being* *(ens),* which was applied in the same sense to him and to the created order, as with respect to his attributes and the concept of person* (analogy*); in this context negations were merely a way of denying the imperfection of created things and affirming divine perfection. God was distinguished from the created order by his infinity. His different attributes were distinguished from one another by their formal non-identity—what the historians call "formal distinction" (God is truly justice and truly mercy, but justice in God remains fundamentally separate from his mercy: *see* Boulnois 1988). The processions of the Trinity formed a strict sequence: the Word was engendered by means of nature, and the Spirit (Holy* Spirit) by means of will. Thus charity was the summit of deity* and was applied to one person (the Spirit) at the same time as defining God in his supreme essence.

Beyond the divine persons, necessary theology dealt with inward and outward emanations, with "instants of nature," moments of the divine thought—self-reflection and the scheme of salvation*. In a first instant, God conceived himself (as infinite*); then he produced finite essences (the divine ideas), then supposed them as in part imitating his perfection, and finally conceived compatible combinations of essences (*Ord.* I, d. 43, §14 . 16; transl. Boulnois 1994), the "compossibles," from among which his will chose a world, freely producing creation* outside himself. All that was created came after these necessary emanations and was thus contingent. But at the same time God had eternal foreknowledge of it: there was in God a science of the contingent—itself contingent because dependent upon the consent of his will.

c) Order of Ends and the Primacy of Christ. The second and contingent part of theology originated in the divine will. For Scotus, indeed, the contingency of the world did not result in short from the secondary causes but from the self-determination of the divine will. So, at the very moment when a thing was created, it could be non-existent. God's absolute power could therefore intervene at any moment in the world to make another possible arise; the ordered power of God was forever revocable (Knuuttila, in Boulnois 1994). But the divine will was structurally good: it desired, of necessity, the infinite good* that was God himself and, contingently, all the other finite goods—doing so gradually, however, since it sought in them the greatest possible good.

The divine will was ordered and as such desired the end before the means. Since God was the final end "he loved himself first" in his three Persons, including that of the Word who was joined with humanity. The union of divine nature with human nature in Christ* was thus the final end in pursuit of which God desired creation: "*Primo,* God loves himself; *secundo,* he loves himself for others *(amat se aliis),* and this is pure love *(amor castus); tertio,* he wishes to be loved by the other who, in the highest degree, can love him outside himself; *quarto,* he has foreseen the union of that nature which was to love him to the highest degree, even if nobody sinned" (*Rep.* III, d. 7, q. 4, §5; Wadding [W.] XI). In a Neoplatonic movement of procession and return, God extended his infinite love* by degrees through his creation and in return was loved by Christ with an infinite love. Christ was the end of all things (Rom 9), in him all people were predestined (Eph 1), for him all had been created (Col 1:15ff.). In the order of ends, Christ was willed for himself (as being alone capable of loving with an infinite love), man was willed next, and then creation. So the Incarnation* was willed and would have taken place even if Adam had not sinned. Thus Scotus responded to the question raised by Anselm*, *Why a God who is man?,* but in quite a different manner: God had to make himself man, independently of sin.

Nonetheless, in actuality Adam*'s sin had taken place. God had not wished it, but he had permitted it. He had also foreseen it and had planned a redemptive Incarnation, which would encounter the Passion and death (*Rep.* III, d. 7, q. 4, §4; W. XI, 451). But in the divine plan this meaning only arose after the event: in the first place God desired hypostatic* union, and after that the salvation* of all mankind; then he foresaw the fall of the latter and the corresponding remedy, "redemption through a mediator" (§3). The two meanings were linked: in point of fact the Son's incarnation did have humanity's redemption as its end, but "it would have taken place even if man had not sinned" (*Opus Oxoniense* = *Ox.* III, d. 7, q. 3, §3; W. VII, 202). The Incarnation was a metaphysical "and not a fortuitous" manifestation of divine generosity (*Ox.* III, d. 19, q. 1, §6; W. VII, 415). The *motive* for the Incarnation was not sin: in so much as he had foreseen and predestined Christ in the flesh and all the elected for grace and for glory, before he foresaw Christ's Passion as a remedy for sin—in the same way that a doctor first desires a man's health before prescribing a medicine for him (ibid.).

The Immaculate Conception (Mary*) ensued from Christ's primacy. In the first place, original sin* was not transmitted as an infection of the flesh (concupiscence) but resided in the immaterial will (*Ox.* II, d. 30, q. 2, §2; W. VI, 936). Moreover, God had the power necessary to keep the Virgin from all sin in her soul. Finally, the order of ends was not chronological: in God's plan it was appropriate that the most perfect mediator should mediate in the most perfect way; and so, by preserving Christ's Mother first of all, the first link between Christ and humanity (*Ox.* III, d. 3, q. 1, §4; W.

VII, 92), God had given him the same grace, from the moment he came to life, as he gave to other human beings by means of baptism* (ibid., §9; W. VII, 94). And so he would not have been the most perfect redeemer "if he had not warranted Mary's preservation from original sin" (ibid., §4; W. VII, 92). Christ's primacy and the Immaculate Conception followed from the same principle of economy.

d) Grace and Predestination. Due to the identity between will and charity in God, the primacy of the divine will was that of grace—in complete contradiction of Pelagianism*. An action was meritorious only if God accepted it as such, by free will: therefore no finite action could oblige God to accept it (voluntarism*). God owed nothing to anyone, and grace was nothing but "the unforced will of God" (*Ox.* II, d. 2, q. 2, §15; W. VII, 83), without which no act had merit: it was a "God-shaped form" (*Quodl.* q. 17, §[5], 12; Alluntis, 616), which gave its status to every human action, a "participation in God" (*Ox.* III, d. 13, q. 4, §14; W. VII, 270), the indwelling of the Holy* Spirit in the human person. God's assistance to human actions thus consisted of two concurrent causes contributing to the same effect (and making it more powerful): grace did not alter the nature of the act, for example the virtuous act, but it increased its intensity and marked it with divine acceptance. The human intellect and will pursued their objects naturally, but grace made these actions easier, more effective, and above all pleasing to God. Human thought was thus perfectly autonomous with respect to faith and action and will with respect to charity.

Divine freedom* was not arbitrary and desired only to bring about good things that would imitate its goodness (*Rep.* I, d. 47, q. 2, §[2]; XI, 237 *a*). The only necessary acceptance was that of the infinite good that was God by the infinite will that was God. The created order, for its part, was the object of a contingent and effective will, by which divine acceptance impelled it to exist (*Quodl.* q. 16, §[7], 29; Alluntis, 595): this was the second moment of acceptance. A third moment followed, by which God led the finite to eternal beatitude (*Rep.* I, d. 17, q. 2, §[4], W. XI, 96 *b; see Ox.* III, d. 32, §[2]; W. VII, 689). True beatitude was not acquired, like that of the philosophers, but received (*Ord.* Prol., §18). No human act was the exclusive *cause* of beatitude. Nothing was due, nothing was meritorious before God on its own account, except what he freely consented to recognize as such: human actions were therefore only an essential condition of beatitude, needing to be ratified by the divine will before the human person could receive the final bliss. "The reason for merit will derive completely from the divine will, which ordains each act to a recompense" (*Ord.* I, d. 17, §144—perhaps in response to Eckhart, *Sermons* 14 and 15). The act only became meritorious when it had been ratified by the free will both of God and of the finite intellectual subject: the *act* was within man's power, since he had the use of his free will, but still he only prepared himself to receive the status of *merit;* a free divine dispensation would come to complete this disposition. Merit was therefore "an act of free power, realized in accordance with a gift of grace, and accepted by God as worthy of the recompense of beatitude" (*Ord.* I, d. 17, §146). And even though Scotus accentuated their opposition, free will and predestination* were perfectly compatible in his eyes, as were the contingency of the world and divine foreknowledge (*Lect.* I, d. 39).

e) Ethics and the Sacraments. God related to nature only by way of his freedom. Nothing of what was in nature*, neither moral excellence nor the sacraments*, could therefore bring about divine grace of necessity. The finite act did no more than seek the consent of the divine liberty. God was subject to no necessity, but he pledged his liberty in a covenant* or pact with mankind, in which he accepted certain signs and moral acts as worthy of receiving grace. The search for virtue* was necessary, but virtue and the observance of the natural law did not in themselves constitute merits: they became so only if they were inspired by charity (*Ox.* II, d. 7, q. 1, §11; W. VI, 566; *Quodl.* 17, §[5–9]; Alluntis, 615–22). As long as they acted with charity in mind, human beings could therefore be saved by conforming to the laws that God had set forth as conditions of grace and charity—the Ten Commandments. Only the first three, for that matter, belonged to the natural law, since their truth* was imposed on the divine intellect by an internal necessity, while the others were contingent, fixed by a divine will that could give exemption from them (*Ox.* III, d. 37, q. 1; W. VII, 857 *Sq*).

In the same way, sacramental formulae possessed no intrinsic virtue and were merely an essential condition, conferring grace in accordance with the free consent of the divine will, which had pledged to accompany such a sign of its grace (*Ox.* IV, d. 1, q. 4–5, §4; W. VIII, 81–82). What made penance* a sacrament was not the three human acts (contrition, confession, atonement) that were its conditions but the divine will to absolve, fulfilled when the priest (priesthood*) pronounced the formula of absolution—the priest for his part being in ignorance of God's judgment* and of the penance appropriate to a given sin (*Ox.* IV, d. 16, q. 1, §7; W. IX, 247). In eucharistic theology, Scotus particularly criticized the theological concept of "transubstantiation."

In his view, faith confined itself to the "conversion" of the bread into the body of Christ: there was no elimination of the first and production of the second but rather a "transformation" *(translatio);* there was no new substance but rather a new presence of God (*Ox.* IV, d. 11, q. 3, §13, 14, 22; W. VIII, 616–17, 618, 625–26).

3. Scotus's Legacy and the Scotist School

The vigor of Scotus's thought and the fame of his teaching made him the great Franciscan doctor of the 14th century, and his opponents—whether Thomists or nominalists—referred constantly to him. More than Scotus's own responses, which are abstruse and hard to interpret, what stands out is the shift in the questions asked. Ockham confirmed his importance by frequently taking a view directly opposed to his (nominalism*). Scotus's immediate followers, meanwhile, tried first and foremost to fill in the gaps in his uncompleted oeuvre. William of Alnwick (†1333) attempted to coordinate his theories on the object of divine thought. The greatest of these followers attempted to go further, but only the philosophical aspects of their work have been made the object of studies and editions. Peter Aureol (†1322) pondered the theory of knowledge as derived from the appearance of phenomena *(notitia apparentium).* Francis of Meyronnes (†1327), drawing on Pseudo-Dionysius*, emphasized God's transcendence, which according to him was no longer to be seen as part of "common being": God was no longer the infinite being but the infinity outside being. Meyronnes also offered a vigorous interpretation of formal distinction and went so far as to posit truly distinct "formalities" that composed the nature of simple things. John of Ripa (mid-14th century) attempted to incorporate the proof of God as infinite into a cosmology that accepted the infinity of the created world: God must consequently be referred to as immense, and his immensity must comprise a multiplicity of infinities.

So there arose a Scotist school, with its manuals, its tradition, its working tools, and its bitter and bilious feuds. It distinguished itself in disputation (the confrontation between Cajetan and Trombeta, *see* Boulnois 1993). Because it made Christ's incarnation an end in itself, it influenced the French school of spirituality (Bérulle*). The doctrine of the Immaculate Conception spread through the Franciscan Order, then to the Catholic Church as a whole (Council of Basel*, 1439—albeit in a session held to be schismatic) until it was proclaimed in 1854. Because the Scotist school allowed the existence of an autonomous natural theology that dealt with God metaphysically, it influenced the structure of metaphysics from Suarez* to Kant* (Honnefelder 1979, 1990). Because it opposed the two theological poles of grace and nature, it formed a background against which Luther was able to bring about his theological upheaval (Vignaux 1934). And because it considered practical reason as belonging to the sphere of will, with no other consequence than to make human beings worthy of being blessed, it was a structural forerunner of the work of Kant (Möhle 1995).

• *Opera omnia,* Ed. Wadding, Lyon, 1639, repr. Hildesheim, 1968.

Opera omnia editio nova juxta editionem Waddingi, Ed. Vivès, 1891 *Sq* (in these two editions, use: *Quaestiones super universalia Porphyrii*; *Quaestiones in libros Elenchorum*; *Quaestiones in I et II librum Peri hermeneias*; *Quaestiones in librum Praedicamentorum*; *Quaestiones de anima*; *Quaestiones subtilissimae super libros Metaphysicorum Aristotelis* [up to Book IX]; *Collationes*; *Theoremata*; *Reportata Parisiensia*).

Critical edition: *Opera omnia, cura et studio commissionis scotisticae,* Ed. C. Balic, Vatican, 1950 *Sq*: *Ordinatio* I–II, d. 3; *Lectura* I–II (t. XVI–XIX parus). Plus two other editions.

G. Guarrae, J. Duns Scoti, P. Aureoli, *Quaestiones disputatae de Immaculata Conceptione,* Quaracchi, 1904.

Additiones magnae secundi libri, Ed. C. Balic, *Les commentaires de Jean Duns Scot sur les quatre livres des "Sentences," Appendice,* Louvain, 1927.

Scotist School: François de Meyronnes, *Doctoris illuminati passus super universalia,* Bologne, 1479; *Opera,* Venice, 1520; *Quaestiones quodlibetales,* Venice, 1507; *Sent.* I, Basel, 1489; II–IV, Venice, 1505–7.

Quaestio de cognitione Dei, Ed. C.R.S. Harris, *Duns Scotus,* vol. 2, *The Philosophical Doctrines of Duns Scotus, Appendix,* Oxford, 1927.

Guillaume d'Alnwick, *Quaestiones de esse intelligibili et de quodlibet,* Florence, 1937.

Tractatus de primo principio, Ed. E. Roche, St. Bonaventure, N.Y., 1949.

Jean de Ripa, *Conclusiones,* Ed. A. Combes, 1957; *Lectura super primum sententiarum,* 1961; *Quaestio de gradu supremo,* Ed. A. Combes, 1964; "De modo inexistendi divine essentiae in omnibus creatures," Ed. A. Combes, F. Ruello, Tr 23 (1967), 191–209; *Lectura super primum Sententiarum, Prologi quaestiones ultimae,* Ed. A. Combes, Paris, 1970.

Cuestiones cuodlibetales, Ed. Alluntis, Madrid, 1968.

Translations: A. de Muralt, "Signification et portée de la pensée de Jean Duns Scot, Intr., trans. and commentary of the distinction 17 of the *Opus Oxoniense* II", *StPh* 33 (1973), 113–49; "Pluralité des formes et unité de l'être, Intr., trans. and commentary of two texts from Duns Scotus, *Sentences* IV, d. 11, q. 3; *Sentences* II, d. 16, q. 1," *StPh* 34 (1974), 57–92; *Traité du premier principe,* CR.Th.Ph, no 10, R. Imbach et al., 1983.

Reportatio I A, d. 2, Ed. A.B. Wolter, M. McCord Adams, "Duns Scotus' Parisian Proof for the Existence of God," *FrSA,* 42 (1982), 249–321.

A.B. Wolter, *Duns Scotus on the Will and Morality,* Washington, D.C., 1986; *Duns Scotus' Political and Economic Philosophy,* Santa Barbara, 1989; *Duns Scotus' Early Oxford Lecture on Individuation,* Santa Barbara, 1992.

A. de Muralt, "Commentary of the First Book of *Sentences,* d. 3, p. 3 (with an introduction on *esse objectivum*)," *Philosophes médiévaux des XIIIe et XIVe siècles,* 1986, 167–206.

O. Boulnois, *Sur la connaissance de Dieu et l'univocité de l'étant,* Paris, 1988.
G. Sondag, *Le principe d'individuation* (*Ord.* II, d. 3, p. 1), Paris, 1992; id., *L'image* (*Ord.* I, d. 3, p. 3, q. 1–4), Paris, 1993; id., *La théologie comme science pratique* (Prologue de la *Lectura*), Paris, 1996.
♦ P. Vignaux (1934), *Justification et prédestination au XIVe siècle: Duns Scot, Pierre d'Auriole, Guillaume d'Occam, Grégoire de Rimini,* Paris; id. (1972), "Infini, liberté et histoire du salut," StSS 5, Rome, 495–507; id. (1978), "Lire Duns Scot aujourd'hui," *Regnum hominis et regnum Dei,* Acta Quarti Congressus Scotistici Internationalis, Rome (= *Philosophie au Moyen Age,* 1987, 243–65).
J. Owens (1948), "Up to What Point Is God Included in the Metaphysics of Duns Scotus?," *MS* 10, 165–71.
É. Gilson (1952), *Jean Duns Scot, Introduction à ses positions fondamentales,* Paris.
A. Magrini (1952), *Johannis Duns Scoti doctrina de scientifica theologiae natura,* Rome.
W. Pannenberg (1954), *Die Prädestinationslehre des Duns Scotus in Zusammenhang der scholastischen Lehrentwicklung,* Göttingen.
J. Finkenzeller (1961), *Offenbarung und Theologie nach der Lehre des Johannes Duns Skotus,* BGPhMA 38.
W. Dettloff (1963), *Die Entwicklung der Akzeptations- und Verdienstlehre von Duns Scotus bis Luther,* Münster.
E. Wölfel (1965), *Seinsstruktur und Trinitätsproblem: Untersuchungen zur Grundlegung der natürlicher Theologie bei Johannes Duns Scotus,* Münster.
L. Veuthey (1967), *Jean Duns Scot, pensée théologique,* Paris.
F. Wetter (1967), *Die Trinitätslehre des Johannes Duns Scotus,* Münster.
L. Walter (1968), *Das Glaubenverständnis bei Johannes Duns Scotus,* Munich.
M. Pellegrini (1970), *La rivelazione nell'insegnamento di Duns Scoto,* Rome.
A. Ghisalberti (1972), "Il Dio dei teologi e il Dio dei filosofi secondo Duns Scoto," StSS 5, 153–64.
L. Honnefelder (1979), *Ens inquantum ens: Der Begriff des Seienden als solchen als Gegenstand der Metaphysik nach der Lehre des Johannes Duns Scotus,* Münster; id. (1990), *Scientia transcendens: Die formale Bestimmung der Seiendheit und Realität in der Metaphysik des Mittelalters und der Neuzeit,* Hamburg.
C. Bérubé (1983), *De l'homme à Dieu selon Duns Scot, Henri de Gand et Olivi,* Rome.
A. B. Wolter (1990), *The Philosophical Theology of John Duns Scotus,* Ithaca.
O. Boulnois (1993), "Puissance neutre et puissance obédientielle: De l'homme à Dieu selon Duns Scot et Cajetan," in B. Pinchard, S. Ricci (Ed.), *Rationalisme analogique et humanisme théologique, la culture de Thomas de Vio "Il Gaetano,"* Naples, 31–70; id. (1994) (Ed.), *La puissance et son ombre,* Paris; id. (1995), "Quand commence l'ontothéologie? Aristote, Thomas d'Aquin et Duns Scot," in S.-T. Bonino (Ed.), *Saint Thomas et l'ontothéologie, RThom,* 95, 85–108; id. (1997), *Duns Scot. La rigueur de la charité,* Paris; id. (Ed.) (1999), *Duns Scot, de la métaphysique à l'éthique, Philosophie,* no. 61.
M. Burger (1994), *Personalität in Horizont absoluter Prädestination: Untersuchungen zur Christologie des Johannes Duns Scotus und ihrer Reception in modernen theologischen Ansätze,* Münster.
H. Möhle (1995), *Ethik als* scientia practica *nach Johannes Duns Scotus, Eine philosophische Grundlegung,* Münster.

Bibliographies

O. Schäfer (1950), *Bibliographia de vita operibus et doctrina Iohannis Duns Scoti,* Rome.
S. Gieben (1965), *Bibliographia scotistica recentior* [1953–65], Rome.

Olivier Boulnois

See also **Bonaventure; Justification; Predestination; Scholasticism; Thomas Aquinas; Thomism; Voluntarism**

Easter. *See* **Resurrection of Christ**

Ecclesiastical Discipline

The expression *ecclesiastical discipline* refers to a group of laws, rules, and statutes that concern the organization and the activities of churches* and religious communities. It has an exact meaning in Protestant churches, but it also has its own sense in the Catholic Church, where there is a canonical law made of canons grouped in a code or in corpus. In canon law*, the expression *ecclesiastical discipline* refers to the part of law (sometimes called *penal law*) in which the exercise of the coercive power of the church over followers is organized, with excommunication as the ultimate realization. The churches of the Reformation, however, have strong reservations with regard to excommunication, although it appears in the founding texts.

a) Discipline in Protestant Churches. The term *discipline* is especially used in the reformed churches. For example, the Reformed Church of France publishes *Statuts, discipline et règlement général d'application* (Statutes, Disciplines, and General Rules of Application). More broadly, the term can designate in general the ecclesiastical law of the churches of the Reformation. In opposition to the canon law of the Roman Church, which many commentators try to base on or explain from the doctrine, discipline or ecclesiastical law, in this way, is based only on the need for organization. Thus, these churches make a fundamental distinction between doctrine and discipline. This organization must be just to meet the role the church should play in societies*, a responsibility that falls onto the communities themselves, especially through the processes of deliberation. This law contains the organizational rules for the local churches, catechesis, ministries*, the organization of the synods*, and so forth, all provisions that regulate and allow communal life and are therefore susceptible to revision and adaptation.

b) Ecclesiastical Discipline and Canon Law. An entire book of the code of canon law (1. VI) and a title of the code of canon of the Catholic Eastern Churches are devoted to sanctions in the Catholic Church. In the code of 1917, this law was called penal and, as in today's code, its rules were mostly technical. The principles it outlined explained how to apply this law. Canon 1317, for example, states that "penalties are to be established only in so far as they are really necessary for the better maintenance of ecclesiastical discipline." But no explanation on the ecclesiastical meaning of this right can be found. The beginning of book VI of the code of 1983 states: "The church has its own inherent right to constrain with penal sanctions Christ's faithful who commit offences." Commentators are needed to understand this meaning. Some base the conception of "innate law" on the fact that the church is organized like a society that must regulate the activities of the faithful while protecting the institution and its realm of action against all acts that harm it. Without fully covering it, this position is in line with the ecclesiology* of the *societas juridice perfecta* that developed in reaction against the modern states that wanted power over their subjects themselves subjected to the church. Other commentators, without denying the necessity of having a body of rules guaranteeing discipline inside the church, questioned the exercise of an ecclesiastical power of coercion. To them it seemed exceeded by the existence of an ecclesiastical communion* stated in the texts of Vatican* II, and consequently they asked that a law of a retributive nature be replaced by a "penal system sui generis."

Thus, these commentators ask us to look back to history and the formation of the church's coercive power. Early and medieval church historians have shown that, since its beginnings, the church has had recourse to judicial practices to sanction faults (Mt 18:15–18; 2 Cor 2:6; 1 Cor 5:11 ff.). Before the 12th century, however, such practices developed without penal processes and the imposition of canonical punishment (excommunications, suspensions, depositions) was totally distinct. From the 12th to the 14th century, there is mention of "the interpenetration of penal and coercive aspects of ecclesiastical discipline," as well as of "their progressive differentiation toward secular penal law" (Meunier 1975). The distinction made by canon law and the theology* of power of jurisdiction* alongside a power of order would allow for the building of a framework for the disciplinary power of the church and for differentiating it from penitential discipline. It was this power of jurisdiction that the Catholic Church would claim from the states, thus defining the church's innate right to impose punishments. But the distinction made between coercive actions of the church on an external level and its action on an internal level or at the level of conscience* (by the sacrament of penance*, notably by virtue of the principle that "all offense is a sin*") shows that, for the actual judicial system, penal law and penitential discipline still complete each other.

• C. Munier (1975), "Discipline pénitentielle et droit pénal ecclésial: Alliances et différenciation," *Concilium: Revue internationale de théologie* 107, 23–32.

A. Borras (1987), *L'excommunication dans le nouveau Code de droit canonique,* Paris.

B. Reymond (1992), *Entre la grâce et la loi: Introduction au droit ecclésial protestant,* Geneva.

PATRICK VALDRINI

See also **Canon Law; Jurisdiction; Law and Christianity; Law and Legislation; Penance**

Ecclesiology

Ecclesiology is the study of the church*. It is an important aspect of dogmatic theology*, as significant as Christology*, pneumatology, eschatology*, anthropology*, and so on. It is the theological arena in which the church considers itself, the point of convergence of systematic, historical, and practical research, which it develops and expresses to today's community of believers, who live and confess their faith* in diverse cultural and sociological contexts. The keynotes of ecclesiological discourse are the actualization and concretization of the biblical message in the daily lives of God's people.

1. Historical Development

Although they mention the church and most of the themes on which ecclesiology would be based, biblical texts offer no ecclesiological treatise. Ecclesiological thought first appears in the works of the Fathers*. Ignatius of Antioch, for example, saw the church as a cosmic entity encompassing heaven and earth (*Letter to the Ephesians* 9, 1; *Letter to the Smyrniotes* 7, 2); Hippolytus of Rome understood it as a holy community prefiguring eschatological reality (*Commentary on Daniel* I, 14–18); Irenaeus* of Lyons spoke of a church founded on the Spirit and on truth*, from which the characteristics of the church derive (*Against Heresies* III, 24). Later, Cyprian* of Carthage maintained the necessity of the church for salvation* (*De ecclesiae catholicae unitate* 6) and the special place of the episcopal ministry (ibid., 17). Augustine*, meanwhile, proposed a distinction between the visible church and the invisible Church (*De civitate dei* XI-XXII) that would become central to later ecclesiology. These remarks cannot, however, be taken as constituting a comprehensive and systematically presented ecclesiology. The period was characterized by a variety of ecclesiological currents reflecting different ecclesial structures*, but no particular form of ecclesiology was positively adopted by the councils*.

In the West, the unification of canon law* under Gratian in the 12th century brought with it more systematic ecclesiological thought. The first complete theological treatises devoted to the church as institution soon appeared (*See* Jacques de Viterbe *Christian Government* or Giles of Rome's *The Power of the Church,* which was the inspiration for Boniface VIII's Bull *Unam Sanctam* of 1302; *DS* 870 *Sq*). The most important treatise was probably the one produced by the Spanish Dominican Juan de Torquemada around 1450 (*Summa de ecclesia; see DThC* XV/I, 1235 *Sq*).

Unlike the ecclesiological works of the later Middle Ages, which are generally commentaries on canon law, the ecclesiology developed by the 16th-century Reformation was more dogmatic and catechetic in scope. The reformers saw ecclesiology as a theological statement that gave an account of the faith of believers confessing the one holy catholic and apostolic Church. This emphasis would be taken up by Catholic theology, which after the 18th century distinguished between an ecclesiology within fundamental* theology, a discourse that developed a vision of the church as the means and instrument of transmission of divine revelation*, and an ecclesiology within dogmatic theology, whose key topics were the origin of the church, its nature, structures and organization; its work and mission*; its mediation, its sacraments* and ministries*; its worship, liturgy* and preaching*; its piety and its future (eschatology).

The 19th century saw a number of comprehensive ecclesiological statements, initially from individual theologians such as J. A. Möhler or M. J. Scheeben*. It was intended to propose a comprehensive ecclesiology at Vatican* I, but only chapter nine of its *Schema de ecclesia,* the dogmatic constitution *Pastor aeternus* (*DS* 3050 *Sq*), was approved in 1870. The encyclicals *Satis cognitum* by Leo XIII (1896; *DS* 3300 *Sq*) and *Mystici corporis* by Pius XII (1943; *DS* 3800 *Sq*) marked important new stages. It was not until Vatican* II, however, that the Catholic Church put forward its first complete ecclesiological treatise to be authorized by the magisterium*, the dogmatic constitution on the Catholic Church *Lumen Gentium.*

By virtue of its desire for Church unity*, contemporary ecumenical dialogue is logically focused on ecce-siological issues. This dialogue has led most of the major denominational families to rethink and reformulate their ecclesiology. One might cite as an example the European Lutheran and Reformed Churches, which in 1994 approved and adopted "The Church of Jesus Christ," their first joint ecclesiological text since the 16th century (*Accords and Dialogues* II, 81 *Sq*); or the work of the Commission on Faith and Constitution of the Ecumenical Council of Churches, which recently presented an important ecclesiological study, *The Church and the World* (1991).

2. A Special Difficulty of Ecclesiology

Seen from the standpoint of the theory of knowledge, ecclesiology belongs to a distinctive genre. The church is, generally speaking, both the subject and the object of its research, since the special preserve of ecclesiological research is the church itself. The main problem arises however from the difficulty of defining the church as an object of research. The same term *church* commonly denotes a spiritual entity as well as a number of very different realities: from matters of worship to ecclesiastical structures and authorities, from the local community to national and international organizations, from the worldly mission to sociological data, or even the simple designation of buildings. This multiplicity of meanings is significant, and flows inevitably from the fitting of the Church, as a spiritual reality, into the material life of human society*. If ecclesiological research limits itself to topics visible and accessible to human logic, namely the institution and forms of the institutional church and its history* and sociology, it risks losing sight of the unique characteristic of the Church (as community of believers throughout time), its link with the divine reality of grace* that is its true foundation. If research is focused on this last aspect, it can no longer resort to its usual scientific approach, and must instead employ images and analogies*—just as, for example, Scripture* and tradition* emphasize conceptions of the Church as "God's people," "the bride of the Savior," "the body of Christ*," or "the temple of the Spirit." None of these images can fully express the unique nature of the Church, which transcends each of them, indeed all of them together.

Generally speaking, modern ecclesiology begins with biblical testimony and takes its cue from the Church's confession of faith over the centuries. The Christian faith lives by the certainty that the Holy* Spirit arouses faith and gathers believers into the one holy catholic and apostolic Church, the communion* of saints. This Church, originating with faith, appears in material forms that differ from century to century and from place to place. Starting with these two dimensions, ecclesiology attempts to make the theological approach and empirical research complementary.

3. Ecclesiology As a Subject of Debate

Ecclesiology inevitably takes a critical view of contemporary ecclesial pronouncements, which it analyzes and with whose development it must keep pace. It inevitably gives rise to reassessments that can cause conflicts at every level. This observation holds true for each separate ecclesiastical tradition (e.g., the debate aroused within the Catholic Church by the theology of H. Küng or L. Boff). It is also relevant to modern ecumenical dialogue, where ecclesiological issues remain the principal stumbling blocks in the search for Church unity. The difficulty becomes apparent as soon as there is any attempt to connect the Church as object of faith with the church as empirical reality. It gives rise to contradictory definitions that find expression for the most part in three closely connected areas, around which the great debates of modern ecclesiology are focused.

a) The first issue is the relationship between the Church as object of faith and the church as ecclesiastical institution. It is generally agreed that the communion of believers could not exist without an institutional structure, but not everyone accords the same importance to the latter. So, for the churches born of the 16th-century Reformation, the Church of Jesus Christ transcends any institutional form—no concrete expression of the church in this world can claim to be a full realization of the Church instituted by Christ. The ecclesiastical institution is a matter of human law; it is imperfect and always in need of reform. The Catholic and Orthodox Churches are reluctant to view their structural and institutional expressions in relative terms, considering them indeed to be as willed by God—even if, since Vatican II, the Catholic Church no longer considers itself the only possible expression of the Church of Christ (*See* ecumenism*). A similar approach in ecclesiology has obvious consequences for the view of hierarchy*, of church government*, and of authority* within the church, or for the understanding of the various ministries. This is not merely an interdenominational question, but a subject of debate within every Christian community. It is not simply a matter of time and place, but an expression of divergent systems of ecclesiology.

b) The second major difficulty of ecclesiology arises from the place accorded to the church within the divine mystery* as a whole. Some see ecclesiology as deriving from Christology and soteriology (Schmaus 1958; *MySal* 1972–73). For others it is a part of pneumatology (Pannenberg 1993), while still others hold it to be the keystone of all dogmatic theology (Tillard 1987; Siegwalt 1986). These individual interpretations reflect a fundamental choice, which Vatican II approached by asserting "that there is an order or 'hierarchy' of the truths of Catholic doctrine, by reason of their different relationships with the basis of the Christian faith" (decree on ecumenism, *UR* 11). Even though the council did not specify this "hierarchy," the Catholic Church is undeniably a central element in it, as the ecclesiological constitution *Lumen Gentium* makes clear.

Some strands within Protestantism, following Schleiermacher*, have considered ecclesiology to be a mere appendix to dogmatics, since for them the Church, as a society of believers, is above all an empirical reality. Contemporary dialogues have enabled clear progress to be made, and the churches that began with the 16th-century Reformation today state that communion within the church cannot be dissociated from the justification* of the believer (*The Church of Jesus Christ* II, 87). Nonetheless, the church's place in God's work of salvation remains an open question in ecumenical dialogue, in which some attribute to the church and its mediations an importance that others cannot accept (*See* Birmelé 1986). These different approaches have resulted in a divergence in ecclesiology, leading some Christian traditions to consider themselves as the one true expression of the Church as body of Christ.

c) A third issue central to ecclesiology is the relationship between the church and contemporary society. All factions agree in emphasizing that the church must engage itself in the affairs of this world*, but they differ in their definitions of the terms of this mission and its consequences for the church. Some advocate a separation between the holy Church and the secular world (Zizioulas 1981), while others call for an osmosis (e.g., Rendtorff 1969). With its insistence on human dignity and on the need for interaction between the church and the world for the good of all humanity, the pastoral constitution put forward by Vatican II, "The Pastoral constitution on the church in the modern world" *(GS),* developed a comprehensive vision to a large extent shared by other Christian traditions. Nevertheless, the relations between church and state*, the understanding of the laity (lay*), questions of culture (inculturation*), and relations with other religions, as well as more sociological aspects such as minority-majority relations, all remain ecclesiological issues—and frequently sources of controversy, not only between the Christian churches but within each one of them. In all these fields, ecclesiology must try to offer solutions that will permit the church to fulfill its vocation; and it is obliged to take a stand. No systematic consideration of the church could remain neutral.

• Augustine, *De civitate dei* (PL 41).
Cyprian of Carthage, *De ecclesiae catholicae unitate* (CChr.SL 3).
Hyppolitus of Rome, *Commentarium in Danielem* (SC 14).
Ignatius of Antioch, *Letters to the Churches of Ephesus, Magnesia, Rome, Tralles, Smyrna* (SC 10).
Irenaeus of Lyons, *Against Heresies I-III* (SC 263, 264, 293, 294, 210 and 211).
Vatican II, decrees: *COD* 817–1135 (*DCO* II/2, 1661–2300).
Église et monde: L'unité de l'Église et le renouveau de la communauté humaine (text from *Foi et Constitution,* COE), Paris, 1993.
L'Église de Jésus-Christ, in A. Birmelé, J. Terme (Ed.), *Accords et dialogues œcuméniques,* Paris, 1995.
♦ Y. Congar (1941), *Esquisse du mystère de l'Église,* Paris (2nd Ed. 1966).
H. de Lubac (1953), *Méditation sur l'Église,* Paris (2nd Ed. 1975).
M. Schmaus (1958), *Katholische Dogmatik* III/1, Munich.
H. Rahner (1964), *Symbole der Kirche: Die Ekklesiologie der Väter,* Salzburg.
H. Küng (1967), *Die Kirche,* Freiburg-Munich (2nd Ed. 1980).
T. Rendtorff (1969), *Christentum außerhalb der Kirche,* Hamburg.
Coll. (1972, 1973), *MySal* IV/1 (contributions by H. Schlier, W. Beinert, H. Fries, O. Semmelroth, and Y. Congar) and IV/2 (contributions by P. Huizing and B. Dupuy).
A. Dulles (1976), *Models of the Church: A Critical Assessment of the Church in All Its Aspects,* Dublin.
W. Kreck (1981), *Grundfragen der Ekklesiologie,* Munich.
H. Rikhof (1981), *The Concept of the Church: A Methodological Inquiry into the Use of Metaphors in Ecclesiology,* London-Shepherdstown.
L. Boff (1985), *Église, charisme et pouvoir,* Paris.
J. Zizioulas (1985), *Being As Communion,* Crestwood, N.Y.
A. Birmelé (1986), *Le salut en Jésus-Christ dans les dialogues œcuméniques,* CFi 141.
H. Döring (1986), *Grundriss der Ekklesiologie,* Darmstadt.
G. Siegwalt (1986–), *Dogmatique pour la catholicité évangélique,* Paris-Geneva.
J.-M. Tillard (1987), *Église d'Églises,* CFi 143.
W. Pannenberg (1993), *Systematische Theologie,* vol. III, Göttingen.
B. Forte (1995), *La Chiesa Icona della Trinitá,* Milan.
K. Rahner (1995), *Selbstvollzug der Kirche, SW* 19, Düsseldorf-Freiburg.
J.-M. Tillard (1995), *L'Église locale,* CFi 191.

ANDRÉ BIRMELÉ

See also **Authority; Church; Church and State; Communion; Council; Ecclesiastical Discipline; Ecumenism; Eucharist; Government, Church; Hierarchy; Indefectibility of the Church; Infallibility; Local Church; Magisterium; Ministry; Regional Church; Structures, Ecclesial; Unity of the Church**

Eckhart von Hohenheim (Meister).

See **Rhineland-Flemish Mysticism**

Ecology

Ecology is the study of the natural world as an interconnected whole in which all things, including human beings, are related in complex interdependence. Scientifically, all living things constitute an ecosphere that includes many ecosystems. On a philosophical, religious, or ethical level, ecosystems principally lead to notions that stress the intrinsic value and interdependence of all living things and nature. Of late there has been a growing awareness that human intervention disregards and destroys the interdependence of ecosystems and is responsible for a global ecological crisis, which endangers humanity by endangering nature. This calls for theological reflection, which needs to criticize and rethink the Christian view of the place of human beings in creation* and their responsibility toward other creatures. Ecological theology* and ecological ethics* in this sense are recent disciplines, but they incorporate earlier theological thought.

The biblical resources for Christian ecological thought comprise four main themes. 1) Human dominion: At the Creation, human beings were commanded by God* to "subdue" the earth and to "have dominion" over other living creatures (Gn 1:28; Ps 8:6–8). They have a unique role within creation. Their creation in the divine image is unique (Gn 1:26, 9:6), which enables them to represent God and rule over creation. However, there is no suggestion in the Bible* that the entire creation exists *for* humanity. 2) The community of creation: Human beings may stand above all other creatures, they are creatures themselves, who share the earth with all the beings that God has created. Thus, after the Flood God makes a covenant with all human beings and all animals (Gn 9:8–17). According to Psalm 104:23, human beings are just one of the living creatures for whom God provides; the earth is the habitat for living creatures, and each holds a God-given place. The same understanding is embodied in laws that restrict exploitation of the land (Ex 23:11; Lv 25:7), and in the teaching of Jesus* (Mt 6:25 f.). 3) Creation as theocentric reality: Creation exists not for humanity, but for the glory of God. All creatures, inanimate and animate, praise and adore him (Ps 148; Rev 5:13). Therefore each creature has worth, which is given by the Creator and offered back to him in praise. 4) The redemption of all creation: Biblical soteriology does not separate human beings from the rest of the world but recognizes their solidarity with all that was created (Col 1:20). The hope* of salvation* is extended to all creation, which in the end will be delivered from corruption (Rom 8:20–21) and be made new (2 Pt 3:13; Rev 21:1). Human beings have no future independent of the rest of creation.

In the theological tradition* up to the early modern period, the notion of human dominion over nature was interpreted through ideas drawn from the Stoics and Aristotle. This brought up the idea of a creation made for human beings, an idea that leads to a tendentious reading of Genesis. To dominate then meant that human beings had the right to use all creatures to meet their own needs. Many contemporary critics, following Lynn White (1967), have seen in this the ideological source of the exploitation of nature that has produced today's ecological crisis, but this is very scant. Up to the Reformation, there was no sense of dominion as an obligation to extend human mastery over nature; further, people had no idea that nature could be completely transformed. To dominate nature simply meant the right to use it in the limited way that was then possible. Moreover, the view that the world exists for human benefit was balanced by the very idea of creation that made human beings creatures of God alongside other creatures.

The modern project of technological domination of nature has its direct roots not in the theological tradition itself, but in the way that it was modified by Renaissance* humanism and by Francis Bacon (1561–1626). For the humanists, dominion over the world was so sovereign and creative that human beings had both the ability and the right to refashion nature as they chose. Any sense of limitations inherent to the creature disappeared and was replaced by a limitless aspiration to master and to create. The Renaissance thus provided the vision that inspired the modern project of dominating nature, while Francis Bacon drew from Genesis a program of scientific and technological enterprise, in which mastery of nature's laws was to be the means of subjecting nature entirely to human needs.

However, this was not the only way in which the role of human beings in the universe could be conceived. In the Middle Ages, an alternative conception appeared, for example, in hagiographies portraying human being living in paradisiacal harmony with all creatures, with a powerful eschatological symbolism. Here, dominion is benevolent rule with a strong sense of what all creatures have in common. This is shown in Saint Francis of Assisi (1181–1226) and the *Canticle of the Creatures.* An idea that first appeared in 17th-century England and that has become influential today (e.g., Wilkinson 1980) turns human beings into stewards of creation. In this light, human beings have received the task of managing God's work on his behalf, and are responsible to God for how they do it. This view recognizes value in nonhuman creation, other than its usefulness to humanity, and gives human beings obligations to treat it accordingly. However, this implies that nature needs the active intervention of human beings. A truly ecological theology, on the other hand, holds that human beings have so little importance within the universe that it limits any notion of a rule over creation. Recent variations on the theme include ideas of human beings as priests of creation, enabling creation to be itself to the praise of God (e.g., Gunton 1992), or as servants of creation, participating in Christ's salvific role of delivering creation from human oppression (e.g., Linzey 1994).

Recent theology includes varied attempts to conceive the relationships of God, human beings, and the rest of the world in ways that replace the idea of hierarchical domination with that of ecological interconnectedness. These include Moltmann's strongly christological and pneumatological interpretation of these connections (1985, 1989); ecofeminist theologies that see the domination of nature as an aspect of patriarchy (e.g., Ruether 1993); the creation spiritualities of Matthew Fox (1988) or Thomas Berry (*See* Berry and Swimme 1992); and, finally, a trend moving away from anthropocentrism to return to the notion of "respect for life" of Albert Schweitzer (1885–1965), for example by L. K. Daly (in Birch, et al. 1990). There have even been attempts to show that the intrinsic value of nonhuman creatures forces human beings to recognize their responsibility toward them, and also implies that animals have rights (e.g. Linzey 1994), or of all participants in the ecosphere (Moltmann 1989).

• L. White, Jr. (1967), "The Historical Roots of our Ecological Crisis," in I. G. Barbour (Ed.) (1973), *Western Man and Environmental Ethics,* Reading, Mass.
D. S. Wallace-Hadrill (1968), *The Greek Patristic View of Nature,* Manchester.
L. Wilkinson (Ed.) (1980), *Earthkeeping: Christian Stewardship of Natural Resources,* Grand Rapids, Mich.
J. Moltmann (1985), *Gott in der Schöpfung: Ökologische Schöpfungslehre,* 2nd Rev. Ed., Munich.
M. Fox (1988), *The Coming of the Cosmic Christ,* San Francisco.
R. D. Sorrell (1988), *St. Francis of Assisi and Nature,* Oxford.
J. Moltmann (1989), *Der Weg Jesu Christi,* Munich.
R. F. Nash (1989), *The Rights of Nature: A History of Environmental Ethics,* Madison, Wis.
C. Birch, W. Eakin, J. B. Daniel (Ed.) (1990), *Liberating Life: Contemporary Approaches to Ecological Theology,* New York.
T. Berry, B. Swimme (1992), *The Universe Story,* San Francisco.
C. E. Gunton (1992), *Christ and Creation,* Carlisle.
Com(F) XVIII/3 (1993), *L'écologie.*
R. R. Ruether (1993), *God and Gaia: An Ecofeminist Theology of Earth Healing,* London.
Éthique (1994/3), *L'écologie: Humanisme ou naturalisme?*
A. Linzey (1994), *Animal Theology,* London.
M. Oeschlager (1994), *Caring for Creation: An Ecumenical Approach to the Environmental Crisis,* New Haven.
J. B. Callicott (1996), "Environnement," *DEPhM,* 498–501.

RICHARD BAUCKHAM

See also **Adam; Anthropology; Cosmos; Spirituality, Franciscan; Woman**

Economy of Salvation. *See* **Salvation**

Ecumenical Dialogue. *See* **Ecumenism**

Ecumenical Movement. *See* **Ecumenism**

Ecumenism

1. Origin and Significance

Oikoumenè, the past participle of the Greek verb *oikein* (to inhabit), was used by Herodotus (c. 490–425/420 B.C.) to designate the inhabited world. The biblical writings seldom use this term, although it was popular in the Hellenistic world of the era. The Septuagint (the first Greek translation of the Bible*, started in the third century B.C.) uses it to translate some passages of the Psalms*. In the New Testament, Luke 2:1 and Matthew 24:14 use it to designate the Roman Empire, and in Hebrews 2:5 *Oikoumenè* refers to the unity of humanity and God* in eschatology*.

In the ancient church*, *Oikoumenè* had both a political meaning (the Roman world) and church meaning (the totality of Christians). In Constantine's reign (306–37), the two meanings were confused. A decisive role was played by the synods* or councils* called *ecumenical,* for their decisions were applied to all of Christendom and to the whole empire. By the end of the Roman and Byzantine Empires, *Oikoumenè* was stripped of its political meaning, and only had church significance: the *Oikoumenè* was the universal Church. During the sixth century, the patriarchate of Constantinople was called "ecumenical" in order to signify its preeminence over several Eastern Churches. This preeminence had already been acknowledged by Emperor Constantine. This usage triggered animated reactions from pope* Gregory I (590–604). In the West the Reformation, which was reticent about the term *catholic,* generally a synonym for *Roman Catholic,* gave a new topicality to *Oikoumenè.* The notion then designated the fullness and unity* of the universal Church, the Christendom of all countries, brought together and guided by the Holy* Spirit. The Church is ecumenical, because, when announcing the gospel to the whole world, it is one and catholic, it is the Church in its fullness given by God.

It was only in the 20th century that the Swedish bishop N. Soederblom (1866–1930) gave *Oikoumenè* and the adjective *ecumenical* the sense that they have today in theology*: everything that relates to bringing together, to the reconciliation and to the unity of churches within what is called the Ecumenical Movement. The noun *ecumenism* was introduced in 1937 by the French Dominican, Yves Congar, and then was adopted and confirmed by Vatican* II in the Decree on Ecumenism, *Unitatis Redintegratio.* In a fundamental study (*Geschichte und Sinn des Wortes "ökumenisch,"* 1953), W. A. Visser't Hooft (1900–1985), the first secretary general of the World* Council of Churches (WCC), notes seven meanings of the adjective *ecumenical* over the course of history*. They are: 1) "what belongs to the inhabited world or represents it," 2) "what belongs to the Roman Empire or represents it," 3) "what has a universal Church value," 4) "what concerns the universal missionary task" (mission*), 5) "what involves the relationships between churches or Christians of different confessional origins," 6) "the spiritual consciousness of belonging to the world communion* of Christian churches," and 7) "the availability of committing oneself to the unity of the Church."

The use of the word *ecumenical* today goes beyond the single church category. Some use it to refer to the dialogue that churches have with other religions; others see it as a qualitative term for all efforts of consensus or unity between individuals or groups.

2. Churches' Commitment to Ecumenism

At first, ecumenism was the concern of Protestant churches. Around the end of the 19th century, the need for a better cooperation among churches led to the creation of the first international organizations, and these would lead to the birth of the WCC in 1948. This step was facilitated by the ecclesiological approach to Protestantism*. While understanding itself as the full and true expression of the unique church of Christ*, a church born of the Reformation nevertheless did not pretend to be the only authentic expression of the one, holy, catholic, and apostolic Church. The Church of Christ, moreover, existed in other forms and traditions. The division and mutual nonrecognition of churches were, however, unacceptable. Communion in the celebration of the Word* and sacraments* was the necessary and sufficient condition for two churches to become one, without, all the while, being uniform.

The concerns of Anglican, Lutheran, Reformed, Methodist, and Baptist Churches, among others, were twofold. On one hand, doctrinal controversy, which had brought about mutual condemnation, had to be transcended. On the other hand, a common form of commitment within society* had to be found. These two concerns were adopted by the Faith and Order Movement, as well as by the Life and Work Movement. Because these movements did not always have the same priorities, there was a certain tension—even opposition—in the two ecumenical options proposed by the churches born of the Reformation. Today, this tension is still perceptible, both within the WCC and within individual churches. Certain traditions, such as the Anglican Communion and Lutheran Churches, give more weight to the Church's communal character in the Ecumenical Movement, the common commitment being the consequence of rediscovered unity. Other Protestant denominations give less importance to ecclesiology* and prioritize common social, ethic, and political initiatives. The visible unity of the Church would be one of the consequences of this ecumenism. The Protestant understanding of ecumenism is still marked by these various approaches, even if all involved agree that the unity of the Church could not be separated from the revival and unity of all humanity.

Insisting on the self-government of sister churches, the Orthodox Churches have always been committed to a council vision of the one Church, based on the unbroken tradition of the seven Ecumenical Councils—from Nicaea* I (325) to Nicaea II (787). While seeing themselves as belonging to the only true Church of Christ, they do not dismiss the presence of a church life beyond their limits. This option allows them to seek dialogue and cooperation with other Christian communities without, all the while, coming to a conclusion about their community qualities. In a 1920 encyclical, the patriarch of Constantinople called for a universal communion of churches. As early as 1927 several self-governed churches and a few formerly Eastern churches participated in the first international conference of the Faith and Order Movement in Lausanne. Orthodoxy* regards doctrinal consensus as preliminary to all ecumenical progress. Considering the obstacles that lie in the way of such a consensus, Orthodoxy has often adopted a prudent, wait-and-see policy. The churches in this tradition nevertheless joined the WCC in 1961, even though they still had various reservations, and, when necessary, expressed dissent.

The Roman Catholic Church and the Eastern churches that recognize the primacy of the pope joined the Ecumenical Movement at a later date. At first, all ideas about ecumenism were rejected. The 1896 encyclical of Leon XIII (1878–1903), *Satis Cognitum* (in *Acta Apostolicae sedis,* 1895–96) specifies that there is only one Church of Jesus Christ, the Church for which the Roman pontiff is responsible. To leave this Church means straying from the path of salvation* *(Satis Cogitum).* The 1928 encyclical circulated by Pius XI (1922–39), *Mortalium animos* (in *Acta Apostolicae sedis,* 1928) forbids any relationship with other Christian communities and all contact with the Ecumenical Movement.

The breakthrough came with Vatican II and was concretized when the Decree on Ecumenism was published. The Dogmatic Constitution on the Church, *Lumen Gentium,* made this evolution possible by specifying that "the one Church of Christ... subsists in the Catholic Church, which is governed by the successor of Peter and by the bishops in communion with him" (*LG* 8). This *subsistit in* is the traditional *is* and it allowed the council to note about the Catholic Church that "many elements of sanctification and of truth* are found outside of its visible structure" (*LG* 8 and *UR* 3). While insisting on the uniqueness of the Catholic Church bound to the pope, the only Church in full, the council proposed common prayer*, doctrinal dialogue for a better mutual understanding, and reestablishment of unity, as well as collaboration in service in this world (*UR* 4–12).

This commitment to ecumenism was confirmed repeatedly in the years after the council—for example, in John Paul II's 1995 encyclical *Ut unum sint.* The Catholic Church participated in several ecumenical dialogues under the charge of the Secretariat for Unity (today, the Pontifical Council for Unity). Councils of churches were established in several countries, and cults* and ecumenical gatherings have become regular occurrences. The Catholic Church's self-understanding as the only Church in full, however, does not allow it to recognize separate churches and communities as "equivalent" partners. This point still lies in the way of its full participation in the WCC.

3. Multiple Forms of Ecumenism

Ecumenism—like all Church life—is a complex and multifaceted reality. Its integrity and indivisibility make it so that it cannot be reduced to a single aspect. One can, however, distinguish a few fundamental thrusts that interact to form the whole.

a) Doctrinal Ecumenism. Because the division of churches was condemned doctrinally, particular importance has been given to theological dialogues between churches. The majority of confessional families (family*, confessional) have participated and have been able to reach remarkable consensus that have allowed them to go beyond traditional controversy. The most significant results were obtained through the multilateral work of the Faith and Order Commission of the WCC and in bilateral dialogues, essentially between Roman Catholics and Anglicans, between Roman Catholics and Lutherans, and between the various traditions that came out of the Reformation. Among these, the consensus was such that, in many areas, full communion was reestablished, with communities mutually recognizing each other as the full and authentic expression of the one Church of Christ.

In the dialogues launched between the churches of the Reformation and the Roman Catholic Church there has been real progress, even if the final stage, that of full mutual recognition, has not been fully achieved. The remaining disagreements mostly concern the understanding of the role of the church in the saving act of God, the nature of ministries*, the exercise of authority*, and the primacy and infallibility* of the pope. Several classical differences of opinion—such as those concerning the understanding of salvation, faith* and works*, and reference to the Holy* Scripture—have, however, been overcome, and a mutual lifting of historical condemnations is no longer a utopian idea.

It should be noted, however, that this doctrinal ecumenism developed more specifically in the Western world. Coming to a mutual understanding is more difficult when partners do not have the same cultural roots. The dialogue between the Catholic and Orthodox Churches has already shown this. These important unions have not yet yielded the desired consequences and possibilities.

b) Spiritual Ecumenism. Every January since 1941, Catholics, Orthodox, and Protestants have celebrated a week of prayer for unity. All the churches emphasize the need for common prayer and liturgy, the unity of the Church being above all the work of the Holy Spirit, a spiritual reality offered by God. There are translations of the Bible that are common to all the churches of different languages. Prayer groups and common or shared Bible studies have developed in all countries, and these have allowed ecumenism to take root in local community realities. This spiritual ecumenism, closely tied to the life of local parishes and to initiatives launched by Christians of different origins in a given area, gives meaning to all the other dimensions of ecumenism. This "local ecumenism" is often at odds with the national or international ecumenical leadership of churches. Slow progress and prudence have proven to be irksome to local bodies.

c) Ecumenism in Witnessing and Service. Ecumenism in witnessing and service has been central from the very beginning of modern ecumenism, as shown by the Life and Work Movement; this dimension stresses the common action of churches in the face of the needs of the contemporary world. Local, national, and international ecumenism cannot ignore this common ethical and social commitment, for concern about renewing, reconciling, and overcoming all human misery, and the unity of all humanity, is part of the mission of all churches. The history and various programs of the WCC concretely illustrate this common commitment of churches—for example, the programs that fight against racism, education programs, aid to refugees, the fight against exclusion, the role of women (woman*) and youth, and the movement for justice*, peace*, and the integrity of creation*.

In many countries this ecumenism is also called "contextual ecumenism," especially in Third World regions, where it is most urgent. Unfortunately, it has often been seen in opposition to the other forms of ecumenism, such as the champions of "secular ecumenism" around 1968. The same kind of unilateral vision neglects the complex nature of ecumenism and undermines its integrity.

d) Institutional Ecumenism. The contemporary Ecumenical Movement was born on the fringes of member churches. At first, it was the concern of a few pioneers. At present, most churches have integrated ecumenical concerns and have even grounded them institutionally. This anchoring has happened at the local level, in national instances that have established several ecumenical commissions, and on the level of large worldwide organizations. Such an evolution was wished for and necessary. It can, however, be accompanied by a certain ponderousness that slows down the movement by trapping it in administrative structures. This development helps give the impression that ecumenism is currently stagnating. It is true that the period of spectacular breakthroughs has passed and that we are now at a point of acceptance of what has been gained over the past years.

In seeking to overcome denominational, national, social, cultural, and ethical barriers, and thus seeking to promote the unity of the Church and of humanity, ecumenism has experienced the ups and downs that characterize all Church life.

• Y. Congar (1937), *Chrétiens désunis: Principes d'un œcuménisme catholique,* Paris.

Actes du concile Vatican II, Paris, 1966.

W. A. Visser't Hooft (1967), "Geschichte und Sinn des Wortes 'ökumenisch,'" *Ökumenischer Aufbruch: Hauptschriften II,* Stuttgart-Berlin, 11–28.

Coll. (1970), "L'œcuménisme séculier," *PosLuth* 18, 48–61.

E. Fouilloux (Ed.) (1976), "L'œcuménisme contemporain," *2,000 ans de christianisme,* vol. X, Paris.

Coll. (1983), "L'œcuménisme au plan local," *PosLuth* 31, 3–51.

H. J. Urban (1985–87) (Ed.), *Handbuch der Oekumenik I-III,* Paderborn.

K. Lehmann, W. Pannenberg (Ed.) (1986), *Lehrverurteilungen-Kirchentrennend?* Freiburg-Göttingen.

J.-P. Willaime (Ed.) (1989), *Vers de nouveaux œcuménismes,* Paris.

N. Lossky, et al. (Ed.) (1991), *Dictionary of the Ecumenical Movement,* Geneva.

R. Frieling (1992), *Der Weg des ökumenischen Gedankens,* Göttingen.

Coll. (1994), "Crise et défi du mouvement œcuménique: Intégrité et indivisibilité," *PosLuth* 42, 289–331.

A. Birmelé, J. Terme (Ed.) (1995), *Accords et dialogues œcuméniques,* Paris.

Jean-Paul II (1995), *Ut unum sint,* Vatican City.

ANDRÉ BIRMELÉ

See also **Family, Confessional; Protestantism; Unity of the Church; World Council of Churches**

Edwards, Jonathan

(1703–58)

Born in Connecticut, Jonathan Edwards studied at Yale College where, in addition to reading the classics and Puritan* manuals, he discovered the writings of Newton and Locke. Appointed pastor in Northampton, Massachusetts, in 1727, he played a central role in the Pietist movement of the Great Awakening (1741–42), of which he became the theologian. Following disagreements concerning who should be admitted to Communion*, he was dismissed by his congregation. Sent to Stockbridge in 1750 as a missionary to the Indians, he wrote his major works there. He was then elected president of the College of New Jersey in Princeton, but he died almost immediately after assuming his position there in 1758. Edwards is considered the first philosopher and the greatest Protestant* theologian of the New World. Two major doctrinal elements of his thought merit particular consideration.

a) Sin and Responsibility. Edwards starts with the following difficulty: There is no sin* unless one freely chooses evil*; but is there free choice when the will is determined? To resolve this question, both intent to avoid the false sense of guilt that threatened Puritanism and troubled by the growing influence of Arminianism (Calvinism*), Edwards set out, on the one hand, a theory of the will, and, on the other, an explanation based on the identity of the person*.

To make responsibility and the absence of moral autonomy compatible, Edwards distinguishes the determination of the will in time from its nature. The will acts only if its inclination is determined, but because this depends on the perception of a real or imaginary good*, the will can never be truly autonomous. To be autonomous, it would have to determine itself—that is, its acts would have to be determined by a preceding volition, leading to an infinite regression. One of two things is true: Either one does not achieve original volition, or else, if it is original, it is not truly volition because it is determined by something other than a preceding volition. To avoid these contradictions, it must be admitted that the will, while always determined, remains voluntary, as he explains in *Freedom of the Will* (1754). The sinner has not himself chosen to will the sin of Adam*, but because he wills it in fact, he is guilty. Edwards therefore joins together determination of the will and responsibility, which the philosophical tradition had declared incompatible. He can then complete his theory of the will before sin by developing the doctrine of original sin—which he did in *The Great Christian Doctrine of Original Sin,* which was published posthumously—and the analysis of servile will.

If what makes the will of the sinner evil in each act (action*) is obviously its opposition to the good, the continuous exercise of this evil will, which is the only thing that allows it to be attributed to a subject, is due to an external constitution. Good and evil acts are in themselves only isolated acts, and the identity of the subject who carries them out depends on a continuous creation*. Theology* teaches us that our condition as moral subjects (with temporal continuity) is founded by a divine act, which establishes a relationship of identity between the personality of Adam and that of each one of his descendants. We are, of course, the responsible authors of our volitions, but we are ourselves only by virtue of the foundational act that connects us to Adam. God*, on the contrary, while he is at every moment the author of our establishment "in" Adam, remains foreign to the evil that we ourselves will. Beyond his original hypothesis on the transmission of original sin, Edwards thus rediscovered the classic thesis that distinguishes within evil a material element attributable to God and a formal element imputable to man.

b) Religious Feelings. Uncovering the spiritual condition of the believer is a central preoccupation of Puritanism. Good works* are the fruits of justification* (the doctrine of justification by faith* alone is one of the great commonplaces of Edwards's preaching*), but they are not unequivocal signs of justification. As for belief, purely intellectual adhesion to the Christian mysteries* is always within reach of the hypocrite. Nourished by the Calvinist spiritual tradition* that had been revivified by the immense spiritual uplift of the Great Awakening, Edwards thus recognizes true religion through certain "affections," the first of which is love*. The devil may imitate the process of conversion*, but he is incapable of counterfeiting its nature, love.

A whole range of signs—Edwards enumerates 12 of them—helps the believer to discern his condition inwardly, but these signs are for others only objective universal criteria, and they do not make it possible to formulate a public judgment* on the faith of a believer. The highest result of conversion is the advent of a spiritual beauty that reflects "the holy beauty of God." This is why 2 Peter 1:4 is the favorite Biblical reference of Edwards. In his *Treatise Concerning Religious Affections* (1746) Edwards holds that the "grace* which is in the heart of the saints is of the same nature although of a lesser degree with the divine holiness."

An ecclesiology* immediately flows from this concern for coherence and authenticity. The founders of Congregationalism* in New England had required the expression of an experience* of personal conversion in order to be admitted to Communion. This principle had gradually fallen into disuse. But Edwards, refusing to surrender to the prevailing laxity, came to require that communicants confess their conversion.

What has been called the New Theology represents the posterity of Edwards. His disciples, systematizing his thought, present a unique example in Protestantism of a fruitful synthesis of dogmatic orthodoxy with evangelical pietism. These disciples include E. and J. Bellamy (1719–70), S. Hopkins (1721–1803), N. Emmons (1744–1840), and the most important preacher of the Second Great Awakening, Timothy Dwight (1752–1817), Edwards's grandson. Edwards's writings were also a considerable influence on John Wesley and George Whitefield.

• *The Works of President Edwards,* London, 1817–47, 10 vols., New Ed., New York, 1968.

The Works of Jonathan Edwards, vol. 2: *Religious Affections,* Ed. John E. Smith, New Haven, 1959.

♦ F.H. Foster (1907), *A History of New England Theology,* Chicago.

J. Ridderbos (1907), *De Theologie van Jonathan E.*, The Hague.

J. Haratounian (1932), *Piety versus Moralism,* New York.

P. Miller (1949), *Jonathan E.*, New York.

C. Cherry (1966), *The Theology of Jonathan E.: A Reappraisal,* Garden City.

J.P. Carse (1967), *Jonathan E. and the Visibility of God,* New York.

A. Delattre (1968), *Beauty and Sensibility in the Thought of Jonathan E.,* New Haven.

T. Erdt (1980), *Jonathan E., Art and the Sense of the Heart,* Amherst.

N. Fiering (1981), *Jonathan E.'s Moral Thought and Its British Context,* Chapel Hill.

M.X. Lesser (1981), *Jonathan E., a Reference Guide,* Boston.

N. Manspeaker (1981), *Jonathan E.: A Bibliographical Synopses,* New York.

M. Vetö (1987), *La pensée de Jonathan E.*, Paris.

R. W. Jenson (1988), *America's Theologian: A Recommendation of Jonathan E.*, New York.

A. V. G. Allen (1989), *Jonathan E.*, Boston.

Miklos Vetö

See also **Calvinism; Congregationalism; Liberty; Lutheranism; Methodism; Puritanism; Sin, Original**

Enhypostasy.

See **Anhypostasy**

Enlightenment

The Enlightenment signifies today the dominant rationalist and liberal cultural movement that occurred in Europe from roughly 1690 to the French Revolution (1789). The term can be traced to a sentence by Bernard Le Bovier de Fontenelle (1657–1757) in the preface to his 1702 *History of the Renewal of the Royal Academy of Sciences,* where it primarily denotes the progress which Fontenelle expected to see during "a century that will become more enlightened day by day." Fontenelle was referring to the natural sciences, but the French term *lumières* (in the plural), and the equivalents in German *(Aufklärung)* and English (Enlightenment), became established to cover the major developments in all the arts, and above all in philosophy*.

The Enlightenment was primarily characterized by its commitment to empirical investigation in the sciences, its optimism about progress in all realms of life, and its belief in human perfectibility. It tried to replace authority by rational investigation, preferred rationally structured order to nature or sentiment in the arts, and made the critical examination of evidence the means of establishing truth* in matters of history* and theology*. Its philosophical core, articulating broader cultural changes, moved from the early rationalism of the Catholic Descartes* to the critical analysis of human intellection and morality of the Protestant Kant*, who, preoccupied with "the starry heavens above and the moral law within," attempted to lay the foundations both for the certainty of modern science and for the possibility of human freedom.

The spirit of the Enlightenment is doubtless best summed up in the tentative and often amusing ironies of the after-dinner pieces of Voltaire (1694–1778), later worked up into *contes* (tales) such as *Candide,* which focused on Voltaire's dislike of dogma (because it bred intolerance) and of rites (because they bred superstition). Voltaire wavered, but he cautiously advocated that organized Christianity be as unstructured as possible without compromising the sanction of posthumous divine remunerative justice, a belief that he still held necessary for the cohesiveness of human society. The possibility of an ethic unsupported by divine retribution after death* had, however, already been canvassed by the Protestant Pierre Bayle (1647–1706) in his 1683 *Pensées diverses sur la comète,* originally a pamphlet attacking as superstitious the view that the advent of comets presaged the occurrence of events on Earth.

The movement's great monument was the 17-volume *Encyclopédie,* edited by Denis Diderot (1713–84) from 1751 to 1765. The *Encyclopédie,* although at first relying on contributions from ecclesiastics and purporting to provide only a systematization of contemporary knowledge, turned progressively in its later volumes into a vehicle for religiously skeptical propaganda.

a) Philosophy. The lifelong attempt of Descartes to provide apodictic metaphysical certainty for metaphysics, physics, medicine, mechanics, and ethics* had been apologetic in intention but it necessarily subverted the need for authority* in philosophy. Buoyed up by the optimism of France after the religious wars and fearful of the religious skepticism they had generated, Descartes sought to establish both the immortality of the human spiritual principle and the path by which human beings might attain to the highest virtue and happiness of which they were capable. He started with a purely methodical universal doubt of all that was not undeniably self-evident, exempting only the truths of revelation, and produced a system that was therefore a purely rational construct.

From that theory, Baruch Spinoza (1632–77) developed his deterministic pantheism, dangerously viewing the mind and body as expressing different attributes of the same substance. It was also against a Cartesian background that the desire for a rationalist explanation of human experience paradoxically led the Oratorian Nicholas Malebranche (1638–1715) and the Protestant Gottfried Wilhelm Leibniz* (1646–1716) to assign to God* a direct intervention in human cognition, an idea that provoked a reaction among the English empiricists. For Malebranche, "we see all things in God." The mind perceives only ideas representing material objects, and these ideas are themselves "the efficacious substance of the divinity." For Leibniz, the appearance of interaction of substances is the result of a harmony preestablished by God. Jacques-Bénigne Bossuet (1627–1704), who thought of himself as a controversialist of Augustinian* stature in defense of Catholicism*, was sufficiently frightened by the writings of both Spinoza and Malebranche to turn against Cartesianism, writing on 7 December 1691 a famous letter on the subject to Pierre Nicole (1625–95), a Jansenist moralist who inspired Pascal*.

Directly opposed to the epistemologies deriving from a Cartesian background was the thought of the Protestant John Locke (1632–1704). His reference to the possibility of thinking matter, abolishing the absolute Cartesian separation of matter and spirit, was to inspire Voltaire's attack on Descartes and was a significant step on the path to materialism. Since the Middle Ages the immortality of the soul had appeared to be contingent on its spirituality. David Hume (1711–76) attacks not only revealed theology but also natural religion, and he grants an even bigger role than Locke to sensory perception in our understanding of the world, increasing the difficulty of defending immortality, which in private even Voltaire doubted.

b) Theology. There was a specifically theological Enlightenment tradition, most prominent in Germany. It derived from Christian Thomasius (1655–1728), a Leipzig professor chiefly famous for his hostility to prejudice and superstition. His religious views led to the withdrawal of his license to teach, and he moved to Halle, which was soon to become the center of Pietism*. Also associated with Halle was Christian Wolff (1679–1754), who was for a while dismissed from his teaching post on account of his theology, largely derived from Leibniz, which was an attempt to base theological truths on evidence of mathematical certitude. Wolff was reinstated and ennobled when Frederick the Great (1712–86) succeeded to the Prussian throne, but his thought was replaced in public esteem by that of Kant, whom it had much influenced.

Like Locke and Leibniz, Johann Gottfried von Herder (1744–1803) was influenced by recent scientific investigation. Court preacher at Wiemar from 1776, Herder's chief interest was the nature of language. Stimulated by Kant at Könisberg to critical inquiry, and prefiguring Hegel, whose dialectical theory of human history he inspired, he moved from early attacks on universal reason and happiness to a genuinely Enlightenment belief in the unicity of the world soul, "the one human reason, the one human truth." Herder combined his religious commitment with his belief in the progress of humanity, his status as a poet, his view that poetry was the original language, and his interest in the history of humanity, but his importance derives partly from his close relationships with such major literary giants of the Enlightenment as Gotthold Ephraim Lessing (1729–81), Johann Wolfgang von Goethe (1749–1832), Christoph Martin Wieland (1733–1813), and Jean Paul [Richter] (1763–1825). An admirer of Jean-Jacques Rousseau (1712–78), Herder finally repudiated the influence of Kant in his *Ideen zur Philosophie der Geschichte der Menschheit* (1784–91). Although often regarded as a freethinker, he represents not so much the rationalist side of the Enlightenment as the interest in art, poetry, and literature that was to bear fruit in the Sturm und Drang movement and in the preromantic exploration of human harmony with nature in its wildness and its majesty.

Enlightenment rationalism replaced authority, whether that of revelation or that of Aristotle, with human reason as the principal criterion of truth. It was frequently on account of the theological implications, sometimes left merely implicit, of 17th-century discoveries in the natural science, notably in optics, medicine, and astronomy, that the Enlightenment came into conflict with the church. It was not the strongly skeptical and sometimes blasphemous satire that was new, but the attack on authority in the name of scientific experiment. Descartes himself had resisted both the discovery of the circulation of the blood by William Harvey (1578–1657) and the obvious conclusions to be drawn from the experiments with the vacuum of Evangelista Torricelli (1608–47), but these matters were mostly left to scientists, or made merely the subject of amused comment. When the teaching of Cartesianism in France was being widely prohibited, Nicolas Boileau-Despréaux (1636–1711) published in 1671 an *Arrêt burlesque* forbidding Reason to enter the schools of the University of Paris. Galileo Galilei (1564–1642) made numerous discoveries about the pendulum, specific gravity, gravitational force, optics, and the measurement of heat before he adopted the Copernican view that the earth revolved around the sun. It was largely on account of his publication of that view, which appeared to be incompatible with the account of the Creation* in Genesis, that scientific advance was made to appear incompatible with divine revelation.

The most important attack on ecclesiastical authority came when the Oratorian biblical scholar Richard Simon (1638–1712) declared that Moses* could not possibly be the author of all the works attributed to him. The whole run of 1,300 copies of Simon's *Histoire critique du Vieux Testament* was destroyed and had to be republished outside France in 1685, although the Protestant authorities were as enraged as the Catholics. After Simon it is primarily to oblique criticisms of authority that we must turn for evidence of a growing skepticism. The tone was often light, as in the satirical *Lettres persanes* (1721), anonymously published by Charles de Secondat, baron de Montesquieu (1689–1755), purporting to describe Paris as seen through the eyes of travelers from the East, or in Pierre Bayle's tongue-in-cheek use of contradictory historical sources to cast doubt on received views in his great 1696 *Dictionnaire historique et critique,* or in Fontenelle's insinuations about the credibility of miracles in his history of oracles and his book on the history of fables. The first works of more or less open atheism such as *L'homme machine* by Julien-Jean Offray de la Mettrie (1709–51), written in 1747, have a comparatively slender thread of provocative argument beneath an only semiserious surface. Like Paul-Henri Thiry, baron d'Holbach (1723–89) author of the atheistic *Le Système de la nature* (1770), La Mettrie was regarded by Diderot as dangerously compromising to what had become a secularizing campaign.

c) The Enlightenment also manifested itself in national literatures, the visual arts, and music. Other constitutive elements included the development of constitutional liberalism* by Locke, the adoption by Montesquieu in *The Spirit of Laws* (1748) of the natural law theory adopted from Grotius (1583–1645), the economic theories of Adam Smith (1723–90), and the philosophy of Giovanni Battista Vico (1668–1744) for his distinction between scientific and historical explanation. Like all major cultural movements, the Enlightenment contained within itself the seeds of its own disintegration, but it was the last period in European culture when a harmonious synthesis between thought and feeling was still generally possible, even if only among a literate social elite.

• P. Hazard (1954), *European Thought in the Eighteenth Century: From Montesquieu to Lessing,* London.
L.G. Crocker (1959), *An Age of Crisis: Man and World in Eighteenth-Century French Thought,* Baltimore-London.
L.G. Crocker (1964), *Nature and Culture: Ethical Thought in the French Enlightenment,* Baltimore.
P. Gay (1966–70), *The Enlightenment,* 2 vols., London.
A. G. Lehmann (1984), *The European Heritage: An Outline of Western Culture,* London.
J. McManners (1998), *Church and Society in Eighteenth-Century France,* 2 vols., Oxford.

ANTHONY LEVI

See also **Humanism, Christian**

Ephesus, Council of

(A.D. 431)

a) Occasion and the Issue at Stake. The third ecumenical council*, in large part, was born from the tension between two major Christological* movements—that of Antioch, Syria, and that of Alexandria, Egypt. Represented by Athanasius at the Council of Nicaea* (325), the Alexandrian* school especially stressed the divinity and the unity* of the Person of Jesus*, the Word* begotten by the Father* and consubstantial* with the Father. The Antiochene school, which fought strongly against Apollinarius (and Apollinarianism*), stressed the full humanity of the Son of God* and the duality of his nature. This tension was exacerbated after 428, when use of the title *Mother of God (theotokos),* for Mary*, was questioned. Although the name *theotokos* was traditional, Nestorius, the new patriarch of Constantinople, insisted that Mary could be named the mother of *Christ** or the mother of *Jesus,* but not the mother of *God* (Loofs 1905). The association of the Word with Christ was one of conjunction *(sunapheia),* imparting dignity and authority, and not a strict unity *(henôsis)* of "a one and the same" (*ACO* I, 5:1, 29–31).

Cyril*, patriarch of Alexandria, defended the title *theotokos* in the name of the strict unity of Jesus with the incarnate Word (*DCO* II, 1:107). Before the end of 429, there was an exchange of letters, and Pope* Celestine soon became involved as arbitrator. A Roman council demanded that Nestorius retract his views within ten days (*ACO* I, 2:7–12). A synod* in Alexandria in November 430 sent the third letter to Constantinople from Cyril to Nestorius, as well as a list of 12 anathemas (*DCO* II/1:124–26).

b) Events of the Council. On 19 November Emperor Theodosius II warned Cyril and the other metropolitans that he was calling a council at Ephesus during Pentecost, 7 June 431 (*ACO* I, 1, 1:114–16). Instructions for the council's procedure were based on those of the senate and took into consideration the goal of the debates (ibid., 120–21). After 15 days, on 22 June, Cyril opened the council before 154 bishops*, without waiting for the bishops from Syria and the Roman legates, who had sent word that they would arrive soon, and over the objections of Count Candidien, the emperor's delegate, and 68 bishops—of whom only 17 were of Eastern origin (*ACO* I, 4:25–30).

The detailed minutes of the 22 June session are available. After reading documents from the proceedings, upon Cyril's request, and after Nestorius was unsuccessfully summoned to the assembly, a second letter from Cyril to Nestorius was read, as was the response of the accused (*DCO* II/1: 104–12 and 112–24). Afterward, the bishops were asked to approve Cyril's letter and condemn Nestorius, in light of the Nicene doctrine. The vote in favor was unanimous, and Nestorius was deposed from his see: "[W]e have been compelled of necessity...to issue this sad condemnation against him, though we do so with many tears. Our Lord Jesus Christ, who has been blasphemed by him, has determined through this most holy synod that the same Nestorius should be stripped of his episcopal dignity and removed from the college of priests" (DCO II/1: 146–8).

Disorder transpired once the Eastern bishops arrived on 26 June. Their assembly, consisting of more than 50 bishops, excommunicated Cyril and Memnon, the bishop of Ephesus (*ACO* I:1, 5, and 119–24). A rescript from the emperor cancelled the 22 June meeting and ordered the reopening of the council (*ACO* I:1, 3, and 9–10). The Roman legates, who had been given the order to conform to the acts of Cyril, arrived on 10 July. Five sessions were held in the presence of the legates, from 10 to 22 July. At this time, Cyril and Celestine were acclaimed, and the condemnations announced by the Eastern bishops' assembly were voided (*ACO* I:1, 3, 15–26, 53–63, and I:1, 7, 84–117). At the beginning of August Theodosius dissolved the council (*ACO* I:1,7, 142).

c) Assessment of the Council. Over the centuries, all kinds of opinions have been advanced on the canonical value and doctrinal impact of these events, and there have been both "systematic defamation" and "easy apologies" (Camelot 1962). Cyril's great haste and actions, as well as the excesses and sensibilities of the Eastern bishops, make it even more difficult to evaluate these unpleasant gatherings. Cyril, however, had been named president of the council by Pope Celestine (*ACO* I, 2:5–6), and the Roman legates joined together with him as soon as they arrived in Ephesus, delivering letters from the pope (ibid., 22–24). Cyril's council was openly approved by Pope Sixtus III, Celestine's successor, in July 432 (*see ACO* I:1, 7, and 143–45).

Cyril had first turned the council into a "heresy* trial" for Nestorius (De Halleux 1993). However, if the votes for Nestorius's deposition had a formal disciplinary character, Nestorius was censured for reasons of doctrine. To take a position, one had to focus on the Nicene Creed. What was at stake was the doctrine of the unity of the Person* of Christ (the hypostatic* union) and, consequently, Mary's divine maternity. The possibility of "adding anything to the Nicene Creed was systematically rejected. Opinion, nevertheless, hardly ever wavered, and the decisions of the council were considered equivalent to a definition" (Jouassard, *Maria,* 1949).

At Ephesus great importance was attached to the tradition* of the Fathers* and particularly to the Nicene Creed, a confession to which the council forbade any additions (*DCO* II:152–56). The authority* of Rome* was also decisively ascertained because of the calls of Nestorius and Cyril to Celestine in 429, the judgement of the synod of Rome, and the sending of the legates and their role in the council's denouement.

Epilogue: The 433 Formula of Union. After an incredible exchange of letters sent back and forth between the Cyrilians and the Easterners, Ephesus had a happy ending in 433. At the invitation of Emperor Theodosius II, John of Antioch wrote a profession of faith, and this "formula of union" was enthusiastically championed by Cyril of Alexandria (PG 83, 1420): "We confess then our lord Jesus Christ, the only begotten Son of God, perfect God and perfect man of a rational soul and body, begotten before all ages from the Father in his godhead, the same in the last days, for us and for our salvation, born of Mary the virgin, according to his humanity, one and the same consubstantial with the Father in godhead and consubstantial with us in humanity, for a union *(henôsis)* of two natures took place. Therefore we confess one Christ, one Son, one Lord. According to this understanding of the unconfused union, we confess the holy Virgin to be the Mother of God *(theotokos),* because God the Word took flesh and became man and from his very conception, united to himself the temple he took from her" (DCO II/1:164–72).

There are three mentions of the Cyrilian term *henôsis* in the formula. Nestorius's word *sunapheia* is not used to designate the pure union of natures in the unique *prosôpon.* As for Cyril, he spoke clearly of two natures after union and renounced the formulas in the letter to the excommunicated.

• F. Loofs (1905), *Nestoriana,* Halle.
Acts: *ACO* I.
A.J. Festugière (1982), *Éphèse et Chalcédoine: Actes des conciles,* Paris.

Decrees: *COD* 37–74 (*DCO* II/1, 97–174).
N. J. Tanner, Ed. (1990), *Decrees of the Ecumenical Councils,* vol. I, London-Washington, D.C.
♦ P.-T. Camelot (1962), *Éphèse et Chalcédoine,* Paris.
J. Liébaert (1963), "Éphèse (concile d')," *DHGE* 15, 561–74.
A. de Halleux (1993), "La première session du concile d'Éphèse (22 juin 431)," *EThL* 69, 48–87; (1995), "L'accord christologique de 433: Un modèle de réconciliation ecclésiale?" *Communion et réunion: Mélanges J.-M.R. Tillard,* Louvain, 293–300.

GILLES LANGEVIN

See also **Chalcedon, Council of; Christ and Christology; Cyril of Alexandria; Hypostatic Union; Idioms, Communication of; Nestorianism**

Epiclesis

The Biblical notion of epiclesis was understood as a religious tribute and a recourse to God* and his name*. In the Christian tradition* after the New Testament it came to mean either an address to the Trinity*—as in the baptismal act and also perhaps in the more ancient perspective of the eucharistic prayer* (Casel)—or, progressively, as a request, an invocation to God the Father* (to whom the eucharistic prayer is most often addressed) that he send the Holy* Spirit. In the eucharistic prayer of the *Apostolic Tradition,* attributed to Hippolytus of Rome (third century), the Spirit is invoked for the unity* of the Church*. In the fourth and fifth centuries, in the eucharistic prayers of Antioch (Taft 1992) and then of Jerusalem*, it is invoked at the beginning—and for the purpose—of blessing the bread and the wine. In Egypt during the same period, the prayer known as the eucharistic prayer of Serapion includes an epiclesis that calls on the Logos instead of the Spirit. Historians cannot say with certainty if this was a tradition proper to Egypt. More likely, it was an isolated attempt to claim to be under the patronage of Serapion, bishop* of Thmuis, who, along with Athanasius* of Alexandria, was a champion of orthodoxy, an act that probably would have been an attempt to avoid confessing the divinity of the Spirit.

Whatever the case may be, the epiclesis in the Antiochene eucharistic prayers is placed after Christ*'s words at the Last Supper, whereas in the Egyptian eucharistic prayers it comes before those words, except for the double epiclesis, which is placed before and after Christ's words. In the Roman tradition prior to Vatican* II the eucharistic prayer did not include an invocation of the Spirit. However, it was comparable to the Egyptian eucharistic prayers in that, from the fourth century, the account of the institution of the Eucharist* was preceded by a paragraph of request that might be understood as an epiclesis in a broad sense.

In the eucharistic prayers of the Antiochene type (Antioch, Constantinople), the doctrine of the conversion of the bread and wine into the body and blood of Christ developed as an interpretation of the words of the epiclesis, pronounced after the account of the institution, whereas in the Roman eucharistic prayer, from the time of Ambrose* of Milan, it was Christ's words at the Last Supper that were understood as having the effect of consecration. In the second part of the Middle Ages (letter of Benedict XII [1341] on the subject of the Armenians, *DS* 1017), the Antiochene and Roman perspectives no longer seemed compatible, even though the celebration of the Greek eucharistic prayers has never been abandoned in the Communion* of the Roman Church.

Since Vatican II the new eucharistic prayers II, III, and IV in the Roman Mass include a double epiclesis. The Holy Spirit is invoked first before the words of Christ, for the transformation of the bread and wine into the body and blood of Christ; and a second time after the anamnesis, for the sanctification of the communicants. Whatever the historical justifications invoked on this subject in the liturgical traditions of Rome and Egypt, this provision had the merit of giving a place to the Holy Spirit in Roman eucharistic devotion at a time when it was seeking to refocus on the eucharistic prayer.

All of the Protestant eucharistic liturgies* currently include an epiclesis.

• O. Casel (1923), "Zur Epiklese," *JLW3,* 100–102; (1924), "Neue Beiträge zur Epiklese-Frage," ibid. 4, 169–78.
E.J. Kilmartin (1984), "The Active Role of Christ and the Holy

Spirit in the Sanctification of the Eucharistic Elements," *TS* 45, 225–53.
J.H. McKenna (1992), "Eucharistic Prayer: Epiclesis," in A. Heinz, H. Rennings (Ed.), *Gratias agamus: Mélanges B. Fischer,* Fribourg, 283–91.
R. Taft (1992), "From Logos to Spirit: On the Early History of the Epiclesis," ibid., 489–502.

PIERRE-MARIE GY

See also **Holy Spirit; Prayer**

Epieikeia

The term *epieikeia* comes from the Greek *epieikeia* (adj. *epieikes*); it designates a virtue* that is difficult to define: ordinary or everyday virtue, virtue that has nothing heroic or exceptional about it. In the New Testament and patristic writings, it is the virtue expected of Christians. The texts provide us with a full description of epieikeia: one who has it is cool-headed, sensible, and balanced; good, tolerant, and understanding; restrained, down-to-earth, and disdains ostentation. Epieikeia is, essentially, moderation, understanding, and discretion. The epithet *decent* comes closest to capturing the nuances of epieikeia.

Epieikeia became a technical term in the 13th century with the translation of the *Ethica Nicomachea (Nicomachean Ethics),* making available a discussion (1137 *a* 31–1138 *a* 2) of how epieikeia relates to justice*. The two are distinct, but not heterogeneous. Epieikeia is just, but not with regard to law*. It corrects legal justice and is thus superior to it. Law is necessarily limited to prescriptions suited to the generality of cases; it can therefore fail to encompass a special case. Epieikeia, on the other hand, provides the correction that the lawgiver himself would have made if he could have been present. The individual who displays epieikeia does not press legal claims to the limit but accepts reasonable compromises.

The impression that this passage made upon medieval thinkers is suggested by the appeal made to epieikeia by Robert Grosseteste (c. 1175–1253), a translator of Aristotle and a commentator on the *Nicomachean Ethics,* in the course of a denunciation of the excesses of the papal curia delivered before Innocent IV at Lyons in 1250. Epieikeia is "halfway between natural justice and legal justice, and is shown in a judge's unwillingness to punish infringements of positive law that do not offend natural justice, as when legal but unreasonable exactions for ecclesiastical visitations are resisted." The reference to natural justice shows how epieikeia fitted into a train of thought already present in western jurisprudence, the notion of "equity." This gives the use of epieikeia in Western Christendom a context in law that is not present in Aristotle. Thus, epieikeia is never conflated with conscience*: although both relate to the application of a law, conscience does so from the point of view of one who acts, epieikeia from the point of view of one who judges actions. Thomas* Aquinas explicitly equates epieikeia with equity (*ST* IIa IIae, q. 120, a. 1). There are occasions when the law fails to meet the case, and true respect for the law is shown at these times by not taking the law literally, but by doing what justice and the common good require. Epieikeia therefore belongs to the virtue of justice rather than to that of temperance (ibid., a. 2); and it thus contributed to that mingling of jurisprudence and moral theology that produced casuistry*.

With the Renaissance* and Reformation, a shift in emphasis occurred, from moderation to leniency. Seneca's *De clementia,* widely read at that time, describes clemency as an "inclination...to mildness" characteristic of the best judges. It is not a question of pardoning or showing "compassion" (which Seneca thought was a vice), for the goal is to identify precisely what justice demands, remaining within the realm of law. Clemency so conceived was readily identified with epieikeia, which gave rise to a stronger criticism of "strict" justice: not only the occasional special case, but every case requires examining the context, which will moderate the severity with which one views an offense. In the growing Augustinianism* of the 16th century, this context included, as a matter of course, a sense of the judge's own dependence upon the mercy* of God*. The story of the adulterous woman (Jn 7:53–8:11), mediated through mystery plays, was combined with the Reformation emphasis on justification* by faith* to define epieikeia/equity/clemency as a humble moderation in passing judgment, such as befits those who know their own sinfulness (*See* Shakespeare, *Measure for Measure* and *The Merchant of Venice*). Thus, William Perkins (1558–1602), basing his discussion of epieikeia on Philippians 4:5 ("Let your epieikeia be known to all men. The Lord is at hand"), takes the latter part of the text as the clue to the whole. The nearness of divine judgment* demands that we are humble when judging others, since we hope to be treated with mercy ourselves. We are "flesh and blood, and full of infirmities," and society* cannot endure if we judge with the rigor that an angel* might use. This is certainly not a reason to abandon justice, but justice must shake hands with mercy (*See* Ps 85 [84]:11, a text traditionally applied to the crucifixion.) The prince's laws cannot be "perfect and absolute" as God's laws are, but the prince may practice a merciful judgment witnessing to the divine work of reconciliation.

The power of dispensation from law thus came to be seen as an expression of epieikeia. Popes had always strongly maintained their right to deviate from universal ecclesiastic legislation (*DS* 731). Richard Hooker thought that a case could be made for the right of secular powers to dispense with law if absolutely necessary (*Laws of Ecclesiastical Polity* V, 9). Some evils cannot be eliminated, but their effects can be eased by equitable measures (V, 9), since "precepts do always propose perfection" (V, 81, 4)—thus reversing the traditional contrast of precepts* and counsel. The interpretation of epieikeia as higher justice found a new expression in Grotius's contrast between justice "in the strict sense" and justice "in the larger sense," also named "expletive" and "attributive." The latter is concerned with deciding "what things are agreeable or harmful (as to both things present and things to come) and what can lead to either alternative," and with "prudent management in expanding the goods proper to individuals and communities" (prol. 9 *Sq;* chap. I, 1, 8).

• R. Grosseteste, Ed. S. Gieben, "Robert Grosseteste at the Papal Curia: Edition of the Documents," CFr 41 (1971), 340–93.

Hugo Grotius, *De iure belli ac pacis,* Ed. P. C. Molhuysen, Leyden, 1919. (English trans., *The Law of War and Peace*, Tr. F. W. Kelsey, Indianapolis, 1962.)

Richard Hooker, *Laws of Ecclesiastical Polity,* in *Works,* Ed. W. S. Hill, Cambridge, Mass., 1977–93.

William Perkins, *Epieikeia; or, a Treatise of Christian Equitie,* in *Works,* London, 1608.

Thomas Aquinas, *ST* IIa IIae, q. 120; q. 80, a. 1, ad 5; Ia IIae, q. 96, a. 6.

♦ P. G. Caron (1971), *"Aequitas" Romana, "Misericordia" Patristica Ed "Epicheia"Aristotelica Nella Dottrina Dell' "Aequitas" Canonica,* Milan.

F. d'Agostino (1976), *La tradizione dell'epikeia nel Medioevo latino,* Milan.

J. D. Cox (1989), *Shakespeare and the Dramaturgy of Power,* Princeton.

R. W. Southern (1992), *Robert Grosseteste: The Growth of an English Mind in Medieval Europe,* Oxford.

OLIVER O'DONOVAN

See also **Casuistry; Justice; Law and Christianity; Law and Legislation; Virtues**

Epistle of Barnabas. *See* **Apostolic Fathers**

Epistle to Diognetus. *See* **Apostolic Fathers**

Equiprobabilism. *See* **Alphonsus Liguori**

Equivocity. *See* **Analogy**

Erasmus, Desiderius

(1469–1536)

Although Erasmus did not present himself as a theologian belonging to a particular school, he had an immense theological influence at the dawn of the Reformation through his theses in defense of free will (in 1524 against Luther*), a return to evangelic and patristic teachings, the reduction in number of the articles of faith* required for salvation*, Christocentrism, and the primacy of orthopraxy over orthodoxy*. In order to defend what he called "the philosophy of Christ*," Erasmus rejected the Scholastic method of argumentation and its neologisms and used all of the literary genres, including prefaces to his translations or editions of the Scriptures and the Fathers* of the Church, philological *Annotations,* his *Paraphrases* of the Bible*, *Colloquia,* and *Adages.*

The ironic style of his prolific correspondence easily veers into digressions, often allowing Erasmus to defend, as though it were a mere aside, a Christocentric theology* (which was more moral than speculative) without trapping himself in rigid, dogmatic positions. It was in 1516, the year his New Testament was published, that he first used the expression *philosophia Christi:* "Now the philosophy of Christ, which he himself called a rebirth, what is it but the restoration of the nature that was created good?" *(Paraclesis).* The expression—which he afterward sometimes varied as *Christian, evangelical,* or *celestial philosophy*—would henceforth signal in abundance his Christocentric biblism.

a) Life. The illegitimate son of a priest, he was baptized under the first name of Gerhardus Gerhardi; he would later Latinize this to Desiderius and adopt the name of Erasmus. Educated in traditional Scolasticism, and then in the spirit of the *devotio moderna,* as a monk from Steyn, Erasmus set out to study theology at Paris in 1495, then in England under John Colet, who initiated him into the works of Paul and into Florentine Platonism. Erasmus earned a doctorate of theology at Turin in 1506, and in 1516 he published his edition of the Greek New Testament, along with his own translation into classical Latin, dedicating it to Pope Leo X.

Erasmus applied his independent and flexible mind with his unswerving fidelity to the faith and unity* of the Church*. He also had a great love of humanist letters and philological matters, and insisted on inner religion and on the primacy of love* over knowledge. In his *Manual,* he writes "You like the arts? That is good if it is for Christ's sake.... Better to know less and love more." But all these things earned him harsh criticism from the Faculties of Paris and Louvain, who classed him among those *humanisticae theologizantes* whom they reproved.

Erasmus devoted his last years in Basel to the edition of the Fathers of the Church. His editions of Augustine*, Jerome, and Origen* were to remain the authoritative texts for a long time. First censured, and later rehabilitated by natural religion and Enlightenment* thought, Erasmus resurfaced in the 20th century—in his true role of Catholic theologian, irenic, and moralist—as one of the masters of 16th-century humanism.

b) Works and Thought. The Christ-centered thought of Erasmus is based on Holy Scripture and especially on the New Testament. The "philosophy of Christ"—the love of Christ as wisdom*—is developed in the whole of his output. His exhortation to a Christian life proposed in his *Enchiridion Militis Christiani*—or *Manual* (dagger) *of the Christian Soldier* (1503, 2nd Ed. 1518)—constitutes a free commentary on Ephesians 6:11–17. Erasmus defends Paul's tripartite philosophy and some rules of true Christianity. The rules can be summed up as: "Love nothing, admire nothing, expect nothing but Christ or because of him." True piety lies in so doing, and that encompasses religion, theology, and a Christian life.

Erasmus wrote *The Praise of Folly* (1511), which he dedicated to his friend Thomas More, in a playful and paradoxical style. That style allowed him to take digs at all the institutions (including universities, religious orders, and ecclesiastical structures*), plead in favor of the teaching of the Beatitudes, and address his comments to children and simple folk rather than to scholars—for in them weakness becomes strength, and the ignominious death* on the cross transforms into the glorious Resurrection*. He asks: "What do all those Scriptural texts cry out constantly but that all mortals are madmen, even the devout ones, if not that Christ, in order to come and succor the madness of mortals, to a certain extent became a madman" by taking on human nature and by saving mankind through the madness of the cross? In order to symbolize mystical (mysticism*) ecstasy, his speech then amounts to a commentary on Paul, who is also presented as mad (2 Cor 2:16 ff.).

In his *Discourse on Free Will* (1524) Erasmus also gives a theological definition of free will as "a power of will that allows man to use what leads him to salvation," and he stacks up the scriptural references favorable to free will in order to defend a synergy of divine grace* and human will. Erasmus holds that grace bends, then leads the will, which has responded to its call. Incapable since the Fall of finding the good by itself, free will nonetheless cooperates with the good as soon as grace directs it and stimulates it. If that were not the case, Erasmus adds, then sin would not be imputable and God would be nothing but a tyrant.

His *Paraclesis,* one of the prefaces to his edition of the New Testament, harks back to the source of this message by specifying a theological method: "The pure and authentic philosophy of Christ is nowhere presented more felicitously than in the Gospels*, than in the Epistles of the apostles*...; by philosophizing piously, praying more than arguing, seeking to transform ourselves rather than to arm ourselves...if we seek an ideal life, why would we find another example preferable to the model, Christ himself?"

Christian philosophy is nothing other than the Gospels, or rather, in the New Testament, the doctor Christ himself teaching *(ipse Christus).*

Erasmus's theology is, therefore, closer to a pious reading of the Scriptures than to speculations or controversy. It is closer to imitation* of the Gospels and of Christ than to observation of the "Judaic laws"—that is, fixed rituals. And yet, except for certain points where his theoretical audacity is based on a strong sense of the historicity of doctrinal positions, or when he debates the role of mutual love as a condition of the indissolubility of Christian marriage*, it is difficult to find Erasmus lacking in doctrinal fidelity. In the debate against Erasmus over the question of free will, Luther saw very clearly that his opponent had managed to place himself at the center of the theological debate and that he revealed a firm attachment to the Catholic tradition*.

A practitioner of an evangelical and patristic theology, often moved to propose a witty and even an allegorical exegesis* (after all, his masters were Origen, Augustine, and Jerome), skillful at always reconciling it with a scholarly knowledge of the text, Erasmus gives an example of a fruitful alliance of erudite knowledge (historical and philological) and Christian wisdom.

• *Opera omnia,* Ed. J. Le Clerc, 1703–6, Leyden (repr. Olms, 1961).

Opera omnia Desiderii Erasmi Rotterdami, Amsterdam Critical Ed., 1969–.

♦ A. Renaudet (1926), *Érasme, sa pensée religieuse et son action d'après sa Correspondance (1518–1521),* Paris.

E. Gilson (1932), "Le Moyen Age et le naturalisme antique," in *Héloïse et Abélard,* Paris, 1938, 183–224.

H. de Lubac (1964), *Exégèse médiévale,* II, 2, Paris.

L. Halkin (1969), *Érasme et l'humanisme chrétien,* Paris.

J.-P. Massaut (1969), "Humanisme et spiritualité chez Érasme," *DSp* 7/1, 1006–28.

M. A. Screech (1980), *Erasmus: Ecstasy and The Praise of Folly.*

G. Chantraine (1981), *Érasme et Luther, libre et serf arbitre,* Paris-Namur.

A. Godin (1982), *Érasme, lecteur d'Origène,* Geneva.

L. Halkin (1991), *Érasme,* Paris.

P. Walter, *Theologie aus dem Geist der Rhetorik,* Mayence.

P. Jacopin, J. Lagrée (1996), *Érasme, humanisme et langage,* Paris.

Guy Bedouelle

See also **Holy Scripture; Humanism, Christian; Liberty; Luther, Martin; Philosophy; Platonism, Christian**

Erastianism

It is somewhat accidental that the name of the physician Thomas Erastus (Luber), 1523–83, became attached in English-speaking lands to a version of a late medieval tradition* of politico-ecclesiastical thought.

a) Thomas Erastus. A native of Basel, in 1558 Erastus became a professor of medicine in Heidelberg, where Elector Frederick III was shortly to introduce a Reformed Confession. Luber was a prominent opponent of the Genevan model of church government* with independent jurisdiction and successfully advocated the subordination of the presbytery to the civil government. His *Explicatio Gravissimae Quaestiones,* which denied to church authorities even the independent practice of excommunication, anticipated Bodin in its argument for an indivisible civil sovereignty. Attracting the attention of Archbishop Whitgift of Canterbury as a potential apology for royal supremacy, it was published posthumously in London in 1589. Among the Reformed churches, those under the British crown, in Scotland and the English Church of the Westminster Confession (1643), followed an Erastian position, as in the Netherlands did the Remonstrants, whose power was crushed at the Synod of Dort (1619).

b) History of Erastian Theory. While the concept of civil sovereignty over church affairs had remote historical roots in the Roman doctrine of imperium and its Christianized Byzantine and Carolingian expressions, its subsequent development arose from medieval quarrels of royal and imperial powers with the papacy. By the turn of the 14th century, extreme papal claims to temporal and spiritual "plenitude of power" *(plenitudo potestatis)* were eliciting strident counterclaims. In the disputes between Philip IV of France and Pope* Boniface VIII over ecclesiastical property and privileges, royal apologists came close to affirming the king's jurisdictional supremacy, thus preparing the way for the full-blown theory of indivisible civil sovereignty propounded in 1324 by Marsiglio of Padua (another physician), just prior to his becoming embroiled in Ludwig of Bavaria's war with Pope John XXII.

Marsiglio's exposition of indivisible civil sovereignty had three foundational principles, only the second of which was shared by Erastus and Bodin: namely, popular sovereignty*, the identical membership of ecclesiastical and civil polity, and the sharp distinction within the human moral-political community between this-worldly and other-worldly ends. According to Marsiglio, the common will of the people *(populus, universitas)* is the original and perpetual source of political authority* and law*; rulers govern as its chosen representatives, and their actions are instrumental to and dependent upon the corporate body politic. As the citizen body in a Christian polity is also the body of believers, its unified will on ecclesiastical as on secular matters must be expressed in a single coercive jurisdiction. The ecclesiastical matters that lie within the jurisdictional competence of the body of believers and its governing agent pertain to this-worldly, or public and institutional, aspects of Christian faith* and practice, and include the selection, education, and appointment of clergy, the disposition of church* finances and property, the authoritative determination of church doctrine and practice, and the punishment of heresy* and other grave violations of divine law. The matters of faith and morals belonging exclusively to priestly authority pertain to Christ's judgment and the salvation* of believers in "the next world" and involve no human jurisdictional competence in this one.

Marsiglio's theory of unitary sovereignty contributed an influential laicizing strand to the conciliarist movement of the late 14th and 15th centuries, in that he invested the authority to define doctrine and practice in the universal body of believers represented at a general church council, to be convoked not by the pope but by the imperial government, which would also (along with lesser civil rulers) enforce conciliar decisions. Throughout the late medieval, Renaissance* and early Reformation periods, royal and imperial powers looked upon general church councils as tools to restrain the jurisdictional pretensions of the papacy, which the Councils of Constance* (1414–18) and Basel* (1431–49) and the conciliabulum of Pisa (1511–12) attempted to do.

The tradition of Sorbonnist conciliarism*, from d'Ailly and Gerson to Almain and Mair, provided crucial formulations of a natural-law basis for church polity into the 16th century, thereby fostering both Erastian and Gallican ecclesiologies. The English reform under Henry VIII and Edward VI asserted the monarch's authority as "Supreme head in earth, nexte under Christe, of the Churche," yet preserved a dualism of jurisdiction under the crown through the role of convocation alongside Parliament. In the Elizabethan era, as the rhetoric was curtailed (giving the queen "the cheefe government"), so the jurisdiction was unified, and Parliament assumed the dominant role. The most formative exposition of the Erastian position in the English church, Richard Hooker's *Laws of Ecclesiastical Polity,* accomplished its defense of the Elizabethan Settlement through the interweaving of natural-law and biblical theological models in a manner characteristic of the Paris masters. However, his insistence on the identical membership of ecclesiastical and civil polity in a Christian commonwealth and on the solely sacramental powers of the priesthood brings him closer to Marsiglio than to his Sorbonnist predecessors.

- G. de Lagarde (1934–46), *La naissance de l'esprit laïque au déclin du moyen âge,* Paris.

H. Kressner (1953), *Schweizer Ursprünge des anglikanischen Staatskirchentums,* Gütersloh.
R. Wesel-Roth (1954), *Thomas Erastus: Ein Beitrag zur Geschichte der reformierten Kirche und zur Lehre von der Staatssouveränität,* Lahr-Baden.
W. Speed Hill (Ed.) (1972), *Studies in Richard Hooker: Essays Preliminary to an Edition of His Works,* Cleveland.
M. Löffelberger (1992), *Marsilius von Padua: Das Verhältnis zwischen Kirche und Staat im "defensor pacis,"* Berlin.
A. S. McGrade (Ed.) (1997), *Richard Hooker and the Construction of Christian Community,* Tempe, Ariz.
C. Russell (2000), "Parliament, the Royal Supremacy and the Church," *Parliamentary History* 19, 27–37.

JOAN LOCKWOOD O'DONOVAN
AND OLIVER O'DONOVAN

See also **Calvinism; Church and State; Conciliarism; Council; Gallicanism; Political Theology; Society**

Eros. *See* **Love**

Eschatology

1. Concept

The term *eschatology*—literally, "doctrine of the last thing" *(eschaton)*—appeared in the 17th century, but it is only since Schleiermacher* that it has been used increasingly to refer to the problematic (the "treatise") that comes last in the theological curriculum. Previously, this had been customarily entitled *De novissimis* (On the Last Things). In general, eschatology is concerned with the goal and fulfillment of creation*, and the history* (individual and universal) of salvation*. Here, fulfillment not only means completion with time*, and an ending within space, but addresses the theme of Christian hope*. Everything that God* has created to be called to "fullness of life" does not return to nothingness*, but attains, in its totality and in each of its parts, the internal and lasting fullness of its essence, by being admitted to participation in the eternal life* of God. This presupposes, however, that the world* as we apprehend it has ceased to exist in time and space, or, better, that our present world is liberated from its fragility within the spatial and temporal order. It is indeed impossible to conceive of this fulfillment, that is, of the integral and lasting fullness of the whole, with all its components, under spatial and temporal conditions.

2. History of Eschatology

a) Early Church. In the first two centuries A.D., the end of the world and the return of Christ* were generally regarded as imminent. For this reason, the New Testament's proclamation of Christ's Resurrection*—which both realized and intensified the promises of the Old Testament—did not prompt any far-reaching reflection on the fulfillment that was promised. Instead, this was envisaged as a direct consequence, or even as a simple "extension," of Christ's Resurrection. The first major theological systems, which emerged from the early third century onward, tended to integrate eschatology into a vast theology* of history, seen through the prism of Christology*. Irenaeus* of Lyon, for example, writes of the "recapitulation and fulfillment of the history of salvation in Christ," and Augustine* addresses the theme of fulfillment with the formulation "from Christ alone *(Christus solus)* to the whole Christ *(Christus totus),* head and body." Alongside these large-scale perspectives, we also find some detailed eschatological statements and reflections on the "how," the "when," and the "where" of the fulfillment. These were developed by bringing together, often in a forced manner, scriptural passages related to these questions, intertestamental and apocalyptic* treatments of the end of the world, and philosophical considerations on the fulfillment of the ages. Some authors also invoked specific themes of eschatology, such as the resurrection of the dead, in order to combat gnosis* and its disembodied spiritualism, or, in the form of the coming of judgment* and the pains of hell*, in order the better to exhort human beings to act in a morally responsible manner. Both these themes appear, most notably, in the writings of Irenaeus and Tertullian*.

In addition, there was a tension to be resolved between, on the one hand, a conception of fulfillment as the *internal result* of the dynamic present in the history of salvation, and, on the other hand, a conception of fulfillment that related it to the notion of a ready-made salvation waiting in the afterlife which human beings only had to rejoin. Whenever this latter, ultimately nonhistorical conception prevailed—fulfillment as a sort of transition from this world to a celestial beyond—the development of millenarian ideas about the establishment of an earthly and messianic kingdom, before the world ended, was not unusual. These were intended to do justice to the idea, advanced notably in the Old Testament, that there would be an age of salvation, belonging (also) to historical time, to which the internal dynamic of the kingdom* of God, now being prepared, was leading (Justin, Papias, Irenaeus). This conception was developed into an eschatology by the early church*, despite the many questions and contradictions inherent in it: "Only the extreme spiritualization of eschatology, on the one hand, and complete millenarianism, on the other, were finally rejected" (E. May, *TRE* 10, 300).

b) Middle Ages. This situation began to change with medieval theology, which concluded the dogmatic theology with a treatise specifically concerned with eschatology.

From the time of Peter Lombard onward, the systematic framework for such treatises was usually provided by the doctrine of the sacraments* (Alexander of Hales), but there were also other approaches: eschatological themes were introduced into theologies of creation and/or grace* (Thomas* Aquinas, Bonaventure*). As in the early church, however, eschatology was envisaged above all as the conclusion to, or as an integral part of, Christology. These perspectives, pertinent in and of themselves, were not, however, integrated into an overarching, complete, and coherent conception of eschatology.

It was Scholasticism* that determined the later development of eschatology by incorporating it into a cosmological ontology dominated by the Aristotelian "scientific" ideal, and thus cutting it off from any foundation in the eschatological and apocalyptic beliefs that still flourished as part of popular piety. The result was to enclose eschatology within a doctrine of future events and places, more or less seen as *things* that were bound to be realized at the end of history and beyond it. Eschatology was almost assimilated to a "judicial inquiry" into ephemeral earthly realities, the future that would go beyond them, and the events that were to be involved in the transition from one sphere to the other. Yet there was no clear delineation of the essential internal link between history and eschatological fulfillment, other than the idea of a strict correspondence between the individual's behavior during his or her earthly existence and his or her dispatch to heaven or hell. All the eschatological statements in the Bible* (Christ's return, the end of the world, resurrection, and the rest) were interpreted exclusively in relation to the future end and to what lay beyond the whole of history; and, following *Benedictus Deus,* the dogmatic constitution of 29 January 1336 (*DS* 1000–1002), there was a particular emphasis on the fulfillment of the individual soul*. There was, then, at least a fear that eschatology would become a matter of less and less concern in this world; and Christian hope was in danger of losing sight of the present reality of everyday life and the need to confront history. Late Scholasticism and, in its wake, Neoscholasticism, kept up this reifying approach, which degenerated into a veritable "physics of *eschata* [last things]" (Y. Congar).

c) Early Modern Period. Reformation theology marked the emergence of a more "existential" and Christocentric approach to eschatology: for Luther*, for example, the faith that justifies was a *truly eschatological* reality (*see* Asendorf). However, what we may appropriately call Reformation orthodoxy went on to join with more traditional approaches. During the Enlightenment*, eschatology, whether Catholic or Protestant, came to be focused on the question of the immortality of the soul, and thus became part of the purely functional perspective of teaching on the rewards and punishments for moral conduct. Accordingly, to a large extent theological eschatology made itself responsible for its own secularization*, for if the central theme of eschatology is morality, then every transcendental dimension is eventually and decisively shown to be superfluous. The main question then becomes whether humanity can be "humanized" and thus establish the "kingdom of God on Earth." The eschatology of the Enlightenment gave rise to the modern utopias that eventually culminated in Marxism (Marx*).

It was only with Schleiermacher, and after him, that broader conceptions were asserted once again, both within Protestant theology and in the Catholic school of Tübingen* in the 19th century. These new approaches, influenced by idealist philosophy*, were based on the conviction that history has an internal teleology, relating it to a kingdom of God that develops and progresses toward its final form. Such perspectives were eliminated from Catholic theology by the Neoscholastics' understanding of eschatology, which conformed in this respect to late Scholasticism. By contrast, within the churches born out of the Reformation, and notably in "liberal Protestantism," the idea of the kingdom of God was reduced to a moral reality given in the present state of the cultural existence of humanity (A. Ritschl). This interpretation distorted a crucial biblical concept in a completely anti-eschatological way.

d) 20th-Century Theology. An authentic renewal of eschatology took place in the early years of the 20th century among the representatives of what has been called "consistent eschatology" (J. Weiss, A. Schweitzer), who protested against the "reduction" of eschatology and argued that the expectation of an imminent irruption of the *eschaton* into history was a determining trait of primitive Christianity. The irrevocable sense of imminence in which the New Testament had been written was integrated programmatically, but not without far-reaching reinterpretation, into dialectical theology. Barth* certainly states that if Christianity were not absolutely and completely eschatology then it would be absolutely and completely foreign to Christ (*Der Römerbrief,* 1922). For the early Barth, however, biblical statements were no more than arguments and conceptual means for rejecting liberal Protestantism's synthesis between the kingdom of God and the world of human culture, and for reestablishing an antithetical relationship between God and humanity: all eschatological statements are no more than *ciphers* for the sovereign transcendence of God in relation to the contingency and futility of created beings, who are touched by God only tangentially, at the moment of their encounter. In this *kairos,* the *eschaton* is present at every moment, as the transcendental meaning of all moments. Consequently, the end that is called for in the New Testament is not a temporal event, not a fabulous "end of the world"; it bears no relation to any hypothetical historical catastrophes, be they earthly or cosmic (ibid.). Barth then distanced himself from this conception and, with hindsight, had to make the following confession (*KD* II/1, 716): "It appears... that, having taken seriously the transcendental nature of the kingdom of God that is to come, I put myself at risk of not taking at all seriously his coming as such.... It may be seen... how, with skill and eloquence, I neglected the teleology that it [Scripture] ascribes to time, and the idea of its progression toward a real end."

Bultmann* went in a different direction, adopting the perspective of existential analytics developed by the early Heidegger* to describe the New Testament *kerugma* (proclamation) as an "eschatological event," in the sense that the proclamation of the Word* of God tears human beings away from their lack of liberty in order to make them achieve liberty*. This new liberty is the *eschaton,* given and realized in the present, and every notion of a future that is still held in reserve within time is radically relativized (*Geschichte und Eschatologie,* 1958): "Do not look around you in universal history; on the contrary, you must look within your own personal history.... In each moment the possibility that it will be the eschatological moment lies dormant. You must awaken it from its sleep."

This "axiological" eschatology of dialectical and existential theology entailed a general broadening of the concept, to the extent that *eschatological* has since come to mean "definitively or supremely valid." These attempts retain their importance: for the first time, there had been an endeavor to arrive at a coherent understanding of the imagery in eschatological formulas and to expound their theological meaning. However, those who remained loyal to traditional eschatology (notably O. Cullmann) responded to these attempts by arguing that, in reinterpreting the temporal future as a theological or existential opening to the future, they had evaded or eliminated the very dimension of the concrete future that the world and history still contain for us. It is precisely this deficit that has shaped the contemporary reorientation of eschatology.

3. Contemporary Problems and Priorities in Eschatology

a) Eschatology in the Theologies of Grace and History. In the second half of the 20th century, eschatology has primarily been shaped by the desire to understand, from the perspective of a theology of grace and a theology of history, what the Bible and tradition* have to say about the end of time.

The "new theology" (notably, Lubac*) has described how God's grace is present throughout reality, tending dynamically toward its own fulfillment. Both as a whole, and through its specific statements, eschatology tells us something about the fulfillment of what is now at work within creation and history: the dynamic of God's grace.

The treatment of eschatology from the point of view of the theology of history can be traced to two scholars above all others—W. Pannenberg and J. Moltmann—and, in Moltmann's case, to his dialogue with Marxism (E. Bloch). Both these theologians argued, each in his own way, that the history of salvation, culminating in Jesus Christ, is made known through certain anticipations of the promised fulfillment, which thus become a stimulus to our understanding of universal history (Pannenberg) as well as to human action* (Moltmann). According to Moltmann, God no longer is the "wholly other" *(der ganz Ändere)* situated *above* history but, because he asks for the historical commitment of humankind, he is the one who "makes everything other" *(der ganz Ändernde) within* history. Thus, the promised *eschaton* is always also a renewed and critical questioning of all the forces that reject the future that God has promised (eschatology as social critique). Within Catholicism, it has principally been Karl Rahner* and, in his wake, Johann Baptist Metz, who have emphasized this critical function and responded to the challenge of Marxism by articulating the future of the divine promise with the future of human action within history. Here, the "absolute future" of God is brought to bear against intrahistorical utopias, but it leaves human beings free to shape their own futures adequately, for Rahner and Metz reject the idea of a *totalitarian* human programming of the future, and place every action under an "eschatological reservation." On the other hand, believers may perceive a contradiction between the biblical promises* and their present condition of loss and lack of liberty, in such a way that the concrete critical negations implicit in eschatological proclamations open up to them possibilities and motives for action. As against this conception of a fairly indirect and dialectical link between a transcendent eschatological future and an immanent future, South American liberation* theology has sought to order these two dimensions of the future in a more direct manner, where it has not simply identified them with each other. G. Gutiérrez (1971), for example, writes: "The growth of the kingdom is a process that is realized historically *within* liberation, to the extent that liberation means a better realization of humanity and the condition for a new society. Yet it goes beyond this, for it is realized in historical facts that have the potential for liberation, it denounces their limits and their ambiguities, it announces its complete fulfillment, and it impels it forward, in effect, toward total communion. We are not faced with an identification: without liberatory historical events, there can be no growth of the kingdom."

It was on the basis of very different premises that Pierre Teilhard de Chardin attempted to reconcile history (and the cosmos*) with eschatology. He understood the whole of reality, from inanimate nature to humanity and its cultural expression, as a process of continuous evolution* toward the absolute future of "the omega point," where the Whole is united with God, who is its motor, the point of convergence, the guarantee—in a word, the principle—of evolution (Teilhard 1955). However, this attempt has remained somewhat isolated, not to say marginal, within the framework of the most recent developments in eschatology, doubtless also because of the scientific questions and problems of interpretation that it raises.

b) Eschatological Hermeneutics. Aside from the perspectives opened up by the theology of grace and the theology of history, since the middle of the 20th century we have witnessed the development of various attempts to construct a specific hermeneutics* for eschatological texts. These attempts offer a new understanding of the *eschata,* opposed to the "reification" and "historicization" to which they were subjected by late Scholasticism. It is generally agreed that such a hermeneutics obeys the following "principles":

1) Eschatological statements are concerned with the fulfillment promised by God and hoped for by humanity, which is the goal of the whole of creation, and toward which history is still progressing at the present moment. From this point of view, these texts are prophetic *indications* of the coming of God and the realization of his promise, and they call on human beings to prepare themselves and to place themselves hopefully on the road. However, they are not apocalyptic *predictions* capable of informing us about the unfolding of a goal that has been programmed in advance within the divine plan, or about a future that is already in a finished state in the beyond, toward which creation does nothing other than move forward.
2) The hope for the fulfillment of individual and universal history beside God, in God, and with God—indeed, the whole content of eschatology—should be interpreted in a resolutely personal sense, rather than in objective or spatial

terms. Augustine remarked long ago that our "place," after death, is God himself. Eschatology in this sense has nothing to do with the dramatic production of a "Last Judgment," nor with heavenly felicity and the like, but is related to God who *exists* "as the heaven that we have gained, as the hell from which we have escaped, as the tribunal that examines us, and as the purgatory that purifies us" (Balthasar* 1960). However, as God is the mystery* that infinitely surpasses human beings, all statements related to fulfillment are essentially connected with the core of this mystery, and should be read as having been shaped by a negative* theology rather than an affirmative one.

3) It must not be forgotten that eschatological formulas are to be taken as figurative. To the extent that hope is turned toward something that is humanly "impossible," it is precisely the function of an image to open up the imagination and to prepare for what is to come from God, beyond human possibilities. Yet the images of Christian hope are not simply "dream visions": they are "extrapolations," that is, "extensions" into the future, of experiences of salvation, or perdition, that have already been acquired. God does not come only "at the end" to complete the creation of the external world: it is the whole of history that bears the mark of the salvific coming of God, whose every act goes beyond himself to an absolute fulfillment. That is why the history of salvation recorded in Scripture* already provides "documentation" from which it is possible to extrapolate the future fulfillment and its structures. It is in this way alone, as extrapolated images and not as "reports from the future," that eschatological formulas must be interpreted in order to reveal their true "content."

There are two projects within contemporary theology that, although they have different emphases, are both aimed at developing a more precise and systematic interpretation of this hermeneutic operation. According to Hans Urs von Balthasar, eschatology is above all an "extended Christology": all eschatological statements are primarily concerned with Christ, and only then, by extrapolation, with ourselves as well. It is therefore necessary to "read" what happens at death, and what judgment, heaven, and fulfillment are, first of all in relation to Christ, before extending them to ourselves, but in such a way that Christ is, and always remains, the indispensable mediator of the fulfillment of created beings. By contrast, Rahner sees eschatology as being principally an "extended anthropology," even though it may find its condensed expression in the figure of Christ: the *eschaton* fulfils what has already been given to us in our present experiences of grace. Accordingly, these experiences constitute the basis from which we can extrapolate toward a future fulfillment, and thus connect the eschatological images in the Bible and tradition to their real content. These two ways of putting a specific hermeneutics of eschatology to work are not mutually exclusive, but are strictly coordinated.

4. Central Eschatological Statements in Context

While the fulfillment promised by God is certainly unitary, it is related to creation, in all its multiplicity and temporality, and therefore takes on a multiple and temporal form.

a) Eschatological fulfillment concerns human beings as individuals and as members of communities. That is why eschatology speaks as much of the end of the individual, in death*, and of individual fulfillment—the immortality of the soul, or resurrection, purification (purgatory), felicity with God—as of the end of humanity, and its universal fulfillment as an entity endowed with "solidarity," in the end of the world, the resurrection of the dead, the last judgment, heaven, and hell. Since creation also has both material and spiritual dimensions, eschatology must also take care to distinguish their respective modes of fulfillment: "the separated soul," the resurrection of the body, the new heaven and the new earth.

b) The fulfillment of the soul is not simply a matter of progressive and harmonious development in God. On the contrary, history is marked by antagonisms, born out of evil* and impiety, suffering and futility. This is why eschatology speaks of judgment, in which what is capable of being fulfilled is "separated" from what is not.

c) In fulfillment, it is God himself who realizes the fullness of humanity, but within the "time of pilgrimage" of this life human liberty can come into conformity with God or reject him. Accordingly, eschatology should speak not only of heaven, as the fulfillment of felicity, but also of hell, as the *immanent consequence* to which a liberty that radically rejects God is exposed. However, heaven and hell are not to be understood as being on the same plane, as two essentially symmetrical possibilities of fulfillment. God has done everything to bring about the salvation of humanity, and human beings themselves, such as they have been created, tend more toward Yes than toward No. That is why hope for a positive fulfillment, that is, hope for heaven, prevails absolutely over fear of hell. Radical rejection, and therefore also hell, remain possibilities nonetheless, and are inseparable from human liberty.

d) Although eschatology speaks of the definitive future of creation in the presence of God at the end of time, it is true, nevertheless, that God has already been communicating with the world throughout the whole span of time, in the external events of the history of salvation, which culminated in Christ, in the sacramental acts of the church, and in the communication of grace to human beings. From this point of view, eschatology is not merely the specific treatise in dogmatics relating to the future, it is also a decisive dimension of theology taken as a whole. Indeed, it exists in numerous forms of "present eschatology," in which the final and the definitive are projected in anticipation, and human beings are encouraged to support and shape the "penultimate" reality of the world and history in the light of the "ultimate" reality. Earthly existence and history thus become, as Vatican* II declared, the "antechamber" in which human beings can already catch "a glimpse of the world to come"; what is more, it is in earthly existence and history that the "material of the heavenly kingdom" is formed, which human beings must carry, as the product of their history, into the fulfillment that is to come (*GS* 38, 39).

Such a conception retains some of the central meanings of millenarianism and worldly utopianism: the insistence on the fulfillment of the earthly quest for justice*, peace*, and humanization, and therefore on the fulfillment of earthly history. However, it would be a mistake to suppose that the potential for hope within creation is thus exhausted, or to lose sight of the lasting antagonism that pervades history. The fulfillment of creation can only be produced beyond the world as it now exists, with God himself, through the admission of humanity, as the communion* of saints, into participation in the life of communion of the triune God.

• P. Teilhard de Chardin (1955), *Le phénomène humain,* Paris.

H. U. von Balthasar (1960), "Umrisse der E.," *Verbum Caro,* Einsiedeln, 276–300.

K. Rahner (1960), "Theologische Prinzipien der Hermeneutik eschatologischer Aussagen," *Schr. zur Th.* 4, 401–28, Einsiedeln-Zurich-Köln.

J. Mouroux (1962), *Le Mystère du temps,* Paris.

J. Moltmann (1964), *Theologie der Hoffnung,* Munich.

K. Rahner (1965), "Marxistische Utopie und christliche Zukunft des Menschen," *Schr. zur Th.* 6, 77–88, Einsiedeln-Zurich-Köln.

W. Pannenberg (1967), *Grundfragen systematischer Theologie,* Göttingen, 91–185.

G. Greshake (1969), *Auferstehung der Toten,* Essen.

K. Rahner (1970), "Die Frage nach der Zukunft," *Schr. zur Th.* 9, 519–40, Einsiedeln-Zurich-Köln.

G. Gutiérrez (1971), *Teología de la liberación,* Lima.

D. Wiederkehr (1974), *Perspektiven der E.,* Einsiedeln-Zurich-Köln.

G. Greshake, G. Lohfink (1975), *Naherwartung-Auferstehung-Unsterblichkeit,* Freiburg-Basel-Vienna, 1982.

G. Martelet (1975), *L'au-delà retrouvé,* Paris (New Ed. 1995).

C. Schütz (1976), "Allgemeine Grundlegung der E.," *MySal* V, 553–700.

J. Ratzinger (1977), *E.: Tod und ewiges Leben,* Regensburg, 1990.

U. Asendorf (1982), "E.," *TRE* 10, 310–34.

H. U. von Balthasar (1983), *Theodramatik* IV, Einsiedeln.

G. Greshake, J. Kremer (1986), *Resurrectio Mortuorum,* Darmstadt (repr. 1992).

M. Kehl (1986), *E.,* Würzburg.

Gisbert Greshake

See also **Beatitude; Hell; History; Hope; Life, Eternal; Limbo; Parousia; Vision, Beatific**

Esoterism. *See* **Theosophy**

Essence. *See* **Being; Deity; Nature**

Eternity of God

The Eternal is my rock, my shepherd, my light, the Psalms* say. For a long time, it seemed completely natural that this adjective substituted for the name of YHWH in more than one translation of the Bible*. In his *Consolation of Philosophy,* Boethius* said that any man of sense recognizes that God* is eternal. But what does he recognize exactly?

1. The Bible

The term that is often translated as "eternal" or "eternity" is *'olâm*—or *aiôn* in the Septuagint (the first Greek translation of the Hebrew Bible, begun in the third century B.C.). It did not originally designate the pure timelessness of God, but at first simply attributed an immense duration to him. It recognized in him an immemorial and indestructible existence. This existence is contrasted to the precariousness of the world* in Psalm 102 [101]:26 ff., a text that is applied to Christ by Hebrews 1:10 ff. It is also contrasted to the mortality of humanity—for example, in Psalm 90 [89] and Deuteronomy 5:23–26, God is the living God; in Deuteronomy 32:40, he says, "As I live forever." His presence and action dominate time*. In his eyes, "a thousand years…are but as yesterday when it is past, or as a watch in the night" (Ps 90:4; 2 Pt 3:8). Furthermore, God remembers his Covenant* "forever" (*lé 'olâm*)—or literally, for "a thousand generations," (Ps 105 [104]:8). He is "from everlasting"—(*mé'olâm,* Ps 93:2), and he was God before he had "formed the earth and the world, from everlasting to everlasting" (Ps 90:2). In this sense, as early as second Isaiah, eternity is clearly a divine attribute (Sasse 1933). This theme is reinforced by that of the preexistence of Wisdom* (Prv 8:22–31; Sir 1:1 [*eis ton aiôna*], 24:9) and of Christ* (e.g., Jn 1; Phil 2:6).

2. Theology

a) Classic Conception. In the Bible eternity is first and foremost a time without end and it cannot be imagined in another way, as is said again and again (*See* al-Razi in Arnaldez 1986; Sasse; Ernst 1995). This does not mean that God is attributed the same kind of duration as our duration, even if unlimited. Even this unlimited quality should be thought about, and can only be considered using the resources of philosophy*. This is why it seems vain to regret the Hellenization* of Christianity regarding this point, as Oscar Cullmann does. It is not certain, moreover, that the first Christians had a "naïve" view of the eternity of God as a time prolonged indefinitely (Cullmann 1946). It may even have been their faith* in an eternal God that allowed them to feel affinity with Platonism (Pannenberg 1988), particularly in the form it took with Plotinus.

For Plotinus, when one says that the eternal is "forever," it is an image to say that it is *veritably* (*Enneads* III. 7. 6). Plotinus did not restrict himself to opposing a timeless eternity to a time that is not related to it; he turns eternity into the fullness of a life that is totally present to itself. "Eternity is God himself exposed…as he is" (*Enneads* III. 7. 5), the one "in whom nothing is missing and to whom nonbeing could not be added" (*Enneads* III. 7. 4); or, as Bossuet would say with regard to the eternity of God, "the one in whom nonbeing has no place" (*Élévations sur les mystères,* I. 3). Plotinus also talks about the relationship of time to eternity, even if only in the mythical form of the fall of the soul* that produces time in its anxiety (*Enneads* III. 7. 11). These elements would inevitably serve theological reflection. We find them, at least until the 17th century, modified accordingly, in what can be called classic considerations of the question (e.g., Petau 1644). Augustine* draws a close parallel between the eternity of God and his immutability*, and radically opposes time, created (*Confessions* XI. xiii, e.g.) and characteristic of the changing creature (*Enarrationes in Psalmos 121,* PL 37, 1623), with eternity, "the very substance of God, in which there is no change" (*Enarrationes in Psalmos 101 [102],* PL 37, 1311).

Boethius is more similar to Plotinus, as can be seen in his definition of eternity: "the complete, simultaneous, and perfect possession of life without end" (*interminabilis vitae tota simul et perfecta possessio; Consolation* V. 6). The word *interminabilis,* here, does not mean "interminable" in the usual sense, which connotes the whole experience and all the impatience of time; its rather designates the positive infinity of the being* of God, which we only understand negatively (*see ST* Ia, q. 10, a. 1, ad. 1). Boethius clearly defines the difference between a life that is simply "interminable" and the fullness of presence of life to itself to which a duration cannot be assigned *(aliud est... per interminabilem duci vitam... aliud interminabilis vitae totam pariter complexum esse praesentiam).* The world is perhaps "perpetual," but only God is "eternal."

These thoughts would be adopted and systematized by Thomas* Aquinas, for whom it is certainly not the fact of having neither beginning nor end that defines eternity with regard to time (*ST* Ia, q. 10, a. 4), but the simultaneity of presence to oneself (Ia, q. 13, a. 11). In this sense, God is not in time, but time is in God (ibid., a. 2, ad. 4, a. 4; Ia, q. 14, a. 13; q. 57, a. 3). Thus, Thomas explains the paradox of God's knowledge of future contingents, which he does not anticipate, but rather sees as present (*prout sunt in sua praesentialitate,* Ia, q. 14, a. 13), since "at every moment in time, eternity is present" (*CG* I, 66).

b) Modernity. This classic conception was adopted again at the end of the 19th century by Vatican* I, which included eternity in the list of divine attributes (*DS* 3001; *see* Lateran* IV, *DS* 800). Yet, it was already not as fitting, contrary to what Boethius thought. Certainly, the negative aspect of eternity prevailed over its positive aspect in academic theology*, and eternity was no longer seen as simple timelessness. However, philosophies on future and on the evolution of the Holy Spirit and the Absolute (Hegel*, Schelling*) dominated at the time, and therefore first enhanced historicity. The eternity that Zarathustra loved was different from the one Augustine held dear (*cara aeternitas; Conf*essions VII. x). It was, rather, an exalted absolute version of the future, of the "eternal return" to which Nietzsche* often turned. All of this made it difficult to see in immutability, impassiveness, the eternity of the positive attributes of divinity. It seemed more appropriate to define death* than life, of which Boethius spoke. There was only life if there was dynamism, future, progress, and conflict perhaps, and this had to be true of the living par excellence. This point of view still thrives: today, the word *static* is clearly pejorative, as opposed to the positive sense that ancient philosophy lent to *nunc stans.* To answer Augustine's question *vis tu... stare?* (PL 37, 1623), we would tend resolutely to say "no." Thus, contemporary theology, in many cases, aims to think about the "dynamism" of God, or at least his close connection to temporality and history*, which seems indispensable in understanding his love* for humanity. In extreme cases, as in "process* theology," eternity is diluted in the undefined future of "events" that do not even form a world. In more classical theologies, thoughts of the past are not dismissed, but they are considered in new terms, by going back to biblical categories. Thus Karl Barth* comes to consider the eternity of God as a duration—"the time of God" *(KD* II/1, 691). It is so full that it has none of the limitations, instability, or disjunctions of created time (691); in a certain way, it constitutes the shape of Trinitarian life (693–4); it contains time (698)—God "has time for us," and "he has time because he has eternity" (689)—and it is possible that it becomes temporal in Jesus Christ (695–6). One would even have to define it as pre-, super-, and post-temporality (698).

This lordship of God over time that Barth recognizes (692) is also asserted by Joseph Ratzinger (1959). Ratzinger is not satisfied either with a negative conception of eternity. This lordship takes shape in the Incarnation*, in which God participated in time to bring man to participate in his eternity (ibid.). One understands that, from this point of view, "eternal" life promised to men is in no way a simple life forever, bearing nothing of the eternity of God—and here we come back to Boethius. This, moreover, is where the interest lies in the notion of *aevum,* which was developed by Scholasticism* in order to try to consider the duration of angels* and souls—that is, in seeking to define a paradisiacal duration that is neither the world's time, nor eternity, which belongs to God alone, but which involves both. "Eviternal" beings are fixed in their essence, but their acts are successive. (*ST* Ia, q. 10, a. 5 and 6).

• Boethius, Anicius Manlius Torquatus Severinus, *De Consolatione Philosophiae* V, 6 (LCL 74).
K. Barth, *KD* II/1, §31.3 (*Dogmatique,* Geneva, 1957).
Plotinus, *Enneads* III. 7.
Thomas Aquinas, *ST* Ia, q. 10.
♦ D. Petau (1644), *Theologica Dogmata,* vol. I. l. III (Ed. Vivès, Paris, 1865).
J. Guitton (1933), *Le temps et l'éternité chez Plotin et saint Augustin,* Paris (3rd Ed. 1959).
H. Sasse (1933), "Aiôn," *ThWNT* 1, 197–209.
O. Cullmann (1946), *Christus und die Zeit,* Zurich.
J. Schierse, J. Ratzinger, K. Jüssen (1959), "Ewigkeit," "Ewigkeit Gottes," *LThK*2 3, 1267–71.
E. Jüngel (1976), *Gottes Sein ist im Werden,* Tübingen.
R. Arnaldez (1986), "Kidam," *EI (F),* New Ed., 5, 97 *b*-101.
D.H. Preuß (1986), "'Olâm,'" *ThWAT* 5, 1144–59.
W. Pannenberg (1988), *Systematische Theologie,* vol. 1, chap. 6, §6, Göttingen.
W. Hasker (1989), *God, Time and Knowledge,* Ithaca-London.
A. Paus, J. Ernst, P. Walter (1995), "Ewigkeit, Ewigkeit Gottes," *LThK*3 3, 1082–84.

IRÈNE FERNANDEZ

See also **Attributes, Divine; Immutability/Impassibility, Divine; Justice, Divine; Knowledge, Divine; Life, Eternal; Omnipresence, Divine; Omnipotence, Divine; Platonism, Christian; Predestination; Providence; Simplicity, Divine**

Ethics

Every society* maintains its identity, coherence, and continuity through a set of values, rules, and practices that constitute its moral tradition. This is possible because human beings are social beings that depend on one another and have other interests beyond their own private concerns; it is necessary because human beings are also selfish beings with an inclination to pursue their own interests at the expense of others. One of the functions of moral traditions is to allow human beings to extend themselves by providing them with an authoritative system of acceptable practice. Such traditions also provide the context in which individuals determine their own aspirations and ideals.

Ethics generally refers to the systematic study of morality. It can be normative, seeking to set rules, or descriptive, seeking to systematize a society's virtues*, values, and obligations by placing them back in the context of the society's historical traditions, and in the light of some fundamental and authoritative principle or set of principles. Christian ethics is the study of that which constitutes the moral life in the light of belief in God* as Creator and Redeemer. Hence, whatever function it may ascribe to human moral intuition and reason*, it is fundamentally a "theological ethics," grounded in the will and wisdom* of God. In the Catholic tradition it is generally known as "moral theology*." Christian ethics is rooted in Scripture* and tradition*, but draws from philosophy*; during its early history it was, like the rest of Christian doctrine, much indebted to the Greco-Roman heritage.

1. Greco-Roman Heritage

a) Morality and Religion. Many mythological stories were far from edifying, and philosophers contended that they could not be taught as moral examples. Thus, explicitly or implicitly, philosophical ethics had a measure of autonomy in relation to religion and offered an independent criterion for testing the truth* of religious beliefs.

b) Law and Nature. If morality was not determined by the will of the gods, was it then determined by the will of human beings? And if so, of which human beings? In *Antigone,* Sophocles (c. 496–406 B.C.) portrays the moral conflict between Creon, who for reasons of state* has forbidden the burial of Polyneices, and Antigone, who disobeys Creon in order to pay her last respects to her brother. In thus observing the piety due to the family*, she appeals to a law* that is deeper and more authoritative than the law imposed by the state.

c) Right and Might. Debates about the source of moral authority* raised questions about the nature of that authority. The Sophists maintained that a moral pronouncement has the authority only of the person who makes it, since moral opinions reflect only the interests of those who hold them. Thus, the morality of a community reflects the interests of those who hold power. This view is ascribed by Plato* to Thrasymachus in the first book of *The Republic* (338 a–348 b). It appears, on the other hand, that Socrates spent much of his life contesting such views, on the grounds that the dialectic of moral argument implies the reality of a constant and unchanging norm, and not merely an infinite variety of opinions.

d) Time and Eternity. Plato continued the reflections of Socrates by giving them a metaphysical foundation. Ethical norms can exist only if they are grounded in transcendent Forms, each of which is unchanging and eternal. The crown of these Forms is the Form of the Good*, which is beyond all being* and knowledge, and is accessible to intellectual intuition only after a sustained period of education.

e) Morality and Happiness. Aristotle rejected the doctrine of the Good because it sheds no light on the practical moral problems of human existence. In its place, he undertook an investigation of what it is that human beings really want and how they might achieve their goal. Everyone, he assumes, wants happiness *(eudaimonia).* By "happiness," he means not simple subjective satisfaction, but a fulfillment of life that embraces both subjective feelings and objective elements. Such happiness depends upon the active and lifelong exercise of characteristically human virtues in accordance with human nature. Supreme among these virtues is the intellectual virtue of contemplation*, which offers the greatest happiness since it most nearly approaches the activity of the divine.

f) Pleasure and Duty. The Hellenistic period saw new ethical developments. The individual replaced the citizen, and values that had previously been associated with membership in a distinctive community were superseded by values associated either with the individual or with universal humanity. Epicureans emphasized individual feeling, and extolled a quiet life of pleasure and contentment, while Stoics emphasized universal rationality, which, they maintained, provides the norms of human behavior. To act in accordance with reason is to act in accordance with the ultimate nature of things, human nature included.

This whole tradition of philosophical reflection provided early Christian theologians with a conceptual framework for the exposition of ethics. The moral beliefs of Christians were largely derived from Jewish origins, although their social relationships were also influenced by the Hellenistic world (e.g., "household codes" regulating relationships between husbands and wives, parents and children, masters and slaves, in such writings as 1 Pt 2:18–25 and 3:1–17; Col 3:18–4:1; Eph 5:21–6:9). The ethical issues were the same as those of the Greek philosophers: the nature, source, and grounds of the moral claim; the relationship between individual, community, and human beings in general; the relationship between the conventional, the natural, and the metaphysical; the dialectic of liberty* and obedience, or virtue and happiness; and, especially important for theology, the relationship between morality according to reason and morality according to revelation*.

2. Judeo-Christian Tradition

At the heart of biblical ethics is faith* in the one God as Creator and Redeemer, and acknowledgment of the Covenant* that God has made with his people*: the Covenant with the Israelites after their departure from Egypt, and then the New Covenant with all who put their trust in Jesus* Christ raised from the dead. For a covenantal ethics, the basic concepts are the gift and the call, the promise* and the command.

a) The Mosaic Covenant. According to the terms of the Covenant made with Moses, God's promise is a new life in a new and prosperous land, while God's command is that his people respect the law, as summarized in the Decalogue* and explained in the Pentateuch. Thus, the ethics of the Covenant is a prescriptive ethics of obedience to God's law as the way of salvation*: if the people respect the law, they will surely "live"; if they break the law, they will surely "die" (Dt 30:15–20; *See* Ex 20:1–21; Dt 5–7).

b) The Two Ages and the New Covenant. The history of Israel*'s obedience and disobedience gave rise after the exile to the imagery of the "two ages": the present age, in which there is a continuing struggle between God and the forces of evil*, and the age to come, a messianic age in which God will establish a universal rule, and God's people will live in holiness*, justice*, and peace*. At the heart of Jesus' proclamation is the message that the kingdom is now at hand, and that people should pray and prepare for its coming. At that period, there were a variety of ways of representing the nature of this kingdom, and the precise intention of the preaching* of Jesus is open to more than one interpretation (*See* the phrase in Lk 17:20 on the kingdom of God, variously translated as "within you," "in your midst," or "in your grasp"). In any case, the effect of such preaching was twofold. First, it confirmed the basis of the Christian life in obedience to God, an obedience that is thankful for God's love*, and called men and women to imitate such love in their relationships with one another. Second, it relativized the claims of all human institutions, such as the family and the state. The disciple should be characterized by love of God and love of neighbor, and the category of "neighbor" was expanded to include everyone in need whom the disciple was in a position to help (Lk 10:25–37).

Shortly before his death, Jesus anticipated the coming of the kingdom, and at the Last Supper he established a New Covenant (Mk 14:22–25 par.). After his death and Resurrection*, the expectation of the coming of the kingdom persisted (Parousia*). The disciples continued to accept social institutions and practices, but recognized that these belonged to the passing age and that, while they should be obeyed, they must now be obeyed "in Christ*" or "in the Lord." This way of thinking doubtless left things as they were, but it also contained the seeds of radical criticism and transformation.

c) The Church and the World. The tension between living under the pressures and constraints of the present age, and anticipating the new life of the age to come, continued long after the expectation of Parousia had moved from the center of Christian consciousness. It can be discerned, for example, in the dialectic between desert and city*, between outright condemnation of riches and concern for their proper use, between celibacy and marriage*, and between an abnegation of coercive force and its employment in maintaining order and safety. Before the conversion* of Constantine (c. 274–337) and the establishment of Christianity as the state religion, Christian ethics could afford to remain an ethics of dissidence, but afterward, in one way or another it had to come to terms with the demands of social and political life. The aspiration to the perfect life of the new age was therefore confronted by the realism of the present age, with its moral and social needs. This situation called forth, on the one hand, an ascetic theology (asceticism*), as exemplified by the earlier documents of the *Philokalia,* and, on the other, a carefully considered social ethics appropriate to the political life of an imperial regime.

d) Augustine and the Two Cities. In *De civitate Dei* (*The City of God*), Augustine* combines a philosophy of history* with a philosophical basis for ethics. In line with Aristotle, Augustine assumes that all human beings seek happiness (*CD.* 10, 11). Because they have been created by God and for God, their true happiness, or blessing*, is to be found in God, who alone can satisfy their deepest longing. Thus, an ethics of self-fulfillment and an ethics of obedience are revealed to be one and the same. Loves for lesser objects are stepping-stones toward the ultimate love (*CD* 15, 22; *Doc. chr.* 1, 27). However, the sin* of love of self has perverted and displaced love of God, thus creating the earthly city in which the citizens of the city of God, on pilgrimage*, are also present until the end of history (e.g., *CD* 14, 28). In the present age, the law of God not only sets forth the true end of human beings and the way to achieve that end, but it also establishes moral boundaries that they must not transgress. Under the rule of God, the earthly city maintains order through restraint and coercion (e.g., *Ep.* 153, 6, 16), while the city of God is ruled by the grace* and persuasion of love (e.g., *CD* 19, 23). Since God wishes that evil should be repressed, Christians are justified in resorting to coercive force, in certain circumstances, but only if they hold political responsibility for the welfare of the community (*CD* 5, 24; cf. *Ep.* 93 and 185, where Augustine lays the foundations for what later became the doctrine of the just war*). Since Christians continue to be engaged in the two cities, an ethics that is intended to be Christian generally seeks some middle way between two extremes: the total rejection of the use of force, on the one hand, and the use of force for spiritual ends, on the other. The tension between the demands of law, order, and justice, and the counsels of patience, forgiveness, and love provides a recurrent theme of Christian ethics, and this tension finds expression in teachings such as the medieval doctrine of the "two swords" or Luther*'s doctrine of the "two kingdoms," as well as in the espousal of nonviolence by some Christian sects and the justification of revolutionary force (revolution*) by some theologians of liberation*.

e) Thomas Aquinas and the Ethics of the Law. According to Thomas* Aquinas, the ultimate fulfillment of human beings and the daily ordering of human life are both grounded in the divine wisdom, the unchanging structure of which is the eternal law. This eternal law is reflected in the world through a triple law: natural, divine, and human (*ST* Ia IIae, q. 91). The new law of the gospel is the presence in the believer's heart of the Spirit of Jesus Christ, who evokes a free response of wisdom and love, and gives spiritual discernment (ibid., q. 106, a. 1). Law is the expression of order, harmony, and fulfillment, and conformity with the law is the work of practical reason. Thus, love and wisdom form the mainstay of the good life, and the particular will of God is to be discerned as much by the Spirit of love as by the precepts* enshrined in written law. In a sense, Aquinas, while developing a different approach, is closer here to the Orthodox Church (orthodoxy*), with its emphasis on the divine "economy," than are some other strains of Western Christianity, such as the penitentiaries, with their fixed tariffs for fixed categories of sin.

f) Conscience, Community, and Christ. The harmony achieved by Aquinas between the immediacy of spiritual discernment and the abstract mediations of the application of principles was not easy for everyone, and there was a great danger of privileging either intuitive reliance on the guidance of the Spirit or detailed casuistry*. The danger was accentuated by the disputes of the Reformation and Counter-Reformation. In the churches of the Reformation, with their condemnation of the hierarchical structures of the medieval church, their emphasis on the immediate access of the believer to the grace of God through Jesus Christ, and their consequent suspicion of any ethical system that smacked of legalism, there was increasing emphasis on the freedom of believers to make their own judgments on the basis of Scripture and the inward prompting of the Spirit. The Council of Trent* sought to respond to this tendency by a renewed practice of auricular confession. As a result, the work of the moral theologian was increasingly restricted to prescribing the minimal requirements of law, while mystical or ascetic theology concerned itself with the deeper aspects of spirituality as lived (life*, spiritual).

The teaching that conscience* is the supreme subjective authority, always to be obeyed but needing to be formed and informed by the objective moral order, must always guard against two dangers: that of relativism*, in which the individual conscience is given an objective authority that does not pertain to it, and that of legalism, in which the abstractions of an impersonal order are preferred to the real problems of human beings.

3. Age of the Enlightenment and the Challenge of Secularization

The Enlightenment and its aftermath saw the radical questioning of traditional ecclesiastical authority. Tradition as the justification of moral and religious belief was rejected in favor of reason, as with Kant*, or feeling, as with Hume (1711–76): an unquestionable foundation for morality was to be discovered in human nature. Sometimes, morality was assimilated to mathematics and its self-evident principles; sometimes, by contrast, it was assimilated to the apparent immediacy of the senses; sometimes, too, it was assimilated to a principle of maximization of interest. In any case, these proposals for grounding morality ascribed to it autonomy in relation to religion, and belief or disbelief in God was thus rendered ethically irrelevant. It would be difficult to find a more forthright assertion of the autonomy of ethics than Kant's celebrated remark: "Even the Holy One of the Gospels must first be compared with our ideal of moral perfection before we can recognize him as such" *(Grundlegung)*.

The notion of the autonomy of ethics was intended to overcome the arbitrariness of religious ideology and to do justice to the freedom, dignity, and moral responsibility of the human agent. The human spirit was put in the place of God, and an innate sense of duty was substituted for obedience to divine law. However, the movement away from the moral object to the moral subject—that is, from moral law to the moral agent—carried within it the seeds of a more radical subjectivism, which rejected the whole idea of an objective morality. Growing awareness of the wide range of disparate and often conflicting beliefs and practices suggested that the idea of an essential humanity and a universal morality was an illusion. It seemed that there were many moralities, but no single morality, and that differing conceptions of morality were incommensurable. In such a situation, total moral anarchy is held in check solely by the fact that human beings must live together and therefore require a social morality, which brings order into their conflicting interests and is based on their common interests. Apart from this social morality, it is for individuals to choose their own values and style of life. Consequently, the primary virtue is no longer obedience to the universal moral law and a sense of obligation to one's fellow human beings, but sincerity and authenticity. In relation to society, it is no longer a question of responsibility, but of rights (*See* Sartre 1943 or Nozick 1974).

The radical subjectivism of contemporary ethics has often been criticized, and there is renewed interest among philosophers and theologians in the concepts of community and duty. However, the debate continues between those who believe that there are universal moral norms and those who believe that such norms are relative to specific systems of beliefs and values. In Christian ethics, the debate focuses on the relationship between natural and revealed morality, between that which is, in principle, the property of all human beings as made in the image of God, and that which is derived from Scripture and Christian tradition. However, although Christian ethics is concerned first and foremost with the community of the redeemed, it also aims at the fulfillment of the "true" humanity of human beings, and therefore, in principle, has a universal scope.

4. Future of Ethics

The clash of cultures and ideologies that threatens to take the place of conflicts between nations has made the advent of a universal ethics all the more urgent. Is such an ethics possible, however, or even, as the most radical pluralists would ask, desirable? If it is, will it be no more than a "negative" ethics, proscribing behavior that infringes against certain basic rights? Or will it include a "positive" ethics, prescribing certain virtues, values, and practices that contribute to human well-being? If the latter, how will this well-being be defined? And should this include the well-being of animals* and even of the environment (ecology*)?

In the second half of the 20th century, not least because of Vatican* II, there was a renewal of moral theology and of theological ethics. The council declared (*Optatam Totius* 16) that: "special attention needs to be given to the development of moral theology. Its scientific exposition should be more thoroughly nourished by scriptural teaching. It should show the nobility of the Christian vocation of the faithful, and their obligation to bring forth fruit in charity for the life of the world." This is a call for a new theological anthropology*, and a deeper understanding of the link between freedom and obedience, which will combine the faith that human beings are made in the image of God with all the insights into what makes human beings truly human. The idea of a "true" humanity need not result in a stereotype.

• Augustine, *De civitate Dei,* BAug 33–37; *De doctrina christiana,* BAug 11, 149–541; *Epistula* 153, CSEL 44.
H. Bergson, *Les deux sources de la morale et de la religion,* Paris, 1932.
E. Kant, *Grundlegung der Metaphysik der Sitten,* AA 4, Berlin, 1910.
J.-P. Sartre, *L'être et le néant,* Paris, 1943.
Thomas Aquinas, *ST* Ia IIae, q. 91–94; 100; 106–8.
♦ K. Barth (1951), *KD* III/4 (*Dogmatique,* Geneva, 1964–65).
H.R. Niebuhr (1951), *Christ and Culture,* New York.
H. Thielicke (1951–58), *Theologische Ethik,* 3 vols., Tübingen.
B. Häring (1954), *Das Gesetz Christi,* Freiburg.
P. Ramsey (1967), *Deeds and Rules in Christian Ethics,* New York.
G.H. Outka, P. Ramsey (Ed.) (1968), *Norm and Context in Christian Ethics,* London.
K. Barth (1973–78), *Ethik,* 2 vols., Zurich.
R. Nozick (1974), *Anarchy State and Utopia,* New York.
J.-M. Hennaux (1975), "Cours de morale fondamentale," course notes, Institut d'études théologiques, Brussels.

J. Gustafson (1979), *Protestant and Roman Catholic Ethics,* London.
R.M. Hare (1981), *Moral Thinking: Its Levels, Methods and Point,* London.
W. Schrage (1982), *Ethik des Neuen Testaments,* Göttingen.
J.M. Finnis (1983), *Fundamental of Ethics,* Oxford.
S. Hauerwas (1984), *The Peaceable Kingdom: A Primer in Christian Ethics,* London.
J. McClendon (1986), *Ethics,* Nashville, Tenn.
J. Macquarrie, J. Childress (Ed.) (1986), *A New Dictionary of Christian Ethics,* London.
O. O'Donovan (1986), *Resurrection and Moral Order,* Leicester.
B. Chilton, J. McDonald (1987), *Jesus and the Ethics of the Kingdom,* London.
A. MacIntyre (1990), *Three Rival Versions of Moral Enquiry,* London.
R. Spaemann (1990), *Glück und Wohlwollen,* Stuttgart.
C. Pinto de Oliveira (1992), *Éthique chrétienne et dignité de l'homme,* Fribourg-Paris.
R. McInerny (1993), *The Question of Christian Ethics,* Washington.
C.E. Curran (1996), "Théologie morale," *DEPhM,* 1511–17.

PETER BAELZ

See also **Asceticism; Conscience; Ethics, Autonomy of; Ethics, Medical; Ethics, Sexual; Good; Market Economics, Morality of; Society**

Ethics, Autonomy of

1. Antiquity

It is said that Pythagoras was the first person to compare human life to the Olympic Games, at which one finds athletes, business people, and spectators. Counter to what we would do spontaneously, Pythagoras classifies them in *ascending* order, for they represent, respectively, those who devote themselves to the body, to action, and to contemplation*. Plato, who was the student of a Pythagorean, took up this value system when he gave the highest standing to contemplation. As with Pythagoras, this preference is explained by belief in the immortality of the soul* and in reincarnation. In Plato's mature work, the period of the *Phaedo* and *Republic,* for example, practical reason* has no independence from theoretical reason. Moreover, there is no terminological distinction. The virtue of both is wisdom* *(phronesis).* Wisdom, both theoretical and practical, is achieved in the grasp of the Forms, and the world of the Forms is unified under the Form of Good*. This world is accessible to the soul separate from the body. During incarnations, it loses touch with this world, under the clouding influence of the senses, but education can bring back reminiscences of it. In this case, reason then guides us into knowledge both of the nature of things and of the right principles of action. The whole of the soul, including the appetites and the spirit, comes under its control. This does not mean, however, that we cannot act contrary to reason. *Republic* (439 *e* 7–440 *a* 3) describes the case of Leontius, torn between his impulse to look at corpses, and his reason, which tells him not to, but still yields to his impulse. Here, Plato is different from Socrates, at least as the latter is represented in the *Protagoras:* according to Socrates, reason is always in control and cannot be "tugged all about like a slave" (352 *b* 3–*c* 2; 358 *b* 6–*d* 2).

Aristotle gives an account of the relation between theoretical and practical reason in which we discern the beginning of the autonomy of ethics. He makes a distinction between two intellectual virtues, theoretical wisdom *(sophia)* and practical wisdom *(phronesis).* Like Plato, he believes that there is something in us, the *noûs,* that survives the death* of the body, but the texts (especially *De anima* III. 5. 430 *a* 10–25) are obscure on this point. Moreover, Aristotle takes up neither reminiscence and reincarnation, nor the idea of Good. We achieve practical wisdom by an outward and inward path, similar to the track that starts and ends at the same place after retracing one's steps. We start from a mixture of desire and second-hand principles, taught to us by our parents and instructors. If we are fortunate, this starting point will enable us to proceed on the outward path, which is a sustained reflection on this mixture and which, at the turning point, reaches a consistent vision of good and of happiness *(eudaimonia).* This will be "truth in accordance with right desire," whereas the goal of theoretical reason is simply truth. The inward path is where this vision is put into practice, so that desire and thought are unified, leaving no frustration. It is important to note that phronesis is not purely intellectual for Aristotle, but also includes balanced desire (*Ethica Nicomachea [EN]* VI. 5. 1140 *b* 28–30). He makes contemplation *(theoria)* of the highest unchangeable realities, such as God* and human nature, an essential ingredient in human happiness, but because we are human and not divine, this is not the whole of our happiness. On the subject of the weakness of the will, Aristotle comes close to Socrates. If practical reason is fully engaged in both the general perception of the good and in its application to individual cases, the power of desire has already been encompassed, and reason cannot be "tugged all about."

2. Christianity

a) Scripture. The Old Testament and the New Testament see ethics centrally as a matter of the law* or of the commandments given by God to his people. It is true that there is also in the Scriptures* the tradition of Wisdom, and that Christ* is both the Word* and Wisdom (1 Cor 1:24–30). Moreover, in Paul's letters, the law is not seen as standing alone in mediating God's will to us, but in a complex relation with grace* and faith* (Rom 7–8). Nevertheless, the emphasis on divine commandment gives Christian ethics a very distinct character.

b) Augustine. Augustine* came to Christianity by way of Platonism and, despite the evolution of his thought, Platonism remained for him a "preparation for the gospel." He agrees with Plato's postulation of an intelligible world of Forms, and follows the tradition that identified this world with the divine mind. Accordingly, he makes a distinction between two forms of mental activity and two forms of excellence, wisdom *(sapientia)* and knowledge (*scientia*). The intellectual cognizance of eternal things belongs to wisdom, but the rational cognizance of temporal things to knowledge (*De Trinitate* XII. xv). Action, in which we use temporal things well, therefore belongs in the domain of knowledge, and contemplation of eternal things in the domain of wisdom. At first glance, this seems like Aristotle's division (*EN* 6, 1, 1139 *a* 6–8), but Augustine's view is different in several respects. First, the eternal things are defined in terms of Christian theology*, especially God's eternity* and our eternal life* with God. Second, Augustine sees the distinction between wisdom and knowledge in terms of another distinction, pervasive in his thought, between use *(usus)* and enjoyment *(fruitio)*. We are to use changeable and corporeal things, which are good, but without taking them as our only objective or endpoint: "Whatever we do rationally in the using of temporal things, we may do it with contemplation of attaining eternal things, passing through the former, but cleaving to the latter" (op. cit., 12, 13). Enjoyment is man's proper attitude to God, and use is his proper relation to everything else. Human deterioration is the tendency to treat as our end what we should be merely using. The reason that has knowledge, in his sense, has appetite very close to it. Augustine compares knowledge to Eve, who alone spoke with the serpent and then gave the fruit to Adam*. In this same way, *scientia* has the capacity to be moved in the direction of the enjoyment of bodily things, and becomes conformed thereby to the image of the animals* rather than the image of God. What makes the difference as to the direction it moves is the presence or absence of faith. In this picture, practical reason is distinguished from theoretical reason, but ordered toward it teleologically. When this ordering is disturbed, the mind becomes estranged from itself, "stuck by the glue of its attachments" (10, 5).

c) Middle Ages. The *Nicomachean Ethics* was known by the great Arabic commentators but disappeared in Christian Europe until the 12th century. Abelard*, for example, shows no knowledge of the work. Its rediscovery was complicated by the fact that the first Latin translations covered only the first three books, which gave a misleading impression of Aristotle's views. Indeed, without Books VI and X, which deal with the superiority of theoretical wisdom and locate the dominant place of contemplation in happiness, the autonomy of philosophical ethics from theology stands out more starkly. Aquinas had the whole of the *Nicomachean Ethics,* as well as Albert* the Great's commentary, but like his 12th-century predecessors, he advocated a certain autonomy of ethics (*ST* IIa IIae, q. 47, a. 4): "The role of practical wisdom (*prudentia,* translating *phronesis*) is to charge our conduct with right reason *(applicatio rationis ad opus),* and this cannot be done without rightful desire. Prudence is therefore not only an intellectual virtue but a moral virtue." Here, Aquinas goes further than Aristotle, who concedes that practical wisdom requires the moral virtues and vice versa, but does not count *phronesis* itself among the moral virtues. Aquinas's philosophical ethics has a place for practical wisdom between theology and the immediate causation of moral behavior. Human beings can arrive at some knowledge of the natural moral law by the light of reason. This limited autonomy is consistent with the idea that "natural law is nothing else but a participation of a rational creature in eternal law, [for] the light of natural reason, whereby we discern what is good and what is evil... is nothing else than an imprint on us of the divine light" (*ST* Ia IIae, q. 91, a. 2). Even though natural moral law is a reflection of eternal law, or of God's plan that directs all things to their ends, it does not need to be the object of a revelation*. Every human being possesses the capacity to reflect by theoretical reason on the fundamental inclinations of human nature, and to reach the universal rules of moral life. For Aquinas, however, philosophical ethics is limited in scope. Perfect happiness or beatitude* is for him the vision of the divine essence, and therefore a heavenly activity belonging to contemplative reason, not an activity of practical reason in action on earth. For Aquinas, the *Nicomachean Ethics* describes the two aspects of imperfect happiness—the happiness of the theoretical or contemplative life and the happiness of social life—that are distinct on this earth. This means, furthermore, that the domain of practical wisdom has a certain priority on earth. In this life, the will, by which we can love God, is superior to the understanding, since we cannot see God, even though, in itself and in the next life, the intellect is nobler (*ST* Ia, q. 82, a. 3). The Franciscan philosophers (Bonaventure*, Duns* Scotus, William of Ockham [c. 1285–1347]) gave an even greater priority to the will. For them, volitional activity and affective experience are more distinctive of humanity than any activity of the intellect, and moral values are dependent upon the free will of God, limited only by the bounds of logical possibility.

d) Reformation and Enlightenment. The synthesis of the authority of Aristotle and the authority of the church* was threatened by the Reformation and the new science of Copernicus (1473–1543) and Galileo (1564–1642). The rationalist philosophers, like Descartes* or Spinoza (1632–77), responded by trying to found knowledge and ethics more securely on the basis of reason. But reason itself was in turn critiqued by the empiricists, especially Hume (1711–76), who attacks the very idea of natural law. Distinguishing descriptive judgments *(is, is not)* from prescriptive judgments *(you must, you must not),* Hume asks how the second can be deduced from the first, since they are not of the same order (*Treatise of Human Nature* III, 1, 1). No term should appear in the conclusion that has not appeared in the premises: one cannot, therefore, make a valid transition from being to having to be, or from fact to value. Nevertheless, even if Hume is right about this, the point is not devastating to Aquinas's project of deriving the precepts of the natural law from reflection about human nature and human inclinations, for he has resources for supplying in the premises the "ought" that Hume requires. More important is another of Hume's arguments, that reason is inert, and it is only passion that moves us to action. He says that it is impossible that reason and passion can ever oppose each other, or vie for the government of the will and actions; but since morality *can* oppose the passions* and move us to action, morality is a matter of passion (albeit of calm passions such as benevolence), not of reason. Hume is not denying here that reason has an effect on action, but he claims (in order to bury Socrates) that reason's proper role is to be the slave of the moral passions, showing them the way to reach satisfaction. Here, he echoes Aristotle, for whom "thought by itself moves nothing; what moves us is thought aiming at some goal and concerned with action" (*EN* 6, 2, 1139 *a* 35f). Thought gets to action through desire, but Aristotle does not say that desire is independent of thought, since it might be (and will be in a virtuous person) what he calls a rational wish *(boulesis).*

Kant*'s response to Hume takes us to an influential view about the autonomy of ethics. Kant wants to show that, contrary to what Hume thinks, reason can be practical, or binding, in the form of the categorical imperative. In order to do this, he has to limit the pretensions of theoretical reason. According to his famous phrase, it was necessary for him to "abolish knowledge to make room for belief" (preface to the *Critique of Pure Reason,* 2nd edition). The Greeks had thought that the objects of contemplation *(theoria)* are by their nature the most valuable (*EN* 6, 7, 1141 b 3), because, unlike the objects of *praxis,* they are eternally and necessarily what they are. Kant turns this argument on its head. It is because the objects of practical reason are superior that when cognition involves pure speculative reason and pure practical reason, the latter prevails *(Critique of Practical Reason).* Speculative reason can only use ideas of immortality, liberty*, and God as regulative or heuristic devices; it cannot make any conclusions about the existence of the objects of these ideas, since it can judge only what can be experienced with the senses. Practical reason, however, relies upon what Kant calls "the fact of reason"—the fact that there is a moral law; it can therefore transcend these limitations and use the ideas of immorality, liberty, and God as constitutive, proofs of the reality of their objects. In saying that reason can be practical, Kant is not denying Hume's claim that humans must be moved to action by something "on the side of inclination," but he says that we can be moved by respect for the moral law. He is also not denying theoretical reason a right of veto over belief. If reason in its speculative use could show that something was impossible, then practical reason could not legitimate our postulating its existence. However, Kant severely limits what speculative reason can show by way of possibility and impossibility. Finally, Kant does not extend the autonomy of ethics into independence of theology, although not all his interpreters agree with this. In the preface to the second edition of *Religion within the Limits of Reason Alone,* he proposes that we look at the pure religion of reason, which contains morality, as the inner of two concentric circles; the outer circle contains historical faith and revelation. He concedes that morality requires belief in some items in the outer circle, even though these items cannot be used in the maxims of speculative or practical reason. In particular, morality requires belief in God's grace in order to explain how human beings, in their condition of submission to radical evil, can ever please God. (op. cit., 61).

3. 19th and 20th Centuries

In the 19th century, Kant was interpreted in several manners, including by "right-wing" and "left-wing" Hegelians, and by opponents of Hegel*. Kierkegaard*, for example, reacted against Hegel by separating three kinds of life, the esthetic, the ethical, and the religious. The ethical life is reached by a mysterious revolution of the will within the esthetic life, but the ethical life itself fails and requires a leap of faith into the religious life, within which a "second ethics" is possible, by God's assistance, and we become able to live as God intends us to.

In 20th-century moral philosophy, the autonomy of ethics has grown as the prestige of speculative reason has declined. Thus, to give one example, the pragmatists follow Kant's dictum that "every interest is ultimately practical." For Charles Sanders Peirce (1839–1914), to be a pragmatist is to find a theory's meaning in the practical consequences that would necessarily result if the theory were true (*Collected Papers* V, §9). John Dewey (1859–1952) thought that there were no final ends and that we should therefore look at "ends in view," all of which may become means for further "ends in view." The existentialists urged that existence precedes essence, denying the role of natural law. Following Kierkegaard, but denying faith, Sartre (1905–80) insisted that we make ourselves what we are by our choice; our nature is not given to us. George Moore (1873–1958) objected to what he called "the naturalistic fallacy" of identifying "good" with any natural property. For emotivists (like Charles Stevenson) and prescriptivists (like Richard Hare), moral judgments are not assertions, but imperatives or means of influencing others; they do not deny, however, that practical judgments have their own kind of objectivity. Finally, some writers have taken up Kant's idea of the unity of nature, but denied the existence of freedom. As more has become known about the structure of the brain, artificial intelligence, and genetics, it has become tempting to think of morality and the freedom that it presupposes as illusions of common sense, just as the physicist can regard the ordinary concepts of tables and chairs as illusory in the light of what physics knows about the structure of matter. The paradoxical logic of this line of thought would lead to the disappearance of not only the autonomy of ethics, which would be absorbed within the scientific conception of nature, but also of the very value of reason, and therefore of science itself.

• Aristotle, *Ethica Nicomachea; De anima.*
Augustine, *De Trinitate,* BAug 15 and 16.
D. Hume, *A Treatise of Human Nature,* Ed. L. A. Selby-Brigge, Oxford, 1888.
E. Kant, *Kritik der reinen Vernunft,* AA 3, 522–38; *Kritik der praktischen Vernunft,* AA 5.
S. Peirce, *Collected Papers* 5, Ed. C. Hartshorne, P. Weiss, A. W. Burks, Cambridge, Mass., 1931–58.
Plato, *Protagoras, Phaedo, Respublica.*
Thomas Aquinas, *ST* Ia IIae, q. 94; IIa IIae, q. 47–50.
♦ É. Gilson (1948), *Le thomisme: Introduction à la philosophie de saint Thomas d'Aquin,* Paris.
R. A. Gauthier, J. Y. Jolif (1970), *L'*Éthique à Nicomaque: *Introduction, traduction et commentaire,* Louvain-Paris.
J. Harrison (1976), *Hume's Moral Epistemology,* Oxford.
O. O'Donovan (1980), *The Problem of Self-Love in St. Augustine,* New Haven.
A. W. Price (1995), *Mental Conflict,* London.
J. E. Hare (1996), *The Moral Gap: Kantian Ethics, Human Limits and God's Assistance,* Oxford.

John E. Hare

See also **Aristotelianism, Christian; Authority; Platonism, Christian; Sciences of Nature**

Ethics, Medical

Jesus* was a healer, and in his healing miracles* the kingdom* of God already made its presence felt (e.g., Lk 11:20). Concern with the sick was therefore one of the traits of Christianity from the beginning.

a) Miracles, Magic, and Medicine. Against the cults* that practiced thaumaturgy, such as those of Asclepius or Serapis, the church* always insisted that the God* who healed was the God of Creation* and Covenant*, and that Jesus was the mediator of God's healing power. The confidence that God would act miraculously to heal was sometimes guarded: miracles are mentioned infrequently in the literature of the second and third centuries. In the fourth century, however, especially in the hagiographic literature, there were frequent reports of miracles (Marty and Vaux 1982). The cult of saints and relics*, and associated miracles, was important in the conversion* of western Europe (Numbers and Amundsen 1986), but it was also influenced by pre-Christian practices, so that it sometimes became difficult to distinguish miracle from magic.

Magical practices had been popular in late antiquity and had often been assimilated into healing communities. Religious figures, including Christ, are invoked in the magical papyruses (Kee 1986). Generally, however, the church, like Augustine*, associated magic with the "deceitful rites of demons" and rejected it as a reliance upon "incantations and charms" rather than upon God, even when the name of Jesus was invoked (*City of God* 10. 9, BAug 34). Voices within the medieval church were regularly raised against the mingling of pagan magical practices with the veneration of saints (Numbers and Amundsen 1986).

Christianity could, however, accommodate Greek medicine without surrendering the conviction that all healing comes from God. Most Christians followed the advice of Jesus ben Sirach, who regarded physicians and their medicines as instruments of God (Eccl 38:1–14). There were some who regarded the use of medicine as faithlessness (e.g., Tatian, *Ad Graecos* 18, PTS, 1995). Most, however, commended the use of medicine (e.g., Clement of Alexandria, *Strom.* 6, 17, PG 9, 379 C-394), while insisting that healing comes from God and must serve God's cause. The Reformers repudiated the popular and magical aspect of the cult of the saints (Thomas 1971). Their suspicion of any magical manipulation of a sovereign God, and their conviction that nature, no less than miracle, comes to us from God, helped secure the primacy of medicine.

b) Christian Medical Ethics. The church's acceptance of medicine did not mean that anything and everything medical was approved. When the church called Jesus "the great physician" (Temkin 1991), it honored physicians, especially those of the school of Hippocrates (c. 460 B.C.–c. 377 B.C.), commending their compassion and their commitment to the patient's good, but it also provided a model for medicine and set it in the context of the history of salvation*. Health thus became part of a larger good* and sickness part of a larger evil, the disorder introduced by sin* (*see.* e.g., example, *City of God* 14, 3; 22, 22, BAug 35 and 37). Although physical affliction was an evil, it might, by the grace* of God, remind people of their finitude, their dependence, their sinfulness, and the disorder that characterized a person's relations with his or her body, with one another, and with God. To care for the sick was a reflection of God's care for sinners, and to heal the sick was a sign of God's triumph over sin. Both sickness and health served God. In short, health was not the sovereign good for Christians, who had to "take great care to employ this medical art…as redounding to the glory of God" (Basil*, *Rules* 55, PG 31, 1043 C–1052). This did not require Christians to undertake a complete rethinking of the basis of the practice of physicians, and they could therefore adopt and adapt the medical ethics epitomized by the Hippocratic Oath. The ascendancy of the oath itself was probably a result of the rise of Christianity (Edelstein 1943). There is a 10th-century version of the oath that is evidence for this adaptation. It begins not by invoking Apollo or Asclepius, but with a doxology, "Blessed be the God and Father of our Lord Jesus Christ." It omits the filial obligations of pupil to teacher; instead, there is a commitment to teach the art "willingly and without an indenture." There are, however, many provisions that stand in continuity with the original oath: fidelity to the sick, and prohibitions of euthanasia, abortion*, and sexual relationships with patients or members of their households.

This version also affirms the obligation of medical confidentiality. Patients, like penitents, were often required to reveal what they might prefer to keep secret, and the physician, like the priest, was forbidden to use such revelations for any other purpose than professional. Jerome (c. 342–420) notes the analogy in a letter in which he instructs a priest that it is his duty to visit the sick and commends the behavior of the Hippocratic physician who respects the intimacy of the households and the secrets of the sick (*Ep.* 52, 15, CSEL 54). The confidentiality of the confessional reinforced confidentiality in medical practice, but also helped identify its limits. Most medieval theologians agreed that secrets could be revealed when they involved serious threats to the public good or to innocent third parties; for example, in the case of a patient suffering from venereal disease who does not intend to disclose this fact to a potential partner (but only the person threatened should be warned, and one should not reveal more than necessary to prevent harm; Regan 1943).

One modification to the Hippocratic tradition was a greater concern about truth-telling. Some in the early church supported the "therapeutic lie" (e.g., Clement of Alexandria, *Strom.* 7, 8, PG 9, 471–74). Augustine, however, rigorously rejected the lie told in order to help or spare the patient (*Against Lying* 18, 36, BAug 2). "The most revolutionary change," however, was the preferential position granted to the sick (Sigerist 1943). The sick were seen as the very image of the Lord and caring for them reflected how one cared for Christ. Matthew 21:31–45 is cited in the instruction of the *Rule* of St. Benedict to care for the sick as if it were Christ himself whom one served (36, SC 182), and echoed in the vow of the Knights Hospitallers of St. John of Jerusalem to "serve our lords the sick" (Amundsen 1995).

Care for the sick also required competence and diligence. The penitential literature prompted by the decree of Lateran* IV (1215) imposed an annual confession, and physicians were expected to confess incompetence and negligence (Amundsen 1982). Both the lack of prudence* and excessive prudence were regarded as sins if it harmed patients or was useless. Exposing a patient, especially a poor one, to unnecessary risk for the sake of an experiment was also a sin. Care for the sick could not be reduced to medical care. Lateran IV also decreed that "physicians of the body [must] admonish the sick to call the physicians of the soul" (*COD* 245, §22). Because life and health are not the greatest goods, the means to preserve them must not violate the greater good. Physicians were forbidden to advise a patient to have recourse to "sinful means" to recover health (ibid.). Such "sinful means" included fornication, masturbation, magic, and breaking the church's fasts.

By means of the requirement of confession and the penitential literature that guided it, the post-Tridentine Catholic Church exercised a remarkable control over every part of life, including medicine. Within the Protestant* tradition, medicine was still considered a vocation oriented to the service of God, but reflection about medical ethics was frequently marked by a suspicion of casuistry* and an emphasis on the liberty* of physician and patient.

c) Caring for the Poor. If one considers that Jesus was also a preacher of "good news to the poor" (Lk 4:18), one will understand why the clergy frequently took the lead in providing medical assistance for the sick and poor. From the early Middle Ages to the modern era, clergy members (Catholic, Orthodox, or Protestant) thus devoted themselves to caring for the sick poor. The tradition was discouraged, but not completely ended, both by the development of guilds and licensure in the late Middle Ages, and by suspicion within the church that some clergy were practicing medicine "for the sake of temporal gain" and "neglecting the care of souls" (Lateran II, *COD* 198, §9). Concern for the sick poor prompted the publication of medical texts such as John XXI's *Thesaurus pauperum* in the 13th century, a list of simple herbal remedies available to the poor, or John Wesley's *Primitive Physick* (1747), and also of treatises exhorting physicians to care for rich and poor alike (Marty and Vaux 1982).

The hospital has its origin in this same concern. In 372, Basil of Caesarea founded a vast *xenodokheion,* or hospice, to care for the sick poor, with separate buildings for contagious and noncontagious diseases, and a staff that included physicians. It quickly became the prototype for many other such institutions. The early hospitals were funded by bishops* themselves, but soon bishops raised funds by calling upon various benefactors. In the 11th century, the Pantokrator hospital in Constantinople had 17 physicians, 34 nurses, and 6 pharmacists; it served patients in five specialized wards, and also treated outpatients. Hospitals developed more slowly in the West, but followed the same pattern.

d) Retrieval of Medical Ethics. When, in the middle of the 20th century, hospitals became showcases for medical technology and patient care became increasingly "medicalized," theologians retrieved important elements of this tradition and thus played a major role in the emergence of modern medical ethics. They opposed extravagant idolatry* of health and the idea that one could expect everything from medicine. Against reducing patients to their pathologies, they stressed the professional commitment of dedication to patients (and research subjects) as persons, and underscored consent as a fundamental component of this fidelity (Ramsey, *The Patient as Person,* New Haven, Conn., 1970). Against reducing people to their capacities for action, they insisted on corporeal existence (ibid.). They also reiterated the importance of concern for the poor in debates about access to health care.

Advances in medical science and technology have prompted a series of dramatic questions. Experimentation on human subjects, transplantation and the definition of death*, the allocation of scarce medical resources (e.g., dialysis), prenatal diagnosis, genetic counseling, reproductive technologies, gametes donations: such questions are not just scientific but also moral. Efforts to answer such questions necessarily invoke value judgments about the ends to be sought with the powers that medicine gives, about the moral appropriateness of certain means, and about how to respect the human being on whom they work. Thus, the new questions lead quickly to some very old questions about life, death, suffering, freedom, and embodiment, to which the Christian tradition should offer its own elements of response.

• Hippocrates, *Serment,* J. Jouanna (Ed.), in *Storia e ecdotica dei testi medici greci,* Ed. A. Garzia, Naples, 1996, 269–70.

♦ W.H.S. Jones (1924), *The Doctor's Oath: An Essay in the History of Medicine,* Cambridge.

L. Edelstein (1943), "The Hippocratic Oath: Text, Translation and Interpretation," *Bulletin of the History of Medicine,* suppl. 5, vol. 1, 1–64.

R.E. Regan (1943), *Professional Secrecy in the Light of Moral Principles,* Washington, D.C.

H. Sigerist (1943), *Civilization and Disease,* Ithaca, N.Y.

L. Edelstein (1967), "The Relation of Ancient Philosophy to Medicine," in O. Temkin and C.L. Temkin (Ed.), *Ancient Medicine: Selected Papers of Ludwig Edelstein,* Baltimore, 349–66.

K. Thomas (1971), *Religion and the Decline of Magic,* New York.

H. Jonas (1974), *Philosophical Essays,* Chicago, essays 1–7.

C. Bruaire (1978), *Une éthique pour la médecine,* Paris.

D.W. Amundsen (1982), "Casuistry and Professional Obligations: The Regulations of Physicians by the Court of Conscience in the Late Middle Ages," in *Transactions and Studies of the College of Physicians of Philadelphia* 3, 22–39, 93–112.

M.E. Marty, K.L. Vaux (1982), *Health/Medicine and the Faith Traditions,* Philadelphia.

H. Jonas (1984), "Technique, morale et génie génétique," *Com(F)* IX/6, 46–65.

H. Jonas (1985), *Technik, Medizin und Ethik,* Frankfurt.

T.S. Miller (1985), *The Birth of the Hospital in the Byzantine Empire,* Baltimore.

H.C. Kee (1986), *Medicine, Miracle and Magic in New Testament Time,* Cambridge.

R.L. Numbers, D.W. Amundsen (Ed.) (1986), *Caring and Curing: Health and Medicine in the Western Religious Traditions,* New York.

O. Temkin (1991), *Hippocrates in a World of Pagans and Christians,* Baltimore.

J. Jouanna (1992), *Hippocrate,* Paris.

M. Grmek (Ed.) (1993), *Histoire de la pensée médicale en Occident, Antiquité et Moyen Age,* vol. I, Paris (bibl.).

Coll. (1994), *Est-il indigne de mourir? Autour de Paul Ramsey, Éthique* 11.

D.W. Amundsen (1995), "History of Medical Ethics: Europe: Ancient and Medieval," in *Encyclopedia of Bioethics,* Rev. Ed., New York, 1509–37.

J.-C. Sournia (1996), "Médicale (éthique)," *DEPhM,* 947–52.

Journals

Hastings Center Report, New York, 1971–.

Journal of Medical Ethics, London, 1975–.

Journal of Medicine and Philosophy, Dordrecht, 1976–.

Ethik in der Medizin, Heidelberg, 1989–.

Éthique, Paris, 1991–96.

ALLEN VERHEY

See also **Death; Ethics; Resurrection of the Dead; Soul-Heart-Body**

Ethics, Sexual

Augustine* was not the first Christian theologian to concern himself with sexual ethics, but he is the key figure in fixing and systematizing the main lines of the pattern of Western Christian teaching on this subject: the commendation of marriage* and celibacy as complementary vocations, and the requirement of chastity for all. Augustine's achievement lies in his attempt to understand the meaning and place of sexuality, in faithfulness to the teaching of the Bible* and within the history* of creation*, reconciliation, and redemption. All Christian thought in this area stands, whether consciously or unconsciously, in relation to Augustine, examining a single element in his analysis, perhaps shifting the emphasis between the elements, or, in more recent times, rejecting that analysis altogether.

a) The Bible and the Early Church Fathers. The New Testament gives an account of sexual sins* that differs very little from that of the Old Testament. Thus, in continuity with the latter (*See* Lv 18–20), Paul includes in his list of those who will not inherit the kingdom* of God (1 Cor 6:9), *pornoi* (the sexually immoral or fornicators), *moikhoi* (adulterers), *malakoi* (effeminates), and *arsenokoitai* (sodomites). The New Testament's regard for marriage also suggests continuity with Judaism*, but this is crucially qualified by a recognition of a vocation to celibacy (e.g., Mt 19:12). It was this qualification that was to cause the immediate divergence between the two traditions*. In the early patristic period, the ascetic movement commended celibacy, and Encratism, associated especially with Tatian (second century), even made celibacy into a requirement by denying baptism* to the married. Despite the condemnation of this movement, the treatment of marriage among its opponents (such as Tertullian* and Clement of Alexandria* [c. 150–215]) was significantly influenced by it. If marriage is accepted, it is placed in a hierarchy that has virginity at its summit. Moreover, continence is desirable after the childbearing years, and second marriages for those who have been widowed are suspect. In short, it is desirable that sexual activity should be very limited.

b) Augustine. There are three important strands of argument in Augustine's thought.

First, Augustine takes up a position against the disparagement of marriage by the Manicheans*, but also by those, such as Tertullian and more especially Jerome (c. 342–420), who were so vigorous in their espousal of continence or celibacy as to forget that, as Augustine has it, virginity is simply the "better of two good things." He insists that marriage is good*, following especially Mark 10:6–9 and an increasingly literal reading of Genesis. Sexual union between man and woman* is natural, as presupposed in their very creation in sexual differentiation. Here, Augustine differs from Gregory* of Nyssa (*De opificio mundi,* SC 6), who taught that sex is an activity made possible after the Fall, by a divine dispensation intended to moderate the bitterness of death*. Among the goods of marriage are not only progeny, but also fidelity and, according to Ephesians 5:32, the sacrament* or sign of indissolubility, whereby it is a figure of the union between Christ* and the church*. These arguments add something to those of Clement of Alexandria (*Strom.* 3, PG 8), who had answered an extreme asceticism by presenting marriage as preeminently a collaboration with the work of the Creator: Augustine finds other goods in marriage besides procreation*. This implicitly involves an account of sexual sin: all sexual relations that do not take this form and serve these ends are held to be contrary to reason* and sinful.

Second, if human sexuality belongs to the created order, it is not to be supposed, with Pelagianism*, that it lies outside the consequences of the Fall. In his controversy with Julian of Eclanum (c. 386–454) in particular, Augustine maintains that even intercourse for the sake of procreation—the only use of marriage that is not a sin, although intercourse for other reasons is merely venial—is still touched by concupiscence, that division of the self against the self, or flesh* against the spirit, that is, since the Fall, "both a consequence and a cause of sin" (Bonner 1986), and is here expressed in disorderly desire. Intercourse for the sake of offspring makes good use of concupiscence, but, before the Fall, Adam* and Eve engaged in sexual intercourse at the bidding of their wills alone, untouched by the disorderly lust that now animates and afflicts even marital union, and renders sexuality a force for unreason, distracting us from our pursuit of the *summum bonum* (highest Good).

Third—and here Augustine owes much to Paul—if marriage is good, virginity is nonetheless to be preferred, not as a recapturing of a prefallen condition, but as founded upon a hope* for the coming kingdom, the service of which, since the birth of Christ, no longer requires procreation. Celibacy witnesses that marriage, if good, is a good of creation that will yet be surpassed, as too does the qualified permission of remarriage.

c) Monastic Tradition and Eastern Christianity. Augustine's contemporary Cassian thought of the problems of human sexuality quite differently. In a way that was influenced by the spiritual and monastic tradition of the Desert Fathers, especially Evagrius (346–99), he made the stilling of the passions* the aim of the spiritual life. By this means, temptation could be overcome and the ladder to perfection climbed; but the temptation to unchastity was but one among these temptations, with greed typically regarded as fundamental. This pattern of thought, also characteristic of later Eastern Orthodox theology (e.g., Maximus the Confessor), continued to conceive of the opposition between flesh and spirit as a conflict to be overcome, and did not follow Augustine in his radical understanding of the self as disabled and wholly incapable, of itself, of loving and serving God*. Nor did it follow Augustine in his tendency to treat sexuality, albeit while stressing the significance of concupiscence, as peculiarly revelatory of the human condition.

(d) Middle Ages and the Reformation. Theologians of the Middle Ages and the Reformation maintained the broad lines of the Augustinian picture, but, while they overcame some of the tension implicit in it, they lost something of its subtlety and balance.

Gregory* the Great, for example, seems to have converted Augustine's suspicion of pleasure into a straightforward condemnation. According to Augustine, marital intercourse for the sake of procreation is not in need of pardon, even though the concupiscence by which it is affected is a result and a cause of sin. For Gregory, however, sin is to be found in every act of intercourse by virtue of the very pleasure that it causes (*Registri epistolarum,* PL 77, 1,193–1,198). Certainly, such a notion may have been instilled by the penitentials (the guides for confessors current from the sixth to the 11th centuries), with their various prohibitions of all sexual intercourse during liturgically significant days and seasons.

It is often said that Thomas* Aquinas had a more favorable view of sexuality, holding that sexual pleasure is natural and that ordinate desire for this pleasure is permissible. It is true that he maintains that the act of intercourse is not sinful simply on account of the fact that it prevents contemplation* of God (*ST Suppl.,* q. 41, a. 3, ad 3); but it does bar such contemplation, and it is "ordinate" when the pursuit of it is related to one of the matrimonial goods. Now, while these goods may require sexual relations and thereby render them licit, they do not, of course, include the sexual relationship as such. Indeed, Aquinas holds, following Augustine, that the marriage of Mary* and Joseph contained all three matrimonial goods, although there was no sexual intercourse between the spouses (IIIa, q. 29, a. 2). Thus for Aquinas, as for Augustine, the goods of fidelity and sacrament relate to the sexual act only negatively. There is fidelity where there is no adultery (although fidelity may oblige a partner to "render the [conjugal] debt" [1 Cor 7:3]), and the sacrament where there is no divorce. The celebration of the marriage of the Virgin, a theme that had reached its apogee in the writings of Hugh of Saint-Victor (Saint*-Victor, school of), symbolizes the unwillingness even of Aquinas to make sense of sexual relations as a marital good. Moreover, the very notion that sexual desire and pleasure are natural goods is called into question by his explanation, essentially Augustinian, of the need for the virgin birth in order to avoid the transmission of original sin* (IIIa, q. 28, a. 1). In the light of this teaching, it would not be unreasonable to suppose that the perfection of the marriage of Mary and Joseph obtains, not in spite of, but because of, their lack of sexual relations. In that case, Augustine's contention that marriage is the lesser of two *goods* seems threatened. This question was being raised even at the time when the notion that marriage is a sacrament conveying grace* was being formalized at the Councils of Florence and Trent*.

If the Reformers reacted against the Catholic suspicion of marriage, it can hardly be said that they made a major contribution to the resolution of the implicit problems in the shared Augustinian heritage. There is no doubt that Luther* and Calvin* inverted the ancient perspective and developed a certain suspicion (though not a repudiation) of celibacy. They taught that it could not be required even of ministers. It is a burden too great for almost all to bear, and, even if it is observed, it is not a means of winning divine favor. Neither Luther nor Calvin, however, engaged in a serious rethinking of Augustine's concept of concupiscence, which had unbalanced the medieval picture of sexuality. Furthermore, their praise of marriage and family* could become essentially worldly, or at least forgetful of the eschatological direction of human existence to which celibacy might be a witness. The Reformers' respect for marriage did, however, encourage the according of greater significance to sexual satisfaction within the marital relationship. The English Puritan W. Perkins (1558–1602), for example, counsels against marriages where there is an excessive disparity of age, for fear that this satisfaction may be lacking. Here we see the beginning of a revision of the Augustinian account of pleasure, which both Protestants and Catholics were to pursue up to our own time.

e) Modern Catholic and Protestant Ideas. For Augustine and Aquinas, procreation alone is a lawful purpose of marital intercourse, although intercourse for the sake of the quelling of concupiscence is merely a venial sin. Catholics have increasingly distanced themselves from these views and accepted that intercourse serves to nurture and demonstrate conjugal love. The encyclical *Casti Connubii* (1930) speaks of the "fostering of mutual love" as among the "secondary ends" of marriage, holding that procreation is the primary end to which the secondary ends are subordinate. Vatican* II, in *Gaudium et Spes,* does not refer to hierarchically ordered ends of marriage, but, noting that the love between husband and wife is "uniquely expressed and perfected through the marital act," speaks of the unitive and procreative meanings that belong to sexual intercourse. This way of thought is taken up and confirmed by Paul VI in *Humanae Vitae,* by John Paul II in *Familiaris Consortio,* and by the Congregation for the Doctrine of the Faith in *Donum Vitae.* It has not led to radical changes in practice, and has indeed been the basis for the renewed condemnation of contraception, but it does represent a reconception of Augustine's "good of fidelity" in terms of loving union. This in turn allows an understanding of sexual intercourse and sexual pleasure not so much as warranted by, but as constitutive of, marriage.

A more thorough and theological reappraisal of the Augustinian pattern is contained in Barth*'s treatment of creation in volume III of *Die Kirchliche Dogmatik.* Understanding creation in the light of the Covenant* to which it is directed, it is necessary, so Barth argues, to understand human beings as beings in communion*, interdependent rather than independent. Thus, we may make sense of sexual differentiation, which is the focus of both the accounts of Creation in Genesis, as the creaturely counterpart to the determination of humankind for God that is known in Jesus Christ. Thus, if human beings are beings in communion, they are specifically and concretely man or woman, or, more accurately, man *and* woman. The command of God is that we should live out the differentiation and connection in which we are created, and which is ordered by, and attests to, the union of Christ and the Church.

Here, one is quite far removed from Augustine's conception, but not in the same way as in recent Catholic thought (e.g., Häring 1979) that rethinks the natural in personalist terms. That is, it finds the meaning of sexual relations, no longer solely in their generative role, but also in their unitive capacity. It is thereby able to consider sexual relations that were essentially questionable for Augustine, with his largely negative conception of the good of fidelity, as unproblematic. For Barth, however, the natural does not simply take on a new and personalist dimension, but is radically transformed by the insistence that the Covenant is the basis for creation, that is, by the idea that the natural or created good is inherently eschatologically ordered. According to Barth, the *sacramentum* of sexual relations is not added to them, but is their essence; it belongs to them not in the indissolubility of marriage alone, but in the incorporation of sexual relations within the community of the life of man and woman, a being in fellowship, or covenant, that witnesses to its prototype. In consequence, the question of the acceptance or refusal of procreation ceases to hold the central place that it has had in the definition of sexual sin both in the thought of Augustine and in recent Catholic pronouncements, although it is still important.

f) Contemporary Critiques. If there are obvious differences between Barth's interpretation of the Augustinian tradition and the interpretation in official Catholic teaching, it remains the case that there is agreement on the first element in Augustine's synthesis, namely, that the goodness of sexual relations is to be understood within the community of husband and wife. This element has been subject to criticism on two fronts in recent debate. Some who allow that sexual relations should occur within a covenantal relationship hold that such a relationship need not be founded on sexual differentiation: thus they challenge traditional thinking on homosexuality. Others maintain, often together with the first thesis, that sexual experience can be good even outside a covenantal relationship, thereby challenging the established teaching, which stems from the biblical treatment of sexual sins, and forbids, for example, fornication, adultery, prostitution, and masturbation.

The main contention of those (e.g., Bailey 1955) who regard homosexual practices as licit is that, in condemning them, the tradition is unaware of modern theories that hold that homosexuality is a deep-seated orientation of the personality, not a matter of choice. This knowledge, they think, places a hermeneutic question mark over the biblical texts that condemn homosexual relations (Lv 18:22 f., 20:13; Rom 1: 26 f.; 1 Cor 6:9 f.; 1 Tm 1: 8–11), and subverts the traditional distinction between natural and unnatural on which the condemnation is based. Whether this knowledge is as decisive as is supposed is open to question, but so too is its status as knowledge. Michel Foucault (1926–84) argued that homosexuality is an invention, by which he meant that the very experience of sexual desire in a particular form is historically or socially determined. Such a claim ought at least to remind us that the key Christian notion is created order, not natural order, and that knowledge of the former is by no means a matter of empirical observation. According to Barth, as already pointed out, knowledge of the creation is first of all knowledge in Jesus Christ. This knowledge shows us that we were created for covenant. In the light of this knowledge, the symbolic significance that the Old and New Testaments find in the bond between man and woman becomes comprehensible. The determination of the male to the female and of the female to the male is the creaturely counterpart to the determination of humankind for God. The question that therefore arises for those who attempt to justify homosexuality is this: On the basis of what anthropology, or what doctrine of creation, do they set aside sexual differentiation, and how does this setting aside relate to the biblical witness?

There is something ironic in the contention that sexual experience can be good even outside a covenantal relationship, for it threatens to introduce again, in a different form, the very fault that beset the Augustinian tradition: its inability to discern the human significance of sexual desire and pleasure. If this significance escaped Augustine, some of his modern critics seem to deal with the problem not by advancing beyond him, but by declaring the problem not to be a problem. Sexual desire and pleasure are not to be accommodated within any deep conception of human good or flourishing, but instead are to be treated simply as functions of bodies, as they are treated in "sex education," consisting in the imparting of purely biological information, or in "sex therapy," consisting in the teaching of techniques of gratification. As Augustine would have realized, this is to remove sexuality altogether from the history of salvation* in relation to which one must understand Christian sexual ethics.

• Augustine, *Contra Faustum manichaeum,* PL 42, 207–518; *Contra Julianum,* PL 44, 641–880; *De bono conjugali,* BAug 2, 15–99; *De bono viduitatis,* BAug 3, 229–305; *De civitate Dei,* BAug 33–37; *De conjugiis adulterinis* BAug 2, 101–233; *De Genesi ad litteram,* BAug 48–49; *De nuptiis et concupiscentia,* PL 44, 413–74; *De sancta virginitate,* BAug 3, 103–227.

K. Barth, *KD* III (*Dogmatique,* Geneva, 1960–65).

J. Calvin, *Inst.,* Ed. J. Benoît, Paris, 1957–63, IV, 12, 23–28.

J. Cassien, *Institutions,* SC 109.

Congrégation pour la doctrine de la foi, *Donum Vitae,* 1988, *AAS* 80, 70–102.

Hugh of Saint-Victor, *De B. Mariae Virginitate,* PL 176, 857–76.

Jean-Paul II, *Familiaris Consortio,* 1988, *AAS* 74, 81–191.

Jerome, *Adversus Rufinum,* SC 303.

M. Luther, *Ein Sermon von dem ehelichen Stand, WA* 2, 166–71; *Vom ehelichen Leben, WA* 10–2, 275–304; *Von den Ehesachen, WA* 30–3, 205–48.

Paul VI, *Humanae Vitae,* 1968, *AAS* 60, 481–503.

W. Perkins, *Christian Oeconomie,* Kingston, 1618.

Pius XI, *Casti Connubii,* 1930, *AAS* 22, 539–92.

Tertullian, *Exhortation to Chastity,* SC 319.

Thomas Aquinas, *ST Suppl.,* q. 41–49, 63–65.

Vatican II, *GS.*

♦ S. Bayley (1955), *Homosexuality and the Western Christian Tradition,* London.

S. Bayley (1959), *The Man-Woman Relation in Early Christian Thought,* London.

J.-D. Broudehoux (1970), *Mariage et famille chez Clément d'Alexandrie,* Paris.

A. Chapelle (1971), *Sexualité et sainteté,* Brussels.

P. Ramsey (1975), *One Flesh: A Christian View of Sex Within, Outside and Before Marriage,* Bramcote, Notts, U.K.

M. Foucault (1976), *La volonté de savoir,* Paris.

B. Häring (1979), *Free and Faithful in Christ,* vol. 2, New York, 493–538.

E. Schmitt (1983), *Le mariage chrétien dans l'œuvre de saint Augustin,* Paris.

M. Foucault (1984), *Le souci de soi;* (1984), *L'usage des plaisirs,* Paris.

G. Bonner (1986), *St. Augustine of Hippo: Life and Controversies,* 2nd Ed., Norwich.

P. Brown (1988), *The Body and Society: Men, Women and Sexual Renunciation in Early Christianity,* London.

P. Ramsey (1988), "Human Sexuality in the History of Redemption," *JRE* 16, 56–86.

A. Soble (1996), "Sexualité," *DEPhM,* 1,387–91.

Michael Banner

See also **Asceticism; Augustinianism; Manicheanism; Sin, Original; Virtues**

Eucharist

A. Biblical Theology

The term *Eucharist* (thanksgiving) comes from Luke 22:19 and 1 Corinthians 11:24. "The Lord's Supper" (1 Cor 11:20) and "breaking [sharing] of the bread" (Acts 2:42; *see* 20:7) refer to the Last Supper of Jesus* with his disciples before his death. It took place on the last evening ("no more": Lk 22:18; *see* Mt 26:29; Mk 14:25), "when the hour came" (Lk 22:14–20), "the night when Jesus was betrayed" (1 Cor 11:23–27). According to John 13 the meal was also taken at night, but the eucharistic words are mentioned in the speech of John 6: 51–58.

1. Literary Forms and Origin

a) Two Traditions. Mark, Matthew, Luke, and 1 Corinthians place at the forefront a *liturgical* tradition*, with the text of the institution of the eucharistic Lord's Supper. Jesus gives his body and his "blood of the Covenant*" to communicate his life. According to these texts, the form that Jesus gives to this supper is liturgical, in the sense that it is turned toward the future, the "memory of the future" in which there will be a communion* of life (particularly in 1 Cor). This liturgy* is structured along three axes: Jesus and God*, Jesus and the disciples, the orientation of the present toward the future.

The other tradition, mostly represented by John, is in a *testamentary* form, in the style of a farewell speech; the synoptic Gospels* (Luke in particular) also retain traces of this. This tradition keeps the memory of what Jesus accomplished by offering himself "for the multitude" (which is a better translation than "for many"). The Johannine milieus celebrate the Eucharist as well (6:51–58). But, in the course of a long farewell speech pronounced one day before Passover*, John 13 replaces the gestures and the words of the institution of the Lord's Supper with the institution of the washing of the feet.

These two traditions represent ways of reaching the Risen One and of sharing his life today (Léon-Dufour 1982).

b) Original Sites. The four texts with a liturgical priority do not have the same origin: 1 Corinthians is the oldest text mentioned (A.D. 55). Paul quotes from it and may have received it in Antioch around A.D. 40. The accounts in Paul and Luke have many points in common, body and Covenant instead of body and blood, the anamnesis formula ("in memory of me"), and a more Hellenistic vocabulary. This is the *Antiochene* tradition. Mark and Matthew, on the other hand, with the exact parallelism of words: "This is my body," "This is my blood," with their more Semitic language, with the formula "for the multitude," represent a *Palestinian* or a *Marcan* tradition originating perhaps in Caesarea, even in Jerusalem* (Mark). Matthew has some Syriac characteristics. The exact places of origin are, however, difficult to ascertain. Although older in its composition, the Antiochene formula is of a more recent tradition.

2. Was the Eucharist a Paschal Supper?

Mark 14:12, Matthew 26:17, and Luke 22:7 set the meal on the day (Mark, Matthew: "first day") of the unleavened bread (Dt 16:1–8: celebration of the unleavened bread), but Matthew omits Mark's and Luke's specificity about the day "when the paschal lamb was sacrificed." On the evening starting the 14th day of Nisan, all traces of leaven had to be taken out of the homes, and the paschal lamb* had to be sacrificed "between the two evenings" (at twilight). The supper took place, therefore, in a paschal atmosphere, without the absolute certainty that the ritual followed was exactly that of a paschal supper. It could well be that it took place a day before the Jewish Passover.

For the synoptic Gospels the date of the Lord's Supper is the Passover vigil, which is the beginning of the day of Easter. For John, on the contrary, Jesus dies at the moment when the lamb is sacrificed for the paschal supper. According to that account, therefore, the Last Supper could not have been a paschal meal. The thesis of A. Jaubert (1957) assumes that, since the Essenian solar calendar always places Passover on a Wednesday, Jesus may have followed that same calendar and may thus have had his paschal supper on the Tuesday evening; his crucifixion took place on Friday, which, according to John, was the official Jewish Passover eve that particular year.

All the accounts give the impression of a supper of the Old Covenant transformed into a supper of the New Covenant. It is the result of Jesus' initiative. It is Jesus' death and Resurrection* that bestow upon this supper all its meaning.

3. Analysis of the Traditions

a) Paul-Luke. (Antiochene liturgical tradition, with a testamentary vestige in Luke). Luke 22:15 ff. is the only tradition to recount and to rewrite the Lord's Supper as the Passover meal: "I have earnestly desired to eat this Passover with you before I suffer. For I tell you I will not eat it until it is fulfilled in the kingdom of God." Luke 22:17 continues: "And he took a cup, and when he had given thanks he said, 'Take this, and divide it among yourselves.'" Jesus then passes around a cup, which represents a future meeting in the kingdom of God. First Corinthians, Mark, and Matthew have omitted this prophetic account.

Luke 22:19–20 offers a long recension, which appears in most of the manuscripts, and a short recension in the text that is known as the "Occidental" text. The latter omits the continuation after "this is my body." In the short text Luke does not have the cup of the Eucharist, but only the cup of the future meeting. The short text may correspond to the accounts that include only the sharing of the bread (Lk 24 and Acts) and it may perhaps date back to an old tradition with the cup coming before the bread, in the order followed by 1 Corinthians 10:16 ff.: "The cup of blessing that we bless, is it not a participation in the blood of Christ*? The bread that we break, is it not a participation in the body of Christ?"

Paul, in 1 Corinthians 11:24, and Luke use the expression "thanksgiving" *(eukharistèsas),* which is more Hellenistic than "blessing" (*eulogèsas,* more Semitic: Mark and Matthew). In 1 Corinthians 11:25, in the formula "in the same way also he took the cup, after supper," the adverb "in the same way" does not occupy the same place as in Luke 22:20. In the perspective suggested by Paul, the paschal meal, which has become the Lord's Supper, would be included within the two eucharistic rites (bread and cup), which would explain the formula used by Paul. Paul and Luke have in common: "for you." "This is my body which is (given: Luke) for you (Paul and Luke)." Finally, after the bread (as in Luke), and another time after the cup, Paul places the formula of anamnesis: "Do this… in remembrance of me." "This cup is *the new covenant in my blood*" ("my": 1 Corinthians; "of me": Luke) clearly takes up the formula of Mark and Matthew:

"This is *my blood of the covenant.*" In 1 Corinthians and Luke the parallelism body/blood is broken in favor of the parallelism body/New Covenant."

The two traditions of Paul and of Luke present similarities. Luke, with: "Take" (Mark and Matthew) and "given to you" (Paul: "which is for you") creates with the formula "this is my body" something other than an objective report: *take* is a word that inks and engages the person who speaks and gives with the person who listens and receives. Whoever eats the bread enters into a communion of life with Jesus. The tradition of Luke and that of Paul are marked by the theology* in which Jesus is the one who gives of and offers himself and who produces the New Covenant (*See* Jer 31:31 ff.).

b) Mark-Matthew (Palestinian Liturgical Tradition, with Some Testamentary Traces). The two texts are closely related. In Matthew Jesus gives the consecrated and broken bread only to the disciples. Mark 14:7 has already indicated that Jesus was eating with "the Twelve." Matthew adds the word "eat" to the word "take" in Mark. There is something original in Matthew: the addition of the words "for the forgiveness of sins*" to the prayer of thanksgiving over the cup (Mt 26:28). Thus is evoked the Covenant that implies the forgiveness of sins. The word *for,* expressed by the preposition *huper,* "in favor and in place of" in Paul, Luke, and Mark (*see* Rom 5:1–10: "Christ died for"), is expressed with the weaker *peri* in Matthew 26:28.

The new Passover takes place within the framework of the old one. The phrase "as they were eating," taken over from 26:21 by Matthew 26:26, indicates that the second part of the paschal meal is starting. Jesus then innovates: 1) With "This is my body;" the liturgy roots this element in the story of the suffering and death of Jesus. 2) The verb *to be,* used in Greek, is not expressed in the corresponding Aramaic sentence, which would be "This my body." These words link together Christ to his disciples and engage him with them. 3) The disciples do not bring anything; rather, it is they who receive. The blood, always placed in relation with the Covenant, is shed for the multitude, and in this way is given as an offering/sacrifice by Christ, as a sign of Covenant and not as atonement. It seals the forgiveness expressed by "in forgiveness of sins." The reaction of the Old Testament against the practices of neighboring religions had already been reflected in the growing spiritualization of sacrificial rites; what was becoming essential among the Israelites was the "sacrifice* of praise*" (*See* Léon-Dufour 1982). The emphasis placed on "blessing" or "thanksgiving" is a reminder that Christ constantly transports believers from death to life.

Thus, 1 Corinthians, Luke, Mark, and Matthew presuppose the liturgical existence of this supper of Communion, which takes place for the multitude. Nothing is said of its frequency or its rhythm. They do not specify who will be empowered to preside. All must drink from the cup. Even if "new" does not appear in front of "covenant" in Mark and Matthew, that is indeed what the reference to covenant actually means, a meaning explicitly stated in 1 Corinthians and Luke (sacrament*).

4. Conclusion

Taking inspiration from the essay of X. Léon-Dufour (1982), which is briefer (our additions or changes are in italics) in order to get to the words spoken by Jesus himself, we obtain:

At the time of Passover, when evening came, Jesus had a last supper with his disciples. When the main course started, Jesus took some bread, and, having blessed it, he broke it, gave it to the disciples and said: "Take this and eat it, this is my body *given* for you. *Do this in memory of me.*" Moreover he took the cup at the end of the supper *(after the supper),* he offered thanks, gave the cup to the disciples and said to them: "*Drink some, all of you.* This is the *cup* of the New Covenant, it is my blood spilled *(shed for the multitude)* for you. *Do this in memory of me.*" And he told them: "I shall never drink from the fruit of the vine, not until the day when I can drink it, new, in the kingdom *(realm)* of God."

It is to be noted that "last supper" should be qualified as "before his death," because there had been other suppers taken with the Risen One. Thus, in the speech of Acts 10:39 ff., Peter* says: "we who ate and drank with him after his resurrection from among the dead." In addition, mention must be made of the sharing of the bread with the disciples he met on the road to Emmaus (Lk 24:30 f.) and the meal that was shared with seven disciples in John 21:13.

The words spoken over the bread and the cup of the Covenant accompany two movements with which they are indissolubly connected. Jesus gives the bread: he thus shows "that he gives himself for" the recipient. He passes the cup around: in this way he shows that he is shedding his blood. All the dynamism of the life of Christ is represented and communicated by the eucharistic supper (Dussaut 1972).

• F.-J. Leenhardt (1955), *"Ceci est mon corps": Explication de ces paroles de Jésus-Christ,* Cth 37.

A. Jaubert (1957), *La date de la Cène: Calendrier biblique et liturgie chrétienne,* Paris.

R. Le Déaut (1963), *La Nuit pascale: Essai sur la signification de la Pâque juive à partir du Targum d'Exode XII 42, AnBib* 22.

J. Coppens (1964), "L'Eucharistie, sacrement et sacrifice de la

Nouvelle Alliance, fondement de l'Église," in (coll.) *Aux origines de l'Église,* RechBib. VII, 125–58.
J.-J. von Allmen (1966), *Essai sur le repas du Seigneur,* Cth 55.
J. Jeremias (1967), *Die Abendmahlsworte Jesu,* 4th Ed., Göttingen.
L. Dussaut (1972), *L'Eucharistie, Pâques de toute la vie,* LeDiv 74.
Coll. (1982), *La Pâque du Christ, mystère du salut: Mélanges offerts au Père Durrwell,* LeDiv 112.
X. Léon-Dufour (1982), *Le partage du pain eucharistique selon le NT,* Paris.
S. Légasse (1994), "Jours et Heures," in *Le procès de Jésus, l'histoire,* LeDiv 56, 113–20.
A. Marx (1994), *Les offrandes végétales dans l'Ancien Testament: Du tribut d'hommage au repas eschatologique,* Leyden.

MAURICE CARREZ

See also **Blessing; Communion; Cult; Expiation; Jesus, Historical; Liturgy; Passover; Passion; Sacrifice; Soul-Heart-Body**

B. Historical Theology

Concept: *Eucharistia.* The word is attested since the end of the apostolic age, or slightly after, by the *Didache* (9, 1 . 5), by the epistles of Ignatius of Antioch (*Sm.* 7, 1; 8, 1; *Eph.* 13, 1; *Philad.* 4, 1) and by Justin (*I Apol.* 65–66). It indicates at the same time the eucharistic action consisting of thanksgiving for bread and wine, as well as that bread and that wine once they have been consecrated (an act expressed by the Greek verb *eucharistein,* which is transitive in Christian Greek). We should note two points:

a) The Christian Eucharist operates at a remove from the Jewish category of blessing* *(berakah);* post-Christian Judaism* developed a lesser insistence on thanksgiving, whereas Christians fairly early placed Christian Eucharist and Jewish blessing in opposition. Thus in the Hippolytan treatise *Refutation of All Heresies:* "the Jews have not honored the Father*, but they have not practiced thanksgiving, because they have not recognized the Son." To this we should add that *eucharistein* is close to *anapherein,* "to offer," which in the sixth century would lead to the giving of the name of anaphoras to the Greek eucharistic prayers.

b) In Latin the eucharistic action was to be called *gratiarum actio,* whereas the Greek term *eucharistia* would be retained in order to designate the consecrated bread and wine. The connection between *eucharistia* and thanksgiving would soon be forgotten; and after Isidore of Seville, all the Latin Middle Ages would believe that *eucharistia* meant "good grace," *bona gratia.* On the other hand, the Latin Middle Ages gave the eucharistic action the name of *missa,* "mass," which appeared around the fifth or sixth century, at a time when this term had gone from its original meaning of "sending" to mean "part of the liturgical action." In reaction against any sacrificial interpretation of the *missa,* and eager to stick to the New Testament, the Reformers of the 16th century borrowed from Paul the name *supper* to replace that of mass; and for the Book of Common Prayer of the Anglican liturgy, Cranmer adopted the term *Holy Communion.*

1. The Eucharist and Its Theology in Early Christianity

a) Second to Fourth Centuries. The fundamental elements of the eucharistic celebration, which brought together, mainly on Sunday*, the bishop* and the ecclesial community, started to appear in the second century. The Eucharist, henceforth separated from the fraternal meal to which the name of agape* has been given, was preceded by a liturgy* of the word (which had possibly been taken over from Jewish synagogal worship). The baptized who were present, except for the penitents, received Holy Communion* every Sunday, and Communion was also taken to the sick who could not attend. The corpus of the New Testament texts was formed in the second century; similarly, during the same period or a little later, a corpus of sacramental practices may have gradually been formed, through processes of exchange and accumulation. This is attested by the collection bearing the name of *Apostolic Tradition;* it is attributed by some historians to Hippolytus, a Roman priest* of the first third of the third century, though the attribution and the date are challenged by others. It is a collection that presents itself as being in the tradition* descending from the apostles*.

According to the earliest documents that mention it, the eucharistic prayer* neither comes as a text transmitted word by word, nor is it endowed with a uniform structure; it comes, on the contrary, in a relative diversity of structures. The eucharistic prayer of the *Apostolic Tradition,* whose text forms a unit in itself, first gives thanks to God the Father for the salvation he has brought about in history* and completed in the redeeming work of Christ*. This thanksgiving leads to the account of the Last Supper and to the words of Christ over the bread and the wine. His words are followed by a paragraph that at once expresses that we remember him for his death* and for his Resurrection*, and that we offer the Father the consecrated bread and wine. Then there is a request for the sending of the Holy* Spirit on the offering and on the communicants (epiclesis*) and glory is rendered. That prayer does not include either the Sanctus (introduced into the eucharistic prayer around the same period, in Egypt or in Syria), or other secondary developments.

In Syria there is another eucharistic prayer, called the anaphora of Addeus and Maris. These were founders of the church* of Edessa. The prayer is close to that of the *Apostolic Tradition* as far as the period is concerned. But it differs from it in several respects, mainly because it appears to be made up of several juxtaposed prayers (a fact that brings it closer to the Jewish prayer patterns) and because it does not quote specifically the words of Christ during the Last Supper, although it does refer to them in the passage mentioning his death and Resurrection. This second point gave rise to some questioning among specialists: was the text in the same state before the seventh century? Is there a reason to consider this as being perhaps a primitive state of the eucharistic prayer, what E. Mazza has called the "preanaphora"? Is it possible to think that the words of Christ had their place at another moment of the celebration? Or, in an opposite direction, should we not grant a greater importance to the fact—as F. Hamm has shown in several examples—that the words of the Eucharist, in the course of the early centuries, were principally transmitted orally?

In its principal but not exclusive form, the eucharistic celebration is a celebration presided over by the bishop, surrounded, depending on the event, by priests and deacons*, and gathering together a whole Christian community. As far as we know about ancient practices, the priests showed, with a gesture, that they shared in what the bishop was doing, and they occupied their own distinct place in the assembly. It is not until the seventh or eighth century that, in Rome*, we see the priests *(Ordo Romanus III)* saying the eucharistic prayer with the pope*: this is a practice of which no similar example is known in the Eastern liturgies until after the Middle Ages, even for the words of Christ. Modern Christians speak here of "concelebration," while wondering retrospectively about the exact significance of the concelebrants' act. On the other hand, until the Middle Ages the church in Rome practiced the rite of the "ferment:" a consecrated eucharistic element was brought from the papal celebration to the other celebrations in town, in order to be mixed with the consecrated breads, as a sign of ecclesial communion, before the distribution of these breads to the faithful.

In the fourth century, at the very latest, the rule was established not to have either food or drink before Communion, the only exceptions being the Communion of Maundy Thursday and generally in the case of the dying. This rule has been considerably relaxed in the 20th century by the Catholic Church.

b) Principal Eucharistic Prayers of the Fourth Century and Their Catecheses. Owing to their rarity, the eucharistic prayers of the first three centuries constitute documents of exceptional historical importance. On the other hand, our knowledge of the fourth and fifth centuries is well documented, so much so that it is not possible to give a complete account here. It is therefore necessary to limit ourselves only to some of the major examples of Christian eucharistic practice and theology*: the Roman eucharistic prayer (which the manuscripts call the "canon of the Mass"), commented in Milan by Ambrose*; and the two eucharistic prayers of Basil* and John Chrysostom*, both of whom can now be safely considered to have rewritten or completed the eucharistic prayers of their respective churches—Caesarea of Cappadocia (Basil) and Antioch (Chrysostom). We could add to this the catecheses* on Christian initiation* (including therefore on the eucharistic action) of Chrysostom, those of Theodore of Mopsuestia, and those of the bishop of Jerusalem*, Cyril, or of his successor, John. In spite of their importance, however, these catecheses would not be sufficient, on their own, to allow us to reconstitute the text of the corresponding eucharistic prayers: the catecheses of Ambrose, for instance (namely the *De Sacramentis* for which we have the listeners' notes and the *De Mysteriis,* the text of which Ambrose himself reworked), interpret in a personal manner the text of the Roman prayer.

At that time the Greek and Latin eucharistic prayers were in agreement on three points: 1) A central place is given to the account of the institution; 2) immediately after this account a paragraph says that the paschal mystery* is being remembered (at least the death and the Resurrection of Christ)—modern liturgists mention anamnesis here (the Greek word corresponding to memory); and 3) mention is made of an offering, at least in the anamnesis. On other points, however, important differences of emphasis can be noted among the local eucharistic traditions: 1) The Antiochene tradition gives ample thanksgiving for the unfolding of the story of salvation, whereas the Roman canon concentrates its attention on the Eucharist considered as sacrifice*. 2) The eschatological perspective of the Eucharist (already present in Ignatius of Antioch, *Éph.* 20, 2, the idea that the Eucharist is "remedy of immortality," *pharmakon athanasias*) is expressed in different ways: in Antioch by means of an anamnesis that mentions simultaneously the death and the Resurrection of Christ, and evokes also his Parousia*; in Rome in the paragraph of the canon regarding the celestial altar *(Supplices),* as well as in the variable prayers of the Mass. 3) Finally, starting with Ambrose, Christ's own words are brought into greater relief in the eucharistic prayer: it is not only the priest who pronounces them, but Christ himself, *ipse clamat* (*De Mysteriis,* 54); these words sanctify or consecrate the bread and the wine by changing them into the body and the blood of Christ. At Antioch the eucharistic prayer of John Chrysostom, who was an approximate contemporary of Ambrose, says in the very text of its epiclesis that the bread and the wine have been changed.

Among the Fathers of the Church it is Augustine* who attributes the greatest importance to the effects of the Eucharist on the Church, the mystical body of Christ. This doctrinal theme, brilliantly studied by H. de Lubac* (1944), is certainly present in the whole of Christian tradition, and in the thinking of medieval theologians, but it does not occupy much space in liturgical prayers. It would be a mistake, however, to think that the manner in which Augustine perceives the effects of the Eucharist is remote from the eschatological perspective to which other Fathers, for example Theodore of Mopsuestia, attach so much importance.

2. The Eucharist in Medieval Christianity

a) Medieval Eucharistic Practice. The eucharistic celebration (the Divine Liturgy for the Greeks, the Mass for the Latins) did not experience a change of structure in the Middle Ages. In the West, however, as had been the case earlier in the East, the eucharistic prayer came to be uttered in a whisper; and during those centuries when the celebration of the priest in private became more frequent, the *ordo missae* was complemented by a body of private prayers, particularly for use at the moment of the offertory. From the time of the Carolingian liturgist Amalaire, and under the influence of Greek liturgists, the details of the Latin Mass started to be interpreted symbolically. This symbolic interpretation referred to the different moments in the life of Christ. It lasted, in the West, until after the Middle Ages; and large parts of this interpretation have survived up to the present time in the Byzantine liturgy.

Just as the actual forms of eucharistic celebration changed in the Middle Ages, so did the theology associated with it. It was during the Carolingian era, or shortly after, that unleavened bread was adopted in the West for the Eucharist, and that the priest started giving Communion in the mouth. The Communion of the faithful, as far as historians are able to assess, seems to have become clearly less frequent than attendance at Mass, which of course affected the manner in which the Eucharist was understood. In the West at least, sacramental confession became for centuries the compulsory prerequisite for Communion, which appeared to sanction a high level of Christian life. From the practices of the previous period the Greeks decided to retain young children's access to Communion of bread as well as Communion of the chalice; but in the West, Communion of the chalice and Communion of young children gradually fell into disuse around the 12th century. At that time attention to the apostle Paul's recommendation that one ought to test oneself before taking Communion (1 Cor 11:28–31) assumed so much importance in Christian consciousness that this brought about the renunciation of Communion for children and the insistence on confession prior to Communion. It was in that perspective that canon 21 of Lateran* IV (*DS* 812) decided what the minimal rule should be for the practice, starting at the age of moral discernment, of annual confession and the Easter Communion; in the list of church commandments that was formulated at the end of the Middle Ages, they came to be called the third (the confession) and the fourth (the Easter Communion). The general rarity of Communion also explains the insistence on a duty to take Communion at the moment of dying, as a viaticum (a term meaning "money for a journey") to assist one's passage to the kingdom*. Moreover, the Council of Constance* found that the custom of taking Communion only with bread was legitimate (*DS* 1198–1200).

Despite the infrequency of Communions, or perhaps in a certain way as a compensation for it, as well as a reaction against the heresy of Berengarius of Tours (*see* b below), and under the effect of a growing devotion to the humanity of Christ, the devotion to the real presence underwent an important development in several ways: at the moment of the elevation during the Mass, and in a cult of the Eucharist outside the mass, crowned by the celebration of the feast of Corpus Christi. The elevation of the host (from around the tenth century, "host" was the name given to the bread meant for the Eucharist), then that of the chalice, was introduced. These elevations took place immediately after the words of consecration and were introduced at request of the faithful, so that although they were behind the priest, they might have the possibility of seeing and adoring the eucharistic elements. This practice started at the beginning of the 13th century, first in Paris but spreading quickly from there. The feast of Corpus Christi owed its institution in part to the fact that the liturgy of Maundy Thursday gave more attention to the betrayal of Jesus* by Judas than to the institution of the Eucharist, and also partly to the devotion of the Christian women of the region of Liège in the second quarter of the 13th century (Julienne du Mont-Cornillon). In 1264 Pope Urban IV, who had been a priest in Liège, instituted (*DS* 646–847) the celebration of Corpus Christi for all the Latin Church, with an office composed by Thomas* Aquinas. This feast, with its eucharistic procession, grew in importance in the period before the Protestant Reformation, and continued to do so after it; similarly for the adoration of the Blessed Sacrament outside the Mass.

The Carolingian era saw the development in the West of masses that were called "private" (the attendance was reduced to one server or a small number of persons). Their celebration was motivated either by the personal desire of the priest to offer the Eucharist, or by some particular intention; this meant that the mass was not offered, as it is on Sunday, by the ecclesial assembly itself, and for its own self, but specifically for a living or a deceased person. The later centuries of the Middle Ages in particular saw the increase of what were called mass foundations, and numerous priests were entrusted with the duty of servicing them.

b) Medieval Eucharistic Theology. In a cultural situation that was different from that of the patristic era, the eucharistic theology of Augustine ran the risk of being misunderstood and of appearing to contradict the theology of Ambrose, which corresponded largely to the liturgy and to the common way of practicing piety. That threat was realized in the ninth century, in the land of the Franks, in an initial controversy that pitted Paschasius Radbert, abbot of Corbie, against the Augustinian monk Ratramnus. In the 11th century the great debate aroused by the dialectician Berengarius of Tours, who placed symbolical and realistic interpretation in opposition to one another instead of synthesizing them, had the effect (Lubac 1944) of forcing theology to take sides in favor of realism only (as in the profession of faith* imposed upon Berengarius in 1059 [*DS* 690]), and it provoked a strong reaction among adherents to eucharistic piety. But it must also be said that the Augustinian formulations of the *sacramentum* assembled by Berengarius during this debate greatly contributed to the research on the concept of sacrament* conducted by the generations of theologians that followed, and they therefore helped to shed light on the sacramental septenary.

The second profession of faith imposed on Berengarius in 1079 (*DS* 700) holds that through the consecration, the bread and wine are "substantially changed" into the body and blood of Christ. Faith in the eucharistic change is already present within the early church; and as far as the category of the "substantial" is concerned, it has here a prephilosophical meaning, which was also to be true of the notion of "transubstantiation" when it made its appearance in the middle of the 12th century, and it seems not to have been different when it was taken up again (1215) in the profession of faith of Lateran IV (*DS* 802). The term *transubstantiation* did not at that time have the importance that would be attributed to it during the denominational debate of the 16th century. Thomas Aquinas prefers to use rather the term *conversion.* Nevertheless, Aristotle's *Metaphysics,* which became known to Western theologians during the second half of the 12th century, would supply them, in the form of the distinction between substance and accidents, with the conceptual tool that would allow them to clarify the ultrarealism of the confession of faith of 1059—strictly speaking, the teeth of the communicant are chewing the "accidents" (*see DS* 690), whereas the substantial change pertains to an absolute affirmation of being*. In any case, theologians did not use the Aristotelian philosophical instrument in its original form: the negative reaction of the Averroists against Thomas Aquinas, on this very matter, makes this clear.

The profession of faith *Firmiter credimus* of Lateran IV expresses the eucharistic dogma* when it says (*DS* 802) that "the body and the blood of Christ are really *(veraciter)* present under the appearance *(species)* of transubstantiated bread and wine." Did this formulation mean that one was perforce led to believe that the eucharistic conversion was total? Or did it mean it was simply possible to imagine that the reality of bread and wine was still there? Thomas Aquinas, who commented on this document (opuscule *In Primam Decretalem*), holds that his terms (which inspire the prayer of the celebration of Corpus Christi) preclude the fact of bread and Christ's body being both present in the sacrament. In the 14th century John Duns* Scotus, followed by the nominalists, may have been tempted to accept this simultaneity (the "consubstantiation"), had it not been because of the authority* of the council. This helps us understand the position Luther* would later adopt.

The distinction between substance and accidents influenced Thomas's eucharistic theology in a different way. Since the time of Hugh of Saint-Victor, theologians have been speaking of the "corporal presence" of Christ in the Eucharist, in reference to Matthew 28:20: "I am with you always, to the end of the age." But Thomas rejects the eucharistic interpretation of that text, and he considers that the presence comes under the category of localization. In the document instituting the feast of Corpus Christi (the bull *Transiturus*), Urban IV put into circulation the notion of "real presence" (*DS* 846), but the liturgy of the feast does not mention it, nor does it refer to Matthew 28:20. Until the Council of Trent*, while standing by the dogmatic formulas of Lateran IV, theologians did occasionally have recourse to the notion of "real presence."

In the Roman eucharistic prayer it is the words of Christ that are the keystone. Their importance was strongly emphasized by Ambrose, and his influence was enormous, for both the devotion of the faithful and for sacramental theology: theologians believed that they actually knew, thanks to a text of Gregory* the Great on the Our Father (*Register* 9, 26), that Christ had consecrated the Eucharist with these brief words, and that the canon of the Mass was added to them at a later stage. From the theological viewpoint Thomas Aquinas thought he could completely isolate the consecrating efficacy of the words of Christ from the rest of the eucharistic prayer, a point on which other theologians did not follow him. But aside from this, another of Thomas's ideas was routinely accepted: the priest pronounces the consecrating words *in persona Christi,* by assuming sacramentally the role of Christ.

3. Reformation, the Council of Trent and Modern Theology

Before the Reformers of the 16th century, we should mention the two requirements of Hussism (Hus*) regarding the Eucharist: the chalice Communion of the faithful and the Communion of young children.

a) Doctrine of the Reformers in the 16th Century The Reformers were in agreement among themselves about taking the words of the Scripture* as the exclusive reference, but their disagreements on the Eucharist were also an essential factor in the debates that opposed them to each other. This was particularly so in the case of Luther's debate with the Swiss Reformers, and with Zwingli* above all. Luther (*Captivity of Babylon* [1520]) demands chalice Communion and denies that the Eucharist is a sacrifice (*Formula of Concord,* Epitome VII, *BSLK* 801): what he understands from the word *sacrifice* is a "good deed" performed by man, whereas the Eucharist is purely divine grace*. He refuses the notion of transubstantiation (ibid.), because it involves an undue recourse to Aristotle. But he does care for the real presence, and in that respect he considers himself closer to the Catholics than to the Swiss Reformers (*CA* 10, *BSLK* 64–65; *see* Calvin* *Inst.* IV, 17). On the other hand, he insists on the liturgy of the word, and he condemns the private mass.

b) Council of Trent. The previous state of Catholic practices, as well as the circumstances of the council, were such that Trent dealt with the Eucharist in several distinct documents and dealt separately with the sacrament, Communion, and the sacrifice of the Mass.

To start with, in session XIII (1551) the council reaffirmed the faith of Lateran IV against the Swiss Reformer (decree on the Eucharist, chap. 1 [*DS* 1636] and canon 1 [*DS* 1651]), and it excluded the term *consubstantiation* in favor of *transubstantiation,* the use of which was said to be most appropriate (can. 2 [*DS* 1652]). Whereas Lateran IV was saying that the body and the blood are "truly contained," the Fathers favored (1547) a wider formulation: "truly and really contained," which they completed later (1551) with the term *substantially.* They also stated that Christ is "present sacramentally." Subsequent to this, the notion of real presence became common in Catholic theology and catechesis. The council also claimed the legitimacy of the worship rendered to the real presence. Among other practices regarding the Eucharist, it reminded the faithful that sacramental confession of grave sins is prescribed before receiving Communion—but it did not present that point as a basic truth* of faith (*DS* 1661).

Ten years later, in session XXI (1562), the council stated that Communion from the chalice and the Communion of young children are not part of what is necessary for salvation*: the church exercises in such things the power with which it is entrusted regarding sacraments; the essential thing is that their substance be safe (*DS* 1728, 1731, 1734). Two months later, the council referred back to the pope the question of the concession of the chalice, whenever it was a need (*DS* 1760). The concession made in 1564 to the metropolitans of the German-speaking countries and of Hungary lasted 20 years; Communion from the chalice had already become a sign of denominational differentiation.

In session XXII (also in 1562) the council defined the content of the Catholic faith regarding the Mass: it is a nonbloody sacrifice, offered for the living and the dead, in which is made present the sacrifice of the cross; and the ministry* of that sacrifice was instituted in the Last Supper at the same time as the Eucharist (*DS* 1740, 1751–1754). On that occasion the council dismissed the wish that the Mass be celebrated in the vernacular language, but it recommended that it be explained to the faithful (*DS* 1747).

c) Roman Missal of 1570. The reform of the missal and of the breviary had been entrusted to the pope by the council. The missal reformed by Pius V, "according to the norm of the Fathers," that is, according to the early church, generally confined itself to the state in which the liturgy of the Mass had been four or five centuries earlier. But in accordance with 16th-century practice it adopted as a fundamental form the Mass said by the priest with a small congregation, instead of the celebration in the ecclesial assembly. Although it had not originally been imposed on those churches that had their own liturgical tradition, in the course of the succeeding centuries this missal became the quasi-exclusive form of eucharistic celebration in the Western Catholic Church.

d) Eucharistic Theology after Trent. For more than three centuries Catholic theologians considered the way in which the Eucharist was realized as sacrifice. The history of doctrines attempted to group the diverse explanations (Lepin 1926): theories of the "real immutation" of Christ (thus Robert Bellarmine* and Alphonsus* Liguori), theories of his "mystical immutation," and theories of oblation (French School, Bérulle* and the French Oratorians, as well as Bossuet). In the 20th century, with Casel and his circle of influence, there was a return to an idea close to Thomas Aquinas, the idea of the "mysterious presence" *(Mysteriengegenwart)* of Christ's own action in the sacrifice of the Mass—an idea that seemed to allow Lutheran theologians to overcome the difficulties experienced in the 16th century.

4. Doctrine and Liturgical Reform of Vatican II

Vatican* II produced no document dealing specifically with the Eucharist. However, its texts make abundant mention of it, regarding its connection with the mystery of the Church, ecumenism*, the ministry of the priesthood, and particularly in the framework of the liturgy and liturgical reform. The following points are given particular emphasis: 1) Correlation between the respective tables of the Word and the Eucharist (*SC* 48, 51, etc.); 2) establishing the connection of the Eucharist, not only with the sacrifice of the cross (*SC* 47), but with the whole paschal mystery; 3) the place occupied by the Eucharist among the sacraments of Christian initiation* (*SC* 71, etc.); 4) interaction between church and Eucharist (*see LG* 26), in the perspective opened up by H. de Lubac, with a change of emphasis that signals a move from a theology of the church viewed primarily as an organized society* (e.g., with Bellarmine) to a theology of the church as sacrament; 5) the importance of the active participation of the faithful in the eucharistic celebration, following the line developed since Pius X *(SC);* 6) the Eucharist seen simultaneously as source and summit of Christian life (*LG* 11). The *Eucharisticum Mysterium* of 1967 was to sum up the teachings of the council on the Eucharist.

The reform of the Roman liturgy, determined and set in motion by the council, dealt in particular with the following questions about the celebration of the Eucharist: 1) The possibility of using the vernacular language; 2) the creation of a greatly enlarged cycle of readings to include, on Sunday, a supplementary reading from the Old Testament and a new insistence on the homily; 3) restoration of the universal prayer; 4) simplification of the offertory prayers; 5) concelebration by priests; 6) recitation aloud of the eucharistic prayer and the suggestion of several eucharistic prayers, including in particular an epiclesis; 7) Communion from the chalice along with the consecrated bread.

5. Latest Tendencies in Theology

It is certainly much too early to attempt a synthesis of the tendencies in contemporary eucharistic theology. We shall at least take note of the attention paid by theologians (claimed by Bouyer 1966) to the fundamental form of the action, whether it is a matter of comparing the *memorial* to the Hebrew *zikkaron* or of attempting to bring out the *Sinngestalt* from the action, its fundamental form (Lies 1978; Ratzinger 1981). What is underscored is the following: the connection of the Eucharist to the paschal mystery, to the history of salvation and to eschatology* (e.g., Tillard 1964; Durrwell 1980); its pneumatological dimension (impor-tance of the epiclesis). In the problematics of the real presence, new concepts have been proposed, some of which were found gravely insufficient by Paul VI's encyclical *Mysterium fidei* ("transfinalization," "transignification"). Similarly, attempts have been made to employ the language of the presence in new philosophical contexts (*see* Marion 1982) or by resorting to the philosophy* of language (Ladrière 1984). Eucharistic theology has been used as a core around which to organize ecclesiology, as part of a particularly creative current in Orthodox theology (Afanassieff 1975; Zizioulas 1985; *see* McPartlan 1993); it has also been possible to link it to a sort of anthropology* (Martelet 1972), or to suggest a perspective borrowed from morality (Lacoste 1984). Last, ecumenical reflection endeavors to remove the misunderstanding remaining from the debates of the 16th century (Thurian 1981).

• **Concept:** G. Dix (1945), *The Shape of the Liturgy,* London.

J.-A. Jungmann (1949), *Missarum Sollemnia,* Freiburg (5th Ed. 1962).

C. Mohrmann (1965), *Études sur le latin des chrétiens,* vol. III, Rome, 351–76 (on *missa*).

H. B. Meyer (1989), *Eucharistie: Geschichte, Theologie, Pastoral,* Regensburg.

P.-M. Gy (1990), *La liturgie dans l'histoire,* Paris; (1992 *a*), "De l'Euch.: Prière au pain et au vin eucharistiés," in A. Heinz, H. Rennings (Ed), *Gratias agamus: Studien zum eucharistischen Hochgebet: Mélanges B. Fischer,* Freiburg, 111–16; (1992 *b*), "Le 'nous' de la prière eucharistique," *MD* 191, 7–14.

T. J. Talley (1992), "Structures des anaphores anciennes et modernes," *MD* 191, 15–43.

1.

A. Hänggi, I. Pahl (1968), *Prex Eucharistica: Textus e variis liturgiis antiquioribus selecti,* Fribourg.

B. Botte (1972), *La Tradition apostolique de saint Hippolyte,* 4th Ed., Münster.

G. Kretschmar (1977), "Abendmahlsfeier I. Die alte Kirche, " *TRE* 1, 59-89; "Abendmahl III. 1. Die alte Kirche," *TRE* 1, 229–78.

A. Verheul (1980), "La prière eucharistique d'Addaï et Mari," *QuLi* 61, 19–27.

P. Bradshaw (1995), *La liturgie chrétienne en ses origines,* Paris, 151–81.

1 . a)

F. Hamm (1928), *Die liturgischen Einsetzungsberichte im Sinne vergleichender Liturgieforschung untersucht,* Münster.

B. Botte (1953), "Note historique sur la concélébration dans l'Église ancienne," *MD* 35, 9–23.

E. Cutrone (1990), "The Liturgical Setting of the Institution Narrative in the Early Syrian Tradition," in J. N. Alexander (Ed.), *Time and Community: Mélanges Talley,* Washington, D.C., 105–14.

E. Mazza (1992), *L'anafora eucaristica: Studi sulle origini,* Rome.

T. J. Talley (1993), "Word and Sacrament in the Primitive Eucharist," in E. Carr, et al. (Ed.), *Eulogèma: Mélanges Taft,* Rome, 497–810.

P.-M. Gy (1995), *"The Shape of the Liturgy de Dom Gregory Dix (1945),"* *MD* 204, 31–50.

1 . b)

J. Betz (1955–63), *Die Eucharistie in der Zeit der griechischen Väter,* Freiburg.

Lies (1978), "Eulogia: Überlegungen zur formalen Sinngestalt der Eucharistie," *ZKTh* 100, 69–120.

2 . a)

M. Rubin (1991), *Corpus Christi: The Eucharist in Late Medieval Culture,* Cambridge.

2 . b)

H. de Lubac (1944), *Corpus Mysticum: L'Eucharistie et l'Église au Moyen Age: Étude historique,* Paris.

H. Jorissen (1965), *Die Entfaltung der Transsubstantiationslehre bis zum Beginn der Hochscholastik,* Münster.

I. Furberg (1968), *Das* Pater noster *in der Messe,* Lund.

J. de Montclos (1971), *Lanfranc et Bérenger: La controverse euchar. du XIe s,* Louvain.

B.-D. Marliangeas (1978), *Clés pour une théologie du ministère:* In persona Christi, in persona Ecclesiae, Paris.

D. Burr (1984), *Eucharistic Presence and Conversion in Late Thirteenth-Century Franciscan Thought,* Philadelphia.

G. Macy (1984), *The Theologies of the Eucharist in the Early Scholastic Period: A Study of the Salvific Function of the Sacrament according to the Theologians c. 1080–c. 1220,* Oxford.

R. Imbach (1993), "Le traité de l'Eucharistie de Thomas d'Aquin et les averroïstes," *RSPhTh* 77, 175–94.

3. a)

K. Lehmann, W. Pannenberg (Ed.) (1986), *Lehrverurteilungen-Kirchentrennend?* Freiburg-Göttingen.

3. b)

M. Lepin (1926), *L'idée du sacrifice de la messe d'après les théologiens depuis l'origine jusqu'à nos jours,* 3rd Ed., Paris.

A. Härdelin (1965), *The Tractarian Understanding of the Eucharist,* Uppsala.

J. Wohlmuth (1975), *Realpräsenz und Transsubstantiation im Konzil von Trient,* Berne-Frankfurt.

4.

Instruction *Eucharisticum Mysterium* (1967), *DC* 64, 1091–22.

R. Kaczynski (1976, 1988, 1997), *Enchiridion documentorum instaurationis liturgicae* I (1963–73), Turin; II (1973–83), Rome; III (1993–1993), Rome.

5.

Bibliography of recent publications in M. Zitnik (1992), *Sacramenta. Bibliographia Internationalis,* 4 vols., Rome.

J.-M. R. Tillard (1964), *L'eucharistie, Pâque de l'Église,* Paris.

L. Bouyer (1966), *Eucharistie: Théologie et spiritualité de la prière eucharistique,* Paris.

N. Lash (1968), *His Presence in the World,* London.

L. Ligier (1971), *Il sacramento dell'Eucharistia,* Rome.

G. Martelet (1972), *Résurrection, eucharistie, genèse de l'homme,* Paris.

N. Afanassieff (1975), *L'Église du Saint-Esprit,* CFi 83.

F. X. Durrwell (1980), *L'eucharistie sacrement pascal,* Paris.

J. Ratzinger (1981), *Das Fest des Glaubens,* Einsiedeln.

M. Thurian (1981), *Le mystère de l'eucharistie, une approche œcuménique,* Paris.

J.-L. Marion (1982), "Le présent et le don," *Dieu sans l'être,* Paris, 225–58.

J.-Y. Lacoste (1984), "Sacrements, éthique, eucharistie," *RThom* 84, 212–42.

J. Ladrière (1984), "Approche philosophique d'une réflexion sur l'eucharistie," *L'articulation du sens,* vol. 2, CFi 125, 308–34.

J. D. Zizioulas (1985), *Being As Communion,* Crestwood, N.Y.

H. B. Meyer (1989), *Eucharistie, Geschichte, Theologie, Pastoral,* Regensburg, 441–63.

P. McPartlan (1993), *The Eucharist Makes the Church: Henri de Lubac and John Zizioulas in Dialogue,* Edinburgh.

W. Pannenberg (1993), *Systematische Theologie* 3, Göttingen, 314–69.

O. González de Cardedal (1997), *La entraña del cristianismo,* Salamanca, 463–522.

PIERRE-MARIE GY

See also **Anointing of the Sick; Baptism; Being; Communion; Confirmation; Marriage; Mass, Sacrifice of the; Mystery; Ordination/Order; Penance; Sacrament**

Eucharistic Conversion. *See* **Being; Eucharist**

Eucharistic Presence. *See* **Being; Eucharist**

Euchites. *See* **Messalianism**

Eudes, John. *See* **Heart of Christ**

Euthanasia. *See* **Death**

Eutyches. *See* **Chalcedon, Council of; Monophysitism**

Evagrius Ponticus. *See* **Asceticism**

See **Asceticism**

Evangelicalism. *See* **Anglicanism; Methodism; Protestantism**

Evangelization. *See* **Mission/Evangelization**

Evil

A. Fundamental Theology

a) Classical Theory. Does evil have a being? All the theoretical instincts of classical antiquity encouraged thinkers to respond to this question by attenuating the ontological status of that which contravened the harmonious order of things. Aristotle denies that there is anything evil among the eternal realities (*Met.* VIII, 9, 1051 a). According to Plotinus, evil cannot be present either in that which is, or in that which is beyond being; it is present only in material realities, because they are mingled with nonbeing (*Enneads* I, VIII, 3). Evil is therefore concealed within beauty* "in order that its reality should remain invisible to the gods" (*Enneads* I, VIII, 15).

However, the question appeared to be more pressing with regard to the coherence of theology* than it was for philosophical reasoning. If the world is indeed the work of a good and omnipotent God*, what status is to be assigned to evil? The classical response was adopted in response to the Gnostics (gnosis*), for whom the world was nothing other than the imperfect work of a demiurge, rather than of the supreme God. Above all, it was also adopted in response to the Manicheans (Manicheanism*), who asserted that evil has just as substantial an existence as good: from the beginning, and as a matter of principle, the combat between good and evil has informed history* with meaning. Christianity was able to articulate its response at an early stage, as in this passage from Origen* (*Princ.* II, 9, 2, *In Joh.* II, 17, PG 14, 137; *see also* Basil* of Caesarea, PG 31, 341): "Do not imagine that God is the cause of the existence of evil, or that evil has its own substance [*hupostasis*]. Perversity does not exist as if it was some living thing; one can never place its substance [*ousia*] before one's eyes as if it truly existed." In the writings of Augustine*, accepting the reality of evil seems still more of a concession to dualism: depriving evil of any reality becomes an elementary theological tactic for rendering dualism impracticable (e.g., *Conf.* III. vii. 12). Evil has no being in reality; it has no status other than as "privation of good" *(privatio boni);* it is the absence of that which should be; and God is not capable of being the cause of nonbeing (*De quaest.* 83, q. 21).

In the Middle Ages, the ontology of the transcendentals provided an ample framework within which to treat the nonreality of evil. If that which is, by virtue of being that which is, is one, true, and good, and if *ens et bonum convertuntur* ("being and good are interchangeable"), then evil in all its forms must be excluded from any ontological inventory of the world, in which it appears only as the limit of being. As L.-B. Geiger wrote (1969): "The realm of the good therefore extends as far as that of being, since the only positive element that distinguishes evil itself from nothingness pure and simple—that is to say, the requirement of being, the having to be—is still a good, and for that reason it is the indispensable foundation for whatever there is of evil." To the extent that there is anything beautiful and good in evil, it was generally agreed that God, "the universal moderator of everything that is" (*universalis provisor totius entis:* Thomas* Aquinas, *ST* Ia, q. 22, a. 2), "has judged it better," as Augustine puts it (*Enchir.* chap. 27), "to draw good from evil than not to permit the existence of any evil." It was believed that God chastises, that he desires the evil of punishment*, but that his responsibility does not extend to moral evil or "sackcloth and ashes." It was possible to give a brief response to the question of physical evil, although that response could also be expanded, or complicated, by adding that the fallen angels*, the demons*, are responsible to some extent for the physical evils that human beings suffer. On the other hand, it was possible to provide an elegant solution to the question of moral evil by attributing to humanity the privilege of being the first cause (Aquinas, *ST* Ia IIae, q. 112, a. 3, ad 2), even while adding that humanity does not thus create anything. Maritain, in his original reinterpretation of Aquinas's themes, was thus able to interpret sin as "the annihilating initiative of the created will" (1946, passim). In the terms adopted by Journet, moral evil is strictly speaking not a matter of action, but of "disaction" or deficient action (1961). In both cases, therefore, the denial that evil has any reality requires that an effort be made toward a rational discourse on nonbeing. Ontology cannot offer any hospitality to evil, but it can attempt to give it an appropriate "non-ontology."

The classical theory cannot avoid addressing the problem of providence*. Once it is accepted that God is good and that he alone is God, two tasks must be accomplished: to remove from God the burden of responsibility for evil, and to place that burden on those who are created and endowed with liberty*. Yet if human beings are the primary cause of moral evil, is the fate of creation* out of the hands of God? Maritain sets up his argument by conceding to human beings the capacity to place obstacles in the way of divine grace*: a human being who enters into the logic of evil through "not considering the moral rule" receives divine motions, but these motions can be broken. One might then object (Nicolas 1960) that on this view God loses his sovereignty and ceases to be the author of the drama, becoming instead its principal player. Against the idea of a grace that sinners are able to resist, but that is accomplished as "unbreakable motion" in those whose wills do not falter, one could also have recourse to a concept derived from Aquinas, that of the "antecedent permissive decree," and link it to the Thomist (Bañezian) notion of "physical pre-motion" (Bañezianism*-Molinism-Baianism, Thomism*). The same objections could also be raised in response to a more recent defense of God's innocence (Garrigues 1982), which is based on the Thomist principle that God, being aware of his creatures only to the extent that he causes them, is incapable of forming the idea of evil (*see* Aquinas, *ST* Ia, q. 15, a. 3, ad 1). If one seeks a radical guarantee of the innocence of God, one will come to think that God is so transcendent that he has lost control of his creation (Nicolas, *RThom* 83, 649–59).

b) The Best of Worlds. Evil, even when deprived of any foundation in reality, does not cease to figure in any experiential inventory of the world: "to set forth the negative nature of evil is not to set forth its negation" (Geiger 1969). Accordingly, depriving evil of reality in principle does not settle any question. Perhaps because dualism no longer confronts modern thought as a real enemy—as it confronted Aquinas in the form of Catharism*—modern thought does not hesitate to accept that evil exists, and saves itself the trouble of asking whether this "existing" is or is not endowed with being. Instead, it handles the problem within the modern framework of theodicy. Should the world be accused of imperfection because of the presence of suffering and of evil wills? Can one consistently affirm that a good and omnipotent God has created this world in which there is evil? Leibniz* responds that in the lawsuit that human beings bring against God, he must be acquitted, because the world, as it is, is the best of all possible worlds. The evil in the world is not unreal, whether it is metaphysical evil (the limitation inherent in the creation, taken as such), physical evil, or moral evil. Evil is necessary for the promotion of the greatest possible created good. God could have created a world from which evil was absent, but such a world would necessarily have been a world from which every free creature was also absent. It would also have been less perfect than our world, in which we are free to will evil, but also to will good. This argument can be found as early as Augustine and has continued in use for a very long time (e.g., Swinburne 1979).

A. Plantinga deserves credit for having provided a significantly revised version of the argument in the course of recent discussions of the question. On the one hand, Leibniz's argument is shown to be invalid, because the concept of "the best of all possible worlds" contains the same type of contradiction as the concept of "the greatest prime number": however many worlds exist, one can always conceive a better one. On the other hand, by making use of the discussions about "possible worlds" within the contemporary logic, one can identify worlds that, in strict logic, God could not have "actualized." Finally, the examination of moral evil makes it possible to identify "transworld depravity," a form of malice that is valid not only for this world but for other possible worlds, and that shows up the inconsistency in the idea that Peter, while remaining Peter, might not have acted as he did act in this world. Accepting the logical necessities that weigh down on God himself thus allows us to affirm, within a framework that is not theodicy but a "defense of free will," that the existence of evil does not contradict either God's knowledge* or his power (*see* the summaries given in chaps. 4–8 of *The Nature of Necessity,* Oxford, 1974).

Thus, the modern treatment of evil does not prevent evil from continuing to be an ontological scandal. One must return to the theology of providence for an account of it, as well as to Hegel*. His concept of the negative provides a way of thinking about the contribution of evil to the history of the spirit as a necessary term in the dialectic, and thus endows thought with a theoretical instrument that is capable of ratifying the reality of evil, within the framework of an ontology that is concerned to get beyond the elementary opposition between being and nothingness, without placing the responsibility on God—who himself puts the negative to the test—and without permitting any drift into dualism.

c) Evil and Meaning. Evil is deprived of being in the classical theory, and is not necessarily present in the modern theory, except to promote the greatest good; however, it does not follow that the experience of evil is deprived of any meaning. The suffering of human beings—already omnipresent in the critiques leveled at Christian theories, such as Leibniz's, by Enlightenment thinkers such as Hume or Voltaire—is theoretically noteworthy in that it is capable of acquiring a meaning. Nevertheless, it acquires this meaning, not within the limits of its own experience, but from the human suffering and death assumed by God in Jesus Christ. Theology can shed no light on the scandalous experience of evil—whether it be the Lisbon earthquake, as for Enlightenment thinkers, or Auschwitz in contemporary thought—except by measuring it against the event at Golgotha. God on the cross did not take all suffering upon himself, since human beings have continued to suffer even after the crucified one suffered, but he does allow all human suffering to take on a degree of christological significance. Not only is suffering educational for human beings, but the suffering of believers achieves "what is lacking in Christ's afflictions" (Col 1:24). Without claiming to "explain" evil, a theology of creation could also perceive in the act of the creator a divine "self-limitation" (Jüngel 1990), which is not identical with a pure and simple kenosis* of divine omnipotence (as is the case in Jonas 1984), but permits a distancing of Christian theory from the God of metaphysics—and therefore also from metaphysical interpretations of evil.

The theological meaning of evil may also be radicalized in a different way when theologians attempt to introduce pathos with respect to God himself. The idea of a God who is the "companion of the sufferings" of human beings (A. N. Whitehead), and the range of systematic treatments of this idea in the various theologies of the suffering of God, in theopaschite Christologies*, and elsewhere, complete the project of theodicy within a mode of hyperbole. There is no need for any "lawsuit," for in a certain sense the test of suffering sets the seal on a communion* between God and humanity. The suffering that this world contains is not an expedient, permitting the engendering of a greater good: it is presented as the most human of experiences, being an experience that God undergoes within his own being.

Finally, is it necessary to rationalize evil (*see* Phillips 1986 versus Swinburne 1979 and Hick 1966)? Doubtless, following G. Marcel's distinction, we should accept that there is not exactly a problem of evil—for the existence of a problem implies the possibility of a complete solution—but rather, a mystery* of evil (Geiger 1969). In this regard, it is possible to accuse every theory of being cynical (e.g., G. Baudler, *Wahrer Gott als wahrer Mensch,* Munich, 1977). To deny that evil has any reality, or to integrate it into the productive logic that generates history, may lead us to forget that the question is less theoretical than practical: first and foremost, evil requires not to be understood, but to be combated. Dostoyevsky's Ivan Karamazov based his reasoned atheism* on the suffering of the innocent, but the only response that he receives is provided, indirectly, by the spiritual experience* of the *starets* Zozimus. The presence of evil is "radical" within humanity, according to Kant*, but good will can exist. The suffering of human beings is obvious, but we have a duty to relieve it. Pope Pius XII avoided a number of theoretical pitfalls when he declared that it is morally legitimate to give birth without pain and to use analgesics (*DC*, vol. 53, 87; vol. 54, 326–40). It is a commonplace truth that even the most intelligent morality or holiness* cannot hunt all the evil out of the world, yet theology operates on the presupposition that God gives a "response" to evil that is wholly action* rather than a use of words (Bouyer 1946). Humanity cannot come to the end of every evil, but the Resurrection* of Christ manifests God's power and capacity. The question of the ontological status of evil in this world may therefore be left, wholly deliberately, in suspense. Even if God is no longer a hidden God, his work in the world remains a "hidden work" *(opus absconditum).*

• F. Billicsich (1936, 1952, 1959), *Das Problem des Übels in der Philosophie des Abendlandes,* 3 vols., Vienna.
L. Lavelle (1940), *Le mal et la souffrance,* Paris.
C. S. Lewis (1940), *The Problem of Pain,* London.
L. Bouyer (1946), "Le problème du mal dans le christianisme antique," *Dieu vivant* 6, 17–42.
J. Maritain (1946), *Court traité de l'existence et de l'existant,* Paris, repr. in *OC* IX, esp. 98–118.
A. G. Sertillanges (1948, 1951), *Le problème du mal,* 2 vols., Paris.
K. Barth (1950), *KD* III/3 (*Dogmatique,* Geneva, 1962–63).
B. Welte (1959), *Über das Böse,* Freiburg-Basel-Vienna.
J.-H. Nicolas (1960), "La permission du péché," *RThom* 60, 5–37, 185–206, 509–46.
C. Journet (1961), *Le Mal,* Paris-Bruges.
J. Maritain (1963), *Dieu et la permission du mal,* Paris (3rd Ed. 1993).
J. Hick (1966), *Evil and the God of Love,* London.
L.-B. Geiger (1969), *L'expérience humaine du mal,* Paris.
D. Sölle (1973), *Leiden,* Stuttgart-Berlin.
A. Plantinga (1974), *God, Freedom and Evil,* New York, 7–64.
R. Swinburne (1979), *The Existence of God,* Oxford, 200–224.
H. U. von Balthasar (1980), *Theodramatik* III, Einsiedeln, 125–86.
Y. Labbé (1980), *Le sens et le mal,* Paris.
W. Sparn (Ed.) (1980), *Leiden: Erfahrung und Denken, Materialien zum Theodizeeproblem,* Munich.
J.-M. Garrigues (1982), *Dieu sans idée du mal,* Limoges (New Ed., Paris, 1990).
H. Jonas (1984), "Der Gottesbegriff nach Auschwitz," in O. Hofius (Ed.), *Reflexionen finsterer Zeit,* Frankfurt, 61–86.
D. Z. Phillips (1986), "The Challenge of What We Know: The Problem of Evil," *Belief, Change and Forms of Life,* London, 52–78.
E. Jüngel (1990), "Gottes ursprüngliches Anfangen als schöpferische Selbstbegrenzung," *Wertlose Wahrheit,* BEvTh 107, 151–62.

JEAN-YVES LACOSTE

See also **Being; Good; Peace; Violence; War**

B. Moral Theology

The concept of moral evil attributes evil to the sphere of action. It presupposes the denial of ontic status to evil, and it situates evil entirely within the sphere of history.

In the course of its struggles with the Gnostics (gnosis*), Christianity identified as heresy* the notion that evil is attributable to the materiality of the world, and specifically of the body. Ascetic hostility to the actions of bodily life—eating, drinking, sexual intercourse, and so on—is suspect in the New Testament, as impugning the creation* (e.g., 1 Tm 3:3 f.). When New Testament authors speak of "flesh" to express the disposition of the moral agent to evil, they point not to the body as such, but to a state of moral psychology, *phronema sarkos* (Rom 6:6), in which one is dominated by material need and unable to act freely.

Evil may be considered under one of two descriptions, active or passive *(malum actionis, malum passionis),* as sin* or suffering. The Judeo-Christian theological tradition*, in which faith* in the purposiveness of divine providence* is fundamental, has maintained that suffering must be subsumed under the intentional interaction of God* and humanity. The inarticulate suffering of animals cannot be attributed to human beings. Suffering must speak of some divine purpose if it is to be comprehended within the history of a moral agent. "Does disaster come to a city, unless the Lord has done it?" (Am 3:6). Suffering thereupon becomes moralized as the occasion for responsive action, evil or good: patience or impatience under temptation*, honesty or dissimulation under punishment*, courage or cowardice before danger, and so on.

In making use of the concept of sin, one recognizes that evil is part of the evil action itself and is not to be imputed to circumstances or conditions. However, evil may be attributed objectively, to the form of the act, or subjectively, to the disposition of the agent. These two starting points have sometimes been contrasted with each other, but they are both necessary, and are mutually corrective in defining moral evil.

In an objective attribution, an evil action is an action that is not what it should be. This is the meaning of sin as "transgression" or "wrong," terms that point to the idea of failure to accomplish. The Greek term *hamartia,* sometimes thought to encapsulate this idea, is often contrasted with a supposedly Jewish sense of "radical sin," but this is misleading, since the most that can be demonstrated is a difference of emphasis. One might even say that precisely this notion of sin as transgression characterized the morality of the Pharisees, which Jesus* criticizes ("Now you Pharisees cleanse the outside of the cup and the dish, but inside you are full of greed and wickedness," Lk 11:39), and that it belongs to the legalistic culture of ancient Judaism*. Here belongs much of traditional ethics* as a deliberative science, with its notion of moral law*, the distinction between sins of omission and sins of commission, and so on. The "manifold" character of *hamartia,* to which Aristotle draws attention in the *Nicomachean Ethics* (1106 *b* 28), springs from the manifold possibilities for action afforded by the complexities of the world. When one seeks the rules of action, evil acts have to be studied according to their different types, for they are not yet part of any subject's history, and their formal relations to specific moral laws are all that there is to be considered. Such an ethics cannot, therefore, dispense with casuistry*.

According to Jesus' critique of the Pharisaic exposition of the law, starting from such a point can never bring us to confront the personal and historical dimensions of evil. It views sin only as a possibility, and past sin only as a contingent accident. Yet behind every evil act there lies a subjective reality of evil: "For from within, out of the heart of man, come evil thoughts" (Mk 7:21). This is the meaning of sin as "guilt," a subjective evil inherent in the moral orientation of the agent. To recognize evil as belonging to one's acts, one must acknowledge not merely error or failure in performance, but disorder in one's agency as such.

Jesus' doctrine of the "heart" must not be confused with the modern (18th-century) concept of "motive," a purely "possible" act of the mind supposed to lie behind each external act but not a root-source for *all* acts. The notion of "heart" lies, rather, somewhere between the notion of character* and the idea of original sin*, an involvement of the whole of humanity in evil. Whatever different forms sins may take objectively—Jesus lists a number of them—the decisive factor is their common source (Mk 7:1–23). Augustine* describes this root of sin as the love* of self, in contrast to the love of God (*City of God* 14, 28). As there is no real alternative to God that the heart may love, it turns on itself, negating the whole world of real existence to conjure up a solipsistic universe.

The complementarity of the two starting points can be seen as each takes on certain emphases of the other. On the one hand, the law in Jesus' teaching is unified by a sovereign command of love, which undergirds all the rules, identifies one failure in which all possible failures are comprised: "If I speak in the tongues of men and angels, but have not love" (1 Cor 13:1; *see* Mk 12:28–31). On the other hand, the idea of a root source of evil is developed by differentiation into a specification of the corruptions to which the moral agent is liable. An analysis of the disorders of the soul in terms of "capital vices" has been common in the Evagrian tradition of spiritual* theology (e.g., in Maximus* the Confessor).

To recognize the evil of one's action requires that one enter into this dialectic of objective and subjective attribution. Otherwise, in considering the idea of responsibility *of* moral evil, one is reduced to the pure incomprehensibility of "dumb" suffering. On the purely objective side, transgression dissolves into a failure of execution that befalls an act accidentally, without engaging the responsibility of the agent, as when an athlete fails to break a speed record because of a contrary wind. On the purely subjective side, the root of evil becomes so deeply hidden that it in no way characterizes the forms of objective action, which thereby become morally indifferent. The acceptance of responsibility for the evil of the action is lost sight of. Critics of Stoicism* in the ancient world thought that this followed from its doctrine of "things indifferent," while in recent times proportionalism* has incurred the same objection because of its sharp differentiation of pre-evil and moral evil, the former being of no moral account, the latter lurking so deep in the depths of the "fundamental option" as to be discerned only in the anxious conscience* and never in categorically evil acts. Between the two, the guilty party, hunted by the philosophers of every continent, slips through undetected.

• Augustine, *City of God,* BAug 33–37; *The Nature of the Good,* BAug 1, 437–509.

J. Edwards, *On the Nature of True Virtue,* in *Ethical Writings,* P. Ramsey (Ed.), New Haven, 1989.

E. Kant, *Die Religion innerhalb der Grenzen der blossen Vernunft,* AA 6, 1968.

Thomas Aquinas, *De malo.*

♦ K. Barth (1950), *KD* III/3 (*Dogmatique,* Geneva, 1962–63).

I. Hausherr (1952), *Philautie,* Rome.

B. Welte (1959), *Über das Böse,* Freiburg-Basel-Vienna.

P. Ricœur (1960), *Finitude et culpabilité,* Paris.

O. O'Donovan (1979), *The Problem of Self-Love in St. Augustine,* New Haven.

G.R. Evans (1982), *Augustine on Evil,* Cambridge.

L. Thunberg (1995), *Microcosm and Mediator,* 2nd Ed., Chicago.

OLIVER O'DONOVAN

See also **Action; Conscience; Ethics; Good; Sin**

Evolution

1. Viewpoint of the Natural Sciences

a) Biological Evolution. In whatever way they might interpret it, no scientists contest the fact of evolution. Paleontological proofs are sufficient in themselves to establish its reality: the dating of fossils makes it possible to confirm the gradual increase in complexity and diversification of forms in the whole of the animal and plant kingdoms. A cluster of convergent supplementary arguments, drawn from embryology, comparative anatomy, and molecular biology, bolster these proofs. The fact of evolution also encompasses the appearance of the human race. In a nutshell, the first "chemical fossils" are contemporaneous with the earliest known sedimentary rocks, going back some three and one-half billion years. They are supposedly due to the action of immense colonies of bacteria, then to the action of Cyanophyceae (blue-green algae). The first eukaryotes (Protozoa and Protophyta) appeared about one and one-half billion years ago. Toward the end of the Pre-Cambrian era, the multicellular Metazoa arrived. In the Mid-Cambrian period the first chordates (animals with nonbony spinal cords) made their appearance, then the vertebrates came on the scene in the Silurian era. Starting at the beginning of the Mesozoic period, the age of reptiles, came the first mammals, which would develop in the Tertiary era at the same time as the birds. The first primates go back as far as the Cretaceous period, at the time when the dinosaurs were dying out.

b) Explanatory Theories. Unanimity evaporates as soon as explanatory theories of evolution come into play. No single one of these seems really satisfactory as an answer to Popper's criterion of scientific "refutability" (or falsifiability). The synthetic or neo-Darwinian theory held sway for a long time, and its problematic nature stands out even more clearly today. The earliest evolutionary theorist was not Darwin (1809–82) but Lamarck (1744–1829), later discredited by the English biologist and his followers. Lamarck sketched out his theory in 1802. There, for the first time, the continuity, diversification, and complexity of animal species in their natural gradations were observed and understood as a kinship in which the most complex had descended from the simplest. However, his explanation of the mechanism of evolution could never be confirmed experimentally. It is based on two laws: in any animal*, use of an organ strengthens it "and gives it power in proportion to the length of that use," while disuse causes its atrophy; and second, acquired characteristics are transmitted through heredity. This second law is the Achilles's heel of Lamarckism.

The Darwinian theory of natural selection was established in 1858 by C.R. Darwin and A.R. Wallace (1823–1913). No doubt it was influenced by T.R. Malthus's *Essay on the Principle of Population* (1798). Then it received the useful support of A. Weismann (1834–1914), who distinguished the *Germen* (germ-plasm), which includes inherited characteristics, from the *Soma,* the perishable body that has no influence on heredity—a distinction that dealt the death blow to Lamarckism. The synthetic theory was gradually developed in the years 1930–50, by merging the Darwinian principle with the hereditary laws of G. Mendel (1822–84) and with Hugo de Vries's (1848–1935) theory of mutations.

Once it was fashioned in this way, for quite some time neo-Darwinism enjoyed the support of the great majority of biologists. Nonetheless, "Whatever form it takes, 'Darwinism' does not explain the great evolution that the organizational plan and the phylae, or branchings of classes and orders, involves" (Grassé). Even at the level of the formation of species, we possess no more than a system of plausible hypotheses, and up to now we lack any decisive experimental test. As for the necessary duration of time* that would explain evolutionary diversity, not to mention the evolution of symbiotic systems, the time span that the synthetic theory supposedly indicates seems to be of an entirely different magnitude from the incredibly short duration of actual evolution. In the case of the "neutrality theory of molecular evolution" or the "non-Darwinian" theory of M. Kimura et al. (1971), which studies, in a selective manner, neutral enzymatic variants linked to vast phenomena of genetic drift, these expectations have hardly been confirmed by experiment. It seems therefore that *no* explanatory theory to date has received any real experimental confirmation.

c) Emergence of Man. The paleontology of the great apes shows the gradual emergence of species that by degrees reached modern man, according to a schema that fits naturally into the evolution of the species of animals. In western and southern Africa the hominoids must have clearly distinguished themselves from the other anthropoidal primates about five million years ago. The oldest known fossils belong to the group of Australopithicidae of the *gracilis* type—the *robustus* type appeared two and one-half million years ago, only to disappear about one million years ago. These hominoids had a bipedal gait and an upright stature, but were not of the genus *Homo*. The first hominids made their appearance in western Africa in the form of *Homo habilis,* of which there are fossils going back from 2.3 million to 1.6 million years. The latter was the first hominid to make stone tools. Then *Homo erectus* appeared, between 1.6 million to less than 300,000 years ago. Starting out from western Africa, this species seems to have colonized Asia (especially Java and China), then Europe. Discovered in Java in 1886 and at that time given the name "Pithecanthropus," *Homo erectus* managed to master fire (indisputable traces of that advance are found in Chou-Kou-Tien, near Beijing, dating from more than 500,000 years ago). In turn, *H. erectus* would make way (by progressive transformation?) for *Homo sapiens neanderthalis,* with a big brain of 1,500 cubic centimeters. This species, which may go back as far as 200,000 years, lived for the most part in western Europe and the Middle East. The Neanderthals were the first to bury their dead (death*), this burial being accompanied by symbolic actions. Did these have a religious significance? About 35,000 years ago the Neanderthals vanished entirely to leave the way open for *Homo sapiens sapiens* or Cro-Magnon man, our present species. Our direct ancestors probably came from western Africa by way of Palestine—where remains have been dated from 100,000 years ago—to arrive in Europe 35,000 years ago, at the time of the extinction of the Neanderthals. The two populations, which must have lived alongside each other for a long time in the Middle East, do not seem ever to have interbred. All human beings living today are only of the *sapiens sapiens* type. They reached America and Australia around 25,000 years ago.

2. Philosophico-Theological Viewpoint

a) Definition of Man. In order to judge the theological impact of evolutionary theories, a precise definition of "human" is required. Indeed, the positivist or materialist prerequisites defined by certain varieties of evolutionary theory make them unacceptable to all Christian theology* and explain certain overreactions. Although Cartesian dualism hardly seems capable of solving the problem, a pure monism would reduce us, through evolution, to pure and simple animality, which is not really compatible with the status of being *imago Dei* (in the image of God). How can one achieve a common ground in the division between the biological view, by which we belong to the order of primates, and a "spiritual" view, which transcends the former in a real way? But, are not the biological data enough to define without arbitrariness at which point the human truly begins? In this area, none of the traditional criteria seems to be conclusive. The ownership of a connected and symbolic language seems to be one decisive factor, but leaves no fossil traces. And it remains to be seen whether the evolution of the species is sufficient to explain it.

According to G. Isaye (1987), whose research lies within the framework of a critical proof at the level of basic knowledge, it is possible to establish two specific characteristics peculiar to human beings, irreducible to biological materiality: first, the consciousness of moral obligation; and second, the possibility of proving, without entering a vicious circle, the first principles of knowledge (according to the Aristotelian argument of retortion). In this context biological evolution would provide only the *material conditions for the possibility*—necessary conditions, but not sufficient—of the advent of a conscious and free man. The mastery of language that makes possible the development of culture would then come to *humanize* the hominid that had been formed by this evolution, though this development is not accounted for convincingly by the physiological transformations that made it possible. For Christian theology, the *imago Dei,* the fruit of a specific creative act (creation*), would have appeared complete with language, which opened the way to consciousness and freedom (liberty*).

b) 19th-Century Conflict about the Concepts and Its 20th-Century Resolution. During the 19th century, in the absence of agreement on the definition of man, conflict about these concepts could not avoid a head-on collision. Despite A. R. Wallace's very laudable efforts to make an appropriate distinction between the biological and cultural aspects of man, Darwin and his successors in fact developed a form of biological materialism contrary to the conceptions of all the Christian churches*. Militant agnostics such as T. H. Huxley (1825–95) and E. Haeckel (1834–1919) found themselves in heated argument with churchmen such as the Anglican bishop S. Wilberforce (1805–73), who were determined to defend the Christian faith*. Although there was no official condemnation from the Roman magisterium*, in 1860 the provincial council of Köln declared "transformism," when applied to the human body, to be contrary to the Scriptures and to the Catholic faith. As for Vatican* I, it contented itself with serenely recalling that it was not possible for the truths of the faith and reason* to contradict each other (*Dei Filius,* chap. 4, *DS* 3015–20).

In the same period, a series of attempts were made to reach agreement, such as the one by S. G. J. Mivart (1827–1900) that aimed to reconcile science and the literal interpretation of the Bible*. These attempts were destined to fail for lack of respecting the differences on the two respective planes. In large measure the real solution to the crisis was to come, on the contrary, from the renewal of biblical studies that began in the nonrationalist Protestant circles of the end of the 19th century, then emerged later in the Catholic world with the works of Father M.-J. Lagrange (1855–1938). The differences in literary* genres in the Scriptures, the real character of biblical Revelation*, which is not at all the same as that of the natural sciences*, combined with a more precise evaluation of the latter, was to lead to the resolution of the conflict, sanctioned in the Catholic Church by the declarations of the magisterium—starting with Pius XII's encyclical letter, *Divino afflante Spiritu,* about the principles of biblical exegesis*, continuing with various constitutions and declarations of Vatican* II, and up to John Paul II's speech on 22 October 1996 at the Pontifical Academy of Sciences (*OR,* 29 October). Meanwhile, a book was published that was to be particularly important for the assimilation of evolutionary theory by Christian thought. The book was by Pierre Teilhard de Chardin, who deserves a brief discussion.

c) Teilhard de Chardin (1881–1955). Quite contrary to his intentions, Teilhard found himself in the midst of interminable controversies. For a long time he was suspected of heterodoxy, or even of pantheism*. He was never officially condemned but found himself "invited" to publish nothing outside his field of scientific competence in the strict sense, and he has been badly served by the faulty interpretations of his admirers as much as of his adversaries. All in all, therefore, it is not easy to arrive at a balanced judgment on him, especially in a few lines. H. de Lubac* (1962) rightly proved his religious orthodoxy; but the fact remains that the philosophical community, just like that of the theologians, still refuses to recognize him as one of its own.

Having been admitted to the novitiate of the Society of Jesus in Jersey—where he had as a companion and friend Auguste Valensin, a disciple of Maurice Blondel*—Pierre Teilhard de Chardin was above all a scientist, geologist, and paleontologist, with a well-earned international reputation. He occupied the chair of geology at the Institut Catholique in Paris, following his thesis on the mammals of the high Eocene period (1922) and after having contributed in a decisive way to the discovery of the *Homo erectus* of Chou-Kou-Tien. But he could not help thinking about the essential philosophical and theological implications of such discoveries. Turning away from the overly abstract and deductive Scholastic* philosophy* that he had been taught during his ecclesiastical studies, Teilhard aimed to incorporate his evolutionist concepts into a cosmic vision of universal scope, conceived as a "hyperscience," to draw together the irreversible growth of unity in complexity at all the "biface" levels of becoming of matter and of the mind. In this way he did indeed construct a realist *cosmology,* certainly more dogmatic* than critical: the law of complexity-consciousness, the ascending convergence where "differentiated unity" took on the function of the necessary engine.

Although he was familiar, especially through Edouard Le Roy (1870–1954), with the evolutionary theory of Bergson (1859–1941), which was extremely different from his own, Teilhard was indebted for certain essential aspects of his own thought to that of Blondel, brought to his attention by Auguste Valensin. Two interconnected aspects of it should be mentioned: first, the one beneath the ambiguity of the expression "panchristism," linked to the Leibnizian hypothesis (Leibniz*) of the *vinculum substantiale* (substantial bond); second, Blondel's dialectics of action, which Teilhard would transport to the more naturalist level in his *Energétique intégrale de l'Univers.* Although Teilhard thereby lost Blondel's critical rigor, he brought evolutionary theory into Christian thought on an equal footing, a status that the former has continued to occupy to the present day.

• J.-B. de Lamarck (1809), *La philosophie zoologique,* Paris; (1972), *Inédits,* Paris.
C. Darwin (1859), *The Origin of Species.*
A. R. Wallace (1870), *Contribution to the Theory of Natural Selection.*
J. Huxley (1942), *Evolution, the Modern Synthesis,* London.
E. C. Messenger (Ed.) (1952), *Theology and Evolution,* London.
D. L. Lack (1957), *Evolutionary Theory and Christian Belief,* London.
P. G. Fothergill (1961), *Evolution and Christians,* New York.
R. J. Nogar (1963), *The Wisdom of Evolution,* New York.
M. Kimura, T. Ohta (1971), *Theoretical Aspects of Population Genetics,* Princeton.
P.-P. Grassé (1973), *L'évolution du vivant,* Paris.
F. C. Lewontin (1974), *The Genetic Basis of Evolutionary Change,* New York-London.
E. Mayr (1974), *Populations, espèces, évolution,* Paris.
F. Ayala (1976), *Molecular Evolution,* Sinauer.
C. Petit, E. Zuckerhandl (1976), *Évolution,* Paris.
P.-P. Grassé (1978), *Biologie moléculaire, mutagenèse, évolution,* Paris.

M. J. D. White (1978), *Modes of Speciation,* Freeman.
P.-P. Grassé (1980), *L'homme en accusation,* Paris.
L. Szyfman (1982), *Lamarck et son époque,* Paris.
J. Ruffié (1986), *Traité du vivant,* Paris.
G. Isaye (1987), *L'affirmation de l'être et les sciences positives,* Ed. M. Leclerc, Paris-Namur.
H. de Saint Blanquat (1987), *Les premiers Français,* Tournai.
A. Scott (1988), *The Creation of Life,* Oxford.
J. Reichholf (1990), *Das Rätsel des Menschwerdung,* Munich; (1992), *Der Schöpferische Impuls, eine neue Sicht der Evolution,* Munich.
M. Denton (1992), *Évolution, une théorie en crise,* Paris.
S. Parker (1992), *L'aube de l'humanité,* Fribourg.
L. Duquesne de La Vinelle (1994), *Du Big Bang à l'homme,* Brussels.
P. Tort (Ed.) (1996), *Dictionnaire du darwinisme et de l'évolution,* 3 vols., Paris.
J. Arnould (1998), *Dire la création après Darwin,* Paris.
G. Martelet (1998), *Évolution et création,* vol. I: *Sens ou nonsens de l'homme dans la nature,* Paris.
♦ P. Teilhard de Chardin (works published in Paris) (1955), *Le phénomène humain*; (1956), *L'apparition de l'homme*; (1956), *Le groupe zoologique humain*; (1957), *Le milieu divin*; (1959), *L'avenir de l'homme*; (1962), *L'énergie humaine*; (1965), *Science et Christ*; (1965), *Écrits du temps de guerre, 1916–1919*; (1976), *Le cœur de la matière*; (1961), *Lettres de voyage (1923–1955)*; (1974), *Lettres intimes à Aug. Valensin, etc., 1919–1955*; (1965), Blondel and Teilhard de Chardin, corresp. by H. de Lubac, Paris.
C. Cuénot (1958), *Teilhard de Chardin: Les grandes étapes de son évolution,* Paris.
H. de Lubac (1962), *La pensée religieuse du P. T. de Chardin,* Paris.
M. Barthélemy-Madaule (1963), *Bergson et T. de Chardin*; (1967), *La personne et le drame humain chez T. de Chardin,* Paris.
H. de Lubac (1968), *L'éternel féminin,* followed by *T. de Chardin et notre temps,* Paris.
C. Cuénot (1972), *Ce que T. de Chardin a vraiment dit,* Paris.

MARC LECLERC

See also **Adam; Exegesis; Sciences of Nature**

Exegesis

Exegesis is a set of procedures for establishing the meaning of a text. The need for it arises whenever a text continues to arouse interest or to be regarded as important, as in the case of laws*, treaties, or literary classics. It is not a requirement of the text at the moment of composition: authors and drafters aspire to make their meaning perfectly clear. Nor is it a private transaction between text and individual reader, permitting an unlimited range of interpretation. It is a product of the needs of the community that makes use of or cherishes the text.

Exegesis is of particular importance in a religious community that bases its doctrine, its moral norms, and its spirituality on texts believed to be inspired. Such a community will have an interest both in the elaboration of procedures for finding hitherto unsuspected meanings and applications in the text, and also in the control of types of exegesis that might influence the beliefs and the conduct of its members. For this article, the relevant communities are a) Jewish, b) ecclesiastical, and c) academic.

a) Jewish Exegesis. In principle, all Jewish exegesis presupposes a body of scriptural texts that is fixed, canonical, and authoritative. In reality, the Hebrew Scriptures evolved over many centuries, and the need to bring exegesis to bear on their older parts is already apparent in its later ones. Laws originally relating to a variety of sanctuaries were reinterpreted as prescribing a single centralized cult* (Ex 20:24; Dt 12:5–14). Warnings and prophecies* originally directed to a particular moment of decision were perceived to apply to longer-term historical developments (Is 1–23, 24–27). Narratives* were rewritten to bring out the moral and religious significance of previously recorded history* (1 and 2 Sm; 1 and 2 Kgs; 1 and 2 Chr). One particular form of exegesis, found in writings classified in modern times as apocalyptic*, begins in Deuteronomy (9:1 f.) with the reinterpretation of former prophecies in the light of later events; it continued for several centuries after the close of the Hebrew canon*. It also inspired many of the sectarian writings preserved in the Dead Sea Scrolls. A notable example is the Habakkuk commentary (1QpHab), where the recurrent formula *pesher* could be rendered "the exegesis of this is." In exegesis of this genre, the fulfillment of ancient prophecies is discerned in events of the present or the near future.

Exegesis of this kind, though not unknown in the Greco-Roman world, is peculiarly Jewish. A more international style was also practiced in Jewish communities, particularly in Alexandria and most notably in the voluminous works of Philo (c. 20 B.C.–A.D. 30). Its principal tool, allegorical interpretation, was already known in the pagan world (Theagenus [sixth to fifth centuries B.C.], the Stoics), and had, in part, a similar motivation. Read literally, the behavior of the gods in Homer could seem shocking to cultivated sensibilities; read as allegory, it could be found to convey important truths. Similarly, with the Hebrew Scriptures, the earthiness of many narratives and the apparently crude anthropomorphism* of much of the language about God could be a deterrent to pagan sympathizers and disquieting for reflective Jews. We do not know for certain to which of these categories Philo's readers belonged, but both would be reassured if allegorical exegesis could reveal a congruence between inspired writings and truths discerned through pagan philosophy*.

Yet there were limits to the use of this exegetical technique. Philo himself (*De Migratione Abrahami*, §89–93) criticizes those whose practice of allegorical interpretation led them to neglect those observances that gave the Jewish people their identity—Sabbaths*, dietary laws, and festivals. It was indeed as a corpus of law that the Hebrew Scriptures exercised their greatest influence over the Jewish people. The most characteristic form of Jewish exegesis was the continuous tradition, mostly transmitted orally until the second century A.D., of interpreting legal texts in such a way as to show their bearing on every new circumstance of personal and social life. This began in the time of Ezra, and finds its fullest development in the Mishnah and the Talmud. In Rabbinic literature, *halakha*—the correct way of "walking"—was the primary goal of scriptural exegesis. By the application of simple rules of logic, and by endlessly bringing one text to bear on the meaning of another, the sages aspired to give honor to their sacred law-book, the Torah. They deduced rules from it to govern every eventuality of contemporary life, and also extracted directives from it to authorize those aspects of the Jewish code of conduct that, although established by long usage, were not directly ordained in Scripture.

Not that this was the only form of exegesis practiced by the rabbis. There was more to Scripture than law and moral instruction: there were riches waiting for "investigation" (one of the meanings of the word *midrash*) that could lead to a deeper knowledge* of God and his will for human beings. By now, the Hebrew Scriptures were a closed system. All resources for their interpretation could be found within them. Every detail had to be scrutinized for clues to a correct or more satisfying interpretation; any word or text within the canon could be used to elucidate any other; inconsistencies and obscurities could be resolved by minute comparison with other instances, regardless of original intention or context. However, attractive and endlessly creative though this nonlegal exegesis *(haggada)* might seem, *halakha* remained the paramount form of exegesis.

b) Ecclesiastical Exegesis. "These things took place as examples for us": so Paul (1 Cor 10:6) describes the significance of a series of key events that befell the Israelites in the desert. For Paul, the word *example* is virtually synonymous with *allegory* (Gal 4:24), but it serves to convey the particular thrust of the new Christian exegesis of Old Testament texts. A new factor had appeared in history in the person* and achievement of Jesus Christ. Yet it was also not new, in that it could be found to have been foretold and prefigured in the Hebrew Scriptures. The truth* of the Christian claims for Jesus was confirmed by Old Testament "types" of his salvific destiny; by the same token, Christians now possessed an exegetical key with which to discern hitherto unsuspected meanings in scriptural texts. The congruence of Old Testament prophecies and "types" with the new realities experienced by Christians was a source of profound encouragement (*paraklesis,* Acts 13:15; Rom 15:4) and edification (2 Tm 3:15 f.).

This congruence was also an important resource for the defense of the new faith* against its enemies and critics. The bitter opposition of the synagogue was a factor in the life of the church for the first two centuries of its history. The claim that Jesus was the Messiah* of Jewish expectation, if it was to be made plausible to Jews, had to be presented as a fulfillment of the true meaning of Old Testament texts. Exegesis was therefore central to the debate. Christological interpretation became a staple feature of Christian anti-Jewish apologetic, not only of prophecies accepted as messianic by Jewish exegetes, but also of many other texts that now seemed to take on new meaning as prefigurations of Jesus' Passion*, death*, and Resurrection* (e.g., Ps 22, 118:22 f.; Is 53). Such an interpretation already formed the substance of the argument in Pseudo-Barnabus and Justin. With the exception of a very few authors, this typological or allegorical form of exegesis became a standard feature of Christian writing in the post-apostolic and patristic periods.

In the second century, the church was challenged not only by Judaism but also by Gnosticism (gnosis*): its elaborate speculative systems were supported by allegorical interpretations of Scripture that ranged far wider than those of Christian orthodoxy did. To combat this threat, it was necessary for Christian exegetes to impose limits on the use of allegory and to insist, sometimes on the literal meaning of the text, at other times on Christian allegories in opposition to those of the Gnostics. A notable instance is the interpretation by a number of Church Fathers* (Justin, Irenaeus*, Tertullian*, Theophilus of Antioch) of Genesis 1–3, which they tended to take as a straight record of fact by way of contesting the cosmological speculations of the Gnostics. In the writers of this period, we see already a tension between the need to find christological meanings in Old Testament texts, through the use of typological and allegorical techniques, and the need to oppose the exaggerated use of allegory by the heretics, through an insistence on the literal meaning of certain texts. This tension was to characterize exegesis throughout the patristic period and beyond. In the absence of any clear principle of hermeneutics* that could serve as a guide, these writers were ready to fall back on the principle, already enunciated in the New Testament (e.g., Ti 3:9 f.), that any exegesis not authorized by the church is heretical.

Thus far, Christian exegesis has been primarily a tool for other purposes: apologetics, catechesis*, liturgy*. With a commentary on John by the Valentinian heretic Heracleon (second century) and another, on Deuteronomy, by Hippolytus (204), a new form appeared that was to recur again and again in the patristic period, that of the consecutive commentary on a biblical text. In this new phase, the Bible* was seen not so much as a resource for establishing and defending the faith of Christians, as a treasury capable of yielding untold wealth for the faithful through the diligence of the skilled interpreter. Yet the same tension persisted between literal and nonliteral exegesis. In the case of the Old Testament, it was taken for granted that behind the literal meaning there lay at least one deeper or more edifying meaning. In the case of the New Testament, the literal meaning was more often taken as paramount, especially in opposition to Gnostic allegorizations, which tended to discount the historicity of the Gospels*. Nevertheless, some details, notably in the parables, received elaborate allegorical treatment. The possibilities of allegory were exploited with unrestrained brilliance by Clement († before 215) and Origen* in Alexandria. A more disciplined and literal approach was practiced by the school of Antioch* (Diodorus in the fourth century, Theodore of Mopsuestia [352–428], John Chrysostom*). Overall, however much or little importance was ascribed to the literal meaning, exegesis in the patristic period always rested upon the presupposition that, in almost every case, the true meaning of Scripture was to be found at a deeper level than that of a literal reading of the text. This conception of Scripture as a collection of divine oracles, of which the true sense must be elucidated by disciplined yet imaginative exegesis, remained fundamental until at least the end of the Middle Ages.

c) Scholarly Exegesis. One consequence of this preoccupation with nonliteral exegesis was the additional assumption that Scripture could be interpreted from within. No information was needed from outside, for the Bible itself held all the necessary clues for discerning the meaning of any passage. Not that exegetes had always been blind to the resources offered by linguistic or historical study: ever since Jerome (c. 347–419/20), there had been those who, despite the anti-Semitic prejudices of the church, saw the advantage of consulting Jewish scholars for the elucidation of difficult Old Testament texts. However, it was the influence of Renaissance scholarship that delivered the fatal blow to allegorical exegesis with the introduction of criteria and information from outside the Bible. One of the most frequently cited justifications for reading a text as an allegory was that its literal sense was unintelligible, unedifying, or absurd. However, if scholars could not find parallels or comparable instances in other ancient literature, this alleged strangeness could be shown to be illusory, and recourse to an allegorical interpretation appeared to be unjustified. A series of commentaries therefore began to appear, laden with the fruits of research into comparative material in pagan and Jewish literature. J. B. Lightfoot in England (*Horae Hebraicae et Talmudicae,* 1658–78), J. Wettstein in the Netherlands (*Novum Testamentum Graecum,* 1751–52), P. Billerbeck in Germany (H. Strack and P. Billerbeck, *Kommentar zum Neuer Testament aus Talmud und Midrasch,* 1922–28), J. Bonsirven in France (*Textes rabbiniques... à l'intelligence du Nouveau Testament,* 1955), and, most recently, S. Lachs in the United States (*A Rabbinic Commentary on the New Testament,* 1987) represent a type of commentary in which the progress of exegesis is related to the growth of knowledge about the ancient world. This knowledge was not confined to literature. Other disciplines also began to form essential parts of the exegete's equipment: archeology (e.g., in relation to Old Testament history or to the journeys of Saint Paul); philology (enlarging the possibilities of interpreting rare Hebrew words or applying knowledge of *koine* Greek, gained from papyrus finds, to New Testament texts); and, above all, historical research into neighboring cultures. This, in turn, had another very important consequence: exegesis ceased to be a task performed within and controlled by the church. It used resources and disciplines freely available in the academic world, and was practiced by scholars for whom freedom of inquiry took priority over scrupulous obedience to the church. Hence, the most rapid progress was made by Protestant exegetes. The difficulties caused for the Catholic Church by the tension between the authority of the magisterium* and the necessity to participate in the academic enterprise can be charted in a series of papal and conciliar pronouncements (e.g., *Divino afflante Spiritu* [1943], or the constitution *Dei Verbum* issued by Vatican* II [1965]), as well as in the struggles of conscience of Catholic scholars (M.-J. Lagrange [1855–1938] 1967; P. Grelot 1994). The official evaluation of exegetical methods in the Catholic Church document of 1993, *The Interpretation of the Bible within the Church,* published by the Pontifical Bible Commission, displays a more open approach, although it still insists upon the ultimate authority of the magisterium in all exegetical questions.

The exegetical use of nonbiblical sources is well represented by the "History of Religions" school *(religionsgeschichtliche Schule),* which included J. Weiss (1863–1914), W. Bousset (1865–1920), and H. Gunkel (1862–1932). This group of mainly German scholars argued that many features of New Testament religion are best explained as deriving from the influence of pagan Hellenistic religions. This view was fiercely criticized at the time, and was subsequently found to be valid, if at all, only in the case of the Old Testament, where the influence of Canaanite religion is undeniable. This led to a certain reaction in favor of intratextual exegesis: the Bible itself once again became the prime source of knowledge. Now, however, whereas allegorists had regarded oddities or inconsistencies in the text as signs of deeper meaning, modern critics saw them as indications of its preliterary history. The presence of two barely compatible Creation* stories in Genesis must be the result of a compiler working with material from more than one source. Inconsistency in the use of the divine name* *YHWH* versus *Elohim* indicated that material from different traditions had been amalgamated into a single text. By separating out these strands, it was possible to discern particular tendencies in each, as, for example, in the priestly(P) tradition, a marked interest in ritual matters.

In the early days of this "source criticism" (Old Testament: theory of the four documents, K. H. Graf [1866] and J. Wellhausen [1876–84]; New Testament: theory of the two sources, H.J. Holtzmann [1863], etc.), it was assumed that the underlying materials consisted of written documents (book*). Entirely new possibilities of interpretation followed the recognition that much of this material—laws, narratives, songs of worship—was first handed down by word of mouth. Studies of oral tradition in other cultures made it apparent that transmission required established *forms* (literary* genres) according to the circumstances in which the material was used. Laws, for example, generally tended to have a casuistic form when cited in law courts but an exhortatory or apodictic form when recited in worship. The coexistence of such forms was a sign that they originated in different "life-situations" *(Sitz im Leben)* in society*. These in turn could yield precious information about the religious and cultural history of the people.

The "history of forms" *(Formgeschichte),* as it came to be called, originated in the study of the Old Testament, and achieved notable success, for example, in H. Gunkel's work on the Psalms* (*Commentary,* 1926; H. Gunkel and J. Begrich, *Einleitung in die Psalmen,* 1928–33). However, it had its greatest influence on the study of the gospels (M. Dibelius, *Die Formgeschichte des Evangeliums,* 1919; R. Bultmann, *Die Geschichte der synoptischen Tradition,* 1921). It was not difficult to notice that certain short sections of text *(pericopae)*—such as a saying, a parable*, or an account of an exorcism—occur in different contexts from one Gospel to another. It could then be inferred that each must have existed independently of any context before it was incorporated into a Gospel. The correct way to study a Gospel, therefore, was to see it, no longer as the literary or inspired creation of a single writer, but as an editorial compilation of small scraps that owed their preservation to a period of oral transmission. Examined separately, these *pericopae* were found to have a number of distinct forms. From these forms, and from the pattern of their distribution in the Gospels (some occurring more frequently than others), it was possible to infer their original *Sitz im Leben,* and hence the interests and concerns of the churches in which these materials had been preserved.

This attention to an assumed preliterary phase in the compilation of a Gospel in due course created an interest in the character of the final compiler. Was he simply an editor, doing the best he could with a mass of jumbled material? Or had he a mind of his own, and the capacity to impose a distinctive character on his narrative? By noticing the subtle changes that each evangelist appears to have made in the treatment of such an element (whenever this comparison is possible), and by discerning a pattern emerging in these changes such as might indicate a particular interest of the author, it seemed possible to build up a profile of each evangelist, and to regard them, no longer merely as competent editors, but as creative writers, even—the ultimate accolade—as "theologians" in their own right.

This procedure has been given the name *Redaktionsgeschichte,* the study of the stages and aims of redaction: W. Marxsen on Mark (1956), G. Bornkamm on Matthew (1948), H. Conzelmann on Luke: *Die Mitte der Zeit* (1953). Along with *Formgeschichte,* it has had two consequences that their first practitioners could hardly have foreseen. First, by directing attention away from the Gospel narratives (of Jesus) to the factors that have determined the present forms of these narratives—the concerns of the church *(Formgeschichte)* or the interest and skills of the evangelists *(Redaktionsgeschichte)*—they have relegated the "quest of the historical Jesus" to secondary status (cf. A. Schweitzer, *Von Reimarus zu Wrede,* 1906; E. Käsemann, *ZThK* 51, 1954; J.M. Robinson, *A New Quest of the Historical Jesus,* 1959). Admittedly, the application of these critical methods had begun to cast doubt on the possibility of any reconstruction of "things concerning Jesus" that could claim to be historically reliable. Even the more critically sophisticated "new quest of the historical Jesus" characteristic of the third quarter of the 20th century yielded no scholarly consensus on which a generally accepted life of Jesus could be founded, even though it found reasons to challenge the extreme skepticism of the principal representatives of *Formgeschichte.* Today, many specialists seem ready to accept that the only proper focus of exegetical interest is to be found in the writers and the writings of the New Testament. Jesus, who wrote nothing and has allegedly been shown to be historically inaccessible, seems barely worthy of serious attention. The second consequence has been a notable narrowing, until recently, of the field of inquiry, to the extent that the gospels are interpreted mainly in terms of biblical texts and a relatively small range of intertestamental writings. The most influential representatives of *Formgeschichte,* M. Dibelius and R. Bultmann, brought to their task a wealth of knowledge derived from a thorough education in classical culture, supplemented by an extensive study of relevant Jewish writings. Their followers, not having had the advantage of such a broad culture, certainly developed their critical techniques to a fine point, but they had little that was new to bring to their exegesis. As a result, their work, being concentrated on ever smaller areas of disagreement, began to show signs of diminishing returns and to lose the confidence of those who rely on scholarly exegesis to strengthen and enrich the teaching and preaching* of the Christian faith.

This apparent alienation of critical exegesis from the needs of any community of the faithful was in part responsible for the movement known as "canonical criticism" (research on the function assigned to a text in the elaboration of a corpus intended to be complete—a canon). This was inspired, and is still mainly represented, by the work of B. Childs (*see* especially his *Exodus,* 1974). According to Childs, although the stages antecedent to the formation of a biblical text and the historicity of the events it refers to remain legitimate objects of study, a more important consideration for exegesis is the fact that the text forms part of the canon of Scripture, which evolved within a community of faith. Thus, the fact that the Exodus narrative was given a prime place in the structure of the Old Testament, and the fact that there are frequent references to it in other canonical texts, constitute for Childs at least as important a factor for the understanding and exegesis of the narrative as the conclusions of any historical inquiry into what may actually have happened, or any critical reconstruction of the way in which the biblical accounts reached their present form.

Canonical criticism has won respect, but has not gained wide acceptance (cf. J. Barr 1983). There was a danger that modern critical techniques might have the result of reducing the interest of exegesis to ever finer points of detail within a generally agreed paradigm of interpretation. This danger was to some extent averted by the arrival on the scene of disciplines developed in other fields. Despite the very small sample of evidence available in the New Testament, models of interpretation borrowed from sociology made it seem possible to reconstruct the social and economic conditions prevailing either in Old Testament times (Max Weber 1923) or in the milieus of Jesus and the early church (G. Theissen, *ZThK* 70, 245–71; W. Meeks, *The First Urban Christians,* 1983). Similarly, certain techniques of literary criticism could be used to direct exegesis more securely in the direction of the meaning and the impact originally intended by the author or implied by the structure of the text (structuralism and the set of methods inspired by the functioning of verbal ensembles: the journals *Semeia* or *Sémiotique et Bible,* and other publications of Centre pour l'analyse du discours religieux [CADIR], under the direction of J. Delorme, Lyon; D. Patte 1983). Research into the literary genres and rhetorical devices (J. Muilenburg 1968, G. Kennedy 1984, R. Meynet 1989) consciously or unconsciously used by ancient Greek authors could be used to elucidate the argument of, say, a Pauline letter.

However, even if these and other new arrivals have introduced some fresh air into the somewhat fetid space of modern biblical scholarship, it may be doubted whether they have yet fulfilled all the conditions for making great advances in exegesis in its wider sense. In and of itself, neither a sociological reconstruction of the biblical environment, nor a close analysis of literary form and structure, necessarily promotes understanding of the meaning of Scripture and its relevance for today. Many church members may be tempted to persist in the notion that exegesis has today become an exercise of interest only to scholars. It is no accident that, in many churches today, the most popular form of exegesis is one allegedly based on a "simple" reading of the text, without the encumbrance or the diversion of critical procedures. This approach makes a slogan out of the principle that "the meaning lies on the surface" (R. Gundry, *Mark,* 1993).

Research into the principles of interpretation has aroused new interest in modern times. Some exegetes have profited from the work of Hans Georg Gadamer and Paul Ricoeur, but probably the most significant, though less often recorded, influence on exegesis has been that of the sociology of knowledge (Jürgen Habermas 1987). Albert Schweitzer's famous dictum that anyone seeking to reconstruct the life of Jesus is like a man looking down a deep well and seeing only a reflection of his own face has been found to apply far more widely. Modern theory of knowledge has called into question the possibility of an objective interpretation of *any* ancient text. Each culture, each generation, brings to the task its own presuppositions, its own priorities, and its own agenda. This has been brought to light in a particularly challenging way by liberation* theology (J. Miguez Bonino, *Revolutionary Theology Comes of Age,* 1975). In the past, almost without exception, exegetes have been persons of at least moderate education, personal security, and material well-being. Now, however, exegesis is also in the hands of scholars who have identified themselves and shared their lives with the poor, the oppressed, and the marginalized. Under their scrutiny, and in the light of their presuppositions and priorities, the texts can yield new meanings and new applications (Rowland and Corner 1990). The same goes for black, feminist, and Asian theologians (inculturation*), indeed for any group whose experience and worldview are different from those of people trained in a traditional theological environment. Each of these may develop a distinctive style of exegesis and challenge traditional interpretations; each in due course will reveal its own bias; all must renounce any claim to be able to provide a definitive reading of the sacred text. Exegesis can never be either halted or finalized. This work of continual exploration and revision is a sign of the vitality of the community of faith with which exegesis must engage.

• J. Guillet (1947), "Les exégèses d'Alexandrie et d'Antioche, conflit ou malentendu?" *RSR* 34, 257–302.

H.J. Kraus (1956), *Geschichte der historisch-kritischen Erforschung des Alten Testaments,* Neukirchen.

H.J. Kraus (1967), *Au service de la Bible:. Souvenirs personnels,* Paris.

Cambridge History of the Bible 1 (Early Church) (1970), 412–53; 2 (Middle Ages) (1969), 155–219.

W. Kümmel (1970), *Das NT im 20. Jahrhundert: Ein Forschungsbericht,* Stuttgart.

R. Kieffer (1972), *Essais de méthodologie néotestamentaire,* Gleerup-Lund.

J.F.A. Sawyer (1972), *Semantics in Biblical Research,* London.

F. Dreyfus (1975), "Exégèse en Sorbonne, exégèse en Église," *RB* 82, 321–59.

Sémiotique et Bible: Bulletin d'études et d'échanges publié par le Centre d'analyse des discours religieux (CADIR) (1975–), Lyons.

G. Vermes (1975), "Bible and Midrash," *Post-Biblical Jewish Studies* 59–91 (bibl.), Leyden.

D. and A. Patte (1978), *Structural Analysis: From Theory to Practice,* Philadelphia.

B.S. Childs (1979), *Introduction to the Old Testament As Scripture,* Philadelphia.

B. de Margerie (1980–83), *Introduction à l'histoire de l'exégèse,* 3 vols., Paris.

A. Gibson (1981), *Biblical Semantic Logic: A Preliminary Analysis,* Oxford.

M. Simonetti (1981), *Profilo storico dell'esegesi patristica,* Rome.

J. Barr (1983), *Holy Scripture: Canon, Authority, Criticism,* Oxford.

J. Barton (1984), *Reading the OT: Methods in Biblical Study,* London.

M.-A. Chevallier (1984), *L'exégèse du Nouveau Testament: Initiation à la méthode,* Geneva.

M. Fishbane (1985), *Biblical Interpretation in Ancient Israel,* Oxford.

P. Guillemette, M. Brisebois (1987), *Introduction aux méthodes historico-critiques,* Québec.

A. de Pury (Ed.) (1989), *Le Pentateuque en question: Les origines et la composition des cinq premiers livres de la Bible à la lumière des recherches récentes,* Geneva.

B. Holmberg (1990), *Sociology and the New Testament: An Appraisal,* Minneapolis.

C. Rowland, M. Corner (1990), *Liberating Exegesis,* London.

J. Delorme (1992), "Sémiotique," *DBS* 12, 281–333 (important bibl.).

C. Coulot (Ed.) (1994), *Exégèse et herméneutique: Comment lire la Bible?* Paris.

P. Grelot (1994), *Combats pour la Bible en Église,* Paris.

P. Ricœur (1994), *Lectures 3: Aux frontières de la philosophie,* Paris.

Anthony E. Harvey

See also **Bible; Biblical Theology; Book; Fathers of the Church; Fundamentalism; Gospels; Hermeneutics; History; Holy Scripture; Jesus, Historical; Literary Genres in Scripture; Magisterium; Narrative Theology; Scripture, Senses of; Tradition; Translations of the Bible, Ancient**

Exemplarism. *See* **Bonaventure**

Exinanition. *See* **Kenosis**

Existence of God, Proofs of

By "proofs of the existence of God" is meant the totality of the intellectual procedures by which human reason* strives to affirm God*. They lie within a theological tradition* (particularly vibrant within Catholicism*) that derives in part from the Scriptures (above all Rom 1:18–25, which takes up Wis 13:1–9). The First Vatican* Council reiterated that "God, the source and end of all things, may be known with certainty by the natural light of human reason on the basis of created things" *(Dei Filius).* The antimodernist oath would subsequently reinforce this affirmation: if God could be known with certainty *(cognosci potest),* it followed that he could also be demonstrated *(demonstrari potest)* by "the visible works of the creation*, as a cause by its effects." In the most general sense, the historical development of proofs of the existence of God is probably inseparable from the impulse that faith* imparts to human intelligence in its search for truth*.

1. History of the Proofs

a) Proofs of the existence of God have a prehistory in ancient thought. To justify the belief in the gods, Plato took up the lessons of Socrates—echoed in Xenophon's *Memorabilia* (I, 4 and IV, 3)—and of a whole earlier body of literature, in particular Diogenes of Apollonia; he mentioned or developed at least three arguments based on the antecedence of the "self-moving" soul, the regular order of the universe and the universal consent of the races of humanity (*see Laws* XII, 966 e, as well as the *Philebus,* the *Sophists,* the *Phaedrus* and the *Timaeus* for the first two arguments, and *Laws* X, 886 for the third). But it was above all the themes of the hierarchy of beings and of the universe of the Forms, which, reinterpreted in particular by Augustine* and Anselm*, would leave their mark on the formulation of proofs of the existence of God.

In his *Physics* VII-VIII and *Metaphysics,* Λ, Aristotle advanced an argument that would find great success: a consideration of movement led him to posit the existence of an "unmoved mover." While the *Physics* defines this only in a negative sense, the *Metaphysics* conceives it positively as something living and intelligent (Λ7, 1072 a, 20–25). This immobile prime mover, which moves all things in a desirable and good* manner, as a final cause, being both life and intelligence, is God, a thought that thinks itself and rejoices in itself. God is an eternal and perfect living being (ibid., 1072 b, 27–30).

Alongside Plato and Aristotle, mention may be made of Cicero, not so much for the originality of his thought as for the influence he exerted through his *De natura deorum,* his *De oratore,* and Macrobius's commentary on Cicero's *Dream of Scipio.* For example, one of the first dialectical arguments developed during the Middle Ages, that of Candidus of Fulda, makes use of the ideas of Chrysippus as set forth in the *De natura deorum* (II, VI), combining them with the Augustinian hierarchy of being*, life, and thought *(Dicta Candidi).*

b) The movement of Augustinian thought, as presented in the *De libero arbitrio* and the *De vera religione* (two texts strongly inspired by Plotinus), approaches God in two stages: *ab exterioribus ad interiora* and *ab inferioribus ad superiora* or, as Gilson glosses it, "from that which is inferior in interior things to the higher realities." The *De libero arbitrio,* after reiterating that "we must first believe the great and divine truths that we wish to understand" (1. II, II, 6), offers a series of arguments whose power to prove rests on reason.

The point of departure of the proof is the certainty of having a personal existence and the breaking down of this into existence, life, and intelligence, thus establishing three properties of the human individual. The best of the three, which belongs to humanity alone, is the starting point for a new progression—from the external senses (which apprehend perceptible qualities) and the inner sense (which perceives and judges the external senses) to reason itself (which judges the inner sense). Reason is the best part of human nature, and it is on the basis of reason that the question of God can be posed. However, a difficulty is raised by Evodius: "If I am able to discover something better than what is best in my own nature, I will not immediately label it God. For it seems to me that I should name as God not the being to whom my reason is inferior, but him to whom nobody is superior."

Augustine attempts to resolve this by showing that, if "by itself reason perceives something eternal" and immutable, then it must "recognize at the same time that it is inferior to this being and that this being is its God" (ibid., VI. 14). This thing that goes beyond reason, this thing independent of the soul, and which rules and transcends it, is the eternal, immutable, and necessary Truth; and the Truth, recognized in this way, testifies to the existence of God. It is therefore enough to go inside oneself to discover the Truth, that is to say God.

Augustinianism* permeated the whole of medieval theology, and is particularly noticeable in the work of Anselm. Reviving the Platonic approach to the Forms, the *Monologion* uses the experience* of good things, of great things, and of things that are, to affirm the existence of a being preeminent in Good, Being and Greatness, and one through whom all other things are good and great. Nevertheless, what posterity has undoubtedly retained is the sole argument of the *Proslogion.* Its simple formulation needs to be set out with precision.

The fool, he who has said in his heart that "God does not exist," must nonetheless recognize that he has in his heart *aliquid quo nihil maius cogitari potest* (something than which nothing greater can be conceived). Now this being than whom nothing greater can be conceived ("the insurpassable," C. Hartshorne) cannot reside in the intelligence alone—indeed intelligence can conceive of a being who would reside both in the intelligence and in reality; and hence *id quo maius cogitari non potest* would not correspond to his conception if he resided only in intelligence and not in reality. It is impossible, without contradiction, to conceive of a being than whom "nothing greater can be conceived" but who exists in the intelligence alone: in this case he would not in fact be the being than whom nothing greater can be conceived. The negative premise of the argument is essential: Anselm says explicitly, in response to Gaunilo, that the argument would not be immediately conclusive if the premise were affirmative and if the name* of God from which one began were "that which is greater than everything" *(Quod est maius omnibus).*

In his reassertion of Anselm's argument, in particular in the disputed questions *De mysterio Trinitatis,* Bonaventure* sees it as "an absolutely evident truth" that the "first and supreme [Being] exists" (q. 1, a. 1, concl.). This obviousness, granted to the soul that allows itself to be purified by faith and lifted up by grace*, is not an intuition of the divine essence, but rather a contuition of its necessary presence in the creation. The *Itinerarium mentis in Deum,* meanwhile, places intellectual reflection in the context of a spiritual quest, where it becomes less a matter of proving the existence of God than of lifting the soul toward him to the point of mystical experience. Thus, just as the six days of the Creation were followed by a seventh day of rest, six illuminations, or enlightenments, prepare the way for the loving contemplation* of the Trinity*.

Thomas* Aquinas, who distinguished more clearly between the mystery* of the life of the Trinity and the considerations relating to the principle, denied Anselm's argument the status of a proof. The existence of God was not evident to us; it had to be demonstrated, which presumed that it was actually demonstrable. The proof *(probari)* was to be effected by five means.

The first part of the process was as follows. Since everything that moves is moved by something else, if the source of the movement moves in turn, then it must be moved by something else; as it is impossible to carry on in this way to infinity, it is necessary to arrive at a prime mover that is not in itself moved; this prime mover is God. The second method refers to the concept of the efficient cause: it is necessary to suppose a first cause, for fear of doing away with the whole system of causes and effects, since no cause can be its own cause. The third method is based on the analysis of the possible and the necessary: if the possible refers to that which can either be or not be, then there cannot exist the possible alone, but some necessity must be allowed in things; and since infinite regression is impossible among necessary things in other fields, so there must be recognized a thing necessary of itself, which is God. The fourth method proceeds by way of the degrees to be observed in things: the more or less good, the more or less true, the more or less noble, are all assessed against the supremely Good, the supremely True, and the supremely Noble, which is also supreme in terms of Being, and which is God. Finally the fifth method approaches God by considering the ordering of things: there is in the world an intelligent Being who guides those things that lack understanding toward their purpose, which is the Good.

A. Wohlmann (1988) has pointed out that Aquinas's first three methods correspond to the first three speculations of Maimonides. Maimonides served as a link between Aquinas and Avicenna. It was Avicenna who had originally developed the concepts of the possible and the necessary later employed by the two thinkers. Equally, the importance in the history of the proofs of the existence of God of Averroes, who was the commentator par excellence of Aristotle and a critic of Avicenna, should not be overlooked.

For Duns* Scotus, as for Aquinas, the proposition "God is" was self-evident, but its obviousness escaped human beings because they lacked a distinct understanding of its terms. It was therefore necessary to prove the proposition. Scotus's proofs, as presented in the *Opus Oxoniense* and the *Tractatus de Primo principio* (probably among the last works of the *Doctor subtilis*), are proofs a posteriori (even though they proceed *more geometrico*), but in a different sense to those of Aquinas. Scotus takes as his starting point the metaphysical properties of being given by experience, in other words not its particular contingent properties but the conditions of its possibility—what Scotus calls "quiddity," or the possible-real. There is an essential order in things that expresses the intelligibility of the existing order while depending on it, and it is on this essential order that Scotus relies. In metaphysical terms, God is considered as the infinite* Being. The proof of God, the demonstration of the existence of an infinite Being, is therefore developed in two stages. One must first prove the existence of a first Being, and then prove that this first Being is infinite. To these two stages is added a final proof, based on the primacy of the infinite Being's will and liberty*. Three arguments borrowed from the analysis of the causal order (efficient causality, final causality, and order of eminence) lead to the affirmation of the first Being. Then, seven arguments referring to the nature of the intellect, the simplicity of the essence, eminence, finality, and efficiency enable Scotus to establish that this singular Being, who is primary, is in fact infinite.

c) Mainstream philosophy*, by developing the proofs of the existence of God into a purely rational form of argument, was to separate (or at least would claim to separate) metaphysics from any theological preconception. Descartes*'s *Méditations* advances three arguments in which the idea of God, considered as an innate idea, plays a fundamental, though in each case a slightly different, role. The third *Méditation* proceeds back from the idea of God as a supremely perfect and infinite Being to the being of God as its necessary cause; and then from the contingent being who conceives the idea of God to God as the Being who creates that contingent being and keeps him in existence. The fifth *Méditation* relies on the model of mathematical truth, and shows that existence, which is a perfection, belongs of necessity to the essence of the supremely perfect Being. Leibniz* would consider completing Descartes's proof by showing that the idea of God is a genuine one: the uncontradictory nature of the divine attributes* made it possible to establish that God was a possible being and consequently that he existed, since *Deus est ens ex cujus essentia sequitur existentia.*

Leibniz also offered a priori as well as a posteriori proofs. The *Theodicy,* which sees in God the final reason of a contingent world, singles out the attributes—understanding, will, and power—of a personal God whose perfection is not only metaphysical but also moral. The *Monadology* approaches God from the perspective of the possible, emphasizing that God is the actual condition of what is real within the possible (§43). In his pre-*Critique* period, Kant* would take up this argument and reflect upon the *One Possible Basis for a Demonstration of the Existence of God,* without perhaps giving sufficient consideration to Leibniz's concept of the reality of possibility.

By bringing out the speculative character of the proofs and claiming to establish their invalidity, the Kantian critique caused a decisive break in the history of proofs of the existence of God. On the one hand Kant underlined the systematic linking of the proofs (physico-theological, cosmological, and ontological) and applied his term "ontological" to the argument a priori. On the other hand he showed that the validity of the proofs was dependent on the ontological proof, which was itself invalid. There was no passage from essence to existence, or from concept to being, and it was not enough for God to be possible in order for him to exist, since existence is not a real attribute. The *Critique of Practical Reason* would nonetheless posit the existence of God as a postulate of moral reason: the will, in the ethical sense of the word, requires the possibility of a Supreme Good in the world. The *Opus postumum* was perhaps to go further, linking the affirmation of God directly to the categorical imperative (fascicle VII).

Hegel*, who toward the end of his life devoted some *Lessons* to the *Proofs of the Existence of God,* submitted Kant's critique of the speculative proofs to severe criticism. Hegel did not limit himself to reestablishing the metaphysical significance of the classical argumentation; he attempted to endow it with a new meaning. He therefore asserted that the cosmological proof contained no paralogism and did not assume the ontological proof; but, in order to be entirely convincing, the cosmological proof did assume two steps (being *is* infinite, and the infinite *is*) whose necessary connectedness referred to the nature of the Concept properly understood, in accordance with a speculative logic. He further asserted that the criticisms Kant had aimed at the physico-theological argument were baseless, if the end and the absolute Good were understood as Spirit. Finally, regarding the ontological argument, a genuine proof that transcended the many finite proofs, Hegel showed that the proof was as one with the development of the Concept itself, in that it provides its own definitions and its own objectivity. With the ontological proof we come to understand the activity of the Concept that eternally gives itself being and life. And by contemplating the idea of God in the ether of pure thought, Logic—which is as one with metaphysical theology—is revealed as the absolute discourse, in other words the discourse of the Absolute, which raises contradictions only to uphold and transcend them.

Schelling* reflected on the meaning of the ontological argument throughout his philosophical career, and offered an interesting clarification in his *Philosophy of Revelation.* He distinguishes what is irrefutable in the ontological argument—the "necessarily existent, insofar as it is nothing but this," in other words, the existent needs no proof of its existence—and what is contestable, which is the fact that God exists. Schelling does not then set out to prove God's existence by beginning with the concept of God, but rather to see how "one may arrive at the divinity by beginning with the existent pure and simple." The presupposition *(prius)* of Schelling's God is the act *(actus);* thus his divinity is seen to reside in power, the *potentia universalis,* and he is consequently revealed as the Super-Being, the Lord of existence (*SW* XIII, 159–60). In tandem with his distinction between rational or negative philosophy and positive philosophy, Schelling's line of reasoning thus inverts the ontological argument in two linked steps. In terms of negative philosophy the Supreme Being, if he exists, must be taken as the necessary existent; and in terms of positive philosophy, the necessary existent must be regarded (not of necessity but in fact) as the Being existing necessarily in a necessary manner, in other words, God. So positive philosophy opens the way to a philosophy of revelation. It reaches its fulfillment in an understanding of singular existence that goes beyond what can be comprehended by pure reason and by virtue of conceptual necessity alone.

d) Among contemporary thinkers, two authors have renewed the philosophical tradition. H. Duméry (1957) used technical concepts from Husserl's phenomenology in a revival of the Neoplatonist tradition. For Duméry, the mind's elevation toward God is not of the order of proof but rather of reduction. Reduction is "an act or movement that aims to cut across the various levels of consciousness in order gradually to arrive at their foundation." This regression is not uniform. Indeed, Husserl distinguishes between eidetic reduction, phenomenological reduction, and constituent reduction. But this last transcendental gesture itself, while constituent and productive of essences, is not the final instance, since it is both one and multiple. A final reduction is therefore needed, which may be termed "henological," and which gives the Principle, the transordinal One, beyond all determination. Reduction expresses the spiritual need for a pursuit of simplicity and unity. Here Husserl is in agreement with Plotinus.

This search for an indeterminate Absolute, taken up from Neoplatonism, was to find its most incisive critic in C. Bruaire (1964 and 1974), the author of a profound reworking of the ontological proof, for whom negative* theology came close to a negation of theology. According to Bruaire, the affirmation of God is demanded by the very logic of existence and arises once man understands that the desire to be God, which leads him to death* and annihilation, must be transformed into a desire for God, expressed in expectation and invocation. And this desire for God, formulated in terms addressed to God, is in turn conditioned by a language of God: in other words, by the discovery of a God able to express and reveal himself, and whose naming within philosophical discourse marks the limit of philosophy as such.

R. Swinburne (1979) is more concerned to maintain some contact with the scientific practice and meaning of proof, and attempts to assess the proofs of the existence of God in terms of the standards of the logic of proof. He bases his approach on the formalization of procedures for measuring the probability of a hypothesis (confirming or invalidating it) and develops the idea of a balancing of the cumulative effects of the different inductive arguments. If one considers the cumulative probability of the various arguments (cosmological, teleological, moral, etc.), putting to one side the counterarguments (e.g., the existence of evil*), it becomes clear, on the one hand, that a personalist explanation is required, to the extent that a purely scientific explanation is incapable of explaining why the laws of the universe are as they are, and, on the other hand, that the existence of a Creator God is more probable than any other personalist explanation of the universe. The explanatory force of theism is thus superior to that of any scientific hypothesis. Measured in the light of the epistemology of the experimental sciences, the a posteriori proofs of the existence of God stand up well to the criticism. The affirmation of God, as an explanatory hypothesis, has as much objective probability as the generally accepted scientific hypotheses.

2. *Logic of the Proofs*

a) The word *proof* denotes in judicial terms the establishing of a fact, in the experimental sciences the verification of a hypothesis, and in mathematics the demonstration of a theorem. "Proofs of the existence of God" can be taken in any of these three senses. Empirical investigation, the experimental method, and rational deduction constitute three methods of proof that make the affirmation of God probable or necessary. Swinburne does not consider deductive proof but restricts himself to a posteriori arguments. Insofar as he interprets induction according to the rules of experimental verification, he is led back to positivism and overlooks, in the sciences* of nature themselves, the epistemological limitations of empirical proof.

On the one hand, the development of any empirical proof already goes beyond sensory experience and its content. Kant recognized this when he attempted to invalidate a posteriori proofs, even though conceptual thought is always preceded by a movement of transcendence that makes it possible: the exercise of language. On the other hand, the taking as axiomatic of physical hypotheses and theoretical representations actually leads scientific thought to go beyond induction and the purely experimental method.

If mathematical deduction is the highest form of scientific proof, it might be supposed that the most significant proof of the existence of God would take a mathematical and a priori form, such as the formulation attempted by the ontological proof. The analysis of formal systems has nonetheless made it possible to establish rigorously what philosophy has known since Aristotle's time—that any theory of demonstration necessarily refers to undemonstrable principles. The most rigorous scientific proof can justify neither its presuppositions nor its method, and consequently cannot be taken as a model for metaphysical proof. Proofs of the existence of God cannot therefore be proofs in the usual sense of the term; they are not lesser proofs, but aim higher. The proofs here considered are insufficient as *proofs* but not as proofs of *God.* Indeed a proof of the existence of God cannot but refer to the linguistic resources required for a general proof to be possible. Thus Hegel's critique of Kant presupposes that the linguistic resources employed are those of speculative thought, which uses and goes beyond the contradictions of finite understanding. The proof of the existence of God then becomes the very logic of absolute discourse, the circular movement of the Concept determining itself by its own negativity and, as did the *Logic,* transcending metaphysics and theology. Substancc, transformed into Subject, is realized and expressed as Totality.

b) This conclusion, though strictly Hegelian, probably does not do full justice to Hegel's project. The *Philosophy of Religion* argues that the ontological proof, the proof par excellence, is the translation into metaphysics of the Christian conception of God. The ontological argument implies the truth of the Christian revelation: God is Spirit, presenting himself freely and fulfilling himself in the action by which he becomes manifest. K. Barth* (1931) has clearly established that the historical sense of Anselm's argument presumed an adherence to the Word* of God. If Anselm was able to recognize and prove the existence of God, this was because he philosophized from the standpoint of faith, because "God permitted him to know him and because he was able to know God" (GA II, p.158). With Hegel this historical truth becomes a speculative proposition: the ternary structure of the *Logic* expresses God's Trinitarian existence as revealed in history*. But while this is the case for Hegel, the contingency of revelation and the essential duality of reason should perhaps be accorded more recognition than he gives them. Indeed, if there is "revelation," it can only be conceived of as a radical act of liberty, manifest within creation and able to be apprehended by the intelligence. God's supreme liberty is in fact constantly presupposed by the Christian affirmation, according to which God simultaneously both reveals and conceals himself within his revelation. When Schelling distinguishes between negative and positive philosophy (whatever the meaning that he assigns to this distinction might be), he clearly shows that intelligence and its sources have a dual structure. In affirming the existence of God, reason combines two intersecting movements. There is the upward movement of an intelligence seeking to make sure of its purpose in the necessary Being, driven by the desire to go beyond all limits. Then there is a downward movement by means of which the intelligence receives the Word* of an Absolute that freely determines, distinguishes, and objectifies itself. Proof then takes the form of allowing the divine liberty to unfold and fulfill itself within the human mind. In a world that contains the vestiges (traces*) of the Creator, man, the image of God, is able to receive his Word as a supreme gift. Blondel, who in *L'Action* saw the ontological argument as the Trinity's approach to us, was reluctant to close the circle of thought into a definitive discourse.

c) The concept of the proof of the existence of God can be subjected to a twofold criticism. The idea of proof is incompatible with the object of theology, which is not precisely an object, while existence, not being a real attribute, is not susceptible of proof. There is an answer to these objections: on the one hand, proof in this instance is more than a proof, in the sense of a definite process; and on the other hand, existence is the affirmation of a freedom that defines its own right and expresses itself in a particular language. Proof is always preceded by the movement of speech, and speech is the very word of liberty. A foundational act, speech does not contain totality as a completed and closed totality, but as the horizon of a transcendence. And by situating the totality of conceptual definitions in a movement that engages with the perceptible in order to put it into perspective, and detaches itself from the perceptible in order to consider it, speech contains the possibility of a metaphysical discourse aware both of its limits and of the infinity of which it is composed.

Lévi-Strauss's reflections on language (1950) are all the more interesting in that they seem removed from any preoccupation with metaphysics. He opposes "symbolism," which "is characteristically discontinuous," and "knowledge," which is "characterized by continuity," showing how "the two categories of the signifier and the signified came to be constituted simultaneously and interdependently, as complementary units; whereas knowledge, that is, the intellectual process that enables us to identify certain aspects of the signifier and certain aspects of the signified... only got started very slowly."

It is thus a characteristic of the symbolic thought at work in our natural languages that there should be a permanent disparity between signifier and signified, resulting from "a superabundance of signifier," a "surplus of signification." This excess, which bears on the exercise of thought as expressed in speech, can be encompassed only by the "divine understanding." G. Fessard's commentary on these passages (1984) locates in this disparity between the two complementary units of signifier and signified the basis for a metaphysics of language in which the floating signifier—the symbolizing power at work in all language—expresses and brings into play a transcendental, supernatural* dimension. This dimension goes beyond both nature and humankind in such a way that, in order to conceive of the link between humanity and nature, Lévi-Strauss is inevitably drawn to invoke divine understanding: God as the perfect unity of Being (signifier) and Thought (signified). Thus the least judgment expressed by means of language "contains an ontological argument." In the most insignificant speech act, which opens onto an infinite dialogue, language situates in God not merely the formal but the real condition of its exercise. I *speak,* therefore God *is.* God, engaged in the destiny of Speech, can *be said* by whomever seeks him in Creation, and can *speak himself* to humankind in the context of a story that becomes meaningful. The proof of God is the intersection or "the cross" of this double utterance.

• É. Gilson (1922), *La philosophie au Moyen Age,* Paris.
K. Barth (1931), Fides quaerens intellectum: *Anselms Beweis der Existenz Gottes im Zusammenhang seines theologischen Programms, GA* II, Zurich, 1981.
É. Gilson (1949), *Introduction à saint Augustin,* Paris.
C. Lévi-Strauss (1950), "Introduction à l'œuvre de Marcel Mauss," in M. Mauss, *Sociologie et Anthropologie,* Paris (2nd Ed.1968), IX-LII. (English trans., *Introduction to the Work of Marcel Mauss,* Tr. Felicity Baker, London, 1987.)
É. Gilson (1952), *Jean Duns Scot: Introduction à ses positions fondamentales,* Paris.
H. Duméry (1957), *Le problème de Dieu en philosophie de la religion,* Bruges.
D. Henrich (1960), *Der ontologische Gottesbeweis,* Tübingen.
C. Bruaire (1964), *L'affirmation de Dieu: Essai sur la logique de l'existence,* Paris.
A. Plantinga (1967), *God and Other Minds: A Study of the Rational Justification of Belief in God,* Ithaca-London (6th Ed. 1990).
J. Moreau (1971), *Le Dieu des philosophes,* Paris.
J. Vuillemin (1971), *Le Dieu d'Anselme et les apparences de la Raison,* Paris.
A. Dies (1972), *Autour de Platon,* Paris.
C. Bruaire (1974), *Le Droit de Dieu,* Paris.
R. Swinburne (1977), *The Coherence of Theism,* Oxford.
R. Swinburne (1979), *The Existence of God,* Oxford.
J. Mackie (1982), *The Miracle of Theism: Arguments for and against the Existence of God,* Oxford.
G. Fessard (1984), *La dialectique des exercices spirituels de saint Ignace,* vol. 3: *Symbolisme et historicité,* Paris-Namur, 115–212, 494–513.
N. Samuelson, et al. (1984), "Gottesbeweise," *TRE* 13, 708–84 (bibl.).
D. Braine (1988), *The Reality of Time and the Existence of God: The Project of Proving God's Existence,* Oxford.

A. Wohlman (1988), *Thomas d'Aquin et Maïmonide: Un dialogue exemplaire,* Paris.
B. Sève (1994), *La question philosophique de l'existence de Dieu,* Paris.
E. Scribano (1994), *L'esistenza di Dio: Storia della prova ontologica da Descartes a Kant,* Bari.
O. Muck, F. Ricken (1995), "Gottesbeweise," *LThK* 4, 878–86.
J. Seifert (1996), *Gott als Gottesbeweis: Eine phänomenologische Neubegründung des ontologischen Arguments,* Heidelberg.
R. Messer (1997), *Does God's Existence Need Proof?* Oxford.

PAUL OLIVIER

See also **Knowledge of God; Natural Theology; Philosophy; Reason; Revelation; Truth**

Exorcism

From the Greek *exorkizô* (to ward off), "to exorcise" means to avert a devil by warding it off with signs of divine power: the name* of God*, the sign of the cross, laying on of hands, holy water, and so forth. "Imperative" exorcisms contain injunctions addressed to the demon; "deprecating" exorcisms are prayers* asking God to ward off an evil*, whether personified or not. A distinction can be made between the following kinds of exorcisms: baptismal exorcisms practiced on catechumens (baptism*); ancient exorcisms of inanimate objects (blessing*); exorcisms of the possessed, that is, of individuals considered to be invaded by a devil. Exorcisms are practically absent from the Old Testament; in the New Testament, the curing of possessed individuals by Jesus*—in a nonritual manner—are signs of his divine filiation* and of the coming of the rule of God (e.g., Mt 8:16 f., 12:28, 28–34). Frequent in the early church*, the practice of exorcism became scarce following abuses, criticisms, and changes in perception of the world.

Catholics and the Orthodox have never abandoned exorcism, but only the Catholic Church has a liturgical and canonical codification to set the norms of sacramental exorcism (sacrament*). Protestants have a wide variety of approaches concerning this matter. Exorcism is particularly frequent in the milieus of a fundamentalist or Pentecostal type, and in those milieus that are permeated by magic; its pertinence and its modalities remain the object of theological discussions.

The understanding of exorcism is closely linked to anthropology* and to soteriology (salvation*). Deliverance from evil, in all its dimensions, touches on the essence of Christianity: it is thus the church's duty to make salvation known to all those who are possessed by a spiritual conflict related to their psychosomatic condition, and which they cannot overcome through their own resources (recovery). Exorcism must be attentive to the modalities of incarnation* and grace*, and, more precisely, to inculturation* and the specific articulation—without confusion or exclusion—of the psychological and the spiritual.

• W. Kasper, K. Lehmann (Ed.) (1978), *Teufel, Dämonen, Besessenheit,* Mayence.
H. A. Kelly (1985), *The Devil at Baptism,* Ithaca.
A. Vergote (1992), "Anthropologie du diable: L'homme séduit en proie aux puissances ténébreuses," in coll., *Figures du démoniaque hier et aujourd'hui,* Brussels, 83–110.
D. Trunk (1994), *Der messianische Heiler,* Freiburg.
M. Ott, et al. (1995), "Exorzismus," *LThK*3 3, 1125–28.
P. Dondelinger (1997), *L'exorcisme des possédés selon le Rituel romain,* Paris.

PATRICK DONDELINGER

See also **Demons; Healing**

Experience

a) Concept. As a primitive, fundamental fact, experience is contact with the real, a condition of all knowledge and all action. This contact must be distinguished from the knowledge that results from it *(empeiria, Erfahrung),* as well as from the experiences acquired from ordinary living *(Erlebnis)* and from the experiment guided by particular inquiry or hypothesis *(experiment).* Certain scholars (Jankélévitch, Dufrenne) propose a distinction between empirical and meta-empirical, with the former designating the everyday course of life, the latter that which unexpectedly perturbs it, such as grace or inspiration.

As contact, experience is consciousness of a relationship with the world, with the other, with God*—of an encounter with otherness. More than simple knowledge, experience means to sense, feel, and perceive. But while the world is unconscious of itself and of the individual, the experience of the other implies an exchange of incarnated consciousness.

Aristotle stressed that experience is memory: like knowledge, it is born of a stock of manifold perceptions (*Metaphysica* I, 1). Experience condenses the "experiences of consciousness," transcends their duration, anticipates the event, recognizes it in the moment, and comes back through memory and thought. It is not true experience unless there is the possibility of reflective return: death*, the suppression of that possible reflection, is not an experience.

Furthermore, I must be involved in duration through my body. The experience of one's body (cenesthesia, kinesthesia, diverse sensations, pleasure, sorrow, etc.) underlies and conditions all experience of others, of the world, and even of God.

Experience as a whole has a yet more profound condition: the presence of the self to the self that constitutes consciousness. But this is not something that is present in its perfection from the outset: rather, it continues to grow through external experience. Otherness promotes consciousness of the self.

Therefore, despite the diverse forms of empiricism, experience is not mere endurance, a pure state of submission. Yet idealism tends only to see a spontaneity, a creation of the mind: if the only reality is the mind, experience is reduced to the experience of the self and its representations. In such a perspective, otherness constitutes an insoluble problem. In fact, experience is both reception and creation, acceptance and spontaneity in indefinitely variable proportions.

Mouroux (1952) distinguished several degrees of depth in experience. The *empirical* designates an experience that is undergone without critical reflection. The *experimental* experience is challenged by the experiencer, who coordinates elements of experience in order to constitute science. The *experiential* marks the most complete commitment of the person*; the person abandons himself to it along with his being* and his resources, his reflection and liberty*. It should be added that the person gives singular meaning to the event, and this new "meaning" can provide further evidence. "In this sense," Mouroux emphasizes, *"all authentic spiritual experience is experiential."* Thus, experience, born of what is simply lived, rises in the realm of science to the rational, and in special moments to the existential, or meta-empirical. Religious experience stems from this last type.

b) Experiencing the Sacred. Feeling the sacred is a criterion of humanity, a primitive fact that is therefore "archaic" and universal. Beyond all reference to personal transcendence, the sense of the sacred expects that beyond the perceptible, the utilitarian, there is a different order of reality that surpasses and envelops the former, granting it a mysterious meaning. The sacred is beyond my grasp, an invisible, inaudible, intangible reality. Direct contact with it would make me run the supreme risks: death, or even damnation.

However, this reserved "essence" paradoxically multiplies its "manifestations" (Van der Leeuw 1955) or "hierophanies" (Éliade 1965, 1968). Whether it involves the "natural" sacred linked to cosmic facts (mountains, storms, etc.) or the "existential" sacred, perceived at certain key moments in life (birth, marriage*, death, etc.), the sacred unites qualities that seem opposed, but are in fact inseparable: transcendence and immanence. It is because the sacred dominates the entire human spectrum that it penetrates it. This is true for both poles of the sacred: the divine, the holy, the majestic, the "consecrated"; and the diabolical, which is perverse, cursed, "execrable."

Despite Girard (1972), the sacred is not essentially linked to violence*. It has an irradiant character, extends across multiple experiences, colors them, unites them, and constitutes one of their dimensions. Thus esthetic experience is the experience of an excess of reality and value that envelops the tangible object, removes it from the level of the utilitarian, and offers it for the happy contemplation* of the senses and spirit. The destruction of beauty is a profanation, a negation of the sacred as such. Moral experience is the experience of the absolute. The Good*, which judges not only my actions but also my feelings and most secret thoughts, imposes itself with extreme sacral force; it can lead me to the sacrifice of my possessions, my affections, or even my life. As for the connection between ontological experience and the sacred, this is noted by Éliade. The profane involves a degree of uncertainty within being, but the sacred *is* in the absolute sense; throughout the flow of events and the vicissitudes of history*, it remains immutable. It is also a principle of value, and so has a "hermeneutic*" aspect as giver of meaning. This is why societies* devoid of the sacred suffer from existential meaninglessness and vainly resort to a ritual of substitution.

The experience of the sacred seems to be a necessary condition, a "preamble" to the religious experience strictly speaking, in that the former is surpassed or amplified in the latter but remains separate from it: this would be the case with certain forms of animism, of humanism—*res sacra homo*—or the civic religion of Greco-Roman antiquity. It seems, however, that beyond traditional mythology, astral religion—including Plato's God: the Idea of the Good (*Republic* VI); Aristotle's God: Thought of thought (*Metaphysica* XII); and the One of Plotinus (*Enneads* VI)—the pagan soul* was in search of an ever higher and purer transcendence. Stoicism, especially among representatives of the imperial era—Epictetus, Seneca, Marcus Aurelius—offers the illogical aspect of uniting pantheistic affirmation (pantheism*) of an impersonal and material god with a religious feeling of true dependence. Epictetus's religion, in particular, consists of praise, of giving thanks to an omniscient, provident, quasi-personal God.

c) Religious Experience. Express reflection on this form of experience is linked to the growing interest that Western culture has in its regard. Although, in the Protestant* movement, faith* was situated in will and affectivity, and although, on the other hand, during the romantic period, the strict deism* of the Enlightenment was rejected, religion and religious emotion were equated in Schleiermacher* (1958). It was intuition and feeling, inextricably linked, that constituted religion, without reference to any dogmatic objectivity received through a revelation*. It was in themselves that people would find religion. The believer was invited—and this not without a certain leaning toward pantheism—to perceive God as present in all things, to become one with the universe, understood as the divine. The same fundamental orientations can be found in W. James (*The Varieties of Religious Experience,* New York, 1902; *Religious Experience,* 1931). He reduces religion to an internal fact of experience and excludes all institutions or dogmatic elements. The affirmation of God is recognized as having only a practical value: it brings the believer the comfort of religious emotions, the tonic of a joy that transfigures existence and renders suffering and sacrifice acceptable. In sum, this pragmatism is less about serving God than about using him. As indicated by the word *varieties* in the title itself, the specifics of religion are dissolved in a fog of emotion and feeling. This specific aspect does indeed present the two elements of fear* (the *tremendum*) and seduction (the *fascinosum*), as distinguished by Otto (1917). But the religious attitude greatly surpasses these elements: it is characterized by a feeling of total dependence on the transcendent God. It is from him that the religious man acknowledges receiving the whole of his being, his essence and existence, the norm of his actions, as well as the sense and goal of his destiny. I call him "my God" not because I own him, but, on the contrary, because he gives me entirely to myself and because I find joy in this dependence. The "place" of this acknowledgement is prayer*, private or ritual, in the dialogue between the human *I* and the divine *Thou.* Within the complexity of the religious act—bodily attitude, the mind's contemplation, offerings, and sacrifices—human beings express, through their whole being, their radical contingency, their reverential admiration for the Absolute of being, value, and meaning. In Jewish monotheism* the religious experience is specified by decisive elements: God, the Creator, has spoken in history. He has chosen a people, has liberated them from slavery in Egypt, has made a Covenant* of salvation* with them as codified in the Law on Mount Sinai. He has revealed his sanctity to Israel, his glory*, the blinding light of his mystery*. Through the voice of the prophets*, whose inspiration cannot be reduced to the expression, however privileged, of a personal experience (*See* Pius X, *Pascendi,* 1907, *DS* 3490–91), as well as through positive or negative events, God, the author of salvation and the one who reveals, sustains the messianic hope* of his people, corrects their infidelities, and prevents them from succumbing to the supreme infidelity that is idolatry*. But deep in the religious consciousness of Israel there is a division. On the one hand there is the desire to attain a greater knowledge of the holy God and of his glory, the desire to see him (Ps 63[62], 84[83]), but on the other hand, there is the suffering that comes from the impossibility of this: as creature and sinner, man cannot see the face of God and live (Gn 28:16 f.; Ex 3:4 ff., 19:12, 33:18–23). Furthermore, in the encounter of the Covenant, the parties are too unequal: the uncertain fidelity of human beings confronts the unfailing fidelity of God.

d) Christian Religious Experience. With belief in the Incarnation* of the Son of God, a decisive transformation takes place in religious experience. The believer can henceforth see the divine glory in the humanity of Jesus* and live on (Jn 1:14, 14:9). Man no longer hears the Word* of God through prophets, but through the Son (Heb 1:1 f.). One can even feel the flesh of the Risen One in order to convince oneself of its reality (Lk 24:39 f.; Jn 20:24–28); sensory experiences are coordinated, examined, and reiterated (1 Jn 1:1 ff.), especially during the post-Easter meals (Lk 24:26–43; Jn 21:9–14; Acts 1:3 f., 10:41). These experiences are intended to elicit and nourish faith. They do not limit it, since what is involved is a summons in the form of signs: the ambiguity of the sign preserves the freedom of the act of faith. Around Jesus, people divide into adversaries and disciples. But for the latter, the experience is so privileged that it inevitably engenders, after Pentecost, the duty and the act of witnessing, even at the cost of imprisonment, flagellation, and also death (Acts 1:6, 4:1–32, 5:15–41, 6:8–15, 7, etc.).

There is another type of Christian experience: one that, following the Ascension, is fed only by apostolic preaching*. In this case the "experience of Jesus" is had through the person and the words of direct witnesses; he is seen, heard, and touched through them and the vigor of their presence. The is a mediated experience, the experience of encountering Jesus "in others"—as in the experience of Polycarp, the disciple of John the Apostle.

After the death of the Twelve we find another type of experience. The Church* nourishes its faith through its only verbal witness, transmitted to tradition through the Scriptures. This is an experience, then, of faith alone. It is necessarily more austere, but there is a promise that it will bring to those who never knew either Jesus or the apostles the full benefit of a specific beatitude*: "Blessed are those who have not seen and yet have believed" (Jn 20:29).

This experience is an integral part of ecclesial communion*. Supported by the institution, it is the matrix of Christian existence. It is an experience of the realities of faith under the guidance of the Holy* Spirit (Jn 14, 15 ff. and 26, 16:12; Rom 8:16; 1 Cor 12) and the protection of the magisterium*. At once human and supernatural, it is made possible through baptismal grace* and comprises a dialogue with God in prayer, a certain vision (1 Cor 13:12; 2 Pt 1:19), and a certain presence (Mt 28:20). To this are added the experience of the daily struggle against sin*, with the law of the body constantly revolting against the law of the Spirit (Rom 6:12–19, 7:14–25; 1 Cor 9:24–27); the experience of struggle against the false evidence of the world*, which opposes the light of faith (1 Cor 1:17–2:16); the experience of alternation between blind faith and sensible fervor (2 Cor 1:3–11, 12:1–10), the impulses of religious affectivity being neither the source nor the measure of theological faith; the experience of persecution through blood, contradiction, and contempt (Mt 5:11 ff., 10:23; Lk 21:12–19; Jn 15:18–16:4); above all, the experience of an intimate and personal relationship between the believer and the triune God (1 Jn 5:5–12), between the human *I* and the divine *Thou;* the experience of a specific exchange between believing man and the man-God Christ (Jn 14:19 ff.); the experience of Christian assembly, of liturgical prayer, of ritual action, of the sacramental meeting between God the Savior and the person to be saved, of the eucharistic Communion with the sacrifice of the risen and glorified Lamb*; the experience of being in the world, of being in solidarity with all those to be saved, and yet without being *of* the world (Jn 15:18–21,17:14–18; 1 Jn 3:13); the experience of Christian unity that is always to be perfected in the love* of God and the brethren (Jn 13:34 f., 17:11, 17:21–26); the experience of mission* (Mt 28:20) and witness (Acts 1:8); the experience of God's patience (Rom 2:4, 3:26, 9:22), and of the impatient but blessed hope: "Come, Lord Jesus!" (Rev 22:20).

• E. Cramausel (1908), *La philosophie religieuse de Schleiermacher,* Montpellier.

H. Pinard de La Boullaye (1913), "Exp. religieuse," *DThC* V/2, 1786–1868.

R. Otto (1917), *Das Heilige: Ueber das Irrationale in der Idee des Göttlichen und sein Verhältnis zum Rationalen,* Munich.

H. Pinard de La Boullaye (1921), "La théorie de l'exp. religieuse de Luther à James," *RHE* 63 *Sq;* 306 *Sq;* 547 *Sq.*

A.J. Festugière (1932), *L'idéal religieux des Grecs et l'Évangile,* Paris.

L. Cristiani (1939), "Schleiermacher," *DThC*14/1, 1495–1508.

R. Lenoble (1943), *Essai sur la notion d'expérience,* Paris.

J. Mouroux (1952), *L'exp. chrétienne: Introduction à une théologie,* Paris.

L. Bourgey (1955), *Observation et expérience chez Aristote,* Paris.

G. Van der Leeuw (1955), *Phénoménologie de la religion,* Paris.

H.D. Lewis (1959), *Our Experience of God,* London.

H.U. von Balthasar (1961), "Die Glaubenserfahrung," *Herrlichkeit* I, Einsiedeln, 211–410.

M. Éliade (1965), *Le sacré et le profane,* Paris.

F. Alquié (1966), *L'expérience,* Paris.

M. Éliade (1968) *Traité d'histoire des religions,* Paris.

R. Girard (1972), *La violence et le sacré,* Paris.

P. Miquel (1972), "La place et le rôle de l'expérience dans la théologie de saint Thomas," *RThAM* 39, 63–70.

M. Simon (1974), *La philosophie de la religion dans l'œuvre de Schleiermacher,* Paris.
P. Miquel (1977), *L'exp. de Dieu,* Paris.
E. Herms (1978), *Theologie: Eine Erfahrungswissenschaft,* Munich.
J. B. Lotz (1978), *Transzendentale Erfahrung,* Freiburg-Basel-Vienna.
J.-P. Torrell (1981), "Dimension ecclésiale de l'exp. chrétienne," *FZPhTh* 28, 3–25.
R. Schaeffler (1982), *Fähigkeit zur Erfahrung: Zur transzendentalen Hermeneutik des Sprechens von Gott,* QD 94.
L. Bouyer (1990), "Exp.," *Dictionnaire théologique,* Paris.
W. P. Alston (1991), *Perceiving God: The Epistemology of Religious Experience,* Ithaca-London.
E. Barbotin (1991), "Témoignage," *DSp* 15, 134–41.
J. Rudhart (1992), *Notions fondamentales de la pensée religieuse et actes constitutifs du culte dans la Grèce classique,* Paris.
P. Rostenne (1993), *Homo religiosus ou l'homme vertical,* Bordeaux.
J.-Y. Lacoste (1994), *Exp. et Absolu,* Paris.
E. Barbotin (1995), *Le témoignage,* Turnhout.
C. Berner (1995), *La philosophie de Schleiermacher,* Paris.
R. Schaeffler (1995), *Erfahrung als Dialog mit der Wirklichkeit,* Freiburg-Munich.
J. I. Gellman (1997), *Experience of God and the Rationality of Theistic Belief,* Ithaca-London.

EDMOND BARBOTIN

See also **Credibility; Mysticism; Pietism; Religion, Philosophy of**

Expiation

I. Old Testament

1. Expiation among Human Beings

a) Compositio. Expiation means the settlement of conflicts by compensation instead of punishment* or violence* (Gn 32:21; Prv 6:35, 16:14). Spontaneous (e. g., Gn 32:21), or institutionalized by law* ("Code of the Covenant*": Ex 21:18–36), it is excluded in the case of premeditated murder (Ex 21:12 ff.; Nm 35:31). The exclusion of a settlement procedure *(compositio)* for voluntary homicide distinguishes Hebrew law from other forms of ancient law. The goal of expiation is reconciliation through the recognition of a (civil) responsibility and the provision of compensation. Expiation replaces conflict with mutual understanding and punishment with compensation.

Expiation as such does not imply a substitution, but a mediator (intercessor, arbiter, judge) may contribute to the *compositio* (Ex 21:22, 32:30; Mk 12:1–11 and parallel passages). The advantage of compensation offered and accepted (Gn 33:8–11) is the balanced distribution of negative effects: to the damage suffered corresponds the restitution claimed and granted. This is the satisfaction that compensates material and moral losses. Expiation is: 1) negotiated: the two parties seek a balance with one another; 2) directed toward the interest of all, that is, the parties in conflict and society*, which needs peace in order to prosper; 3) rational: instead of there being two negativities (damage inflicted and violent punishment), the positive character of reparation softens the damage inflicted; and 4) more durable than punishment because it is not hurtful.

b) Ethos of Expiation. Expiation presupposes moderation and gentleness by excluding vengeance and excess, by preferring peace* and equity to violence (Prv 16:14; Ps 103:9 f.), in the general interest. It resolves conflicts with clemency and by accommodating the parties: it calls for magnanimity from the wronged party and requires from the guilty party the intention to make reparation. It is creative: refusing to destroy, it creates compensation and peace. These qualities explain why *compositio* among human beings was transposed to the relationship between God* and humanity.

2. Religious Expiation

Before P (the "priestly" text; *see* Bible*), expiation is seldom mentioned, but 1 Samuel 6, 26:19; 2 Samuel 21:3, and other passages evidence its existence in an early period. In P, expiation is organized into a complex sacrificial system. The principal expiatory sacrifices*: *chattât* (Greek *hamartia*) *'âshâm* (Greek *plèmmeleia*), and others, are distinguished by a particular rite of the sprinkling of blood (Lv 4–5). But the burnt offering is also expiatory (Lv 1:4).

Together with the Day of Atonement (*yôm [ha-]kippoûrîm,* Greek *hèmera [ex-]hilasmou*), these sacrifices make up a system of forgiveness for different categories of sins*. In the P narratives* there are other means of expiation: incense (Nm 17:11 ff.), the image of the serpent (Nm 21:8 ff.), zeal (in the sense of "jealousy for God") (Nm 25:10–13; Ps 106:30), intercession (Ex 32:30; Ps 106:23), a sacred personal tax during a census (Ex 30:11–16; 2 Sm 24), and votive offerings (Nm 31:50). But it is especially the blood of an animal—or, for the poor, flour (Lv 5:11 ff.)—that accomplishes expiation (Lv 17:10 ff.; *See* Heb 9:22).

3. Interpretation

Historically, the most widespread interpretation explains expiation as a substitution for the guilty person, replaced by an innocent victim who suffers death* in his place. It is based on a conception of sacrifice defined as the immolation of an animal victim, especially after the rite of the laying on of hands *(semîkâ)* by the sinner on the head of the victim, this rite being explained as an identification of the guilty one with the victim or a transfer of the sin to the victim. The theory of vicarious punitive substitution (the innocent victim punished in place of the guilty one) is seldom defended today, but the identification of the human subject with the victim (Gese, Janowski) or the diversion of social violence onto a scapegoat are variants of the theory. Milgrom interprets the sacrifices of expiation and of *Yôm kippoûrîm* as rites of purification. It seems that these interpretations have neglected the secular analogy of the ritual of expiation: the offering as compensation offered and accepted restores peace. The particular blood rites of expiatory sacrifices and of the Day of Atonement cause blood to splash in the direction of the veil of the sanctuary and enter into the Holy of Holies (Lv 16:14 f.), into the presence of YHWH. This rite seems to signify the presentation of blood by sinful human beings as symbolic compensation, prescribed by YHWH. The rite of the scapegoat* on the Day of Atonement (Lv 16:20 ff.) expresses the removal of sins and impurities (*see* the sacrificial bird, Lv 14:7, 53). The laying on of both hands (Lv 16:21) is distinct from the laying on of only one hand, which precedes all sacrifices (Lv 1:4, 3:2). This gesture *(semîkâ)* seems to signify that the victim becomes the possession of YHWH, or that the celebrant is its owner.

4. Biblical Theology of Expiation

Ritual expiation represents in liturgical symbols the reconciliation between God and human beings (individuals and community). In it, sin is understood as negativity and damage inflicted, producing a break in relation and a "responsibility" (an obligation to make reparation) in the sinner, God being the person harmed in this case. God renounces punishment by offering the possibility of a reconciliation through a ritual sign, that is, through the liturgy* of expiation and blood (Lv 17:10 ff.), which are expressions of his grace*. The offering of sacrifices brought by the sinner corresponds to a compensation that signifies regret for the evil* caused and the desire to accept the reconciliation offered by God. Expiation is an exchange in which God takes the initiative; the sinner responds to it. Hence, punishment or vindictive violence, effects of God's anger, are replaced by a reparation that is both designated and accepted by him, thanks to his gentleness. Expiation is a nonviolent divine response. It is not the term *satisfaction* that is biblical, but the idea of the replacement of divine punishment *(poena)* by a compensation designated, given, and received with a view to a peaceful and definitive reconciliation.

II. New Testament

The reconciliation between God and human beings is thematized in narratives (parables*) and in the use of the Old Testament ritual terminology of expiation.

1. Parables

Mark 12:1–11, Matthew 5:25 f., and Luke 15:11–32 recount conflicts over money in which the protagonists may accept or reject an amicable settlement, favoring mutual understanding and favorable to the guilty or indebted party. In Mark 12:1–11, the owner's son intercedes between the father* and the tenants to secure a negotiated and nonviolent reconciliation. The punishment of the rebellious debtors is delayed because of the owner's kindness, to leave room for an amicable settlement, which fails. In Luke 15:11–32 the father chooses a smooth reconciliation with the prodigal son over punishing him for wasting his money, while the elder son thinks that his younger brother should be disciplined for that loss. In these three parables, secular *compositio,* a human though difficult solution, is the image of reconciliation with God, who prefers peace to strict justice* or violent punishment.

2. Logion of the Ransom (Mark 10:45 and Parallel Passages; 1 Timothy 2:6) and the Logion of the Cup (Mark 14:24 and Parallel Passages; 1 Corinthians 11:25).

The logion of the ransom is an embryonic parable: the "Son* of man" serves the "multitude" (the peoples?; *see* Dn 7; Is 53) by paying on its behalf and in its place the "ransom," that is, the compensation necessary for the *compositio.* The terminology is not ritual but legal.

The metaphor of the "payment of a price" for the gift of life indicates that the "Son of man" fully commits himself (Mk 8:35 f. and parallel passages) in favor of the reconciliation of the multitude with God. The logion of the cup retains the expression "for *(huper)* the multitude" and replaces the life to be paid as compensation by the "blood to be shed," a metaphorical designation of martyrdom* and an evocation of ritual expiation. Taken together, these two logia suggest the idea of the martyrdom of the "Son of man," in view of a reconciliation between God and "the multitude," by metaphorically using the language of secular *compositio* and ritual expiation (Is 53).

3. Terminology of Ritual Expiation

In Ephesians (5:2), Colossians (1:24), 1 John (2:2, 4:10), Hebrews (9 f.), 1 Peter (1:2), and Revelations (5:95 f.), the Old Testament ritual expressions of expiation serve to interpret the meaning of the violent death of Jesus Christ*. *Blood* evokes the ritual of blood, which is typical of liturgical expiation *(yôm kippoûrîm).* Romans 3:25 and Hebrews 9 f. establish a typological relation between the Old Testament ritual of expiation and the death and Resurrection* of Christ. Second Corinthians 5:21 can be read as an allusion to the sacrifice for sin *(chattât, hamartia).* The basis for the New Testament terminology of ritual expiation seems to be the metaphor of "blood spilled" for martyrdom. The metaphor also suggests the blood offered by YHWH on the altar to accomplish forgiveness (Lv 17:11). For martyrdom, in Israel*, reconciles God with his people* (2 Macc 7:37 f.) and takes the place of sacrifices (Dn 3:38 ff.). A martyr is a just person submitted to an extreme ordeal, obtaining as intercessor the salvation* of sinners and of Israel. The New Testament terminology of expiation combines the theology* of the martyr-intercessor with that of ritual reconciliation. The death of Jesus is understood in this context as the martyrdom of a just man, and the martyrdom of the just, persecuted from the second century B.C. on, is added, as another path of reconciliation, to the ritual expiation suppressed under persecution.

4. Conclusion

The New Testament links expiation to martyrdom because both accomplish reconciliation between God and the community. The vocabulary of "martyrdom" is based on the historical execution of Jesus the Just One, that of "expiation" on the grace of reconciliation. The martyrdom of a just person obtains that grace for the people as a whole ("the multitude"), but ritual expiation, the symbolic expression of the grace of reconciliation offered by God to the individual or collective sinner, has the same effect. One difference may be noted: ritual expiation is celebrated with no intermediary except the priest* (*see* the sacerdotal typology of Hebrews), but the martyr is an intercessor for others. The mediation of Christ Jesus, whereby he reconciles human beings with God, is rooted in his death as martyrdom, not in expiation. The terminology of expiation serves to underscore the grace of that reconciliation with God, who prefers gentleness to violence, peaceful understanding to punishment.

• K. Bähr (1839), *Symbolik des mosaischen Cultus,* vol. 2, Heidelberg.
J. Herrmann (1905), *Die Idee der Sühne im AT,* Leipzig.
A. Médebielle (1924), *L'expiation dans l'Ancien et le Nouveau Testament,* Rome.
A. Büchler (1929), *Studies in Sin and Atonement in the Rabbinic Literature of the First Century,* New York.
D. Schötz (1930), *Schuld- und Sündopfer im AT,* Breslau.
J. Herrmann, F. Büchsel (1938), *"hileôs, hilaskomai,* etc.," *ThWNT* 3, 300–324.
L. Moraldi (1956), *Espiazione sacrificale e riti espiatori nell'ambiente biblico e nell'AT,* Rome.
L. Sabourin (1961), *Rédemption sacrificielle,* Bruges.
E. Lohse (1963), *Märtyrer und Gottesknecht,* Göttingen.
R.J. Thompson (1963), *Penitence and Sacrifice in Early Israel Outside the Levitical Law,* Leyden.
R. de Vaux (1964), *Les sacrifices de l'AT,* Paris.
K. Elliger (1966), *Leviticus,* Tübingen.
S. Lyonnet, L. Sabourin (1970), *Sin, Redemption and Sacrifice.* Rome.
R. Girard (1972), *La violence et le sacré,* Paris.
K. Kertelge (Ed.) (1976), *Der Tod Jesu im NT,* Freiburg.
J. Milgrom (1976), *Cult and Conscience: The ASHAM and the Priestly Doctrine of Repentance,* Leyden.
H. Gese (1977), *Zur biblischen Theologie,* Munich.
H. Schürmann (1977), *Comment Jésus a-t-il vécu sa mort?* Paris.
R.J. Daly (1978), *Christian Sacrifice,* Washington.
M. Hengel (1981 *a*), *The Atonement: The Origins of the Doctrine in the NT,* London; (1981 *b*), *La crucifixion dans l'Antiquité et le message de la folie de la croix,* Paris.
F. Vattioni (Ed.) (1981), *Sangue e Antropologia Biblica,* vols. 1–2, Rome.
A. Wallenkampf (Ed.) (1981), *The Sanctuary and the Atonement,* Washington.
B. Janowski (1982), *Sühne als Heilsgeschehen,* Neukirchen.
A. Schenker (1982), "Substitution du châtiment ou prix de la paix?" in M. Benzerath, et al. (Ed.), *La Pâque du Christ Mystère de salut: Mélanges Durwell,* Paris, 75–90.
J. Milgrom (1983), *Studies in Cultic Theology and Terminology,* Leyden.
B. Lang (1984), *"kipper,"* *ThWAT* 4, 303–18.
R. Rendtorff (1985–), *Leviticus,* BK, Neukirchen.
P. Bovati (1986), *Ristabilire la giustizia: Procedure, vocabolario, orientamenti,* Rome.
N. Kiuchi (1987), *The Purification Offering in the Priestly Literature,* Sheffield.
A. Schenker (1987), *Chemins bibliques de la non-violence,* Chambray-lès-Tours.
B. Levine (1989), *Leviticus,* Philadelphia.
J. Milgrom (1990), *Numbers,* Philadelphia; (1991), *Leviticus* I-XVI, New York.
A. Schenker (1991), *Text und Sinn im AT,* Fribourg-Göttingen.
F. Crüsemann (1992), *Die Tora,* Munich.

A. Schenker (1992), "Die Anlässe zum Schuldopfer Ascham," in A. Schenker (Ed.), *Studien zu Opfer und Kult im AT,* Tübingen, 45–66.
R. Péter-Contesse (1993), *Lévitique* 1–16, Geneva.

ADRIAN SCHENKER

See also **Cult; Eucharist; Passion; Purity/Impurity; Sacrifice; Scapegoat; Servant of YHWH; Sin; Vengeance of God; Wrath of God**

Extreme Unction. *See* **Anointing of the Sick**

F

Faith

A. Biblical Theology

Faith is the inner attitude of one who believes. The words of the Bible that we translate as "faith" or "fidelity" *('èmunâh, 'émèt),* and as "believe" *(hé'èmîn),* come from the same Hebrew root *('mn);* Greek shows the same relationship in *pistis,* "faith," and *pisteuein,* "believe." The underlying idea in Hebrew is that of firmness; in Greek, that of persuasion.

1. Old Testament

In English, "believe" can denote either an uncertain opinion or a strong conviction, based on an interpersonal relationship. The latter meaning is the one that is found in the Bible*; hence the frequency of the vocabulary of faith in the Psalms* (84 times); see also Deuteronomy (23 times), Isaiah (34 times), and Jeremiah (21 times).

a) Trust in God. The verb "believe" makes its first appearance in Genesis 15:6, a fundamental text. God* has made Abraham an improbable promise*, "And he believed the Lord, and he counted it to him as righteousness." When God asks him to offer the son of the promise, Abraham's faith is subjected to an ordeal (Gn 22:1), which he endures in obedience (22:2f., 22:18) and with confidence: "God will provide" (22:8, 22:14). Faith, confidence, and obedience are constantly linked. The converse is also true: faced with the land promised to them, the people refuse to enter it (Nm 13–14; Dt 1:19–45; Heb 3:7–4:11); they "despised the pleasant land, having no faith in his promise" (Ps 106:24). In the desert, instead of believing God at his word (Ps 78:22 and vv. 32, 37), they "tempted" him (vv. 18, 41, 56) (temptation*), that is, they wished to force him to act (Ps 95:7b–10; Ex 17:1–7; Nm 20:2–13).

Adherence to God, faith, is only possible to the extent that God makes himself known. God speaks to human beings. He opens Job's eyes to the works of creation* (Jb 38:1–42:6). He addresses an assembly (Dt 5:22ff.), but more often a single person* (Gn 12:1; Ex 3:4ff.) with whom he establishes an intimate relation (Jer 15:16) by giving him a mission* for the benefit of others (Gn 12:1ff.; Ex 3:10; Is 6:8–13; Jer 1:9f.).

b) Trust in Men of God. The envoy in turn must be believed. On what basis? In many cases his message is recognized because it is similar to previous divine interventions. In other cases, God confirms it by wonders, as in the case of Moses (Ex 4:1–9, 14:31; *see* 19:9) or that of Elijah (1 Kgs 17:1–24). But miracles* are ambiguous (*see* Ex 7:11; Dt 13:2ff.) and discernment remains necessary. By accepting the mediation of accredited messengers, believers enter into a community of faith. This is what the Israelites formed because "they believed in the Lord and in his servant Moses" (Ex 14:31) after their liberation from Egypt. This is the path of the covenant* (Ex 19:5f., 24:3–8), in which fidelity and obedience predominate, the basis remaining the generous and gratuitous initiative of God. The recognition of such benefits for Israel* and for all human beings will always remain the Old Testament's essential "confession" of faith.

c) Faith, Religion, Ethics. Beginning with Elijah, the champion of faith in YHWH against the Canaanite cult* of Baal, the prophets struggled against idolatry* (Hos 8:4ff.; Jer 2:26ff., 10:2–5; Ez 9–12 and against a ritualistic conception of religion accompanied by what amounted in real, practical terms to disobedience of God. They gave vitality to the bond between faith and the practice of justice. The very politics of the city* had to have faith as a basis. This led to a refusal to rely either on military strength or alliance with major powers. Isaiah in particular followed this line: "If you are not firm in faith, you will not be firm at all" (Is 7:9, 28:16). The ordeal of the exile paradoxically led Israel to strengthen its monotheistic faith (Is 40:12–41:29, 44:6–46:13). But the message concerning the Servant* of YHWH was thought by Deutero-Isaiah to have come up against a refusal to believe: "Who has believed what they heard from us?" (Is 53:1; *see* Jn 12:38; Rom 10:16). The door opened onto what would later become the great apocalyptic revelations* (Dn 7–12), including that of the resurrection* of the dead (Dn 12:2; 2 Macc 7:9–29; Wis 5:1–5).

2. New Testament

a) Synoptic Gospels. In this historical context Jesus* proclaimed the imminent coming of the Kingdom* of God (Mt 3:17 and parallel passages). Mark summarizes his message in the terms of the first Christian preaching*: "Believe in the gospel" (1:15). But Jesus had already brought to the fore the fundamental significance of faith. He says to the person whom he has cured: "Your faith has made you well" (Mt 9:22 and parallel passages; Mk 10:52 and parallel passages; Lk 7:50). "All things are possible for one who believes" (Mk 9:23; *see* Mt 7:20 and parallel passages; 21:21 and parallel passages). In general he does not specify in whom one should have faith. He does not say, "Believe in me," but the circumstances reveal that the faith in God that he wants to encourage is linked to a faith in his own person. "He was teaching them as one who had authority*" (Mt 7:29 and parallel passages), as a fully accredited envoy. The expression "Amen, I say to you" is peculiar to Jesus (the Hebrew *'amen* affirms certainty). The signs and wonders that accompany his speaking are above all cures, which are asked for with faith (*see* Mt 9:2 and parallel passages, 9:28ff., 13:58). Peter* acquired the conviction that Jesus was the Messiah* (Mk 8:29). But Jesus foresaw for himself a fate that seemed unworthy of the Messiah. His death on the cross provoked a refusal to believe that is reported in terms evoking the defiance of the people in the desert (Mk 15:32 and parallel passages; *see* Ps 78:18–22). It also provoked an adherence of faith (Mk 15:39 and parallel passages). The Good News was proclaimed in order to be believed by the entire world (Mk 16:15ff.).

b) Acts of the Apostles. For this narrative*, faith and baptism* "in the name of Jesus Christ" ensure for believers the forgiveness of sins* (Acts 2:38, 26:18), the purification of the heart (15:9), justification* (13:39), and salvation* (16:31). The first to be called to Christian faith are the Jews (3:26), and after them the Gentiles (13:46ff.). "Now the full number of those who believed were of one heart and soul*" (4:32). United by faith, they constituted the Church* (9:31).

c) Johannine Writings. They contain the verb "believe" 98 times. Unlike the synoptic Gospels, John's writings about Jesus often speak of belief *in him* (Jn 2:11, 3:16, 3:18). Jesus himself invites this belief (14:1), explaining that belief in him is belief in God, who sent him (12:44). The *interpersonal aspect* of faith is emphasized (1:35–51, 4:7–26), particularly through the parallelism between "come to" and "believe in" (6:35, 6:64f., 7:37f.). Faith establishes Jesus and the believer in a reciprocal inwardness (15:15; *see* 6:56, 17:20). A significant *doctrinal aspect* also appears, as witnessed in the profusion of the vocabulary of knowledge* and truth*. The word of Jesus reveals who he is (4:26, 6:35). It is supported by divine "works" that evidence his union with the Father* (5:36, 10:30, 10:38) and are "signs" likely to give rise to faith (2:11, 2:23, 20:30f.). The attachment to "signs and wonders" (4:48) impedes belief in Jesus on the basis of his words and, later, belief in the witnesses who have seen him risen (20:25): blessed is the one who believes without having seen (20:29)! Faith is expressed in explicit confessions of belief (6:69, 11:27). The declared aim of the writing of the gospel is to bring readers to "believe that Jesus is the Christ*, the Son of God" (20:31). Johannine faith encompasses simultaneously the gospel and the Scriptures of the Old Testament (Jn 2:22, 5:46, 20:8f.; cf. Luke 24:25, 44–47). It is a source of life (Jn 20:31, 11:25f.).

d) The letters of Paul give strong emphasis to faith ("believe" occurs 54 times; "faith," 152 times) and to its interpersonal aspect. Christ lives in the believer (Gal 2:20; Eph 3:17); the believer is "in Christ" (2 Cor 5:17; Phil 3:9) and is crucified with Christ (Gal 2:19, 5:24; Rom 6:6) in order to live with him as risen (Rom

6:4, 6:11). The doctrinal aspect is no less prominent: adherence to the message (1 Cor 15:3f.; Rom 10:5).

Apostle* to the Gentiles, Paul understood that human beings are "justified" by faith in Christ and not by observance of the Law* of Moses (Gal 2:16; Rom 3:28). Paul thereby defined the basis of Christian life. Whoever believes in Christ, who "died for our sins," is freed from his sin "as a gift" (Rom 3:24). Paul rightly refuses to accept two heterogeneous bases for this fundamental justification, namely, faith in Christ and the "works* of the Law." Galatians 3:6 and Romans 4 derive support from Genesis 15:6, reread in the light of the Christian situation. Perhaps to correct misunderstandings provoked by Paul's paradoxes, the Letter of James (Jas 2:14–26) demonstrates that justification is not obtained by faith without works. James's point of view is different: he is not concerned with initial justification but with the last judgment* and speaks not of the works of the Law but of those "of faith" (2:22). Paul, too, requires that faith not remain sterile: the last judgment will be made on each person "according to his works" (Rom 2:6; *see* 2 Cor 5:10; Gal 6:7–10).

In the letters written in captivity there is a notable emphasis on "the wisdom* and understanding" procured by faith (Eph 1:8, 1:17–20; Col 1:9) and on "mystery*" (Eph, six times; Col, four times). The pastoral letters are concerned with preserving faith from collapse (1 Tm 1:19, 6:20; 2 Tm 2:18), warning against "fables" (1 Tm 1:4, 4:7), and inviting the believer to embrace a "healthy" faith and doctrine (eight times).

e) The Epistle to the Hebrews presents the glorified Christ as our "merciful and faithful [Gr. *pistos*] high priest in the service of God" (Heb 2:17, 3:2; *see* Nm 12:7 Septuagint); it warns against the disastrous "lack of faith" (3:12–19) and invites the believer to a "full assurance of faith" (10:22). Hebrews 11:1–40, a splendid hymn in praise of faith and of the great believers of the Old Testament, shows faith at the origin of all worthwhile accomplishments, of triumphs achieved and of ordeals overcome. Along with the interpersonal aspect (11:6 and vv. 8, 11, 26f.) appear certain doctrinal aspects (11:3 and vv. 6, 19, 35), but the opening sentence defines faith by its effects. Neither specifically Christian nor even religious, this definition brings together two perspectives: one existential and biblical (accepting a promise with faith is "a way of already possessing what is hoped for"), the other intellectual and Hellenistic (accepting the word of a competent person with faith is "a way of knowing what cannot be seen"). The two perspectives recur in the rest of the chapter.

f) Pistis Christou. This Greek expression (Gal 2:16c; Phil 3:9) and several similar ones have provoked discussion because of their ambiguity. In fact, the act of believing, so often mentioned in the New Testament (Greek *pisteuein:* 241 times), is never attributed in the text to Jesus. On the other hand, the New Testament often speaks of "believing in him" (42 3) or "faith in him" (9 3). As a consequence, *pistis Christou* may be translated "faith in Christ," as *pistis Theou* (Mk 11:22) is translated "faith in God." But it may also be translated "fidelity of Christ." Finally, reference can be made to Romans 3:3, where *pistis* corresponds to the Hebrew *'èmét* and designates the absolute "faithfulness" of God.

• P. Antoine (1938), "Foi (dans l'Écriture)," *DBS* 3, 276–312; (1955), "Qu'est-ce que la foi? Données bibliques," *LV(L)* 22, 425–531.

A. Weiser, R. Bultmann (1959), "*Pisteuô, pistis,*" *ThWNT* 6, 174–230 (*Foi,* Geneva, 1976).

P. Vallotton (1960), *Le Christ et la foi,* Geneva.

E.D. O'Connor (1961), *Faith in the Synoptic Gospels,* Notre Dame, Ind.

H. Ljungman (1964), *Pistis,* Lund.

E. Grässer (1965), *Der Glaube im Hebräerbrief,* Marbourg.

H. Wildberger (1968), "Glauben im AT," *ZThK* 65, 129–59.

F.M. Braun (1969), "La foi selon saint Jean," *RThom* 69, 357–77.

Colloque œcuménique (1970), *Foi et salut selon saint Paul,* Rome.

A. Jepsen (1973), "*'âman,*" *ThWAT* 1, 313–48.

W. Mundle (1973), *Der Glaubensbegriff des Paulus,* Leipzig.

J.-M. Faux (1977), *La foi du NT,* Brussels.

J. Guillet (1980), *La foi de Jésus Christ,* Paris.

F. Hahn, H. Klein (1982), *Glaube im Neuen Testament,* Neukirchen.

R.B. Hays (1983), *The Faith of Jesus Christ,* Chicago.

C.D. Marshall (1987), *Faith as a Theme in Mark's Narrative.*

A.R. Dulles (1994), *The Assurance of Things Hoped For,* New York.

Albert Vanhoye

See also **Dogma; Fideism; Grace; Justification; Knowledge of God; Law and Christianity; Liberty; Luther, Martin; Pauline Theology; Preaching; Revelation; Salvation; Truth; Works**

B. Historical and Systematic Theology

1. Patristics

The first theology* inherted from the Scriptures (which it saw as canonical) images and concepts of faith that were rich and flexible. This theology did not systematize such images and concepts but is remarkable by its choice of perspectives. It made these choices on both missionary and exegetical grounds.

Christianity was rather quickly classified, according to the sociological taxonomy of late antiquity, among the schools of thought *(haireseis)* and was never tempted to identify itself with a particular ethnic group; it had an essentially missionary vocation as a community sent by the one whom the Father* had sent. This mission was carried out in a totally exoteric manner. There was a Christian cult* and there were Christian "mysteries*," just as there were at the time a cult and mysteries of Mithra. Hence, there was a Christian initiation* and liturgical actions to which only believers were admitted. But unlike Mithraism and any other mystery religion, Christianity saw itself from the beginning as the bearer of a true word that could be proclaimed in the agora or the forum as well as in Jewish synagogues, a word to which only Jewish theology and pagan philosophy* were capable of responding. No apologetics were necessary to defend the idea of faith in the face of Israel, since faith was a biblical concept: the *pistis* of which the Christians spoke articulated in Greek a form of conduct without Greek equivalent (*contra* Buber 1950). But distinctions were required with respect to Hellenism, and Clement of Alexandria* was the first to provide them.

Indeed, in the Platonic conceptual framework, "faith," in comparison to true knowledge *(epistemè, gnôsis),* represented an impoverished form of knowledge. Clement adopted a dual strategy. 1) His first step was to rely on Aristotelianism against Platonism. Aristotle had in fact suggested a concept of faith that lent itself to theological acceptance. To be sure, faith was different from rigorous knowledge on the model of syllogistic reasoning based on experience. But although different, it was not of lesser value; rather, defined as the grasp of self-evident truths, it was more certain than reason* itself. Thus Clement in turn was able to define it by playing Hellenism against itself: "Faith, which the Greeks disparage because they consider it vain and barbarous, is a voluntary anticipation, a religious assent" (*Strom.* II. 2. 8. 4). 2) It was thereby possible to see faith as a near-synonym of knowledge (gnosis), and this second term made Christian experience* fully intelligible (and thus able to be used) in a mission* to the Greeks. Heterodox Gnosticism, to be sure, laid claim to "knowledge" (and also to faith); but for Clement, as was later true for Origen*, the fulfillment of Christian life in the contemplative experience of gnosis created no ambiguity. Gnosis did not abolish *pistis;* it was simply the full exercise of that faith.

Against Celsus, Origen enriched the theory with a reflection on the faith of simple people: the act of faith possessed the same dignity as the entry into philosophy, but it placed experience of a philosophical kind within the reach of everyone. Also against Celsus, he shed light on the believer's trust in God with an analysis of the role played by confidence generally in interpersonal life. In the school of Antioch, and also relying on Aristotle, Theodoret of Cyr provided a new version of the theory. For him too, faith was the foundation on which one built gnosis, and gnosis was interpreted as a form of knowledge that *exceeded* the philosophical rather than being simply nonphilosophical; and he too contrasted the intuitive character of the grasp of faith with discursive reasoning. Theodoret offered the following definition: "Faith is the voluntary assent *(ekousios sugkatathesis)* of the soul, or else the contemplation* *(theôria)* of an invisible object, or the taking of a position with respect to what is *(peri to on stasis),* as well as a direct grasp *(katalèpsis)* of the invisible world, in harmony with our nature, or else an unambiguous disposition *(diathesis)* rooted in the soul* of those who possess it" (*Therapeutics* 1. 91, SC 57/1).

From the fourth century onward, *pistis* frequently became a synonym of "confession of faith" in Greek patristics, as, for example, in the expression "faith of Nicaea." The most remarkable contributions to the doctrine of faith came in fact from monastic-mystical theology. Two major currents came into conflict, and the reconciliation of the two tendencies was to remain one of the permanent problems of Christian thought. A neo-Origenist tradition (Evagrius) thought of the life of faith in strictly intellectualist terms, while the Macarian tradition expressed it in purely affective terms. In addition, the noetics of Pseudo-Dionysius* provided a conceptual framework in which it was possible to articulate precisely the excess of ordinary reason in terms of the dialectical interplay of knowledge and unknowing that is characteristic of faith.

The Alexandrian concept of faith was not accepted as such by all of the Latin Fathers. Tertullian*, for example, sees faith as a relation to truth*, but the rationality of what is believable is denied, with celebrated rhetorical verve: the death* of the Son of God* "is believable because it is absurd"; and his resurrection* "is certain because it is impossible (*credibile est, quia ineptum est...certum est, quia impossibile, De carne Christi* 5). The theoretical contribution of the Latin Fathers was, however, composed of important assertions: that of the link between faith and the church's *regula veritas* in the case of Ireneaus*; the affirmation of the *free* character of faith in the case of Zeno of Verona; the affirmation by Ambrose* of the *virtuous* quality of faith; and by Hilary of the clear distinction between belief and understanding *(intelligere).* It was left to Augustine* to create a synthesis out of these disparate elements. Setting himself to consider the relation between belief and knowledge, he sees faith as the prerequisite for any knowledge: Isaiah 7:9 (Vulgate), *si non credideritis, non intellegetis,* "if you do not believe, you will not understand," is one of his favorite scriptural quotations. And in searching for the reasons for faith, he refers to grounds for credibility*—the fulfillment of the prophecies* in Christ*, miracles*, the success of Christianity—and bases the acceptance of faith on a theology of the authority* of the church ("For my part, I would not believe the Gospel if it were not transmitted through the authority of the Catholic Church," CSEL 25. 197). The rationality of faith is complete, but in a mode that transcends the earthly uses of reason. Finally, Augustine formulated two distinctions that have remained canonical. On the one hand, he distinguished between the content of faith and the act of faith: *aliud sunt ea quae creduntur, aliud fides qua creduntur* (*Trin.* 13. 2. 5). And on the other, in the access to faith he distinguished a sequence of three acts: "believing God," "having faith in God," and "believing in God" *(credere Deum, credere Deo, credere in Deum),* of which only the third characterizes Christian experience.

In 529 the Second Council of Orange, assembled and inspired by Caesar of Arles and ratified by Pope* Boniface II, canonized the principal theses of Augustine on original sin*, grace*, and faith. At the end of the patristic age, the Christian West thus dogmatically confessed that "we must, with the help of God, preach and believe that the sin of the first man so diverted and weakened free will that no one since can love God as he should, nor do good for God, if divine grace and mercy* have not shown him the way" (*DS* 396).

The Christian East, although it had not had to refute Pelagianism*, and thus had not sharpened its formulations to this extent, would probably have accepted these assertions. And because it experienced no real debate about faith, the history of its theology of faith is that of a peaceful persistence of patristic conceptions.

2. Medieval Theology

Most medieval theologies of faith were also organized around a speculative exegesis* of Isaiah 7:9. In Anselm*, the leitmotif of a faith in search of understanding, *fides quaerens intellectum,* should be understood as what he says it is. The arguments and the apparently exorbitant desire to find "necessary reasons," *rationes necessariae,* follow from beginning to end a believing process (*see* Barth* 1931), carried out by a reason to which the very act of believing has granted through grace the competence that it possessed before the Fall. Anselm's primary purpose was not apologetic, but rather to articulate the logic of the language of faith. But because that logic unfolds under the presupposed aegis of harmony between rationality and faith, it is also the logic of a weakened (but not annihilated) reason, whose inherent dynamism leads it to seek faith (and hence, in a second stage, to seek and find itself).

In Abelard*, by contrast, we encounter a new missionary theology. Nurtured by the "arts of language" *(artes sermonicales)* that the Latin West was in the process of rediscovering (logic, rhetoric, grammar), this theology had as its goal the transmission of faith to simple people or its defense and illustration against heretics and non-Christians (for example, in the *Dialogue between a Philosopher, a Jew, and a Christian*). Like almost all theologians of faith and reason, Abelard commented on Hebrews 11:1 (Vulgate)—*Fides est substantia rerum sperandarum, argumentum non apparentium,* "faith is the substance of things hoped for, the evidence of things not seen"—and places the emphasis of the commentary on his interpretation of *argumentum,* which he glosses as *existimatio,* "evaluation." This presupposed an exalted idea of reason: the believer who addresses nonbelievers or other believers in these terms must himself possess an *intellectus fidei* capable of proving that the language of faith is fully invested with meaning. Abelard, however, knew the limits of discursive rationality: true knowledge* of God, *cognitio,* is without location in the world and the church; it is a purely eschatological reality.

Abelard's theory found a relentless adversary in Bernard* of Clairvaux. Bernard did have an Anselmian conception of reason healed by faith, and this might have made possible a positive appreciation of Abelard's work. But his monastic theology, focused as it was on spiritual experience, could hardly find a place for the instrumentalization of philosophical theories, and Bernard's emphasis on the will and the emotions, like that of his disciple William of Saint-Thierry, led to a different understanding of the act of faith and of the life of faith.

We owe to the theologians of Saint*-Victor several original concepts and propositions. Also interested in the problem of the faith of simple people, Hugh of Saint-Victor interpreted it by reference to the solidarity of believers. The faith of the simple, like that of the just of the Old Testament (whose christological faith was only implicit), was carried by the faith of the clergy and the monks. Hugh elsewhere sketched a theory of knowledge illustrated by the model of the "three eyes": the eye of the flesh making possible knowledge of the world, the eye of reason making possible knowledge of the self, and the eye of contemplation making possible knowledge of God. The eye of the flesh was not blinded by sin, so that it has the ability to ascend from the world* to God; and the three modes of knowledge are in addition interdependent, so that faith, by making contemplation possible, also affects knowledge of the self and the world.

Commenting on Hebrews 11:1, Hugh places the emphasis of his commentary on *substantia,* and posits that it is already eschatological goods that "subsist" in the experience of the believer. Finally, he provides his own definition: faith is *certitudio quaedam animi de rebus absentibus, supra opinionem et infra scientiam,* "an intellectual certainty concerning absent things, superior to opinion and inferior to science" (*De sacram.*, PL 176. 330). And he contributed to thought about the balance between rational and emotional factors in positing that *fides quae* was governed by reason and *fides qua* by the powers of emotion, that the "matter" of faith lies in knowledge but its "substance" in *affectio.*

For Richard of Saint-Victor, commentary on Isaiah 7:9 did not lead to a theory of theological knowledge, as was the case for Anselm, but immediately to a theory of mystical knowledge. And for him, faith grasps the *rationes necessariae* in the framework of a mystical contemplation, in a manner rather close to that of Anselm. Peter Lombard was the first to articulate a problem that was to reappear in all later theologians, that of the faith of devils (*Sent.* III. d. 23, *see* Jas 2:19). If we must concede that devils believe, then we must admit the existence of a faith that is dead and of no use to salvation*, reduced to a pure act of knowledge. To demonstrate by contrast the true nature of *credere in,* Peter Lombard was then led to broaden the field of the *quaestio de fide* to encompass all theological experience (faith-hope*-charity). And it was in *caritas,* which he identified with the Holy* Spirit, that he saw the foundation of theological life, a foundation that was guaranteed by what was akin to an inspiration.

For his part, reflecting on the relation between faith and reason, Gilbert de la Porrée noted a reversal: in the things of this world, reason precedes faith; in the things of God, faith precedes reason. Gilbert was primarily a theoretician of the scientific practice of theology, for whom *intellectus fidei* was identical to theological knowledge. But, like Anselm, he described a labor of reason entirely pursued under the protection of the act of faith. He thus modified a classic Augustinian formulation: where Augustine defined faith as a *cum assentione cogitare,* a "thought with assent," Gilbert defined it as a *cum assentione percipere,* a "perception with assent." An early interest in what would later become the *analysis fidei* was beginning to surface. Finally, there was another beginning in Nicholas of Amiens, the first thinker to conceive of reason as entrusted with providing "preambles to faith."

Two major tasks were thus bequeathed to the theologians of the 13th century: that of précising the place of faith in all cognitive experiences and that of integrating faith into the general economy of the Christian experience. The wish to accomplish both tasks was universally evident. In William of Auxerre, for example, we encounter a theory of theological knowledge in which the articles of faith make up the set of axioms on which a rigorous theology must be based; but speculative experience can nonetheless not be abstracted from Christian life as a whole, for faith also gives rise to the love* of God. For William of Auvergne, the weakness of reason in its worldly use is asserted with such force that faith in it becomes improbable, *improbabilis,* but the grace of faith is also asserted with similar force, and theological experience gives evidence of reason going beyond itself, making possible the dissolution of all improbability. In the *Summa halensis,* the theory of faith is first of all a theory of the bases for a science, but a science that attains its object by "tasting" it, *secundum gustum,* within an experience whose cohesion is ensured by emotional factors and the work of the will.

For Bonaventure*, the theory of faith is rooted in a theology of history* in which the preambles to Christian experience are not provided by philosophical work* (he constantly saw philosophy primarily as the legacy of a dead past) but by the history of Israel. It is incumbent on a theology of the Old Testament to provide the concrete precomprehensions and pre-experiences of Christian faith. At the center of his interpretation, the triad of "memory," "intelligence," and "will" composes an "image of the Trinity*," *imago creationis,* in human beings. Sin has almost erased this image, but theological life restores it in the exalted mode of an *imago recreationis.* Faith is consequently an event that occupies the entire space of consciousness. Because human beings do not enjoy eschatological immediacy in their relation to God, their faith requires the speculative services of discursive knowledge—but on the path that leads the mind to God, faith is focused on mystical experience and is fulfilled in that experience as an immediate relation. A disciple of Bonaventure, Matthew of Acquasparta particularized the relation of will to intellect in terms that had a long-lasting influence: faith is related *causaliter* to will, it is related to intellect *formaliter* and *essentialiter.* He also produced a theory of knowledge according to which faith and knowledge can coexist in the same person.

The analysis proposed by Thomas* Aquinas remains the most straightforward, the least encumbered with nuances. The presupposition is intellectualist: "believe" is said of an assent to truths guaranteed by primordial Truth itself. But if there is room in the Thomist structure of knowledge for purely rational assent (for a pure and simple constraint exercised by truth on the intelligence), the natural operation of reason cannot go beyond a metaphysical affirmation of God, for which Thomas provides a model in the first questions of the *Summa Theologica.* The logic of belief is distinguished from a logic of pure intellection in that it is intellectual assent moved by the will; thus it is both a process of knowledge in the strict sense (its order is that of *theôria*) and a work of liberty* (hence meritorious). Because no one believes except by reason of an attraction exercised by God on him (Jn 6:44), faith is an *innate* virtue. And because it does not consist of a momentary act but of the permanence of a way of being, it is a *habitus* and an innate *virtue.* Christian experience, however, is not limited to the experience of faith; charity in fact is the "form of the virtues*," of the theological virtues (faith and hope) as of the others. Faith, on the other hand, acquiesces to truths proposed in a linguistic form that make up a system, but its spiritual dynamism goes beyond—*actus credentis non terminatur ad enuntiabile sed ad rem* ("the act of believing ends not at the expressible but at the deed"; *ST* IIa IIae. q.1. a. 2. ad 2)—and aims toward God himself through what it causes us to say truthfully about him. And in the framework of an intellectualist eschatology* in which the absolute future of humanity is a plenitude of knowledge, faith itself takes on a certain eschatological coloration: on this side of death it is like a "foretaste of the future vision" (*In Sent.* III. d. 23. q.2. a. 1. ad 4) that it promises to human beings. The necessity of belief is finally rooted in the created nature of human beings (before the Fall, Adam* must have believed) and not in the concrete conditions of sinful existence.

Beginning with Duns* Scotus, followed by Ockham, medieval theology underwent a reorganization. The clearest result of this was a reduction of the field of philosophical knowledge and hence an enlargement of the realm of faith. When the order of things no longer appeared to be the product of a divine will conceived on the model of arbitrary will, Anselm's idea of a discernment of "necessary reasons" was doomed to disappear in favor of other concepts: that of faith defined as "learned ignorance" or as an "incomprehensible grasp of the incomprehensible" (Nicholas* of Cusa); or that of a confidence that refused to base itself on any form of credibility* or to ally itself with any form of philosophy.

3. Reformation and Modern Theology

a) The theology of Luther* carried out a work of concentration: a christological concentration on the one hand, and a concentration on the living experience of faith on the other. A certain number of refusals followed: a refusal to accept the existence of a "dead faith" (the only mortal sin is the sin against the Holy Spirit, and its consequence is the disappearance of all faith); a rejection of the Augustinian distinction between *fides quae* and *fides qua* and of the distinction made by Peter Lombard between *fides catholica* and *fides cum caritate;* and a rejection of the distinction between *acquired faith* and *innate faith* (*WA* 6. 84–86). These refusals were the result of positions taken. Luther understood faith primarily as a salvific process that is worked out in human beings by the Holy Spirit. It is also understood as the birth certificate of the new person—*fides facit personam* (*WA* 39/1. 283. 1)—and as the focus of a theological experience (faith-hope-charity) from which it cannot be abstracted and in which, moreover, it appropriates traits characteristic of hope and charity. Faith also is born from the Word*—*fides ex auditu* (Rom 10:17)—and requires no legitimation.

Because it is based in Jesus Christ and is lived as faith *in* him *(credere in),* it is not possible to isolate the contents of faith that individuals might meditate upon in a first stage and then assent to in a second stage. In the end, only faith makes it possible to recognize the divinity of God, and Luther found provocative language for this assertion: "*Fides est creatrix divinitatis, non in persona, sed in nobis*—Faith creates divinity not in itself but in us; outside of faith, God loses his justice, his glory, etc.; where faith is lacking, there remains nothing of his majesty and his divinity" (*WA* 40/1. 360. 5ff.).

The Lutheran *sola fide* is intelligible only on the condition that we recognize that it depends on a new arrangement of the realm of faith by virtue of which "belief" receives an unprecedented extension. By refusing to distinguish in the act of faith between the work of reason and the work of will (and the emotions), Luther in fact posits that faith is a gift of the Holy Spirit to the entire person* and an offering of the entire person to God. The concept deserves to be called "existential," something also shown in Luther's lack of interest in protological (on the faith or the knowledge of Adam) or eschatological speculations. Faith is an act of the whole person, and it is so in a manner not susceptible to analysis. Finally, although the logic of confidence, *fiducia,* is also a logic of knowledge, since the particularity of faith is to recognize God given to humanity on the cross of Jesus*, it has no rational preamble and does not open onto a new use of speculative reason. The problem of the faith of simple people therefore does not arise, for the act of faith is the same in all, and in the world there is nothing beyond the act of faith.

The theory nevertheless required adjustments when the rebellion of a single man against medieval Catholicism took the form of a mass movement that was finally organized into a church. Lived faith had to be inscribed in symbolic books, and Reformation confessions of faith revived in Protestantism* the notion of *fides quae.* The experience of preaching* and especially the experience of confessional polemics also demonstrated that recourse to the purity of the gospel in fact required the development of a theology. It thus fell to Luther's best disciple, Melanchthon, to systematize the founding teachings of the Reformation in didactic form. The first important characteristic of this systematic organization was the reemphasis on the content of faith: "*Fides est assentio, qua accipis omnes articulos fidei, et est fiducia acquiescens in Deo propter Mediatorem*—Faith is the assent of whoever accepts all the articles of faith, and it is the confidence of whoever accepts God by reason of the Mediator" (CR 23. 456).

The act of faith is broken down into three stages: "perception" *(notitia),* "assent" *(assensus),* and "confidence" *(fiducia).* Perception and assent are the work of reason, confidence the work of the will. This conception might be called neoclassical. It does not distort the governing idea of faith alone as justification, and its general outline was adopted by Calvin*. However, Calvin introduced a new factor into the analysis, incredulity, of which he asserts that it is "always mixed with faith" (*Inst.* 1536, 3. 2. 4). Protestant theology of the 17th century did not modify this balance.

It was in its decree on justification* that the Council of Trent* responded to Protestant theologies of faith. First of all, Trent rejected the earlier concentration on the question of faith and reaffirmed the doctrine of the theological virtues: the union of human person and God could not be accomplished in the single element of faith but required hope and charity (*DS* 1531). It then rejected the concept of *fiducia,* which could lead to belief in the possibility of a *subjective certainty* of salvation: *cum nullus scire valeat certitudine fidei, cui non potest subesse falsum, se gratiam Dei esse consecutum* (*DS* 1534). The council further recalled that theological life is a response in man to prevenient grace (*DS* 1553), which enables free will to cooperate with the work of the God who "calls" him. Lastly, the grace of God does not revive a free will that original sin has abolished ("slave will"), but brings about its restoration.

b) From Trent to the early 20th century, two separate but linked problems were to occupy most of the attention of Catholic theology: the analysis of the act of faith and of the (rational) preambles to faith. In a complex history, two major tendencies stand out.

1) In response to the suspicions that the Reformation had brought to bear on the capacities of reason, there was a reorganization of apologetics from which was to arise a "fundamental* theology" endowed with an ambitious program: to demonstrate the "truth of religion," "Christian truth," and "Catholic truth" *(demonstratio religiosa, demonstratio christiana, demonstratio catholica).* New missionary necessities were added to the needs of confessional polemics. In the face of the libertines, arguments had to be made in favor of religion as such. A "new world" had to be evangelized. The duty of speaking presupposed the possibility of an intelligible and true discourse. Without the notion of a reason universally imparted to everyone, always present in sinful human beings who innately aspired to belief, this program could not be carried out. It is not without significance that the spearhead of missionary Catholicism, the Society of Jesus, chose as its official theologian Thomas Aquinas, one of the medieval thinkers most confident in the powers of reason. But while the arguments of medieval theologians, including Thomas, proposed first to explore the field of rational experience opened up by faith, and only secondarily to pick out the rational preambles to faith, modern apologetics was paradoxically constructed so as to delay the moment of belief in order to provide a better basis for the rationality of that belief. The central christological and Trinitarian affirmations of Christian discourse, were, of course, never subsumed under the authority of an apologetic demonstration—it is because G. Hermes assigned excessive tasks to its apolegetic

that he was accused of "rationalism*" in 1835. But in support of its preaching the church could rely either on *facts* (fulfillment of prophecies and miracles, with the resurrection of Jesus as the supreme miracle) or on universal truths of reason, above all the existence of God. And with perfect coherence, Vatican* I finally set the entire authority of the church behind a definition of the prerogatives of a nontheological knowledge of God in aid of faith—the prerogatives of a nontheological theoretical enterprise conducted under the supervision of theology.

During the same period there appeared in Catholic thought the form of irrationalism known as *fideism**. In the form it assumed in the work of Bautain, and which was condemned, fideism was not identical to a rejection of all forms of credibility and of any preambles to faith. But it replaced the leitmotif of an intellect in search of faith with the idea of a *cor quaerens fidem,* the logic of which necessarily led to the diminution of the claims of rationality and a neglect of the tools of rational apologetics. A major point, however, is worth noting. The condemnation of fideism was made by positing the *possibility* of a certain knowledge of God through natural reason (*DS* 2751; repeated by Vatican* II, *DV* §6) and later (in the antimodernist Oath) even the possibility of a *demonstrative* proof of the existence* of God (*DS* 3538). But the documents do not at all suggest that this knowledge is achieved anywhere in a normative form. They speak rather of a perpetual labor of reason by saying that it can in principle be accomplished.

2) These concerns also led to new questions concerning the act of faith. The motive force of faith, its "formal object," is the "authority of the God who reveals [himself]"; it is because there is free obedience that there is faith, which is a consent to *believe* where one does not *see.* A problem followed for the theoreticians of the *analysis fidei:* how to think of the personal contribution of the person to his or her act of faith. There was certainly no question of reconsidering the strictly supernatural character of faith as defined by the Council of Orange. But after those reversals in theory and in the church that were caused by the Reformation, it was, on the other hand, necessary to restate in new terms that the act of faith was—also—the meritorious result of a free decision.

The concerns of Christian humanism, as Erasmus* had defended them against Luther, were then taken over by the missionary concerns of the 16th and 17th centuries. In this case, too, the predominant role played by the Jesuits in the pastoral enterprises of the time, whether in the intellectual and spiritual training of the elite of the old world or in the evangelization (conversion*) of newly discovered cultures, largely explains the concern to grant to human beings, as creatures called on to believe, the greatest freedom that theology could countenance. Greek theology had resolved this problem in the patristic age by making use of the concept of cooperation between God and human beings *(sunergeia),* so that divine activity did not lessen human activity but made it fully possible. This concept, however, had never been articulated in a system (which probably explains its persisting suggestive power). The Catholicism of the Counter Reformation, on the contrary, wished to systematize, which led both to heterodox constructions (the "Augustinians gone astray" [Lubac*]: Baius and Jansenius) and to competing constructions among which the Roman magisterium* finally admitted it was unable to decide: Bañezianism* and Molinism. The debates had to do not only with faith: in fact, predestination* and the divine presence, together with the status of evil* and God's permitting of it, were the most discussed questions. But whether one defended a theory of grace in which a divine gesture—"physical premotion"—was a precondition for any human spiritual decision (Bañez), or a theory of "concord" between nature* and grace (Molina), the question of the act of faith soon appeared in the debate. The intentions governing its appearance were no doubt pure. But the kinds of theological analysis to which they led (and to which they led all the parties to the debate)—breaking down the act of faith into moments, the distribution of intellectual and voluntary-affective factors according to the moments at which they came into play, the localization of the help provided by grace—had the result of putting theories into circulation, or creating a theoretical climate, in which faith lost all its lived unity. And the assimilation of the content of faith to a system of true propositions, a constant temptation of post-Tridentine theology, added a depersonalizing aspect to the doctrines that were proposed.

c) In the same period, Protestant theology had simultaneously to integrate the exigencies of an irrationalism—Pietism*—and those of rationalism—the *Aufklärung* or German Enlightenment.

1) Pietism was more a theology of Christian life than a theology of the access to Christianity, and its first distinctive note was the orchestration on a large scale of a traditional theme that the reformers had not forgotten, that of Christian expe-

rience as a new or a regenerated life. The Pietists affirmed this by linking justification with sanctification, by emphasizing the in-dwelling of the Holy Spirit in human beings, but also by dismissing any merely imputational concept of justification in favor of a conception of faith as the "life of Christ in us," as the experience of a *Christus inhabitans* (already present in Weigl). Making its appearance later, the second distinctive note of Pietism was the assignment of Christian experience to the realm of the "heart." The enterprise of Pietist theology was then to carry out an "affective transposition of doctrine" (Pelikan) in which the contents of faith were articulated in such a manner that they called for the assent of the heart rather than of reason, and in which faith in turn committed the believer to a life of "piety" and sanctification entirely governed by feeling. This theology intended to be "experiential" (Oetinger), understanding by that the immediate experience of the Holy Spirit. And it revealed its real provocative force when it asserted that the only ones who possessed *fiducia* (bluntly, the only ones who really had faith) were those who had known such an experience. These premises did not prevent Pietism from taking on missionary activities. In the late 18th century the *Discourses* of Schleiermacher* and the *Génie du christianisme* of Chateaubriand demonstrated that the religion of feeling could also be organized in apologetic form, and then Schleiermacher's *Christian Faith* offered a dogmatics that is from beginning to end dominated by religious feeling.

2) It was principally as a response to the Enlightenment that the apologetics of feeling was conceived, and the faith it proposed was one that knew, or thought it knew, that reason no longer led to God. In the voice of Kant*, the moderate wing of the *Aufklärung* had said both that theoretical reason knew nothing of God and that that left the field open to faith. On the other hand, Enlightenment philosophy had also had its radicals, who had asserted that the limits of the rational were the limits of the knowable. The consequences were many: a grammar of belief translated into postulates of practical reason (Kant); a Christianity devoid of mystery (Toland); a first historicist "demythologization" of Christian origins (Reimarus); and a skeptical rationalism that knew no access to God other than the "leap" of faith (Lessing); among others. A faith not in search of reason and a reason not in search of faith, simplistic a dilemma as it may seem, does not overly distort the spirit of the age. Two theological tactics were possible and were followed: that of a rationalist theology principally concerned with justifying all its statements by the standards of enlightened reason (theological "rationalism," in the technical sense of the term), and that of a systematic theology of feeling for which emotion alone is the organ of knowledge in religious matters (Schleiermacher and his posterity). The 19th century, however, saw the opening of a third path, a redefinition of the reciprocal positions of "reason" and "faith."

d) Destined to have no theological influence—or at least none that was faithful to their intentions—before the 20th century, the works of Hegel* and Schelling* contain a more or less revolutionary contribution to the *disputatio de fide.* The contents of faith, in Hegel's *Phenomenology* and *Logic* and in Schelling's *Philosophy of Revelation,* actually become philosophical objects in their own right. Christian exoterism is thus pushed to its highest point. The positivity of Christianity and the inscription of what is believable in Christianity in a history and in facts are all offered to the operation of the intelligence, on the sole condition that rationality sets itself no a priori limit, that is, on condition that it truly intends to perform a work of reason *(Vernunft)* and not to content itself, like the Enlightenment, with a work of understanding *(Verstand).* A hint of rationalism readily arises. If in Hegel there is still room for religious faith in the journey of the knowing mind, this journey concludes with a full experience of the rational, an "absolute knowledge" that knows faith better than faith knows itself; and knows the contents of faith better than faith itself knows them, because it knows them by means of conceptualization and faith knows them by means of "representation." However, the idea of a reason essentially capable of thinking what faith believes corresponds in part to Anselm's interest in "necessary reasons." Furthermore, the idea of a philosophy that assigns central positions to a Christology* and a Trinitarian theology breaks down a barrier between philosophy and theology that had only been constructed in the 13th century and that Bonaventure himself had not really known. The question of a knowledge *(gnôsis)* that knows more and better than faith nevertheless raises objections that the texts cannot resolve satisfactorily. This is a culmination of theological intellectualism,* in the context of which the faith of simple people cannot be seen as embodying a fullness of experience. This position prohibits in advance someone like Theresa of Lisieux from playing a magisterial role in the church.

e) On the fringes of the debates of his time, the work of Kierkegaard also had to await the 20th century (namely, the appearance of "dialectical theology") before it exercised real influence. It contains two aspects, the first of which easily masks the second. Against Hegelian intellectualism (the "system"), Kierkegaard is first of all the theoretician of a strict voluntarism* that frequently recalls Lessing's "leap of faith." Conceived in a strictly apophatic manner as an "absolute paradox," separated from man by an "infinite qualitative difference," the God of Kierkegaard makes impossible the traditional interplay between *intellectus quaerens fidem* and *fides quaerens intellectum.* On the one hand, faith does nothing but accomplish a break in relation to any other human act (intellectual or emotional). On the other hand, it is not defined as something that restores a reason weakened by sin (Bonaventure), or as establishing a reason even more reasonable than that of Adam—nothing lies beyond the pure act of belief. As rigorous a fideism as possible is linked, however, to a reorganization of knowledge in which, in a very paradoxical way, Kierkegaard accomplishes by other means a part of Hegel's and Schelling's program. In this instance too, a division of labor that had become canonical is abolished in favor of a unified field in which the logic of "existence" is given at bottom only a single duty, the defense and illustration of the Lutheran *fides facit personam.* The reasons governing the *Philosophical Fragments* are those of Christology. A dialectic of existence, clearly aimed at founding faith in no other way than on the paradox of the God who has come incognito among human beings, unfolds, however, in such a way that the Christian experience effects a horde of meanings. There is no "system of existence," says Kierkegaard. The question of faith, moreover, does not have to do with a body of truths to be believed, but with the person of the God who invites us to follow him. The coincidence of access to Christianity and access to the self (to the truth of subjectivity), however, makes possible a recapitulation of the whole person in the life lived before God. And finally, by denying that belief was easier for the disciple of the first generation than it is for modern man, Kierkegaard is led to form a concept of "contemporaneity" that provides a first profound response to the challenges of the historical critique of the foundations of faith, whether that critique came from the Enlightenment or from the Hegelians of the left.

Protestant theology of the 19th century was divided among the various influences mentioned above. Schleiermacher's idea of a faith coextensive with feeling was predominant. The work of the *Aufklärung* was also continued in the form of a historical-critical demolition of Christian sources that was to culminate in Schweitzer's judgment that Jesus was totally unknowable, and his proposition of an act of faith that could no longer even claim certainly to derive from a gospel. Finally, Liberal Protestantism called into question the christological structure that the principal current of Christianity had always recognized in faith. Distinguishing faith *in* Jesus from the faith *of* Jesus (e.g., Harnack, *Das Wesen des Christentums,* 1900), and favoring the latter, made possible the appearance of a new *notitia* (entrusted with determining what critical history had left intact in Christianity) and a new *assensus* (entrusted with acquiescing to the Good News of God the Father); and although *fiducia* survived, it was only in the form of a certain piety.

From the Restoration to the First Vatican Council, the interventions of the Roman magisterium in theological life made it possible to lay out a path—that of a faith without fideism and a reason without rationalism—and the appearance of a triumphant Neoscholasticism sometimes seemed to indicate the appropriate way of following that path. The modernist crisis, however, was to demonstrate that more significant readjustments would be necessary. The crisis arose first from the repercussions of Protestant exegesis among the Catholic intelligentsia, and when it broke out, the Catholic tradition* and the Protestant tradition were on the point of once again taking up a common history.

4. Contemporary Theology

"New Thought," the title of an article in which the Jewish philosopher Rosenzweig summarized the arguments of his *Star of Redemption,* also expressed the general ambition of contemporary forms of Christianity. Throughout various schools and confessions, common needs had in fact appeared, and new possibilities had surfaced.

1) The needs were linked to the appearance of philosophies "of the person." Employed to designate the concrete individual engaged in the operation of all his or her faculties, the concept of person could render appreciable service by avoiding the subtle divisions between rational, voluntary, and affective factors characteristic of classical theology. In this context the merit of Rousselot (1878–1915) was to propose the first description of the access to faith that proceeded by means of a concrete integration of all the dynamics at work (credibility). Rousselot himself was influenced by the *Grammar of Assent* of Newman*, a book of 1870 that was nevertheless ahead of its time. Instead of treating assent as the final moment of an intellective-discursive process, Newman linked it to a complex intuition

based on a "sense of inference," the *illative sense.* It was only after Rousselot that Newman's epistemology became common currency.

2) The lexicon of the "personal" appeared elsewhere to criticize the representation of an "objective" and disinterested rational activity, a representation that was extremely difficult to use in a theory of the act of faith. The important book on this question was *Personal Knowledge* by the chemist and epistemologist Polanyi (1958). Devoted to bringing to the fore the uncriticized presuppositions of any intellectual work and the tacit beliefs that such work presupposed, to showing the element of self-implication (hence of "nonobjectivity") that it involved, and to demonstrating the need for a certain theoretical aptitude *(skills)* that can derive only from concrete contact with reality, the book put an end to a caricature of scientific rationality. In doing so, it made possible a clearer perception that the act of faith is not rational *despite* what it contains of self-implication and decision (*see* Torrance, Ed., *Belief in Science and Christian Life: The Relevance of M. Polanyi's Thought for Christian Faith and Life,* Edinburgh, 1980).
3) Another related event was the theological acceptance of Gadamer's hermeneutics*. *Truth and Method* by Gadamer (1960) carried out a critique in high style of "prejudices against prejudice," which made possible a clearer apprehension of the ("hermeneutic") logic according to which the act of faith included an act of comprehension, itself relying on precomprehensions. And because it included a rejection of all individualist theories and situated every work of interpretation within interpretive traditions, it also made possible the location of the act of faith within the total interpretive work of the Christian community.
4) The ecclesial status of faith was also to become a major concern. Theologies dealt with it in different ways. In *Catholicisme* by H. de Lubac (1938), "to believe" is conjugated in the plural by showing the presence of ecclesiological elements in the entire architecture of Christian dogma*. In the same period, philosophies of the person attempted to propose a concept of the "we" (e.g., G. Marcel). Later, J.D. Zizioulas was to emphasize the strictly "ontological" novelty of belonging to the church. As for narrative* theologies, they provided a useful description of faith as an entry into a community that affirms its identity by telling its founding stories and as a personal appropriation of those stories.
5) After a long tradition of indifferent silence, it was thus impossible not to ask what "believe" means biblically. To be sure, it was still possible in 1952 to write a treatise on faith in which the present experience of faith is not thought of as a reactualization of acts normatively rooted in the experience of Israel and of the first Christian generation (Guérard des Lauriers, *Dimensions de la foi*), but as acquiescence to a doctrine, and thereby to ratify the opposition proposed by Buber (1950) between Jewish faith ("historical") and Christian faith ("doctrinal"). Against Buber, however, the main current of theology was able to establish that in this domain continuity won out over discontinuity (*see* Flusser 1994; Werblowsky 1988), so that Israel's capacities for the experience of God also entered into a Christian experience taken in its complete existential dimensions. Christian faith is not a Greek attitude.
6) Also recuperated were patristic sources, and with them a concept of "knowledge" enriched with all the overtones of the *gnôsis* of Clement of Alexandria and Origen. The concept of *fides quaerens intellectum* consequently ceased to be that of a faith seeking to give itself conceptual tools, and could again designate an innate impulse of faith; "intellection" ceased to be understood primarily as the production of knowledge and revealed a more complex (and more experiential) logic of knowledge.
7) A more flexible idea of rationality imposed itself all the more in the 20th century because belief frequently lost its status as an image of the irrational and was positively integrated into the logic of knowledge. In Husserl it could be learned that consciousness lives innately in the element of belief. By focusing on ordinary language and the experiences that it expresses, analytical philosophy was also able to observe that the border between belief and knowledge is less certain than the old models of reason suggested. The "Wittgensteinian fideism" of which D.Z. Phillips is considered the earliest proponent (*see* Nielsen, *Philosophy,* 1967) is the most brilliant example in the Anglo-American world of a philosophy that affirms the full legitimacy of belief while at the same time prohibiting any foundational maneuver.
8) The disappearance of the propositional theory of revelation* (a product of post-Tridentine dogmatics) also made possible any dissociation between "believe in" and "believe that" (*see* Price 1965), in favor of the latter. In the principal theo-

logical currents of all confessions, the act of faith then appears less as an acquiescence to a body of truths (which it still is as late as Rousselot) than as the discovery of a divine Thou. An apologetics of *proof* necessarily tends to yield place to a pedagogy of spiritual experience aimed at providing a unified initiation into a *Christian experience* whose possibility it knows to be rooted a priori in every human person: for example, in the "transcendental Thomism" derived from Maréchal (Lotz, Rahner*, Coreth, and others); in Schaeffler (*Fähigkeit zur Erfahrung,* 1982), within the framework of a hermeneutics of meaning; and in J. Mouroux, in an approach that combines Thomist inspiration with personalist influences (*L'expérience chrétienne,* 1954).

9) Finally, we can note a new interest in the language of faith. The question was classically that of the contents of faith, of the true language used by the one who believes. The influence of research on self-involving languages (Evans, *The Logic of Self-involvement,* 1963) has, however, led contemporaries to be more willing to interpret the language of confessions of faith, of prayer*, and of the liturgy* (Bruaire 1977; Ladrière 1984). As for the secular philosophical research devoted in Great Britain to the phenomenon of faith (Price, Cohen, Helm, etc.), they are awaiting their theological reception from which could emerge a new evaluation of the *fides quae* as well as a new perception of the relationships between theological faith, belief, and knowledge.

Two common characteristics are shared by most of these tendencies. 1) The first is an interpretation of faith that sees it first as a reality that is destined to survive. Attributing to faith an eschatological or pre-eschatological dimension is not really theologically original. But whereas medieval theology placed primary emphasis on the distance separating faith and "vision," contemporary theology is more willing to emphasize a continuity. This emphasis is expressed in radical form by von Balthasar*, who paradoxically maintains that faith is a divine mode of existence (1984). Another radical form is provided by the realized eschatology of Bultmann*, for whom a present faith today grasps the truth of existence in such a way that nothing remains to be hoped for. In any event, and excepting such extreme cases, theologies of the 20th century agree in describing the experience of faith as establishing in human beings modes of being that characterize their humanity in a definitive manner.

2) A theology concerned with distinguishing the factors—intellectual, affective, voluntary—that enter in the form of a sequence into the genesis of the act of faith has been replaced by a theology more concerned to describe the simultaneous cooperation of everything that makes up human beings (or the "person"). In the theory of faith proposed by Balthasar, the preeminence accorded to the concept of *evidence* and the choice of an aesthetic model bind truth and experience together in a meaningful way (evidence is the experience of truth) and give to experience a twofold content, intellectual and affective. What is given to be believed, insofar as it is given to be believed, is also given to be loved and so provides grounds for hope. An integral theory of faith does not seem to be thinkable if it is not in fact organized as a theological anthropology*.

• K. Barth (1931), Fides quaerens intellectum, *Anselms Beweis des Existenz Gottes im Zusammenhang seines theologischen Programms,* Zürich, GA II/2, 1981.

M. Buber (1950), *Zwei Glaubensweisen,* Zürich, Gerlingen (2nd Ed. 1994).

R. Bultmann (1953), *Theologie des Neuen Testaments,* Göttingen, §35–37 (8th Ed. 1980).

J. Hick (1957), *Faith and Knowledge,* London (3rd Ed. 1988).

H. D. Lewis (1959), *Our Experience of God,* London.

K. Jaspers (1962), *Der philosophische Glaube angesichts der Offenbarung,* Munich.

H. H. Price (1965), "Belief 'in' and Belief 'that,' " *RelSt* 1, 1–27.

H. U. von Balthasar (1967), "Bewegung zu Gott," in *Spiritus Creator, Skizzen zur Theologie* 3, Einsiedeln, 13–50.

J. Mouroux (1968), *A travers le monde de la foi,* CFi 31.

L. Malevez (1969), *Pour une théologie de la foi,* ML.T 63.

H. de Lubac (1970), *La foi chrétienne: Essai sur le symbole des apôtres,* 2nd Rev. Ed., Paris, 149–407.

C. Bruaire (Ed.) (1977), *La confession de la foi,* Paris, 231–76 (article by G. Kalinowski, M. Constantini, and J.-L. Marion).

W. Pannenberg (1980), "Wahrheit, Gewißheit und Glaube," in *Grundfr. syst. Th.* 2, Göttingen, 226–64.

G. E. M. Anscombe (1981), "Faith," in *Ethics, Religion, and Politics: Collected Philosophical Papers* 3, Oxford, 113–20.

R. Swinburne (1981), *Faith and Reason,* Oxford.

J. Ratzinger (1982), *Theologische Prinzipienlehre,* Munich, 15–87.

H. U. von Balthasar (1984), "Die Einheit der theologischen Tugenden," *IKaZ* 13, 306–14.

I. U. Dalferth (1984), *Existenz Gottes und christlicher Glaube,* BEvTh 93, §134–74.

J. Ladrière (1984), *L'articulation du sens,* CFi 125 and 126.

G. Lanczkowski et al. (1984), "Glaube," *TRE* 13, 275–365.

H. Fries (1985), *Fundamentaltheologie,* Graz, 17–103.

G. Picht (1991), *Glauben und Wissen,* Stuttgart.

D. Flusser (1994), "Buber's 'Zwei Glaubensweisen,' " annex to M. Buber, *Zwei Glaubensweisen,* Gerlingen, 186–247.

W. Lad Sessions (1994), *The Concept of Faith: A Philosophical Investigation,* Ithaca-London.

Jean-Yves Lacoste and Nicolas Lossky

See also **Credibility; Hope; Love; Philosophy; Reason; Revelation; Truth**

Faith of Christ. *See* **Christ's Consciousness**

Fall. *See* **Sin, Original**

Family

A religious conception of the family has been obvious since the epoch of the patriarchs in Israel*: the family is made for procreation* and is intended to transmit inheritance and secure the protection of its members, whether they be related by blood, marriage*, or adoption. These presuppositions are no longer accepted. Knowing that family and structures of kinship take many forms across cultures, we are tempted to say that the family is only a social construction. Some have gone further, stating that this construction is the enemy of individual liberty*, emotional fulfillment, or gender equality. It remains the case, however, that no known society* has left human sexuality to function in a purely anarchic way, and that the multiplicity of familial structures shares one common feature: the universal existence of rules of marriage and systems of kinship. The contemporary context is, in Western society, that of a crisis of the so-called "traditional" family, and economic globalization is tending to promote a similarly critical situation within other cultures. In the face of this crisis, and of the fact that it is not a development external to the church*, one might at least expect that moral theology* would be of service. In a situation of total uncertainty in secular discourses on the family, it might provide theologically exact coordinates for a Christian response to this crisis. The present crisis proves, perhaps, that the family is "a new idea, yet to be discovered" (Chapelle 1996).

a) Family in the Bible. In the Old Testament, family presupposes a patriarchal, largely patrilineal and endogamous kinship system, in which the production of male heirs is a chief concern. Israel needs sons: to ensure continuity of the people's faith* and traditions* (Ex 13:14f.; Dt 6:20–25) and, in the pre-exilic period, to pass on family holdings (but *see* Nm 27:1–11 and 36:1–14 on female inheritance in default of a male line). Women* find their social and religious identity primarily as mothers. This is the basic purpose of marriage, even though, ideally, spouses should also be partners and friends linked by mutual fidelity (Gn 1–3). Marriage was sometimes polygamous in the patriarchal period and until about the time of the monarchy (Gn 29:21–30; 2 Sm 5:13–16; 1 Kgs 11:1f.). Concubinage was also permitted (Gn 16:1–4 and 30:1–13). Levirate marriage, requiring a man to marry his brother's widow and beget sons in his name, provided protection to the bereaved woman and furthered continuation of the family line (Gn 38:8; Dt 25:5–10). Only husbands could initiate divorce (Dt 24:1–4; but *see* Mal 2:14f. for a critique of this situation). Sex outside marriage was prohibited, but much more stringently for women than for men (Lv 20:10; Dt 22:22–29; Prv 5:7, 5:27), since female promiscuity threatened patrilineal inheritance.

In the New Testament, this family-centered ethic is perceptibly amended, if not subverted outright. Marriage and family are the background for many of the sayings and parables* of Jesus*, and in them he takes up at least one position against Israelite family law*, in the form of his rejection of divorce (Mt 5:27f. and 19:9; Mk 10:11f.; Lk 16:18; 1 Cor 7:10f.). Of more importance, however, is the call to join the community of disciples, which is structured in a way that owes nothing to marital or familial status. Not only does the founding experience of individual call and individual response occur outside the institution of the family, but family loyalties can create an obstacle to the demands of the gospel (Mt 10:37 and 12:46–50; Mk 3:31–35 and 10:29; Lk 8:19f. and 14:26; Gal 3:28). It was certainly possible for late medieval theology to take the "holy family"—Jesus, Mary, and Joseph—as a model for every family of believers. However, in order to find scriptural legitimization for this model, it must be perceived as what it was, a family that God's initiative had caused to deviate from all other received models.

In the Roman Empire, where Christianity first spread, the family, *familia,* was placed under the authority of the *paterfamilias* and included not only relatives in the strict sense but also slaves, servants, and property. In the form of marriage most common in the first century A.D., the wife remained under the authority of her natal *familia* and hence was not a member of that of her husband, though they shared a common domicile. Conversely, married children of the *paterfamilias* remained members of his *familia,* but usually occupied separate residences. Membership in a particular family considerably influenced a person's identity and social role. Adoption (of an adult male, preferably from among kin) was a common means of transmitting and controlling a name, a patrimony, or a line of succession. Marriage served the same aim, and also served to increase a family's influence and wealth. A hierarchical friendship between spouses and a long-lasting marriage were the ideal, but such an ideal was rarely realized, especially in the upper classes. Older men were usually married to younger women (girls married at 12), which often precluded egalitarian relationships; sexual activity outside marriage was accepted for men but prohibited for citizen women. Divorce and remarriage were frequent, for political as well as personal reasons; consequently, precariousness was an important feature of familial experience. In this context, the appearance of a group, the Christians, who downplayed the importance of family roles and regarded themselves as primarily a community of brothers, clearly called the patriarchal institution into question.

In the earliest Christian communities, the lively expectation of a Parousia* that was believed to be imminent certainly led to doubts as to whether it was appropriate to found a family. This reluctance dissipated as the Parousia was deferred into the future. Nevertheless, it left a trace, in the attribution of eschatological significance to celibacy chosen "for the sake of the kingdom." More important, no doubt, was the very rapid appearance of "domestic codes" intended for married Christians. These codes were generally adaptations from Greek philosophical models and revealed a church eager to articulate norms for family life, partly because of the threat of persecution. They address the members of households in hierarchical relationships (husband/wife, father/children, master/slave) and urge submission on the subordinate party while exhorting the *paterfamilias* to love* and restraint (Eph 5:21–6:9; Col 3:18–4:1; 1 Pt 2:18–3:7). Abstracted from all the New Testament testimony, these texts have undeniably been used throughout the centuries to assert within the family a man's authority and a woman's submission, a practice that stands in tension with the egalitarian thrust of the preaching* of the Kingdom. A major theoretical task thus made its appearance: because the *eschaton* had not been realized in the "event of Jesus Christ," the right of family structures to have a legitimate place among Christian realities had to be guaranteed; but because the *eschaton* had been well and truly anticipated, the fraternal experience of the disciples had to be permitted to become the measure and the norm for the family experience.

b) Family in Christian Tradition. The Encratite tendency to place a wholly negative value on the physical dimension of existence was very quickly rejected by the church, but it survived in a minor mode among patristic authors. Thus, some Fathers*, most notably Jerome (c. 342–420), came close to condemning marriage in their praise of virginity. The mainstream, represented, for example, by Clement of Alexandria (c. 150–215), saw marriage, lived in a spirit of self-control and aimed at producing children, as compatible with the Christian life (*Stromata* 2, 23, SC 38; *Paedagogus* 2, 10, SC 108). The family possessed theological legitimacy because it was a site for the transmission of faith: the religious education and spiritual good* of children was its true raison d'être. John Chrysostom*, who compared the family to a small church, urged married couples to turn aside from wealth and luxury, and to educate the members of their families for lives of prayer* and service (*Hom. in Eph.* 20, PG 62, 135–48).

The indissolubility of marriage was gradually imposed in theology and canon* law. By protecting women against divorce initiated by their husbands or fathers, indissolubility promoted equality within the couple* and gave couples some leverage against paternal power. With the reforms of Gregory VII (c. 1015–85), canon law prohibited remarriage after divorce. Since the theory of the purposes of marriage included the licit exercise of sexuality, each of the marital partners had the right to demand that the other perform his or her "conjugal duty." On the other hand, men and women of all social classes could always enter into the religious life in the name of an ideal of virginity that trumped the demands of family life.

The position of the Reformers was partly a response to the abuses to which church regulation of marriage had given rise and partly a reaction against the celibacy that the church had not succeeded in imposing on clerics* in a satisfactory way. The logic of the Reformist reaction held that marriage and family were ordinary and blessed states of life, ordained by God for human benefit, and in relation to which the church had no function other than to attest God's blessing*. Luther viewed the family as the basic unit of society, a privileged realm where a Christian bore the cross and served God and neighbor. Subsequently, Puritanism* established an exceptionally strong connection between the family and religious identity. God made a "covenant of grace" with believers and their descendants, in which children were not guaranteed salvation* but could be made more open to it by efforts of their parents. This benefit accrued even to servants who shared in the family's religious discipline. The assimilation of the family to a basic form of Christian community was still to be found in the writings of F. D. Maurice (1805–72), the most important Anglican moralist of the 19th century. It was even at the center of the "cult of domesticity" as advocated by authors such as Alexander Campbell (1788–1866). Within Catholicism*, the 20th century has witnessed a notable development in the treatment of the purposes of marriage: the documents of Vatican* II and the revised Code of Canon Law (1983) henceforth identify the community of love and mutual aid *(mutuum adjutorium)* as being of the most importance.

c) Modernity. The ideas and the reality of the modern world could not fail to have an impact on the family in general, and on the Christian idea of the family. Modern ideas included the ideals of the Enlightenment: individual dignity, personal responsibility, and individual freedom. Modern reality was that of an industrialized and urbanized world that separated the private sphere of women (the home and the education of children) from the public sphere of men (waged labor and politics). With the advent of a cash economy, a situation arose in which children's marriages no longer depended on inherited property and (hence) on parental approval. In industrialized countries, fertility declined rapidly near the end of the 19th century, at the same time as the right to education and the right to vote were becoming accessible to women. Life spans increased, posing the problem of the care of elderly family members. The fact that the modern family is mobile, often due to circumstances of employment, has fragmented the networks of extended kin in which children, the sick, and the aged were cared for in previous generations. (One should, however, avoid overgeneralization on this point; it has been shown that the nuclear family did not make its first appearance during industrialization.) These new circumstances demonstrate that it is not sufficient to wish to obey the injunction to honor one's parents; one must also have the support of a social system. Since the forms of the family are changing, the exercise of family responsibilities is also required to take on a new aspect.

In practice, Europe and North America, heirs to an already ancient intellectual tradition that privileges contractual relations to the detriment of family relations, display little dexterity in the theoretical and practical treatment of family realities: if authentic interpersonal bonds are born only from consent, then biological bonds become almost irrelevant. Accordingly, we witness the rejection of the patriarchal family and the appearance of "nontraditional" family relations between heterosexuals or homosexuals. Medical techniques aimed at providing remedies for sterility permit couples to buy, sell, or trade gametes and embryos, creating new relationships between parents and children. Consequently, the biological relationship of parents and children seems no longer to have any meaning in itself. The facts of nature seem to be totally absorbed into totally cultural practices. The family is no longer a given, to be presupposed, but a plastic reality, completely in the hands of humanity.

The consistency of education also poses a grave problem. Western laws authorize serial marriages, but, after divorce, men in Western cultures hold less responsibility for their children than in African or Asian societies that permit polygamy or institutionalized concubinage. Economic, social, and emotional insecurity, especially for women and children, has been a major and troubling consequence of rising divorce rates. In certain countries, the state has taken over some of the functions of support and education once the domain of the family. However, it is unclear whether children can become responsible adults without a strong family network.

d) The Christian Position. A Christian discourse on the family must be organized around a number of doctrines. The theories of creation*, original sin*, and incarnation* provide the base for all possible theologies of the body, and they imply an ethic of corporeal realities that perceives procreation and kinship as strong determinants of family ties. At the same time, the position that love occupies in the logic of virtues*—it is both the "form" of all things and the qualifier of interpersonal relationships, as well as of the relationship with God—obviously prohibits us from regarding the family as a biologically grounded social mechanism for the efficient organization of reproduction, material life, and protection. And because, logically, human love must see in the beloved a gift of God, which calls for fidelity, it is not possible for Christians to accept the idea of an indeterminate series of contracts that one may freely choose or break to maximize one's own best interests.

In its recent teaching, the Catholic Church has revived a concept from the patristic era, calling the family a "domestic church" (Vatican II, *LG* 11, *GS* 48; *see* John Paul II, *Familiaris consortio* 21). A similar view has been proposed by Protestants, like Erich Fuchs (1995). The idea reaches back to the house churches of the New Testament, which gathered in individuals' homes to celebrate the cult and for the agape (Rom 16:3–5). The concept has certainly retained its force, both descriptive and prescriptive, even though it demands to be more finely determined. For example, family relations cannot consistently claim to have a strictly ecclesial dignity unless greater equality within the family—especially between men and women—has been established. Moreover, if the Christian family should be a place of evangelization, it can only do so by allowing its members to acquire social and civic virtues as well as familial virtues. The idea of the "domestic church" is not that of a private moral and religious haven, set apart from the city*, but that of a school for faith, peace*, and hope* in the service of the common good. All the Christian churches have at their disposal the ecclesiological resources that are needed to permit the family to take on, in a coherent way, the task of coexistence lived out as communion* and service. All the churches also have an experience of tradition capable of shedding its light on familial mediations.

Unlike the church, the family doubtless has no eschatological future. Its order is that of divine "mandates" that humanity accomplishes within worldly historical time*. Nevertheless, theology knows that provisional realities receive a new meaning in the Christian experience*; the family must therefore appear as a reality "before and after" (Bonhoeffer), destined to be erased, but capable of engendering that which shall not pass away.

• Augustine, *De bono conjugali,* BAug 2, 15–99.
Augustine, *De nuptiis et concupiscentia,* BAug 23, 41–289.
Augustine, *Ep.* 188, CSEL 57.
Jean-Paul II, *Familiaris Consortio, AAS* 74, 81–191.
M. Luther, *Genesisvorlesung, WA* 44.
M. Luther, *Vom Ehelichen Leben, WA* 10/2.
Cotton Mather, *Cares about the Nursery,* 1702.
F. D. Maurice, *The Church a Family,* London, 1850.
♦ E. S. Morgan (1944, 1966), *The Puritan Family: Religion and Domestic Relations in Seventeenth-Century New England,* New York.
P. Ariès (1960), *L'enfant et la vie familiale sous l'Ancien Régime,* Paris.
N. Davies (1975), *Society and Culture in Early Modern France,* London.
L. Stone (1977), *Family, Sex, and Marriage in England, 1500–1800,* New York.
J.L. Flandrin (1979), *Families in Former Times: Kinship, Household, and Sexuality,* Cambridge–New York.
Coll. (1981), "Pour une théologie de la famille," *EeT* 12.
D. Schneider (1984), *A Critique of the Study of Kinship,* Ann Arbor, Mich.
J. Brundage (1987), *Law, Sex, and Christian Society in Medieval Europe,* Chicago.
S. Okin (1989), *Justice, Gender, and the Family,* New York.
B. Fox (Ed.) (1993), *Family Patterns, Gender Relations,* Toronto-Oxford-New York.
L. Cahill and D. Mieth (Ed.) (1995), *La famille, Conc(F)* 261.
Coll. (1995), *La famille: Des sciences à l'éthique* (Acts from the European Colloquia for the Institute of Family Studies, Lyons, April 1994), Paris.
É. Fuchs (1995), "La famille: Réflexions théologiques et éthiques," *EeT* 26/1, 43–60.
W. Right (1995), *The Moral Animal: The New Science of Evolutionary Psychology,* London.
M. Banner (1996), " 'Who Are My Mother and My Brothers?': Marx, Bonhoeffer, and Benedict and the Redemption of the Family," *Studies in Christian Ethics* 9/1, 1–22.
A. Chapelle (1996), "La famille dans la pensée moderne," *NRTh* 118, 398–409.
Coll. (1996), *Famille en crise, Éthique,* no. 21.
É. Fuchs (1996), "Amour familial et conjugalité," *DEPhM,* 51–55.

LISA SOWLE CAHILL

See also **Couple; Ethics, Sexual; Marriage; Procreation; Woman**

Family, Confessional

a) Meaning and Usage. In the early 19th century the Catholic theologian J.A. Moehler (*Symbolik* 1832) gave the name "confessions" to the various church currents internal to Christianity, which until than had been called "religions," "religious parties," or "Christian societies." "Confession," which already had various complementary meanings in theology*, has since then been the technical term used to designate a particular Christian tradition, a confessional family.

This usage can be explained historically and theologically against the background of the Reformation. Having challenged the magisterial and ministerial structures of the church*, as well as the centralized exercise of authority*, as being the glue and the expression of the unity* of the church, most of the communities that came out of the Reformation defined themselves in relation to doctrinal references set out in confessions of faith*. For example, the Augsburg Confession of 1530 became the common charter of the Lutheran churches; the Thirty-nine Articles that of the Anglican community; the Confession of Faith of La Rochelle (1559) that of the French Reformed churches. At their ordination*, pastors* committed themselves on the basis of these documents. Although their intentions were universal, these confessions defined the faith and identity of particular churches, and for that reason, when several of these churches made reference to a single document, they were called "confessions" or "confessional families". In the late 19th century, geographical expansion led confessional families to organize themselves into world churches and to establish international structures. For example, in 1867 the Anglican Church organized the first meeting of the Lambeth Conference, which brought together all the bishops of that confessional family. In 1877, the Reformed churches founded the World Alliance of Reformed Churches; in 1881, the Methodist churches set up the World Methodist Council. The World Baptist Alliance was created in 1905, and the World Lutheran Federation in 1947.

Catholicism* and Orthodoxy* have always refused to be considered as confessional families. These churches do not see themselves as church traditions alongside others, but each one considers itself to be the sole full expression of the single Church of Jesus Christ. A more sociological approach to "confession" as the expression of a particular church identity would however lead to the inclusion of these churches within the group of confessional families. This notion is indirectly confirmed by the regular participation of the Orthodox patriarchate* and the Pontifical Council for Unity (Vatican) in meetings of the leadership of confessional families, which, since 1979, have preferred the title World Christian Communities.

b) Character and Structure of Confessional Families. For confessional families, it is understood that the one, holy, catholic, and apostolic church takes on concrete existence in this world in plural forms. Each confessional family sees itself as an expression of that one church. Many consider themselves as world churches and are structured accordingly. This is the case for the Anglican communion and the communion of Lutheran churches, who each, in this way, approach the self-understanding of the Catholic and Orthodox churches. Others, by contrast, emphasize their character as free associations or federations of churches. Within a single confessional family, participating churches are conscious of belonging to the same spiritual family sharing a single historical heritage. Forms of piety and liturgical celebrations, doctrinal references, church structures*, as well as visions and priorities are the same, or at least very similar, for all. Member churches of a particular confessional family generally live in full church communion: communion in the celebration of the word* of God and of the sacraments*, as well as mutual recognition of ministries*. Their international bodies have analogous structures (regular general assemblies, executive committees, presidents and secretaries-general, commissions for theology, mutual aid, and education, etc.). The authority of international structures, however, remains limited. Member churches, generally organized into regional or national communities, insist on their autonomy, giving them the power of decision. After a difficult period during which many considered the Ecumenical Council of Churches (ECC) as a place in which distinctions between confessional families would be overcome, solid cooperation has now been established between the ECC and confessional families, almost all of whose churches are members of the ECC. Confessional families are the privileged locations for theological dialogue among

Christian traditions. The reconciliation that has already taken place between various confessional families is essential for the unity of the whole church.

• H.E. Fey (1970), "Confessional Families and the Ecumenical Movement," in id. (Ed.), *A History of the Ecumenical Movement,* vol. 2: *1948–1968,* Geneva, 115–42 (2nd Ed. 1986).
Y. Ischida, H. Meyer, and E. Perret (1979), *The History and Theological Concerns of World Confessional Families, LWF.R* 14.

ANDRÉ BIRMELÉ

See also **Anglicanism; Baptists; Calvinism; Catholicism; Creeds; Lutheranism; Methodism; Ecumenism; Orthodoxy; Pentecostalism; Unity of the Church; World Council of Churches**

Father

A. Biblical Theology

a) Old Testament. The Hebrew word *'av* means "father," but it is often also applied to a broader relationship across generations, for example, with the ancestor of a tribe (Gn 10:21, 17:4, 19:37), and, by extension, to the inventor of a skill or a mode of existence (Gn 4:20f.; Jer 35:6), a king (1 Sm 24:12), a prophet* (2 Kgs 2:12), a priest* (Jgs 17:10), a protector (Jb 29:16; Sir 4:10), a counselor (Gn 45:8), or the creator of rain (Jb 38:28, "Has the rain a father… ?").

Fathers and mothers are to transmit instruction in wisdom* (Prv 1:8, 6:20), the narrative of Israel*, and the commandments (Ps 44:2, 78:3–8; Ex 12:26f., 13:14f.; Dt 6:20–25). The Law* prescribes duties in this domain (Ex 20:12, 21:15, 21:17; Dt 5:16; Lv 19:3). The rebellious son is to be punished with death*, but according to Deuteronomy 21:18–21, not by decision of his father alone, but after appearing before the elders (*see* Prv 30:17).

The predominantly patrilineal genealogies are an expression in time* of the union of the tribes in space (Gn 1–12; 1 Chr 1–9): they interpret God*'s plan. In relation to persons (A. Alt) or places (O. Eissfeldt), "the God of Abraham your father" (Gn 26:24 and, already in the sense of "ancestor," in Gn 28:13, 31:5, and 32:10) tends to become the "God of your father, the God of Abraham, the God of Isaac, and the God of Jacob" (Ex 3:6, 3:13). Deuteronomy (1:11, 1:21, 6:3) uses this formula to underline continuity from generation to generation. In Chronicles, it is a stereotype equivalent to YHWH (2 Chr 13:12), used in the struggle for conversion* (2 Chr 19:4) and against apostasy (2 Chr 34:33).

God is compared (analogy*) to a father who loves his children (Ps 103:13; Prv 3:12, 14:26). The filial status of the people is proclaimed (Dt 14:1; Is 1:2; Jer 3:19) as early as the eighth century B.C. (Hos 11:1). The assertion that Israel is the "firstborn son" of YHWH (Ex 4:22) is of uncertain date: according to Eissfeldt ("L"), this formula is part of the oldest stratum of the narrative, but according to Noth it may be Yahwist. It is set forth as the key to the whole narrative* of the departure from Egypt.

YHWH is also the father of the king. The notion of adoption, which was to play a major role in New Testament Messianism*, appears in Psalms* 2:7 (*see* 2 Sm 7:14 and 1 Chr 28:6). The king addresses YHWH as his "father," "the Rock of my salvation" (Ps 89:26). It is only later that God is more commonly invoked as a father (Sir 23:1 and 23:4 [Greek], 51:10 [Hebrew]; Wis 14:3), and that the just are described as "son of God" (Wis 2:16, 2:18, 5:5). The invocation "*'avinou malkenou*" ("our father, our king"), in the second blessing* in the Jewish liturgy*, probably dates from the first century A.D.

Finally, a symbolic feminine (Hos 11:8; Jer 31:20; Is 49:15) expresses God's tenderness toward Israel (Briend 1992).

b) New Testament. In the New Testament, the Greek word *theos,* "God," always means the Father (Rahner* 1954). Jesus* is aware of being his Son before his crucifixion.

The use of the familiar Aramaic *'abba,* a term of family intimacy, to address the Father is peculiar to Jesus himself and has few Jewish parallels (Jeremias 1966; *see* the discussion in Schlosser 1987). In the

Gospels*, Jesus always addresses God as his Father (Mt 17:3; Jn 17:3), with the sole exception of "Eli, Eli..." (Mt 27:46). However, it is thanks to his death (Mk 15:39) and resurrection* (Mt 28:19) that Jesus is confessed as the Son of God. Matthew inserts Christ*, born of God, in the lineage of David (Mt 1:16), and Luke relates him to God through Adam* (Lk 3:23–38). The book of Mark is the "gospel of Jesus Christ, the Son of God" (Mk 1:1).

Jesus reveals the Father to those around him in giving them knowledge of himself. He does not establish a household, or secure any progeny, but he insists on the commandment (Decalogue*) to honor one's father and mother (Mt 15:4ff.) and on the Creator's arrangements for establishing the human couple* (Mt 19:4ff.); yet one cannot follow him without being free from family* ties (Mk 1:16–20).

The Sermon on the Mount introduces the expression "Our Father" (Mt 6:7–13) in the midst of a series of "The Lord's Prayer" (10:3, above 13:3 in Mt.). In the "hymn of jubilation" (Mt 11:25ff.), Jesus speaks of the mutual knowledge of the Father and the Son, and his joy in seeing his children receive his revelation*. All believers are called upon to use "*abba*" themselves, thanks to the Spirit, who makes them sons of God and co-heirs with the Son (Gal 4:6; *see* Rom 8:14–17). Finally, Acts (3:13 and 13:32) makes a connection between the Christian faith* and the Jewish heritage of "our fathers."

The Father shows himself through Jesus in his solidarity with sinners following his baptism* (Mt 3:13–17). Peter's confession (Mt 16:17) is attributed to "my Father who is in heaven." The transfiguration illuminates the synoptic prefigurings of the Passion* and the resurrection by advancing the communication of the Father to the disciples by the Son (Mt 17:1–5). In his agony, Jesus still cries "*abba*" (Mk 14:36). In Luke's Gospel, the mercy* of the Father (*see* Lk 15:11–32, 6:36) is that of Jesus on the cross (Lk 23:34 and vv. 43 and 46). John (Johannine* theology) presents for our contemplation a Son who is the Father's only child (*monogenès;* 1:14 and 1:18) and who was present "in the beginning" (1:1; *see* Gn 1:1). This filiation* implies a distinction between the Father and the Son, on the one hand, and, on the other, God's paternity in relation to all believers, "born...of God" (1:13), "one" all together, as the Father and the Son are "one" (17:11 and 17:20–23). By contrast, to fail to believe in the Son is to fail to love him while hearing his word*, to have as one's father the Devil (demons*), "a murderer from the beginning," liar and father of lies, and to carry out his wishes (8:44), instead of performing the works* of Abraham (8:39), whose faith has made him become "the father of us all" (Rom 4:16–25). John reveals the unique fatherhood of God, exposing his imitators without falling into dualism.

• K. Rahner (1954), "Theos im Neuen Testament," *Schr. zur Th.* 1, Einsiedeln-Zürich-Köln, 91–167.

J. Jeremias (1966), *Abba: Untersuchungen zur neutestamentlichen Theologie und Zeitgeschichte,* Göttingen.

H. Ringgren (1973), *"'Av," ThWAT* 1, 2–19.

G. Schelbert (1981), "Sprachgeschichtliches zu Abba," in P. Casetti, O. Keel, A. Schenker (Ed.), *Mélanges Dominique Barthélemy,* Fribourg-Göttingen, 395–447.

M.I. Gruber, "The Motherhood of God in Second Isaiah," *RB* 90, 351–59.

J. Schlosser (1987), *Le Dieu de Jésus,* Paris, 179–212.

J. Briend (1992), "La maternité de Dieu dans la Bible," in *Dieu dans l'Écriture,* Paris.

Yves Simoens

See also **Creation; Family; Filiation; Knowledge of God; Monotheism; Trinity**

B. Systematic and Historical Theology

a) Definition. The term "Father" when referring to God can signify the following: 1) priority in the order of creation*; 2) universal authority*; 3) benevolence toward his creatures; 4) an adoptive or familial relationship to man; 5) the begetting of the Son; 6) essential masculinity. Traditional Christianity has resisted meaning number 6, while distinguishing the three divine functions of creation (1–3), adoption (4), and generation (5).

b) Greek and Roman Antiquity. Zeus, conceived as masculine, is the "father of gods and men" in Homer (e.g., *Iliad* 1, 544), the title denoting authority over other gods rather than temporal priority. "Jupiter" contains the root *pater,* "father," and is a title of Aeneas (*Jupiter Indiges*), who was often called father of the Roman nation. Augustus reinforced the divine sanction of his principate (27 B.C.–14 A.D.) by assuming the title "father of the fatherland" *(pater patriae).*

From the third century B.C., the Stoics employed the term to assert an affinity between gods and men, calling men the offspring of Zeus (Cleanthes, *Hymn to Zeus;* Aratus, *Phaenomena* 5; *see* Acts 17:28). This kinship was believed to reside in intellect, but Seneca (*De providentia* I, 5) declares that it lies in virtue*, being acquired by imitation rather than inherited. Epictetus (*Discourses* II, 10, 7) reminds us that fatherhood still implies authority: just as all a son's things are at the disposal of his father, so all a man's things are at the disposal of God.

Plato calls the Good* the father of the Beautiful (*Republic* 509 *b*), and the Demiurge father and maker of the world* (*pater kai poietes, Timaeus* 28 *c*), adding that he is difficult to discover and impossible to reveal to all. Plutarch urges that no affinity between the highest God and the material world is implied: the Demiurge is father of the soul*, but only maker of the body (*Moralia* 1001 C). Numenius (middle of the second century A.D.) distinguishes the Demiurge from the transcendent deity*, calling the latter the "Father of the Demiurge" (Fr. 21 Des Places). Borrowing the language of archaic poets, he styles the first God "grandfather," the second his "son," and the world their "grandchild." Plotinus applies the term "father" to the mind in relation to soul, and to the One in relation to mind (e.g., *Enneads* III, 5, V, 5). The cardinal point is usually resemblance, since the lower reality is an image of the higher reality, and even matter is an emanation of divinity in his view. At the same time, the transcendence of the higher reality is implied, so that those who desert the Good for the Beautiful are styled undutiful sons (*Enn.* V, 5, 12). Plotinus holds that, although both the world and Mind are eternal, they are not consubstantial* with each other, or with the One.

In mystery religions, the savior God is often called the father of his initiates, obviously by adoption, and the Mithraic initiate may himself attain the rank of father. Finally, Platonists assert an intellectual affinity between all men and the gods, but progress in virtue can make a man a "father of gods" (Plotinus, *Enn.* VI, 9; Porphyry, *Sententiae* 32).

c) Judaism, Hermeticism, and Gnosticism. In Philo's *De opificio mundi,* the terms "father" and "maker," clearly derived from Plato, are at first interchangeable, denoting both the benevolence and the authority of God. In relation to man, his image, however, God is Father in a special sense, and the term "maker" disappears. The logos (Word*) is his firstborn, and the man whose reason* obeys it is "the heir of divine things" in the treatise of that name. Abraham is a father, not only biologically, but through a secret allegory: as the "chosen father of the sound" (*De mutatione*..., §65–68), he begets rational language.

Rabbis were called "Abba," but Jesus* may have been unique in using the term habitually of God. In Gnostic (gnosis*) and Hermetic literature, both of which have associations with Judaism, the secret teaching is passed from father to son, although it is not clear, in the *Allogenes* and *Hermeticum* 13, whether the relation is natural or nominal. Although the author of being is often called Father in Hermetic literature (e.g., II, 17), and is supposed to be an intellect, his transcendence is continually stressed, with allusion to both *Timaeus* (28 *c*) and the Jewish notion of God's inscrutability. Ibn Gabirol's teaching that matter is an emanation from the Godhead is therefore highly unusual.

Irenaeus* (*Adv. Haer.* I, 1), the Gnostic Valentinus (c. middle of the second century), averring that no name* is truly predicable of the highest principle, styled it *propator* ("ancestor"). For the Gnostics, the divine is often a combination (syzygy) of feminine and masculine, although the masculine principle always remains dominant. In their view, the Father of the Old Testament is a lesser divine being (the Demiurge), feminine or asexual rather than masculine, and limited in knowledge (e.g., Epiphanius, *Panarion* XXIII, 3–8). The true paternal being is the source of spiritual existence, but exercises neither authority nor providence* in the world. Nevertheless, the world is said to emanate from him, sometimes through the feminine power Sophia (*see* Prv 8:22).

d) Patristic. Early theologians inherited three conceptions of the fatherhood of God, who could be 1) Father of the world, according to one reading of Plato; 2) Father of the elect, according to Judaism and the New Testament; or 3) Father of the Son, according to the Gospels* and, presumably, the liturgy* (*see* Mt 28 finis; 2 Cor 13 finis). Three points defined orthodoxy*: to deny any natural affinity between creature and Creator, while affirming the adoptive relation that holds between the elect and their redeemer, and distinguishing this from the eternal generation of the Son. Nevertheless, these terms are not exactly synonyms, as the Son is both creator and redeemer of the world, and John 1:13 was read in some manuscripts as applying to Jesus.

Proclamations of God's fatherhood in apologetic texts, often based on Plato, illustrate his unity, his transcendence, and his providential government. Between 150 and 250, *Timaeus* 28*c* was quoted by Justin, Minucius Felix, Athenagoras, Tertullian*, Clement of Alexandria*, and Origen*. While the Gnostics and Numenius distinguished between the father of the intellectual realm and the maker of this world, Irenaeus asserted the unity of God's Kingdom over both matter and spirit. Where Jews maintained the unity of the Godhead, Justin (apologists*), in his *Dialogue with Trypho* (c. A.D. 140) also credits him with a Son who created, educates, and redeems humanity.

Trinitarian speculation in the third century led to a strong differentiation of dignity between Father and Son; this subordinationism* reached its extreme form in monarchianism, which denied internal relations in the Godhead, and therefore made the Father himself suffer on the cross (e.g., Tertullian, *Adv. Praxean* 2). Even for Tertullian, however, the Son becomes hypostatic only for the creation of the world, and his power is delegated from a "monarchic" Father. Origen was the first to affirm that fatherhood is inherent in the Trinity*, Son and Spirit being coeternal with the Father; yet he protests against the practice of addressing prayer* to the Son. Prayer is addressed to the Father alone (*De oratione* 15), by the Son. In his *Dialogue with Heraclides,* Origen styles the Son a second God *(heteros theos),* but if, in a sense, there are two gods, both are one single God. Origen uses *genesis* ("genesis") and *ktisma* ("foundation") interchangeably with *gennesis* ("procreation") as names for a productive activity peculiar to God, which is distinguished from human *poiesis* ("making"). Nevertheless, the subordination of the Son is clearly implied, as is also the case in Hippolytus of Rome (c. 170–235), who argues in his *Contra Noetum* and *Refutatio* X for a position like Tertullian's, but calls the Son *genomenos* ("brought into being").

After the Arian controversy, in the fourth century, orthodox writers generally distinguished between the genesis of the world and the eternal generation of the Son. Athanasius* makes no reference to Plato in his constant use of the term "Father," and introduces the adjective *idios* ("proper") to denote the Son's possession of his Father's essence (*Contra Arianos* I). Human beings obtain adoption only by partaking of the Son, to whom prayers are rightly offered by the church*. The extreme Arianism of Eunomius allowed for still more detail. According to Eunomius, the divine essence is fully knowable, and he identifies it as the quality of being ungenerated *(agenneron):* because the Son is generated *(gennetos),* he cannot therefore be God. The Cappadocians (Gregory* of Nyssa, *Contra Eunomium,* and Basil*, *Ad Ablabium*) replied that the divine essence is unknowable; that the division of the persons is one of operation rather than nature; and that the fatherhood of God is merely the priority of eternal cause over eternal effect. Their idiosyncratic contemporary Marius Victorinus (*Contra Arianos* I, 51) holds that the Spirit is (figuratively speaking) the mother of the Son.

Origen, who sometimes seems to allow only a moral union between Father and Son, postulates a natural affinity between man's mind and God's (e.g., *De principiis* I, 1; I, 3, 5). Gregory of Nyssa maintains (*De opificio hominis* 11) that the human mind is so like God that it is equally inscrutable, but the full affinity is possessed only by abstract humanity, before the Fall and the division of the sexes. The image, like all three Persons, transcends the categories of male and female (*In Canticum canticorum; see* Gregory* of Nazianzus, *Oratio* 31). Others insist that man achieves the image by adoption; thus Cyril* of Alexandria locates it in acquired virtue *(Ad Calosirium).* For Epiphanius (†403), the meaning of the term "image" is inscrutable (*Ancoratus* 56). The divine Fatherhood itself in relation to us is defined by Hilary* of Poitiers as "invisible, incomprehensible, eternal, self-existent, self-originating, self-sustained" (*De Trinitate* II, 7).

e) Mediaeval and Byzantine Period. The Lord's Prayer and, since the mid–second century, baptismal creeds connect the title Father with God's lordship over the world. In the Greek Church, the doctrine that the Father is the sole fountainhead of the Trinity remains a cardinal point of disagreement with the West, in whose creed the Spirit proceeds from both Father and Son (Filioque*). John the Scot Eriugena (ninth century), in his *Peri physeon,* makes matter an emanation from the Godhead; Gnostic views were also echoed by Joachim of Fiore (millenarianism*), who argued that a kingdom of the Son had replaced that of the Father, and that a kingdom of the Spirit would supersede that of the Son.

Thomas* Aquinas holds that the Father is so called both essentially and personally: in the latter sense, he is peculiarly the Father of the Son, but in the former he is the Father of all, in the sense that all receive from him (*ST* Ia, q. 33, a. 3).

f) Modern and Contemporary Era. Protestantism* has generally conceived of God as Father of his creatures rather than of the Trinity. Criticism of the idea of divine fatherhood has come from liberal theology*, psychological anthropology*, and political radicalism, and in each case criticism has led to a renewal of interest in Trinitarian speculation among orthodox theologians.

Luther* identified creation with fatherhood, but traditional Protestantism reserves the term "sons" for the elect. The liberal theologian Adolf von Harnack (1851–1930) finds the heart of the Gospel in God's paternal (i.e., benevolent) relation to all men (*Wesen des*

Christentums, 1899–1900). Extreme liberals have argued that the concept of a personal God, implied by the term Father, is untenably anthropomorphic. Thus, Paul Tillich* prefers to call God the ground of being. The omission of the term "Father" is already notable in Schleiermacher*'s *The Christian Faith* (1830), where such terms as "creator" and "governor" are preferred, and the Trinity is relegated to a brief appendix.

Psychological theories see the notion of God as an extension of the attitude of children to their fathers. Ludwig Feuerbach (*Wesen des Christianums,* 1841) holds that Judaism and Christianity confer on a paternal God the infinite possession of those qualities that the worshippers find lacking in themselves. Freud* (1913–14) derives religion from the guilt incurred by the sons of a primeval ancestor who murdered him and then tried to retrieve his powers through the sacrifice* of a totemic animal. Jung (1952) sees the Bible* as the history of the slow education of a tyrannical father figure.

Political criticism of the concept of God as Father asserts that patriarchal theology justifies inequality in society* and the church. Authoritarian ideals have been supported by such works as Robert Filmer's *Patriarcha* (1680, rebutted by Locke), which derives kingship from the absolute rights conferred by God on Adam and transmitted by primogeniture. Feminist theologians contend that the exclusively male priesthoods* of the Orthodox and Catholic churches are combined with an authoritarian structure, and have campaigned for both women's ordination and the liturgical use of female terms with application to God. J. Bachofen and others have maintained that the worship of the Goddess was the original religion.

Barth* combines the Calvinist notion of elective fatherhood with Trinitarian theology in a powerful set of structures. The Father's liberty* is a property of his Trinitarian nature, and as the Father of the Son he elects mankind to salvation. Moltmann, who believes that only Trinitarian theology can prevent the use of God's name to support authoritarianism, presents the generation of the Son as the source of the Father's liberty and benevolence, since it enables him perpetually to act with regard to an Other. Nicholas Berdyaev offers a similar explanation for the creation of the world, since he makes the whole Trinity an emanation from a nameless ground of being. For all these writers, the fatherhood of God is both the guarantee of his ineffability and the clue to his relation with other beings. Catholic theology asserts the same paradox of concealment in revelation. Karl Rahner* frequently calls the Son the symbol of the hidden Father, while Hans Urs von Balthasar* (1967) says that the glory* of the Father is manifested through the *kenosis** of the Son in his incarnation* and, above all, on the cross. Thus, the Trinitarian title that expresses God's omnipotence* and sufficiency is also the revelation of his inalienable love*.

One contemporary reconstruction, influenced by J.D. Zizioulas, has had an impact on the theology of the Trinity, as well as on other matters. Zizioulas, who is an exemplar of the "Greek model" of Trinitarian theology studied in his own time by Thomas de Régnon, conceives the Trinity on the basis of the kingship of the Father, without making use of the concept of divine *ousia.* God is without cause, but, in God, the Father is the cause of being, by communicating his being to the Son. Roman theology, which also understands the Father as the *fons et origo totius divinitatis,* should also show that it is capable of avoiding any construction of the Trinity on the basis of a divine essence.

• E. Norden (1913), *Agnostos Theos,* Leipzig.
S. Freud (1913–14), *Totem und Tabu,* Vienna.
C.C.J. Webb (1918), *God and Personality,* Edinburgh.
J. Bachofen (1927), *Mutterrecht und Urreligion,* Basel.
N. Berdiaeff (1935), *De la destination de l'homme,* Paris (trans. from Russian).
C.G. Jung (1952), *Antwort auf Hiob,* Zürich.
A.J. Festugière (1954), *Le Dieu inconnu et la gnose,* Paris.
K. Barth (1945–50), *Die kirchliche Dogmatik* III/1–3, Zollikon (*Dogmatique,* Geneva, 1960–63).
H.U. von Balthasar (1967), *Herrlichkeit: Eine theologische Ästhetik* III, 2, Einsiedeln.
M.J. Le Guillou (1972), *Le mystère du Père,* Paris.
L. Bouyer (1976), *Le Père invisible,* Paris.
R.R. Ruether (1983), *Sexism and God-talk,* London.
S. Pétrement (1984), *Le Dieu séparé,* Paris.
J. Moltmann (1985), *Gott in der Schöpfung,* Munich.
J.D. Zizioulas (1985), *Being as Communion,* Crestwood, N.Y., 67–122.
T.F. Torrance (1993), *The Trinitarian Faith,* Edinburgh, 47–109.
P. Widdicombe (1993), *The Fatherhood of God from Origen to Athanasius,* Oxford.

Mark J. Edwards

See also **Consubstantial; God; Hypostatic Union; Monotheism; Nicaea I, Council of; Subordinationism; Trinity; Word**

Fathers of the Church

a) Origins of the Expression. Until the beginning of the fourth century the term *Father* was used sporadically in the texts as a sign of deference and gratitude to designate individuals whose teachings the author had followed—for example, Alexander of Jerusalem's remarks about Pantaenus and Clement of Alexandria* (recorded by Eusebius in his *History of the Church* VI, 14:9) and, more generically, comments by Clement himself (in *Stromata,* I, 1, 3) and Irenaeus (in *Adversus haereses* VI, 14:9), who refers to the term's being used by "one of his predecessors." In the fourth century, even before "Father" began to be used in the plural to designate the members of the Council of Nicaea* (Basil* of Caesarea's *Letters,* 52, II and 140, 2) or, more generally, to designate past links in Christian tradition (by Athanasius* in *Ad Afros* 6, and Gregory of Nazianzus—*see Orientalia,* 33:15), an approximation of the complete expression can be read in Eusebius.

Being fond of the epithet *ecclesiastic,* Eusebius included it in the titles of at least two of his works (*Ecclesiastical History*—or *History of the Church*—and *Ecclesiastical Theology*) and attached it (c. 336) at least three times to a mention of the Fathers in the course of his polemic with Marcellus of Ancyra (*Contra Marcellus* I:4 and II:4 and *Ecclesiastical Theology* I:14—in vol. 14 of *Die griechischen christlichen Schriftsteller der ersten drei Jahhunderte*). In addition to the term "Father," the expression "Ecclesiastical Fathers" is already sometimes applied to the bishops* at the council*, and sometimes applied to the whole body of those who, in earlier generations, accomplished a mission of explanation and transmission of church* doctrine.

Given the interchangeable character of the adjective and of the genitive case in the Greek and Latin of that epoch, it could be expected that our expression "father of the church" was already about to be born. But it was far from receiving immediate adoption. Although fifth-century writers continued, with increasing frequency, to refer to the Fathers, it was only at the Lateran Council of 649 that the expression was found simultaneously in both Greek and Latin. The proceedings of that council, written in Latin, were translated immediately into Greek by Maximus* the Confessor; they include the phrases: "All the recognized Fathers of the Church," in canon 18, and, in canon 20, "the Fathers of the Holy Catholic Church" (J. D. Mansi's *Sacrorem Conciliorum nova et amplissima collectio,* 10:1157–1158A and 1159–1160E, and *Denchiridion symbolorum,* 518 and 522). In both canons these mentions of the Fathers are linked together with the mention of the five Ecumenical Councils. The intention was probably to link the findings of the council to the teachings of the Fathers, as they appear in their individual writings, when they are completely consonant with the ones given in the council.

The more common expression *the holy fathers* appears in canons 1–11 and then again in canons 17–19 of the Lateran Council. Other contemporaneous documents use similar expressions, which suggests that the term "father of the church" was used almost haphazardly. Pope* Agatho spoke of "the Holy Fathers that the Apostolic Church of Christ receives" in 680, and there was mention of "the holy and acknowledged Fathers" at the Third Council of Constantinople* in 680.

From 392 to 393 Jerome had put into circulation a more flexible and comprehensive expression. Although the title of his work, through emulation of Suetonius, spoke of "illustrious men," his prologue stated the intention of "drawing up a list of the writers of the Church"; and even though the first intention incited him to create the broadest listing, which included among these "illustrious men" Philo and Seneca, the second list provided a more useful criterion. It was "to introduce rapidly all those who published something on the Holy Scriptures*" (*see* Richardson, Ed., *TU,* XIV). Jerome's continuator, Gennadius of Marseilles, cited the work under the title *De viris illustribus (Of Illustrious Men);* however, in his first introduction, he called Jerome's book "*catalogus scribarum*" ("a catalogue of writers").

b) The Expression's Entry into the Canon. At the beginning of the sixth century, probably in Italy or in southern Gaul, an anthology was published known as *Decretum Gelasianum.* After giving lists of the canonical books of the Bible, the three Apostolic Sees, and the three Ecumenical Councils, this anthology adds a list of "short treatises of the holy fathers received into the Catholic Church." These short treatises are by 12 authors—six are in Greek, six are in Latin, and a single piece is by Pope Leo I (IV, §2 and 3; 36–38). Following these lists, without a roll of names, comes a more inclusive definition: "in the same way, major and minor treatises of all the orthodox fathers who, without having deviated from a single tenet of the Holy Roman Church, without having left the faith* and its preaching*, participated in its communion*, by the grace of God, until the last day of their lives" (38–39).

The Council of Trent* used the traditional conciliar vocabulary when it referred to the "example of the orthodox fathers" at the moment that it accepted all the books of both Testaments (*Conciliorum œcumenicorum decreta,* 663:15ff.). What is even more important, it mentioned "a unanimous consent of the Fathers," which should not be violated when interpreting the Scriptures (*Conciliorum œcumenicorum decreta,* 664:22ff.). The latter expression did not, however, lead Melchior Cano (1509–60) to identify in that statement a specific *locus classicus* or theological theme. Cano's sixth such theme is, in fact, "the authority* of the saints," and not that of the Fathers. In addition, Cano distinguishes this authority from a seventh one, which is "the authority of the scholastic doctors*" (*De locis theologicis,* 1563). Only in the edition obtained by Serry (1659–1738), which was reprinted innumerable times, are the titles in which the word "Father" occurs added to the chapter heads of Book VII. Sixtus of Siena (1520–69), another post-Tridentine theologian as well as a historian of exegeses*, uses the expression here and there. For example, he holds that the "most illustrious Fathers of the Church" had witnessed in favor of Origen (1566, I, IV, 439) and that certain writings from the New Testament had been held to be apocryphal* by the "earliest Fathers of the Church" (l. I, 2, 32). Sixtus also drew up a list of the authors who had written commentaries on the Scriptures. This very comprehensive list is much more in the line of the hieronymic "ecclesiastical writers."

It would seem that it was in the 17th century that the big names in "Positive Theology" tended to distinguish more clearly "the Fathers" from more recent ecclesiastical authors. Perhaps this was due to the influence of the Protestant idea of a gradual corruption of the message of faith, for, until the Reformation, there was a tendency to recede ever further from the source. At least according to a survey, Petau (*Theologica dogmata,* 1644–59) prefers to speak of *Patres et magistri* ("Fathers and teachers of the Church") or of *Patres antiqui* ("Ancient Fathers"); Thomassin (*Dogmata theologica,* 1680–89) speaks outright of *Patres Ecclesiae* ("Fathers of the Church"). But, since the communal nature of the Fathers' statements is the most important point in this type of theology*, they hardly concerned themselves at this date with specifying what a father of the church was as an individual. Tillemont (1637–98) stands essentially for the tradition of Jerome's *De viris illustribus* (Of Illustrious Men) and of his list of "ecclesiastical writers."

In the revised *Dictionnaire de Trévoux* (1752) a still quite elastic definition occurs: "*Father,* or *Father of the Church,* is said of ecclesiastical authors who preserve for us in their writings the tradition of the Church.... The name of *Father* or of *Father of the Church* is given to those who lived in the Church's first 12 centuries. Those who wrote since the 12th century are called Doctors, not Fathers."

C.L. Richard's almost contemporary *Dictionnaire* gives no chronological limits, but it distinguishes the "former doctors of the Church who have preserved the tradition in their writings" from "the bishops assembled at Councils." It must be noted that, as in the first usages, both expressions essentially concern collectives. Littré gives the same chronological limit as does the *Dictionnaire de Trévoux:* "The Fathers of the Church or, absolutely, the Fathers (capitalized), the holy doctors from before the 13th century, from whom the Church received and approved the decisions on matters of faith." Then follow examples drawn from Pascal*, Fléchier, and La Bruyère (among which none contain the determiner "of the church"). Under the heading of "Father," Larousse in his *Grand dictionnaire universel du XIXe siècle* gives a definition inspired by Littré, shortening it by a few words; but in the entry "Patrology," Larousse gives another and fuller definition, which is all the more remarkable for its different time-limit from the earlier entry: "The Fathers," he holds, "can be split into two periods," the first going from "the establishment of Christianity to the end of the sixth century"—and the names cited immediately afterwards confirm that indeed that was his end-date. Larousse also indicates that Catholics, such as Ellies du Pin and Bellarmine, after the example of Protestants, such as Cave and Oudin, list all the authors among the "ecclesiastical writers." The *Dictionnaire de patrologie* (Dictionary of Patrology), in the series *Bibliothèque du clergé,* which was published between 1851 and 1859 under the general editorship of Migne, and edited by Sevestre, is in fact another *De scriptoribus ecclesiasticis* (On Ecclesiastical Writers). It goes as far as the 12th century and includes Abelard* just as readily as Origen* or other likely people.

It was in the manuals of Catholic patrology (from the ninth and 20th centuries) that attempts were first made to draw up a list of characteristic features that would determine the acceptance of such and such an ecclesiastic among the Fathers of the Church. J. Fessler gives three of them in his *Institutiones patrologiae* (1850): a) An orthodox doctrine and a knowledge that is essentially sacred; b) a saintly life; and. c) antiquity. But on the point of antiquity, the limits are quite loose. Fessler would gladly go forward as far as Bonaventure* and Thomas (25), while acknowledging that after Mabillon, Bernard* (who died in 1153) is most often called the "last of the Fathers." To Fessler's mind, the title of bishop is not indispensable, nor is that of priest*—he is anxious in fact to include Prosper of Aquitaine.

Without quite adopting them, O. Bardenhewer numbers four characteristics in his *Geschichte der altkirchlichen Literatur* (1913): a) Orthodox doctrine; b) a saintly life; c) approval by the church; and d) antiquity. Earlier (I, 16) Bardenhewer mentions that a certain agreement had been reached in fixing the limits of that "antiquity" in the East, at John of Damascus (who died before 754), and in the West, at Gregory* the Great (who died in 604). On two occasions *(DthC,* 12/1, 1933) E. Amann gives this definition: "The Fathers of the Church are ecclesiastical writers from Christian Antiquity who should be considered particularly authoritative witnesses to the faith." Amann then lists the four "attributes by which one recognizes a Father of the Church," which are identical to those proposed by Bardenhewer, including the chronological limit, even though Amann points out that "even today, one still hears 'Saint Bernard, the last of the Fathers,' " (ibid., 1197). Even though he adopts these attributes, Amann has to concede that each one is only usable with a certain margin of flexibility.

The same four attributes are found again in German Catholic publications, such as in the three editions of the *LthK* (1933, 1961, and 1997) and *HTTL.* On the other hand, dictionaries of Protestant inspiration (*RE, TRE,* and *RGG*) do not include an entry on *Kirchenvater* ("Father of the Church"). The *ODCC* (1957) remarks that the term forms part of the popular language rather than of the technical language.

c) Present-day Usage of the Expression. The instruction of 10 November 1989 of the Congregation for Catholic Education, while going to some trouble to restore the distinction between *patristic* and *patrology,* gives no definition of the expression "father of the church." It includes Clement of Alexandria and Origen among the Fathers cited, thereby tacitly abandoning some attributes that seem to be a 19th-century invention, restricted to the Catholic confession alone. Joseph Cardinal Ratzinger, in his *Theologische Prinzipienlehre* (1982), concedes that serious questions arise from demanding orthodoxy and antiquity as characteristics for Fathers of the Church. He suggests a more theological and less historical definition: "The Fathers are doctors of the Church indivisible." One problem would then remain: determining to what extent the rarity of the communications, often one-way, between the various parts of the Christian world, made it possible for any Father at all to practice a really ecumenical teaching role.

Benoît (1961) recalls the *DThC's* definition, then proposes three others. The first, which in fact defines *patristics,* translates a text by Overbeck and depends on a conception that distinguishes radically between the Christian writings that have literary forms separate from the Greco-Roman models and those that adhere to them: "Patristics is the study of Greco-Roman literature of Christian confession and of Christian interest." The Fathers are thus the authors of this type of Christian writing. After this first rather literary definition, the second revises a phrase by the historian Mandouze: "The Fathers are the authors of the first Christian centuries, who were universally involved as direct or indirect witnesses of the Christian doctrine or of the life of the Church at this epoch." Lastly Benoît furnishes his own definition, more in conformity with the Protestant conception of the Christian message: "A Father of the Church [can be defined] as an interpreter or a writer of exegeses on the Scriptures… . A Father is defined by his attachment to the Church's tradition, which itself is measured against the Scriptures, that is, in the last analysis by its faithfulness to the Scriptures."

Faced with this wealth of choices, however, a Protestant author, Lods (1988), observed that "it is really impossible to give a definition of Father of the Church that satisfies everyone." Indeed it seems that one risks indulging in a quite futile exercise with an attempt, by restricting the plural, to define the group very narrowly, or, by using in the singular an expression which designates a collective, to award to such and such an individual, to the exclusion of such and such another, the epithet of "father of the church," treated as a sort of precocious ascendant of the title of doctor. The most useful word is no doubt the adjective "patristic," a parallel to "monastic," "scholastic," and "Baroque," which allows us—just as they do—to designate conveniently a certain period of theological and literary production. Otherwise, it would be better to stop at "ecclesiastical writers," which is just as traditional a designation (or, if needed, given the equivalence noted, at "writers of the church," writers who have tried as best they could to work and to produce within the bosom of the church). That policy avoids the ridiculous stance of having to exclude people like Origen or Hippolytus, or even Tertullian* or Lactantius. And the example given by Augustine* in the West, just as the one given in lesser measure by Cyril* in the East, shows the danger that might lurk in separating too thoroughly a Father, in the singular, from the whole of the group.

• M. Cano (1st Ed. 1563; 1704), *De locis theologicis,* Lyon.
Sixtus of Siena (1st Ed. 1566; 1742), *Bibliotheca sancta,* Naples.
Dictionnaire universel français et latin... vulgairement appelé le Dictionnaire de Trévoux (1752), Rev. Ed., Paris.
C.L. Richard (Ed.) (1759–61), *Dictionnaire canonique, historique, géographique et chronologique des sciences ecclésiastiques,* Paris.
J. Fessler (1850), *Institutiones patrologiae,* Innsbruck.
F. Overbeck (1882), "Über die Anfänge der patristischen Literatur," *HZ* 48, 417–72, New Ed. Basel, 1966.
O. Bardenhewer (1913), *Geschichte der altkirchlichen Literatur,* 2nd Ed., vol. I, Freiburg.
A. Benoît (1961), *L'actualité des Pères de l'Église,* CTh, no. 47.
F.L. Cross and E.A. Livingstone (Eds.) (1974), *ODCC,* 2nd Ed., Oxford (3rd Ed. 1997).
J. Ratzinger (1982), "Die Bedeutung der Väter im Laufbahn des Glaubens," in *Theologische Prinzipienlehre,* Munich, 139–59.
M. Lods (1988), "La patristique comme discipline de la théologie protestante," in J.-N. Pérès and J.-D. Dubois (Ed.), *Protestantisme et tradition de l'É.,* Paris, 317–31.
Congrégation pour l'éducation catholique (1989), Instruction du 10 novembre 1989: *L'étude des P. de l'É. dans la formation sacerdotale.*
Coll. (1997), *Les Pères de l'Église au XXe siècle,* Paris.

GEORGES M. DE DURAND †

See also **Apologists; Apostolic Fathers; Doctor of the Church; Tradition**

Fear of God

In the Bible*, fear gets hold of the human being whose life is threatened by a death* threat. But the expression "fear of God" covers a wider spectrum of meanings, some of which are known in the Egyptian, Mesopotamian, and Canaanitic religions.

The terminology of fear is rich in Hebrew: *yâré'* (and its derivatives) is the most commonly used, but the following roots are also used: *phd* and *'ym* (tremor, terror), *chrd* (tremor), *chtt* and *'rç* (fright), *gwr* III (fright), to quote only the most frequent. In Greek, the verb *phobeô* and its derivatives are by far the most frequent, but the fear of God may be expressed with the *sebomai* group.

a) From Dread to Reverential Fear. The origin of the expression "fear of God" is probably to be found in the terror provoked by certain manifestations of God*, by which a human being experiences sanctity*, transcendence: theophany* (Ex 20:18), vision or dream (Gn 28:17), demonstration of force in creation* (Jer 5:22 and Ps 65:9), spectacle of a dignitary arrayed with his authority (Ex 34:30 and 1 Sm 12:18), and history* (Ex 15:15–16 and Ps 64:10)—in particular, in the wars* of YHWH (1 Sm 11:7 and 2 Chr 20:29) and his kingship (Ps 47:3 and 96:4).

The noun *môrâ'* ("Terrible") is a divine title (Ps 76:12) and the adjective with the same meaning, *nôrâ'*, in parallel with the predicates "great" and "saint," describes YHWH (Neh 1:5), his Name* (Mal 1:14 and Ps 111:9), his Works* (Ex 34:10), his Day (Jl 2:11). Likewise, the high actions* of God are called *nôrâ'ôt* (Ps 106, 22) or *môrâ'îm* (Dt 4:34).

In the Gospels* and the Acts of the Apostles, the fear of the beneficiaries or witnesses of apparitions (Lk 1:12 and 24:37), of miracles* (Mk 4:41 and 5:15; Lk 7:16; and Acts 2:43), and of the signs of resurrection* (Mk 9:6 and 16:8) must reflect the same respectful and admiring experience of recoiling in front of the Kingdom*'s signs.

Even in the Old Testament, and in particular in the texts quoted, one seldom finds unalloyed terror in front of the numinous; the notion takes on most often meanings of respect, of reverential fear, and of trust toward that God who saves man from death (Jer 32:39f.–40), even if the prospect of the Last Judgment* raises the fear of punishment* (Is 2:10; Ps 9:20f.; and 2 Cor 5:10f.).

b) "Do Not Fear!" The frequent formula "Do not fear" is used to reassure, to comfort, and to encourage in a moment of fear, of crisis, or of necessity (secular context: Gn 43:23 and 1 Sm 22:23). It is often pronounced by God himself or by his authorized representative. Thus, at the time of an encounter with God, particularly if the beneficiary knows he is a sinner, this formula means that God does not come for death, but for life, and as a result fear may change into respectful trust (Ex 20:20; 1 Sm 12:18–24; and Mk 6:50).

For those facing difficult circumstances and adversity, particularly war, the invitation not to fear is followed by a promise* of success or by a victory (Dt 31:6–8; Jos 10:25; Is 35:4; and Mt 10:26–31), which will arouse the fear of God (Ex 14:10 and vv. 13 and 31). The formula "do not fear" is also frequently used in the oracles of salvation* (Is 41:10 and Jer 30:10, and *see also* Gn 15:1 and Mt 28:5).

c) Developments of the Concept. In Deuteronomy and the deuteronomic literature, the fear of God is a key concept of the theology* of alliance. It designates loyalty toward YHWH and it materializes in observance of the Law*. The synonyms are significant: to serve God (Jos 24:14), to listen to his voice (1 Sm 12:14), to keep or practice his commandments (Dt 5:29), to love him and to become attached to him (Dt 10:12f. and 10:20), and to walk behind (Dt 13:4) or in the way of God (Dt 8:6). The opposite of the fear of God is idolatry* (Dt 6:13ff.).

In the biblical wisdom literature* (except for Ecclesiastes), the fear of God is close to wisdom* (Jb 28:28). It is its beginning (Prv 9:10), its early signs (Ps 111:10 and Prv 1:7), the schooling leading to it (Prv 15:33), and its root, fulfillment, and crowning (Sir 1:11–21). Linked to intelligence and knowledge* (Prv 1:29 and 2:1–6), the fear of God underscores the religious aspect of wisdom. It is experienced in ethical rectitude and in the refusal of evil* (Ps 34:12–15 and Prv 3:7 and 14:2), as seen in Job (1:8). Such a behavior leads to life (Prv 10:27 and 14:26f. and Sir 6:16).

The expression "God-fearing" is in keeping with the preceding developments, but it has various meanings. In the Psalms*, the God-fearing man is the just man whose behavior is honest. The plural of the same expression, the God-fearing men, designates the community assembled for worship* (Ps 22:23f.), all the people* of God (Ps 85:8f.), or only the believers (Ps 25:14). Switching to the Acts of the Apostles in the New Testament, when used with the term "worshipper" *(sebomenos),* "God-fearing" serves to describe pagans* who are close to Judaism* (Acts 10: 2 and 13:16).

Addressing the Philippians and exhorting them to "work out your own salvation" (Phil 2:12), Paul coined the phrase "fear and trembling" *(phobos kai tromos),* but said that if we follow the Spirit, we will be sons of God and so free from "fear" (Rom 8:12–15; *see also* 1 Jn 4:18). It is thus possible to see that the expression "fear of God" moves us somehow away from the ordinary meaning of the word "fear."

• J. Becker (1965), *Gottesfurcht im AT,* Rome.
L. Derousseaux (1970), *La crainte de Dieu dans l'AT,* Paris.
H. Balz, G. Wanke (1973), *"phobeô, etc.," ThWNT* 9, 186–216.
H.P. Stähli (1978), *"jr'* fürchten," *THAT* 1, 765–78.
E.H. Fuchs (1982), *"jârê'," ThWAT* 3, 869–93.
B. Costacurta (1988), *La vita minacciata: Il tema della paura nella Bibbia Ebraica,* Rome.
H.P. Müller (1989), *"pâhad?" ThWAT* 6, 552–62.

André Wénin

See also **Decalogue; Filiation; Law and Christianity; Prayer; Spiritual Theology; Theophany; Word; Wrath of God**

Febronianism

A German episcopal doctrine, analogous to Gallicanism*, the manifesto for which was *De statu ecclesiae et legitima potestate Romani Pontificis liber singularis* published in 1763 by J. Febronius (pseudonym of J.N. von Hontheim, auxiliary bishop of Trier and spokesman for the archbishop electors of Germany), Febronianism presented itself as a reform of the Catholic Church,* taking the primitive church as a model, preserving for the pope* only a primacy of honor, advocating greater power for bishops* and more autonomy for secular authorities. Febronian ideas expressed the wishes of a good number of the bishops and princes of the Holy Roman Empire. A new reform program was proposed by the archbishops of the Empire in 1786. Among other things, it proposed the end of exemptions for and the diminution of the powers of papal nuncios, but it had no effect. The political transformations resulting from the French Revolution changed the state of mind of German bishops; the age of Febronianism was followed by an age of ultramontanism*.

• W. Pitzer (1983), "Febronius/Febronianismus," *TRE* 11, 67–69 (bibl.).
R. Reinhardt (1995), "Episkopalismus," *LThK3,* 3, 726–28.

The Editors

See also **Gallicanism; Ultramontanism**

Felicity. *See* **Beatitude; Supernatural**

Feminist Theology. *See* **Woman**

Ferrara, Council of. *See* **Basel-Ferrara-Florence, Council of**

Fessard, Gaston. *See* **History**

Fideism

Fideism, as the word indicates, attributes to faith* *(fides)* the principal role in religious knowledge, which, when taken to the extreme, however, leads it to question the very possibility of an authentic access to faith. Reacting to the exclusive rationalism* of the Enlightenment*, fideism is nevertheless dependent on certain fundamental presuppositions of the position that it challenges. Not only does it perpetuate the opposition between "reason*" and "faith," conceived as two independent entities, it also accepts the technical-mathematical conception of "reason" that prevailed in the 18th century, and sets against it a global vision of knowledge that gives prominent status to immediate intuition, concrete historical reality, and affective and psychological dimensions. It also relies on the mediation of authority* and tradition*, denounced by Enlightenment rationalism. These themes make it possible to understand the development of fideism in the early 19th century and the importance it assumed, after the failure of the French Revolution and the Napoleonic wars, in the context of the restoration of a system of Catholic theological teaching. Its influence was felt not only in France but also, to a lesser degree, in other countries (schools of Tübingen*).

The best known representatives of this movement were, under the label of "traditionalism*," L. de

Bonald (1754–1840) and H.-F.-R. de Lammenais (1782–1854), and under the label of "fideism," Ph.-O. Gerbet (1798–1864), L.-E.-M. Bautain (1796–1867), and A. Bonnety (1798–1879). Their attacks against the Scholasticism of their time, which they regarded as rationalist, provoked controversies that focused essentially on the status of knowledge within the framework of a fundamental* theology.

Under the influence of F.X. von Baader, Hegel*, Schelling*, and F.H. Jacobi, the Strasbourg professor L. Bautain accentuated the opposition to rationalism by relying on Augustine*'s distinctions and by defining true philosophy* as a quest for wisdom*, which was identified with religion itself. However, the positions he took caused difficulties, firstly with his bishop*, Mgr. de Trévern, which finally led to serious discussions in Rome*. At the conclusion of these discussions in 1840 Bautain had to subscribe to a series of theses (*DS* 2751–56) that accepted the possibility of reaching knowledge* of the existence* of God by inductive means, indicating that reason could precede or even lead to faith. These propositions were placed at the beginning of the German edition of the documents of the magisterium on the faith of the church (Regensburg 1938), so as to emphasize the decisive import of the questions that had been debated. And, to provide even more emphasis, extracts from the letter *Qui pluribus* of 1846 were attached, in which Pope* Pius IX had taken a position on fideism and traditionalism on the one hand, and on rationalism in Catholic thought on the other (G. Hermes). The magisterium* thereby attempted to remove the dangers of both sides by defining a moderate position between the two extremes. Other doctrinal statements followed, including the Syllabus of 1864 and the decrees of the First Vatican* Council in 1870.

The name "fideism" was also claimed around this time by a group of French Protestants represented by A. Sabatier and E. Ménégoz, who applied the principles of Schleiermacher* and adopted positions derived from the school of the history* of religions. It was of course possible to attempt to resolve these problems in the 19th century by adopting an intermediate formulation, dismissing the extremes while preserving the "parcel of truth," which in fideism lies in the emphasis on the supernatural dimension of Christian truth* and its knowledge. But it is difficult to be satisfied with positions consisting of a superficial juxtaposition of different propositions that merely assigns to each one a positive or negative value. (This is the criticism that should be leveled at the declarations of the magisterium, as well as at the foundational work of Blondel*, *Histoire et dogma* [1904], even though the latter's philosophical-theological approach was aimed at going beyond a purely extrinsic juxtaposition of the competing arguments.)

To the extent that they put into play the relations between revelation* and reason, these controversies have continued in current ecumenical debates. Can human beings accede to or open themselves to revelation, and can the means that are universally available to them (ideas; concepts; language; acquired knowledge; logical or systematic associations; historical, social, legal, and cultural determinations; and so on) be used to express this kind of truth? The controversies necessarily raise the question of Christian anthropology*, and particularly the concept of knowledge that it presupposes. However indispensable distinctions in this area may be, it would, therefore, hardly be credible to defend a unilateral position that satisfied itself with challenging the presence in gospel truth either of a rational element or, on the other hand, a supernatural* element going beyond mere reason. Similarly, it is no longer acceptable to isolate each of the two components in a way that would exclude any articulation between them. Christianity, in fact, understands its message and the faith that responds to it as realities that are also rooted in the order of reason, as facts that certainly point beyond a purely rational world* but can in no way be conceived as contrary to reason. This is what makes that truth communicable, without in any way being detrimental to its specific content or altering its profound essence. For not only do the very dignity of human beings and the meaning of existence depend on this possibility of communication, but so too does the meaning of the history that unites God with humanity and with the world. In this respect, we cannot accept the existence of one all-embracing truth, endowed with its own logic, without introducing an open conception of reality. In this reality, the components are organized according to positive relations that themselves determine real differences, without making these differences into autarkical entities locked in their antagonism or reciprocal exclusion.

Fideism should thus be seen as an attempt to do justice at the level of human experience to what there is in concrete and immediate reality that is irreducible to the analyses of reason. It represents the quest for a wisdom superior to pure learning, the desire to keep reality open to a possible transcendence and everything that that implies. All these themes have met with increasing interest in our time. We can sense in them the attraction for a certain irrationalism (which, if its influence were to grow, would in turn require a reaffirmation of the rational factors in Christianity). It would, however, be better to define an approach that keeps a balance between the two poles, and so makes the pendulum swings between them unnecessary. A "logic of faith" should simultaneously do justice to human existence and to the meaning of the gospel. It will probably reach this goal if it is able to resist the restrictive approaches that ultimately contradict the very reality of man and expose him, individually and socially, to unnecessary dangers. Reason is a constituent part of a Christian faith that also contains human elements of a nonrational character. It should therefore be possible, even before fully formulating the idea of what Christian faith is, to carry out a consistent articulation of the rational and the nonrational, thereby providing spiritual access to supernatural faith.

• E. Doumergue (1892), *L'autorité en matière de foi et la nouvelle école,* Paris.
M. Blondel (1904), "Histoire et dogme," *La Quinzaine* 56, repr. in *Les premiers écrits de M. Blondel,* Paris, 1956, 149–222.
E. Doumergue (1906), *Les étapes du fidéisme,* Paris.
E. Doumergue (1907), *Le dernier mot du fidéisme,* Paris.
H. Haldimann (1907), *Der Fideismus,* Paderborn.
W.F. Hogan (1957), *A. Bonnetty and the Problem of Faith and Reason,* Washington.
P. Poupard (1961), *Un essai de philosophie chrétienne au XIXe siècle: L'abbé L. Bautain,* Paris.
N. Hötzel (1962), *Uroffenbarung im französischen Traditionalismus,* Munich.
H. Bouillard (1964), *Logique de la foi,* Paris.
P. Walter (1980), *Die Frage der Glaubensbegründung aus innerer Erfahrung auf dem I Vatikanum,* TTS 16.
E. Coreth et al. (Ed.) (1987), *Christliche Philosophie im katholischen Denken des XIX. und XX. Jahrhunderts,* vol. 1: *Neue Ansätze im XIX. Jahrhundert,* Graz.

KARL-HEINZ NEUFELD

See also **Credibility; Faith; Modernism; Rationalism; Reason; Traditionalism; Wittgenstein**

Filiation

In the Bible* the term *son* (*bén* in Hebrew and *huios* in Greek) is used to designate origin, dependence, or belonging, as well as the relationship of a father and mother with their offspring. The naming of Jesus* as God*'s only son and the adoptive filiation that follows for the believer occupy a central place in the New Testament.

I. Filiation in the Old Testament

1. Physical Parenthood and Figurative Senses

In the narrow sense, a son (or daughter) is anyone born from a father* and a mother. In a wider sense, sons include other descendants (Gn 29:5 and 31:28), and the Israelites are designated as "sons of Israel*" (Gn 32, 33; Ex 1:7 and 3:10), whereas the term "sons of men" designates humanity in general (Ps 12:1). (The English Standard Version of the Bible, however, renders these phrases as "people of Israel," "children of Israel," and "children of man.") According to the Law* of Moses, the family*'s firstborn male is consecrated to the Lord (Ex 13:1). Designated also as sons in the Old Testament are companions, disciples, servants, whoever is connected to a group, and whoever is a native of such and such a place.

2. Filiation with God

The angels* are sometimes called sons of God (Wis 5:5; Jb 1:6, 2:1, and 38:7). This expression comes from surrounding religions, and it has a figuratively weaker sense; it means that in the hierarchy of beings, the angels occupy a position close to being divine, without God being considered their father.

When Israel is called son of God, the intention is to translate in terms of human relationship the connection between God and his people*, as in the statement that the people whom Egypt had treated as slaves were adopted by God as sons (Ex 4:22; Hos 11:1; Jer 3:19; and Wis 18:13). Israel has done nothing to deserve such a filiation; it lives for receiving the Law and for remaining faithful to it. By extension, the members of the people who will remain faithful to the covenant* concluded in the Sinai are called "sons of the Lord" (Dt 14:1). The psalmist who keeps his heart pure does not betray the generation of the children of God (Ps 73:15). The just is persecuted for having called himself "God's son" (Wis 2:18). Conversely, God may bemoan the fact that the sons he reared up "have rebelled" against him (Is 1:2): they have become "rebellious children" (Is 30:1) or "faithless children" (Jer 3:14). The hope* remains however that the people remember having been adopted, and they go back toward their Father (Is 63:7–16, especially vv. 8 and 16).

If a founding oracle presents King David in a relationship of son to God (2 Sm 7:14 and Ps 89:26–27), it is never in the sense of the surrounding monarchies: David is never deified. It is, rather, a matter of insisting on the particular place he occupies, with his descendants, in the economy of election: the Messiah*, descended from David, will also be adopted by God and recognized as son (*see* Ps 2:2–8).

II. Filiation in the New Testament

1. Outside Christology

The same semantic universe of the expression that appears in the Old Testament is found in the New Testament. Sonship is used to describe family relationships in the literal sense, and is also widely used in the figurative sense, as in "sons of the Kingdom*" (Mt 8:12), "son of peace*" (Lk 10:6), "sons of this world" and "sons of light" (Lk 16:8), "son of perdition" (Jn 17:12), and "sons of the prophets*" (Acts 3:25).

2. Filiation of Jesus

The originality of the New Testament resides in the presentation of the filiation of Jesus.

a) Synoptic Gospels (Matthew, Mark, and Luke) If Jesus is the son of Mary* (Mk 6:3), the childhood narratives* (Mt 1–2 and Lk 1–2) highlight the particular nature of his filiation: the angel Gabriel announces to Mary that her son will be called "Son of the Most High" (Lk 1:32) and "Son of God" (Lk 1:35). Matthew 1:20 and Luke 1:35 translate into their narratives a theological affirmation: the double nature of Christ*, son of a woman* and only Son of God. The account of Jesus' baptism* (Mk 1:9–11) and that of the Transfiguration (Mk 9:2–10) highlight the quality of this divine filiation of Christ: Jesus is Son of the Father in a unique relationship of communion*, that of "beloved Son," of only Son.

The expression "Son of God" gives an account of the relationship of Jesus with his Father in a manner that is not devoid of ambiguity. In the account of the temptation* (Mt 4:1–11), Satan uses the title as a sign of omnipotence as do the devils expelled by Jesus (Mk 3:11 and 5:7). The evangelical narrative makes us discover that Jesus is "Son of God" in the humbling and acceptance of finiteness: it is the passage through death* that is the true sign of his divine filiation, a perspective that is unacceptable for the disciples who also form a notion of the divine filiation under the sign of omnipotence (*see* Mk 8:27–33 and Mt 16:13–23). Peter*, after his confession at Caesarea, is called Satan by Jesus because he refuses the perspective of the cross. Finally, at Gethsemane, in total obedience to the will of God (Mk 14:32–42), Jesus shows fully his unique filiation. By calling upon God as Father *(Abba)* and accepting death, Jesus reveals another comprehension of God. The confession of the Roman centurion (Mk 15:39) highlights this new discovery of the divine filiation of Jesus to the cross.

Finally, the use of the traditional messianic title "Son of David" is to be noted. This title is being used in spite of the fact the Gospels* have shown its insufficiency to account for what is new in Christ (*see* Mk 12:35–37).

b) Paul. If Jesus was born from a woman, it was as Son of God (*see* Gal 4:4, where biological and divine filiation coexist). This divine filiation of Jesus is recognized thanks to his resurrection* (Rom 1:3–4 and 1:9). This means that with God revealing himself to the world through the death of his Son, he is contesting the usual image that mankind has of him (*see* 1 Cor 1:18–25). In an altogether different language (that of the Son's vocation), the Epistle to the Hebrews extends the paradoxical rapprochement anticipated by the Gospels and by Paul between filiation and sacrificing the Son for death (*see* Heb 1:2, 1:5–8, 5:1–8, 7:3, and 7:28).

c) John's Gospel, the presentation of Jesus as the only Son, who reveals the Father, is of fundamental importance. All there is that must be known about God is from then on knowable in the meeting of faith* with the Son, the messenger who fully reveals to man the love* of his Father (Jn 1:18, 3:16–18, 3:35–36, and 5:19–30). Like elsewhere in the New Testament, this revelation* comes through via Jesus' death, which is regarded as a glorification (Jn 12:16, 12:23, 12:28, and 13:31–32).

3. Filiation of the Believers

Starting with the particular filiation of Jesus, the New Testament develops the notion of the adoptive filiation of the Christians.

a) Synoptic Gospels. The relationship between the "sons" and the "Father" is often described through the intermediary of the language of parables (*see* Mt 21:28–32 and Lk 15:11–32). In the words of Jesus, God reveals himself as a compassionate Father of his children.

b) Paul. The major texts in which the theme of adoption *(huiothesia)* is developed are Galatians 4:1–7 and Romans 8:14–17. The new condition of the believer is that of adopted son, heir to the Father and no longer a slave (in Gal 4:21–31, the believer is not son of the slave Hagar, but son of the free woman Sarah). It is faith in Christ and no longer obedience to the Law (Rom 3:21–31) that makes adoption possible, and it is the Spirit that makes us adopted sons and makes us cry out: "Abba! Father!" (Rom 8:15). By associating the believer with the death of Christ, baptism is the sign par excellence of his new condition (Rom 6:1–14).

c) John's Gospel. The believer "must be born anew" (Jn 3:7), which means that he must find his origin in God, the Father. Freedom characterizes this newborn, who is like the wind—nobody knows where he comes from or where he is going (*see* Jn 3:8). Conversely, slavery characterizes those who have not recognized Jesus as the messenger of the words* of the Father, and who are sons of the devil in spite of their claim to be sons of Abraham (Jn 8:31–59). It is thus underscored that man is always son of someone, always in a state of dependency and never autonomous. Only those who are set free by the Son are really free (Jn 8:36). John's epistles extend the same theological intuition: whoever confesses the Son "has the Father" and is "in the Son and in the Father" (1 Jn 2:22–24).

III. Conclusion: From the Only Son to the Adoptive Sons

According to the total corpus of New Testament evidence, the filiation of Jesus, if it preexists Creation* (Jn 1:1–10), is fulfilled and can be seen in the Incarnation*. It is through finitude in Jesus that God calls all men to filiation. Jesus reveals to mankind the new face of a God unveiling his voluntary limitation—not the face of a mighty Father who judges and condemns, but the face of a loving Father who is welcoming and willing to adopt mankind. Such a Father opens to mankind the road to a freedom, which, though finite, or in other words human, will still be one of the main attributions of a filiation that has been regained (Gal 5:1f., 5:13).

• O. Cullmann (1957), *Die Christologie des Neuen Testaments,* Tübingen.

F. Hahn (1963, 3rd Ed. 1966), *Christologische Hoheitstitel,* Göttingen.

A. George (1965), "Jésus Fils de Dieu dans l'Évangile selon saint Luc," *RB* 72, 185–209.

H. Conzelmann (1967), *Grundriss der Theologie des Neuen Testaments,* Munich.

W. von Martitz et al. (1969), *"Huios," ThWNT* 8, 334–402; 482–92.

C. Burger (1970), *Jesus als Davidssohn,* Göttingen.

J. Jeremias (1971), *Neutestamentliche Theologie,* I: *Die Verkündigung Jesu.*

A. Descamps (1974), "Pour une histoire du titre Fils de Dieu," in M. Sabbé (Ed.), *L'Évangile selon Marc,* Louvain, 529–71 (2nd Ed. 1988).

M. Hengel (1975), *Der Sohn Gottes,* Tübingen.

J.D. Kingsbury (1975), "The Title *Son of God* in Matthew's Gospel," *BTB* 5, 3–31.

J.D. Kingsbury (1976), "The Title *Son of David* in Matthew's Gospel," *JBL* 95, 591–602.

J. Ansaldi (1980), *La paternité de Dieu: Libération ou névrose,* Montpellier.

F. Hahn (1983), *"Huios," EWNT* 3, 911–38.

W. Loader (1989), *The Christology of the Fourth Gospel,* Frankfurt.

C. Breytenbach (1991), "Grundzüge markinischer Gottessohn-Christologie," in C. Breytenbach and H. Paulsen (Ed.), *Anfänge der Christologie,* Göttingen, 169–84.

C. Dietzfelbinger (1991), "Sohn und Gesetz: Überlegungen zur paulinischen Christologie," ibid., 111–29.

J.M. Scott (1992), *Adoption as Sons of God: An Exegetical Investigation into the Background of "UIOTHESIA" in the Pauline Corpus,* Tübingen.

ÉLIAN CUVILIER

See also **Adam; Adoptionism; Anthropology; Arianism; Consubstantial; Couple; Family; Father; Messianism/Messiah; Prayer; Son of Man; Trinity; Woman; Word**

Filioque

As the term itself suggests—*filioque* "and the Son"—the controversy known as the *Filioque* centered on the Latin theological doctrine expressed in the Nicene Creed: *qui ex patre fiolioque procedit,* referring to the Holy* Spirit "which proceeds from the Father* and from the Son."

a) From the Scriptural Evidence to the Schism of 1054. In the Gospel of John, Jesus speaks of "the Spirit of truth, who proceeds from the Father" (Jn 15:26) *(para tou Patros ekporeuomenon)* and who "will take what is mine and declare it to you" (Jn 16:14). Paul speaks of the Spirit "of the Son" or "of Christ*" (Rom 8:4; 2 Cor 3:18; Gal 4:6; etc.). The creed of the First Council of Constantinople* states that the Spirit "proceeds from [*ek*] the Father." A baptismal confession of faith* collected in the *Ancoratus* of Epiphanius (374) speaks of the Spirit that "proceeds from the Father and receives from the Son" (Hahn).

Toward the end of the fourth century, Latin theology* began to assert that the Holy Spirit proceeded from the Father and the Son. The beginnings of this assertion are to be found in the work of Hilary* (whose preferred formula is, however, that the Spirit proceeds "from the Father by the Son"). The doctrine also appears in the work of Ambrose*, although he uses the formula only with respect to the mission (Trinity*) of the Spirit (PL 16, 762, 783, 800, 810). The only place where it is fully set out is Augustine*'s *De Trinitate.* After Augustine it became widespread in Latin theology. Leo the Great adopted it in a vague form (SC 74, 150), and then explicitly in 447 (PL 54, 680—possibly apocryphal*). The *Filioque* appears in the so-called Athanasian Creed.

The doctrine is absent from Greek patristics. A few formulae of Epiphanius and Cyril* of Alexandria resemble it. Cyril even employs words close to those of Latin theology (e.g., PG 75, 585*b*): he talks of the Spirit "proper" *(idion)* to the Son (PG 71, 377*d*), and states that the Spirit "derives from" *(proeisi)* and "extends in front of" *(prokheitai)* the Son (PG 76, 173*a–b*). The Greek Fathers*' preferred formula confines itself to the words of the Bible: the Spirit proceeds from the Father and receives from the Son (e.g., Pseudo-Cyril, PG 94, 1140*b,* John of Damascus PG 94, 821*b*). "From the Father *by* the Son" is in fact uncommon (but found as early as Origen*, *In Joan.* II, 73–75, *dia tou logou;* Gregory* of Nyssa, Jaeger III/1, 56; VIII/2, 760).

The discrepancy between the Latin and Greek theologies was first analyzed by Maximus* the Confessor in his letter to Marinus, in which he observes that the *Filioque,* confessed by Pope* Martin I, is equivalent to "from the Father by the Son." Maximus restricts himself to a procession of the Spirit "by means of the Logos" *(dia mesou tou Logou)* (PG 91, 136). John of Damascus (c. 645–ca. 749) explicitly denied the *Filioque:* the Spirit "is the Spirit of the Son not because it comes from him *(ouk ôs ek autou)* but because it comes by him *(all'ôs di'autou)* from the Father, for the Father alone is cause *(monos aitios ho Patèr)*" (PG 90, 849*b*).

The insertion of the *Filioque* into an official confession of faith was undoubtedly a Spanish initiative intended to combat Arianism* (while emphasizing the equality of Father and Son) and Priscillianist modalism*. The confession of faith of King Recared at the Third Council of Toledo (589) affirmed the *Filioque.* It was repeated by Toledo IV (633), and again in the profession of faith of Toledo XI (675). In 787 the Third Council of Nicaea* (images*) affirmed that the Spirit proceeded "from the Father by the Son" (Mansi 12, 1122). The Council of Frankfurt, called by Charlemagne in 794, refused this point: "by" the Son was not equivalent to "from" the Son (PL 98, 1117). The authority* of this last council, however, was not great.

In the ninth century a liturgical problem was added to the differences between the Greek and Latin theologies. Greek eucharistic liturgy* seems to have included a confession of faith since the fifth century (the practice was apparently initiated by the Patriarch of Antioch, Peter the Fuller), but the insertion of a similar confession into the Mass of the Latin Church came later. Toledo III called for the Creed of Nicaea and Constantinople to be sung in the course of the liturgy. Its use became widespread. In 794 Charlemagne had it sung (with the addition of the *Filioque*) at Aix-la-Chapelle. In 807 the abbot of the Mount of Olives introduced the practice to Jerusalem*; but the addition of the *Filioque* gave rise to a dispute with the Greek monks of Saint Sabas. The matter was referred to Pope Leo III and Charlemagne. The emperor's theologians wrote a number of treatises on the Holy Spirit (Theodulf, Smaragdus, a pseudo-Alcuin). Leo III confessed the *Filioque* (PL 102, 1030–32) but refused to insert it into the Roman liturgical texts and called for its suppression from all liturgical formularies (PL 102, 971–76). His demand was in vain: the insertion of the *Filioque* was finally accepted by Benedict VIII in 1014 (at which date the Credo became part of the Roman eucharistic liturgy). The 16th-century reformers would retain the addition.

The charge of liturgical innovation was to recur constantly in Greek polemics against the *Filioque.* The Council of Ephesus* had declared the creed (the "faith," *pistis*) of Nicaea-Constantinople inviolable (*COD* 65, 16 *Sq*), and the Council of Chalcedon* had repeated this declaration (*COD* 87, 3 *Sq*), so Latin liturgical practice was in violation of church* discipline. It appears, however, that this argument did not feature in the earliest debates. Photius did not use it; and it was only when Cardinal Humbert of Silva Candida, in his discussions with Nicetas Stethatos in 1054, accused the Greeks of deleting the *Filioque* from the creed that the patriarch Michael Cerularius realized that the Latins had added it.

In the meantime the Greeks' objections had been expressed more extremely by Photius, patriarch of Constantinople, who in 867 put forward an opposing theology according to which the Holy Spirit proceeded "from the Father alone" (monopatrism) (PG 102, 292; *also* 721–42). The problem of the *Filioque* was to be among the causes of the schism* and would be central to all the debates between East and West; indeed it was probably more important than the issue of Peter*'s primacy.

b) Theological Development and Ecumenical Initiatives. From the 11th century onward, Latin theology was unwavering in its affirmation of the *Filioque.* In the Greek world, Gregory of Cyprus suggested a qualified wording: "[...] the Spirit accompanies the Word*, and it is by the Word that it proceeds, radiates, and appears in its eternal and pre-eternal splendor" (PG 142, 290*c*). Gregory* Palamas took up some of Gregory of Cyprus's ideas, and contrived a possible place for the *Filioque* in the order of "energetic manifestation": the Spirit—not as hypostasis, but giving hypostasis to the divine energy—pours forth from the Father "by the Son" *(dia tou Huiou),* and even "from the Son" *(ek tou Huiou)* (PG 147, 269–300). The *Filioque* was ratified by the Fourth Lateran* Council in 1215, reaffirmed at the unionist Council of Lyons* II (1274), and again at the council of union at Florence (1439). The latter declared it to be equivalent to the formula "from the Father by the Son"—giving preference to the *Filioque,* but without insisting that the Greeks incorporate it into the creed.

The union of Florence was short-lived, but it was again the desire for reunion that provided the impetus for a fresh consideration of the subject in the late 19th and the 20th centuries. In 1874–75, a conference in Bonn gathered together representatives of Russian Orthodoxy* and of the Old Catholic Church: the latter accepted Greek theology in its entirety. Some important theses by B. Bolotov, relating to this conference, were published in 1898. According to Bolotov, Photius's formula ("from the Father alone") was a theologoumenon, not a dogma*. Moreover, "The Filioque, as a particular theological opinion, cannot [...] be an *impedimentum dirimens* to the reestablishment of ecclesiastical communion" (thesis 27): this thesis was accepted in the 20th century by S. Bulgakov, P. Evdokimov, and L. Voronov, but rejected by V. Lossky. The Anglican Church, which was represented at the Bonn conference, has repeatedly declared itself ready to remove the *Filioque* from the creed, "whatever the merits or demerits of its doctrinal content" (*Iren.* 48 (1975), 362). K. Barth* was a notable defender of the *Filioque* in modern Protestant theology (*KD* I/2, 273 *Sq*), though the Protestant churches as a whole are prepared to abandon its liturgical use. The Catholic episcopate in Greece dropped it in 1973.

c) Reconciliation of Latin and Greek Views. The search for a solution to the problem of the *Filioque* took a number of forms in the history of theology after 1054. It seemed inconceivable to Duns* Scotus that there could be heresy* involved, in either Latin or Greek pneumatology (*I Sent.,* dist. 11, q. 1). Bonaventure* distinguished between the faith common to all, the clarifications that had given rise to the divergence, and the formulae that stoked the controversy. Thomas* Aquinas pointed out that the Holy Spirit does not proceed from the Father *by the mediation of the Son,* since the Son receives from the Father (*I Sent.,* dist. 12, q. 1, a. 3), and noted that the Greek *ek* is not equivalent to the Latin *ab* (ibid., a. 2, ad. 3). However, the most significant progress has been the fruit of recent research. The Greek concept of *ekporesis* is one thing, and the Latin concept of *procession* (which entered theology with Tertullian) is another. Greek theology has two verbs, *ekporeuesthai* and *proienai,* to describe the (eternal) relationship of the Spirit to the Father and its eternal relationship to the Father and Son, while Latin dogmatics employs only *procedere.* Greek Trinitarian theology, on the other hand, is structured around the concept of the Father's "monarchy": the Father alone is the "principle" *(arkhè)* and cause *(aitia).* Thus Latin theology is able to say that "the Spirit proceeds in principle from the Father and, by means of the latter's immaterial gift to the Son, from both in communion* *(communiter)*" (Augustine, *De Trin.* XV, 25, 47, PL 42, 1095). It can even say that the Father and the Son are "a single principle" in relation to the Spirit (Augustine, PL 42, 921), and that the Spirit proceeds from the Father and the Son "as from a single principle," *tamquam ex uno principio* (*COD* 314, 10; 526, 40–42)—which would be an absurdity within the conceptual framework of Greek theology.

A formula that will do justice to both Eastern and Western theology must therefore respect these conceptual differences. J.-M. Garrigues has proposed the following formulation: "I believe in the Holy Spirit, the Lord and giver of life, who issuing from the Father *(ek tou Patros ekporeuomenon),* proceeds from the Father and the Son *(ex Patre Filioque procedit, ek tou Patros kai tou Huiou proion)*" (1981). An Orthodox reception* of the *Filioque* is not inconceivable (Lossky 1967), and nor, even, is a Catholic reception of monopatrism (Halleux 1990). The *Catechism of the Catholic Church* (1992) may be overoptimistic when it speaks of a "legitimate complementarity" that, "provided it does not become rigid, does not affect the identity of faith in the reality of the same mystery* confessed" (§248). All the same, more than one Orthodox theologian acknowledges that the Son "is not uninvolved" in the ekporesis of the Holy Spirit (Bobrinskoy, Zizioulas).

• H. B. Swete (1876), *On the History of the Doctrine of the Procession of the Holy Spirit from the Apostolic Age to the Death of Charlemagne,* Cambridge.
B. Bolotov (1898), "Thesen über das 'Filioque,' "*RITh* 3, 89–95.
S. Boulgakov (1946), *Le Paraclet,* Paris.
J. N. D. Kelly (1950), *Early Christian Creeds,* London (3rd Ed. 1972).
"Où en est la théologie du 'Filioque'?" (1950), *Russie et chrétienté,* 123–244.
Vl. Lossky (1967), *A l'image et à la ressemblance de Dieu,* Paris, 67–93.
S. Bilalis (1972), *Hè hairesis tou Filioque,* Athens.
Y. Congar (1980), *Je crois en l'Esprit Saint,* vol. 3, Paris.
J.-M. Garrigues (1981), *L'Esprit qui dit "Père" et le problème du Filioque,* Paris.
L. Vischer (Ed.) (1981), *La théologie du Saint-Esprit dans le dialogue œcuménique entre l'Orient et l'Occident,* Paris-Cluny.
Th. Stylianopoulos (1986), "The Filioque: Dogma, Theologoumenon, or Error?" *GOTR* 31, 255–88.
H. U. von Balthasar (1987), *Theologik 3, Der Geist der Wahrheit,* Einsiedeln.
A. de Halleux (1990), *Patrologie et œcuménisme,* Louvain (studies 8 to 12).
Th. Stylianopoulos (1991), "An Ecumenical Solution to the Filioque Question?" *JES* 28, 260–80.
Conseil pontifical pour la promotion de l'unité des chrétiens (1995), "Les traditions grecque et latine concernant la procession du Saint-Esprit," *DC* 2125, 941–45.

THE EDITORS

See also **Ethics; Father; Trinity; Word**

Finitude. *See* **Death; Infinite; Nothingness**

Flesh

I. Old Testament

1. Field of Reference

In the Old Testament, *flesh* signifies in a fairly general way human beings, man, humanity ("all flesh," as in Gn 6:12), the animal*, food (Ex 21:10), and, in a more restricted sense, man's fragility (Ps 56:4), or even the sexual organs (Ex 28:42). In the Old Testament, the most common meaning is concentrated on man as an individual or even as a collective. Three main axes mark the roughly 6,270 occurrences of *flesh* (*bâsâr* in Hebrew and *sarx* in Greek). They are: totality, vitality, and relationship. Because of the wealth of the topic, the lexicons of the original languages and those of translations align even less often than in other cases.

a) Idea of Totality. To express the completeness of the human being as an *individual,* biblical authors refer freely to the various parts of the human person (body, mind, blood, soul*, heart, bones, skin, kidneys, etc.,); these terms accompany "flesh" in a synonymous parallelism, or they replace it. "Flesh" also refers to the collective, in order to stress the solidarity of earthly creatures. The syntagm *kol-bâsâr* ("all flesh"), which appears 40 times in the Bible*, takes into account either the whole gamut of creatures, including humans and animals (Gn 6:17, etc.), or the more restricted group of mankind (Is 40:5, etc.). This solidarity of the flesh and in the flesh expresses even more particularly the ties of blood, the union of spouses in a single flesh (Gn 2:24, or in Gn 2:23, where the concept is expressed as "flesh of my flesh"), and so on.

b) Vitality of the Human Being. This quality is recounted in various ways. In the Second Book of Kings, the leprous flesh of Naaman the Syrian becomes healthy and alive like a child's after his healing (2 Kgs 5:14). Ezekiel sees the Creator "cause flesh to come upon" a valley full of dry bones, which spring back to life (Ez 37:6).

c) Relationship. Lastly and above all, *flesh* implies the idea of a relationship. Man is understood in his condition as a creature in relation with God*, but also in his dialogue with other beings made of flesh.

2. From the Hebrew to the Greek of the Septuagint
Translating from one language into another (the Septuagint, or LXX) caused important semantic differences in the anthropological domain as well as in the theological interpretation.

a) The Hebrew *bâsâr* is rendered quite often (about 145 times) as *sarx.* Among other terms, the most frequently used is *sôma* (body).

b) The synonymic practice of the LXX differs from that of the Hebrew (see below). It tends, in fact, to create a distinction between flesh, body, mind, and so on, more in conformity with Greek anthropology*. The *sôma* (body) constitutes the human envelope; this latter is thereby distinguished from the *pneuma* (spirit), which therefore refers to an independent, more spiritual part of the human being. In the LXX, the stress is placed less on the whole; it expresses more the complexity of the being made of flesh.

II. New Testament

Paul's epistles and the Gospels* are the chief books to consider.

1. Authentic Epistles of Paul
Paul gives increasing importance to "flesh," about which he often creates a theological theme. Three stages are apparent:

a) Corinthians. In the First Letter of Paul to the Corinthians, it does not seem at first glance that Paul has yet organized any theological thoughts about the theme of the flesh. The word *flesh* takes on various meanings, in fact, which are quite commonplace. All the same, the milestones of his later development can already be discerned. This development has its origins in phrases such as *kata sarka* ("according to the flesh") in 1 Corinthians 10:18. Even if "flesh" is not mentioned directly in 1 Corinthians 6 (except in the citation from Gn 2:24 in 6:16), the first elements of the depreciation of the flesh begin to show there. In the Second Letter to the Corinthians, these sketches grow clearer, and the beginning of a more thematic theological meditation can be seen. Paul does not yet contrast the flesh and the spirit, but the terms *kata sarka* ("according to the flesh") and *en sarki* ("in the flesh") take on more definitive meanings.

b) Galatians. The Letter to the Galatians seemingly represents a very active period in Paul's meditations on the flesh. Indeed, these epistles contain the various meanings of flesh, including the human viewpoint indicated by flesh and blood and the weakness of the flesh that results in Paul's illness (Gal 4:13). But chapters 3 and 4 of Galatians constitute the letter's real center, and it is there that the theme is expressed. Paul accentuates the link between the flesh and sin*, either as a return to the pre-Christian era, or as desire for the sinful flesh *(epithumia).*

The apostle attacks violently those who want to turn from the spirit to the flesh and follow a path in opposition to the Gospel (Gal 3:3). The homily on the two unions, based on the allegory of Hagar, the slave whose son "was born according to the flesh," and Sarah, the free woman, whose son was born "through promise*" (Gal 4:23) brilliantly illustrates Paul's thought. The contrasting of the flesh *(kata sarka)* with the spirit *(kata pneuma)* begins to take on greater and greater definition. Finally, the quotation from Psalm 143:2 in Galatians 2:16 plays an important role in this period of theological maturation. Paul would take it up again in Romans 3:20. The Pauline version of this line from the psalmist states, "by works of the law shall no one [actually, *pasa sarx,* which means, literally, "all flesh"] be justified"—which distances itself from the Hebrew and from the LXX—and it is not a matter of chance. The steps have been marked already in Galatians; the route has been signposted for the theological treatise in the Epistle to the Romans.

c) Romans. In the Letter to the Romans, Paul takes up again the ideas sketched in 1 and 2 Corinthians, and especially the contrast between the flesh and the spirit, which was already developed systematically in Galatians. A violent inner struggle had taken possession of the apostle. He tries to explain it to himself from a theological point of view in his thematic perusal of the flesh and the spirit, Romans 7 to 9, the watershed of the two big sections of the first part of Romans (chapters 1 to 8 and 9 to 11), which preserves the traces of the apostle's inner struggle, specifically in his use of "flesh." Other thematic links are woven, with the theme of justification*, on the one hand, and with the theme of the salvation of Israel* on the other.

As an overture to the theme, the indictment in Romans 7 contrasts life in the flesh *(en tè sarki)*, a place of sin, of aging, of death*, to the newness of the spirit (Rom 7:5, 7:6, 7:18, and 7:25). We are told that by "sending his own Son in the likeness of sinful flesh and for sin, [God] condemned sin in the flesh" (Rom 8:3). Paul stresses the contradictions between the authority of the Law* and that of the Spirit, and he gradually introduces a theology* of the filial spirit, the gift of God for life. The word *flesh* invades the beginning of chapter 8, appearing in verses 3, 4, 5, 6, 7, 8, 9, 12, and 13. In these verses the apostle affirms the perishability—even more, the death-dealing power—of the flesh. But, nevertheless, Paul in no way devalues Christ*'s coming in the flesh. Chapters 9 to 11 emphasize the coming into the flesh of the Son born of David's line (Rom 1:3). Focused on the problem of Israel's abandonment, chapters 9 to 11 are framed by the question of the Salvation, which came in the flesh (9.3, 9:5, 9:6, and 11:14). As an introduction to this dramatic question, Paul lists the privileges of the Children of Israel (Rom 9:4–5), placing at the summit the supreme privilege of the Incarnation*—*ho Christo te kata sarka* ("Christ, according to the flesh"). In this way, Paul demonstrates the importance of the progression from the flesh to the promise (Rom 9:8).

2) In the Gospels

While the Gospel According to Mark and the Gospel According to Matthew, which follows Mark, give hardly any emphasis to the theme of the flesh, the Gospels of Luke and John—each in their own way—enhance this motive theologically.

a) Mark and Matthew. Mark's three mentions of "flesh" are all placed within the words of Jesus*: In Mark 10:8 and Matthew 19:5, while addressing the question of divorce, Jesus cites Genesis 24. In Mark 13:20 and Matthew 24:22, the Greek word for *flesh* is used for *life* or *person.* Finally, in Mark 14:38 and Matthew 26:41, at the moment of the agony, Jesus recalls the weakness of the flesh. In addition to picking up these three traditional sayings from Mark, Matthew adds to the pericope of Peter*'s confession of faith, Jesus' remark that the Father in heaven had revealed to Peter what he had confessed, and not "flesh and blood" (Mt 16:17). "Flesh and blood" is rooted in the Hebrew idiom *bâsâr-wa-dâm,* which recalls the limits of the human condition compared to divine revelation.*

b) Luke. Luke's Gospel uses the word *flesh* in an original way. Near the beginning and at the end of his Gospel, Luke establishes an inclusive relation between the two common usages of *flesh.* In the quotation from Isaiah 40:5—"all flesh shall see the salvation of God" (Lk 3:6)—he uses *flesh* to mean *humans.* Then, in the words of the risen Jesus, he brings out the Greek contrast between the spirit and the flesh—"a spirit has not flesh and bones as you see that I have" (Lk 34:30). Luke also mentions the flesh three times in the second part of his work, the Acts of the Apostles. All three references (Acts 2:17, 2:26, and 2:31) come in Peter's homily at Pentecost and are marked by the theme of hope* in the resurrection of all flesh.

c) The Fourth Gospel. The originality of the theology of the Gospel of John lies essentially in two passages in John 6 and in the prologue. In chapter 6, where Jesus speaks about the bread of life, the word *flesh* is used seven times. The first six occurrences (in vv. 51, 52, 53, 54, 55, and 56) refer to the eucharistic* flesh of Christ, which he is offering as a food that will give everlasting life. The last use of the word *flesh* in this passage (6:63) accompanies the other six in order to explain the role of the Holy Spirit. It reflects back to another use of the word in Jesus' dialogue with Nicodemus (Jn 3:6).

Verse 14 of the prologue of the Fourth Gospel has delivered to Christian theology a confession of faith in the incarnation of Christ—"and the Word became flesh" *(ho logos sarx egeneto).* Today the phrase remains at the heart of Christian faith*. It is a unique occurrence, but it encompasses the whole of John's theology. The manifestation in the flesh becomes one of the privileged themes of the glory* of Christ. John's epistles tell of the importance that his communities gave to the recognition of Christ's having come in the flesh (2 Jn 7).

A study of the context in which the word *flesh* is used should thus not be neglected and care should be taken not to come to hasty conclusions when determining the meaning of *flesh* in its different occurrences. In particular, the way in which the Bible sees *flesh* should be distinguished, in many instances, from the way in which it sees the body. But when all is said and done, several passages, especially in the New Testament (including 1 Cor 5:5, Col 2:23, and 1 Pt 3:21), still remain obscure.

E. Schweizer, R. Meyer (1964), "*sarx,*" *ThWNT,* 7, 98–145.
D. Lys (1967), *La chair dans l'Ancien Testament.* Paris.
R. Jewett (1971), *Paul's Anthropological Terms,* AGJU 10.
• N.P. Bratsiotis (1973), "*bâsâr,*" *ThWAT,* 1, 850–67.
V. Guénel (Ed.) (1983), *Le corps et le corps du Christ dans la première épître aux Corinthiens* (Congrès de l'ACFEB, Tarbes, 1981), Paris.
J. Scharbert, P. Trummer (1991), "Fleisch," *NBL* 4, 677–82 (bibl.).

Michèle Morgen

See also **Adam; Animals; Anthropology; Cosmos; Johannine Theology; Law and Christianity; Pauline Theology; Resurrection of Christ; Resurrection of the Dead; Sin; Soul-Heart-Body; World**

Florence, Council of. *See* **Basel-Ferrara-Florence, Council of**

Forgiveness. *See* **Mercy**

Formgeschichte. *See* **Literary Genres in Scripture**

Formulas of Faith. *See* **Creeds**

Francis de Sales. *See* **Spirituality, Salesian**

Francis of Assisi. *See* **Spirituality, Franciscan**

Franzelin, Johann Baptist. *See* **Tradition**

Freedom, Religious

Religious freedom is an aspect of political freedom and should be distinguished from the idea of freedom found in the New Testament. Like other freedoms, religious freedom involves the rights and privileges of citizens within an organized political community, concurrent with the guarantee that the states will protect such rights. In Western democracies*, religious freedom is essentially the negative freedom to practice or not one's religion, to meet and assemble for religious purposes, and to change religion.

Until the fourth century, theological reflection had no occasion to address the questions that would divide Christians later: whether the civil authorities* ought to give active support to the Christian religion, abolish paganism*, give official recognition to ecclesiastical authorities, or punish heresy*. Scripture says nothing about religious freedom, but the early apologists* and martyrs liked to quote Peter*: "We must obey God* rather than men" (Acts 5:29). By obeying Christ's injunction to refuse to grant unto Caesar what was God's, they gave witness to the possibility of an alternative society* capable of resisting an empire with totalitarian pretensions.

Out of its early struggle for freedom from imperial domination, the church* gradually developed the notion of two different orders of authority. Later, this was articulated as the theory of the two powers: that church and state are each autonomous in their own spheres. The clearest statement of this doctrine is in the often cited letter of Pope* Gelasius (492–96) to the Emperor Anastasius I, written in 494: "There are two powers... by which this world is ruled, the sacred authority *(auctoritas)* of priests and the royal power *(potestas)*" (PL 59, 41–47). Centuries of debate followed over the relation between the two powers, particularly over the precise meaning of the "superiority" of the spiritual. Nevertheless, it is obvious that adopting the distinction ended the concept that dominated antiquity for which religion and city were interdependent. The modern concept of religious freedom could not have emerged without such controversies.

Following the Edict of Milan (313, in SC 39), which proclaimed universal toleration for all religious convictions within the empire, Christianity was soon placed in a privileged status, to the detriment of paganism. It is understandable that in the eyes of a church that had been persecuted for two centuries, and that had always been convinced, even in the midst of the harshest persecution, that rulers were "instituted by God" or "appointed by God" (Rom 13), Constantine could have appeared sent by God. However, it soon became clear that the support of the emperor confronted the church with new problems that potentially threatened its freedom. The state increasingly intervened in church affairs; from this followed the danger that crucial doctrines might be compromised for reasons of state. In the fourth century, for example, the empire temporarily supported Arianism*.

Constantine was indifferent to the theological controversy over the consubstantiality (consubstantial*) of the Word* with the Father* and considered all such disputes to be forms of childishness (Eusebius, *Vita Constantini,* GCS I, 67–71). However, it was also his conviction that he was a colleague of the bishops* (*Vita,* GCS I, 84, 20–23) and a "bishop of external affairs" (*Vita,* GCS I, 124, 9, 11). Because the theological dissension threatened the unity of the empire, he could not avoid the Trinitarian controversies and often counseled orthodox bishops to compromise with the Arians, threatening sanctions if they refused. When his son Constantius sought to impose Arianism, the church realized the threat to its independence.

The church was also forced to reflect on the proper relation between orthodox rulers and various heresies, especially those that threatened the unity of the empire. This issue came to a head at the time of the Donatist crisis (Donatism*), which was to have an influence for centuries because of the role played by Augustine*. At first, Augustine advocated leniency toward the Donatists and rejected recourse to the secular power to bring them back forcibly into communion* with the church. He did change his views, however, and accepted the intervention of legitimate authorities *(ordinatae a Deo potestates),* thinking that coercion led to the return to the truth and salvation of many Donatists who would have remained so by force of habit (Markus 1970): "We see many who have renounced their former blindness; how could I begrudge them their salvation by dissuading my colleagues from exercising their fatherly care, by which this has been brought about?" (*Ep.* 93, CSEL 34–2). Augustine legitimized the use of force to compel heretics back into the church by appealing to Luke 14:23, "compel people to come in."

Given other emphases in Augustine's political theology* that mitigate the triumphalistic defense of a "Christian empire," one wonders why it did not occur to Augustine, when he was thinking about religious coercion, to restrict the scope of the state's actions. Perhaps it was because he did not consider Christian rulers and civil servants as members of the governmental machine, but as members of the church, through which the church uses their power for just ends. Augustine thus continued "to speak without inhibition of Christian emperors long after he had abandoned all talk about a Christian empire" (Markus).

Augustine's view found ready application in the prefeudal world of the early Middle Ages, in which the distinction between civil and ecclesiastical authorities was acknowledged in principle but, in practice, it was much easier to think of political realities in terms of princes and officials than in terms of abstract political concepts such as "state" or "government." Augustine believed that coercion was to be used only in exceptional cases, but its use was eventually given general validity, in no small measure because of Augustine's authority.

According to Thomas* Aquinas, faith* is by nature an act of freedom, and it is therefore wrong to force infidels—Jews, Moslems, or pagans—to become Christians (*ST* IIa IIae, q. 10, a. 8). This does not imply that their religious practices should be tolerated within a Christian *res publica.* Such tolerance is permissible only if it leads to some great good* or prevents some great evil (ibid., a. 11). While Jews (Judaism*) may be permitted to practice their religion, since they prefigure the Christian faith and in a sense bear witness to it, other religions should not be tolerated except to prevent some greater evil (a. 11). As for the heretic who persists in his heresy, Aquinas articulates the common view in saying (*ST* IIa IIae, q. 11, a. 3) that "the church gives up hope of his conversion and takes thought for the safety of others by separating him from the church by sentence of excommunication; and further leaves him to the secular court, to be exterminated from the world by death." Indeed, heresy appeared to medieval theologians to be a culpable error, an example of insincerity and bad faith, an error that should not be permitted to spread like a cancer through a morally and religiously unified body politic.

This view persisted after the breakup of Christendom into nations and after the fracturing of Western Christian unity in the Reformation. The views of the Reformers are accurately summarized in the *Confessio belgica* (1619, *BSKORK* 119–36): concerning civil magistrates, it is said that their office is not only to have regard to the welfare of the state, but also to protect the ministry*, and remove and prevent all idolatry* and false religion (article 36). Similarly, the Westminster Confession (1647) states (ch. 23) that it is the duty of the magistrate "to take order, that unity and peace be preserved in the church, and that the truth of God be kept pure and entire, that all blasphemies and heresies be suppressed, all corruptions and abuses in worship and discipline prevented or reformed, and all the ordinances of God duly settled, administered and observed."

The two heresies penalized by death in the Code of Justinian (482–565), the denial of the Trinity* and the repetition of baptism* (originally targeted at Arians and Donatists), were taken to justify action against anti-Trinitarians (e.g., Michael Servetus, 1511–53) and Anabaptists*. Luther*, Melanchthon (1497–1560), and Calvin* all appealed to the imperial law. Only the Anabaptists were exceptional in rejecting all coercion in matters of faith, believing that compromise and worldliness inevitably result from church establishments.

The ideal of a society unified by a common faith and baptism remained long after heresy came to be seen as inculpable error. *Cuius regio, eius et religio:* this principle was imposed at the Peace of Augsburg (1555). When remedies to religious discord were supposedly found by adopting a skeptical or relativistic position, religious freedom was still not approved of, or it would even be suppressed for reasons of state as with Hobbes (1588–1679), or by the establishment of a "civil religion," as with Rousseau (1712–78). If certain religious claims or forms of worship were by nature indifferent, they could easily be penalized or proscribed for the sake of political unity.

Before Vatican* II, the Catholic position was expressed by means of notions of thesis and hypothesis: religious pluralism was tolerated *in hypothesi* and rejected *in thesi,* in favor of a Catholic confessional state. This doctrine was still being defended by Leo XIII in *Immortale Dei* (1885). Largely through the efforts of the American Jesuit John Courtney Murray, this doctrine was rejected in the conciliar declaration on religious freedom, *Dignitatis Humanae,* which ranks among the most important ecclesiastical documents on the problem. While it clearly affirms the principle of religious freedom, it is very much a compromise document, which embodies a number of different arguments in support of the principle. These include, for example, alongside arguments from scripture, the idea of the right and duty to follow one's conscience* and seek the truth, as well as the constitutional principle of limited government. Murray, who was the defender of the "constitutional argument," found the other arguments less convincing.

• M. A. Huttmann (1914), *Establisment of Christianity and the Proscription of Paganism,* New York.
W. K. Jordon (1932–46), *The Development of Religious Toleration in England,* 4 vols., Cambridge, Mass.
H. Rommen (1945), *The State in Catholic Thought,* New York.
J. Lecler (1946), *L'Église et la souveraineté de l'État,* Paris.
R. H. Bainton (1951), *The Travail of Religious Liberty,* New York.
S. L. Guterman (1951), *Religious Toleration and Persecution in Ancient Rome,* London.
G. H. Williams (1951), "Christology and Church-State Relations in the Fourth Century," *ChH* 20 (September), 3–33.
W. H. C. Frend (1952), *The Donatist Church,* Oxford.
J. Lecler (1955), *Histoire de la tolérance au siècle de la Réforme,* 2 vols., Paris.
M. Bevenot (1954), "Thesis and Hypothesis," *TS* 15, 440–46.
A. F. Carillo de Albornoz (1959), *Roman Catholicism and Religious Liberty,* Geneva.
H. Rahner (1961), *Kirche und Staat im frühen Christentum,* Munich.
G. H. Williams (1962), *The Radical Reformation,* Philadelphia.
H. A. Deane (1963), *The Political and Social Ideas of St. Augustine,* New York.
W. H. C. Frend (1965), *Martyrdom and Persecution in the Early Church,* Oxford.
E. A. Goerner (1965), *Peter and Caesar: Political Authority and the Catholic Church,* New York.
J. C. Murray (1965), *The Problem of Religious Freedom,* Westminster, Md.
J. C. Murray (Ed.) (1966), *Religious Liberty: An End and a Beginning,* New York.
G. Leff (1967), *Heresy in the Middle Ages,* 2 vols., New York.
R. Regan (1967), *Conflict and Consensus,* New York.
R. Markus (1970), *Saeculum: History and Society in the Theology of St. Augustine,* Cambridge.
N. H. Baynes (1972), *Constantine the Great and the Christian Church,* London.
P. R. Brown (1972), "St. Augustine's Attitude to Religious Coercion," in *Religion and Society in the Age of St. Augustine,* London, 260–78.
J. H. Yoder (1985), *The Priestly Kingdom: Social Ethics as Gospel,* Notre Dame, Ind.
D. Gonnet (1994), *La liberté religieuse à Vatican II: La contribution de John Courtney Murray,* Paris.
K. J. Pavlischek (1994), *John Courtney Murray and the Dilemma of Religious Toleration,* Kirksville, Mo.
O. O'Donovan (1997), *The Desire of the Nations,* Cambridge.

KEITH J. PAVLISCHEK

See also **Anabaptists; Church and State; Donatism; Martyrdom; Orthodoxy; Relativism; Revolution**

Free Spirit. *See* **Beguines; Rhineland-Flemish Mysticism; Vienna, Council of**

Free Will. *See* **Liberty**

Freud, Sigmund

1856–1938

a) Psychoanalysis of Religion and Theory of Culture. Freud is known for having asserted ever more confidently an association between religion and obsessional neurosis. "[O]ne might venture to regard obsessional neurosis as a pathological counterpart of the formation of a religion," he wrote in 1907 ("Obsessive Actions and Religious Practices"). This association, which appears throughout Freud's work, is not a diagnosis drawn from clinical experience and observation of certain constants (endless repetition of rituals, magical expectation of their effectiveness, proliferating fabrications about their origin); it rather has to do with a theory of religion and a concomitant interpretation of culture. At the intersection of prehistory, ethnology, and psychoanalysis, Freud asserts that the establishment of collective ritual practices and the recognition of fellow human beings have a common foundation in the dissolution of social organization caused by a sexual impulse that also engenders neurosis.

During the founding events of collective life, this impulse is said to have destroyed the imaginary and megalomaniacal identification of the members of the primal horde with the supposed sexual omnipotence of their leader. This identification, by subjecting them to the authority* of the "archaic Father*," and to the constraints guaranteeing the life of the group, provided them with sexual satisfaction only by means of the expectation of an imaginary legacy. The archaic Father is said to have been put to death in circumstances that excluded his customary replacement. The organization of the group is then supposed to have collapsed and required the establishment of a fraternal pact: that is, a new social organization based on a new distribution of sexual energy. The sons now have access to women and recognize one another as alike and equal; but because the catastrophe was just barely avoided, sexual energy is in part turned against the self. Anxiety therefore infuses sexuality and organizes its expression (incest taboo, exogamy, prohibition of killing the rival); anxiety is produced individually in the form of obsessions, and collectively in the form of a totemic cult, which oscillates between expiation for the primal murder, nostalgia for a return to the authority of the archaic Father, and exaltation over his removal. The establishment of the totem is interpreted to mean that the archaic Father is not dead and that his protective power has survived. The burdensome veneration he receives restores the former submission and deserves some recompense. As for the periodic sacrifice and eating of the totem, they symbolically repeat the action of the conspirators and confirm their descendants' possession of the stolen omnipotence of the archaic Father. Totemism thus works to maintain the fraternal bond but allows guilt to spread and to be repeated.

All religions thus obsessionally bring together a demand for sexual pleasure and the desire to reconnect with an omnipotence that has been overcome by proliferating sacrificial practices. Establishing a link between recognition of fellow human beings, religion, and neurosis, religion becomes an ambiguous partner of culture. It tames asocial instincts and participates in the psychic development of fear. Moreover, it evades the critique inevitably provoked by the conflict between illusory hopes and real sacrifices only by imposing itself on people at an early age and thereby limiting their intellectual development.

This analysis applies to Judaism* and to a lesser extent to Christianity. With respect to the Jewish religion, Freud thought it possible to establish that Moses was put to death by Egyptian slaves who had been led across the Red Sea. Evoking the unconscious memory of the primal murder, this crime violently divided Jewish consciousness between the expectation of the highest election and the necessity of subjecting themselves to divine law*. The result was an unequaled ethical tension finding its counterpart in an identity entirely based on the exaltation and the work of intelligence. Christianity is also rooted in the climate of totemism. In the Eucharist*, what is involved is an omnipotent hero, his putting to death, and the symbolic incorporation of his power. But by reason of the historical proximity of the death of Jesus*, Paul, the creator of this "new religion," was unable to identify the omnipotence of Christ* with that of the archaic Father. Reviving fantasies that preceded totemism and are detectable in the cults of mother goddesses, he made Christianity into a "religion of the Son," in which Jesus is the repository of an omnipotence that is to be shared, not challenged. This religion proposed a regression that was likely to reactivate polytheistic tendencies (the cult of Mary* and of the saints) but that would not have, theoretically, any cultural influence. Freud, however, took note of the cultural importance of Christianity, largely attributing the credit for this to the Reformation.

b) Reception of the Freudian Critique. Freud's analysis has lost the points of support on which it originally relied. Protohistorians soon abandoned the hypothesis of the primal horde, and ethnologists that of the descent of all religions from a totemic cult. Biologists have challenged the possibility of cultural heredity, and psychoanalysts have expressed surprise at Freud's silence on the position of women. Moreover, the Freudian theory of Christianity develops a second theory of religion hardly compatible with the first, neglects the developments of Trinitarian theology (Trinity*), and overemphasizes the cult of the Virgin.

Furthermore, Freudian analysis appears to have had little effect on many thinkers. Badly received in Jewish cultural circles, it was considered an unfortunate deviation (O. Pfister, R. Laforgue). Although some disciples (E. Jones, G. Roheim) drew on it in order to study myths*, these individuals' work made little impact on specialists in the history of mythology. As for other readers of Freud, either they did not attempt to articulate with reference to a particular point their general reservations concerning psychoanalysis, or they paid more attention to the relations between religion and psychoanalysis as articulated by Lacan (C. Lévi-Strauss, D. Vasse).

We might then conclude that the Freudian theory of religion is merely an extrapolation, outside its field of operation, of the *nil nisi sexuale* dear to Freud, unless we consider that it sheds interesting light on the occupation with and contamination of religion by neurosis.

But we can go further. The Freudian approach to totemism under the categories of the archaic, the sexual, and the infantile certainly constitutes a myth (Freud himself calls it a "scientific myth"); it nevertheless produced a major shift with regard to the positivist interpretation of religion. By making the Parousia of the positive spirit the structuring axis of history*, A. Comte (1798–1857) had in fact strengthened the positions of rationalism* against religion: since humanity must necessarily move away from belief, it is appropriate to endure the rhythm of that movement. Far from flatly reiterating the positivist credo, *The Future of an Illusion* asserts that if there is indeed an illusion and its prompt dissipation is to be desired, its pure and simple disappearance cannot be expected. There is at work in it, even if awkwardly, a psychic dynamism that lies at the very foundation of our culture. *Civilization and Its Discontents* again considers the incapacity of the *logos* to provide an account of human development that has any immediacy. An irritating thorn is thus set in the heart of rationalist conviction, and it is not gratuitous. Classical philosophy* was interested in representation as a repository of knowledge; those representations were called religious that were devoid of any identifiable knowledge content. This simplistic definition of the religious was, however, challenged under the pressure of a critical movement internal to rationality. The advent of the natural sciences, and the role played in them by perception, led to the idea that representations do not come from two sources, one rational, the other affective, but that everything comes together in a representational process operating at the juncture of individual inclinations and stimuli emanating from reality. Taking up this argument, psychoanalysis investigates the dialectic of desire developing in religious representations and in their ritual staging. Without accepting everything that it says on the subject, we can agree that it does not dishonor religion by seeking to understand how the sexual, understood as the stimulus to an unavoidable interest in others, is at work in it; and how it serves, even awkwardly, the joint development of sociability and culture. Psychoanalysis would thus attempt to understand the transmutation of *éros* into *agapè* (love*).

• S. Freud, *GW*, London, then Frankfurt, 1947–87, 19 vols., 18 vols. (*OC*, Paris, 1989–).

S. Freud (1907), "Zwangshandlungen und Religionsübungen," *GW* VII, 129–39 ("Obsessive Actions and Religious Practices," *The Standard Edition of the Complete Psychological Works of Sigmund Freud,* vol. IX, 1959, 115–27).

S. Freud (1908), "Die 'kulturelle' Sexualmoral und die moderne Nervosität," *GW* VII, 143–67.

S. Freud (1909), "Bemerkungen über einen Fall von Zwangsneurose," *GW* VII, 381–463.

S. Freud (1910), "Psychoanalytische Bemerkungen über einen autobiographisch berschriebenen Fall von paranoia (Dementia Paranoides)," *GW* VIII, 239–320 (*OC* X, 225–304).

S. Freud (1911), "Gross ist die Diana der Epheser," *GW* VIII, 359–61.

S. Freud (1913), "Totem und tabou," *GW* IX.

S. Freud (1921), "Massenpsychologie und Ich-Analyse," *GW* XIII, 71–161 (*OC* XVI, 1–83).

S. Freud (1927), "Die Zukunft einer Illusion," *GW* XIV, 323–80 (*OC* XVIII, 141–98).

S. Freud (1929), "Das Unbehagen in der Kultur," *GW* XIV, 421–506 (*OC* XVIII, 245–333).

S. Freud (1939), "Der Mann Moses und die monotheistische Religion," *GW* XVI, 101–246.

♦ O. Pfister (1919), *Au vieil Évangile par un chemin nouveau,* Bern.

O. Pfister (1928), "Die Illusion einer Zukunft," *Imago* XIV, 2–3.

R. Bienefeld (1938), *Die religion des religionslosen Juden,* Vienna.

C. Lévi-Strauss (1949), *Les structures élémentaires de la parenté,* Paris.

G. Roheim (1950), *Psychoanalysis and Anthropology,* London.

E. Jones (1951), *Essays in Applied Psycho-Analysis* II, London.

C. Lévi-Strauss (1951), *Le totémisme aujourd'hui,* Paris.
R. Laforgue (1963), "Freud et le monothéisme," in *Au-delà du scientisme,* Geneva, 93–117.
P. Ricœur (1965), *De l'interprétation: Essai sur Freud,* Paris.
D. Vasse (1969), *Le temps du désir,* Paris.
A. Vergote (1974), *Dette et désir,* Paris.
J. Gagey (1982), *Freud et le christianisme,* Paris.
H. Schott (1997), "Psychiatrie," *TRE* 27, 672–76.
K. Winkler (1997), "Psychoanalyse/Psychotherapie," ibid., 677–84.

JACQUES GAGEY

See also **Ethics, Sexual; Hermeneutics; Marx, Karl; Nietzsche, Friedrich Wilhelm; Pauline Theology; Sin**

Fundamental Choice

Fundamental choice is a theory according to which the sequence of acts performed by an individual is underpinned by a fundamental choice for or against God*, for or against the good*. The theory makes the concept of "mortal sin*" impossible, that is, an individual sinful act that is enough in itself to separate man from God. The theory has a certain force: it compels us to evaluate every existence through the totality of its decisions and its developments. It also has a certain weakness: it presupposes the existence of an underlying coherence, both in the present and over time—but moral choices, in the plural, may very well be incoherent, both synchronically and diachronically.

JEAN-YVES LACOSTE

Fundamental Theology

Christianity is a religion of revelation, and this gives fundamental theology its primary and constant mission as well as its very content. "So faith comes from hearing" (Rom 10:17). But in what way is the proclaimed or well-understood announcement credible? Who guarantees it? The right to take a position freely before the challenge of the Christian preaching* entails the duty of being accountable for this decision to oneself and to others, as much as is rationally possible. The Bible defines the program of fundamental theology: "Always being prepared to make a defense to anyone who asks you for a reason for the hope that is in you" (1 Pt 3:15; *see also* Phil 1:7 and 1:16).

I. History of Fundamental Theology

The history of fundamental theology is first of all one of its content, and second, one of the names it has been given.

1. Stages of Apology and Apologetics

a) Antiquity and Middle Ages. In antiquity and the Middle Ages, Christian apologetics targeted, on the one hand, Judaism* and on the other, the Greek "pagan" environment where the first Christians lived. Later, it targeted Islam. The writings of the New Testament already sought to highlight their own consistency with the Old Testament, which could be read as typologically foreshadowing the arrival of the Messiah, Jesus*. Justin's *Dialogue with Trypho* (v. 160) opened a millennium of polemic literature, *Adversus Iudaeos.* A dozen or more classical apologists* in the second century A.D. raised their voices against the accusations and errors of the "Hellenes" (*see* F. Morel's *Corpus Apologetarum,* Paris, 1615). Subsequent times saw the development of great polemics against the "Mohammedans" or the "Moors," as in, for example, *Pugio fidei adversus Mauros et Iudaeos,* written by Raymond Martini in about 1220–1284.

b) From the Reformation to the Enlightenment. It was during this period that Christian apologetics underwent a sufficiently systematic development to earn its name, which did not appear until the 18th century, and then in Protestant literature! (*See* Ebeling 1970.) Marsilio Ficino (1433–99) shows the transition from circumstantial apologetics to a more fundamental one, which flourished later in the historic upheavals of the 16th, 17th, and 18th centuries (*see* Niemann's *From Medieval Apology to Modern Apologetics,* 1983). Precursors of the Reformation, such as John Wyclif (†1384) and Jan Hus*, had already questioned the legitimacy of the papal church* and its hierarchy*. The reaction to these criticisms engendered the first *Tractatus de Ecclesia* (Jean de Raguse, 1431; Juan de Turrecremata, 1486.)

Subsequently, the great Reformation of the Western Latin Church (Luther*, Zwingli*, Calvin*) enhanced the need for urgently defining the "True Church" by its essential characteristics, *notae ecclesiae.* Among all the qualities attributed to the Church of Jesus, four traits took shape based on the ancient symbols: unity*, sanctity*, catholicity (in the etymological sense of universality), and apostolicity. (For the Catholic Church, *see* Thils 1937, and for the Protestant churches, Steinacker 1982.) The Church of Rome* claimed exclusive ownership over these, and a very systematic part of its apologetics—the *demonstratio catholica*—was mostly devoted to justifying this claim.

Pierre Charron (1541–1603) in his apology of the *Trois verités…,* published in 1593, divided into three parts the issues that were to preoccupy theologians far beyond the Age of Enlightenment*. Here are the treatises corresponding to the three truths in question (2nd expanded edition, Paris, 1595):

1. *Religion* in general: "There is a religion accessible to all and to everyone, as against all atheists and nonreligious persons" (1).
2. *Christianity:* "Christianity is the best religion of all: opposing all nonbelievers, Gentiles, Jews and Mohammedans" (113).
3. The *Catholic Church:* "Of all the divisions existing in Christianity, the Roman Catholic is the best: opposing all heretics and schismatics" (193 and up to 607).

In his *Triumphus Crucis* (1497) Savonarola had already treated the triple issue of religion, Christianity, and the church, although he had only touched on ecclesiology* in a marginal way. On the other hand, the Huguenot Philippe Duplessis-Mornay (1549–1623), arguing against Catholicism*, devoted a special work to ecclesiology, the *Traité de l'Église* (1578), while the fundamental question of God* and Christianity from the perspective of Revelation* provided the subject for yet another book, *De la vérité de la religion chrétienne* (1581.)

In the tripartite structure of apologetics, strictly confessional defense is preceded by two other parts, devoted respectively to *demonstratio religiosa* and *demonstratio christiana,* and it is the latter that theologists of the Enlightenment emphasized. The issue was no longer the differences between Christians but Christianity as a religion of Revelation, which Deism* wanted to replace by a religion of nature* and reason*. Opposing that, the theologists evoked the miracles* of Jesus and the actualization of the messianic prophesies* of the Old Testament to prove Jesus' "supernatural*" and divine mission. Thus, a whole new subdivision devoted to revelation appeared within *demonstratio christiana,* and the issues of whether revelation was possible and necessary were most often discussed in rational terms, regardless of the fact that it had occurred in Jesus.

There was abundant apologetic literature of the 18th century (*see* Niemann 1983), and much of it illustrates the principle of the tripartite division—for example, in the *Vertheidigung der natürlichen, christlichen und katholischen Religion nach den Bedürfnissen unserer Zeiten* (1787–89), by Beda Mayr, O.S.B. The middle part of this work in its turn is divided into two volumes. The Irishman Hook, who taught at the Sorbonne, also wrote a *Religionis naturalis et revelatae principia* (1754) based on the model "natural religion–religion of Revelation–church."

c) 19th and 20th Centuries. The 19th and 20th centuries saw the spread of late-Enlightenment radical atheism* in the form of vulgar materialism, of dogmatic "dialectical" materialism, and even of a pathos of freedom based on existential precepts. The time had come for the third systematic part of apologetics, *demonstratio religiosa,* establishing the existence of God as a precondition for a possible revelation and discussing his qualities, as well as his relation with the world* and with humanity as the Creator. These fundamental questions took a place of prominence in voluminous works appearing in German around 1900 under the title of *Christian Apologetics*—for example, the works of Schanz, Hettinger, and Weiss. Neoscholastic thought had risen to the ranks of an official doctrine of the Catholic Church since the time of Leo XIII, and Leo's encyclical *Aeternis Patris* of 1879, and was grounded in the teachings of Thomas* Aquinas, who would inspire a number of manuals right up to the 20th century, such as those by Garrigou-Lagrange (Le Saulchoir, Belgique, 1929–31, 3rd Ed.), Dieckmann S.J. (Valkenburg, 1925–30), and Tromp S.J. (Rome, 1937).

Mention should be made of Lang, who wrote three books in Germany: one on religion (1957), another on the mission of Jesus, and the third on church ministry (1954, 1967–68, 4th Ed.). Also of note are the treatises on religion, revelation, and the church in the first three volumes of the four-volume *Handbuch der Fundamentaltheologie* (1985–88) by Kern et al.

2. Fundamental Theology: Term and Content

The first work to use the title *Fundamental Theology* was a two-volume manual by Ehrlich (1810–64), published in Prague in 1859 and 1862. The author added to that two notebooks of *Apologetic Supplements* (1863–64), emphasizing in §34 that the task of fundamental theology "is the same as that of apologetics" (*see also* §16).

Prior to that, Schwetz's work *Theologia generalis* had appeared in Latin (Vienna, 1850) and would subsequently be republished with revealing changes of title: *Theologia generalis seu fondamentalis* (1854), then *Theologia fundamentalis seu generalis* (1858–82).

Similarly, there was A. Knoll's *Institutiones theologiae dogmaticae generalis seu fondamentalis* (Innsbruck, 1852) and Guzmics's *Theologia christiana fundamentalis* (Turin, 1828). The general metaphor of "fundament" (basis) appeared in apologetic literature of the early 18th century, and "Fundamental Theology" seemed to echo the then frequent title of *Fundamental Philosophy* (*see HistorischesWörterbuch der Philosophie* 2, 1972).

Ehrlich aims to show that salvation through revelation, as it appeared with Jesus, is the turning point of all human history*. This belies the strong influence of the Catholic School of Tübingen (from the first half of the 19th century)—specifically, that of Drey (1777–1853) and of the Freiburg professor Staudenmaier (1800–56); and through their influence Ehrlich would reveal himself to be an heir of Friedrich Daniel Ernst Schleiermacher*. Drey's main work, *Die Apologetik als wissenschaftliche Nachweisung der Göttlichkeit des Christentums in seiner Erscheinung* (1838–47) comprises three volumes: I, *Philosophy of Revelation;* II, *Religion in Its Historical Development and Its Fulfillment in the Revelation of Christ;* and III, *Christian Revelation in the Catholic Church.* Thus, Christianity is situated in the context of the universal history of religions, which finds in Christianity its culmination, and constitutes in its internal coherence and organic whole a history of divine revelation. For Drey, all religion is based on "man's [natural] contact and link with God," an "internal revelation" (I), and an inspiration bestowed in the very act of creation. But there is also a need for an "*external* revelation" (*see* I), so that the "internal image" of God in the human being can acquire an explicit form. Just as creation is subdivided spirit and nature into two areas, divine revelation works by inspiration and miracle. Reality can only be proven through reality (*see* I). Thus, apologetics (whose name Drey retained) actually became fundamental theology.

Neoscholastics and the First Vatican* Council put an end to the spread of the ideas of the Tübingen School. Yet, manuals, even when following a more traditional apologetic line, continued to appear, preferably under the modern title of *Fundamental Theology,* which referred simultaneously to the justification of faith as a decision and the basis of theology*.

3. Fundamental Doctrine

In theology the term *fundamental doctrine* has a global concept that may refer to two areas: 1) a formal and epistemological approach to theological sources and methods, and (2) a materialistic and hermeneutic approach to the fundamental questions of the Christian faith.

a) Theory of Theological Knowledge. Works that sought to lay the foundations of a scientific study of theology were often given the title *Theory of Theological Knowledge.* Other titles given to such works included *Encyclopédie théologique, Theologia generalis, Introduction…,* and *Prolégomènes de la dogmatique.* Pierre Annat (1638–1715) accepted in 1700 that his *Theologia positiva,* devoted to these issues, be called *Fundamentalis Theologia*—the oldest occurrence of this term found to date (Stirnimann 1977).

In the beginning, the *encyclopedic* nature of these works was promoted. Schleiermacher's *Brief Outline on the Study of Theology* (1811) had a determining influence on Catholic theologists Drey in his *Brief Introduction…* (1819) and Staudenmaier in his *Encyclopedia…* (1834). In Pelt's *Theologische Encyklopddie* (1843) fundamental theology, or "the fundamental doctrine" (the first part of a systematic theology), is devoted to a discussion of the "principles of the unique Christian Church... and the principles underlying various confessions."

It is in this framework that Gerhard Ebeling's works (1970; 1975) aroused a new interest in fundamental theology in the Protestant world, even though it had long been considered "a Catholic specificity." Here it was approached as the science of the basic principles underlying the whole of theology and all particular theological disciplines (1970). In 1974 Wilfrid Joest accomplished Ebeling's program in his own way by publishing the first Protestant work under the title of *Fundamentaltheologie;* it was subtitled *Theological Problems about Basis and Methods.* The methodological part deals with theology's function and (exclusively scriptural) sources; its hermeneutic, logical, and semantic problems; and, finally, its scientific character.

On the Catholic side, the theory of theological knowledge claims to have its roots in Melchior Cano's *Loci theologici.* The classical scholastic work is Scheeben*'s *Theory of Theological Knowledge* (1874.) The evolution of Catholic thought in the last century—affected, among other things, by Vatican* II—has influenced theological epistemology, which is the subject of the fourth treatise of the *Handbuch der Fundamentaltheologie.* Its topics are: God's word* and faith, the Holy* Scripture, tradition*, catechesis*, and theology as a science of faith and its scientific practice.

b) Toward a Fundamental Theory of Christianity. The need for such a theory has been largely felt. As Seckler (1988) has pointed out, "we are lacking genuine advanced research into the essential content of Christianity" on its basis and its central message. The Tübingen School largely opened the way in this direction. Recently there have been some landmark advances in the area of the so-called "fundamental items" (since the 17th and 18th centuries): the "essence of the Scripture," the "essence of Christianity," the "hierarchy of truths" (Vatican II, *Unitatis Redintegratio* 11) and the "abbreviated formulae of the faith." Rahner*'s *Grundkurs des Glaubens* (1976; translated into English in 1978 as *Foundations of Christian Faith*) has sought to play the role of an introduction to "the concept of Christianity." Söhngen revived an older project of Rahner's (*see* the *Lexikon für Theologie und Kirche* 2, 1960). It sought to construct a noology of revelation as a primary and rigorously formal science. (It would have been unfortunate to give this discipline the initially planned name of *Fundamentale Theologie,* since it would have been indistinguishable from *Fundamentaltheologie* except by means of an untranslatable graphic device.)

Joest reflects upon the "basis of faith" (26) and the "ultimate confidence underlying the faith" (50) in the part of his *Fundamental Theology* devoted to the principles of theology (*see* Seckler 1975). This primary foundation is Jesus Christ in whom "God Himself is present among humankind" (50.) But *how* he is present is only described *within* faith: the primary question of the *justification* remains to be answered, not that of faith itself but of the credibility* of its proclamation.

II. Understanding Revelation and Justifying Its Credibility

1. Traditional Approach of Vatican I

In its constitution, *Dei Filius,* promulgated on 24 April 1870, Vatican I made the following declaration against fideism* and traditionalism*: "God, who is the end and origin of everything, can be known with certainty through the natural light of the mind from all things created" *(1991 Enchiridion Symbolorum* 3004; *see* Rom 1:20). "Natural (or philosophic) theology" manifesting this knowledge is part of the "preambles of faith." The council opposed rationalism*, specifically, the semirationalism of Hermes and Günther *(Lexikon für Theologie und Kirche),* who, following Kant* and Hegel* respectively, admitted that even the "mysteries*" of supernatural revelation could be grasped by reason in their internal possibility, once their reality was recognized. The council affirmed that there were terms of faith "totally surpassing human intelligence *(humanae mentis intelligentiam omnino superant)*" in such a way that their revelation by God is "absolutely necessary" *(1991 Enchiridion Symbolorum* 3005). These mysteries are believed, therefore, "not because of their intrinsic truth, acknowledged by the light of natural reason *(non propter... intrinsecam veritatem)* but by virtue of the authority of God himself as the author of revelation" (*Enchiridion Symbolorum* 3008). These are "secrets hidden in God," *propria dicta mysteria,* among which theological education places highest the Trinity*, Incarnation*, and the Eucharist*.

Knowledge of (supernatural) revelation is justified above all by the miracles*, which are considered "absolutely certain signs, understandable to everyone," as well as by the accomplishment of prophecies (*Enchiridion Symbolorum* 3033). The church "itself is a powerful and constant source of credibility... by virtue of its marvelous propagation, its eminent sanctity, and its inexhaustible generation of good" (the council borrowed this idea from Cardinal Dechamps). It is possible, moreover, that "reason enlightened by faith may yield the mysteries of faith to a certain intelligence that is sometimes extremely productive *(aliquam... mysteriorum intelligentiam),* relying just as much on the analogy* with objects of natural knowledge as on the consistency of the mysteries among themselves and with the ultimate human goal." Thus, side by side with external criteria, Vatican I admitted both *objective* and *internal* criteria justifying the credibility of revelation.

2. New Approach of Vatican II

The transformation of Vatican I into Vatican II is marked by the influence of Pascal* and Newman*, through the intermediary of what is usually called the "apologetics of immanence"—*see* Blondel*, but also *De la certitude morale* (1919, 8th Ed.) by Ollé-Laprune (1839–98), Laberthonnière (1860–1932), and Gardeil (1859–1931). For this approach, it is not only the intellect but human beings as a whole, with their will and emotion, who must seek access to the revelation (*see* Aubert 1958 and Waldenfels 1969).

The old apologetics, which had been reproached with adhering almost exclusively to criteria external to the revelation, had been mostly derived from manuals of theology still subscribing to the demonstrative scheme of Thomas Aquinas's *Summa Theologica* (III, q. 43, a.e 1): "For those things which are of faith surpass human reason, hence they cannot be proved by human arguments" but only "by the argument of Divine power: so that when a man does works that God alone can do, we may believe that what he says is from God." This was followed by a comparison: "Just as when a man is a bearer of letters sealed with the king's ring, it is to be believed that what they contain expresses the king's will."

a) Perfect Intelligence of Revelation. Aquinas's comparison shows how much the event of revelation was reduced to the expression of a formal doctrinal authority, which, once legitimized, was to be accepted without questioning, whatever teaching it might proclaim. This presupposes, first of all, that it is possible to fundamentally *separate* the *fact* of a revelation from its *content.* However, that is not at all the case. According to Vatican II's constitution, *Dei Verbum,* "It pleased God...to reveal himself and to make known the mystery of his will thanks to which men, through Christ...become sharers in divine nature; [in this revelation, the invisible God talks to men] to invite and receive them in communion with Him. The economy of Revelation is realized by deeds and words, which are intrinsically bound up with each other." Revelation consists neither of words only, nor of various *truths*—in the plural—alone, concerning the mysteries, but in the *reality* of the *unique* mystery of the act by which God communicates his presence to the people. It is in the "fact" of revelation that his essential content—God himself—offers himself to us. The fact implies the content; the content renders the fact explicit. That is why no one can know the fact of revelation without being existentially confronted with its content.

b) Cumulative Justification. Revelation thus understood cannot be subjected to traditional demonstration. If it is impossible to separate the fact from the content of revelation, then it is imperative to abandon the second precept of Aquinas's citation and deny that revelation, as a fact, can and must be the object of a direct and rigorous argument, based on the historical reality of miracles that can only be attributed to the actual power of God. This would mean taking the content of revelation, the global mystery of the faith, to the level of natural truths accessible to human reason.

This necessarily leads to rethinking the apologetic call for *miracles,* which should no longer be perceived as a break in the laws of nature by the sublime power of the Almighty but, in Augustine's words, as an act "which contradicts not nature but only our *experience of nature,*" an act "going against the *generally known* course of nature" (*De civitatae Dei* 1:21 and *Contra Faustum* 29:4). Therefore, miracles should be defined as unusual events in the structure of global meaning that religion establishes, as events, which one understands, while remaining open to them, as accomplished by God in a particular manner (through the intermediary of "secondary," interworld reasons).

The Resurrection* of Jesus Christ surpasses by far all "physical miracles." Paul lists in 1 Corinthians 15:5–8 those who witnessed the apparition of the Crucified whom they recognized as living. As for the *via empirica,* the empirical justification of the credibility of revelation through the practice of the actual church (according to Vatican I—*see* above), it can be obtained only through "the contribution of Christianity to a more human world" (*Handbuch der Fundamentaltheologie* IV); the defense of human dignity; and the affirmation of the rights of all human beings to freedom and equality; but also through such peaks of literary apology as *Le génie du christianisme* (1802) by Chateaubriand (1768–1848), along with *Les martyrs ou le triomphe de la religion* (1809), and such official church documents as the pastoral constitution *The Church in the Modern World* (*Gaudium et Spes* 5) by Vatican II and Pope Jean-Paul II's inaugural encyclical *Redemptor hominis.* The "external" criteria, in their multiplicity and diversity, contribute by their global convergence—in Newman's "illative sense" (*Grammar of Assent,* Chapter IX)—to creating a "moral" certainty with regard to the divine legitimacy of Jesus and the church, which lives and proclaims His Gospel.

c) "Internal Logos" of Revelation. "The miracles of Jesus also demonstrate that the kingdom has already come on: 'But if it is by the finger of God that I cast out demons, then the kingdom of God has come upon you' (Luke 11:20; *see* Matt. 12:28)." With this passage (from *Lumen Gentium* 5), Vatican II established that miracles are *not only external signs*. God's Kingdom is manifested first and foremost "in the person* of Christ himself" (*Lumen Gentium* 5). His church constitutes "the sign and the instrument of the most intimate union with God, as the unity of the entire human race" (*Lumen Gentium* 5.1). Its members must be a "sign that renders Christ visible in a way that is perfectly adapted to our times" (*Apostolicam Actuositatem* 16.) All of this indicates that at the *very heart* of the person and work of Jesus one can find revelation, which he not only proclaimed but truly incarnated.

Vatican I accepted that the *teachings* of Jesus—as collected in the writings of the New Testament and interpreted by the councils* of the early centuries through the characteristic dogmas* of Christianity—also allow an individual *in himsef* to attain a certain understanding of the mysteries of faith (*Enchiridion Symbolorum* 3016). How far can one go in this direction that fundamental theology has not yet exploited to the full? What is the boundary of the program of *fides quaerens intellectum,* the "faith seeking rational intelligence"?

Fundamental theology can and must adhere to this program: "The human reason, in its attempt to understand the content of faith, can find 'material reasons' that help satisfy the demands of justification" (Pottmeyer 1988). We must show "*the internal coherence* of the message of Revelation and the faithful interpretation that it is possible to give, through this message, of our experience* of reality"; we must bring to the fore its "internal rationality." But can the internal coherence of the faith in the Trinity be proven—as Hegel undertook to do—"in the medium of intersubjective rationality" (Seckler 1988)? Can it even be "integrated into other non-Christian cognitive frameworks to find *itself in them*?" The *Handbuch der Fundamentaltheologie* contains examples (I:189–93 and II:71–83; *see also,* on a more "material" level, II:197–222) ascribing to fundamental theology the task of "opening to knowledge" (IV:486) the "content of faith" (487)—to the extent that truth "given media coverage through faith can open itself to reason as governed by God" (477)! This is the task that a treatise on the "theory of Christianity" would have to fulfill (see above). But that would mean betraying its legitimate intention to expect answers from it that it could not provide.

d) Justification by Witnessing. Someone who represents a credible authority, worthy of confidence, is called a "witness." He is the "appropriate intermediary of the message of Revelation" (Pottmeyer 1988). According to Vatican II, every Christian "must be a witness before the world to the resurrection and life of the Lord Jesus" (*Lumen Gentium* 38) and "must learn to give witness to the hope that is in them (1 Peter 3:15)" (*Gravissimum Educationis* 2). Over and above verbal testimony, the council promotes testimony from experience. Certainly, what matters in the long run is what the testimony tells of God and his Kingdom and thus of the eternal destiny of every human being. But "the testimony cannot be separated from what it testifies to, nor can the certificate be separated from its certified content" (Ratzinger, in the *Lexickon für Theologie und Kirche* II, 511; cited in Pottmeyer 1988). The witnesses give to the Kingdom of God a physical reality and a human face in concrete history. Thus, the testimony appears as an indispensable means of making revelation credible through experience, because truth acquires a convincing presence and an immediate transparency in the one testifying. This representation of the truth *within* and *through* the witness makes patently clear the conjunction of internal and external reasons on which faith in the revelation is founded, still without any doubt, and in varying proportions.

III. Toward Building a Fundamental Theology

The history of fundamental theology and the debate on the central articulation of revelation and credibility suggest the following agenda:

A. Fundamental theology as a science of foundations ("material part"):
   1. Religion of the one God
   2. Revelation in and by Jesus
   3. Structures of the church

B. Fundamental theology as a science of the basis ("reflexive part"):
   4. Theological epistemology
   5. Reflection on fundamental theology
   6. Theory of Christianity

Let us briefly explain this agenda: *Part A* preserves the tripartition of apologetics as it has appeared since the beginning of modernity and has been maintained throughout all changes of approach. By *apologetics* is meant not only the defense of Christianity "toward the exterior" but first and foremost the responsibility of Christians toward themselves and their companions in faith. In *Part B.4:* Theological epistemology discusses not only the sources and methods of theology as a science (see above) and its subdivision into various disciplines, but also poses in depth the question of how the church as a community of faith acquires specific knowledge (*see* Seckler in *Theologische Quartalschrift,* 1983). *B.5* reflects more precisely—as we have tried to do here, however briefly and imperfectly—on the discipline of fundamental theology.

• K. Werner (1861–76), *Die Geschichte der apologetischen und polemischen Literatur der christlichen Theologie,* 5 vols., Schaffhouse (Catholic).
O. Zöckler (1903), *Geschichte der Apologie des Christentums,* Gütersloh (Protestant).
A. Gardeil (1908), *La crédibilité et l'apologétique,* Paris.
X.M. Le Bachelet (1910), "Apologétique: Apologie," *DAFC* 1, 189–251.
P. Rousselot (1910), "Les yeux de la foi," *RSR* 1, 241–59 and 244–75.
G. Thils (1937), *Les notes de l'Église dans l'apologétique catholique depuis la Réforme,* Gembloux.
R. Aubert (1958), *Le problème de l'acte de la foi,* 3rd Ed., Louvain.
H. Bouillard (1964), *Logique de la foi,* Paris.
J.-P. Torrell (1964–84), "Chronique de théologie fondamentale," *RThom.*
H.J. Pottmeyer (1968), *Der Glaube vor dem Anspruch der Wissenschaft,* Freiburg.
J. Schmitz (1969), "Die Fundamentaltheologie im 20. Jahrhundert," in *Bilanz der Theologie*... II, Freiburg.
H. Waldenfels (1969), *Offenbarung (Vat. II "auf dem Hintergrund der neueren Theologie"),* Munich.
G. Ebeling (1970), "Erwägungen zu einer evangelischen Fundamentaltheologie," *ZThK* 67, 479–524.
A. Dulles (1971), *A History of Apologetics,* London.
H. Bouillard (1972), "La tâche actuelle de la théologie fondamentale," *Le point théol.* 2, 7–49.
E. Castelli (Ed.) (1972), *Le témoignage,* Paris.
W. Joest (1974), *Fundamentaltheologie: Theologische Grundlagen-und Methodenprobleme,* Stuttgart.
G. Ebeling (1975), *Das Studium der Theologie: Eine enzyklopädische Orientierung,* Tübingen (esp. 162–75).
M. Seckler (1975), "Evangelische Fundamentaltheologie," *ThQ* 155, 281–99.
H. Stirnimann (1977), "Erwägungen zur Fundamentaltheologie," *FZPhTh* 24, 291–365 and 460–76.
L.W. Barnard, K.G. Steck, H.-R. Müller-Schwefe (1978), "Apologetik," *TRE* 3, 371–429 (omit the VIe-XVe c.).
J.-P. Torrell (1979), "Questions de théologie fondamentale," *RThom* 87, 273–314.
G. O'Collins (1981), *Fundamental Theology,* Ramsey, N.J., and London.
J. Doré (1982, 1983, 1985, 1986, 1990, 1991, 1995), "Bulletin de théologie fondamentale," *RSR.*
P. Latourelle, G. O'Collins (Ed.) (1982), *Problèmes et perspectives de théologie fondamentale,* Paris-Montreal.
P. Steinacker (1982), *Die Kennzeichen der Kirche,* Berlin.
F.-J. Niemann (1983), *Jesus als Glaubensgrund in der Fundamentaltheologie der Neuzeit,* Innsbruck.
H. Wagner (1983), "Fundamentaltheologie," *TRE* 11, 738–52.
R. Fisichella (1985), *La rivelazione: Evento e credibilità,* Bologne.
H. Fries (1985), *Fundamentaltheologie,* Graz.
W. Kern, H.J. Pottmeyer, M. Seckler (Ed.) (1985–88), *Handbuch der Fundamentaltheologie (HFTh),* 4 vols., Freiburg.
H. Waldenfels (1985), *Kontextuelle Fundamentaltheologie,* Paderborn.
G. Ruggieri (Ed.) (1987), *Enciclopedia di Teologia Fondamentale I,* Genoa.
R. Fisichella (Ed.) (1988), *Gesù Rivelatore,* Piemme.
A.P. Kustermann (1988), *Die Apologetik J.S. Dreys,* Tübingen.
H.J. Pottmeyer (1988), "Zeichen und Kriterien der Glaubwürdigkeit des Christentums," ibid., 373–413.
J. Reikerstorfer (1988), "Fundamentaltheologische Modelle der Neuzeit," *HFTh* 3, 347–72.
M. Seckler (1988), "Die Fundamentaltheologie: Aufgaben und Aufbau, Begriff und Namen," ibid., 450–514.
S. Pié y Ninot (1989), *Tratado de Teología Fundamental,* Salamanca.
H. Bouillard (1990), *Vérité du christianisme,* Paris.
R. Latourelle, R. Fisichella (Ed.) (1990), *DTF.*
F.-J. Niemann (1990), *Jesus der Offenbarer* (texts), 2 vols., Graz.
H. Verweyen (1991), *Gottes letztes Wort: Grundriß der Fundamentaltheologie,* Düsseldorf.
M. Kessler, W. Pannenberg, H.J. Pottmeyer (Ed.) (1992), *Fides quaerens intellectum,* Tübingen.
G. O'Collins (1993), *Retrieving Fundamental Theology,* New York.
E. Schockenhoff, P. Walter (Ed.) (1993), *Glaube-Dogma: Bausteine zu einer theologische Erkenntnislehre,* Mainz.
O. González de Cardedal (1997), *La entraña del cristianismo,* Salamanca (2nd Ed. 1998).

WALTER KERN

See also **Dogmatic Theology; Hermeneutics; Theology; Truth**

Fundamentalism

Fundamentalism is a type of religious reaction to all forms of modernity. Within Christianity this phenomenon is mostly characteristic of Protestantism* but is also found in Catholicism*. In fact, the term *fundamentalism* was coined in the United States at the beginning of the 20th century, but it was only toward the end of that century that the term began to be applied to some Catholic movements.

a) Protestantism. Between 1900 and 1915 a group of conservative evangelical Protestants published a series of brochures entitled *The Fundamentals.* These brochures responded to a certain number of discussions that had been animating American Protestantism over the preceding half a century. In the beginning, Protestant evangelical churches*, although they had their differences, shared a certain common perspective, but toward the end of the 19th century three debates tore them apart. The first one occurred as a number of liberal- and modern-minded Protestants accepted Darwinian theories of evolution*. The second one was due to the teaching of biblical criticism (exegesis*) in some major seminaries. The final disagreement resulted from the progressive view of history* that was characteristic of liberal Protestantism: a view whereby an immanent God* was bringing forth his Kingdom* with the help of human effort. These ideas gained a lot of support at a time when many evangelists were ardent followers of millenarian and apocalyptic* views of the imminent end of the world*.

During the First World War, different churches fought for power. The conservatives (especially among some Baptists* and Presbyterians*) sought to keep their power when they had it or to regain it if they had lost it. They fought mostly about the teaching of theology* and the locations for sending out missions*. In 1919, a global association, the World's Christian Fundamentals Association, became the common mouthpiece for all churches concerned. In July 1920, a Baptist journalist, Curtis Lee Laws, editor-in-chief of *Baptist Watchman-Examiner,* appealed to all those who thought like him to call themselves *fundamentalists,* and the term prevailed. Laws criticized the conservatives' passivity: the church needed people who were ready to fight for the Lord. Thus, all who rallied to fundamentalism were considered fighters against modernity*. They practiced a literal interpretation of the Bible*: for them, Mary*'s immaculate conception had actually taken place, as had the punishment of Christ* for our sins (expiation*); real, too, were the physical resurrection* of bodies and the Second Coming. And underneath all this lay a literal conception of the infallibility of the Bible.

At the time of these debates fundamentalism received a certain amount of unwelcome publicity through a Tennessee trial about the teaching of evolution in schools. The moderates and liberals retained control over their churches while the defeated fundamentalists left the churches to establish their own confessional groups, biblical colleges, papers, radio stations, and so on. Opposing their extremist positions, in 1942 the moderates created a World Evangelical Association that the fundamentalists attacked. The fundamentalists became visible again in the last third of the 20th century, reacting against the liberal trends in major Protestant churches.

In the United States the first fundamentalist movement was generally apolitical; but the most recent movements, conversely, are openly and aggressively political. Building alliances with some more moderate evangelical conservatives, they have organized to seek political power. After 1980 they became very influential among the Republicans. About the same time identical, although less politicized, forces gained ground in Canadian Protestantism and, finally, in Latin America and other countries where the United States has been sending missionaries. This is how a fundamentalist party came to power repeatedly in Guatemala.

b) Catholicism. The fundamentalist movement in the Catholic Church has not been significant. The infallibility of the Bible is not a dogma* for Catholics, thus offering little ground for fundamentalism. Catholicism allows some leeway for developing dogma (John Henry Newman*) as well as for the importance of tradition* and, in contrast to the fundamentalists, it does not consider the Bible to be the only authority*.

Yet one can observe some Catholic movements today that are quasi-fundamentalist. They emphasize the conservative pontifical documents from the last few centuries and are wary of the more moderate decrees of Vatican* II (Monsignor Lefèbvre's anti–Vatican II movement in France is a vivid example). These movements did not draw undue attention from the hierarchy*, but they did influence certain informal developers of fundamentalism among some Catholics. Some such influences came from relations with Protestants—such as through charismatic movements that crossed denominational borders.

c) Main Characteristics of Fundamentalism. The array of conservative, orthodox*, and other traditional* movements are not necessarily fundamentalist. Their attitudes must be transformed for them to become fundamentalism. First of all, they have to become a lot more militant than they normally are. Fundamentalists claim orthodoxy, but they have a tendency to choose doctrines and practices that they qualify as fundamental. Feeling threatened by the destructive forces of modernity, they avidly grab at anything that might help them eliminate the threat to their faith* and their personal and social identity.

Being determined to defend themselves, fundamentalists take their position from a particular document (most often the Bible), which serves them as a rule to discern what is really "fundamental." They have a tendency to constitute separate groups and clearly distinguish themselves, sometimes even in a Manichean way, from the rest of the Christians and the world around them. They leave no territory for agreement with others and no room for moderates. "True believers" find the moderates a lot more dangerous than the moderns or the "unfaithful." Equipped with their principles, they apply Laws's command: fight for God. They consider themselves specially chosen to accomplish the divine designs while confidently approaching the apocalyptic end of history. Indeed, moderate evangelical, pentecostal, and conservative movements are more popular than the fundamentalists; still, the fundamentalists have been thriving in the times of secular and ecclesiastic upheaval that are centered on the end of the second millennium. They appear authoritative to people who do not know what to hope for and easily accept the model of a church that would protect them from all others and would allow them to combat the forces deemed hostile to God.

- E.R. Sandeen (1970), *The Roots of Fundamentalism: British and American Millenarianism, 1800–1930,* Chicago.

G.M. Marsden (1980), *Fundamentalism and American Culture,* New York.

N.T. Ammermann (1987), *Bible Believers: Fundamentalists in the Modern World,* New Brunswick, N.J.

B.B. Lawrence (1989), *Defenders of God: The Fundamentalist Revolt against the Modern Age,* San Francisco.

M.E. Marty and R.S. Appleby (1991), *Fundamentalism Observed,* Chicago.

MARTIN E. MARTY

See also **Choice; Eschatology; Literary Genres in Scripture; Messianism/Messiah; Millenarianism; Myth; Salvation; Secularization; Theology; Traditionalism**